LAROUSSE

MINI
DICCIONARIO

ESPAÑOL-INGLÉS
INGLÉS-ESPAÑOL

LAROUSSE

ISBN 2-03-402062-6
Larousse, Paris

ISBN 2-03-420900-1
Distribución/Sales : Larousse Kingfisher Chambers Inc., New York
Library of Congress Catalog Card Number
94-72845

ISBN 2-03-430900-6
Distribución/Sales : Larousse plc, London

Printed in France

El diccionario MINI Larousse está pensado para principiantes y viajeros.

Con más de 30.000 voces y 40.000 traducciones, esta nueva obra presenta una amplia cobertura del vocabulario básico, así como un tratamiento exhaustivo del léxico propio de carteles, letreros y menús de restaurante.

El texto incluye una gran cantidad de indicadores de sentido claros y precisos. Se ha puesto especial cuidado en la redacción de las palabras más básicas, con numerosos ejemplos de uso y una atractiva presentación.

De consulta rápida y eficaz, esta obra práctica y completa será la herramienta indispensable para estudiantes y turistas. Esperamos que disfruten con él y no duden en ponerse en contacto con nosotros si tienen cualquier observación que hacernos.

EL EDITOR

The Larousse MINI dictionary has been designed with beginners and travellers in mind.

With over 30,000 references and 40,000 translations, this new dictionary gives thorough coverage of general vocabulary plus extensive treatment of the language found on street signs and menus.

Clear sense markers are provided throughout, while special emphasis has been placed on basic words, with many examples of usage and a particularly user-friendly layout.

Easy to use and comprehensive, this handy book packs a lot of wordpower for users at school, at home and on the move. We hope you enjoy using this dictionary, and don't hesitate to send us your comments.

THE PUBLISHER

ABBREVIATIONS		**ABREVIATURAS**
abbreviation	*abbr/abrev*	abreviatura
adjective	*adj*	adjetivo
adverb	*adv*	adverbio
American English	*Am*	inglés americano
Latin American Spanish	*Amér*	español latinoamericano
anatomy	*ANAT*	anatomía
before noun	*antes de s*	antes de sustantivo
article	*art*	artículo
automobile, cars	*AUT(OM)*	automóviles
auxiliary	*aux*	auxiliar
British English	*Br*	inglés británico
commerce, business	*COM(M)*	comercio
comparative	*compar*	comparativo
computers	*COMPUT*	informática
conjunction	*conj*	conjunción
continuous	*cont*	continuo
culinary, cooking	*CULIN*	cocina
sport	*DEP*	deporte
juridical, legal	*DER*	derecho, jurídico
pejorative	*despec*	despectivo
economics	*ECON*	economía
school, education	*EDUC*	educación
exclamation	*excl*	interjección
feminine noun	*f*	sustantivo femenino
informal	*fam*	familiar
figurative	*fig*	figurado
finance, financial	*FIN*	finanzas
formal	*fml*	formal, culto
inseparable	*fus*	inseparable
generally	*gen*	generalmente
grammar	*GRAM(M)*	gramática
informal	*inf*	familiar

LAROUSSE

MINI

SPANISH-ENGLISH
ENGLISH-SPANISH

DICTIONARY

LAROUSSE

Realizado por / Produced by

LAROUSSE

Redacción/Editors

JOAQUÍN BLASCO, ISABEL BROSA SÁBADA
CARMEN ZAMANILLO, ZÖE PETERSEN
ANA CARBALLO VARELA, ELENA PARSONS
MALIHE FORGHANI-NOWBARI, LESLEY KINGSLEY
CALLUM BRINES, WENDY LEE

computers	*INFORM*	informática
exclamation	*interj*	interjección
invariable	*inv*	invariable
juridical, legal	*JUR*	derecho, jurídico
masculine noun	*m*	sustantivo masculino
mathematics	*MATH*	matemáticas
medicine	*MED*	medicina
military	*MIL*	militar
music	*MUS/MÚS*	música
noun	*n*	sustantivo
nautical, maritime	*NAUT*	náutica, marítimo
numeral	*num/núm*	número
oneself	*o.s.*	
pejorative	*pej*	despectivo
plural	*pl*	plural
politics	*POL(IT)*	política
past participle	*pp*	participio pasado
preposition	*prep*	preposición
pronoun	*pron*	pronombre
past tense	*pt*	pasado, pretérito
registered trademark	®	marca registrada
religion	*RELIG*	religión
noun	*s*	sustantivo
someone, somebody	*sb*	
school education	*SCH*	educación
Scottish English	*Scot*	inglés escocés
separable	*sep*	separable
singular	*sg*	singular
something	*sthg*	
subject	*subj/suj*	sujeto
superlative	*superl*	superlativo
technology	*TECH/TECN*	tecnología
television	*TV*	televisión
transport	*TRANS(P)*	transportes
verb	*vb/v*	verbo
intransitive verb	*vi*	verbo intransitivo

impersonal verb	*v impers*	verbo impersonal
pronominal verb	*vpr*	verbo pronominal
transitive verb	*vt*	verbo transitivo
vulgar	*vulg*	vulgar
cultural equivalent	≃	equivalente cultural

SPANISH ALPHABETICAL ORDER

This dictionary follows international alphabetical order. Thus entries with **ch** appear after **cg** and not at the end of **c**. Similarly, entries with **ll** appear after **lk** and not at the end of **l**. Note, however, that **ñ** *is* treated as a separate letter and follows **n**.

LA ORDENACIÓN ALFABÉTICA EN ESPAÑOL

En este diccionario se ha seguido la ordenación alfabética internacional. Esto significa que las entradas con **ch** aparecerán después de **cg** y no al final de **c**; del mismo modo las entradas con **ll** vendrán después de **lk** y no al final de **l**. Adviértase, sin embargo, que la letra **ñ** *sí* se considera letra aparte y sigue a la **n**.

ENGLISH COMPOUNDS

A compound is a word or expression which has a single meaning but is made up of more than one word, e.g. **point of view**, **kiss of life**, **virtual reality** and **West Indies**. It is a feature of this dictionary that English compounds appear in the A-Z list in strict alphabetical order. The compound **blood test** will therefore come after **bloodshot** which itself follows **blood pressure**.

LOS COMPUESTOS EN INGLÉS

En inglés se llama compuesto a una locución sustantiva de significado único pero formada por más de una palabra; p.ej. **point of view**, **kiss of life**, **virtual reality** o **West Indies**. Uno de los rasgos distintivos de este diccionario es la inclusión de estos compuestos con entrada propia y en riguroso orden alfabético. De esta forma **blood test** vendrá después de **bloodshot**, el cual sigue a **blood pressure**.

mos, partiréis, partirán, **E** partiría, partirías, partiría, partiríamos, partiríais, partirían, **F** parta, partas, parta, partamos, partáis, partan, **G** partiera, partieras, partiera, partiéramos, partierais, partieran, **H** parte, parta, partamos, partid, partan, **I** partiendo, **J** partido, -da

pedir: **A** pido, pedimos, etc., **C** pidió, pedimos, pidieron, etc., **F** pida, pidamos, etc., **G** pidiera, pidiéramos, etc., **H** pide, pida, pidamos, pedid, etc., **I** pidiendo

poder: **A** puedo, podemos, etc., **C** pude, pudimos, etc., **D** podré, podremos, etc., **E** podría, podríamos, etc., **F** pueda, podamos, etc., **G** pudiera, pudiéramos, etc., **H** puede, pueda, podamos, poded, etc., **I** pudiendo

poner: **A** pongo, pone, ponemos, etc., **C** puse, pusimos, etc., **D** pondré, pondremos, etc., **E** pondría, pondríamos, etc., **F** ponga, pongamos, etc., **G** pusiera, pusiéramos, etc., **H** pon, ponga, pongamos, poned, etc., **J** puesto, -ta

querer: **A** quiero, queremos, etc., **C** quise, quisimos, etc., **D** querré, querremos, etc., **E** querría, querríamos, etc., **F** quiera, queramos, etc., **G** quisiera, quisiéramos, etc., **H** quiere, quiera, queramos, quered, etc.

reír: **A** río, reímos, etc., **C** rió, reímos, rieron, etc., **F** ría, riamos, etc., **G** riera, riéramos, etc., **H** ríe, ría, riamos, reíd, etc., **I** riendo

saber: **A** sé, sabe, sabemos, etc., **C** supe, supimos, etc., **D** sabré, sabremos, etc., **E** sabría, sabríamos, etc., **F** sepa, sepamos, etc., **G** supiera, supiéramos, etc., **H** sabe, sepa, sepamos, sabed, etc.

salir: **A** salgo, sale, salimos, etc., **D** saldré, saldremos, etc., **E** saldría, saldríamos, etc., **F** salga, salgamos, etc., **H** sal, salga, salgamos, salid, etc.

sentir: **A** siento, sentimos, etc., **C** sintió, sentimos, sintieron, etc., **F** sienta, sintamos, etc., **G** sintiera, sintiéramos, etc., **H** siente, sienta, sintamos, sentid, etc., **I** sintiendo

SER: **A** soy, eres, es, somos, sois, son, **B** era, eras, era, éramos, erais, eran, **C** fui, fuiste, fue, fuimos, fuisteis, fueron, **D** seré, serás, será, seremos, seréis, serán, **E** sería, serías, sería, seríamos, seríais, serían, **F** sea, seas, sea, seamos, seáis, sean, **G** fuera, fueras, fuera, fuéramos, fuerais, fueran, **H** sé, sea, seamos, sed, sean, **I** siendo, **J** sido, -da

sonar: **A** sueno, sonamos, etc., **F** suene, sonemos, etc., **H** suena, suene, sonemos, sonad, etc.

TEMER: **A** temo, temes, teme, tememos, teméis, temen, **B** temía, temías, temía, temíamos, temíais, temían, **C** temí, temiste, temió, temimos, temisteis, temieron, **D** temeré, temerás, temerá, temeremos, temeréis, temerán, **E** temería, temerías, temería, temeríamos, temeríais, temerían, **F** tema, temas, tema, temamos, temáis, teman,

G temiera, temieras, temiera, temiéramos, temierais, temieran, **H** teme, tema, temamos, temed, teman, **I** temiendo, **J** temido, -da

tender: A tiendo, tendemos, etc., **F** tienda, tendamos, etc., **H** tiende, tendamos, etc.

tener: A tengo, tiene, tenemos, etc., **C** tuve, tuvimos, etc., **D** tendré, tendremos, etc., **E** tendría, tendríamos, etc., **F** tenga, tengamos, etc., **G** tuviera, tuviéramos, etc., **H** ten, tenga, tengamos, tened, etc.

traer: A traigo, trae, traemos, etc., **C** traje, trajimos, etc., **F** traiga, traigamos, etc., **G** trajera, trajéramos, etc., **H** trae, traiga, traigamos, traed, etc., **I** trayendo

valer: A valgo, vale, valemos, etc., **D** valdré, valdremos, etc., **E** valdría, valdríamos, etc., **F** valga, valgamos, etc., **H** vale, valga, valgamos, valed, etc.

venir: A vengo, viene, venimos, etc., **C** vine, vinimos, etc., **D** vendré, vendremos, etc., **E** vendría, vendríamos, etc., **F** venga, vengamos, etc., **G** viniera, viniéramos, etc., **H** ven, venga, vengamos, venid, etc., **I** viniendo

ver: A veo, ve, vemos, etc., **C** vi, vio, vimos, etc., **G** viera, viéramos, etc., **H** ve, vea, veamos, ved, etc., **I** viendo, etc., **J** visto, -ta

VERBOS IRREGULARES INGLESES

Infinitive	Past Tense	Past Participle	Infinitive	Past Tense	Past Participle
arise	arose	arisen	blow	blew	blown
awake	awoke	awoken	break	broke	broken
be	was/ were	been	breed	bred	bred
			bring	brought	brought
bear	bore	born(e)	build	built	built
beat	beat	beaten	burn	burnt /burned	burnt /burned
begin	began	begun			
bend	bent	bent	burst	burst	burst
bet	bet /betted	bet /betted	buy	bought	bought
			can	could	–
bid	bid	bid	cast	cast	cast
bind	bound	bound	catch	caught	caught
bite	bit	bitten	choose	chose	chosen
bleed	bled	bled	come	came	come

Infinitive	Past Tense	Past Participle	Infinitive	Past Tense	Past Participle
cost	cost	cost	kneel	knelt	knelt
creep	crept	crept		/kneeled	/kneeled
cut	cut	cut	know	knew	known
deal	dealt	dealt	lay	laid	laid
dig	dug	dug	lead	led	led
do	did	done	lean	leant	leant
draw	drew	drawn		/leaned	/leaned
dream	dreamed	dreamed	leap	leapt	leapt
	/dreamt	/dreamt		/leaped	/leaped
drink	drank	drunk	learn	learnt	learnt
drive	drove	driven		/learned	/learned
eat	ate	eaten	leave	left	left
fall	fell	fallen	lend	lent	lent
feed	fed	fed	let	let	let
feel	felt	felt	lie	lay	lain
fight	fought	fought	light	lit	lit
find	found	found		/lighted	/lighted
fling	flung	flung	lose	lost	lost
fly	flew	flown	make	made	made
forget	forgot	forgotten	may	might	–
freeze	froze	frozen	mean	meant	meant
get	got	got	meet	met	met
		(Am gotten)	mow	mowed	mown
give	gave	given			/mowed
go	went	gone	pay	paid	paid
grind	ground	ground	put	put	put
grow	grew	grown	quit	quit	quit
hang	hung	hung		/quitted	/quitted
	/hanged	/hanged	read	read	read
have	had	had	rid	rid	rid
hear	heard	heard	ride	rode	ridden
hide	hid	hidden	ring	rang	rung
hit	hit	hit	rise	rose	risen
hold	held	held	run	ran	run
hurt	hurt	hurt	saw	sawed	sawn
keep	kept	kept	say	said	said

Infinitive	Past Tense	Past Participle	Infinitive	Past Tense	Past Participle
see	saw	seen	spoil	spoiled /spoilt	spoiled /spoilt
seek	sought	sought	spread	spread	spread
sell	sold	sold	spring	sprang	sprung
send	sent	sent	stand	stood	stood
set	set	set	steal	stole	stolen
shake	shook	shaken	stick	stuck	stuck
shall	should	–	sting	stung	stung
shed	shed	shed	stink	stank	stunk
shine	shone	shone	strike	struck	struck /stricken
shoot	shot	shot			
show	showed	shown	swear	swore	sworn
shrink	shrank	shrunk	sweep	swept	swept
shut	shut	shut	swell	swelled	swollen /swelled
sing	sang	sung			
sink	sank	sunk	swim	swam	swum
sit	sat	sat	swing	swung	swung
sleep	slept	slept	take	took	taken
slide	slid	slid	teach	taught	taught
sling	slung	slung	tear	tore	torn
smell	smelt /smelled	smelt /smelled	tell	told	told
			think	thought	thought
sow	sowed	sown /sowed	throw	threw	thrown
			tread	trod	trodden
speak	spoke	spoken	wake	woke /waked	woken /waked
speed	sped /speeded	sped /speeded			
			wear	wore	worn
spell	spelt /spelled	spelt /spelled	weave	wove /weaved	woven /weaved
spend	spent	spent	weep	wept	wept
spill	spilt /spilled	spilt /spilled	win	won	won
			wind	wound	wound
spin	spun	spun	wring	wrung	wrung
spit	spat	spat	write	wrote	written
split	split	split			

SPANISH VERBS

Key: **A** = present indicative, **B** = imperfect, **C** = preterite,
D = future, **E** = conditional, **F** = present subjunctive,
G = imperfect subjunctive, **H** = imperative, **I** = gerund,
J = past participle

N.B. All forms of the **imperfect subjunctive** can also take the endings: -se, -ses, -se, -semos, -seis, -sen

acertar: A acierto, acertamos, etc., **F** acierte, acertemos, etc., **H** acierta, acertemos, acertad, etc.

adquirir: A adquiero, adquirimos, etc., **F** adquiera, adquiramos, etc., **H** adquiere, adquiramos, adquirid, etc.

AMAR: A amo, amas, ama, amamos, amáis, aman, **B** amaba, amabas, amaba, amábamos, amabais, amaban, **C** amé, amaste, amó, amamos, amasteis, amaron, **D** amaré, amarás, amará, amaremos, amaréis, amarán, **E** amaría, amarías, amaría, amaríamos, amaríais, amarían, **F** ame, ames, ame, amemos, améis, amen, **G** amara, amaras, amara, amáramos, amarais, amaran, **H** ama, ame, amemos, amad, amen, **I** amando, **J** amado, -da

andar: C anduve, anduvimos, etc., **G** anduviera, anduviéramos, etc.

avergonzar: A avergüenzo, avergonzamos, etc., **C** avergoncé, avergonzó, avergonzamos, etc., **F** avergüence, avergoncemos, etc., **H** avergüenza, avergüence, avergoncemos, avergonzad, etc.

caber: A quepo, cabe, cabemos, etc., **C** cupe, cupimos, etc., **D** cabré, cabremos, etc., **E** cabría, cabríamos, etc., **F** quepa, quepamos, cabed, etc., **G** cupiera, cupiéramos, etc., **H** cabe, quepa, quepamos, etc.

caer: A caigo, cae, caemos, etc., **C** cayó, caímos, cayeron, etc., **F** caiga, caigamos, etc., **G** cayera, cayéramos, etc., **H** cae, caiga, caigamos, caed, etc., **I** cayendo

conducir: A conduzco, conduce, conducimos, etc., **C** conduje, condujimos, etc., **F** conduzca, conduzcamos, etc., **G** condujera, condujéramos, etc., **H** conduce, conduzca, conduzcamos, conducid, etc.

conocer: A conozco, conoce, conocemos, etc., **F** conozca, conozcamos, etc., **H** conoce, conozca, conozcamos, conoced, etc.

dar: A doy, da, damos, etc., **C** di, dio, dimos, etc., **F** dé, demos, etc., **G** diera, diéramos, etc., **H** da, dé, demos, dad, etc.

decir: A digo, dice, decimos, etc., **C** dije, dijimos, etc., **D** diré, diremos, etc., **E** diría, diríamos, etc., **F** diga, digamos, etc., **G** dijera, dijéramos, etc., **H** di, diga, digamos, decid, etc., **I** diciendo, **J** dicho, -cha.

dormir: A duermo, dormimos, etc., **C** durmió, dormimos, durmieron, etc., **F** duerma, durmamos, etc., **G** durmiera, durmiéramos, etc., **H** duerme, duerma, durmamos, dormid, etc., **I** durmiendo

errar: A yerro, erramos, etc., **F** yerre, erremos, etc., **H** yerra, yerre, erremos, errad, etc.

estar: A estoy, está, estamos, etc., **C** estuve, estuvimos, etc., **F** esté, estemos, etc., **G** estuviera, estuviéramos, etc., **H** está, esté, estemos, estad, etc.,

HABER: A he, has, ha, hemos, habéis, han, **B** había, habías, había, habíamos, habíais, habían, **C** hube, hubiste, hubo, hubimos, hubisteis, hubieron, **D** habré, habrás, habrá, habremos, habréis, habrán, **E** habría, habrías, habría, habríamos, habríais, habrían, **F** haya, hayas, haya, hayamos, hayáis, hayan, **G** hubiera, hubieras, hubiera, hubiéramos, hubierais, hubieran, **H** he, haya, hayamos, habed, hayan, **I** habiendo, **J** habido, -da

hacer: A hago, hace, hacemos, etc., **C** hice, hizo, hicimos, etc., **D** haré, haremos, etc., **E** haría, haríamos, etc., **F** haga, hagamos, etc., **G** hiciera, hiciéramos, etc., **H** haz, haga, hagamos, haced, **J** hecho, -cha

huir: A huyo, huimos, etc., **C** huyó, huimos, huyeron, etc., **F** huya, huyamos, etc., **G** huyera, huyéramos, etc., **H** huye, huya, huyamos, huid, etc., **I** huyendo

ir: A voy, va, vamos, etc., **C** fui, fue, fuimos, etc., **F** vaya, vayamos, etc., **G** fuera, fuéramos, etc., **H** ve, vaya, vayamos, id, etc., **I** yendo

leer: C leyó, leímos, leyeron, etc., **G** leyera, leyéramos, etc., **I** leyendo

lucir: A luzco, luce, lucimos, etc., **F** luzca, luzcamos, etc., **H** luce, luzca, luzcamos, lucid, etc.

mover: A muevo, movemos, etc., **F** mueva, movamos, etc., **H** mueve, mueva, movamos, moved, etc.

nacer: A nazco, nace, nacemos, etc., **F** nazca, nazcamos, etc., **H** nace, nazca, nazcamos, naced, etc.

oír: A oigo, oye, oímos, etc., **C** oyó, oímos, oyeron, etc., **F** oiga, oigamos, etc., **G** oyera, oyéramos, etc., **H** oye, oiga, oigamos, oíd, etc., **I** oyendo

oler: A huelo, olemos, etc., **F** huela, olamos, etc., **H** huele, huela, olamos, oled, etc.

parecer: A parezco, parece, parecemos, etc., **F** parezca, parezcamos, etc., **H** parece, parezca, parezcamos, pareced, etc.,

PARTIR: A parto, partes, parte, partimos, partís, parten, **B** partía, partías, partía, partíamos, partíais, partían, **C** partí, partiste, partió, partimos, partisteis, partieron, **D** partiré, partirás, partirá, partire-

PHONETIC TRANSCRIPTION

English vowels

[ɪ] pit, big, rid
[e] pet, tend
[æ] pat, bag, mad
[ʌ] run, cut
[ɒ] pot, log
[ʊ] put, full
[ə] mother, suppose
[i:] bean, weed
[ɑ:] barn, car, laugh
[ɔ:] horn, lawn
[u:] loop, loose
[ɜ:] burn, learn, bird

English diphthongs

[eɪ] bay, late, great
[aɪ] buy, light, aisle
[ɔɪ] boy, foil
[əʊ] no, road, blow
[aʊ] now, shout, town
[ɪə] peer, fierce, idea
[eə] pair, bear, share
[ʊə] poor, sure, tour

Semi-vowels

you, spaniel   [j]
wet, why, twin   [w]

Consonants

pop, people   [p]
bottle, bib   [b]
                      [β]
train, tip   [t]
dog, did   [d]
come, kitchen   [k]
gag, great   [g]
                      [ɣ]

TRANSCRIPCIÓN FONÉTICA

Vocales españolas

[i] piso, imagen
[e] tela, eso
[a] pata, amigo
[o] bola, otro
[u] luz, una

Vocales catalanas

[ɛ] fresc

Diptongos españoles

[ei] ley, peine
[ai] aire, caiga
[oi] soy, boina
[au] causa, aula
[eu] Europa, deuda

Semivocales

hierba, miedo
agua, hueso

Consonantes

papá, campo
vaca, bomba
curvo, caballo
toro, pato
donde, caldo
que, cosa
grande, guerra
aguijón, bulldog

chain, wre**tch**ed	[tʃ]	o**ch**o, **ch**usma
jet, fri**dg**e	[dʒ]	
fib, **ph**ysical	[f]	**f**ui, a**f**án
vine, li**v**e	[v]	
think, fif**th**	[θ]	**c**era, pa**z**
this, wi**th**	[ð]	ca**d**a, par**d**o
seal, pea**c**e	[s]	**s**olo, pa**s**o
zip, hi**s**	[z]	
sheep, ma**ch**ine	[ʃ]	
u**s**ual, mea**s**ure	[ʒ]	
	[x]	**g**emir, **j**amón
how, per**h**aps	[h]	
metal, co**mb**	[m]	**m**adre, ca**m**a
night, di**nn**er	[n]	**n**o, pe**n**a
su**ng**, parki**ng**	[ŋ]	
	[ɲ]	ca**ñ**a
little, he**lp**	[l]	a**l**a, **l**uz
right, ca**rr**y	[r]	a**t**ar, pa**r**o
	[rr]	pe**rr**o, **r**osa
	[ʎ]	**ll**ave, co**ll**ar

The symbol ['] indicates that the following syllable carries primary stress and the symbol [,] that the following syllable carries secondary stress.

Los símbolos ['] y [,] indican que la sílaba siguiente lleva un acento primario o secundario respectivamente.

The symbol [ʳ] in English phonetics indicates that the final "r" is pronounced only when followed by a word beginning with a vowel. Note that it is nearly always pronounced in American English.

El símbolo [ʳ] en fonética inglesa indica que la "r" al final de palabra se pronuncia sólo cuando precede a una palabra que comienza por vocal. Adviértase que casi siempre se pronuncia en inglés americano.

a *prep* 1. *(tiempo):* **a las pocas semanas** a few weeks later; **al mes de casados** a month after marrying; **a las siete** at seven o'clock; **a los once años** at the age of eleven; **dos veces al año** twice a year; **al oír la noticia se desmayó** on hearing the news, she fainted.

2. *(frecuencia)* per, every; **cuarenta horas a la semana** forty hours a week.

3. *(dirección)* to, **voy a Sevilla** I'm going to Seville; **llegó a Barcelona/la fiesta** he arrived in Barcelona/at the party.

4. *(posición, lugar, distancia):* **a la salida del cine** outside the cinema; **está a cien kilómetros** it's a hundred kilómetres away; **a la derecha/izquierda** on the right/left.

5. *(con complemento indirecto)* to; **dáselo a Juan** give it to Juan; **dile a Juan que venga** tell Juan to come.

6. *(con complemento directo):* **quiere a su hijo** she loves her son.

7. *(cantidad, medida, precio):* **a cientos/docenas** by the hundred/dozen; **¿a cuánto están las peras?** how much are the pears?; **vende las peras a 150 pesetas** he's selling pears for 150 pesetas; **ganaron por tres a cero** they won three nil.

8. *(modo, manera):* **a la gallega** Galician style; **escribir a máquina** to type; **a mano** by hand.

9. *(finalidad)* to; **entró a pagar** he came in to pay; **aprender a nadar** to learn to swim.

abad, -desa *m, f* abbot (*f* abbess).

abadía *f* abbey.

abajo *adv (de situación)* below; *(en edificio)* downstairs; *(de dirección)* down; **allí ~** down there; **aquí ~** down here; **más ~** further down; **para ~** downwards; **de ~** *(piso)* downstairs.

abalear *vt (Amér)* to shoot.

abandonado, -da *adj* abandoned; *(lugar)* deserted.

abandonar *vt (persona, animal, proyecto)* to abandon; *(coche, lugar, examen)* to leave; *(prueba)* to drop out of ◻ **abandonarse** *vpr* to let o.s. go.

abandono *m (dejadez)* neglect.

abanicarse *vpr* to fan o.s.

abanico *m* fan.

abarcar *vt (incluir)* to include; *(ver)* to have a view of.

abarrotado, -da *adj* packed.

abarrotero, -ra *m, f (Amér)* grocer.

abarrotes *mpl (Amér)*

ceries.

abastecer vt to supply □ **abastecerse de** v + prep to get, to buy.

abatible adj folding.

abatido, -da adj (desanimado) dejected.

abatir vt (muro) to knock down; (árbol) to flatten.

abdicar vi to abdicate.

abdomen m abdomen.

abdominales mpl sit-ups.

abecedario m (alfabeto) alphabet.

abeja f bee.

abejorro m bumblebee.

aberración f (disparate) stupid thing.

abertura f (agujero) opening.

abeto m fir.

abierto, -ta adj open; (de ideas) open-minded; **estar ~ a** to be open to.

abismo m abyss.

ablandar vt (materia) to soften; (persona) to mollify.

abofetear vt to slap.

abogado, -da m, f lawyer.

abolición f abolition.

abolir vt to abolish.

abollar vt to dent.

abonado, -da adj (tierra) fertilized; **está ~ a la televisión por cable** he subscribes to cable TV.

abonar vt (tierra) to fertilize; (cantidad, precio) to pay □ **abonarse** a v + prep (revista) to subscribe to; (teatro, fútbol) to have a season ticket for.

abono m (del metro, autobús) sea-

son ticket; (para tierra) fertilizer.

abordar vt to tackle.

aborrecer vt to loathe.

abortar vi (espontáneamente) to have a miscarriage; (intencionadamente) to have an abortion.

aborto m (espontáneo) miscarriage; (intencionado) abortion; (fam: persona fea) freak.

abrasador, -ra adj burning.

abrasar vt (suj: incendio) to burn down; (suj: sol) to burn.

abrazadera f brace.

abrazar vt to hug □ **abrazarse** vpr to hug.

abrazo m hug.

abrebotellas m inv bottle opener.

abrecartas m inv paper knife.

abrelatas m inv tin opener (Br), can opener (Am).

abreviar vt (texto) to abridge; (discurso) to cut.

abreviatura f abbreviation.

abridor m opener.

abrigar vt (del frío) to keep warm □ **abrigarse** vpr to wrap up.

abrigo m (prenda) coat; **al ~ de** (roca, árbol) under the shelter of.

abril m April, → setiembre.

abrillantador m polish.

abrillantar vt to polish.

abrir vt to open; (grifo, gas) to turn on; (curso) to start; (agujero) to make; (ir delante de) to lead ♦ vi (comercio) to open □ **abrirse** vpr: **~se a alguien** to open up to sb.

abrochar vt to do up □ **abrocharse** vpr: **~se el pantalón** to do up one's trousers; **abróchen-**

class *(used of Indians)*.

ácido, -da *adj (sabor)* sour ♦ *m* acid.

acierto *m (respuesta, solución)* right answer; *(habilidad)* skill.

aclamar *vt* to acclaim.

aclarar *vt (ropa, cabello, platos)* to rinse; *(dudas, problemas)* to clear up; *(situación)* to clarify ♦ *v impers (tiempo)* to clear up ❑ **aclararse** *vpr (entender)* to understand.

aclimatación *f* acclimatization.

aclimatar *vt* to acclimatize ❑ **aclimatarse** *vpr* to become acclimatized.

acogedor, -ra *adj (lugar)* cosy.

acoger *vt (suj: persona)* to welcome; *(suj: lugar)* to shelter ❑ **acogerse a** *v + prep (ley)* to have recourse to; *(excusa)* to resort to.

acogida *f* welcome.

acomodado, -da *adj (rico)* well-off.

acomodador, -ra *m, f* usher (f usherette).

acomodarse *vpr (aposentarse)* to make o.s. comfortable ❑ **acomodarse a** *v + prep (adaptarse a)* to adapt to.

acompañamiento *m (en música)* accompaniment.

acompañante *mf* companion.

acompañar *vt (hacer compañía)* to accompany; *(adjuntar)* to enclose; **le acompaño en el sentimiento** my condolences.

acomplejado, -da *adj* with a complex.

acondicionado, -da *adj (establo, desván)* converted.

acondicionador *m (en peluquería)* conditioner.

acondicionar *vt (establo, desván)* to convert; *(local)* to fit out.

aconsejable *adj* advisable.

aconsejar *vt* to advise.

acontecer *v impers* to happen.

acontecimiento *m* event.

acoplar *vt (encajar)* to fit together; *(adaptar)* to adapt.

acordar *vt* to agree on; ~ **hacer algo** to agree to do sthg ❑ **acordarse** *vpr* to remember; **~se de hacer algo** to remember to do sthg.

acorde *adj (conforme)* in agreement ♦ *m* chord; **~ con** in keeping with.

acordeón *m* accordion.

acortar *vt* to shorten.

acosar *vt (perseguir)* to hound; *(molestar)* to harass.

acoso *m* harassment.

acostar *vt* to put to bed ❑ **acostarse** *(pr: irse a dormir)* to go to bed; **~se con alguien** *(fam)* to sleep with sb.

acostumbrar *vt:* **~ a alguien a** *(habituar)* to get sb used to; **no acostumbro a hacerlo** I don't usually do it ❑ **acostumbrarse** *vpr:* **~se a** to get used to.

acreditado, -da *adj (con buena reputación)* reputable.

acreditar *vt (con documentos)* to authorize.

acrílico, -ca *adj* acrylic.

acrobacia *f* acrobatics *(pl)*.

acróbata *mf* acrobat.

acta *f (de reunión)* minutes *(pl)*.

actitud *f (del ánimo)* attitude;

(postura) posture.

activar vt to activate.

actividad f activity ❑ **actividades** fpl activities.

activo, -va adj active.

acto m act; **~ seguido** straight after; **en el ~** *(llaves, arreglos)* while you wait; *(multar)* on the spot; **"paga sus consumiciones en el ~"** sign indicating that customers should pay for their order immediately.

actor, -triz m, f actor (f actress).

actuación f *(conducta)* behaviour; *(en el cine, teatro)* performance.

actual adj current, present.

actualidad f *(momento presente)* present time; **de ~** topical; **en la ~** nowadays.

actualizar vt to bring up to date.

actualmente adv *(en este momento)* at the moment; *(hoy día)* nowadays.

actuar vi to act.

acuarela f watercolour.

acuario m aquarium ❑ **Acuario** m Aquarius.

acuático, -ca adj *(animal, planta)* aquatic; *(deporte)* water *(antes de s)*.

acudir vi *(ir)* to go; *(venir)* to come; **~ a alguien** to turn to sb.

acueducto m aqueduct.

acuerdo m agreement; **de ~** all right; **estar de ~** to agree; **ponerse de ~** to agree.

acumulación f accumulation.

acumular vt to accumulate.

acupuntura f acupuncture.

acusación f *(increpación)* accusation; *(DER)* charge.

acusado, -da m, f: **el/la ~** the accused.

acusar vt: **~ a alguien (de)** to accuse sb (of).

acústica f *(de un local)* acoustics *(pl)*.

adaptación f adaptation.

adaptador m adapter.

adaptarse: adaptarse a v + prep *(medio, situación)* to adapt to; *(persona)* to learn to get on with.

adecuado, -da adj suitable, appropriate.

adecuar vt to adapt ❑ **adecuarse** vpr *(acostumbrarse)* to adjust.

a. de J.C. *(abrev de antes de Jesucristo)* BC.

adelantado, -da adj advanced; *(pago)* advance; **ir ~** *(reloj)* to be fast; **por ~** in advance.

adelantamiento m overtaking.

adelantar vt *(sobrepasar)* to overtake; *(trabajo, cita, reunión)* to bring forward; *(reloj)* to put forward ◆ vi *(reloj)* to be fast ❑ **adelantarse** vpr *(anticiparse)* to be early.

adelante adv ahead ◆ interj *(pase)* come in!; **más ~** later; **en ~** from now on.

adelanto m advance; *(en carretera)* overtaking.

adelgazante adj slimming.

adelgazar vt to lose ◆ vi to lose weight.

además adv *(también)* also; *(encima)* moreover; **~ de** as well as.

adentro *adv* inside.

adherente *adj* adhesive.

adherir *vt* to stick ❑ **adherirse a** *v* + *prep (propuesta, idea, opinión, etc)* to support; *(asociación, partido)* to join.

adhesión † *(unión)* sticking; *(apoyo)* support; *(afiliación)* joining.

adhesivo, -va *adj* adhesive ◆ *m (pegatina)* sticker.

adicción *f* addiction.

adición *f* addition.

adicional *adj* additional.

adicto, -ta *adj:* **~ a** addicted to.

adiós *m* goodbye ◆ *interj* goodbye!

adivinanza *f* riddle.

adivinar *vt (solución, respuesta)* to guess; *(futuro)* to foretell.

adivino, -na *m, f* fortuneteller.

adjetivo *m* adjective.

adjuntar *vt* to enclose.

administración *f (de productos)* supply; *(de oficina)* administration ❑ **Administración** *f:* **la Administración** the Government *(Br)*, the Administration *(Am)*.

administrar *vt (organizar, gobernar)* to run; *(medicamento)* to give.

administrativo, -va *adj* administrative ◆ *m, f* office worker.

admiración *f (estimación)* admiration; *(sorpresa)* amazement.

admirar *vt (estimar)* to admire; *(provocar sorpresa)* to amaze.

admisible *adj* acceptable.

admitir *vt* to admit.

admón. *(abrev de administración)* admin.

adobe *m* adobe.

adolescencia *f* adolescence.

adolescente *adj & mf* adolescent.

adonde *adv* where.

adónde *adv* where.

adopción *f (de un hijo)* adoption.

adoptar *vt* to adopt.

adoptivo, -va *adj (padre)* adoptive; *(hijo)* adopted.

adoquín *m* cobblestone.

adorable *adj* adorable.

adoración *f (culto)* worship; *(amor, pasión)* adoration.

adorar *vt (divinidad)* to worship; *(persona, animal, cosa)* to adore.

adornar *vt* to decorate.

adorno *m* ornament.

adosado, -da *adj:* **~ a** against; **casa adosada** semi-detached house; **chalé ~** semi-detached house.

adquirir *vt (comprar)* to purchase; *(conseguir)* to acquire.

adquisición *f* purchase.

adquisitivo, -va *adj* purchasing.

adrede *adv* deliberately.

aduana *f* customs *(sg);* **pasar por la ~** to go through customs.

aduanero, -ra *adj* customs *(antes de s)* ◆ *m, f* customs officer.

adulterio *m* adultery.

adúltero, -ra *adj* adulterous.

adulto, -ta *adj & m, f* adult.

adverbio *m* adverb.

adversario, -ria *m, f* adversary.

adverso, -sa *adj* adverse.

advertencia *f* warning.

advertir *vt (avisar)* to warn; *(notar)* to notice.

aéreo, -a *adj* air *(antes de s)*.

aerobic (æˈroβik) *m* aerobics *(sg)*.

aeromodelismo *m* airplane modelling.

aeromoza *f (Amér)* air hostess.

aeronave *f* aircraft.

aeropuerto *m* airport.

aerosol *m* aerosol.

afán *m (deseo)* urge.

afear *vt* to make ugly.

afección *f (formal: enfermedad)* complaint.

afectado, -da *adj (afligido)* upset; *(amanerado)* affected; **~ de** o **por** *(enfermedad)* suffering from.

afectar *vt* to affect ❑ **afectar a** *v + prep* to affect; **afectarse** *vpr:* **~se por** o **con** to be affected by.

afectivo, -va *adj (sensible)* sensitive.

afecto *m* affection.

afectuoso, -sa *adj* affectionate.

afeitado, -da *adj (barba)* shaven; *(persona)* clean-shaven ❖ *m* shave.

afeitarse *vpr* to shave.

afeminado, -da *adj* effeminate.

afiche *m (Amér)* poster.

afición *f (inclinación)* fondness; *(partidarios)* fans *(pl)*.

aficionado, -da *adj (amateur)* amateur; **~ a** *(interesado por)* fond of.

aficionarse: aficionarse a *v + prep (interesarse por)* to become keen on; *(habituarse a)* to become fond of.

afilado, -da *adj* sharp.

afilar *vt* to sharpen.

afiliado, -da *adj:* **estar ~ a** to be a member of.

afiliarse: afiliarse a *v + prep* to join.

afín *adj* similar.

afinar *vt (instrumento)* to tune; *(puntería)* to perfect ❖ *vi* to be in tune.

afinidad *f* affinity.

afirmación *f* statement.

afirmar *vt (decir con seguridad)* to assert ❑ **afirmarse en** *v + prep (postura, idea)* to reaffirm.

afirmativo, -va *adj* affirmative.

afligido, -da *adj* upset.

afligir *vt (apenar)* to upset ❑ **afligirse** *vpr* to get upset.

aflojar *vt (cuerda)* to slacken; *(nudo)* to loosen ❖ *vi (en esfuerzo)* to ease off; *(ceder)* to die down.

afluencia *f (de gente)* crowds *(pl)*.

afluente *m* tributary.

afónico, -ca *adj:* **quedar ~** to lose one's voice.

aforo *m* seating capacity.

afortunadamente *adv* fortunately.

afortunado, -da *adj (con suerte)* lucky, fortunate; *(oportuno)* happy; **~ en** lucky in.

África *s* África.

africano, -na *adj & m, f* African.

afrodisíaco m aphrodisiac.

afrutado, -da adj fruity.

afuera adv outside ❑ **afueras** fpl: **las ~s** the outskirts.

agacharse vpr to crouch down.

agarrar vt (con las manos) to grab; (fam: enfermedad) to catch ❑ **agarrarse** vpr (pelearse) to fight; **agarrarse a** v + prep (oportunidad) to seize.

agencia f agency; **~ de viajes** travel agency.

agenda f (de direcciones, teléfono) book; (personal) diary; (actividades) agenda.

agente mf agent; **~ de policía** police officer.

ágil adj (movimiento) agile; (pensamiento) quick.

agilidad f (del cuerpo) agility; (de la mente) sharpness.

agitación f restlessness.

agitado, -da adj (líquido) shaken; (persona) restless.

agitar vt (líquido) to shake; (multitud) to stir up ❑ **agitarse** vpr (aguas) to get choppy; (persona) to get restless.

agnóstico, -ca adj agnostic.

agobiado, -da adj overwhelmed.

agobiar vt to overwhelm ❑ **agobiarse** vpr to be weighed down.

agosto m August, → **setiembre**.

agotado, -da adj (cansado) exhausted; (edición, existencias) sold-out; **el dinero está ~** the money has run out.

agotador, -ra adj exhausting.

agotamiento m (cansancio) exhaustion.

agotar vt (cansar) to exhaust; (dinero, reservas) to use up; (edición, existencias) to sell out of ❑ **agotarse** vpr (cansarse) to tire o.s. out; (acabarse) to run out.

agradable adj pleasant.

agradar vi to be pleasant.

agradecer vt (ayuda, favor) to be grateful for; **agradecí su invitación** I thanked her for her invitation.

agradecido, -da adj grateful.

agradecimiento m gratitude.

agredir vt to attack.

agregado, -da adj added ◆ m, f (en embajada) attaché (f attachée).

agregar vt to add.

agresión f attack.

agresivo, -va adj aggressive.

agresor, -ra m, f attacker.

agreste adj (paisaje) wild.

agrícola adj agricultural.

agricultor, -ra m, f farmer.

agricultura f agriculture.

agridulce adj sweet-and-sour.

agrio, agria adj sour.

agrupación f group.

agrupar vt to group.

agua f (líquido) water; (lluvia) rain; **~ de colonia** eau de cologne; **~ corriente** running water; **~ mineral** mineral water; **~ mineral con/sin gas** sparkling/still mineral water; **~ oxigenada** hydrogen peroxide; **~ potable** drinking water; **~ tónica** tonic water ❑ **aguas** fpl (mar) waters.

aguacate m avocado.

aguacero m shower.

aguafiestas *m inv* wet blanket.
aguamiel *f (Amér)* drink of water and cane sugar.
aguanieve *f* sleet.
aguantar *vt (sostener)* to support; *(soportar)* to bear; *(suj: ropa, zapatos)* to last for; **no lo aguanto** I can't stand it □ **aguantarse** *vpr (risa, llanto)* to hold back; *(resignarse)* to put up with it.
aguardar *vt* to wait for ◆ *vi* to wait.
aguardiente *m* liquor.
aguarrás *m* turpentine.
agudeza *f (de ingenio)* sharpness.
agudo, -da *adj (persona, dolor)* sharp; *(sonido)* high; *(ángulo)* acute; *(palabra)* oxytone.
águila *f* eagle.
aguinaldo *m* Christmas box.

---

i AGUINALDO

In Spain, it is traditional for deliverymen and postmen to go from house to house over the Christmas period with Christmas cards for the occupiers. In return, they receive an "aguinaldo": a gift or a small amount of money in recognition of their services over the year.

---

aguja *f (de coser)* needle; *(de reloj)* hand; *(de pelo)* hairpin; ~ **hipodérmica** hypodermic needle.
agujerear *vt* to make holes in.
agujero *m* hole.
agujetas *fpl:* **tener** ~ to feel stiff *(after running)*.

ahí *adv* there; **por** ~ *(en un lugar indeterminado)* somewhere or other; *(fuera)* out; *(aproximadamente)* something like that; **de** ~ **que** that's why.
ahijado, -da *m, f (de un padrino)* godson *(f goddaughter)*; *(en adopción)* adopted son *(f adopted daughter)*.
ahogado, -da *adj (sin respiración)* breathless ◆ *m, f* drowned man *(f drowned woman)*.
ahogarse *vpr (en el agua)* to drown; *(jadear)* to be short of breath; *(por calor, gas, presión)* to suffocate.
ahora *adv* now; **por** ~ for the time being; ~ **bien** however; ~ **mismo** right now.
ahorcar *vt* to hang □ **ahorcarse** *vpr* to hang o.s.
ahorita *adv (Amér)* right now.
ahorrar *vt* to save.
ahorro *m* saving □ **ahorros** *mpl (dinero)* savings.
ahuecar *vt (vaciar)* to hollow out; *(pelo, colchón, almohada)* to fluff up.
ahumado, -da *adj* smoked.
aire *m* air; *(viento)* wind; *(gracia, garbo)* grace; *(parecido)* resemblance; **al** ~ *(descubierto)* exposed; **al** ~ **libre** in the open air; **se da** ~**s de artista** *(despec)* he fancies himself as a bit of an artist; **estar/quedar en el** ~ to be in the air; **hace** ~ it's windy; ~ **acondicionado** air conditioning.
airear *vt* to air.
airoso, -sa *adj (gracioso)* graceful; *(con éxito)* successful.
aislado, -da *adj* isolated.

aislamiento *m* isolation.

aislante *adj* insulating.

aislar *vt* (*persona, animal*) to isolate; (*local*) to insulate ◻ **aislarse** *vpr* to cut o.s. off.

ajedrez *m* chess.

ajeno, -na *adj*: **eso es ~ a mi trabajo** that's not part of my job; **~ a** (*sin saber*) unaware of; (*sin intervenir*) not involved in.

ajetreo *m* bustle.

ají *m* (*Amér*) (*pimiento picante*) chilli; **ponerse como un ~** (*fam: ruborizarse*) to go red.

ajiaco *m* (*Amér*) chilli, meat and vegetable stew.

ajillo *m*: **al ~** in a garlic and chilli sauce.

ajo *m* garlic; **estar en el ~** to be in on it.

ajuar *m* trousseau.

ajustado, -da *adj* (*cantidad, precio*) reasonable; (*ropa*) tight-fitting.

ajustar *vt* (*adaptar*) to adjust; (*puerta, ventana*) to push to; (*precios, condiciones, etc*) to agree ◻ **ajustarse a** *v* + *prep* (*condiciones*) to comply with; (*circunstancias*) to adjust to.

al → **a**, **el**.

ala *f* wing; (*de sombrero*) brim.

alabanza *f* praise.

alabar *vt* to praise.

alabastro *m* alabaster.

alacena *f* recess for storing food.

alambrar *vt* to fence with wire.

alambre *m* (*de metal*) wire; (*Amér: brocheta*) shish kebab.

alameda *f* (*paseo*) tree-lined avenue.

álamo *m* poplar.

alardear: **alardear de** *v* + *prep* to show off about.

alargar *vt* (*falda, pantalón, etc*) to lengthen; (*situación*) to extend; (*acercar*) to pass ◻ **alargarse** *vpr* (*en una explicación*) to speak at length.

alarma *f* alarm; **dar la (voz de) ~** to raise the alarm.

alarmante *adj* alarming.

alarmar *vt* to alarm ◻ **alarmarse** *vpr* to be alarmed.

alba *f* dawn.

albañil *m* bricklayer.

albarán *m* delivery note.

albaricoque *m* apricot.

albatros *m inv* albatross.

albedrío *m*: **elija el postre a su ~** choose a dessert of your choice.

alberca *f* (*Amér*) swimming pool.

albergar *vt* (*personas*) to put up; (*odio*) to harbour; (*esperanza*) to cherish ◻ **albergarse** *vpr* to stay.

albergue *m* (*refugio*) shelter; **~ juvenil** youth hostel.

albóndiga *f* meatball; **~s a la jardinera** meatballs in a tomato sauce with peas and carrots.

albornoz (*pl* -ces) *m* bathrobe.

alborotado, -da *adj* (*persona*) rash; (*cabello*) ruffled.

alborotar *vt* to stir up ♦ *vi* to be rowdy ◻ **alborotarse** *vpr* to get worked up.

alboroto *m* (*jaleo*) fuss.

albufera *f* lagoon.

álbum *m* album; **~ familiar** family album; **~ de fotos** photo album.

alcachofa f (planta) artichoke; (de ducha) shower head; **~s con jamón** artichokes cooked over a low heat with chopped "jamón serrano".

alcaldada f (abuso) abuse of authority.

alcalde, -desa m, f mayor.

alcaldía f (cargo) mayoralty.

alcalino, -na adj alkaline.

alcance m (de misil) range; (repercusión) extent; **a su ~** within your reach; **dar ~ a** to catch up; **fuera del ~ de** out of reach of.

alcanfor m camphor.

alcantarilla f (cloaca) sewer; (boca) drain.

alcanzar vt (autobús, tren) to manage to catch; (persona) to catch up with; (meta, cima, dimensiones) to reach; (suj: disparo) to hit; **~ a** (lograr) to be able to; **~ algo a alguien** to pass sthg to sb ❑ **alcanzar para** v + prep (ser suficiente para) to be enough for.

alcaparra f caper.

alcayata f hook.

alcázar m fortress.

alcoba f bedroom.

alcohol m alcohol; **sin ~** alcohol-free.

alcohólico, -ca adj & m, f alcoholic.

alcoholismo m alcoholism.

alcoholizado, -da adj alcoholic.

alcoholizarse vpr to become an alcoholic.

alcornoque m cork oak.

aldea f small village.

aldeano, -na m, f villager.

alebestrarse vpr (Amér) (po-nerse nervioso) to get worked up; (enojarse) to get annoyed.

alegrar vt (persona) to cheer up; (fiesta) to liven up ❑ **alegrarse** vpr to be pleased; **~se de** to be pleased about; **~se por** to be pleased for.

alegre adj happy; (local) lively; (color) bright; (fam: borracho) tipsy; (decisión, actitud) reckless.

alegremente adv (con alegría) happily; (sin pensar) recklessly.

alegría f happiness.

alejar vt to move away ❑ **alejarse** vpr: **~se de** to move away from.

alemán, -ana adj, m, f German.

Alemania s Germany.

alergia f allergy; **tener ~ a** to be allergic to.

alérgico, -ca adj allergic; **ser ~ a** to be allergic to.

alero m (de tejado) eaves (pl).

alerta adv & f alert ◆ interj watch out!; **estar ~** to be on the lookout; **~ roja** red alert.

aleta f (de pez) fin; (de automóvil) wing; (de nariz) flared part ❑ **aletas** fpl (para nadar) flippers.

alevín m (de pez) fry; (en deportes) beginner.

alfabético, -ca adj alphabetical.

alfabetización f (de personas) literacy.

alfabetizar vt (personas) to teach to read and write; (palabras, letras) to put into alphabetical order.

alfabeto m alphabet.

alfarero, -ra m, f potter.

alférez (pl -ces) m = second lieutenant.

alfil m bishop (in chess).

alfiler m (aguja) pin; (joya) brooch; ~ **de gancho** (Amér) safety pin.

alfombra f (grande) carpet; (pequeña) rug.

alfombrilla f (de coche) mat; (felpudo) doormat; (de baño) bathmat.

alga f seaweed.

álgebra f algebra.

algo pron (alguna cosa) something; (en interrogativas) anything ♦ adv (un poco) rather; ~ **de** a little; **¿~ más?** is that everything?; **por ~** for some reason.

algodón m cotton; **de ~** cotton; **~ hidrófilo** cotton wool.

alguien pron (alguna persona) someone, somebody; (en interrogativas) anyone, anybody.

algún → alguno

alguno, -na adj (indeterminado) some; (en interrogativas, negativas) any ♦ pron (alguien) somebody, some people (pl); (en interrogativas) anyone, anybody; **no hay mejora alguna** there's no improvement.

alhaja f (joya) jewel; (objeto) treasure.

aliado, -da adj allied.

alianza f (pacto) alliance; (anillo de boda) wedding ring; ~ **matrimonial** marriage.

aliarse: aliarse con v + prep to ally o.s. with.

alicates mpl pliers.

aliciente m incentive.

aliento m (respiración) breath; **quedarse sin ~** to be out of breath; **tener mal ~** to have bad breath.

aligerar vt (peso) to lighten; (paso) to quicken.

alijo m contraband.

alimentación f (acción) feeding; (regimen alimenticio) diet.

alimentar vt (persona, animal) to feed; (máquina, motor) to fuel ♦ vi (nutrir) to be nourishing ❑ **alimentarse de** v + prep to live on.

alimenticio, -cia adj nourishing.

alimento m food.

alinear vt to line up ❑ **alinearse** vpr (DEP) to line up.

aliñar vt (carne) to season; (ensalada) to dress.

aliño m (para carne) seasoning; (para ensalada) dressing.

alioli m garlic mayonnaise.

aliviar vt (dolor, enfermedad) to alleviate; (trabajo, carga, peso) to lighten.

alivio m relief.

allá adv (de espacio) over there; (de tiempo) back (then); ~ **él** that's his problem; **más ~** further on; **más ~ de** beyond.

allegado, -da m, f (pariente) relative; (amigo) close friend.

allí adv (de lugar) there, ~ **mismo** right there.

alma f soul.

almacén m (para guardar) warehouse; (al por mayor) wholesaler ❑ **almacenes** mpl (comercio grande) department store (sg).

almacenar vt (guardar) to store; (acumular) to collect.

almanaque *m* almanac.

almejas *fpl* clams; ~ **a la marinera** clams cooked in a sauce of onion, garlic and white wine.

almendra *f* almond.

almendrado *m* round almond paste sweet.

almendro *m* almond tree.

almíbar *m* syrup; **en** ~ in syrup.

almidón *m* starch.

almidonado, -da *adj* starched.

almidonar *vt* to starch.

almirante *m* admiral.

almohada *f (para dormir)* pillow; *(para sentarse)* cushion.

almohadilla *f* small cushion.

almorranas *fpl* piles.

almorzar *vt (al mediodía)* to have for lunch; *(a media mañana)* to have for brunch ♦ *vi (al mediodía)* to have lunch; *(a media mañana)* to have brunch.

almuerzo *m (al mediodía)* lunch; *(a media mañana)* brunch.

aló *interj (Amér)* hello! *(on the telephone)*.

alocado, -da *adj* crazy.

alojamiento *m* accommodation.

alojar *vt* to put up ❏ **alojarse** *vpr (hospedarse)* to stay.

alondra *f* lark.

alpargata *f* espadrille.

Alpes *mpl*: **los** ~ the Alps.

alpinismo *m* mountaineering.

alpinista *mf* mountaineer.

alpino, -na *adj* Alpine.

alpiste *m* birdseed.

alquilar *vt (casa, apartamento, oficina)* to rent; *(coche, TV, bicicleta)*

to hire; **"se alquila"** "to let".

alquiler *m (de casa, apartamento, oficina)* renting; *(de coche, TV, bicicleta)* hiring; *(precio de casa, etc)* rent; *(precio de TV)* rental; *(precio de coche, etc)* hire charge; **de** ~ *(coche)* hire *(antes de s)*; *(casa, apartamento)* rented; ~ **de coches** car hire.

alquitrán *m* tar.

alrededor *adv*: ~ **(de)** *(en torno a)* around; ~ **de** *(aproximadamente)* about ❏ **alrededores** *mpl*: **los** ~**es** the surrounding area *(sg)*.

alta *f (de enfermedad)* (certificate of) discharge; *(en una asociación)* admission; **dar de** ~ to discharge.

altar *m* altar.

altavoz *(pl* -**ces**) *m (para anuncios)* loudspeaker; *(de tocadiscos)* speaker.

alteración *f (cambio)* alteration; *(trastorno)* agitation.

alterado, -da *adj (trastornado)* agitated.

alterar *vt (cambiar)* to alter; *(trastornar, excitar)* to agitate ❏ **alterarse** *vpr (excitarse)* to get agitated.

altercado *m* argument.

alternar *vt*: ~ **algo con algo** to alternate sthg with sthg ❏ **alternar con** *v + prep (relacionarse con)* to mix with.

alternativa *f* alternative.

alterno, -na *adj* alternate.

Alteza *f*: **su** ~ His/Her Highness.

altibajos *mpl (de comportamiento, humor)* ups and downs; *(de terreno)* unevenness *(sg)*.

altillo *m (de vivienda)* mezzanine; *(de armario)* small cupboard to use up the space near the ceiling.

altiplano *m* high plateau.

altitud *f (altura)* height; *(sobre el nivel del mar)* altitude.

altivo, -va *adj* haughty.

alto, -ta *adj* high; *(persona, edificio, árbol)* tall ◆ *m (interrupción)* stop; *(lugar elevado)* height ◆ *adv (hablar)* loud; *(encontrarse, volar)* high ◆ *interj* halt!; **a altas horas de la noche** in the small hours; **en lo ~ de** at the top of; **mide dos metros de ~** *(cosa)* it's two metres high; *(persona)* he's two metres tall.

altoparlante *m (Amér)* loudspeaker.

altramuz *(pl* **-ces)** *m (fruto)* lupin seed *(formerly eaten as snack).*

altruismo *m* altruism.

altruista *adj* altruistic.

altura *f (medida)* height; *(elevación)* altitude; **tiene dos metros de ~** *(cosa)* it's two metres high; *(persona)* he's two metres tall; **estar a la ~ de** to match up to ❑ **alturas** *fpl:* **me dan miedo las ~s** I'm scared of heights; **a estas ~s** now.

alubias *fpl* beans.

alucinación *f* hallucination.

alucinar *vi* to hallucinate.

alud *m* avalanche.

aludido, -da *adj:* **darse por ~** *(ofenderse)* to take it personally.

aludir: aludir a *v + prep* to refer to.

alumbrado *m* lighting.

alumbrar *vt (iluminar)* to light up ◆ *vi (parir)* to give birth.

aluminio *m* aluminium.

alumno, -na *m, f (de escuela)* pupil; *(de universidad)* student.

alusión *f* reference; **hacer ~ a** to refer to.

alza *f* rise; **en ~** *(que sube)* rising.

alzar *vt* to raise ❑ **alzarse** *vpr (levantarse)* to rise; *(sublevarse)* to rise up.

a.m. *(abrev de ante meridiem)* a m.

amabilidad *f* kindness.

amable *adj* kind.

amablemente *adv* kindly.

amaestrado, -da *adj* performing.

amaestrar *vt* to train.

amamantar *vt (animal)* to suckle; *(bebé)* to breastfeed.

amanecer *m* dawn ◆ *vi (en un lugar)* to wake up ◆ *v impers:* **amaneció a las siete** dawn broke at seven.

amanerado, -da *adj* affected.

amansar *vt (animal)* to tame; *(persona)* to calm down.

amante *mf (querido)* lover; **ser ~ de** *(aficionado)* to be keen on.

amapola *f* poppy.

amar *vt* to love.

amargado, -da *adj* bitter.

amargar *vt* to make bitter ◆ *vi* to taste bitter ❑ **amargarse** *vpr (alimento, bebida)* to go sour; *(persona)* to become embittered.

amargo, -ga *adj* bitter.

amarillear *vi* to turn yellow.

amarillo, -lla *adj & m* yellow.

amarrar *vt (embarcación)* to moor.

amarre m mooring.

amasar vt (pan) to knead; (fortuna) to amass.

amateur (ama'ter) adj & mf amateur.

amazona f horsewoman.

Amazonas m: **el ~** the Amazon.

amazónico, -ca adj Amazonian.

ámbar m amber.

ambición f ambition.

ambicioso, -sa adj ambitious.

ambientador m air freshener.

ambiental adj (ecológico) environmental.

ambiente m (aire) air; (medio social, personal) circles (pl); (animación) atmosphere; (Amér: habitación) room.

ambigüedad f ambiguity.

ambiguo, -gua adj ambiguous.

ámbito m confines (pl).

ambos, -bas adj pl both ♦ pron pl both (of them).

ambulancia f ambulance.

ambulante adj travelling.

ambulatorio m state-run surgery.

amén adv amen; **decir ~ (a todo)** to agree (with everything) unquestioningly.

amenaza f threat; **~ de bomba** bomb scare.

amenazar vt to threaten ♦ vi impers: **amenaza lluvia** it's threatening to rain; **~ a alguien (con** o **de)** to threaten sb (with).

amenizar vt to liven up.

ameno, -na adj entertaining.

América s America.

americana f jacket.

americanismo m Latin Americanism.

americano, -na adj & m, f American ♦ m (lengua) Latin American Spanish.

ametralladora f machine gun.

ametrallar vt to machinegun.

amígdalas fpl tonsils.

amigo, -ga m, f friend; **ser ~s** to be friends.

amistad f friendship □ **amistades** fpl friends.

amnesia f amnesia.

amnistía f amnesty.

amo, ama m, f (dueño) owner; **ama de casa** housewife; **ama de llaves** housekeeper.

amodorrado, -da adj drowsy.

amoldarse: amoldarse a v + prep to adapt to.

amoníaco m ammonia.

amontonar vt to pile up □ **amontonarse** vpr (problemas, deudas) to pile up.

amor m love; **hacer el ~** to make love; **~ propio** pride □ **amores** mpl love affair (sg).

amordazar vt (persona) to gag; (animal) to muzzle.

amoroso, -sa adj loving.

amortiguador m shock absorber.

amortiguar vt (golpe) to cushion; (ruido) to muffle.

amparar vt to protect □ **ampararse en** v + prep to have recourse to.

amparo m protection; **al ~ de** under the protection of.

ampliación f (de local) extension; (de capital, negocio) expansion; (de fotografía) enlargement.

ampliar vt (estudios, conocimientos) to broaden; (local) to add an extension to; (capital, negocio) to expand; (fotografía) to enlarge.

amplificador m amplifier.

amplio, -plia adj (avenida, calle) wide; (habitación, coche) spacious; (extenso, vasto) extensive.

amplitud f (de avenida, calle) width; (de habitación, coche) spaciousness; (extensión) extent.

ampolla f (en la piel) blister; (botella) phial.

amueblado, -da adj furnished.

amueblar vt to furnish.

amuermarse vpr (fam) to get bored.

amuleto m amulet.

amurallar vt to build a wall around.

analfabetismo m illiteracy.

analfabeto, -ta adj & m, f illiterate.

analgésico m analgesic.

análisis m inv (de problema, situación) analysis; (de frase) parsing; **~ (de sangre)** blood test.

analítico, -ca adj analytical.

analizar vt (problema, situación) to analyse; (frase) to parse.

analogía f similarity.

análogo, -ga adj similar.

ananás m inv (Amér) pineapple.

anaranjado, -da adj orange.

anarquía f (en política) anar-

chism; (desorden) anarchy.

anárquico, -ca adj anarchic.

anarquista adj anarchist.

anatomía f anatomy.

anatómico, -ca adj anatomical.

anca f haunch.

ancho, -cha adj wide ◆ m width; **tener dos metros de ~** to be two metres wide; **a sus anchas** at ease; **quedarse tan ~** not to bat an eyelid; **venir ~** (prenda de vestir) to he too big.

anchoa f anchovy.

anchura f width.

anciano, -na adj old ◆ m, f old man (f old woman).

ancla f anchor.

anda interj gosh!

Andalucía s Andalusia.

andaluz, -za adj & m, f Andalusian.

andamio m scaffold.

andar vi 1. (caminar) to walk.
2. (moverse) to move.
3. (funcionar) to work; **el reloj no anda** the clock has stopped; **las cosas andan mal** things are going badly.
4. (estar) to be; **anda atareado** he is busy; **creo que anda por ahí** I think she's around somewhere; **~ haciendo algo** to be doing sthg.
◆ vt (recorrer) to travel.
◆ m (de animal, persona) gait.
❑ **andar en** v + prep (ocuparse) to be involved in; **andar por** v + prep: **anda por los cuarenta** he's about forty; **andarse con** v + prep: **~se con cuidado** to be careful; **andares** mpl (actitud) gait (sg).

ándele *interj (Amér) (vale)* all right; *(venga)* come on!

andén *m* platform.

Andes *mpl:* los ~ the Andes.

andinismo *m (Amér)* mountaineering.

andinista *mf (Amér)* mountaineer.

andino, -na *adj* Andean.

anécdota *f* anecdote.

anecdótico, -ca *adj* incidental.

anemia *f* anaemia.

anémico, -ca *adj* anaemic.

anémona *f* anemone.

anestesia *f* anaesthesia.

anestesista *mf* anaesthetist.

anexo, -xa *adj (accesorio)* attached ◆ *m* annexe.

anfetamina *f* amphetamine.

anfibios *mpl* amphibians.

anfiteatro *m (de teatro)* circle; *(edificio)* amphitheatre.

anfitrión, -ona *m, f* host *(f* hostess).

ángel *m* angel.

angelical *adj* angelic.

angina *f:* tener ~s to have a sore throat; ~ de pecho angina (pectoris).

anglosajón, -ona *adj & m, f* Anglo-Saxon.

anguila *f* eel.

angula *f* elver.

angular *adj* angular.

ángulo *m* angle.

angustia *f* anxiety.

angustiado, -da *adj* distressed.

angustiarse *vpr* to get

worried.

angustioso, -sa *adj (momentos)* anxious; *(noticia)* distressing.

anhelar *vt (ambicionar)* to long for.

anhelo *m* longing.

anidar *vi* to nest.

anilla *f* ring ☐ **anillas** *fpl (en gimnasia)* rings.

anillo *m* ring.

ánima *m o f* soul.

animación *f (alegría)* liveliness.

animado, -da *adj (divertido)* lively; ~ a *(predispuesto)* in the mood for.

animal *m* animal ◆ *adj (bruto, grosero)* rough; *(exagerado)* gross; ~ de compañía pet; ~ doméstico *(de granja)* domestic animal; *(de compañía)* pet.

animar *vt (alegrar)* to cheer up; *(alentar)* to encourage ☐ **animarse** *vpr (alegrarse)* to cheer up; ~se a *(decidirse a)* to finally decide to.

ánimo *m (humor)* mood; *(valor)* courage ◆ *interj* come on!

aniñado, -da *adj* childish.

aniquilar *vt* to annihilate.

anís *m (grano)* aniseed; *(licor)* anisette.

aniversario *m (de acontecimiento)* anniversary; *(cumpleaños)* birthday.

ano *m* anus.

anoche *adv* last night.

anochecer *m* dusk ◆ *v impers* to get dark; al ~ at dusk.

anomalía *f* anomaly.

anómalo, -la *adj* anomalous.

anonimato *m* anonimity.

anónimo, -ma *adj* anonymous ◆ m anonymous letter.

anorak m anorak.

anorexia f anorexia.

anotar vt to note down.

ansia f (deseo, anhelo) yearning; (inquietud) anxiousness.

ansiedad f (inquietud) anxiety.

ansioso, -sa adj; ~ **por** impatient for.

Antártico m: el ~ the Antarctic.

ante prep (en presencia de) before; (frente a) in the face of ◆ m (piel) suede.

anteanoche adv the night before last.

anteayer adv the day before yesterday.

antebrazo m forearm.

antecedentes mpl: **tener ~ (penales)** to have a criminal record

anteceder vt to precede.

antecesor, -ra m, f predecessor.

antelación f: **con ~** in advance.

antemano: de antemano adv beforehand.

antena f (de radio, TV) aerial; (de animal) antenna; ~ **parabólica** satellite dish.

anteojos mpl (Amér) glasses.

antepasados mpl ancestors.

antepenúltimo, -ma adj last but two.

anterior adj (en espacio) front; (en tiempo) previous.

antes adv 1. (en el tiempo) before; ~ **se vivía mejor** life used to be better; **¿quién llamó ~?** who rang earlier?; **mucho/poco ~** much/a bit

earlier; **lo ~ posible** as soon as possible; ~ **de hacerlo** before doing it; **llegó ~ de las nueve** she arrived before nine o'clock.
2. (en el espacio) in front; **la farmacia está ~** the chemist's is in front; ~ **de** o **que** in front of; **la zapatería está ~ del cruce** the shoe shop is before the crossroads.
3. (primero) first; **yo la vi ~** I saw her first.
4. (en locuciones): **iría a la cárcel ~ que mentir** I'd rather go to prison than lie; ~ **(de) que** (prioridad en el tiempo) before; ~ **de nada** first of all.
◆ adj previous; **llegó el día ~** she arrived on the previous day.

antesala f waiting room.

antiabortista mf antiabortionist.

antiarrugas m inv anti-wrinkle cream.

antibiótico m antibiotic.

anticición m anticyclone

anticipado, -da adj (prematuro) early; (pago) advance.

anticipar vt (noticias) to tell in advance; (pagos) to pay in advance □ **anticiparse** vpr: ~**se a alguien** to beat sb to it.

anticipo m (de dinero) advance.

anticoncepción f contraception.

anticonceptivo m contraceptive.

anticuado, -da adj old-fashioned.

anticuario m antique dealer.

anticuerpo m antibody.

antidepresivo m antidepressant.

antier adv (Amér: fam) the day before yesterday.

antifaz (pl **-ces**) m mask.

antiguamente adv formerly.

antigüedad f (en el trabajo) seniority; (época): **en la ~** in the past ❑ **antigüedades** fpl (muebles, objetos) antiques.

antiguo, -gua adj (viejo) old; (inmemorial) ancient; (pasado de moda) old-fashioned; (anterior) former.

antihistamínico m antihistamine.

antiinflamatorio m antiinflammatory drug.

Antillas s: **las ~** the West Indies.

antílope m antelope.

antipatía f dislike.

antipático, -ca adj unpleasant.

antirrobo adj antitheft ❖ m (en coche) antitheft device; (en edificio) burglar alarm.

antiséptico m antiseptic.

antitérmico m antipyretic.

antojitos mpl (Amér) Mexican dishes such as tacos served as snacks.

antojo m (capricho) whim; **tener ~ de** to have a craving for.

antología f anthology.

antónimo m antonym.

antorcha f torch.

antro m (despec) dump.

anual adj annual.

anuario m yearbook.

anulado, -da adj (espectáculo) cancelled; (tarjeta, billete, etc) void; (gol) disallowed.

anular m ring finger ❖ vt (espectáculo) to cancel; (partido) to call off; (tarjeta, billete) to validate; (gol) to disallow; (personalidad) to repress.

anunciar vt to announce; (en publicidad) to advertise.

anuncio m (notificación) announcement; (en publicidad) advert; (presagio, señal) sign.

anzuelo m (fish) hook.

añadidura f addition; **por ~** what is more.

añadir vt to add.

añicos mpl: **hacerse ~** to shatter.

año m year; **hace ~s** years ago; **¿cuántos ~s tienes?** how old are you?; **tengo 17 ~s** I'm 17 (years old); **~ nuevo** New Year; **los ~s 50** the fifties.

añoranza f (del pasado) nostalgia; (del hogar) homesickness.

añorar vt to miss.

aorta f aorta.

apache adj & mf Apache.

apacible adj (persona, carácter) gentle; (lugar) pleasant; (tiempo) mild.

apadrinar vt (en bautizo) to act as godparent to; (proteger, ayudar) to sponsor.

apagado, -da adj (luz, fuego) out; (aparato) off; (persona, color) subdued; (sonido) muffled.

apagar vt (luz, lámpara, televisión, etc) to turn off; (fuego) to put out; (fuerzas) to sap ❑ **apagarse** vpr (morirse) to pass away.

apagón m power cut.

apaisado, -da adj oblong.

apalabrar vt to make a verbal

agreement regarding.

apalancado, -da *adj* comfortably installed.

apañado, -da *adj* clever.

apañarse *vpr* to manage; **apañárselas** to manage.

apapachado, -da *(adj) (Amér)* pampered.

apapachar *vt (Amér)* to stroke fawningly.

aparador *m* sideboard.

aparato *m (máquina)* machine; *(de radio, televisión)* set; *(dispositivo)* device; *(electrodoméstico)* appliance; *(avión)* plane; *(digestivo, circulatorio, etc)* system; *(ostentación)* ostentation.

aparcamiento *m (lugar)* car park; *(hueco)* parking place; *(de un vehículo)* parking; "~ **público**" "car park".

aparcar *vt (vehículo)* to park; *(problema, decisión, etc)* to leave to one side; "**no ~**" "no parking"; "~ **en batería**" *sign indicating that cars must park at right angles to the pavement*.

aparecer *vi (de forma repentina)* to appear; *(lo perdido)* to turn up; *(publicación)* to come out.

aparejador, -ra *m, f* quantity surveyor.

aparejar *vt (embarcación)* to rig.

aparejo *m (de embarcación)* rigging.

aparentar *vt (fingir)* to feign; *(edad)* to look.

aparente *adj (fingido)* apparent; *(vistoso)* showy.

aparición *f* appearance; *(de lo sobrenatural)* apparition.

apariencia *f* appearance; **en ~** outwardly; **guardar las ~s** to keep up appearances.

apartado, -da *adj (lejano)* remote; *(separado)* separated ◆ *m* paragraph; ~ **de correos** P.O. Box.

apartamento *m* apartment; "**~s de alquiler**" "apartments (to let)".

apartar *vt (separar)* to separate, *(quitar)* to remove; *(quitar de en medio)* to move out of the way; *(disuadir)* to dissuade ❑ **apartarse** *vpr (retirarse)* to move out of the way; **~se de** *(alejarse de)* to move away from.

aparte *adv (en otro lugar)* to one side; *(separadamente)* separately; *(además)* besides ◆ *adj (privado)* private; *(diferente)* separate; ~ **de** *(además de)* besides; *(excepto)* apart from.

aparthotel *m* holiday apartments *(pl)*.

apasionado, -da *adj* passionate; ~ **por** *(aficionado)* mad about.

apasionante *adj* fascinating.

apasionar *vi*: **le apasiona el teatro** he loves the theatre ❑ **apasionarse** *vpr (excitarse)* to get excited; **apasionarse por** *v + prep (ser aficionado a)* to love.

apdo. *(abrev de apartado)* P.O. Box.

apechugar *vi*: ~ **con** *(fam)* to put up with.

apego *m*: **tener ~ a** to be fond of.

apellidarse *vpr*: **se apellida Gómez** her surname is Gómez.

apellido *m* surname.

apenado, -da *adj (Amér)* embarrased.

apenar *vt* to sadden.

apenas *adv* hardly; *(escasamente)* only; *(tan pronto como)* as soon as.

apéndice *m* appendix.

apendicitis *f inv* appendicitis.

aperitivo *m (bebida)* aperitif; *(comida)* appetizer.

---

i APERITIVO

Before their main midday meal, Spanish people often go to a bar, where they sit outside and have a glass of vermouth, wine or some other drink and some "tapas", to whet their appetite. It is also common for them to have an aperitif at home, whilst finishing the cooking.

---

apertura *f (inauguración)* opening.

apestar *vi* to stink.

apetecer *vi*: ¿te apetece un café? do you fancy a coffee?

apetecible *adj* appetizing.

apetito *m* appetite; **abrir el ~** to whet one's appetite; **tener ~** to feel hungry.

apetitoso, -sa *adj* appetizing.

apicultura *f* beekeeping.

apiñado, -da *adj* packed.

apiñarse *vpr* to crowd together.

apio *m* celery.

apisonadora *f* steamroller.

aplanar *vt* to level.

aplastar *vt (chafar)* to flatten.

aplaudir *vt & vi* to applaud.

aplauso *m* round of applause;

~s applause *(sg)*.

aplazar *vt* to postpone.

aplicación *f* application.

aplicado, -da *adj (alumno, estudiante)* diligent; *(ciencia, estudio)* applied.

aplicar *vt* to apply ❑ **aplicarse** *vpr*: **~se en** to apply o.s. to.

aplique *m* wall lamp.

aplomo *m* composure.

apoderarse: apoderarse de *v* + *prep* to seize.

apodo *m* nickname.

apogeo *m* height; **estar en su ~** to be at its height.

aportación *f* contribution.

aportar *vt* to contribute.

aposta *adv* on purpose.

apostar *vt & vi* to bet ❑ **apostar por** *v* + *prep* to bet on.

apóstol *m* apostle.

apóstrofo *m* apostrophe.

apoyar *vt (animar)* to support; *(fundamentar)* to base; *(respaldar)* to lean ❑ **apoyarse** *vpr (arrimarse)*: **~se (en)** to lean (on).

apoyo *m* support.

apreciable *adj (perceptible)* appreciable; *(estimable)* worthy.

apreciación *f* appreciation.

apreciado, -da *adj (estimado)* esteemed.

apreciar *vt (sentir afecto por)* to think highly of; *(valorar)* to appreciate; *(percibir)* to make out.

aprecio *m* esteem.

apremiar *vt (dar prisa)* to urge ♦ *vi (tiempo)* to be short.

aprender *vt* to learn ♦ *vi*: **~ a** to learn to.

aprendiz (pl -ces) m apprentice.

aprendizaje m (proceso) learning.

aprensión f (miedo) apprehension; (escrúpulo) squeamishness.

aprensivo, -va adj (miedoso) apprehensive; (escrupuloso) squeamish; (hipocondríaco) hypochondriac.

apresurado, -da adj hurried.

apresurarse vpr to hurry; ~ a to hurry to.

apretado, -da adj (cinturón, ropa, etc) tight; (victoria, triunfo) narrow; (agenda) full

apretar vt (presionar) to press; (gatillo) to pull; (ajustar) to tighten; (ceñir) to be too tight for; (con los brazos) to squeeze ♦ vi (calor, hambre) to intensify ❑ **apretarse** vpr (apiñarse) to crowd together; **~se el cinturón** to tighten one's belt.

apretujar vt (fam) to squash ❑ **apretujarse** vpr to squeeze together.

aprisa adv quickly.

aprobado m pass.

aprobar vt (asignatura, examen, ley) to pass; (actitud, comportamiento) to approve of.

apropiado, -da adj suitable.

apropiarse: apropiarse de v + prep (adueñarse de) to appropriate.

aprovechado, -da adj (tiempo) well-spent; (espacio) well planned.

aprovechar vt (ocasión, oferta) to take advantage of; (tiempo, espacio) to make use of; (lo inservible) to put to good use ♦ vi: ¡que

aproveche! enjoy your meal! ❑

aprovecharse de v + prep to take advantage of.

aproximación f (acercamiento) approach; (en cálculo) approximation.

aproximadamente adv approximately.

aproximar vt to move closer ❑ **aproximarse** vpr: **~se a** to come closer to.

apto, -ta adj: **~ para** (capacitado) capable of; **~ para menores** suitable for children; **no ~ para menores** unsuitable for children.

apuesta f bet.

apuesto, -ta adj dashing.

apunarse vpr (Amér) to get altitude sickness.

apuntador, -ra m, f prompter.

apuntar vt (escribir) to note down; (inscribir) to put down; (arma) to aim; (con el dedo) to point at ❑ **apuntarse** vpr (inscribirse) to put one's name down; **apuntarse a** v + prep (participar en) to join in with.

apunte m (nota) note; (boceto) sketch ❑ **apuntes** mpl notes; **tomar ~s** to take notes.

apuñalar vt to stab.

apurar vt (agotar) to finish off; (preocupar) to trouble ❑ **apurarse** vpr (darse prisa) to hurry; **~se por** (preocuparse por) to worry about.

apuro m (dificultad) fix; (escasez económica) hardship; **me da ~** (hacerlo) I'm embarrassed (to do it); **estar en ~s** to be in a tight spot.

aquel, aquella adj that.

aquél, aquélla pron (lejano en

el espacio) that one; *(lejano en el tiempo)* that; ~ **que** anyone who.

aquello *pron neutro* that; ~ **de su mujer es mentira** all that about his wife is a lie.

aquellos, -llas *adj pl* those.

aquéllos, -llas *pron pl* those.

aquí *adv (en este lugar); (ahora)* now; ~ **arriba** up here; ~ **dentro** in here.

árabe *adj & mf* Arab ◆ *m (lengua)* Arabic.

Arabia Saudí *s* Saudi Arabia.

arado *m* plough.

arandela *f* washer.

araña *f* spider.

arañar *vt* to scratch.

arañazo *m* scratch.

arar *vt* to plough.

arbitrar *vt (partido)* to referee; *(discusión)* to arbitrate.

árbitro *m* referee.

árbol *m* tree; ~ **de Navidad** Christmas tree.

arbusto *m* bush.

arca *f (cofre)* chest.

arcada *f* arcade ❏ **arcadas** *fpl (náuseas)* retching *(sg).*

arcaico, -ca *adj* archaic.

arcángel *m* archangel.

arcén *m (en carretera)* verge; *(de autopista)* hard shoulder.

archipiélago *m* archipelago.

archivador *m* filing cabinet.

archivar *vt* to file.

archivo *m (lugar)* archive; *(documentos)* archives *(pl).*

arcilla *f* clay.

arcilloso, -sa *adj* clayey.

arco *m (de flechas)* bow; *(en arqui-*

tectura) arch; *(en geometría)* arc; *(Amér: en deporte)* goal; ~ **iris** rainbow; ~ **de triunfo** triumphal arch.

arder *vi* to burn; **está que arde** *(fam)* he's fuming.

ardiente *adj (que arde)* burning; *(líquido)* scalding; *(apasionado)* ardent.

ardilla *f* squirrel.

área *f* area; **"~ de descanso"** "rest area"; **"~ de recreo"** ≃ "picnic area".

arena *f* sand; ~s **movedizas** quicksand.

arenoso, -sa *adj* sandy.

arenque *m* herring.

aretes *mpl (Amér)* earrings.

Argelia *s* Algeria.

Argentina *s* Argentina.

argentino, -na *adj & m, f* Argentinian.

argolla *f (Amér: fam)* ring.

argot *m (popular)* slang; *(técnico)* jargon.

argumentar *vt (alegar)* to allege.

argumento *m (razón)* reason; *(de novela, película, etc)* plot.

aria *f* aria.

árido, -da *adj* dry.

Aries *m* Aries.

arista *f* edge.

aristocracia *f* aristocracy.

aristócrata *mf* aristocrat.

aritmética *f* arithmetic.

arlequín *m* harlequin.

arma *f* weapon; **ser de ~s tomar** *(tener mal carácter)* to be a nasty piece of work.

armada *f (fuerzas navales)* navy.

armadillo *m* armadillo.

armadura *f (coraza)* armour.

armamento *m (armas)* arms *(pl)*.

armar *vt (ejército)* to arm; *(pistola, fusil)* to load; *(mueble)* to assemble; *(tienda)* to pitch; *(alboroto, ruido)* to make ❏ **armarse** *vpr* to arm o.s.; **armarse de** *v + prep (valor, paciencia)* to summon up.

armario *m (de cajones)* cupboard; *(ropero)* wardrobe; **~ empotrado** fitted cupboard/wardrobe.

armazón *f (de cama, tienda de campaña)* frame; *(de coche)* chassis.

armisticio *m* armistice.

armonía *f* harmony.

armónica *f* harmonica.

armonizar *vt* to match.

aro *m (anilla)* ring; *(juguete)* hoop.

aroma *m (olor)* aroma; *(de vino)* bouquet; **~ artificial** artificial flavouring.

arpa *f* harp.

arqueología *f* archeology.

arqueólogo, -ga *m, f* archeologist.

arquero *m (Amér)* goalkeeper.

arquitecto, -ta *m f* architect.

arquitectónico, -ca *adj* architectural.

arquitectura *f* architecture.

arraigar *vi* to take root.

arrancar *vt (del suelo)* to pull up; *(motor)* to start; *(de las manos)* to snatch ♦ *vi (iniciar la marcha)* to set off; *(vehículo)* to start up; **~ de** to stem from.

arranque *m (ímpetu)* drive; *(de ira, pasión)* fit.

arrastrar *vt (por el suelo)* to drag; *(convencer)* to win over ❏ **arrastrarse** *vpr (reptar)* to crawl; *(humillarse)* to grovel.

arrastre *m* dragging; **estar para el ~** to have had it.

arrebatar *vt* to snatch.

arrebato *m (de ira, pasión)* outburst.

arreglar *vt (ordenar)* to tidy up; *(reparar)* to repair; *(casa)* to do up ❏ **arreglarse** *vpr (solucionarse)* to smarten up; *(solucionarse)* to sort itself out; **arreglárselas** to manage.

arreglo *m (reparación)* repair; *(de ropa)* mending; *(acuerdo)* agreement.

arrendatario, -ria *m, f* tenant.

arreos *mpl* harness *(sg)*.

arrepentirse: arrepentirse de *v + prep* to regret.

arrestar *vt* to arrest.

arriba *adv (de situación)* above; *(de dirección)* up; *(en edificio)* upstairs; **allí ~** up there, **aquí ~** up here; **más + further** up; **para ~** upwards, **de ~** *(piso)* upstairs; **de ~ abajo** *(detenidamente)* from top to bottom; *(con desdén)* up and down.

arriesgado, -da *adj* risky.

arriesgar *vt* to risk ❏ **arriesgarse** *vpr:* **~se a** to dare to.

arrimar *vt* to move closer; **~ el hombro** to lend a hand ❏ **arrimarse** *vpr:* **~se a** to move closer to.

arrodillarse *vpr* to kneel down.

arrogancia *f* arrogance.

arrogante *adj* arrogant.

arrojar *vt (lanzar)* to hurl; *(vomi-*

tar) to throw up; **~ a alguien de** *(echar)* to throw sb out of ❑ **arrojarse** *vpr (al vacío)* to hurl o.s.; *(sobre una persona)* to leap.

arroyo *m* stream.

arroz *m* rice; **~ blanco** boiled rice (with garlic); **~ a la cazuela** *dish similar to paella, but cooked in a pot*; **~ chaufa** *(Amér)* chop suey; **~ a la cubana** *boiled rice with fried egg, tomatoes and fried banana*; **~ con leche** rice pudding; **~ negro** *rice cooked with squid ink.*

arruga *f (en piel)* wrinkle; *(en tejido)* crease.

arrugado, -da *adj (piel)* wrinkled; *(tejido, papel)* creased.

arrugar *vt* to crease ❑ **arrugarse** *vpr* to get creased.

arruinar *vt* to ruin ❑ **arruinarse** *vpr* to be ruined.

arsénico *m* arsenic.

arte *m o f* art; **tener ~ para** to be good at; **con malas ~s** using trickery; **por ~ de magia** as if by magic ❑ **artes** *fpl* arts.

artefacto *m* device.

arteria *f* artery.

artesanal *adj* handmade.

artesanía *f* craftsmanship; **de ~** handmade.

artesano, -na *m, f* craftsman *(f* craftswoman).

ártico *adj* arctic ❑ **Ártico** *m*: **el Ártico** the Arctic.

articulación *f* joint; *(de sonidos)* articulation.

articulado, -da *adj* articulated.

articular *vt* to articulate.

articulista *mf* journalist.

artículo *m* article; *(producto)* product; **~s de consumo** consumer goods; **~s de lujo** luxury goods.

artificial *adj* artificial.

artificio *m (dispositivo)* device; *(habilidades)* trick.

artista *mf* artist; *(de espectáculo)* artiste.

artístico, -ca *adj* artistic.

arveja *f (Amér)* pea.

arzobispo *m* archbishop.

as *m* ace.

asa *f* handle.

asado, -da *adj & m* roast; **carne asada** *(al horno)* roast meat; *(a la parrilla)* grilled meat; **pimientos ~s** baked peppers.

asador *m* roaster.

asalariado, -da *adj* salaried ♦ *m, f* wage earner.

asaltar *vt (robar)* to rob; *(agredir)* to attack.

asalto *m (a banco, tienda, persona)* robbery; *(en boxeo, judo, etc)* round.

asamblea *f (de una asociación)* assembly; *(en política)* mass meeting.

asar *vt (al horno)* to roast; *(a la parrilla)* to grill ❑ **asarse** *vpr* to be boiling hot.

ascendencia *f (antepasados)* ancestors *(pl).*

ascendente *adj* ascending.

ascender *vt (empleado)* to promote ♦ *vi (subir)* to rise ❑ **ascender a** *v + prep (suj: cantidad)* to come to.

ascendiente *mf* ancestor.

ascenso *m (de sueldo)* rise *(Br)*, raise *(Am)*; *(de posición)* promotion.

ascensor *m* lift *(Br)*, elevator *(Am).*

asco *m* revulsion; **ser un ~** to be awful; **me da ~** I find it disgusting; **¡qué asco!** how disgusting!; **estar hecho un ~** *(fam)* to be filthy.

ascua *f* ember; **estar en ~s** to be on tenterhooks.

aseado, -da *adj* clean.

asear *vt* to clean □ **asearse** *vpr* to get washed and dressed.

asegurado, -da *adj* insured ◆ *m, f* policy-holder.

asegurar *vt (coche, vivienda)* to insure; *(cuerda, nudo)* to secure; *(prometer)* to assure □ **asegurarse de** *v + prep* to make sure that.

asentir *vi* to agree.

aseo *m (limpieza)* cleaning; *(habitación)* bathroom; **"~s"** "toilets".

aséptico -ca *adj* aseptic.

asequible *adj (precio, producto)* affordable.

asesinar *vt* to murder.

asesinato *m* murder.

asesino, -na *adj* murderer.

asesor, -ra *adj* advisory ◆ *m, f* consultant.

asesorar *vt* to advise □ **asesorarse** *vpr* to seek advice.

asesoría *f* consultant's office.

asfaltado, -da *adj* tarmacked ◆ *m* road surface.

asfaltar *vt* to surface.

asfalto *m* asphalt.

asfixia *f* suffocation.

asfixiante *adj (olor)* overpowering; *(calor)* suffocating.

asfixiar *vt* to suffocate □ **asfixiarse** *vpr* to suffocate.

así *adv & adj inv* like this; **~ de**

grande this big; **~ como** just as; **~ es** that's right; **~ es como** that is how; **~ y todo** even so; **y ~ sucedió** and that is exactly what happened.

Asia *s* Asia.

asiático, -ca *adj & m, f* Asian.

asiento *m* seat.

asignatura *f* subject.

asilado, -da *adj* living in a home.

asilo *m (para ancianos)* old people's home; **~ político** political asylum.

asimilación *f* assimilation.

asimilar *vt (conocimientos)* to assimilate; *(cambio, situación)* to take in one's stride.

asistencia *f (a clase, espectáculo)* attendance; *(ayuda)* assistance; *(público)* audience.

asistir *vt (suj: médico, enfermera)* to attend to □ **asistir a** *v + prep (clase, espectáculo)* to attend

asma *f* asthma.

asmático, -ca *adj* asthmatic.

asno, -na *m, f* ass.

asociación *f* association.

asociar *vt* to associate □ **asociarse a** *v + prep* to become a member of; **asociarse con** *v + prep* to form a partnership with.

asolar *vt* to devastate.

asomar *vi* to peep up ◆ *vt* to stick out □ **asomarse** *vpr*: **~se a** *(ventana)* to stick one's head out of; *(balcón)* to go out onto.

asombrar *vt (causar admiración)* to amaze; *(sorprender)* to surprise □ **asombrarse de** *v + prep (sentir admiración)* to be amazed at; *(sor-*

prenderse) to be surprised at.

asombro m *(admiración)* amazement; *(sorpresa)* surprise.

asorocharse *vpr (Amér)* to get altitude sickness.

aspa f *(de molino de viento)* arms *(pl)*.

aspecto m *(apariencia)* appearance; **tener buen/mal ~** *(persona)* to look well/awful; *(cosa)* to look nice/horrible.

aspereza f roughness.

áspero, -ra *adj (al tacto)* rough; *(voz)* harsh.

aspiradora f vacuum cleaner.

aspirar *vt (aire)* to breathe in ❏ **aspirar a** v + *prep* to aspire to.

aspirina® f aspirin.

asqueado, -da *adj* disgusted.

asquerosidad f filthiness.

asqueroso, -sa *adj* filthy.

asta f *(de lanza)* shaft; *(de bandera)* flagpole; *(de toro)* horn; *(de ciervo)* antler.

asterisco m asterisk.

astillero m shipyard.

astro m star.

astrología f astrology.

astrólogo, -ga m, f astrologer.

astronauta mf astronaut.

astronomía f astronomy.

astronómico, -ca *adj* astronomical.

astrónomo, -ma m, f astronomer.

astuto, -ta *adj (sagaz)* astute; *(ladino)* cunning.

asumir *vt (problema)* to cope with; *(responsabilidad)* to assume.

asunto m *(tema general)* subject;

(tema específico) matter; *(problema)* issue; *(negocio)* affair.

asustar *vt* to frighten ❏ **asustarse** *vpr* to be frightened.

atacar *vt* to attack.

atajo m *(camino)* short cut; *(despec: grupo de personas)* bunch; **un ~ de** a string of.

ataque m *(agresión)* attack; *(de ira, risa, etc)* fit; *(de fiebre, tos, etc)* bout; **~ al corazón** heart attack.

atar *vt (con cuerda, cadena, etc)* to tie; *(ceñir)* to tie up.

atardecer m: **al ~** at dusk.

atareado, -da *adj* busy.

atasco m *(de tráfico)* traffic jam.

ataúd m coffin.

ate m *(Amér)* quince jelly.

ateísmo m atheism.

atención f *(interés)* attention; *(regalo, obsequio)* kind gesture; **~ al cliente** customer service; **llamar la ~** to be noticeable ❏ **atenciones** fpl *(cuidados)* attentiveness *(sg)*.

atender *vt (solicitud, petición, negocio)* to attend to; *(clientes)* to serve; *(enfermo)* to look after ♦ *vi (escuchar)* to pay attention; **¿le atienden?** are you being served?

atentado m attempt *(on sb's life)*.

atentamente *adv (en cartas)* Yours sincerely.

atento, -ta *adj (con atención)* attentive; *(amable)* considerate.

ateo, -a m, f atheist.

aterrizaje m landing; **~ forzoso** emergency landing.

aterrizar *vi* to land.

aterrorizar *vt* to terrify.

atestado, -da *adj* packed.

atestiguar vt to testify to.

ático m penthouse.

atinar vi to guess correctly.

atípico, -ca adj atypical.

Atlántico m: el ~ the Atlantic.

atlas m inv atlas.

atleta mf athlete.

atlético, -ca adj athletic.

atletismo m athletics.

atmósfera f atmosphere.

atmosférico, -ca adj atmospheric.

atole m (Amér) thick drink of maize flour boiled in milk or water.

atolondrarse vpr to get flustered.

atómico, -ca adj nuclear.

átomo m atom.

atónito, -ta adj astonished.

atontado, -da adj dazed.

atorado, -da adj (Amér) (atascado) blocked; (agitado, nervioso) nervous.

atorar vt (Amér) to block □ **atorarse** vpr (Amér) (atascarse) to get blocked; (atragantarse) to choke.

atracador, -ra m, f (de banco, tienda) armed robber; (de persona) mugger.

atracar vt (banco, tienda) to rob; (persona) to mug ◆ vi (barco) to dock □ **atracarse de** v + prep to eat one's fill of.

atracción f attraction □ **atracciones** fpl fairground attractions.

atraco m robbery.

atractivo, -va adj attractive ◆ m (de trabajo, lugar) attraction; (de persona) attractiveness.

atraer vt to attract ◆ vi to be attractive.

atragantarse vpr to choke.

atrapar vt to catch.

atrás adv (de posición) behind; (al moverse) backwards; (de tiempo) before.

atrasado, -da adj (trabajo, tarea, proyecto) delayed; (pago) overdue; (en estudios) backward; ir ~ (reloj) to be slow.

atrasar vt (llegada, salida) to delay; (proyecto, cita, acontecimiento) to postpone; (reloj) to put back ◆ vi (reloj) to be slow □ **atrasarse** vpr (persona) to be late; (tren, avión, etc) to be delayed; (proyecto, acontecimiento) to be postponed.

atraso m (de evolución) backwardness □ **atrasos** mpl (de dinero) arrears.

atravesar vt (calle, río, puente) to cross; (situación difícil, crisis) to go through; (objeto, madero, etc) to penetrate □ **atravesarse** vpr to be in the way.

atreverse vpr: ~ a to dare to.

atrevido, -da adj (osado) daring; (insolente) cheeky; (ropa, libro) risqué; (propuesta) forward.

atribución f (de poder, trabajo) responsibility.

atribuir vt to attribute; (poder, cargo) to give.

atributo m attribute.

atrio m (de palacio) portico; (de convento) cloister.

atropellar vt (suj: vehículo) to run over; (con empujones) to push out of the way □ **atropellarse** vpr (hablando) to trip over one's words.

atropello *m* running over.

ATS *mf (abrev de Ayudante Técnico Sanitario)* qualified nurse.

atte *abrev* = atentamente.

atún *m* tuna; **~ en aceite** tuna in oil.

audaz *(pl -ces) adj* daring.

audiencia *f* audience.

audiovisual *adj* audiovisual ◆ *m* audiovisual display.

auditivo, -va *adj* ear *(antes de s)*.

auditor *m* auditor.

auditoría *f (trabajo)* auditing; *(lugar)* auditor's office.

auditorio *m (público)* audience; *(local)* auditorium.

auge *m* boom; **en ~** booming.

aula *f (de universidad)* lecture room; *(de escuela)* classroom.

aullar *vi* to howl.

aullido *m* howl.

aumentar *vt* to increase; *(peso)* to put on.

aumento *m* increase; *(en óptica)* magnification.

aun *adv* even ◆ *conj:* **~ estando enferma, vino** she came, even though she was ill; **~ así** even so.

aún *adv* still; **~ no han venido** they haven't come yet.

aunque *conj* although.

aureola *f (de santo)* halo; *(fama, éxito)* aura.

auricular *m (de teléfono)* receiver ❑ **auriculares** *mpl (de radio, casete)* headphones.

ausencia *f* absence.

ausente *adj (de lugar)* absent; *(distraído)* absent-minded.

austeridad *f* austerity.

austero, -ra *adj* austere.

Australia *s* Australia.

australiano, -na *adj & m, f* Australian.

Austria *s* Austria.

austríaco, -ca *adj & m, f* Austrian.

autenticidad *f* authenticity.

auténtico, -ca *adj (joya, piel)* genuine; *(verdadero, real)* real.

auto *m (automóvil)* car.

autobiografía *f* autobiography.

autobús *m* bus.

autocar *m* coach; **~ de línea** (long-distance) coach.

autocontrol *m* self-control.

autóctono, -na *adj* indigenous.

autoescuela *f* driving school.

autógrafo *m* autograph.

automáticamente *adv* automatically.

automático, -ca *adj* automatic.

automóvil *m* car.

automovilismo *m* motoring.

automovilista *mf* motorist.

autonomía *f* autonomy; **~ de vuelo** range.

autonómico, -ca *adj (región, gobierno)* autonomous; *(ley)* devolution.

autónomo, -ma *adj (independiente)* autonomous; *(trabajador)* freelance.

autopista *f* motorway; **~ de peaje** toll motorway *(Br)*, turnpike *(Am)*.

autopsia *f* autopsy.

autor, -ra *m, f (de libro)* author; *(de cuadro, escultura)* artist; *(de acción, hecho)* perpetrator.

autoridad *f* authority; **la ~ the** authorities *(pl)*.

autoritario, -ria *adj* authoritarian.

autorización *f* authorization.

autorizado, -da *adj* authorized.

autorizar *vt* to authorize.

autorretrato *m* self-portrait.

autoservicio *m* self-service.

autostop *m* hitch-hiking; **hacer ~** to hitch-hike.

autostopista *mf* hitch-hiker.

autosuficiente *adj* self-sufficient.

autovía *f* dual carriageway *(Br)*, divided road *(Am)*.

auxiliar *adj* auxiliary ♦ *mf* assistant ♦ *vt* to assist; **~ administrativo** office clerk; **~ de vuelo** flight attendant.

auxilio *m* help ♦ *interj* help!; **primeros ~s** first aid *(pl)*.

aval *m (persona)* guarantor; *(documento)* guarantee.

avalador, -ra *m, f* guarantor.

avalancha *f* avalanche.

avalar *vt (crédito)* to guarantee; *(propuesta, idea)* to endorse.

avance *m (de tecnología, ciencia, etc)* advance; *(de noticia)* summary; *(de película)* preview.

avanzado, -da *adj* advanced.

avanzar *vi* to advance.

avaricioso, -sa *adj* avaricious.

avaro, -ra *adj* miserly.

avda *(abrev de avenida)* Ave.

AVE *m (abrev de Alta Velocidad Española)* Spanish high-speed train.

ave *f* bird.

avellana *f* hazelnut.

avellano *m* hazel tree.

avena *f* oats *(pl)*.

avenida *f* avenue.

aventar *vt (Amér)* to throw.

aventón *m (Amér)* shove; **dar un ~ a alguien** to give sb a lift.

aventura *f* adventure; *(de amor)* affair.

aventurarse *vpr*: **~ a hacer algo** to risk doing sthg.

aventurero, -ra *adj* adventurous ♦ *m, f* adventurer *(f* adventuress).

avergonzado, -da *adj (abochornado)* embarrassed; *(deshonrado)* ashamed.

avergonzarse: **avergonzarse de** *v + prep (por timidez)* to be embarrassed about; *(por deshonra)* to be ashamed of.

avería *f (de coche)* breakdown; *(de máquina)* fault.

averiado, -da *adj (coche)* broken-down; *(máquina)* out of order.

averiarse *vpr* to break down.

averiguar *vt* to find out.

aversión *f* aversion.

avestruz *(pl -ces) m* ostrich.

aviación *f (navegación)* aviation; *(cuerpo militar)* airforce.

AVIACO *f* charter flight division of Iberia, the Spanish state airline.

aviador, -ra *m, f* aviator.

avión *m* plane; **en ~** by plane; **por ~** *(carta)* airmail.

avioneta *f* light aircraft.

avisar vt (llamar) to call ❑ **avisar de** v + prep (comunicar) to inform of; (prevenir) to warn of.

aviso m (noticia) notice; (advertencia) warning; (en aeropuerto) call; **hasta nuevo ~** until further notice; **sin previo ~** without notice.

avispa f wasp.

avituallarse vpr to get provisions.

axila f armpit.

ay interj (expresa dolor) ouch!; (expresa pena) oh!

ayer adv yesterday; **~ noche** last night; **~ por la mañana** yesterday morning.

ayuda f (en trabajo, tarea, etc) help; (a otros países, etc) aid.

ayudante mf assistant.

ayudar vt: **~ a alguien a** to help sb to; **~ a alguien en** to help sb with.

ayunar vi to fast.

ayuntamiento m (edificio) town hall; (corporación) town council.

azada f hoe.

azafata f air hostess; **~ de vuelo** air hostess.

azafrán m (condimento) saffron.

azar m chance; **al ~** at random.

azotea f terraced roof.

azúcar m o f sugar; **~ glass** icing sugar; **~ moreno** brown sugar.

azucarado, -da adj sweet.

azucarera f sugar bowl.

azucena f white lily.

azufre m sulphur.

azul adj & m blue; **~ marino** navy (blue).

azulado, -da adj bluish.

azulejo m (glazed) tile.

azuloso, -sa adj (Amér) bluish.

B

baba f saliva.

babero m bib.

babor m port.

babosa f slug.

baboso, -sa adj (caracol) slimy; (bebé) dribbling; (fam: infantil) wet behind the ears; (Amér: tonto) stupid.

baca f roof rack.

bacalao m cod; **~ a la llauna** dish of salt cod cooked in a metal pan with garlic, parsley, tomato, oil and salt; **~ al pil-pil** Basque dish of salt cod cooked slowly in an earthenware dish with olive oil and garlic; **~ con sanfaina** Catalan dish of salt cod in a ratatouille sauce; **~ a la vizcaína** Basque dish of salt cod baked with a thick sauce of olive oil, garlic, paprika, onions, tomato and red peppers.

bacán adj (Amér) elegant ♦ m (Amér) dandy.

bachillerato m (former) course of secondary studies for academically orientated 14 to 16-year-olds.

bacinica f (Amér) chamber pot.

bádminton m badminton.

bafle m loudspeaker.

bahía f bay.

bailar vt & vi to dance; **el pie me baila en el zapato** my shoe is too big for me.

bailarín, -ina *m, f (de ballet)* ballet dancer; *(de otras danzas)* dancer.

baile *m (danza)* dance; *(fiesta)* ball.

baja *f (por enfermedad)* sick leave; **dar de ~** *(en empresa)* to lay off; *(en asociación, club)* to expel; **darse de ~** to resign; **estar de ~** to be on sick leave.

bajada *f* descent; **~ de bandera** minimum fare.

bajar *vt (lámpara, cuadro, etc)* to take down; *(cabeza, mano, voz, persiana)* to lower; *(música, radio, volumen)* to turn down; *(escalera)* to go down* ♦ *vi (disminuir)* to go down □ **bajar de** *v + prep (de avión, tren)* to get off; *(de coche)* to get out of.

bajío *m (Amér)* low-lying land.

bajo, -ja *adj (persona)* short; *(objeto, cifra, precio)* low; *(sonido)* soft* ♦ *m (instrumento)* bass* ♦ *adv (hablar)* quietly* ♦ *prep (físicamente)* under; *(con temperaturas)* below □ **bajos** *mpl (de un edificio)* ground floor *(sg)*.

bala *f* bullet.

balacear *vt (Amér)* to shoot.

balacera *f (Amér)* shootout.

balada *f* ballad.

balance *m (de asunto, situación)* outcome; *(de un negocio)* balance; **hacer ~ de** to take stock of.

balancín *m (mecedora)* rocking chair; *(en el jardín)* swing hammock.

balanza *f (para pesar)* scales *(pl)*.

balar *vi* to bleat.

balcón *m* balcony.

balde *m* bucket; **de ~** free (of charge); **en ~** in vain.

baldosa *f (en la calle)* paving stone; *(en interior)* floor tile.

Baleares *fpl:* **las (islas) ~** the Balearic Islands.

balido *m* bleat.

ballena *f* whale.

ballet [baˈle] *m* ballet.

balneario *m (con baños termales)* spa; *(Amér: con piscinas, etc)* = lido.

---

i BALNEARIO

In South America, a "balneario" is a place where there are several open-air swimming pools and cheap facilities for sunbathing, eating and drinking etc.

---

balón *m* ball.

baloncesto *m* basketball.

balonmano *m* handball.

balonvolea *m* volleyball.

balsa *f (embarcación)* raft; *(de agua)* pond.

bálsamo *m* balsam.

bambú *m* bamboo.

banana *f* banana.

banca *f (institución)* banks *(pl)*; *(profesión)* banking; *(en juegos)* bank.

banco *m (para dinero)* bank; *(para sentarse)* bench; *(de iglesia)* pew; *(de peces)* shoal; **~ de arena** sandbank.

banda *f (cinta)* ribbon; *(franja)* stripe; *(lado)* side; *(en fútbol)* touchline; *(de músicos)* band; *(de delincuentes)* gang; **~ sonora** soundtrack.

bandeja f tray.

bandera f flag.

banderilla f (en toros) banderilla, barbed dart thrust into bull's back; (para comer) hors d'oeuvre on a stick.

banderín m pennant.

bandido m (ladrón) bandit; (fam: pillo) rascal.

bando m (en partido) side; (de alcalde) edict.

banjo m banjo.

banquero m banker.

banqueta f stool.

bañador m (para mujeres) swimsuit; (para hombres) swimming trunks (pl).

bañar vt (persona) to bath; (cosa) to soak; (suj: luz) to bathe; (suj: mar) to wash the coast of □ **bañarse** vpr (en río, playa, piscina) to go for a swim; (en el baño) to have a bath.

bañera f bath (tub).

bañista f bather.

baño m (en bañera, de vapor, espuma) bath; (en playa, piscina) swim; (espacio, habitación) bathroom; (de oro, pintura) coat; (de chocolate) coating; **al ~ maría** cooked in a bain-marie; **darse un ~** to have a bath □ **baños** mpl (balneario) spa (sg).

bar m bar; **~ musical** bar with live music.

baraja f pack (of cards).

BARAJA ESPAÑOLA

The Spanish deck contains 48 cards divided into 4 suits of 12 cards each. The symbols of the four suits are gold coins, wooden clubs, swords and goblets. In each suit, the cards called "sota", "caballo" and "rey" correspond roughly to the jack, queen and king in a standard deck.

barajar vt (naipes) to shuffle; (posibilidades) to consider; (datos, números) to marshal.

baranda f handrail.

barandilla f handrail.

baratija f trinket.

barato, -ta adj cheap ♦ adv cheaply.

barba f beard; **por ~** per head.

barbacoa f barbecue; **a la ~** barbecued.

barbaridad f (crueldad) cruelty; (disparate) stupid thing; **una ~** loads; **¡qué ~!** how terrible!

barbarie f (incultura) barbarism; (crueldad) cruelty.

bárbaro, -ra adj (cruel) cruel; (fam: estupendo) brilliant.

barbería f barber's (shop).

barbero m barber.

barbilla f chin.

barbudo, -da adj bearded.

barca f small boat; **~ de pesca** fishing boat.

barcaza f lighter.

Barcelona s Barcelona.

barco m (más pequeño) boat; (más grande) ship; **~ de vapor** steamboat; **~ de vela** sailing ship.

barítono m baritone.

barman m barman.

barniz (pl -ces) m varnish.

barnizado, -da adj varnished.

barnizar vt (madera) to varnish; (loza, cerámica) to glaze.

barómetro m barometer.

barquillo m cone.

barra f bar; (de turrón, helado, etc) block; ~ **de labios** lipstick; ~ **de pan** baguette; ~ **libre** unlimited drink for a fixed price.

barraca f (chabola) shack; (para feria) stall.

barranco m (precipicio) precipice.

barrendero, -ra m, f road sweeper.

barreño m washing-up bowl.

barrer vt to sweep.

barrera f (obstáculo) barrier; (de tren) crossing gate; (en toros) low wall encircling central part of bullring.

barriada f area.

barriga f belly.

barril m barrel.

barrio m (de población) area; (Amér: suburbio) poor area; ~ **chino** red light district; ~ **comercial** shopping district.

barro m (fango) mud; (en cerámica) clay.

barroco, -ca adj & m baroque.

bártulos mpl things, stuff (sg).

barullo m racket.

basarse: basarse en v i prep to be based on.

bascas fpl (náuseas) nausea (sg).

báscula f scales (pl).

base f (de cuerpo, objeto) base; (de edificio) foundations (pl); (fundamento, origen) basis; **a ~ de** by (means of); ~ **de datos** database.

básico, -ca adj basic.

basta interj that's enough!

bastante adv (suficientemente) enough; (muy) quite, pretty ♦ adj (suficiente) enough; (en cantidad) quite a few.

bastar vi to be enough; **basta con decírselo** it's enough to tell him; **basta con estos dos** these two are enough ❑ **bastarse** vpr: ~**se para hacer algo** to be able to do sthg o.s.

bastardo, -da adj bastard.

bastidores mpl: **entre ~** behind the scenes.

basto, -ta adj coarse ❑ **bastos** mpl (naipes) suit in Spanish deck of cards bearing wooden clubs.

bastón m (para andar) walking stick; (de mando) baton.

basura f rubbish (Br), garbage (Am).

basurero, -ra m, f dustman (f dustwoman) (Br), garbage collector (Am) ♦ m rubbish dump.

bata f (de casa) housecoat; (para baño, etc) dressing gown; (de médico, científico) coat.

batalla f battle; **de ~** everyday.

batería f battery; (en música) drums (pl); ~ **de cocina** pots and pans (pl).

batido m milkshake.

batidora f mixer.

batín m short dressing gown.

batir vt (nata) to whip; (marca, huevos) to beat; (récord) to break.

batuta f baton.

baúl m (caja) trunk; (Amér: maletero) boot (Br), trunk (Am).

bautismo m baptism.

bautizar vt (en religión) to baptize; (dar un nombre) to christen.

bautizo m (ceremonia) baptism; (fiesta) christening party.

baya f berry.

bayeta f cloth.

bayoneta f bayonet.

bazar m bazaar.

beato, -ta adj (santo) blessed; (piadoso) devout; (fam: tonto) simple-minded.

beba f (Amér: fam) little girl.

bebé m baby.

beber vt & vi to drink.

bebida f drink.

bebido, -da adj drunk.

bebito, -ta m, f (Amér) new-born baby.

beca f (del gobierno) grant; (de fundación privada) scholarship.

becario, -ria m, f (del gobierno) grant holder; (de fundación privada) scholarship holder.

becerro, -rra m, f calf.

bechamel f béchamel sauce.

bedel m caretaker (Br), janitor (Am).

begonia f begonia.

beige [beiʃ] adj inv beige.

béisbol m baseball.

belén m crib.

belga adj & mf Belgian.

Bélgica s Belgium.

bélico, -ca adj war (antes de s).

belleza f beauty.

bello, -lla adj (hermoso) beautiful; (bueno) fine.

bellota f acorn.

bendecir vt to bless.

bendición f blessing.

bendito, -ta adj holy ♦ m, f (bobo) simple soul.

beneficencia f charity.

beneficiar vt to benefit ❑ **beneficiarse de** v + prep to do well out of.

beneficio m (bien) benefit; (ganancia) profit; **a ~ de** (concierto, gala) in aid of.

benéfico, -ca adj (gala, rifa) charity (antes de s); (institución) charitable.

benevolencia f benevolence.

benévolo, -la adj benevolent.

bengala f flare.

berberechos mpl cockles.

berenjena f aubergine; **~s rellenas** stuffed aubergines (usually with mince or rice).

bermudas mpl Bermuda shorts.

berrinche m tantrum.

berza f cabbage.

besar vt to kiss ❑ **besarse** vpr to kiss.

beso m kiss; **dar un ~** to give a kiss.

bestia adj (bruto) rude; (ignorante) thick ♦ mf brute ♦ f (animal) beast.

besugo m sea bream.

betún m (para calzado) shoe polish.

biberón m (baby's) bottle.

Biblia f Bible.

bibliografía f bibliography.

biblioteca f library.

bibliotecario, -ria m, f librarian.

bicarbonato m bicarbonate of soda.

bíceps m inv biceps.

bicho m (animal pequeño) creature, beast; (insecto) bug; (pillo) little terror.

bici f (fam) bike.

bicicleta f bicycle.

bicolor adj two-coloured.

bidé m bidet.

bidón m can.

bien m 1. (lo que es bueno) good. 2. (bienestar, provecho) good; **hacer el ~** to do good.

♦ adv 1. (como es debido, correcto) well; **has actuado ~** you did the right thing; **habla ~ inglés** she speaks English well. 2. (expresa opinión favorable) well; **estar ~** (de salud) to be well; (de aspecto) to be nice; (de calidad) to be good; (de comodidad) to be comfortable. 3. (suficiente): **estar ~** to be enough. 4. (muy) very; **quiero un vaso de agua ~ fría** I'd like a nice, cold glass of water. 5. (vale, de acuerdo) all right.

♦ adj inv (adinerado) well-to-do.

♦ conj 1.: **~ ... ~** either ... or; **entrega el carta ~ a mi padre, ~ a mi madre** give the receipt to either my father or my mother. 2. (en locuciones): **más ~** rather; **¡está ~ (vale)** all right then!; (es suficiente) that's enough; **¡muy ~!** very good!

❑ **bienes** mpl (patrimonio) property (sg); (productos) goods; **~es de consumo** consumer goods; **~es inmuebles** O **raíces** real estate (sg).

bienal adj biennial.

bienestar m wellbeing.

bienvenida f welcome.

bienvenido, -da adj welcome

♦ interj welcome!

bife m (Amér) steak.

bifocal adj bifocal.

bigote m moustache.

bigotudo, -da adj moustachioed.

bigudí m curler.

bilingüe adj bilingual.

billar m (juego) billiards; (sala) billiard hall; **~ americano** pool

billete m (de dinero) note (Br), bill (Am); (de transporte) ticket; (de lotería) lottery ticket; **~ de ida y vuelta** return (ticket) (Br), round-trip (ticket) (Am); **~ sencillo** single (ticket) (Br), one-way (ticket) (Am).

billetero m wallet.

billón m billion (Br), trillion (Am).

bingo m (juego) bingo; (sala) bingo hall.

biodegradable adj biodegradable.

biografía f biography.

biográfico, -ca adj biographical.

biología f biology.

biopsia f biopsy.

bioquímica f biochemistry.

biquini m bikini.

birlar vt (fam) to swipe.

birra f (fam) beer.

birria f (fam: persona) sight; (fam: cosa) monstrosity; (Amér: carne) barbecued meat.

bisabuelo, -la m, f great-grandfather (f great-grandmother).

biscuit m sponge; **~ con chocolate** chocolate sponge cake; **~ glacé** ice cream made with eggs, milk, *flour and sugar.*

bisexual *adj* bisexual.

bisnieto, -ta *m, f* great-grandson (f great-granddaughter).

bisonte *m* bison.

bistec *m* steak; ~ **a la plancha** grilled steak; ~ **de ternera** veal cutlet.

bisturí *m* scalpel.

bisutería *f* imitation jewellery.

bíter *m* bitters.

bizco, -ca *adj* cross-eyed.

bizcocho *m* sponge.

blanca *f:* **estar sin** ~ *(fam)* to be broke, → **blanco.**

blanco, -ca *adj & m, f* white ♦ *m (color)* white; *(diana, objetivo)* target; **dar en el** ~ *(acertar)* to hit the nail on the head; **en** ~ *(sin dormir)* sleepless; *(sin memoria)* blank.

blando, -da *adj* soft; *(carne)* tender; *(débil)* weak.

blanquear *vt (pared)* to whitewash; *(ropa)* to bleach.

blindado, -da *adj (puerta, edificio)* armour-plated; *(coche)* armoured.

blindar *vt* to armour-plate.

bloc *m (de notas)* notepad; *(de dibujo)* sketchpad.

bloque *m* block; ~ **de pisos** block of flats.

bloquear *vt (cuenta, crédito)* to freeze; *(por nieve, inundación)* to cut off; *(propuesta, reforma)* to block ❑

bloquearse *vpr (mecanismo)* to jam; *(dirección)* to lock; *(persona)* to have a mental block.

bloqueo *m (mental)* mental block; *(económico, financiero)* blockade.

blusa *f* blouse.

bluyines *mpl (Amér)* jeans.

bobada *f* stupid thing; **decir** ~**s** to talk nonsense.

bobina *f (de automóvil)* coil; *(de hilo)* reel.

bobo, -ba *adj (tonto)* stupid; *(ingenuo)* naïve.

boca *f* mouth; ~ **a** ~ mouth-to-mouth resuscitation; ~ **de incendios** hydrant; ~ **de metro** tube entrance *(Br)*, subway entrance *(Am)*; ~ **abajo** face down; ~ **arriba** face up.

bocacalle *f (entrada)* entrance (to a street); *(calle)* side street.

bocadillo *m* sandwich.

bocado *m (comida)* mouthful; *(mordisco)* bite.

bocata *m (fam)* sarnie.

boceto *m (de cuadro, dibujo, edificio)* sketch; *(de texto)* rough outline. ♦

bochorno *m (calor)* stifling heat; *(vergüenza)* embarrassment.

bochornoso, -sa *adj (caluroso)* muggy; *(vergonzoso)* embarrassing.

bocina *f (de coche)* horn; *(Amér: de teléfono)* receiver.

boda *f* wedding; ~**s de oro** golden wedding *(sg)*; ~**s de plata** silver wedding *(sg)*.

bodega *f (para vinos)* wine cellar; *(tienda)* wine shop; *(bar)* bar; *(de avión, barco)* hold; *(Amér: almacén)* warehouse.

bodegón *m (pintura)* still life.

bodrio *m (despec: porquería)* rubbish; *(comida)* pigswill.

bofetada *f* slap (in the face).

bogavante *m* lobster.

bohemio, -mia *adj* bohemian.

bohío m (Amér) hut.

boicot (pl boicots) m boycott; **hacer el ~ a** to boycott.

boicotear vt to boycott.

boina f beret.

bola f (cuerpo esférico) ball; (fam: mentira) fib; (Amér fam: rumor) racket; (Amér: fam: lío) muddle; **hacerse ~s** (Amér: fam) to get into a muddle.

bolera f bowling alley.

bolero m bolero.

boletería f (Amér) box office.

boletín m (informativo) bulletin; (de suscripción) subscription form.

boleto m ticket.

boli m (fam) Biro®.

bolígrafo m Biro®.

Bolivia s Bolivia.

boliviano, -na adj & m, f Bolivian.

bollería f (tienda) cake shop.

bollo m (dulce) bun; (de pan) roll.

bolos mpl (juego) skittles.

bolsa f (de plástico, papel, tela) bag; (en economía) stock market; **~ de basura** bin liner; **~ de viaje** travel bag.

bolsillo m pocket; **de ~** pocket (antes de s).

bolso m (de mujer) handbag.

boludez f (Amér) stupid thing.

boludo, -da m, f (Amér) idiot.

bomba f (explosivo) bomb; (máquina) pump; **~ atómica** nuclear bomb; **pasarlo ~** to have a great time

bombardear vt to bombard.

bombardeo m bombardment.

bombero m fireman.

bombilla f light bulb.

bombo m (de lotería, rifa) drum; (tambor) bass drum; **a ~ y platillo** with a lot of hype.

bombón m (golosina) chocolate; (persona) stunner.

bombona f cylinder; **~ de butano** gas cylinder.

bombonería f sweetshop.

bonanza f (de tiempo) fair weather; (de mar) calm at sea; (prosperidad) prosperity.

bondad f goodness; **tenga la ~ de** (formal) please be so kind as to.

bondadoso, -sa adj kind.

bonificación f discount.

bonificar vt to give a discount of.

bonito, -ta adj (persona, cosa) pretty; (cantidad) considerable ◆ m (pescado) tuna; **~ con tomate** tuna in a tomato sauce.

bono m (vale) voucher.

bonobús m multiple-journey ticket.

bonoloto f Spanish lottery.

---

i | BONOLOTO

In this Spanish state-run lottery, participants try to guess a combination of six numbers between one and forty-nine. A ticket contains eight grids of forty-nine boxes, each grid being equivalent to one entry. The "bonoloto" is drawn four times a week.

---

bonsai m bonsai.

boñiga f cowpat.

boquerones *mpl* (fresh) anchovies.

boquete *m* hole.

boquilla *f* (del cigarrillo) cigarette holder; (de flauta, trompeta, etc) mouthpiece; (de tubo, aparato) nozzle; **de ~** insincere.

borda *f* gunwale.

bordado, -da *adj* embroidered ♦ *m* embroidery; **salir ~** to turn out just right.

bordar *vt* (en costura) to embroider; (ejecutar perfectamente) to play to perfection.

borde *m* (extremo) edge; (de carretera) side; (de vaso, botella) rim ♦ *adj* (despec) grouchy, miserable; **al ~ de** on the verge of.

bordear *vt* (rodear) to border.

bordillo *m* kerb.

bordo *m*: **a ~ (de)** on board.

borla *f* (adorno) tassel; (para maquillaje) powder puff.

borrachera *f* drunkenness; **coger una ~** to get drunk.

borracho, -cha *adj & m, f* drunk.

borrador *m* (boceto) rough draft; (goma) rubber (Br), eraser (Am).

borrar *vt* (con goma) to rub out (Br), to erase (Am); (en ordenador) to delete; (en casete) to erase; (dar de baja) to strike off.

borrasca *f* thunderstorm.

borrón *m* blot.

borroso, -sa *adj* blurred.

bosque *m* (pequeño) wood; (grande) forest.

bostezar *vi* to yawn.

bostezo *m* yawn.

bota *f* (calzado) boot; (de vino) small leather container in which wine is kept; **~s de agua** wellington boots; **ponerse las ~s** to stuff o.s.

botana *f* (Amér) snack, tapa.

botánica *f* botany.

botánico, -ca *adj* botany.

bote *m* (de vidrio) jar; (de metal) can; (de plástico) bottle; (embarcación) boat; (salto) jump; **~ salvavidas** lifeboat; **tener a alguien en el ~** to have sb eating out of one's hand.

botella *f* bottle.

botellín *m* small bottle.

botijo *m* earthenware jug.

botín *m* (calzado) ankle boot; (tras un robo, atraco) loot.

botiquín *m* (maletín) first-aid kit; (mueble) first-aid cupboard.

botón *m* button ❏ **botones** *m inv* bellboy.

bouquet [bu'ke] *m* bouquet.

boutique [bu'tik] *f* boutique.

bóveda *f* vault.

bovino, -na *adj* (en carnicería) beef (antes de s).

boxear *vi* to box.

boxeo *m* boxing.

boya *f* (en el mar) buoy.

bragas *fpl* knickers.

braguetu *f* flies (pl) (Br), zipper (Am).

bramar *vi* to bellow.

brandada *f*: **~ de bacalao** thick fish soup made with cod and milk.

brandy *m* brandy.

brasa *f* ember; **a la ~** barbecued.

brasero *m* brazier.

brasier *m* (Amér) bra.

Brasil s Brazil.

brasilero, -ra adj & m, f (Amér) Brazilian.

bravo, -va adj (toro) wild; (persona) brave; (mar) rough ◆ interj bravo!

braza f (en natación) breaststroke.

brazalete m bracelet.

brazo m arm; (de lámpara, candelabro) branch; **con los ~s abiertos** with open arms; **de ~s cruzados** without lifting a finger; **~ de gitano ~** swiss roll.

brebaje m concoction.

brecha f (abertura) hole; (herida) gash.

brécol m broccoli.

breve adj brief; **en ~** shortly.

brevedad f shortness.

brevemente adv briefly.

brezo m heather.

bricolaje m do-it-yourself.

brida f bridle.

brigada f (de limpieza) team; (de la policía) brigade.

brillante adj (material, shiny; (persona, trabajo, actuación) brilliant ◆ m (sur) diamond.

brillantina f Brylcreem®.

brillar vi to shine.

brillo m shine; **sacar ~** to polish.

brilloso, -sa adj (Amér) shiny.

brindar vi to drink a toast ◆ vt to offer; **~ por** to drink to ▢ **brindarse** vpr: **~se a** to offer to.

brindis m inv toast.

brío m spirit.

brisa f breeze.

británico, -ca adj British ◆ m,

f British person; **los ~s** the British.

brizna f (de hierba) blade.

broca f (drill) bit.

brocal m parapet (of well).

brocha f (para pintar) brush; (para afeitarse) shaving brush.

broche m (joya) brooch; (de vestido) fastener.

brocheta f (plato) shish kebab; (aguja) skewer.

broma f (chiste) joke; (travesura) prank; **gastar una ~ a alguien** to play a joke on sb, **ir en ~** to be joking; **tomar algo a ~** not to take sthg seriously; **~ pesada** bad joke.

bromear vi to joke.

bromista adj fond of playing jokes ◆ mf joker.

bronca f (jaleo) row; **echar una ~ a alguien** to tell sb off.

bronce m bronze.

bronceado m tan.

bronceador m suntan lotion.

broncearse vpr to get a tan.

bronquios mpl bronchial tubes.

bronquitis f inv bronchitis.

brotar vi (plantas) to sprout; (lágrimas, agua) to well up.

brote m (de planta) bud; (de enfermedad) outbreak.

bruja f (fam: fea y vieja) old hag, → **brujo**.

brujería f witchcraft.

brujo, -ja m, f wizard (f witch).

brújula f compass.

brusco, -ca adj (repentino) sudden; (grosero) brusque.

brusquedad f (imprevisión) suddenness; (grosería) brusqueness.

brutal adj (salvaje) brutal; (enorme) huge.

brutalidad f (brusquedad) brutishness; (salvajada) brutal act.

bruto, -ta adj (ignorante) stupid; (violento) brutish; (rudo) rude; (peso, precio, sueldo) gross.

bucear vi to dive.

buche m (de ave) crop.

bucle m (de cabello) curl; (de cinta, cuerda) loop.

bucólico, -ca adj country (antes de s).

bueno, -na (compar, superl mejor) adj good ◆ adv (conforme) all right ◆ interj (Amér: al teléfono) hello!; ¡buenas! hello!; ¡buen día! (Amér) hello!; ¡buenas noches! (despedida) good night!; ¡buenas tardes! (hasta las cinco) good afternoon!; (después de las cinco) good evening!; ¡~ días! (hola) hello!; (por la mañana) good morning!; hace buen día it's a nice day.

buey m ox; ~ de mar spider crab.

búfalo m buffalo.

bufanda f scarf.

bufete m (despacho) lawyer's practice.

buffet m buffet; "~ libre" "eat as much as you can from the buffet".

buhardilla f (desván) attic; (ventana) dormer (window).

búho m owl.

buitre m vulture.

bujía f (de coche) spark plug; (vela) candle.

bula f (papal) bull.

bulbo m bulb.

bulerías fpl Andalusian song with lively rhythm accompanied by clapping.

bulevar m boulevard.

Bulgaria s Bulgaria.

bulla f racket.

bullicio m (actividad) hustle and bustle; (ruido) hubbub.

bullicioso, -sa adj (persona) rowdy; (lugar) busy.

bulto m (volumen) bulk; (paquete) package; (en superficie) bump; (en piel, cabeza) lump; "un solo ~ de mano" "one item of hand luggage only".

bumerang [bume'raŋ] m boomerang.

bungalow [buŋga'lo] m bungalow.

buñuelo m = doughnut; ~ de bacalao type of cod dumpling; ~ de viento = doughnut.

BUP m (abrev de Bachillerato Unificado Polivalente) academically-orientated secondary school course taught in Spain for pupils aged 14-17.

buque m ship.

burbuja f (de gas, aire) bubble; (flotador) rubber ring.

burdel m brothel.

burgués, -esa adj middle-class ◆ m, f middle class person.

burguesía f middle class.

burla f taunt.

burlar vt (eludir) to evade; (ley) to flout ❏ **burlarse de** v + prep to make fun of.

buró m (Amér) bedside table.

burrada f stupid thing.

burro, -rra m, f (animal) donkey; (persona tonta) dimwit.

buscar *vt* to look for; **ir a ~** *(personas)* to pick up; *(cosas)* to go and get.

busto *m (en escultura, pintura)* bust; *(parte del cuerpo)* chest.

butaca *f (asiento)* armchair; *(en cine, teatro)* seat.

butano *m* butane (gas).

butifarra *f type of Catalan pork sausage;* **~ con judías** barbecued "butifarra" with haricot beans.

buzo *m (persona)* diver; *(traje)* overalls *(pl)*.

buzón *m* letterbox.

c/ *(abrev de calle)* St; *(abrev de cuenta)* a/c.

cabales *mpl*: **no está en sus ~** he's not in his right mind.

cabalgada *f* mounted expedition.

cabalgar *vi* to ride.

cabalgata *f* procession.

caballa *f* mackerel.

caballería *f (cuerpo militar)* cavalry; *(animal)* mount.

caballero *m (persona, cortés)* gentleman; *(formal: señor)* Sir; *(de Edad Media)* knight; **"~s"** *(en aseos)* "gents"; *(en probadores)* "men"; *(en tienda de ropa)* "menswear".

caballete *m (para mesa, tabla)* trestle; *(para cuadro, pizarra)* easel.

caballito *m*: **~ de mar** sea horse; **~ de totora** *(Amér)* small fishing boat made of reeds used by Peruvian and Bolivian Indians □ **caballitos** *mpl (tiovivo)* merry-go-round *(sg)*.

caballo *m (animal)* horse; *(en la baraja)* ≃ queen; *(en ajedrez)* knight; **~s de vapor** horsepower.

cabaña *f* cabin.

cabaret *m* cabaret.

cabecear *vi (negando)* to shake one's head; *(afirmando)* to nod one's head; *(durmiéndose)* to nod off; *(barco)* to pitch; *(coche)* to lurch.

cabecera *f (de la cama)* headboard; *(en periódico)* headline; *(en libro, lista)* heading; *(parte principal)* head.

cabecilla *mf* ringleader.

cabellera *f* long hair.

cabello *m* hair; **~ de ángel** *sweet consisting of strands of pumpkin coated in syrup.*

caber *vi* to fit; *(ser posible)* to be possible; **no cabe duda** there is no doubt about it; **no me caben los pantalones** my trousers are too small for me.

cabestrillo *m* sling.

cabeza *f* head; **~ de ajos** head of garlic; **~ de familia** head of the family; **~ rapada** skinhead; **por ~** per head; **perder la ~** to lose one's head; **sentar la ~** to settle down; **traer de ~** to drive mad

cabezada *f*: **dar una ~** to have a nap.

cabida *f*: **tener ~** to have room.

cabina *f (booth)* booth; **~ telefónica** phone box *(Br)*, phone booth.

cable *m* cable; **por ~** by cable; **~**

eléctrico electric cable.
cabo m (en geografía) cape; (cuerda) rope; (militar, policía) corporal; **al ~ de** after; **atar ~s** to put two and two together; **~ suelto** loose end; **de ~ a rabo** from beginning to end; **llevar algo a ~** to carry sthg out.

cabra f goat; **estar como una ~** to be off one's head.

cabré v → caber.

cabrear vt (vulg) to piss off ❏
cabrearse vpr (vulg) to get pissed off.

cabreo m (vulg): **coger un ~** to get pissed off.

cabría v → caber.

cabrito m kid (goat).

cabrón m (vulg) bastard (f bitch).

cabronada f (vulg) dirty trick.

caca f (excremento) pooh; (suciedad) dirty thing.

cacahuete m peanut.

cacao m (chocolate) cocoa; (fam: jaleo) racket; (de labios) lip salve.

cacarear vi to cluck.

cacería f hunt.

cacerola f pot.

cachalote m sperm whale.

cacharro m (de cocina) pot; (fam: trasto) junk; (fam: coche) banger.

cachear vt to frisk.

cachemir m cashmere.

cachete m slap.

cachivache m knick-knack.

cacho m (fam: trozo) piece; (Amér: cuerno) horn.

cachondearse: cachondearse de v + prep (fam) to take the mickey out of.

cachondeo m (fam): **estar de ~** to be joking; **ir de ~** to go out on the town.

cachondo, -da adj (fam: alegre) funny.

cachorro, -rra m, f puppy.

cacique m local political boss.

cactus m cactus.

cada adj (para distribuir) each; (en frecuencia) every; **~ vez más** more and more; **~ vez más corto** shorter and shorter; **~ uno** each one.

cadáver m corpse.

cadena f chain; (de televisión) channel; (de radio) station; (de música) sound system; (de montañas) range; **en ~** (accidente) multiple.

cadencia f rhythm.

cadera f hip.

cadete m cadet.

caducar vi (alimento) to pass its sell-by date; (ley, documento, etc) to expire.

caducidad f expiry.

caduco, -ca adj (persona) very old-fashioned; **de hoja caduca** deciduous.

caer vi to fall; (día, tarde, verano) to draw to a close; **~ bien/mal** (comentario, noticia) to go down well/badly; **me cae bien/mal** (persona) I like/don't like him; **cae cerca de aquí** it's not far from here; **dejar ~ algo** to drop sthg ❏ **caer en** v + prep (respuesta, solución) to hit on, to find; (caer) to be on; (mes) to be in; **~ en la cuenta** to realize; **caerse** vpr (persona) to fall down.

café m (bebida, grano) coffee;

(establecimiento) cafe; ~ **descafeina-**
do decaffeinated coffee; ~ **irlandés**
Irish coffee; ~ **con leche** white coffee; ~ **molido** ground coffee; ~
solo black coffee.

ℹ️ CAFÉ

Spanish coffee is usually of the
strong, expresso variety, served
in very small cups. A small cup of
black coffee is called "un solo". A
"solo" with a tiny amount of milk
added is called "un cortado". "Un
carajillo" is a black coffee with a
dash of liqueur. "Café con leche" is a
large cup filled half with coffee and
half with hot milk and is usually
drunk at breakfast. In South
America, "café de olla", which contains sugar, cinnamon and other
spices, is also common.

cafebrería f *(Amér)* cafe cum
bookshop.

ℹ️ CAFEBRERÍA

The South American "cafebrería"
is a cafe which, in addition
to serving drinks and snacks, also
sells books, magazines and records.
"Cafebrerías" are often the venue for
"tertulias", poetry readings, confer-
ences and concerts.

cafeína f caffeine.
cafetera f *(para servir)* coffee
pot; *(en bares)* expresso machine;
(eléctrica) coffee machine.
cafetería f cafe.

cagar vi *(vulg)* to shit ◆ vt *(vulg)*
to fuck up.
caída f fall.
caído, -da adj *(abatido)* down-
hearted; los ~s the fallen.
caiga v → **caer.**
caimán m alligator.
caja f *(recipiente)* box; *(para trans-*
porte, embalaje) crate; *(de banco)*
cashier's desk; *(de supermercado)*
till, *(de instrumento musical)* body; ~
de ahorros savings bank; ~ **de**
cambios gearbox; ~ **de herramien-**
tas tool-box; "~ **rápida**" ≃ "hand-
baskets only", *sign at till for cus-*
tomers with any a small number of
items; ~ **registradora** cash register.
cajero, -ra m, f *(de banco)* teller;
(de tienda) cashier; ~ **automático**
cash point
cajetilla f packet ◆ m *(Amér:*
despec) city slicker.
cajón m *(de mueble)* drawer; ~ **de**
sastre muddle.
cajonera f chest of drawers.
cajuela f *(Amér)* boot *(Br)*, trunk
(Am).
cal f lime.
cala f *(ensenada)* cove.
calabacín m courgette *(Br)*,
zucchini *(Am)*; ~ **relleno** courgette
stuffed with mince.
calabaza f pumpkin.
calabozo m cell.
calada f drag.
calamar m squid; ~**es a la plan-**
cha grilled squid; ~**es a la romana**
squid rings fried in batter; ~**es en su**
tinta squid cooked in its own ink.
calambre m *(de un músculo)*
cramp; *(descarga eléctrica)* shock.

calamidad f calamity; **ser una ~** (persona) to be a dead loss.

calar vt (suj: lluvia, humedad) to soak; (suj: frío) to penetrate ❑ **calar en** v + prep (ideas, sentimiento) to have an impact on; **calarse** vpr (mojarse) to get soaked; (suj: vehículo) to stall; (sombrero) to jam on.

calato, -ta adj naked.

calaveras fpl (Amér) rear lights.

calcar vt (dibujo) to trace; (imitar) to copy.

calcáreo, -a adj lime.

calcetín m sock.

calcio m calcium.

calcomanía f transfer.

calculador, -ra adj calculating.

calculadora f calculator.

calcular vt (cantidad) to calculate; (suponer) to reckon.

caldear vt (local) to heat; (ambiente) to liven up.

caldera f boiler.

calderilla f small change.

caldo m broth; **~ gallego** thick soup made with meat.

calefacción f heating; **~ central** central heating.

calefactor m heater.

calendario m calendar; (de actividades) timetable.

calentador m heater.

calentamiento m (en deporte) warm-up.

calentar vt (agua, leche, comida) to heat up; (fig: pegar) to hit; (fig: incitar) to incite ❑ **calentarse** vpr (en deporte) to warm up; (excitarse) to get turned on.

calesitas fpl (Amér) merry-go-round (sg).

calibrar vt to gauge.

calibre m (importancia) importance.

calidad f quality; (clase) class; **de ~** quality; **en ~ de** in one's capacity as.

cálido, -da adj warm; (agradable, acogedor) friendly.

caliente adj hot; **en ~** in the heat of the moment.

calificación f (en deportes) score; (de un alumno) mark.

calificar vt (trabajo, examen) to mark; **~ a alguien de algo** to call sb sthg.

caligrafía f (letra) handwriting.

cáliz m (de flor) calyx; (de misa) chalice.

callado, -da adj quiet.

callar vi to be quiet ♦ vt (secreto) to keep; (respuesta) to keep to o.s. ❑ **callarse** vpr (no hablar) to keep quiet; (dejar de hablar) to be quiet.

calle f (de población) street; (de carretera, en natación) lane; **dejar a alguien en la ~** to put sb out of a job; **~ abajo/arriba** down/up the street.

callejero, -ra adj street (antes de s) ♦ m street map.

callejón m (calle estrecha) alley; (en toros) passageway behind low wall encircling bullring; **~ sin salida** cul-de-sac.

callejuela f side street.

callo m (de pies) corn; (de manos) callous ❑ **callos** mpl tripe (sg); **~s a la madrileña** tripe cooked with black pudding, smoked pork sausage, onion *and peppers.*

calloso, -sa *adj* calloused.

calma *f* calm.

calmado, -da *adj* calm.

calmante *m* sedative.

calmar *vt* to calm ❑ **calmarse** *vpr* to calm down.

calor *m o f (temperatura elevada, sensación)* heat; *(tibieza, del hogar)* warmth; **hace ~** it's hot; **tener ~** to be hot.

caloría *f* calorie.

calumnia *f (oral)* slander; *(escrita)* libel.

calumniar *vt (oralmente)* to slander; *(por escrito)* to libel.

caluroso, -sa *adj (caliente)* hot; *(tibio, afectuoso, cariñoso)* warm.

calvario *m (sufrimiento)* ordeal.

calvicie *f* baldness.

calvo, -va *adj* bald ◆ *m* bald man.

calzada *f* road (surface); **"~ irregular"** "uneven road surface".

calzado *m* footwear; **"reparación de ~s"** "shoe repairs".

calzador *m* shoehorn.

calzar *vt (zapato, bota)* to put on; **¿qué número calza?** what size (shoe) do you take? ❑ **calzarse** *vpr* to put on.

calzoncillos *mpl* underpants.

calzones *mpl (Amér)* knickers.

cama *f* bed; **guardar ~** to be confined to bed; **~ individual** single bed; **~ de matrimonio** double bed.

camaleón *m* chameleon.

cámara[1] *f (para filmar)* camera; *(de diputados, senadores)* chamber; *(de neumático)* inner tube; **~ fotográfica** camera; **~ de vídeo**

video (camera).

cámara[2] *m* cameraman *(f* camerawoman).

camarada *mf (en el trabajo)* colleague.

camarero, -ra *m, f (de bar, restaurante)* waiter *(f* waitress); *(de hotel)* steward *(f* chambermaid).

camarón *m* shrimp.

camarote *m* cabin.

camastro *m* rickety bed.

cambiar *vt* to change; *(ideas, impresiones, etc)* to exchange ◆ *vi* to change; **~ de *(coche, vida)*** to change; *(domicilio)* to move ❑ **cambiarse** *vpr (de ropa)* to change; **~se de *(casa)*** to move; **~se de camisa** to change one's shirt

cambio *m* change; *(de ideas, propuestas, etc)* exchange; *(valor de moneda)* change rate; **en ~** on the other hand; **~ de marchas** gear change; **"~ (de moneda)"** "bureau de change"; **"~ de sentido"** sign *indicating a sliproad allowing drivers to change direction on a motorway.*

camello *m* camel.

camellón *m (Amér)* central reservation.

camembert ['kamember] *m* camembert.

camerino *m* dressing room.

camilla *f (para enfermo, herido)* stretcher.

caminante *mf* walker.

caminar *vi* to walk ◆ *vt* to travel.

caminata *f* long walk.

camino *m (vía)* road; *(recorrido)* path; *(medio)* way; **a medio ~** halfway; **~ de** on the way to; **ir**

por buen/mal ~ (ruta) to be going the right/wrong way; **ponerse en ~** to set off.

camión m (de mercancías) lorry (Br), truck (Am); (Amér: autobús) bus.

camionero, -ra m, f lorry driver (Br), trucker (Am).

camioneta f van.

camisa f shirt.

camisería f outfitter's (shop).

camisero, -ra adj with buttons down the front.

camiseta f (de verano) T-shirt; (ropa interior) vest.

camisola f (Amér) shirt.

camisón m nightdress.

camomila f camomile.

camorra f trouble.

campamento m camp.

campana f (de iglesia) bell; (de chimenea) chimney breast; (de cocina) hood.

campanario m belfry.

campaña f campaign.

campechano, -na adj goodnatured.

campeón, -ona m, f champion.

campeonato m championship; **de ~** terrific.

campera f (Amér) jacket.

campesino, -na m, f (agricultor) farmer; (muy pobre) peasant.

campestre adj country.

camping ['kampin] m (lugar) campsite; (actividad) camping; **ir de ~** to go camping.

campista mf camper.

campo m field; (campiña)

countryside; (de fútbol) pitch; (de golf) course; **~ de deportes** sports ground; **dejar el ~ libre** to leave the field open.

Campsa f Spanish state petrol company.

campus m campus.

camuflar vt to camouflage.

cana f grey hair; **tener ~s** to be going grey.

Canadá m: **(el) ~** Canada.

canadiense adj & mf Canadian.

canal m (para regar) canal; (en geografía) strait; (de televisión) channel; (de desagüe) pipe.

canalla mf swine.

canapé m canapé.

Canarias fpl: **(las islas) ~** the Canary Islands.

canario, -ria adj of/relating to the Canary Islands ◆ m, f Canary Islander ◆ m (pájaro) canary.

canasta f basket; (en naipes) canasta.

canastilla f (de recién nacido) layette.

cancela f wrought-iron gate.

cancelación f cancellation.

cancelar vt to cancel; (cuenta, deuda) to settle.

cáncer m cancer ❏ **Cáncer** m Cancer.

cancerígeno, -na adj carcinogenic.

cancha f court.

canciller m chancellor.

canción f song.

cancionero m songbook.

candado m padlock.

candela f (Amér) fire.

candelabro m candelabra.

candidato, -ta m, f: ~ (a) candidate (for).

candidatura f candidacy.

candil m (lámpara) oil lamp; (Amér: araña) chandelier.

candilejas fpl footlights.

caneca f (Amér) rubbish bin (Br), trashcan (Am).

canela f cinnamon.

canelones mpl cannelloni.

cangrejo m crab.

canguro m (animal) kangaroo ♦ mf (persona) babysitter.

caníbal mf cannibal.

canica f marble ❑ **canicas** fpl (juego) marbles.

canijo, -ja adj sickly.

canilla f (Amér) (grifo) tap; (pierna) leg.

canje m exchange.

canjeable adj exchangeable.

canjear vt to exchange; ~ algo por to exchange sthg for.

canoa f canoe.

canon m (de belleza, perfección) ideal.

canónico, -ca adj canon.

canoso, -sa adj grey-haired.

cansado, -da adj (fatigado, aburrido) tired; (pesado) tiring; **estar ~ (de)** to be tired (of).

cansador, -ra adj (Amér) tiring.

cansancio m tiredness.

cansar vt to tire ❑ **cansarse** vpr: ~se (de) (fatigarse) to get tired (from); (hastiarse) to get tired (of).

cantábrico, -ca adj Cantabrian ❑ **Cantábrico** m; **el Cantá-**brico the Cantabrian Sea.

cantante mf singer.

cantaor, -ra m, f flamenco singer.

cantar vt (canción) to sing; (premio) to call (out) ♦ vi to sing; (fig: confesar) to talk.

cántaro m large pitcher; **llover a ~s** to rain cats and dogs.

cantautor, -ra m, f singer-songwriter.

cante m: ~ flamenco o jondo flamenco singing.

cantera f (de piedra) quarry; (de profesionales) source.

cantidad f (medida) quantity; (importe) sum; (número) number ♦ adv a lot; **en ~** in abundance.

cantimplora f water bottle.

cantina f (en fábrica) canteen; (en estación de tren) buffet, station café.

canto m (arte) singing; (canción) song; (borde) edge, **de ~** edgeways; ~ rodado boulder.

canturrear vt & vi to sing softly.

caña f (tallo) cane; (de cerveza) small glass of beer; ~ **de azúcar** sugarcane; ~ **de pescar** fishing rod.

cáñamo m hemp.

cañaveral m sugar-cane plantation.

cañería f pipe.

caño m (de fuente) jet; (tubo) pipe; (Amér: grifo) tap.

cañón m (arma moderna) gun; (arma antigua) cannon; (de fusil) barrel; (entre montañas) canyon.

cañonazo m gunshot.

caoba f mahogany.

caos *m inv* chaos.

caótico, -ca *adj* chaotic.

capa *f (manto)* cloak; *(de pintura, barniz, chocolate)* coat; *(de la tierra, sociedad)* stratum; *(de torero)* cape; **~ de ozono** ozone layer; **a ~ y espada** *(defender)* tooth and nail; **andar de ~ caída** to be doing badly.

capacidad *f (de envase, aforo)* capacity; *(habilidad)* ability.

capacitado, -da *adj:* **estar ~ para** to be qualified to.

caparazón *m* shell.

capataz *(pl -ces) mf* foreman (f forewoman).

capaz, -ces *adj* capable; **ser ~ de** to be capable of.

capazo *m* large wicker basket.

capellán *m* chaplain.

capicúa *adj inv* reversible.

capilar *adj* hair *(antes de s).*

capilla *f* chapel.

capital *adj (importante)* supreme ♦ *m & f* capital.

capitalismo *m* capitalism.

capitalista *adj & mf* capitalist.

capitán, -ana *m, f* captain.

capitanía *f (edificio)* = field marshal's headquarters.

capitel *m* capital *(in architecture).*

capítulo *m* chapter.

capó *m* bonnet *(Br)*, hood *(Am).*

capón *m (animal)* capon; *(golpe)* rap.

capota *f* hood *(Br)*, top *(Am).*

capote *m (de torero)* cape.

capricho *m* whim; **darse un ~** to treat o.s.

caprichoso, -sa *adj* capricious.

Capricornio *m* Capricorn.

cápsula *f* capsule.

captar *vt (sonido, rumor)* to hear; *(persona)* to win over; *(explicación, idea)* to grasp; *(señal de radio, TV)* to receive.

capturar *vt* to capture.

capucha *f (de prenda de vestir)* hood; *(de pluma, bolígrafo)* cap.

capuchino, -na *adj & m, f* Capuchin ♦ *m* cappuccino.

capullo *m (de flor)* bud; *(de gusano)* cocoon.

cara *f (rostro)* face; *(de página, tela, luna, moneda)* side; **~ a ~** face to face; **de ~ a** *(frente a)* facing; **~ o cruz** heads or tails; **echar algo a ~ o cruz** to toss a coin for sthg; **dar la ~** to face the consequences; **echar en ~ algo a alguien** to reproach sb for sthg; **esta comida no tiene buena ~** this meal doesn't look very good; **plantar ~ a** to stand up to; **tener (mucha) ~** to have a cheek.

carabela *f* caravel.

carabina *f (arma)* rifle; *(fam: persona)* chaperone.

caracol *m* snail; **~es a la llauna** snails cooked in a pan with oil, garlic and parsley.

caracola *f* conch.

caracolada *f* dish made with snails.

carácter *m (modo de ser)* character; *(tipo)* nature; **tener mal/buen ~** to be bad-tempered/good-natured; **tener mucho/poco ~** to have a strong/weak personality.

característica *f* characteristic.

característico, -ca *adj* characteristic.

caracterizar *vt (identificar)* to characterize; *(representar)* to portray ❑ **caracterizarse por** *v + prep* to be characterized by.

caradura *adj inv (fam)* cheeky.

carajillo *m coffee with a dash of liqueur.*

caramba *interj (expresa sorpresa)* good heavens!; *(expresa enfado)* for heaven's sake!

carambola *f (in billiards);* **de ~** *(de casualidad)* by a fluke; *(de rebote)* indirectly.

caramelo *m (golosina)* sweet; *(azúcar fundido)* caramel.

carátula *f (de libro, revista)* front cover; *(de disco)* sleeve; *(de casete)* inlay card.

caravana *f (en carretera)* tailback; *(remolque)* caravan; **hacer ~** to sit in a tailback.

caravaning [karaβaniŋ] *m caravanning.*

caray *interj (expresa sorpresa)* good heavens!; *(expresa enfado, daño)* damn it!

carbón *m* coal.

carboncillo *m* charcoal.

carbono *m* carbon.

carburador *m* carburettor.

carburante *m* fuel.

carcajada *f* guffaw; **reír a ~s** to roar with laughter.

cárcel *f (prisón)* prison; **en la ~** in prison.

carcoma *f* woodworm.

cardenal *m (en religión)* cardinal; *(morado)* bruise.

cardíaco, -ca *adj* cardiac.

cardinal *adj* cardinal.

cardiólogo, -ga *m, f* cardiologist.

cardo *m (planta)* thistle; *(fam: persona)* prickly customer.

carecer: carecer de *v + prep* to lack.

carencia *f (ausencia)* lack; *(defecto)* deficiency.

careta *f* mask.

carey *m (de tortuga)* tortoiseshell.

carga *f (de barco, avión)* cargo; *(de tren, camión)* freight; *(peso)* load; *(para bolígrafo, mechero, pluma)* refill; *(de urna, explosivo, batería)* charge; *(responsabilidad)* burden; **"~ y descarga"** "loading and unloading".

cargado, -da *adj (cielo)* overcast; *(habitación, ambiente)* stuffy, *(bebida, infusión)* strong; **~ de** *(lleno de)* loaded with.

cargador, -ra *m, f* loader ♦ *m (de arma)* chamber; *(de batería)* charger.

cargar *vt (mercancía, bulto)* to load; *(bolígrafo, pluma, mechero)* to refill; *(tener capacidad para)* to hold; *(factura, deudas, batería)* to charge ♦ *vi (molestar)* to be annoying; **~ algo de** *(llenar)* to fill sthg with ❑ **cargar con** *v + prep (paquete)* to carry; *(responsabilidad)* to bear; *(consecuencia)* to accept; **cargar contra** *v + prep* to charge; **cargarse** *vpr (fam: estropear)* to break; *(fam: matar)* to bump off; *(fam: suspender)* to fail; *(ambiente)* to get stuffy; **cargarse de** *v + prep (llenarse de)* to fill up with.

cargo *m (cargo; (empleo, función)* post; **estar a ~ de** to be in charge of; **hacerse ~ de** *(responsabilizarse)* to take care of; *(asumir el control)* to take charge of; *(comprender)* to understand.

cargosear *vt (Amér)* to annoy.

cargoso, -sa *adj (Amér)* annoying.

cariado, -da *adj* decayed.

Caribe m: el ~ the Caribbean.

caribeño, -ña *adj* Caribbean.

caricatura *f* caricature.

caricia *f (a persona)* caress; *(a animal)* stroke.

caridad *f* charity.

caries *f inv* tooth decay.

cariño m *(afecto)* affection; *(cuidado)* loving care; *(apelativo)* love.

cariñoso, -sa *adj* affectionate.

carisma m charisma.

caritativo, -va *adj* charitable.

cariz m appearance.

carmín m *(para labios)* lipstick.

carnal *adj (pariente)* first.

Carnaval m Shrovetide.

carne *f (alimento)* meat; *(de persona, fruta)* flesh; ~ **de cerdo** pork; ~ **de cordero** lamb; ~ **de gallina** goose pimples *(pl)*; ~ **picada** mince *(Br)*, mincemeat *(Am)*; ~ **de ternera** veal; ~ **de vaca** beef.

carné m *(de club, partido)* membership card; ~ **de conducir** driving licence *(Br)*, driver's license *(Am)*; ~ **de identidad** identity card.

carnear *vt (Amér: reses)* to slaughter; *(fig: reses, personas)* to butcher.

carnero m ram.

carnicería *f (tienda)* butcher's

(shop); *(matanza)* carnage.

carnicero, -ra *f* butcher.

carnitas *fpl (Amér)* snack of spicy, fried meat in taco or bread.

caro, -ra *adj* expensive ♦ *adv* at a high price; **costar** ~ to be expensive.

carpa *f (de circo)* big top; *(para fiestas)* marquee; *(pez)* carp.

carpeta *f* file.

carpintería *f (oficio)* joinery; *(arte)* carpentry; *(taller)* joiner's workshop.

carpintero m *(profesional)* joiner; *(artista)* carpenter.

carrera *f (competición)* race; *(estudios)* degree course; *(profesión)* career; *(en medias, calcetines)* ladder *(Br)*, run *(Am)*; **a la** ~ at full speed.

carrerilla *f (carrera corta)* run-up; **de** ~ *(fam)* by heart.

carreta *f* cart.

carrete m *(de fotografías)* roll; *(de hilo)* reel.

carretera *f* road; ~ **de circunvalación** ring road; ~ **comarcal** minor road; ~ **de cuota** *(Amér)* toll road; ~ **nacional** = A road *(Br)*, = state highway *(Am)*.

carretilla *f* wheelbarrow.

carril m *(de carretera, autopista)* lane; *(de tren)* rail; ~ **de aceleración** fast lane; ~ **bici** cycle lane; ~ **bus** bus lane; ~ **de los lentos** *(fam)* crawler lane.

carrito m *(de la compra)* trolley; *(para bebés)* pushchair *(Br)*, buggy *(Am)*.

carro m *(carruaje)* cart; *(Amér: coche)* car; ~ **comedor** *(Amér)* dining car; ~ **de la compra** trolley.

carrocería f bodywork.

carromato m covered wagon.

carroña f carrion.

carroza f coach, carriage.

carruaje m carriage.

carrusel m (de feria) carousel.

carta f (escrito) letter; (de restaurante, bar) menu; (de la baraja) card; ~ **de vinos** wine list.

cartabón m set square.

cartearse vpr to correspond.

cartel m poster.

cartelera f (de espectáculos) entertainments section; (tablón) hoarding (Br), billboard (Am); **estar en** ~ (película) to be showing; (obra de teatro) to be running.

cartera f (para dinero) wallet; (de colegial) satchel; (para documentos) briefcase; (sin asa) portfolio; (de mujer) clutch bag.

carterista mf pickpocket.

cartero, -ra m, f postman (f postwoman).

cartilla f (para aprender a leer) first reading book; ~ **de ahorros** savings book; ~ **de la Seguridad Social** National Insurance card.

cartón m (material) cardboard; (de cigarrillos) carton.

cartucho m cartridge.

cartulina f card.

casa f (edificio) house; (vivienda, hogar) home; (familia) family; (empresa) company; **en** ~ at home; **ir a** ~ to go home; ~ **de campo** country house; ~ **de huéspedes** guesthouse.

casadero, -ra adj marriageable.

casado, -da adj married.

casamiento m marriage, wedding.

casar vt to marry ❏ **casar con** v + prep (colores, tejidos) to go with; **casarse** vpr. **~se (con)** to get married (to).

cascabel m bell.

cascada f waterfall.

cascado, -da adj (fam: persona, ropa) worn-out; (voz) hoarse.

cascanueces m inv nutcracker.

cascar vt (romper) to crack; (fam: golpear) to thump.

cáscara f (de huevo, frutos secos) shell; (de plátano, naranja) peel.

casco m (para la cabeza) helmet; (envase) empty (bottle); (de caballo) hoof; (de barco) hull; ~ **antiguo** old (part of) town; ~ **urbano** town centre; **~s azules** Blue Berets.

caserío m (casa de campo) country house.

caserita f (Amér) housewife.

casero, -ra adj (hecho en casa) home-made; (hogareño) home-loving ◆ m, f (propietario) landlord (f landlady).

caseta f (de feria) stall; (para

perro) kennel; *(en la playa)* bathing hut.

casete *m (aparato)* cassette player ◆ *m o f (cinta)* cassette, tape.

casi *adv* nearly, almost; ~ **nada** almost nothing, hardly anything; ~ **nunca** hardly ever.

casilla *f (de impreso)* box; *(de tablero, juego)* square; *(de mueble, caja, armario)* compartment; ~ **de correos** *(Amér)* P.O. Box.

casillero *m (mueble)* set of pigeonholes; *(casilla)* pigeonhole.

casino *m* casino.

caso *m* case; **en** ~ **de** in the event of; **(en)** ~ **de que venga** if he comes; **en todo** ~ in any case; **en cualquier** ~ in any case; **hacer** ~ **a alguien** to take notice of sb; **ser un** ~ *(fam)* to be a case; **no venir al** ~ to be irrelevant.

caspa *f* dandruff.

casquete *m* skullcap.

casquillo *m (de bala)* cartridge case; *(de lámpara)* socket.

casta *f (linaje)* stock; *(en la India)* caste.

castaña *f (fruto)* chestnut; *(fam: golpe)* bash.

castaño, -ña *adj (color)* chestnut ◆ *m (árbol)* chestnut tree.

castañuelas *fpl* castanets.

castellano, -na *adj & m, f* Castilian ◆ *m (lengua)* Spanish.

castidad *f* chastity.

castigar *vt* to punish.

castigo *m* punishment.

castillo *m* castle.

castizo, -za *adj* pure.

casto, -ta *adj* chaste.

castor *m* beaver.

castrar *vt* to castrate.

casualidad *f* coincidence; **por** ~ by chance.

catacumbas *fpl* catacombs.

catalán, -ana *adj, m, f* Catalan.

catálogo *m* catalogue.

Cataluña *s* Catalonia.

catamarán *m* catamaran.

catar *vt* to taste.

cataratas *fpl (de agua)* waterfalls, falls; *(en los ojos)* cataracts.

catarro *m* cold.

catástrofe *f* disaster.

catastrófico, -ca *adj* disastrous.

catear *vt (fam)* to flunk.

catecismo *m* catechism.

cátedra *f (en universidad)* chair; *(en instituto)* post of head of department.

catedral *f* cathedral.

catedrático, -ca *m, f* head of department.

categoría *f* category; **de** ~ top-class.

catequesis *f inv* catechesis.

cateto, -ta *m, f (despec)* dimwit.

catire, -ra *adj (Amér)* blond (blonde).

catolicismo *m* Catholicism.

católico, -ca *adj & m, f* Catholic.

catorce *núm* fourteen, → **seis**.

catre *m* campbed.

cauce *m (de río)* riverbed; *(de lluvia, artificial)* channel.

caucho *m* rubber.

caudal *m (de un río)* volume,

flow; ~es (dinero) wealth (sg).

caudaloso, -sa adj with a large flow.

caudillo m leader.

causa f cause; a ~ de because of.

causante m (Amér) taxpayer.

causar vt to cause.

cáustico, -ca adj caustic.

cautela f caution; con ~ cautiously.

cautivador, -ra adj captivating.

cautivar vt (seducir) to captivate.

cautiverio m captivity; en ~ in captivity.

cautivo, -va adj & m, f captive.

cauto, -ta adj cautious.

cava f (bodega) wine cellar ◆ m Spanish champagne-type wine; al ~ in a sauce of single cream, shallots, "cava" and butter; ~ brut brut "cava".

cavar vt to dig.

caverna f (cueva) cave, (más grande) cavern.

caviar m caviar.

cavidad f cavity.

cavilar vi to ponder.

cayera v → caer

caza f (actividad) hunting; (presa) game, andar o ir a la ~ de to chase; dar ~ to hunt down.

cazador, -ra m, f hunter (f huntress).

cazadora f (bomber) jacket, → cazador.

cazar vt (animales) to hunt; (fam: marido, esposa) to get o.s.; (captar, entender) to catch.

cazo m (vasija) saucepan; (cucharón) ladle.

cazuela f (de barro) earthenware pot; (guiso) casserole; a la ~ casseroled.

cazurro, -rra adj (obstinado) stubborn.

CC (abrev de código civil) civil code in Spanish law.

c/c (abrev de cuenta corriente) a/c.

CE f (abrev de Comunidad Europea) EC.

cebar vt (animales) to fatten up ▯ **cebarse en** v + prep to take it out on.

cebo m bait.

cebolla f onion.

cebolleta f spring onion.

cebra f zebra.

cecear vi to lisp.

ceder vt (sitio, asiento, etc) to give up ◆ vi (puente) to give way; (cuerda) to slacken; (viento, lluvia, etc) ▯ abate; "ceda el paso" "give way".

cedro m cedar.

cédula f (document; ~ de identidad) identity card.

cegato, -ta adj (fam) short-sighted.

ceguera f blindness.

ceja f eyebrow.

celda f cell.

celebración f celebration.

celebrar vt (cumpleaños, acontecimiento, misa) to celebrate; (asamblea, reunión) to hold.

célebre adj famous.

celebridad f fame; ser una ~ be famous.

celeste adj (del cielo) of

celestial adj celestial.

celo m (cinta adhesiva) Sellotape®; (en el trabajo, etc) zeal; **estar en ~** to be on heat ❏ **celos** mpl jealousy (sg); **tener ~s** to be jealous.

celofán® m Cellophane®.

celoso, -sa adj (en el amor) jealous.

célula f cell.

celulitis f inv cellulitis.

cementerio m cemetry; **~ de coches** breaker's yard.

cemento m cement; **~ armado** reinforced concrete.

cena f dinner.

cenar vt to have for dinner ♦ vi to have dinner.

cencerro m cowbell; **estar como un ~** (fig) to be mad.

cenefa f border.

cenicero m ashtray.

ceniza f ash ❏ **cenizas** fpl (restos mortales) ashes.

censado, -da adj recorded.

censar vt to take a census of.

censo m census; **~ electoral** electoral roll.

censor m censor.

censura f (de película, libro, etc) censorship.

censurar vt (película, libro, etc) to censor; (conducta, etc) to censure.

centena f hundred; **una ~ de** a hundred.

centenar m hundred; **un ~ de** a hundred.

centenario, -ria adj (persona) hundred-year-old ♦ m centenary.

centeno m rye.

centésimo, -ma núm hundredth, → **sexto**.

centígrado, -da adj centigrade.

centímetro m centimetre.

céntimo m (moneda) cent; **no tener un ~** not to have a penny.

centinela mf sentry.

centollo m spider crab.

centrado, -da adj (en el centro) in the centre; (persona) well-balanced; (derecho) straight; **~ en** (trabajo, ocupación) focussed on.

central adj central ♦ f (oficina) head office; **~ eléctrica** power station.

centralismo m centralism.

centralita f switchboard.

centrar vt (cuadro, mueble) to centre; (miradas, atención) to be the centre of ❏ **centrarse en** v + prep to focus on.

céntrico, -ca adj central.

centrifugar vt (suj: lavadora) to spin.

centro m centre; (de ciudad) (town) centre; **en el ~ de** in the middle of; **ir al ~** to go to town; **ser el ~ de** to be the centre of; **~ comercial** shopping centre; **~ juvenil** youth club; **~ social** community centre; **~ turístico** tourist resort; **~ urbano** town centre.

Centroamérica s Central America.

centuria f century.

ceñido, -da adj tight.

ceñir vt (ajustar) to tighten; (rodear) to surround ❏ **ceñirse a** v + prep to stick to.

ceño m frown.

cepa f (vid) vine.

cepillar vt (pelo, traje, etc) to brush; (fam: elogiar) to butter up □

cepillarse vpr (fam) (acabar) to polish off; (matar) to bump off.

cepillo m brush; ~ **de dientes** toothbrush.

cepo m (de animales) trap; (de coches) wheelclamp.

CEPSA f Spanish petrol company.

cera f wax.

cerámica f (objeto) piece of pottery; (arte) pottery; **de** ~ ceramic.

ceramista mf potter.

cerca f (valla) fence ◆ adv near; ~ **de** (en espacio) near; (casi) nearly; **son** ~ **de las cuatro** it's nearly four o'clock; **de** ~ from close up.

cercanías fpl (alrededores) outskirts.

cercano, -na adj (en espacio) nearby; (en tiempo) near.

cercar vt (vallar) to fence off; (rodear) to surround.

cerco m (de vallas) fence.

cerda f (hilillo,) cerdo.

cerdo, -da m, f (animal) pig (f sow); (despec: persona) pig ◆ adj (despec) filthy ◆ m (carne) pork.

cereal m cereal □ **cereales** mpl (para desayuno) breakfast cereal (sg).

cerebro m (del cráneo) brain; (persona inteligente) brainy person; (organizador, responsable) brains (pl); ~ **electrónico** computer.

ceremonia f ceremony.

ceremonioso, -sa adj ceremonious.

cereza f cherry.

cerezo m (árbol) cherry tree.

cerilla f match.

cerillo m (Amér) match.

cero m núm (número) zero, nought; (en fútbol) nil; (en tenis) love; **bajo** ~ below zero; **sobre** ~ above zero; **ser un** ~ **a la izquierda** (fam: ser un inútil) to be useless, → **seis**.

cerquillo m (Amér) fringe (Br), bangs (Am) (pl).

cerrada f (Amér) cul-de-sac (on estate).

cerrado, -da adj (espacio, local, etc) closed; (tiempo, cielo) overcast; (introvertido) introverted; (intransigente) narrow-minded; (curva) sharp; "~ **por vacaciones**" "closed for the holidays".

cerradura f lock.

cerrajería f locksmith's (shop).

cerrajero m locksmith.

cerrar vt to close; (con llave) to lock; (grifo, gas) to turn off; (local, negocio, fábrica) to close down; (ir detrás de) to bring up the rear of; (impedir) to block; (pacto, trato) to strike ◆ vi (comercio) to close □ **cerrarse** vpr (en uno mismo) to close o.s. off; **cerrarse a** v + prep (propuestas, innovaciones) to close one's mind to.

cerro m hill.

cerrojo m bolt.

certamen m (concurso) competition; (fiesta) awards ceremony.

certeza f certainty; **tener la** ~ **de** to be sure that.

certidumbre f certainty.

certificado, -da adj (carta, paquete) registered ◆ m certifica[...]

certificar vt (documento) to [...]tify; (carta, paquete) to reg[...]

cervecería *f (establecimiento)* bar.

cerveza *f* beer; ~ **con Casera®** ≈ shandy; ~ **sin alcohol** alcohol-free beer; ~ **negra** stout; ~ **rubia** lager.

cesar *vi* to stop ♦ *vt*: ~ **a alguien de** *(cargo, ocupación)* to sack sb from; **no** ~ **de hacer algo** to keep doing sthg; **sin** ~ non-stop.

cesárea *f* Caesarean (section).

cese *m (de empleo, cargo)* sacking; *(de actividad)* stopping.

cesión *f* transfer.

césped *m (superficie)* lawn; *(hierba)* grass.

cesta *f* basket; ~ **de la compra** cost of living.

cesto *m* large basket.

cetro *m* sceptre.

cg *(abrev de centigramo)* cg.

chabacano, -na *adj* vulgar ♦ *m (Amér) (fruto)* apricot; *(árbol)* apricot tree.

chabola *f* shack; **barrios de ~s** shanty town *(sg)*.

chacarero, -ra *m, f (Amér) (agricultor)* farmer; *(hablador)* chatterbox.

chacha *f (fam) (criada)* maid; *(niñera)* nanny.

cháchara *f* chatter.

chacolí *m* light, dry wine from the North of Spain.

chacra *f (Amér)* smallholding.

chafar *vt (aplastar)* to flatten; *(plan, proyecto)* to ruin; *(fam: desmoralizar)* to depress.

chal *m* shawl.

chalado, -da *adj (fam)* crazy; **estar ~ por** *(estar enamorado)* to be crazy about.

chalé *m (en ciudad)* detached house; *(en el campo)* cottage; *(en alta montaña)* chalet.

chaleco *m* waistcoat; ~ **salvavidas** life jacket.

chamaco, -ca *m, f (Amér)* lad *(f* lass).

chamba *f (Amér: fam)* job.

chambear *vi (Amér: fam)* to work.

champán *m* champagne.

champiñón *m* mushroom; **champiñones con jamón** mushrooms fried slowly with garlic and cured ham.

champú *m* shampoo.

champurrado *m (Amér)* cocktail.

chamuscado, -da *adj (madera)* scorched.

chamuscarse *vpr (barba, pelo, tela)* to singe.

chamusquina *f*: **oler a ~** *(fig)* to smell fishy.

chance *f (Amér)* chance.

chanchada *f (Amér) (fig: grosería)* rude thing; *(porquería)* filth.

chancho *m (Amér)* pig.

chancleta *f (de playa)* flip-flop; *(de vestir)* low sandal.

chanclo *m (de madera)* clog; *(de goma)* galosh.

chándal *m* tracksuit.

changarro *m (Amér)* small shop.

changurro *m* spider crab.

chantaje *m* blackmail.

chantajista *mf* blackmailer.

chapa *f (de metal)* plate; *(de botella)* top; *(Amér: cerradura)* lock; ~ **de madera** veneer.

chapado, -da *adj (con metal)*

plated; *(con madera)* veneered; **~ a la antigua** old-fashioned.

chapar *vt (con metal)* to plate; *(con madera)* to veneer.

chaparrón *m* cloudburst.

chapucería *f* botch (job).

chapucero, -ra *adj (trabajo, obra)* shoddy; *(persona)* bungling.

chapuza *f* botch (job).

chaqué *m* morning coat.

chaqueta *f* jacket.

chaquetilla *f* short jacket.

chaquetón *m* three-quarter length coat.

charca *f* pond.

charco *m* puddle.

charcutería *f (tienda)* ≈ delicatessen, *(productos)* cold cuts *(pl)* and cheese.

charla *f (conversación)* chat; *(conferencia)* talk.

charlar *vi* to chat.

charlatán, -ana *adj (hablador)* talkative; *(indiscreto)* gossipy.

charola *f (Amér)* tray.

charro *adj (Amér) típico de* Mexican cowboys ◆ *m (Amér)* Mexican cowboy.

chárter *m inv* charter flight.

chasco *m (decepción)* disappointment; *(broma)* practical joke.

chasis *m inv* chassis.

chatarra *f (metal)* scrap; *(objetos, piezas)* junk.

chatarrero, -ra *m, f* scrap dealer.

chato, -ta *adj (nariz)* snub; *(persona)* snub-nosed ◆ *m (apelativo)* love ◆ *m (de vino)* small glass of wine.

chau *interj (Amér)* bye!

chaucha *f (Amér) (patata)* new potato; *(vaina)* pod; *(moneda)* small coin.

chavo, -va *m, f (Amér: fam)* lad (f lass).

che *interj (Amér)* pah!

Checoslovaquia *s* Checoslovakia.

chef *m* chef.

cheque *m* cheque; **~ de viaje** traveller's cheque.

chequeo *m (médico)* check-up.

chequera *f (Amér)* cheque book.

chévere *adj (Amér)* great.

chic *adj inv* chic.

chica *f (muchacha)* girl; *(criada)* maid.

chicha *f (fam)* meat; *(Amér: bebida)* fermented maize liquor.

chícharo *m (Amér)* pea.

chicharrones *mpl* pork crackling *(sg)*.

chicho *m (Amér) (chuchería)* knick-knack; *(fam: teta)* tit.

chichón *m* bump.

chicle *m* chewing gum.

chico, -ca *adj* small ◆ *m (muchacho)* boy.

chicote *m (Amér) (látigo)* whip; *(colilla)* cigarette butt.

chifa *m (Amér)* Chinese restaurant.

chiflado, -da *adj (fam)* crazy.

chiflar *vi (Amér: aves)* to sing; **me chifla** *(fam)* I love it ❏ **chiflarse** *vpr (fam)* to go crazy.

chiflido *m (Amér)* whistle.

Chile *s* Chile.

chileno, -na adj & m, f Chilean.

chillar vi (gritar) to scream.

chillido m scream.

chillón, -ona adj (voz, sonido) piercing; (color) loud.

chimenea f (de casa) chimney; (de barco) funnel; (hogar) hearth.

chimpancé m chimpanzee.

china f (piedra) pebble; (Amér: criada) Indian maid; **le tocó la ~** he drew the short straw.

China f: **la ~** China.

chinche f (insecto) bedbug ◆ adj (pesado) annoying.

chincheta f drawing pin (Br), thumbtack (Am).

chinchín m (en brindis) toast; (sonido) clash (of a brass band) ◆ excl cheers!

chingado, -da adj (Amér: vulg: estropeado) fucked.

chingar vt (Amér: vulg: estropear) to fuck up.

chino, -na adj, m, f Chinese.

chip m chip.

chipirón m baby squid; **chipirones en su tinta** baby squid served in its own ink.

chirimoya f custard apple.

chirucas fpl canvas boots.

chisme m (habladuría) piece of gossip; (fam: objeto, aparato) thingy.

chismoso, -sa adj gossipy.

chispa f spark; (pizca) bit; (de lluvia) spot.

chiste m joke.

chistorra f cured pork and beef sausage typical of Aragon and Navarre.

chistoso, -sa adj funny.

chivarse vpr (fam) (niño) to tell; (delincuente) to grass.

chivatazo m (fam) tip-off.

chivato, -ta m, f (fam: acusica) telltale; (fam: delator) grass ◆ m (Amér: hombre valioso) brave man; (Amér: aprendiz) apprentice.

chocar vi (coche, camión, etc) to crash; (enfrentarse) to clash ◆ vt (las manos) to shake; (copas, vasos) to clink; (sorprender) to shock.

chocho, -cha adj (viejo) senile; (encariñado) doting.

choclo m (Amér) maize (Br), corn (Am).

chocolate m (alimento) chocolate; (bebida) drinking chocolate; **~ amargo** dark chocolate.

chocolatería f bar which serves drinking chocolate.

chocolatina f chocolate bar.

chófer m (de coche) chauffeur; (de autobús) driver.

chollo m (fam) (ganga) bargain; (trabajo) cushy number.

chompa f (Amér) jumper.

chongo m (Amér) bun.

chopitos mpl baby squid in batter (sg).

chopo m poplar.

choque m (colisión) crash; (pelea, riña) clash.

chorizo m (embutido) spiced, smoked pork sausage; (fam: ladrón) thief.

choro m (Amér) mussel.

chorrada f (fam) stupid thing.

chorrear vi (ropa) to drip.

chorro m (de líquido) jet; **salir a ~s** to gush out.

choto, -ta m, f (cabrito) kid.

choza f hut.

christma m Christmas card.

chubasco m (heavy) shower.

chubasquero m raincoat.

chúcaro, -ra adj (Amér) (bravío) wild; (huraño) surly.

chuchería f (golosina) sweet; (trivialidad) trinket.

chucho, -cha m, f (fam) mutt.

chueco, -ca adj (Amér) (torcido) twisted; (patizambo) bow-legged.

chufa f tiger nut.

chuleta f (de carne) chop; (de examen) crib note; **~ de cerdo** pork chop; **~ de ternera** veal cutlet.

chuletón m large cutlet.

chulo, -la adj (engreído) cocky; (fam: bonito) lovely ♦ m (de prostituta) pimp.

chumbera f prickly pear.

chupachup® m lollipop.

chupado, -da adj (fig: flaco) skinny; (fam: fácil) dead easy; **está ~ fam** it's a cinch.

chupar vt (caramelo, fruta, etc) to suck; (suj: esponja, papel) to soak up; **~le algo a alguien** (fam: quitar) to milk sb for sthg.

chupe m (Amér) stew made with potato and meat or fish; **~ de camarones** thick potato and prawn soup.

chupete m (de bebé) dummy (Br), pacifier (Am); (de biberón) teat.

chupito m (de licor) tot.

churrasco m barbecued meat.

churrería f stall selling "churros".

churro m (dulce) stick of dough fried in oil, usually eaten with sugar or thick drinking chocolate; (fam: chapuza) botch.

chusma f mob.

chutar vt to kick.

chute m (fam: en fútbol) shot.

Cía (abrev de compañía) Co.

cicatriz (pl -ces) f scar.

cicatrizar vi to heal ❑ **cicatrizarse** vpr to heal.

ciclismo m cycling.

ciclista m f cyclist.

ciclo m (periodo de tiempo) cycle; (de actos, conferencias) series.

ciclomotor m moped.

ciclón m cyclone.

ciego, -ga adj blind ♦ m, f blind person; **~ de** (pasión, ira, etc) blinded by; **los ~** the blind.

cielo m (de la tierra) sky; (de casa, habitación, etc) ceiling; (en religión) heaven; (apelativo) darling; **como llovido del ~** (fig) out of the blue ❑ **cielos** interj good heavens!

ciempiés m inv centipede.

cien núm one O a hundred, → **ciento**.

ciencia f (disciplina) science; (saber, sabiduría) knowledge; **~ ficción** science fiction; **~s económicas** economics (sg); **~s naturales** natural sciences ❑ **ciencias** fpl (en educación) science (sg).

científico, -ca adj scientific ♦ m, f scientist.

ciento núm one O a hundred, → **seis; ~ cincuenta** one hundred and fifty; **cien mil** one hundred thousand; **por ~** percent.

cierre m (mecanismo) fastener; (de local, tienda, negociación) closing; (de trato) striking; (de actividad, acto) closure; **~ centralizado** central locking.

cierto, -ta *adj* certain; *(seguro, verdadero)* true; ~ **hombre** a certain man; **cierta preocupación** a degree of unease; **por** ~ by the way.

ciervo, -va *m, f* deer.

CIF *m Spanish tax code.*

cifra *f* figure.

cigala *f* Dublin Bay prawn.

cigarra *f* cicada.

cigarrillo *m* cigarette.

cigarro *m (cigarrillo)* cigarette.

cigüeña *f* stork.

cilindrada *f* cylinder capacity.

cilíndrico, -ca *adj* cylindrical.

cilindro *m* cylinder.

cima *f (de montaña)* summit.

cimiento *m (de edificio)* foundations *(pl)*; *(principio, raíz)* basis.

cinco *núm* five, → **seis**.

cincuenta *núm* fifty, → **seis**.

cine *m* cinema.

cineasta *mf (film)* director.

cinematografía *f* cinematography.

cinematográfico, -ca *adj* film *(antes de s)*.

cínico, -ca *adj* cynical.

cinismo *m* cynicism.

cinta *f (de tela)* ribbon; *(de papel, plástico)* strip; *(para grabar, medir)* tape; ~ **adhesiva** adhesive tape; ~ **aislante** insulating tape; ~ **magnética** recording tape; ~ **de vídeo** videotape.

cintura *f* waist.

cinturón *m* belt; ~ **de seguridad** seat belt.

cipote, -ta *m, f (Amér) (muchacho)* boy *(f* girl); *(persona rechoncha)* chubby person.

ciprés *m* cypress.

circo *m* circus.

circuito *m (recorrido)* tour; *(en competiciones)* circuit; ~ **eléctrico** electrical circuit.

circulación *f (de automóviles)* traffic; *(de la sangre)* circulation.

circular *adj & f* circular ♦ *vi (automóvil)* to drive (along); *(persona, grupo)* to move along; *(información, noticia)* to circulate.

círculo *m* circle; ~ **polar** polar circle.

circunferencia *f* circumference.

circunscribir *vt*: ~ **algo a** to restrict sthg to.

circunscrito, -ta *pp* → **circunscribir**.

circunstancia *f* circumstance; **las** ~**s** the circumstances.

circunstancial *adj* chance.

cirio *m* large candle.

cirrosis *f inv* cirrhosis.

ciruela *f* plum.

ciruelo *m* plum tree.

cirugía *f* surgery; ~ **plástica** plastic surgery.

cirujano, -na *m, f* surgeon.

cisma *m (en religión)* schism.

cisne *m* swan.

cisterna *f (de agua)* tank.

cita *f (con médico, jefe, etc)* appointment; *(de novios)* date; *(nota)* quotation; **tener una** ~ **con alguien** to have arranged to meet sb.

citación *f* summons.

citar *vt (convocar)* to summons; *(mencionar)* to quote ❏ **citarse** *vpr* to arrange to meet.

cítrico, -ca adj citric ❏ **cítricos** mpl citrus fruits.

ciudad f (población no rural) town; (población importante) city; ~ **universitaria** (university) campus.

ciudadanía f citizenship.

ciudadano, -na adj city/town (antes de s) ◆ m, f citizen.

cívico, -ca adj (de la ciudad, ciudadano) civic; (educado, cortés) public-spirited.

civil adj civil; (de la ciudad) civic.

civilización f civilization.

civilizado, -da adj civilized.

civismo m (educación, cortesía) civility.

cl (abrev de centilitro) cl.

clan m clan.

clara f (de huevo) white; (bebida) shandy.

claraboya f skylight.

clarear vt to make lighter ◆ vi to brighten up ◆ v impers (amanecer): **empezaba a ~** dawn was breaking.

claridad f (en el hablar) clarity; (sinceridad) sincerity.

clarinete m clarinet.

clarividencia f farsightedness.

claro, -ra adj clear; (con luz) bright; (color) light; (sincero, franco) straightforward ◆ m (de tiempo) bright spell; (en el bosque) clearing ◆ adv clearly ◆ interj of course!; **poner en ~** to clear up; **sacar en ~** to make out.

clase f class; (variedad, tipo) kind; (aula) classroom; **dar ~s** to teach; **de primera** ~ first-class; **toda** ~ **de** all sorts of; ~ **media** middle class; ~ **preferente** club class; ~ **turista**

tourist class; **primera/segunda** ~ first/second class.

clásico, -ca adj classical.

clasificación f (lista) classification; (DEP) league table.

clasificador m (carpeta) divider (for filing); (mueble) filing cabinet.

clasificar vt to classify ❏ **clasificarse** vpr (en competición) to qualify.

claudicar vi (rendirse) to give up.

claustro m (de iglesia, convento, etc) cloister; (de profesores) senate.

claustrofobia f claustrophobia.

cláusula f clause.

clausura f (de acto) closing ceremony; (de curso) end.

clausurar vt (acto, celebración) to close; (curso) to finish; (local, establecimiento) to close down.

clavado, -da adj (en punto) on the dot; **ser ~ a** (fam) to be the spitting image of.

clavar vt (clavo, palo) to drive in; (cuchillo) to thrust; (alfiler) to stick; (sujetar, fijar) to fix; (fam: en el precio) to rip off.

clave f (explicación, solución) key; (de enigma, secreto) code ◆ adj inv key.

clavel m carnation.

clavícula f collar bone.

clavija f (de madera) peg; (de metal) pin.

clavo m (para sujetar) nail; (especia) clove; **dar en el ~** to hit the nail on the head.

claxon m horn.

clérigo m clergyman.

clero m clergy.

cliché m (de fotografía) negative; (frase, actuación) cliché.

cliente mf (de médico, abogado) client; (de tienda, comercio) customer; (de hotel) guest.

clima m climate.

climático, -ca adj climatic.

climatizado, -da adj air-conditioned.

climatología f (tiempo) weather.

clímax m inv climax.

clínica f clinic.

clínico, -ca adj clinical.

clip m (para papeles) paper clip; (para pelo) hairclip.

cloaca f sewer.

cloro m chlorine.

club m club; ~ **náutico** yacht club.

cm (abrev de centímetro) cm.

coacción f coercion.

coaccionar vt to coerce.

coartada f alibi.

coba f: **dar** ~ to suck up to.

cobarde adj cowardly ◆ mf coward.

cobardía f cowardice.

cobertizo m (tejado) lean-to; (barracón) shed.

cobija f (Amér) blanket.

cobijar vt (suj: edificio) to house; (suj: persona) to put up; (proteger) to shelter ❑ **cobijarse** vpr to (take) shelter.

cobra f cobra.

cobrador, -ra m, f (de autobús) conductor (f conductress).

cobrar vt (dinero) to charge;

(cheque) to cash; (en el trabajo) to earn; (importancia, fama) to acquire; **¿me cobra, por favor?** could I have the bill, please?

cobre m copper; **no tener un** ~ (Amér) not to have a penny.

cobro m (de dinero) collection; (de talón) cashing; **llamar a** ~ **revertido** to reverse the charges (Br); to call collect (Am).

coca f (planta) coca; (fam: cocaína) coke.

cocaína f cocaine.

cocainómano, -na m, f cocaine addict.

cocción f (en agua) boiling; (en horno) baking.

cocear vi to kick.

cocer vt (guisar) to cook; (en agua) to boil; (en horno) to bake ◆ vi (hervir) to boil ❑ **cocerse** vpr (fig: idea, plan) to be brewing.

cochayuyo m (Amér) seaweed.

coche m (automóvil) car; (de tren, caballos) carriage; ~ **de alquiler** hire car; ~ **cama** sleeper; ~ **restaurante** dining car.

cochinillo m: ~ **al horno** roast suckling pig, a speciality of Segovia.

cochino, -na adj filthy ◆ m, f (animal) pig (f sow).

cocido, -da adj boiled ◆ m stew; ~ **madrileño** stew made with meat, chickpeas, bacon and root vegetables, typical of Madrid.

cocina f (estancia, habitación) kitchen; (aparato) cooker; (arte, técnica) cooking; ~ **española** Spanish cuisine; ~ **de butano** butane gas cooker; ~ **eléctrica** electric cooker; ~ **de gas** gas cooker.

cocinar vt & vi to cook.

cocinero, -ra m, f cook.

coco m (fruto) coconut; (árbol) coconut palm; (fam: cabeza) nut.

cocodrilo m (animal) crocodile; (piel) crocodile skin.

cocotero m coconut palm.

cóctel m (bebida) cocktail; (reunión, fiesta) cocktail party.

coctelera f cocktail shaker.

codazo m poke with the elbow.

codiciar vt to covet.

codificado, -da adj coded.

código m code; ~ **de barras** bar code; ~ **de circulación** highway code; ~ **penal** penal code; ~ **postal** post code (Br), zip code (Am).

codo m elbow; ~ **a** ~ side by side.

codorniz (pl -ces) f quail.

coeficiente m coefficient; ~ **intelectual** I.Q.

coetáneo, -a adj contemporary.

coexistencia f coexistence.

coexistir: coexistir con v + prep to coexist with.

cofia f (de tendera, camarera) cap; (de monja) coif.

cofradía f religious fraternity.

cofre m (arca) chest.

coger vt to take; (ladrón, pez, enfermedad, oír) to catch; (frutos) to pick; (suj: toro) to gore; (entender) to get ◆ vi (planta, árbol) to take; (caber) to fit; ~ **algo a alguien** to take sthg (away) from sb; **coge cerca de aquí** it's not far from here; ~ **a la derecha** to turn right ❑ **cogerse** vpr: ~**se** (agarrarse de) to hold on to.

cogida f (de toro) goring.

cogollos mpl (brotes) shoots.

cogote m nape (of the neck).

cohabitar vi to live together.

coherencia f coherence.

coherente adj coherent.

cohete m rocket.

COI m (abrev de Comité Olímpico Internacional) IOC.

coima f (Amér: fam) bribe.

coincidencia f coincidence.

coincidir vi (en un lugar) to meet; (ser igual) to coincide ❑ **coincidir con** v + prep (ser de la misma opinión que) to agree with; (ocurrir en el mismo momento que) to coincide with.

coito m (sexual) intercourse.

cojear vi (persona) to limp; (mueble) to wobble.

cojín m cushion.

cojo, -ja adj (persona, animal) lame; (mesa, silla) wobbly ◆ m, f lame person.

cojón m (vulg: testículo) ball ❑ **cojones** interj (vulg) balls!

cojonudo, -da adj (vulg) bloody brilliant.

cojudear vt (Amér: fam) to mess about.

cojudez f (Amér: fam) silly thing.

cojudo, -da adj (Amér: fam) silly.

col f cabbage; ~ **de Bruselas** Brussels sprout.

cola f (rabo, de avión) tail; (fila) queue (Br), line (Am); (de tren) back; (de vestido) train; (para pegar) glue; (bebida) cola; ~ **de caballo** ponytail; **hacer** ~ to queue (Br), to stand in line (Am); **traer** ~ (fig) to

have repercussions.
colaboración f *(en trabajo, tarea)* collaboration; *(en publicación)* article.
colaborador, -ra m, f *(en trabajo)* collaborator; *(en periódico)* writer.
colaborar vi: ~ **en** *(trabajo, tarea)* to collaborate on; *(periódico)* to write for.
colada f *(de ropa)* laundry.
colado, -da adj: **estar ~ por** *(fam)* to have a crush on.
colador m *(para líquidos)* strainer; *(para verduras)* colander.
colar vt *(líquido)* to strain; *(café)* to filter; *(lo falso, lo ilegal)* to slip through *(it won't wash* □ **colarse** vpr *(en cine, metro)* to jump the queue *(Br)*, to jump the line *(Am)*; *(equivocarse)* to get it wrong.
colcha f bedspread.
colchón m mattress; ~ **inflable** air bed.
colchoneta f *(en la playa)* beach mat.
colección f collection.
coleccionar vt to collect.
coleccionista mf collector.
colecta f collection.
colectivo, -va adj collective ♦ m group.
colega mf colleague.
colegiado, -da m, f referee.
colegial, -la m, f schoolchild.
colegio m *(de estudiantes)* school; *(de profesionales)* professional association.
cólera m *(enfermedad)* cholera ♦ f *(enfado)* rage.

colérico, -ca adj bad-tempered.
colesterol m cholesterol.
coleta f pigtail.
colgador m hanger.
colgar vt to hang; *(la ropa)* to hang out; *(fam: abandonar)* to give up ♦ vi *(pender)* to hang; *(al teléfono)* to hang up; ~ **el teléfono** to hang up.
coliflor f cauliflower.
colilla f butt.
colina f hill.
colirio m eyewash.
colitis f inv diarrhea.
collage m collage.
collar m *(joya)* necklace; *(para animales)* collar.
collarín m surgical collar.
colmado m grocer's (shop).
colmar vt *(cuchara, vaso, etc)* to fill to the brim; ~ **a alguien de** to shower sb with.
colmena f beehive.
colmillo m *(de persona)* eyetooth; *(de elefante)* tusk.
colmo m: **ser el ~ de** to be the height of; **¡eso es el ~!** that's the last straw!
colocación f position.
colocado, -da adj *(fam)* *(drogado)* high; *(bebido)* plastered.
colocar vt to place; ~ **a alguien** *(proporcionar empleo)* to give sb a job □ **colocarse** vpr *(fam: drogarse)* to get stoned.
Colombia s Colombia.
colombiano, -na adj & m, f Colombian.
colonia f *(perfume)* (eau de) cologne; *(grupo de personas, territo-*

río) colony; *(Amér: barrio)* area; **~ proletaria** *(Amér)* slum area; **~ de verano** summer camp ❑ **colonias** *fpl (para niños)* holiday camp *(sg)*; **ir de ~s** to go to a holiday camp.

colonización *f* colonization.

colonizar *vt* to colonize.

colono *m* settler.

coloquial *adj* colloquial.

coloquio *m* debate.

color *m* colour; *(colorante)* dye; *(aspecto)* tone; **en ~** colour *(antes de s).*

colorado, -da *adj (rojo)* red; **ponerse ~** to go red.

colorante *m* colouring.

colorete *m* blusher.

colorido *m (conjunto de colores)* colours *(pl)*; *(animación)* colour.

colosal *adj (extraordinario)* extraordinary; *(muy grande)* colossal.

columna *f* column; *(de objetos)* stack; **~ vertebral** spinal column.

columpiarse *vpr* to swing.

columpio *m* swing.

coma *f (signo ortográfico)* comma; *(signo matemático)* decimal point ◆ *m:* **estar en ~** to be in a coma; **cinco ~ dos** five point two.

comadreja *f* weasel.

comadrona *f* midwife.

comandante *mf* major.

comando *m* commando.

comarca *f* area.

comba *f (juego)* skipping.

combate *m* fight ❑ **combates** *mpl* fighting *(sg)*.

combatir *vi* to fight ◆ *vt* to combat.

combinación *f* combination; *(de transportes)* connections *(pl)*; *(prenda femenina)* slip.

combinado *m (cóctel)* cocktail.

combinar *vt (unir, mezclar)* to combine; *(bebidas)* to mix ◆ *vi:* **~ (con)** *(colores, ropa etc)* to go together (with); **~ algo con** *(compaginar)* to combine sthg with.

combustible *m* fuel.

combustión *f* combustion.

comecocos *m inv (juego)* brainteaser.

comedia *f (obra humorística)* comedy; *(obra en general)* play; **hacer ~** *(fam)* to pretend.

comediante *mf (actor)* actor *(f* actress); *(farsante)* fraud.

comedor *m (habitación)* dining room; *(muebles)* dining room furniture.

comensal *mf* fellow diner.

comentar *vt* to comment on.

comentario *m (observación)* comment; *(análisis)* commentary.

comentarista *mf* commentarist.

comenzar *vt & vi* to begin, to start; **~ a** to begin to, to start to.

comer *vt* to eat ◆ *vi (alimentarse)* to eat; *(almorzar)* to have lunch.

comercial *adj* commercial.

comercializar *vt* to market.

comerciante *mf (negociante)* trader; *(tendero)* shopkeeper.

comerciar *vi:* **~ (con)** to trade (with).

comercio *m (negocio)* trade; *(tienda)* shop; *(actividad comercial)* business.

comestible *adj* edible.

cometa m (astro) comet ◆ f (juguete) kite.

cometer vt (delito) to commit; (error) to make.

cometido m task.

cómic m comic.

comicios mpl (formal) elections.

cómico, -a adj (gracioso) comical; (de la comedia) comedy (antes de s) ◆ m, f comedian (f comedienne).

comida f (alimento) food; (almuerzo, cena, etc) meal; (almuerzo) lunch; ~ **rápida** fast food; ~s **caseras** home-made food (sg); ~s **para llevar** takeaway food (sg).

comienzo m beginning, start; a ~s de at the beginning of.

comillas fpl inverted commas; **entre** ~ in inverted commas.

comilón, -ona adj greedy.

comilona f (fam) blow-out.

comino m cumin; **me importa un** ~ (fam) I couldn't care less.

comisaría f police station.

comisario, -ria m, f (de policía) police superintendent; (de exposición, museo) curator.

comisión f (grupo de personas) committee; (cantidad de dinero) commission.

comisura f (de labios) corner of the mouth.

comité m committee.

comitiva f retinue.

como adv as; (comparativo) like; (aproximadamente) roughly, more or less ◆ conj (ya que) as; (si) if; **tan ... ~ ... as ... as ...;** ~ **si** as if.

cómo adv how ◆ m: **el ~ y el porqué** the whys and wherefores;

¡~ es? what's it like?; **¡~?** (¿qué dices?) sorry?; **¡~ no!** of course!

cómoda f chest of drawers.

cómodamente adv comfortably.

comodidad f comfort ❏ **comodidades** fpl (ventajas) advantages; **con todas las ~es** all mod cons.

comodín m joker.

cómodo, -da adj comfortable.

comodón, -ona adj comfortloving.

compa mf (Amér: fam) mate.

compacto, -ta adj compact ◆ m compact disc.

compadecer vt to feel sorry for ❏ **compadecerse de** v + prep to feel sorry for.

compadrear vi (Amér: fam) to brag.

compadreo m (Amér: fam) friendship.

compaginar vt: ~ **algo con** to reconcile sthg with.

compañerismo m comradeship.

compañero, -ra m, f (acompañante) companion; (de clase) classmate; (de trabajo) colleague; (de juego) partner; (amigo) partner.

compañía f company; **de** ~ (animal) pet; **hacer** ~ **a alguien** to keep sb company.

comparación f comparison.

comparar vt to compare ❏ **compararse con** vpr: ~**se con** to compare with.

comparsa f (de fiesta) group of masked revellers at carnival; (de teatro) extras (pl) ◆ mf extra.

compartimiento *m* compartment.

compartir *vt* to share; ~ **algo con alguien** to share sthg with sb.

compás *m* (*en dibujo*) pair of compasses; (*ritmo*) beat.

compasión *f* compassion.

compasivo, -va *adj* compassionate.

compatible *adj* compatible; ~ **con** compatible with.

compatriota *mf* compatriot.

compenetrarse *vpr* to be in tune.

compensación *f* compensation.

compensar *vt* to compensate for ◆ *vi* (*satisfacer*) to be worthwhile; ~ **algo con** to make up for sthg with.

competencia *f* (*rivalidad*) competition, (*incumbencia*) area of responsibility; (*aptitud*) competence.

competente *adj* competent.

competición *f* competition.

competir *vi* to compete.

competitivo, -va *adj* competitive.

complacer *vt* to please ◆ *vi* to be pleasing ❑ **complacerse** *vpr*: ~**se en** to take pleasure in

complaciente *adj* obliging.

complejidad *f* complexity.

complejo, -ja *adj & m* complex.

complementar *vt* to complement ❑ **complementarse** *vpr* to complement one another.

complementario, -ria *adj* complementary.

complemento *m* (*accesorio*) complement; (*en gramática*) complement, object.

completamente *adv* completely.

completar *vt* to complete.

completo, -ta *adj* (*con todas sus partes*) complete; (*lleno*) full; **por** ~ completely; **"completo"** "no vacancies".

complexión *f* build.

complicación *f* complication.

complicado, -da *adj* complicated.

complicar *vt* (*hacer difícil*) to complicate; ~ **a alguien en** (*implicar*) to involve sb in ❑ **complicarse** *vpr* (*situación, problema*) to get complicated; (*enfermedad*) to get worse.

cómplice *mf* accomplice.

complot *m* plot.

componente *m* component.

componer *vt* (*obra literaria*) to write; (*obra musical*) to compose; (*lo roto*) to repair; (*lo desordenado*) to tidy up ❑ **componerse de** *v + prep* to consist of; **componérselas** to manage.

comportamiento *m* behaviour.

comportar *vt* to involve ❑ **comportarse** *vpr* to behave.

composición *f* composition.

compositor, -ra *m, f* composer.

compostura *f* (*buena educación*) good behaviour.

compota *f* stewed fruit; ~ **de manzana** stewed apple.

compra *f* purchase; **hacer la ~**

to do the shopping; **ir de ~s** to go shopping; **~ a plazos** hire purchase.

comprador, -ra *m, f* buyer.

comprar *vt* to buy; **~ algo a alguien** to buy sthg from sb.

comprender *vt (entender)* to understand; *(abarcar)* to comprise.

comprensible *adj* understandable.

comprensión *f (de ejercicio, texto)* comprehension; *(de problema, situación)* understanding.

comprensivo, -va *adj* understanding.

compresa *f (para higiene femenina)* sanitary towel; *(para uso médico)* compress.

comprimido, -da *adj* compressed ◆ *m* pill.

comprimir *vt* to compress.

comprobación *f* checking.

comprobar *vt (verificar)* to check; *(demostrar)* to prove.

comprometer *vt* to compromise ❑ **comprometerse** *vpr (novios)* to get engaged; **~se (a)** to commit o.s. (to); **~se (con)** to commit o.s. (to).

comprometido, -da *adj (empeñado)* committed; *(apuro)* difficult situation; **sin ~** uncompromising.

compromiso *m (obligación)* commitment; *(acuerdo)* compromise; *(apuro)* difficult situation; **sin ~** uncompromising.

compuerta *f* sluice gate.

compuesto, -ta *adj (por varios elementos)* composed; *(reparado)* repaired ◆ *m* compound.

compungido, -da *adj* remorseful.

comulgar *vi* to take communion ❑ **comulgar con** *v + prep (ideas, sentimientos)* to agree with.

común *adj (frecuente)* common; *(compartido)* shared.

comuna *f* commune.

comunicación *f (entre personas, animales)* communication; *(escrito)* communiqué; *(por carretera, tren, etc)* communications *(pl)*; **se cortó la ~** I was cut off.

comunicado, -da *adj* connected ◆ *m* statement; **bien/mal ~** *(pueblo, ciudad)* with good/bad connections.

comunicar *vt* to communicate ◆ *vi (al teléfono)* to get through; **está comunicando** *(teléfono)* the line's engaged.

comunicativo, -va *adj* communicative.

comunidad *f* community; **~ autónoma** Spanish autonomous region; **Comunidad Europea** European Community.

> **i COMUNIDAD AUTÓNOMA**
>
> In Spain, the "comunidad autónoma" is a region consisting of one or more provinces which enjoys a degree of autonomy in administrative matters. There are 17 "comunidades autónomas": Andalusia, Aragon, the Principality of Asturias, the Balearic Islands, the Canary Islands, Cantabria, Castile and León, Castile and La Mancha, Catalonia, Extremadura, La Rioja, Madrid, Murcia, Navarre, Valencia, Galicia and the Basque Country.

comunión f communion.

comunismo m communism.

comunista mf communist.

comunitario, -ria adj community (antes de s).

con prep 1. (modo, medio) with; **hazlo ~ el martillo** do it with the hammer; **lo ha conseguido ~ su esfuerzo** he has achieved it through his own efforts. 2. (compañía) with; **trabaja ~ su padre** he works with his father. 3. (junto a) with; **una cartera ~ varios documentos** a briefcase containing several documents. 4. (a pesar de) in spite of; **~ lo aplicado que es lo han suspendido** for all his hard work, they still failed him; **~ todo iremos a su casa** we'll go to her house anyway. 5. (condición) by; **~ salir a las cinco será suficiente** it we leave at five we'll have plenty of time. 6. (en locuciones): **~ (tal) que** as long as.

conato m (de agresión) attempt; (de incendio) beginning of.

cóncavo, -va adj concave.

concebir vt to conceive; **no ~** (no entender) to be unable to conceive of.

conceder vt (dar) to grant; (premio) to award; (asentir) to admit.

concejal, -la m, f councillor.

concentración f (de personas) gathering; (de líquido) concentration.

concentrado, -da adj (reunido) gathered; (espeso) concentrated ◆ m: **~ de ...** concentrated ...

concentrar vt (interés, atención) to concentrate; (lo desunido) to bring together □ **concentrarse** vpr: **~se en** (estudio, trabajo, etc) to concentrate on; (lugar) to gather in.

concepción f conception.

concepto m (idea) concept; (opinión) opinion; **en ~ de** by way of.

concernir; **concernir a** v + prep to concern.

concertación f agreement.

concertado, -da adj agreed.

concertar vt (precio) to agree on; (cita, entrevista) to arrange; (acuerdo) to reach.

concesión f award.

concesionario, -ria adj concessionary ◆ m licensee.

concha f (caparazón) shell; (material) tortoiseshell.

conchudo, -da adj (Amér: vulg) bloody stupid.

conciencia f (conocimiento) awareness; (moral) conscience; **a ~** conscientiously; **tener ~ de** to be aware of.

concienzudo, -da adj conscientious.

concierto m (actuación musical) concert; (composición musical) concerto; (convenio) agreement.

conciliación f reconciliation.

conciliar vt to reconcile; **~ el sueño** to get to sleep □ **conciliarse** con v + prep to be reconciled with.

concisión f conciseness.

conciso, -sa adj concise.

concluir vt to conclude ◆ vi to (come to an) end.

conclusión *f* conclusion.

concordancia *f* agreement.

concordar *vt* to reconcile ♦ *vi (de género)* to agree; *(de número)* to tally; ~ **con** *(coincidir con)* to agree with.

concordia *f* harmony.

concretar *vt (especificar)* to specify; *(reducir)* to cut down.

concreto, -ta *adj (no abstracto)* concrete; *(específico)* specific ♦ *m:* ~ **armado** *(Amér)* concrete.

concubina *f* concubine.

concurrencia *f (público)* audience; *(de hechos)* concurrence; *(asistencia)* attendance.

concurrente *adj* concurrent.

concurrido, -da *adj* crowded.

concurrir *vi (asistir)* to attend; *(coincidir)* to meet.

concursante *mf* contestant.

concursar *vi* to compete.

concurso *m (de deportes, literatura)* competition; *(en televisión)* game show.

condado *m* county.

condal *adj* county *(antes de s)*.

conde, -desa *m, f* count *(f* countess).

condecoración *f* medal.

condena *f* sentence.

condenado, -da *adj* convicted ♦ *m, f* convicted criminal.

condenar *vt (suj: juez)* to sentence; *(desaprobar)* to condemn.

condensación *f* condensation.

condensar *vt* to condense.

condición *f (supuesto)* condition; *(modo de ser)* nature; *(estado*

social) status ❑ **condiciones** *fpl (situación)* conditions; **estar en buenas/malas condiciones** to be/not to be in a fit state.

condicional *adj* conditional.

condimentar *vt* to season.

condimento *m* seasoning.

condominio *m (Amér: viviendas)* block of flats *(Br)*, apartment block *(Am)*; *(oficinas)* office block.

conducción *f (de vehículos)* driving; *(cañerías)* pipes *(pl)*.

conducir *vt (vehículo)* to drive; *(llevar)* to lead; *(dirigir)* to conduct ♦ *vi* to drive.

conducta *f* behaviour.

conducto *m (tubo)* pipe; *(vía)* channel.

conductor, -ra *m, f* driver.

conectar *vt* to connect ❑ **conectar con** *v + prep (contactar con)* to get in touch with; *(comprender)* to get on well with.

conejera *f (madriguera)* warren.

conejo, -ja *m, f* rabbit; ~ **a la cazadora** *rabbit cooked in olive oil, with onion, garlic and parsley.*

conexión *f* connection.

confección *f (de vestido)* dressmaking ❑ **confecciones** *fpl (tienda)* clothes shop *(sg)*.

confederación *f* confederation.

conferencia *f (disertación)* lecture; *(por teléfono)* long-distance call.

conferenciante *mf* speaker *(at conference)*.

confesar *vt* to confess ❑ **confesarse** *vpr* to take confession.

confesión *f (de los pecados)* confession; *(religión)* religion.

confesionario *m* confessional.

confesor *m* confessor.

confeti *m* confetti.

confiado, -da *adj (crédulo)* trusting.

confianza *f (seguridad)* confidence; *(fe)* faith; *(trato familiar)* familiarity.

confiar *vt (secreto)* to confide; *(persona, cosa)* to entrust ❏ **confiar en** *v + prep (persona)* to trust; *(esperar en)* to have faith in; **~ en que** to be confident that; **confiarse** *vpr* to be overconfident.

confidencia *f* confidence.

confidencial *adj* confidential.

confidente *mf (de un secreto)* confidante; *(de la policía)* informer.

configuración *f* configuration.

configurar *vt* to shape.

confirmación *f* confirmation.

confirmar *vt* to confirm.

confiscar *vt* to confiscate.

confitado, -da *adj* crystallized.

confite *m* sweet *(Br)*, candy *(Am)*.

confitería *f (tienda)* sweet shop *(Br)*, candy store *(Am)*.

confitura *f* preserve.

conflictivo, -va *adj* difficult.

conflicto *m (desacuerdo)* conflict; *(situación difícil)* difficulty.

confluencia *f (lugar)* intersection; *(de ríos)* confluence.

confluir: confluir en *v + prep* to meet at.

conformarse: conformarse

con *v + prep* to settle for.

conforme *adj* in agreement ◆ *adv* as; **~ a** o **con** in accordance with.

conformidad *f:* **dar la ~** to give one's consent.

conformismo *m* conformism.

conformista *mf* conformist.

confort *m* comfort; **"todo ~"** "all mod cons".

confortable *adj* comfortable.

confrontación *f* confrontation.

confundir *vt* to confuse; **~ algo/a alguien con** to confuse sthg/sb with ❏ **confundirse** *vpr (equivocarse)* to make a mistake; *(al teléfono)* to get the wrong number; **~te de casa** to get the wrong house; **confundirse con** *v + prep (mezclarse con)* to merge into.

confusión *f (equivocación)* mixup; *(desorden)* confusion.

confuso, -sa *adj (persona)* confused; *(no diferenciado)* unclear.

congelación *f* freezing.

congelado, -da *adj (alimentos, productos)* frozen; *(persona)* freezing ❏ **congelados** *mpl (alimentos)* frozen foods.

congelador *m* freezer.

congelar *vt* to freeze ❏ **congelarse** *vpr (persona)* to be freezing.

congeniar: congeniar con *v + prep* to get on with.

congénito, -ta *adj* congenital.

congestión *f* congestion.

conglomerado *m (de madera)* hardboard.

congregar *vt* to gather together ❏ **congregarse** *vpr* to gather.

congresista *mf* delegate.

congreso *m* (de especialistas) conference; (de diputados) parliament; **el ~ de diputados** the lower house of the Spanish Parliament.

conjetura *f* conjecture.

conjugación *f* (de verbos) conjugation; (de colores, estilos, etc) combination.

conjugar *vt* (verbos) to conjugate; (unir) to combine.

conjunción *f* (GRAM) conjunction; (unión) combining.

conjuntamente *adv* jointly.

conjuntivitis *f inv* conjunctivitis.

conjunto *m* (grupo, de rock) group; (ropa) outfit; (en matemáticas) set; **en ~** as a whole.

conmemoración *f* commemoration.

conmemorar *vt* to commemorate.

conmigo *pron* with me.

conmoción *f* shock; **~ cerebral** concussion.

conmover *vt* (impresionar) to move, to touch.

conmutador *m* (de electricidad) switch; (Amér: centralita) switchboard.

cono *m* cone.

conocer *vt* to know; (persona por primera vez) to meet; (distinguir) to recognize ❑ **conocerse** *vpr* (tratarse) to know one another; (por primera vez) to meet; (reconocerse) to recognize one another; (uno mismo) to know o.s.

conocido, -da *adj* well-known ♦ *m, f* acquaintance.

conocimiento *m* (entendimiento) knowledge; (MED) consciousness ❑ **conocimientos** *mpl* knowledge (sg).

conque *conj* so.

conquista *f* conquest.

conquistador, -ra *adj* seductive ♦ *m, f* conqueror.

conquistar *vt* (país, territorio) to conquer; (puesto, trabajo, etc) to obtain; (persona) to win over.

consagrado, -da *adj* (en religión) consecrated; (dedicado) dedicated.

consagrar *vt* (monumento, calle, etc) to dedicate; (acreditar) to confirm.

consciente *adj*: **estar ~** to be conscious; **ser ~ de** to be aware of.

consecuencia *f* consequence; **en ~** consequently.

consecuente *adj* (persona) consistent; (hecho) resultant.

consecutivo, -va *adj* consecutive.

conseguir *vt* (lograr) to obtain; (objetivo) to achieve.

consejo *m* (advertencias) advice; (advertencia concreta) piece of advice; (organismo) council; (reunión) meeting.

consenso *m* consensus.

consentido, -da *adj* spoilt.

consentir *vt* (permitir) to allow.

conserje *m* caretaker.

conserjería *f* reception (desk).

conserva *f*: **en ~** tinned ❑ **conservas** *fpl* tinned food (sg).

conservador, -ra *adj* (en ideología) conservative; (en política)

Conservative; *(que mantiene)* preservative.

conservadurismo *m* conservatism.

conservante *m* preservative.

conservar *vt (mantener, cuidar)* to preserve; *(guardar)* to keep ❏ **conservarse** *vpr (persona)* to look after o.s.; *(alimentos, productos)* to keep.

conservatorio *m* conservatoire.

considerable *adj (grande)* considerable; *(hecho)* notable.

consideración *f (respeto)* respect; **de ~** considerable.

considerar *vt* to consider; *(valorar)* to value.

consigna *f (orden)* instructions *(pl)*; *(depósito)* left-luggage office; **~ automática** (left-)luggage locker.

consignación *f* consignment.

consigo *pron (con él, con ella)* with him (*f* with her); *(con usted)* with you; *(con uno mismo)* with o.s.

consiguiente: por consiguiente *adv* therefore.

consistencia *f* consistency.

consistente *adj (sólido)* solid.

consistir: consistir en *v + prep (componerse de)* to consist of; *(estar fundado en)* to be based on.

consistorio *m* town council.

consola *f (mesa)* console table; *(de videojuegos)* console.

consolar *vt* to console ❏ **consolarse** *vpr* to console o.s.

consolidación *f* consolidation.

consolidar *vt* to consolidate.

consomé *m* consommé; **~ al**

jerez *consommé* made with sherry.

consonante *f* consonant.

consorcio *m* consortium.

consorte *mf* spouse.

conspiración *f* conspiracy.

conspirar *vi* to conspire.

constancia *f (tenacidad)* perseverance.

constante *adj (que dura)* constant; *(tenaz)* persistent ♦ *f* constant; **~s vitales** signs of life.

constantemente *adv* constantly.

constar: constar de *v + prep* to be made up of ❏ **constar en** *v + prep (figurar en)* to appear in; **me consta que** I know that; **que conste que** let there be no doubt that.

constelación *f* constellation.

constipado *m (formal)* cold.

constiparse *vpr (formal)* to catch a cold.

constitución *f (forma)* make-up; *(ley)* constitution.

constitucional *adj* constitutional.

constituir *vt (formar)* to make up; *(componer, fundar)* to form; *(ser)* to be ❏ **constituirse** *vpr (formarse)* to form; **~se de** *(estar compuesto de)* to be made up of.

construcción *f (edificio)* building; *(arte)* construction.

constructivo, -va *adj* constructive.

constructor *m* builder.

constructora *f* construction company.

construir *vt* to build; *(máquina)* to manufacture.

consuelo *m* consolation.

cónsul *mf* consul.

consulado *m (lugar)* consulate; *(cargo)* consulship.

consulta *f (aclaración, examen médico)* consultation; *(pregunta)* question; **~ (médica)** surgery.

consultar *vt (persona, libro)* to consult; *(dato)* to look up; **~ algo a alguien** to consult sb about sthg.

consultorio *m (de médico)* surgery; *(de revista)* problem page; *(de radio)* programme which answers listeners' questions.

consumición *f (alimento)* food; *(bebida)* drink; **"~ obligatoria"** "minimum charge".

consumidor, -ra *m, f* consumer.

consumir *vt (gastar)* to use; *(acabar totalmente)* to use up ♦ *vi (gastar dinero)* to spend ❏ **consumirse** *vpr (extinguirse)* to burn out.

consumismo *m* consumerism.

consumo *m* consumption.

contabilidad *f (cuentas)* accounts *(pl)*.

contable *mf* accountant.

contacto *m* contact; *(de coche)* ignition.

contador, -ra *m, f (Amér) (prestamista)* moneylender; *(contable)* accountant ♦ *m* meter.

contagiar *vt (persona)* to infect; *(enfermedad)* to pass on, to give.

contagio *m* infection; **transmitirse por ~** to be contagious.

contagioso, -sa *adj* infectious.

container *m (de mercancías)* container; *(de basuras)* wheely bin

for rubbish from blocks of flats etc.

contaminación *f* pollution.

contaminado, -da *adj* polluted.

contaminar *vt* to pollute ❏ **contaminarse** *vpr* to become polluted.

contar *vt* to count; *(explicar)* to tell ♦ *vi* to count ❏ **contar con** *v + prep (tener en cuenta)* to take into account; *(tener)* to have; *(confiar en)* to count on.

contemplaciones *fpl* indulgence *(sg)*; **sin ~** without standing on ceremony.

contemplar *vt* to contemplate.

contemporáneo, -a *adj* contemporary.

contenedor *m* container; **~ de basura** wheely bin for rubbish from blocks of flats etc.

contener *vt (llevar)* to contain; *(impedir)* to hold back ❏ **contenerse** *vpr* to hold back.

contenido, -da *adj* restrained ♦ *m* contents *(pl)*.

contentar *vt* to please ❏ **contentarse con** *v + prep* to make do with.

contento, -ta *adj (alegre)* happy; *(satisfecho)* pleased.

contestación *f* answer.

contestador *m:* **~ automático** answering machine.

contestar *vt* to answer ♦ *vi (responder)* to answer; *(responder mal)* to answer back.

contexto *m* context.

contigo *pron* with you.

contiguo, -gua *adj* adjacent.

continental *adj* continental.

continente *m* continent.

continuación *f* continuation; **a ~** then.

continuamente *adv* (*sin interrupción*) continuously; (*repetidamente*) continually.

continuar *vt* to continue; **continúa en la casa** it's still in the house.

continuo, -nua *adj* (*sin interrupción*) continuous; (*repetido*) continual.

contorno *m* (*silueta*) outline.

contra *prep* against ♦ *m*. **los pros y los ~s** the pros and cons; **en ~** against; **en ~ de** against.

contrabajo *m* (*instrumento*) double bass.

contrabandista *mf* smuggler.

contrabando *m* (*de mercancías, droga*) smuggling; (*mercancías*) contraband.

contracorriente *f* cross current; **a ~** against the flow.

contradecir *vt* to contradict ◻ **contradecirse** *vpr* to be inconsistent.

contradicción *f* contradiction.

contradicho, -cha *pp* → **contradecir**.

contradictorio, -ria *adj* contradictory.

contraer *vt* to contract; (*deuda*) to run up; **~ matrimonio** to marry.

contraindicado, -da *adj* not recommended.

contraluz *m* picture taken against the light; **a ~** against the light.

contrapartida *f* compensation; **en ~** as compensation.

contrapelo *m*: **a ~** against the grain.

contrapeso *m* counterbalance.

contrariar *vt* (*disgustar*) to upset.

contrario, -ria *adj* (*opuesto*) opposite; (*equipo, etc*) opposing; (*negativo*) contrary ♦ *m, f* opponent; **al ~** on the contrary; **por el ~** on the contrary; **llevar la contraria** to always take an opposing view.

contraseña *f* password.

contrastar *vi* (*comparar*) to contrast; (*comprobar*) to check ♦ *vi* to contrast.

contraste *m* contrast.

contratar *vt* to hire.

contratiempo *m* mishap.

contrato *m* contract.

contribuir *vi* to contribute; **~ a** to contribute to; **~ con** to contribute.

contrincante *mf* opponent.

control *m* (*comprobación*) inspection; (*dominio*) control; **~ de pasaportes** passport control.

controlar *vt* (*comprobar*) to check; (*dominar*) to control ◻ **controlarse** *vpr* to control o.s.

contusión *f* bruise.

convalidar *vt* (*estudios*) to recognize.

convencer *vt* to convince ◻ **convencerse de** *v* + *prep* to convince o.s. of.

convención *f* convention.

convencional *adj* conventional.

conveniente *adj (oportuno)* suitable; *(hora)* convenient; *(aconsejable)* advisable; *(útil)* useful.

convenio *m* agreement.

convenir *vt* to agree on ♦ *vi (ser adecuado)* to be suitable; **conviene hacerlo** it's a good idea to do it.

convento *m (de monjas)* convent; *(de monjes)* monastery.

conversación *f* conversation.

conversar *vi* to have a conversation.

convertir *vt*: ~ **algo/a alguien en** to turn sth/sb into ❑ **convertirse** *vpr*: ~**se a** *(religión, ideología)* to convert to; ~**se en** *(transformarse en)* to turn into.

convicción *f* conviction.

convidado, -da *m, f* guest.

convidar *vt* to invite.

convincente *adj* convincing.

convite *m* banquet.

convivencia *f* living together.

convivir convivir con *v + prep* to live with.

convocar *vt (reunión)* to convene; *(huelga, elecciones)* to call.

convocatoria *f (de exámenes)* diet.

convulsión *f (espasmo)* convulsion; *(conmoción, revolución)* upheaval.

cónyuge *mf* spouse.

coña *f (vulg: guasa)* joke; **estar de** ~ to be pissing around.

coñac *m* brandy.

coñazo *m (vulg)* pain (in the arse).

coño *interj (vulg)* fuck!

cooperar *vi* to cooperate.

cooperativa *f* cooperative.

coordinación *f* coordination.

coordinar *vt* to coordinate.

copa *f (para beber)* glass; *(trofeo)* cup; *(de árbol)* top; **invitar a alguien a una** ~ to buy sb a drink; **tomar una** ~ to have a drink; **ir de** ~**s** to go out drinking ❑ **copas** *fpl (de la baraja)* suit with pictures of goblets in Spanish deck of cards.

copeo *m*: **ir de** ~ *(fam)* to go out drinking.

copia *f* copy.

copiar *vt* to copy.

copiloto *m* copilot.

copioso, -sa *adj* copious.

copla *f (estrofa)* verse; *(canción)* popular song.

copo *m* flake.

coquetear *vi* to flirt.

coqueto, -ta *adj (que flirtea)* flirtatious.

coraje *m (valor)* courage; **dar** ~ to make angry.

coral *vt* coral ♦ *f (coro)* choir.

coraza *f (de soldado)* cuirass.

corazón *m* heart; *(de fruta)* core; **corazones** *mpl (de la baraja)* hearts.

corbata *f* tie.

corchea *f* quaver.

corchete *m (cierre)* hook and eye; *(signo)* square bracket.

corcho *m* cork.

cordel *m* cord.

cordero, -ra *m, f* lamb; ~ **asado** roast lamb.

cordial *adj* cordial.

cordialmente *adv* cordially.

cordillera *f* mountain range; **la** ~ **Cantábrica** the Cantabrian Mountains *(pl)*.

cordón m (cuerda) cord; (de zapato) lace; (cable eléctrico) flex; ~ **umbilical** umbilical cord.

Corea s Korea; ~ **del Norte** North Korea; ~ **del Sur** South Korea.

coreografía f choreography.

corista mf chorus singer.

cornada f goring.

cornamenta f (de toro) horns (pl); (de ciervo) antlers (pl).

córnea f cornea.

corneja f crow.

córner m corner (kick).

cornete m cone.

cornflakes® [ˈkɒnfleɪks] mpl Cornflakes®.

cornisa f cornice.

coro m choir; **a** ~ in unison.

corona f (de rey) crown; (fig: trono) throne; (de flores) garland.

coronar vt to crown.

coronel m colonel.

coronilla f crown (of the head); **estar hasta la** ~ to be fed up to the back teeth.

corporal adj (olor) body (antes de s).

corpulento, -ta adj corpulent.

Corpus m Corpus Christi.

corral m (para animales) pen.

correa f (de bolso, reloj) strap, (de pantalón) belt; (de animal) lead.

corrección f (de errores) correction; (de comportamiento) correctness.

correctamente adv correctly.

correcto, -ta adj (sin errores) correct; (educado) polite.

corredor, -ra m, f (en deporte) runner; (intermediario) agent ◆ m (pasillo) corridor.

corregir vt (error, comportamiento) to correct; (exámenes) to mark ❑ **corregirse** vpr to mend one's ways.

correo m post, mail; ~ **aéreo** airmail; ~ **certificado** = registered post; ~ **urgente** = special delivery ❑ **Correos** m inv the Post Office; **"Correos y Telégrafos"** sign outside a major post office indicating telegram service.

correr vi (persona, animal) to run; (río) to flow; (tiempo) to pass; (noticia, rumor) to go around ◆ vt (mesa, silla, etc) to move up; (cortinas) to draw; **dejar** ~ **algo** to let sthg be ❑ **correrse** vpr (tintas, colores) to run.

correspondencia f correspondence; (de transporte) connection; **"~s"** (en metro) "to other lines".

corresponder vi: ~ **a alguien (con algo)** to repay sb (with sthg); **te corresponde hacerlo** it's your responsibility to do it.

correspondiente adj corresponding.

corresponsal mf correspondent.

corrida f (de toros) bullfight.

corriente adj (agua) running; (común) ordinary; (día, mes, año) current ◆ f (de aire) draught; (de mar) current; **estar al** ~ **de** to be up to date with; **ponerse al** ~ **de** to bring o.s. up to date with; ~ **(eléctrica)** (electric) current.

corro m circle.

corromper vt (pervertir) to corrupt; (sobornar) to bribe; (pudrir) to rot.

corrupción f (perversión) corruption; (soborno) bribery.

corsé m corset.

corsetería f ladies' underwear shop.

cortacésped m lawnmower.

cortado, -da adj (leche) off; (salsa) curdled; (labios, manos) chapped; (fam: persona) inhibited ♦ m small coffee with a drop of milk.

cortante adj (cuchilla, etc) sharp; (persona) cutting; (viento, frío) bitter.

cortar vt to cut; (calle) to block off; (conversación) to cut short; (luz, gas, etc) to cut off; (piel) to chap ♦ **cortarse** vpr (herirse) to cut o.s.; (avergonzarse) to become tonguetied; (leche, salsa) to curdle.

cortaúñas m inv nailclippers (pl).

corte m (herida) cut; (en vestido, tela, etc) tear; (de corriente eléctrica) power cut; (vergüenza) embarrassment; ~ **y confección** (para mujeres) dressmaking; ~ **de pelo** haircut.

Cortes fpl: Las ~ the Spanish parliament.

cortés adj polite.

cortesía f politeness.

corteza f (de árbol) bark; (de pan) crust; (de queso, limón) rind; (de naranja) peel; ~s **de cerdo** pork scratchings.

cortijo m farm.

cortina f curtain.

corto, -ta adj (breve) short; (fam: tonto) thick; **quedarse** ~ (al

calcular) to underestimate; ~ **de vista** short-sighted.

cortometraje m short (film).

cosa f thing; ¿**alguna** ~ **más?** is that everything?; **ser** ~ **de alguien** to be sb's business; **como si tal** ~ as if nothing had happened.

coscorrón m bump on the head.

cosecha f harvest; (de vino) vintage.

cosechar vt to harvest ♦ vi to bring in the harvest.

coser vt & vi to sew.

cosmopolita adj cosmopolitan.

cosmos m cosmos.

cosquillas fpl: **hacer** ~ to tickle; **tener** ~ to be ticklish.

cosquilleo m tickling sensation.

costa f (orilla) coast; **a** ~ **de** at the expense of.

costado m side.

costar vi (valer) to cost; **me cuesta (mucho) hacerlo** it's (very) difficult for me to do it; ¿**cuánto cuesta?** how much is it?

Costa Rica s Costa Rica.

costarriqueño, -ña adj & m, f Costa Rican.

coste m (de producción) cost; (de producto, mercancía) price.

costero, -ra adj coastal.

costilla f rib; ~s **de cordero** lamb chops.

costo m (de producción) cost; (de producto, mercancía) price.

costoso, -sa adj expensive.

costra f (de herida) scab.

costumbre f habit; **tener la** ~

de to be in the habit of.

costura f (labor) sewing; (de vestido) seam.

costurera f seamstress.

costurero m sewing box.

cota f (altura) height (above sea level).

cotejo m comparison.

cotidiano, -na adj daily.

cotilla mf (fam) gossip.

cotilleo m (fam) gossip.

cotillón m New Year's Eve party.

cotización f (de la moneda) price.

cotizar vt (en la Bolsa) to price; (cuota) to pay.

coto m (terreno) reserve; ~ **(privado) de caza** (private) game preserve.

cotorra f (pájaro) parrot; (fam: charlatán) chatterbox

COU m (abrev de curso de orientación universitaria) optional year of Spanish secondary education in which 17-18 year olds prepare for university entrance exams; a mixture of compulsory and optional subjects is studied.

coyuntura f current situation.

coz f tick.

cráneo m skull.

cráter m crater.

crawl [krol] m crawl.

creación f creation.

creador, -ra m, f creator.

crear vt (inventar) to create; (fundar) to found.

creatividad f creativity.

creativo, -va adj creative.

crecer vi to grow; (río) to rise;

(luna) to wax.

crecimiento m growth.

credencial f identification.

crédito m (préstamo) loan; (disponibilidad) credit; (confianza) confidence.

credo m (oración) Creed.

creencia f (en religión) faith; (convicción) belief.

creer vt (dar por verdadero) to believe; (suponer) to think; **¡ya lo creo!** I should say so! □ **creer en** v + prep to believe in.

creído, -da adj (presuntuoso) vain.

crema f (nata, cosmético) cream; (betún) polish; ~ **de ave** cream of chicken soup; ~ **de belleza** beauty cream; ~ **de cangrejos** crab bisque; ~ **catalana** Catalan dessert similar to crème caramel; ~ **de espárragos** cream of asparagus soup; ~ **de gambas** shrimp bisque; ~ **de marisco** seafood bisque; ~ **(pastelera)** custard.

cremallera f zip (Br), zipper (US).

crepe [krep] f crepe.

cresta f crest.

cretino, -na adj (estúpido) stupid.

creyente mf believer.

cría f (de ganado) breeding; (hijo de animal) young, → **crío.**

criadero m farm.

criadillas fpl bull's testicles.

criado, -da m, f servant (f maid).

crianza f (de animales) breeding; (educación) bringing up; (de vino) vintage.

criar vt (animales) to breed; (educar) to bring up ◆ vi to breed.

criatura f creature.

crimen m crime.

criminal mf criminal.

crío, -a m, f kid.

criollo, -lla m, f Latin American of Spanish extraction.

crisis f inv (en política) crisis; (económica) recession; (en enfermedad) breakdown.

cristal m (sustancia) glass; (vidrio fino) crystal; (de ventana) pane.

cristalería f (tienda) glassware shop; (objetos) glassware.

cristalino, -na adj crystalline.

cristianismo m Christianity.

cristiano, -na adj & m, f Christian.

Cristo m Christ.

criterio m (regla, norma) criterion; (opinión) opinion.

crítica f (de arte, cine, etc) review; (censura) criticism, → **crítico**.

criticar vt (obra, película, etc) to review; (censurar) to criticize ◆ vi to criticize.

crítico, -ca adj critical ◆ m, f critic.

croar vi to croak.

croissant [krwa'san] m croissant.

croissantería f shop selling filled croissants.

crol m (front) crawl.

cromo m (estampa) transfer.

crónica f (de historia) chronicle; (en periódico) column.

cronometrar vt to time.

cronómetro m stopwatch.

croqueta f croquette.

croquis m inv sketch.

cros m inv cross-country (running).

cruce m (de calles, caminos) crossroads; (en el teléfono) crossed line.

crucero m (en barco) cruise; (de iglesia) transept.

crucial adj crucial.

crucifijo m crucifix.

crucigrama m crossword.

crudo, -da adj (no cocido) raw; (novela, película) harshly realistic; (clima) harsh.

cruel adj cruel.

crueldad f cruelty.

crujido m creak.

crujiente adj (alimento) crunchy.

crustáceo m crustacean.

cruz f cross; (de la moneda) tails; (fig: carga) burden.

cruzada f crusade.

cruzar vt to cross ❑ **cruzarse** vpr: ~se de brazos (fig) to twiddle one's thumbs; **cruzarse con** v + prep (persona) to pass.

cta. (abrev de cuenta) a/c.

cte. (abrev de corriente) inst.

CTNE (abrev de Compañía Telefónica Nacional de España) Spanish state telephone company.

cuaderno m (libreta) notebook; (de colegial) exercise book.

cuadra f (lugar, conjunto) stable; (Amér: esquina) corner; (Amér: de casas) block.

cuadrado, -da adj & m square.

cuadriculado, -da adj squared.

cuadrilla f group, team.

cuadro m (cuadrado) square; (pintura) picture, painting; (gráfico) diagram; **a o de ~s** checked.

cuajada f curd; **~ con miel** dish of curd covered in honey.

cual pron: **el/la ~** (persona) who; (cosa) which; **lo ~** which; **sea ~ sea su nombre** whatever his name may be.

cuál pron (qué) what; (especificando) which; **¿~ te gusta más?** which do you prefer?

cualidad f quality.

cualificado, -da adj skilled.

cualquier adj → **cualquiera**.

cualquiera adj any ◆ pron anybody ◆ mf nobody; **cualquier día iré a verte** I'll drop by one of these days.

cuando adv when ◆ conj (si) if ◆ prep: **~ la guerra** when the war was on; **de ~ en ~** from time to time; **de vez en ~** from time to time.

cuándo adv when.

cuantía f amount.

cuanto, -ta adj 1. (todo): **despilfarra ~ dinero gana** he squanders all the money he earns.

2. (compara cantidades): **cuantas más mentiras digas, menos te creerán** the more you lie, the less people will believe you.

◆ pron 1. (de personas): everyone who; **dio las gracias a todos ~s le ayudaron** he thanked everyone who helped him.

2. (todo lo que): everything; **come ~/~s quieras** eat as much/as many as you like; **todo ~ dijo era verdad** everything she said was true.

3. (compara cantidades): **~ más se tiene, más se quiere** the more you have, the more you want.

4. (en locuciones): **~ antes** as soon as possible; **en ~** (tan pronto como) as soon as; **en ~ a** as regards; **unos ~s** a few.

cuánto, -ta adj (interrogativo singular) how much; (interrogativo plural) how many; (exclamativo) what a lot of ◆ pron (interrogativo singular) how much; (interrogativo plural) how many; **¿~ quieres?** how much do you want?

cuarenta núm forty, → **seis**.

cuaresma f Lent.

cuartel m barracks (pl); **~ de la Guardia Civil** headquarters of the "Guardia Civil".

cuartelazo m (Amér) military uprising.

cuarteto m quartet.

cuartilla f sheet of (quarto) paper.

cuarto, -ta núm fourth ◆ m (parte, periodo) quarter; (habitación) room, → **sexto**; **~ de baño** bathroom; **~ de estar** living room; **un ~ de hora** a quarter of an hour; **un ~ de kilo** a quarter of a kilo.

cuarzo m quartz.

cuate mf inv (Amér. fam) mate.

cuatro núm four, → **seis**.

cuatrocientos, -tas núm four hundred, → **seis**.

Cuba s Cuba.

cubalibre m rum and Coke.

cubano, -na adj & m, f Cuban.

cubertería f cutlery.

cubeta f (Amér) bucket.

cúbico, -ca adj cubic.

cubierta f (de libro) cover; (de barco) deck.

cubierto, -ta pp irreg → **cubrir** ♦ adj (tapado) covered; (cielo) overcast ♦ m (pieza para comer) piece of cutlery; (para comensal) place setting; **a ~ under cover.**

cubito m: ~ **de hielo** ice cube.

cúbito m ulna.

cubo m (recipiente) bucket; (en geometría, matemáticas) cube; ~ **de la basura** rubbish bin (Br), trash can (Am).

cubrir vt to cover; (proteger) to protect ☐ **cubrirse** vpr to cover o.s.

cucaracha f cockroach.

cuchara f spoon.

cucharada f spoonful.

cucharilla f teaspoon.

cucharón m ladle.

cuchilla f blade; ~ **de afeitar** razor blade.

cuchillo m knife.

cuclillas fpl: **en ~** squatting.

cucurucho m cone.

cuello m (del cuerpo) neck; (de la camisa) collar.

cuenca f (de río, mar) basin.

cuenco m bowl.

cuenta f (cálculo) sum; (factura) bill; (de banco) account; (de collar) bead; **la ~, por favor** could I have the bill, please?; **caer en la ~** to catch on; **darse ~ de** to notice; **tener en ~** to take into account.

cuentagotas m inv dropper; **en ~** in dribs and drabs.

cuentakilómetros m inv (de distancia) = mileometer; (de veloci-dad) speedometer.

cuento m (relato) short story; (mentira) story.

cuerda f (fina, de instrumento) string; (gruesa) rope; (del reloj) spring; **~s vocales** vocal cords; **dar ~ a** (reloj) to wind up.

cuerno m horn; (de ciervo) antler.

cuero m (piel) leather; ~ **cabelludo** scalp; **en ~s** stark naked.

cuerpo m body; (de policía) force; (militar) corps.

cuervo m raven.

cuesta f slope; ~ **arriba** uphill; ~ **abajo** downhill; **a ~s** on one's back.

cuestión f question; **ser ~ de** to be a question of.

cuestionario m questionnaire.

cueva f cave.

cuidado m care ♦ interj be careful!; **¡~ con la cabeza!** mind your head!; **de ~** dangerous; **estar al ~ de** to be responsible for; **tener ~** to be careful.

cuidadosamente adv carefully.

cuidadoso, -sa adj careful.

cuidar vt to look after ♦ vi: ~ **de** to look after ☐ **cuidarse** vpr to look after o.s.; **cuidarse de v + prep (encargarse de)** to look after.

culata f (de arma) butt; (de motor) cylinder head.

culebra f snake.

culebrón m (fam) soap opera.

culo m (fam) (de persona) bum (Br), butt (Am); (de botella, etc) bottom.

culpa f fault; **echar la ~ a alguien**

to blame sb; **tener la ~** to be to blame.

culpabilidad f guilt.

culpable mf guilty party ◆ adj: **~ de** guilty of.

culpar vt (echar la culpa) to blame; (acusar) to accuse; **~ a algo/a alguien de** to blame sthg/sb for.

cultivar vt (plantas) to grow; (tierra) to farm.

cultivo m (plantas) crop.

culto, -ta adj (persona) educated; (estilo) refined; (lenguaje) literary ◆ m worship.

cultura f (actividades) culture; (conocimientos) knowledge.

cultural adj cultural.

culturismo m body-building.

cumbre f summit.

cumpleaños m inv birthday.

cumplido m compliment.

cumplir vt (ley, orden) to obey; (promesa) to keep, (condena) to serve ◆ vi (plazo) to expire; **~ con** (deber) to do; (promesa) to keep; **hoy cumple 21 años** he's 21 today.

cúmulo m (de cosas) pile (de nubes) cumulus.

cuna f (cama) cot; (origen) cradle; (natal) birthplace.

cuneta f (en carretera) ditch; (en la calle) gutter.

cuña f (calza) wedge; (en radio, televisión) commercial break.

cuñado, -da m, f brother-in-law (f sister-in-law).

cuota f (a club, etc) membership fee; (a Hacienda) tax (payment); (precio) fee.

cuplé m type of popular song.

cupo v → caber ◆ m (cantidad máxima) quota; (cantidad proporcional) share.

cupón m (vale) coupon; (de sorteo, lotería) ticket.

cúpula f (de edificio) dome.

cura¹ m (sacerdote) priest.

cura² f (restablecimiento) recovery; (tratamiento) cure; **~ de reposo** rest cure.

curandero, -ra m, f quack.

curar vt to cure; (herida) to dress; (pieles) to tan ❑ **curarse** vpr to recover.

curiosidad f curiosity; **tener ~ por** to be curious about.

curioso, -sa adj (de noticias, habladurías, etc) curious; (interesante, raro) strange ◆ m, f onlooker.

curita f (Amér) (sticking) plaster.

curry m curry, **al ~** curried.

cursi adj (persona) pretentious; (vestido, canción) naff.

cursillo m (curso breve) short course; (de conferencias) series of talks.

curso m course; (año académico, alumnos) year; **en ~** (año) current.

cursor m cursor.

curva f curve; (de camino, carretera, etc) bend.

curvado, -da adj curved.

custodia f (vigilancia) safekeeping; (de los hijos) custody.

cutis m inv skin, complexion.

cutre adj (fam: sucio) shabby; (fam: pobre) cheap and nasty.

cuy m (Amér) guinea-pig.

cuyo, -ya adj (de quien) whose; (de que) of which.

D. *abrev* = **don**.

dado *m* dice.

daga *f* dagger.

dalia *f* dahlia.

dama *f* lady ❑ **damas** *fpl (juego)* draughts *(sg)*.

danés, -esa *adj & m* Danish ◆ *m, f* Dane.

danza *f* dance.

danzar *vt & vi* to dance.

dañar *vt (persona)* to harm; *(cosa)* to damage.

dañino, -na *adj (sustancia)* harmful; *(animal)* dangerous.

daño *m (dolor)* pain; *(perjuicio)* damage; *(a persona)* harm; **hacer ~** *(producir dolor)* to hurt; **la cena me hizo ~** the meal didn't agree with me.

dar *vt* 1. *(entregar, regalar, decir)* to give; **da clases en la universidad** he teaches at the university; **me dio las gracias/los buenos días** she thanked me/said good morning to me.
2. *(producir)* to produce.
3. *(causar, provocar)* to give; **me da vergüenza/sueño** it makes me ashamed/sleepy; **me da risa** it makes me laugh.
4. *(suj: reloj)* to strike; **el reloj ha dado las diez** the clock struck ten.
5. *(encender)* to turn on; **por favor, da la luz** turn on the lights, please.
6. *(comunicar, emitir)* to give.
7. *(película, programa)* to show; *(obra de teatro)* to put on.
8. *(mostrar)* to show; **su aspecto daba señales de cansancio** she was showing signs of weariness.
9. *(expresa acción)* to give; **~ un grito** to give a cry; **le dio un golpe** he hit him.
10. *(banquete, baile)* to hold; **van a ~ una fiesta** they're going to throw a party.
11. *(considerar)*: **~ algo/a alguien por algo** to consider sthg/sb to be sthg.
◆ *vi* 1. *(horas)* to strike; **han dado las tres en el reloj** the clock struck three.
2. *(golpear)*: **le dieron en la cabeza** they hit her on the head; **la piedra dio contra el cristal** the stone hit the glass.
3. *(sobrevenir)*: **le dieron varios ataques al corazón** he had several heart attacks.
4.: **~ a** *(balcón, ventana)* to look out onto; *(pasillo)* to lead to; *(casa, fachada)* to face.
5. *(proporcionar)*: **~ de comer** to feed; **~ de beber a alguien** to give sb something to drink.
6.: **~ en** *(blanco)* to hit.
7. *(en locuciones)*: **~ de sí** to stretch; **~ que hablar** to set people talking; **da igual** ○ **lo mismo** it doesn't matter; **¡qué más da!** what does it matter!
❑ **dar a** *v + prep (llave)* to turn; **dar con** *v + prep (encontrar)* to find; **darse** *vpr (suceder)* to happen; *(dilatarse)* to stretch; **~se contra** to bump into; **se le da bien/mal el latín** she is good/bad at Latin; **~se prisa** to hurry; **se las da de listo** he

likes to make out that he's clever; **~se por vencido** to give in; **darse a** v + prep (entregarse) to take to.

dardo m dart ❏ **dardos** mpl (juego) darts (sg).

dátil m date.

dato m fact, piece of information; **~s** information (sg); **~s personales** personal details.

dcha. (abrev de derecha) r.

d. de J.C. (abrev de después de Jesucristo) AD.

de prep 1. (posesión, pertenencia) of; **el coche ~ mi padre/mis padres** my father's/parents' car; **la casa es ~ ella** the house is hers.

2. (materia) (made) of; **un reloj ~ oro** a gold watch.

3. (contenido) of; **un vaso ~ agua** a glass of water.

4. (en descripciones): **~ fácil manejo** user-friendly; **la señora ~ verde** the lady in green; **difícil ~ creer** hard to believe; **una bolsa ~ deporte** a sports bag.

5. (asunto) about; **háblame ~ ti** tell me about yourself; **libros ~ historia** history books.

6. (en calidad de) as; **trabaja ~ bombero** he works as a fireman.

7. (tiempo): **trabaja ~ nueve a cinco** she works from nine to five; **trabaja ~ noche y duerme ~ día** he works at night and sleeps during the day; **a las tres ~ la tarde** at three in the afternoon; **llegamos ~ madrugada** we arrived early in the morning; **~ pequeño** as a child.

8. (procedencia, distancia) from; **vengo ~ mi casa** I've come from home; **soy ~ Zamora** I'm from Zamora; **del metro a casa voy a pie** I walk home from the under-

ground.

9. (causa, modo) with; **morirse ~ frío** to freeze to death; **llorar ~ alegría** to cry with joy; **~ una (sola) vez** in one go.

10. (con superlativos): **el mejor ~ todos** the best of all.

11. (cantidad): **más/menos ~** more/less than.

12. (condición) if; **~ querer ayudarme, lo haría** if she wanted to help me, she would.

dé v → dar.

debajo adv underneath; **~ de** under.

debate m debate.

debatir vt to debate.

deber m duty.

♦ vt 1. (expresa obligación): **debes dominar tus impulsos** you should control your impulses; **nos debemos ir a casa a las diez** we must go home at ten.

2. (adeudar) to owe; **me debes doce mil pesetas** you owe me twelve thousand pesetas; **¿cuánto o qué le debo?** how much does it come to?

3. (en locuciones): **debido a** due to. ❏ **deber de** v + prep: **debe de llegar a las nueve** she should arrive at nine; **deben de ser las doce** it must be twelve o'clock; **deberse a** v + prep (ser consecuencia de) to be due to; (dedicarse a) to have a responsibility towards; **deberes** mpl (trabajo escolar) homework (sg).

debido, -da adj proper; **~ a** due to.

débil adj (sin fuerzas) weak; (voz, sonido) faint; (luz) dim.

debilidad f weakness.

debilitar vt to weaken.

debut m (de artista) debut.

década f decade.

decadencia f (declive) decline.

decadente adj decadent.

decaer vi (fuerza, energía) to fail; (esperanzas, país) to decline; (ánimos) to flag.

decaído, -da adj (deprimido) gloomy.

decano, -na m, f (de universidad) dean; (el más antiguo) senior member.

decena f ten.

decente adj (honesto) decent; (limpio) clean.

decepción f disappointment.

decepcionar vt to disappoint □ **decepcionarse** vpr to be disappointed.

decidido, -da adj determined.

decidir vt to decide □ **decidirse** vpr: ~se a to decide to.

decimal adj decimal.

décimo, -ma núm tenth ◆ m (en lotería) tenth share in a lottery ticket, → **sexto**.

decir vt (enunciar) to say; (contar) to tell; ~ **a alguien que haga algo** to tell sb to do sthg; ~ **que sí** to say yes; ¡**diga?**, ¿**dígame?** (al teléfono) hello?; **es** ~ that is; ¿**cómo se dice** ...? how do you say ...?; **se dice** ... they say ...

decisión f (resolución) decision; (de carácter) determination; **tomar una** ~ to take a decision.

declaración f statement; (de amor) declaration; **prestar** ~ to give evidence; **tomar** ~ to take a statement; ~ **de la renta** tax return.

declarado, -da adj declared.

declarar vt to state; (afirmar, bienes, riquezas) to declare ◆ vi (dar testimonio) to give evidence □ **declararse** vpr (incendio, epidemia, etc) to break out; (en el amor) to declare o.s.; **me declaro a favor de** ... I'm in favour of ...

declinar vt to decline.

decoración f (de casa, habitación) décor; (adornos) decorations (pl).

decorado m (en teatro, cine) set.

decorar vt to decorate.

decretar vt to decree.

decreto m decree.

dedal m thimble.

dedicación f dedication.

dedicar vt (tiempo, dinero, energía) to devote; (obra) to dedicate □ **dedicarse a** v + prep (actividad, tarea) to spend time on; ¿**a qué se dedica Vd?** what do you do for a living?

dedo m (de mano, bebida) finger; (de pie) toe; (medida) centimetre; **hacer** ~ (fam) to hitchhike; ~ **corazón** middle finger; ~ **gordo** thumb.

deducción f deduction.

deducir vt (concluir) to deduce; (restar) to deduct.

defecar vi (formal) to defecate.

defecto m (físico) defect; (moral) fault.

defender vt to defend □ **defenderse** vpr (protegerse) to defend o.s.; ~**se de** (ataque, insultos) to defend o.s. against.

defensa f defence.

defensor, -ra m, f defender; (abogado) counsel for the defence.

deficiencia f (defecto) deficiency; (falta, ausencia) lack.

deficiente adj (imperfecto) deficient.

déficit m inv (en economía) deficit; (escasez) shortage.

definición f definition.

definir vt to define □ **definirse** vpr (fig) to take a position.

definitivo, -va adj (final, decisivo) definitive; (terminante) definite; **en definitiva** in short.

deformación f deformation.

deformar vt to deform.

defraudar vt (decepcionar) to disappoint; (estafar) to defraud.

defunción f (formal) death.

degenerado, -da m, f degenerate.

degenerar vi to degenerate.

degustación f tasting.

dejadez f neglect.

dejar vt 1 (colocar, poner) to leave; **deja el abrigo en la percha** leave your coat on the hanger; **"deje aquí su compra"** sign indicating lockers where bags must be left when entering a supermarket.
2. (prestar) to lend; **me dejó su pluma** she lent me her pen.
3. (no tomar) to leave; **deja lo que no quieras** leave whatever you don't want; **deja un poco de café para mí** leave a bit of coffee for me.
4. (dar) to give; **déjame la llave** give me the key; **dejé el perro a mi madre** I left the dog with my mother.

5. (vicio, estudios) to give up; (casa, novia) to leave; (familia) to abandon; **dejó su casa** he left home.
6. (producir) to leave; **este perfume deja mancha en la ropa** this perfume stains your clothing.
7. (permitir) to allow, to let; **~ a alguien hacer algo** to let sb do sthg; **"dejen salir antes de entrar"** (en metro, tren) "let the passengers off the train first, please"; **sus gritos no me dejaron dormir** his cries prevented me from sleeping.
8. (olvidar, omitir) to leave out; **~ algo por o sin hacer** to fail to do sthg; **déjalo para otro día** leave it for another day.
9. (no molestar) to leave alone; **¡déjame!** let me be!
10. (esperar): **dejó que acabara de llover para salir** he waited until it stopped raining before going out.
11. (en locuciones): **~ algo aparte** to leave sthg to one side; **~ algo/a alguien atrás** to leave sthg/sb behind; **~ caer algo** (objeto) to drop sthg.

♦ vi 1. (parar): **~ de hacer algo** to stop doing sthg.
2. (no olvidar): **no ~ de hacer algo** to be sure to do sthg.
□ **dejarse** vpr (olvidarse) to leave; (descuidarse, abandonarse) to let o.s. go; **~se llevar por** to get carried away with; **apenas se deja ver** we hardly see anything of her; **dejarse de** v + prep: **¡déjate de tonterías!** stop that nonsense!

del → de, el.

delantal m apron.

delante adv (en primer lugar) in front; (en la parte delantera) at the front; (enfrente) opposite; **~ de** in front of.

delantera f *(de coche, avión, etc)* front; **coger** o **tomar la ~** to take the lead.

delantero, -ra adj front ♦ m *(en deporte)* forward.

delatar vt *(persona)* to denounce; *(suj: gesto, acto)* to betray.

delco® m distributor.

delegación f *(oficina)* (local) office; *(representación)* delegation.

delegado, -da m, f delegate; **~ de curso** student elected to represent his/her classmates.

delegar vt to delegate.

deletrear vt to spell.

delfín m dolphin.

delgado, -da adj thin; *(esbelto)* slim.

deliberadamente adv deliberately.

deliberado, -da adj deliberate.

deliberar vt to deliberate.

delicadeza f *(atención, miramiento)* consideration; *(finura)* delicacy; *(cuidado)* care.

delicado, -da adj delicate; *(respetuoso)* considerate.

delicia f delight.

delicioso, -sa adj *(exquisito)* delicious; *(agradable)* lovely.

delincuencia f crime.

delincuente mf criminal; **~ común** common criminal.

delirante adj *(persona)* delirious; *(idea)* mad.

delirar vi *(por la fiebre)* to be delirious; *(decir disparates)* to talk rubbish.

delirio m *(perturbación)* ravings *(pl)*.

delito m crime.

delta m delta.

demanda f *(petición)* request; *(reivindicación, de mercancías)* demand; *(en un juicio)* action.

demandar vt *(pedir)* to request; *(reivindicar)* to demand; *(en un juicio)* to sue.

demás adj other ♦ pron: **los/las ~** the rest; **lo ~** the rest; **por lo ~** apart from that.

demasiado, -da adj *(con sustantivos singulares)* too much; *(con sustantivos plurales)* too many ♦ adv too much; **~ rápido** too fast; **hace ~ frío** it's too cold.

demencia f insanity.

demente adj *(formal)* insane.

democracia f democracy.

demócrata adj democratic ♦ mf democrat.

democráticamente adv democratically.

democrático, -ca adj democratic.

demoledor, -ra adj *(máquina, aparato)* demolition *(antes de s)*; *(argumento, crítica)* devastating.

demoler vt to demolish.

demonio m devil; **¿qué ~s ...?** what the hell ...?

demora f delay.

demostración f *(de hecho)* proof; *(de afecto, sentimiento, etc)* demonstration.

demostrar vt *(probar)* to prove; *(indicar)* to demonstrate, to show.

denominación f: **~ de origen** appellation d'origine.

densidad f density.

denso, -sa *adj* dense.

dentadura *f* teeth *(pl)*; **~ postiza** dentures *(pl)*.

dentífrico *m* toothpaste.

dentista *mf* dentist.

dentro *adv (en el interior)* inside; **~ de** *(en el interior)* in; *(en el plazo de)* in, within.

denunciante *mf* person who reports a crime.

denunciar *vt (delito, persona)* to report (to the police); *(situación irregular, escándalo)* to reveal.

departamento *m (de empresa, organismo)* department; *(de armario, maleta)* compartment.

dependencia *f (subordinación)* dependence; *(habitación)* room; *(sección, departamento)* branch.

depender *vi.* **depende ...** it depends ...; □ **depender de** *v + prep* to depend on.

dependiente, -ta *m, f* shop assistant.

depilarse *vpr* to remove hair from; **~ las cejas** to pluck one's eyebrows.

depilatorio, -ria *adj* hair-removing.

deporte *m* sport; **hacer ~** to do sport; **~s de invierno** winter sports.

deportista *mf* sportsman *(f* sportswoman).

deportivo, -va *adj (zapatillas, pantalón, prueba)* sports *(antes de s)*; *(persona)* sporting ◆ *m* sports car.

depositar *vt (en un lugar)* to place; *(en el banco)* to deposit.

depósito *m (almacén)* store; *(de dinero)* deposit; *(recipiente)* tank; **~ de agua** water tank; **~ de gasolina** petrol tank *(Br)*, gas tank *(Am)*.

depresión *f* depression.

depresivo, -va *adj (MED)* depressive.

deprimido, -da *adj* depressed.

deprimir *vt* to depress □ **deprimirse** *vpr* to get depressed.

deprisa *adv* quickly.

depuradora *f* purifier.

depurar *vt (sustancia)* to purify.

derecha *f:* **la ~** *(mano derecha)* one's right hand; *(lado derecho, en política)* the right; **a la ~** on the right; **gira a la ~** turn right; **ser de ~s** to be right wing.

derecho, -cha *adj (lado, mano, pie)* right; *(recto)* straight ◆ *m (privilegio, facultad)* right; *(estudios)* law; *(de tela, prenda)* right side ◆ *adv* straight; **todo ~** straight on; **¡no hay ~!** it's not fair!

derivar: derivar de *v + prep* to derive from; **derivar en** *v + prep* to end in.

dermoprotector, -ra *adj* barrier *(antes de s)*.

derramar *vt (por accidente)* to spill; *(verter)* to pour □ **derramarse** *vpr* to spill.

derrame *m* spillage; **~ cerebral** brain haemorrhage.

derrapar *vi* to skid.

derretir *vt* to melt □ **derretirse** *vpr (hielo, mantequilla)* to melt; *(persona)* to go weak at the knees.

derribar *vt (casa, muro, adversario)* to knock down; *(gobierno)* to overthrow.

derrochar vt to waste.
derroche m (de dinero) waste; (de esfuerzo, simpatía) excess.
derrota f defeat.
derrotar vt to defeat.
derrumbar vt (casa, muro) to knock down ❑ **derrumbarse** vpr (casa, muro) to collapse; (moralmente) to be devastated.
desabrochar vt to undo ❑ **desabrocharse** vpr: **~se la camisa** to unbutton one's shirt. ~
desacreditar vt to discredit.
desacuerdo m disagreement.
desafiar vt (persona) to challenge; (elementos, peligros) to defy; **~ a alguien a** to challenge sb to.
desafinar vi to be out of tune ❑ **desafinarse** vpr to go out of tune.
desafío m challenge.
desafortunadamente adv unfortunately.
desafortunado, -da adj (sin suerte) unlucky; (inoportuno) unfortunate.
desagradable adj unpleasant.
desagradecido, -da adj (persona) ungrateful; (trabajo, tarea) thankless.
desagüe m (de bañera, fregadero, piscina) drain; (cañería) drainpipe.
desahogarse vpr to pour one's heart out.
desaire m snub.
desajuste m: **~ horario** jet lag.
desaliñado, -da adj (persona) unkempt.
desalojar vt (por incendio, etc) to evacuate; (por la fuerza) to evict; **~ a alguien de** to evict sb from.
desamparado, -da adj abandoned.

desangrarse vpr to lose a lot of blood.
desanimar vt to discourage ❑ **desanimarse** vpr to be discouraged.
desaparecer vi to disappear.
desaparecido, -da m, f missing person.
desaparición f disappearance.
desapercibido, -da adj: **pasar ~** to go unnoticed.
desaprovechar vt to waste.
desarmador m (Amér) screwdriver.
desarrollado, -da adj developed; (persona) well-developed.
desarrollar vt to develop ❑ **desarrollarse** vpr to develop; (suceder) to take place.
desarrollo m development.
desasosiego m anxiety.
desastre m disaster; (objeto de mala calidad) useless thing.
desatar vt to untie; (sentimiento) to unleash.
desatino m (equivocación) mistake.
desavenencia f disagreement.
desayunar vt to have for breakfast ♦ vi to have breakfast.
desayuno m breakfast.
desbarajuste m disorder.
desbaratar vt to ruin.
desbordarse vpr (río, lago) to overflow; (sentimiento, pasión) to erupt.
descabellado, -da adj mad.
descafeinado adj decaffeinated ♦ m decaffeinated coffee; **café ~** decaffeinated coffee.

descalificar vt (jugador) to disqualify; (desacreditar) to discredit.

descalzarse vpr to take one's shoes off.

descalzo, -za adj barefoot; **ir ~** to go barefoot.

descampado m open ground.

descansar vi (reposar) to rest; (dormir) to sleep.

descansillo m landing.

descanso m (reposo) rest; (pausa) break; (intermedio) interval; (alivio) relief.

descapotable m convertible.

descarado, -da adj (persona) cheeky; (intento, mentira) blatant.

descarga f (de mercancías) unloading; **~ eléctrica** electric shock.

descargar vt (camión, mercancías, equipaje) to unload; (arma) to fire ❑ **descargarse** vpr (batería) to go flat; (encendedor) to run out; (desahogarse) to vent one's frustration.

descaro m cheek.

descarrilar vi to be derailed.

descartar vt (ayuda) to reject; (posibilidad) to rule out.

descendencia f (hijos) offspring.

descender vi to go down.

descendiente mf descendent.

descenso m (bajada) drop; (de un río, montaña) descent.

descifrar vt to decipher.

descolgar vt (cortina, ropa, cuadro) to take down; (teléfono) to take off the hook ◆ vi to pick up the receiver.

descolorido, -da adj faded.

descomponer vt (Amér) to break ❑ **descomponerse** vpr (Amér) to break down.

descomposición f (de un alimento) decomposition; **~ (de vientre)** (formal) diarrhea.

descompuesto, -ta pp → **descomponer** ◆ adj (Amér) broken.

desconcertante adj disconcerting.

desconcertar vt to disconcert.

desconfianza f distrust.

desconfiar: desconfiar de v + prep to distrust.

descongelar vt (alimentos) to thaw; (nevera) to defrost ❑ **descongelarse** vpr (alimentos) to thaw; (nevera) to defrost.

descongestionarse vpr to clear.

desconocer vt not to know.

desconocido, -da adj → stranger.

desconocimiento m ignorance.

desconsiderado, -da adj inconsiderate.

desconsolado, -da adj distressed.

desconsuelo m distress.

descontar vt to deduct.

descrédito m discredit.

describir vt to describe.

descripción f description.

descrito, -ta pp → **describir**.

descuartizar vt to quarter.

descubierto, -ta pp → **descubrir** ◆ adj (sin tapar) uncovered; (sin nubes) clear; **al ~** in the open.

descubrimiento m discovery.

descubrir vt to discover; (averiguar, destapar) to uncover.

descuento m discount.

descuerar vt (Amér: fig) to pull to pieces.

descuidado, -da adj (persona, aspecto) untidy; (lugar) neglected.

descuidar vt to neglect □ **descuidarse de** v + prep (olvidarse de) to forget to.

descuido m (imprudencia) carelessness; (error) mistake.

desde prep (tiempo) since; (espacio) from; ~ ... hasta ... from ... to ...; **vivo aquí ~ hace dos años** I've been living here for two years; ~ **luego** of course; ~ **que** since.

desdén m disdain.

desdentado, -da adj toothless.

desdicha f (pena) misfortune.

desdoblar vt (papel, servilleta) to unfold.

desear vt (querer) to want; (anhelar) to wish for; (amar) to desire; **¿qué desea?** what can I do for you?

desechable adj disposable.

desechar vt (tirar) to throw away.

desechos mpl (basura) rubbish (sg); (residuos) waste (sg).

desembarcar vi to disembark.

desembocadura f (de río) mouth; (de calle) opening.

desembocar: **desembocar en** v + prep (río) to flow into; (calle) to lead into; (situación, problema) to end in.

desempeñar vt (funciones) to

carry out; (papel) to play; (objeto empeñado) to redeem.

desempleo m unemployment.

desencadenar vt (provocar) to unleash □ **desencadenarse** v impers (tormenta) to break; (tragedia) to strike.

desencajarse vpr (piezas) to come apart; (rostro) to become distorted.

desencanto m disappointment.

desenchufar vt to unplug.

desenfadado, -da adj (persona) easy-going; (ropa) casual; (estilo) light.

desenfrenado, -da adj (ritmo) frantic.

desengañar vt to reveal the truth to □ **desengañarse** vpr: ~se de to become disillusioned with.

desengaño m disappointment.

desenlace m ending.

desenmascarar vt to expose.

desenredar vt (pelo, madeja, ovillo) to untangle; (situación) to unravel.

desentenderse: **desentenderse de** v + prep to refuse to have anything to do with.

desenvolver vt to unwrap □ **desenvolverse** vpr (persona) to cope.

desenvuelto, -ta pp → desenvolver.

deseo m desire.

desequilibrado, -da adj (formal: loco) (mentally) unbalanced.

desesperación f desperation.

desesperarse vpr to lose hope.

desfachatez *f* cheek.

desfallecer *vi (debilitarse)* to flag; *(desmayarse)* to faint.

desfigurarse *vpr* to be disfigured.

desfiladero *m* (mountain) pass.

desfile *m (de militares)* parade; *(de carrozas, etc)* procession; *(de modelos)* fashion show.

desgana *f (falta de apetito)* lack of appetite; *(falta de interés)* lack of enthusiasm; **con ~** unwillingly.

desgastar *vt (objeto)* to wear out; *(fuerza)* to wear down.

desgracia *f (suerte contraria)* bad luck, *(suceso trágico)* disaster; **por ~** unfortunately.

desgraciadamente *adv* unfortunately.

desgraciado, -da *m, f* poor wretch.

desgraciar *vt (estropear)* to spoil.

desgreñado, -da *adj* tousled; **ir ~** to be dishevelled.

deshacer *vt (lo hecho)* to undo, *(cama)* to mess up; *(quitar las sábanas de)* to strip; *(las maletas)* to unpack; *(destruir)* to ruin; *(disolver)* to dissolve □ **deshacerse** *vpr (disolverse)* to dissolve; *(derretirse)* to melt; *(destruirse)* to be destroyed; **deshacerse de** *v + prep (desprenderse de)* to get rid of.

deshecho, -cha *pp* → **deshacer** ◆ *adj (nudo, paquete)* undone; *(cama)* unmade; *(maletas)* unpacked; *(estropeado)* ruined; *(triste, abatido)* shattered.

desheredar *vt* to disinherit.

deshidratarse *vpr* to be dehydrated.

deshielo *m* thaw.

deshonesto, -ta *adj (inmoral)* indecent; *(poco honrado)* dishonest.

deshonra *f* dishonour.

deshuesar *vt (carne)* to bone; *(fruta)* to stone.

desierto, -ta *adj (lugar)* deserted ◆ *m* desert.

designar *vt (persona)* to appoint; *(lugar)* to decide on.

desigual *adj (no uniforme)* different; *(irregular)* uneven.

desigualdad *f* inequality.

desilusión *f* disappointment.

desilusionar *vt* to disappoint.

desinfectante *m* disinfectant.

desinfectar *vt* to disinfect.

desinflar *vt (balón, globo, rueda)* to let down.

desintegración *f* disintegration.

desinterés *m* lack of interest.

desinteresado, -da *adj* unselfish.

desistir: desistir de *v + prep* to give up.

desliz *(pl -ces)* *m* slip.

deslizar *vt* to slide □ **deslizarse** *vpr (resbalar)* to slide.

deslumbrar *vt* to dazzle.

desmadrarse *vpr (fam)* to go over the top.

desmaquillador *m* make-up remover.

desmaquillarse *vpr* to take one's make-up off.

desmayarse *vpr* to faint.

desmayo *m (desvanecimiento)*

fainting fit.

desmentir vt (negar) to deny.

desmesurado, -da adj excessive.

desmontar vt (estructura) to take down; (aparato) to take apart ♦ vi to dismount.

desmoralizar vt to demoralize.

desnatado, -da adj (leche) skimmed; (yogur) low-fat.

desnivel m (del terreno) unevenness.

desnudar vt to undress ❏ desnudarse vpr to get undressed.

desnudo, -da adj (sin ropa) naked; (sin adorno) bare.

desnutrición f undernourishment.

desobedecer vt to disobey.

desobediente adj disobedient.

desodorante m deodorant.

desorden m (de objetos, papeles) mess; en ~ in disarray.

desordenar vt to mess up.

desorganización f disorganization.

desorientar vt (confundir) to confuse ❏ desorientarse vpr (perderse) to lose one's bearings; (confundirse) to get confused.

despachar vt (vender) to sell; (despedir) to sack.

despacho m (oficina) office; (estudio) study; ~ de billetes ticket office.

despacio adv slowly ♦ interj slow down!

despampanante adj stunning.

desparpajo m self-assurance.

despecho m bitterness.

despectivo, -va adj disdainful.

despedida f goodbye.

despedir vt (decir adiós) to say goodbye to; (del trabajo) to sack; (arrojar) to fling; (producir) to give off ❏ despedirse vpr (decir adiós) to say goodbye; (del trabajo) to hand in one's notice.

despegar vt to remove ♦ vi (avión) to take off.

despegue m take-off.

despeinarse vpr to mess up one's hair.

despejado, -da adj (cielo, día, camino) clear; (persona) alert; (espacio) spacious.

despejar vt (lugar) to clear; (incógnita, dudas) to clear up ❏ despejarse vpr (cielo, día, noche) to clear up; (persona) to clear one's head.

despensa f larder.

despeñadero m precipice.

desperdiciar vt to waste.

desperdicio m waste ❏ desperdicios mpl (basura) waste (sg); (de cocina) scraps.

desperezarse vpr to stretch.

desperfecto m (daño) damage; (defecto) fault.

despertador m alarm clock.

despertar vt (persona) to wake up; (sentimiento) to arouse ❏ despertarse vpr to wake up.

despido m dismissal.

despierto, -ta adj (que no duerme) awake; (listo) alert.

despistado, -da adj absent-minded.

despistarse vpr (desorientarse) to get lost; (distraerse) to get confused.

despiste m (olvido) absent-mindedness; (error) mistake.

desplazarse vpr (moverse) to move; (viajar) to travel.

desplegar vt (tela, periódico, mapa) to unfold; (bandera) to unfurl; (alas) to spread; (cualidad) to display.

desplomarse vpr to collapse.

despojos mpl (de animal) offal (sg); (de persona) remains; (sobras) leftovers.

despreciar vt (persona, cosa) to despise; (posibilidad, propuesta) to reject.

desprecio m contempt.

desprender vt (desenganchar) to unfasten; (soltar) to give off ❑ **desprenderse** vpr (soltarse) to come off; **desprenderse de** v + prep (deshacerse de) to get rid of; (deducirse de) to be clear from.

desprendimiento m (de tierra) landslide.

despreocuparse: despreocuparse de v + prep (no atender) to neglect.

desprevenido, -da adj unprepared.

desproporcionado, -da adj disproportionate.

después adv 1. (más tarde) afterwards; (entonces) then; (justo lo siguiente) next; **lo haré ~** I'll do it later; **yo voy ~** it's my turn next; **años ~** years later; **poco/mucho ~** soon/ a long time after.

2. (en el espacio) next; **¿qué calle viene ~?** which street comes next?; **hay una farmacia y ~ está mi casa** there's a chemist's and then you come to my house.

3. (en una lista) further down.

4. (en locuciones): **~ de** after; **~ de que** after; **~ de todo** after all.

destacar vt to emphasize ◆ vi (resaltar) to stand out.

destajo m: **trabajar a ~** to do piecework.

destapar vt (caja, botella, etc) to open.

destello m (de luz) flash.

destemplado, -da adj (persona) out of sorts.

desteñir vt to bleach ◆ vi to run.

desterrar vt (persona) to exile; (pensamiento, sentimiento) to banish.

destierro m exile.

destilación f distillation.

destilar vt to distil.

destilería f distillery.

destinar vt (objeto) to earmark; (persona) to appoint; (programa, medidas) to aim.

destinatario, -ria m, f addressee.

destino m (azar) destiny; (de viaje) destination; (finalidad) use; (trabajo) job; **vuelos con ~ a Londres** flights to London.

destornillador m screwdriver.

destornillar vt to unscrew.

destrozar vt (objeto) to smash; (plan, proyecto) to ruin; (persona) to shatter.

destrucción f destruction.

destruir vt to destroy; *(plan, proyecto)* to ruin.

desuso m disuse; **caer en ~** to become obsolete.

desvalijar vt *(persona)* to rob; *(casa)* to burgle.

desván m attic.

desvanecimiento m *(desmayo)* fainting fit.

desvariar vi to rave.

desvelar vt *(persona)* to keep awake; *(secreto)* to reveal ❑ **desvelarse** vpr *(no dormir)* to be unable to sleep; *(Amér: quedarse levantado)* to have a late night.

desventaja f disadvantage.

desvergonzado, -da adj shameless.

desvestirse vpr to get undressed.

desviar vt *(de un camino)* to divert ❑ **desviarse** vpr: **~se de** *(camino)* to turn off; *(propósito)* to be diverted from.

desvío m diversion.

detallar vt to describe in detail.

detalle m *(pormenor, minucia)* detail; *(delicadeza)* kind gesture; **al ~** *(minuciosamente)* in detail.

detallista adj *(minucioso)* painstaking.

detectar vt to detect.

detective mf detective.

detener vt *(parar)* to stop; *(retrasar)* to hold up; *(arrestar)* to arrest ❑ **detenerse** vpr *(pararse)* to stop.

detenido, -da m, f prisoner.

detergente m detergent.

determinación f *(decisión)* decision; **tomar una ~** to take a

decision.

determinado, -da adj *(concreto)* specific; *(en gramática)* definite.

determinante adj decisive ♦ m determiner.

determinar vt *(fijar)* to fix; *(decidir)* to decide; *(causar, motivar)* to cause.

detestable adj detestable.

detestar vt to detest.

detrás adv *(en el espacio)* behind; *(en el orden)* then; **el interruptor está ~** the switch is at the back; **~ de** behind; **por ~** at/on the back.

deuda f debt; **contraer ~s** to get into debt.

devaluación f devaluation.

devaluar vt to devalue.

devoción f devotion.

devolución f *(de dinero)* refund; *(de objeto)* return.

devolver vt *(objeto, regalo comprado, favor)* to return; *(dinero)* to refund; *(cambio, objeto prestado)* to give back; *(vomitar)* to bring up ♦ vi to be sick; **"devuelve cambio"** "change given".

devorar vt to devour.

devoto, -ta adj *(en religión)* devout; *(aficionado)* devoted.

devuelto, -ta pp → **devolver**.

dg *(abrev de decigramo)* dg.

DGT abrev = **Dirección General de Tráfico**.

di v → **dar, decir**.

día m day; **es de ~** it's daytime; **de ~** in the daytime; **al ~ siguiente** the next day; **del ~** *(fresco)* fresh; **el ~ seis** the sixth; **por ~** daily; **¿qué tal ~ hace?** what's the weather like today?; **todos los ~s** every day; **~ azul** day for cheap travel on trains; **~ del espectador** day on which cinema tickets are sold at a discount; **~ festivo** (public) holiday; **Día de los inocentes** 28 December, = April Fools' Day; **~ laborable** working day; **~ libre** day off; **Día de los Muertos** Day of the Dead; **~ del santo** saint's day.

---

i **DÍA DE LOS INOCENTES**

On 28 December, it is traditional for Spanish people to play tricks and practical jokes known as "inocentadas" on each other, the most typical of which is to stick a paper doll to somebody's back without them realizing. It is also common for the media to run false stories aimed at duping the public.

---

i **DÍA DE LOS MUERTOS**

In Mexico, "Day of the Dead" is the name given to All Saints' Day. Officially, the Day of the Dead is 2 November, although the celebrations start on 1 November. Children dress up as skeletons, mummies, vampires etc, and the shops sell brightly-coloured sugar and chocolate skulls bearing the name of a dead person. These will form part of an offering to dead friends and relatives which may also include "pan de muerto", a type of large, round cake coated in sugar.

---

diabetes *f inv* diabetes.
diabético, -ca *m, f* diabetic.

diablo *m* devil.
diablura *f* prank.
diabólico, -ca *adj* diabolical.
diadema *f* Alice band.
diagnosticar *vt* to diagnose.
diagnóstico *m* diagnosis.
dialecto *m* dialect.
diálogo *m* (conversación) conversation.
diamante *m* diamond □ **diamantes** *mpl* (palo de la baraja) diamonds.
diana *f* (blanco) bull's-eye.
diapositiva *f* slide.
diario, -ria *adj* daily ♦ *m* (daily) newspaper; **a ~** every day.
diarrea *f* diarrhea.
dibujar *vt* to draw.
dibujo *m* drawing; **~s animados** cartoons.
diccionario *m* dictionary.
dice *v* → **decir**.
dicha *f* (felicidad) joy.
dicho, -cha *m* → **decir** ♦ *m* saying; **~ y hecho** no sooner said than done; **mejor ~** rather.
diciembre *m* December, → **setiembre**.
dictado *m* dictation.
dictador *m* dictator.
dictadura *f* dictatorship.
dictamen *m* opinion.
dictar *vt* (texto) to dictate; (decreto) to issue; (ley) to enact.
dictatorial *adj* dictatorial.
diecinueve *núm* nineteen, → **seis**.
dieciocho *núm* eighteen, → **seis**.
dieciséis *núm* sixteen, → **seis**.

diecisiete *núm* seventeen, → seis.

diente *m* tooth; **~ de ajo** clove of garlic; **~ de leche** milk tooth.

diera *v* → dar.

diéresis *f inv* diaeresis.

dieron *v* → dar.

diesel *m* diesel.

diestro, -tra *adj (de la derecha)* right-hand; *(experto)* skilful ◆ *m* matador.

dieta *f* diet ❑ **dietas** *fpl (honorarios)* expenses.

dietética *f* dietetics *(sg)*; **tienda de ~** health food shop.

diez *núm* ten, → seis.

diferencia *f* difference; **a ~ de** in contrast to.

diferenciar *vt* to distinguish.

diferente *adj* different ◆ *adv* differently.

diferido, -da *adj*: **en ~** recorded.

diferir *vt* to defer ❑ **diferir de** *v* + *prep* to differ from.

difícil *adj* difficult.

dificultad *f (complejidad)* difficulty; *(obstáculo)* problem.

difundir *vt (calor, luz)* to diffuse; *(noticia, idea)* to spread; *(programa)* to broadcast.

difunto, -ta *m, f*: **el ~** the deceased.

difusión *f (de noticia, idea)* dissemination; *(de programa)* broadcasting.

diga *v* → decir.

digerir *vt* to digest.

digestión *f* digestion; **hacer la ~** to digest.

digital *adj (en electrónica)* digital; *(de los dedos)* finger *(antes de s)*.

dígito *m* digit.

dignarse *vpr* to deign.

dignidad *f (decoro)* dignity; *(cargo)* office.

digno, -na *adj (merecedor)* worthy; *(apropiado)* appropriate; *(honrado)* honourable.

digo *v* → decir.

dilema *m* dilemma.

diligente *adj* diligent.

diluviar *v impers*: **diluvió** it poured with rain.

diluvio *m* flood.

dimensión *f (medida)* dimension; *(importancia)* extent.

diminuto, -ta *adj* tiny.

dimitir *vi*: **~ (de)** to resign (from).

dimos *v* → dar.

Dinamarca *s* Denmark.

dinámico, -ca *adj* dynamic.

dinamita *f* dynamite.

dinastía *f* dynasty.

dinero *m* money; **~ de bolsillo** pocket money; **~ suelto** loose change.

dinosaurio *m* dinosaur.

dio *v* → dar.

diócesis *f inv* diocese.

dios *m* god ❑ **Dios** *m* God; **como Dios manda** properly; **¡Dios mío!** my God!; **¡por Dios!** for God's sake!

diploma *m* diploma.

diplomacia *f* diplomacy.

diplomado, -da *m, f* qualified man *(f qualified woman)*.

diplomarse: diplomarse en *v* + *prep* to get a qualification in.

diplomático, -ca adj diplomatic ◆ m, f diplomat.

diplomatura f degree awarded after three years of study.

diptongo m diphthong.

diputación f (edificio) building that houses the "diputación provincial"; ~ **provincial** governing body of each province of an autonomous region in Spain, = county council (Br).

diputado, -da m, f = MP (Br), = representative (Am).

dique m dike; ~ **seco** dry dock.

dirá v → decir.

dirección f (rumbo) direction; (domicilio) address; (de empresa) management; (de vehículo) steering; **calle de ~ única** one-way street; ~ **asistida** power steering; **Dirección General de Tráfico** Spanish traffic department

direccionales mpl (Amér) indicators.

directa f (en el coche) top gear.

directo, -ta adj direct; **en ~** live.

director, -ra m, f (de empresa) director; (de hotel) manager (f manageress); (de orquesta) conductor; (de colegio) head.

directorio m directory.

diría v → decir.

dirigente mf (de partido) leader; (de empresa) manager.

dirigir vt (destinar) to address; (conducir, llevar) to steer; (gobernar) to run; (película, obra de teatro, enfocar) to direct; (orquesta) to conduct; (periódico) to edit; (guiar, orientar) to guide; ~ **la palabra a alguien** to

speak to sb ☐ **dirigirse a** v + prep (ir, marchar) to head for; (hablar a) to speak to.

discar vt (Amér) to dial.

disciplina f discipline.

discípulo, -la m, f disciple.

disco m (en música) record; (cilindro) disc; (semáforo) (traffic) light; (en informática) disk; (en deporte) discus; ~ **compacto** compact disc.

disconformidad f disagreement.

discoteca f disco.

discotequero, -ra adj (fam) disco (antes de s).

discreción f discretion.

discrepancia f difference.

discreto, -ta adj (diplomático) discreet; (mediano) modest.

discriminación f discrimination.

discriminar vt to discriminate against.

disculpa f (pretexto) excuse; (al pedir perdón) apology; **pedir ~s** to apologize.

disculpar vt to excuse ☐ **disculparse** vpr: **~se (por algo)** to apologize (for sthg).

discurrir vi (pensar) to reflect.

discurso m speech.

discusión f (debate) discussion; (riña) argument.

discutible adj debatable

discutir vt (debatir) to discuss; (contradecir) to dispute ◆ vi (reñir) to argue.

disecar vt (planta) to dry; (animal) to stuff.

diseñador, -ra m, f designer.

diseñar vt to design.

diseño m design; **de ~** designer.

disfraz (pl **-ces**) m disguise.

disfrazar vt & vi to disguise □ **disfrazarse**: **~se (de)** to dress up (as).

disfrutar vi to enjoy o.s. □ **disfrutar de** v + prep to enjoy.

disgustar vt to upset □ **disgustarse** vpr to get upset.

disgusto m annoyance; **llevarse un ~** to be upset.

disidente mf dissident.

disimular vt to hide ♦ vi to pretend.

disminución f decrease.

disminuir vt to decrease.

disolvente m solvent.

disolver vt to dissolve.

disparar vt & vi to shoot □ **dispararse** vpr (actuar precipitadamente) to go over the top; (precios) to shoot up.

disparate m stupid thing.

disparo m shot.

dispensar vt: **~ a alguien de** to excuse sb from.

dispersar vt to scatter.

disponer vt (colocar) to arrange; (preparar) to lay on; (suj: ley) to stipulate □ **disponer de** v + prep (tener) to have; (usar) to make use of; **disponerse** vpr: **~se a** to get ready to.

disponible adj available.

disposición f (colocación) arrangement; (estado de ánimo) mood; (orden) order; **a ~ de** at the disposal of.

dispositivo m device.

dispuesto, -ta pp → disponer ♦ adj (preparado) ready; **~ a** prepared to.

disputa f dispute.

disputar vt (competición) to compete in; (premio) to compete for ♦ vi to argue □ **disputarse** vpr (competir por) to dispute.

disquete m diskette.

disquetera f disk drive.

distancia f distance; (en tiempo) gap; **¿a qué ~?** how far away?

distanciarse vpr (perder afecto) to grow apart.

distante adj (lugar) far away; (persona) distant.

diste v → dar.

distinción f (diferencia) distinction; (elegancia) refinement.

distinguido, -da adj (elegante) refined; (notable, destacado) distinguished.

distinguir vt (diferenciar) to distinguish; (lograr ver) to make out; (destacar) to pick out.

distintivo m distinctive.

distinto, -ta adj different.

distracción f (falta de atención) absent-mindedness; (descuido) slip; (diversión) entertainment.

distraer vt (entretener) to entertain □ **distraerse** vpr (descuidarse) to get distracted; (no prestar atención) to let one's mind wander; (entretenerse) to enjoy o.s.

distraído, -da adj (entretenido) entertaining; (despistado) absentminded.

distribución f (de correo, mercancías) delivery; (comercial) distribution.

distribuir vt (repartir) to distribute; (correo, mercancías) to deliver.

distrito m district; ~ **postal** postal district.

disturbio m (tumulto) disturbance; (del orden público) riot.

disuelto, -ta pp → **disolver**.

diurno, -na adj daytime.

diva f diva.

diván m couch.

diversidad f diversity.

diversión f entertainment.

diverso, -sa adj diverse; ~s various.

divertido, -da adj (entretenido) enjoyable; (que hace reír) funny.

divertirse vpr to enjoy o.s.

dividir vt to divide.

divino, -na adj divine.

divisar vt to spy.

divisas fpl foreign exchange (sg).

división f division.

divorciado, -da m, f divorcé (f divorcée).

divorciarse vpr to get divorced.

divorcio m divorce.

divulgar vt (secreto) to reveal; (noticia) to spread; (información) to disseminate.

DNI m (abrev de documento nacional de identidad) ID card.

DNI

All Spaniards over the age of 14 are required to have an identity card which they must carry at all times. The card has a photograph of the holder, their full name, date and place of birth, home address and tax number. Failure to present one's identity card when stopped by the police may result in a fine.

---

dobladillo m hem.

doblaje m dubbing.

doblar vt (plegar) to fold; (duplicar) to double; (flexionar) to bend; (en cine) to dub; ~ **la esquina** to go round the corner.

doble adj & mf double ◆ m: **el ~ (de)** twice as much □ **dobles** mpl (en tenis) doubles.

doce núm twelve, → **seis**.

docena f dozen.

docente adj teaching.

dócil adj obedient.

doctor, -ra m, f doctor.

doctorado m doctorate.

doctorarse vpr to get a doctorate.

doctrina f doctrine.

documentación f (papeles (pl)); ~ **del coche** registration documents (pl).

documental m documentary.

documento m (escrito) document; (de identidad) identity card; (en historia) record.

dogma m dogma.

dogmático, -ca adj dogmatic.

dólar m dollar.

doler vi to hurt; **me duele la pierna** my leg hurts; **me duele la garganta** I have a sore throat.

dolor m (daño) pain; (pena) sorrow; **tener ~ de cabeza** to have a headache; **tener ~ de estómago** to have a stomachache; **tener ~ de muelas** to have toothache.

doloroso, -sa *adj* painful.

domador, -ra *m, f* tamer.

domar *vt* to tame.

domesticar *vt* to tame.

doméstico, -ca *adj* domestic.

domicilio *m (casa)* residence; *(dirección)* address; **servicio a ~** home delivery.

dominante *adj* dominant.

dominar *vt (persona, panorama)* to dominate; *(nación)* to rule; *(situación)* to be in control of; *(nervios, pasiones, etc)* to control; *(incendio)* to bring under control; *(idioma)* to be fluent in; *(divisar)* to overlook ♦ *vi (sobresalir, destacar)* to stand out; *(ser característico)* to predominate ❑ **dominarse** *vpr* to control o.s.

domingo *m* Sunday; **~ de Pascua** Easter Sunday; **~ de Ramos** Palm Sunday, → **sábado**.

dominguero, -ra *m, f (fam)* Sunday tripper.

dominical *m* Sunday supplement.

dominio *m (control)* control; *(autoridad)* authority; *(de una lengua)* command; *(territorio)* domain; *(ámbito)* realm.

dominó *m (juego)* dominoes *(sg)*.

don *m (regalo, talento)* gift; *(tratamiento)* = Mr.

donante *mf* donor.

donativo *m* donation.

donde *adv* where; **el bolso está ~ lo dejaste** your bag is where you left it; **de/desde ~** from where; **por ~** wherever.
♦ *pron* where; **la casa ~ nací** the house where I was born; **la ciudad de ~ vengo** the town I come from; **por ~** where.

dónde *adv* where; **¿~ está el niño?** where's the child?; **no sé ~ se habrá metido** I don't know where she can be; **¿de ~ eres?** where are you from?; **por ~** where.

donut® ['donut] *m* (ring) doughnut.

doparse *vpr* to take artificial stimulants.

doping ['dopiŋ] *m* doping.

dorado, -da *adj* golden.

dormir *vi* to sleep ♦ *vt (niño)* to put to bed; **~ con alguien** to sleep with sb ❑ **dormirse** *vpr (persona)* to fall asleep; *(parte del cuerpo)* to go to sleep.

dormitorio *m (habitación)* bedroom; *(mobiliario)* bedroom suite.

dorsal *adj* back *(antes de s)*.

dorso *m* back; **~ de la mano** back of the hand.

dos *núm* two; **cada ~ por tres** every five minutes, → **seis**.

doscientos *núm* two hundred, → **seis**.

dosis *f inv* dose.

dotado, -da *adj* gifted; **~ de** *(persona)* blessed with; *(edificio, instalación)* equipped with.

dotar *vt (equipar, proveer)* to provide; *(suj: naturaleza)* to endow.

doy *v* → **dar**.

Dr. *(abrev de doctor)* Dr.

Dra. *(abrev de doctora)* Dr.

dragón *m* dragon.

drama *m (obra)* play; *(género)* drama; *(desgracia)* tragedy.

dramático, -ca *adj* dramatic.

dramaturgo, -ga *m, f* playwright.

droga *f* drug; **la ~ drugs** (*pl*).

drogadicción *f* drug addiction.

drogadicto, -ta *m, f* drug addict.

droguería *f* shop selling paint, cleaning materials etc.

dto. *abrev* = **descuento**.

dual *adj* (*emisión*) that can be listened to either dubbed or in the original language version.

ducha *f* shower; **darse una ~ to have a shower.**

ducharse *vpr* to have a shower.

duda *f* doubt; **sin ~ doubtless.**

dudar *vi* to be unsure ❏ **dudar de** *v + prep* to have one's doubts about.

duelo *m* (*pelea*) duel; (*en deporte*) contest; (*pena*) grief.

duende *m* (*de cuentos infantiles*) goblin; (*gracia, encanto*) charm; **tener ~ to have a certain something.**

dueño, -ña *m, f* (*propietario*) owner; (*de piso*) landlord (*f* landlady).

dulce *adj* sweet; (*agua*) fresh ♦ *m* (*caramelo, postre*) sweet; (*pastel*) cake; **~ de membrillo** quince jelly.

dulzura *f* sweetness.

duna *f* dune.

dúo *m* duet.

dúplex *m inv* duplex.

duplicar *vt* to double.

duración *f* length.

durante *adv* during; **~ toda la semana** all week; **lo estuve haciendo ~ dos horas** I was doing it for two hours.

durar *vi* (*prolongarse*) to last;

(*resistir*) to wear well.

durazno *m* (*Amér*) peach.

dureza *f* hardness; (*callosidad*) callus; (*de carácter*) harshness.

duro, -ra *adj* hard; (*carácter, persona, clima*) harsh; (*carne*) tough ♦ *m* (*moneda*) five-peseta piece ♦ *adv* hard.

E

ébano *m* ebony.

ebrio, ebria *adj* (*formal*) drunk.

ebullición *f* boiling.

echado, -da *adj* (*acostado*) lying down.

echar *vt* 1. (*tirar*) to throw; **echó la pelota** she threw the ball.

2. (*añadir*) **~ algo a** (*sal, azúcar*) to add sthg to; (*vino, agua*) to pour sthg into.

3. (*reprimenda, discurso*) to give; **me echaron la buenaventura** I had my fortune told

4. (*carta, postal*) to post.

5. (*expulsar*) to throw out; (*del trabajo*) to sack; **lo echaron del colegio** they threw him out of school.

6. (*humo, vapor, chispas*) to give off.

7. (*accionar*): **~ la llave/el cerrojo** to lock/bolt the door; **~ el freno** to brake.

8. (*flores, hojas*) to sprout.

9. (*acostar*) to lie (down); **echa al niño en el sofá** lie the child down on the sofa.

10. *(calcular):* **¿cuántos años me echas?** how old would you say I am?

11. *(fam: en televisión, cine)* to show; **¿qué echan esta noche en la tele?** what's on telly tonight?

12. *(en locuciones):* ~ **abajo** *(edificio)* to pull down; *(gobierno)* to bring down; *(proyecto)* to ruin; ~ **de menos** to miss.

♦ *vi* **1.** *(dirigirse):* **echó por el camino más corto** he took the shortest route.

2. *(empezar):* ~ **a hacer algo** to begin to do sthg; ~ **a correr** to break into a run.

❏ **echarse** *vpr (lanzarse)* to throw o.s.; *(acostarse)* to lie down; **nos echamos a la carretera** we set out on the road; **~se a hacer algo** *(empezar)* to begin to do sthg.

echarpe *m* shawl.

eclesiástico, -ca *adj* ecclesiastical.

eclipse *m* eclipse.

eco *m* echo; **tener ~** to arouse interest.

ecología *f* ecology.

ecológico, -ca *adj* ecological.

economía *f (administración)* economy; *(ciencia)* economics ❏ **economías** *fpl (ahorros)* savings.

económico, -ca *adj (situación, crisis)* economic; *(barato)* cheap; *(motor, dispositivo)* economical.

economista *mf* economist.

ecosistema *m* ecosystem.

ecu *m* ecu.

ecuación *f* equation.

ecuador *m* equator.

Ecuador *m:* **(el)** ~ Equador.

ecuatoriano, -na *adj & m, f* Equadorian.

edad *f* age; **tengo 15 años de** ~ I'm 15 (years old); **la Edad Media** the Middle Ages *(pl).*

edición *f (publicación)* publication; *(ejemplares)* edition.

edificante *adj* exemplary.

edificar *vt* to build.

edificio *m* building.

editar *vt (publicar)* to publish; *(disco)* to release.

editor, -ra *m, f* publisher.

editorial *f* publishing house.

edredón *m* duvet.

educación *f (formación)* education; *(cortesía, urbanidad)* good manners *(pl).*

educado, -da *adj* polite; **bien ~** polite; **mal ~** rude.

educar *vt (hijos)* to bring up; *(alumnos)* to educate; *(sensibilidad, gusto)* to refine.

educativo, -va *adj* educational; *(sistema)* education *(antes de s).*

EEUU *mpl (abrev de Estados Unidos)* USA.

efectivo *m* cash; **en ~** in cash.

efecto *m (resultado)* effect; *(impresión)* impression; **en ~** indeed; **~s personales** personal belongings; **~ secundarios** side effects.

efectuar *vt (realizar)* to carry out; *(compra, pago, viaje)* to make.

eficacia *f (de persona)* efficiency; *(de medidas, plan)* effectiveness.

eficaz *(pl* **-ces)** *adj (persona)* efficient; *(medidas, plan)* effective.

eficiente *adj (medicamento, solu-*

ción, etc) effective; (*trabajador*) efficient.

EGB *f* (*abrev de Enseñanza General Básica*) Spanish primary education system for pupils aged 6-14.

Egipto *s* Egypt.

egoísmo *m* selfishness.

egoísta *adj* selfish.

egresado, -da *m, f* (*Amér*) graduate.

egresar *vi* (*Amér*) to graduate.

egreso *m* (*Amér*) graduation.

ej. (*abrev de ejemplo*) eg.

eje *m* (*de rueda*) axle; (*centro, en geometría*) axis.

ejecución *f* (*de condenado*) execution.

ejecutar *vt* (*realizar*) to carry out; (*matar*) to execute.

ejecutivo, -va *m, f* executive.

ejemplar *adj* exemplary ◆ *m* (*de especie, raza*) specimen; (*de libro*) copy; (*de revista*) issue.

ejemplo *m* example; **poner un ~** to give an example; **por ~** for example.

ejercer *vt* (*profesión, actividad*) to practise; (*influencia, autoridad*) to have.

ejercicio *m* exercise; (*de profesión, actividad*) practising; **~ físico** physical exercise.

ejército *m* army.

ejote *m* (*Amér*) green bean.

el, la (*pl* los, las) *art* 1. (*con sustantivo genérico*) the; **~ coche** the car; **las niñas** the girls; **~ agua/hacha/águila** the water/axe/eagle.

2. (*con sustantivo abstracto*) **~ amor** love; **la vida** life; **los celos** jealousy (*sg*).

3. (*indica posesión, pertenencia*): **se rompió la pierna** he broke his leg; **tiene ~ pelo oscuro** she has dark hair.

4. (*con días de la semana*): **vuelven ~ sábado** they're coming back on Saturday.

5. (*antes de adj*): **prefiero la blanca** I prefer the white one.

6. (*en locuciones*): **cogeré ~ de atrás** I'll take the one at the back; **mi hermano y ~ de Juan** my brother and Juan's; **~ que** (*persona*) whoever; (*cosa*) whichever (one); **~ que más me gusta** the one I like best.

él, ella (*pl* ellos, ellas) *pron* 1. (*sujeto, predicado*) he (*f* she), they (*pl*); (*animal, cosa*) it, they (*pl*); **mi hermano es ~** he's my brother; **ella es una amiga de la familia** she's a friend of the family.

2. (*complemento*) him (*f* her), them (*pl*); (*animal, cosa*) it, them (*pl*); **voy a ir de vacaciones con ellos** I'm going on holiday with them.

3. (*posesivo*): **de ~** his; **de ella** hers.

elaborar *vt* (*preparar*) to make; (*idea*) to work out; (*plan, lista*) to draw up.

elasticidad *f* elasticity.

elástico, -ca *adj* elastic ❏ **elásticos** *mpl* (*para pantalones*) braces.

elección *f* (*de regalo, vestido, etc*) choice; (*de presidente, jefe, etc*) election ❏ **elecciones** *fpl* elections.

electricidad *f* electricity.

electricista *mf* electrician.

eléctrico, -ca *adj* electric.

electrocutar *vt* to electrocute.

electrodoméstico *m* electrical household appliance.

electrónica *f* electronics.

electrónico, -ca *adj* electronic.

elefante *m* elephant.

elegancia *f* elegance; *(de comportamiento)* dignity.

elegante *adj* elegant; *(comportamiento)* dignified.

elegir *vt (escoger)* to choose; *(en votación)* to elect.

elemental *adj (sencillo)* obvious; *(fundamental)* basic.

elemento *m* element; *(factor)* factor ❏ **elementos** *mpl (fuerzas de la naturaleza)* elements.

elevación *f* rise.

elevado, -da *adj* high; *(edificio, monte)* tall.

elevador *m (Amér)* lift (Br), elevator (Am).

elevadorista *mf (Amér)* lift attendant (Br), elevator operator (Am).

elevar *vt* to raise; *(ascender)* to promote ❏ **elevarse** *vpr (subir)* to rise.

eliminación *f* elimination.

eliminar *vt* to eliminate.

élite *f* elite.

ello *pron neutro* it.

ellos, ellas *pron pl (sujeto)* they; *(complemento)* them; **de ~/ellas** theirs.

elocuencia *f* eloquence.

elocuente *adj* eloquent.

elogiar *vt* to praise.

elogio *m* praise.

elote *m (Amér)* cob.

eludir *vt* to avoid.

emancipado, -da *adj* emancipated.

emanciparse *vpr* to become emancipated.

embajada *f (lugar)* embassy; *(cargo)* ambassadorship.

embajador, -ra *m, f* ambassador.

embalar *vt* to wrap up ❏ **embalarse** *vpr* to race away.

embalsamar *vt* to embalm.

embalse *m* reservoir.

embarazada *adj f* pregnant.

embarazo *m (de mujer)* pregnancy; *(dificultad)* obstacle.

embarcación *f* boat.

embarcadero *m* jetty.

embarcar *vi* to board ❏ **embarcarse** *vpr (pasajeros)* to board; *(en asunto, negocio)* to get involved.

embargar *vt (bienes, propiedades)* to seize.

embargo *m (de bienes)* seizure; **sin ~** however.

embarque *m (de pasajeros)* boarding; *(de equipaje)* embarkation.

embestir *vt* to attack.

emblema *m (símbolo)* symbol; *(distintivo)* emblem.

emborracharse *vpr* to get drunk.

emboscada *f* ambush.

embotellado, -da *adj (vino, licor)* bottled; *(calle, circulación)* blocked.

embotellamiento *m (de tráfico)* traffic jam; *(de vino, agua)* bottling.

embotellar vt (líquido) to bottle.

embrague m clutch.

embrión m embryo.

embromar vt (Amér) to annoy.

embrujar vt to bewitch.

embudo m funnel

embustero, -ra m, f liar.

embutidos mpl cold, cured meat (sg).

emergencia f emergency.

emigración f (de familia, pueblo) emigration; (de animales) migration.

emigrante mf emigrant.

emigrar vi (persona, pueblo) to emigrate; (animal) to migrate.

eminente adj eminent.

emisión f (de sonido) emission; (del mensaje) transmission; (programa) broadcast; (de juicio, opinión, etc) expression.

emisor, -ra adj broadcasting.

emisora f radio station.

emitir vt (palabras) to utter; (sonido) to emit; (programa, música, etc) to broadcast; (juicio, opinión, etc) to express.

emoción f emotion; ¡qué ~! how exciting!

emocionado, -da adj excited.

emocionante adj exciting.

emocionarse vpr to get excited.

empacho m (de comida) upset stomach

empanada f pasty; ~ gallega pasty containing tomato, tuna and peppers.

empanadilla f small pasty.

empañarse vpr to steam up.

empapado, -da adj (mojado) soaked.

empapar vt (mojar) to soak ❏ **empaparse** vpr to get soaked.

empapelar vt to paper.

empaquetar vt to pack; "empaquetado para regalo" "gift-wrapped"

empastar vt to fill.

empaste m filling.

empatar vi to draw ♦ vt (Amér) to connect.

empate m (en juego, deporte) draw; (Amér: empalme) connection; ~ a dos two-two draw.

empeñar vt (joyas, bienes) to pawn ❏ **empeñarse** vpr (endeudarse) to get into debt; **empeñarse en** v + prep (insistir en) to insist on.

empeño m (constancia) determination.

empeorar vi to make worse ♦ vt to get worse.

emperador, -triz (fpl -ces) m, f emperor (f empress) ♦ m (pez) swordfish.

empezar vt & vi to begin, to start; ~ a hacer algo to begin to do sthg, to start to do sthg.

empinado, -da adj steep.

empleado, -da m, f employee; ~ de banco bank clerk.

emplear vt (trabajador) to employ; (objeto, herramienta) to use; (dinero, tiempo) to spend ❏ **emplearse en** v + prep (empresa, oficina) to get a job in.

empleo m (trabajo en general)

employment; *(puesto)* job; *(uso)* use.

emplomadura f *(Amér)* filling.

emplomar vt *(Amér)* to fill.

empotrado, -da adj built-in; **armario ~** fitted cupboard.

emprender vt *(tarea, negocio, etc)* to start; *(viaje)* to set off on.

empresa f company.

empresario, -ria m, f businessman *(f businesswoman)*.

empujar vt to push; **~ alguien a hacer algo** to push sb into doing sthg.

empujón m shove; **a empujones** *(bruscamente)* by pushing; *(de forma discontinua)* in fits and starts.

en prep 1. *(en el interior de)* in; **viven ~ la capital** they live in the capital.
2. *(sobre la superficie de)* on; **~ el plato/la mesa** on the plate/table.
3. *(en un punto concreto de)* at; **~ casa/el trabajo** at home/work.
4. *(dirección)* into; **el avión cayó ~ el mar** the plane fell into the sea; **entraron ~ la habitación** they came into the room.
5. *(tiempo)* in; *(día)* on; *(período, momento)* at; **llegará ~ mayo/Navidades** she will arrive in May/at Christmas; **nació ~ 1940/sábado** he was born in 1940/on a Saturday; **~ un par de días** in a couple of days.
6. *(medio de transporte)* by; **ir ~ coche/tren/avión/barco** to go by car/train/plane/boat.
7. *(modo)* in; **lo dijo ~ inglés** she said it in English; **todo se lo gasta ~ ropa** he spends it all on clothes; **~ voz baja** in a low voice; **aumentar ~ un 10%** to increase by 10%.
8. *(precio)* in; **las ganancias se calculan ~ millones** profits are calculated in millions; **te lo dejo ~ 5.000 pesetas** I'll let you have it for 5,000 pesetas.
9. *(tema)*: **es un experto ~ matemáticas** he's an expert on mathematics; **es doctor ~ medicina** he's a doctor of medicine.
10. *(cualidad)*: **rápido ~ actuar** quick to act; **le supera ~ inteligencia** she is more intelligent than he is.

enaguas fpl petticoat *(sg)*.

enamorado, -da adj: **~ (de)** in love (with).

enamorarse vpr: **~ (de)** to fall in love (with).

enano, -na adj *(verdura)* baby *(antes de s)* ♦ m, f dwarf.

encabezar vt *(lista, carta, escrito)* to head; *(grupo)* to lead.

encadenar vt *(atar)* to chain; *(enlazar)* to link ❑ **encadenarse** vpr *(hechos, sucesos)* to happen one after the other.

encajar vt *(meter)* to fit; *(aceptar)* to take ♦ vi *(caber)* to fit; *(cuadrar)* to square.

encaje m *(tejido)* lace; *(de vestido, camisa)* lace trim.

encalar vt to whitewash.

encamotarse vpr *(Amér: fam)* to fall in love.

encantado, -da adj *(satisfecho)* delighted; *(lugar, edificio)* haunted; *(persona)* bewitched ♦ interj: **~ de conocerle** pleased to meet you.

encantador, -ra adj delightful.

encantar vt *(hechizar)* to cast a spell on; **me encanta bailar** I love

encontrar

dancing; ¡me encanta! I love it! ❏
encantarse vpr (distraerse) to be entranced.

encanto m (atractivo) charm; (hechizo) spell.

encapotado, -da adj overcast.

encapricharse vpr: ~ con (obstinarse) to set one's mind on.

encaramarse encaramarse a v + prep to climb up onto.

encarar vt (problema, riesgo) to face up to ❏ **encararse** vpr: ~se a to confront.

encarcelar vt to imprison.

encarecer vt (precio) to make more expensive.

encargado, -da m, f (responsable) person in charge; (de tienda, negocio) manager (f manageress).

encargar vt (pedir) to order, (poner al cuidado) to put in charge ❏ **encargarse de** v + prep to see to, to take care of.

encargo m (pedido) order; (tarea) task; (recado) errand.

encariñarse encariñarse con v + prep to become fond of.

encarnado, -da adj (rojo) red; (personificado) incarnate.

encausar vt to prosecute.

encendedor m lighter.

encender vt (fuego, cigarrillo) to light; (luz, gas, aparato eléctrico) to turn on.

encendido m (de motor) ignition.

encerado m (pizarra) blackboard; (del suelo) polishing.

encerrar vt (recluir) to lock up; (contener) to contain ❏ **encerrarse**

vpr to shut o.s. away.

encestar vi to score a basket.

enchilarse vpr (Amér) (con chile) to eat a mouthful of very hot food; (fig: enfadarse) to get angry.

enchinar vt (Amér) to curl.

enchufar vt (aparato eléctrico) to plug in; (fam: a una persona) to pull strings for.

enchufe m (de aparato) plug; (de pared) socket; (fam: recomendación) connections (pl)

encía f gum.

enciclopedia f encyclopedia.

encierro m (de personas) sit-in; (de toros) running of the bulls to the enclosure where they are kept before a bullfight.

encima adv (arriba) on top; (en edificio) upstairs; (además) on top of that; **no llevo dinero** ~ I haven't got any money on me; ~ **de** (en lugar superior) above; (en edificio) upstairs from; (sobre) on (top of) ❏ **por** ~ (superficialmente) superficially, por ~ de (más arriba de) over; **por** ~ **de sus posibilidades** beyond his means; **por** ~ **de todo** more than anything.

encimera f worktop.

encina f holm oak.

encinta adj f pregnant.

encoger vt (piernas) to pull in ◆ vi to shrink ❏ **encogerse** vpr (tejido, ropa) to shrink; (persona) to get scared; ~**se de hombros** to shrug one's shoulders.

encolar vt (pegar) to glue.

encolerizarse vpr to get angry.

encontrar vt to find; (persona)

to meet; **~ trabajo** to find work ❑

encontrarse *vpr (coincidir)* to meet; *(hallarse)* to be; **~se con alguien** to meet sb.

encrespado, -da *adj (pelo)* curly; *(mar)* rough.

encrucijada *f* crossroads *(sg)*.

encuadernar *vt* to bind.

encuadre *m (de foto)* composition.

encubierto, -ta *pp* → **encubrir**.

encubrir *vt* to conceal.

encuentro *m (con persona)* meeting; *(partido)* match.

encuesta *f* survey.

encuestador, -ra *m, f* pollster.

enderezar *vt (lo torcido)* to straighten; *(lo caído)* to put upright; *(persona, negocio, trabajo)* to set right.

endeudado, -da *adj* in debt.

endivia *f* endive; **~s al roquefort** endives in a Roquefort sauce.

enemigo, -ga *m, f* enemy; **ser ~ de** to hate.

energía *f (en física, etc)* energy; *(de persona)* strength; **~ atómica** nuclear power.

enérgico, -ca *adj* energetic.

enero *m* January, → **setiembre**.

enfadado, -da *adj* angry.

enfadarse *vpr* to get angry.

enfado *m* anger.

enfermar *vi* to fall ill ❑ **enfermarse** *vpr (Amér)* to fall ill.

enfermedad *f (caso concreto)* illness; *(morbo)* disease.

enfermería *f* sick bay.

enfermero, -ra *m, f* nurse.

enfermizo, -za *adj* unhealthy.

enfermo, -ma *adj* ill, sick ◆ *m, f (persona enferma)* sick person; *(en el hospital)* patient; **ponerse ~** to fall ill.

enfocar *vt (luz, foco)* to shine; *(cámara)* to focus; *(tema, cuestión, problema)* to look at.

enfoque *m (de cámara)* focus; *(de cuestión, problema)* approach.

enfrentamiento *m* confrontation.

enfrentarse *vpr* to clash; **~se a** *(oponerse a)* to confront.

enfrente *adv* opposite; **~ de** opposite; **la casa de ~** the house across the road.

enfriamiento *m* cold.

enfriarse *vpr (comida, bebida)* to get cold; *(relación)* to cool down; *(resfriarse)* to catch a cold.

enganchar *vt (objeto, papel)* to hang up; *(caballos, caravana, coche)* to hitch up ❑ **engancharse** *vpr (ropa, persona)* to get caught.

enganche *m (Amér: depósito)* deposit; *(mecanismo, pieza)* hook; **$50 de ~** *(Amér)* a $50 deposit.

engañar *vt (decir mentiras a)* to deceive; *(timar)* to cheat; *(a cónyuge)* to cheat on ❑ **engañarse** *vpr (equivocarse)* to be wrong.

engaño *m (mentira)* deceit; *(timo)* swindle; *(infidelidad)* cheating.

engañoso, -sa *adj (apariencia)* deceptive; *(mirada, palabra)* deceitful.

engendrar *vt (persona, animal)* to give birth to; *(sentimiento)* to give rise to.

englobar *vt* to bring together.

engordar vi *(persona)* to put on weight; *(alimento)* to be fattening ❑ **engordarse** vpr to put on weight.

engorde m *(Amér)*: **(carne de) ~** meat from domestic animals (not birds) reared for slaughter.

engranaje m *(de coche)* gears *(pl)*.

engrasar vt *(mecanismo, pieza)* to lubricate, *(ensuciar)* to make greasy.

engreído, -da adj conceited.

enhorabuena f congratulations *(pl)* ♦ interj congratulations!; **dar la ~** to congratulate.

enigma m enigma.

enjabonar vt *(ropa)* to soap; *(fig: persona)* to butter up ❑ **enjabonarse** vpr to soap o.s. down.

enjuagar vt to rinse ❑ **enjuagarse** vpr *(boca)* to rinse out one's mouth.

enlace m *(de trenes)* connection; *(de mercancías) link; (formal: matrimonio)* marriage ♦ mf *(intermediario)* go-between.

enlazar vt *(conectar)* to tie; *(relacionar)* to connect ♦ vi: **~ con** to connect with.

enlosar vt to pave.

enmendar vt *(corregir)* to correct ❑ **enmendarse** vpr to mend one's ways.

enmienda f *(corrección)* correction; *(de ley)* amendment.

enmudecer vi to be struck dumb.

enojado, -da adj annoyed.

enojar vt *(enfadar)* to anger; *(molestar)* to annoy ❑ **enojarse** vpr *(enfadarse)* to get angry; *(molestarse)* to get annoyed.

enojo m *(enfado)* anger; *(molestia)* annoyance.

enorme adj huge.

enredadera f creeper.

enredar vt *(lana, hilo, pelo)* to tangle; **~ a alguien en** *(complicar)* to involve sb in.

enredo m *(de lana, hilo, etc)* tangle; *(situación difícil, desorden)* mess.

enriquecer vt to make rich ❑ **enriquecerse** vpr to get rich.

enrojecer vt to redden ♦ vi *(sonrojarse)* to blush.

enrollar vt to roll up ❑ **enrollarse** vpr *(fam) (hablar mucho)* to go on and on, *(ligar)* to get off with each other.

ensaimada f cake made of sweet, coiled pastry.

ensalada f salad; **~ catalana** salad of lettuce, tomato, onion and old meats; **~ de lechuga** lettuce salad; **~ mixta** mixed salad; **~ variada** o **del tiempo** salad of lettuce, tomato, carrot and onion; **~ verde** green salad.

ensaladera f salad bowl.

ensaladilla f: **~ (rusa)** Russian salad.

ensanchar vt *(camino)* to widen; *(falda, pantalón)* to let out.

ensayar vt *(espectáculo)* to rehearse; *(mecanismo, invento)* to test.

ensayo m *(de espectáculo)* rehearsal; *(de mecanismo, invento)* test; *(escrito)* essay.

enseguida adv *(inmediatamente)* immediately; *(pronto)* very soon.

ensenada f cove.

enseñanza f (método, sistema) education; (profesión) teaching.

enseñar vt (en escuela, universidad) to teach; (indicar, mostrar) to show.

enseres mpl belongings.

ensopar vt (Amér) to soak.

ensuciar vt to make dirty ❑ **ensuciarse** vpr to get dirty.

ente m (ser) being; (asociación) organization.

entender vt to understand; (opinar) to think ◆ vi to understand ❑ **entender de** v + prep (saber de) to be an expert on; **entenderse** vpr (comprenderse) to understand each other; (llegar a un acuerdo) to reach an agreement; (fam: estar liado) to be involved; **~se bien/mal con** to get on well/badly with.

entendido, -da m, f expert.

enterarse: enterarse de v + prep (noticia, suceso) to find out about; (fam: darse cuenta de) to realize.

entero, -ra adj whole; (de carácter) composed; **por ~** entirely.

enterrar vt to bury.

entidad f (asociación) body.

entierro m burial.

entlo abrev = **entresuelo**.

entonces adv then; **desde ~** since then.

entrada f (lugar) entrance; (puerta) doorway; (de espectáculo) ticket; (plato) starter; (anticipo) down payment; **"entrada"** "way in"; **"~ libre"** "admission free"; **"~ por la otra puerta"** "enter by other door"; **"prohibida la ~"** "no

entry"; **de ~** (en principio) from the beginning; **¡qué quiere de ~?** what would you like for starters?

entrantes mpl (entremeses) hors d'œuvres.

entrañable adj (digno de afecto) likeable; (afectuoso) affectionate.

entrañas fpl (vísceras) entrails.

entrar vt 1. (introducir) to bring in; **están entrando el carbón** they're bringing in the coal; **ya puedes ~ el coche en el garaje** you can put your car in the garage now.
2. (INFORM) to enter.
◆ vi 1. (introducirse) to enter, to come/go in; **la pelota entró por la ventana** the ball came in through the window; **entramos en el bar** we went into the bar.
2. (penetrar) to go in; **el enchufe no entra** the plug won't go in; **el clavo ha entrado en la pared** the nail went into the wall.
3. (caber) to fit; **este anillo no te entra** this ring doesn't fit you; **en el garaje entran dos coches** you can fit two cars in the garage.
4. (incorporarse) to join; **para ~ has de hacer un test** you have to do a test to get in; **entró en el partido en abril** she joined the party in April; **entró de secretaria** she started out as a secretary.
5. (entender): **no le entra la geometría** he can't get the hang of geometry.
6. (estado físico o de ánimo): **me entró mucha pena** I was filled with pity; **me entraron ganas de hablar** I suddenly felt like talking.
7. (estar incluido): **~ (en)** to be included (in); **la consumición no**

entra *(en discoteca)* drinks are not included.

8. *(participar):* ~ **(en)** to participate (in).

9. *(cantidad):* **¿cuántas peras entran en un kilo?** how many pears do you get to the kilo?

10. *(AUTOM)* to engage; **no entra la quinta** you can't get into fifth.

11. *(empezar):* ~ **a hacer algo** to start doing sthg.

entre *prep* **1.** *(en medio de dos términos)* between; **aparcar ~ dos coches** to park between two cars; **vendré ~ las tres y las cuatro** I'll come between three and four.

2. *(en medio de muchos)* among; **estaba ~ los asistentes** she was among those present; **~ hombres y mujeres somos cien** there are a hundred of us, taking men and women together.

3 *(participación, cooperación)* between; **~ todos lo consiguieron** between them they managed it; **~ nosotros** *(en confianza)* between you and me.

4. *(lugar)* among; **encontré tu carta ~ los libros** I found your letter among the books.

entreabierto, -ta *adj (puerta, ventana)* ajar.

entreacto *m* interval.

entrecejo *m* space between the brows.

entrecot *m* entrecôte; **~ a la pimienta verde** entrecôte in a green peppercorn sauce; **~ al roquefort** entrecôte in a Roquefort sauce.

entrega *f (acto)* handing over; *(de pedido)* delivery; *(dedicación)* devotion; *(fascículo)* instalment.

entregar *vt (dar)* to hand over; *(pedido, paquete)* to deliver ❑ **entregarse a** *v + prep (rendirse)* to surrender to; *(abandonarse a)* to surrender to; *(dedicarse a)* to devote o.s. to.

entrelazar *vt* to interlace.

entremeses *mpl* hors d'œuvres.

entrenador, -ra *m, f* coach.

entrenamiento *m* training.

entrenar *vt* to train ❑ **entrenarse** *vpr* to train.

entrepierna *f* crotch.

entresuelo *m* mezzanine.

entretanto *adv* meanwhile.

entretecho *m (Amér)* attic.

entretener *vt (divertir)* to entertain; *(hacer retrasar)* to hold up ❑ **entretenerse** *vpr (divertirse)* to amuse o.s.; *(retrasarse)* to be held up.

entretenido, -da *adj (divertido)* entertaining; *(que requiere atención)* time-consuming.

entretenimiento *m (diversión)* entertainment.

entretiempo *m*: **de ~** mildweather.

entrever *vt (ver)* to glimpse; *(sospechar)* to suspect.

entreverar *vt (Amér)* to mix up ❑ **entreverarse** *vpr (Amér)* to be mixed up.

entrevero *m (Amér)* muddle.

entrevista *f* interview.

entrevistador, -ra *m, f* interviewer.

entrevistar *vt* to interview.

entrevisto, -ta *pp* → **entrever.**

entristecer vt to make sad ❑
entristecerse vpr to become sad.
entrometerse vpr to interfere.
entusiasmado, -da adj full of enthusiasm.
entusiasmar vt: me entusiasma I love it ❑ **entusiasmarse** vpr to get excited.
entusiasmo m enthusiasm.
entusiasta adj enthusiastic.
envasar vt to pack.
envase m (recipiente) container; ~ sin retorno non-returnable bottle.
envejecer vi to grow old.
envenenamiento m poisoning.
envenenar vt to poison.
envergadura f (importancia) extent.
enviar vt to send.
envidia f envy.
envidiar vt to envy.
envidioso, -sa adj envious.
envío m (acción) delivery; (paquete) package.
enviudar vi to be widowed.
envolver vt (regalo, paquete) to wrap (up).
envuelto, -ta pp → envolver.
enyesar vt (pared, muro) to plaster; (pierna, brazo) to put in plaster.
epidemia f epidemic.
episodio m (suceso) event; (capítulo) episode.
época f (periodo) period; (estación) season.
equilibrado, -da adj balanced.

equilibrar vt to balance.
equilibrio m balance; (de persona) level-headedness.
equilibrista mf tightrope walker.
equipaje m luggage (Br), baggage (Am); ~ de mano hand luggage.
equipar vt (proveer) to equip.
equipo m (de personas) team; (de objetos) equipment; (de prendas) kit.
equitación f horse riding.
equivalente adj & m equivalent.
equivaler: equivaler a v + prep to be equivalent to.
equivocación f mistake.
equivocado, -da adj wrong.
equivocar vt (confundir) to mistake ❑ **equivocarse** vpr (cometer un error) to make a mistake; (no tener razón) to be wrong; ~ de nombre to get the wrong name; me he equivocado (al teléfono) sorry, wrong number.
era v → **ser** ✦ f era.
eres v → **ser**.
erguido, -da adj erect.
erizo m hedgehog; ~ de mar sea urchin.
ermita f hermitage.
erótico, -ca adj erotic.
erotismo m eroticism.
errante adj wandering.
errar vi (equivocarse) to make a mistake.
erróneo, -a adj wrong.
error m mistake, error.
eructar vi to belch.
eructo m belch.

erudito, -ta *m, f* erudite.

erupción *f (de la piel)* rash; *(de volcán)* eruption.

es *v* → ser.

esbelto, -ta *adj* slim.

esbozo *m (dibujo)* sketch; *(resumen, guión)* outline.

escabeche *m*: **en ~** marinated.

escala *f* scale; *(de barco, avión)* stopover; **a gran ~** *(fam)* on a large scale; **~ musical** scale; **hacer ~ en** to stop over at.

escalador, -ra *m, f* climber.

escalar *vt* to climb.

escalera *f (de casa, edificio)* staircase, stairs *(pl)*; *(portátil)* ladder; **~ de caracol** spiral staircase; **~ de incendios** fire escape; **~ mecánica** escalator ☐ **escaleras** *fpl* stairs *(pl)*.

escalerilla *f* stairs *(pl)*.

escalofrío *m* shiver.

escalón *m* step.

escalope *m* escalope.

escalopín *m*. **escalopines de ternera** escalope of veal *(sg)*.

escama *f (de pez, reptil)* scale; *(en la piel)* flake.

escampar *vi* to clear up.

escandalizar *vt* to shock ☐ **escandalizarse** *vpr* to be shocked.

escándalo *m (inmoralidad)* scandal; *(alboroto)* uproar.

escaño *m (de diputado)* seat *(in parliament)*.

escapar *vi*. **~ (de)** to escape (from) ☐ **escaparse** *vpr (persona)* to escape; *(líquido, gas)* to leak.

escaparate *m (shop)* window.

escape *m (de líquido, gas)* leak; *(de coche)* exhaust; **a ~ in** a rush.

escarabajo *m* beetle.

escarbar *vt* to scratch.

escarcha *f* frost.

escarmentar *vi* to learn (one's lesson) ♦ *vt*: **~ a alguien** to teach sb a lesson.

escarola *f* endive.

escasear *vi* to be scarce.

escasez *f (insuficiencia)* shortage; *(pobreza)* poverty.

escaso, -sa *(recursos, número)* limited; *(víveres)* scarce, *(tiempo)* short; *(visibilidad)* poor; **un metro ~** barely a metre; **andar ~ de dinero** to be short of money.

escayola *f* plaster.

escayolar *vt* to put in plaster.

escena *f* scene; *(escenario)* stage.

escenario *m (de teatro)* stage; *(de un suceso)* scene.

escepticismo *m* scepticism.

escéptico, -ca *adj* sceptical.

esclavitud *f* slavery.

esclavo, -va *m, f* slave.

esclusa *f* lock.

escoba *f* broom.

escobilla *f* brush.

escocer *vi* to sting.

escocés, -esa *adj* Scottish ♦ *m, f* Scot.

Escocia *s* Scotland.

escoger *vt* to choose ♦ *vi*: **~ entre** to choose between

escolar *adj* school *(antes de s)* ♦ *mf* schoolboy *(f* schoolgirl).

escolaridad *f* schooling.

escollo *m (roca)* reef.

escolta *f* escort.

escombros *mpl* rubble *(sg)*.

esconder *vt* to hide ☐ **escon-**

derse *vpr* to hide.

escondidas: a escondidas *adv* in secret.

escondite *m (lugar)* hiding place; *(juego)* hide-and-seek.

escopeta *f* shotgun.

escorpión *m* scorpion ❑ **Escorpión** *m* Scorpio.

escotado, -da *adj* low-cut.

escote *m (de vestido)* neckline.

escotilla *f* hatch.

escribir *vt & vi* to write; **~ a mano** to write by hand; **~ a máquina** to type ❑ **escribirse** *vpr (tener correspondencia)* to write to one another; **¿cómo se escribe …?** how do you spell …?

escrito, -ta *pp → escribir ♦ m (texto)* text; *(documento)* document.

escritor, -ra *m, f* writer.

escritorio *m* desk.

escritura *f (letra)* script; *(documento)* deed.

escrúpulo *m* scruple ❑ **escrúpulos** *mpl (reservas)* qualms.

escuadra *f (en dibujo)* set square; *(de barcos)* squadron; *(del ejército)* squad.

escuchar *vt* to listen to ♦ *vi* to listen; **~ la radio** to listen to the radio.

escudella *f:* **~ catalana** Catalan dish similar to "cocido madrileño".

escudo *m (arma defensiva)* shield; *(moneda)* escudo.

escuela *f* school; **~ privada/pública** private/state school; **~ universitaria** university which awards degrees after three years' study.

esculpir *vt* to sculpt.

escultor, -ra *m, f* sculptor *(f sculptress).*

escultura *f* sculpture ♦.

escupir *vt* to spit out ♦ *vi* to spit.

escurrir *vt (ropa)* to wring out; *(platos)* to drain; *(deslizar)* to slide ❑ **escurrirse** *vpr (deslizarse)* to slip.

ese, esa *adj* that.

ése, ésa *pron* that one.

esencia *f* essence.

esencial *adj* essential.

esfera *f (en geometría)* sphere; *(del reloj)* face; *(ámbito)* circle.

esférico, -ca *adj* spherical.

esforzarse *vpr* to make an effort.

esfuerzo *m* effort.

esfumarse *vpr* to vanish.

esgrima *f* fencing.

esguince *m* sprain.

eslabón *m* link.

eslálom *m* slalom.

eslip *(pl* **eslips)** *m (pieza interior)* briefs *(pl);* *(bañador)* swimming trunks *(pl).*

Eslovaquia *s* Slovakia.

esmalte *m* enamel; **~ de uñas** nail varnish.

esmeralda *f* emerald.

esmerarse *vpr* to take great pains.

esmero *m* great care.

esmoquin *m* dinner jacket *(Br),* tuxedo *(Am).*

esnob *(pl* **esnobs)** *mf* person who wants to be trendy.

eso *pron neutro* that; **~ que tienes en la mano** that thing in your hand; **a ~ de** (at) around; **por ~ te**

lo digo that's why I'm telling you; **y ~ que** even though.

esos, esas adj pl those.

espacial adj space (antes de s).

espacio m space; (de tiempo) period; (programa) programme; **~ aéreo** air space; **~ publicitario** advertising spot.

espacioso, -sa adj spacious.

espada f sword ❑ **espadas** fpl (naipes) suit in a Spanish deck of cards bearing swords.

espaguetis mpl spaghetti (sg).

espalda f back ♦ f inv (en natación) backstroke ❑ **espaldas** fpl back (sg); **a ~s de** behind.

espantapájaros m inv scarecrow.

espanto m fright.

espantoso, -sa adj (que asusta) horrific; (muy feo, desagradable) horrible, (enorme) terrible.

España s Spain.

español, -la adj & m Spanish ♦ m, f Spaniard.

esparadrapo m (sticking) plaster.

esparcir vt (extender) to spread; (azúcar) to sprinkle; (semillas, papeles) to scatter.

espárrago m asparagus; **~s trigueros** wild asparagus.

espasmo m spasm.

espátula f (en cocina) spatula.

especia f spice.

especial adj special; (fam: persona) odd; **~ para** specially for.

especialidad f speciality (Br), specialty (Am); **~ de la casa** house speciality.

especialista mf specialist.

especializado, -da adj specialized.

especializarse: especializarse en v + prep to specialize in.

especialmente adv especially.

especie f (familia) species; (fig: tipo) type; **en ~** in kind; **~ protegida** protected species.

especificar vt to specify.

específico, -ca adj specific.

espectáculo m (en teatro, circo, etc) performance, show.

espectador, -ra m, f (en deporte) spectator; (en cine, teatro) member of the audience.

especulación f speculation.

espejismo m mirage.

espejo m mirror.

espera f wait; **en ~ de** waiting for.

esperanza f (deseo) hope; (confianza) expectation.

esperar vt (aguardar) to wait for; (confiar) to expect; (recibir, buscar) to meet; (en el futuro) to await ♦ vi (aguardar) to wait; **~ que** to hope (that); **¡eso espero!** I hope so!; **¡espera y verás!** wait and see!; **espérate sentado** (fig) you're in for a long wait ❑ **esperarse** vpr (figurarse) to expect; (aguardar) to wait.

esperma m sperm.

espeso, -sa adj thick.

espesor m (grosor) thickness; (densidad) density.

espía mf spy.

espiar vt to spy on.

espiga f (de trigo) ear.

espina f (de planta) thorn; (de pez) bone.

espinacas fpl spinach (sg).

espinilla f (de la pierna) shin; (en la piel) blackhead.

espionaje m espionage.

espiral f spiral; **en ~** spiral.

espirar vi to breathe out.

espiritismo m spiritualism.

espíritu m (alma) spirit; (en religión) soul.

espiritual adj spiritual.

espléndido, -da adj (magnífico) splendid; (generoso) lavish.

esplendor m splendour.

espliego m lavender.

esponja f sponge.

esponjoso, -sa adj spongy.

espontaneidad f spontaneity.

espontáneo, -a adj spontaneous ♦ m spectator who takes part in bullfight on the spur of the moment.

esposas fpl handcuffs.

esposo, -sa m, f husband (f wife).

espray m spray.

esprint m sprint.

esprínter mf sprinter.

espuma f (burbujas) foam; (de jabón) lather; (de cerveza) head; ~ **para el pelo** (styling) mousse.

esqueleto m skeleton.

esquema m (esbozo) outline; (gráfico) diagram.

esquematizar vt to outline.

esquí m (patín) ski; (deporte) skiing; ~ **acuático** water skiing.

esquiador, -ra m, f skier.

esquiar vi to ski.

esquilar vt to shear.

esquimal adj & mf Eskimo.

esquina f corner.

esquivar vt to avoid.

estabilidad f stability.

estable adj stable.

establecer vt (fundar) to establish; (suj: ley, decreto) to stipulate ❑ **establecerse** vpr (con residencia) to settle.

establecimiento m (acto) setting up; (local) establishment.

establo m cowshed.

estaca f (de tienda de campaña) peg.

estación f (de tren, autobús, etc) station; (del año, temporada) season; "~ **de servicio**" "service station".

estacionamiento m (aparcamiento) parking; ~ **indebido** parking offence; "~ **limitado**" "restricted parking".

estacionar vt to park; **"no ~"** "no parking" ❑ **estacionarse** vpr to park.

estadio m (de deporte) stadium.

estadística f (censo) statistics (pl).

estado m state; **estar en ~** to be expecting; **en buen/mal ~** in good/bad condition; ~ **civil** marital status; ~ **físico** physical condition ❑ **Estado** m: **el Estado** the State.

Estados Unidos mpl: **(los) ~** the United States.

estadounidense adj United States ♦ mf United States citizen.

estafa f swindle.

estafador, -ra m, f swindler.

estafar vt (engañar) to swindle; (robar) to defraud.

estalactita f stalactite.

estalagmita f stalagmite.

estallar vi (bomba) to explode; (guerra, revolución) to break out; ~ **en sollozos** to burst into tears.

estallido m (explosión) explosion.

estambre m stamen.

estamento m class.

estampado, -da adj printed ♦ m (cotton) print.

estampida f stampede.

estampilla f (Amér) (sello) stamp; (cromo) transfer.

estancado, -da adj (agua, río, etc) stagnant; (mecanismo) jammed.

estancarse vpr (agua, río, etc) to stagnate; (mecanismo) to jam.

estancia f (periodo) stay; (cuarto) room; (Amér: hacienda de campo) cattle ranch.

estanciero, -ra m, f (Amér) ranch owner.

estanco m tobacconist's (shop)

estand (pl estands) m stand, stall.

estándar adj standard.

estanque m (alberca) pond; (para riego) reservoir.

estante m shelf.

estantería f (estantes) shelves (pl); (para libros) bookcase.

estaño m tin.

estar vi 1. (hallarse) to be; ¿está Juan? is Juan in?; estaré allí a la hora convenida I'll be there at the agreed time.

2. (con fechas). ¿a qué estamos hoy? what's the date today?; hoy estamos a martes 13 de julio today is Tuesday the 13th of July; estamos en febrero/primavera it's February/spring.

3. (quedarse) to stay; **estaré un par de horas y me iré** I'll stay a couple of hours and then I'll go; **estuvo toda la tarde en casa** he was at home all afternoon.

4. (hallarse listo) to be ready; **la comida estará a las tres** the meal will be ready at three.

5. (expresa duración) to be; **están golpeando la puerta** they're banging on the door.

6. (expresa valores, grados): **la libra está a 200 pesetas** the pound is at 200 pesetas; **estamos a 20 grados** it's 20 degrees here.

7. (servir): ~ **para** to be (there) for.

8. (faltar): **eso está por descubrir** we have yet to discover that.

9. (hallarse a punto de): ~ **por hacer algo** to be on the verge of doing sthg

♦ v copulativo 1. (expresa cualidad, estado) to be; ¿cómo estás? how are you?; **esta calle está sucia** this street is dirty; ~ **bien/mal** (persona) to be well/unwell; **el cielo está con nubes** the sky is cloudy; **estoy sin dinero** I'm out of money; **el jefe está que muerde** the boss is furious.

2. (sentar): **el traje te está muy bien** the suit looks good on you.

3. (expresa situación, ocupación, acción): ~ **como camarero** to be a waiter; ~ **de suerte** to be in luck; ~ **de viaje** to be on a trip.

4. (expresa permanencia). ~ **en uso** to be in use.

5. (consistir): ~ **en** to lie in.

❑ **estarse** vpr (permanecer) to stay.

estárter m starter.

estatal adj state.

estático, -ca adj (inmóvil)

stock-still.

estatua f statue.

estatura f height.

estatus m status.

estatuto m (de compañía) article (of association); (de comunidad autónoma) by-law.

este¹, esta adj this.

este² m east ❑ **Este** m: **el Este** (de Europa) Eastern Europe.

éste, ésta pron (cercano en espacio) this one; (cercano en el tiempo) this.

estera f mat.

estéreo m stereo.

estéril adj (persona, animal) sterile; (envase, jeringuilla) sterilized.

esterilizar vt to sterilize.

esternón m breastbone.

estética f (aspecto) look.

estibador, -ra m, f stevedore.

estiércol m (excremento) dung; (abono) manure.

estilo m style; (de natación) stroke; **algo por el ~** something of the sort.

estilográfica f fountain pen.

estima f esteem.

estimación f (aprecio) esteem; (valoración) valuation.

estimado, -da adj (querido) esteemed; (valorado) valued; **Estimado señor** Dear Sir.

estimulante adj (alentador) encouraging ◆ m stimulant.

estimular vt (animar) to encourage; (excitar) to stimulate.

estímulo m incentive.

estirado, -da adj (orgulloso) haughty; (ropa) stretched.

estirar vt to stretch ◆ vi to pull ❑ **estirarse** vpr (desperezarse) to stretch.

estirpe f stock.

esto pron neutro this; **~ que dices** what you're saying.

estofado m stew.

estoico, -ca adj stoical.

estómago m stomach.

estorbar vt (obstaculizar) to hinder; (molestar) to bother ◆ vi (estar en medio) to be in the way; (molestar) to be a bother.

estorbo m (obstáculo) hindrance.

estornudar vi to sneeze.

estornudo m sneeze.

estos, -tas adj pl these.

éstos, -tas pron pl (cercano en espacio) these (ones); (cercano en el tiempo) these.

estoy v → estar.

estrafalario, -ria adj (fam) eccentric.

estrangulador, -ra m, f strangler.

estrangular vt to strangle.

estratega mf strategist.

estrategia f strategy.

estratégico, -ca adj strategic.

estrechar vt (camino, calle) to narrow; (ropa) to take in; (amistad, relación) to make closer; **~ la mano a alguien** to shake sb's hand ❑ **estrecharse** vpr (apretarse) to squeeze up.

estrecho, -cha adj (calle, camino, etc) narrow; (zapato, ropa, etc) tight; (amistad) close ◆ m strait; **estar ~** (en un lugar) to be cramped.

estrella f star; ~ **de cine** film star; ~ **fugaz** shooting star; ~ **de mar** starfish.

estrellarse vpr (chocar) to crash.

estremecerse: estremecerse de v + prep to tremble with.

estrenar vt (ropa) to wear for the first time; (espectáculo) to première; (coche, vajilla, sábanas) to use for the first time.

estreno m (de espectáculo) première.

estreñimiento m constipation.

estrepitoso, -sa adj (ruido, caída, etc) noisy.

estrés m stress.

estría f groove.

estribillo m (de canción) chorus.

estribo m (del jinete) stirrup; (del automóvil) step; **perder los ~s** to fly off the handle.

estribor m starboard.

estricto, -ta adj strict.

estrofa f verse.

estropajo m scourer.

estropeado, -da adj (coche) broken down; (máquina) out of order.

estropear vt (proyecto, plan, comida, etc) to spoil; (averiar) to break; (dañar) to damage ❑ **estropearse** vpr (máquina, aparato) to break down.

estructura f structure.

estuario m estuary.

estuche m case.

estudiante mf student.

estudiar vt & vi to study.

estudio m study; (de artista) studio; (piso) studio apartment ❑ **estudios** mpl (de radio, televisión) studios; (educación) education (sg).

estudioso, -sa adj studious.

estufa f heater.

estupefacto, -ta adj astonished.

estupendo, -da adj great ♦ interj great!

estupidez f (calidad) stupidity; (dicho, acto) stupid thing.

estúpido, -da adj stupid.

estuviera v → estar.

ETA f (abrev de Euskadi ta Askatasuna) ETA (terrorist Basque separatist organization).

etapa f stage.

etarra mf member of "ETA".

etc. (abrev de etcétera) etc.

etcétera adv etcetera.

eternidad f eternity; **una ~** (fam) ages (pl).

eterno, -na adj (perpetuo) eternal; (fam: que dura mucho, que se repite) interminable.

ética f ethics (pl).

ético, -ca adj ethical.

etimología f etymology.

etiqueta f (de paquete, vestido) label; (normas) etiquette; **de ~** formal.

étnico, -ca adj ethnic.

eucalipto m eucalyptus.

eucaristía f Eucharist.

eufemismo m euphemism.

eufórico, -ca adj elated.

Europa s Europe.

europeo, -a adj & m, f European.

Euskadi s the Basque Country.

euskera *adj & m* Basque.
eutanasia *f* euthanasia.
evacuación *f* evacuation.
evacuar *vt* to evacuate.
evadir *vt* to avoid □ **evadirse** *vpr:* ~**se de** to escape from.
evaluación *f (de trabajo, examen, etc)* assessment; *(de casa, terreno, etc)* valuation.
evaluar *vt (trabajo, examen, etc)* to assess; *(casa, terreno, etc)* to value.
evangelio *m* gospel.
evangelización *f* evangelization.
evaporarse *vpr* to evaporate.
evasión *f (distracción)* amusement; *(fuga)* escape; ~ **de capitales** capital flight.
eventual *adj (posible)* possible; *(trabajador)* casual.
eventualidad *f (posibilidad)* possibility.
evidencia *f (seguridad)* obviousness; *(prueba)* evidence.
evidente *adj* evident.
evidentemente *adv* evidently.
evitar *vt* to avoid; *(desastre, peligro)* to avert.
evocar *vt* to evoke.
evolución *f (desarrollo)* development; *(cambio)* evolution; *(movimiento)* manoeuvre.
evolucionar *vi (progresar)* to evolve; *(cambiar)* to change; *(hacer movimientos)* to carry out manoeuvres.
exactamente *adv* exactly.
exactitud *f (fidelidad)* accuracy; *(rigurosidad)* exactness.

exacto, -ta *adj (riguroso)* exact; *(preciso)* accurate; *(correcto)* correct; *(cantidad, hora, etc)* precise; *(igual)* exactly the same.
exageración *f* exaggeration.
exagerado, -da *adj (poco razonable)* exaggerated; *(precio)* exorbitant.
exagerar *vt & vi* to exaggerate.
exaltarse *vpr* to get excited.
examen *m (prueba, ejercicio)* exam; *(inspección)* examination.
examinar *vt* to examine □ **examinarse** *vpr:* ~**se (de)** to take an exam (in).
excavación *f (en arqueología)* dig.
excavadora *f* (mechanical) digger.
excavar *vt (en arqueología)* to excavate.
excedencia *f* leave (of absence).
exceder *vt* to exceed □ **excederse** *vpr (propasarse)* to go too far.
excelencia *f (calidad superior)* excellence; *(tratamiento)* Excellency; **por ~** par excellence.
excelente *adj* excellent.
excentricidad *f* eccentricity.
excéntrico, -ca *m, f* eccentric.
excepción *f* exception; **a** ○ **con** ~ **de** except for; **de** ~ exceptional.
excepcional *adj* exceptional.
excepto *adv* except (for).
excesivo, -va *adj* excessive.
exceso *m* excess; **en** ~ excessively; ~ **de peso** excess weight; ~ **de velocidad** speeding □ **excesos** *mpl (abusos)* excesses.

excitar vt (provocar nerviosismo) to agitate; (ilusionar) to excite ❑

excitarse vpr (ponerse nervioso) to get agitated; (ilusionarse) to get excited.

exclamación f (grito) cry.

excluir vt (descartar) to rule out; (no admitir) to exclude.

exclusivo, -va adj exclusive.

excursión f trip; "excursiones" "day trips".

excusa f (pretexto) excuse; (disculpa) apology.

excusar vt (disculpar) to excuse ❑ **excusarse** vpr to apologize.

exento, -ta adj exempt.

exhaustivo, -va adj exhaustive.

exhibición f (demostración) display; (deportiva, artística) exhibition; (de películas) showing.

exhibir vt (productos) to display; (cuadros, etc) to exhibit; (película) to show.

exigencia f (petición) demand; (pretensión) fussiness.

exigente adj demanding.

exigir vt (pedir) to demand; (requerir) to require.

exiliar vt to exile ❑ **exiliarse** vpr to go into exile.

exilio m exile.

existencia f existence ❑ **existencias** fpl stock (sg).

existir vi to exist; **existen varias razones** there are several reasons.

éxito m success; (canción) hit; **tener ~** to be successful.

exitoso, -sa adj (Amér) successful.

exótico, -ca adj exotic.

expedición f expedition; (de carné) issuing.

expediente m (de trabajador, empleado) file; (documentación) documents (pl); (de alumno) record.

expedir vt (paquete, mercancía, etc) to send; (documento) to draw up; (pasaporte, carné) to issue.

expendedor, -ra m, f (comerciante) dealer; (de lotería) vendor; **~ automático** vending machine; **"expendedora de billetes"** "ticket machine".

expensas fpl expenses; **a ~ de** at the expense of.

experiencia f experience; (experimento) experiment.

experimentado, -da adj experienced.

experimental adj experimental.

experimentar vt (en ciencia) to experiment with; (probar) to test; (sensación, sentimiento) to experience.

experimento m experiment.

experto, -ta m, f expert; **~ en** expert on.

expirar vi (formal) to expire.

explicación f explanation.

explicar vt to explain; (enseñar) to teach ❑ **explicarse** vpr (hablar) to explain o.s.; (comprender) to understand.

explícito, -ta adj explicit.

explorador, -ra m, f explorer.

explorar vt to explore.

explosión f (de bomba, artefacto) explosion; (de alegría, tristeza) outburst.

explosivo, -va adj & m explosive.

explotación *f (de petróleo)* drilling; *(agrícola)* farming; *(de mina)* mining; *(de negocio)* running; *(de trabajador, obrero)* exploitation; ~ **agrícola** *(instalación)* farm.

explotar *vi* to explode ◆ *vt (mina)* to work; *(negocio)* to run; *(terreno)* to farm; *(obreros)* to exploit.

exponente *m (ejemplo)* example.

exponer *vt (explicar)* to explain; *(exhibir)* to display; *(arriesgar)* to risk ❑ **exponerse a** *v + prep* to expose o.s. to.

exportación *f* export.

exportar *vt* to export.

exposición *f (de pinturas)* exhibition; *(en fotografía)* exposure; *(en escaparate)* display; *(de automóviles)* show; *(de tema, asunto)* explanation; ~ **de arte** art exhibition.

expositor, -ra *m, f (persona)* exhibitor ◆ *m (mueble)* display cabinet.

exprés *adj (tren)* express; *(café)* espresso.

expresar *vt* to express ❑ **expresarse** *vpr* to express o.s.

expresión *f* expression.

expresivo, -va *adj (elocuente)* expressive; *(afectuoso)* affectionate.

expreso, -sa *adj (claro)* clear; *(tren)* express ◆ *m (tren)* express train.

exprimidor *m* squeezer.

exprimir *vt (limón, naranja)* to squeeze.

expuesto, -ta *pp →* **exponer** ◆ *adj:* **estar ~ a** to be exposed to.

expulsar *vt (de clase, local)* to throw out; *(de colegio)* to expel; *(jugador)* to send off.

expulsión *f (de local)* throwing-out; *(de colegio)* expulsion; *(de jugador)* sending-off.

exquisitez *(pl* -ces*) f* delicacy.

exquisito, -ta *adj (comida)* delicious.

éxtasis *m inv* ecstasy.

extender *vt (desplegar)* to spread (out); *(brazos, piernas)* to stretch; *(influencia, dominio)* to extend; *(documento)* to draw up; *(cheque)* to make out; *(pasaporte)* to issue ❑ **extenderse** *vpr (ocupar)* to extend; *(durar)* to last; *(hablar mucho)* to talk at length; *(difundirse)* to spread.

extensión *f (en espacio)* area; *(en tiempo)* length; *(alcance)* extent; *(de teléfono)* extension.

extenso, -sa *adj (espacio)* extensive; *(duración)* long.

exterior *adj (de fuera)* outside; *(capa)* outer; *(extranjero)* foreign ◆ *m (parte exterior)* outside.

exterminar *vt* to exterminate.

externo, -na *adj* outer ◆ *m, f* day boy *(f* day girl*);* **"uso ~"** "for external use only".

extinguirse *vpr (luz, fuego)* to go out; *(vida, amor)* to come to an end.

extintor *m* fire extinguisher.

extirpar *vt (formal: órgano)* to remove.

extra *adj (de calidad superior)* top-quality; *(de más)* extra ◆ *m* extra.

extracción *f (formal: de órgano)* removal; *(de petróleo)* drilling; *(de* *mineral)* mining.

extracto *m (resumen)* summary; *(sustancia)* extract; **~ de cuentas** bank statement.

extractor *m* extractor (fan).

extradición *f* extradition.

extraer *vt (formal: órgano)* to remove; *(petróleo)* to drill for.

extranjero, -ra *adj* foreign ◆ *m, f* foreigner ◆ *m* foreign countries *(pl)*; **en el/al ~** abroad.

extrañar *vt (echar de menos)* to miss; *(sorprender)* to surprise □ **extrañarse de** *v + prep* to be surprised at.

extrañeza *f* surprise.

extraño, -ña *adj* strange ◆ *m, f* stranger.

extraordinario, -ria *adj* extraordinary.

extraterrestre *mf* extraterrestrial.

extravagante *adj* eccentric.

extraviar *vt (formal: perder)* to mislay □ **extraviarse** *vpr (formal) (objeto)* to go missing; *(persona)* to get lost.

extremar *vt* to go to extremes with.

extremidades *fpl* extremities.

extremista *mf* extremist.

extremo, -ma *adj (último)* furthest; *(exagerado)* extreme ◆ *m (final)* end; *(punto máximo)* extreme; **en ~** extremely.

extrovertido, -da *adj* extrovert.

F

fabada *f:* **~ (asturiana)** Asturian stew made of beans, pork sausage and bacon.

fábrica *f* factory.

fabricante *mf* manufacturer.

fabricar *vt* to make, to manufacture; **"fabricado en"** "made in".

fábula *f (relato)* fable.

fabuloso, -sa *adj (extraordinario)* fabulous; *(irreal)* mythical.

faceta *f* facet.

fachada *f (de edificio)* façade.

fácil *adj* easy; *(dócil)* easy-going; *(probable)* likely.

facilidad *f (aptitud)* aptitude; *(sencillez)* ease; **tener ~ para** to have a gift for; **~es de pago** easy *(payment)* terms.

facilitar *vt (hacer fácil)* to make easy; *(hacer posible)* to make possible; *(proporcionar)* to provide.

factor *m (elemento, condición)* factor; *(empleado)* luggage clerk.

factura *f (de gas, teléfono, hotel)* bill; *(por mercancías, etc)* invoice.

facturación *f (de equipaje)* checking-in; *(de empresa)* turnover; **"facturación"** "check-in".

facturar *vt (equipaje)* to check in; *(cobrar)* to bill.

facultad *f* faculty; *(poder)* right; **~ de ciencias/letras** faculty of science/arts.

faena *f (tarea, trabajo)* task; *(en los*

toros) bullfighter's performance.
faisán *m* pheasant.
faja *f (ropa interior)* corset; *(para cintura)* sash.
fajo *m (de billetes)* wad.
falange *f (hueso)* phalanx.
falda *f (prenda de vestir)* skirt; *(de montaña)* mountainside; *(de persona)* lap ▪ **faldas** *fpl (fam: mujeres)* girls.
falla *f (de terreno)* fault; *(de cartón) cardboard figure burned during "Fallas"* ▪ **Fallas** *fpl celebrations in Valencia on 19 March during which "fallas" are burned.*

---

i FALLAS

Valencia is famous for the festival known as "las Fallas". Throughout the year, people prepare grotesque papier-mâché giants ("ninots") which are decorated with ornaments called "fallas". These are displayed in the streets and squares of Valencia from 16–19 March, and a jury decides which will be spared from being burned in the "cremà" at midnight on 19 March.

---

fallar *vi (equivocarse)* to get it wrong; *(no acertar)* to miss; *(fracasar, no funcionar)* to fail.
fallecer *vi (formal)* to pass away.
fallo *m (equivocación)* mistake; *(de frenos, etc)* failure; *(sentencia)* verdict.
falsedad *f* falseness.
falsete *m* falsetto.
falsificar *vt* to forge.
falso, -sa *adj (afirmación, noticia)*

false; *(puerta, salida)* hidden; *(joya, piel)* fake; *(dinero, cuadro)* forged; *(hipócrita)* deceitful.
falta *f (carencia)* lack; *(necesidad)* need; *(error)* mistake; *(de asistencia, puntualidad)* absence; *(en fútbol, etc)* foul; *(en tenis)* fault; *(infracción)* offence; **echar en ~ algo/a alguien** *(echar de menos)* to miss sthg/sb; *(notar la ausencia de)* to notice sthg/sb is missing; **hacer ~** to be necessary; **me hace ~ suerte** I need some luck; **~ de educación** rudeness.
faltar *vi (no haber)* to be lacking; *(estar ausente)* to be absent; **falta aire** there isn't enough air; **falta sal** it needs some salt; **me falta un lápiz** I need a pencil; **le falta interés** she lacks interest; **falta una semana** there's a week to go; **faltan 15 km para Londres** we're 15 km away from London; **~ a clase** not to attend one's classes; **¡no faltaba más!** that's all I/we *etc* needed! ▪ **faltar a** *v + prep (obligación)* to neglect; *(palabra, promesa)* to break; *(cita, trabajo)* not to turn up at; *(ofender)* to offend.
fama *f (renombre)* fame; *(reputación)* reputation.
familia *f* family; **~ numerosa** large family.
familiar *adj (de familia)* family *(antes de s)*; *(conocido)* familiar; *(llano)* informal ◆ *mf* relative.
familiarizarse: familiarizarse con *v + prep* to familiarize o.s. with.
famoso, -sa *adj* famous.
fanatismo *m* fanaticism.
fandango *m* fandango.

fanfarrón, -ona *adj* boastful.

fantasía *f (imaginación)* imagination; *(imagen, ilusión)* fantasy.

fantasma *m (aparición)* ghost; *(fam: persona presuntuosa)* show-off.

fantástico, -ca *adj* fantastic.

farmacéutico, -ca *m, f* chemist.

farmacia *f* chemist's (shop) *(Br)*, pharmacy *(Am)*; "**~ de guardia**" "duty chemist's".

faro *m (torre)* lighthouse ❑ **faros** *mpl (de coche)* headlights.

farol *m (lámpara)* street light; *(en los toros)* movement in which bull-fighter throws cape towards bull before passing it over his head to rest on his shoulders.

farola *f (poste)* lamppost; *(farol)* street light.

farolillo *m* paper lantern.

farsa *f* farce.

farsante *adj (impostor)* fraudulent; *(hipócrita)* deceitful.

fascismo *m* fascism.

fascista *mf* fascist.

fase *f* phase.

fastidiar *vt (molestar)* to annoy; *(fiesta, planes)* to ruin; *(máquina, objeto)* to break ❑ **fastidiarse** *vpr (toes) (persona)* to put up with it, *(plan, proyecto)* to be ruined.

fastidio *m (molestia)* bother.

fatal *adj (trágico)* fatal; *(inevitable)* inevitable; *(malo)* awful ◆ *adv (fam)* awfully; **me siento ~** I feel awful.

fatalidad *f (desgracia)* misfortune; *(destino, suerte)* fate.

fatiga *f (cansancio)* fatigue.

fatigarse *vpr* to get tired.

fauna *f* fauna.

favor *m* favour; **estar a ~ de** to be in favour of; **hacer un ~ a alguien** to do sb a favour; **pedir un ~ a alguien** to ask sb a favour; **por ~** please.

favorable *adj* favourable.

favorecer *vt (quedar bien)* to suit; *(beneficiar)* to favour.

favorito, -ta *adj* favourite.

fax *m inv* fax.

fayuquero *m (Amér)* contra-band dealer.

fe *f* faith; **de buena/mala ~** *(fig)* in good/bad faith.

fealdad *f* ugliness.

febrero *m* February, → **setiembre**.

fecha *f* date; **~ de caducidad** *(de carné etc)* expiry date; *(de alimentos)* sell-by date; *(de medicamentos)* "use-by" date; **~ de nacimiento** date of birth ❑ **fechas** *fpl (período, época)* time *(sg)*.

fechar *vt* to date.

fecundo, -da *adj (mujer)* fertile; *(productivo, creativo)* prolific.

federación *f* federation.

felicidad *f* happiness ❑ **felicidades** *interj (enhorabuena)* congratulations!; *(en cumpleaños)* happy birthday!

felicitación *f (de palabra)* congratulations *(pl)*; *(tarjeta)* greetings card.

felicitar *vt* to congratulate.

feligrés, -esa *m, f* parishioner.

feliz *adj* happy; *(viaje, trayecto, día)* pleasant; **¡felices Pascuas!** Happy Easter!; **¡~ Año Nuevo!**

Happy New Year; ¡~ cumpleaños! Happy Birthday; ¡~ **Navidad!** Merry Christmas.

felpudo *m* doormat.

femenino, -na *adj* feminine.

feminismo *m* feminism.

feminista *mf* feminist.

fémur *m* thighbone.

fenomenal *adj (estupendo)* wonderful; *(fam: muy grande)* huge.

fenómeno *m* phenomenon ◆ *adv (fam)* brilliantly.

feo, -a *adj (rostro, decoración)* ugly; *(actitud, comportamiento, tiempo)* nasty.

féretro *m* coffin.

feria *f* fair; ~ **de muestras** trade fair ❑ **ferias** *fpl (fiestas)* festival *(sg)*.

---

i FERIA DE ABRIL

The "feria de abril" in Seville is Spain's most famous festival. People gather in an open-air compound to look at the hundreds of stalls and to drink, talk and dance the "sevillanas". At the same time, the first bullfights of the season are held in Seville's bullrings.

---

fermentación *f* fermentation.

feroz, -ces *adj (animal)* fierce; *(cruel)* savage.

ferretería *f* ironmonger's (shop) *(Br)*, hardware store *(Am)*.

ferrocarril *m* railway.

ferroviario, -ria *adj* rail *(antes de s)*.

ferry *m* ferry.

fértil *adj* fertile.

fertilidad *f* fertility.

festival *m* festival; ~ **de cine** film festival.

---

i FESTIVALES

The most important theatre festivals in Spain are the "Festival Internacional de Teatro de Mérida", the "Fira de Teatre al carrer de Tàrrega" and the "Sitges Teatre Internacional". Film festivals are usually held in September and October, the most important being the "Festival Internacional de Cine de San Sebastián", the "Semana Internacional de Cine de Valladolid (SEMINCI)", the "Festival de Cinema Fantàstic de Sitges" and the "Festival de Cine Iberoamericano de Huelva".

---

festividad *f* festivity.

festivo, -va *adj (traje)* festive; *(humorístico)* funny.

feto *m* foetus.

fiambre *m* cold meat *(Br)*, cold cut *(Am)*.

fiambrera *f* lunch box.

fianza *f (de alquiler, venta)* deposit; *(de preso)* bail.

fiar *vt (vender a crédito)* to sell on credit ❑ **fiarse de** *v + prep* to trust.

fibra *f* fibre.

ficción *f* fiction.

ficha *f (de datos)* card; *(de datos personales)* file; *(de guardarropa, parking)* ticket; *(de casino)* chip; *(de dominó, parchís, etc)* counter.

fichar *vt (contratar)* to sign up; *(delincuente)* to put on police files ◆

vi (empleado) to clock in/out.
fichero *m* file.
ficticio, -cia *adj* fictitious.
fidelidad *f (lealtad)* loyalty;
(exactitud) accuracy.
fideos *mpl* noodles.
fiebre *f* fever; **tener ~** to have a
temperature.
fiel *adj (amigo, seguidor)* loyal;
(cónyuge) faithful; *(exacto)* accurate
◆ *m (cristiano)* believer.
fieltro *m* felt.
fiera *f (animal)* wild animal.
fiero, -ra *adj* savage.
fierro *m (Amer)* iron.
fiesta *f (de pueblo, etc)* festivities
(pl); (reunión) party, *(día festivo)*
public holiday; *(alegría)* delight; **~
mayor** local celebrations for the festival of a town's patron saint.

FIESTA MAYOR

All Spain's towns and villages
hold a "fiesta mayor", which
consists of celebrations and cultural
activities in honour of their patron
saint. Dances are usually held every
evening of the fiesta which may last
from a weekend up to 10 days.

FIESTAS PATRIAS

This is the name given to the
national celebrations held across
all of Spanish-speaking America to
mark the day on which each country
gained independence from Spain.
The independence day celebrations
usually last two days.

figura *f (forma exterior)* shape;
(representación) figure.
figurar *vt (representar)* to represent; *(simular)* to feign ◆ *vi (constar)*
to appear; *(ser importante)* to be
important ❑ **figurarse** *vpr (imaginarse)* to imagine.
figurativo, -va *adj* figurative.
figurín *m (dibujo)* fashion
sketch; *(revista)* fashion magazine.
fijador *m (de pelo)* hairspray;
(crema) hair gel.
fijar *vt tv* tix ❑ **fijarse** *vpr (prestar
atención)* to pay attention; **~se en**
(darse cuenta de) to notice.
fijo, -ja *adj* fixed; *(sujeto)* secure;
(fecha) definite.
fila *f (hilera)* line.
filatelia *f* philately.
filete *m* fillet; *(de carne)* steak; **~
de ternera** fillet of veal; **~ de
lenguado** fillet of sole.
filiación *f (datos personales)*
record; *(procedencia)* relationship.
filial *adj* filial ◆ *f* subsidiary.
Filipinas *fpl:* **(las) Filipinas** the
Philippines.
filmar *vt & vi* to film.
filoso, -sa *adj (Amér)* sharp.
filosofar *vi (fam)* to philoso-
phize.
filosofía *f* philosophy.
filósofo, -fa *m, f* philosopher.
filtrar *vt (líquido)* to filter; *(noticia, información)* to leak.
filtro *m* filter; **bronceador con 15
~s** factor 15 suntan lotion.
filudo, -da *adj (Amér)* sharp.
fin *m* end; *(objetivo)* aim; **a ~ de
que** in order that; **a ~es de** at the
end of; **en ~** anyway; **por ~** final-

ly; **~ de semana** weekend; **"~ zona de estacionamiento"** "end of parking zone".

final adj & f final ♦ m end.

finalidad f purpose.

finalista mf finalist.

finalizar vt & vi to finish.

financiación f financing.

financiar vt to finance.

financista mf (Amér) financier.

finanzas fpl finance (sg).

finca f (bienes inmuebles) property; (casa de campo) country residence.

finger m (de aeropuerto) jetway.

fingir vt to feign.

finlandés, -esa adj Finnish ♦ m, f Finn.

Finlandia s Finland.

fino, -na adj (delgado) thin; (suave) smooth; (esbelto) slim; (restaurante, hotel) posh; (persona) refined; (de calidad, sabor, olor) fine; (sutil) subtle ♦ m dry sherry; **finas hierbas** fines herbes.

fiordo m fjord.

firma f (de persona) signature; (empresa) firm.

firmar vt to sign.

firme adj firm; (bien sujeto) stable; (carácter) resolute.

firmemente adv firmly.

firmeza f (solidez) stability; (constancia) firmness; (de carácter) resolution.

fiscal adj tax (antes de s) ♦ mf public prosecutor (Br), district attorney (Am).

fiscalía f (oficio) post of public prosecutor (Br), post of district attorney (Am); (oficina) public prosecutor's office (Br), district attorney's office (Am).

física f physics (sg), → **físico**.

físico, -ca adj physical ♦ m, f physicist ♦ m (aspecto exterior) physique.

fisioterapeuta mf physiotherapist.

fisonomía f appearance.

fisonomista adj good at remembering faces.

flaco, -ca adj thin.

flamante adj (llamativo) resplendent; (nuevo) brand-new.

flamenco, -ca adj (de Flandes) Flemish ♦ m (ave) flamingo; (cante andaluz) flamenco.

flan m crème caramel; **~ con nata** crème caramel with whipped cream.

flaqueza f weakness.

flash [flaʃ] m (en fotografía) flash.

flauta f flute.

flecha f arrow.

fleco m (de cortina, mantel) fringe ❑ **flecos** mpl (de pantalón, camisa) frayed edges.

flemón m gumboil.

flequillo m fringe.

flexibilidad f flexibility.

flexible adj flexible.

flexión f (ejercicio) press-up.

flojera f (fam) lethargy.

flojo, -ja adj (cuerda, clavo) loose; (carácter, persona) weak; (de poca calidad) poor.

flor f flower.

flora f flora.

florecer vi (planta) to flower; (prosperar) to flourish.

florero m vase.

florido, -da adj (árbol) blossoming; (jardín) full of flowers.

florista mf florist.

floristería f florist's (shop).

flota f fleet.

flotador m (para la cintura) rubber ring; (para los brazos) arm band.

flotar vi to float.

flote: a flote adv afloat; **salir a ~** (fig) to get back on one's feet.

fluido, -da adj (líquido) fluid; (lenguaje, estilo) fluent ♦ m fluid.

fluir vi to flow.

flúor m (en dentífrico) fluoride.

FM f (abrev de frecuencia modulada) FM.

foca f seal.

foco m (en teatro) spotlight; (en campo de fútbol) floodlight; (de infección, epidemia) centre; (Amér: bombilla) light bulb.

foie-gras m inv foie-gras.

folio m sheet (of paper).

folklore m folklore.

folklórico, -ca adj (tradición, baile) traditional, popular; (fam. ridículo) absurd.

follaje m foliage.

folleto m (turístico, publicitario) brochure; (explicativo, de instrucciones) leaflet.

fomentar vt to encourage.

fonda f boarding house.

fondo m bottom; (de dibujo, fotografía) background; (dimensión) depth; **a ~** thoroughly; **al ~ de** (calle) at the end of; (habitación) at the back of □ **fondos** mpl (dinero) funds; (de archivo, biblioteca) catalogue (sg).

fono m (Amér) receiver.

fontanero, -ra m, f plumber.

footing ['futin] m jogging; **hacer ~** to go jogging.

forastero, -ra m, f stranger.

forense mf pathologist.

forestal adj forest (antes de s).

forfait f ski pass.

forjar vt (hierro) to forge; (crear) to build up.

forma f (figura externa) shape; (modo, manera) way; **en ~ de** in the shape of, **estar en ~** to be fit □ **formas** fpl (modales) social conventions.

formación f formation; (educación) training; **~ profesional** Spanish vocational training for pupils aged 14-18 who do not do "BUP"; it is possible to go on to study technical subjects at university.

formal adj (de forma) formal; (de confianza) reliable; (serio) serious.

formalidad f (seriedad) seriousness; (requisito) formality.

formar vt (crear) to form; (educar) to train □ **formarse** vpr (educarse) to be trained.

formidable adj (estupendo) amazing; (grande) tremendous.

fórmula f formula.

formular vt to formulate.

formulario m form.

forrar vt (libro) to cover; (ropa) to line □ **forrarse** vpr (fam) to make a pile.

forro m (de prenda de vestir) lining; (de libro) cover.

fortaleza f (fuerza) strength; (recinto) fortress.

fortuna f (suerte) (good) luck; (riqueza) fortune.

forzado, -da adj forced.

forzar vt to force; ~ **a alguien a hacer algo** to force sb to do sthg.

forzosamente adv necessarily.

fósforo m (cerilla) match.

fósil m fossil.

foso m (de castillo) moat; (de orquesta) pit; (hoyo) ditch.

foto f (fam) photo; **sacar una** ~ to take a photo.

fotocopia f photocopy.

fotocopiadora f photocopier.

fotocopiar vt to photocopy.

fotografía f (imagen) photograph; (arte) photography.

fotografiar vt to photograph.

fotográfico, -ca adj photographic.

fotógrafo, -fa m, f photographer.

fotomatón m passport photo machine.

FP abrev = **formación profesional**.

fra. (abrev de factura) inv.

fracasar vi to fail.

fracaso m failure.

fracción f fraction.

fractura f fracture.

fragancia f fragrance.

frágil adj: "**frágil**" "fragile".

fragmento m (pedazo) fragment; (de obra) excerpt.

fraile m friar.

frambuesa f raspberry.

francamente adv (sinceramente) frankly; (muy) really.

francés, -esa adj & m French ◆ m, f Frenchman (f Frenchwoman); **los franceses** the French.

Francia s France.

franco, -ca adj (sincero) frank; (sin obstáculos) free ◆ m (moneda) franc.

francotirador, -ra m, f sniper.

franela f flannel.

franja f (en bandera, ropa) stripe.

franqueo m postage.

frasco m small bottle.

frase f sentence.

fraternal adj fraternal.

fraternidad f brotherhood.

fraude m fraud.

fray m brother.

frazada f (Amér) blanket; ~ **eléctrica** electric blanket.

frecuencia f frequency; **con** ~ often.

frecuente adj (repetido) frequent; (usual) common.

fregadero m (kitchen) sink.

fregado, -da adj (Amér: fam) annoying.

fregar vt (limpiar) to wash; (frotar) to scrub; (Amér: fam: molestar) to bother; ~ **los platos** to do the washing-up.

fregona f (utensilio) mop; (despec: mujer) skivvy.

freír vt to fry.

frenar vt (parar) to brake; (contener) to check ◆ vi to brake.

frenazo m: **dar un** ~ to slam on the brakes.

frenético, -ca adj (rabioso) furious; (exaltado) frantic.

freno m brake; ~ **de mano** hand brake (Br), parking brake (Am); ~ **de urgencia** (en tren) emergency cord.

frente[1] m front; **estar al ~ de** (dirigir) to be at the head of.

frente[2] f (de la cara) forehead; **de ~ head on**; ~ **a** opposite; ~ **a ~** face to face.

fresa f strawberry.

fresco, -ca adj fresh; (frío) cool; (desvergonzado) cheeky; (tejido, ropa) light ♦ m, f (desvergonzado) checky person ♦ m (frío suave) cool; (pintura) fresco; **hare ~** it's chilly; **tomar el ~** to get a breath of fresh air.

fresno m ash (tree).

fresón m large strawberry.

fricandó m fricandeau.

frigorífico m refrigerator.

frijol m (judía) bean; (Amér: tipo de judía) pinto bean.

frío, -a adj & m cold; **hace ~** it's cold; **tener ~** to be cold.

fritada f fried dish; ~ **de pescado** dish of fried fish.

frito, -ta pp → **freír** ♦ adj fried.

fritura f fried dish.

frívolo, -la adj frivolous.

frondoso, -sa adj leafy.

frontera f border.

fronterizo, -za adj (cerca de la frontera) border (antes de s); (vecino) neighbouring.

frontón m (juego) pelota; (de edificio) pediment.

frotar vt to rub.

fruncir vt: ~ **el ceño** to frown.

frustración f frustration.

frustrar vt (plan, proyecto) to thwart ❑ **frustrarse** to get frustrated; (plan, proyecto) fail.

fruta f fruit; ~ **del tiempo** fruit in season.

frutal m fruit tree.

frutería f fruit shop.

frutero, -ra m, f (persona) fruiterer ♦ m (plato) fruit bowl.

frutilla f (Amér) strawberry.

fruto m fruit; (nuez, avellana, etc) nut ❑ **frutos** mpl produce (sg); ~**s del bosque** fruits of the forest; ~**s secos** dried fruit and nuts.

fue v → **ir, ser**.

fuego m fire; **a ~ lento** over a low heat; **¿tienes ~?** do you have a light?; ~**s artificiales** fireworks.

fuelle m (de aire) bellows (pl); (entre vagones) concertina vestibule.

fuente f (manantial) spring; (en la calle) fountain; (recipiente) dish; (origen) source.

fuera v → **ir, ser** ♦ adv (en el exterior) outside; (en otro lugar) away ♦ interj get out!; **sal ~** go out; **por ~** (on the outside); **por ~** **borda** outboard motor; ~ **de** (a excepción de) except for; ~ **de combate** (en boxeo) knocked out; "~ **de servicio**" "out of order".

fuerte adj strong; (frío, dolor) intense; (lluvia) heavy; (golpe, colisión) hard; (alimento) rich; (voz, sonido) loud ♦ m (fortaleza) fort; (afición) strong point ♦ adv (con fuerza, intensidad) hard; (gritar) loudly.

fuerza f force; (de persona, animal, resistencia) strength; **a ~ de** by dint of; **a la ~** by force; **por ~** (por

...gación) by force; (por necesidad) ...t necessity; **las ~s armadas** the armed forces.

fuese v → **ir, ser**.

fuga f (de persona) escape; (de gas) leak.

fugarse vpr to escape; **~ de casa** to run away (from home).

fugaz, -ces adj fleeting.

fugitivo, -va m, f fugitive.

fui v → **ir**.

fulana f (tart, → **fulano**.

fulano, -na m, f what's his/her name.

fulminante adj (muy rápido) sudden.

fumador, -ra m, f smoker; "**~es**" "smokers"; "**no ~es**" "non-smokers".

fumar vt & vi to smoke; **~ en pipa** to smoke a pipe; "**no ~**" "no smoking".

función f (utilidad) function; (de teatro) show.

funcionar vi to work; **funciona con diesel** it runs on diesel; "**no funciona**" "out of order".

funcionario, -ria m, f civil servant.

funda f (cubierta) cover; (de almohada) pillowcase.

fundación f foundation.

fundador, -ra m, f founder.

fundamental adj fundamental.

fundamento m (base) basis ❑ **fundamentos** mpl (conocimientos) basics.

fundar vt (crear) to found; (apoyar) to base ❑ **fundarse en** v + prep to be based on.

fundición f (de metal) smelting; (fábrica) foundry.

fundir vt (derretir) to melt; (aparato) to fuse; (bombilla, dinero) to blow; (unir) to merge ❑ **fundirse** vpr (derretirse) to melt.

funeral m funeral.

fungir vi (Amér) to act.

funicular m (por tierra) funicular railway; (por aire) cable car.

furgón m (coche grande) van; (vagón de tren) wagon.

furgoneta f van.

furia f fury.

furioso, -sa adj (lleno de ira) furious; (intenso) intense.

furor m (furia) rage; **hacer ~** (fam) to be all the rage.

fusible m fuse.

fusil m rifle.

fusilar vt to shoot.

fusión m (de metal, cuerpo sólido) melting; (de empresas) merger.

fustán m (Amér) (enaguas) petticoat; (falda) skirt.

fútbol m football; **~ sala** indoor five-a-side.

futbolín m table football.

futbolista mf footballer.

futuro, -ra adj & m future.

g (abrev de gramo) g.

g/ abrev = **giro**.

gabán m overcoat.

gabardina f raincoat.

gabinete m (sala) study; (gobierno) cabinet.

gafas fpl glasses; ~ **de sol** sunglasses.

gaita f bagpipes (pl); **ser una** ~ (fam) to be a pain in the neck.

gala f (actuación) show; **de** ~ black tie (antes de s) ❏ **galas** fpl (vestidos) best clothes.

galán m (hombre atractivo) handsome man; (actor) leading man; (mueble) clothes stand.

galaxia f galaxy.

galería f gallery; (corredor descubierto) verandah; ~ **de arte** art gallery ❏ **galerías** fpl (tiendas) shopping arcade (sg).

Gales s Wales.

galés, -esa adj & m Welsh ◆ m, f Welshman (f Welshwoman); **los galeses** the Welsh.

Galicia s Galicia.

gallego, -ga adj & m, f Galician.

galleta f biscuit.

gallina f (animal) hen ◆ mf (cobarde) chicken.

gallinero m (corral) henhouse; (de teatro) gods (pl).

gallo m (ave) cock; (pescado) John Dory; (fam: nota falsa) false note.

galopar vi to gallop.

galope m gallop.

gama f range.

gamba f (prawn; ~s al ajillo prawns cooked in an earthenware dish in a sauce of oil, garlic and chilli; ~s a la plancha grilled prawns.

gamberro, -rra m, f hooligan.

gamonal m (Amér) village chief.

gamuza f (piel, para limpiar el coche, etc) chamois; (para quitar el polvo) duster.

gana f (apetito) appetite; **de buena** ~ willingly; **de mala** ~ unwillingly; **no me da la** ~ **de hacerlo** I don't feel like doing it ❏ **ganas** fpl: **tener** ~**s de** to feel like.

ganadería f (ganado) livestock; (actividad) livestock farming; (en toros) breed.

ganadero, -ra m, f (dueño) livestock farmer; (cuidador) cattle hand.

ganado m (animales de granja) livestock; (vacuno) cattle.

ganador, -ra m, f winner.

ganancias fpl profit (sg).

ganar vt to win; (obtener) to earn; (beneficio) to make; (aumentar) to gain; (derrotar) to beat ◆ vi (ser vencedor) to win, (mejorar) to benefit ❏ **ganarse** vpr (conseguir) to earn; ~**se la vida** to earn a living.

ganchillo m (aguja) crochet hook; (labor) crochet.

gancho m (para colgar) hook; (atractivo) sex appeal; (Amer: percha) coat hanger.

gandul, -la adj lazy.

ganga f bargain.

ganso m goose.

garabato m scribble.

garaje m garage.

garantía f guarantee.

garbanzo m chickpea.

garfio m hook.

garganta f (de persona) throat; (entre montañas) gorge.

gargantilla f (short) necklace.

gárgaras fpl: **hacer** ~ to gargle.

garra f (de animal) claw.

garrafa f large bottle usually in a wicker holder.

garrapata f tick.

garúa f (Amér) drizzle.

gas m gas ◆ **gases** mpl (del estómago) wind (sg).

gasa f gauze.

gaseosa f lemonade.

gaseoso, -sa adj fizzy.

gasfitería f (Amér) plumber's (shop).

gasfitero m (Amér) plumber.

gasóleo m diesel oil.

gasolina f petrol (Br), gas (Am); ~ **normal** = two-star petrol; ~ **sin plomo** unleaded petrol; ~ **súper** = four-star petrol.

gasolinera f petrol station (Br), gas station (Am).

gastar vt (dinero) to spend; (usar) to use; (talla, número) to use; (acabar) to use up ❑ **gastarse** vpr (acabarse) to run out; (desgastarse) to wear out.

gasto m (acción de gastar) expenditure; (cosa que pagar) expense ❑ **gastos** mpl expenditure (sg).

gastritis f inv gastritis.

gastronomía f gastronomy.

gastronómico, -ca adj gastronomic.

gatear vi to crawl.

gatillo m trigger.

gato, -ta m, f cat ◆ m (aparato) jack; **a gatas** on all fours.

gauchada f (Amér: fig) shrewd action.

gaucho m gaucho.

gavilán m sparrowhawk.

gaviota f seagull.

gazpacho m: ~ **(andaluz)** gazpacho, Andalusian soup made from tomatoes, peppers, cucumbers and bread, served chilled.

gel m gel.

gelatina f (para cocinar) gelatine; (postre) jelly.

gemelo, -la adj & m, f twin ◆ m (músculo) calf ❑ **gemelos** mpl (botones) cufflinks; (anteojos) binoculars.

gemido m moan.

Géminis m inv Gemini.

gemir vi to moan.

generación f generation.

generador m generator.

general adj & m general; **en ~** in general; **por lo ~** generally.

generalizar vt to make widespread ◆ vi to generalize.

generalmente adv generally.

generar vt to generate.

género m (mercancía) goods (pl); (clase, especie) type; (GRAM) gender; (en literatura) genre; ~**s de punto** knitwear.

generosidad f generosity.

generoso, -sa adj generous.

genial adj brilliant.

genio m (carácter) character; (mal carácter) bad temper; (persona inteligente) genius; **tener mal ~** to be bad-tempered.

genitales mpl genitals.

gente f people (pl); (fam: familia) folks (pl).

gentil adj (cortés) kind; (elegante) elegant.

gentileza f (cortesía) kindness; (elegancia) elegance.

genuino, -na *adj* genuine.

geografía *f* geography; **la ~ nacional** the country.

geometría *f* geometry.

geométrico, -ca *adj* geometric.

geranio *m* geranium.

gerente *mf* manager (*f* manageress).

germen *m* germ.

gestión *f* (*diligencia*) step; (*administración*) management.

gestionar *vt* (*tramitar*) to work towards; (*administrar*) to manage.

gesto *m* (*con las manos*) gesture; (*mueca*) grimace, face.

gestor, -ra *m, f* (*de gestoría*) agent who deals with public bodies on behalf of private individuals; (*de empresa*) manager.

gestoría *f* (*establecimiento*) office of a "gestor".

Gibraltar *s* Gibraltar.

gibraltareño, -na *adj & m, f* Gibraltarian.

gigante, -ta *adj & m, f* giant.

gigantesco, -ca *adj* gigantic.

gimnasia (*deporte*) gymnastics (*pl*); (*ejercicio*) exercises (*pl*).

gimnasio *m* gymnasium.

gimnasta *mf* gymnast.

ginebra *f* gin.

ginecólogo, -ga *m, f* gynaecologist.

gin tonic [ʒin'tonik] *m* gin and tonic.

gira *f* tour.

girar *vt* (*hacer dar vueltas*) to turn; (*rápidamente*) to spin; (*letra, cheque*) to draw; (*paquete*) to send; (*dinero*)

to transfer ◆ *vi* (*dar vueltas*) to turn; (*rápidamente*) to spin.

girasol *m* sunflower.

giro *m* turn; (*de letra, cheque*) draft; (*expresión, dicho*) saying; **~ postal** postal order; **~ urgente** *postal order delivered by the Post Office to the payee on the following day.*

gitano, -na *adj & m,* f gypsy.

glaciar *m* glacier.

gladiolo *m* gladiolus.

glándula *f* gland.

global *adj* overall.

globo *m* (*para jugar, volar*) balloon; (*cuerpo esférico*) sphere; (*la Tierra, de lámpara*) globe; **~ terráqueo** globe.

glóbulo *m* corpuscle.

gloria *f* glory; (*fam: placer*) bliss; (*persona*) star.

glorieta *f* (*plaza*) square; (*redonda*) = roundabout (*Br*), = traffic circle (*Am*); (*de jardín*) bower

glorioso, -sa *adj* glorious.

glotón, -ona *adj* gluttonous, greedy.

glucosa *f* glucose.

gluten *m* gluten

gobernador, -ra *m, f* governor.

gobernante *mf* leader.

gobernar *vt* (*nación, país*) to govern; (*nave, vehículo*) to steer.

gobierno *m* (*de país*) government; (*edificio*) governor's office; (*de nave, vehículo*) steering.

goce *m* pleasure.

godo, -da *m, f* Goth.

gol *m* goal.

goleador, -ra *m, f* scorer.

golf

golf m golf.

golfa f (prostituta) whore, → golfo.

golfo, -a m, f (gamberro) lout; (pillo) rascal ♦ m (en geografía) gulf.

golondrina f swallow.

golosina f (dulce) sweet.

goloso, -sa adj sweet-toothed.

golpe m (puñetazo, desgracia) blow; (bofetada) smack; (en puerta) knock; (choque) bump; (DEP) shot; (gracia) witticism; (atraco, asalto) raid; **de ~** suddenly; **~ de Estado** coup.

golpear vt to hit ♦ vi to bang.

goma f (pegamento) gum; (material) rubber; (banda elástica) elastic; (gomita) elastic band; **~ de borrar** rubber (Br), eraser (Am).

gomero m (Amér) rubber tree.

gomina f hair gel.

góndola f (Amér) bus.

gordo, -da adj (obeso) fat; (grueso) thick; (grave) big; (importante) important ♦ m, f fat person ♦ m: el **~ (de la lotería)** first prize.

i EL GORDO

This is the name given to first prize in the Spanish National Lottery, especially the one in the Christmas draw, where all the winning numbers are sung out by children on national radio.

gordura f fatness.

gorila m (animal) gorilla; (fam: guardaespaldas) bodyguard; (fam: en discoteca) bouncer.

gorjeo m chirping.

gorra f cap; **de ~** for free.

gorrión m sparrow.

gorro m cap.

gota f drop; (enfermedad) gout; **no quiero ni ~** I don't want anything ❏ **gotas** fpl (para nariz, ojos) drops.

gotera f leak; (mancha) stain (left by leaking water).

gótico, -ca adj Gothic ♦ m (en arte) Gothic (art).

gozar vi to enjoy o.s. ❏ **gozar de** v + prep (disponer de) to enjoy.

gozo m joy.

gr (abrev de grado) deg.

grabación f recording.

grabado m (arte) engraving; (lámina) print.

grabar vt to engrave; (canción, voz, imágenes, etc) to record.

gracia f (humor) humour; (atractivo) grace; (don) talent; (chiste) joke; **no me hace ~** (no me gusta) I'm not keen on it; **tener ~** to be funny ❏ **gracias** fpl thanks ♦ interj thank you; **dar las ~ a** to thank; **~s a** thanks to; **~s por** thank you for; **muchas ~s** thank you very much.

gracioso, -sa adj (que da risa) funny; (con encanto) graceful.

grada f (de plaza de toros) row; (peldaño) step; **las ~s** the terraces.

gradería f (de plaza de toros) rows (pl); (de estadio) terraces (pl); (público) crowd.

grado m (medida) degree; (fase) stage; (de enseñanza) level; (del ejército) rank; **de buen ~** willingly.

graduación f (de bebida) = proof; (de militar) rank; (acto) grading.

graduado, -da adj (persona) graduate; (regla, termómetro) graduated ◆ m, f (persona) graduate ◆ m (título) degree; **~ escolar** qualification received on completing primary school.

GRADUADO ESCOLAR

This is the qualification received on successful completion of primary education in Spain. It is needed in order to go to secondary school and is also one of the requirements for people over the age of 25 who wish to go to university.

---

gradual adj gradual
gradualmente adv gradually.
graduar vt (calefacción, calentador) to regulate □ **graduarse** vpr (militar) to receive one's commission; **~se (en)** (estudiante) to graduate (in).
graffiti m graffiti.
grafía f written symbol.
gráfico, -ca adj graphic ◆ m o f (dibujo) graph.
gragea f pill.
gramática f grammar.
gramatical adj grammatical.
gramo m gram.
gran adj → **grande**.
granada f (fruto) pomegranate, (proyectil) grenade.
granadilla f (Amér) passion fruit.
granate adj inv deep red ◆ m garnet.
Gran Bretaña s Great Britain.

grande adj (de tamaño) big; (de altura) tall; (importante) great ◆ m (noble) grandee; **le va ~** (vestido, zapato) it's too big for him; **~s almacenes** department store (sg).
grandeza f (importancia) grandeur; (tamaño) (great) size.
grandioso, -sa adj grand.
granel: a granel adv (arroz, judías, etc) loose; (líquidos) by volume; (en abundancia) in abundance.
granero m granary.
granito m granite.
granizada f hailstorm.
granizado m ≃ Slush Puppie®, drink consisting of crushed ice with lemon juice, coffee etc.
granizar v impers: **está granizando** it's hailing.
granja f (en el campo) farm; (bar) milk bar.
granjero, -ra m, f farmer.
grano m (de cereal) grain; (de la piel) spot; (de fruto, planta) seed; (de café) bean; **ir al ~** (fam) to get to the point.
granuja mf (chiquillo) rascal.
grapa f staple.
grapadora f stapler.
grapar vt to staple.
grasa f grease; (de persona, animal) fat.
grasiento, -ta adj greasy.
graso, -sa adj greasy.
gratificar vt (recompensar) to reward; **"se gratificará"** "reward".
gratinado m gratin.
gratinar vt to cook au gratin.
gratis adv free.
gratitud f gratitude.

grato, -ta adj pleasant.

gratuito, -ta adj (gratis) free; (sin fundamento) unfounded.

grave adj serious; (voz) deep; (tono) low; (palabra) with the stress on the penultimate syllable.

gravedad f (importancia) seriousness; (de la Tierra) gravity.

gravilla f gravel.

Grecia s Greece.

gremio m (profesión) profession, trade.

greña f mop of hair.

griego, -ga adj & m, f Greek.

grieta f crack.

grifero, -ra m, f (Amér) petrol-pump attendant.

grifo m (de agua) tap; (Amér: gasolinera) petrol station (Br), gas station (Am).

grill [gril] m grill.

grilla f (Amér: fam) plot to oust sb from their post.

grillo m cricket.

gripa f (Amér) flu.

gripe f flu.

gris adj & m grey.

gritar vi (hablar alto) to shout; (chillar) to scream.

grito m (de dolor, alegría) cry; (palabra) shout; **a ~s** at the top of one's voice.

grosella f redcurrant; **~ negra** blackcurrant.

grosería f (dicho) rude word; (acto) rude thing.

grosero, -ra adj (poco refinado) coarse; (maleducado) rude.

grosor m thickness.

grotesco, -ca adj grotesque.

grúa f (máquina) crane; (para averías) breakdown truck; (para aparcamientos indebidos) towaway truck.

grueso, -sa adj (persona) fat; (objeto) thick ◆ m (espesor, volumen) thickness; (parte principal) bulk.

grumo m lump.

gruñido m grunt.

gruñir vi to grunt.

grupa f hindquarters (pl).

grupo m group; **en ~** in a group; **~ de riesgo** high risk group; **~ sanguíneo** blood group.

gruta f grotto.

guaca f (Amér) Indian tomb.

guacal m (Amér) basket.

guacamole m (Amér) guacamole.

guachimán m (Amér) security guard.

guacho, -cha adj (Amér) (huérfano) orphaned; (solitario) solitary ◆ m, f (Amér: hijo ilegítimo) illegitimate child.

guaco m (Amér) object of pre-Colombian pottery.

guagua f (Amér) (fam: autobús) bus; (bebé) baby.

guaiño m (Amér) melancholy Indian song.

guajiro, -ra m, f (Amér: fam) peasant.

guano m (Amér) manure.

guante m glove.

guantera f glove compartment.

guapo, -pa adj (mujer) pretty; (hombre) handsome; (fam: objeto, ropa, etc) nice.

guardabarros m inv mudguard.

guardacoches m inv car park attendant.

guardaespaldas m inv bodyguard.

guardameta m goalkeeper.

guardapolvo m (prenda) overalls (pl); (funda) dust cover.

guardar vt to keep; (poner) to put (away); (cuidar) to look after; (suj: guardia) to guard; (ley) to observe □ **guardarse** vpr: ~**se de** (abstenerse de) to be careful not to

guardarropa m (de local) cloakroom; (armario) wardrobe.

guardería f (escuela) nursery (school); (en el trabajo) crèche.

guardia mf (policía) police officer ◆ f (vigilancia) guard; (turno) duty; ~ **civil** member of the "Guardia Civil"; ~ **municipal** □ **urbano** local police officer who deals mainly with traffic offences; ~ **de seguridad** security guard; **farmacia de** ~ duty chemist's □ **Guardia Civil** f Spanish police who patrol rural areas, highways and borders

guardián, -ana m, f guardian.

guarida f lair.

guarnición f (de comida) garnish; (del ejército) garrison.

guarro, -rra adj (despec) filthy.

guasa f (fam) (ironía) irony; (gracia) humour.

guasca f (Amér) (látigo) whip; (vulg: pene) prick.

Guatemala s Guatemala.

guatemalteco, -ca adj & m, f Guatemalan.

guateque m party.

guayaba f guava.

guayabo m guava tree.

güero, -ra adj (Amér: fam) blond (f blonde).

guerra f war; ~ **civil** civil war; ~ **mundial** world war.

guerrera f (chaqueta) military-style jacket, → guerrero.

guerrero, -ra m, f warrior.

guerrilla f guerilla group.

guerrillero, -ra m, f guerrilla.

guía mf (persona) guide ◆ f (libro, folleto, indicación) guide; ~ **de ferrocarriles** train timetable; ~ **telefónica** telephone directory; ~ **turística** tourist guide.

guiar vt (mostrar dirección) to guide; (vehículo) to steer □ **guiarse por** v + prep to be guided by.

guijarro m pebble.

guillotina f guillotine.

guinda f morello cherry.

guindilla f chilli pepper.

guiñar vt: ~ **un ojo** to wink

guiñol m puppet theatre.

guión m (argumento) script; (esquema) outline; (signo) hyphen.

guionista mf scriptwriter.

güiri m (fam) bloody foreigner.

guirnalda f garland.

guisado m stew.

guisante m pea; ~**s salteados** □ **con jamón** peas fried with "jamón serrano".

guisar vt & vi to cook.

guiso m dish (food).

guitarra f guitar.

guitarrista mf guitarist.

gusano m worm.

gustar vi: **me gusta** I like it; **me gustan los pasteles** I like cakes; **no**

gusto
144

me gusta ese libro I don't like that book.

gusto *m* taste; *(placer)* pleasure; **a tu ~** as you wish; **vivir a ~** *(bien)* to live comfortably; **un filete al ~** a steak done the way you like it; **con mucho ~** with pleasure; **mucho ~** pleased to meet you.

h. *(abrev de hora)* h.

ha *v → haber.*

ha. *(abrev de hectárea)* ha.

haba *f* broad bean; **~s a la catalana** stew of broad beans, bacon, "butifarra" and wine.

habano *m* Havana cigar.

haber *m (bienes)* assets *(pl)*; **tiene tres pisos en su ~** he owns three flats.

◆ *v aux* 1. *(en tiempos compuestos)* to have; **los niños han comido** the children have eaten; **habían desayunado antes** they'd had breakfast earlier.

2. *(expresa reproche):* **¡lo dicho!** why didn't you say so?

◆ *v impers* 1. *(existir, estar, tener lugar):* **hay** there is, there are *(pl)*; **¿qué hay hoy para comer?** what's for dinner today?; **¡no hay nadie en casa?** isn't anyone at home?; **el jueves no habrá reparto** there will be no delivery on Thursday.

2. *(expresa obligación):* **~ que hacer**

algo to have to do sthg; **habrá que soportarlo** we'll have to put up with it.

3. *(en locuciones):* **habérselas con alguien** to confront sb; **¡hay que ver!** well I never!; **no hay de qué** don't mention it.

❏ **haber de** *v + prep* to have to.

habichuela *f* bean.

hábil *adj (diestro)* skilful; *(astuto)* clever; **día ~** working day.

habilidad *f (destreza)* skill; *(astucia)* cleverness.

habiloso, -sa *adj (Amér)* shrewd.

habitación *f (cuarto)* room; *(dormitorio)* bedroom; **~ doble** *(con cama de matrimonio)* double room; *(con dos camas)* twin room; **~ individual** single room.

habitante *mf* inhabitant.

habitar *vi* to live ◆ *vt* to live in.

hábito *m* habit.

habitual *adj (acostumbrado)* habitual; *(cliente, lector)* regular.

habitualmente *adv (generalmente)* usually; *(siempre)* regularly.

hablador, -ra *adj* talkative.

habladurías *fpl* gossip *(sg).*

hablar *vi* to talk, to speak ◆ *vt (saber)* to speak; *(tratar)* to discuss; **~ de** to talk about; **~ por teléfono** to talk on the telephone; **~ por ~** to talk for the sake of it; **¡ni ~!** no way! ❏ **hablarse** *vpr (relacionarse)* to speak (to each other); **"se habla inglés"** "English spoken".

habrá *v → haber.*

hacer *vt* 1. *(elaborar, crear, cocinar)* to make; **~ planes/un vestido** to make plans/a dress; ~ **un poema** to write a poem; ~ **la comida** to make the meal.

2. *(construir)* to build.

3. *(generar)* to produce; **la carretera hace una curva** there's a bend in the road; **el fuego hace humo** fire produces smoke; **llegar tarde hace mal efecto** arriving late makes a bad impression.

4. *(realizar)* to make; **hizo un gesto de dolor** he grimaced with pain; **le hice una señal con la mano** I signalled to her with my hand; **estoy haciendo segundo** I'm in my second year; **haremos una excursión** we'll go on a trip.

5. *(practicar)* to do; **deberías ~ deporte** you should start doing some sport.

6. *(colada)* to do; *(cama)* to make.

7. *(dar aspecto)*: **este traje te hace más delgado** this suit makes you look slimmer.

8. *(transformar)* to make; **hizo pedazos el papel** she tore the paper to pieces; **~ feliz a alguien** to make sb happy.

9 *(en cine y teatro)* to play; **hace el papel de reina** she plays (the part of) the queen.

10. *(mandar)*: **haré que tiñan el traje** I'll have this dress dyed.

11. *(comportarse como)*: ~ **el tonto** to act the fool.

12. *(ser causa de)*: **no me hagas reír/llorar** don't make me laugh/cry.

13. *(en cálculo, cuentas)* to make; **éste hace cien** this one makes (it) a hundred.

♦ **v i 1.** *(intervenir)*: **déjame ~ a mí** let me do it.

2. *(en cine y teatro)*: ~ **de malo** to play the villain.

3. *(trabajar, actuar)*: ~ **de cajera** to be a checkout girl.

4. *(aparentar)*: ~ **como si** to act as if.

♦ **v impers 1.** *(tiempo meteorológico)*: **hace frío/calor/sol** it's cold/hot/sunny; **hace buen/mal tiempo** the weather is good/bad.

2. *(tiempo transcurrido)*: **hace un año que no lo veo** it's a year since I saw him; **no nos hablamos desde hace un año** we haven't spoken for a year.

❑ **hacerse** *vpr (convertirse en)* to become; *(formarse)* to form; *(desarrollarse, crecer)* to grow; *(cocerse)* to cook; *(resultar)* to get, to become; **~se el rico** to pretend to be rich; **hacerse a** v + prep *(acostumbrarse)* to get used to; **hacerse con** v i + prep *(apropiarse)* to take.

hacha f axe.

hachís m hashish.

hacia *prep (de + acción)* towards; *(en el tiempo)* about; ~ **abajo** downwards; ~ **arriba** upwards; **gira ~ la izquierda** turn left.

hacienda f *(finca)* farm; *(bienes)* property ❑ **Hacienda** f *the Spanish Treasury.*

hada f fairy.

haga v → **hacer.**

Haití s Haiti.

hala *interj (para dar prisa)* hurry up!; *(expresa contrariedad)* you're joking!

halago m flattery.

halcón m falcon.

hall [xol] m foyer.

hallar vt *(encontrar)* to find;

(inventar) to discover ❏ **hallarse** *vpr* to be.

halógeno, -na *adj* halogen *(antes de s)*.

halterofilia *f* weightlifting.

hamaca *f (en árbol, etc)* hammock; *(en la playa)* deck chair.

hambre *f* hunger; **tener ~** to be hungry.

hambriento, -ta *adj* starving.

hamburguesa *f* hamburger.

hamburguesería *f* hamburger joint.

hámster ['xamster] *m* hamster.

hangar *m* hangar.

hará *v* → **hacer**.

hardware ['xarwar] *m* hardware.

harina *f* flour.

hartar *vt (saciar)* to fill up; *(cansar)* to annoy ❏ **hartarse de** *v* + *prep (cansarse de)* to get fed up with; **~se de algo** *(hacer en exceso)* to do sthg non-stop.

harto, -ta *adj (saciado)* full; **estar ~ de** *(cansado)* to be fed up with.

hasta *prep (en el espacio)* as far as; *(en el tiempo)* until ♦ *adv (incluso)* even; **el agua llega ~ el borde** the water comes up to the edge; **desde ... ~ ...** from ... to ...; **~ luego** see you later; **~ mañana** see you tomorrow; **~ pronto** see you soon; **~ que** until.

haya *v* → **haber** ♦ *f* beech.

haz *(pl* **-ces)** *v* → **hacer** ♦ *m (de luz)* beam; *(de hierba, leña)* bundle.

hazaña *f* exploit.

he *v* → **haber**.

hebilla *f* buckle.

hebra *f (de hilo)* thread; *(de legumbres)* string.

hebreo, -a *adj & m, f* Hebrew.

hechizar *vt* to bewitch.

hechizo *m (embrujo)* spell; *(fascinación)* charm.

hecho, -cha *pp* → **hacer** ♦ *adj (carne)* done ♦ *m (suceso)* event; *(dato)* fact; *(acto)* action; **muy ~** well-done; **poco ~** rare; **~ de** *(material)* made of; **de ~** in fact.

hectárea *f* hectare.

helada *f* frost.

heladería *f (tienda)* ice-cream parlour; *(quiosco)* ice-cream stall.

helado, -da *adj (muy frío)* freezing; *(congelado)* frozen; *(pasmado)* astonished ♦ *m* ice-cream; **"~s variados"** "assorted ice-creams".

helar *vt* to freeze ♦ *v impers*: **heló** there was a frost ❏ **helarse** *vpr* to freeze.

hélice *f (de barco, avión)* propeller.

helicóptero *m* helicopter.

hematoma *m* bruise.

hembra *f (animal)* female; *(de enchufe)* socket.

hemorragia *f* haemorrhage.

heno *m* hay.

hepatitis *f inv* hepatitis.

herboristería *f* herbalist's (shop).

heredar *vt* to inherit.

heredero, -ra *m, f* heir *(f* heiress).

hereje *mf* heretic.

herejía *f (en religión)* heresy; *(disparate)* silly thing.

herencia *f* inheritance.

herida *f (lesión)* injury; *(en lucha,*

atentado) wound, → **herido**.

herido, -da *adj (lesionado)* injured; *(en lucha, atentado)* wounded; *(ofendido)* hurt ◆ *m, f*: **hubo 20 ~s** 20 people were injured.

herir *vt (causar lesión)* to injure; *(en lucha, atentado)* to wound; *(ofender)* to hurt.

hermanastro, -tra *m, f* stepbrother *(f* stepsister).

hermano, -na *m, f* brother *(f* sister).

hermético, -ca *adj* airtight.

hermoso, -sa *adj (bello)* beautiful; *(hombre)* handsome; *(fam: grande)* large.

hermosura *f* beauty; *(de hombre)* handsomeness.

héroe *m* hero.

heroico, -ca *adj* heroic.

heroína *f (persona)* heroine; *(droga)* heroin.

heroinómano, -na *m, f* heroin addict.

heroísmo *m* heroism.

herradura *f* horseshoe.

herramienta *f* tool.

herrería *f (taller)* forge.

herrero *m* blacksmith.

hervir *vt & vi* to boil.

heterosexual *mf* heterosexual.

hice *v* → **hacer**.

hidalgo *m* nobleman.

hidratante *adj* moisturizing.

hidratar *vt* to moisturize.

hiedra *f* ivy.

hielo *m* ice.

hiena *f* hyena.

hierba *f (césped)* grass; *(planta)*

herb; **mala ~** weed.

hierbabuena *f* mint.

hierro *m* iron.

hígado *m* liver.

higiene *f (aseo)* hygiene; *(salud)* health.

higiénico, -ca *adj* hygienic.

higo *m* fig.

higuera *f* fig tree.

hijastro, -tra *m, f* stepson *(f* stepdaughter).

hijo, -ja *m, f* son *(f* daughter); **~ de la chingada** *(Amér: vulg)* son of a bitch; **~ político** son-in-law; **hija política** daughter-in-law; **~ de puta** *(vulg)* son of a bitch ▢ **hijos** *mpl* children

hilera *f* row.

hilo *m (de coser, de conversación)* thread; *(tejido)* linen; *(alambre, cable)* wire; **~ musical**® piped music.

hilvanar *vt (coser)* to tack.

hincapié *m*: **hacer ~ en algo** *(insistir)* to insist on sthg; *(subrayar)* to emphasize sthg.

hincha *mf* fan.

hinchado, -da *adj (globo, colchón)* inflated; *(parte del cuerpo)* swollen.

hinchar *vt* to blow up ▢ **hincharse** *vpr (parte del cuerpo)* to swell up; **hincharse de** *v + prep (hartarse de)* to stuff o.s. with.

hinchazón *f* swelling.

híper *m (fam)* hypermarket.

hipermercado *m* hypermarket.

hipermetropía *f* longsightedness.

hipertensión *f* high blood

pressure.

hipertenso, -sa *adj* suffering from high blood pressure.

hípica *f (carreras de caballos)* horseracing; *(de obstáculos)* show-jumping.

hipnotizar *vt* to hypnotize.

hipo *m* hiccups *(pl)*.

hipocresía *f* hypocrisy.

hipócrita *adj* hypocritical.

hipódromo *m* racecourse.

hipopótamo *m* hippopotamus.

hipoteca *f* mortgage.

hipótesis *f inv (supuesto)* theory.

hipotético, -ca *adj* hypothetical.

hippy [ˈxipi] *mf* hippy.

hispánico, -ca *adj* Hispanic, Spanish-speaking.

hispano, -na *adj (hispanoamericano)* Spanish-American; *(español)* Spanish.

Hispanoamérica *s* Spanish-speaking Latin America.

hispanoamericano, -na *adj & m (persona)* Spanish-American.

hispanohablante *mf* Spanish speaker.

histeria *f* hysteria.

histérico, -ca *adj* hysterical.

historia *f (hechos pasados)* history; *(narración)* story.

histórico, -ca *adj (real, auténtico)* factual; *(de importancia)* historic.

historieta *f (relato)* anecdote; *(cuento con dibujos)* comic strip.

hizo *v → hacer.

hobby [ˈxoβi] *m* hobby.

hocico *m (de cerdo)* snout; *(de perro, gato)* nose.

hockey [ˈxokej] *m* hockey.

hogar *m (casa)* home; *(de chimenea)* fireplace.

hogareño, -ña *adj (persona)* home-loving.

hoguera *f* bonfire.

hoja *f (de plantas)* leaf; *(de papel)* sheet; *(de libro)* page; *(de cuchillo)* blade; **~ de afeitar** razor blade.

hojalata *f* tinplate.

hojaldre *m* puff pastry.

hola *interj* hello!

Holanda *s* Holland.

holandés, -esa *adj & m* Dutch ♦ *m, f* Dutchman *(f* Dutchwoman).

holgado, -da *adj (ropa)* loose-fitting; *(vida, situación)* comfortable.

holgazán, -ana *adj* lazy.

hombre *m (de man)* ♦ *interj* wow!; **~ de negocios** businessman.

hombrera *f (almohadilla)* shoulder pad.

hombro *m* shoulder.

homenaje *m* tribute; **en ~ a** in honour of.

homeopatía *f* homeopathy.

homicida *mf* murderer.

homicidio *m* murder.

homosexual *mf* homosexual.

hondo, -da *adj (profundo)* deep; *(intenso)* deep.

Honduras *s* Honduras.

hondureño, -ña *adj & m, f* Honduran.

honestidad *f (sinceridad)* honesty.

honesto, -ta *adj (honrado)*

hoy

honest.

hongo *m (comestible)* mushroom; *(no comestible)* toadstool.

honor *m* honour; **en ~ de** in honour of.

honorario *adj* honorary ☐ **honorarios** *mpl* fees.

honra *f* honour; **¡a mucha ~!** and (I'm) proud of it!

honradez *f* honesty.

honrado, -da *adj* honest.

honrar *vt* to honour.

hora *f (periodo de tiempo)* hour; *(momento determinado)* time; **¿a qué ~ ...?** what time ...?; **¿qué ~ es?** what's the time?; **media ~** half an hour; **pedir ~ para** to ask for an appointment for; **tener ~ (con)** to have an appointment (with); **a última ~** at the last minute; **"~s convenidas"** "appointments available"; **~s de visita** visiting times; **~ punta** rush hour.

horario *m* timetable; **"~ comercial"** "opening hours".

horca *f (de ejecución)* gallows *(pl)*; *(en agricultura)* pitchfork.

horchata *f* cold drink made from ground tiger nuts, milk and sugar.

horchatería *f* "horchata" bar.

horizontal *adj* horizontal.

horizonte *m* horizon.

horma *f (molde)* mould; *(para zapatos)* last.

hormiga *f* ant.

hormigón *m* concrete; **~ armado** reinforced concrete.

hormigonera *f* concrete mixer.

hormiguero *m* anthill.

hormona *f* hormone.

hornear *vt* to bake.

hornillo *m (para cocinar)* camping stove.

horno *m* oven; **al ~** *(carne)* roast; *(pescado)* baked.

horóscopo *m* horoscope.

horquilla *f (para el pelo)* hairgrip.

hórreo *m* type of granary, on stilts, found in Galicia and Asturias.

horrible *adj (horroroso)* horrible; *(pésimo)* awful.

horror *m* terror; **¡qué ~!** that's awful!

horrorizar *vt* to terrify.

horroroso, -sa *adj* horrible.

hortaliza *f (garden)* vegetable.

hortelano, -na *m, f* market gardener.

hortensia *f* hydrangea.

hortera *adj (fam)* tacky.

hospedarse *vpr* to stay.

hospital *m* hospital.

hospitalario, -ria *adj (persona)* hospitable.

hospitalidad *f* hospitality.

hospitalizar *vt* to put in hospital.

hostal *m* = two-star hotel.

hostelería *f* hotel trade.

hostia *f (en religión)* host; *(vulg: golpe)* whack ◆ *interj (vulg)* bloody hell!; **darse una ~** *(vulg)* to have a smash-up.

hostil *adj* hostile.

hotel *m* hotel; **~ de lujo** luxury hotel.

hotelero, -ra *adj* hotel *(antes de s)*.

hoy *adv (día presente)* today;

(momento actual) nowadays; **~ en día** nowadays; **~ por ~** at the moment.

hoyo *m* hole.

hoz *f* sickle.

huachafería *f (Amér)* tacky thing.

huachafo, -fa *adj (Amér)* tacky.

huachinango *m (Amér)* porgy.

hubiera *v →* haber.

hucha *f* moneybox.

hueco, -ca *adj (vacío)* hollow ♦ *m (agujero)* hole; *(de tiempo)* spare moment.

huelga *f* strike.

huella *f (de persona)* footprint; *(de animal)* track; **~s dactilares** fingerprints.

huérfano, -na *m, f* orphan.

huerta *f* market garden.

huerto *m (de hortalizas)* vegetable patch; *(de frutales)* orchard.

hueso *m (del esqueleto)* bone; *(de una fruta)* stone.

huésped, -da *m, f* guest.

huevada *f (Amér: fam)* stupid thing.

huevear *vi (Amér: fam)* to be stupid.

huevo *m* egg; **~ de la copa** o **tibio** *(Amér)* hard-boiled egg; **~ duro** hard-boiled egg; **~ escalfado** poached egg; **~ estrellado** *(Amér)* fried egg; **~ frito** fried egg; **~ pasado por agua** soft-boiled egg; **~s a la flamenca** *"huevos al plato"* with fried pork sausage, black pudding and a tomato sauce; **~s al plato** eggs cooked in the oven in an earthenware dish; **~s revueltos** scrambled eggs.

huevón *m (Amér)* idiot.

huida *f* escape.

huir *vi (escapar)* to flee; *(de cárcel)* to escape; **~ de algo/alguien** *(evitar)* to avoid sthg/sb.

humanidad *f* humanity ❑ **humanidades** *fpl* humanities.

humanitario, -ria *adj* humanitarian.

humano, -na *adj (del hombre)* human; *(benévolo, compasivo)* humane ♦ *m* human (being).

humareda *f* cloud of smoke.

humedad *f (de piel)* moisture; *(de atmósfera)* humidity; *(en la pared)* damp.

humedecer *vt* to moisten.

húmedo, -da *adj (ropa, toalla, etc)* damp; *(clima, país)* humid; *(piel)* moist.

humilde *adj* humble.

humillación *f* humiliation.

humillante *adj* humiliating.

humillar *vt* to humiliate.

humo *m (gas)* smoke; *(de coche)* fumes *(pl)* ❑ **humos** *mpl* airs.

humor *m (estado de ánimo)* mood; *(gracia)* humour; **estar de buen ~** to be in a good mood; **estar de mal ~** to be in a bad mood.

humorismo *m* comedy.

humorista *mf* comedian *(f* comedienne).

humorístico, -ca *adj* humorous.

hundir *vt (barco)* to sink; *(edificio)* to knock down; *(techo)* to bash in; *(persona)* to devastate ❑ **hundirse** *vpr (barco)* to sink; *(edificio, techo)* to collapse; *(persona)* to be devastated.

húngaro, -ra *adj & m, f* Hungarian.

Hungría *s* Hungary.

huracán *m* hurricane.

hurtadillas: a hurtadillas *adv* stealthily.

hurto *m* theft.

iba *v → ir.*

IBERIA *f* IBERIA *(Spanish national airline).*

ibérico, -ca *adj* Iberian.

Ibiza *s* Ibiza.

iceberg *m* iceberg.

ICONA *m* Spanish national conservation organization.

icono *m* icon.

id *v → ir.*

ida *f* outward journey; **(billete de) ~ y vuelta** return (ticket).

idea *f* idea; *(propósito)* intention; *(opinión)* impression; **no tengo ni ~** I've no idea.

ideal *adj & m* ideal.

idealismo *m* idealism.

idealista *mf* idealist.

idéntico, -ca *adj* identical.

identidad *f* identity.

identificación *f* identification.

identificar *vt* to identify ❑

identificarse *vpr (mostrar documentación)* to show one's identifi-

cation.

ideología *f* ideology.

idilio *m* love affair.

idioma *m* language.

idiota *adj (despec)* stupid ✦ *mf* idiot.

ídolo *m* idol.

idóneo, -a *adj* suitable.

iglesia *f* church.

ignorancia *f* ignorance.

ignorante *adj* ignorant.

ignorar *vt (desconocer)* not to know; *(no hacer caso)* to ignore.

igual *adj (idéntico)* the same; *(parecido)* similar; *(cantidad proporción)* equal; *(ritmo)* steady ✦ *adv* the same; **ser ~ que** to be the same as; **da ~** it doesn't matter; **me da ~** I don't care; **es ~** it doesn't matter; **al ~ que** just like; **por ~** equally.

igualado, -da *adj* level.

igualdad *f* equality.

igualmente *adv* likewise.

ilegal *adj* illegal.

ilegítimo, -ma *adj* illegitimate.

ileso, -sa *adj* unhurt.

ilimitado, -da *adj* unlimited.

ilógico, -ca *adj* illogical.

iluminación *f (alumbrado)* lighting.

iluminar *vt (suj: luz, sol)* to light up.

ilusión *f (esperanza)* hope; *(espejismo)* illusion; **el regalo me ha hecho ~** I liked the present; **me hace ~ la fiesta** I'm looking forward to the party; **hacerse ilusiones** to get one's hopes up.

ilusionarse *vpr (esperanzarse)* to get one's hopes up; *(emo-*

cionarse) to get excited.

ilustración f illustration.

ilustrar vt to illustrate.

ilustre adj illustrious.

imagen f image; (en televisión) picture.

imaginación f imagination.

imaginar vt (suponer) to imagine; (inventar) to think up ❑ **imaginarse** vpr to imagine.

imaginario, -ria adj imaginary.

imaginativo, -va adj imaginative.

imán m magnet.

imbécil adj (despec) stupid ◆ mf idiot.

imitación f (de persona) impression; (de obra de arte) imitation.

imitar vt to imitate.

impaciencia f impatience.

impaciente adj impatient; ~ **por** impatient to.

impar adj odd.

imparable adj unstoppable.

imparcial adj impartial.

impasible adj impassive.

impecable adj impeccable.

impedimento m obstacle.

impedir vt (no permitir) to prevent; (obstaculizar) to hinder.

impensable adj unthinkable.

imperativo m (en gramática) imperative.

imperceptible adj imperceptible.

imperdible m safety pin.

imperdonable adj unforgivable.

imperfecto, -ta adj (incomple-

to) imperfect; (defectuoso) faulty ◆ m imperfect tense.

imperial adj imperial.

imperio m (territorio) empire; (dominio) rule.

impermeable adj waterproof ◆ m raincoat.

impersonal adj impersonal.

impertinencia f (insolencia) impertinence; (comentario) impertinent remark.

impertinente adj impertinent.

ímpetu m (energía) force.

implicar vt to involve; (significar) to mean.

implícito, -ta adj implicit.

imponer vt (obligación, castigo, impuesto) to impose; (obediencia, respeto) to command ◆ vi to be imposing.

importación f (producto) import.

importancia f importance.

importante adj (destacado) important; (cantidad) large.

importar vt (mercancías) to import ◆ vi (interesar) to matter; **¿le importa que fume?** do you mind if I smoke?; **¿le importaría venir?** would you mind coming?; **no importa** it doesn't matter; **no me importa** I don't care.

importe m (precio) price; (en cuenta, factura) total; "~ **del billete**" "ticket price".

imposibilidad f impossibility.

imposible adj impossible ◆ interj never! ◆ m: **pedir un** ~ to ask the impossible.

impostor, -ra m, f impostor.

impotencia f impotence.
impotente adj impotent.
impreciso, -sa adj vague.
impregnar vt (humedecer) to soak.
imprenta f (arte) printing; (taller) printer's (shop).
imprescindible adj indispensable.
impresión f (de un libro) edition; (sensación) feeling; (opinión) impression.
impresionante adj impressive.
impresionar vt to impress ◆ vi (causar admiración) to be impressive.
impreso, -sa pp → imprimir ◆ m (formulario) form.
impresora f printer.
imprevisto m unexpected event.
imprimir vt to print.
improvisación f improvisation.
improvisado, -da adj improvised.
improvisar vt to improvise.
imprudente adj rash.
impuesto, -ta pp → imponer ◆ m tax.
impulsar vt (empujar) to drive; ~ a alguien a to drive sb to.
impulsivo, -va adj impulsive.
impulso m (empuje) momentum, (estímulo) stimulus.
impuro, -ra adj impure.
inaceptable adj unacceptable.
inadecuado, -da adj unsuitable.

inadmisible adj unacceptable.
inaguantable adj unbearable.
inauguración f inauguration, opening.
inaugurar vt to inaugurate, to open.
incapacidad f (incompetencia) incompetence; (por enfermedad) incapacity.
incapaz, -ces adj incapable; ser ~ de to be unable to.
incendio m fire, contra ~s (medidas) fire-fighting; (seguro, brigada) fire (antes de s).
incentivo m incentive.
incidente m incident.
incineradora f incinerator.
incinerar vt to incinerate.
incitar vt (animar) to encourage; (a la violencia) to incite.
inclinación f (saludo) bow; (tendencia) tendency; (afecto) fondness.
inclinarse vpr: ~ por (preferir) to favour; (decidirse por) to decide on.
incluido, -da adj included.
incluir vt (contener) to include; (adjuntar) to enclose.
inclusive adv inclusive.
incluso adv even.
incógnita f (cosa desconocida) mystery.
incoherente adj (contradictorio) inconsistent.
incoloro, -ra adj colourless.
incómodo, -da adj uncomfortable.
incomparable adj incomparable.
incompatibilidad f incompatibility.

incompetente adj incompetent.

incomprensible adj incomprehensible.

incomunicado, -da adj (pueblo) cut off.

incondicional adj (apoyo, ayuda) wholehearted; (amigo) staunch.

inconfundible adj unmistakable.

inconsciencia f (irresponsabilidad) thoughtlessness.

inconsciente adj (sin conocimiento) unconscious; (insensato) thoughtless.

incontable adj countless.

inconveniente m (dificultad) difficulty; (desventaja) disadvantage.

incorporación f (unión) inclusion.

incorporar vt (agregar) to incorporate; (levantar) to sit up ◻ **incorporarse** vpr (levantarse) to sit up; ~**se a** (ingresar en) to join.

incorrecto, -ta adj (erróneo) incorrect; (descortés) impolite.

incorregible adj incorrigible.

incrédulo, -la adj sceptical.

increíble adj (inverosímil) hard to believe; (extraordinario) incredible.

incremento m increase.

incubadora f incubator.

incubar vt to incubate.

inculpado, -da m, f accused.

inculto, -ta adj (persona) uneducated.

incumbir vi: **no te incumbe hacerlo** it's not for you to do it.

incurable adj incurable.

incurrir: incurrir en v + prep (error) to make; (delito) to commit.

indecente adj indecent.

indeciso, -sa adj (falta de iniciativa) indecisive; (falto de decisión) undecided; (poco claro) inconclusive.

indefenso, -sa adj defenceless.

indefinido, -da adj indefinite; (impreciso) vague.

indemnización f compensation.

indemnizar vt to compensate.

independencia f independence.

independiente adj independent.

independizarse: independizarse de v + prep to become independent of.

indeterminado, -da adj indefinite.

India f: **la ~** India.

indicación f (señal) sign ◻ **indicaciones** fpl (instrucciones) instructions; (para llegar a un sitio) directions.

indicador m indicator; ~ **de dirección** indicator.

indicar vt (señalar) to indicate; (lugar, dirección) to show; (suj: señal, reloj) to read.

indicativo, -va adj indicative.

índice m (de libro, precios) index; (de natalidad, mortalidad) rate; (de la mano) index finger.

indicio m (señal) sign.

indiferencia f indifference.

indiferente adj indifferent; **es**

~ it makes no difference.
indígena *mf* native.
indigestión *f* indigestion.
indigesto, -ta *adj* hard to digest.
indignación *f* indignation.
indignado, -da *adj* indignant.
indignante *adj* outrageous.
indio, -dia *adj & m, f* Indian.
indirecta *f* hint.
indirecto, -ta *adj* indirect.
indiscreto, -ta *adj* indiscreet.
indiscriminado, -da *adj* indiscriminate.
indiscutible *adj* indisputable.
indispensable *adj* indispensable.
indispuesto, -ta *adj* unwell.
individual *adj (del individuo)* individual; *(cama, habitación)* single; **~es** *(DEP)* singles.
individuo *m* individual.
índole *f (tipo)* type.
Indonesia *s* Indonesia.
indudablemente *adv* undoubtedly.
indumentaria *f* clothes *(pl).*
industria *f (actividad)* industry; *(fábrica)* factory.
industrial *adj* industrial ◆ *mf* industrialist.
industrializado, -da *adj* industrialized.
inédito, -ta *adj (desconocido)* unprecedented.
inepto, -ta *adj* inept.
inequívoco, -ca *adj (clarísimo)* unequivocal; *(inconfundible)* unmistakable.
inesperado, -da *adj* unexpected.

inestable *adj* unstable.
inevitable *adj* inevitable.
inexperto, -ta *adj (sin experiencia)* inexperienced.
infalible *adj* infallible.
infancia *f* childhood.
infanta *f* princess.
infantería *f* infantry.
infantil *adj (para niños)* children's; *(despec: inmaduro)* childish.
infarto *m* heart attack.
infección *f* infection.
infeccioso, -sa *adj* infectious.
infectar *vt* to infect ▢ **infectarse** *vpr* to become infected.
infelicidad *f* unhappiness.
infeliz *(pl* **-ces)** *adj* unhappy ◆ *mf (desgraciado)* wretch; *(fam: ingenuo)* naïve person.
inferior *adj (de abajo, menos importante, cantidad)* lower; *(de menos calidad)* inferior ◆ *mf* inferior.
inferioridad *f* inferiority.
infidelidad *f* infidelity.
infiel *adj (a la pareja)* unfaithful ◆ *mf (no cristiano)* infidel
infierno *m* hell.
ínfimo, -ma *adj* very low.
infinito, -ta *adj* infinite ◆ *m* infinity.
inflación *f* inflation.
inflar *vt (de aire)* to inflate; *(globo)* to blow up ▢ **inflarse de** *v + prep (comer, beber)* to stuff o.s. with.
inflexible *adj* inflexible.
influencia *f* influence; **tener ~** to have influence.
influenciar *vt* to influence.

influir: influir en v + prep to influence.

influjo m influence.

influyente adj influential.

información f (datos) information; (noticias) news; (oficina) information office; (mostrador) information desk; (de teléfono) directory enquiries (pl) (Br), directory assistance (Am).

informal adj (persona) unreliable; (lenguaje, traje) informal.

informalidad f (irresponsabilidad) unreliability.

informar vt to tell ❑ **informarse** vpr to find out.

informática f information technology, computing, → **informático**.

informático, -ca m, f computer expert.

informativo m news bulletin.

informe m report ❑ **informes** mpl (referencias) references.

infracción f (delito) offence.

infundir vt to inspire.

infusión f infusion; ~ **de tila** lime blossom tea.

ingeniería f engineering.

ingeniero, -ra m, f engineer.

ingenio m (agudeza) wit; (inteligencia) ingenuity; (máquina) device.

ingenioso, -sa adj (agudo) witty; (inteligente) ingenious.

ingenuidad f naivety.

ingenuo, -nua adj naive.

Inglaterra s England.

ingle f groin.

inglés, -esa adj & m English ◆ m, f Englishman (f English-

woman); **los ingleses** the English.

ingrato, -ta adj (trabajo) thankless; (persona) ungrateful.

ingrediente m ingredient.

ingresar vt (dinero) to deposit ◆ vi (en hospital) to be admitted; (en sociedad) to join; (en universidad) to enter.

ingreso m (entrada, en universidad) entry; (de dinero) deposit; (en hospital) admission; (en sociedad) joining ❑ **ingresos** mpl (sueldo) income (sg).

inhabitable adj uninhabitable.

inhalar vt to inhale.

inhibición f inhibition.

inhumano, -na adj inhumane.

iniciación f (comienzo) beginning.

inicial adj & f initial.

iniciar vt (empezar) to begin, to start ❑ **iniciarse en** v + prep (conocimiento, práctica) to learn.

iniciativa f initiative; **tener ~** to have initiative.

inicio m beginning, start.

inimaginable adj unimaginable.

injerto m graft.

injusticia f injustice.

injusto, -ta adj unfair.

inmaduro, -ra adj (persona) immature; (fruta) unripe.

inmediatamente adv immediately.

inmediato, -ta adj (tiempo) immediate; (contiguo) next; **de ~** immediately.

inmejorable adj unbeatable.

inmenso, -sa adj immense.

inmigración f immigration.

inmigrante *mf* immigrant.

inmigrar *vi* to immigrate.

inmobiliaria *f* estate agency *(Br)*, real-estate office *(Am)*.

inmoral *adj* immoral.

inmortal *adj* immortal.

inmóvil *adj (persona)* motionless; *(coche, tren)* stationary.

inmovilizar *vt* to immobilize.

inmueble *m* building.

inmune *adj* immune.

inmunidad *f* immunity.

innato, -ta *adj* innate.

innecesario, -ria *adj* unnecessary.

innovación *f* innovation.

inocencia *f* innocence.

inocentada *f (bobada)* foolish thing; *(broma)* practical joke.

inocente *adj* innocent.

inofensivo, -va *adj* harmless.

inolvidable *adj* unforgettable.

inoportuno, -na *adj (inadecuado)* inappropriate; *(molesto)* inconvenient; *(en mal momento)* untimely.

inoxidable *adj (material)* rustproof; *(acero)* stainless.

inquietarse *vpr* to worry.

inquieto, -ta *adj (preocupado)* worried; *(aventurero)* restless.

inquietud *f* worry.

inquilino, -na *m, f* tenant.

Inquisición *f*: la ~ the (Spanish) Inquisition.

insaciable *adj* insatiable.

insalubre *adj* unhealthy.

insatisfacción *f* dissatisfaction.

insatisfecho, -cha *adj* dissatisfied.

inscribir: inscribirse en *v + prep* to enrol on.

inscripción *f (de moneda, piedra, etc)* inscription; *(en registro)* enrolment.

inscrito, -ta *pp* → **inscribir**.

insecticida *m* insecticide.

insecto *m* insect.

inseguridad *f (falta de confianza)* insecurity; *(peligro)* lack of safety.

inseguro, -ra *adj (sin confianza)* insecure; *(peligroso)* unsafe.

insensato, -ta *adj* foolish.

insensible *adj (persona)* insensitive; *(aumento, subida, bajada)* imperceptible.

inseparable *adj* inseparable.

insertar *vt* to insert; ~ **algo en** to insert sthg into.

inservible *adj* useless.

insignia *f (distintivo)* badge; *(de militar)* insignia; *(estandarte)* flag.

insignificante *adj* insignificant.

insinuar *vt* to hint at ❑ **insinuarse** *vpr* to make advances.

insípido, -da *adj* insipid.

insistencia *f* insistence.

insistir *vi*: ~ **(en)** to insist (on).

insolación *f (indisposición)* sunstroke.

insolencia *f (dicho, hecho)* insolent thing.

insolente *adj (desconsiderado)* insolent; *(orgulloso)* haughty.

insólito, -ta *adj* unusual.

insolvente *adj* insolvent.

insomnio *m* insomnia.

insonorización f soundproofing.

insoportable adj unbearable.

inspeccionar vt to inspect.

inspector, -ra m, f inspector; **~ de aduanas** customs official.

inspiración f (de aire) inhalation; (de un artista) inspiration.

inspirar vt (aire) to inhale; (ideas) to inspire □ **inspirarse en** v + prep to be inspired by.

instalación f (acto) installation; (equipo) installations (pl); **~ eléctrica** wiring □ **instalaciones** fpl (edificios) facilities; **instalaciones deportivas** sports facilities.

instalar vt (teléfono, antena, etc) to install; (gimnasio, biblioteca, etc) to set up; (alojar) to settle □ **instalarse** vpr (en nueva casa) to move in.

instancia f (solicitud) application.

instantánea f snapshot.

instantáneo, -a adj instantaneous.

instante m instant; **al ~** straight away.

instintivo, -va adj instinctive.

instinto m instinct.

institución f institution □ **instituciones** fpl institutions.

institucional adj institutional.

instituir vt to set up.

instituto m institute; (centro de enseñanza) state secondary school.

institutriz (pl **-ces**) f governess.

instrucción f (formación) education □ **instrucciones** fpl (indicaciones) instructions.

instruir vt (enseñar) to teach; (enjuiciar) to prepare.

instrumental m instruments (pl).

instrumento m instrument.

insuficiente adj insufficient ♦ m fail.

insufrible adj insufferable.

insultante adj insulting.

insultar vt to insult □ **insultarse** vpr to insult each other.

insulto m insult.

insuperable adj (inmejorable) unsurpassable; (problema) insurmountable.

intacto, -ta adj intact.

integración f integration.

integrarse: integrarse en v + prep to become integrated in.

íntegro, -gra adj (cosa) whole; (persona) honourable.

intelectual mf intellectual.

inteligencia f intelligence.

inteligente adj intelligent.

intemperie f: **a la ~** in the open air.

intención f intention; **con la ~ de** with the intention of; **tener la ~ de** to intend to.

intencionado, -da adj deliberate; **bien ~** well-meaning; **mal ~** ill-intentioned.

intensivo, -va adj intensive.

intenso, -sa adj intense; (luz) bright; (lluvia) heavy.

intentar vt to try; **~ hacer algo** to try to do sthg.

intento m (propósito) intention; (tentativa) try.

intercalar vt to insert.

intercambio *m* exchange.

interceder: interceder por *v* + *prep* to intercede on behalf of.

interceptar *vt* to intercept.

interés *m* interest; *(provecho)* self-interest ❏ **intereses** *mpl (dinero)* interest *(sg)*; *(fortuna, aspiraciones)* interests.

interesado, -da *adj (que tiene interés)* interested; *(egoísta)* self-interested.

interesante *adj* interesting.

interesar *vi* to interest; ¿te interesa la música? are you interested in music? ❏ **interesarse en** *v* + *prep* to be interested in; **interesarse por** *v* + *prep* to take an interest in

interferencia *f* interference.

interina *f (criada)* cleaning lady.

interino, -na *adj (trabajador)* temporary.

interior *adj* inner; *(mercado, política)* domestic ♦ *m (parte de dentro)* inside; *(fig: mente)* inner self; *(en deporte)* inside forward; **el ~ de España** inland Spain.

interlocutor, -ra *m, f* speaker.

intermediario, -ria *m, f* middleman.

intermedio, -dia *adj* intermediate ♦ *m* interval.

interminable *adj* endless.

intermitente *m* indicator.

internacional *adj* international.

internado *m* boarding school.

interno, -na *adj* internal ♦ *m, f (en colegio)* boarder; *(en hospital)* intern.

interponerse *vpr* to intervene.

interpretación *f (en teatro, cine, etc)* performance; *(traducción)* interpreting.

interpretar *vt (en teatro, cine, etc)* to perform; *(traducir)* to interpret.

intérprete *mf (en teatro, cine, etc)* performer; *(traductor)* interpreter.

interpuesto, -ta *pp* → **interponer.**

interrogación *f (pregunta)* question; *(signo)* question mark.

interrogante *m o f* question mark.

interrogar *vt* to question.

interrogatorio *m* questioning.

interrumpir *vt* to interrupt.

interrupción *f* interruption.

interruptor *m* switch.

interurbano, -na *adj* long-distance.

intervalo *m (tiempo)* interval; *(espacio)* gap.

intervención *f (discurso)* speech; **~ quirúrgica** operation.

intervenir *vt (en medicina)* to operate on; *(confiscar)* to seize ♦ *vi (tomar parte)* to participate.

interviú *f* interview.

intestino *m* intestine.

intimidad *f (vida privada)* private life.

íntimo, -ma *adj (cena, pensamiento, etc)* private; *(amistad, relación)* close; *(ambiente, restaurante)* intimate.

intocable *adj* untouchable.

intolerable *adj* intolerable.

intolerante *adj* intolerant.

intoxicación *f* poisoning; ~ **alimenticia** food poisoning.

intoxicarse *vpr* to be poisoned.

intranquilo, -la *adj (nervioso)* restless; *(preocupado)* worried.

intransigente *adj* intransigent.

intransitable *adj* impassable.

intrépido, -da *adj* intrepid.

intriga *f (maquinación)* intrigue; *(trama)* plot.

intrigar *vt & vi* to intrigue.

introducción *f* introduction.

introducir *vt* to introduce; *(meter)* to put in; "~ **monedas**" "insert coins".

introvertido, -da *adj* introverted.

intruso, -sa *m, f* intruder.

intuición *f* intuition.

inundación *f* flood.

inundar *vt* to flood.

inusual *adj* unusual.

inútil *adj* useless; *(no provechoso)* unsuccessful; *(inválido)* disabled.

invadir *vt (país, territorio)* to invade; *(suj: alegría, tristeza)* to overwhelm.

inválido, -da *m, f* disabled person.

invasión *f* invasion.

invasor, -ra *m, f* invader.

invención *f* invention.

inventar *vt* to invent.

inventario *m* inventory.

invento *m* invention.

invernadero *m* greenhouse.

inversión *f (de dinero)* investment; *(de orden)* reversal.

inversionista *mf (Amér)* investor.

inverso, -sa *adj* opposite; **a la inversa** the other way round.

invertir *vt (dinero, tiempo)* to invest; *(orden)* to reverse.

investigación *f (de delito, crimen)* investigation; *(en ciencia)* research.

investigador, -ra *m, f* researcher.

investigar *vt (delito, crimen)* to investigate; *(en ciencia)* to research.

invidente *mf* blind person.

invierno *m* winter; **en ~** in (the) winter.

invisible *adj* invisible.

invitación *f* invitation; **es ~ de la casa** it's on the house.

invitado, -da *m, f* guest.

invitar *vt (a fiesta, boda, etc)* to invite; **os invito** *(a café, copa, etc)* it's my treat; **te invito a cenar fuera** I'll take you out for dinner; **~ a alguien a** *(incitar)* to encourage sb to.

involucrar *vt* to involve ❑ **involucrarse en** *v + prep* to get involved in.

invulnerable *adj* invulnerable.

inyección *f* injection.

ir *vi* 1. *(desplazarse)* to go; **fuimos andando** we went on foot; **iremos en coche** we'll go by car; **¡vamos!** let's go!
2. *(asistir)* to go; **nunca va a las juntas** he never goes to meetings.
3. *(extenderse)* to go; **la carretera va hasta Valencia** the road goes as far

as Valencia.
4. *(funcionar)* to work; **la televisión no va** the television's not working.
5. *(desenvolverse)* to go; **le va bien en su trabajo** things are going well (for him) in his job; **los negocios van mal** business is bad; **¿cómo te va?** how are you doing?
6. *(vestir):* **~ en o con** to wear; **~ de azul/de uniforme** to wear blue/a uniform.
7. *(tener aspecto físico)* to look like; **tal como voy no puedo entrar** I can't go in looking like this.
8. *(valer)* to be; **¿a cuánto va el pollo?** how much is the chicken?
9. *(expresa duración gradual):* **~ haciendo algo** to be doing sthg; **voy mejorando mi estilo** I'm working on improving my style.
10. *(sentar):* **le va fatal el color negro** black doesn't suit him at all; **le irían bien unas vacaciones** she could do with a holiday.
11. *(referirse):* **~ por o con alguien** to go for sb.
12. *(en locuciones):* **ni me va ni me viene** *(fam)* I don't care; **¡qué va!** you must be joking!; **vamos, no te preocupes** come along, don't worry; **¿vamos bien a Madrid?** is this the right way to Madrid?
❏ **ir a** v + prep *(expresa intención)* to be going to; **ir de** v + prep *(película, libro)* to be about; **ir por** v + prep *(buscar)* to go and fetch, **voy por la mitad del libro** I'm halfway through the book; **irse** vpr to go; **~se abajo** *(edificio)* to fall down; *(negocio)* to collapse; *(proyecto)* to fall through.

ira f fury, rage.

Irak s Iraq.

Irán s Iran.

Irlanda s Ireland; **~ del Norte** Northern Ireland.

irlandés, -esa adj Irish ◆ m, f Irishman (f Irishwoman); **los irlandeses** the Irish.

ironía f irony.

irónico, -ca adj ironic.

IRPF m *(abrev de Impuesto sobre la Renta de las Personas Físicas)* Spanish income tax.

irracional adj irrational.

irrecuperable adj irretrievable.

irregular adj irregular, *(objeto, superficie)* uneven.

irregularidad f irregularity; *(de superficie, contorno)* unevenness.

irresistible adj *(inaguantable)* unbearable; *(apetecible)* irresistible.

irresponsable adj irresponsible.

irreversible adj irreversible.

irrigar vt to irrigate.

irritable adj *(persona)* irritable; *(piel, ojos)* itchy.

irritación f irritation.

irritante adj irritating.

irritar vt to irritate ❏ **irritarse** vpr to get irritated.

isla f island.

islam m Islam.

islandés, -esa adj Icelandic ◆ m, f Icelander.

Islandia s Iceland.

islote m islet.

Israel s Israel.

istmo m isthmus.

Italia s Italy.

italiano, -na *adj, m, f* Italian.

itinerario *m* itinerary.

IVA *m* (*abrev de impuesto sobre el valor añadido*) VAT.

izda (*abrev de izquierda*) l.

izquierda *f*: **la ~** (*lado izquierdo*) the left; (*mano izquierda*) one's left hand; **a la ~** on the left; **girar a la ~** to turn left; **ser de ~s** to be left-wing.

izquierdo, -da *adj* left.

J

jabalí *m* wild boar.

jabalina *f* javelin.

jabón *m* soap.

jabonera *f* soap dish.

jacal *m* (*Amér*) shack.

jacuzzi® *m* Jacuzzi®.

jade *m* jade.

jadear *vi* to pant.

jaguar *m* jaguar.

jaiba *f* (*Amér*) crayfish.

jalea *f* jelly; **~ real** royal jelly.

jaleo *m* (*barullo*) row; (*lío*) mess.

Jamaica *s* Jamaica.

jamás *adv* never; **lo mejor que he visto ~** the best I've ever seen.

jamón *m* ham; **~ de bellota** *cured ham from pigs fed on acorns;* **~ de jabugo** *type of top-quality cured ham from Jabugo;* **~ serrano** *cured ham;* **= Parma ham;** **~ (de) York** boiled ham.

Japón *s* Japan.

japonés, -esa *adj, m, f* Japanese.

jarabe *m* syrup; **~ para la tos** cough mixture.

jardín *m* garden; **~ botánico** botanical gardens (*pl*); **~ de infancia** nursery school; **~ público** park.

jardinera *f* (*recipiente*) plant pot holder, → **jardinero**.

jardinero, -ra *m, f* gardener; **a la jardinera** garnished with vegetables.

jarra *f* jug; **en ~s** (*posición*) hands on hips.

jarro *m* jug.

jarrón *m* vase.

jaula *f* cage.

jazmín *m* jasmine.

jazz [ʒas] *m* jazz.

jefatura *f* (*lugar*) headquarters (*pl*); (*cargo*) leadership; **~ de policía** police headquarters.

jefe, -fa *m, f* (*de trabajador*) boss; (*de empresa*) manager; (*de partido, asociación*) leader; (*de departamento*) head; **~ de gobierno** head of state.

jerez *m* sherry.

jerga *f* (*argot*) slang; (*lenguaje difícil*) jargon.

jeringuilla *f* syringe.

jeroglífico *m* (*pasatiempo*) rebus.

jersey *m* sweater; **~ de cuello alto** polo neck.

Jesucristo *s* Jesus Christ.

jesús *interj* (*después de estornudo*) bless you!; (*de asombro*) good heavens!

jícama *f* (*Amér*) large, onion-shaped tuber.

jinete *m* rider.

163

juntar

jirafa *f* giraffe.

jirón *m (Amér)* avenue.

jitomate *m (Amér)* tomato.

JJOO *abrev* = **juegos olímpicos**.

joder *vt (vulg: fastidiar)* to fuck up ♦ *vi (vulg: copular)* to fuck ♦ *interj (vulg)* fucking hell!

Jordania *s* Jordan.

jornada *f (de trabajo)* working day; *(de viaje, trayecto)* day's journey.

jornal *m* day's wage.

jornalero, -ra *m, f* day labourer.

jota *f (baile)* popular dance of Aragon.

joven *adj* young ♦ *mf* young man *(f young woman)* □ **jóvenes** *mpl (juventud)*: **los jóvenes** young people.

joya *f* jewel; *(fig: persona)* gem.

joyería *f* jeweller's (shop).

joyero, -ra *m, f* jeweller ♦ *m* jewellery box.

joystick *m* joystick.

jubilación *f (retiro)* retirement; *(pensión)* pension.

jubilado, -da *m, f* pensioner.

jubilarse *vpr* to retire.

judaísmo *m* Judaism.

judía *f* bean; ~ **tierna** young, stringless bean; ~**s blancas** haricot beans; ~**s pintas** kidney beans; ~**s verdes** green beans, → **judío**.

judío, -a *adj* Jewish ♦ *m, f* Jew.

judo [ˈʒudo] *m* judo.

juego *m (entretenimiento, en tenis)* game; *(acción)* play; *(con dinero)* gambling; *(conjunto de objetos)* set; **hacer ~ (con algo)** to match (sthg); ~ **de azar** game of chance; ~ **de**

manos *(conjuring)* trick; ~**s de sociedad** parlour games; ~**s olímpicos** Olympic Games.

juerga *f* party; **irse de ~** to go out on the town.

jueves *m inv* Thursday; **Jueves Santo** Maundy Thursday, → **sábado**.

juez *(pl* -**ces***) mf* judge; ~ **de línea** *(en fútbol)* linesman.

jugador, -ra *m, f (participante)* player; *(de dinero)* gambler.

jugar *vi (entretenerse)* to play; *(con dinero)* to gamble ♦ *vt* to play □ **jugar a** *v + prep (fútbol, parchís, etc)* to play; **jugar con** *v + prep (no tomar en serio)* to play with; **jugarse** *vpr (arriesgar)* to risk; *(apostar)* to bet.

jugo *m (líquido)* juice; *(interés)* substance.

jugoso, -sa *adj* juicy.

juguete *m* toy.

juguetería *f* toy shop.

juguetón, -ona *adj* playful.

juicio *m (sensatez)* judgment; *(cordura)* sanity; *(ante juez, tribunal)* trial; *(opinión)* opinion; **a mi ~** in my opinion.

julio *m* July, → **setiembre**.

junco *m* reed.

jungla *f* jungle.

junio *m* June, → **setiembre**.

junta *f* committee; *(sesión)* meeting.

juntar *vt (dos cosas)* to put together; *(personas)* to bring together; *(fondos, provisiones)* to get together □ **juntarse** *vpr (ríos, caminos)* to meet; *(personas)* to get together; *(pareja)* to live together.

junto, -ta *adj (unido)* together ♦ *adv* at the same time; ~ **a** *(al lado de)* next to; *(cerca de)* near; **todo** ~ all together.

jurado *m (de juicio)* jury; *(de concurso, oposición)* panel of judges.

jurar *vt & vi* to swear.

jurídico, -ca *adj* legal.

justicia *f* justice; *(organismo)* law.

justificación *f* justification.

justificar *vt* to justify; *(persona)* to make excuses for; *(demostrar)* to prove ❑ **justificarse** *vpr (excusarse)* to excuse o.s.

justo, -ta *adj (equitativo)* fair; *(exacto)* exact; *(adecuado)* right; *(apretado)* tight ♦ *adv* just; ~ **en medio** right in the middle.

juvenil *adj (persona)* youthful.

juventud *f (etapa de la vida)* youth; *(jóvenes)* young people *(pl)*.

juzgado *m* court; *(territorio)* jurisdiction.

juzgar *vt (procesar)* to try; *(considerar, opinar)* to judge.

karaoke *m (juego)* karaoke; *(lugar)* karaoke bar.

kárate *m* karate.

kg *(abrev de kilogramo)* kg.

kilo *m (fam)* kilo; **un cuarto de ~ de ...** a quarter of a kilo of ...

kilogramo *m* kilogram.

kilómetro *m* kilometre; **~s por hora** kilometres per hour.

kimono *m* silk dressing gown.

kiwi *m* kiwi fruit.

kleenex® *m inv* tissue.

km *(abrev de kilómetro)* km.

KO *m (abrev de knock-out)* KO.

l *(abrev de litro)* l.

la → **el, lo.**

laberinto *m* labyrinth.

labio *m* lip.

labor *f (trabajo)* work; *(tarea)* task; *(en agricultura)* farmwork; *(de costura)* needlework.

laborable *adj (día)* working ♦ *m:* "**sólo ~s**" "working days only".

laboral *adj* labour *(antes de s)*.

laboratorio *m* laboratory; ~ **fotográfico** developer's (shop).

laborioso, -sa *adj (trabajador)* hard-working; *(complicado, difícil)* laborious.

labrador, -ra *m, f (agricultor)* farmer.

labrar *vt (tierra)* to farm; *(madera, piedra, etc)* to carve.

laca *f (de cabello)* hairspray; *(barniz)* lacquer.

lacio, -cia *adj (cabello)* straight.

lacón *m* shoulder of pork; ~ **con grelos** *Galician dish of shoulder of* *pork with turnip tops.*

lácteo, -a *adj (de leche)* milk *(antes de s); (producto)* dairy *(antes de s).*

ladera *f (de cerro)* slope; *(de montaña)* mountainside.

lado *m* side; *(sitio)* place; **al ~** *(cerca)* nearby; **al ~ de** beside; **al otro ~ de** on the other side of; **de ~ a ~** to one side; **en otro ~** somewhere else; **la casa de al ~** the house next door.

ladrar *vi* to bark.

ladrido *m* bark.

ladrillo *m* brick.

ladrón, -ona *m, f* thief ♦ *m (enchufe)* adapter.

lagartija *f (small)* lizard.

lagarto *m* lizard.

lago *m* lake.

lágrima *f* tear.

laguna *f (de agua)* lagoon; *(de ley)* loophole; *(de memoria)* gap.

lamentable *adj* pitiful.

lamentar *vt* to be sorry about ❑ **lamentarse** *vpr:* **~se (de)** to complain (about).

lamer *vt* to lick.

lámina *f (de papel, metal, etc)* sheet; *(estampa)* plate.

lámpara *f* lamp.

lampista *m* plumber.

lana *f* wool, *(Amér: fam: dinero)* dough.

lancha *f* boat; **~ motora** motorboat.

langosta *f (crustáceo)* lobster; *(insecto)* locust.

langostino *m* king prawn; **~s al ajillo** *king prawns cooked in an earthenware dish in garlic and chilli sauce;* **~s a la plancha** grilled king prawns.

lanza *f (arma)* spear.

lanzar *vt (pelota, dardo, etc)* to throw; *(producto, novedad)* to launch ❑ **lanzarse** *vpr (al mar, piscina, etc)* to dive; *(precipitarse)* to rush into it.

lapa *f* limpet.

lápida *f* memorial stone.

lápiz *(pl* **-ces)** *m* pencil; **~ de labios** lipstick; **~ de ojos** eyeliner.

largo, -ga *adj* long ♦ *m* length; **tiene 15 metros de ~** it's 15 metres long; **a la larga** in the long run; **a lo ~ de** *(playa, carretera, etc)* along; *(en el transcurso de)* throughout; **de ~ recorrido** long-distance.

largometraje *m* feature film

laringe *f* larynx.

las → **el, lo.**

lástima *f (compasión)* pity; *(disgusto, pena)* shame; **¡qué ~!** what a pity!

lata *f (envase, lámina)* tin; *(de bebidas)* can; **ser una ~** *(fam)* to be a pain.

latido *m* beat.

látigo *m* whip.

latín *m* Latin.

Latinoamérica *s* Latin América.

latinoamericano, -na *adj & m, f* Latin American.

latir *vi* to beat.

laurel *m (hoja)* bay leaf; *(árbol)* laurel.

lava *f* lava.

lavabo *m (cuarto de baño)* toilet; *(pila)* washbasin.

lavadero *m (de coches)* carwash.

lavado m wash; ~ automático automatic wash.

lavadora f washing machine; ~ automática automatic washing machine.

lavanda f lavender.

lavandería f (establecimiento) launderette; (de hotel, residencia) laundry.

lavaplatos m inv (máquina) dishwasher ◆ mf inv (persona) dishwasher.

lavar vt (limpiar) to wash; (dientes) to clean; ~ la ropa to do the washing ❑ **lavarse** vpr to wash; ~se las manos to wash one's hands; ~se los dientes to clean one's teeth.

lavavajillas m inv (máquina) dishwasher; (detergente) washing-up liquid.

laxante m laxative.

lazo m (nudo) bow; (para animales) lasso; (vínculo) tie, link.

le pron (a él) him; (a ella) her; (a usted) you.

leal adj loyal.

lealtad f loyalty.

lección f lesson.

lechal adj: cordero ~ baby lamb.

leche f milk; (vulg: golpe) whack ◆ interj shit!; ~ condensada condensed milk; ~ desnatada o descremada skimmed milk; ~ entera full-cream milk (Br), whole milk; ~ frita sweet made from fried milk, cornflour and lemon rind; ~ limpiadora cleansing milk.

lechera f (jarra) milk jug, → lechero.

lechería f dairy.

lechero, -ra m, f milkman (f milkwoman).

lecho m bed.

lechuga f lettuce.

lechuza f owl.

lector, -ra m, f (persona) reader; (profesor) language assistant ◆ m (aparato) scanner.

lectura f reading.

leer vt & vi to read.

legal adj legal.

legalidad f (cualidad) legality; (conjunto de leyes) law.

legible adj legible.

legislación f legislation.

legislatura f term (of office).

legítimo, -ma adj (legal) legitimate; (auténtico) genuine.

legumbre f pulse.

lejano, -na adj distant.

lejía f bleach.

lejos adv (en el espacio) far (away); (en el pasado) long ago; (en el futuro) far away; ~ de far from; a lo ~ in the distance; de ~ from a distance.

lencería f (ropa interior) lingerie; (tienda) draper's (shop).

lengua f (órgano) tongue; (idioma) language; ~ de gato = chocolate finger (biscuit); ~ materna mother tongue; ~ oficial official language.

lenguado m sole; ~ menier sole meunière.

lenguaje m language.

lengüeta f tongue.

lentamente adv slowly.

lente m o f lens; ~s de contacto contact lenses ❑ **lentes** mpl (formal: gafas) spectacles.

lenteja f lentil; **~s estofadas** lentil stew (with wine) (sg).
lentitud f slowness.
lento, -ta adj slow ♦ adv slowly.
leña f firewood.
leñador, -ra m, f woodcutter.
leño m log.
Leo m Leo.
león, -ona m, f lion (f lioness).
leopardo m (animal) leopard; (piel) leopard skin.
leotardos mpl thick tights.
lépero, -ra adj (Amér) (vulg: malicioso) spiteful; (astuto) sharp.
les pron (a ellos, ellas) them; (a ustedes) you.
lesbiana f lesbian.
lesión f (herida) injury.
letal adj lethal.
letra f (signo) letter; (de persona) handwriting; (de canción) lyrics (pl); (de una compra) bill of exchange; **~ de cambio** bill of exchange ☐ **letras** fpl (en enseñanza) arts.
letrero m sign.
levantamiento m (sublevación) uprising; **~ de pesos** weightlifting.
levantar vt to raise; (caja, peso, prohibición) to lift; (edificio) to build ☐ **levantarse** vpr (de la cama) to get up; (ponerse de pie) to stand up; (sublevarse) to rise up.
levante m (este) east; (viento) east wind ☐ **Levante** m the east coast of Spain between Castellón and Cartagena.
léxico m vocabulary.
ley f law; (parlamentaria) act.
leyenda f legend.
liar vt (atar) to tie up; (envolver) to

roll up; (fam: complicar) to muddle up ☐ **liarse** vpr (enredarse) to get muddled up; **~se a** (comenzar a) to start to.
Líbano s Lebanon.
libélula f dragonfly.
liberal adj liberal.
liberar vt to free.
libertad f freedom ☐ **libertades** fpl (atrevimiento) liberties.
libertador, -ra m, f liberator.
Libia s Libya.
libra f (moneda, unidad de peso) pound; **~ esterlina** pound (sterling) ☐ **Libra** m (zodiaco) Libra.
librar vt (de trabajo) to free; (de peligro) to save; (letra, orden de pago) to make out ♦ vi (tener fiesta) to be off work ☐ **librarse de** v + prep (peligro, obligación) to escape from.
libre adj free; (no ocupado) vacant; (asiento) available; **"libre"** (taxi) "for hire"; **~ de** free from; **~ de impuestos** tax-free.
librería f (establecimiento) bookshop; (mueble) bookcase.
librero m (Amér) bookshelf.
libreta f (cuaderno) notebook; (de ahorros) savings book.
libro m book; **~ de bolsillo** paperback; **~ de cheques** cheque book; **~ de reclamaciones** complaints book; **~ de texto** textbook.
licencia f licence.
licenciado, -da m, f graduate.
licenciarse vpr (en universidad) to graduate; (de servicio militar) to be discharged.
licenciatura f degree.
licor m liquor.

licorería f (tienda) = off-licence (Br), = liquor store (Am).

licuadora f liquidizer.

líder mf leader.

lidia f (corrida) bullfight; **la** = bullfighting.

liebre f hare.

lienzo m (tela) canvas; (pintura) painting.

liga f league; (para medias) suspender.

ligar vt (atar) to tie; (relacionar) to link ◆ vi: ~ **con** (fam) to get off with.

ligeramente adv (poco) slightly.

ligero, -ra adj light; (rápido) quick; (ágil) agile; (leve) slight; (vestido, tela) thin; **a la ligera** lightly.

light adj inv (comida) low-calorie; (bebida) diet (antes de s); (cigarrillo) light.

ligue m (fam: relación) fling.

liguero m suspender belt (Br), garter belt (Am).

lija f (papel) sandpaper.

lijar vt to sandpaper.

lila adj inv & f lilac.

lima f (herramienta) file; (fruto) lime; ~ **para uñas** nail file.

límite m limit; (línea de separación) boundary; ~ **de velocidad** speed limit.

limón m lemon.

limonada f lemonade.

limonero m lemon tree.

limosna f alms (pl); **pedir** ~ to beg.

limpiabotas m inv shoeshine.

limpiacristales m inv (detergente) window-cleaning fluid ◆ mf inv (persona) window cleaner.

limpiador, -ra m, f cleaner.

limpiaparabrisas m inv (de automóvil) windscreen wiper (Br), windshield wiper (Am) ◆ mf inv (persona) windscreen cleaner (Br), windshield cleaner (Am).

limpiar vt (quitar suciedad) to clean; (zapatos) to polish; (con trapo) to wipe; (mancha) to wipe away; (fam: robar) to pinch; ~ **la casa** to do the housework.

limpieza f (cualidad) cleanliness; (acción) cleaning; (destreza) skill; (honradez) honesty; **hacer la** ~ to do the cleaning.

limpio, -pia adj (sin suciedad) clean; (pulcro) neat; (puro) pure; (correcto) honest; (dinero) net; **en** ~ (escrito) fair.

linaje m lineage.

lince m lynx.

lindo, -da adj pretty; **de lo** ~ a great deal.

línea f line; (pauta) course; (aspecto) shape; ~ **aérea** airline; ~ **telefónica** (telephone) line.

lingote m ingot; ~ **de oro** gold ingot.

lingüística f linguistics (sg).

lingüístico, -ca adj linguistic.

lino m (tejido) linen; (planta) flax.

linterna f (utensilio) torch (Br), flashlight (Am).

lío m (paquete) bundle; (fam: desorden, embrollo) mess; (fam: relación amorosa) affair; **hacerse un** ~ to get muddled up.

lionesa f large profiterole filled with cream or chocolate.

liquidación f (de cuenta) settlement; (de mercancías, género) clearance sale; "**~ total**" "closing down sale".

liquidar *vt (cuenta)* to settle; *(mercancías, existencias)* to sell off; *(fam: matar)* to bump off.

líquido *m* liquid.

lira *f (instrumento)* lyre.

lirio *m* iris.

liso, -sa *adj (llano)* flat; *(sin asperezas)* smooth; *(vestido, color)* plain; *(pelo)* straight ♦ *m, f (Amér)* rude person.

lista *f (enumeración)* list; *(de tela)* strip; **~ de boda** wedding list; **~ de correos** poste restante; **~ de espera** waiting list; **~ de precios** price list; **~ de vinos** wine list.

listín *m* directory; **~ telefónico** telephone directory.

listo, -ta *adj (inteligente, astuto)* clever; *(preparado)* ready ♦ *interj* I'm/we're/it's ready!

listón *m (de madera)* lath; *(en deporte)* bar.

lisura *f (Amér)* swearword.

litera *f (de tren) couchette; (de barco)* berth; *(mueble)* bunk (bed).

literal *adj* literal.

literario, -ria *adj* literary.

literatura *f* literature.

litro *m* litre.

llaga *f* wound.

llama *f (de fuego)* flame; *(animal)* llama.

llamada *f* call; **hacer una ~ a cobro revertido** to reverse the charges *(Br)*, to call collect *(Am)*; **~ automática** direct-dialled call; **~ interprovincial** national call; **~ interurbana** long-distance call; **~ metropolitana** local call; **~ provin-**

cial = local area call; **~ telefónica** telephone call.

llamar *vt* to call ♦ *vi (a la puerta)* to knock; *(al timbre)* to ring; **~ por teléfono** to phone □ **llamarse** *vpr* to be called; **¿cómo te llamas?** what's your name?

llano, -na *adj (superficie, terreno)* flat; *(amable)* straightforward ♦ *m* plain.

llanta *f (de rueda)* rim; *(Amér: rueda de coche, camión)* wheel.

llanura *f* plain.

llave *f* key; *(para tuercas)* spanner; *(signo ortográfico)* curly bracket; **echar la ~** to lock up; **~ de contacto** ignition key; **~ inglesa** monkey wrench; **~ maestra** master key; **~ de paso** mains tap.

llegada *f (de viaje, trayecto, etc)* arrival; *(en deporte)* finish □ **llegadas** *fpl (de tren, avión, etc)* arrivals; **"~s internacionales"** "international arrivals".

llegar *vi (a un lugar)* to arrive; *(fecha, momento)* to come; *(ser suficiente)* to be enough; **~ a** o **hasta** *(extenderse)* to reach; **~ a hacer algo** *(expresa conclusión)* to come to do sthg; *(expresa esfuerzo)* to manage to do sthg □ **llegar a** *v + prep (presidente, director)* to become; *(edad, altura, temperatura)* to reach; **~ a ser** to become; **~ a conocer** to get to know.

llenar *vt (recipiente, espacio)* to fill; *(impreso)* to fill out □ **llenarse** *vpr (lugar)* to fill up; *(hartarse)* to be full; **llenarse de** *v + prep (cubrirse)* to get covered with.

lleno, -na *adj (ocupado)* full; *(espectáculo, cine)* sold out ♦ *m (en* *espectáculo)* full house; **de ~** *(totalmente)* completely.

llevar *vt* 1. *(transportar)* to carry; **el barco lleva carga y pasajeros** the boat carries cargo and passengers. 2. *(acompañar)* to take; **llevó al niño a casa** she took the child home; **me llevaron en coche** they drove me there. 3. *(prenda, objeto personal)* to wear; **lleva gafas** he wears glasses; **no llevamos dinero** we don't have any money on us. 4. *(coche, caballo)* to handle. 5. *(conducir)*: **~ a alguien a** to lead sb to. 6. *(ocuparse, dirigir)* to be in charge of; **lleva muy bien sus estudios** he's doing very well in his studies. 7. *(tener)* to have; **~ el pelo largo** to have long hair; **llevas las manos sucias** your hands are dirty. 8. *(soportar)* to deal with. 9. *(con tiempo)*: **lleva tres semanas de viaje** he's been travelling for three weeks; **me llevó mucho tiempo hacer el trabajo** I took a long time to get the work done. 10. *(sobrepasar)*: **te llevo seis puntos** I'm six points ahead of you; **le lleva seis años** she's six years older than him.
◆ *vi* 1. *(dirigirse)* to lead; **este camino lleva a Madrid** this road leads to Madrid. 2. *(haber)*: **llevo leída media novela** I'm halfway through the novel. 3. *(estar)*: **lleva viniendo cada día** she's been coming every day.
❏ **llevarse** *vpr (coger)* to take; *(conseguir, recibir)* to get; *(estar de moda)* to be in (fashion); **~se bien/mal (con)** to get on well/badly (with).

llorar *vi* to cry ◆ *vt* to mourn.

llorón, -ona *m, f* crybaby.

llover *v impers*: **está lloviendo** it's raining ◆ *vi (ser abundante)* to rain down; **~ a cántaros** to rain cats and dogs.

llovizna *f* drizzle.

lloviznar *v impers*: **está lloviznando** it's drizzling.

lluvia *f* rain; *(fig: de preguntas)* barrage.

lluvioso, -sa *adj* rainy.

lo, la *pron (cosa)* it, them *(pl)*; *(persona)* him *(f* her), them *(pl)*; *(usted, ustedes)* you ◆ *pron neutro* it ◆ *art*: **~ mejor** the best; **~ bueno del asunto** the good thing about it; **ella es guapa, él no ~ es** she's good-looking, he isn't; **siento ~ de tu padre** I'm sorry about your father; **~ que** what.

lobo, -ba *m, f* wolf.

local *adj* local ◆ *m (lugar)* premises *(pl)*.

localidad *f (población)* town; *(asiento)* seat; *(entrada)* ticket.

localización *f* location.

localizar *vt (encontrar)* to locate; *(limitar)* to localize ❏ **localizarse** *vpr (situarse)* to be located.

loción *f* lotion; **~ bronceadora** suntan lotion.

loco, -ca *adj* mad ◆ *m, f* madman *(f* madwoman) ◆ *por (aficionado)* mad about; **a lo ~** *(sin pensar)* hastily; **volver ~ a alguien** to drive sb crazy.

locomotora *f* engine, locomotive.

locura *f (falta de juicio)* madness; *(acción insensata)* folly; **tener ~ por**

to be mad about.

locutor, -ra *m, f* presenter.

locutorio *m (de emisora)* studio; *(de convento)* visiting room.

lodo *m* mud.

lógica *f* logic.

lógico, -ca *adj* logical.

logrado, -da *adj (bien hecho)* accomplished.

lograr *vt (resultado, objetivo)* to achieve; *(beca, puesto)* to obtain; ~ **hacer algo** to manage to do sthg; ~ **que alguien haga algo** to manage to get sb to do sthg.

logro *m* achievement.

lombriz *(pl* -**ces***) f* earthworm.

lomo *m (de animal)* back; *(carne)* loin; *(de libro)* spine; ~ **de cerdo** pork loin; ~ **embuchado** pork loin *stuffed with seasoned mince;* ~ **ibérico** *cold, cured pork sausage;* ~**s de merluza** hake steak *(sg)*.

lona *f* canvas.

loncha *f* slice.

lonche *m (Amér)* lunch.

Londres *s* London.

longaniza *f type of spicy, cold pork sausage.*

longitud *f* length.

lonja *f (edificio)* exchange; *(loncha)* slice.

loro *m* parrot.

lote *m (porción)* share.

lotería *f* lottery; ~ **primitiva** *twice-weekly state-run lottery.*

---

i LOTERÍA PRIMITIVA

In this Spanish state-run lottery, participants try to guess a combination of six numbers between one and forty-nine. A ticket contains eight grids of forty-nine boxes, each grid being equivalent to one entry. The "lotería primitiva" is drawn twice a week.

lotero, -ra *m, f* lottery ticket seller.

loza *f (material)* earthenware; *(porcelana)* china; *(vajilla)* crockery.

ltda. *(abrev de limitada)* Ltd.

lubina *f* sea bass.

lubricante *m* lubricant.

lucha *f (pelea)* fight; *(oposición)* struggle; ~ **libre** all in wrestling.

luchador, -ra *m, f* fighter.

luchar *vi (pelear)* to fight; *(esforzarse)* to struggle.

luciérnaga *f* glow-worm.

lucir *vt (llevar puesto)* to wear ◆ *vi* to shine; *(Amér: verse bien)* to look good* ❑ **lucirse** *vpr (quedar bien)* to shine; *(exhibirse)* to be seen; *(fam: hacer el ridículo)* to mess things up.

lucro *m* profit.

lúdico, -ca *adj:* **actividades lúdicas** fun and games.

luego *adv (justo después)* then; *(más tarde)* later; *(Amér: pronto)* soon ◆ *conj* so; **desde** ~ *(sin duda)* of course; *(para reprochar)* for heaven's sake; **luego luego** *(Amér)* straight away

lugar *m* place; **tener** ~ to take place; **en** ~ **de** instead of.

lujo *m* luxury; *(abundancia)* profusion; **de** ~ luxury *(antes de s)*.

lujoso, -sa *adj* luxurious.

lujuria *f* lust.

lumbago *m* lumbago.

luminoso, -sa *adj* bright.

luna *f (astro)* moon; *(de vidrio)* window *(pane)*.

lunar *m (de la piel)* mole ❏

lunares *mpl (estampado)* spots.

lunes *m inv* Monday, → **sábado**.

luneta *f (de coche)* windscreen *(Br)*, windshield *(Am)*; ~ **térmica** demister.

lupa *f* magnifying glass.

lustrabotas *m inv (Amér)* bootblack.

lustrador *m (Amér)* bootblack.

luto *m* mourning.

luz *(pl -ces) f* light; *(electricidad)* electricity; ~ **solar** sunlight; **dar a** ~ to give birth ❏ **luces** *fpl (de coche)* lights.

lycra® *f* Lycra®.

M

m *(abrev de metro)* m.

macana *f (Amér) (garrote)* club; *(fig: disparate)* stupid thing.

macanudo *adj (Amér: fam)* great.

macarrones *mpl* macaroni *(sg)*.

macedonia *f*: ~ **(de frutas)** fruit salad.

maceta *f* flowerpot.

machacar *vt* to crush.

machismo *m* machismo.

machista *mf* male chauvinist.

macho *adj (animal, pieza)* male; *(hombre)* macho ♦ *m (animal)* male.

macizo, -za *adj* solid ♦ *m (de montañas)* massif; *(de flores)* flowerbed.

macramé *m* macramé.

macuto *m* backpack.

madeja *f* hank.

madera *f* wood; *(pieza)* piece of wood; **de** ~ wooden.

madrastra *f* stepmother.

madre *f* mother; ~ **política** mother-in-law; **¡~ mía!** Jesus!

madreselva *f* honeysuckle.

Madrid *s* Madrid; ~ **capital** (the city of) Madrid.

madriguera *f (de tejón)* den; *(de conejo)* burrow.

madrileño, -ña *adj* of/relating to Madrid ♦ *m, f* native/inhabitant of Madrid.

madrina *f (de bautizo)* god-mother; *(de boda)* bridesmaid; *(de fiesta, acto)* patroness.

madrugada *f (noche)* early morning; *(amanecer)* dawn.

madrugador, -ra *adj* early-rising.

madrugar *vi* to get up early.

madurar *vt (proyecto, plan, idea)* to think through ♦ *vi (fruto)* to ripen; *(persona)* to mature.

madurez *f (sensatez)* maturity; *(edad adulta)* adulthood; *(de fruto)* ripeness.

maduro, -ra *adj (fruto, grano)* ripe; *(sensato, mayor)* mature; *(proyecto, plan, idea)* well thought-out.

maestría *f (habilidad)* mastery.

maestro, -tra *m, f (de escuela)* teacher; *(de arte, oficio)* master;

malo

(músico) maestro.

mafia *f* mafia.

magdalena *f* fairy cake.

magia *f* magic.

mágico, -ca *adj (maravilloso)*
magical; *(de la magia)* magic.

magistrado, -da *m, f (de justicia)* judge.

magistratura *f (tribunal)* tribunal; *(cargo)* judgeship.

magnate *m* magnate.

magnesio *m* magnesium.

magnético, -ca *adj* magnetic.

magnetófono *m* tape recorder.

magnífico, -ca *adj* magnificent.

magnitud *f* magnitude.

magnolia *f* magnolia.

mago, -ga *m, f (en espectáculo)*
magician; *(personaje fantástico)* wizard.

magro, -gra *adj (carne)* lean.

maguey *m (Amér)* agave, maguey.

maicena *f* cornflour *(Br)*, cornstarch *(Am)*.

maillot *m (de ballet, deporte)*
maillot.

maitre *m* maître.

maíz *m* maize *(Br)*, corn *(Am)*.

majestuoso, -sa *adj* majestic.

majo, -ja *adj (agradable)* nice;
(bonito) pretty.

mal *m (daño)* harm; *(enfermedad)*
illness ◆ *adv (incorrectamente)*
wrong; *(inadecuadamente)* badly ◆
adj → **malo**; **el ~** evil; **encontrarse
~** to feel ill; **oír/ver ~** to have poor
hearing/eyesight; **oler ~** to smell
bad; **saber ~** to taste bad; **sentar ~**

a alguien *(ropa)* not to suit sb;
(comida) to disagree with sb;
(comentario) to upset sb; **ir de ~ en
peor** to go from bad to worse.

Malasia *s* Malaysia.

malcriar *vt* to spoil.

maldad *f (cualidad)* evil; *(acción)*
evil thing.

maldición *f* curse.

maldito, -ta *adj* damned;
¡maldita sea! damn it!

maleable *adj* malleable.

malecón *m (atracadero)* jetty;
(rompeolas) breakwater.

maleducado, -da *adj* rude.

malentendido *m* misunderstanding.

malestar *m (inquietud)* uneasiness; *(dolor)* discomfort.

maleta *f* suitcase; **hacer las ~s**
to pack (one's bags).

maletero *m* boot *(Br)*, trunk
(Am).

maletín *m* briefcase.

malformación *f* malformation.

malgastar *vt (dinero, esfuerzo,
tiempo)* to waste.

malhablado, -da *adj* foul-mouthed.

malhechor, -ra *adj* criminal.

malicia *f (maldad)* wickedness;
(mala intención) malice; *(astucia)*
sharpness.

malintencionado, -da *adj*
malicious.

malla *f (tejido)* mesh; *(traje)* leotard ❑ **mallas** *fpl (pantalones)* leggings.

Mallorca *s* Majorca.

malo, -la *(compar & superl peor)*

adj bad; *(travieso)* naughty; **estar ~** *(enfermo)* to be ill; **estar de malas** to be in a bad mood; **por las malas** by force.

malograr *vt (Amér)* to waste ❑
malograrse *(Amér)* to fail.

malpensado, -da *m, f* malicious person.

maltratar *vt (persona)* to illtreat; *(objeto)* to damage.

mamá *f (fam)* mum; *(Amér)* grandma.

mamadera *f (Amér) (biberón)* (baby's) bottle; *(tetilla)* teat.

mamar *vt & vi* to suckle.

mamey *m (Amér)* mammee.

mamífero *m* mammal.

mamita *f (Amér: fam)* mum.

mampara *f* screen.

manada *f (de vacas)* herd.

mánager *m* manager.

manantial *m* spring.

mancha *f* stain.

manchar *vt (ensuciar)* to make dirty; *(con manchas)* to stain ❑
mancharse *vpr* to get dirty.

manco, -ca *adj* one-handed.

mancuerna *f (Amér)* cufflink.

mandar *vt (suj: ley, orden)* to decree; *(ordenar)* to order; *(dirigir)* to be in charge of; *(enviar)* to send; **~ hacer algo** to have sthg done; **¿mande?** *(Amér)* eh?

mandarina *f* mandarin.

mandíbula *f* jaw.

mando *m (autoridad)* command; *(jefe)* leader; *(instrumento)* control; **~ a distancia** remote control.

manecilla *f* hand *(of clock)*.

manejable *adj* manageable.

manejar *vt (herramienta, persona)* to handle; *(aparato)* to operate; *(dinero)* to manage; *(Amér: conducir)* to drive.

manejo *m (de instrumento)* handling; *(de aparato)* operation; *(de dinero)* management; *(engaño, astucia)* intrigue.

manera *f* way; **de cualquier ~** *(mal)* any old how; *(de todos modos)* anyway; **de esta ~** *(así)* this way; **de ninguna ~** certainly not; **de ~ que** *(así que)* so (that) ❑ **maneras** *fpl (comportamiento)* manners.

manga *f (de vestido)* sleeve; *(tubo flexible)* hosepipe; *(de campeonato)* round.

mango *m (asa)* handle; *(fruto)* mango.

manguera *f* hosepipe.

maní *m (Amér)* peanut.

manía *f (obsesión)* obsession; *(afición exagerada)* craze; *(antipatía)* dislike.

maniático, -ca *adj (tiquismiquis)* fussy ❖ *m, f*: **es un ~ del fútbol** he's football crazy.

manicomio *m* mental hospital.

manicura *f* manicure; **hacerse la ~** to have a manicure.

manifestación *f (de personas)* demonstration; *(muestra)* display; *(declaración)* expression.

manifestante *mf* demonstrator.

manifestar *vt (declarar)* to express; *(mostrar)* to show ❑ **manifestarse** *vpr* to demonstrate.

manifiesto, -ta *adj* clear ❖ *m* manifesto.

manillar *m* handlebars *(pl)*.

maniobra f (de coche, barco, tren) manoeuvre; (astucia) trick.

manipular vt (con las manos) to handle; (persona, información) to manipulate.

maniquí m (muñeco) dummy ◆ mf (persona) model.

manito m (Amér: fam) pal.

manivela f crank.

mano f hand; (capa) coat ◆ m (Amér) pal; a ~ (sin máquina) by hand; (cerca) to hand; a ~ derecha on the right; de segunda ~ second hand; dar la ~ a alguien to shake hands with sb; echar una ~ a alguien to lend sb a hand; ~ de obra (trabajadores) workforce.

manoletina f (zapato) type of open, low-heeled shoe, often with a bow.

manopla f mitten.

manosear vt to handle roughly.

mansión f mansion.

manso, -sa adj (animal) tame; (persona) gentle.

manta f blanket.

manteca f (de animal) fat; (de cerdo) lard; (de cacao, leche) butter.

mantecado m (dulce) short-cake; (sorbete) ice-cream made of milk, eggs and sugar.

mantel m tablecloth.

mantelería f table linen.

mantener vt to keep; (sujetar) to support; (defender) to maintain; (relación, correspondencia) to have ❑ **mantenerse** vpr (edificio) to be standing; (alimentarse) to support o.s.

mantenimiento m (de per-

sona) sustenance; (de edificio, coche) maintenance.

mantequería f dairy.

mantequilla f butter.

mantilla f (de mujer) mantilla

mantón m shawl.

manual adj & m manual.

manualidad f manual labour.

manuscrito m manuscript.

manzana f (fruto) apple; (de casas) block; ~ al horno baked apple.

manzanilla f (infusión) camomile tea; (vino) manzanilla (sherry).

manzano m apple tree.

mañana f morning ◆ adv & m tomorrow; las dos de la ~ two o'clock in the morning; ~ por la ~ tomorrow morning; por la ~ in the morning.

mañanitas fpl (Amér) birthday song (sg).

mapa m map.

maqueta f model.

maquillaje m (producto) make-up; (acción) making-up.

maquillar vt to make up ❑ **maquillarse** vpr to put on one's make up.

máquina f (aparato) machine; (locomotora) engine; (Amér: coche) car; a ~ by machine; ~ de afeitar electric razor, ~ de coser sewing machine; ~ de escribir typewriter; ~ fotográfica camera.

maquinaria f (conjunto de máquinas) machinery.

maquinilla f razor.

maquinista mf (de metro, tren) engine driver (Br), engineer (Am).

mar *m* o *f* sea ❑ **Mar** *m*: **el Mar del Norte** the North Sea.

maracas *fpl* maracas.

maratón *m* (*carrera*) marathon; (*fig: de cine*) three or more films by the same director or on the same subject, shown consecutively.

maravilla *f* (*cosa extraordinaria*) marvel; (*impresión*) wonder.

maravilloso, -sa *adj* marvellous.

marc *m*: ~ **de champán** champagne brandy.

marca *f* (*señal, huella*) mark; (*nombre*) brand; (*en deporte*) record; **de** ~ (*ropa, producto*) designer (*antes de s*); ~ **registrada** registered trademark.

marcado, -da *adj* marked.

marcador *m* (*panel*) scoreboard; (*rotulador*) marker pen.

marcapasos *m inv* pacemaker.

marcar *vt* (*poner señal*) to mark; (*anotar*) to note down; (*un tanto*) to score; (*suj: termómetro, contador*) to read; (*suj: reloj*) to say; (*número de teléfono*) to dial; (*pelo*) to set; (*con el precio*) to price; ~ **un gol** to score a goal; ~ **un número** to dial a number.

marcha *f* (*partida*) departure; (*de vehículo*) gear; (*desarrollo*) progress; (*fam: animación*) life; (*pieza musical*) march; **dar** ~ **atrás** to reverse; **en** ~ (*motor*) running; **poner en** ~ to start.

marchar *vi* (*aparato, mecanismo*) to work; (*asunto, negocio*) to go well; (*soldado*) to march ❑ **marcharse** *vpr* (*irse*) to go; (*partir*) to leave.

marchitarse *vpr* to wither.

marchoso, -sa *adj* (*fam*) lively.

marco *m* frame; (*límite*) framework.

marea *f* tide; ~ **negra** oil slick.

mareado, -da *adj* (*con náuseas*) sick; (*en coche*) carsick; (*en barco*) seasick; (*en avión*) airsick; (*aturdido*) dizzy.

marearse *vpr* (*en coche*) to be carsick; (*en barco*) to be seasick; (*en avión*) to be airsick; (*aturdirse*) to get dizzy.

marejada *f* heavy sea.

marejadilla *f* slight swell.

maremoto *m* tidal wave.

mareo *m* (*náuseas*) sickness; (*aturdimiento*) dizziness.

marfil *m* ivory.

margarina *f* margarine.

margarita *f* daisy.

margen *m* (*de página, beneficio*) margin; (*de camino*) side; (*de río*) bank; (*tiempo, de actuar*) leeway.

marginación *f* exclusion.

marginado, -da *m, f* outcast.

mariachi *m* (*orquesta*) mariachi band.

$\boxed{i}$ MARIACHI

Mariachi bands are groups of Mexican musicians who wear traditional Mexican dress and play their music at local "fiestas", in restaurants and in the streets. They are often hired for private functions such as birthdays or weddings.

---

maricón *m* (*vulg*) poof.

marido *m* husband.

marihuana f marijuana.

marina f (armada) navy; (cuadro) seascape.

marinero, -ra adj (ropa) sailor (antes de s); **a la marinera** cooked in a white wine and garlic sauce.

marino m sailor.

marioneta f (muñeco) puppet □ **marionetas** fpl (teatro) puppet show (sg).

mariposa f butterfly.

mariquita f ladybird (Br), ladybug (Am).

mariscada f seafood dish.

mariscos mpl seafood (sg).

marisma f salt marsh.

marítimo, -ma adj (paseo) seaside (antes de s); (barco) sea-going.

mármol m marble.

marqués, -esa m, f marquis (f marchioness).

marquesina f (de puerta, andén) glass canopy; (parada de autobús) bus shelter.

marrano, -na adj (sucio) filthy; (inmoble) contemptible ◆ m, f (cerdo) pig.

marrón adj inv brown.

marroquí adj & mf Moroccan.

Marruecos s Morocco.

martes m inv Tuesday, → sábado.

martillo m hammer.

mártir mf martyr.

marzo m March, → setiembre.

más adv 1. (comparativo) more; Pepe es ~ alto/ambicioso Pepe is taller/more ambitious; **tengo** ~ **hambre** I'm hungrier; ~ **de/que** more than; ~ ... **que** ... more ...

than ...; **de** ~ (de sobra) left over.
2. (superlativo): **el/la** ~ ... the most ...; **el** ~ **listo** the cleverest.
3. (en frases negativas) any more; **no necesitas** ~ **trabajo** you don't need any more work.
4. (con pron interrogativo o indefinido) else; ¿**quién/qué** ~? who/what else?; **nadie** ~ no one else.
5. (indica intensidad): ¡**qué día** ~ **bonito!** what a lovely day!; ¡**es** ~ **tonto!** he's so stupid!
6. (indica suma) plus; **dos** ~ **dos igual a cuatro** two plus two is four.
7. (indica preferencia): ~ **vale que te quedes en casa** it would be better for you to stay at home.
8. (en locuciones): **es** ~ what is more; ~ **bien** rather; ~ **o menos** more or less; **poco** ~ little more; **por** ~ **que** however much; **por** ~ **que lo intente** however hard she tries; ¿**qué** ~ **da?** what difference does it make!
◆ m inv: **tiene sus** ~ **y sus menos** it has its good points and its bad points.

masa f mass; (de pan, bizcocho) dough; (Amér: dulce) small cake.

masaje m massage.

masajista mf masseur (f masseuse).

mascar vt to chew.

máscara f mask.

mascarilla f (crema, loción) face pack; (para nariz y boca) mask.

mascota f mascot.

masculino, -na adj (sexo) male; (viril) manly; (en gramática) masculine.

masía f farm (in Aragon or Catalonia).

masticar vt to chew.

mástil m (de barco) mast.

matadero m slaughterhouse.

matador m matador.

matambre m (Amér) cut of cold meat from between the hide and the ribs of a cow.

matamoscas m inv (palo) flyswat; (espray) flyspray.

matanza f (de personas, animales) slaughter; (de cerdo) pig-killing.

matar vt to kill; (hacer sufrir) to drive mad; (brillo, color) to tone down; (en juegos, cartas) to beat ❑ **matarse** vpr (tomarse interés, trabajo) to go to great lengths.

matarratas m inv (insecticida) rat poison; (bebida mala) rotgut.

matasellos m inv postmark.

mate adj matt ◆ m (en ajedrez) mate; (planta, infusión) maté.

ℹ️ MATE

Maté is a herbal infusion from the southern part of South America. It is drunk from a small cup, also known as a maté, which is made from a small, hollowed-out gourd.

---

matemáticas fpl mathematics.

matemático, -ca adj mathematical.

materia f (sustancia, tema) matter; (material) material; (asignatura) subject; ~ **prima** raw material.

material adj (de materia) material; (físico) physical ◆ m (compo-

nente) material; (instrumento) equipment.

maternidad f (cualidad) motherhood; (clínica) maternity hospital.

materno, -na adj (de madre) maternal; (lengua) mother (antes de s).

matinal adj morning (antes de s).

matiz m (pl -ces) (de color) shade; (leve diferencia) nuance.

matizar vt (colores) to tinge; (concepto, idea, proyecto) to explain in detail.

matón m (guardaespaldas) bodyguard; (asesino) hired assassin.

matorral m thicket.

matrícula f (de colegio) registration; (de universidad) matriculation; (de vehículo) numberplate; ~ **de honor** top marks (pl).

matricular vt to register ❑ **matricularse** vpr to register.

matrimonio m (ceremonia) marriage; (pareja) married couple.

matutino, -na adj morning (antes de s).

maullar vi to miaow.

maullido m miaow.

máxima f (temperatura) highest temperature; (frase) maxim.

máximo, -ma superl → **grande** ◆ adj (triunfo, pena, frecuencia) greatest; (temperatura, puntuación, galardón) highest ◆ m maximum; **como** ~ at the most.

maya adj Mayan ◆ mf Maya Indian ◆ m (lengua) Maya.

mayo m May, → **setiembre**.

mayonesa f mayonnaise.

mayor adj (en tamaño) bigger; (en

medio

número) higher; (*en edad*) older; (*en importancia*) greater; (*adulto*) grown-up; (*anciano*) elderly ◆ *m* (*en el ejército*) major; **el/la ~** (*en tamaño*) the biggest; (*en número*) the highest; (*en edad*) the oldest; (*en importancia*) the greatest; **al por ~** wholesale; **la ~ parte** (*of*): **ser ~ de edad** to be an adult ☐ **mayores** *mpl*: **los ~es** (*adultos*) grown-ups; (*ancianos*) the elderly.

mayoreo *m* (*Amér*) wholesale.

mayoría *f* majority; **la ~ de** most of.

mayúscula *f* capital letter; **en ~s** in capitals.

mazapán *m* marzipan.

mazo *m* (*de madera*) mallet; (*de cartas*) balance (of the deck).

me *pron* (*complemento directo*) me; (*complemento indirecto*) (to) me; (*reflexivo*) myself; **~ voy** I'm going.

mear *vi* (*fam*) to piss.

mecánica *f* (*mecanismo*) mechanics (*pl*).

mecánico, -ca *adj* mechanical ◆ *m* mechanic.

mecanismo *m* (*funcionamiento*) procedure; (*piezas*) mechanism.

mecanografía *f* typing.

mecanógrafo, -fa *m, f* typist.

mecedora *f* rocking chair.

mecer *vt* to rock.

mecha *f* (*de vela*) wick; (*de explosivo*) fuse; (*de pelo*) streak; (*de tocino*) strip of meat used as stuffing for chicken etc.

mechero *m* (cigarette) lighter.

mechón *m* (*de pelo*) lock.

medalla *f* medal.

medallón *m* medallion; **meda-**

llones de rape médaillons of angler fish; **medallones de solomillo** médaillons of sirloin steak.

media *f* (*calcetín*) stocking; (*punto*) average ☐ **medias** *fpl* tights.

mediado, -da *adj*: **a ~s de** in the middle of.

mediana *f* (*de autopista*) central reservation (*Br*), median (*Am*).

mediano, -na *adj* (*en tamaño*) medium; (*en calidad*) average.

medianoche *f* midnight.

mediante *prep* by means of.

mediar *vi* (*llegar a la mitad*) to be halfway through; (*transcurrir*) to pass; (*interceder*) to intercede; **~ entre** to be between.

medicamento *m* medicine.

medicina *f* medicine.

medicinal *adj* medicinal.

médico, -ca *m, f* doctor; **~ de guardia** duty doctor.

medida *f* (*dimensión*) measurement; (*cantidad, disposición*) measure; (*intensidad*) extent; **tomar ~s** to take measures; **~s de seguridad** safety measures; **a la ~** (*ropa*) made-to-measure; **a ~ que** as; **en cierta ~** to some extent.

medieval *adj* medieval.

medio, -dia *adj* half; (*tamaño, estatura*) medium; (*posición, punto, clase*) middle; (*de promedio*) average ◆ *m* (*centro*) middle; (*entorno, ambiente*) environment; (*manera, medida, de transporte*) means; (*en matemáticas*) average ◆ *adv* half; **en ~ de** (*entre dos*) between; (*entre varios, en mitad de*) in the middle of; **a medias** (*partido entre dos*) half each; **hacer algo a medias** to half-do something; **~ ambiente** environment; **media hora** half an hour; **~ kilo (de)** half a kilo (of); **media docena/libra (de)** half a dozen/pound (of); **un vaso y ~ a** glass and a half; **media pensión** half board ❑ **medios** *mpl (económicos)* resources; **los ~s de comunicación** the media.

mediocre *adj* mediocre.

mediocridad *f* mediocrity.

mediodía *m* midday.

mediopensionista *mf* child who has lunch at school.

medir *vt (dimensión, intensidad)* to measure; *(comparar)* to weigh up; *(fuerzas)* to compare; *(palabras, acciones)* to weigh; **¿cuánto mides?** how tall are you?

meditar *vt* to ponder ♦ *vi* to meditate.

mediterráneo, -a *adj* Mediterranean ❑ **Mediterráneo** *m*: **el (mar) Mediterráneo** the Mediterranean (Sea).

médium *mf inv* medium.

medusa *f* jellyfish.

megáfono *m* megaphone.

mejilla *f* cheek.

mejillón *m* mussel; **mejillones a la marinera** moules marinières.

mejor *adj & adv* better; **el/la ~** the best; **a lo ~** maybe.

mejora *f* improvement.

mejorar *vt* to improve; *(superar)* to be better than; *(enfermo)* to make better ♦ *vi (enfermo)* to get better; *(tiempo, clima)* to improve ❑ **mejorarse** *vpr (persona)* to get better; *(tiempo, clima)* to improve.

mejoría *f* improvement.

melancolía *f* melancholy.

melancólico, -ca *adj* melancholic.

melena *f (de persona)* long hair; *(de león)* mane.

mella *f (en metal)* nick; *(en diente)* chip; **hacer ~** *(causar impresión)* to make an impression.

mellizo, -za *adj* twin *(antes de s)* ❑ **mellizos** *mpl* twins.

melocotón *m* peach; **~ en almíbar** peaches *(pl)* in syrup.

melocotonero *m* peach tree.

melodía *f* tune.

melodrama *m* melodrama.

melodramático, -ca *adj* melodramatic.

melón *m* melon; **~ con jamón** *melon with "serrano" ham*.

membrillo *m (fruto)* quince; *(dulce)* quince jelly.

memorable *adj* memorable.

memoria *f* memory; *(estudio)* paper; *(informe)* report; **de ~** by heart ❑ **memorias** *fpl (de persona)* memoirs.

memorizar *vt* to memorize.

menaje *m (de cocina)* kitchenware.

mención *f* mention.

mencionar *vt* to mention.

mendigo, -ga *m, f* beggar.

menestra *f*: **~ (de verduras)** vegetable stew.

menor *adj (en edad)* younger; *(en tamaño)* smaller; *(en número)* lower; *(en calidad)* lesser ♦ *m (persona)* minor; **el/la ~** *(en tamaño)* the smallest; *(en edad)* the youngest; *(en número)* the lowest; **~ de edad** under age.

Menorca *s* Minorca.

menos *adv* 1. *(comparativo)* less; **está ~ gordo** he's not as fat; **tengo ~ hambre** I'm not as hungry; **~ leche** less milk; **~ manzanas** fewer apples; **~ de/que** fewer/less than; **~ ... que ...** fewer/less ... than ...; **me han dado 25 pesetas de ~** they've given me 25 pesetas too little.
2. *(superlativo)*: **el/la ~ ...** the least ...; **lo ~ que puedes hacer** the least you can do.
3. *(indica resta)* minus; **tres ~ dos igual a uno** three minus two is one.
4. *(con las horas)*: **son las cuatro ~ diez** it is ten to four.
5. *(en locuciones)*. **a ~ que** unless; **poco ~ de** just under; **¡~ mal!** thank God!; **eso es lo de ~** that's the least of it.
♦ *prep (excepto)* except (for); **acudieron todos ~ él** everyone came except him; **todo ~ eso** anything but that.
♦ *m inv*: **al** O **por lo ~** at least.

menospreciar *vt (despreciar)* to despise; *(apreciar poco)* to undervalue.

menosprecio *m (desprecio)* scorn; *(poco aprecio)* undervaluing.

mensaje *m* message.

mensajero, -ra *m, f (de paquetes, cartas)* courier; *(de comunicados)* messenger.

menstruación *f* menstruation.

mensual *adj* monthly.

menta *f* mint; **a la ~** with mint.

mental *adj* mental.

mente *f (inteligencia)* mind; *(forma de pensar)* mentality.

mentir *vi* to lie.

mentira *f* lie.

mentiroso, -sa *m, f* liar.

mentón *m* chin.

menú *m* menu; *(de precio reducido)* set menu; **~ de degustación** *meal consisting of several small portions of different dishes*; **~ (del día)** set meal.

menudeo *m (Amér)* retail.

menudo, -da *adj* small; **a ~** often; **¡~ gol!** what a goal!

meñique *m* little finger.

mercadillo *m* flea market.

mercado *m* market.

mercancía *f* merchandise.

mercantil *adj* commercial.

mercería *f* haberdasher's (shop) *(Br)*, notions store *(Am)*.

mercurio *m* mercury.

merecer *vt* to deserve ❑ **merecerse** *vpr* to deserve.

merendar *vt* = to have for tea
♦ *vi* = to have tea.

merendero *m* open air café or bar in the country or on the beach.

merengue *m* meringue.

meridiano, -na *adj (evidente)* crystal-clear; *(del mediodía)* midday *(antes de s)* ♦ *m* meridian.

meridional *adj* southern.

merienda *f (de media tarde)* tea *(light afternoon meal)*, *(para excursión)* picnic.

mérito *m* merit.

merluza *f* hake; **~ a la plancha** grilled hake; **~ a la romana** hake fried in batter.

mermelada *f* jam.

mero *m* grouper; **~ a la plancha**

grilled grouper.

mes m month; (salario mensual) monthly salary; **en el ~ de** in (the month of).

mesa f table; (escritorio) desk; (de personas) committee; **poner la ~** to lay the table; **quitar la ~** to clear the table.

mesero, -ra m, f (Amér) waiter (f waitress).

meseta f plateau.

mesilla f: **~ de noche** bedside table.

mesón m (restaurante) old, country-style restaurant and bar.

mestizo, -za m, f person of mixed race.

meta f goal; (de carrera) finishing line.

metáfora f metaphor.

metal m metal.

metálico, -ca adj (de metal) metal ♦ m cash; **en ~** in cash.

meteorito m meteorite.

meteorología f meteorology.

meter vt 1. (introducir, ingresar, invertir) to put in; **~ algo/a alguien en algo** to put sthg/sb in sthg; **lo han metido en la cárcel** they've put him in prison.
2. (hacer partícipe): **~ a alguien en algo** to get sb into sthg.
3. (fam: hacer soportar): **nos meterá su discurso** she'll make us listen to her speech.
4. (fam: imponer, echar) to give; **me han metido una multa** they've given me a fine; **le metieron una bronca** they told him off.
5. (causar): **~ miedo/prisa a alguien** to scare/rush sb.

meterse vpr (entrar) to get in; (estar) to get to; (entrometerse) to meddle; **~se a** (dedicarse a) to become; (empezar) to start; **~se en** (mezclarse con) to get involved in; **meterse con** v + prep (molestar) to hassle; (atacar) to go for.

método m (modo ordenado) method; (de enseñanza) course.

metralla f (munición) shrapnel; (fragmento) piece of shrapnel.

metro m (unidad de longitud) metre; (transporte) underground (Br), subway (Am); (instrumento) tape measure.

metrópoli f metropolis.

mexicano, -na adj & m, f Mexican.

México s Mexico.

mezcla f mixture.

mezclar vt to mix; (confundir, involucrar) to mix up ☐ **mezclarse en** v + prep to get mixed up in.

mezquino, -na adj mean.

mezquita f mosque.

mg (abrev de miligramo) mg.

mi (pl **mis**) adj my.

mí pron (después de preposición) me; (reflexivo) myself; **¡a ~ qué!** so what!; **por ~ ...** as far as I'm concerned ...

mico m monkey.

microbio m germ.

micrófono m microphone.

microondas m inv microwave (oven).

microscopio m microscope.

miedo m fear; **tener ~ de** to be afraid of.

miedoso, -sa adj fearful.

miel f honey.

miembro m (de grupo, asociación) member; (extremidad) limb.

mientras conj (a la vez) while; ~ **no se apruebe** until it has been approved; ~ **(que)** whilst; ~ **(tanto)** in the meantime.

miércoles m inv Wednesday, → **sábado**.

mierda f (vulg) shit ◆ interj (vulg) shit!

mies f (cereal) ripe corn; (siega) harvest time.

miga f crumb; (parte sustanciosa) substance ⊔ **migas** fpl (guiso) fried breadcrumbs.

migaja f crumb.

mil núm a thousand; **dos** ~ two thousand, → **seis**.

milagro m miracle; **de** ~ miraculously.

milenario, -ria adj ancient ◆ m millennium.

milenio m millennium.

milésimo, -ma adj thousandth.

mili f (fam) military service; **hacer la** ~ (fam) to do one's military service.

miligramo m milligram.

mililitro m millilitre.

milímetro m millimetre.

militante mf militant.

militar adj military ◆ m soldier.

milla f (en tierra) mile; (en mar) nautical mile

millar m thousand.

millón núm million; **dos millones** two million, → **seis**.

millonario, -ria m, f millionaire (f millionairess).

mimado, -da adj spoilt.

mimar vt to spoil.

mímica f mime.

mimosa f mimosa.

min (abrev de minuto) min.

mina f mine; (de lápiz) lead.

mineral adj & m mineral.

minero, -ra m, f miner.

miniatura f miniature.

minifalda f mini skirt.

mínimo, -ma superl → **pequeño** ◆ adj & m minimum; **como** ~ at the very least.

ministerio m ministry.

ministro, -tra m, f minister.

minoría f minority.

minoritario, -ria adj minority (antes de s).

minucioso, -sa adj (persona) meticulous; (trabajo) very detailed.

minúscula f small letter; **en** ~ in lower-case letters.

minúsculo, -la adj (muy pequeño) minute.

minusválido, -da m, f disabled person.

minutero m minute hand.

minuto m minute.

mío, mía adj mine ◆ pron: **el** ~, **la mía** mine; **lo** ~ (lo que me gusta) my thing; **un amigo** ~ a friend of mine.

miope adj shortsighted.

miopía f shortsightedness.

mirada f look; (rápida) glance; **echar una** ~ **a** to have a quick look at.

mirador m (lugar) viewpoint; (balcón cerrado) enclosed balcony.

mirar vt (ver) to look at; (observar, vigilar) to watch; (considerar) to consider ♦ *vi (buscar)* to look; **~ a** *(estar orientado)* to face; **estoy mirando** *(en tienda)* I'm just looking ❏ **mirarse** *vpr* to look at o.s.

mirilla *f* spyhole.

mirlo *m* blackbird.

mirón, -ona *m, f (espectador)* onlooker.

misa *f* mass; **~ del gallo** midnight mass.

miserable *adj (muy pobre)* poor; *(desgraciado, lastimoso)* wretched; *(mezquino)* mean.

miseria *f (pobreza)* poverty; *(poca cantidad)* pittance.

misericordia *f* compassion.

misil *m* missile.

misión *f* mission; *(tarea)* task.

misionero, -ra *m, f* missionary.

mismo, -ma *adj (igual)* same ♦ *pron*: **el ~, la misma** the same; **el ~ que vi ayer** the same one I saw yesterday; **ahora ~** right now; **lo ~ (que)** the same thing (as); **da lo ~** it doesn't matter; **en este ~ cuarto** in this very room; **yo ~** I myself.

misterio *m (secreto)* mystery; *(sigilo)* secrecy.

misterioso, -sa *adj* mysterious.

mitad *f (parte)* half; *(centro, medio)* middle; **a ~ de camino** halfway there; **a ~ de precio** half-price; **en ~ de** in the middle of.

mitin *m* rally.

mito *m* myth.

mitología *f* mythology.

mitote *m (Amér: fam)* racket; **armar un ~** to make a racket.

mixto, -ta *adj (colegio, vestuario)* mixed; *(comisión, agrupación)* joint ♦ *m* ham and cheese toasted sandwich.

ml *(abrev de mililitro)* ml.

mm *(abrev de milímetro)* mm.

mobiliario *m* furniture.

mocasín *m* moccasin.

mochila *f* backpack.

mocho *m (fregona)* mop.

mochuelo *m* little owl.

moco *m* mucus; **tener ~s** to have a runny nose.

moda *f* fashion; **a la ~** fashionable; **estar de ~** to be fashionable; **pasado de ~** unfashionable.

modalidad *f (variante)* type; *(en deporte)* discipline.

modelo *m* model; *(vestido)* number ♦ *mf* model.

modem *(pl* **modems)** *m* modem.

modernismo *m (en arte)* Modernismo.

modernista *adj (en arte)* Modernista.

moderno, -na *adj* modern.

modestia *f* modesty.

modesto, -ta *adj* modest.

modificación *f* alteration.

modificar *vt* to alter.

modisto, -ta *m, f (sastre)* tailor *(f* dressmaker).

modo *m (manera)* way; *(en gramática)* mood; **de ~ que** in such a way that; **de ningún ~** in no way; **de todos ~s** in any case; **en cierto ~** in some ways; **~ de empleo** instructions *(pl)*.

moflete *m* chubby cheek.

mogollón *m (fam: cantidad)* loads *(pl)*.

montaje

moho m (hongo) mould.

mojado, -da adj (empapado) wet; (húmedo) damp.

mojar vt (empapar) to wet; (humedecer) to dampen; (pan) to dunk ❑ **mojarse** vpr to get wet.

molde m mould.

moldeado m (en peluquería) soft perm.

moldear vt (dar forma) to mould; (en peluquería) to give a soft perm to.

mole m (Amér) chilli sauce containing green tomatoes, spices and sometimes chocolate and peanuts.

molestar vt (incordiar) to annoy; (disgustar) to bother; (doler) to hurt ❑ **molestarse** vpr (enfadarse, ofenderse) to take offence; (darse trabajo) to bother.

molestia f (fastidio) nuisance; (dolor) discomfort.

molesto, -ta adj (fastidioso) annoying; **estar ~** (enfadado) to be annoyed.

molino m mill, **~ de viento** windmill.

molusco m mollusc.

momento m moment; (época) time; **hace un ~** a moment ago; **por el ~** for the moment; **al ~** straightaway; **de un ~ a otro** any minute now; **¡un ~!** just a moment!

momia f mummy.

mona: **mona de Pascua** f round sponge cake coated in chocolate with a chocolate egg on top, → **mono.**

monada f (fam) (cosa) lovely thing; (niño) little darling.

monaguillo m altar boy.

monarca m monarch.

monarquía f monarchy.

monasterio m monastery.

Moncloa f: **la ~** the Moncloa palace.

ⓘ LA MONCLOA

The Moncloa palace has been the official residence of the Spanish premier and the seat of the Spanish government since 1977. It is situated in the northwest of Madrid, near the Complutense university campus. It forms part of a complex of government buildings and has been rebuilt several times, most notably after the Spanish Civil War.

---

moneda f (pieza) coin; (divisa) currency; **~ de duro** five-peseta coin.

monedero m purse.

monitor, -ra m, f (persona) instructor ♦ m monitor.

monja f nun.

monje m monk.

mono, -na adj lovely ♦ m, f (animal) monkey ♦ m (con peto) dungarees (pl); (con mangas) overalls (pl); **¡qué ~!** how lovely!

monólogo m monologue.

monopatín m skateboard.

monopolio m monopoly.

monótono, -na adj monotonous.

monstruo m monster.

montacargas m inv goods lift (Br), freight elevator (Am).

montaje m (de una máquina) assembly; (de espectáculo) staging;

(de película) editing; *(estafa)* put-up job.

montaña *f* mountain; **~ rusa** roller coaster.

montañismo *m* mountaineering.

montañoso, -sa *adj* mountainous.

montar *vt (caballo, burro)* to ride; *(tienda de campaña)* to put up; *(máquina, instalación)* to assemble; *(negocio, tienda)* to set up; *(clara de huevo)* to beat; *(nata)* to whip; *(película)* to edit ♦ *vi (subir)*: **~ en** *(animal, bicicleta)* to get on; *(coche)* to get into; **~ en bicicleta** to ride a bicycle; **~ a caballo** to ride a horse.

monte *m (montaña)* mountain; *(bosque)* woodland.

montera *f* bullfighter's cap.

montón *m* heap; **un ~ de** *(fam)* loads of.

montura *f (de gafas)* frame; *(caballo, burro, etc)* mount.

monumental *adj (lugar, ciudad)* famous for its monuments; *(enorme)* monumental.

monumento *m* monument.

moño *m* bun.

MOPU *m (abrev de Ministerio de Obras Públicas y Urbanismo) Spanish ministry of public works and town planning.*

moqueta *f* (fitted) carpet.

mora *f* blackberry, → **moro**.

morado, -da *adj* purple ♦ *m (color)* purple; *(herida)* bruise.

moral *adj* moral ♦ *f* morality; *(ánimo)* morale.

moraleja *f* moral.

moralista *mf* moralist.

morcilla *f* = black pudding *(Br)*, = blood sausage *(Am)*.

mordaza *f* gag.

mordedura *f* bite.

morder *vt* to bite.

mordida *f (Amér: fam)* bribe.

mordisco *m* bite.

moreno, -na *adj (por el sol)* tanned; *(piel, pelo)* dark.

moribundo, -da *adj* dying.

morir *vi* to die ❑ **morirse** *vpr (fallecer)* to die; *(fig: tener deseo fuerte)* to be dying.

moro, -ra *adj* Moorish ♦ *m, f* Moor.

morocho, -cha *adj (Amér) (fam: robusto)* tough; *(moreno)* dark.

moroso, -sa *m, f* defaulter.

morralla *f (fig)* change.

morro *m (de animal)* snout; *(vulg: de persona)* thick lips *(pl)*; **por el ~** *(fam)* without asking.

morsa *f* walrus.

mortadela *f* Mortadella, *type of cold pork sausage.*

mortal *adj (vida)* mortal; *(herida, accidente)* fatal; *(fig: aburrido)* deadly.

mortero *m* mortar.

mosaico *m* mosaic.

mosca *f* fly; **por si las ~s** just in case.

moscatel *m* Muscatel.

mosquito *m* mosquito.

mostaza *f* mustard.

mostrador *m (en tienda)* counter; *(en bar)* bar; **"~ de facturación"** "check-in desk".

mostrar *vt* to show ❑ **mostrarse** *vpr*: **se mostró muy interesado** he expressed great interest.

motel m motel.

motivación f (motivo) motive.

motivar vt (causar) to cause.

motivo m (causa, razón) reason; (en música, pintura) motif; **con ~ de** (a causa de) because of; (con ocasión de) on the occasion of.

moto f motorbike, motorcycle; **~ acuática** jet-ski.

motocicleta f motorbike, motorcycle.

motociclismo m motorcycling.

motociclista mf motorcyclist.

motocross m inv motocross.

motor m engine, motor; **~ de arranque** starter.

motora f motorboat.

motorista mf motorcyclist.

mountain bike f mountain biking.

mousse f mousse; **~ de chocolate** chocolate mousse; **~ de limón** lemon mousse.

mover vt to move; (hacer funcionar) to drive. **□ moverse** vpr (fam: realizar gestiones) to make an effort.

movida f (fam) scene.

movido, -da adj (persona) restless.

móvil adj mobile ◆ m (motivo) motive.

movimiento m movement; (circulación) activity; (de cuenta corriente) transactions (pl).

mozárabe adj Mozarabic ◆ m Mozarabic style.

mozo, -za m, f young boy (f young girl) ◆ m (de hotel, estación) porter; (recluta) conscript; (Amér:

camarero) waiter.

mucamo, -ma m, f (Amér) servant.

muchacha f (fam: criada) maid, → muchacho.

muchachada f (Amér) crowd of young people.

muchacho, -cha m, f boy (f girl).

muchedumbre f crowd.

mucho, -cha adj a lot of ◆ pron a lot ◆ adv a lot; (indica comparación) much; **tengo ~ sueño** I'm very sleepy; **~ antes** long before; **~ gusto** (saludo) pleased to meet you; **como ~** at most; **¡con ~ gusto!** (encantado) with pleasure!; **vinieron ~s** a lot of people came; **ni ~ menos** by no means; **por ~ que** no matter how much.

mudanza f (de casa) move.

mudar vt (piel, plumas) to moult □ **mudarse** vpr (de ropa) to change; **~se (de casa)** to move (house).

mudéjar adj Mudejar ◆ m Mudejar style.

mudo, -da adj (que no habla) dumb; (película, letra) silent ◆ m, f mute.

mueble m piece of furniture; **los ~s** the furniture.

mueca f (gesto) face; (de dolor) grimace.

muela f (diente) tooth.

muelle m (de colchón) spring; (de puerto) dock.

muerte f (fallecimiento) death; (homicidio) murder.

muerto, -ta pp → morir ◆ adj dead ◆ m, f dead person; **~ de frío**

freezing; ~ **de hambre** starving.

muestra f *(de mercancía)* sample; *(señal)* sign; *(demostración)* demonstration; *(exposición)* show; *(prueba)* proof.

mugido m moo.

mugir vi to moo.

mujer f woman; *(esposa)* wife.

mulato, -ta m, f mulatto.

muleta f *(bastón)* crutch; *(de torero)* muleta, red cape hanging from a stick used to tease the bull.

mulo, -la m, f mule.

multa f fine.

multar vt to fine.

multicine m multiscreen cinema.

multinacional f multinational.

múltiple adj multiple ❏ **múltiples** adj pl *(numerosos)* numerous.

multiplicación f multiplication.

multiplicar vt to multiply ❏ **multiplicarse** vpr *(persona)* to do lots of things at the same time.

multitud f *(de personas)* crowd.

mundial adj world *(antes de s)*.

mundo m world; **un hombre de ~** a man of the world; **todo el ~** everyone.

munición f ammunition.

municipal adj municipal ◆ m, f local police officer who deals mainly with traffic offences.

municipio m *(territorio)* town; *(organismo)* town council.

muñeca f *(de la mano)* wrist, → **muñeco**.

muñeco, -ca m, f doll.

muñeira f type of music and dance from Galicia.

muñequera f wristband.

mural m mural.

muralla f wall.

murciélago m bat.

muro m wall.

musa f muse.

músculo m muscle.

museo m museum; ~ **de arte** art gallery.

musgo m moss.

música f music; ~ **ambiental** background music; ~ **clásica** classical music; ~ **pop** pop music, → **músico**.

musical adj musical.

músico, -ca m, f musician.

muslo m thigh; ~ **de pollo** drumstick.

musulmán, -ana adj & m, f Muslim.

mutilado, -da m, f cripple.

mutua f mutual benefit society.

muy adv very.

nabo m turnip.

nacer vi *(persona, animal)* to be born; *(vegetal)* to sprout; *(arroyo, río)* to rise.

nacimiento m *(de persona, animal)* birth; *(de vegetal)* sprouting; *(de río, arroyo)* source; *(belén)* Nativity scene.

nación f nation.

nacional *adj* national; *(vuelo, mercado)* domestic.

nacionalidad *f* nationality.

nada *pron (ninguna cosa)* nothing; *(en negativas)* anything ♦ *adv*: **no me gustó ~** I didn't like it at all; **de ~** *(respuesta a "gracias")* you're welcome; **~ más** nothing else; **~ más llegar** as soon as he arrived.

nadador, -ra *m, f* swimmer.

nadar *vi* to swim.

nadie *pron* nobody; **no se lo dije a ~** I didn't tell anybody.

nailon® ['nailon] *m* nylon.

naipe *m* (playing) card.

nalga *f* buttock □ **nalgas** *fpl* backside *(sg)*.

nana *f* lullaby.

naranja *adj inv, m & f* orange; **~ exprimida** freshly-squeezed orange juice.

naranjada *f* orange squash.

naranjo *m* orange tree.

narcotraficante *mf* drug trafficker.

narcotráfico *m* drug trafficking.

nariz *(pl -ces) f* nose.

narración *f (relato)* story.

narrador, -ra *m, f* narrator.

narrar *vt* to tell.

narrativa *f* narrative.

nata *f* cream; **~ montada** whipped cream.

natación *f* swimming.

natillas *fpl* custard *(sg)*.

nativo, -va *m, f* native.

natural *adj* natural; *(alimento)* fresh; **ser ~ de** to come from; **al ~** *(fruta)* in its own juice.

naturaleza *f* nature; **por ~** by nature.

naufragar *vi* to be wrecked.

naufragio *m* shipwreck.

náuseas *fpl* nausea *(sg)*; **tener ~** to feel sick.

náutico, -ca *adj (de navegación)* nautical; *(DEP)* water *(antes de s)*.

navaja *f (pequeña)* penknife; *(más grande)* jackknife; *(de afeitar)* razor; *(molusco)* razor clam.

naval *adj* naval.

nave *f (barco)* ship; *(de iglesia)* nave; *(en una fábrica)* plant; **~ espacial** spaceship.

navegable *adj* navigable.

navegar *vi (un barco)* to sail.

Navidad *f* Christmas (Day) □ **Navidades** *fpl* Christmas *(sg)*.

nazareno *m* man dressed in hood and tunic who takes part in Holy Week processions.

neblina *f* mist.

necedad *f (cualidad)* stupidity; *(dicho)* stupid thing.

necesario, -ria *adj* necessary.

neceser *m* toilet bag.

necesidad *f* need; **de primera ~** essential □ **necesidades** *fpl*: **hacer sus ~es** to answer the call of nature.

necesitar *vt* to need; **"se necesita ..."** "... wanted".

necio, -cia *adj* foolish.

nécora *f* fiddler crab.

necrológicas *fpl* obituaries.

negación *f (desmentido)* denial; *(negativa)* refusal.

negado, -da *adj* useless.

negar *vt* to deny □ **negarse** *vpr*: **~se (a)** to refuse (to).

negativa f (negativa) refusal; (desmentido) denial.

negativo, -va adj & m negative.

negociable adj negotiable.

negociación f negotiation.

negociador, -ra m, f negotiator.

negociar vt to negotiate ♦ vi (comerciar) to do business; ~ **en** to deal in.

negocio m business; (transacción) deal; (beneficio) good deal; **hacer ~s** to do business.

negro, -gra adj & m black ♦ m, f (persona) black man (f black woman).

nene, -na m, f (fam) baby.

nenúfar m water lily.

nervio m (de persona) nerve; (de planta) vein; (de carne) sinew; (vigor) energy ❑ **nervios** mpl (estado mental) nerves.

nerviosismo m nerves (pl).

nervioso, -sa adj nervous; (irritado) worked-up.

neto, -ta adj (peso, precio) net; (contorno, línea) clean.

neumático m tyre.

neurosis f inv neurosis.

neutral adj neutral.

neutro, -tra adj neutral.

nevada f snowfall.

nevado, -da adj snowy.

nevar v impers: **está nevando** it's snowing.

nevera f fridge (Br), icebox (Am).

ni conj: **no ... ~ ...** neither ... nor ...; **no es alto ~ bajo** he's neither tall nor short; **~ mañana ~ pasado** neither tomorrow nor the day

after; **~ un/una ...** not a single ...; **~ siquiera lo ha probado** she hasn't even tried it; **~ que** as if.
♦ adv not even; **está tan atareado que ~ come** he's so busy he doesn't even eat.

Nicaragua s Nicaragua.

nicaragüense adj & mf Nicaraguan.

nicho m niche.

nido m nest.

niebla f (densa) fog; (neblina) mist; **hay ~** it's foggy.

nieto, -ta m, f grandson (f granddaughter).

nieve f snow.

NIF m (abrev de número de identificación fiscal) = National Insurance number (Br), identification number for tax purposes.

ningún adj → ninguno.

ninguno, -na adj no ♦ pron (ni uno) none; (nadie) nobody; **no tengo ningún abrigo** I don't have a coat; **~ me gusta** I don't like any of them; **~ de los dos** neither of them.

niña f (del ojo) pupil, → niño.

niñera f nanny.

niñez f childhood.

niño, -ña m, f (crío) child, boy (f girl); (bebé) baby; **los ~s** the children.

níquel m nickel.

níspero m medlar.

nítido, -da adj clear.

nitrógeno m nitrogen.

nivel m level; **al ~ de** level with; **~ de vida** standard of living.

no adv (de negación) not; (en respuestas) no; **¿~ vienes?** aren't you coming?; **estamos de acuerdo ¿~?** so, we're agreed then, are we?; **~ sé** I don't know; **~ veo nada** I can't see anything; **¿cómo ~?** of course; **eso sí que ~** certainly not; **¡qué ~!** I said no!

nº (abrev de número) no.

noble adj (metal) precious; (honrado) noble ♦ mf noble.

nobleza f nobility.

noche f (más tarde) night; (atardecer) evening; **ayer por la ~** last night; **esta ~** tonight; **por la ~** at night; **las diez de la ~** ten o'clock at night.

Nochebuena f Christmas Eve.

nochero m (Amér) (vigilante nocturno) night watchman; (trasnochador) night owl; (mesita de noche) bedside table.

Nochevieja f New Year's Eve.

ⓘ NOCHEVIEJA

New Year's Eve traditions in Spain include the dancing of the "cotillón" to see out the old year and the eating of twelve grapes, one for each of the twelve chimes of midnight, which supposedly brings good luck for the coming year.

---

noción f notion ❑ **nociones** fpl: **tener nociones de** to have a smattering of.

nocivo, -va adj harmful.

noctámbulo, -la m, f night owl.

nocturno, -na adj (tren, vuelo, club) night (antes de s); (clase) evening (antes de s).

nogal m walnut.

nómada mf nomad.

nombrar vt (mencionar) to mention; (para un cargo) to appoint.

nombre m name; (en gramática) noun; **a ~ de** (cheque) on behalf of; (carta) addressed to; **~ de pila** first name; **~ y apellidos** full name.

nomeolvides m inv forget-me-not.

nómina f (lista de empleados) payroll; (sueldo) wages (pl).

nopal m (Amér) prickly pear.

nórdico, -ca adj (del norte) northern; (escandinavo) Nordic.

noroeste m north-east.

noria f (de feria) Ferris wheel, big wheel (Br).

norma f (principio) standard; (regla) rule.

normal adj normal.

normalmente adv normally.

noroeste m north-west.

norte m north.

Norteamérica s North America.

norteamericano, -na adj & m, f (North) American.

Noruega s Norway.

noruego, -ga adj, m, f Norwegian.

nos pron (complemento directo) us; (complemento indirecto) (to) us; (reflexivo) ourselves; (recíproco) each other; **~ vamos** we're going.

nosotros, -tras pron (sujeto) we; (complemento) us.

nostalgia f (de país, casa) homesickness.

nostálgico, -ca adj (de país, casa) homesick.

nota f note; (en educación) mark; (cuenta) bill; **tomar ~ de** to note down.

notable adj remarkable.

notar vt (darse cuenta de) to notice; (sentir) to feel.

notario, -ria m, f notary.

noticia f piece of news ◻ **noticias** fpl (telediario) news (sg).

novatada f (broma) joke (played on new arrivals).

novato, -ta m, f beginner.

novecientos, -tas núm nine hundred, → **seis**.

novedad f (cualidad) newness; (suceso) new development; (cosa) new thing; "**~es**" (discos) "new releases"; (ropa) "latest fashion" (sg).

novela f novel; **~ de aventuras** adventure story; **~ policíaca** detective story; **~ rosa** romantic novel.

novelesco, -ca adj fictional.

novelista mf novelist.

noveno, -na núm ninth, → **sexto**.

noventa núm ninety, → **seis**.

noviazgo m engagement.

noviembre m November, → **setiembre**.

novillada f bullfight with young bulls.

novillero m apprentice bull-fighter.

novillo, -lla m, f young bull (f young cow) (2-3 years old).

novio, -via m, f (prometido) fiancé (f fiancée); (amigo) boyfriend (f girlfriend) ◻ **novios** mpl (recién casados) newly weds.

nubarrón m storm cloud.

nube f cloud.

nublado, -da adj cloudy.

nublarse v impers: **se está nublando** it's clouding over.

nubosidad f cloudiness.

nuboso, -sa adj cloudy.

nuca f nape.

nuclear adj nuclear.

núcleo m (parte central) centre.

nudillos mpl knuckles.

nudismo m nudism.

nudista mf nudist.

nudo m (de cuerda, hilo) knot; (de comunicaciones) major junction; (en argumento) crux.

nuera f daughter-in-law.

nuestro, -tra adj conj ◆ pron: **el ~, la nuestra** ours; **lo ~** (lo que nos gusta) our thing; **un amigo ~** a friend of ours.

nuevamente adv again.

Nueva Zelanda s New Zealand.

nueve núm nine, → **seis**.

nuevo, -va adj new; **de ~** again.

nuez (pl -ces) f (fruto seco en general) nut; (de nogal) walnut; (del cuello) Adam's apple.

nulidad f (anulación) nullity; (persona) useless idiot.

nulo, -la adj (sin valor legal) null and void; (inepto) useless.

núm. (abrev de número) no.

numerado, -da adj numbered.

número m number; (de lotería) ticket; (de una publicación) issue; (talla) size; **~ de teléfono** telephone number.

numeroso, -sa adj numerous.

numismática f coin-collecting.

nunca adv never; (en negativas) ever.

nupcial adj wedding (antes de s).

nupcias fpl wedding (sg).

nutria f otter.

nutrición f nutrition.

nutritivo, -va adj nutritious.

ñandú m rhea.

ñato, -ta adj (Amér) snub.

ñoñería f insipidness.

ñoño, -ña adj (remilgado) squeamish, (quejica) whining; (soso) dull.

ñoqui m gnocchi (pl).

ñudo: al ñudo adv (Amér) in vain.

o conj or; **~ sea** in other words.

oasis m inv oasis.

obedecer vt to obey ❑ **obedecer a** v + prep (ser motivado por) to be due to.

obediencia f obedience.

obediente adj obedient.

obesidad f obesity.

obeso, -sa adj obese.

obispo m bishop.

objeción f objection.

objetividad f objectivity.

objetivo, -va adj objective ◆ m (finalidad) objective; (blanco) target; (lente) lens.

objeto m object; (finalidad) purpose; **con el ~ de** with the aim of; **"~s perdidos"** "lost property".

obligación f (deber) obligation; (de una empresa) bond.

obligar vt to force ❑ **obligarse a** v + prep (comprometerse a) to undertake to.

obligatorio, -ria adj compulsory.

obra f (realización) work; (en literatura) book; (en teatro) play, (en música) opus; (edificio en construcción) building site; **~ de caridad** charity; **~ (de teatro)** play ❑ **obras** fpl (reformas) alterations; **"obras"** (en carretera) "roadworks".

obrador m workshop.

obrero, -ra m, f worker.

obsequiar vt: **~ a alguien con algo** to present sb with sthg.

obsequio m gift.

observación f observation

observador, -ra adj observant.

observar vt to observe; (darse cuenta de) to notice.

observatorio m observatory.

obsesión f obsession.

obsesionar vt to obsess ❑ **obsesionarse** vpr to be obsessed.

obstáculo m obstacle.

obstante: no obstante conj nevertheless.

obstinado, -da adj (persistente) persistent; (terco) obstinate.

obstruir vt to obstruct ❑ **obstruirse** vpr (agujero, cañería) to get blocked (up).

obtener vt to get.

obvio, -via adj obvious.

oca f (ave) goose; (juego) board game similar to snakes and ladders.

ocasión f (momento determinado) moment; (vez) occasion; (oportunidad) chance; **de ~** (rebajado) bargain (antes de s).

ocasional adj (eventual) occasional; (casual) accidental.

ocaso m (de sol) sunset; (fig: decadencia) decline.

occidental adj western.

occidente m west ❑ Occidente m the West.

océano m ocean.

ochenta núm eighty, → **seis**.

ocho núm eight, → **seis**.

ochocientos, -tas núm eight hundred, → **seis**.

ocio m leisure.

ocioso, -sa adj (inactivo) idle.

ocre adj inv ochre.

octavo, -va núm eighth, → **sexto**.

octubre m October, → **setiembre**.

oculista mf ophthalmologist.

ocultar vt (esconder) to hide; (callar) to cover up.

oculto, -ta adj hidden.

ocupación f occupation, (oficio) job.

ocupado, -da adj (plaza, asiento) taken; (aparcamiento) full; (lavabo) engaged; (atareado) busy; (invadido) occupied; **"ocupado"** (taxi) sign indicating that a taxi is not for hire.

ocupar vt to occupy; (habitar) to live in; (mesa) to sit at; (en tiempo)

to take up; (cargo, posición, etc) to hold; (dar empleo) to provide work for ❑ **ocuparse de** v + prep (encargarse de) to deal with; (persona) to look after.

ocurrir vi to happen ❑ **ocurrirse** vpr: **no se me ocurre la respuesta** I can't think of the answer.

odiar vt to hate.

odio m hatred.

oeste m west.

ofensiva f offensive.

oferta f (propuesta) offer; (en precio) bargain; (surtido) range.

oficial adj official ♦ m, f (militar) officer.

oficina f office; **~ de correos** post office; **~ de objetos perdidos** lost property office; **~ de turismo** tourist office.

oficinista mf office worker.

oficio m (profesión) trade; (empleo) job; (misa) service.

ofrecer vt to offer; (mostrar) to present ❑ **ofrecerse** vpr (ser voluntario) to volunteer.

oftalmología f ophthalmology.

ogro m ogre.

oído m (sentido) hearing; (órgano) ear; **hablar al ~ a alguien** to have a word in sb's ear.

oír vt (ruido, música, etc) to hear; (atender) to listen to; **¡oiga, por favor!** excuse me!

ojal m buttonhole.

ojalá interj if only!

ojeras fpl bags under the eyes.

ojo m eye; (de cerradura) keyhole ♦ interj watch out!; **~ de buey** porthole; **a ~** (fig) roughly.

OK [o'kej] *interj* OK.

okupa *mf (fam)* squatter.

ola *f* wave; **~ de calor** heatwave; **~ de frío** cold spell.

ole *interj* bravo!

oleaje *m* swell.

óleo *m* oil (painting).

oler *vt & vi* to smell; **~ bien** to smell good; **~ mal** to smell bad ❑ **olerse** *vpr* to sense.

olfato *m (sentido)* sense of smell; *(astucia)* nose.

olimpíadas *fpl* Olympics.

olímpico, -ca *adj* Olympic.

oliva *f* olive.

olivo *m* olive tree.

olla *f* pot, **~ a presión** pressure cooker.

olmo *m* elm (tree).

olor *m* smell.

olvidar *vt* to forget; *(dejarse)* to leave ❑ **olvidarse de** *v + prep (dejarse)* to leave.

olvido *m (en memoria)* forgetting; *(descuido)* oversight.

ombligo *m (de vientre)* navel; *(fig: centro)* heart.

omitir *vt* to omit.

once *núm* eleven, → **seis**.

ONCE *f Spanish association for the blind.*

---

i **ONCE**

The ONCE is an independent organization which was originally set up to help the blind, although it now covers other disabled people as well. One of its main aims is to provide work for its members, and to this end it runs a daily national lottery, tickets for which are sold by the blind. The lottery is the ONCE's main source of income.

---

onda *f* wave.

ondulado, -da *adj* wavy.

ONU *f* UN.

opaco, -ca *adj* opaque.

opción *f* option; **tener ~ a** to be eligible for.

ópera *f* opera.

operación *f* operation; *(negocio)* transaction; **~ retorno/salida** *police operation to assist travel of holidaymakers to/from city homes, minimizing congestion and maximizing road safety.*

operadora *f (de teléfonos)* operator.

operar *vt (enfermo)* to operate on; *(realizar)* to bring about ❑ **operarse** *vpr (del hígado, etc)* to have an operation.

operario, -ria *m, f* worker.

opinar *vt* to think ◆ *vi* to give one's opinion.

opinión *f* opinion; **la ~ pública** public opinion.

oponer *vt (obstáculo, resistencia)* to use against; *(razón, argumento, etc)* to put forward ❑ **oponerse** *vpr (contrarios, fuerzas)* to be opposed; **oponerse a** *v + prep (ser contrario a)* to oppose; *(negarse a)* to refuse to.

oportunidad *f* opportunity; **"~es"** "bargains".

oportuno, -na *adj (adecuado)* appropriate; *(propicio)* timely;

oposición f (impedimento) opposition; (resistencia) resistance; **la ~** the opposition ❏ **oposiciones** fpl (para empleo) public entrance examinations.

oprimir vt (botón) to press; (reprimir) to oppress.

optar: optar a v + prep (aspirar a) to go for ❏ **optar por** v + prep: **~ por algo** to choose sthg; **~ por hacer algo** to choose to do sthg.

optativo, -va adj optional.

óptica f (ciencia) optics; (establecimiento) optician's (shop).

optimismo m optimism.

optimista m optimistic.

óptimo, -ma superl → **bueno**.

opuesto, -ta pp → **oponer** ♦ adj (contrario) conflicting; **~ a** contrary to.

oración f (rezo) prayer; (frase) sentence.

orador, -ra m, f speaker.

oral adj oral.

órale interj (Amér) that's right!

orangután m orangutan.

órbita f (de astro) orbit; (de ojo) eye socket; (ámbito) sphere.

orca f killer whale.

orden[1] m order; **en ~** (bien colocado) tidy; (en regla) in order.

orden[2] f order.

ordenación f (colocación) arrangement; (de sacerdote) ordination.

ordenado, -da adj (en orden) tidy.

ordenador m computer.

ordenar vt (colocar) to arrange; (armario, habitación) to tidy up;

(mandar) to order; (sacerdote) to ordain.

ordeñar vt to milk.

ordinario, -ria adj (habitual) ordinary; (basto, grosero) coarse.

orégano m oregano.

oreja f ear; (de sillón) wing.

orgánica, -ca adj organic.

organillo m barrel organ.

organismo m (de ser vivo) body; (institución) organization.

organización f organization.

organizador, -ra m, f organizer.

organizar vt to organize; (negocio, empresa) to set up.

órgano m organ.

orgullo m pride.

orgulloso, -sa adj proud; **~ de** proud of.

oriental adj (del este) eastern; (del Lejano Oriente) oriental ♦ mf oriental.

orientar vt (guiar) to direct; **~ algo hacia algo** to place sthg facing sthg.

oriente m (punto cardinal) east; (viento) east wind ❏ **Oriente** m: **el Oriente** the East.

orificio m hole.

origen m origin; (motivo) cause; (ascendencia) birth.

original adj original; (extraño) eccentric.

originario, -ria adj (país, ciudad) native; (inicial) original; **ser ~ de** to come from.

orilla f (de mar, lago) shore; (de río) bank; (borde) edge.

orillarse vpr (Amér) to move to one side.

orina f urine.

orinal m chamberpot.

orinar vi to urinate.

oro m (metal) gold; (riqueza) riches (pl) ❏ **oros** mpl (de la baraja) suit of Spanish cards bearing gold coins.

orquesta f (de música) orchestra; (lugar) orchestra pit.

orquestar vt to orchestrate.

orquídea f orchid.

ortiga f (stinging) nettle.

ortodoxo, -xa adj orthodox.

oruga f caterpillar.

os pron (complemento directo) you; (complemento indirecto) (to) you; (reflexivo) yourselves; (recíproco) each other.

oscilar vi (moverse) to swing; ~ (entre) (variar) to fluctuate (between).

oscuridad f (falta de luz) darkness; (confusión) obscurity.

oscuro, -ra adj dark; (confuso) obscure; (nublado) overcast; **a oscuras** in the dark.

oso, osa m, f bear; ~ **hormiguero** anteater.

osobuco m osso bucco.

ostra f oyster ❏ **ostras** interj (fam) wow!

OTAN f NATO.

otoño m autumn (Br), fall (Am).

otorrino, -na m, f (fam) ear, nose and throat specialist.

otorrinolaringólogo, -ga m, f ear, nose and throat specialist.

otro, otra adj another (sg), other (pl) ♦ pron (otra cosa) another (sg), other (pl); (otra persona) someone else; **el** ~ the other one; **los** ~**s** the others; ~ **vaso** another

glass; ~**s dos vasos** another two glasses; **el** ~ **día** the other day; **la otra tarde** the other evening.

ovalado, -da adj oval.

ovario m ovary.

oveja f sheep.

ovni ['oβni] m UFO.

óxido m (herrumbre) rust.

oxígeno m oxygen.

oyente mf listener.

ozono m ozone.

p. (abrev de paseo) Av.

pabellón m (edificio) pavilion; (de hospital) block; (tienda de campaña) bell tent; (de oreja) outer ear.

pacer vi to graze.

pachamama f (Amér) (mother) earth.

pacharán m liqueur made from brandy and sloes.

paciencia f patience; **perder la** ~ to lose one's patience; **tener** ~ to be patient.

paciente adj & mf patient.

pacificación f pacification.

pacífico, -ca adj peaceful ❏ **Pacífico** m: **el Pacífico** the Pacific.

pacifista mf pacifist.

pack m pack.

pacto m (entre personas) agreement.

padecer vt (enfermedad) to suf-

fer from; *(soportar)* to endure ◆ *vi*
to suffer; **padece del hígado** she
has liver trouble.

padrastro *m (pariente)* stepfather; *(pellejo)* hangnail.

padre *m* father ◆ *adj (Amér: fam:
estupendo)* brilliant ❏ **padres** *mpl
(de familia)* parents.

padrino *m (de boda)* best man;
(de bautizo) godfather ❏ **padrinos**
mpl godparents.

padrísimo *adj (Amér: fam)* brilliant.

padrote *m (Amér)* pimp.

paella *f* paella.

pág. *(abrev de página)* p.

paga *f (sueldo)* wages *(pl)*.

pagadero, -ra *adj:* ~ **a 90 días**
payable within 90 days.

pagano, -na *m, f* pagan.

pagar *vt (cuenta, deuda, etc)* to
pay; *(estudios, gastos, error)* to pay
for; *(corresponder)* to repay ◆ *vi* to
pay; **"pague en caja antes de retirar su vehículo"** "please pay before
leaving" *(sign in car park)*.

página *f* page.

pago *m* payment; *(recompensa)*
reward.

paila *f (Amér) (sartén)* frying pan;
(charco pequeño) small pool.

país *m* country.

paisaje *m* landscape; *(vista panorámica)* view.

paisano, -na *m, f (persona no
militar)* civilian; *(de país)* compatriot; *(de ciudad)* person from the
same city.

Países Bajos *mpl:* **los** ~ the
Netherlands.

País Vasco *m:* **el** ~ the Basque

country.

paja *f* straw; *(parte desechable)*
padding.

pajarita *f (corbata)* bow tie; ~
de papel paper bird.

pájaro *m* bird.

paje *m* page.

pala *f (herramienta)* spade; *(de
ping-pong)* bat; *(de cocina)* slice; *(de
remo, hacha)* blade.

palabra *f* word; **dar la** ~ **a
alguien** to give sb the floor; **de** ~
(hablando) by word of mouth ❏
palabras *fpl (discurso)* words.

palacio *m* palace; ~ **municipal**
(Amér) town hall.

ℹ️ PALACIO DE LA MONEDA

The Palacio de la Moneda is the
official residence of the Chilean
president and the seat of the Chilean
government. It is here that the president holds Cabinet meetings and
receives State visits.

ℹ️ PALACIO DE LA ZARZUELA

This is the current residence of
the Spanish monarch and is
situated in the El Pardo hills to the
northwest of Madrid. It was built
during the reign of Philip IV, who
used it as a country retreat and a
hunting lodge. A neoclassical building which consists of a single floor
built around an interior courtyard, it
was rebuilt in the 18th century and
redecorated in the rococo style.

---

paladar *m* palate.

paladear *vt* to savour.

palanca *f* lever; ~ **de cambio** gear lever.

palangana *f* (*para fregar*) washing-up bowl; (*para lavarse*) wash bowl.

palco *m* box (*at theatre*).

paletilla *f* shoulder blade; ~ **de cordero** shoulder of lamb.

pálido, -da *adj* pale.

palillo *m* (*para dientes*) toothpick; (*para tambor*) drumstick.

paliza *f* (*zurra, derrota*) beating; (*esfuerzo*) hard grind.

palma *f* (*de mano, palmera*) palm; (*hoja de palmera*) palm leaf ❑ **palmas** (*pl*) applause (*sg*); **dar ~s** to applaud.

palmada *f* (*golpe*) pat; (*ruido*) clap.

palmera *f* (*árbol*) palm (tree).

palmitos *mpl* (*de cangrejo*) crab sticks; ~ **a la vinagreta** crab sticks in vinegar.

palo *m* (*de madera*) stick; (*de golf*) club; (*de portería*) post; (*de tienda de campaña*) pole; (*golpe*) blow (with a stick); (*de barco*) mast; (*en naipes*) suit.

paloma *f* dove, pigeon.

palomar *m* dovecote.

palomitas *fpl* popcorn (*sg*).

palpitar *vi* (*corazón*) to beat; (*sentimiento*) to shine through

palta *f* (*Amér*) avocado.

pamela *f* sun hat.

pampa *f* pampas (*pl*).

pan *m* (*alimento*) bread; (*hogaza*) loaf; ~ **dulce** (*Amer*) (*sweet*) pastry; ~ **integral** wholemeal bread; ~ **de**

molde sliced bread; ~ **de muerto** (*Amér*) sweet pastry eaten on All Saints' Day; ~ **rallado** breadcrumbs (*pl*); ~ **con tomate** bread rubbed with tomato and oil; ~ **tostado** toast.

panadería *f* bakery.

panadero, -ra *m, f* baker.

panal *m* honeycomb.

Panamá *s* Panama.

panameño, -ña *adj & m, f* Panamanian.

pancarta *f* banner.

pandereta *f* tambourine.

pandilla *f* gang.

panecillo *m* (bread) roll.

panel *m* panel.

panera *f* (*cesta*) bread basket; (*caja*) bread bin.

pánico *m* panic.

panorama *m* (*paisaje*) panorama; (*situación*) overall state.

panorámica *f* panorama.

panorámico, -ca *adj* panoramic.

pantaletas *fpl* (*Amér*) knickers.

pantalla *f* (*de cine, televisión*) screen; (*de lámpara*) lampshade.

pantalones *mpl* trousers; ~ **cortos** shorts; ~ **vaqueros** jeans.

pantano *m* (*embalse*) reservoir; (*ciénaga*) marsh.

pantanoso, -sa *adj* marshy.

pantera *f* panther.

pantimedias *fpl* (*Amér*) tights.

pantorrilla *f* calf.

pantys *mpl* tights.

pañal *m* nappy (*Br*), diaper (*Am*); ~**es higiénicos** disposable nappies.

paño *m* cloth; ~ **de cocina** tea towel.

pañuelo m (para limpiarse) handkerchief; (de adorno) scarf.

Papa m: el ~ the Pope.

papá m (fam) dad; ~ **grande** (Amér) grandad ❑ **papás** mpl (fam: padres) parents.

papachador, -ra adj (Amér) pampering.

papachar vt (Amér) to spoil.

papagayo m parrot.

papalote m (Amér) kite.

papel m paper; (hoja) sheet of paper; (función, de actor) role; ~ **higiénico** toilet paper; ~ **pintado** wallpaper ❑ **papeles** mpl (documentos) papers.

papeleo m red tape.

papelera f wastepaper basket.

papelería f stationer's (shop).

papeleta f (de votación) ballot paper; (de examen) slip of paper with university exam results; (fig: asunto difícil) tricky thing.

paperas fpl mumps.

papilla f (alimento) baby food.

paquete m (postal) parcel; (de cigarrillos, klínex, etc) pack; ~ **turístico** package tour.

Paquistán m: el ~ Pakistan.

paquistaní adj & mf Pakistani.

par adj (número) even ◆ m (de zapatos, guantes, etc) pair; (de veces) couple; **abierto de ~ en ~** wide open; **sin ~** matchless; **un ~ de ...** a couple of ...

para prep 1. (finalidad) for; **esta agua no es buena ~ beber** this water isn't fit for drinking; **lo he comprado ~ ti** I bought it for you; **te lo repetiré ~ que te enteres** I'll repeat it so you understand.

2. (motivación) (in order) to; **lo he hecho ~ agradarte** I did it to please you.

3. (dirección) towards; **ir ~ casa** to head (for) home; **salir ~ el aeropuerto** to leave for the airport.

4. (tiempo) for; **lo tendré acabado ~ mañana** I'll have it finished for tomorrow.

5. (comparación) considering; **está muy delgado ~ lo que come** he's very thin considering how much he eats.

6. (inminencia, propósito): **la comida está lista ~ servir** the meal is ready to be served.

parabólica f satellite dish.

parabrisas m inv windscreen (Br), windshield (Am).

paracaídas m inv parachute.

parachoques m inv bumper (Br), fender (Am).

parada f stop; ~ **de autobús** bus stop; ~ **de taxis** taxi rank, → **parado**.

parado, -da adj (coche, máquina, etc) stationary; (desempleado) unemployed; (sin iniciativa) unenterprising ◆ m, f unemployed person.

paradoja f paradox.

paradójico, -ca adj paradoxical.

parador m (mesón) roadside inn; ~ **nacional** state-owned luxury hotel.

---

i **PARADOR NACIONAL**

A "parador nacional" is a building of artistic or historic interest which has been converted into a luxury four-star hotel and is run by the Spanish state. Although some may be found in cities, they are usually situated in the countryside, in places of outstanding natural beauty.

---

paraguas *m inv* umbrella.

Paraguay *s* Paraguay.

paraguayo, -ya *adj & m, f* Paraguayan.

paraíso *m* paradise.

paraje *m* spot.

paralelas *fpl* parallel bars.

paralelo, -la *adj & m* parallel.

parálisis *f inv* paralysis.

paralítico, -ca *m, f* paralytic.

paralizar *vt* to paralyze.

parapente *m* parasailing.

parar *vt* to stop; *(Amér: levantar)* to lift ◆ *vi (detenerse)* to stop; *(hacer huelga)* to go on strike; **~ de hacer algo** to stop doing sthg; **"para en todas las estaciones"** "stopping at all stations"; **sin ~** non-stop ❑ **pararse** *vpr (detenerse)* to stop; *(Amér: ponerse de pie)* to stand up.

pararrayos *m inv* lightning conductor.

parasol *m* parasol.

parchís *m inv* ludo.

parcial *adj* partial; *(injusto)* biased ◆ *m (examen)* end-of-term examination.

pardo, -da *adj* dun-coloured.

parecer *m (opinión)* opinion ◆ *v copulativo* to look, to seem ◆ *v impers:* **me parece que ...** I think (that) ...; **parece que va a llover** it looks like it's going to rain; **¿qué te parece?** what do you think?; **de**

buen ~ good-looking ❑ **parecerse** *vpr* to look alike; **~se a** to resemble.

parecido, -da *adj* similar ◆ *m* resemblance.

pared *f (muro)* wall.

pareja *f (conjunto de dos)* pair; *(de casados, novios)* couple; *(compañero)* partner.

parentesco *m* relationship.

paréntesis *m inv (signo de puntuación)* bracket; *(interrupción)* break; **entre ~** in brackets.

pareo *m* wraparound skirt.

pariente, -ta *m, f* relative.

parking ['parkin] *m* car park.

parlamentario, -ria *m, f* member of parliament.

parlamento *m (asamblea legislativa)* parliament; *(discurso)* speech.

parlanchín, -ina *adj* talkative.

paro *m (desempleo)* unemployment; *(parada)* stoppage; **(huelga)** strike; **estar en ~** to be unemployed.

parpadear *vi (ojos)* to blink.

párpado *m* eyelid.

parque *m (jardín)* park; *(de niños)* playpen; *(de automóviles)* fleet; **~ acuático** waterpark; **~ de atracciones** amusement park; **~ de bomberos** fire station; **~ infantil** children's playground; **~ nacional** national park; **~ zoológico** zoo.

---

i **PARQUE NACIONAL**

S panish national parks are areas of natural beauty that are protected by the government. Although admission is free, there are strict regulations governing what visitors may do, to minimize the damage they may cause to the surroundings. The best-known national parks are the Coto de Doñana in Huelva, the Ordesa national park in Huesca and the Delta del Ebro park in Tarragona.

---

parqué *m* parquet.

parquear *vt (Amér)* to park.

parquímetro *m* parking meter.

parra *f* vine.

párrafo *m* paragraph.

parrilla *f (para cocinar)* grill; *(Amér: baca)* roof rack; **a la ~** grilled.

parrillada *f* mixed grill; **~ de carne** selection of grilled meats; **~ de pescado** selection of grilled fish.

parroquia *f (iglesia)* parish church; *(conjunto de fieles)* parish; *(fig: clientela)* clientele.

parte *f* part; *(bando, lado, cara)* side ♦ *m* report; *(de)* to report sthg; **de ~ de** *(en nombre de)* on behalf of; **¿de ~ de quién?** *(en el teléfono)* who's calling?; **en alguna ~** somewhere; **en otra ~** somewhere else; **en ○** partly; **en todas ~s** everywhere; **~ meteorológico** weather forecast; **por otra ~ (además)** what is more.

participación *f (colaboración)* participation; *(de boda, bautizo)* notice; *(en lotería)* share.

participar *vi:* **~ (en)** to participate (in) ♦ *vt:* **~ algo a alguien** to notify sb of sthg.

partícula *f* particle.

particular *adj (privado)* private; *(propio)* particular; *(especial)* unusual; **en ~** in particular.

partida *f (marcha)* departure; *(en el juego)* game; *(certificado)* certificate; *(de género, mercancías)* consignment.

partidario, -ria *m, f* supporter; **ser ~ de** to be in favour of.

partidista *adj* partisan.

partido *m (en política)* party; *(en deporte)* game; **sacar ~ de** to make the most of; **~ de ida** away leg; **~ de vuelta** home leg.

partir *vt (dividir)* to divide; *(romper)* to break; *(nuez)* to crack; *(repartir)* to share ♦ *vi (ponerse en camino)* to set off; **a ~ de** from □ **partir de** *v + prep (tomar como base)* to start from.

partitura *f* score.

parto *m* birth.

parvulario *m* nursery school.

pasa *f* raisin.

pasable *adj* passable.

pasada *f (con trapo)* wipe; *(de pintura, barniz)* coat; *(en labores de punto)* row; **de ~** in passing.

pasado, -da *adj (semana, mes, etc)* last; *(viejo)* old; *(costumbre)* old-fashioned; *(alimento)* off, bad ♦ *m* past; **el año ~** last year; **bien ~** *(carne)* well-done; **de moda** old-fashioned; **~ mañana** the day after tomorrow.

pasaje *m (de avión, barco)* ticket; *(calle)* alley; *(conjunto de pasajeros)* passengers *(pl)*; *(de novela, ópera)* passage; **"~ particular"** "pedestrianized zone".

pasajero, -ra *adj* passing ◆ *m, f* passenger; "**~s sin equipaje**" "passengers with hand luggage only".

pasamanos *m inv (barandilla)* handrail.

pasaporte *m* passport.

pasar *vt* 1. *(deslizar, filtrar)* to pass; **me pasó la mano por el pelo** she ran her hand through my hair; **~ algo por** to pass sthg through.
2. *(cruzar)* to cross; **~ la calle** to cross the road.
3. *(acercar, hacer llegar)* to pass; **¿me pasas la sal?** would you pass me the salt?
4. *(contagiar)*: **me has pasado la tos** you've given me your cough.
5. *(trasladar)*: **~ algo a** to move sthg to.
6. *(llevar adentro)* to show in; **nos pasó al salón** he showed us into the living room.
7. *(admitir)* to accept.
8. *(rebasar)* to go through; **no pases el semáforo en rojo** don't go through a red light.
9. *(sobrepasar)*: **ya ha pasado los veinticinco** he's over twenty-five now.
10. *(tiempo)* to spend; **pasó dos años en Roma** she spent two years in Rome.
11. *(padecer)* to suffer.
12. *(adelantar)* to overtake.
13. *(aprobar)* to pass.
14. *(revisar)* to go over.
15. *(en cine)* to show.
16. *(en locuciones)*: **~lo bien/mal** to have a good/bad time; **~ lista** to call the register; **~ visita** to see one's patients.
◆ *vi* 1. *(ir, circular)* to go; **el autobús**
pasa por mi casa the bus goes past my house; **el Manzanares pasa por Madrid** the Manzanares goes through Madrid; **~ de largo** to go by.
2. *(entrar)* to go in; "**no ~**" "no entry"; **¡pase!** come in!; "**pasen por caja**" "please pay at the till".
3. *(poder entrar)* to get through; **déjame más sitio, que no paso** move up, I can't get through.
4. *(ir un momento)* to pop in; **pasaré por tu casa** I'll drop by (your place).
5. *(suceder)* to happen; **¿qué (te) pasa?** what's the matter (with you?); **¿qué pasa aquí?** what's going on here?; **pase lo que pase** whatever happens.
6. *(terminarse)* to be over; **cuando pase el verano** when the summer's over.
7. *(transcurrir)* to go by; **el tiempo pasa muy deprisa** time passes very quickly.
8. *(cambiar de acción, tema)*: **~ a** to move on to.
9. *(servir)* to be all right; **puede ~** it'll do.
10. *(fam: prescindir)*: **paso de política** I'm not into politics.
❏ **pasarse** *vpr (acabarse)* to pass, *(comida)* to go off; *(flores)* to fade; *(fam: propasarse)* to go over the top; *(tiempo)* to spend; *(omitir)* to miss out; **se me pasó decírtelo** I forgot to mention it to you; **no se le pasa nada** she doesn't miss a thing.

pasarela *f (de barco)* gangway; *(para modelos)* catwalk.

pasatiempo *m* pastime.

Pascua *f (en primavera)* Easter ❏

Pascuas *fpl (Navidad)* Christmas *(sg)*.

pase *m* pass.

pasear *vt* to take for a walk ◆ *vi* to go for a walk ❑ **pasearse** *vpr* to walk.

paseíllo *m opening procession of bullfighters.*

paseo *m (caminata)* walk; *(calle ancha)* avenue; *(distancia corta)* short walk; **dar un ~** to go for a walk; **ir de ~** to go for a walk; **~ marítimo** promenade.

pasillo *m* corridor.

pasión *f* passion.

pasiva *f (en gramática)* passive voice.

pasividad *f* passivity.

pasivo, -va *adj* passive ◆ *m (deudas)* debts *(pl).*

paso *m* step; *(acción de pasar)* passing; *(manera de andar)* walk; *(ritmo)* pace; *(en montaña)* pass; **de ~** in passing; **estar de ~** to be passing through; **a dos ~s** *(muy cerca)* round the corner; **~ de cebra** zebra crossing; **~ a nivel** level crossing; **~ de peatones** pedestrian crossing; **~ subterráneo** subway *(Br)*, underpass *(Am).*

pasodoble *m* paso doble.

pasta *f (macarrones, espagueti, etc)* pasta; *(para pastelería)* pastry; *(pastelillo)* cake; *(fam: dinero)* dough; **~ de dientes** toothpaste.

pastel *m (tarta)* cake; *(salado)* pie; *(en pintura)* pastel.

pastelería *f (establecimiento)* cake shop; *(bollos)* pastries *(pl).*

pastelero, -ra *m, f* cake shop owner.

pastilla *f (medicamento)* pill; *(de chocolate)* bar.

pastor, -ra *m, f (de ganado)* shepherd *(f shepherdess)* ◆ *m (sacerdote)* minister.

pastoreo *m* shepherding.

pata *f (pierna, de mueble)* leg; *(pie)* foot; *(de perro, gato)* paw ◆ *m (Amér)* mate; **~ negra** *type of top-quality cured ham;* **estar ~s arriba** *(fig)* to be upside-down; **meter la ~** to put one's foot in it; **tener mala ~** *(fig)* to be unlucky, → **pato.**

patada *f* kick.

patata *f* potato; **~s fritas** *(de sartén)* chips *(Br)*, French fries *(Am)*; *(de bolsa)* crisps *(Br)*, chips *(Am).*

paté *m* paté.

patente *adj* obvious ◆ *f* patent.

paterno, -na *adj* paternal.

patilla *f (de barba)* sideboard *(Br)*, sideburn *(Am)*; *(de gafas)* arm.

patín *m (de ruedas)* skate; *(de hielo)* ice skate; **~ (de pedales)** pedal boat.

patinaje *m* skating; **~ sobre hielo** ice skating.

patinar *vi (con patines)* to skate; *(resbalar)* to skid; *(fam: equivocarse)* to put one's foot in it.

patinazo *m (resbalón)* skid; *(fam: equivocación)* blunder.

patinete *m* scooter.

patio *m (de casa)* patio; *(de escuela)* playground; **~ de butacas** stalls *(pl)*; **~ interior** courtyard.

pato, -ta *m, f* duck; **~ a la naranja** duck à l'orange.

patoso, -sa *adj* clumsy.

patria *f* native country.

patriota *mf* patriot.

patriótico, -ca *adj* patriotic.

patrocinador, -ra *m, f* sponsor.

patrón, -ona *m, f (de pensión)* landlord *(f* landlady); *(jefe)* boss; *(santo)* patron saint ♦ *m (de barco)* skipper; *(en costura)* pattern; *(fig: modelo)* standard.

patronal *f (de empresa)* management.

patrono, -na *m, f (jefe)* boss; *(protector)* patron *(f* patroness).

patrulla *f* patrol; ~ **urbana** vigilante group.

pausa *f* break.

pauta *f* guideline.

pavimento *m* road surface.

pavo, -va *m, f* turkey; ~ **real** peacock.

payaso, -sa *m, f* clown.

paz *(pl* -ces) *f* peace; **dejar en** ~ to leave in peace; **hacer las paces** to make it up; **que en** ~ **descanse** may he/she rest in peace.

pazo *m* Galician country house.

PC *m (abrev de personal computer)* PC.

PD *(abrev de posdata)* PS.

peaje *m* toll.

peatón *m* pedestrian.

peatonal *adj* pedestrian *(antes de s).*

peca *f* freckle.

pecado, -ra *m, f* sinner.

pecar *vi* to sin.

pecera *f (acuario)* fish tank.

pecho *m (en anatomía)* chest; *(de la mujer)* breast.

pechuga *f* breast *(meat).*

pecoso, -sa *adj* freckly.

peculiar *adj (propio)* typical; *(extraño)* peculiar.

pedagogía *f* education.

pedagogo, -ga *m, f (profesor)* teacher.

pedal *m* pedal.

pedalear *vi* to pedal.

pedante *adj* pedantic.

pedazo *m* piece; **hacer** ~s to break to pieces.

pedestal *m* pedestal.

pediatra *mf* pediatrician.

pedido *m* order.

pedir *vt (rogar)* to ask for; *(poner precio)* to ask; *(en restaurante, bar)* to order; *(exigir)* to demand ♦ *vi (mendigar)* to beg; ~ **a alguien que haga algo** to ask sb to do sthg; ~ **disculpas** to apologize; ~ **un crédito** to ask for a loan; ~ **prestado algo** to borrow sthg.

pedo *m (vulg: ventosidad)* fart.

pedregoso, -sa *adj* stony.

pedrisco *m* hail.

pega *f (pegamento)* glue; *(fam: inconveniente)* hitch; **poner** ~s to find problems.

pegajoso, -sa *adj (cosa)* sticky; *(fig: persona)* clinging.

pegamento *m* glue.

pegar *vi (sol)* to beat down; *(armonizar)* to go (together) ♦ *vt (adherir, unir)* to stick; *(cartel)* to put up; *(golpear)* to hit; *(contagiar)* to give, to pass on; *(grito, salto)* to give; ~ **algo a algo** *(arrimar)* to put sthg up against sthg ❑ **pegarse** *vpr (chocar)* to hit o.s.; *(adherirse)* to stick; *(a una persona)* to attach o.s.

pegatina f sticker.

peinado m hairstyle.

peinar vt to comb ❑ **peinarse** vpr to comb one's hair.

peine m comb.

peineta f ornamental comb.

p.ej. (abrev de por ejemplo) e.g.

peladilla f sugared almond.

pelar vt (patatas, fruta) to peel; (ave) to pluck ❑ **pelarse** vpr: **~se de frío** to be freezing cold.

peldaño m step.

pelea f fight.

pelear vi to fight ❑ **pelearse** vpr to fight.

peletería f (tienda) furrier's (shop).

pelícano m pelican.

película f film.

peligro m (riesgo) risk; (amenaza) danger; **correr ~** to be in danger.

peligroso, -sa adj dangerous.

pelirrojo, -ja adj red-haired.

pellejo m skin.

pellizcar vt to pinch.

pellizco m pinch.

pelma mf (fam) pain.

pelo m hair; (de animal) coat; (fig: muy poco) tiny bit; **con ~s y señales** in minute detail; **por un ~** by the skin of one's teeth; **tomar el ~ a alguien** to pull sb's leg; **~ rizado** curly hair.

pelota f ball ♦ mf (fam) crawler; **jugar a la ~** to play ball; **hacer la ~** to suck up; **~ (vasca)** (juego) pelota.

pelotari mf pelota player.

pelotón m (de gente) crowd; (de soldados) squad.

pelotudo, -da adj (Amér: fam)

thick.

peluca f wig.

peludo, -da adj hairy.

peluquería f (local) hairdresser's (salon); (oficio) hairdressing; **"~-estética"** "beauty salon".

peluquero, -ra m, f hairdresser.

pelvis f inv pelvis.

pena f (lástima) pity; (tristeza) sadness; (desgracia) problem; (castigo) punishment; (condena) sentence; (Amér: vergüenza) embarrassment; **me da ~** (lástima) I feel sorry for him; (vergüenza) I'm embarrassed about it; **a duras ~s** with great difficulty; **vale la ~** it's worth it; **¡qué ~!** what a pity!

penalti m penalty.

pendiente adj (por hacer) pending ♦ m earring ♦ f slope.

péndulo m pendulum.

pene m penis.

penetrar: **penetrar en** v + prep (filtrarse por) to penetrate; (entrar en) to go into; (perforar) to pierce.

penicilina f penicillin.

península f peninsula.

peninsular adj (de la península española) of/relating to mainland Spain.

penitencia f penance; **hacer ~** to do penance.

penitente m (en procesión) person in Holy Week procession wearing penitent's clothing.

penoso, -sa adj (lamentable) distressing; (dificultoso) laborious; (Amér: vergonzoso) shy.

pensador, -ra *m, f* thinker.

pensamiento *m* thought.

pensar *vi* to think ♦ *vt (meditar)* to think about; *(opinar)* to think; *(idear)* to think up; ~ **hacer algo** to intend to do sthg; ~ **en algo** to think about sthg; ~ **en un número** to think of a number.

pensativo, -va *adj* pensive.

pensión *f (casa de huéspedes)* = guesthouse; *(paga)* pension; **media** ~ half board; ~ **completa** full board.

peña *f (piedra)* rock; *(acantilado)* cliff; *(de amigos)* group.

peñasco *m* large rock.

peón *m (obrero)* labourer; *(en ajedrez)* pawn.

peonza *f* (spinning) top.

peor *adj & adv* worse ♦ *interj* too bad!; **el/la** ~ the worst; **el que lo hizo** ~ the one who did it worst.

pepino *m* cucumber.

pepita *f (de fruta)* pip; *(de metal)* nugget.

pepito *m (f. mini) grilled meat sandwich.*

pequeño, -ña *adj* small, little; *(cantidad)* low; *(más joven)* little.

pera *f* pear.

peral *m* pear tree.

percebe *m* barnacle.

percha *f* (coat) hanger.

perchero *m (de pared)* clothes' rail; *(de pie)* coat stand.

percibir *vt (sentir, notar)* to notice; *(cobrar)* to receive.

perdedor, -ra *m, f* loser.

perder *vt* to lose; *(tiempo)* to waste; *(tren, oportunidad)* to miss ♦ *vi (en competición)* to lose; *(empeo-*

rar) to get worse; **echar a** ~ *(fam)* to spoil ❑ **perderse** *vpr (extraviarse)* to get lost.

pérdida *f* loss.

perdigón *m* pellet.

perdiz *(pl* -**ces**) *f* partridge.

perdón *m* forgiveness ♦ *interj* sorry!

perdonar *vt (persona)* to forgive; ~ **algo a alguien** *(obligación, castigo, deuda)* to let sb off sthg; *(ofensa)* to forgive sb for sthg.

peregrinación *f (romería)* pilgrimage.

peregrino, -na *m, f* pilgrim.

perejil *m* parsley.

pereza *f (gandulería)* laziness; *(lentitud)* sluggishness.

perezoso, -sa *adj* lazy.

perfección *f* perfection.

perfeccionista *mf* perfectionist.

perfectamente *adv (sobradamente)* perfectly; *(muy bien)* fine

perfecto, -ta *adj* perfect.

perfil *m (contorno)* outline; *(de cara)* profile; **de** ~ in profile.

perforación *f (MED)* puncture.

perforar *vt* to make a hole in.

perfumar *vt* to perfume ❑ **perfumarse** *vpr* to put on perfume.

perfume *m* perfume.

perfumería *f* perfumery; "~-cosmética" "beauty products".

pergamino *m* parchment.

pérgola *f* pergola.

periferia *f (de ciudad)* outskirts *(pl).*

periódico, -ca *adj* periodic ♦ *m* newspaper.

periodismo *m* journalism.

periodista *mf* journalist.

período *m* period.

periquito *m* parakeet.

peritaje *m* expert's report.

perito, -ta *m, f (experto)* expert; *(ingeniero técnico)* technician.

perjudicar *vt* to harm.

perjuicio *m* harm.

perla *f* pearl; **me va de ~s** it's just what I need.

permanecer *vi (seguir)* to remain; **~ (en)** *(quedarse en)* to stay (in).

permanencia *f* continued stay.

permanente *adj* permanent ◆ *f* perm.

permiso *m (autorización)* permission; *(documento)* permit; *(de soldado)* leave; **~ de conducir** driving licence *(Br)*, driver's license *(Am)*.

permitir *vt* to allow.

pernoctar *vi* to spend the night.

pero *conj* but; **~ ¡no lo has visto?** you mean you haven't seen it?

perpendicular *adj* perpendicular ◆ *f* perpendicular line; **~ a** at right angles to.

perpetuo, -tua *adj* perpetual.

perplejo, -ja *adj* bewildered.

perra *f (rabieta)* tantrum; *(dinero)* penny, → **perro**.

perrito *m:* **~ caliente** hot dog.

perro, -rra *m, f* dog *(f* bitch).

persa *adj & mf* Persian.

persecución *f (seguimiento)* pursuit.

perseguir *vt* to pursue.

persiana *f* blind.

persona *f* person; **cuatro ~s** four people; **en ~** in person.

personaje *m (celebridad)* celebrity; *(en cine, teatro)* character.

personal *adj* personal ◆ *m (empleados)* staff; *(fam: gente)* people *(pl)*; **"sólo ~ autorizado"** "staff only".

personalidad *f* personality.

perspectiva *f (vista, panorama)* view; *(aspecto)* perspective; *(esperanzas, porvenir)* prospect.

persuadir *vt* to persuade.

persuasión *f* persuasion.

pertenecer *vi:* **~ a** to belong to; *(corresponder a)* to belong in.

perteneciente *adj:* **~ a** belonging to.

pertenencias *fpl (objetos personales)* belongings.

pértiga *f (deporte)* pole vault.

Perú *m:* **(el) ~** Peru.

peruano, -na *adj & m, f* Peruvian.

pesa *f* weight ❑ **pesas** *fpl (en gimnasia)* weights.

pesadez *f (molestia)* drag; *(sensación)* heaviness.

pesadilla *f* nightmare.

pesado, -da *adj (carga, sueño)* heavy; *(broma)* bad; *(agotador)* tiring; *(aburrido)* boring; *(persona)* annoying.

pesadumbre *f* sorrow.

pésame *m:* **dar el ~** to offer one's condolences.

pesar *m (pena)* grief ◆ *vt* to weigh ◆ *vi (tener peso)* to weigh; *(ser pesado)* to be heavy; *(influir)* to carry weight; **me pesa tener que**

hacerlo it grieves me to have to do it; **a ~ de** in spite of.

pesca f (actividad) fishing; (captura) catch.

pescadería f fishmonger's (shop).

pescadero, -ra m, f fishmonger.

pescadilla f whiting.

pescado m fish.

pescador, -ra m, f fisherman (f fisherwoman).

pescar vt (peces) to fish for; (fam: pillar) to catch.

pesebre m (establo) manger; (belén) crib.

posero m (Amer) small bus used in towns.

peseta f peseta.

pesimismo m pessimism.

pesimista adj pessimistic.

pésimo, -ma superl → **malo** ♦ adj awful.

peso m weight; (moneda) peso.

pesquero, -ra adj fishing ♦ m (barco) fishing boat.

pestañas fpl eyelashes.

peste f (mal olor) stink; (enfermedad) plague.

pesticida m pesticide.

pestillo m (cerrojo) bolt; (en verjas) latch.

petaca f (para bebidas) hip flask.

pétalo m petal.

petanca f boules, form of bowls using metal balls, played in public areas.

petardo m firecracker.

petición f (solicitud) request.

peto m (vestidura) bib.

petróleo m oil.

petrolero, -ra adj oil (antes de s) ♦ m (barco) oil tanker.

petrolífero, -ra adj oil (antes de s).

petulancia f (comentario) opinionated remark.

petulante adj opinionated.

petunia f petunia.

peúco m bootee.

pez m (pl -ces) m fish; **~ espada** swordfish.

pezón m (de mujer) nipple.

pezuña f hoof.

pianista mf pianist.

piano m piano; **~ bar** piano bar.

piar vi to tweet.

pibe, -ba m, f (Amér: fam) boy (f girl).

picador, -ra m, f (torero) picador.

picadora f mincer, → **picador**.

picadura f (de mosquito, serpiente) bite; (de avispa, ortiga) sting; (tabaco picado) (loose) tobacco.

picante adj (comida) spicy; (broma, chiste) saucy.

picantería f (Amér) stall selling spicy food.

picar vt (suj: mosquito, serpiente, pez) to bite; (suj: avispa, ortiga) to sting; (al toro) to goad; (piedra) to hack at; (carne) to mince; (verdura) to chop; (billete) to clip ♦ vi (comer un poco) to nibble; (sal, pimienta, pimiento) to be hot; (la piel) to itch; (sol) to burn ❏ **picarse** vpr (vino) to go sour; (muela) to decay; (fam: enfadarse) to get upset.

pícaro, -ra adj (astuto) crafty.

picas fpl (palo de la baraja)

spades.
pichincha f (Amér) bargain.
pichón m (young) pigeon.
picnic m picnic.
pico m (de ave) beak; (de montaña) peak; (herramienta) pickaxe; .**cincuenta y ~** fifty-odd; **a las tres y ~** just after three o'clock.
picor m itch.
picoso, -sa adj (Amér) spicy.
pie m foot; (apoyo) stand; **a ~** on foot; **en ~** (válido) valid; **estar de ~** to be standing up; **no hacer ~** (en el agua) to be out of one's depth; **~s de cerdo** (pig's) trotters.
piedad f pity.
piedra f stone; (granizo) hailstone; **~ preciosa** precious stone.
piel f (de persona, animal, fruta) skin; (cuero) leather; (pelo) fur.
pierna f leg; **estirar las ~s** to stretch one's legs; **~ de cordero** leg of lamb.
pieza f piece; (en mecánica) part; (en pesca, caza) specimen; **~ de recambio** spare part.
pijama m pyjamas (pl).
pila f (de casete, radio, etc) battery; (montón) pile; (fregadero) sink; **~ alcalina** alkaline battery.
pilar m pillar.
píldora f pill.
pillar vt (agarrar) to grab hold of; (atropellar) to hit; (dedos, ropa, delincuente) to catch; **~ una insolación** (fam) to get sunstroke; **~ un resfriado** (fam) to catch a cold.
pilotar vt (avión) to pilot; (barco) to steer.
piloto mf (de avión) pilot; (de barco) navigator ♦ m (luz de coche)

tail light; **~ automático** automatic pilot.
pimentón m paprika.
pimienta f pepper (for seasoning); **a la ~ verde** in a green peppercorn sauce.
pimiento m (fruto) pepper (vegetable); **~ del piquillo** type of hot red pepper eaten baked.
pin m pin (badge).
pincel m paintbrush.
pinchar vt (con aguja, pinchos) to prick; (rueda) to puncture; (globo, balón) to burst; (provocar) to annoy; (fam: con inyección) to jab ❑ **pincharse** vpr (fam: drogarse) to shoot up.
pinchazo m (de rueda) puncture; (en la piel) prick.
pinche adj (Amér: fam) damned.
pincho m (punta) point; (tapa) aperitif on a stick, or a small sandwich; **~ moruno** shish kebab.
pinga f (Amér: vulg) cock.
ping-pong® [pin'pon] m table tennis.
pingüino m penguin.
pino m pine tree; **los Pinos** official residence of the Mexican president.

---

i **LOS PINOS**

Los Pinos is the official residence of the Mexican president and the seat of the Mexican government. It is here that the president holds Cabinet meetings and receives State visits.

pintada f graffiti.

pintado, -da adj (coloreado) coloured; (maquillado) made-up; "recién ~" "wet paint".

pintalabios m inv lipstick.

pintar vt to paint ❑ **pintarse** vpr to make o.s. up.

pintor, -ra m, f painter.

pintoresco, -ca adj picturesque.

pintura f (arte, cuadro) painting; (sustancia) paint.

pinza f (de tender ropa) peg; (pliegue) pleat ❑ **pinzas** fpl (para depilar) tweezers; (para utilizar tongs) (de cangrejo) pincers.

piña f (ananás) pineapple; (del pino) pine cone; (fam: de gente) close-knit group; **~ en almíbar** pineapple in syrup; **~ natural** fresh pineapple.

piñata f pot of sweets.

PIÑATA

This is an earthenware pot filled with sweets and small gifts which blindfolded children break open with a stick at birthday parties. In Latin America, a papier-mâché doll is used instead of a jar.

---

piñón m (semilla) pine nut.

piojo m louse.

pipa f (de fumar) pipe; (semilla) seed ❑ **pipas** fpl (de girasol) sunflower seeds coated in salt.

pipí m (fam) wee.

pique m (fam: enfado) bad feeling; **irse a ~** (barco) to sink.

piragua f canoe.

piragüismo m canoeing.

pirámide f pyramid.

piraña f piranha.

pirata adj & m pirate.

piratear vt (programa informático) to hack.

Pirineos mpl: **los ~** the Pyrenees.

pirómano, -na m, f pyromaniac.

piropo m flirtatious comment.

pirueta f pirouette.

pisada f (huella) footprint; (ruido) footstep.

pisar vt to step on.

piscina f swimming pool.

Piscis m Pisces.

pisco m (Amér) strong liquor made from grapes, popular in Chile and Peru; **~ sour** (Amer) cocktail with "pisco".

piso m (vivienda) flat (Br), apartment (Am); (suelo, planta) floor; (Amér: influencia) influence; **~ bajo** ground floor.

pisotón m stamp (on sb's foot).

pista f track; (indicio) clue; **~ de aterrizaje** runway; **~ de baile** dance floor; **~ de esquí** ski slope; **~ de tenis** tennis court.

pistacho m pistachio.

pistola f pistol.

pistolero m gunman.

pitar vi (tocar el pito) to blow a whistle; (tocar la bocina) to toot one's horn; **salir pitando** (fig) to leave in a hurry.

pitillera f cigarette case.

pitillo m cigarette.

pito m whistle.

pitón m (del toro) tip of the horn; (de botijo, jarra) spout; (serpiente) python.

pizarra f (encerado) blackboard; (roca) slate.

pizza ['pitsa] f pizza.

pizzería [pitse'ria] f pizzeria.

placa f (lámina) plate; (inscripción) plaque; (insignia) badge.

placer m pleasure; **es un ~** it's a pleasure.

plan m (proyecto, intención) plan; (programa) programme; hacer ~es to make plans; ~ **de estudios** syllabus.

plancha f (para planchar) iron; (para cocinar) grill; (de metal) sheet; (fam: error) boob; **a la ~** grilled.

planchar vt to iron.

planeta m planet.

plano, -na adj flat ♦ m (mapa) plan; (nivel) level; (en cine, fotografía) shot; (superficie) plane.

planta f (vegetal, fábrica) plant; (del pie) sole; (piso) floor; ~ **baja** ground floor; **segunda ~** second floor.

plantar vt (planta, terreno) to plant; (poste) to put in; (tienda de campaña) to pitch; (persona) to stand up ❏ **plantarse** vpr (ponerse) to plant o.s.; (en naipes) to stick.

planteamiento m (exposición) raising; (perspectiva) approach.

plantear vt (plan, proyecto) to set out; (problema, cuestión) to raise ❏ **plantearse** vpr to think about.

plantilla f (personal) staff; (de zapato) insole; (patrón) template.

plástico, -ca adj & m plastic; **de ~** plastic.

plastificar vt to plasticize.

plastilina® f Plasticine®.

plata f silver; **de ~** silver.

plataforma f (tarima) platform; (del tren, autobús, etc) standing room.

plátano m (fruta) banana; (árbol platanáceo) plane tree.

platea f stalls (pl).

plateresco, -ca adj plateresque.

plática f (Amér) chat.

platicar vi (Amér) to have a chat.

platillo m (plato pequeño) small plate; (de taza) saucer; (de balanza) pan ❏ **platillos** mpl (en música) cymbals.

plato m (recipiente) plate; (comida) dish; (parte de una comida) course; ~ **combinado** single-course meal usually of meat or fish with chips and vegetables; ~ **del día** today's special; ~ **principal** main course; ~**s caseros** home-made food (sg); **primer ~** starter.

platudo, -da adj (Amér: fam) loaded.

playa f beach; **ir a la ~ de vacaciones** to go on holiday to the seaside; ~ **de estacionamiento** (Amér) car park.

play-back ['pleiβak] m: **hacer ~** to mime (the lyrics).

playeras fpl (de deporte) tennis shoes; (para la playa) canvas shoes.

plaza f (en una población) square; (sitio, espacio) space; (puesto, vacante) job; (asiento) seat; (mercado) market; ~ **de toros** bullring.

|

plazo m (de tiempo) period; (pago) instalment; **hay 20 días de ~ the** deadline is in 20 days; **a corto ~** in the short term; **a largo ~** in the long term; **a ~s** in instalments.

plegable adj (silla) folding.

pleito m (en un juicio) lawsuit.

plenamente adv completely.

plenitud f (apogeo) peak.

pleno, -na adj complete ◆ m plenary (session); **en ~ día** in broad daylight; **en ~ invierno** in the middle of the winter.

pliegue m (en tela) pleat.

plomería f (Amér) plumbing.

plomero m (Amér) plumber.

plomo m (metal) lead; (bala) bullet; (fam: persona pesada) pain; (fusible) fuse.

pluma f (de ave) feather; (para escribir) pen; **~ estilográfica** fountain pen.

plumaje m (de ave) plumage; (adorno) plume.

plumero m (para el polvo) feather duster; (estuche) pencil case; (adorno) plume.

plumier (pl plumiers) m pencil case.

plumilla f nib.

plumón m down.

plural adj & m plural.

pluralidad f (diversidad) diversity.

plusmarca f record.

plusmarquista mf record holder.

p.m. (abrev de post meridiem) p.m.

PM (abrev de policía militar) MP.

p.n. (abrev de peso neto) nt. wt.

p.o. (abrev de por orden) by order.

población f (habitantes) population; (ciudad) town; (más grande) city; (pueblo) village.

poblado, -da adj populated ◆ m (ciudad) town; (pueblo) village.

poblar vt (establecerse en) to settle.

pobre adj poor ◆ mf (mendigo) beggar.

pobreza f (miseria) poverty; (escasez) scarcity.

pochismo m (Amér: fam) English spoken by Californian Mexicans.

pocho, -cha adj (Amér) (fam) (mejicano) Mexican American; (rechoncho) plump.

pocilga f pigsty.

poco, -ca adj & pron (en singular) little, not much; (en plural) few, not many ◆ adv (con escasez) not much; (tiempo corto) not long; **tengo ~ dinero** I don't have much money; **unos ~s días** a few days; **tengo ~** I don't have many; **como ~** he doesn't eat much; **dentro de ~** shortly; **hace ~** not long ago; **~ a ~** bit by bit; **por ~** almost; **un ~ (de)** a bit (of).

poda f (acto) pruning.

podar vt to prune.

poder m 1. (facultad, gobierno) power; **~ adquisitivo** purchasing power; **estar en el ~** to be in power.

2. (posesión): **estar en ~ de alguien** to be in sb's hands.

◆ v aux 1. (tener facultad para) can, to be able to; **puedo hacerlo** I can do it.

2. (tener permiso para) can, to be allowed to; **¿se puede fumar aquí?** can I smoke here?; **no puedo salir**

poderoso   214

por la noche I'm not allowed to go out at night.
3. *(ser capaz moralmente de)* can; **no podemos abandonarle** we can't abandon him.
4. *(tener posibilidad)* may, can; **puedo ir en barco o en avión** I can go by boat or by plane; **podías haber cogido el tren** you could have caught the train.
5. *(expresa queja, reproche)*: **¡hubiera podido invitarnos!** she could have invited us!
6. *(en locuciones)*: **es tonto a o hasta más no ~** he's as stupid as can be; **no ~ más** *(estar lleno)* to be full (up); *(estar enfadado)* to have had enough; *(estar cansado)* to be too tired to carry on; **¿se puede?** may I come in?
◆ *v impers (ser posible)* may; **puede ser que llueva** it may rain; **no puede ser verdad** it can't be true; **¿vendrás mañana? - puede** will you come tomorrow? - I may do.
◆ *vt (tener más fuerza que)* to be stronger than.
❏ **poder con** *v + prep (enfermedad, rival)* to be able to overcome; *(tarea, problema)* to be able to cope with; **no puedo con los celos** I can't stand jealousy.

poderoso, -sa *adj* powerful.
podio *m* podium.
podrá *v → poder*.
podría *v → poder*.
podrido, -da *pp → pudrir* ◆ *adj* rotten.
poema *m* poem.
poesía *f (poema)* poem; *(arte)* poetry.
poeta *mf* poet.

poético, -ca *adj* poetic.
polar *adj* polar.
polaroid® *f* Polaroid®.
polea *f* pulley.
polémica *f* controversy.
polémico, -ca *adj* controversial.
polen *m* pollen.
polichinela *m (títere)* marionette.
policía *f (cuerpo)* police ◆ *mf* policeman *(f* policewoman)*; ~ **municipal o urbana** local police who deal mainly with traffic offences and administrative matters; ~ **nacional** national police.
policíaco, -ca *adj* police *(antes de s)*.
polideportivo *m* sports centre.
poliéster *m* polyester.
políglota *mf* polyglot.
polígono *m*: ~ **industrial** industrial estate.
politécnica *f* university faculty devoted to technical subjects.
política *f (arte de gobernar)* politics; *(modo de gobernar)* policy, → **político**.
político, -ca *m, f* politician ◆ *adj* political; **hermano ~** brother-in-law.
póliza *f (de seguros)* policy; *(sello)* stamp on a document proving payment of tax.
pollera *f (Amér)* loose skirt worn by Peruvian and Bolivian Indians.
pollito *m* chick.
pollo *m* chicken; ~ **al ajillo** chicken pieces fried in garlic until crunchy; ~ **asado** roast chicken; ~ **a l'ast**

chicken roasted on a spit; **~ al curry** chicken curry; **~ a la plancha** grilled chicken.

polluelo *m* chick.

polo *m (helado)* ice lolly; *(de una pila)* pole; *(jersey)* polo shirt; *(juego)* polo.

pololo, -la *m, f (Amér: persona impertinente)* cheeky person ♦ *m (Amér: galán)* ladies' man.

Polonia *s* Poland.

Polo Norte *m*: **el ~ the** North Pole.

Polo Sur *m*: **el ~ the** South Pole.

polución *f* pollution.

polvera *f* powder compact.

polvo *m* dust ❑ **polvos** *mpl (en cosmética, medicina)* powder *(sg)*; **~s de talco** talcum powder *(sg)*.

pólvora *f* gunpowder.

polvoriento, -ta *adj* dusty.

polvorón *m* powdery sweet made of flour, sugar and butter.

pomada *f* ointment.

pomelo *m* grapefruit.

pomo *m* knob.

pómulo *m* cheekbone.

ponchar *vt (Amér)* to puncture ❑ **poncharse** *vpr (Amér)* to get a puncture

poner *vt* **1.** *(colocar, añadir)* to put; **pon el libro en el estante** put the book on the shelf; **pon más azúcar al café** put some more sugar in the coffee. **2.** *(vestir)*: **~ algo** to put sthg on. **3.** *(contribuir, invertir)* to put in; **puso su capital en el negocio** he put his capital into the business. **4.** *(hacer estar de cierta manera)*: **me**

has puesto colorado you've made me blush; **lo puso de mal humor** it put him in a bad mood. **5.** *(radio, televisión, luz, etc)* to switch on; *(gas, instalación)* to put in. **6.** *(oponer)*: **~ inconvenientes** to raise objections. **7.** *(telegrama, fax)* to send; *(conferencia)* to make; **¿me pones con Juan?** can you put me through to Juan? **8.** *(asignar, imponer)* to fix; **le han puesto una multa** they've fined him; **¿qué nombre le han puesto?** what have they called her? **9.** *(aplicar facultad)* to put; **no pone ningún interés** he shows no interest. **10.** *(montar)* to set up; *(casa)* to do up, *(tienda de campaña)* to pitch; **han puesto una tienda nueva** they've opened a new shop. **11.** *(en cine, teatro, televisión)* to show; **¿qué ponen en la tele?** what's on (the) telly? **12.** *(escribir, decir)* to say; **no sé qué pone ahí** I don't know what that says. **13.** *(suponer)* to suppose; **pongamos que sucedió así** (let's) suppose that's what happened. **14.** *(en locuciones)*: **~ en marcha** *(iniciar)* to start. ♦ *vi (ave)* to lay (eggs). ❑ **ponerse** *vpr (ropa, gafas, maquillaje)* to put on; *(estar de cierta manera)* to become; *(astro)* to set; **ponte aquí** stand here; **se puso rojo** he went red; **~se bien** *(de salud)* to get better; **~se malo** to fall ill.

pongo *v* **~ poner.**

poniente *m (oeste)* west.

popa f stern.

popular adj (del pueblo) of the people; (arte, música) folk; (famoso) popular.

popularidad f popularity.

póquer m poker.

por prep 1. (causa) because of; **se enfadó ~ tu comportamiento** she got angry because of your behaviour.
2. (finalidad) (in order) to; **lo hizo ~ complacerte** he did it to please you; **lo compré ~ ti** I bought it for you; **luchar ~ algo** to fight for sthg.
3. (medio, modo, agente) by; **~ mensajero/fax** by courier/fax; **~ escrito** in writing; **el récord fue batido ~ el atleta** the record was broken by the athlete.
4. (tiempo): **~ la mañana/tarde** in the morning/afternoon; **~ la noche** at night; **~ unos días** for a few days; **creo que la boda será ~ abril** I think the wedding will be some time in April.
5. (aproximadamente en): **está ~ ahí** it's round there somewhere; **¿~ dónde vive?** whereabouts does she live?
6. (a través de) through; **pasar ~ la aduana** to go through customs; **entramos en Francia ~ Irún** we entered France via Irún.
7. (a cambio, en lugar de) for; **cambió el coche ~ una moto** he exchanged his car for a motorbike.
8. (distribución) per; **cien pesetas ~ unidad** a hundred pesetas each; **20 km ~ hora** 20 km an hour.
9. (en matemáticas) times; **dos ~ dos igual a cuatro** two times two is four.

porcelana f (material) porce-lain; (vasija) piece of porcelain.

porcentaje m percentage.

porche m porch.

porción f (cantidad) portion; (parte) share.

porno adj (fam) porno.

pornografía f pornography.

pornográfico, -ca adj porno-graphic.

porque conj because.

porqué m reason.

porrón m wine jar with a long spout for drinking.

portada f (de libro) title page; (de revista) cover.

portador, -ra m, f carrier; **al ~** (cheque) to the bearer.

portaequipajes m inv boot (Br), trunk (Am).

portafolios m inv (carpeta) file.

portal m (vestíbulo) hallway; (entrada) main entrance.

portalámparas m inv socket.

portarse vpr to behave; **~ bien/mal** to behave well/badly.

portátil adj portable.

portavoz (pl -ces) mf spokes-man (f spokeswoman).

portazo m slam; **dar un ~** to slam the door.

portería f (conserjería) porter's office; (en deporte) goal.

portero, -ra m, f (conserje) porter; (en deporte) goalkeeper; **~ electrónico** entryphone.

Portugal s Portugal.

portugués, -esa adj & m, f Portuguese.

porvenir m future.

posada f (alojamiento) accommodation; (hostal) guesthouse.

posarse vpr (ave) to perch; (insecto) to settle.

posavasos m inv coaster.

posdata f postscript.

pose f pose.

poseedor, -ra m, f (dueño) owner; (de cargo, récord) holder.

poseer vt (ser dueño de) to own; (tener) to have, to possess.

posesión f possession.

posesivo, -va adj & m possessive.

posibilidad f possibility.

posible adj possible.

posición f position; (social) status; (económica) situation.

positivamente adv positively.

positivo, -va adj positive ◆ m (en fotografía) print.

posmoderno, -na adj postmodern.

poso m sediment.

postal f postcard.

poste m post.

póster m poster.

posterior adj (en tiempo, orden) subsequent; (en espacio) back; ~ a after.

postre m dessert; ~ de la casa chef's special dessert.

póstumo, -ma adj posthumous.

postura f position.

potable adj (agua) drinkable; (fam: aceptable) palatable.

potaje m stew; ~ de garbanzos chickpea stew.

potencia f power.

potenciar vt to foster.

potrillo m (Amér) large glass.

potro m (caballo) colt; (en gimnasia) vaulting horse.

pozo m (de agua) well.

p.p. (abrev de por poder) p.p.

práctica f practice; (de un deporte) playing ❑ **prácticas** fpl (de conducir) lessons.

practicante mf (en religión) practising member; ~ (**ambulatorio**) medical assistant.

practicar vt (ejercer) to practise; (deporte) to play ◆ vt to practise.

práctico, -ca adj practical.

pradera f large meadow, prairie.

prado m meadow.

pral. abrev = principal.

precario, -ria adj precarious.

precaución f (medida) precaution; (prudencia) care.

precintado, -da adj sealed.

precio m price; ¿qué ~ tiene? how much is it?; ~ fijo fixed price; ~ de venta al público retail price; ~s de coste warehouse prices.

preciosidad f (cosa preciosa) beautiful thing.

precioso, -sa adj (bonito) lovely; (valioso) precious.

precipicio m precipice.

precipitación f (imprudencia, prisa) haste; (lluvia) rainfall.

precipitado, -da adj hasty.

precipitarse vpr (actuar sin pensar) to act rashly.

precisamente adv precisely.

precisar vt (especificar) to specify; (necesitar) to need.

preciso, -sa adj (detallado, exacto) precise; (imprescindible) necessary.

precoz *adj (persona)* precocious.
predicar *vt* to preach.
predilecto, -ta *adj* favourite.
predominar *vi* to prevail.
preeminente *adj* preeminent.
preescolar *adj* pre-school.
preferencia *f* preference; *(en carretera)* right of way.
preferible *adj* preferable.
preferir *vt* to prefer.
prefijo *m (en gramática)* prefix; *(de teléfono)* dialling code.
pregón *m (de fiesta)* opening speech.
pregonar *vt (noticia)* to announce; *(secreto)* to spread about.
pregonero *m* town crier.
pregunta *f* question; **hacer una ~** to ask a question.
preguntar *vt* to ask ❑ **preguntar por** *v + prep* to ask after; **preguntarse** *vpr* to wonder.
prehistórico, -ca *adj* prehistoric.
prejuicio *m* prejudice.
prematuro, -ra *adj* premature.
premeditación *f* premeditation.
premiar *vt* to award a prize to.
premio *m* prize; *(recompensa)* reward; **~ gordo** first prize.
premisa *f* premise.
prenatal *adj* antenatal.
prenda *f (vestido)* item of clothing; *(garantía)* pledge.
prensa *f* press; **la ~** the press.
preocupación *f* worry.
preocupado, -da *adj*

worried.
preocupar *vt* to worry ❑ **preocuparse de** *v + prep (encargarse de)* to take care of; **preocuparse por** *v + prep* to worry about.
preparación *f (arreglo, disposición)* preparation; *(formación)* training.
preparar *vt (disponer)* to prepare; *(maletas)* to pack; *(estudiar)* to study for ❑ **prepararse** *vpr (arreglarse)* to get ready.
preparativos *mpl* preparations.
preparatoria *f (Amér)* pre-university course in Latin America.

| *i* | **PREPARATORIA** |

This is the name given to the three years of pre-university education in Latin America. Students usually begin the "prepa", as it is known colloquially, at the age of 16 and finish when they are 19.

---

preponderante *adj* prevailing.
preposición *f* preposition.
prepotente *adj* dominant.
presa *f (de un animal)* prey; *(embalse)* dam, → **preso**.
presbiterio *m* chancel.
prescindir: prescindir de *v + prep (renunciar a)* to do without; *(omitir)* to dispense with.
presencia *f* presence.
presenciar *vt* to attend.
presentable *adj* presentable.
presentación *f* presentation;

(entre personas) introduction.

presentador, -ra *m, f* presenter.

presentar *vt* to present; *(queja)* to lodge; *(a dos personas)* to introduce; *(excusas, respetos)* to offer; *(aspecto, apariencia)* to have ❏ **presentarse** *vpr (comparecer)* to turn up; *(como candidato, voluntario)* to put o.s. forward; **~se a** *(examen)* to sit; *(elección)* to stand for.

presente *adj & m* present; **tener ~** to remember.

presentimiento *m* feeling, hunch.

preservar *vt* to protect.

preservativo *m* condom.

presidencia *f (cargo)* presidency; *(lugar)* president's office; *(grupo de personas)* board.

presidencial *adj* presidential.

presidente, -ta *m, f (de nación)* president; *(de asamblea)* chairperson.

presidiario, -ria *m, f* convict.

presidir *vt (ser presidente de)* to preside over; *(reunión)* to chair; *(predominar)* to dominate.

presión *f* pressure; **~ sanguínea** blood pressure.

preso, -sa *m, f* prisoner.

préstamo *m* loan.

prestar *vt (dinero)* to lend; *(colaboración, ayuda)* to give; *(declaración)* to make; *(atención)* to pay ❏ **prestarse a** *v + prep (ofrecerse a)* to offer to; *(dar motivo a)* to be open to.

prestigio *m* prestige.

presumido, -da *adj* conceited.

presumir *vt* to presume ◆ *vi* to show off; **~ de guapo** to think o.s. good-looking.

presunción *f (suposición)* assumption; *(vanidad)* conceit.

presunto, -ta *adj (delincuente, etc)* alleged.

presuntuoso, -sa *adj* conceited.

presupuesto *m (cálculo)* budget; *(de costo)* estimate.

pretencioso, -sa *adj* pretentious.

pretender *vt (aspirar a)* to aim at; *(afirmar)* to claim; **~ hacer algo** to try to do sthg.

pretendiente *mf (al trono)* pretender; *(a una mujer)* suitor.

pretensión *f (intención)* aim; *(aspiración)* aspiration.

pretexto *m* pretext.

prever *vt (presagiar)* to foresee; *(prevenir)* to plan.

previo, -via *adj* prior.

previsor, -ra *adj* farsighted.

previsto, -ta *adj (planeado)* anticipated.

primaria *f (enseñanza)* primary school.

primario, -ria *adj (primordial)* primary; *(elemental)* primitive.

primavera *f* spring.

primer *núm* → **primero**.

primera *f (velocidad)* first gear; *(clase)* first class; **de ~** first-class, → **primero**.

primero, -ra *núm & adv* first ◆ *m, f*: **el ~ de la clase** top of the class; **a ~s de** at the beginning of; **lo ~** the main thing; **primera clase** first class; **~s auxilios** first aid *(sg)*,

→ **sexto**.

primo, -ma m, f (familiar) cousin; (fam: bobo) sucker.

primogénito, -ta m, f first-born (child).

princesa f princess.

principado m principality.

principal adj main ◆ m first floor.

príncipe m prince.

principiante m beginner.

principio m (inicio) beginning; (causa, origen) origin; (norma) principle; **a ~s de** at the beginning of; **al ~** at the beginning; **en ~** in principle; **por ~s** on principle.

pringoso, -sa adj (pegajoso) sticky.

prioridad f priority.

prisa f (rapidez) speed; (urgencia) urgency; **darse ~** to hurry up; **tener ~** to be in a hurry.

prisión f (cárcel) prison.

prisionero, -ra m, f prisoner.

prisma m prism.

prismáticos mpl binoculars.

privado, -da adj private.

privar vt to deprive ◘ **privarse de** v + prep to go without.

privilegiado, -da adj privileged.

privilegio m privilege.

proa f bows (pl).

probabilidad f (cualidad) probability; (oportunidad) chance.

probable adj probable.

probador m changing room.

probar vt (demostrar) to prove; (examinar) to check; (comida, bebida) to taste ◆ vi to try ◘ **probarse**

vpr (ropa, zapato) to try on.

probeta f test tube.

problema m problem.

problemático, -ca adj problematic.

procedencia f (origen, fuente) origin; **con ~ de** (arriving) from.

procedente adj (oportuno) appropriate; **~ de** from.

proceder m behaviour ◆ vi (actuar) to act; (ser oportuno) to be appropriate ◘ **proceder de** v + prep to come from.

procedimiento m (método) procedure.

procesado, -da m, f accused.

procesar vt (enjuiciar) to try.

procesión f procession.

proceso m process; (transcurso, evolución) course; (juicio) trial.

proclamación f proclamation.

proclamar vt to proclaim; (aclamar) to acclaim ◘ **proclamarse** vpr to proclaim o.s.

procurar vt: **~ hacer algo** to try to do sthg.

prodigarse vpr (esforzarse) to put o.s. out; **~ en algo** to overdo sthg.

producción f production; (producto) products (pl).

producir vt to produce; (provocar) to cause ◘ **producirse** vpr (ocurrir) to take place.

productividad f productivity.

productivo, -va adj (que produce) productive; (que da beneficio) profitable.

producto m product; (de la tierra) produce; (beneficios) profit.

productor, -ra m, f producer.

productora f (en cine) production company, → **productor**.

profecía f prophecy.

profesión f profession.

profesional adj & mf professional.

profesionista mf (Amér) professional.

profesor, -ra m, f teacher.

profeta m prophet.

profiteroles mpl profiteroles.

profundidad f depth; **tiene dos metros de ~** it's two metres deep.

profundo, -da adj deep; (notable) profound.

programa m programme; (de estudios) syllabus; (plan) schedule; (en informática) program.

programación f (en televisión, radio) programmes (pl); (en informática) programming.

programador, -ra m, f programmer.

programar vt (planear) to plan; (en televisión, radio) to put on; (en informática) to program.

progresar vi to (make) progress.

progresivo, -va adj progressive.

progreso m progress.

prohibición f ban.

prohibido, -da adj prohibited; "~ aparcar" "no parking"; "~ el paso" "no entry"; "~ el paso a personas ajenas a la obra" "no entry for unauthorised personnel"; "~ fijar carteles" "billposters will be prosecuted"; "~ fumar" "no smoking"; **"prohibida la entra-**da" "no entry"; **"prohibida la entrada a menores"** "adults only".

prohibir vt (vedar) to forbid; (por ley) to prohibit; (práctica existente) to ban.

prójimo m fellow human being.

proliferación f proliferation.

prólogo m (en libro, revista) introduction.

prolongar vt (alargar) to extend; (hacer durar más) to prolong ❑ **prolongarse** vpr to go on.

promedio m average.

promesa f promise.

prometer vt to promise ♦ vi to show promise ❑ **prometerse** vpr to get engaged.

prometido, -da m, f fiancé (f fiancée).

promoción f (ascenso) promotion; (curso) class.

promocionar vt to promote ❑ **promocionarse** vpr to promote o.s.

promotor, -ra m, f promoter.

pronóstico m (predicción) forecast; (en medicina) prognosis; **~ del tiempo** weather forecast.

pronto adv (temprano) early; (dentro de poco) soon; (rápidamente) quickly; **de ~** suddenly; **tan ~ como** as soon as.

pronunciación f pronunciation.

pronunciar vt to pronounce; (discurso) to make.

propaganda f advertising.

propensión f: ~ **a** a tendency towards.

propenso, -sa adj: **ser ~ a** to

have a tendency to.

propicio, -cia adj favourable.

propiedad f property; (posesión) ownership.

propietario, -ria m, f owner.

propina f tip.

propio, -pia adj (de propiedad) own; (peculiar) characteristic; (apropiado) appropriate; (natural) natural; **el ~ presidente** the president himself.

proponer vt to propose ❑ **proponerse** vpr to intend.

proporcionado, -da adj proportionate.

proporcionar vt (facilitar) to give, to provide; (ser causa de) to add.

proposición f (propuesta) proposal.

propósito m (intención) intention; (objetivo) purpose; **a ~ on** purpose; **a ~ de** with regard to.

propuesta f proposal.

propuesto, -ta pp → proponer.

prórroga f (aplazamiento) extension; (en deporte) extra time.

prorrogar vt to extend.

prosa f prose.

proscrito, -ta m, f exile.

prospecto m (folleto) leaflet; (de medicamento) instructions leaflet.

próspero, -ra adj prosperous.

prostíbulo m brothel.

prostitución f prostitution.

prostituta f prostitute.

protagonista mf (de libro) main character; (en cine, teatro) lead.

protección f protection.

proteger vt to protect ❑ **protegerse** vpr (resguardarse) to shelter.

protegido, -da m, f protegé (f protegée).

proteína f protein.

protesta f protest.

protestante mf Protestant.

protestar vi to protest.

protocolo m protocol.

provecho m benefit; **buen ~** enjoy your meal!; **sacar ~ de** to make the most of.

provechoso, -sa adj advantageous.

provenir: provenir de v + prep to come from.

proverbio m proverb.

provincia f province.

provisional adj provisional.

provocación f provocation.

provocar vt (incitar, enojar) to provoke; (excitar sexualmente) to arouse; (causar) to cause; (incendio) to start; **¿te provoca hacerlo?** (Amér) do you feel like doing it?

provocativo, -va adj provocative.

próximo, -ma adj (cercano) near; (ciudad, casa) nearby; (siguiente) next; **"próximas llegadas"** "arriving next".

proyección f (de película) showing.

proyectar vt (película) to show; (luz) to shine; (sombra, figura) to cast; (idear) to plan.

proyecto m (plan) plan; (propósito) project; (de ley) bill.

proyector m (de cine, diapositivas) projector.

prudencia f (cautela) caution; (moderación) moderation.

prudente adj (cauteloso) cautious; (sensato) sensible.

prueba f (testimonio) proof; (ensayo, examen) test; (competición) event.

psicoanálisis m inv psychoanalysis.

psicología f psychology.

psicológico, -ca adj psychological.

psicólogo, -ga m, f psychologist.

psicópata mf psychopath.

psiquiatra mf psychiatrist.

psiquiátrico m psychiatric hospital.

psíquico, -ca adj psychic.

pta. (abrev de peseta) pta.

púa f (de planta) thorn; (de peine) tooth.

pub [paβ] m upmarket pub.

pubertad f puberty.

pubis m inv pubes (pl).

publicación f publication.

públicamente adv publicly.

publicar vt to publish; (noticia) to make public.

publicidad f (propaganda) advertising; (en televisión) adverts (pl).

publicitario, -ria adj advertising (antes de s).

público, -ca adj public; (colegio) state ♦ m (en cine, teatro, televisión) audience, (en partido) crowd; **en ~** in public.

pucha interj (Amér) good heavens!

pucho m (Amér) cigarette butt.

pudding ['puðiŋ] m pudding.

pudiera v → poder.

pudor m (recato) modesty; (timidez) shyness.

pudrir vt to rot ❑ **pudrirse** vpr to rot.

pueblo m people; (localidad pequeña) village; (más grande) town.

pueda v → poder.

puente m bridge; **hacer ~** to take a day off between two public holidays; **~ aéreo** shuttle.

puerco, -ca adj filthy ♦ m, f pig.

puerro m leek.

puerta f door; (de jardín, ciudad) gate; (en deporte) goal; **~ de embarque** boarding gate; **~ principal** front door.

puerto m (de mar) port; (de montaña) pass; **~ deportivo** marina.

Puerto Rico s Puerto Rico.

pues conj (ya que) since; (así que) so; (uso enfático) well.

puesta f: **~ de sol** sunset.

puesto, -ta pp → poner ♦ adj (elegante) smart ♦ m (lugar) place; (cargo) job; (tienda pequeña) stall; (de la Guardia Civil) station; **~ que** as, since.

pulga f flea.

pulgar m thumb.

pulidora f polisher.

pulir vt to polish.

pulmón m lung.

pulmonía f pneumonia.

pulpa f flesh.

pulpo m octopus; **~ a la gallega** octopus cooked with red pepper and spices.

pulque m (Amér) alcoholic drink made from maguey juice.

pulquería f (Amér) bar where "pulque" is sold.

pulsar vt (timbre, botón) to press; (cuerdas de un instrumento) to play.

pulsera f bracelet.

pulso m (latido) pulse; (firmeza) steady hand.

puma m puma.

punk [pan] mf punk.

punta f (extremo agudo) point; (extremo) end; (de dedo) tip; (de tierra) point; **en la ~ de la lengua** on the tip of one's tongue.

puntapié m kick.

puntera f toecap.

puntería f (habilidad) marksmanship.

puntiagudo, -da adj pointed.

puntilla f point lace.

punto m point; (marca) dot; (signo ortográfico) full stop; (lugar) spot, place; (momento) moment; (grado, intensidad) level; (en cirugía, costura) stitch; **estar a ~ de** to be about to; **en ~** on the dot; **hacer ~** to knit; **dos ~s** colon (sg); **~ de encuentro** meeting point; **~ muerto** neutral; **~ de vista** point of view; **~ y aparte** new paragraph; **~ y coma** semi-colon; **~ y seguido** full-stop; **~s suspensivos** suspension points.

puntuación f (en gramática) punctuation; (en competición) score; (en examen) mark.

puntual adj (persona) punctual; (detallado) detailed.

puntualidad f (de persona) punctuality.

puntualización f detailed explanation.

puntualizar vt to explain in detail.

puntuar vt (texto) to punctuate; (examen) to mark.

punzón m punch.

puñado m handful.

puñal m dagger.

puñalada f (golpe) stab; (herida) stabwound.

puñeta interj damn!

puñetazo m punch.

puñetero, -ra adj (fam) damn.

puño m (mano cerrada) fist; (de arma) hilt; (de camisa) cuff; (de bastón, paraguas) handle.

pupa f (en el labio) blister; (fam: daño) sore.

pupitre m desk.

puré m (concentrado) purée; (sopa) thick soup; **~ de patatas** mashed potatoes (pl).

puritano, -na adj puritanical.

puro, -ra adj pure; (cielo) clear; (verdad) simple ♦ m cigar.

puta f (vulg) whore.

puzzle ['puθle] m jigsaw puzzle.

PVP m abrev = **precio de venta al público**.

pza. (abrev de plaza) Sq.

que *pron* **1.** *(cosa)* that, which; **la moto ~ me gusta** the motorbike (that) I like; **el libro ~ le regalé** the book (that) I gave her; **la playa a la ~ fui** the beach I went to; **el día en ~ me fui** the day I left.

2. *(persona: sujeto)* who, that; **el hombre ~ corre** the man who's running.

3. *(persona: complemento)* whom, that; **el hombre ~ conociste** the man you met; **la chica a la ~ lo presté** the girl to whom I lent it; **la mujer con la ~ hablas** the woman to whom you are talking.

♦ *conj* **1.** *(con oraciones de sujeto)* that; **es importante ~ me escuches** it's important that you listen to me.

2. *(con oraciones de complemento directo)* that; **me ha confesado ~ me quiere** he has told me that he loves me.

3. *(comparativo)* than; **es más rápido ~ tú** he's quicker than you; **antes morir ~ vivir la guerra** I'd rather die than live through a war.

4. *(expresa causa)*: **hemos de esperar, ~ todavía no es la hora** we'll have to wait, as it isn't time yet.

5. *(expresa consecuencia)*: **tanto me lo pidió ~ se lo di** she asked for it so persistently that I gave it to her.

6. *(expresa finalidad)* so (that); **ven aquí ~ te vea** come here so (that) I can see you.

7. *(expresa deseo)* that; **espero ~ te diviertas** I hope (that) you enjoy yourself; **quiero ~ lo hagas** I want you to do it.

8. *(expresa disyunción)* or; **quieras ~ no** whether you want to or not.

9. *(en oraciones exclamativas)*: **¡~ te diviertas!** have fun!; **¡~ sí/no!** I said yes/no!

qué *adj (interrogativo)* what; *(al elegir, concretar)* which ♦ *pron* what ♦ *adv* how; **¡qué!** *(¿cómo?)* sorry?; **¿por ~ (...)?** why (...)?

quebrado *m* fraction.

quebrar *vt* to break ♦ *vi* to go bankrupt.

quedar *vi (permanecer)* to remain, to stay; *(haber suficiente, faltar)* to be left; *(llegar a ser, acabar)* to turn out; *(sentar)* to look; *(estar situado)* to be; **~ en ridículo** to make a fool of o.s.; **~ por hacer** to remain to be done; **~ bien/mal con alguien** to make a good/bad impression on sb; **~ en nada** to come to nothing ❑ **quedar con** *v + prep (citarse)* to arrange to meet; **quedar en** *v + prep (acordar)* to agree to; **quedarse** *vpr (permanecer)* to stay; *(cambio)* to keep; *(comprar)* to take; **se quedó ciego** he went blind; **quedarse con** *v + prep (preferir)* to go for; *(fam: burlarse de)* to take the mickey out of.

quehacer *m* task.

quejarse *vpr (protestar)* to complain; *(lamentarse)* to cry out; **~ de/por** to complain about.

quejido *m* cry.

quemadura *f* burn.

quemar vt to burn ♦ vi to be (scalding) hot ❑ **quemarse** vpr (casa, bosque, etc) to burn down; (persona) to get burnt.

quepa v → caber.

quepo v → caber.

querer m love.

♦ vt 1. (desear) to want; **quiere una bicicleta** she wants a bicycle; **queremos que las cosas vayan bien** we want things to go well; **quiero que vengas** I want you to come; **quisiera hacerlo** I would like to do it; **tal vez él quiera acompañarte** maybe he'll go with you.
2. (amar) to love; **quiere mucho a su hijo** he loves his son very much.
3. (en preguntas formales): **¿quiere pasar?** would you like to come in?
4. (precio) to want; **¿cuánto quiere por el coche?** how much does he want for the car?
5. (requerir) to need; **esta habitación quiere más luz** this room needs more light.

♦ vi 1. (apetecer) to want; **ven cuando quieras** come whenever you like O want; **estoy aquí porque quiero** I'm here because I want to be.
2. (en locuciones): **queriendo** (con intención) on purpose; **~ decir** to mean; **sin ~** accidentally.

♦ v impers: **parece que quiere llover** it looks like rain. ❑ **quererse** vpr to love each other.

querido, -da adj dear.

queso m cheese; **~ de bola** Dutch cheese; **~ manchego** hard, mild yellow cheese made in La Mancha; **~ rallado** grated cheese.

quiebra f (de empresa) bankruptcy.

quien pron (relativo sujeto) who; (relativo complemento) whom; (indefinido) whoever.

quién pron who; **¡~ pudiera verlo!** if only I could have seen it!; **¿~ es?** (en la puerta) who is it?; (al teléfono) who's speaking?

quieto, -ta adj (inmóvil) still; (inactivo) at a standstill; (de carácter) quiet.

quilla f keel.

quilo m = **kilo**.

química f chemistry, → **químico**.

químico, -ca m, f chemist.

quince núm fifteen, → **seis**; → **días** a fortnight.

quincena f fortnight.

quiniela f (juego) (football) pools (pl).

quinientos, -tas núm five hundred, → **seis**.

quinqué m oil lamp.

quinteto m quintet.

quinto, -ta núm fifth ♦ m (recluta) recruit, → **sexto**.

quiosco m (puesto) kiosk; (de periódicos) newspaper stand.

quirófano m operating theatre.

quisquilla f shrimp.

quisquilloso, -sa adj (detallista) pernickety; (susceptible) touchy.

quitamanchas m inv stain remover.

quitar vt (robar) to take; (separar, retirar, suprimir) to remove; (ropa, zapatos) to take off; **~le algo a alguien** to take sthg away from sb

❏ **quitarse** *vpr (apartarse)* to get out of the way; **~se la ropa** to take off one's clothes.

quizá(s) *adv* perhaps.

rábano *m* radish.

rabia *f (ira)* rage; *(enfermedad)* rabies.

rabieta *f* tantrum.

rabioso, -sa *adj (enfermo)* rabid; *(violento)* furious.

rabo *m* tail.

racha *f (de viento, aire)* gust; *(fam: época)* spell; **buena/mala ~** good/bad patch.

racial *adj* racial.

racimo *m* bunch.

ración *f* portion; *(en un bar)* large portion of a particular dish, served as a snack.

racismo *m* racism.

racista *mf* racist.

radar *m* radar.

radiación *f* radiation.

radiador *m* radiator.

radiante *adj* radiant.

radiar *vt (irradiar)* to radiate; *(en la radio)* to broadcast; *(en medicina)* to give X-ray treatment to.

radical *adj* radical.

radio *f* radio ◆ *m* radius; *(de una rueda)* spoke.

radioaficionado, -da *m, f* radio ham.

radiocasete *m o f* radio cassette (player).

radiodespertador *m* clock radio *(with alarm)*.

radiodifusión *f* broadcasting.

radiografía *f (fotografía)* X-ray.

radiólogo, -ga *m, f* radiologist.

radionovela *f* radio soap opera.

radiorreloj *m* clock radio.

radiotaxi *m* minicab.

radioyente *mf* listener.

ráfaga *f (de viento, aire)* gust; *(de luz)* flash; *(de disparos)* burst.

rafia *f* raffia.

rafting *m* white-water rafting.

rail *m* rail.

raíz *f* root; **a ~ de** as a result of.

raja *f (grieta)* crack; *(porción)* slice.

rajatabla: a rajatabla *adv* to the letter.

rallador *m* grater.

rallar *vt* to grate.

rally ['rali] *(pl* **rallys***) m* rally.

rama *f* branch.

ramada *f (Amér)* shed.

rambla *f* avenue.

ramo *m (de flores)* bunch; *(de actividad)* branch.

rampa *f (pendiente)* steep incline; *(para ayudar el acceso)* ramp.

rana *f* frog.

ranchera *f (Amér)* popular Mexican song and dance.

rancho *m (granja)* ranch; *(comida)* mess.

rancio, -cia *adj (vino)* mellow; *(pasado)* rancid.

rango *m (categoría social)* standing; *(en una jerarquía)* rank.

ranura *f (surco)* groove; *(para monedas)* slot.

rape *m* angler fish; **~ a la marinera** *angler fish cooked in a white wine and garlic sauce;* **~ a la plancha** *grilled angler fish.*

rápidamente *adv* quickly.

rapidez *f* speed.

rápido, -da *adj (veloz)* fast; *(que dura poco)* quick ◆ *adv* quickly ◆ *m (tren)* express train □ **rápidos** *mpl* rapids.

raptar *vt* to abduct.

raqueta *f (de tenis)* racquet; *(para la nieve)* snowshoe.

raramente *adv* rarely.

raro, -ra *adj (poco frecuente)* unusual; *(extraño)* strange; *(escaso)* rare; *(extravagante)* odd.

rascacielos *m inv* skyscraper.

rascador *m* scraper.

rascar *vt (con las uñas)* to scratch; *(limpiar)* to scrub; *(pintura)* to scrape (off).

rasgar *vt* to tear.

rasgo *m (de rostro)* feature; *(característica)* characteristic; *(trazo)* stroke.

raso, -sa *adj (superficie)* flat; *(cucharada, etc)* level ◆ *m* satin; **al ~** in the open (air).

rastrillo *m* rake.

rastro *m (huella)* trace; *(mercadillo)* flea market.

RASTRO

A "rastro" is a street market where antiques, second-hand and new goods are sold. The most famous "rastro" is the one in Madrid, although they are to be found in most Spanish cities.

rata *f* rat.

ratero, -ra *m, f* petty thief.

rato *m* while; **a ~s** from time to time; **pasar un buen ~** to have a good time; **pasar un mal ~** to have a hard time of it; **~s libres** spare time *(sg).*

ratón *m* mouse.

rattán *m (Amér)* wicker.

raya *f (línea)* line; *(estampado)* stripe; *(del pelo)* parting; *(de pantalón)* crease; *(arañazo)* scratch; *(pez)* ray; **a** ○ **de ~s** stripy.

rayo *m* ray; *(de tormenta)* bolt of lightning; **~s** lightning *(sg);* **~s-X** X-rays.

rayuela *f* pitch and toss.

raza *f (de personas)* race; *(de animales)* breed; **de ~** pedigree.

razón *f* reason; **dar la ~ a alguien** to say that sb is right; **entrar en ~** to see reason; **"se vende piso: ~ portería"** "flat for sale: enquire at caretaker's office"; **tener ~** to be right.

razonable *adj* reasonable.

razonamiento *m* reasoning.

razonar *vt* to reason out ◆ *vi* to reason.

reacción *f* reaction.

reaccionar *vi (responder)* to react; *(a tratamiento)* to respond.

reactor *m (avión)* jet (plane); *(motor)* jet engine.

real *adj (verdadero)* real; *(de rey)* royal.

realeza f royalty.

realidad f (existencia) reality; (verdad) truth; **en ~** in fact.

realismo m realism.

realización f (de tarea, trabajo) carrying-out; (de proyecto, plan) implementation; (de deseo, sueño) fulfilment; (de película) production.

realizar vt (tarea, trabajo) to carry out; (proyecto, plan) to implement; (deseo, sueño) to fulfil; (película) to produce.

realmente adv (en verdad) actually; (muy) really.

realquilado, -da m, f subtenant.

realquilar vt to sublet.

reanimación f (de fuerzas, energía) recovery; (de enfermo) revival; (del ánimo) cheering-up.

rebaja f (de precio) discount; (de altura, nivel, etc) reduction ❏ **rebajas** fpl sales.

rebajado, -da adj reduced.

rebajar vt (precio) to reduce; (altura, nivel, etc) to lower; (humillar) to humiliate.

rebanada f slice.

rebanar vt to slice.

rebaño m (de ovejas) flock.

rebelarse vpr to rebel.

rebelde adj rebellious; (niño, pelo) unruly; (enfermedad) persistent ◆ mf rebel.

rebeldía f (cualidad) rebelliousness; (acción) rebellion.

rebelión f rebellion.

rebozado, -da adj coated in batter or fried breadcrumbs.

recado m (mensaje) message.

recaer vi (en enfermedad) to have a relapse; (en vicio, error, etc) to relapse.

recalcar vt to stress.

recalentar vt (volver a calentar) to warm up; (calentar demasiado) to overheat ❏ **recalentarse** vpr to overheat.

recámara f (Amér) bedroom.

recamarera f (Amér) maid.

recambio m (pieza) spare (part); (de pluma) refill.

recargar vt (mechero, recipiente) to refill; (batería) to recharge; (arma) to reload; (cargar demasiado) to overload; (impuesto) to increase.

recato m (pudor) modesty; (prudencia) caution.

recepción f reception.

recepcionista mf receptionist.

receptor m receiver.

recesión f recession.

receta f (de guiso) recipe; ~ **(médica)** prescription.

recetar vt to prescribe.

rechazar vt to reject; (físicamente) to push away; (denegar) to turn down.

rechazo m rejection.

recibidor m entrance hall.

recibimiento m reception.

recibir vt to receive; (dar la bienvenida a) to welcome; (ir a buscar) to meet.

recibo m receipt.

reciclado, -da adj recycled.

reciclar vt to recycle ❏ **reciclarse** vpr (persona) to retrain.

recién adv recently; ~ **hecho** fresh; ~ **nacido** newborn baby; "~ **pintado**" "wet paint".

reciente adj recent.

recientemente *adv* recently.

recinto *m* area.

recipiente *m* container.

recital *m (de música pop)* concert; *(de música clásica)* recital.

recitar *vt* to recite.

reclamación *f (queja)* complaint; *(petición)* claim; **"reclamaciones y quejas"** "complaints".

reclamar *vt* to demand.

recluir *vt* to shut away.

reclusión *f (encarcelamiento)* imprisonment; *(voluntaria)* seclusion.

recobrar *vt* to recover ❑ **recobrarse de** *v + prep* to recover from.

recogedor *m* dustpan.

recoger *vt (coger)* to pick up; *(reunir)* to collect; *(fruta)* to pick; *(ir a buscar)* to meet; *(mesa)* to clear; *(acoger)* to take in ❑ **recogerse** *vpr (retirarse)* to withdraw; *(acostarse)* to retire.

recogida *f (de objetos, basura, etc)* collection; *(de frutos)* harvest.

recolección *f (de frutos)* harvesting.

recomendar *vt* to recommend.

recompensa *f* reward.

recompensar *vt* to reward.

reconocer *vt* to recognize; *(examinar)* to examine; *(terreno)* to survey.

reconocimiento *m* recognition; *(agradecimiento)* gratitude; *(en medicina)* examination.

récord ['rekor] *m* record.

recordar *vt* to remember; **~ a alguien a** to remind sb of.

recorrer *vt (país, etc)* to travel across; *(distancia)* to cover.

recorrido *m (trayecto)* route; *(viaje)* journey; **tren de largo ~** intercity train.

recortar *vt (pelo)* to trim; *(papel)* to cut out; *(tela, gastos, precio)* to cut.

recostarse *vpr* to lie down.

recreo *m (diversión)* recreation; *(de escolares)* break.

recta *f* straight line.

rectangular *adj* rectangular.

rectángulo *m* rectangle.

rectitud *f* rectitude.

recto, -ta *adj (camino, línea, etc)* straight; *(severo, honesto)* upright; **todo ~** straight on.

rector, -ra *m, f* vice chancellor *(Br)*, president *(Am)*.

recuerdo *m (del pasado)* memory; *(de viaje)* souvenir ❑ **recuerdos** *mpl (saludos)* regards; **dar ~s a** to give one's regards to.

recuperación *f* recovery.

recuperar *vt* to recover; *(tiempo)* to make up ❑ **recuperarse** *vpr (volver en sí)* to come to; **recuperarse de** *v + prep* to recover from.

recurrir *vi (en juicio)* to appeal; **~ a** *(pedir ayuda)* to turn to.

recurso *m (medio)* resort; *(reclamación)* appeal ❑ **recursos** *mpl* resources; **~s humanos** human resources.

red *f (malla, en deporte)* net; *(de pelo)* hairnet; *(de carreteras, conductos, etc)* network; *(de tiendas, empresas, etc)* chain.

redacción *f (de texto, periódico)* editing; *(en escuela)* essay; *(estilo)* wording; (*conjunto de personas*) editorial team; (*oficina*) editorial office.

redactar *vt* to write.

redactor, -ra *m, f* (*escritor*) writer; (*editor*) editor.

redil *m* pen.

redondeado, -da *adj* (*material, forma, etc*) rounded; (*precio, cantidad, etc*) rounded up/down.

redondel *m* ring.

redondo, -da *adj* round; (*perfecto*) excellent.

reducción *f* reduction.

reducir *vt* to reduce; (*someter*) to suppress ❑ **reducirse a** *v + prep* to be reduced to.

reembolsar *vt* (*gastos*) to reimburse; (*dinero*) to refund; (*deuda*) to repay.

reembolso *m* (*de gastos*) reimbursement; (*de dinero*) refund; (*de deuda*) repayment; **contra ~** cash on delivery.

reemplazar *vt* to replace.

reestrenar *vt* to re-release.

reestreno *m* re-release.

reestructurar *vt* to restructure.

refacción *f* (*Amér*) spare (part).

refaccionar *vt* (*Amér*) to repair.

referencia *f* reference ❑ **referencias** *fpl* references.

referéndum *m* referendum.

referente *adj*: ~ **a** concerning.

referirse: referirse a *v + prep* to refer to.

refinería *f* refinery.

reflector *m* spotlight.

reflejar *vt* to reflect ❑ **reflejarse** *vpr* to be reflected.

reflejo, -ja *adj* (*movimiento*) reflex ◆ *m* (*luz*) gleam; (*imagen*) reflection ❑ **reflejos** *mpl* (*reacción rápida*) reflexes; **hacerse ~s** (*en el pelo*) to have highlights put in.

reflexión *f* reflection.

reflexionar *vi* to reflect.

reforma *f* reform; (*de casa, edificio*) alteration; (*de idea, plan*) change.

reformar *vt* to reform; (*casa, edificio*) to do up; (*idea, plan*) to alter ❑ **reformarse** *vpr* to mend one's ways.

reforzar *vt* to reinforce.

refrán *m* proverb.

refrescante *adj* refreshing.

refresco *m* soft drink; "**~s**" "refreshments".

refrigerado, -da *adj* (*con aire acondicionado*) air-conditioned.

refrigerador *m* refrigerator.

refugiado, -da *m, f* refugee.

refugiar *vt* to give refuge to ❑ **refugiarse** *vpr* to take refuge.

refugio *m* refuge; (*de guerra*) shelter.

regadera *f* (*para plantas*) watering can; (*Amér: ducha*) shower head.

regadío *m* irrigated land.

regalar *vt* (*obsequiar*) to give (as a present); (*dar gratis*) to give away.

regaliz *m* liquorice.

regalo *m* present, gift.

regañar *vt* to tell off ◆ *vi* (*pelearse*) to argue.

regar *vt* (*campos, plantas*) to water; (*suj: río*) to flow through.

regata *f* (*competición*) regatta;

(canal) irrigation channel.

regatear *vt (precio)* to haggle over; *(esfuerzos, ayuda)* to be sparing with; *(en deporte)* to beat, to dribble past.

regazo *m* lap.

regenerar *vt (cosa)* to regenerate; *(persona)* to reform ◻ **regenerarse** *vpr (persona)* to mend one's ways.

regente *m (Amér)* mayor.

régimen *m (de alimentación)* diet; *(conjunto de normas)* rules *(pl)*; *(forma de gobierno)* regime.

región *f* region.

regional *adj* regional.

regir *vt (dirigir)* to run ◆ *vi* to apply.

registrar *vt (inspeccionar)* to search; *(cachear)* to frisk; *(en lista, registro, cinta)* to record ◻ **registrarse** *vpr (ocurrir)* to occur.

registro *m (libro)* register; *(inspección)* search; *(de luz, agua, etc)* cupboard containing electricity/water meter; **~ (civil)** registry office.

regla *f (norma)* rule; *(instrumento)* ruler; *(menstruación)* period; **en ~** in order; **por ~ general** as a rule.

reglamento *m* regulations *(pl)*.

regresar *vt (Amér)* to return ◆ *vi* to return ◻ **regresarse** *vpr (Amér)* to return.

regreso *m* return.

regular *adj (uniforme)* regular; *(de tamaño)* medium; *(vuelo)* scheduled; *(habitual)* normal; *(mediocre)* average ◆ *vt (reglamentar)* to regulate; *(mecanismo)* to adjust ◆ *adv* all right.

regularidad *f* regularity.

rehabilitar *vt (local, casa, etc)* to restore; *(persona)* to rehabilitate.

rehén *mf* hostage.

rehogar *vt* to fry over a low heat.

reina *f* queen.

reinado *m* reign.

reinar *vi* to reign.

reincorporar *vt* to reincorporate ◻ **reincorporarse a** *v + prep* to go back to.

reino *m* kingdom.

Reino Unido *m*: **el ~** the United Kingdom.

reintegro *m (pago)* reimbursement; *(en banco)* withdrawal; *(en lotería)* return of one's stake.

reír *vi* to laugh ◆ *vt* to laugh at ◻ **reírse de** *v + prep* to laugh at.

reivindicación *f* claim.

reivindicar *vt* to claim.

reja *f (de puerta, ventana)* bars *(pl)*.

rejilla *f (para abertura)* grid; *(de ventana)* grille; *(de horno)* gridiron; *(de silla)* wickerwork; *(para equipaje)* luggage rack.

rejuvenecer *vt & vi* to rejuvenate.

relación *f (nexo)* relation; *(trato)* relationship; *(enumeración)* list; *(narración)* account ◻ **relaciones** *fpl (amistades)* relations; *(influencias)* connections; *(noviazgo)* relationship *(sg)*.

relacionar *vt* to relate ◻ **relacionarse** *vpr (ideas, objetos, etc)* to be related; *(personas)* to mix.

relajación *f* relaxation.

relajar *vt* to relax ◻ **relajarse** *vpr* to relax.

relajo *m (Amér)* commotion.

relámpago *m* flash of lightning.

relampaguear *v impers*: **relampagueó** lightning flashed.

relatar *vt* to relate.

relativo, -va *adj (no absoluto)* relative; *(escaso)* limited; **~ a** concerning.

relato *m (cuento)* tale; *(exposición)* account.

relevo *m (sustitución)* relief; *(en deporte)* relay ❑ **relevos** *mpl* relay (race) *(eg)*.

relieve *m* relief, *(importancia)* importance.

religión *f* religion.

religioso, -sa *adj* religious ♦ *m, f (monje)* monk *(f* nun).

relinchar *vi* to neigh.

rellano *m* landing.

rellenar *vt (volver a llenar)* to refill; *(pastel)* to fill; *(pollo, almohada)* to stuff; *(formulario, documento)* to fill in.

relleno, -na *adj* stuffed ♦ *m* stuffing *(de pastel)* filling.

reloj *m* clock; **~ de arena** hourglass; **~ (de pared)** clock; **~ (de pulsera)** watch.

relojería *f (tienda)* watchmaker's (shop); *(taller)* watchmaker's workshop.

relojero, -ra *m, f* watchmaker.

remar *vi* to row.

remediar *vt (solucionar)* to put right; *(problema)* to solve.

remedio *m (solución)* solution; *(auxilio)* help; *(para enfermedad)* remedy; **no queda más ~** there's nothing for it; **no tener más ~** to have no choice; **sin ~** hopeless.

remendar *vt* to mend.

remezón *m (Amér)* earth tremor.

remite *m* sender's name and address.

remitente *mf* sender.

remitir *vt* to send ❑ **remitir a** *v + prep* to refer to.

remo *m* oar.

remojar *vt* to soak.

remojo *m*: **poner en ~** to leave to soak.

remolacha *f* beetroot *(Br)*, beet *(Am)*.

remolcador *m (embarcación)* tugboat; *(camión)* breakdown lorry.

remolcar *vt* to tow.

remolque *m (vehículo)* trailer.

remontar *vt* to go up ❑ **remontarse a** *v + prep* to date back to.

remordimiento *m* remorse.

remoto, -ta *adj* remote.

remover *vt (café, sopa)* to stir; *(tierra)* to dig up; *(recuerdos)* to rake up.

remuneración *f* remuneration.

renacuajo *m* tadpole.

rencor *m* resentment.

rendición *f* surrender.

rendimiento *m (de motor)* performance.

rendir *vt (homenaje)* to pay ♦ *vi (máquina)* to perform well; *(persona)* to be productive; *(negocio, dinero)* to be profitable ❑ **rendirse** *vpr (someterse)* to surrender.

RENFE *f* Spanish state railway network.

reno m reindeer.

renovación f (de decoración, local) renovation; (de contrato, carné) renewal.

renovar vt (decoración, local) to renovate; (contrato, carné, relación) to renew; (vestuario) to clear out.

renta f (ingresos) income; (beneficio) return; (alquiler) rent.

rentable adj profitable.

rentar vt (Amér) to rent.

renunciar: renunciar a v + prep (prescindir de) to give up; (declinar) to refuse to.

reñir vt (reprender) to tell off ◆ vi (pelearse) to argue; (romper relaciones) to fall out.

reo, -a m, f offender.

reparación f (de coche, avería, etc) repair; (de daño, ofensa, etc) reparation.

reparar vt (coche, máquina, etc) to repair; (equivocación, ofensa, etc) to make amends for ❑ **reparar en** v + prep to notice.

repartidor, -ra m, f deliveryman (f deliverywoman).

repartir vt (dividir) to share out; (distribuir) to deliver.

reparto m (de bienes, dinero, etc) division; (de mercancías, periódicos, etc) delivery; (de actores) cast.

repasar vt to go over; (trabajo, lección) to revise; (releer) to go over; (remendar) to mend; **~ apuntes** to go over one's notes.

repaso m revision; (fam: reprensión) telling off.

repelente adj repulsive.

repente: de repente adv suddenly.

repentino, -na adj sudden.

repercusión f repercussion.

repertorio m (catálogo) list; (de actor, compañía, etc) repertoire.

repetición f repetition.

repetidor, -ra m, f (alumno) student repeating a year ◆ m (en telecomunicaciones) repeater.

repetir vt to repeat; (comida, bebida) to have seconds of ◆ vi (sabor) to repeat.

réplica f (copia) replica; (contestación) reply.

replicar vt & vi to answer back.

repoblación f (de ciudad, región, etc) repopulation; (de bosque, campos) replanting; **~ forestal** reafforestation.

repoblar vt (ciudad, región, etc) to repopulate; (bosque, campos, etc) to replant.

reponer vt to replace; (película, obra de teatro) to re-run ❑ **reponerse** vpr to recover.

reportaje m (en radio, televisión) report; (en periódico, revista) article.

reportar vt (Amér) to report ❑ **reportarse** (Amér) to report.

reporte m (Amér) report.

reportero, -ra m, f reporter.

reposera f (Amér) deck chair.

reposo m (descanso) rest; (quietud) calm.

repostería f confectionery.

representación f representation; (de obra de teatro) performance; **en ~ de** on behalf of.

representante mf (de actor, cantante, etc) agent; (vendedor) representative.

representar vt to represent;

(obra de teatro) to perform; (edad) to look; (importar) to mean.

representativo, -va adj representative.

represión f suppression.

reprimir vt to suppress ❑ **reprimirse** vpr to restrain o.s.

reprochar vt to reproach.

reproche m reproach.

reproducción f reproduction.

reproducir vt to reproduce ❑ **reproducirse** vpr (seres vivos) to reproduce.

reptar vi to crawl.

reptil m reptile.

república f republic.

República Dominicana f: la ~ the Dominican Republic.

republicano, -na adj republican.

repuesto, -ta pp ➤ **reponer** ♦ m (recambio) spare (part), de ~ spare.

repugnar vt: me repugna ese **olor** I find that smell disgusting.

reputación f reputation.

requerir vt to require.

requesón m cottage cheese.

resaca f (de borrachera) hangover; (del mar) undertow.

resbalada f (Amér) slip.

resbaladizo, -za adj slippery.

resbalar vi (deslizarse) to slide; (caer) to slip; (equivocarse) to slip up ❑ **resbalarse** vpr to slip.

rescatar vt to rescue.

rescate m (dinero) ransom.

resentimiento m resentment.

reserva¹ f (de habitación, asiento, comedimiento) reservation; (cautela)

discretion; (de alimentos, provisiones, etc) reserves (pl); (de animales) reserve; **de ~ (de repuesto)** in reserve; "~s hoteles y pensiones" "hotel and guest house reservations"; ~ **natural** nature reserve.

reserva² m (vino) vintage.

reservado, -da adj reserved ♦ m (compartimento) reserved compartment.

reservar vt (asiento, billete, etc) to reserve, to book; (callar) to reserve; (noticia, datos) to keep to o.s.; (guardar) to set aside.

resfriado, -da m cold ♦ adj: estar ~ to have a cold.

resfriarse vpr to catch a cold.

resfrío m (Amér) cold.

resguardar vt to protect ❑ **resguardarse de** v + prep to shelter from

resguardo m (documento) receipt.

residencia f (estancia) stay; (casa) residence; (de estudiantes) hall of residence; (de ancianos) old people's home; (pensión) guest house.

residuo m residue ❑ **residuos** mpl waste (sg).

resignarse vpr to resign o.s.

resistencia f resistance; (para correr, etc) stamina; (de pared, material, etc) strength.

resistente adj tough.

resistir vt (carga, dolor, enfermedad) to withstand; (tentación, deseo, ataque) to resist; (tolerar) to stand ♦ vi (durar) to keep going ❑ **resistirse a** v + prep to refuse to.

resolver vt (duda, crisis) to

resolve; *(problema, caso)* to solve.
resonancia f *(de sonido)* resonance; *(repercusión)* repercussions *(pl)*.
resorte m spring.
respaldo m *(de asiento)* back.
respectivo, -va adj respective.
respecto m: al ~ in this respect; (con) ~ a regarding.
respetable adj *(digno de respeto)* respectable; *(considerable)* considerable.
respetar vt to respect.
respeto m respect.
respiración f breathing.
respirar vi to breathe; *(sentir alivio)* to breathe again.
respiro m *(alivio)* relief; **darse un** ~ to have a breather.
resplandor m brightness.
responder vt to answer ♦ vi *(contestar)* to answer; *(replicar)* to answer back; *(reaccionar)* to respond; ~ **a algo** to answer sthg □ **responder a** v + prep *(deberse a)* to be due to; **responder de** v + prep to answer for; **responder por** v + prep to answer for.
responsabilidad f responsibility.
responsable adj responsible; ~ **de** responsible for.
respuesta f *(contestación)* answer; *(reacción)* response.
resta f subtraction.
restar vt *(quitar)* to take away; *(en matemáticas)* to subtract.
restauración f restoration; *(en hostelería)* restaurant trade.
restaurado, -da adj restored.

restaurador, -ra m, f *(de pintura, escultura, etc)* restorer; *(en hostelería)* restaurateur.
restaurante m restaurant.
restaurar vt to restore.
resto m rest □ **restos** mpl remains; *(de comida)* leftovers.
restricción f restriction.
resucitar vt *(persona)* to bring back to life ♦ vi to rise from the dead.
resuelto, -ta pp → **resolver** ♦ adj *(decidido)* determined.
resultado m result.
resultar vi *(acabar en)* to turn out to be; *(tener éxito)* to work out; *(ser)* to be □ **resultar de** v + prep to result from.
resumen m summary.
resumir vt to summarize.
retablo m altarpiece.
retal m remnant.
retención f *(de tráfico)* hold-up; *(de líquidos, grasas)* retention.
retirado, -da adj *(apartado)* secluded; *(jubilado)* retired.
retirar vt *(quitar, recoger)* to remove; *(carné, permiso, dinero, afirmación)* to withdraw □ **retirarse** vpr to retire.
reto m challenge.
retocar vt *(fotografía, pintura)* to touch up; *(trabajo)* to put the finishing touches to.
retorcer vt *(brazo)* to twist; *(ropa)* to wring □ **retorcerse de** v + prep *(dolor)* to writhe in; *(risa)* to double up with.
retórica f rhetoric.
retornable adj returnable.
retorno m return.

retransmisión f broadcast.

retransmitir vt to broadcast.

retrasado, -da adj (tren) delayed; (trabajo) behind; (reloj) slow; (no actual) old-fashioned; (persona) backward.

retrasar vt (aplazar) to postpone; (reloj) to put back; (hacer más lento) to hold up ◻ **retrasarse** vpr (tardar) to be late; (reloj) to lose time; (en el pago) to be behind.

retraso m (de persona, tren, etc) delay; (de reloj) slowness; (de pueblo, cultura, etc) backwardness; (deuda) arrears (pl); **con ~** late; **llevar ~** to be late.

retratar vt (fotografiar) to photograph; (dibujar, pintar) to do a portrait of; (describir) to portray.

retrato m (fotografía) photograph; (dibujo, pintura) portrait; (descripción) portrayal; (imagen parecida) spitting image.

retrete m toilet.

retroceder vi to go back.

retrospectivo, -va adj retrospective.

retrovisor m rear-view mirror.

reuma m o f rheumatism.

reunión f meeting.

reunir vt (personas) to bring together; (dinero, fondos) to raise; (condiciones) to meet ◻ **reunirse** vpr to meet.

revancha f revenge.

revelado m developing; **~ en color/blanco y negro** colour/black and white developing.

revelar vt (secreto, noticia, etc) to reveal; (fotografía) to develop.

reventar vt (romper) to burst; (fam: fastidiar) to bug ◆ vi (cansar) to get exhausted; (bomba) to explode; (globo) to burst; (fam: morir) to kick the bucket ◻ **reventarse** vpr (romperse) to burst.

reventón m puncture.

reverencia f (inclinación) bow.

reversible adj reversible.

reverso m back.

revés m (de moneda, folio, etc) back; (con raqueta) backhand; (con mano) slap; (desgracia) setback; **al ~** (en orden contrario) the other way round; (en mal orden) the wrong way round; (al contrario) on the contrary.

revestimiento m (de pintura) coat.

revisar vt (corregir) to revise; (coche) to service.

revisión f (repaso) revision; (arreglo) amendment.

revisor, -ra m, f (en tren) ticket inspector; (en autobús) conductor.

revista f (publicación) magazine; (espectáculo) revue; (inspección) inspection.

revistero m magazine rack.

revolcarse vpr to roll about.

revoltillo m (confusión) jumble; (guiso) scrambled egg, usually with fried prawns and mushrooms.

revoltoso, -sa adj (travieso) naughty; (rebelde) rebellious.

revolución f revolution.

revolucionario, -ria m, f revolutionary.

revolver vt (mezclar) to mix; (desordenar) to mess up; (líquido) to stir.

revólver m revolver.

revuelta f (rebelión) revolt.
revolver, -ta pp → **revolver**
♦ adj (desordenado) in a mess; (turbio) cloudy; (tiempo) unsettled; (mar) choppy; (alborotado) turbulent ♦ m scrambled eggs (pl).

rey m king; **los Reyes Magos** the Three Wise Men ❑ **Reyes** m (fiesta) Epiphany, 6 January when Spanish children traditionally receive presents.

[i] REYES

On 6 January, Spanish children traditionally receive presents supposedly brought by the Three Wise Men. The "roscón de reyes" is a large ring-shaped bun eaten for dessert on this day, in which a bean and a small figure are hidden. Whoever gets the slice with the bean has to pay for the "roscón", whilst the person who finds the figure is proclaimed "king of the party".

rezar vt to say ♦ vi to pray.
rezo m prayer.
ría f estuary.
riachuelo m stream.
riada f flood.
ribera f (del río) bank; (del mar) shore; (terreno) plain (irrigated by a river).
ribete m (de vestido, zapato, etc) edging; (añadido) touch.
rico, -ca adj rich; (sabroso) tasty; (fam: simpático) cute.
ridículo, -la adj (cómico) ridiculous; (escaso) laughable ♦ m: **hacer el ~** to make a fool of o.s.

riego m irrigation.
rienda f rein.
riesgo m risk; **a todo ~** comprehensive.
rifar vt to raffle.
rigidez f (de palo, tela, etc) stiffness; (de carácter) inflexibility; (de norma, regla) strictness.
rígido, -da adj (palo, tela, etc) stiff; (carácter, persona) inflexible; (norma, regla) strict.
rigor m (exactitud) accuracy; (severidad) strictness; (del clima) harshness; **de ~** essential.
riguroso, -sa adj (exacto) rigorous; (severo, normas, leyes, etc) strict; (frío, calor) harsh.
rima f rhyme.
rímel m mascara.
rincón m corner.
ring m (boxing) ring.
rinoceronte m rhinoceros.
riña f (discusión) quarrel; (pelea) fight.
riñón m kidney ❑ **riñones** mpl (parte del cuerpo) lower back (sg); **riñones al jerez** kidneys cooked in sherry.
riñonera f bum bag (Br), fanny pack (Am).
río m river.
rioja m Rioja (wine).
RIP (abrev of requiescat in pace) RIP.
riqueza f (fortuna) wealth; (cualidad) richness.
risa f laughter.
ristra f string.
ritmo m (armonía) rhythm; (velocidad) pace.
rito m rite; (costumbre) ritual.

ritual *m* ritual.

rival *mf* rival.

rizado, -da *adj (pelo)* curly; *(papel, tela, etc)* crumpled; *(mar)* choppy.

rizo *m (de pelo)* curl.

RNE *(abrev de Radio Nacional de España) Spanish national radio station.*

robar *vt (quitar)* to steal; *(casa)* to burgle; *(cobrar demasiado)* to rob; *(en naipes, dominó)* to draw.

roble *m* oak.

robo *m* robbery; *(en casa)* burglary; *(estafa):* **es un ~** it's daylight robbery.

robot *m (de cocina)* food processor.

robusto, -ta *adj* robust.

roca *f* rock.

roce *m (acción)* rub; *(más suave)* brush; *(desgaste)* wear; *(trato)* close contact; *(desavenencia)* brush.

rociar *vt (mojar)* to sprinkle; *(con spray)* to spray.

rocío *m* dew.

rock *m* rock.

rocoso, -sa *adj* rocky.

rodaballo *m* turbot.

rodaje *m (de película)* shooting; *(de vehículo)* running-in.

rodar *vt (película)* to shoot; *(vehículo)* to run in ♦ *vi (bola, pelota, etc)* to roll; *(coche)* to go, to travel; *(caerse)* to tumble; *(deambular)* to wander.

rodeado, -da *adj* surrounded; **~ de** surrounded by.

rodear *vt (cercar)* to surround; *(dar la vuelta a)* to go around □ **rodearse de** *v + prep* to surround

o.s. with.

rodeo *m (camino largo, vuelta)* detour; *(al hablar)* evasiveness; *(espectáculo)* rodeo; **dar ~s** to beat about the bush.

rodilla *f* knee; **de ~s** on one's knees.

rodillo *m (de máquina)* roller; *(utensilio)* rolling pin.

roedor *m* rodent.

roer *vt (raspar, atormentar)* to gnaw (at); *(desgastar)* to eat away (at).

rogar *vt (pedir)* to ask.

rojo, -ja *adj, m, f* red.

rollito *m:* **~ de primavera** spring roll.

rollo *m (cilindro)* roll; *(película fotográfica)* (roll of) film; *(fam: persona, cosa, actividad aburrida)* bore.

romana *f:* **a la ~** fried in batter.

románico, -ca *adj (lengua)* Romance; *(en arte)* Romanesque ♦ *m* Romanesque.

romano, -na *adj* Roman.

romántico, -ca *adj (sentimental)* romantic; *(en arte)* Romantic.

rombo *m (símbolo)* lozenge.

romería *f (fiesta) popular religious festival combining a religious ceremony and dancing, eating etc.*

romero *m (planta)* rosemary.

romo, -ma *adj* blunt.

rompecabezas *m inv (juego)* jigsaw; *(asunto complicado)* puzzle.

rompeolas *m inv* breakwater.

romper *vt* to break; *(rasgar)* to tear; *(hacer añicos)* to smash; *(terminar)* to break off ♦ *vi (olas, día)* to break; **~ con alguien** to split up with sb; **~ a hacer algo** to suddenly start doing sthg ❏ **romperse** *vpr (partirse)* to break; *(desgarrarse)* to tear.

ron *m* rum.

roncar *vi (persona)* to snore; *(mar, viento, etc)* to roar.

ronco, -ca *adj* hoarse.

ronda *f (paseo)* nighttime walk on which young men serenade young women outside their windows; *(grupo de personas)* group of serenaders; *(vigilancia)* rounds *(pl)*; *(fam: de copas, tapas)* round; *(de circunvalación)* ring road.

rondín *m (Amér)* guard.

ronquido *m (de persona)* snore; *(de motor, máquina)* roar.

ronronear *vi* to purr.

ronroneo *m* purr.

ropa *f* clothes *(pl)*; ~ **interior** underwear.

roquefort [roke'for] *m* Roquefort; **al** ~ in a Roquefort sauce.

rosa *f* rose ♦ *adj inv* pink; ~ **de los vientos** compass.

rosado, -da *adj* pink ♦ *m* rosé.

rosal *m* rose(bush).

rosario *m* rosary.

roscón *m*: ~ **(de reyes)** ringshaped bun eaten on 6 January.

rosetón *m* rose window.

rosquilla *f* ring doughnut.

rostro *m* face.

rotativo *m* newspaper.

roto, -ta *pp* → **romper** ♦ *adj* broken ♦ *m (en ropa)* tear.

rotonda *f (plaza)* circus; *(edificio)* rotunda.

rotulador *m (para dibujar)* felttip pen; *(para marcar)* marker pen.

rótulo *m (letrero)* sign.

rotundo, -da *adj (respuesta, negación)* emphatic.

rozar *vt (frotar)* to rub; *(tocar)* to brush (against) ❏ **rozarse** *vpr (desgastarse)* to get worn.

r.p.m. *(abrev de revoluciones por minuto)* rpm.

Rte. *abrev* = **remitente**.

RTVE *f Spanish state broadcasting company.*

rubí *m* ruby.

rubio, -bia *adj* blond *(f blonde).*

rubor *m (enrojecimiento)* blush; *(vergüenza)* embarrassment.

ruborizarse *vpr* to blush.

rudimentario, -ria *adj* rudimentary.

rudo, -da *adj* rough; *(descortés)* rude.

rueda *f (pieza)* wheel; *(corro)* circle; ~ **de prensa** press conference; ~ **de repuesto** O **de recambio** spare wheel.

ruedo *m (plaza de toros)* bullring; *(de falda)* hem.

ruego *m* request.

rugby *m* rugby.

rugido *m* roar.

rugir *vi* to roar.

rugoso, -sa *adj (áspero)* rough; *(con arrugas)* wrinkled.

ruido *m (sonido desagradable)* noise; *(sonido cualquiera)* sound.

ruidoso, -sa *adj* noisy.

ruin *adj* mean.

ruina *f* ruin ❏ **ruinas** *fpl* ruins.

ruinoso, -sa *adj (edificio, puente)* tumbledown; *(negocio, trabajo)* ruinous.

ruiseñor *m* nightingale.

ruleta f roulette.

rulo m (rizo) curl; (objeto) curler.

ruma f (Amér) pile.

rumba f rumba.

rumbo m (dirección) direction; (con) ~ a heading for.

rumiante m ruminant.

rumiar vt (masticar) to chew; (fig: reflexionar) to chew over.

rumor m (chisme) rumour; (ruido) murmur.

rumorearse v impers: **se rumorea que** ... it is rumoured that ...

ruptura f (de relaciones) breaking-off.

rural adj rural.

Rusia s Russia.

ruso, -sa adj, m, f Russian.

ruta f route.

rutina f routine.

S

s (abrev de segundo) sec.

S (abrev de San) St.

SA f (abrev de sociedad anónima) ~ Ltd, = PLC.

sábado m Saturday; **cada ~, todos los ~s** every Saturday; **caer en ~** to be on a Saturday; **el próximo ~, el ~ que viene** next Saturday; **viene el ~** she's coming on Saturday; **el ~ pasado** last Saturday; **el ~ por la ma-**

ñana/tarde/noche (on) Saturday morning/afternoon/night; **este ~ (pasado)** last Saturday; (próximo) this (coming) Saturday; **los ~s (on) Saturdays.**

sábana f sheet.

sabañón m chilblain.

saber m knowledge ♦ vt (conocer) to know; (entender de) to know about; (poder hablar) to speak ♦ vi: ~ **hacer algo** (ser capaz de) to know how to do sthg, to be able to do sthg; (Amér: soler) to usually do sthg; **¿sabes algo de él?** have you heard from him?; ~ **bien/mal** (alimento, bebida) to taste good/bad; ~ **mal a alguien** to upset sb ❑ **saber a** v + prep to taste of.

sabiduría f (prudencia) wisdom; (conocimiento profundo) knowledge.

sabio, -bia adj (prudente) wise; (con conocimientos profundos) knowledgable ♦ m, f (persona prudente) wise person; (persona sabia) knowledgable person.

sable m sabre.

sabor m (gusto) taste; (variedad) flavour; **tener ~ a** to taste of; **helado con ~ a fresa** strawberry ice cream.

saborear vt to savour.

sabotaje m sabotage.

sabrá v → saber.

sabroso, -sa adj (comida) tasty; (comentario, noticia, etc) juicy; (cantidad) substantial.

sacacorchos m inv corkscrew.

sacapuntas m inv pencil sharpener.

sacar vt (extraer, llevar) to take out; (quitar) to remove; (salvar, información) to get out; (conseguir, *obtener*) to get; (*en el juego*) to play; (*ensanchar*) to let out; (*pecho, barriga*) to stick out; (*crear, fabricar*) to bring out; (*copia*) to make ◆ *vi* (*en tenis*) to serve; **~ billetes** o **entradas** to get tickets; **~ brillo** to polish; **~ dinero** to withdraw money; **~ fotos** to take photos; **~ la lengua** to stick one's tongue out; **~ nota** to get a good mark; **~ buenas/malas notas** to get good/bad marks; **sacan tres puntos a sus rivales** they are three points ahead of their rivals ❑ **sacarse** *vpr* (*carné, permiso*) to get.

sacarina *f* saccharine.

sacerdote *m* priest.

saciar *vt* to satisfy; (*sed*) to quench.

saco *m* sack, bag; (*Amér: chaqueta*) jacket; **~ de dormir** sleeping bag.

sacramento *m* sacrament.

sacrificar *vt* (*renunciar a*) to sacrifice; (*animal*) to slaughter ❑ **sacrificarse** *vpr:* **~se por** to make sacrifices for.

sacrificio *m* sacrifice; (*de animal*) slaughter.

sacristán *m* sacristan.

sacudida *f* (*movimiento brusco*) shake; (*de vehículo*) bump; (*terremoto*) tremor.

sacudir *vt* (*agitar*) to shake; (*alfombra, sábana*) to shake out; (*pegar*) to hit.

safari *m* (*expedición*) safari; (*parque zoológico*) safari park.

Sagitario *m* Sagittarius.

sagrado, -da *adj* sacred.

sal *f* (*condimento*) salt; (*fig: gracia*) wit ❑ **sales** *fpl* (*de baño*) bath salts;

(*para reanimar*) smelling salts.

sala *f* (*habitación*) room; (*de hospital*) ward; (*de cine*) screen, cinema; (*tribunal*) court; **~ de espera** waiting room; **~ de estar** living room; **~ de fiestas** discothèque; **~ de juegos** casino; **"~ climatizada"** "air-conditioning".

salado, -da *adj* (*comida*) salty; (*persona*) funny.

salamandra *f* salamander.

salar *vt* (*comida*) to add salt to; (*para conservar*) to salt.

salario *m* salary.

salchicha *f* sausage.

salchichón *m* = salami.

saldo *m* (*de cuenta*) balance; (*pago*) payment; (*mercancía*) remnant.

salero *m* (*recipiente*) salt cellar; (*gracia*) wit.

salida *f* (*de lugar*) exit; (*de tren, avión, autobús*) departure; (*excursión*) outing; (*ocurrencia*) witty remark; (*recurso*) way out; (*de productos*) output; **"~ sin compra"** *sign in supermarkets etc indicating exit for people who have not bought anything;* **~ de incendios** fire escape; **~ de socorro** o **emergencia** emergency exit; **~s internacionales** international departures.

salina *f* saltmine ❑ **salinas** *fpl* saltworks (*sg*).

salir *vi* 1. (*ir fuera*) to go out; (*venir fuera*) to come out; **salió a la calle** he went out into the street; **¡sal aquí fuera!** come out here!; **~ de** to leave.

2. (*marcharse*) to leave; **el tren sale muy temprano** the train leaves very early; **él ha salido para Madrid**

he's left for Madrid.

3. (ser novios) to go out; **Juan y María salen juntos** Juan and María are going out together.

4. (separarse) to come off; **el anillo no le sale del dedo** the ring won't come off her finger.

5. (resultar) to turn out; **ha salido muy estudioso** he has turned out to be very studious; **ha salido perjudicado** he came off badly; **~ bien/mal** to turn out well/badly; **mi número ha salido premiado** my ticket won a prize.

6. (resolverse): **este problema no me sale** I can't solve this problem.

7. (proceder): **~ de** to come from.

8. (surgir) to come out; **ha salido el sol** (al amanecer) the sun has come up.

9. (aparecer) to appear; (publicación, producto, disco) to come out; **¡qué bien sales en la foto!** you look great in the photo!; **en la película sale tu actor favorito** your favourite actor is in the film.

10. (costar): **la comida le ha salido por diez mil pesetas** the meal worked out at ten thousand pesetas.

11. (sobresalir) to stick out

12. (librarse): **~ de** to get out of.

13. (en locuciones): **~ adelante** (persona, empresa) to get by; (proyecto, propuesta) to be successful.

□ **salirse** vpr (marcharse) to leave; (rebosar) to overflow; **~se de** (desviarse) to come off; (fig: escaparse) to deviate from.

saliva f saliva.

salmón m salmon; **~ ahumado** smoked salmon; **~ fresco** fresh salmon.

salmonete m red mullet.

salón m (de casa) living room; (de edificio público) hall; (muebles) lounge suite; (exposición) show; **~ del automóvil** motor show; **~ recreativo** arcade.

salpicadero m dashboard.

salpicar vt to splash ♦ vi (aceite) to spit.

salpicón m: **~ de marisco** cold dish of chopped seafood with pepper, salt, oil, vinegar and onion.

salpimentar vt to season.

salsa f (para comidas) sauce; (de carne) gravy; (gracia) spice; (baile, música) salsa; **~ bechamel** bechamel sauce; **~ rosa** thousand island dressing; **~ de tomate** tomato sauce; **~ verde** sauce made with mayonnaise, parsley, capers and gherkins.

salsera f gravy boat.

saltamontes m inv grasshopper.

saltar vi to jump; (tapón, corcho) to pop out; (levantarse) to jump (up); (botón, pintura) to come off; (enfadarse) to flare up; (explotar) to explode ♦ vt to jump over □ **saltarse** vpr (omitir) to miss out; (cola, semáforo) to jump; (ley, norma) to break.

salteado, -da adj (discontinuo) unevenly spaced; (frito) sautéed.

saltear vt (freír) to sauté.

salto m jump; (en el tiempo, omisión) gap; **~ de agua** waterfall; **~ de cama** negligée.

salud f health; **tener buena/mala ~** to be healthy/in poor health; **estar bien/mal de ~** to be healthy/in poor health; **¡(a su) ~!**

cheers!

saludable *adj* healthy; *(provechoso)* beneficial.

saludar *vt* to greet ❑ **saludarse** *vpr* to greet each other.

saludo *m* greeting ❑ **saludos** *mpl (recuerdos)* regards.

salvación *f (rescate)* rescue.

Salvador *m*: **El ~** El Salvador.

salvadoreño, -ña *adj & m, f* Salvadoran.

salvaje *adj* wild.

salvamanteles *m inv* tablemat.

salvar *vt* to save; *(persona)* to rescue; *(obstáculo)* to go round; *(peligro, dificultad)* to get through; *(distancia, espacio)* to cover ❑ **salvarse** *vpr (escapar)* to escape.

salvavidas *m inv (chaleco)* lifejacket; *(cinturón)* lifebelt.

salvo *adv* except; **a ~** safe.

san *adj* → **santo**.

sanatorio *m* sanatorium.

sanción *f (castigo)* punishment.

sancochado *m (Amér)* meat and vegetable stew.

sancochar *vt (Amér)* to stew.

sandalia *f* sandal.

sandía *f* watermelon.

sandwich ['sanwitʃ] *m* toasted sandwich.

sanfermines *mpl* Pamplona bullfighting festival.

---

i **SANFERMINES**

Pamplona is famous for the "sanfermines", a week-long festival starting on 7 July, in which bulls are let loose in the streets of the town and young men demonstrate their bravery by running in front of them on the way to the bullring, sometimes receiving fatal wounds in the process. Bullfights are held every afternoon of the festival.

---

sangrar *vi* to bleed ◆ *vt (línea, párrafo)* to indent.

sangre *f (líquido)* blood; **~ azul** blue blood; **~ fría** sangfroid.

sangría *f* sangria.

sangriento, -ta *adj* bloody.

sanidad *f (servicios de salud)* (public) health; *(higiene)* health.

sanitario, -ria *adj* health *(antes de s)* ◆ *m, f* health worker ❑ **sanitarios** *mpl (instalaciones)* bathroom fittings.

sano, -na *adj* healthy; *(sin daño)* undamaged; **~ y salvo** safe and sound.

santiguarse *vpr* to make the sign of the Cross.

santo, -ta *adj* holy ◆ *m, f* saint ◆ *m (festividad)* saint's day.

---

i **SANTO**

Catholic tradition dictates that each day of the year is dedicated to a particular saint. On the day in question, people with the same name as the saint celebrate by buying drinks for their friends and family and, in turn, they are given presents.

---

santuario *m* shrine.

sapo *m* toad.

saque *m (en tenis)* serve.

secuestrar

saquear *vt (tienda)* to loot; *(vaciar)* to ransack.

sarampión *m* measles.

sarcástico, -ca *adj* sarcastic.

sardana *f popular Catalan dance*.

sardina *f* sardine; **~s a la plancha** grilled sardines.

sargento *m* sergeant.

sarna *f (de persona)* scabies.

sarpullido *m* rash.

sarro *m (de dientes)* tartar.

sartén *f* frying pan.

sastre *m* tailor.

sastrería *f (tienda)* tailor's (shop); *(oficio)* tailoring.

satélite *m* satellite.

sátira *f* satire.

satírico, -ca *adj* satirical.

satisfacción *f* satisfaction.

satisfacer *vt* to satisfy; *(deuda)* to pay; *(duda, pregunta, dificultad)* to deal with.

satisfecho, -cha *pp* → **satisfacer** ♦ *adj* satisfied.

sauce *m* willow.

sauna *f* sauna.

saxofón *m* saxophone.

sazonar *vt* to season.

se *pron* 1. *(reflexivo)* himself *(f* herself), themselves *(pl)*; *(usted mismo)* yourself, yourselves *(pl)*; *(de cosas, animales)* itself, themselves *(pl)*; **~ lavó los dientes** she cleaned her teeth.
2. *(recíproco)* each other; **~ aman** they love each other; **~ escriben** they write to each other.
3. *(en construcción pasiva)*: **~ ha suspendido la reunión** the meeting has been cancelled.
4. *(en construcción impersonal)*: "**~**

habla inglés" "English spoken"; "**~ prohíbe fumar**" "no smoking"; **~ dice que** it is said that.
5. *(complemento indirecto)* to him *(f* to her), to them *(pl)*; *(usted, ustedes)* to you; *(de cosa, animal)* to it, to them *(pl)*; **yo ~ lo daré** I'll give it to him/her/etc.

sé *v* → **saber, ser**.

sea *v* → **ser**.

secador *m* dryer; **~ de cabello** hairdryer.

secadora *f (tumble)* dryer.

secano *m* dry land.

secar *vt* to dry; *(sudor, sangre)* to wipe away □ **secarse** *vpr (río, fuente)* to dry up; *(planta, árbol)* to wilt; *(ropa, cabello, superficie)* to dry.

sección *f* section; *(de empresa, oficina)* department.

seco, -ca *adj* dry; *(planta, árbol)* wilted; *(delgado)* lean; *(ruido, sonido)* dull; *(brusco)* brusque; **a secas** just, simply; **parar en ~** to stop dead.

secretaría *f (oficina)* secretary's office; *(cargo)* post of secretary.

secretariado *m (estudios)* secretarial studies *(pl)*; *(profesión)* secretaries *(pl)*.

secretario, -ria *m, f* secretary; *(de ministerio)* Secretary of State.

secreto, -ta *adj* secret ♦ *m* secret; *(reserva)* secrecy; **en ~** in secret.

secta *f* sect.

sector *m* sector.

secuestrador, -ra *m, f (de persona)* kidnapper; *(de avión)* hijacker.

secuestrar *vt (persona)* to kidnap; (avión) to hijack.

secuestro m (de persona) kidnap; (de avión) hijacking.

secundario, -ria adj secondary.

sed v → ser ◆ f thirst; **correr me da ~** running makes me thirsty; **tener ~** to be thirsty.

seda f silk.

sedante m sedative.

sede f headquarters (pl).

sedentario, -ria adj sedentary.

sediento, -ta adj thirsty.

seductor, -ra adj (persona) seductive; (oferta, libro) enticing.

segador, -ra m, f harvester.

segadora f (máquina) reaping machine, → **segador**.

segar vt (hierba) to mow; (cereal) to reap.

segmento m segment.

seguido, -da adj (continuo) continuous; (consecutivo) consecutive ◆ adv (en línea recta) straight on; **dos años ~s** two years in a row; **en seguida** straight away; **todo ~** straight ahead.

seguir vt to follow; (perseguir) to chase; (reanudar) to continue ◆ vi to continue; **~ a algo** to follow sthg; **sigue nevando** it's still snowing.

según prep (de acuerdo con) according to; (dependiendo de) depending on ◆ adv as; **~ yo/tú** in my/your opinion.

segunda f (velocidad) second (gear), → **segundo**.

segundero m second hand.

segundo, -da núm second

◆ m, f second-in-command ◆ m (de tiempo) second, → **sexto**.

seguramente adv (con seguridad) for certain; (probablemente) probably.

seguridad f (falta de peligro) safety; (protección) security; (certidumbre) certainty; (confianza) confidence ❏ **Seguridad Social** f Social Security.

seguro, -ra adj (sin riesgo, peligro) safe; (confiado) sure; (infalible) reliable; (amigo) firm ◆ adv definitely ◆ m (de coche, vida, casa) insurance; (de arma, máquina) safety catch; (de un temor) to be safe; (cierto, confiado) to be sure; **~ Social** (Amér) Social Security.

seis adj inv six ◆ m six; (día) sixth ◆ mpl six; (temperatura) six (degrees) ◆ fpl: **(son) las ~** (it's) six o'clock; **el ~ de agosto** the sixth of August; **doscientos ~** two hundred and six; **treinta y ~** thirty-six; **de ~ en ~** in sixes; **los ~** the six of them; **empataron a ~** they drew six-all; **~ a cero** six-nil.

seiscientos núm six hundred, → **seis**.

selección f selection; (equipo nacional) team.

seleccionador, -ra m, f = manager.

seleccionar vt to pick.

selectividad f (examen) Spanish university entrance examination.

---

i **SELECTIVIDAD**

The "selectividad" is a series of exams which take place over two days at the end of secondary education in Spain. The mark obtained in these exams is one of the factors which determines whether or not a student is admitted to his or her preferred field of study at university.

selecto, -ta adj fine, choice.

selector m selector.

self-service m self-service restaurant.

sello m (de correos) stamp; (tampón) rubber stamp.

selva f (jungla) jungle; (bosque) forest.

semáforo m traffic lights (pl).

semana f week ❑ **Semana Santa** f Easter; (RELIG) Holy Week.

---

i SEMANA SANTA

Throughout Easter week in Spain, a number of processions take place. People line the streets and pray, as statues of Christ and the saints are carried past. The most famous procession is that of Seville.

---

semanal adj (que sucede cada semana) weekly; (que dura una semana) week-long.

semanario m weekly (newspaper).

sembrar vt to sow.

semejante adj (parecido) similar; (tal, uso despectivo) such ◆ m fellow human being; **~ cosa** such a thing.

semejanza f similarity.

semen m semen.

semestre m six-month period.

semidesnatado, -da adj semi-skimmed.

semidirecto, -ta adj: **tren ~** through train, a section of which becomes a stopping train.

semifinal f semifinal.

semilla f seed.

sémola f semolina.

Senado m: **el ~** the Senate.

senador, -ra m, f senator.

sencillo, -lla adj simple; (espontáneo) unaffected; (Amér: monedas) small change.

sendero m track.

seno m (pecho) breast, (interior) heart.

sensación f sensation; (premonición) feeling.

sensacional adj sensational.

sensacionalismo m sensationalism.

sensacionalista adj sensationalist.

sensato, -ta adj sensible.

sensibilidad f (don) feel; (sentimentalismo, de aparato) sensitivity; (de los sentidos) feeling.

sensible adj sensitive.

sensual adj sensual.

sentado, -da adj (persona) sensible; **dar por ~** to take for granted.

sentar vt (basar) to base ◆ vi. **~ bien/mal a alguien** (comida, bebida) to agree/disagree with sb; (ropa, zapatos, joyas) to suit/not to suit sb; (dicho, hecho, broma) to go down well/badly with sb ❑ **sentarse** vpr to sit (down).

sentencia f (de juez, tribunal)

sentence; (frase corta) saying.

sentenciar vt to sentence.

sentido m sense; (dirección) direction; (conocimiento) consciousness; ~ común common sense.

sentimental adj sentimental.

sentimiento m feeling; le acompaño en el ~ my deepest sympathy.

sentir m feeling ♦ vt to feel; (lamentar) to be sorry about, to regret; lo siento I'm sorry □ sentirse vpr to feel; ~se bien/mal (de salud) to feel well/ill; (de ánimo) to feel good/bad.

seña f (gesto) sign; (marca) mark □ señas fpl (domicilio) address (sg); ~s personales description (sg).

señal f sign; (aviso, orden) signal; (fianza) deposit; (cicatriz) mark; (de teléfono) tone; ~ de tráfico road sign.

señalado, -da adj (fecha, día) special; (persona) distinguished.

señalar vt (poner marca, herir) to mark; (con la mano, dedo) to point out; (lugar, precio, fecha) to fix; (nombrar) to pick; (ser indicio de) to indicate.

señor, -ra adj (gran) big ♦ m (hombre) man; (antes de nombre) Mr; (al dirigir la palabra) Sir; (dueño) owner; (caballero) gentleman; muy ~ mío Dear Sir.

señora f (mujer, dama) lady; (antes de nombre) Mrs; (al dirigir la palabra) Madam; (esposa) wife; (dueña) owner; muy ~ mía Dear Madam.

señorita f (maestra) teacher; (mujer joven) young woman; (mujer soltera) Miss.

señorito, -ta adj (despec) lordly ♦ m master.

sepa v → saber.

separación f separation; (espacio, distancia) space.

separado, -da adj (persona, matrimonio) separated.

separar vt to separate; (silla, etc) to move away; (reservar) to put aside □ separarse vpr (persona) to leave; (pareja) to separate.

sepia f cuttlefish; ~ a la plancha grilled cuttlefish.

septentrional adj northern.

septiembre m = setiembre.

séptimo, -ma núm seventh, → sexto.

sepulcro m tomb.

sequía f drought.

ser m being; ~ humano human being.
♦ v aux (forma la voz pasiva) to be; el atracador fue visto the robber was seen.
♦ v copulativo 1. (descripción) to be; mi abrigo es lila my coat is lilac; este señor es alto/gracioso this man is tall/funny; ~ como to be like.
2. (empleo, dedicación) to be; su mujer es abogada his wife is a lawyer.
3.: ~ de (materia) to be made of; (origen) to be from; (posesión) to belong to; (pertenencia) to be a member of.
♦ vi 1. (suceder, ocurrir) to be; la final fue ayer the final was yesterday.
2. (haber, existir) to be.
3. (valer) to be; ¿cuánto es? - son doscientas pesetas how much is it?

- two hundred pesetas, please.

4. *(día, fecha, hora)* to be; **hoy es martes** it's Tuesday today; **¿qué hora es?** what time is it?; **son las tres (de la tarde)** it's three o'clock (in the afternoon).

5. *(en locuciones):* **a no ~ que** unless; **como sea** somehow or other; **o sea** I mean.

◆ *v impers (expresión de tiempo)* to be; **es de día/de noche** it's day-time/night; **es muy tarde** it is very late.

❑ **ser para** *v + prep (servir para, adecuarse a)* to be for.

serenar *vt* to calm ❑ **serenarse** *vpr (persona, ánimo)* to calm down; *(mar)* to become calm; *(tiempo)* to clear up.

serenidad *f* calm.

sereno, -na *adj* calm; *(tiempo)* fine.

serie *f* series; *(en deportes)* heat.

seriedad *f* seriousness; *(formalidad)* responsible nature.

serio, -ria *adj* serious; *(responsable)* responsible; *(sin adornos)* sober; **en ~** seriously; **ir en ~** to be serious; **tomar en ~** to take seriously.

sermón *m* sermon.

serpentina *f* streamer.

serpiente *f* snake.

serrar *vt* to sow.

serrín *m* sawdust.

serrucho *m* handsaw.

servicio *m* service; *(retrete)* toilet; **estar de ~** to be on duty; **~ militar** military service; **~ público** public service; **~ de revelado rápido** = developing in one hour; **~ urgente** express service; **~s míni**-mos skeleton services *(pl)* ❑ **servicios** *mpl (baño)* toilets.

servidumbre *f (criados)* servants *(pl)*; *(dependencia)* servitude.

servilleta *f* serviette.

servir *vt (bebida, comida)* to serve; *(mercancía)* to supply; *(ayudar)* to serve ◆ *vi* to serve; *(ser útil)* to be useful; **no sirven** *(ropa, zapatos)* they're no good; **~ de algo** to serve as sthg; **¿en qué le puedo ~?** what can I do for you? ❑ **servirse** *vpr (bebida, comida)* to help o.s. to; **"sírvase usted mismo"** "please help yourself"; **servirse de** *v + prep* to make use of.

sesenta *núm* sixty, → **seis**.

sesión *f* session; *(de cine)* showing; *(de teatro)* performance; **~ continua** continuous showing; **~ golfa** late-night showing; **~ matinal** matinée; **~ de noche** evening showing; **~ de tarde** afternoon matinée.

sesos *mpl* brains.

seta *f* mushroom; **~s al ajillo** garlic mushrooms; **~s con gambas** *mushrooms filled with prawns and egg.*

setecientos, -tas *núm* seven hundred, → **seis**.

setenta *núm* seventy, → **seis**.

setiembre *m* September; **a principios/mediados/finales de ~** at the beginning/in the middle/at the end of September; **el nueve de ~** the ninth of September; **el pasado/próximo (mes de) ~** last/next September; **en ~** in September; **este (mes de) ~** *(pasado)* last September; *(próximo)* this (coming) September; **para ~** by

September.

seto *m* hedge.

severidad *f* severity.

severo, -ra *adj* severe; *(estricto)* strict.

Sevilla *s* Seville.

sevillanas *fpl (baile)* dance from Andalusia; *(música)* music of the *"sevillanas"*.

sexismo *m* sexism.

sexista *mf* sexist.

sexo *m* sex; *(órganos sexuales)* genitals *(pl)*.

sexto, -ta *adj* sixth ♦ *m*; **el ~, la sexta** *(persona, cosa)* the sixth; *(piso, planta)* the sixth floor ♦ *m*: ~ **(de E.G.B.)** year six of Spanish primary education system; **llegar el ~** to come sixth; **capítulo ~** chapter six; **el ~ día** the sixth day; **en ~ lugar, en sexta posición** in sixth place; **la sexta parte** a sixth.

sexual *adj* sexual.

sexualidad *f* sexuality.

si *conj* if.

sí *(pl* **síes)** *adv* yes ♦ *pron (de personas)* himself *(f* herself*)*, themselves *(pl)*; *(usted)* yourself, yourselves *(pl)*; *(de cosas, animales)* itself, themselves *(pl)*; *(impersonal)* oneself ♦ *m* consent; **creo que ~** I think so.

sida *m* AIDS.

sidecar *m* sidecar.

sidra *f* cider.

siega *f (acción)* harvesting; *(temporada)* harvest.

siembra *f (acción)* sowing; *(temporada)* sowing time.

siempre *adv* always; *(Amér: con toda seguridad)* definitely; **desde ~** always.

sien *f* temple.

sierra *f (herramienta)* saw; *(de montañas)* mountain range.

siesta *f* afternoon nap; **echar una ~** to have an afternoon nap.

siete *núm* seven, → **seis** ♦ *f*: **¡la gran ~!** *(Amér: fam)* Jesus!

sifón *m (botella)* siphon; *(agua con gas)* soda water.

siglas *fpl* acronym *(sg)*.

siglo *m* century; *(fam: periodo muy largo)* ages *(pl)*.

significado *m* meaning.

significar *vt* to mean.

significativo, -va *adj* significant.

signo *m* sign; ~ **de admiración** exclamation mark; ~ **de interrogación** question mark.

siguiente *adj (en el tiempo, espacio)* next; *(a continuación)* following ♦ *mf*: **el/la ~** the next one.

sílaba *f* syllable.

silbar *vi* to whistle ♦ *vt (abuchear)* to boo.

silbato *m* whistle.

silbido *m* whistle.

silenciador *m* silencer.

silencio *m* silence.

silenciosamente *adv* silently.

silencioso, -sa *adj* silent, quiet.

silla *f* chair; ~ **de montar** saddle; ~ **de ruedas** wheelchair.

sillín *m* saddle.

sillón *m* armchair.

silueta *f* figure; *(contorno)* outline.

silvestre *adj* wild.

símbolo *m* symbol.

simétrico, -ca *adj* symmetrical.

similar *adj* similar.

similitud *f* similarity.

simpatía *f* (*cariño*) affection; (*cordialidad*) friendliness.

simpático, -ca *adj* (*amable*) nice; (*amigable*) friendly.

simpatizante *mf* sympathizer.

simpatizar *vi*: ~ (con) (*persona*) to get on (with); (*cosa*) to sympathize (with).

simple *adj* simple; (*sin importancia*) mere ♦ *m* (*en tenis, ping-pong*) singles (*pl*).

simplicidad *f* (*sencillez*) simplicity; (*ingenuidad*) simpleness.

simular *vt* to feign.

simultáneo, -a *adj* simultaneous.

sin *prep* without; **está ~ hacer** it hasn't been done before; **estamos ~ vino** we're out of wine; **~ embargo** however.

sinagoga *f* synagogue.

sinceridad *f* sincerity.

sincero, -ra *adj* sincere.

sincronizar *vt* to synchronize.

sindicato *m* (trade) union.

sinfonía *f* symphony.

sinfónico, -ca *adj* symphonic.

singular *adj* (*único*) unique; (*extraordinario*) strange; (*en gramática*) singular ♦ *m* singular.

siniestro, -tra *adj* sinister ♦ *m* (*accidente, desgracia*) disaster; (*de coche, avión*) crash.

sinnúmero *m*: **un ~ de** countless.

sino *conj* (*para contraponer*) but; (*excepto*) except.

sinónimo *m* synonym.

síntesis *f* (*resumen*) summary.

sintético, -ca *adj* synthetic.

sintetizador *m* synthesizer.

síntoma *m* symptom.

sintonía *f* (*música, canción*) signature tune; (*de televisión, radio*) tuning.

sintonizar *vt* to tune in to.

sinvergüenza *mf* (*descarado*) cheeky person; (*estafador*) scoundrel.

siquiera *adv* at least; **ni ~** not even.

sirena *f* (*sonido*) siren; (*en mitología*) mermaid.

sirviente, -ta *m, f* servant.

sisa *f* (*robo*) pilfering; (*de vestido*) armhole.

sistema *m* system; (*medio, método*) method; **por ~** systematically.

sitiar *vt* to besiege.

sitio *m* (*lugar, plaza, espacio*) space, room; (*de ciudad, pueblo*) siege; (*Amér: de taxis*) rank; **en otro ~** somewhere else; **hacer ~** to make room.

situación *f* (*estado, condición, localización*) position; (*circunstancias*) situation.

situar *vt* (*colocar*) to put; (*localizar*) to locate ❑ **situarse** *vpr* (*establecerse*) to get established.

skin head *mf* skinhead.

SL *f* (abrev de sociedad limitada) = Ltd.

SM (abrev de Su Majestad) HM.

s/n abrev = **sin número**.

sobaco *m* armpit.

sobado, -da adj (vestido) shabby; (libro) dog-eared; (chiste, broma) old.

soberbia f arrogance.

soberbio, -bia adj (orgulloso) arrogant; (magnífico) magnificent.

soborno m bribe.

sobrar vi (haber demasiado) to be more than enough; (estar de más) to be superfluous; (quedar) to be left (over).

sobras fpl (de comida) leftovers.

sobrasada f spicy Mallorcan sausage.

sobre[1] prep 1. (encima de) on (top of); el libro estaba ~ la mesa the book was on the table.
2. (por encima de) over, above; el pato vuela ~ el lago the duck is flying over the lake.
3. (acerca de) about; un libro ~ el amor a book about love.
4. (alrededor de) about; llegaron ~ las diez they arrived at about ten o'clock.
5. (en locuciones): ~ todo above all.

sobre[2] m envelope.

sobreático m penthouse.

sobrecarga f excess weight.

sobredosis f inv overdose.

sobrehumano, -na adj superhuman.

sobremesa f period of time sitting around the table after lunch; hacer la ~ to have a chat after lunch.

sobrenombre m nickname.

sobrepasar vt (exceder) to exceed; (aventajar) to overtake.

sobreponer vt (poner delante) to put first ❑ **sobreponerse a** v + prep to overcome.

sobrepuesto, -ta adj superimposed.

sobresaliente adj outstanding
♦ m (nota) excellent.

sobresalir vi (en altura) to jut out; (en importancia) to stand out.

sobresalto m fright.

sobrevivir vi to survive.

sobrevolar vt to fly over.

sobrino, -na m, f nephew (f niece).

sobrio, -bria adj sober; (moderado) restrained.

sociable adj sociable.

social adj (de la sociedad) social; (de los socios) company (antes de s).

socialista mf socialist.

sociedad f society; (empresa) company.

socio, -cia m, f (de club, asociación) member; (de negocio) partner.

sociología f sociology.

sociólogo, -ga m, f sociologist.

socorrer vt to help.

socorrismo m (primeros auxilios) first aid; (en la playa) lifesaving.

socorrista mf (primeros auxilios) first aid worker; (en la playa) lifeguard.

socorro m help ♦ interj help!

soda f soda water.

sofá m sofa, couch.

sofisticado, -da adj sophisticated.

sofocante adj stifling.

sofoco m (ahogo) breathlessness; (disgusto) fit (of anger); (vergüenza) embarrassment.

sofrito m tomato and onion sauce.

software ['sofwer] m software.

sois v → ser.

sol m sun; (de plaza de toros) seats in the sun which are the cheapest in the bullring; **hace ~** it's sunny; **tomar el ~** to sunbathe.

solamente adv only.

solapa f (de vestido, chaqueta) lapel; (de libro) flap.

solar adj solar ♦ m (undeveloped) plot.

solárium m solarium.

soldado m soldier; **~ raso** private.

soldador m soldering iron.

soldar vt to weld.

soleado, -da adj sunny.

soledad f (falta de compañía) solitude; (tristeza) loneliness.

solemne adj solemn; (grande) utter.

solemnidad f ceremony.

soler vi: **~ hacer algo** to do sthg usually; **solíamos hacerlo** we used to do it.

solicitar vt (pedir) to request; (puesto) to apply for.

solicitud f (petición) request; (de puesto) application; (impreso) application form.

solidaridad f solidarity.

sólido, -da adj (cimientos, casa, muro) solid; (argumento, conocimiento) sound ♦ m solid.

solista mf soloist.

solitario, -ria adj (sin compañía) solitary; (lugar) lonely ♦ m, f loner ♦ m (juego) patience; (joya) solitaire.

sollozar vi to sob.

sollozo m sob.

solo, -la adj (sin compañía, familia) alone; (único) single; (sin añadidos) on its own; (café) black; (whisky) neat; (solitario) lonely; **a solas** on one's own.

sólo adv only.

solomillo m sirloin; **~ a la parrilla** grilled sirloin steak; **~ de ternera** veal sirloin.

soltar vt (de la mano) to let go of; (desatar) to undo; (dejar libre) to set free; (desenrollar) to pay out; (decir) to come out with; (lanzar) to let out.

soltero, -ra adj single ♦ m, f bachelor (f single woman).

solterón, -ona m, f old bachelor (f old maid).

soltura f fluency; **con ~** fluently.

solución f solution.

solucionar vt to solve.

solvente adj solvent.

sombra f (oscuridad) shade; (de un cuerpo) shadow; (de plaza de toros) most expensive seats in the bullring, located in the shade; **a la ~** in the shade; **el árbol da ~** the tree is shady.

sombrero m hat.

sombrilla f sunshade.

someter vt (dominar) to subdue; (mostrar) to submit; **~ a algo** to subject sb to sthg ☐ **someterse** vpr (rendirse) to surrender.

somier m (de muelles) bed springs (pl).

somnífero m sleeping pill.

somos v → ser.

son v → ser.

sonajero m rattle.

sonar vi to sound; (teléfono, timbre) to ring; (ser conocido) to be familiar; (letra) to be pronounced ◆ vt (nariz) to blow; **suena a verdad** it sounds true ❑ **sonarse** vpr to blow one's nose.

sonido m sound.

sonoro, -ra adj resonant; (banda) sound (antes de s); (consonante, vocal) voiced.

sonreír vi to smile ❑ **sonreírse** vpr to smile.

sonriente adj smiling.

sonrisa f smile.

sonrojarse vpr to blush.

soñar vi to dream ◆ vt to dream about; ~ **con** to dream of.

sopa f soup; ~ **de ajo** garlic soup; ~ **de cebolla** onion soup; ~ **de marisco** seafood bisque; ~ **de pescado** fish soup.

sopera f soup tureen.

soplar vi to blow ◆ vt (polvo, migas) to blow away; (respuesta) to whisper.

soplete m blowlamp.

soplido m puff.

soplo m (soplido) puff; (del corazón) murmur; (fam: chivatazo) tip-off.

soportales mpl arcade (sg).

soportar vt (carga, peso) to support; (persona) to stand; (dolor, molestia) to bear.

soporte m support.

soprano f soprano.

sorber vt (beber) to sip; (haciendo ruido) to slurp; (absorber) to soak up.

sorbete m sorbet; ~ **de fram-** buesa raspberry sorbet; ~ **de limón** lemon sorbet.

sordo, -da adj deaf; (ruido, sentimiento) dull ◆ m, f deaf person.

sordomudo, -da m, f deaf-mute.

soroche m (Amér) altitude sickness.

sorprendente adj surprising.

sorprender vt to surprise ❑ **sorprenderse** vpr to be surprised.

sorpresa f surprise; **por** ~ by surprise.

sorpresivo, -va adj (Amér) unexpected.

sortear vt (rifar) to raffle; (evitar) to dodge.

sorteo m (lotería) draw; (rifa) raffle.

sortija f ring.

sosiego m peace, calm.

soso, -sa adj bland.

sospechar vt to suspect ❑ **sospechar de** v + prep to suspect.

sospechoso, -sa adj suspicious ◆ m, f suspect.

sostén m (apoyo) support; (prenda femenina) bra.

sostener vt to support; (defender, afirmar) to defend ❑ **sostenerse** vpr (sujetarse) to stay fixed; (tenerse en pie) to stand up.

sota f = jack.

sotana f cassock.

sótano m basement.

soy v → ser.

squash [esˈkwaʃ] m squash.

Sr. (abrev de señor) Mr.

Sra. (abrev de señora) Mrs.

Sres. *(abrev de señores)* Messrs.

Srta. *abrev* = **señorita**.

SSMM *abrev* = **Sus Majestades**.

Sta. *(abrev de santa)* St.

Sto. *(abrev de santo)* St.

stock [es'tok] *m* stock.

stop *m* stop sign.

su *(pl* **sus)** *adj (de él)* his; *(de ella)* her; *(de cosa, animal)* its; *(de ellos, ellas)* their; *(de usted, ustedes)* your.

suave *adj (agradable al tacto)* soft; *(liso)* smooth; *(cuesta, brisa)* gentle; *(clima, temperatura)* mild.

suavidad *f (al tacto)* softness, *(de cuesta, brisa)* gentleness; *(de clima, temperatura)* mildness.

suavizante *m* conditioner.

subasta *f* auction.

subcampeón, -ona *m, f* runner-up.

subconsciente *m* subconscious.

subdesarrollado, -da *adj* underdeveloped.

subdesarrollo *m* underdevelopment.

subdirector, -ra *m, f* assistant manager *(f* assistant manageress).

súbdito, -ta *m, f (de país)* citizen.

subida *f (de precios, temperatura)* increase; *(pendiente, cuesta)* hill.

subir *vt (escaleras, calle, pendiente)* to go up; *(montaña)* to climb; *(llevar arriba)* to take up; *(brazo, precio, volumen, persiana)* to raise; *(ventanilla)* to close ◆ *vi* to rise; ~ **a** *(piso, desván)* to go up to; *(montaña, torre)* to go up; *(coche)* to get into; *(avión, barco, tren, bicicleta)* to get

onto; *(cuenta, factura)* to come to; ~ **de** *(categoría)* to be promoted from.

súbito, -ta *adj* sudden.

subjetivo, -va *adj* subjective.

subjuntivo *m* subjunctive.

sublevar *vt (indignar)* to infuriate ❑ **sublevarse** *vpr* to rebel.

sublime *adj* sublime.

submarinismo *m* skin-diving.

submarinista *mf* skin-diver.

submarino *m* submarine.

subrayar *vt* to underline.

subsidio *m* benefit.

subsistencia *f* subsistence.

subterráneo, -a *adj* underground ◆ *m* underground tunnel.

subtitulado, -da *adj* with subtitles.

subtítulo *m* subtitle.

suburbio *m* poor suburb.

subvención *f* subsidy.

sucedáneo *m* substitute.

suceder *v impers* to happen ❑ **suceder a** *v* + *prep (en un cargo, trono)* to succeed; *(venir después de)* to follow.

sucesión *f* succession; *(descendencia)* heirs *(pl).*

sucesivo, -va *adj (consecutivo)* successive; **en días ~s** over the next few days.

suceso *m* event.

sucesor, -ra *m, f (en un cargo, trono)* successor; *(heredero)* heir *(f* heiress).

suciedad *f (cualidad)* dirtiness; *(porquería)* dirt.

sucio, -cia *adj* dirty; *(al comer, trabajar)* messy ◆ *adv (en juego)* dirty.

suculento, -ta adj tasty.

sucumbir vi (rendirse) to succumb; (morir) to die.

sucursal f branch.

sudadera f sweatshirt.

sudado m (Amér) stew.

Sudáfrica s South Africa.

Sudamérica s South America.

sudamericano, -na adj & m, f South American.

sudar vi to sweat.

sudeste m southeast.

sudoeste m southwest.

sudor m sweat.

Suecia s Sweden.

sueco, -ca adj & m Swedish ♦ m, f Swede.

suegro, -gra m, f father-in-law (f mother-in-law).

suela f sole.

sueldo m salary, wages (pl).

suelo m (piso) floor; (superficie terrestre) ground; (terreno) soil; (para edificar) land; **en el ~** on the ground/floor.

suelto, -ta adj loose; (separado) separate; (calcetín, guante) odd; (arroz) fluffy ♦ m (dinero) change.

sueño m (acto de dormir) sleep; (ganas de dormir) drowsiness; (imagen mental, deseo) dream; **coger el ~** to get to sleep; **tener ~** to be sleepy.

suero m (en medicina) serum.

suerte f (azar) chance; (fortuna, casualidad) luck; (futuro) fate; (en el toreo) each of the three parts of a bullfight ♦ interj good luck!; **por ~** luckily; **tener ~** to be lucky.

suéter m sweater.

suficiente adj enough ♦ m (nota) pass.

sufragio m suffrage.

sufrido, -da adj (persona) uncomplaining; (color) that does not show the dirt.

sufrimiento m suffering.

sufrir vt (accidente, caída) to have; (persona) to bear ♦ vi to suffer; **~ de** to suffer from; **~ del estómago** to have a stomach complaint.

sugerencia f suggestion.

sugerir vt to suggest; (evocar) to evoke.

suicidio m suicide.

suite [switʃ] f suite.

Suiza s Switzerland.

suizo, -za adj & m, f Swiss ♦ m (bollo) type of plain bun covered in sugar.

sujetador m bra.

sujetar vt (agarrar) to hold down; (asegurar, aguantar) to fasten □ **sujetarse** vpr (agarrarse) to hold on.

sujeto, -ta adj fastened ♦ m subject; (despec: individuo) individual.

suma f (operación) addition; (resultado) total; (conjunto de cosas, dinero) sum.

sumar vt to add together.

sumario m (resumen) summary; (de juicio) indictment.

sumergible adj waterproof.

sumergirse vpr to plunge.

suministrar vt to supply.

suministro m (acción) supplying; (abasto, víveres) supply.

sumiso, -sa adj submissive.

súper *adj (fam)* great ◆ *m (fam)* supermarket ◆ *f (gasolina)* = fourstar.

superación *f* overcoming.

superar *vt (prueba, obstáculo)* to overcome; *(persona)* to beat ❑ **superarse** *vpr (mejorar)* to better o.s.

superficial *adj* superficial.

superficie *f* surface; *(área)* area.

superfluo, -flua *adj* superfluous.

superior *adj (de arriba)* top; *(excepcional)* excellent; ~ **a** *(mejor)* superior to; *(en cantidad, importancia)* greater than ◆ *m* superior.

supermercado *m* supermarket.

superponer *vt (colocar encima)* to put on top.

superpuesto, -ta *pp* → superponer.

superstición *f* superstition.

supersticioso, -sa *adj* superstitious.

superviviente *mf* survivor.

supiera *v* → saber.

suplemento *m* supplement.

suplente *adj (médico)* locum; *(jugador)* substitute.

supletorio *m (teléfono)* extension.

súplica *f* plea.

suplir *vt (falta, carencia)* to compensate for; *(persona)* to replace.

supo *v* → saber.

suponer *vt (creer)* to suppose; *(representar, implicar)* to involve; *(imaginar)* to imagine.

suposición *f* assumption.

supositorio *m* suppository.

suprema *f* chicken breast.

suprimir *vt (proyecto, puesto)* to axe; *(anular)* to abolish; *(borrar)* to delete.

supuesto, -ta *pp* ◗ **suponer** ◆ *adj (presunto)* supposed; *(delincuente)* alleged; *(falso)* false ◆ *m* assumption; **por ~** of course.

sur *m* south; *(viento)* south wind.

surco *m (en la tierra)* furrow; *(de disco)* groove; *(de piel)* line.

sureño, -ña *adj* southern.

surf *m* surfing.

surfista *mf* surfer.

surgir *vi (brotar)* to spring forth; *(destacar)* to rise up; *(producirse)* to arise.

surtido, -da *adj* assorted ◆ *m* range.

surtidor *m (de agua)* spout; *(de gasolina)* pump.

susceptible *adj (sensible)* oversensitive; ~ **de** liable to.

suscribir *vt (escrito)* to sign; *(opinión)* to subscribe to ❑ **suscribirse** *a v + prep* to subscribe to.

suscripción *f* subscription.

suspender *vt (interrumpir)* to adjourn; *(anular)* to postpone; *(examen)* to fail; *(de empleo, sueldo)* to suspend; *(colgar)* to hang (up).

suspense *m* suspense.

suspenso *m* fail.

suspensores *mpl (Amér)* braces.

suspirar *vi* to sigh ❑ **suspirar por** *v + prep* to long for.

suspiro *m* to sigh.

sustancia *f* substance; *(esencia)* essence; *(de alimento)* nutritional value.

sustancial *adj* substantial.

sustantivo *m* noun.

sustituir *vt* to replace; **~ algo/a alguien por** to replace sthg/sb with.

susto *m* fright; **¡qué ~!** what a fright!

sustracción *f* *(robo)* theft; *(resta)* subtraction.

sustraer *vt* *(robar)* to steal; *(restar)* to subtract.

susurrar *vt & vi* to whisper.

suyo, -ya *adj* *(de él)* his; *(de ella)* hers; *(de usted, ustedes)* yours; *(de ellos, de ellas)* theirs ♦ *pron:* **el ~, la suya** *(de él)* his; *(de ella)* hers; *(de usted, ustedes)* yours; *(de ellos, de ellas)* theirs; **lo ~** his/her etc thing; **un amigo ~** a friend of his/hers etc.

T

t *(abrev de tonelada)* t.

Tabacalera *f* State tobacco monopoly in Spain.

tabaco *m* tobacco; *(cigarrillos)* cigarettes *(pl)*.

tábano *m* horsefly.

tabasco® *m* Tabasco®.

taberna *f* country-style bar, usually cheap.

tabique *m* partition (wall).

tabla *f* *(de madera)* plank; *(lista, de multiplicar)* table; *(de navegar,*

surf) board; *(en arte)* panel ❑

tablas *fpl* *(en juego)* stalemate *(sg)*; *(escenario)* stage *(sg)*.

tablao *m:* **~ flamenco** flamenco show.

tablero *m* board.

tableta *f* *(de chocolate)* bar; *(medicamento)* tablet.

tablón *m* plank; **~ de anuncios** notice board.

tabú *m* taboo.

taburete *m* stool.

tacaño, -ña *adj* mean.

tachar *vt* to cross out.

tacho *m* *(Amér)* bin.

tácito, -ta *adj* *(acuerdo, trato)* unwritten.

taco *m* *(para pared)* plug; *(de billar)* cue; *(de jamón, queso)* hunk; *(de papel)* wad; *(fam: palabrota)* swearword; *(fam: lío)* muddle; *(Amér: tortilla)* taco.

tacón *m* heel.

tacto *m* *(sentido)* sense of touch; *(textura)* feel; *(en el trato)* tact.

taekwondo [taj'kwondo] *m* tae kwon do.

Taiwán [tai'wan] *s* Taiwan.

tajada *f* slice; **agarrarse una ~** *(fam)* to get sloshed.

tal *adj* such ♦ *pron* such a thing; **~ cosa** such a thing; **¿qué ~?** how are you doing?; **~ vez** perhaps.

taladradora *f* drill.

taladrar *vt* to drill.

taladro *m* drill.

talco *m* talc.

talento *m* *(aptitud)* talent; *(inteligencia)* intelligence.

talgo *m* Spanish intercity high-speed train.

tapa

talla f (de vestido, calzado) size; (estatura) height; (de piedra preciosa) cutting; (escultura) sculpture.

tallarines mpl tagliatelle (sg).

taller m (de coches) garage; (de trabajo manual) workshop.

tallo m stem.

talón m heel; (cheque) cheque.

talonario m cheque book.

tamal m (Amér) mixture of maize flour and meat wrapped in banana/maize leaf and cooked.

tamaño m size.

también adv also; ~ dijo que ... she also said that ...; yo ~ me too.

tambor m drum.

tampoco adv neither; yo ~ me neither; si a ti no te gusta a mí ~ it you don't like it, then neither do I.

tampón m (sello) stamp; (para la menstruación) tampon.

tan adv → tanto.

tanda f (turno) shift; (serie) series.

tándem m (bicicleta) tandem, (dúo) duo.

tanga m tanga.

tango m tango.

tanque m (vehículo cisterna) tanker; (de guerra) tank.

tanto, -ta adj 1. (gran cantidad) so much, so many (pl); **tiene ~ dinero** he's got so much money; **tanta gente** so many people; ~ ... **que** so much ... that.
2. (cantidad indeterminada) so much, so many (pl); **tantas pesetas al día** so many pesetas a day; **cincuenta y ~s** fifty-something, fifty-odd.
3. (en comparaciones): ~ ... **como** as

much ... as, as many ... as (pl); **tiene tanta suerte como tú** she's as lucky as you.
◆ adv 1. (gran cantidad) so much; **no merece la pena disgustarse ~** it's not worth getting so upset; ~ **que** so much that.
2. (en comparaciones): ~ ... **como** as much ... as; **sabe ~ como yo** she knows as much as I do.
3. (en locuciones): **por (lo) ~** so, therefore; ~ **(es así) que** so much so that.
◆ pron 1. (gran cantidad) so many (pl); **él no tiene ~s** he doesn't have so many.
2. (igual cantidad) as much, as many (pl); **había mucha gente allí, aquí no tanta** there were a lot of people there, but not as many here.
3. (cantidad indeterminada) so much, so many (pl); **supongamos que vengan ~s** let's suppose so many come; **a ~s de agosto** on such-and-such a date in August.
4. (en locuciones): **eran las tantas** it was very late.
◆ m 1. (punto) point; (gol) goal; **marcar un ~** to score.
2. (cantidad indeterminada): **un ~** so much; ~ **por ciento** percentage.

tapa f (de recipiente) lid; (de libro) cover; (de comida) tapa; (de zapato) heel plate; **"~s variadas"** "selection of tapas".

---

i TAPAS

A "tapa" is a small portion of food, usually eaten with a glass of wine or beer in a bar before a main meal. Many bars specialize in "tapas", particularly in the north of Spain and in Andalusia.

---

tapabarro m (Amér) mudguard.

tapadera f (de recipiente) lid; (para encubrir) front.

tapar vt (cofre, caja, botella) to close; (olla) to put the lid on; (encubrir) to cover up; (en la cama) to tuck in; (con ropa) to wrap up ❑ **taparse** vpr (en la cama) to tuck o.s. in; (con ropa) to wrap up.

tapete m runner.

tapia f (stone) wall.

tapicería f (tela) upholstery; (tienda) upholsterer's (shop).

tapiz (pl -ces) m tapestry.

tapizado m upholstery.

tapizar vt to upholster.

tapón m (de botella) stopper; (de rosca) top; (de bañera, fregadero) plug; (para el oído) earplug.

taquería f (Amér) taco bar.

TAQUERÍA

This is a type of café where traditional Mexican food, especially tacos, is eaten. In recent years, taquerías have become popular outside Mexico, especially in the United States.

---

taquigrafía f shorthand.

taquilla f (de cine, teatro) box office; (de tren) ticket office; (armario) locker; (recaudación) takings (pl).

taquillero, -ra adj who/that

pulls in the crowds ◆ m, f ticket clerk.

tara f (defecto) defect; (peso) tare.

tardar vt (tiempo) to take ◆ vi (retrasarse) to be late; **el comienzo tardará aún dos horas** it doesn't start for another two hours.

tarde f (hasta las cinco) afternoon; (después de las cinco) evening ◆ adv late; **las cuatro de la ~** four o'clock in the afternoon; **por la ~** in the afternoon/evening; **buenas ~s** good afternoon/evening.

tarea f (trabajo) task; (deberes escolares) homework.

tarifa f (de electricidad, etc) charge; (en transportes) fare; (lista de precios) price list; **"~s de metro"** "underground fares".

tarima f platform.

tarjeta f card; **"~s admitidas"** "credit cards accepted"; **~ de crédito** credit card; **~ de embarque** boarding pass; **~ postal** postcard; **~ 10 viajes** (en metro) underground travelcard valid for ten journeys.

tarro m jar.

tarta f cake; (plana, con base de pasta dura) tart; **~ de la casa** chef's special cake; **~ de chocolate** chocolate cake; **~ helada** ice cream gâteau; **~ de Santiago** sponge cake filled with almond paste; **~ al whisky** whisky-flavoured ice-cream gâteau.

tartamudo, -da m, f stammerer.

tasa f rate.

tasca f ≈ pub.

tatuaje m tattoo.

taurino, -na adj bullfighting (antes de s).

Tauro m Taurus.
tauromaquia f bullfighting.

i TAUROMAQUIA

Bullfights begin with a procession in which all the participants parade across the bullring in traditional costume. The fight itself is divided into three parts: in the first part, the "picador" goads the bull with a lance; in the second, the "banderillero" sticks barbed darts into it and in the final part, the "matador" performs a series of passes before killing the bull.

taxi m taxi.
taxímetro m taximeter.
taxista mf taxi driver.
taza f cup; (de retrete) bowl.
tazón m bowl.
te pron (complemento directo) you; (complemento indirecto) (to) you; (reflexivo) yourself.
té m tea.
teatral adj (de teatro) theatre (antes de s); (afectado) theatrical.
teatro m theatre.
tebeo® m (children's) comic.
techo m (de habitación, persona, avión) ceiling; (tejado) roof.
tecla f key.
teclado m keyboard.
teclear vi (en ordenador) to type.
técnica f technique; (de ciencia) technology.
técnico, -ca adj technical.
tecnología f technology.
tecnológico, -ca adj techno-

logical.
teja f tile.
tejado m roof.
tejanos mpl jeans.
tejer vt (jersey, labor) to knit; (tela) to weave.
tejido m (tela) fabric; (del cuerpo humano) tissue.
tejo m (juego) hopscotch.
tel. (abrev de teléfono) tel.
tela f (tejido) material, cloth; (lienzo) canvas; (fam: dinero) dough.
telaraña f spider's web.
tele f (fam) telly.
telearrastre m ski-tow.
telecabina f cable-car.
telecomunicación f (medio) telecommunication; (estudios) telecommunications.
telediario m television news.
teledirigido, -da adj remote-controlled.
telefax m inv fax.
teleférico m cable-car.
telefonazo m phone call.
telefonear vt to phone.
Telefónica f Spanish national telephone monopoly.
telefónico, -ca adj telephone (antes de s).
telefonista mf telephonist.
teléfono m telephone; ~ **móvil** mobile telephone.
telégrafo m telegraph.
telegrama m telegram; **poner un** ~ to send a telegram.
telenovela f television soap opera.
teleobjetivo m telephoto lens.

telescopio *m* telescope.

telesilla *f* chair lift.

telespectador, -ra *m, f* viewer.

telesquí *m* ski lift.

teletexto *m* Teletext®.

teletipo *m* teleprinter.

televidente *mf* viewer.

televisado, -da *adj* televised.

televisión *f* television.

televisor *m* television (set).

télex *m inv* telex.

telón *m* curtain.

tema *m* subject; *(melodía)* theme.

temática *f* subject matter.

temático, -ca *adj* thematic.

temblar *vi* to tremble; *(de frío)* to shiver.

temblor *m (de persona)* trembling; *(de suelo)* earthquake.

temer *vt* to fear; **~ por** to fear for ☐ **temerse** *vpr* to fear.

temor *m* fear.

temperamento *m* temperament.

temperatura *f* temperature.

tempestad *f* storm.

templado, -da *adj (líquido, comida)* lukewarm; *(clima)* temperate.

templo *m (pagano)* temple; *(iglesia)* church.

temporada *f (periodo concreto)* season; *(de una actividad)* period; **de ~** seasonal.

temporal *adj* temporary ♦ *m* storm.

temprano, -na *adj & adv* early.

ten *v →* tener.

tenazas *fpl* pliers.

tendedero *m* clothes line.

tendencia *f* tendency.

tender *vt (colgar)* to hang out; *(extender)* to spread; *(tumbar)* to lay (out); *(cable)* to lay; *(cuerda)* to stretch (out); *(entregar)* to hand ☐ **tender a** *v + prep* to tend to; **tenderse** *vpr* to lie down.

tenderete *m* stall.

tendero, -ra *m, f* shopkeeper.

tendón *m* tendon.

tendrá *v →* tener.

tenedor *m* fork.

tener *vt* **1.** *(poseer, contener)* to have; **tiene mucho dinero** she has a lot of money; **tengo dos hijos** I have two children; **~ un niño** *(parir)* to have a baby; **la casa tiene cuatro habitaciones** the house has four bedrooms; **tiene los ojos azules** she has blue eyes.
2. *(medidas, edad)* to be; **la sala tiene cuatro metros de largo** the room is four metres long; **¿cuántos años tienes?** how old are you?; **tiene diez años** he's ten (years old).
3. *(padecer, sufrir)* to have; **~ dolor de muelas/fiebre** to have toothache/a temperature.
4. *(sujetar, coger)* to hold; **tiene la olla por las asas** she's holding the pot by its handles; **¡ten!** here you are!
5. *(sentir)* to be; **~ frío/calor** to be cold/hot; **~ hambre/sed** to be hungry/thirsty.
6. *(sentimiento)*: **nos tiene cariño** he's fond of us.
7. *(mantener)* to have; **hemos tenido una discusión** we've have an

argument.

8. (para desear) to have; **que tengan unas felices fiestas** have a good holiday.

9. (deber asistir a) to have; **hoy tengo clase** I have to go to school today; **el médico no tiene consulta hoy** the doctor is not seeing patients today.

10. (valorar, considerar): ~ **algo/a alguien por algo** to think sthg/sb is sthg; **ten por seguro que lloverá** you can be sure it will rain.

11. (haber de): **tengo mucho que contaros** I have a lot to tell you.

◆ v aux **1.** (haber): **tiene alquilada una casa en la costa** she has a rented house on the coast.

2. (hacer estar): **me tienes loca** you're driving me mad.

3. (obligación): ~ **que hacer algo** to have to do sthg; **tenemos que estar a las ocho** we have to be there at eight.

tenga v → tener.

tengo v → tener.

teniente m lieutenant.

tenis m tennis; ~ **de mesa** table tennis.

tenista mf tennis player.

tenor m tenor.

tensión f tension; (de la sangre) blood pressure; (fuerza) stress; (voltaje) voltage.

tenso, -sa adj (persona) tense; (objeto, cuerda) taut.

tentación f temptation.

tentáculo m tentacle.

tentempié m (bebida, comida) snack.

tenue adj (color, luz) faint; (tela, cortina) fine.

teñir vt to dye.

teología f theology.

teoría f theory; **en ~** in theory.

terapeuta mf therapist.

tercera f (categoría) third class; (velocidad) third (gear).

tercermundista adj third-world.

tercero, -ra núm third ◆ m (persona) third party; (piso) third floor, → **sexto.**

tercio m (tercera parte) third; (de corrida de toros) each of the three parts of a bullfight.

terciopelo m velvet.

terco, -ca adj stubborn.

tergal® m Tergal®.

termas fpl hot baths, spa (sg).

terminado, -da adj finished.

terminal adj (enfermo) terminal; (estación) final ◆ m terminal ◆ f (de aeropuerto) terminal; (de autobús) terminus.

terminar vt to finish ◆ vi to end, (tren) to terminate; ~ **en** to end in; ~ **por hacer algo** to end up doing sthg.

término m end; (plazo) period; (palabra) term; ~ **municipal** district ❑ **términos** mpl terms.

terminología f terminology.

termita f termite.

termo m Thermos® (flask).

termómetro m thermometer.

termostato m thermostat.

ternera f veal; ~ **asada** roast veal.

ternero, -ra m, f calf.

terno m (Amér) suit.

ternura f tenderness.

terraplén m embankment.

terrateniente *mf* landowner.

terraza *f* (*balcón*) balcony; (*techo*) terrace roof; (*de bar, restaurante, cultivo*) terrace.

terremoto *m* earthquake.

terreno *m* (*suelo*) land; (*parcela*) plot (of land); (*fig: ámbito*) field.

terrestre *adj* terrestrial.

terrible *adj* (*que causa terror*) terrifying; (*horrible*) terrible.

territorio *m* territory.

terrón *m* (*de azúcar*) lump.

terror *m* terror.

terrorismo *m* terrorism.

terrorista *mf* terrorist.

tertulia *f* (*personas*) regular meeting of people for informal discussion of a particular issue of common interest; (*lugar*) area in café given over to billiard and card tables.

tesis *f inv* thesis.

tesoro *m* (*botín*) treasure; (*hacienda pública*) treasury.

test *m* test.

testamento *m* will.

testarudo, -da *adj* stubborn.

testículo *m* testicle.

testigo *m* witness.

testimonio *m* (*prueba*) proof; (*declaración*) testimony.

teta *f* (*fam*) tit.

tetera *f* teapot.

tetrabrick *m* tetrabrick.

textil *adj* textile.

texto *m* text; (*pasaje, fragmento*) passage.

textura *f* texture.

ti *pron* (*después de preposición*) you; (*reflexivo*) yourself.

tianguis *m inv* (*Amér*) (open-air)

market.

tibia *f* shinbone.

tibio, -bia *adj* (*cálido*) warm; (*falto de calor*) lukewarm.

tiburón *m* shark.

ticket *m* (*billete*) ticket; (*recibo*) receipt.

tiempo *m* time; (*en meteorología*) weather; (*edad*) age; (*en deporte*) half; (*en gramática*) tense; **a ~** on time; **al mismo ~ que** at the same time as; **con ~** in good time; **del ~** (*bebida*) at room temperature; **en otros ~s** in a different age; **hace ~** a long time ago; **hace ~ que no te veo** it's a long time since I saw you; **tener ~** to have time; **todo el ~** (*todo el rato*) all the time; (*siempre*) always; **~ libre** spare time.

tienda *f* shop; (*para acampar*) tent; **~ de campaña** tent; **~ de comestibles** grocery (shop); **~ de confecciones** clothes shop.

tiene *v* → tener.

tierno, -na *adj* tender; (*pan*) fresh.

tierra *f* land; (*materia*) soil; (*suelo*) ground; (*patria*) homeland; **~ adentro** inland; **tomar ~** to touch down ❑ **Tierra** *f*: **la Tierra** the Earth.

tieso, -sa *adj* (*rígido*) stiff; (*erguido*) erect; (*antipático*) haughty.

tiesto *m* flowerpot.

tigre, -gresa *m, f* tiger (*f* tigress).

tijeras *fpl* scissors.

tila *f* lime blossom tea.

tilde *f* (*acento*) accent; (*de ñ*) tilde.

tiliches *mpl* (*Amér*) bits and pieces.

timbal m kettledrum.

timbre m (aparato) bell; (de voz, sonido) tone; (sello) stamp.

tímido, -da adj shy.

timo m swindle.

timón m rudder.

tímpano m (del oído) eardrum.

tina f (vasija) pitcher; (bañera) bathtub.

tino m (juicio) good judgment; (moderación) moderation.

tinta f ink; **en su ~** cooked in its ink.

tintero m (en pupitre) inkwell.

tinto m red wine.

tintorería f dry cleaner's.

tío, -a m, f (pariente) uncle (f aunt); (fam: compañero, amigo) mate (f darling); (fam: persona) guy (f bird).

tiovivo m merry-go-round.

típico, -ca adj typical; (traje, restaurante) traditional.

tipo m (clase) type; (figura de mujer) figure; (figura de hombre) build; (fam: individuo) guy; (modelo) model; **~ de cambio** exchange rate.

tipografía f (arte) printing.

TIR m (abrev de transport international routier) ≈ HGV.

tira f strip.

tirabuzón m curl.

tirada f (número de ventas) circulation; (en juegos) throw; (distancia grande) long way.

tiradero m (Amer) tip.

tirador m (de puerta, cajón) handle.

tiranía f tyranny.

tirano, -na m, f tyrant.

tirante adj (estirado) taut; (relación, situación) tense ❑ **tirantes** mpl braces (Br), suspenders (Am).

tirar vt (arrojar, lanzar) to throw; (desechar, malgastar) to throw away; (derribar) to knock down; (dejar caer) to drop; (volcar) to knock over; (derramar) to spill; (disparar) to fire ◆ vi (atraer) to be attractive; (desviarse) to head; (fam: durar) to keep going; (en juegos) to have one's go; **~ de** to pull; **voy tirando** I'm O.K., I suppose, "tirar" "pull" ❑ **tirar a** v + prep (parecerse a) to take after; **~ a gris** to be greyish; **tirarse** vpr to throw o.s.; (tiempo) to spend.

tirita® f (sticking) plaster (Br), Bandaid® (Am).

tiritar vi to shiver.

tiro m shot; (actividad) shooting; (herida) gunshot wound; (de chimenea) draw; (de carruaje) team.

tirón m (estirón) pull; (robo) bag-snatching.

tisú m lamé.

títere m puppet ❑ **títeres** mpl (espectáculo) puppet show (sg).

titular adj official ◆ m headline ◆ vt to title ❑ **titularse** vpr (llamarse) to be called; (en estudios) to graduate.

título m title; (diploma) qualification; (licenciatura) degree.

tiza f chalk

tlapalería f (Amér) shop selling paint, cleaning materials, pots and pans etc.

toalla f towel; **~ de ducha** bath towel; **~ de manos** hand towel.

tobillo m ankle.

tobogán m (en parque de atrac-

ciones) helter-skelter; *(rampa)* slide; *(en piscina)* flume; *(trineo)* toboggan.

tocadiscos *m inv* record player.

tocador *m (mueble)* dressing table; *(habitación)* powder room.

tocar *vt* to touch; *(palpar)* to feel; *(instrumento musical)* to play; *(alarma)* to sound; *(timbre, campana)* to ring; *(tratar)* to touch on ◆ *vi (a la puerta)* to knock; *(al timbre)* to ring; *(estar próximo)* to border; **te toca a ti** *(es tu turno)* it's your turn; *(es tu responsabilidad)* it's up to you; **le tocó la mitad** he got half of it; **le tocó el gordo** she won first prize; **"no ~ el género"** "do not touch".

tocino *m* bacon fat; **~ de cielo** *dessert made of sugar and eggs.*

todavía *adv* still; **~ no** not yet.

todo, -da *adj* all; *(cada, cualquier)* every ◆ *pron (para cosas)* everything, all of them *(pl)*; *(para personas)* everybody ◆ *m* whole; **~ el libro** all (of) the book; **~s los lunes** every Monday; **tenemos de ~** we've got all sorts of things; **ante ~** first of all; **sobre ~** above all.

toga *f (de abogado, juez)* gown.

toldo *m (de tienda)* awning; *(de playa)* sunshade.

tolerancia *f* tolerance.

tolerante *adj* tolerant.

tolerar *vt* to tolerate; *(sufrir)* to stand.

toma *f (de leche)* feed; *(de agua, gas)* inlet; *(de luz)* socket.

tomar *vt* to take; *(contratar)* to take on; *(comida, bebida, baño, ducha)* to have; *(sentir)* to acquire; **~ a alguien por** to take sb for; **~**

algo a mal to take sthg the wrong way; **~ algo** *(comer, beber)* to have sthg to eat/drink; **~ el fresco** to get a breath of fresh air; **~ el sol** to sunbathe; **~ prestado** to borrow.

tomate *m* tomato.

tómbola *f* tombola.

tomillo *m* thyme.

tomo *m* volume.

tonel *m* barrel.

tonelada *f* tonne.

tongo *m (Amér) type of bowler hat worn by Bolivian Indians.*

tónica *f (bebida)* tonic water.

tónico, -ca *adj (vigorizante)* revitalizing; *(con acento)* tonic ◆ *m (cosmético)* skin toner.

tono *m* tone; *(de color)* shade.

tontería *f (cualidad)* stupidity; *(indiscreción)* stupid thing; *(cosa sin valor)* trifle.

tonto, -ta *adj* stupid; *(ingenuo)* innocent.

tope *m (punto máximo)* limit; *(pieza)* block.

tópico, -ca *adj (medicamento)* topical ◆ *m (tema recurrente)* recurring theme; *(frase muy repetida)* cliché.

topo *m* mole.

tórax *m inv* thorax.

torbellino *m (de viento)* whirlwind; *(de sucesos, preguntas, etc)* spate.

torcer *vt (retorcer)* to twist; *(doblar)* to bend; *(girar)* to turn; *(inclinar)* to tilt ◆ *vi* to turn □ **torcerse** *vpr (fracasar)* to go wrong; *(no cumplirse)* to be frustrated; **~se el brazo** to twist one's arm; **~se el tobillo** to sprain one's ankle.

torcido, -da *adj (retorcido)* twisted; *(doblado)* bent; *(inclinado)* crooked.

tordo *m* thrush.

torear *vt (toro, vaquilla)* to fight; *(fig: evitar)* to dodge; *(fig: burlarse de)* to mess about ♦ *vi* to fight bulls.

torera *f* bolero (jacket).

torero, -ra *m, f* bullfighter.

tormenta *f* storm.

tormentoso, -sa *adj* stormy.

torneo *m* tournament.

tornillo *m* screw.

torniquete *m (para hemorragia)* tourniquet.

toro *m* bull □ **toros** *mpl (corrida)* bullfight *(sg)*; *(fiesta)* bullfighting *(sg)*.

torpe *adj (poco ágil)* clumsy; *(poco inteligente, lento)* slow.

torpedo *m* torpedo.

torpeza *f (falta de agilidad)* clumsiness; *(falta de inteligencia, lentitud)* slowness.

torre *f* tower; *(de oficinas, etc)* tower block; *(en ajedrez)* castle, rook.

torrente *m* torrent.

torrija *f* French toast.

torta *f (de harina)* cake; *(fam: bofetada)* thump; *(fam: accidente)* bump; **ni ~** *(fam)* not a thing.

tortazo *m (fam) (bofetada)* thump; *(golpe fuerte)* bump.

tortilla *f* omelette; *(Amér: de harina)* tortilla; **~ de atún** tuna omelette; **~ de champiñón** mushroom omelette; **~ (a la) francesa** plain omelette; **~ de gambas**

prawn omelette; **~ de jamón** ham omelette; **~ de patatas** Spanish omelette.

tórtola *f* turtledove.

tortuga *f (terrestre)* tortoise; *(marina)* turtle.

torturar *vt* to torture.

tos *f* cough.

toser *vi* to cough.

tosta *f piece of toast with a topping.*

tostada *f* piece of toast.

tostador *m* toaster.

tostar *vt* to toast □ **tostarse** *vpr (broncearse)* to get brown.

total *adj & m* total ♦ *adv* so, anyway.

totalidad *f:* **la ~ de** all of.

totora *f (Amér)* merry-go-round.

tóxico, -ca *adj* poisonous.

toxicomanía *f* drug addiction.

toxicómano, -na *m, f* drug addict.

trabajador, -ra *adj* hardworking ♦ *m, f* worker.

trabajar *vt & vi* to work; **~ de** to work as; **~ de canguro** to babysit.

trabajo *m* work; *(empleo)* job; *(esfuerzo)* effort; *(en el colegio)* essay; **~s manuales** arts and crafts.

trabalenguas *m inv* tongue-twister.

traca *f* string of firecrackers.

tractor *m* tractor.

tradición *f* tradition.

tradicional *adj* traditional.

tradicionalmente *adv* traditionally.

traducción *f* translation.

traducir vt to translate.

traductor, -ra m, f translator.

traer vt 1. (trasladar) to bring; (llevar) to carry; **me trajo un regalo** she brought me a present; **¿qué traes ahí?** what have you got there?
2. (provocar, ocasionar) to bring; **le trajo graves consecuencias** it had serious consequences for him.
3. (contener) to have; **el periódico trae una gran noticia** the newspaper has an important piece of news in it.
4. (llevar puesto) to wear.
❏ **traerse** vpr: **se las trae** (fam) it's got a lot to it.

traficante mf trafficker.

traficar vi to traffic.

tráfico m (de vehículos) traffic; (de drogas) trafficking.

tragar vt (ingerir) to swallow; (fam: devorar, consumir) to guzzle; (soportar) to put up with ◆ vi to swallow; **no ~ a alguien** (fam) not to be able to stand sb ❏ **tragarse** vpr (fam) to swallow.

tragedia f tragedy.

trágico, -ca adj tragic.

tragicomedia f tragicomedy.

trago m (de líquido) mouthful; (fam: copa) drink; (disgusto) difficult situation.

traición f (infidelidad) betrayal; (delito) treason.

traje m (vestido) dress; (de hombre) suit; (de chaqueta) two-piece suit; (de región, época, etc) costume; **~ de baño** swimsuit; **~ (de) chaqueta** woman's two-piece suit; **~ de luces** matador's outfit.

trama f (de novela, historia) plot; (maquinación) intrigue.

tramar vt to weave.

tramitar vt (suj: autoridades) to process (document); (suj: solicitante) to obtain.

tramo m (de camino, calle) stretch; (de escalera) flight (of stairs).

tramontana f north wind.

tramoya f (en teatro) stage machinery.

tramoyista mf stage hand.

trampa f (para cazar) trap; (engaño) trick; (en juego) cheating; (puerta) trapdoor; **hacer ~** to cheat.

trampolín m (en piscina) diving board; (en esquí) ski jump; (en gimnasia) springboard.

trance m (momento difícil) difficult situation; (estado hipnótico) trance.

tranquilidad f (de lugar) peacefulness; (de carácter) calmness; (despreocupación) peace of mind.

tranquilo, -la adj (lugar) peaceful; (de carácter, mar, tiempo) calm; (libre de preocupaciones) unworried.

transbordador m ferry.

transbordar vt to transfer.

transbordo m change (of train etc); **hacer ~** to change.

transcurrir vi to take place.

transeúnte mf passer-by.

transferencia f transfer.

transformación f transformation.

transformador m transformer.

transformar vt to transform;

~ algo/a alguien en to turn sthg/sb into ☐ **transformarse** *vpr* (*cambiar*) to be transformed; **~se en** to be converted into.

transfusión *f* transfusion.

transición *f* transition.

transigir *vi* (*ceder*) to compromise; (*ser tolerante*) to be tolerant.

transistor *m* transistor.

tránsito *m* (*de vehículos*) traffic.

translúcido, -da *adj* translucent.

transmitir *vt* (*difundir*) to broadcast; (*comunicar*) to pass on; (*contagiar*) to transmit.

transparente *adj* transparent.

transportar *vt* to transport.

transporte *m* transport; ~ **público** public transport.

transversal *adj* (*atravesado*) transverse; (*perpendicular*) cross (*antes de s*).

tranvía *m* tram.

trapear *vt* (*Amér*) to wash.

trapecio *m* trapeze.

trapecista *mf* trapeze artist.

trapo *m* (*trozo de tela*) rag; (*para limpiar*) cloth.

tráquea *f* windpipe.

tras *prep* (*detrás de*) behind; (*después de*) after.

trasero, -ra *adj* back (*antes de s*) ◆ *m* (*fam*) backside.

trasladar *vt* (*mudar*) to move; (*empleado, trabajador*) to transfer; (*aplazar*) to postpone ☐ **trasladarse** *vpr* (*desplazarse*) to go; (*mudarse*) to move.

traslado *m* (*de muebles, libros, etc*) moving; (*de puesto, cargo, etc*) transfer.

traspasar *vt* (*cruzar*) to cross (over); (*atravesar*) to go through; (*suj: líquido*) to soak through; (*negocio*) to sell (as a going concern).

traspiés *m inv* (*tropezón*) trip; (*equivocación*) slip.

trasplantar *vt* to transplant.

trasplante *m* transplant.

traste *m* (*Amér*) (*trasto*) thing; (*trasero*) backside.

trasto *m* (*objeto inútil*) piece of junk; (*fig: persona*) nuisance ☐ **trastos** *mpl* (*equipo*) things.

tratado *m* (*acuerdo*) treaty; (*escrito*) treatise.

tratamiento *m* treatment; (*título*) title.

tratar *vt* to treat; (*discutir*) to discuss; (*conocer*) to come into contact with ☐ **tratar de** *v + prep* (*hablar sobre*) to be about; (*intentar*) to try to.

trato *m* (*de persona*) treatment; (*acuerdo*) deal; (*tratamiento*) dealings (*npl*).

trauma *m* trauma.

través: a través de *prep* (*en espacio*) across; (*en tiempo*) through.

travesaño *m* (*de portería*) crossbar.

travesía *f* (*calle*) cross-street; (*por mar*) crossing; (*por aire*) flight.

travesti *m* transvestite.

travieso, -sa *adj* mischievous.

trayecto *m* (*camino, distancia*) distance; (*viaje*) journey; (*ruta*) route.

trayectoria *f* (*recorrido*) trajectory; (*desarrollo*) path.

trazado *m* (*de carretera, canal*) course; (*de edificio*) design.

trazar vt (línea, dibujo) to draw; (proyecto, plan) to draw up.

trazo m line; (de escritura) stroke.

trébol m (planta) clover; (en naipes) club.

trece núm thirteen, → **seis**.

tregua f (en conflicto) truce; (en trabajo, estudios) break.

treinta núm thirty, → **seis**.

tremendo, -da adj (temible) terrible; (muy grande) enormous; (travieso) mischievous.

tren m train; ~ **de cercanías** local train; ~ **de lavado** car wash.

trenza f plait.

trepar vt to climb.

tres núm three, → **seis**.

tresillo m (sofá) three-piece suite; (juego) ombre, card game for three players.

trial m trial.

triangular adj triangular.

triángulo m triangle.

tribu f tribe.

tribuna f (para orador) rostrum; (para espectadores) stand.

tribunal m court; (en examen, oposición) board of examiners.

triciclo m tricycle.

trigo m wheat.

trilladora f threshing machine.

trillar vt to thresh.

trillizos, -zas m, fpl triplets.

trimestral adj (cada tres meses) quarterly; (de tres meses) three-month.

trimestre m (periodo) quarter, three months (pl); (en escuela) term.

trinchante m (cuchillo) carving knife; (tenedor) meat fork.

trineo m sledge.

trío m trio.

tripa f (barriga) belly; (intestino) gut □ **tripas** fpl (interior) insides.

triple adj triple ♦ m (en baloncesto) basket worth three points; **el** ~ **de** three times as much as.

trípode m tripod.

tripulación f crew.

tripulante mf crew member.

triste adj sad; (color, luz) pale; (insuficiente) miserable.

tristeza f sadness.

triturar vt (desmenuzar) to grind; (mascar) to chew.

triunfal adj triumphant.

triunfar vi (vencer) to win; (tener éxito) to succeed.

triunfo m (victoria) triumph; (en encuentro) victory, win.

trivial adj trivial.

trizas fpl bits; **hacer** ~ (hacer añicos) to smash to pieces; (desgarrar) to tear to shreds.

trocha f (Amér) gauge.

trofeo m trophy.

trombón m trombone.

trombosis f inv thrombosis.

trompa f (de elefante) trunk; (instrumento) horn; **coger una** ~ (fam) to get sloshed.

trompazo m bump.

trompeta f trumpet.

tronar v impers: **tronaba** it was thundering.

tronco m trunk; ~ **de merluza** thick hake steak taken from the back of the fish.

trono m throne.

tropa f (de soldados) troops (pl); (de personas) crowd ❑ **tropas** fpl troops.

tropezar vi to trip; ~ **con** to run into.

tropezón m (tropiezo) trip; (de jamón, pan) small chunk, (equivocación) slip.

tropical adj tropical.

trópico m tropic.

tropiezo m (tropezón) trip; (dificultad) obstacle; (equivocación) slip.

trotar vi (caballo) to trot; (persona) to dash around.

trote m (de caballo) trot; (trabajo, esfuerzo) dashing around.

trozo m piece; **a ~s** in patches; **un ~ de** a piece of.

trucaje m (en cine) trick photography.

trucha f trout.

truco m (trampa, engaño) trick; (en cine) special effect.

trueno m (durante tormenta) (roll of) thunder; (de arma) boom.

trufa f truffle; **~s heladas** frozen chocolate truffles.

trusa f (Amér) (traje de baño) swimming trunks (pl); (braga) knickers (pl).

tu (pl **tus**) adj your.

tú pron you; **hablar** ❑ **tratar de** ~ **a alguien** to address sb as "tú".

tuberculosis f inv tuberculosis.

tubería f pipe.

tubo m (de agua, gas) pipe; (recipiente) tube; ~ **de escape** exhaust pipe.

tuerca f nut.

tuerto, -ta adj (sin un ojo) one-eyed.

tul m tulle.

tulipán m tulip.

tullido, -da adj paralysed.

tumba f grave.

tumbar vt (derribar) to knock down; (fam: suspender) to fail ❑ **tumbarse** vpr to lie down.

tumbona f (en la playa) deck chair; (en el jardín) sun lounger.

tumor m tumour.

tumulto m (disturbio) riot; (confusión) uproar.

tuna f group of student minstrels.

---

i | TUNA

A "tuna" is a musical group made up of university students who wear black capes and coloured ribbons. They wander the streets playing music, singing and dancing, either for pleasure or to collect money.

---

túnel m tunnel.

Túnez s (país) Tunisia.

túnica f tunic.

tupido, -da adj thick.

turbina f turbine.

turbio, -bia adj (líquido, agua) cloudy; (asunto) shady.

turbulencia f turbulence.

turco, -ca adj, m, f Turkish.

turismo m tourism; (coche) private car.

turista mf tourist.

turístico, -ca adj tourist (antes de s).

túrmix® f inv blender.

turno m (momento) turn; (en el trabajo) shift; **"su ~"** "next customer, please".

Turquía s Turkey.

turrón m sweet eaten at Christmas, made with almonds and honey.

tute m (juego) card game similar to whist.

tutear vt to address as "tú" ❑ **tutearse** vpr to address one another as "tú".

tutor, -ra m, f (de bienes, menor) guardian; (de curso) form teacher.

tuviera v → tener.

tuyo, -ya adj yours ◆ pron: **el ~, la tuya** yours; **lo ~** your thing; **un amigo ~** a friend of yours.

TV (abrev de televisión) TV.

U

UCI f (abrev de unidad de cuidados intensivos) ICU.

Ud. abrev = usted.

Uds. abrev = ustedes.

úlcera f ulcer.

ultimar vt (Amér) to kill.

último, -ma adj last; (más reciente) latest; (más bajo) bottom; (más alto) top; **a ~s de** at the end of; **por ~** finally; **última llamada** last call.

ultramarinos m inv (tienda) grocer's (shop).

ultravioleta adj ultraviolet.

umbral m threshold.

un, una art a, an (antes de sonido vocálico) ◆ adj → **uno**; **~ hombre** a man; **una mujer** a woman; **~ águila** an eagle.

unánime adj unanimous.

UNED f Spanish open university.

únicamente adv only.

único, -ca adj (solo) only; (extraordinario) unique; (precio) single; **lo ~ que quiero** all I want.

unidad f unit; (unión, acuerdo) unity.

unido, -da adj (cariñosamente) close; (físicamente) joined.

unifamiliar adj detached.

unificación f unification.

uniforme m uniform ◆ adj even.

unión f union; (coordinación, acuerdo) unity; (cariño) closeness.

unir vt (juntar) to join; (mezclar) to mix; (personas) to unite; (comunicar) to link ❑ **unirse** vpr to join together.

unisex adj inv unisex.

universal adj universal.

universidad f university.

universitario, -ria m, f (estudiante) student; (licenciado) graduate.

universo m universe.

uno, una adj 1. (indefinido) one, some (pl); **un día volveré** one day I will return; **~s coches** some cars. 2. (para expresar cantidades) one; **treinta y un días** thirty-one days. 3. (aproximadamente) around, about; **había unas doce personas** there were around twelve people.

◆ pron 1. (indefinido) one, some (pl); coge ~ take one; dame unas give me some; ~ de ellos one of them; ~ ... otro one ... another, some ... others (pl).
2. (fam: referido a personas) someone; ayer hablé con ~ que te conoce I spoke to someone who knows you yesterday.
3. (yo) one.
4 (en locuciones): de ~ en ~ one by one; ~ a o por ~ one by one; más de ~ many people, → seis.

untar vt (pan, tostada) to spread; (manchar) to smear ❏ **untarse** vpr to smear o.s.

uña f (de persona) nail; (de animal) claw; **hacerse las ~s** to do one's nails.

uralita® f corrugated material made from cement and asbestos, used for roofing.

urbanización f housing estate.

urbano, -na adj urban ◆ m, f local police officer who deals mainly with traffic offences.

urgencia f emergency ❏ **Urgencias** fpl casualty (department) (sg).

urgente adj urgent; **"urgente"** (en cartas) "express".

urgentemente adv urgently.

urinario m urinal.

urna f (de votación) (ballot) box; (para restos mortales) urn; (de exposición) glass case.

urraca f magpie.

urticaria f nettle rash.

Uruguay s Uruguay.

uruguayo, -ya adj & m, f Uruguayan.

usado, -da adj (gastado) worn.

usar vt to use; (llevar) to wear; ¿qué talla usa? what size do you take?

uso m use; (costumbre) custom.

usted (pl -des) pron you.

usual adj usual.

usuario, -ria m, f user.

utensilio m (herramienta) tool; (de cocina) utensil.

útero m womb.

útil adj useful ◆ m tool.

utilidad f (cualidad) usefulness; (provecho) use.

utilitario m run-around car.

utilizar vt to use.

uva f grape; **~s de la suerte** twelve grapes eaten for luck as midnight chimes on New Year's Eve in Spain.

va v → ir.

vaca f (animal) cow; (carne) beef.

vacaciones fpl holidays; **estar de ~** to be on holiday; **ir de ~** to go on holiday.

vacante f vacancy.

vaciar vt to empty; (hacer hueco) to hollow out.

vacilar vi (dudar) to hesitate; (tambalearse) to wobble.

vacilón m (Amér) party.

vacío, -a adj empty ◆ m (espacio) void; (hueco) gap; **envasado al ~**

vacuum-packed.

vacuna f vaccine.

vacunación f vaccination.

vacunar vt to vaccinate.

vado m (en la calle) lowered kerb; (de río) ford; "~ permanente" "keep clear".

vagabundo, -da m, f tramp.

vagamente adv vaguely.

vagina f vagina.

vago, -ga adj (perezoso) lazy; (impreciso) vague.

vagón m (de pasajeros) carriage.

vagoneta f cart.

vaho m (vapor) steam; (aliento) breath ◻ **vahos** mpl inhalation (sg).

vaina f (de guisantes, habas) pod.

vainilla f vanilla.

vajilla f crockery.

valdrá v → valer.

vale m (papel) voucher; (Amér: amigo) mate ◆ interj OK!

valenciana f (Amér) turn-up.

valentía f bravery.

valer vt (costar) to cost; (tener un valor de) to be worth; (originar) to earn ◆ vi (ser eficaz, servir) to be of use; (persona) to be good; (ser válido) to be valid; (estar permitido) to be allowed; ¿**cuánto vale?** how much is it?; ¡**vale?** OK?; **vale la pena** it's worth it ◻ **valerse de** v + prep to make use of.

valeriana f (infusión) valerian tea.

valga v → valer.

validez f validity.

válido, -da adj (documento, ley) valid.

valiente adj (persona) brave; (actitud, respuesta) fine.

valioso, -sa adj valuable.

valla f (cercado) fence; (muro) barrier; (de publicidad) hoarding; (en deporte) hurdle.

valle m valley.

valor m value; (valentía) bravery.

valoración f (de precio) valuation.

valorar vt (tasar) to value; (evaluar) to evaluate.

vals m waltz.

válvula f valve.

vanguardista adj avant-garde.

vanidad f vanity.

vanidoso, -sa adj vain.

vano: en vano adv in vain.

vapor m vapour; (de agua) steam; (barco) steamship; **al ~** steamed.

vaporizador m spray.

vaquero, -ra adj (ropa) denim ◻ **vaqueros** mpl (pantalones) jeans.

vara f (de árbol) stick; (de metal) rod; (de mando) staff.

variable adj changeable.

variado, -da adj (que varía) varied; (bombones, dulces) assorted.

variar vt (cambiar) to change; (dar variedad) to vary ◆ vi: ~ **de** (cambiar) to change; (ser diferente) to be different from.

varicela f chickenpox.

varices fpl varicose veins.

variedad f variety ◻ **variedades** fpl (espectáculo) variety (sg).

varios, -rias adj pl (algunos) several; (diversos) various.

varón m male.

varonil adj (de varón) male; (valiente, fuerte) manly.

vasallo, -lla m, f subject.

vasco, -ca adj, m, f Basque.

vasija f container (earthenware).

vaso m glass; (de plástico) cup.

vasto, -ta adj vast.

Vaticano m: El ~ the Vatican.

vaya v → ir ♦ interj well!

Vda. abrev = viuda.

ve v → ir.

vecindad f (vecindario) community; (alrededores) neighbourhood.

vecindario m community.

vecino, -na adj neighbouring ♦ m, f (de una casa) neighbour; (de barrio) resident; (de pueblo) inhabitant.

vegetación f vegetation.

vegetal adj (planta) plant (antes de s); (sandwich) salad (antes de s) ♦ m vegetable.

vegetariano, -na m, f vegetarian.

vehículo m vehicle; (de infección) carrier.

veinte núm twenty, → seis.

vejez f old age.

vejiga f bladder.

vela f (cirio) candle; (de barco) sail; (vigilia) vigil; **pasar la noche en ~** not to sleep all night.

velero m (más pequeño) sailing boat; (más grande) sailing ship.

veleta f weather vane.

vello m down.

velo m (prenda) veil; (tela) cover.

velocidad f (rapidez) speed; (marcha) gear; **"~ controlada por radar"** = "speed cameras in operation".

velódromo m cycle track.

velomotor m moped.

velorio m (Amér) wake.

veloz adj fast.

ven v → venir.

vena f vein.

venado m (carne) venison.

vencedor, -ra m, f winner.

vencejo m swift.

vencer vt (rival, enemigo) to beat; (dificultad, sueño) to overcome ♦ vi (ganar) to win; (plazo, garantía) to expire; (pago) to be due.

vencido, -da adj beaten; **darse por ~** to give in.

vencimiento m (de plazo, garantía) expiry; (de pago) due date.

venda f bandage.

vendaje m bandaging.

vendar vt to bandage.

vendaval m gale.

vendedor, -ra m, f seller.

vender vt to sell.

vendimia f grape harvest.

vendimiador, -ra m, f grape picker.

vendimiar vt to pick (grapes).

vendrá v → venir.

veneno m poison.

venenoso, -sa adj poisonous.

venezolano, -na adj & m, f Venezuelan.

Venezuela s Venezuela.

venga v → venir.

venganza f revenge.

vengarse vpr to take revenge.

vengo v → venir.

venida f (llegada) arrival

so) return.

venir *vi* 1. *(presentarse)* to come; **vino a verme** he came to see me.
2. *(llegar)* to arrive; **vino a las doce** he arrived at twelve o'clock.
3. *(seguir en el tiempo)* to come; **el año que viene** next year; **ahora viene la escena más divertida** the funniest scene comes next.
4. *(suceder)*: **le vino una desgracia inesperada** she suffered an unexpected misfortune; **vino la guerra** the war came.
5. *(proceder)*: **~ de** to come from.
6. *(hallarse, estar)* to be; **el texto viene en inglés** the text is in English.
7. *(ropa, zapatos)*: **el abrigo le viene pequeño** the coat is too small for her; **tus zapatos no me vienen** your shoes don't fit me.
8. *(en locuciones)*: **¿a qué viene esto?** what do you mean by that?
❑ **venirse** *vpr (llegar)* to come back; **~se abajo** *(edificio, persona)* to collapse; *(proyecto)* to fall through.
venta *f* sale; *(hostal)* country inn; **"~ de billetes"** "tickets on sale here"; **"en ~"** "for sale"; **~ anticipada** advance sale; **~ al detalle** retail; **~ al mayor** wholesale.
ventaja *f* advantage.
ventana *f* window.
ventanilla *f (de oficina, banco)* counter; *(de cine, etc)* ticket office; *(de coche)* window.
ventilación *f* ventilation.
ventilador *m* ventilator, fan.
ventisca *f* blizzard.
ventosa *f* sucker.
ventoso, -sa *adj* windy.
ventrílocuo, -cua *m, f* ven-

triloquist.

ver *vt* 1. *(percibir)* to see; *(mirar)* to look at; *(televisión, partido)* to watch; **desde casa vemos el mar** we can see the sea from our house; **he estado viendo tu trabajo** I've been looking at your work; **~ la televisión** to watch television.
2. *(visitar, encontrar)* to see; **fui a ~ a unos amigos** I went to see some friends.
3. *(darse cuenta de, entender)* to see; **ya veo que estás de mal humor** I see you're in a bad mood; **ya veo lo que pretendes** now I see what you're trying to do.
4. *(investigar)* to see; **voy a ~ si han venido** I'm going to see whether they've arrived.
5. *(juzgar)*: **yo no lo veo tan mal** I don't think it's that bad.
6. *(en locuciones)*: **hay que ~ qué lista es** you wouldn't believe how clever she is; **por lo visto** o **que se ve** apparently; **~ mundo** to see the world.
♦ *vi* to see; **a ~** let's see.
❑ **verse** *vpr (mirarse)* to see o.s.; *(encontrarse)* to meet, to see each other; **desde aquí se ve el mar** you can see the sea from here.
veraneante *mf* (summer) holidaymaker.
veranear *vi* to have one's summer holiday.
veraneo *m* summer holidays *(pl)*.
veraniego, -ga *adj* summer *(antes de s)*.
verano *m* summer; **en ~** in summer.
veras: de veras *adv* really.

verbena f *(fiesta)* street party *(on the eve of certain saints' days)*; *(planta)* verbena.

verbo m verb; **~ auxiliar** auxiliary verb.

verdad f truth; **es ~** it's true; **de ~** *(en serio)* really; *(auténtico)* real; **está bueno ¿~?** it's good, isn't it?

verdadero, -ra adj *(cierto, real)* real; *(no falso)* true.

verde adj inv green; *(obsceno)* blue, dirty ♦ m green.

verdulería f greengrocer's *(shop)*.

verdulero, -ra m, f greengrocer.

verdura f vegetables *(pl)*, greens *(pl)*; **~ con patatas** starter of boiled potatoes and vegetables, usually cabbage and green beans.

vereda f *(Amér)* pavement *(Br)*, sidewalk *(Am)*.

veredicto m verdict.

vergonzoso, -sa adj *(persona)* bashful; *(acción)* shameful.

vergüenza f *(timidez)* bashfulness; *(sofoco)* embarrassment; *(dignidad)* pride; *(pudor)* shame; *(escándalo)* disgrace; **me dio ~** I was embarrassed.

verificar vt *(comprobar)* to check, to verify; *(confirmar)* to confirm.

verja f *(puerta)* iron gate.

vermut m vermouth.

verosímil adj probable.

verruga f wart.

versión f version; **en ~ original** undubbed *(film)*.

verso m *(unidad)* line; *(poema)* poem.

vertedero m *(de basuras)* *(rubbish)* tip.

verter vt *(contenido, líquido)* to pour out; *(recipiente)* to empty; *(derramar)* to spill.

vertical adj vertical.

vertido m *(residuo)* waste.

vertiente f slope.

vértigo m *(mareo)* dizziness; *(fobia)* vertigo.

vestíbulo m *(de casa)* hall; *(de hotel)* foyer.

vestido m *(ropa)* clothes *(pl)*; *(prenda de mujer)* dress.

vestimenta f clothes *(pl)*.

vestir vt *(con ropa)* to dress; *(llevar puesto)* to wear; *(mantener)* to clothe ♦ vi to dress ❑ **vestirse** vpr to get dressed.

vestuario m *(ropa)* wardrobe; *(de gimnasio, etc)* changing room; *(de teatro)* dressing room.

veterano, -na m, f veteran.

veterinario, -ria m, f vet.

vez *(pl* **ces)** f *(ocasión, turno)*; **a veces** sometimes; **¿lo has hecho alguna ~?** have you ever done it?; **cada ~ más** more and more; **de ~ en cuando** from time to time; **dos veces** twice; **en ~ de** instead of; **muchas veces** a lot, often; **otra ~** again; **pocas veces** hardly ever; **tres veces por día** three times a day; **una ~** once; **unas veces** sometimes.

VHF m VHF.

VHS m VHS.

vía f *(rail)* track; *(andén)* platform; *(medio de transporte)* route; *(calzada, calle)* road; *(medio)* channel; **en ~s de** in the process of; **por ~ aérea/marítima** by air/sea; **por ~**

oral orally.

viaducto *m* viaduct.

viajar *vi* to travel.

viaje *m* (*trayecto*) journey; (*excursión*) trip; (*en barco*) voyage; **ir de ~** to go away; **¡buen ~!** have a good trip!; **~ de novios** honeymoon.

viajero, -ra *m, f* (*persona que viaja*) traveller; (*pasajero*) passenger.

víbora *f* viper.

vibrar *vi* to vibrate.

vicepresidente, -ta *m, f* vicepresident.

vichysoisse [biʃi'swas] *f* vichysoisse.

viciarse *vpr* to get corrupted.

vicio *m* (*mala costumbre*) bad habit; (*inmoralidad*) vice.

vicioso, -sa *adj* depraved.

víctima *f* victim; (*muerto*) casualty; **ser ~ de** to be the victim of.

victoria *f* victory.

vid *f* vine.

vida *f* life; (*medios de subsistencia*) living; **de toda la ~** (*amigo, etc*) lifelong; **buena ~** good life; **mala ~** vice; **~ familiar** family life.

vidente *mf* clairvoyant.

vídeo *m* video.

videocámara *f* camcorder.

videocasete *m* video(tape).

videojuego *m* video game.

vidriera *f* (*de iglesia*) stained glass window.

vidrio *m* glass.

vieira *f* scallop.

viejo, -ja *adj* old ♦ *m, f* (*anciano*) old man (*f* old woman); (*Amér: amigo*) mate.

viene *v* → **venir**.

viento *m* wind; **hace ~** it's windy.

vientre *m* stomach.

viera *v* → **ver**.

viernes *s: ~* **del Norte** North Vietnam; **~ del Sur** South Vietnam.
❏ **Viernes Santo** *m* Good Friday.

Vietnam *s: ~* **del Norte** North Vietnam; **~ del Sur** South Vietnam.

viga *f* (*de madera*) beam; (*de hierro*) girder.

vigencia *f* (*de ley, documento*) validity; (*de costumbre*) use.

vigente *adj* (*ley, documento*) in force; (*costumbre*) in use.

vigilante *mf* guard.

vigilar *vt* (*niños, bolso*) to keep an eye on; (*presos, banco*) to guard.

vigor *m* vigour; **en ~** in force.

vigoroso, -sa *adj* vigorous.

vil *adj* despicable.

villancico *m* Christmas carol.

vinagre *m* vinegar.

vinagreras *fpl* cruet set (*sg*).

vinagreta *f*: (*salsa*) **~** vinaigrette; **a la ~** with vinaigrette.

vinculación *f* link.

vincular *vt* to link.

viniera *v* → **venir**.

vino *v* → **venir** ♦ *m* wine; **~ blanco** white wine; **~ de la casa** house wine; **~ corriente** cheap wine; **~ de mesa** table wine; **~ rosado** rosé; **~ tinto** red wine.

viña *f* vineyard.

violación *f* (*de persona*) rape.

violador, -ra *m, f* rapist.

violar *vt* (*ley, acuerdo*) to break; (*mujer*) to rape; (*territorio*) to violate.

violencia f (agresividad) violence; (fuerza) force; (incomodidad) embarrassment.

violento, -ta adj violent; (incómodo) awkward.

violeta f violet.

violín m violin.

violinista mf violinist.

violoncelo m cello.

VIP m VIP.

virgen adj (mujer) virgin; (cinta) blank; (película) new ▫ **Virgen** f. la Virgen the Virgin Mary.

Virgo s Virgo.

virtud f virtue; **en ~ de** by virtue of.

viruela f smallpox.

virus m inv virus.

viruta f shaving; **~s de jamón** small flakes of "serrano" ham.

visa m Visa®.

visado m visa.

víscera f internal organ.

viscosa f viscose.

vísera f (en gorra) peak; (suelta) visor.

visible adj visible.

visillos mpl net curtains.

visita f visit; (persona) visitor; **hacer una ~ a** to visit.

visitante mf visitor.

visitar vt to visit.

vislumbrar vt (entrever) to make out; (adivinar) to get an idea of.

víspera f eve.

vista f (sentido) sight; (ojos) eyes (pl); (panorama) view; (perspicacia) foresight; (juicio) hearing; a

primera ~ at first sight; **a simple ~** at first sight; **¡hasta la ~!** see you!

vistazo m glance; **echar un ~ a** to have a quick look at.

visto, -ta pp → **ver** ◆ adj (pasado de moda) old-fashioned; **estar bien/mal ~** to be approved of/frowned on; **por lo ~** apparently.

vistoso, -sa adj eye-catching.

vital adj (de la vida) life (antes de s); (fundamental) vital; (con vitalidad) lively.

vitalidad f vitality.

vitamina f vitamin.

vitrina f glass cabinet.

viudo, -da m, f widower (f widow).

viva interj hurray!

víveres mpl supplies.

vivienda f (casa) dwelling.

vivir vi to live ◆ vt to experience; **~ de** to live on.

vivo, -va adj alive; (dolor, ingenio) sharp; (detallado) vivid; (ágil, enérgico) lively; (color) bright.

vizcaíno, -na adj: **a la vizcaína** in a thick sauce of olive oil, onion, tomato, herbs and red peppers.

vocabulario m vocabulary.

vocación f vocation.

vocal f vowel.

vodka ['boθka] m vodka.

vol. (abrev de volumen) vol.

volador, -ra adj flying.

volante adj flying ◆ m (de coche) steering wheel; (adorno) frill.

volar vi to fly; (desaparecer) to vanish ◆ vt to blow up.

volcán m volcano.

volcánico, -ca *adj* volcanic.

volcar *vt* (*sin querer*) to knock over; (*vaciar*) to empty out ◆ *vi* (*recipiente*) to tip over; (*camión, coche*) to overturn; (*barco*) to capsize.

voleibol *m* volleyball.

volquete *m* dumper truck.

voltaje *m* voltage.

voltear *vt* (*Amér*) to knock over ❑ **voltearse** *vpr* (*Amér*) to turn.

voltereta *f* (*en el aire*) somersault; (*en el suelo*) handspring.

volumen *m* volume.

voluntad *f* (*facultad, deseo*) will; (*resolución*) willpower.

voluntario, -ria *adj* voluntary ◆ *m, f* volunteer.

voluntarioso, -sa *adj* willing.

volver *vt* 1. (*cabeza, ojos, vista*) to turn; ~ **la mirada** to look round. 2. (*lo de arriba abajo*) to turn over; (*boca abajo*) to turn upside down; (*lo de dentro fuera*) to turn inside out; **vuelve la tortilla** turn the omelette over; **he vuelto el abrigo** I've turned the coat inside out. 3. (*convertir*): **lo volvió un delincuente** it turned him into a criminal; **me vuelve loco** it makes me mad.
◆ *vi* to return; ~ **a** (*tema*) to return to; ~ **a hacer algo** to do sthg again. ❑ **volverse** *vpr* (*darse la vuelta*) to turn round; (*ir de vuelta*) to return; (*convertirse*) to become; **~se loco** to go mad; **~se atrás** (*de decisión*) to back out; (*de afirmación*) to go back on one's word.

vomitar *vt* to vomit.

vos *pron* (*Amér*) you.

VOSE *f* (*abrev de versión original subtitulada en español*) original language version with Spanish subtitles.

vosotros, -tras *pron* you.

votación *f* vote.

votante *mf* voter.

votar *vt* to vote for ◆ *vi* to vote.

voto *m* (*en elecciones*) vote; (*en religión*) vow.

voy *v* → **ir**.

voz (*pl* **-ces**) *f* voice; (*grito*) shout; (*palabra*) word; (*rumor*) rumour; **en ~ alta** aloud; **en ~ baja** softly.

vuelo *m* flight; (*de un vestido*) fullness; ~ **chárter** charter flight; ~ **regular** scheduled flight; **"~s nacionales"** "domestic flights".

vuelta *f* (*movimiento, de llave*) turn; (*acción*) turning; (*regreso*) return; (*monedas*) change; (*paseo*) walk; (*en coche*) drive; (*cambio*) twist; **dar la ~ a** (*rodear*) to go round sthg; **dar una ~** to go for a walk/drive; **dar ~s** to spin; **darse la ~** to turn round; **estar de ~** to be back; **a la ~** (*volviendo*) on the way back; **a la ~ de la esquina** round the corner; **a ~ de correo** by return (of post); **"~ al colegio"** "back to school".

vuelto, -ta *pp* → **volver** ◆ *m* (*Amér*) change.

vuestro, -tra *adj* your ◆ *pron*: **el ~, la vuestra** yours; **lo ~** your thing; **un amigo ~** a friend of yours.

vulgar *adj* (*popular*) ordinary; (*no técnico*) lay; (*grosero*) vulgar.

W

walkman® ['walman] *m* Walkman®.

wáter ['bater] *m* toilet.

waterpolo [water'polo] *m* water polo.

WC *m* WC.

whisky ['wiski] *m* whisky.

windsurf [winsurf] *m* windsurfing; **hacer ~** to windsurf.

X

xenofobia *f* xenophobia.

xilófono *m* xylophone.

Y

y *conj* and; *(pero)* and yet; *(en preguntas)* what about.

ya *adv (ahora, refuerza al verbo)* now; *(ahora mismo)* at once; *(denota pasado)* already; *(denota futuro)*

some time soon ◆ *interj (expresa asentimiento)* that's it!; *(expresa comprensión)* yes! ◆ *conj:* **~ ... ~ ...** whether ... or ...; **~ que** since.

yacimiento *m* deposit.

yanqui *mf (despec)* Yank.

yate *m* yacht.

yegua *f* mare.

yema *f (de huevo)* yolk; *(de dedo)* fingertip; *(de planta)* bud; *(dulce)* sweet made of sugar and egg yolk, similar to marzipan.

yerbatero *m (Amér)* herbalist.

yerno *m* son-in-law.

yeso *m* plaster.

yo *pron* I, **soy ~** it's me; **~ que túél/etc** if I were you/him/*etc*.

yodo *m* iodine.

yoga *m* yoga.

yogur *m* yoghurt.

Yugoslavia *s* Yugoslavia.

yunque *m* anvil.

yunta *f (Amér)* cufflinks *(pl)*.

Z

zafacón *m (Amér)* dustbin *(Br)*, trashcan *(Am)*.

zafiro *m* sapphire.

zafra *f* container for sprinkling oil on food.

zaguán *m* entrance hall.

zambullida *f* dive.

zambullirse *vpr* to dive.

zanahoria f carrot.

zancadilla f trip.

zanco m stilt.

zancudo m (Amér) mosquito.

zanja f ditch.

zapallo m (Amér) pumpkin.

zapateado m type of flamenco foot-stamping dance.

zapatería f (tienda) shoe shop; (taller) shoemaker's (shop).

zapatero, -ra m, f cobbler ♦ m (mueble) shoe cupboard.

zapatilla f slipper; ~ **de deporte** trainer.

zapato m shoe; ~**s de caballero/señora** men's/women's shoes.

zapping m channel-hopping; **hacer** ~ to channel-hop.

zarandear vt to shake.

zarpar vi to set sail.

zarpazo m clawing.

zarza f bramble.

zarzamora f blackberry.

zarzuela f (obra musical) light opera; (guiso) spicy fish stew.

zenit m zenith.

zinc m zinc.

zíper m (Amér) zip (Br), zipper (Am).

zipizape m (fam) squabble.

zócalo m (del edificio) plinth; (de muro, pared) skirting board.

zodíaco m zodiac.

zona f area, zone; (parte) part; ~

azul restricted parking zone; "~ **de estacionamiento limitado y vigilado**" "restricted parking".

i **ZONA AZUL**

In Spain, blue lines on the road surface indicate areas where parking meters are in operation. Parking in "zonas azules" is free between certain hours; these times are displayed on the parking meters.

zonzo, -za adj (Amér) stupid; **hacerse el** ~ to act dumb.

zoo m zoo.

zoología f zoology.

zoológico, -ca adj zoological ♦ m zoo.

zopenco, -ca adj stupid.

zorra f (vulg: prostituta) whore, → **zorro.**

zorro, -rra m, f fox ♦ m (piel) fox(fur).

zueco m clog.

zumbar vt (fam) to thump ♦ vi to buzz.

zumbido m buzzing.

zumo m juice; ~ **de fruta** fruit juice; ~ **de naranja** orange juice.

zurcir vt to darn.

zurdo, -da adj (izquierdo) left; (que usa la mano izquierda) left-handed.

zurrar vt to hit.

GLOSSARY OF
CATALAN
SIGNS AND MENU
ITEMS

I

data

accés [ək'sɛs] *m* access; **"~ tancat festius"** *sign indicating that entrance is closed on public holidays.*

adrogueria [əðruɣə'ɾiə] *f shop selling paint, cleaning materials etc.*

ajuntament [əʒuntə'men] *m town hall.*

alineament [əlineə'men] *m:* **"~ direcció"** *sign indicating that steering alignment is carried out.*

allioli [aʎi'ɔli] *m garlic mayonnaise.*

alvocat [alβu'kɔt] *m* avocado.

amanida [əmə'niðə] *f salad;* **~ verda** green salad; **~ del temps** seasonal salad.

anxova [ən'ʃɔβə] *f anchovy;* **anxoves de L'Escala** *anchovies from the coastal resort of L'Escala.*

arròs [ə'rɔs] *m rice;* **~ negre** *rice cooked with squid ink.*

assortiment [əsuɾti'men] *m* assortment; **~ d'amanides** selection of salads; **~ de formatges** cheeseboard.

bacallà [bəkə'ʎa] *m* cod, amb samfaina *salt cod in a ratatouille sauce.*

bistec [bis'tek] *m* steak.

bitllets [bi'ʎʎets] *mpl* tickets.

botifarra [buti'faɾə] *f type of Catalan pork sausage.*

botiga [bu'tiɣə] *f shop.*

brasa ['bɾazə] *f:* **a la ~** barbecued.

brou [bɾɔw] *m* consommé.

bunyols [bu'ɲɔls] *mpl* = doughnuts; **~ de bacallà** cod dumplings.

bus [bus] *m* bus; **nit ~** night bus.

bústia ['bustiə] *f* postbox.

cabrit [kə'βɾit] *m* kid (goat); **~ al**

forn roast kid (goat).

caixa ['kaʃə] *f:* **~ d'estalvis i de pensions** savings bank.

calamars [kələ'maɾs] *mpl* squid (sg); **~ a la romana** *squid rings fried in batter.*

calçats [kəl'sats] *mpl* shoe shop (sg).

caliu [kə'liw] *m:* **al ~** roast *(cooked on hot coals).*

canelons [kənə'lons] *mpl* cannelloni.

canvi ['kambi] *m* change; **"torna ~"** "change given".

cargols [kəɾ'ɣɔls] *mpl* snails.

càrrega ['karəɣə] *f:* **"excepte ~ i descàrrega"** "except for loading".

cloïsses [klu'isəs] *fpl* clams.

complements [kumplə'mens] *mpl* accessories.

confeccions [kumfəksi'ons] *fpl* clothes shop (sg).

conill [ku'niʎ] *m* rabbit.

conservar [kunsəɾ'βa] *vt:* **"conserveu el tiquet de caixa"** "please keep your receipt".

copisteria [kupistə'ɾiə] *f photocopying shop.*

costella [kus'teʎə] *f* chop; **~ de porc** pork chop; **~ de xai** lamb chop.

costelletes [kustə'ʎetəs] *fpl* spare ribs; **~ de xai** lamb cutlets.

crema ['kɾemə] *f:* **~ catalana** *type of Catalan dessert similar to crème caramel.*

croquetes [kɾu'kɛtəs] *fpl* croquettes; **~ de pernil** ham croquettes; **~ de pollastre** chicken croquettes.

data ['datə] *f* date; **~ d'acaba-**

ment *(de carné etc)* expiry date; *(de alimentos)* sell-by date; *(de medicamentos)* "use-by" date.

daurada [dəu'raðə] *f* gilthead; ~ **al forn** baked gilthead.

descompte [dəs'komtə] *m* discount.

dia ['diə] *m*: **del ~** fresh.

diaris [di'aris] *mpl* newspapers.

dietètica [diə'tɛtikə] *f* dietetics.

direcció [dirəksi'o] *f*: **"~-suspensió-frens"** *sign indicating that steering, suspension and brakes are checked*.

embotits [əmbu'tits] *mpl* cold, cured meat *(sg)*.

empènyer [əm'pɛɲə] *vt*: **"empenyeu" "push"**.

emprovadors [əmpruβə'ðos] *mpl* fitting rooms.

endívies [ən'diβiəs] *fpl* chicory *(sg)*; ~ **al roquefort** *chicory in Roquefort sauce*.

entrada [ən'traðə] *f* entrance; **"~ lliure" "admission free".**

entrecot [əntrə'kɔt] *m* entrecôte; ~ **de vedella** entrecôte of veal.

entrepans [əntrə'pans] *mpl* sandwiches.

escalivada [əskəli'βaðə] *f* grilled peppers, aubergines and onions.

escudella [əsku'ðeʎə] *f*: ~ **barrejada** thick soup made of bacon, meat, chickpeas and vegetables.

espàrrecs [əs'parəks] *mpl* asparagus *(sg)*.

espatlla [əs'paʎʎə] *f* shoulder; ~ **de cabrit** shoulder of kid; ~ **de xai** shoulder of lamb.

esqueixada [əskə'ʃaðə] *f*: ~ **de**

bacallà *shredded salt cod marinated in oil and vinegar with tomatoes, onions and red pepper.*

estanc [əs'taŋ] *m* tobacconist's (shop).

estofat [əstu'fat] *m* stew; ~ **de bou** beef stew; ~ **de vedella** veal stew.

farcit [fər'sit] *adj* stuffed.

fet [fet] *adj*: ~ **a mà** hand-made.

fira ['firə] *f* trade fair.

flam [flam] *m* crème caramel; ~ **amb nata** crème caramel with whipped cream.

fleca ['flɛkə] *f* bakery.

formatgeria [furmədʒə'riə] *f* cheese shop.

forn [forn] *m*: ~ **de pa** bakery; **al ~** baked.

fregit [frə'ʒit] *adj* fried.

fresc [frɛsk] *adj* fresh.

fricandó [frikən'do] *m* meat stew cooked with onions, tomatoes and herbs; ~ **amb moixernons** *"fricandó" with mushrooms.*

fruita [fru'itə] *f* fruit; ~ **del temps** fruit in season.

fumat [fu'mat] *adj* smoked.

funcionar [funsiu'na] *vi*: **"no funciona" "out of order".**

fusteria [fustə'riə] *f* carpenter's (shop).

galeria [gələ'riə] *f* gallery.

gambes ['gambəs] *fpl* prawns.

gaspatxo [gəs'patʃu] *m*: ~ **(andalús)** gazpacho.

gelat [ʒə'lat] *m* ice-cream.

gelateria [ʒələtə'riə] *f* ice-cream parlour.

gènere ['ʒenərə] *m*: ~ **de punt** knitwear.

gos [gos] *m*: "**gossos no**" "no dogs allowed".

graella [grəˈeʎə] *f*: **a la ~** grilled.

graellada [grəeˈʎaðə] *f* mixed grill; **~ de peix** mixed grill of fish.

gual [gwal] *m*: "**~ permanent**" "keep clear for access".

guàrdia [ˈgwarðiə] *f*: **~ urbana** local police officer who deals mainly with traffic offences.

guarnició [gwərnisiˈo] *f* garnish.

horari [uˈrari] *m* opening hours (*pl*).

institut [instiˈtut] *m*: **~ de bellesa** beauty salon.

jocs [ʒoks] *mpl*: **~ i joguines** games and toys.

joieria [ʒuiəˈriə] *f* jeweller's (shop).

laborable [ləβuˈrablə] *m*: "**~ s feiners**" "working days and public holidays".

llagostins [ʎəɣusˈtins] *mpl* king prawns.

llanta [ˈʎantə] *f* wheel rim.

llenguado [ʎəŋˈgwaðu] *m* sole.

llenties [ʎənˈtiəs] *fpl* lentils; **~ estofades** lentil stew (*sg*).

llibreria [ʎiβrəˈriə] *f* bookshop.

llom [ʎom] *m* loin; **~ a la planxa** grilled pork loin.

lluç [ʎus] *m* hake; **~ a la planxa** grilled hake; **~ a la romana** hake cooked in batter.

magatzem [məɣəˈdzem] *m* warehouse.

mel [mel] *f*: **~ i mató** curd cheese served with honey.

mercat [mərˈkat] *m* market.

minusvàlid [minuzˈβalit] *m* disabled person.

musclos [ˈmuskləs] *mpl* mussels; **~ a la marinera** moules marinière; **~ al vapor** steamed mussels.

navalles [nəˈβaʎəs] *fpl* razor clams.

obsequis [upˈsekis] *mpl* gifts.

obtenció [uptənsiˈo] *f*: "**~ de tiquet a l'expenedor**" *sign indicating that passengers should obtain tickets from the ticket machine.*

pas [pas] *m*: "**~ exclusiu veïns**" "(access for) residents only".

passeig [pəˈsetʃ] *m* avenue; **~ maritim** promenade.

pastís [pəsˈtis] *m* cake.

pastisseria [pəstisəˈriə] *f* cake shop.

patata [pəˈtatə] *f* potato; **patates al caliu** potatoes baked on hot coals; **patates fregides** (*de sartén*) chips (*Br*), French fries (*Am*); (*de bolsa*) crisps (*Br*), chips (*Am*).

pebrot [pəˈβrɔt] *m* pepper; **~s farcits** stuffed peppers.

peixet [pəˈʃet] *m*: **~ de platja** whitebait.

pernil [pərˈnil] *m* ham; **~ dolç** boiled ham; **~ salat** cured ham.

perruqueria [pərukəˈriə] *f* hairdresser's (salon).

pèsols [ˈpezuls] *mpl* peas.

planxa [ˈplanʃə] *f*: **a la ~** grilled.

pollastre [puˈʎastrə] *m* chicken; **~ al curry** chicken curry; **~ al forn** roast chicken; **~ rostit** chicken casserole.

porc [pɔrk] *m* pork.

porros [ˈpɔrus] *mpl* leeks.

preu [prɛw] *m* price; **a meitat del seu ~** half-price.

queviures [kəˈβiurəs] *mpl* gro

cer's (shop).

quiosc [ki'osk] *m* newspaper stand.

rap [rap] *m* angler fish; ~ **a l'all cremat** *angler fish fried in garlic*; ~ **a la planxa** grilled angler fish.

rebaixes [rəˈβaʃəs] *fpl* sales.

regals [rəˈvals] *mpl* gifts.

reservat [rəzərˈβat] *adj*: "~ **el dret d'admissió**" "the management reserves the right to refuse admission".

revoltim [rəβulˈtim] *m* scrambled eggs *(pl)*; ~ **de bolets** scrambled eggs with mushrooms.

romana [ruˈmanə] *f*: **a la** ~ fried in batter.

rostit [rusˈtit] *adj* roast.

sabateria [səβətəˈriə] *f* shoe shop.

sala [ˈsalə] *f*: ~ **d'art** art gallery.

salmó [səlˈmo] *m* salmon; ~ **fumat** smoked salmon.

samfaina [səmˈfajnə] *f vegetable sauce similar to ratatouille.*

sardina [sərˈðinə] *f* sardine; **sardines en escabetx** marinated sardines.

sèpia [ˈsɛpiə] *f* cuttlefish.

servei [sərˈβei] *m*: "~ **alimentació**" "supermarket".

sorbet [surˈβet] *m* sorbet; ~ **de llimona** lemon sorbet.

sortida [surˈtiðə] *f* exit; "~ **de socors**" "emergency exit".

soterrani [sutəˈrani] *m* basement.

suc [suk] *m* juice; ~ **de taronja** orange juice.

suís [suˈis] *m thick drinking chocolate with whipped cream.*

suquet [suˈket] *m*: ~ **(de peix)** *seafood stew.*

tancat [təŋˈkat] *adj*: "~ **diumenges i festius**" "closed on Sundays and public holidays".

targeta [tərˈʒetə] *f*: ~ **multiviatge** = travelcard.

temps [tems] *m inv*: **del** ~ in season.

tintoreria [tinturəˈriə] *f* dry-cleaner's (shop).

tomàquet [tuˈmakɛt] *m* tomato.

tonyina [tuˈɲinə] *f* tuna.

truita [truˈitə] *f* omelette; ~ **a la francesa** French omelette; ~ **de patates** Spanish omelette; ~ **(de riu)** trout.

vestuari [bəstuˈari] *m* changing room.

xai [ʃai] *m* lamb.

xampinyons [ʃəmpiˈɲons] *mpl* mushrooms.

xocolata [ʃukuˈlatə] *f* chocolate; ~ **desfeta** hot chocolate.

ENGLISH-SPANISH
INGLÉS-ESPAÑOL

a [stressed eɪ, unstressed ə] indef art
1. (referring to indefinite thing, person)
un (una); **a friend** un amigo; **a table** una mesa; **an apple** una manzana; **to be a doctor** ser médico.
2. (instead of the number one) un (una); **a hundred and twenty pounds** ciento veinte libras; **a month ago** hace un mes; **a thousand** mil; **four and a half** cuatro y medio.
3. (in prices, ratios) por; **they're £2 a kilo** están a dos libras el kilo; **three times a year** tres veces al año.

AA n (Br: abbr of Automobile Association) asociación británica del automóvil, = RACE m.

aback [əˈbæk] adj: **to be taken ~** quedarse atónito(-ta).

abandon [əˈbændən] vt abandonar.

abattoir [ˈæbətwɑːʳ] n matadero m.

abbey [ˈæbɪ] n abadía f.

abbreviation [əˌbriːvɪˈeɪʃn] n abreviatura f.

abdomen [ˈæbdəmən] n abdomen m.

abide [əˈbaɪd] vt: **I can't ~ him** no le aguanto ❏ **abide by** vt fus (rule,

law) acatar.

ability [əˈbɪlətɪ] n (capability) capacidad f, facultad f; (skill) dotes fpl.

able [ˈeɪbl] adj capaz, competente; **to be ~ to do sthg** poder hacer algo.

abnormal [æbˈnɔːml] adj anormal.

aboard [əˈbɔːd] adv a bordo ◆ prep (ship, plane) a bordo de; (train, bus) en.

abolish [əˈbɒlɪʃ] vt abolir.

aborigine [ˌæbəˈrɪdʒənɪ] n aborigen mf de Australia.

abort [əˈbɔːt] vt abortar.

abortion [əˈbɔːʃn] n aborto m; **to have an ~** abortar.

about [əˈbaʊt] adv **1.** (approximately) más o menos; **~ 50** unos cincuenta; **at ~ six o'clock** a eso de las seis.
2. (referring to place) por ahí, **to walk ~** pasearse.
3. (on the point of): **to be ~ to do sthg** estar a punto de hacer algo; **it's ~ to rain** va a empezar a llover.
◆ prep **1.** (concerning) acerca de; **a book ~ Scotland** un libro sobre

Escocia; **what's it ~?** ¿de qué (se) trata?; **what ~ a drink?** ¿qué tal si tomamos algo?
2. *(referring to place)* por; **there are lots of hotels ~ the town** hay muchos hoteles por toda la ciudad.

above [ə'bʌv] *prep* por encima de ♦ *adv (higher)* arriba; **children aged ten and ~** niños mayores de diez años; **the room ~** la habitación de arriba; **~ all** sobre todo.

abroad [ə'brɔːd] *adv (be, live, work)* en el extranjero; *(go, move)* al extranjero.

abrupt [ə'brʌpt] *adj* repentino(-na).

abscess ['æbses] *n* absceso *m*.

absence ['æbsəns] *n* ausencia *f*.

absent ['æbsənt] *adj* ausente.

absent-minded [-'maɪndɪd] *adj* despistado(-da).

absolute ['æbsəluːt] *adj* absoluto(-ta).

absolutely [*adv* 'æbsəluːtlɪ, *excl* ˌæbsə'luːtlɪ] *adv (completely)* absolutamente ♦ *excl* ¡por supuesto!

absorb [əb'sɔːb] *vt (liquid)* absorber.

absorbed [əb'sɔːbd] *adj:* **to be ~ in sthg** estar absorto(-ta) en algo.

absorbent [əb'sɔːbənt] *adj* absorbente.

abstain [əb'steɪn] *vi:* **to ~ (from)** abstenerse (de).

absurd [əb'sɜːd] *adj* absurdo(-da).

ABTA ['æbtə] *n* asociación británica de agencias de viajes.

abuse [*n* ə'bjuːs, *vb* ə'bjuːz] *n (insults)* insultos *mpl*; *(wrong use,*

maltreatment) abuso *m* ♦ *vt (insult)* insultar; *(use wrongly)* abusar de; *(maltreat)* maltratar.

abusive [ə'bjuːsɪv] *adj* insultante.

AC *(abbr of alternating current)* CA.

academic [ˌækə'demɪk] *adj (educational)* académico(-ca) ♦ *n* profesor *m* universitario (profesora *f* universitaria).

academy [ə'kædəmɪ] *n* academia *f*.

accelerate [ək'seləreɪt] *vi* acelerar.

accelerator [ək'seləreɪtə*r*] *n* acelerador *m*.

accent ['æksent] *n* acento *m*.

accept [ək'sept] *vt* aceptar; *(blame, responsibility)* admitir.

acceptable [ək'septəbl] *adj* aceptable.

access ['ækses] *n* acceso *m*.

accessible [ək'sesəbl] *adj* accesible.

accessories [ək'sesərɪz] *npl (extras)* accesorios *mpl*; *(fashion items)* complementos *mpl*.

access road *n* vía *f* de acceso.

accident ['æksɪdənt] *n* accidente *m*; **by ~** por casualidad.

accidental [ˌæksɪ'dentl] *adj* accidental.

accident insurance *n* seguro *m* contra accidentes.

accident-prone *adj* propenso(-sa) a los accidentes.

acclimatize [ə'klaɪmətaɪz] *vi* aclimatarse.

accommodate [ə'kɒmədeɪt] *vt* alojar.

accommodation [əˌkɒmə'deɪʃn] *n* alojamiento *m*.

accommodations [əˌkɒmə-
'deɪʃnz] npl (Am) = **accommodation**.

accompany [ə'kʌmpənɪ] vt
acompañar.

accomplish [ə'kʌmplɪʃ] vt conseguir, lograr.

accord [ə'kɔːd] n: of one's own ~
por propia voluntad.

accordance [ə'kɔːdəns] n: in ~
with conforme a.

according to [ə'kɔːdɪŋ-] prep
según.

accordion [ə'kɔːdɪən] n acordeón m.

account [ə'kaunt] n (at bank,
shop) cuenta f; (spoken report) relato
m; to take into ~ tener en cuenta;
on no ~ bajo ningún pretexto; on
~ of debido a □ **account for** vt fus
(explain) justificar; (constitute) representar.

accountant [ə'kauntənt] n contable mf.

account number n número
m de cuenta.

accumulate [ə'kjuːmjʊleɪt] vt
acumular.

accurate ['ækjʊrət] adj (description, report) veraz; (work, measurement, figure) exacto(-ta).

accuse [ə'kjuːz] vt: to ~ sb of sthg
acusar a alguien de algo.

accused [ə'kjuːzd] n: the ~ el
acusado m (la acusada f).

ace [eɪs] n as m.

ache [eɪk] n dolor m ♦ vi: my leg
~s me duele la pierna.

achieve [ə'tʃiːv] vt conseguir.

acid ['æsɪd] adj ácido(-da) ♦ n
ácido m.

acid rain n lluvia f ácida.

acknowledge [ək'nɒlɪdʒ] vt
(accept) reconocer; (letter) acusar
recibo de.

acne ['æknɪ] n acné m.

acorn ['eɪkɔːn] n bellota f.

acoustic [ə'kuːstɪk] adj acústi-
co(-ca).

acquaintance [ə'kweɪntəns] n
(person) conocido m (-da f).

acquire [ə'kwaɪər] vt adquirir.

acre ['eɪkər] n acre m.

acrobat ['ækrəbæt] n acróbata
mf.

across ['ækrɒs] prep (to, on other
side of) al otro lado de; (from one
side to the other of) de un lado a
otro de ♦ adv (to other side) al otro
lado; it's ten miles ~ tiene diez
millas de ancho; we walked ~ the
road cruzamos la calle; ~ from en
frente de.

acrylic [ə'krɪlɪk] n acrílico m.

act [ækt] vi actuar; (behave) comportarse ♦ n (action) acto m, acción
f; (POL) ley f; (of play) acto; (performance) número m; to ~ as (serve as)
hacer de.

action ['ækʃn] n acción f; to take
~ tomar medidas; to put sthg into
~ poner algo en acción; out of ~
(machine) averiado; (person) fuera
de combate.

active ['æktɪv] adj activo(-va).

activity [æk'tɪvətɪ] n actividad f
□ **activities** npl (leisure events)
atracciones fpl.

activity holiday n vacaciones
organizadas para niños de actividades
deportivas, etc.

act of God n caso m de fuerza
mayor.

actor ['æktər] n actor m.

actress ['æktrıs] n actriz f.

actual ['æktʃʊəl] adj (exact, real) verdadero(-ra); (for emphasis) mismísimo(-ma); (final) final.

actually ['æktʃʊəlı] adv (really) realmente; (in fact) la verdad es que.

acupuncture ['ækjʊpʌŋktʃəʳ] n acupuntura f.

acute [ə'kju:t] adj (feeling, pain) intenso(-sa); (angle, accent) agudo(-da).

ad [æd] n (inf) anuncio m.

AD (abbr of Anno Domini) d.C.

adapt [ə'dæpt] vt adaptar ◆ vi adaptarse.

adapter [ə'dæptəʳ] n (for foreign plug) adaptador m; (for several plugs) ladrón m.

add [æd] vt (put, say in addition) añadir; (numbers, prices) sumar ❑ **add up** vt sep sumar; **add up to** vt fus (total) venir a ser.

adder ['ædəʳ] n víbora f.

addict ['ædıkt] n adicto m (-ta f).

addicted [ə'dıktıd] adj: **to be ~ to sthg** ser adicto(-ta) a algo.

addiction [ə'dıkʃn] n adicción f.

addition [ə'dıʃn] n (added thing) adición f; (in maths) suma f; **in ~** además; **in ~ to** además de.

additional [ə'dıʃənl] adj adicional.

additive ['ædıtıv] n aditivo m.

address [ə'dres] n (on letter) dirección f ◆ vt (speak to) dirigirse a; (letter) dirigir.

address book n agenda f de direcciones.

addressee [ˌædre'si:] n destinatario m (-ria f).

adequate ['ædıkwət] adj (sufficient) suficiente; (satisfactory) acep-

table.

adhere [əd'hıəʳ] vi: **to ~ to** (stick to) adherirse a; (obey) observar.

adhesive [əd'hi:sıv] adj adhesivo(-va) ◆ n adhesivo m.

adjacent [ə'dʒeısənt] adj adyacente.

adjective ['ædʒıktıv] n adjetivo m.

adjoining [ə'dʒɔınıŋ] adj contiguo(-gua).

adjust [ə'dʒʌst] vt ajustar ◆ vi: **to ~ to** adaptarse a.

adjustable [ə'dʒʌstəbl] adj ajustable.

adjustment [ə'dʒʌstmənt] n ajuste m.

administration [ədˌmınıˈstreıʃn] n administración f.

administrator [əd'mınıstreıtəʳ] n administrador m (-ra f).

admiral ['ædmərəl] n almirante m.

admire [əd'maıəʳ] vt admirar.

admission [əd'mıʃn] n (permission to enter) admisión f; (entrance cost) entrada f.

admission charge n entrada f.

admit [əd'mıt] vt admitir ◆ vi: **to ~ to sthg** admitir algo; **"~s one"** (on ticket) "válido para una persona".

adolescent [ˌædə'lesnt] n adolescente mf.

adopt [ə'dɒpt] vt adoptar.

adopted [ə'dɒptıd] adj adoptivo(-va).

adorable [ə'dɔːrəbl] adj adorable.

adore [ə'dɔːʳ] vt adorar.

adult ['ædʌlt] n adulto m (-ta f) ◆ adj (entertainment, films) para

adultos; *(animal)* adulto(-ta).
adult education *n* educación *f* para adultos.
adultery [ə'dʌltərɪ] *n* adulterio *m*.
advance [əd'vɑːns] *n (money)* anticipo *m*; *(movement)* avance *m* ◆ *adj (warning)* previo(-via), *(payment)* anticipado(-da) ◆ *vt* adelantar ◆ *vi* avanzar.
advance booking *n* reserva *f* anticipada.
advanced [əd'vɑːnst] *adj (student, level)* avanzado(-da).
advantage [əd'vɑːntɪdʒ] *n (benefit)* ventaja *f*; **to take ~ of** *(opportunity, offer)* aprovechar; *(person)* aprovecharse de.
adventure [əd'ventʃə'] *n* aventura *f*.
adventurous [əd'ventʃərəs] *adj (person)* aventurero(-ra).
adverb ['ædvɜːb] *n* adverbio *m*.
adverse ['ædvɜːs] *adj* adverso(-sa).
advert ['ædvɜːt] *n* = **advertisement**.
advertise ['ædvətaɪz] *vt (product, event)* anunciar.
advertisement [əd'vɜːtɪsmənt] *n* anuncio *m*.
advice [əd'vaɪs] *n* consejos *mpl*; **a piece of ~** un consejo.
advisable [əd'vaɪzəbl] *adj* aconsejable.
advise [əd'vaɪz] *vt* aconsejar; **to ~ sb to do sthg** aconsejar a alguien que haga algo; **to ~ sb against doing sthg** desaconsejar a alguien que haga algo.
advocate [*n* 'ædvəkət, *vb* 'ædvəkeɪt] *n (JUR)* abogado *m* (-da *f*) ◆ *vt* abogar por.

aerial ['eərɪəl] *n* antena *f*.
aerobics [eə'rəubɪks] *n* aerobic *m*.
aerodynamic [,eərəudaɪ'næmɪk] *adj* aerodinámico(-ca).
aeroplane ['eərəpleɪn] *n* avión *m*.
aerosol ['eərəsɒl] *n* aerosol *m*.
affair [ə'feə'] *n (matter)* asunto *m*; *(love affair)* aventura *f* (amorosa); *(event)* acontecimiento *m*.
affect [ə'fekt] *vt (influence)* afectar.
affection [ə'fekʃn] *n* afecto *m*.
affectionate [ə'fekʃnət] *adj* cariñoso(-sa).
affluent ['æfluənt] *adj* opulento(-ta).
afford [ə'fɔːd] *vt*: **to be able to ~ sthg** *(holiday, new coat)* poder permitirse algo; **I can't ~ it** no me lo puedo permitir; **I can't ~ the time** no tengo tiempo.
affordable [ə'fɔːdəbl] *adj* asequible.
afloat [ə'fləut] *adj* a flote.
afraid [ə'freɪd] *adj*: **to be ~ of** *(person)* tener miedo a; *(thing)* tener miedo de; **I'm ~ so/not** me temo que sí/no.
Africa ['æfrɪkə] *n* África.
African ['æfrɪkən] *adj* africano(-na) ◆ *n* africano *m* (-na *f*)
after ['ɑːftə'] *prep* después de ◆ *conj* después de que ◆ *adv* después; **a quarter ~ ten** *(Am)* las diez y cuarto; **to be ~ sthg/sb** *(in search of)* buscar algo/a alguien; **~ all** *(in spite of everything)* después de todo; *(it should be remembered)* al fin y al cabo.
aftercare ['ɑːftəkeə'] *n* asistencia *f* post-hospitalaria.

aftereffects ['ɑ:ftərɪ,fekts] *npl* efectos *mpl* secundarios.

afternoon [,ɑ:ftə'nu:n] *n* tarde *f*; **good ~!** ¡buenas tardes!

afternoon tea *n* = **merienda** *f*.

aftershave ['ɑ:ftəʃeɪv] *n* colonia *f* de hombre.

aftersun ['ɑ:ftəsʌn] *n* aftersún *m*.

afterwards ['ɑ:ftəwədz] *adv* después.

again [ə'gen] *adv* de nuevo, otra vez; **~ and ~** una y otra vez; **never ~** nunca jamás.

against [ə'genst] *prep* contra; *(in disagreement with)* en contra de; **to lean ~ sthg** apoyarse en algo; **~ the law** ilegal.

age [eɪdʒ] *n* edad *f*; *(old age)* vejez *f*; **under ~** menor de edad; **I haven't seen her for ~s** *(inf)* hace siglos que no la veo.

aged [eɪdʒd] *adj:* **~ eight** de ocho años de edad.

age group *n* grupo *m* de edad.

age limit *n* edad *f* máxima/mínima.

agency ['eɪdʒənsɪ] *n* agencia *f*.

agenda [ə'dʒendə] *n* orden *m* del día.

agent ['eɪdʒənt] *n* agente *mf*.

aggression [ə'greʃn] *n* agresividad *f*.

aggressive [ə'gresɪv] *adj* agresivo(-va).

agile [*Br* 'ædʒaɪl, *Am* 'ædʒəl] *adj* ágil.

agility [ə'dʒɪlətɪ] *n* agilidad *f*.

agitated ['ædʒɪteɪtɪd] *adj* agitado(-da).

ago [ə'gəʊ] *adv:* **a month ~** hace un mes; **how long ~?** ¿cuánto tiempo hace?

agonizing ['ægənaɪzɪŋ] *adj (delay)* angustioso(-sa); *(pain)* atroz.

agony ['ægənɪ] *n* dolor *m* intenso.

agree [ə'gri:] *vi (be in agreement)* estar de acuerdo; *(consent)* acceder; *(correspond)* concordar; **it doesn't ~ with me** *(food)* no me sienta bien; **to ~ to sthg** acceder a algo; **to ~ to do sthg** acceder a hacer algo ❑ **agree on** *vt fus (time, price)* acordar.

agreed [ə'gri:d] *adj* acordado(-da); **to be ~** *(person)* estar de acuerdo.

agreement [ə'gri:mənt] *n* acuerdo *m*; **in ~ with** de acuerdo con.

agriculture ['ægrɪkʌltʃə'] *n* agricultura *f*.

ahead [ə'hed] *adv (in front)* delante; *(forwards)* adelante; **the months ~** los meses que vienen; **to be ~** *(winning)* ir ganando; **~ of** *(in front of)* delante de; *(in better position than)* por delante de; **~ of schedule** por delante de lo previsto; **go straight ~** sigue todo recto; **they're two points ~** llevan dos puntos de ventaja.

aid [eɪd] *n* ayuda *f* ◆ *vt* ayudar; **in ~ of** a beneficio de; **with the ~ of** con la ayuda de.

AIDS [eɪdz] *n* SIDA *m*.

ailment ['eɪlmənt] *n* *(fml)* achaque *m*.

aim [eɪm] *n* *(purpose)* propósito *m* ◆ *vt* apuntar ◆ *vi:* **to ~ (at)** apuntar (a); **to ~ to do sthg** aspirar a hacer algo.

air [eə'] *n* aire *m* ◆ *vt (room)* ventilar ◆ *adj* aéreo(-a); **by ~** *(travel)* en avión; *(send)* por avión.

airbed ['eəbed] *n* colchón *m*

de aire.

airborne ['eəbɔ:n] *adj* en el aire.

air-conditioned [-kən'dɪʃnd] *adj* climatizado(-da).

air-conditioning [-kən'dɪʃnɪŋ] *n* aire *m* acondicionado.

aircraft ['eəkrɑ:ft] (*pl inv*) *n* avión *m*.

aircraft carrier [-,kærɪəʳ] *n* portaaviones *m inv*.

airfield ['eəfi:ld] *n* aeródromo *m*.

airforce ['eəfɔ:s] *n* fuerzas *fpl* aéreas.

air freshener [-,freʃnəʳ] *n* ambientador *m*.

airhostess ['eə,həʊstɪs] *n* azafata *f*.

airing cupboard ['eərɪŋ-] *n* armario de aire caliente para guardar la ropa.

airletter ['eə,letəʳ] *n* aerograma *m*.

airline ['eəlaɪn] *n* línea *f* aérea.

airliner ['eə,laɪnəʳ] *n* avión *m* (grande) de pasajeros.

airmail ['eəmeɪl] *n* correo *m* aéreo; **by ~** por avión.

airplane ['eəpleɪn] *n* (*Am*) avión *m*.

airport ['eəpɔ:t] *n* aeropuerto *m*.

air raid *n* ataque *m* aéreo

airsick ['eəsɪk] *adj* mareado(-da) (*en avión*).

air steward *n* auxiliar *m* de vuelo.

air stewardess *n* azafata *f*.

air traffic control *n* (*people*) personal *m* de la torre de control.

airy ['eərɪ] *adj* espacioso(-sa) y bien ventilado(-da).

aisle [aɪl] *n* (*in church*) nave *f* lateral; (*in plane, cinema, supermarket*)

pasillo *m*.

aisle seat *n* (*on plane*) asiento *m* junto al pasillo; (*record*) elepé *m*.

ajar [ə'dʒɑːʳ] *adj* entreabierto (-ta).

alarm [ə'lɑːm] *n* alarma *f* ◆ *vt* alarmar.

alarm clock *n* despertador *m*.

alarmed [ə'lɑːmd] *adj* (*door, car*) con alarma.

alarming [ə'lɑːmɪŋ] *adj* alarmante.

Albert Hall ['ælbət-] *n*: **the ~** el Albert Hall.

ℹ️ ALBERT HALL

Esta gran sala de conciertos londinense se llama así en honor al príncipe Albert, consorte de la reina Victoria. Además de conciertos, en el Albert Hall se celebran otros espectáculos, incluidos acontecimientos deportivos.

---

album ['ælbəm] *n* (*for photos*) álbum *m*; (*record*) elepé *m*.

alcohol ['ælkəhɒl] *n* alcohol *m*.

alcohol-free *adj* sin alcohol.

alcoholic [,ælkə'hɒlɪk] *adj* alcohólico(-ca) ◆ *n* alcohólico *m* (-ca *f*).

alcoholism ['ælkəhɒlɪzm] *n* alcoholismo *m*.

alcove ['ælkəʊv] *n* hueco *m*.

ale [eɪl] *n* cerveza oscura de sabor amargo y alto contenido en alcohol.

alert [ə'lɜːt] *adj* atento(-ta) ◆ *vt* alertar.

A-level *n examen necesario para acceder a la universidad.*

---

i A-LEVEL

Los exámenes llamados "A-levels" se realizan a los 18 años normalmente y son un requisito obligatorio para acceder a la universidad en Gran Bretaña. En general, los estudiantes se examinan de tres materias, o cuatro como máximo. Las notas de los "A-levels" son muy importantes puesto que determinan si los estudiantes pueden ir a la universidad de su elección.

---

algebra ['ældʒɪbrə] *n* álgebra *f.*

Algeria [æl'dʒɪərɪə] *n* Argelia.

alias ['eɪlɪəs] *adv* alias.

alibi ['ælɪbaɪ] *n* coartada *f.*

alien ['eɪlɪən] *n (foreigner)* extranjero *m* (-ra *f*); *(from outer space)* extraterrestre *m.*

alight [ə'laɪt] *adj* ardiendo ◆ *vi (fml: remove from train, bus):* **to ~ (from)** apearse (de).

align [ə'laɪn] *vt* alinear.

alike [ə'laɪk] *adj* parecido(-da) ◆ *adv* igual; **to look ~** parecerse.

alive [ə'laɪv] *adj* vivo(-va).

all [ɔːl] *adj* **1.** *(with singular noun)* todo(-da); **~ the money** todo el dinero; **~ the time** todo el rato; **~ day** todo el día.

2. *(with plural noun)* todos(-das); **the houses** todas las casas; **~ trains stop at Tonbridge** todos los trenes hacen parada en Tonbridge; **~ three died** los tres murieron.

◆ *adv* **1.** *(completely)* completa-

mente; **~ alone** completamente solo.

2. *(in scores):* **it's two ~** van empatados a dos.

3. *(in phrases):* **~ but empty** casi vacío; **~ over** *adj (finished)* terminado ◆ *prep* por todo.

◆ *pron* **1.** *(everything)* todo *m* (-da *f*); **~ of the work** todo el trabajo; **is that ~?** *(in shop)* ¿algo más?; **the best of ~** lo mejor de todo.

2. *(everybody)* todos *mpl* (-das *fpl*); **~ of us went** fuimos todos.

3. *(in phrases):* **in ~** *(in total)* en total; **can I help you at ~?** ¿le puedo ayudar en algo?

Allah ['ælə] *n* Alá *m.*

allege [ə'ledʒ] *vt* alegar.

allergic [ə'lɜːdʒɪk] *adj:* **to be ~ to** ser alérgico(-ca) a.

allergy ['ælədʒɪ] *n* alergia *f.*

alleviate [ə'liːvɪeɪt] *vt* aliviar.

alley ['ælɪ] *n (narrow street)* callejón *m.*

alligator ['ælɪɡeɪtəʳ] *n* caimán *m.*

all-in *adj (Br: inclusive)* con todo incluido.

all-night *adj (bar, petrol station)* abierto(-ta) toda la noche.

allocate ['æləkeɪt] *vt* asignar.

allotment [ə'lɒtmənt] *n (Br: for vegetables)* parcela municipal arrendada para su cultivo.

allow [ə'laʊ] *vt (permit)* permitir; *(time, money)* contar con; **to ~ sb to do sthg** dejar a alguien hacer algo; **to be ~ed to do sthg** poder hacer algo ❑ **allow for** *vt fus* contar con.

allowance [ə'laʊəns] *n (state benefit)* subsidio *m;* *(for expenses)* dietas *fpl;* *(Am: pocket money)* dinero *m* de bolsillo.

all right adj bien ◆ adv (satisfactorily) bien; (yes, okay) vale.

ally [ˈælaɪ] n aliado m (-da f).

almond [ˈɑːmənd] n almendra f.

almost [ˈɔːlməʊst] adv casi.

alone [əˈləʊn] adj & adv solo(-la); to leave sb ~ dejar a alguien en paz; to leave sthg ~ dejar algo.

along [əˈlɒŋ] prep (towards one end of) por; (alongside) a lo largo de ◆ adv: she was walking ~ iba caminando; to bring sthg ~ traerse algo; all ~ siempre, desde el principio; ~ with junto con.

alongside [əˌlɒŋˈsaɪd] prep junto a ◆ adv: to come ~ ponerse al lado.

aloof [əˈluːf] adj distante.

aloud [əˈlaʊd] adv en voz alta.

alphabet [ˈælfəbet] n alfabeto m.

Alps [ælps] npl: the ~ los Alpes.

already [ɔːlˈredɪ] adv ya.

also [ˈɔːlsəʊ] adv también.

altar [ˈɔːltər] n altar m.

alter [ˈɔːltər] vt & vi cambiar.

alteration [ˌɔːltəˈreɪʃn] n alteración f.

alternate [Br ɔːlˈtɜːnət, Am ˈɔːltərnət] adj alterno(-na).

alternating current [ˈɔːltəneɪtɪŋ-] n corriente f alterna.

alternative [ɔːlˈtɜːnətɪv] adj alternativo(-va) ◆ n alternativa f.

alternatively [ɔːlˈtɜːnətɪvlɪ] adv o bien.

alternator [ˈɔːltəneɪtər] n alternador m.

although [ɔːlˈðəʊ] conj aunque.

altitude [ˈæltɪtjuːd] n altitud f.

altogether [ˌɔːltəˈgeðər] adv (completely) completamente; (in total) en total.

aluminium [ˌæljʊˈmɪnɪəm] n (Br) aluminio m.

aluminum [əˈluːmɪnəm] (Am) = aluminium.

always [ˈɔːlweɪz] adv siempre.

am [æm] → be.

a.m. (abbr of ante meridiem): at 2 ~ a las dos de la mañana.

amateur [ˈæmətər] n aficionado m (-da f).

amazed [əˈmeɪzd] adj asombrado(-da).

amazing [əˈmeɪzɪŋ] adj asombroso(-sa).

Amazon [ˈæməzn] n (river): the ~ el Amazonas.

ambassador [æmˈbæsədər] n embajador m (-ra f).

amber [ˈæmbər] adj (traffic lights) (de color) ámbar, (jewellery) de ámbar.

ambiguous [æmˈbɪgjʊəs] adj ambiguo(-gua).

ambition [æmˈbɪʃn] n ambición f.

ambitious [æmˈbɪʃəs] adj ambicioso(-sa).

ambulance [ˈæmbjʊləns] n ambulancia f.

ambush [ˈæmbʊʃ] n emboscada f.

amenities [əˈmiːnətɪz] npl instalaciones fpl.

America [əˈmerɪkə] n América f.

American [əˈmerɪkən] adj americano(-na) ◆ n (person) americano m (-na f).

amiable [ˈeɪmɪəbl] adj amable.

ammunition [ˌæmjʊˈnɪʃn] n

municiones *fpl*.

amnesia [æm'niːzɪə] *n* amnesia *f*.

among(st) [ə'mʌŋ(st)] *prep* entre.

amount [ə'maʊnt] *n* cantidad *f* ◊ amount to *vt fus* (total) ascender a.

amp [æmp] *n* amperio *m*; **a 13-~ plug** un enchufe con un fusible de 13 amperios.

ample ['æmpl] *adj* más que suficiente.

amplifier ['æmplɪfaɪə'] *n* amplificador *m*.

amputate ['æmpjʊteɪt] *vt* amputar.

Amtrak ['æmtræk] *n* organismo que regula los ferrocarriles en EEUU.

amuse [ə'mjuːz] *vt* (make laugh) divertir; (entertain) entretener.

amusement arcade [ə'mjuːz-mənt-] *n* salón *m* de juegos.

amusement park [ə'mjuːz-mənt-] *n* parque *m* de atracciones.

amusements [ə'mjuːzmənts] *npl* atracciones *fpl*.

amusing [ə'mjuːzɪŋ] *adj* divertido(-da).

an [stressed æn, unstressed ən] → **a**.

anaemic [ə'niːmɪk] *adj* (Br: person) anémico(-ca).

anaesthetic [ˌænɪs'θetɪk] *n* (Br) anestesia *f*.

analgesic [ˌænæl'dʒiːzɪk] *n* analgésico *m*.

analyse ['ænəlaɪz] *vt* analizar.

analyst ['ænəlɪst] *n* (psychoanalyst) psicoanalista *mf*.

analyze ['ænəlaɪz] (Am) = analyse.

anarchy ['ænəkɪ] *n* anarquía *f*.

anatomy [ə'nætəmɪ] *n* anatomía *f*.

ancestor ['ænsestə'] *n* antepasado *m* (-da *f*).

anchor ['æŋkə'] *n* ancla *f*.

anchovy ['æntʃəvɪ] *n* (salted) anchoa *f*; (fresh) boquerón *m*.

ancient ['eɪnʃənt] *adj* antiguo(-gua).

and [strong form ænd, weak form ənd, ən] *conj* y; (before "i" or "hi") e; **~ you?** ¿y tú?; **a hundred ~ one** ciento uno; **more ~ more** cada vez más; **to try ~ do sthg** intentar hacer algo; **to go ~ see** ir a ver.

Andalusia [ˌændə'luːzɪə] *n* Andalucía.

Andes ['ændiːz] *npl*: **the ~** los Andes.

anecdote ['ænɪkdəʊt] *n* anécdota *f*.

anemic [ə'niːmɪk] (Am) = anaemic.

anesthetic [ˌænɪs'θetɪk] (Am) = anaesthetic.

angel ['eɪndʒl] *n* ángel *m*.

anger ['æŋgə'] *n* ira *f*, furia *f*.

angina [æn'dʒaɪnə] *n* angina *f* de pecho.

angle ['æŋgl] *n* ángulo *m*; **at an ~** torcido.

angler ['æŋglə'] *n* pescador *m* (-ra *f*) (con caña).

angling ['æŋglɪŋ] *n* pesca *f* (con caña).

angry ['æŋgrɪ] *adj* (person) enfadado(-da); (words, look, letter) airado(-da); **to get ~ (with sb)** enfadarse (con alguien).

animal ['ænɪml] *n* animal *m*.

aniseed ['ænɪsiːd] *n* anís *m*.

ankle ['æŋkl] *n* tobillo *m*.

annex ['æneks] *n (building)* edificio *m* anejo.

annihilate [ə'naɪəleɪt] *vt* aniquilar.

anniversary [ænɪ'vɜːsərɪ] *n* aniversario *m*.

announce [ə'naʊns] *vt* anunciar.

announcement [ə'naʊnsmənt] *n* anuncio *m*.

announcer [ə'naʊnsə^r] *n (on TV)* presentador *m* (-ra *f*); *(on radio)* locutor *m* (-ra *f*).

annoy [ə'nɔɪ] *vt* molestar, fastidiar.

annoyed [ə'nɔɪd] *adj* molesto(-ta); **to get ~ (with)** enfadarse (con).

annoying [ə'nɔɪɪŋ] *adj* molesto (-ta), fastidioso(-sa).

annual ['ænjʊəl] *adj* anual.

anonymous [ə'nɒnɪməs] *adj* anónimo(-ma).

anorak ['ænəræk] *n* anorak *m*.

another [ə'nʌðə^r] *adj* otro (otra) ◆ *pron* otro *m* (otra *f*); **~ one** otro (otra); **one** ~ el uno al otro (la una a la otra); **they love one ~** se quieren; **with one ~** el uno con el otro (la una con la otra); **one after** ~ uno tras otro (una tras otra).

answer ['ɑːnsə^r] *n* respuesta *f* ◆ *vt (person, question)* contestar a; *(letter, advert)* responder a ◆ *vi* contestar; **to ~ the door** abrir la puerta; **to ~ the phone** coger el teléfono ❑ **answer back** *vi* replicar.

answering machine ['ɑːnsər-ɪŋ-] = **answerphone**.

answerphone ['ɑːnsəfəʊn] *n* contestador *m* automático.

ant [ænt] *n* hormiga *f*.

Antarctic [æn'tɑːktɪk] *n*: **the ~** el Antártico.

antenna [æn'tenə] *n (Am: aerial)* antena *f*.

anthem ['ænθəm] *n* himno *m*.

antibiotics [ˌæntɪbaɪ'ɒtɪks] *npl* antibióticos *mpl*.

anticipate [æn'tɪsɪpeɪt] *vt* prever.

anticlimax [ˌæntɪ'klaɪmæks] *n* anticlímax *m inv*.

anticlockwise [ˌæntɪ'klɒkwaɪz] *adv (Br)* en sentido contrario al de las agujas del reloj.

antidote ['æntɪdəʊt] *n* antídoto *m*.

antifreeze ['æntɪfriːz] *n* anticongelante *m*.

antihistamine [ˌæntɪ'hɪstəmɪn] *n* antihistamínico *m*.

antiperspirant [ˌæntɪ'pɜːspə-rənt] *n* desodorante *m*.

antiquarian bookshop [ˌæntɪ'kweərɪən-] *n* librería *f* en que se encuentran volúmenes antiguos.

antique [æn'tiːk] *n* antigüedad *f*.

antique shop *n* tienda *f* de antigüedades.

antiseptic [ˌæntɪ'septɪk] *n* antiséptico *m*.

antisocial [ˌæntɪ'səʊʃl] *adj (person)* insociable; *(behaviour)* antisocial.

antlers ['æntləz] *npl* cornamenta *f*.

anxiety [æŋ'zaɪətɪ] *n* inquietud *f*, ansiedad *f*.

anxious ['æŋkʃəs] *adj (worried)* preocupado(-da); *(eager)* ansioso(-sa).

any ['enɪ] adj 1. (in questions) algún(-una); **have you got ~ money?** ¿tienes (algo de dinero)?; **have you got ~ postcards?** ¿tienes alguna postal?; **have you got ~ rooms?** ¿tienes habitaciones libres? 2. (in negatives) ningún(-una); **I haven't got ~ money** no tengo (nada de) dinero; **we don't have ~ rooms** no tenemos ninguna habitación. 3. (no matter which) cualquier; **take ~ one you like** coge el que quieras. ◆ pron 1. (in questions) alguno m (-na f); **I'm looking for a hotel - are there ~ nearby?** estoy buscando un hotel ¿hay alguno por aquí cerca? 2. (in negatives) ninguno m (-na f); **I don't want ~ (of them)** no quiero ninguno; **I don't want ~ (of it)** no quiero (nada). 3. (no matter which one) cualquiera; **you can sit at ~ of the tables** puede sentarse en cualquier mesa. ◆ adv 1. (in questions): **is that ~ better?** ¿es así mejor?; **is there ~ more cheese?** ¿hay más queso?; **~ other questions?** ¿alguna otra pregunta? 2. (in negatives): **he's not ~ better** no se siente nada mejor; **we can't wait ~ longer** ya no podemos esperar más.

anybody ['enɪ,bɒdɪ] = anyone.

anyhow ['enɪhaʊ] adv (carelessly) de cualquier manera; (in any case) en cualquier caso; (in spite of that) de todos modos.

anyone ['enɪwʌn] pron (in questions) alguien; (any person) cualquiera; **I don't like ~** no me gusta nadie.

anything ['enɪθɪŋ] pron (in questions) algo; (no matter what) cualquier cosa; **he didn't say ~** no dijo nada.

anyway ['enɪweɪ] adv de todos modos.

anywhere ['enɪweə'] adv (in questions) en/a algún sitio; (any place) en/a cualquier sitio; **I can't find it ~** no lo encuentro en ningún sitio; **~ you like** donde quieras.

apart [ə'pɑːt] adv aparte; **they're miles ~** están muy separados; **to come ~** romperse; **~ from** (except for) salvo; (as well as) además de.

apartheid [ə'pɑːtheɪt] n apartheid m.

apartment [ə'pɑːtmənt] n (Am) piso m, apartamento m.

apathetic [,æpə'θetɪk] adj apático(-ca).

ape [eɪp] n simio m.

aperitif [ə,perɪ'tiːf] n aperitivo m.

aperture ['æpətʃə'] n (of camera) abertura f.

APEX ['eɪpeks] n (plane ticket) APEX f; (Br: train ticket) billete de precio reducido no transferible que se compra con dos semanas de antelación.

apiece [ə'piːs] adv cada uno (una).

apologetic [ə,pɒlə'dʒetɪk] adj lleno(-na) de disculpas.

apologize [ə'pɒlədʒaɪz] vi: **to ~ (to sb for sthg)** disculparse (con alguien por algo).

apology [ə'pɒlədʒɪ] n disculpa f.

apostrophe [ə'pɒstrəfɪ] n

apóstrofo m.

appal [ə'pɔːl] vt horrorizar.

appall [ə'pɔːl] (Am) = appal.

appalling [ə'pɔːlɪŋ] adj horrible.

apparatus [ˌæpə'reɪtəs] n aparato m.

apparently [ə'pærəntlɪ] adv (it seems) por lo visto; (evidently) aparentemente.

appeal [ə'piːl] n (JUR) apelación f; (fundraising campaign) campaña f para recaudar fondos ♦ vi (JUR) apelar; **to ~ to sb (for sthg)** hacer un llamamiento a alguien (para algo); **it doesn't ~ to me** no me atrae.

appear [ə'pɪər] vi (come into view) aparecer; (seem) parecer; (in play, on TV) salir; (before court) comparecer; **it ~s that** parece que.

appearance [ə'pɪərəns] n (arrival) aparición f; (look) aspecto m.

appendicitis [əˌpendɪ'saɪtɪs] n apendicitis f inv.

appendix [ə'pendɪks] (pl -dices) n apéndice m.

appetite [ˈæpɪtaɪt] n apetito m.

appetizer [ˈæpɪtaɪzər] n aperitivo m.

appetizing [ˈæpɪtaɪzɪŋ] adj apetitoso(-sa).

applaud [ə'plɔːd] vt & vi aplaudir.

applause [ə'plɔːz] n aplausos mpl.

apple [ˈæpl] n manzana f.

apple charlotte [-'ʃɑːlət] n postre de manzana con miga de pan envuelto completamente en rebanadas de pan y cocido al horno.

apple crumble n budín de manzana cubierto con una masa de harina, azúcar y mantequilla que se sirve caliente.

apple juice n zumo m de manzana.

apple pie n pastel de hojaldre relleno de compota de manzana.

apple sauce n compota de manzana que se suele servir con chuletas de cerdo.

apple tart n tarta f de manzana.

apple turnover [-'tɜːnˌəʊvər] n bollo de hojaldre relleno de compota de manzana.

appliance [ə'plaɪəns] n aparato m; **electrical/domestic ~** electrodoméstico m.

applicable [ə'plɪkəbl] adj: **to be ~ (to)** ser aplicable (a); **if ~** si corresponde.

applicant [ˈæplɪkənt] n solicitante mf.

application [ˌæplɪ'keɪʃn] n solicitud f.

application form n impreso m de solicitud.

apply [ə'plaɪ] vt (lotion) aplicar; (brakes) pisar ♦ vi: **to ~ to sb for sthg** (make request) solicitar algo a alguien; **to ~ (to sb)** (be applicable) ser aplicable (a alguien).

appointment [ə'pɔɪntmənt] n (with businessman) cita f; (with doctor, hairdresser) hora f; **to have an ~ (with)** (businessman) tener una cita (con); (doctor, hairdresser) tener hora (con); **to make an ~ (with)** (businessman) pedir una cita (con); (doctor, hairdresser) pedir hora (a); **by ~** mediante cita.

appreciable [ə'priːʃəbl] *adj* apreciable.

appreciate [ə'priːʃɪeɪt] *vt (be grateful for)* agradecer; *(understand)* ser consciente de; *(like, admire)* apreciar.

apprehensive [ˌæprɪ'hensɪv] *adj* inquieto(-ta).

apprentice [ə'prentɪs] *n* aprendiz *m* (-za *f*).

apprenticeship [ə'prentɪsʃɪp] *n* aprendizaje *m*.

approach [ə'prəʊtʃ] *n (road)* acceso *m*; *(to problem, situation)* enfoque *m*, planteamiento *m* ◆ *vt (come nearer to)* acercarse a; *(problem, situation)* enfocar ◆ *vi* acercarse.

appropriate [ə'prəʊprɪət] *adj* apropiado(-da).

approval [ə'pruːvl] *n (favourable opinion)* aprobación *f*; *(permission)* permiso *m*.

approve [ə'pruːv] *vi*: **to ~ of sthg/sb** ver con buenos ojos algo/a alguien.

approximate [ə'prɒksɪmət] *adj* aproximado(-da).

approximately [ə'prɒksɪmətlɪ] *adv* aproximadamente.

apricot ['eɪprɪkɒt] *n* albaricoque *m*.

April ['eɪprəl] *n* abril *m*, → **September**.

April Fools' Day *n* ≈ Día *m* de los Santos Inocentes.

---

i APRIL FOOLS' DAY

El primero de abril es el día en que la gente se gasta bromas (trucos,

bromas prácticas, etc). No existe la tradición de los monigotes de papel, y no se permiten más bromas después del mediodía.

---

apron ['eɪprən] *n* delantal *m*.

apt [æpt] *adj (appropriate)* acertado(-da); **to be ~ to do sthg** ser propenso(-sa) a hacer algo.

aquarium [ə'kweərɪəm] *(pl* **-ria** [-rɪə]*) n* acuario *m*.

aqueduct ['ækwɪdʌkt] *n* acueducto *m*.

Arab ['ærəb] *adj* árabe ◆ *n (person)* árabe *mf*.

Arabic ['ærəbɪk] *adj* árabe ◆ *n (language)* árabe *m*.

arbitrary ['ɑːbɪtrərɪ] *adj* arbitrario(-ria).

arc [ɑːk] *n* arco *m*.

arcade [ɑː'keɪd] *n (for shopping)* centro *m* comercial; *(of video games)* salón *m* de juegos.

arch [ɑːtʃ] *n* arco *m*.

archaeology [ˌɑːkɪ'ɒlədʒɪ] *n* arqueología *f*.

archbishop [ˌɑːtʃ'bɪʃəp] *n* arzobispo *m*.

archery ['ɑːtʃərɪ] *n* tiro *m* con arco.

archipelago [ˌɑːkɪ'peləgəʊ] *n* archipiélago *m*.

architect ['ɑːkɪtekt] *n* arquitecto *m* (-ta *f*).

architecture ['ɑːkɪtektʃər] *n* arquitectura *f*.

archive ['ɑːkaɪv] *n* archivo *m*.

Arctic ['ɑːktɪk] *n*: **the ~** el Ártico.

are [*weak form* ər, *strong form* ɑːr] → **be**.

area ['eərɪə] *n (region, space, zone)*

zona f, **área** f; *(surface size)* área f.

area code n *(Am)* prefijo m *(telefónico)*.

arena [əˈriːnə] n *(at circus)* pista f; *(at sportsground)* campo m.

aren't [ɑːnt] = are not.

Argentina [ˌɑːdʒənˈtiːnə] n Argentina.

Argentinian [ˌɑːdʒənˈtɪnɪən] adj argentino(-na) ◆ n argentino m (-na f).

argue [ˈɑːgjuː] vi: **to ~ (with sb about sthg)** discutir (con alguien acerca de algo) ◆ vt: **to ~ (that)** sostener que.

argument [ˈɑːgjəmənt] n *(quarrel)* discusión f; *(reason)* argumento m.

arid [ˈærɪd] adj árido(-da).

arise [əˈraɪz] (pt **arose** [əˈrəʊz], pp **arisen** [əˈrɪzn]) vi: **to ~ (from)** surgir (de).

aristocracy [ˌærɪˈstɒkrəsɪ] n aristocracia f.

arithmetic [əˈrɪθmətɪk] n aritmética f.

arm [ɑːm] n *(of person, chair)* brazo m; *(of garment)* manga f.

arm bands npl *(for swimming)* brazaletes mpl *(de brazos)*.

armchair [ˈɑːmtʃeəʳ] n sillón m.

armed [ɑːmd] adj armado(-da).

armed forces npl: **the ~** las fuerzas armadas.

armor [ˈɑːməʳ] *(Am)* = **armour.**

armour [ˈɑːməʳ] n *(Br)* armadura f.

armpit [ˈɑːmpɪt] n axila f.

arms [ɑːmz] npl *(weapons)* armas fpl.

army [ˈɑːmɪ] n ejército m.

A-road n *(Br)* = carretera f nacional.

aroma [əˈrəʊmə] n aroma m.

aromatic [ˌærəˈmætɪk] adj aromático(-ca).

arose [əˈrəʊz] pt → **arise.**

around [əˈraʊnd] adv *(about, round)* por ahí; *(present)* por ahí/aquí ◆ prep *(surrounding, approximately)* alrededor de; *(to the other side of)* al otro lado de; *(near, all over)* por; **~ here** *(in the area)* por aquí; **to go ~ the corner** doblar la esquina; **to turn ~** volverse; **to look ~** *(turn head)* volver la mirada; *(visit)* visitar; **is Paul ~?** ¿está Paul por aquí?

arouse [əˈraʊz] vt *(suspicion, interest)* suscitar.

arrange [əˈreɪndʒ] vt *(flowers, books)* colocar; *(meeting, event)* organizar; **to ~ to do sthg (with sb)** acordar hacer algo (con alguien).

arrangement [əˈreɪndʒmənt] n *(agreement)* acuerdo m; *(layout)* disposición f; **by ~** sólo con cita previa; **to make ~s (to do sthg)** hacer los preparativos (para hacer algo).

arrest [əˈrest] n detención f ◆ vt detener; **under ~** bajo arresto.

arrival [əˈraɪvl] n llegada f; **on ~** al llegar; **new ~** *(person)* recién llegado m (-da f).

arrive [əˈraɪv] vi llegar; **to ~ at** llegar a.

arrogant [ˈærəgənt] adj arrogante.

arrow [ˈærəʊ] n flecha f.

arson [ˈɑːsn] n incendio m provocado.

art [ɑːt] n arte m ❑ **arts** npl

(humanities) letras *fpl*; **the ~s** *(fine arts)* las bellas artes.

artefact [ˈɑːtɪfækt] *n* artefacto *m*.

artery [ˈɑːtərɪ] *n* arteria *f*.

art gallery *n* · *(commercial)* galería *f* (de arte); *(public)* museo *m* (de arte).

arthritis [ɑːˈθraɪtɪs] *n* artritis *f inv*.

artichoke [ˈɑːtɪtʃəʊk] *n* alcachofa *f*.

article [ˈɑːtɪkl] *n* artículo *m*.

articulate [ɑːˈtɪkjʊlət] *adj* elocuente.

artificial [ˌɑːtɪˈfɪʃl] *adj* artificial.

artist [ˈɑːtɪst] *n* artista *mf*.

artistic [ɑːˈtɪstɪk] *adj (person)* con sensibilidad artística; *(design)* artístico(-ca).

arts centre *n* = casa *f* de cultura.

arty [ˈɑːtɪ] *adj (pej)* con pretensiones artísticas.

as [*unstressed* əz, *stressed* æz] *adv (in comparisons)*: **~ ... ~** tan ... como; **he's ~ tall ~ I am** es tan alto como yo; **twice ~ big ~** el doble de grande que; **~ many ~** tantos como; **~ much ~** tanto como.

♦ *conj* **1.** *(referring to time)* mientras; **~ the plane was coming in to land** cuando el avión iba a aterrizar. **2.** *(referring to manner)* como; **do ~ you like** haz lo que quieras; **~ expected** (tal) como era de esperar. **3.** *(introducing a statement)* como; **~ you know** como sabes. **4.** *(because)* como, ya que. **5.** *(in phrases)*: **~ for** en cuanto a; **~ from** a partir de; **~ if** como si.

♦ *prep (referring to function)* como;

(referring to job) de; **I work ~ a teacher** soy profesor.

asap *(abbr of as soon as possible)* a la mayor brevedad posible.

ascent [əˈsent] *n* ascenso *m*.

ascribe [əˈskraɪb] *vt*: **to ~ sthg to** atribuir algo a.

ash [æʃ] *n (from cigarette, fire)* ceniza *f*; *(tree)* fresno *m*.

ashore [əˈʃɔːr] *adv (be)* en tierra; **to go ~** desembarcar.

ashtray [ˈæʃtreɪ] *n* cenicero *m*.

Asia [*Br* ˈeɪʃə, *Am* ˈeɪʒə] *n* Asia.

Asian [*Br* ˈeɪʃn, *Am* ˈeɪʒn] *adj* asiático(-ca) ♦ *n* asiático *m* (-ca *f*).

aside [əˈsaɪd] *adv* a un lado; **to move ~** apartarse.

ask [ɑːsk] *vt (person)* preguntar; *(question)* hacer; *(request)* pedir; *(invite)* invitar ♦ *vi*: **to ~ about sthg** preguntar acerca de algo; **to ~ sb sthg** preguntar algo a alguien; **to ~ sb about sthg** preguntar a alguien acerca de algo; **to ~ sb to do sthg** pedir a alguien que haga algo; **to ~ sb for sthg** pedir a alguien algo ❑ **ask for** *vt fus (ask to talk to)* preguntar por; *(request)* pedir.

asleep [əˈsliːp] *adj* dormido(-da); **to fall ~** quedarse dormido.

asparagus [əˈspærəgəs] *n* espárragos *mpl*.

asparagus tips *npl* puntas *fpl* de espárragos.

aspect [ˈæspekt] *n* aspecto *m*.

aspirin [ˈæsprɪn] *n* aspirina *f*.

ass [æs] *n (animal)* asno *m* (-na *f*).

assassinate [əˈsæsɪneɪt] *vt* asesinar.

assault [əˈsɔːlt] *n* agresión *f* ♦ *vt* agredir.

assemble [ə'sembl] vt (bookcase, model) montar ◆ vi reunirse.

assembly [ə'sembli] n (at school) reunión cotidiana de todos los alumnos y profesores en el salón de actos.

assembly hall n (at school) salón m de actos.

assembly point n punto m de reunión.

assert [ə'sɜːt] vt (fact, innocence) afirmar; (authority) imponer; **to ~ o.s.** imponerse.

assess [ə'ses] vt evaluar.

assessment [ə'sesmənt] n evaluación f.

asset [æset] n (valuable person, thing) elemento m valioso.

assign [ə'saɪn] vt: **to ~ sthg to sb** ceder algo a alguien; **to ~ sb to do sthg** asignar algo a alguien.

assignment [ə'saɪnmənt] n (task) misión f; (SCH) trabajo m.

assist [ə'sɪst] vt ayudar.

assistance [ə'sɪstəns] n ayuda f; **to be of ~ (to sb)** ayudar (a alguien).

assistant [ə'sɪstənt] n ayudante mf.

associate [n ə'səʊʃɪət, vb ə'səʊʃɪeɪt] n socio m (-cia f) ◆ vt: **to ~ sthg/sb with** asociar algo/a alguien con; **to be ~d with** estar asociado con.

association [ə,səʊsɪ'eɪʃn] n asociación f.

assorted [ə'sɔːtɪd] adj surtido (-da), variado(-da).

assortment [ə'sɔːtmənt] n surtido m.

assume [ə'sjuːm] vt (suppose) suponer; (control, responsibility) asumir.

assurance [ə'ʃʊərəns] n (promise) garantía f; (insurance) seguro m.

assure [ə'ʃʊər] vt asegurar; **to ~ sb (that)** ... asegurar a alguien que ...

asterisk [æstərɪsk] n asterisco m.

asthma [æsmə] n asma f.

asthmatic [æs'mætɪk] adj asmático(-ca).

astonished [ə'stɒnɪʃt] adj estupefacto(-ta), pasmado(-da).

astonishing [ə'stɒnɪʃɪŋ] adj asombroso(-sa).

astound [ə'staʊnd] vt asombrar, pasmar.

astray [ə'streɪ] adv: **to go ~** extraviarse.

astrology [ə'strɒlədʒɪ] n astrología f.

astronomy [ə'strɒnəmɪ] n astronomía f.

asylum [ə'saɪləm] n hospital m psiquiátrico.

at [unstressed ət, stressed æt] prep 1. (indicating place, position) en; **~ the bottom of the hill** al pie de la colina; **~ school** en la escuela; **~ the hotel** en el hotel; **~ home** en casa; **~ my mother's** en casa de mi madre.
2. (indicating direction) a; **to throw sthg ~ sthg** arrojar algo contra algo; **to look ~ sthg/sb** mirar algo/a alguien, **to smile ~ sb** sonreir a alguien.
3. (indicating time) a; **~ Christmas** en Navidades; **~ nine o'clock** a las nueve; **~ night** por la noche.
4. (indicating rate, level, speed) a; **it works out ~ £5 each** sale a 5 libras

cada uno; **~ 60 km/h** a 60 km/h.

5. *(indicating activity)*: **to be ~ lunch** estar comiendo; **I'm good/bad ~ maths** se me dan bien/mal las matemáticas.

6. *(indicating cause)*: **shocked ~ sthg** horrorizado ante algo; **angry ~ sb** enfadado con alguien; **delighted ~ sthg** encantado con algo.

ate [*Br* et, *Am* eɪt] *pt* → **eat**.

atheist ['eɪθɪɪst] *n* ateo *m* (-a *f*).

athlete ['æθliːt] *n* atleta *mf*.

athletics [æθ'letɪks] *n* atletismo *m*.

Atlantic [ət'læntɪk] *n*: **the ~ (Ocean)** el (océano) Atlántico.

atlas ['ætləs] *n* atlas *m inv*.

atmosphere ['ætməsfɪər] *n* atmósfera *f*.

atom ['ætəm] *n* átomo *m*.

A to Z *n (map)* callejero *m*.

atrocious [ə'trəʊʃəs] *adj* atroz.

attach [ə'tætʃ] *vt* sujetar; **to ~ sthg to sthg** sujetar algo a algo.

attachment [ə'tætʃmənt] *n (device)* accesorio *m*.

attack [ə'tæk] *n* ataque *m* ◆ *vt* atacar.

attacker [ə'tækər] *n* atacante *mf*.

attain [ə'teɪn] *vt (fml)* alcanzar, conseguir.

attempt [ə'tempt] *n* intento *m* ◆ *vt* intentar; **to ~ to do sthg** intentar hacer algo.

attend [ə'tend] *vt* asistir a ❑ **attend to** *vt fus* ocuparse de.

attendance [ə'tendəns] *n* asistencia *f*.

attendant [ə'tendənt] *n (in museum)* conserje *mf*; *(in car park)*

attention [ə'tenʃn] *n* atención *f*; **to pay ~ (to)** prestar atención (a).

attic ['ætɪk] *n* desván *m*.

attitude ['ætɪtjuːd] *n* actitud *f*.

attorney [ə'tɜːnɪ] *n (Am)* abogado *m* (-da *f*).

attract [ə'trækt] *vt* atraer.

attraction [ə'trækʃn] *n* atracción *f*; *(attractive feature)* atractivo *m*.

attractive [ə'træktɪv] *adj* atractivo(-va).

attribute [ə'trɪbjuːt] *vt*: **to ~ sthg to** atribuir algo a.

aubergine ['əʊbəʒiːn] *n (Br)* berenjena *f*.

auburn ['ɔːbən] *adj* castaño rojizo.

auction ['ɔːkʃn] *n* subasta *f*.

audience ['ɔːdɪəns] *n (of play, concert, film)* público *m*; *(of TV, radio)* audiencia *f*.

audio ['ɔːdɪəʊ] *adj (store, department)* de sonido.

audio-visual [-'vɪzjʊəl] *adj* audiovisual.

auditorium [ˌɔːdɪ'tɔːrɪəm] *n* auditorio *m*.

August ['ɔːgəst] *n* agosto *m*, → **September**.

aunt [ɑːnt] *n* tía *f*.

au pair [ˌəʊ'peər] *n* au pair *f*.

aural ['ɔːrəl] *adj* auditivo(-va).

Australia [ɒ'streɪlɪə] *n* Australia.

Australian [ɒ'streɪlɪən] *adj* australiano(-na) ◆ *n (person)* australiano *m* (-na *f*).

Austria ['ɒstrɪə] *n* Austria.

Austrian ['ɒstrɪən] *adj* austríaco(-ca) ◆ n (person) austríaco m (-ca f).

authentic [ɔːˈθentɪk] adj auténtico(-ca).

author [ˈɔːθəʳ] n (of book, article) autor m (-ra f); (by profession) escritor m (-ra f).

authority [ɔːˈθɒrɪtɪ] n autoridad f; **the authorities** las autoridades.

authorization [ˌɔːθəraɪˈzeɪʃn] n autorización f.

authorize [ˈɔːθəraɪz] vt autorizar; **to ~ sb to do sthg** autorizar a alguien a hacer algo.

autobiography [ˌɔːtəbaɪˈɒɡrəfɪ] n autobiografía f.

autograph [ˈɔːtəɡrɑːf] n autógrafo m.

automatic [ˌɔːtəˈmætɪk] n (car) coche m automático ◆ adj automático(-ca); **you will receive an ~ fine** Vd. será multado en el acto.

automatically [ˌɔːtəˈmætɪklɪ] adv automáticamente.

automobile [ˈɔːtəməbiːl] n (Am) coche m, automóvil m.

autumn [ˈɔːtəm] n otoño m; **in (the) ~** en otoño.

auxiliary (verb) [ɔːɡˈzɪljən] n verbo m auxiliar.

available [əˈveɪləbl] adj disponible.

avalanche [ˈævəlɑːnʃ] n avalancha f.

Ave. (abbr of avenue) Avda.

avenue [ˈævənjuː] n avenida f.

average [ˈævərɪdʒ] adj medio (-dia); (not very good) regular ◆ n media f, promedio m; **on ~** por tér-

mino medio.

aversion [əˈvɜːʃn] n aversión f.

aviation [ˌeɪvɪˈeɪʃn] n aviación f.

avid [ˈævɪd] adj ávido(-da).

avocado (pear) [ˌævəˈkɑːdəʊ] n aguacate m.

avoid [əˈvɔɪd] vt evitar; **to ~ doing sthg** evitar hacer algo.

await [əˈweɪt] vt esperar, aguardar.

awake [əˈweɪk] (pt awoke, pp awoken) adj despierto(-ta) ◆ vi despertarse.

award [əˈwɔːd] n premio m, galardón m ◆ vt: **to ~ sb sthg** (prize) otorgar algo a alguien; (damages, compensation) adjudicar algo a alguien.

aware [əˈweəʳ] adj consciente; **to be ~ of** ser consciente de.

away [əˈweɪ] adv (move, look, turn) hacia otra parte; (not at home, in office) fuera; **put your toys ~!** ¡recoge tus juguetes!; **to take sthg ~ (from sb)** quitarle algo (a alguien); **far ~** lejos; **it's 10 miles ~ (from here)** está a 10 millas (de aquí); **it's two weeks ~** faltan dos semanas; **to look ~** apartar la vista; **to walk/drive ~** alejarse; **we're going ~ on holiday** nos vamos de vacaciones.

awesome [ˈɔːsəm] adj impresionante.

awful [ˈɔːfl] adj (very bad) fatal; (very great) tremendo(-da); **how ~!** ¡qué horror!

awfully [ˈɔːflɪ] adv (very) tremendamente.

awkward [ˈɔːkwəd] adj (movement) torpe; (position, situation) incómodo(-da); (shape, size) poco manejable; *(time)* inoportuno(-na); *(question, task)* difícil.

awning ['ɔːnɪŋ] *n* toldo *m*.

awoke [ə'wəʊk] *pt* → **awake**.

awoken [ə'wəʊkn] *pp* → **awake**.

axe [æks] *n* hacha *f*.

axle ['æksl] *n* eje *m*.

BA *(abbr of Bachelor of Arts) (titular de una)* licenciatura de letras.

babble ['bæbl] *vi (person)* far-fullar.

baby ['beɪbɪ] *n (newborn baby)* bebé *m*; *(infant)* niño *m* (-ña *f*); **to have a ~** tener un niño; **~ sweetcorn** *pequeña mazorca de maíz usada en la cocina china.*

baby carriage *n (Am)* cochecito *m* de niños.

baby food *n* papilla *f*.

baby-sit *vi* cuidar a niños.

baby wipe *n* toallita *f* húmeda para bebés.

back [bæk] *n (of person)* espalda *f*; *(of chair)* respaldo *m*; *(of room)* fondo *m*; *(of car, book)* parte *f* trasera; *(of hand, banknote)* dorso *m* ♦ *adj* trasero(-ra) ♦ *vi (car, driver)* dar marcha atrás ♦ *vt (support)* respaldar ♦ *adv (towards the back)* hacia atrás; *(to previous position, state)* de vuelta; **to get ~** llegar; **to give ~** devolver; **to put sthg ~** devolver algo a su sitio; **to stand ~** apartarse; **to write ~** contestar; **at the ~ of** detrás de; **in ~ of** *(Am)* detrás de; **~ to front** al revés ❑ **back up** *vt sep (support)* apoyar ♦ *vi (car, driver)* dar marcha atrás.

backache ['bækeɪk] *n* dolor *m* de espalda.

backbone ['bækbəʊn] *n* columna *f* vertebral.

back door *n* puerta *f* trasera.

backfire [,bæk'faɪəʳ] *vi (car)* petardear.

background ['bækgraʊnd] *n (in picture, on stage)* fondo *m*; *(to situation)* trasfondo *m*; *(upbringing)* origen *m*.

backlog ['bæklɒg] *n* acumulación *f*.

backpack ['bækpæk] *n* mochila *f*.

backpacker ['bækpækəʳ] *n* mochilero *m* (-ra *f*).

back seat *n* asiento *m* trasero OR de atrás.

backside [,bæk'saɪd] *n (inf)* trasero *m*.

back street *n* callejuela en una zona periférica y deprimida.

backstroke ['bækstrəʊk] *n* espalda *f (en natación)*.

backwards ['bækwədz] *adv (move, look)* hacia atrás; *(the wrong way round)* al revés.

bacon ['beɪkən] *n* panceta *f*, bacon *m*; **~ and eggs** huevos fritos con bacon.

bacteria [bæk'tɪərɪə] *npl* bacterias *fpl*.

bad [bæd] *(compar* **worse**, *superl* **worst**) *adj* malo(-la); *(accident,* *wound)* grave; *(cold)* fuerte; *(poor, weak)* débil; **not ~** (bastante) bien; **to go ~** echarse a perder.

badge [bædʒ] *n* chapa *f*.

badger [bædʒə*r*] *n* tejón *m*.

badly [bædlɪ] *(compar* **worse,** *superl* **worst)** *adv (poorly)* mal; *(seriously)* gravemente; *(very much)* mucho.

badly paid *adj* mal pagado (-da).

badminton [bædmɪntən] *n* bádminton *m*.

bad-tempered [-tempəd] *adj* de mal genio.

bag [bæg] *n (of paper, plastic)* bolsa *f*; *(handbag)* bolso *m*; *(suitcase)* maleta *f*; **a ~ of crisps** una bolsa de patatas fritas.

bagel [beɪgəl] *n* bollo de pan en forma de rosca.

baggage [bægɪdʒ] *n* equipaje *m*.

baggage allowance *n* equipaje *m* permitido.

baggage reclaim *n* recogida *f* de equipajes.

baggy [bægɪ] *adj* holgado(-da).

bagpipes [bægpaɪps] *npl* gaita *f*.

bail [beɪl] *n* fianza *f*.

bait [beɪt] *n* cebo *m*.

bake [beɪk] *vt* cocer al horno ♦ *vi* (CULIN) gratén *m*.

baked [beɪkt] *adj* asado(-da) al horno.

baked Alaska [-əlæskə] *n* postre de bizcocho y helado, cubierto de merengue y cocinado al horno durante breves minutos.

baked beans *npl* alubias *fpl* cocidas en salsa de tomate.

baked potato *n* patata *f*

asada OR al horno *(con piel).*

baker [beɪkə*r*] *n* panadero *m* (-ra *f*); **~'s** *(shop)* panadería *f*.

Bakewell tart [beɪkwəl-] *n* tarta glaseada consistente en una base de masa quebrada cubierta con bizcocho de sabor a almendra con una capa de mermelada.

balance [bæləns] *n (of person)* equilibrio *m*; *(of bank account)* saldo *m*; *(remainder)* resto *m* ♦ *vt* mantener en equilibrio.

balcony [bælkənɪ] *n (small)* balcón *m*; *(big)* terraza *f*

bald [bɔːld] *adj* calvo(-va).

Balearic Islands [bælɪˈærɪk-] *npl* the ~ (las) Baleares.

ball [bɔːl] *n (in tennis, golf, table tennis)* pelota *f*; *(in football)* balón *m*; *(in snooker, pool, of paper)* bola *f*; *(of wool, string)* ovillo *m*; *(dance)* baile *m*; **on the ~** *(fig)* al tanto de todo.

ballad [bæləd] *n* balada *f*.

ballerina [bæləˈriːnə] *n* bailarina *f*.

ballet [bæleɪ] *n* ballet *m*.

ballet dancer *n* bailarín *m* (-ina *f*).

balloon [bəˈluːn] *n* globo *m*.

ballot [bælət] *n* votación *f*.

ballpoint pen [bɔːlpɔɪnt-] *n* bolígrafo *m*.

ballroom [bɔːlrum] *n* salón *m* de baile.

ballroom dancing *n* baile *m* de salón.

bamboo [bæmˈbuː] *n* bambú *m*.

bamboo shoots *npl (CULIN)* brotes *mpl* de bambú.

ban [bæn] *n* prohibición *f* ♦ *vt*

prohibir; **to ~ sb from doing sthg** prohibir a alguien hacer algo.

banana [bə'nɑːnə] n plátano m.

banana split n banana split m, plátano partido por la mitad y relleno con helado y nata montada.

band [bænd] n (pop group) grupo m; (military orchestra) banda f; (strip of paper, rubber) cinta f.

bandage ['bændɪdʒ] n venda f ◆ vt vendar.

B and B abbr = bed and breakfast.

bandstand ['bændstænd] n quiosco m de música.

bang [bæŋ] n estruendo m ◆ vt (hit loudly) golpear; (shut loudly) cerrar de golpe; **to ~ one's head** golpearse la cabeza.

banger ['bæŋər] n (Br: inf: sausage) salchicha f; **~s and mash** salchichas con puré de patatas.

bangle ['bæŋgl] n brazalete m.

bangs [bæŋz] npl (Am) flequillo m.

banister ['bænɪstər] n barandilla f.

banjo ['bændʒəʊ] n banjo m.

bank [bæŋk] n (for money) banco m; (of river, lake) orilla f, ribera f; (slope) loma f.

bank account n cuenta f bancaria.

bank book n libreta f (del banco).

bank charges npl comisiones fpl bancarias.

bank clerk n empleado m de banco.

bank draft n giro m bancario.

banker ['bæŋkər] n banquero m (-ra f).

banker's card n tarjeta f de identificación bancaria.

bank holiday n (Br) día m festivo.

bank manager n director m (-ra f) de banco.

bank note n billete m de banco.

bankrupt ['bæŋkrʌpt] adj quebrado(-da).

bank statement n extracto m de cuenta.

banner ['bænər] n pancarta f.

bannister ['bænɪstər] = **banister**.

banquet ['bæŋkwɪt] n (formal dinner) banquete m; (at Indian restaurant etc) menú fijo para varias personas.

bap [bæp] n (Br) panecillo m, bollo m.

baptize [Br bæp'taɪz, Am 'bæptaɪz] vt bautizar.

bar [bɑːr] n (pub, in restaurant, hotel) bar m; (counter in pub, metal rod) barra f; (of wood) tabla f; (of soap) pastilla f; (of chocolate) tableta f ◆ vt (obstruct) bloquear.

barbecue ['bɑːbɪkjuː] n barbacoa f ◆ vt asar a la parrilla.

barbecue sauce n salsa f para barbacoa.

barbed wire [bɑːbd-] n alambre m de espino.

barber ['bɑːbər] n barbero m; **~'s** (shop) barbería f.

bar code n código m de barras.

bare [beər] adj (feet) descalzo(-za); (head) descubierto(-ta); (arms) desnudo(-da); (room, cup-

board) vacío(-a); *(facts, minimum)* esencial.

barefoot [ˌbeəˈfʊt] *adv:* **to go ~** ir descalzo.

barely [ˈbeəlɪ] *adv* apenas.

bargain [ˈbɑːgɪn] *n (agreement)* trato *m,* acuerdo *m; (cheap buy)* ganga *f* ♦ *vi* negociar ◻ **bargain for** *vt fus* contar con.

bargain basement *n* sección *f* de oportunidades.

barge [bɑːdʒ] *n* barcaza *f* ◻ **harge in** *vi:* **to ~ in (on sb)** interrumpir (a alguien).

bark [bɑːk] *n (of tree)* corteza *f* ♦ *vi* ladrar.

barley [ˈbɑːlɪ] *n* cebada *f.*

barmaid [ˈbɑːmeɪd] *n* camarera *f.*

barman [ˈbɑːmən] *(pl* -**men** [-mən]) *n* camarero *m.*

bar meal *n* comida sencilla en un *pub o en el bar de un hotel.*

barn [bɑːn] *n* granero *m.*

barometer [bəˈrɒmɪtəʳ] *n* barómetro *m.*

baron [ˈbærən] *n* barón *m.*

baroque [bəˈrɒk] *adj* barroco(-a).

barracks [ˈbærəks] *npl* cuartel *m.*

barrage [ˈbærɑːʒ] *n (of questions, criticism)* lluvia *f,* alud *m.*

barrel [ˈbærəl] *n (of beer, wine, oil)* barril *m; (of gun)* cañón *m.*

barren [ˈbærən] *adj (land, soil)* estéril.

barricade [ˌbærɪˈkeɪd] *n* barricada *f.*

barrier [ˈbærɪəʳ] *n* barrera *f.*

barrister [ˈbærɪstəʳ] *n* abogado *m* (-da *f) (de tribunales superiores).*

bartender [ˈbɑːtendəʳ] *n (Am)* camarero *m* (-ra *f).*

barter [ˈbɑːtəʳ] *vi* hacer trueques.

base [beɪs] *n* base *f* ♦ *vt:* **to ~ sthg on** basar algo en; **to be ~d** *(company)* tener la sede; *(person)* trabajar.

baseball [ˈbeɪsbɔːl] *n* béisbol *m.*

baseball cap *n* gorra *f* de béisbol.

basement [ˈbeɪsmənt] *n* sótano *m.*

bases [ˈbeɪsiːz] *pl* → **basis.**

bash [bæʃ] *vt (door)* dar un porrazo a; **to ~ one's head** darse un porrazo en la cabeza.

basic [ˈbeɪsɪk] *adj (fundamental)* básico(-ca); *(accommodation, meal)* simple ◻ **basics** *npl:* **the ~s** los fundamentos.

basically [ˈbeɪsɪklɪ] *adv* en realidad.

basil [ˈbæzl] *n* albahaca *f.*

basin [ˈbeɪsn] *n (washbasin)* lavabo *m; (bowl)* barreño *m.*

basis [ˈbeɪsɪs] *(pl* -**ses**) *n* base *f;* **on a weekly ~** de forma semanal; **on the ~ of** partiendo de.

basket [ˈbɑːskɪt] *n* cesto *m,* cesta *f.*

basketball [ˈbɑːskɪtbɔːl] *n* baloncesto *m.*

basmati rice [ˌbæzˈmɑːtɪ-] *n* arroz de origen pakistaní utilizado en muchos platos de cocina oriental.

Basque [bɑːsk] *adj* vasco(-ca) ♦ *n (person)* vasco *m* (-ca *f); (language)* euskera *m.*

Basque Country *n:* **the ~** el País Vasco, Euskadi.

bass[1] [beɪs] *n (singer)* bajo *m.*

bass² [bæs] n (fish) lubina f, róbalo m.

bass guitar [beis-] n bajo m.

bassoon [bə'su:n] n fagot m.

bastard ['bɑ:stəd] n (vulg) cabrón m (-ona f).

bat [bæt] n (in cricket, baseball) bate m; (in table tennis) paleta f; (animal) murciélago m.

batch [bætʃ] n lote m.

bath [bɑ:θ] n (tub) bañera f ◆ vt bañar; **to have a ~ bañarse** □ **baths** npl (Br: public swimming pool) piscina f municipal.

bathe [beɪð] vi bañarse.

bathing ['beɪðɪŋ] n (Br) baños mpl.

bathrobe ['bɑ:θrəʊb] n (for bathroom, swimming pool) albornoz m; (dressing gown) bata f.

bathroom ['bɑ:θrʊm] n (room with bath) cuarto m de baño; (Am: toilet) servicio m.

bathroom cabinet n armario m de aseo.

bathtub ['bɑ:θtʌb] n bañera f.

baton ['bætən] n (of conductor) batuta f; (truncheon) porra f.

batter ['bætəʳ] n (CULIN) masa f para rebozar ◆ vt (wife, child) maltratar.

battered ['bætəd] adj (CULIN) rebozado(-da).

battery ['bætərɪ] n (for radio, torch etc) pila f; (for car) batería f.

battery charger [-ˌtʃɑ:dʒəʳ] n aparato m para recargar pilas.

battle ['bætl] n (in war) batalla f; (struggle) lucha f.

battlefield ['bætlfi:ld] n campo m de batalla.

battlements ['bætlmənts] npl almenas fpl.

battleship ['bætlʃɪp] n acorazado m.

bay [beɪ] n (on coast) bahía f; (for parking) plaza f.

bay leaf n hoja f de laurel.

bay window n ventana f salediza.

B & B abbr = bed and breakfast.

BC (abbr of before Christ) a.C.

be [bi:] (pt was, were, pp been) vi 1. (exist) ser; **there is/are** hay; **are there any shops near here?** ¿hay alguna tienda por aquí?
2. (referring to location) estar; **the hotel is near the airport** el hotel está cerca del aeropuerto.
3. (go, come) estar; **have you ever been to Ireland?** ¿has estado alguna vez en Irlanda?; **I'll ~ there in five minutes** estaré ahí dentro de cinco minutos.
4. (occur) ser; **the final is in May** la final es en mayo.
5. (describing quality, permanent condition) ser; **he's a doctor** es médico; **I'm British** soy británico.
6. (describing state, temporary condition) estar; **I'm angry** estoy enfadado; **I'm hot/cold** tengo calor/frío.
7. (referring to health) estar; **how are you?** ¿cómo estás?; **I'm fine** estoy bien; **she's ill** está enferma.
8. (referring to age): **how old are you?** ¿cuántos años tienes?; **I'm 14 (years old)** tengo 14 años (de edad).
9. (referring to cost) valer, costar; **how much is it?** ¿cuánto es?; **it's ten pounds** son diez libras.

10. (referring to time, dates) ser; **what time is it?** ¿qué hora es?; **it's ten o'clock** son las diez; **it's the 9th of April** estamos a 9 de abril.

11. (referring to measurement): **it's 2 metres wide/long** mide 2 metros de ancho/largo; **he's 2 metres tall** mide 2 metros; **I'm 60 kilos** peso 60 kilos.

12. (referring to weather) hacer; **it's hot/cold** hace calor/frío; **it's sunny/windy** hace sol/viento; **it's going to be nice today** hoy va a hacer buen tiempo.

♦ aux vb **1.** (forming continuous tense) estar; **I'm learning French** estoy aprendiendo francés; **we've been visiting the museum** hemos estado visitando el museo; **I was eating when …** estaba comiendo cuando …

2. (forming passive) ser; **to ~ loved** ser amado; **the flight was delayed** el avión se retrasó.

3. (with infinitive to express order): **all rooms are to ~ vacated by ten a.m.** las habitaciones han de ser desocupadas antes de las diez de la mañana.

4. (with infinitive to express future tense): **the race is to start at noon** la carrera empezará a mediodía.

5. (in tag questions): **it's cold, isn't it?** hace frío ¿no?

beach [biːtʃ] n playa f.

bead [biːd] n cuenta f, abalorio m.

beak [biːk] n pico m.

beaker ['biːkəʳ] n taza f (sin asa).

beam [biːm] n (of light) rayo m; (of wood, concrete) viga f ♦ vi (smile) sonreír resplandeciente.

bean [biːn] n (haricot) judía f; (pod) judía f verde; (of coffee) grano m.

bean curd [-kɜːd] n pasta hecha de soja y generalmente en forma de cubo que se usa en la cocina china y vegetariana.

beansprouts ['biːnsprauts] npl brotes mpl de soja.

bear [beəʳ] (pt **bore**, pp **borne**) n (animal) oso m (osa f) ♦ vi aguantar, soportar; **to ~ left/right** torcer a la izquierda/derecha.

bearable ['beərəbl] adj soportable.

beard [biəd] n barba f.

bearer ['beərəʳ] n (of cheque) portador m (-ra f); (of passport) titular mf.

bearing ['beərɪŋ] n (relevance) relación f; **to get one's ~s** orientarse.

beast [biːst] n bestia f.

beat [biːt] (pt **beat**, pp **beaten** ['biːtn]) n (of heart, pulse) latido m; (MUS) ritmo m ♦ vt (defeat) ganar, derrotar; (hit) golpear; (eggs, cream) batir ❑ **beat down** vt sep convencer que rebaje el precio ♦ vi (rain) descargar; (sun) pegar fuerte; **beat up** vt sep dar una paliza a.

beautiful ['bjuːtɪful] adj (in appearance, very good) precioso(-sa); (person) guapo(-pa).

beauty ['bjuːtɪ] n belleza f.

beauty parlour n salón m de belleza.

beauty spot n (place) bello paraje m.

beaver ['biːvəʳ] n castor m.

became [bɪ'keɪm] pt → **become**.

because [bɪ'kɒz] conj porque; **~ of** a causa de.

beckon ['bekən] vi: to ~ (to) hacer señas para atraer la atención (a).

become [bɪ'kʌm] (pt **became**, pp **become**) vi hacerse; (ill, angry, cloudy) ponerse; (champion, prime minister) llegar a ser; **what became of him?** ¿qué fue de él?

bed [bed] n (for sleeping in) cama f; (of river, CULIN) lecho m; (of sea) fondo m; **in ~** en la cama; **to get out of ~** levantarse (de la cama); **to go to ~** irse a la cama; **to go to ~ with sb** acostarse con alguien; **to make the ~** hacer la cama.

bed and breakfast n (Br) casa privada donde se ofrece cama y desayuno a precios asequibles.

BED AND BREAKFAST

Los "B & B" o "guest houses" son casas particulares en lugares turísticos con una o más habitaciones para huéspedes. En el precio de la habitación se incluye el "desayuno inglés", consistente en salchichas, huevos, beicon, tostadas y té o café.

---

bedclothes ['bedkləʊðz] npl ropa f de cama.

bedding ['bedɪŋ] n ropa f de cama.

bed linen n sábanas y fundas de almohada.

bedroom ['bedrʊm] n (en casa) dormitorio m; (en hotel) habitación f.

bedside table ['bedsaɪd-] n mesita f de noche.

bedsit ['bed,sɪt] n (Br) habitación

alquilada con cama e instalaciones para cocinar y lavarse.

bedspread ['bedspred] n colcha f.

bedtime ['bedtaɪm] n hora f de dormir.

bee [biː] n abeja f.

beech [biːtʃ] n haya f.

beef [biːf] n carne f de vaca; ~ **Wellington** ternera f al hojaldre.

beefburger ['biːf,bɜːgəʳ] n hamburguesa f.

beehive ['biːhaɪv] n colmena f.

been [biːn] pp → **be**.

beer [bɪəʳ] n cerveza f; **to have a couple of ~s** tomarse un par de cervezas.

BEER

A grandes rasgos, la cerveza británica se puede dividir en "bitter" y "lager". La "bitter", o "heavy" en Escocia, es oscura y tiene un sabor ligeramente amargo, mientras que la "lager" es la cerveza rubia que se encuentra normalmente en España. "Real ale" es un tipo de "bitter" en barril, normalmente más cara, que frecuentemente se produce en pequeñas cervecerías utilizando métodos y recetas tradicionales. La cerveza en Estados Unidos es casi siempre "lager".

---

beer garden n patio m de bar.

beer mat n posavasos m inv (de bar).

beetle ['biːtl] n escarabajo m.

beetroot ['biːtruːt] n remolacha f.

before [bɪˈfɔːʳ] adv antes ♦ prep (earlier than) antes de; (in order) antes que; (fml: in front of) frente a ♦ conj antes de; **~ you leave** antes de irte; **the day ~** el día anterior; **the week ~ last** la semana pasada no, la anterior.

beforehand [bɪˈfɔːhænd] adv con antelación.

befriend [bɪˈfrend] vt hacer amistad con.

beg [beg] vi mendigar ♦ vt: **to ~ sb to do sthg** rogar a alguien que haga algo.

began [bɪˈgæn] pt → begin.

beggar [ˈbegəʳ] n mendigo m (-ga f).

begin [bɪˈgɪn] (pt **began**, pp **begun**) vt & vi empezar, comenzar; **to ~ doing** OR **to do sthg** empezar a hacer algo; **to ~ by doing sthg** empezar haciendo algo; **to ~ with** (firstly) de entrada; (in restaurant) de primero.

beginner [bɪˈgɪnəʳ] n principiante mf.

beginning [bɪˈgɪnɪŋ] n comienzo m; **at the ~ of** a principios de.

begun [bɪˈgʌn] pp → begin.

behalf [bɪˈhɑːf] n: **on ~ of** en nombre de.

behave [bɪˈheɪv] vi comportarse; **to ~ (o.s.)** (be good) portarse bien.

behavior [bɪˈheɪvjəʳ] (Am) = behaviour.

behaviour [bɪˈheɪvjəʳ] n comportamiento m.

behind [bɪˈhaɪnd] adv detrás ♦ n (inf) trasero m ♦ prep (at the back of) detrás de; **to be ~ sb** (support-

ing) apoyar a alguien; **to be ~ (schedule)** ir retrasado; **to leave sthg ~** dejarse algo (olvidado); **to stay ~** quedarse.

beige [beɪʒ] adj beige (inv).

being [ˈbiːɪŋ] n ser m; **to come into ~** nacer.

belated [bɪˈleɪtɪd] adj tardío(-a).

belch [beltʃ] vi eructar.

Belgian [ˈbeldʒən] adj belga ♦ n belga mf.

Belgian waffle n (Am) gofre m (grueso).

Belgium [ˈbeldʒəm] n Bélgica.

belief [bɪˈliːf] n (faith) creencia f; (opinion) opinión f.

believe [bɪˈliːv] vt creer ♦ vi: **to ~ in** creer en; **to ~ in doing sthg** ser partidario de hacer algo.

believer [bɪˈliːvəʳ] n creyente mf.

bell [bel] n (of church) campana f; (of phone, door) timbre m.

bellboy [ˈbelbɔɪ] n botones m inv.

bellow [ˈbeləʊ] vi rugir.

belly [ˈbeli] n (inf) barriga f.

belly button n (inf) ombligo m.

belong [bɪˈlɒŋ] vi (be in right place) ir; **to ~ to** (property) pertenecer a; (to club, party) ser miembro de.

belongings [bɪˈlɒŋɪŋz] npl pertenencias fpl.

below [bɪˈləʊ] prep por debajo de ♦ adv (lower down) abajo; (in text) más abajo; **the flat ~** el piso de abajo; **~ zero** bajo cero; **children ~ the age of ten** niños menores de diez años.

belt [belt] n (for clothes) cinturón m; (TECH) correa f.

beltway ['belt,weɪ] *n* (*Am*) carretera *f* de circunvalación.

bench [bentʃ] *n* banco *m*.

bend [bend] (*pt & pp* bent) *n* curva *f* ◆ *vt* doblar ◆ *vt* torcerse ◻ **bend down** *vi* agacharse; **bend over** *vi* inclinarse.

beneath [bɪˈniːθ] *adv* debajo ◆ *prep* bajo.

beneficial [,benɪˈfɪʃl] *adj* beneficioso(-sa).

benefit ['benɪfɪt] *n* (*advantage*) ventaja *f*; (*money*) subsidio *m* ◆ *vt* beneficiar ◆ *vi*: **to ~ (from)** beneficiarse (de); **for the ~ of** en atención a.

benign [bɪˈnaɪn] *adj* (*MED*) benigno(-na).

bent [bent] *pt & pp* → **bend**.

bereaved [bɪˈriːvd] *adj* desconsolado(-da).

beret ['bereɪ] *n* boina *f*.

Bermuda shorts [bəˈmjuːdə] *npl* bermudas *fpl*.

berry ['berɪ] *n* baya *f*.

berserk [bəˈzɜːk] *adj*: **to go ~** ponerse hecho(-cha) una fiera.

berth [bɜːθ] *n* (*for ship*) amarradero *m*; (*in ship, train*) litera *f*.

beside [bɪˈsaɪd] *prep* junto a; **it's ~ the point** no viene al caso.

besides [bɪˈsaɪdz] *adv* además ◆ *prep* además de.

best [best] *adj & adv* mejor ◆ *n*: **the ~** el mejor (la mejor); **a pint of ~** (*beer*) una pinta de "bitter" de máxima calidad; **I like it ~** me gusta más; **the ~ thing to do is ...** lo mejor es ...; **to make the ~ of it** apañárselas; **to do one's ~** hacer lo mejor que uno puede; **"~ before**

..." "consúmase preferentemente antes de ...."; **at ~** en el mejor de los casos; **all the ~!** (*in letter*) un abrazo.

best man *n* padrino *m* de boda.

best-seller [-ˈseləʳ] *n* (*book*) éxito *m* editorial.

bet [bet] (*pt & pp* bet) *n* apuesta *f* ◆ *vt* (*gamble*) apostar ◆ *vi*: **to ~ (on)** apostar (por); **I ~ (that) you can't do it** a que no puedes hacerlo.

betray [bɪˈtreɪ] *vt* traicionar.

better ['betəʳ] *adj & adv* mejor; **you had ~ go** más vale que te vayas; **to get ~** mejorar.

betting ['betɪŋ] *n* apuestas *fpl*.

betting shop *n* (*Br*) casa *f* de apuestas.

between [bɪˈtwiːn] *prep* entre ◆ *adv* (*in time*) entremedias; **in ~** *prep* entre ◆ *adv* (*in space*) en medio; (*in time*) entremedias; **"closed ~ 1 and 2"** "cerrado de 1 a 2".

beverage ['bevərɪdʒ] *n* (*fml*) bebida *f*.

beware [bɪˈweəʳ] *vi*: **to ~ of** tener cuidado con; **"~ of the dog"** "ojo con el perro".

bewildered [bɪˈwɪldəd] *adj* desconcertado(-da).

beyond [bɪˈjɒnd] *prep* más allá de ◆ *adv* más allá; **to be ~ doubt** estar fuera de toda duda.

biased ['baɪəst] *adj* parcial.

bib [bɪb] *n* (*for baby*) babero *m*.

bible ['baɪbl] *n* biblia *f*; **the Bible** la Biblia.

biceps ['baɪseps] *n* bíceps *m inv*.

bicycle ['baɪsɪkl] *n* bicicleta *f*.

bicycle path *n* camino *m* para bicicletas.

bicycle pump n bomba f (de bicicleta).

bid [bɪd] (pt & pp **bid**) n (at auction) puja f; (attempt) intento m ♦ vt pujar ♦ vi: **to ~ (for)** pujar (por).

bidet ['biːdeɪ] n bidé m.

big [bɪg] adj grande; **a ~ problem** un gran problema; **my ~ brother** mi hermano mayor; **how ~ is it?** ¿cómo es de grande?

bike [baɪk] n (inf) (bicycle) bici f; (motorcycle) moto f.

biking ['baɪkɪŋ] n: **to go ~** ir en bici.

bikini [bɪ'kiːnɪ] n biquini m.

bikini bottom n bragas fpl de biquini.

bikini top n sujetador m de biquini.

bilingual [baɪ'lɪŋgwəl] adj bilingüe.

bill [bɪl] n (for meal) cuenta f; (for electricity, hotel room) factura f; (Am: bank note) billete m; (at cinema, theatre) programa m; (POL) proyecto m de ley; **can I have the ~, please?** la cuenta, por favor.

billboard ['bɪlbɔːd] n cartelera f.

billfold ['bɪlfəʊld] n (Am) billetera f.

billiards ['bɪljədz] n billar m.

billion ['bɪljən] n (thousand million) millar m de millones; (Br: million million) billón m.

bin [bɪn] n (rubbish bin) cubo m de la basura; (wastepaper bin) papelera f; (for bread) panera f; (for flour) bote m; (on plane) maletero m superior.

bind [baɪnd] (pt & pp **bound**) vt atar.

binding ['baɪndɪŋ] n (of book) encuadernación f; (for ski) fijación f.

bingo ['bɪŋgəʊ] n bingo m.

E l "bingo" es un juego muy popular en Gran Bretaña que consiste en rellenar casillas en una tarjeta con números. El "bingo caller" canta los números elegidos al azar y la primera persona que completa una línea o toda la tarjeta es la que gana. Los premios pueden ser en metálico, pero muchas veces son regalos como osos de peluche o adornos. A menudo se juega en antiguos cines o grandes salas públicas y también en salones de juego en lugares de veraneo.

binoculars [bɪ'nɒkjʊləz] npl prismáticos mpl.

biodegradable [ˌbaɪəʊdɪ'greɪdəbl] adj biodegradable.

biography [baɪ'ɒgrəfɪ] n biografía f.

biological [ˌbaɪə'lɒdʒɪkl] adj biológico(-ca).

biology [baɪ'ɒlədʒɪ] n biología f.

birch [bɜːtʃ] n abedul m.

bird [bɜːd] n (smaller) pájaro m; (large) ave f; (Br: inf: woman) tía f.

bird-watching [-ˌwɒtʃɪŋ] n observación f de aves.

Biro® ['baɪərəʊ] n bolígrafo m.

birth [bɜːθ] n nacimiento m; **by ~** de nacimiento; **to give ~ to** dar a luz.

birth certificate n partida f

de nacimiento.

birth control n control m de natalidad.

birthday ['bɜːθdeɪ] n cumpleaños m inv; **happy ~!** ¡feliz cumpleaños!

birthday card n tarjeta f de cumpleaños.

birthday party n fiesta f de cumpleaños.

birthplace ['bɜːθpleɪs] n lugar m de nacimiento.

biscuit ['bɪskɪt] n (Br) galleta f; (Am: scone) masa cocida al horno que se suele comer con salsa de carne.

bishop ['bɪʃəp] n (RELIG) obispo m; (in chess) alfil m.

bistro ['biːstrəʊ] n = bar-restaurante m.

bit [bɪt] pt → **bite** ♦ n (piece) trozo m; (of drill) broca f; (of bridle) bocado m, freno m; **a ~ of** un poco de; **a ~ un poco; not a ~ interested** nada interesado; **~ by ~** poco a poco.

bitch [bɪtʃ] n (vulg: woman) bruja f; (dog) perra f.

bite [baɪt] (pt bit, pp bitten ['bɪtn]) n (when eating) bocado m; (from insect, snake) picadura f ♦ vt (subj: person, dog) morder; (subj: insect, snake) picar; **to have a ~** to eat comer algo.

bitter ['bɪtər] adj (taste, food) amargo(-ga); (lemon, grapefruit) agrio (agria); (cold, wind) penetrante; (person) resentido(-da); (argument, conflict) enconado(-da) ♦ n (Br: beer) tipo de cerveza amarga.

bitter lemon n bíter m de limón.

bizarre [bɪ'zɑːr] adj extravagante.

black [blæk] adj negro(-gra); (coffee, tea) solo ♦ n (colour) negro m; (person) negro m (-gra f) ❑ **black out** vi desmayarse.

black and white adj en blanco y negro.

blackberry ['blækbrɪ] n mora f.

blackbird ['blækbɜːd] n mirlo m.

blackboard ['blækbɔːd] n pizarra f.

black cherry n variedad de cereza oscura.

blackcurrant [,blæk'kʌrənt] n grosella f negra.

black eye n ojo m morado.

Black Forest gâteau n pastel m (de chocolate) Selva Negra.

black ice n hielo transparente en el suelo.

blackmail ['blækmeɪl] n chantaje m ♦ vt chantajear.

blackout ['blækaʊt] n (power cut) apagón m.

black pepper n pimienta f negra.

black pudding n (Br) = morcilla f.

blacksmith ['blæksmɪθ] n herrero m.

bladder ['blædər] n vejiga f.

blade [bleɪd] n (of knife, saw) hoja f; (of propeller, oar) aleta f; (of grass) brizna f.

blame [bleɪm] n culpa f ♦ vt echar la culpa a; **to ~ sb for sthg** culpar a alguien de algo; **to ~ sthg on sb** echar la culpa de algo a alguien.

bland [blænd] adj soso(-sa).

blank [blæŋk] adj (space, page) en blanco; (cassette) virgen; (expres-

sion) vacío(-a) ◆ *n (empty space)* espacio *m* en blanco.

blank cheque *n* cheque *m* en blanco.

blanket ['blæŋkɪt] *n* manta *f*.

blast [blɑ:st] *n (explosion)* explosión *f*; *(of air, wind)* ráfaga *f* ◆ *excl (inf)* ¡maldita sea!; **at full ~** a todo trapo.

blaze [bleɪz] *n (fire)* incendio *m* ◆ *vi (fire)* arder; *(sun, light)* resplandecer.

blazer ['bleɪzəʳ] *n* chaqueta *de sport generalmente con la insignia de un equipo, colegio, etc.*

bleach [bli:tʃ] *n* lejía *f* ◆ *vt (hair)* decolorar; *(clothes)* blanquear.

bleak [bli:k] *adj (weather)* desapacible; *(day, city)* sombrío(-a).

bleed [bli:d] *(pt & pp* bled [bled]) *vi* sangrar.

blend [blend] *n (of coffee, whisky)* mezcla *f* ◆ *vt* mezclar.

blender ['blendəʳ] *n* licuadora *f*.

bless [bles] *vt* bendecir; **~ you!** ¡¡salud!!

blessing ['blesɪŋ] *n* bendición *f*.

blew [blu:] *pt → blow.*

blind [blaɪnd] *adj* ciego(-ga) ◆ *n (for window)* persiana *f* ◆ *npl:* **the ~** los ciegos.

blind corner *n* curva *f* sin visibilidad.

blindfold ['blaɪndfəʊld] *n* venda *f* (en los ojos) ◆ *vt* vendar los ojos a.

blind spot *n (AUT)* ángulo *m* muerto.

blink [blɪŋk] *vi* parpadear.

blinkers ['blɪŋkəz] *npl (Br)* anteojeras *fpl.*

bliss [blɪs] *n* gloria *f*.

blister ['blɪstəʳ] *n* ampolla *f*.

blizzard ['blɪzəd] *n* ventisca *f (de nieve).*

bloated ['bləʊtɪd] *adj (after eating)* hinchado(-da).

blob [blɒb] *n* gota *f*.

block [blɒk] *n* bloque *m*; *(Am: in town, city)* manzana *f* ◆ *vt* bloquear; **to have a ~ed (up) nose** tener la nariz bloqueada ❏ **block up** *vt sep* obstruir.

blockage ['blɒkɪdʒ] *n* obstrucción *f*.

block capitals *npl* mayúsculas *fpl.*

block of flats *n* bloque *m* de pisos.

bloke [bləʊk] *n (Br: inf)* tipo *m*.

blond [blɒnd] *adj* rubio ◆ *n* rubio *m*.

blonde [blɒnd] *adj* rubia ◆ *n* rubia *f*.

blood [blʌd] *n* sangre *f*.

blood donor *n* donante *mf* de sangre.

blood group *n* grupo *m* sanguíneo.

blood poisoning *n* septicemia *f*.

blood pressure *n* presión *f* sanguínea; **to have high ~** tener la tensión alta; **to have low ~** tener la tensión baja.

bloodshot ['blʌdʃɒt] *adj* inyectado(-da) de sangre.

blood test *n* análisis *m inv* de sangre.

blood transfusion *n* transfusión *f* de sangre.

bloody ['blʌdɪ] *adj (hands, hand-*

kerchief) ensangrentado(-da); *(Br: vulg: damn)* maldito(-ta) ◆ *adv (Br: vulg)* acojonantemente.

Bloody Mary ['-mɛərɪ] *n (drink)* Bloody Mary *m, vodka con zumo de tomate.*

bloom [bluːm] *n* flor *f* ◆ *vi* florecer; **in ~** en flor.

blossom ['blɒsəm] *n* flor *f.*

blot [blɒt] *n* borrón *m.*

blotch [blɒtʃ] *n* mancha *f.*

blotting paper ['blɒtɪŋ-] *n* papel *m* secante.

blouse [blauz] *n* blusa *f.*

blow [bləʊ] *(pt* **blew,** *pp* **blown)** *vt (subj: wind)* hacer volar; *(whistle, trumpet)* tocar; *(bubbles)* hacer ◆ *vi (wind, person)* soplar; *(fuse)* fundirse ◆ *n (hit)* golpe *m;* **to ~ one's nose** sonarse la nariz ❑ **blow up** *vt sep (cause to explode)* volar; *(inflate)* inflar ◆ *vi* estallar.

blow-dry *n* secado *m* (con secador) ◆ *vt* secar (con secador).

blown [bləʊn] *pp →* **blow.**

BLT *n (sandwich)* sándwich *m* de bacon, lechuga y tomate.

blue [bluː] *adj (colour)* azul; *(film)* porno ◆ *n* azul *m* ❑ **blues** *n (MUS)* blues *m inv.*

bluebell ['bluːbel] *n* campanilla *f.*

blueberry ['bluːbərɪ] *n* arándano *m.*

bluebottle ['bluː,bɒtl] *n* moscardón *m.*

blue cheese *n* queso *m* azul.

bluff [blʌf] *n (cliff)* peñasco *m* ◆ *vi* farolear.

blunder ['blʌndəʳ] *n* metedura *f* de pata.

blunt [blʌnt] *adj (knife, pencil)* desafilado(-da); *(fig: person)* franco(-ca).

blurred [blɜːd] *adj* borroso(-sa).

blush [blʌʃ] *vi* ruborizarse.

blusher ['blʌʃəʳ] *n* colorete *m.*

blustery ['blʌstərɪ] *adj* borrascoso(-sa).

board [bɔːd] *n (plank)* tabla *f; (notice board)* tablón *m; (for games)* tablero *m; (blackboard)* pizarra *f; (of company)* junta *f* directiva; *(hardboard)* conglomerado *m* ◆ *vt (plane, ship)* embarcar en; *(bus)* subir a; **~ and lodging** comida y habitación; **full ~** pensión completa; **half ~** media pensión; **on ~** *adv* a bordo ◆ *prep (plane, ship)* a bordo de; *(bus)* dentro de.

board game *n* juego *m* de tablero.

boarding ['bɔːdɪŋ] *n* embarque *m.*

boarding card *n* tarjeta *f* de embarque.

boardinghouse ['bɔːdɪŋhaʊs, *pl* -haʊzɪz] *n* casa *f* de huéspedes.

boarding school *n* internado *m.*

board of directors *n* junta *f* directiva.

boast [bəʊst] *vi:* **to ~ (about sthg)** alardear (de algo).

boat [bəʊt] *n (large)* barco *m; (small)* barca *f;* **by ~** en barco.

boat train *n (Br)* tren de enlace con un barco.

bob [bɒb] *n (hairstyle)* media melena *f* (en una capa).

bobby pin ['bɒbɪ-] *n (Am)* horquilla *f.*

bodice ['bɒdɪs] n cuerpo m.

body ['bɒdɪ] n (of person, wine) cuerpo m; (corpse) cadáver m; (of car) carrocería f; (organization) organismo m.

bodyguard ['bɒdɪgɑːd] n guardaespaldas m inv.

bodywork ['bɒdɪwɜːk] n carrocería f.

bog [bɒg] n cenagal m.

bogus ['bəʊgəs] adj falso(-sa).

boil [bɔɪl] vt (water) hervir; (kettle) poner a hervir; (food) cocer ◆ vi hervir ◆ n pústula f.

boiled egg [bɔɪld-] n huevo m pasado por agua.

boiled potatoes [bɔɪld-] npl patatas fpl cocidas.

boiler ['bɔɪlər] n caldera f.

boiling (hot) ['bɔɪlɪŋ-] adj (inf: person) asado(-da) de calor; (weather) abrasador(-ra); (water) ardiendo.

bold [bəʊld] adj (brave) audaz.

Bolivia [bəˈlɪvɪə] n Bolivia f.

Bolivian [bəˈlɪvɪən] adj boliviano(-na) ◆ n boliviano m (-na f).

bollard ['bɒlɑːd] n (Br: on road) poste m.

bolt [bəʊlt] n (on door, window) cerrojo m; (screw) tornillo m ◆ vt (door, window) echar el cerrojo a.

bomb [bɒm] n bomba f ◆ vt bombardear.

bombard [bɒmˈbɑːd] vt bombardear.

bomb scare n amenaza f de bomba.

bomb shelter n refugio m antiaéreo.

bond [bɒnd] n (tie, connection) lazo m, vínculo m.

bone [bəʊn] n (of person, animal) hueso m; (of fish) espina f.

boned [bəʊnd] adj (chicken) deshuesado(-da); (fish) limpio (-pia).

boneless ['bəʊnləs] adj (chicken, pork) deshuesado(-da).

bonfire ['bɒn,faɪər] n hoguera f.

bonnet ['bɒnɪt] n (Br: of car) capó m.

bonus ['bəʊnəs] (pl -es) n (extra money) paga f extra; (additional advantage) beneficio m adicional.

bony ['bəʊnɪ] adj (fish) lleno(-na) de espinas; (chicken) lleno de huesos.

boo [buː] vi abuchear.

boogie ['buːgɪ] vi (inf) mover el esqueleto.

book [bʊk] n (for reading) libro m; (for writing in) libreta f, cuaderno m; (of stamps) librillo m; (of matches) cajetilla f; (of tickets) talonario m ◆ vt (reserve) reservar ☐ **book in** vi registrarse.

bookable ['bʊkəbl] adj (seats, flight) reservable.

bookcase ['bʊkkeɪs] n estantería f.

booking ['bʊkɪŋ] n (reservation) reserva f.

booking office n taquilla f.

bookkeeping ['bʊk,kiːpɪŋ] n contabilidad f.

booklet ['bʊklɪt] n folleto m.

bookmaker's ['bʊk,meɪkəz] n casa f de apuestas.

bookmark ['bʊkmɑːk] n separador m.

bookshelf ['bʊkʃelf] (pl -shelves

[-ʃelvz]) n (shelf) estante m; (book-case) estantería f.

bookshop [ˈbukʃɒp] n librería f.

bookstall [ˈbukstɔːl] n puesto m de libros.

bookstore [ˈbukstɔːʳ] = book-shop.

book token n vale m para comprar libros.

boom [buːm] n (sudden growth) auge m ♦ vi (voice, guns) retumbar.

boost [buːst] vt (profits, production) incrementar; (confidence, spirits) estimular.

booster [ˈbuːstəʳ] n (injection) inyección f de revacunación.

boot [buːt] n (shoe) bota f; (Br: of car) maletero m.

booth [buːð] n (for telephone) cabina f; (at fairground) puesto m.

booze [buːz] n (inf) bebida f, alcohol m ♦ vi (inf) empinar el codo.

bop [bɒp] n (inf: dance): **to have a ~** mover el esqueleto.

border [ˈbɔːdəʳ] n (of country) frontera f; (edge) borde m; **the Borders** región de Escocia que linda con Inglaterra, especialmente las zonas central y oriental.

bore [bɔːʳ] pt → **bear** ♦ n (person) pelmazo m (-za f); (thing) rollo m ♦ vt (person) aburrir; (hole) horadar.

bored [bɔːd] adj aburrido(-da).

boredom [ˈbɔːdəm] n aburrimiento m.

boring [ˈbɔːrɪŋ] adj aburrido(-da).

born [bɔːn] adj: **to be ~** nacer.

borne [bɔːn] pp → bear.

borough [ˈbʌrə] n municipio m.

borrow [ˈbɒrəʊ] vt: **to ~ sthg (from sb)** tomar algo prestado (de alguien).

bosom [ˈbuzəm] n pecho m.

boss [bɒs] n jefe m (-fa f) ❑ **boss around** vt sep mangonear.

bossy [ˈbɒsɪ] adj mandón(-ona).

botanical garden [bəˈtænɪkl-] n jardín m botánico.

both [bəʊθ] adj ambos(-bas) ♦ pron los dos m/pl (las dos f/pl) ♦ adv: **she speaks ~ French and German** habla francés y alemán; **~ of them** los dos (las dos); **~ of us** los dos (las dos).

bother [ˈbɒðəʳ] vt (worry) preocupar; (annoy, pester) molestar ♦ vi molestarse ♦ n molestia f; **I can't be ~ed** no tengo ganas; **it's no ~!** ¡no es molestia!

bottle [ˈbɒtl] n (container, contents) botella f; (of shampoo) bote m; (of medicine) frasco m; (for baby) biberón m.

bottle bank n contenedor m de vidrio (para reciclaje).

bottled [ˈbɒtld] adj embotellado(-da); **~ beer** cerveza f de botella; **~ water** agua f mineral (embotellada).

bottle opener [-ˌəʊpnəʳ] n abrebotellas m inv.

bottom [ˈbɒtəm] adj (shelf, line, object in pile) inferior; (floor) bajo(-ja); (last, worst) peor ♦ n (of sea, bag) fondo m; (of hill, stairs, ladder) pie m; (of page) final m; (of glass, bin) culo m; (farthest part) final m, fondo m; (buttocks) trasero m.

bought [bɔːt] pt & pp → buy.

boulder [ˈbəʊldəʳ] n canto m

rodado.

bounce [bauns] *vi (rebound)* rebotar; *(jump)* saltar; *(cheque)* ser rechazado por el banco.

bouncer ['baunsər] *n (inf)* matón *m (en discoteca, bar, etc)*.

bouncy ['baunsı] *adj (person)* dinámico(-ca).

bound [baund] *pt & pp →* bind ♦ *vi* ir dando saltos ♦ *adj*: **it's ~ to rain** seguro que llueve; **to be ~ for** ir rumbo a; **to be out of ~s** estar en zona prohibida.

boundary ['baundrı] *n* frontera *f*.

bouquet [bu:'keı] *n (of flowers)* ramo *m*; *(of wine)* buqué *m*.

bourbon ['bɜ:bən] *n* bourbon *m*.

bout [baut] *n (of illness)* ataque *m*; *(of activity)* racha *f*.

boutique [bu:'ti:k] *n* boutique *f*.

bow¹ [bau] *n (of head)* reverencia *f*; *(of ship)* proa *f* ♦ *vi* inclinarse.

bow² [bəu] *n (knot)* lazo *m*; *(weapon, MUS)* arco *m*.

bowels ['bauəlz] *npl* intestinos *mpl*.

bowl [bəul] *n (for salad, fruit, sugar)* bol *m*, cuenco *m*; *(for soup, of soup)* tazón *m*; *(for washing-up)* barreño *m*; *(of toilet)* taza *f* ☐ **bowls** *npl* bochas *fpl*.

bowling alley ['bəulıŋ-] *n* bolera *f*.

bowling green ['bəulıŋ-] *n* campo de cesped para jugar a las bochas.

bow tie [bəu-] *n* pajarita *f*.

box [bɒks] *n (container, contents)* caja *f*; *(of jewels)* estuche *m*; *(on form)* casilla *f*; *(in theatre)* palco *m* ♦ *vi* boxear; **a ~ of chocolates** una caja de bombones.

boxer ['bɒksər] *n* boxeador *m*.

boxer shorts *npl* calzoncillos *mpl* boxer.

boxing ['bɒksıŋ] *n* boxeo *m*.

Boxing Day *n* el 26 de diciembre.

BOXING DAY

El 26 de diciembre, "Boxing Day", es fiesta en toda Gran Bretaña. Tradicionalmente, era el día en el que los comerciantes y criados recibían un dinero extra que se llamaba el "Christmas box". Aún hoy, los repartidores de leche, los basureros y los niños que reparten periódicos reciben este aguinaldo.

---

boxing gloves *npl* guantes *mpl* de boxeo.

boxing ring *n* cuadrilátero *m*.

box office *n* taquilla *f*.

boy [bɔı] *n (male)* chico *m*, niño *m*; *(son)* hijo *m* ♦ *excl (Am. inf)* : **(oh)** ! **¡olín!**

boycott ['bɔıkɒt] *vt* boicotear.

boyfriend ['bɔıfrend] *n* novio *m*.

boy scout *n (boy)* scout *m*.

BR *abbr* = **British Rail**.

bra [brɑ:] *n* sujetador *m*.

brace [breıs] *n (for teeth)* aparato *m* corrector ☐ **braces** *npl (Br)* tirantes *mpl*.

bracelet ['breıslıt] *n* brazalete *m*.

bracken ['brækn] *n* helecho *m*.

bracket ['brækıt] *n (written symbol)* paréntesis *m inv*; *(support)* soporte *m*, palomilla *f*.

brag [bræg] *vi* fanfarronear.

braid [breɪd] n (hairstyle) trenza f; (on clothes) galón m.

brain [breɪn] n cerebro m.

brainy ['breɪnɪ] adj (inf) listo (-ta).

braised [breɪzd] adj cocido(-da) a fuego lento.

brake [breɪk] n freno m ♦ vi frenar.

brake block n zapata f.

brake fluid n líquido m para frenos.

brake light n luz f de freno.

brake pad n pastilla f de frenos.

brake pedal n pedal m de freno.

bran [bræn] n salvado m.

branch [brɑːntʃ] n (of tree, subject) rama f; (of bank, company) sucursal f ❑ **branch off** vi desviarse.

branch line n ramal m.

brand [brænd] n marca f ♦ vt: **to ~ sb (as)** tildar a alguien (de).

brand-new adj completamente nuevo(-va).

brandy ['brændɪ] n coñac m.

brash [bræʃ] adj (pej) insolente.

brass [brɑːs] n latón m.

brass band n banda f de metal.

brasserie ['bræsərɪ] n restaurante m.

brassiere [Br 'bræsɪər, Am brə'zɪr] n sujetador m.

brat [bræt] n (inf) mocoso m (-sa f).

brave [breɪv] adj valiente.

bravery ['breɪvərɪ] n valentía f.

bravo [ˌbrɑː'vəʊ] excl ¡bravo!

brawl [brɔːl] n gresca f.

Brazil [brə'zɪl] n Brasil.

brazil nut n nuez f de Pará.

breach [briːtʃ] vt (contract) incumplir; (confidence) abusar de.

bread [bred] n pan m; **~ and butter** pan con mantequilla.

bread bin n (Br) panera f.

breadboard ['bredbɔːd] n tabla f (de cortar pan).

bread box (Am) = **bread bin**.

breadcrumbs ['bredkrʌmz] npl pan m rallado.

breaded ['bredɪd] adj empanado(-da).

bread knife n cuchillo m de pan.

bread roll n panecillo m.

breadth [bretθ] n anchura f.

break [breɪk] (vt **broke**, pp **broken**) n (interruption) interrupción f; (in transmission) corte m; (in line) espacio m; (rest, pause) descanso m; (SCH: playtime) recreo m ♦ vt (cup, window, record) romper; (machine) estropear; (disobey) violar, infringir; (fail to fulfil) incumplir; (journey) interrumpir; (news) dar ♦ vi (cup, window, chair) romperse; (machine) estropearse; (dawn) romper; (voice) cambiar; **without a ~** sin parar; **a lucky ~** un golpe de suerte; **to ~ one's leg** romperse la pierna ❑ **break down** vi (car, machine) estropearse ♦ vt sep (door, barrier) derribar; **break in** vi entrar por la fuerza; **break off** vt (detach) partir; (holiday) interrumpir ♦ vi (stop suddenly) pararse, detenerse; **break out** vi (fire, war) desencadenarse; (panic) cundir; **he broke out in a rash** le salió un sarpullido; **break up** vi (with spouse, partner) romper;

(meeting) disolverse; *(marriage)* deshacerse; *(school, pupils)* terminar el curso.

breakage ['breɪkɪdʒ] *n* rotura *f*.

breakdown ['breɪkdaʊn] *n (of car)* avería *f*; *(in communications, negotiations)* ruptura *f*; *(acute depression)* crisis *f* nerviosa.

breakdown truck *n* camión *m* grúa.

breakfast ['brekfəst] *n* desayuno *m*; **to have ~** desayunar; **to have sthg for ~** desayunar algo.

breakfast cereal *n* cereales *mpl* (para desayuno).

break-in *n* robo *m* (con allanamiento de morada).

breakwater ['breɪkwɔːtə[r]] *n* rompeolas *m inv*.

breast [brest] *n (of woman)* pecho *m*, seno *m*; *(of chicken, duck)* pechuga *f*.

breastbone ['brestbəʊn] *n* esternón *m*.

breast-feed *vt* dar el pecho a.

breaststroke ['breststrəʊk] *n* braza *f*.

breath [breθ] *n* aliento *m*; **out of ~** sin aliento; **to go for a ~ of fresh air** salir a tomar un poco de aire; **to take a deep ~** respirar hondo.

Breathalyser® ['breθəlaɪzə[r]] *n (Br)* alcoholímetro *m*.

Breathalyzer® ['breθəlaɪzər] *n (Am)* = Breathalyser.

breathe [briːð] *vi & vt* respirar □ **breathe in** *vi* aspirar; **breathe out** *vi* espirar.

breathtaking ['breθ,teɪkɪŋ] *adj* sobrecogedor(-ra).

breed [briːd] *(pt & pp* **bred** [bred]*)*

n (of animal) raza *f*; *(of plant)* especie *f* ♦ *vt* criar ♦ *vi* reproducirse.

breeze [briːz] *n* brisa *f*.

breezy ['briːzɪ] *adj*: **it's ~** hace aire.

brew [bruː] *vt (beer)* elaborar; *(tea, coffee)* preparar ♦ *vi (tea, coffee)* reposar.

brewery ['brʊərɪ] *n* fábrica *f* de cerveza.

bribe [braɪb] *n* soborno *m* ♦ *vt* sobornar.

bric-a-brac ['brɪkəbræk] *n* baratijas *fpl*.

brick [brɪk] *n* ladrillo *m*.

bricklayer ['brɪk,leɪə[r]] *n* albañil *m*.

brickwork ['brɪkwɜːk] *n* enladrillado *m*.

bride [braɪd] *n* novia *f*.

bridegroom ['braɪdgrʊm] *n* novio *m*.

bridesmaid ['braɪdzmeɪd] *n* dama *f* de honor.

bridge [brɪdʒ] *n (across road, river)* puente *m*; *(of ship)* puente *m* de mando; *(card game)* bridge *m*.

bridle ['braɪdl] *n* brida *f*.

bridle path *n* camino *m* de herradura.

brief [briːf] *adj* breve ♦ *vt* informar; **in ~** en resumen □ **briefs** *npl (underpants)* calzoncillos *mpl*, *(knickers)* bragas *fpl*.

briefcase ['briːfkeɪs] *n* cartera *f*.

briefly ['briːflɪ] *adv (for a short time)* brevemente; *(in few words)* en pocas palabras.

brigade [brɪ'geɪd] *n* brigada *f*.

bright [braɪt] *adj (light)* brillante; *(sun, smile)* radiante; *(weather)* despejado(-da); *(room)* luminoso(-sa); *(colour)* vivo(-va); *(clever)* listo(-ta), inteligente; *(idea)* genial.

brilliant ['brɪljənt] *adj (colour)* vivo(-va); *(light, sunshine)* resplandeciente; *(idea, person)* genial; *(inf: wonderful)* fenomenal.

brim [brɪm] *n (of hat)* ala *f*; **it's full to the ~** está lleno hasta el borde.

brine [braɪn] *n* salmuera *f*.

bring [brɪŋ] *(pt & pp* **brought)** *vt* traer; *(cause)* producir ❑ **bring along** *vt sep* traer; **bring back** *vt sep (return)* devolver; *(shopping, gift)* traer; **bring in** *vt sep (introduce)* introducir; *(earn)* ganar; **bring out** *vt sep (new product)* sacar; **bring up** *vt sep (child)* criar; *(subject)* sacar a relucir; *(food)* devolver.

brink [brɪŋk] *n*: **on the ~ of** al borde de.

brisk [brɪsk] *adj (quick)* rápido (-da); *(efficient)* enérgico(-ca).

bristle ['brɪsl] *n (of brush)* cerda *f*; *(on chin)* pelillo *m*.

Britain ['brɪtn] *n* Gran Bretaña.

British ['brɪtɪʃ] *adj* británico(-ca) ◆ *npl*: **the ~** los británicos.

British Rail *n* compañía ferroviaria británica.

British Telecom [-'telɪkɒm] *n* principal empresa británica de telecomunicaciones.

Briton ['brɪtn] *n* británico *m* (-ca *f*).

brittle ['brɪtl] *adj* quebradizo(-za).

broad [brɔːd] *adj (wide)* ancho(-cha); *(wide-ranging)* amplio (-plia); *(description, outline)* general; *(accent)* cerrado(-da).

B road *n (Br)* ≃ carretera *f* comarcal.

broad bean *n* haba *f* de mayo.

broadcast ['brɔːdkɑːst] *(pt & pp* **broadcast)** *n* emisión *f* ◆ *vt* emitir.

broadly ['brɔːdlɪ] *adv* en general; **~ speaking** en líneas generales.

broccoli ['brɒkəlɪ] *n* brécol *m*.

brochure ['brəʊʃəʳ] *n* folleto *m*.

broiled [brɔɪld] *adj (Am)* a la parrilla.

broke [brəʊk] *pt* → **break** ◆ *adj (inf)* sin blanca.

broken ['brəʊkn] *pp* → **break** ◆ *adj (window, glass, leg)* roto(-ta); *(machine)* estropeado(-da); *(English, Spanish)* macarrónico(-ca).

bronchitis [brɒŋ'kaɪtɪs] *n* bronquitis *f inv*.

bronze [brɒnz] *n* bronce *m*.

brooch [brəʊtʃ] *n* broche *m*.

brook [brʊk] *n* arroyo *m*.

broom [bruːm] *n* escoba *f*.

broomstick ['bruːmstɪk] *n* palo *m* de escoba.

broth [brɒθ] *n* caldo *m*.

brother ['brʌðəʳ] *n* hermano *m*.

brother-in-law *n* cuñado *m*.

brought [brɔːt] *pt & pp* → **bring**.

brow [braʊ] *n (forehead)* frente *f*; *(eyebrow)* ceja *f*.

brown [braʊn] *adj (earth, paint, wood)* marrón; *(hair, eyes)* castaño(-ña); *(skin)* moreno(-na); *(tanned)* bronceado(-da) ◆ *n* marrón *m*.

brown bread *n* pan *m* moreno.

brownie ['braʊnɪ] *n (CULIN)* pequeño bizcocho de chocolate y nueces de forma cuadrada.

Brownie ['braʊnɪ] n guía f (de 7-10 años).

brown rice n arroz m integral.

brown sauce n (Br) salsa f inglesa.

brown sugar n azúcar m moreno.

browse [braʊz] vi (in shop) mirar, curiosear; **to ~ through sthg** hojear algo.

browser ['braʊzər] n: **"~s welcome"** "le invitamos a curiosear".

bruise [bruːz] n cardenal m.

brunch [brʌntʃ] n desayuno-almuerzo que se toma por la mañana tarde.

brunette [bruː'net] n morena f.

brush [brʌʃ] n (for hair, teeth) cepillo m; (of artist) pincel m; (for decorating) brocha f ◆ vt (floor) barrer; (clothes) cepillar; (move with hand) quitar; **to ~ one's hair** cepillarse el pelo; **to ~ one's teeth** cepillarse los dientes.

Brussels sprouts ['brʌslz-] npl coles fpl de Bruselas.

brutal ['bruːtl] adj brutal.

BSc n (abbr of Bachelor of Science) (titular de una) licenciatura de ciencias.

BT abbr = **British Telecom**.

bubble ['bʌbl] n burbuja f.

bubble bath n espuma f de baño.

bubble gum n chicle m (para hacer globos).

bubbly ['bʌblɪ] n (inf) champán m.

buck [bʌk] n (Am: inf: dollar) dólar

m; (male animal) macho m.

bucket ['bʌkɪt] n cubo m.

Buckingham Palace ['bʌkɪŋəm-] n el palacio de Buckingham.

ℹ️ BUCKINGHAM PALACE

El palacio de Buckingham, construido en 1703 por el duque de Buckingham, es la residencia oficial en Londres del monarca británico. Se encuentra al final de The Mall, entre Green Park y St James's Park. La ceremonia del cambio de guardia tiene lugar a diario frente al palacio.

---

buckle ['bʌkl] n hebilla f ◆ vt (fasten) abrochar (con hebilla) ◆ vi (warp) combarse.

Buck's Fizz [ˌbʌks'fɪz] n bebida preparada con champán y zumo de naranja.

bud [bʌd] n (shoot) brote m; (flower) capullo m ◆ vi brotar.

Buddhist ['bʊdɪst] n budista mf.

buddy ['bʌdɪ] n (inf) amiguete m (-ta f).

budge [bʌdʒ] vi moverse.

budgerigar ['bʌdʒərɪgɑːr] n periquito m.

budget ['bʌdʒɪt] adj (holiday, travel) económico(-ca) ◆ n presupuesto m; **the Budget** (Br) los presupuestos del Estado ❑ **budget for** vt fus contar con.

budgie ['bʌdʒɪ] n (inf) periquito m.

buff [bʌf] n (inf) aficionado m (-da f).

buffalo ['bʌfələʊ] n búfalo m.

buffalo wings npl (Am) alitas fpl de pollo fritas.

buffer [ˈbʌfər] n (on train) tope m.

buffet [Br ˈbʊfeɪ, Am bəˈfeɪ] n (meal) bufé m; (cafeteria) cafetería f.

buffet car [ˈbʊfeɪ-] n coche m restaurante (sólo mostrador).

bug [bʌg] n (insect) bicho m; (inf: mild illness) virus m inv ◆ vt (inf: annoy) fastidiar.

buggy [ˈbʌgɪ] n (pushchair) silla f de niño; (Am: pram) cochecito m de niño.

bugle [ˈbjuːgl] n corneta f.

build [bɪld] (pt & pp **built**) n complexión f ◆ vt construir □ **build up** vt sep (strength, speed) n aumentando ◆ vi acumularse.

builder [ˈbɪldər] n constructor m (-ra f).

building [ˈbɪldɪŋ] n edificio m.

building site n solar m.

building society n (Br) = caja f de ahorros.

built [bɪlt] pt & pp → build.

built-in adj empotrado(-da).

built-up area n zona f urbanizada.

bulb [bʌlb] n (for lamp) bombilla f; (of plant) bulbo m.

Bulgaria [bʌlˈgeərɪə] n Bulgaria.

bulge [bʌldʒ] vi hacer bulto.

bulk [bʌlk] n: **the ~ of** la mayor parte de; **in ~** a granel.

bulky [ˈbʌlkɪ] adj voluminoso(-sa).

bull [bʊl] n toro m.

bulldog [ˈbʊldɒg] n buldog m.

bulldozer [ˈbʊldəʊzər] n bulldozer m.

bullet [ˈbʊlɪt] n bala f.

bulletin [ˈbʊlətɪn] n boletín m.

bullfight [ˈbʊlfaɪt] n corrida f (de toros).

bull's-eye n diana f.

bully [ˈbʊlɪ] n abusón m (-ona f) ◆ vt intimidar.

bum [bʌm] n (inf: bottom) culo m; (Am: inf: tramp) vagabundo m (-da f).

bum bag n (Br) riñonera f.

bumblebee [ˈbʌmblbiː] n abejorro m.

bump [bʌmp] n (on surface) bulto m; (on road) bache m; (on head, leg) chichón m; (sound, minor accident) golpe m ◆ vt: **to ~ one's head** golpearse la cabeza □ **bump into** vt fus (hit) darse con; (meet) toparse con.

bumper [ˈbʌmpər] n (on car) parachoques m inv; (Am: on train) tope m.

bumpy [ˈbʌmpɪ] adj (road) lleno(-na) de baches; (flight, journey) con muchas sacudidas.

bun [bʌn] n (cake) bollo m; (bread roll) panecillo m; (hairstyle) moño m.

bunch [bʌntʃ] n (of people) grupo m; (of flowers) ramo m; (of grapes, bananas) racimo m; (of keys) manojo m.

bundle [ˈbʌndl] n (of clothes) bulto m; (of notes, papers) fajo m.

bung [bʌŋ] n tapón m.

bungalow [ˈbʌŋgələʊ] n bungalow m.

bunion [ˈbʌnjən] n juanete m.

bunk [bʌŋk] n litera f.

bunk bed n litera f.

bunker [ˈbʌŋkər] n (shelter) búnquer m; (for coal) carbonera f; (in golf) búnker m.

bunny ['bʌnɪ] n conejito m.

buoy [Br bɔɪ, Am 'buːɪ] n boya f.

buoyant ['bɔɪənt] adj (that floats) boyante.

BUPA ['buːpə] n seguro médico privado en Gran Bretaña.

burden ['bɜːdn] n carga f.

bureaucracy [bjʊə'rɒkrəsɪ] n burocracia f.

bureau de change [,bjʊərəʊdə'ʃɒndʒ] n caja f de cambio.

burger ['bɜːgə'] n (hamburger) hamburguesa f; (made with nuts, vegetables etc) hamburguesa vegetariana.

burglar ['bɜːglə'] n ladrón m (-ona f).

burglar alarm n alarma f antirrobo.

burglarize ['bɜːgləraɪz] (Am) = **burgle**.

burglary ['bɜːglərɪ] n robo m (de una casa).

burgle ['bɜːgl] vt robar (una casa).

burial ['berɪəl] n entierro m.

burn [bɜːn] (pt & pp burnt OR burned) n quemadura f ◆ vt quemar ◆ vi (be on fire) arder; to ~ one's hand quemarse la mano ❑ **burn down** vt sep incendiar ◆ vi incendiarse.

burning (hot) ['bɜːnɪŋ-] adj muy caliente.

Burns' Night ['bɜːnz-] n el 25 de enero.

burnt [bɜːnt] pt & pp → burn

burp [bɜːp] vi (inf) eructar.

burrow ['bʌrəʊ] n madriguera f.

burst [bɜːst] (pt & pp burst) n (of gunfire, applause) estallido m ◆ vt & vi reventar; **he ~ into the room** irrumpió en la habitación; **to ~ into tears** romper a llorar; **to ~ open** (door) abrirse de golpe.

bury ['berɪ] vt enterrar.

bus [bʌs] n autobús m; **by ~** en autobús.

bus conductor [-,kən'dʌktə'] n cobrador m (-ra f) de autobús.

bus driver n conductor m (-ra f) de autobús.

bush [bʊʃ] n arbusto m.

business ['bɪznɪs] n (commerce) negocios mpl; (shop, firm, trade) negocio m; (things to do) asuntos mpl, tareas fpl; (affair) asunto m; **mind your own ~!** ¡no te metas donde no te llaman!; **"~ as usual"** "abierto como de costumbre".

business card n tarjeta f de visita.

business class n clase f preferente.

business hours *npl* horario *m* de apertura.

businessman ['bɪznɪsmæn] (*pl* -**men** [-men]) *n* hombre *m* de negocios.

business studies *npl* empresariales *fpl*.

businesswoman ['bɪznɪs,wʊmən] (*pl* -**women** [-,wɪmɪn]) *n* mujer *f* de negocios.

busker ['bʌskəʳ] *n* (*Br*) músico *m* callejero (música *f* callejera).

bus lane *n* carril *m* de autobús.

bus pass *n* abono *m* (de autobús).

bus shelter *n* marquesina *f* (de parada de autobús).

bus station *n* estación *f* de autobuses.

bus stop *n* parada *f* de autobús.

bust [bʌst] *n* (*of woman*) busto *m* ♦ *adj*: **to go ~** (*inf*) quebrar.

bustle ['bʌsl] *n* bullicio *m*.

bus tour *n* excursión *f* (en autobús).

busy ['bɪzɪ] *adj* (*person, telephone, line*) ocupado(-da); (*day*) ajetreado(-da); (*schedule*) lleno(-na); (*street, office*) concurrido(-da); **to be ~ doing sthg** estar ocupado haciendo algo.

busy signal *n* (*Am*) señal *f* de comunicando.

but [bʌt] *conj* pero ♦ *prep* menos; **not just one ~ two** no uno sino dos; **you've done nothing ~ moan** no has hecho más que quejarte; **the last ~ one** el penúltimo; **~ for** de no ser por.

butcher ['bʊtʃəʳ] *n* carnicero *m*

(-ra *f*); **~'s** (*shop*) carnicería *f*.

butt [bʌt] *n* (*of rifle*) culata *f*; (*of cigarette, cigar*) colilla *f*.

butter ['bʌtəʳ] *n* mantequilla *f* ♦ *vt* untar con mantequilla.

butter bean *n* judía *f* blanca.

buttercup ['bʌtəkʌp] *n* ranúnculo *m*.

butterfly ['bʌtəflaɪ] *n* mariposa *f*.

butterscotch ['bʌtəskɒtʃ] *n* dulce hecho hirviendo azúcar y mantequilla.

buttocks ['bʌtəks] *npl* nalgas *fpl*.

button ['bʌtn] *n* (*on clothing, machine*) botón *m*; (*Am: badge*) chapa *f*.

buttonhole ['bʌtnhəʊl] *n* (*hole*) ojal *m*.

button mushroom *n* champiñón *m* pequeño.

buttress ['bʌtrɪs] *n* contrafuerte *m*.

buy [baɪ] (*pt & pp* **bought**) *vt* comprar ♦ *n*: **a good ~** una buena compra; **to ~ sthg for sb, to ~ sb sthg** comprar algo a alguien; **to ~ sthg from sb** comprar algo a alguien.

buzz [bʌz] *vi* zumbar ♦ *n* (*inf: phone call*): **to give sb a ~** dar un telefonazo a alguien.

buzzer ['bʌzəʳ] *n* timbre *m*.

by [baɪ] *prep* **1.** (*expressing cause, agent*) por; **funded ~ the government** subvencionado por el gobierno; **a book ~ Joyce** un libro de Joyce.
2. (*expressing method, means*): **car/train/plane** en coche/tren/

avión; **~ post/phone** por correo/teléfono; **to pay ~ credit card** pagar con tarjeta de crédito; **to win ~ cheating** ganar haciendo trampa.

3. *(near to, beside)* junto a; **~ the sea** junto al mar.

4. *(past)* por delante de; **a car went ~ the house** pasó un coche por delante de la casa.

5. *(via)* por; **exit ~ the door on the left** salgan por la puerta a la izquierda.

6. *(with time)* para; **be there ~ nine** estate allí para las nueve; **~ day/night** de día/noche; **~ now** ya.

7. *(expressing quantity)* por; **prices fell ~ 20%** los precios bajaron en un 20%; **we charge ~ the hour** cobramos por horas.

8. *(expressing meaning)* por; **what do you mean ~ that?** ¿qué quieres decir con eso?

9. *(in division, multiplication)* por; **two metres ~ five** dos metros por cinco.

10 *(according to)* según; **~ law** según la ley; **it's fine ~ me** por mí no hay problema.

11. *(expressing gradual process)*: **one ~ one** uno a uno; **day ~ day** día a día.

12. *(in phrases):* **~ mistake** por equivocación; **~ oneself** *(alone)* solo; **he did it ~ himself** lo hizo él solo; **~ profession** de profesión.

♦ *adv (past).* **to go/drive ~** pasar.

bye(-bye) [baı(baı)] *excl (inf)* ¡hasta luego!

bypass ['baıpɑːs] *n* carretera *f* de circunvalación.

C *(abbr of Celsius, centigrade)* C.

cab [kæb] *n (taxi)* taxi *m*; *(of lorry)* cabina *f*.

cabaret ['kæbəreı] *n* cabaret *m*.

cabbage ['kæbɪdʒ] *n* col *f*.

cabin ['kæbɪn] *n (on ship)* camarote *m*; *(of plane)* cabina *f*; *(wooden house)* cabaña *f*.

cabin crew *n* personal *m* de cabina.

cabinet ['kæbɪnɪt] *n (cupboard)* armario *m*; *(POL)* consejo *m* de ministros.

cable ['keɪbl] *n* cable *m*.

cable car *n* teleférico *m*.

cable television *n* televisión *f* por cable.

cactus ['kæktəs] *(pl* **-tuses** OR **-ti** [-taı]*) n* cactus *m inv*.

Caesar salad [ˌsiːzə-] *n* ensalada verde con anchoas, aceitunas, queso parmesano y croutons.

cafe ['kæfeı] *n* cafetería *f*.

cafeteria [ˌkæfɪ'tɪərɪə] *n* cantina *f*.

cafetière [kæf'tjeə^r] *n* cafetera *f* de émbolo.

caffeine ['kæfiːn] *n* cafeína *f*.

cage [keɪdʒ] *n* jaula *f*.

cagoule [kə'guːl] *n (Br)* chubasquero *m*.

Cajun ['keɪdʒən] *adj* cajún.

Originariamente colonos franceses en Nueva Escocia, la comunidad cajún fue deportada a Luisiana en el siglo XVIII. Allí desarrollaron una lengua y cultura propia cuya cocina, caracterizada por el uso de especias picantes, es hoy muy conocida, así como la música popular cajún que hace uso prominente del violín y acordeón.

cake [keɪk] *n* (sweet) pastel *m*; (savoury) medallón *m* empanado; (of soap) pastilla *f*.

calculate ['kælkjʊleɪt] *vt* calcular.

calculator ['kælkjʊleɪtər] *n* calculadora *f*.

calendar ['kælɪndər] *n* calendario *m*.

calf [kɑːf] (*pl* calves) *n* (of cow) ternero *m* (-ra *f*); (part of leg) pantorrilla *f*.

call [kɔːl] *n* (visit) visita *f*; (phone call, at airport) llamada *f*; (of bird) reclamo *m* ◆ *vt* llamar; (meeting, elections, strike) convocar; (flight) anunciar ◆ *vi* (phone) llamar; **to ~ at** (visit) pasarse (por); **to be ~ed** llamarse; **what is he ~ed?** ¿cómo se llama?; **could I have a ~ for eight o'clock?** por favor, llámeme a las ocho; **on ~** (nurse, doctor) de guardia; **she ~ed my name** me llamó; **to pay sb a ~** hacer una visita a alguien; **this train ~s at ...** este tren para en ...; **who's ~ing?** ¿de parte de quién? ❑ **call back** *vt sep* llamar (más tarde) ◆ *vi* (phone again) llamar (más tarde); (visit again) volver a pasarse; **call for** *vt fus* (come to fetch) ir a buscar; (demand) pedir; (require) requerir; **call on** *vt fus* (visit) visitar; **to ~ on sb to do sthg** pedir a alguien que haga algo; **call out** *vt sep* (name, winner) anunciar; (doctor, fire brigade) llamar ◆ *vi* gritar; **call up** *vt sep* (MIL) llamar a filas a; (telephone) llamar (por teléfono).

call box *n* cabina *f* telefónica.

caller ['kɔːlər] *n* (visitor) visita *f*; (on phone) persona *f* que llama.

calm [kɑːm] *adj* (person) tranquilo(-la); (sea) en calma; (weather, day) apacible ◆ *vt* calmar ❑ **calm down** *vt sep* calmar ◆ *vi* calmarse.

Calor gas® ['kælə-] *n* butano *m*.

calorie ['kælərɪ] *n* caloría *f*.

calves [kɑːvz] *pl* → **calf**.

camcorder ['kæm,kɔːdər] *n* cámara *f* de vídeo.

came [keɪm] *pt* → **come**.

camel ['kæml] *n* camello *m*.

camembert ['kæməmbeər] *n* camembert *m*.

camera ['kæmərə] *n* cámara *f*.

cameraman ['kæmərəmæn] (*pl* -men [-men]) *n* cámara *m*.

camera shop *n* tienda *f* de fotografía.

camisole ['kæmɪsəʊl] *n* picardías *m inv*.

camp [kæmp] *n* (for holidaymakers) colonia de vacaciones para toda la familia, un parque de atracciones, etc; (for soldiers) campamento *m*; (for prisoners) campo *m* ◆ *vi* acampar.

campaign [kæmˈpeɪn] n campaña f ◆ vi: **to ~ (for/against)** hacer campaña (a favor de/contra).

camp bed n cama f de campaña.

camper [ˈkæmpəʳ] n (person) campista mf; (van) caravana f.

camping [ˈkæmpɪŋ] n: **to go ~** ir de camping.

camping stove n cocina f de camping.

campsite [ˈkæmpsaɪt] n camping m.

campus [ˈkæmpəs] (pl -es) n campus m inv.

can[1] [kæn] n (container) lata f.

can[2] [weak form kən, strong form kæn] (pt & conditional **could**) aux vb
1. (be able to) poder; **~ you help me?** ¿puedes ayudarme?; **I ~ see** the sea veo el mar.
2. (know how to) saber; **~ you drive?** ¿sabes conducir?; **I ~ speak Spanish** hablo español.
3. (be allowed to) poder; **~ I speak to the manager?** ¿puedo hablar con el director?
4. (in polite requests) poder; **~ you tell me the time?** ¿me puedes decir la hora?
5. (expressing occasional occurrence): **it ~ get cold at night** a veces hace frío por la noche.
6. (expressing possibility) poder; **I could do it** podría hacerlo; **they could be lost** puede que se hayan perdido.

Canada [ˈkænədə] n Canadá.

Canadian [kəˈneɪdjən] adj canadiense ◆ n canadiense f.

canal [kəˈnæl] n canal m.

canapé [ˈkænəpeɪ] n canapé m.

Canaries [kəˈneərɪz] npl: **the ~** (las islas) Canarias.

Canary Islands [kəˈneərɪ-] npl: **the ~** (las islas) Canarias.

cancel [ˈkænsl] vt cancelar.

cancellation [ˌkænsəˈleɪʃn] n cancelación f.

cancer [ˈkænsəʳ] n cáncer m.

Cancer [ˈkænsəʳ] n Cáncer m.

candidate [ˈkændɪdət] n (for parliament, job) candidato m (-ta f); (in exam) examinando m (-da f).

candle [ˈkændl] n vela f.

candlelit dinner [ˈkændlɪt-] n cena f a la luz de las velas.

candy [ˈkændɪ] n (Am) (confectionery) golosinas fpl; (sweet) caramelo m.

candyfloss [ˈkændɪflɒs] n (Br) algodón m (de azúcar).

cane [keɪn] n (for walking) bastón m; (for punishment) vara f; (for furniture, baskets) caña f.

canister [ˈkænɪstəʳ] n (for tea) bote m; (for gas) bombona f.

cannabis [ˈkænəbɪs] n canabis m.

canned [kænd] adj (food, drink) en lata.

cannon [ˈkænən] n cañón m.

cannot [ˈkænɒt] = can not.

canoe [kəˈnuː] n (SPORT) piragua f.

canoeing [kəˈnuːɪŋ] n piragüismo m.

canopy [ˈkænəpɪ] n (over bed etc) dosel m.

can't [kɑːnt] = cannot.

cantaloup(e) [ˈkæntəluːp] n cantalupo m.

canteen [kænˈtiːn] n cantina f.

canvas ['kænvəs] n (for tent, bag) lona f.

cap [kæp] n (hat) gorra f; (without peak) gorro m; (of pen) capuchón m; (of bottle) tapón m; (contraceptive) diafragma m.

capable ['keɪpəbl] adj (competent) competente, hábil; **to be ~ of doing sthg** ser capaz de hacer algo.

capacity [kə'pæsɪti] n (ability) habilidad f, facultad f; (of stadium, theatre) capacidad f.

cape [keɪp] n (of land) cabo m; (cloak) capa f.

capers ['keɪpəz] npl alcaparras fpl.

capital ['kæpɪtl] n (of country) capital f; (money) capital m; (letter) mayúscula f.

capital punishment n pena f capital.

cappuccino [ˌkæpʊ'tʃiːnəʊ] n capuchino m.

capsicum ['kæpsɪkəm] n pimiento m.

capsize [kæp'saɪz] vi volcar.

capsule ['kæpsjuːl] n cápsula f.

captain ['kæptɪn] n capitán m (-ana f).

caption ['kæpʃn] n pie m, leyenda f.

capture ['kæptʃəᵊ] vt (person, animal) capturar; (town, castle) tomar.

car [kɑːᵊ] n (motorcar) coche m, carro m (Amér); (railway wagon) vagón m.

carafe [kə'ræf] n vasija sin mango para servir vino y agua.

caramel ['kærəmel] n (sweet) tofe m; (burnt sugar) azúcar m quemado.

carat ['kærət] n quilate m; **24-~**

gold oro de 24 quilates.

caravan ['kærəvæn] n (Br) caravana f.

caravanning ['kærəvænɪŋ] n (Br): **to go ~** ir de vacaciones en caravana.

caravan site n (Br) camping m para caravanas.

carbohydrate [ˌkɑːbəʊ'haɪdreɪt] n (in foods) fécula f.

carbon ['kɑːbən] n carbono m.

carbon copy n copia f en papel carbón.

carbon dioxide [-daɪ'ɒksaɪd] n dióxido m de carbono.

carbon monoxide [-mɒ'nɒksaɪd] n monóxido m de carbono.

car boot sale n (Br) mercadillo de objetos usados exhibidos en el maletero del coche.

carburetor [ˌkɑːbə'retər] (Am) = **carburettor**.

carburettor [ˌkɑːbə'retəᵊ] n (Br) carburador m.

car crash n accidente m de tráfico.

card [kɑːd] n tarjeta f; (postcard) postal f; (playing card) carta f, naipe m; (cardboard) cartulina f; **~s** (game) las cartas.

cardboard ['kɑːdbɔːd] n cartón m.

car deck n cubierta f para coches.

cardiac arrest [ˌkɑːdɪæk-] n paro m cardíaco.

cardigan ['kɑːdɪgən] n cárdigan m.

care [keəᵊ] n (attention) cuidado m ◆ vi (mind): **I don't ~** no me importa; **to take ~ of** *(look after)* cuidar de; *(deal with)* encargarse de; **would you ~ to …?** *(fml)* ¿le importaría …?; **to take ~ to do sthg** tener cuidado de hacer algo; **take ~!** *(good-bye)* ¡cuídate!; **with ~** con cuidado; **"handle with ~"** "frágil"; **to ~ about** *(think important)* preocuparse por; *(person)* tener aprecio a.

career [kəˈrɪəʳ] *n* carrera *f*.

carefree [ˈkeəfriː] *adj* despreocupado(-da).

careful [ˈkeəfʊl] *adi (cautious)* cuidadoso(-sa); *(driver)* prudente; *(thorough)* esmerado(-da); **be ~!** ¡ten cuidado!

carefully [ˈkeəflɪ] *adv (cautiously)* cuidadosamente; *(drive)* con prudencia; *(thoroughly)* detenidamente, con atención.

careless [ˈkeələs] *adj (inattentive)* descuidado(-da); *(unconcerned)* despreocupado(-da).

caretaker [ˈkeəˌteɪkəʳ] *n (Br: of school, flats)* conserje *mf*.

car ferry *n* transbordador *m* de coches.

cargo [ˈkɑːgəʊ] *(pl* -es OR -s) *n* cargamento *m*.

car hire *n (Br)* alquiler *m* de coches.

Caribbean [Br ˌkærɪˈbiːən, Am kəˈrɪbɪən] *n:* **the ~** el Caribe.

caring [ˈkeərɪŋ] *adj* solícito(-ta).

carnation [kɑːˈneɪʃn] *n* clavel *m*.

carnival [ˈkɑːnɪvl] *n* carnaval *m*.

carousel [ˌkærəˈsel] *n (for luggage)* cinta *f* transportadora; *(Am: merry-go-round)* tiovivo *m*.

carp [kɑːp] *n* carpa *f*.

car park *n (Br)* aparcamiento *m*.

carpenter [ˈkɑːpəntəʳ] *n* carpintero *m* (-ra *f*).

carpentry [ˈkɑːpəntrɪ] *n* carpintería *f*.

carpet [ˈkɑːpɪt] *n (not fitted)* alfombra *f*; *(fitted)* moqueta *f*.

car rental *n (Am)* alquiler *m* de coches.

carriage [ˈkærɪdʒ] *n (Br: of train)* vagón *m*; *(horse-drawn)* carruaje *m*.

carriageway [ˈkærɪdʒweɪ] *n (Br)* carril *m*.

carrier (bag) [ˈkærɪəʳ-] *n* bolsa *f* (de papel o plástico).

carrot [ˈkærət] *n* zanahoria *f*.

carrot cake *n* pastel de bizcocho hecho con zanahoria rallada y cubierto con azúcar glaseado.

carry [ˈkærɪ] *vt* llevar; *(disease)* transmitir ◆ *vi (voice, sound)* oírse a lo lejos ❑ **carry on** *vi* continuar ◆ *vt fus (continue)* continuar; *(conduct)* realizar; **to ~ on doing sthg** seguir haciendo algo; **carry out** *vt sep (perform)* llevar a cabo; *(fulfil)* cumplir.

carrycot [ˈkærɪkɒt] *n (Br)* moisés *m inv*.

carryout [ˈkærɪaʊt] *n (Am & Scot)* comida *f* para llevar.

carsick [ˈkɑːˌsɪk] *adj* mareado(-da) *(en coche)*.

cart [kɑːt] *n (for transport)* carro *m*; *(inf: video game cartridge)* cartucho *m*; *(Am: in supermarket)* carrito *m*.

carton [ˈkɑːtn] *n* cartón *m*, envase *m*.

cartoon [kɑːˈtuːn] *n (drawing)* chiste *m* (en viñeta); *(film)* película *f* de dibujos animados.

cartridge ['kɑːtrɪdʒ] *n* (for gun) cartucho *m*; (for pen) recambio *m*.

carve [kɑːv] *vt* (wood, stone) tallar; (meat) trinchar.

carvery ['kɑːvərɪ] *n* restaurante donde se sirve un bufé de carne que se trincha delante del cliente.

car wash *n* lavado *m* de coches.

case [keɪs] *n* (Br: suitcase) maleta *f*; (container) estuche *m*; (instance, patient) caso *m*; (JUR: trial) pleito *m*; **in any ~** de todas formas; **in ~ of** en caso de; **(just) in ~** por si acaso; **in that ~** en ese caso.

cash [kæʃ] *n* (coins, notes) efectivo *m*; (money in general) dinero *m* ◆ *vt*: **to ~ a cheque** cobrar un cheque; **to pay ~** pagar en efectivo.

cash desk *n* caja *f*.

cash dispenser *n* cajero *m* automático.

cashew (nut) ['kæʃuː-] *n* anacardo *m*.

cashier [kæ'ʃɪəʳ] *n* cajero *m* (-ra *f*).

cashmere [kæʃ'mɪəʳ] *n* cachemir *m*.

cashpoint ['kæʃpɔɪnt] *n* (Br) cajero *m* automático.

cash register *n* caja *f* (registradora).

casino [kə'siːnəʊ] *n* (*pl* **-s**) casino *m*.

cask [kɑːsk] *n* tonel *m*.

cask-conditioned [-kən'dɪʃnd] *adj* fermentado en tonel.

casserole ['kæsərəʊl] *n* (stew) guiso *m*; **~ (dish)** cacerola *f*.

cassette [kə'set] *n* casete *m*, cinta *f*.

cassette recorder *n* casete *m*.

cast [kɑːst] (*pt* & *pp* **cast**) *n* (actors) reparto *m*; (for broken bone) escayola *f* ◆ *vt* (shadow, light) proyectar; (look) echar; (vote) emitir; **to ~ doubt on** poner en duda ◻ **cast off** *vi* (boat, ship) soltar amarras.

caster ['kɑːstəʳ] *n* ruedecilla *f*.

caster sugar *n* (Br) azúcar *m* extrafino.

Castile [kæs'tiːl] *n* Castilla.

castle ['kɑːsl] *n* (building) castillo *m*; (in chess) torre *f*.

casual ['kæʒʊəl] *adj* (relaxed) despreocupado(-da); (offhand) superficial; (clothes) informal; **~ work** trabajo eventual.

casualty ['kæʒjʊəltɪ] *n* víctima *f*; **~ (ward)** urgencias *fpl*.

cat [kæt] *n* gato *m*.

Catalan ['kætəlæn] *adj* catalán(-ana) ◆ *n* (person) catalán *m* (-ana *f*); (language) catalán *m*.

catalog ['kætəlɒg] (Am) = **catalogue**.

catalogue ['kætəlɒg] *n* catálogo *m*.

Catalonia [,kætə'ləʊnɪə] *n* Cataluña.

Catalonian [,kætə'ləʊnɪən] *adj* catalán(-ana).

catapult ['kætəpʌlt] *n* tirachinas *m inv*.

cataract ['kætərækt] *n* (in eye) catarata *f*.

catarrh [kə'tɑːʳ] *n* catarro *m*.

catastrophe [kə'tæstrəfɪ] *n* catástrofe *f*.

catch [kætʃ] (*pt* & *pp* **caught**) *vt*

coger, agarrar *(Amér)*; *(fish)* pescar; *(bus, train, plane, taxi)* coger, tomar *(Amér)*; *(hear)* coger, escuchar *(Amér)*; *(attract)* despertar ◆ *vi (become hooked)* engancharse ◆ *n (of window, door)* pestillo *m*; *(snag)* pega *f* ❑ **catch up** *vt sep* alcanzar ◆ *vi:* **to ~ up (with)** ponerse a la misma altura (que).

catching ['kætʃɪŋ] *adj (inf)* contagioso(-sa).

category ['kætəgərɪ] *n* categoría *f*.

cater for ['keɪtəf] **: cater for** *vt fus (Br) (needs, tastes)* atender a, satisfacer; *(anticipate)* contar con.

caterpillar ['kætəpɪləʳ] *n* oruga *f*.

cathedral [kə'θiːdrəl] *n* catedral *f*.

Catholic ['kæθlɪk] *adj* católico(-ca) ◆ *n* católico *m* (-ca *f*).

Catseyes® ['kætsaɪz] *npl (Br)* catafaros *mpl*.

cattle ['kætl] *npl* ganado *m* (vacuno).

caught [kɔːt] *pt & pp* → **catch**.

cauliflower ['kɒlɪflaʊəʳ] *n* coliflor *f*.

cauliflower cheese *n* coliflor *en salsa bechamel con queso*.

cause [kɔːz] *n* causa *f*; *(justification)* motivo *m* ◆ *vt* causar; **to ~ sb to do sthg** hacer que alguien haga algo.

causeway ['kɔːzweɪ] *n* carretera *f* elevada.

caustic soda [,kɔːstɪk-] *n* sosa *f* cáustica.

caution ['kɔːʃn] *n (care)* cautela *f*; *(warning)* amonestación *f*.

cautious ['kɔːʃəs] *adj* cauteloso(-sa).

cave [keɪv] *n* cueva *f* ❑ **cave in** *vi* hundirse, derrumbarse.

caviar(e) ['kævɪɑːʳ] *n* caviar *m*.

cavity ['kævətɪ] *n (in tooth)* caries *f inv*.

CD *n (abbr of compact disc)* CD *m*.

CDI *n (abbr of compact disc interactive)* CDI *m*.

CD player *n* reproductor *m* de CD.

CDW *n (abbr of collision damage waiver)* franquicia *f*.

cease [siːs] *vt (fml)* suspender ◆ *vi (fml)* cesar.

ceasefire ['siːsˌfaɪəʳ] *n* alto *m* el fuego.

ceilidh ['keɪlɪ] *n* baile popular en Escocia e Irlanda.

---

i CEILIDH

El "ceilidh" es un espectáculo tradicional escocés o irlandés de carácter informal que consiste en bailes y música popular. Tradicionalmente, un "ceilidh" era una pequeña reunión de amigos y familiares, pero hoy en día son normalmente grandes bailes públicos.

---

ceiling ['siːlɪŋ] *n* techo *m*.

celebrate ['selɪbreɪt] *vt* celebrar ◆ *vi:* **let's ~** ¡hay que celebrarlo!

celebration [,selɪ'breɪʃn] *n (event)* festejo *m* ❑ **celebrations** *npl (festivities)* conmemoraciones *fpl*.

celebrity [sɪ'lebrətɪ] *n (person)*

celebridad f.

celeriac [sɪˈleriæk] n apio m nabo.

celery [ˈselərɪ] n apio m.

cell [sel] n (of plant, body) célula f; (in prison) celda f.

cellar [ˈselər] n sótano m.

cello [ˈtʃeləʊ] n violoncelo m.

Cellophane® [ˈseləfeɪn] n celofán® m.

Celsius [ˈselsɪəs] adj centígrado(-da).

cement [sɪˈment] n cemento m.

cement mixer n hormigonera f.

cemetery [ˈsemɪtrɪ] n cementerio m.

cent [sent] n (Am) centavo m.

center [ˈsentər] (Am) = **centre**.

centigrade [ˈsentɪɡreɪd] adj centígrado(-da); **five degrees ~** cinco grados (centígrados).

centimetre [ˈsentɪˌmiːtər] n centímetro m.

centipede [ˈsentɪpiːd] n ciempiés m inv.

central [ˈsentrəl] adj (in the middle) central; (near town centre) céntrico(-ca).

central heating n calefacción f central.

central locking [-ˈlɒkɪŋ] n cierre m centralizado.

central reservation n (Br) mediana f.

centre [ˈsentər] n (Br) centro m ◆ adj (Br) central; **the ~ of attention** el centro de atención.

century [ˈsentʃʊrɪ] n siglo m.

ceramic [sɪˈræmɪk] adj de cerámica ❑ **ceramics** npl piezas fpl de

cerámica.

cereal [ˈsɪərɪəl] n (breakfast food) cereales mpl.

ceremony [ˈserɪmənɪ] n ceremonia f.

certain [ˈsɜːtn] adj (sure) seguro(-ra); (particular) cierto(-ta); **she's ~ to be late** seguro que llega tarde; **to be ~ of sthg** estar seguro de algo; **to make ~ (that)** asegurarse de que.

certainly [ˈsɜːtnlɪ] adv desde luego.

certificate [səˈtɪfɪkət] n (of studies, medical) certificado m; (of birth) partida f.

certify [ˈsɜːtɪfaɪ] vt (declare true) certificar.

chain [tʃeɪn] n cadena f ◆ vt: **to ~ sthg to sthg** encadenar algo a algo.

chain store n grandes almacenes mpl.

chair [tʃeər] n silla f.

chair lift n telesilla m.

chairman [ˈtʃeəmən] (pl -men [-mən]) n presidente m.

chairperson [ˈtʃeəˌpɜːsn] n presidente m (-ta f).

chairwoman [ˈtʃeəˌwʊmən] (pl -women [-ˌwɪmɪn]) n presidenta f.

chalet [ˈʃæleɪ] n chalé m.

chalk [tʃɔːk] n (for writing) tiza f; (substance) creta f; **a piece of ~** una tiza.

chalkboard [ˈtʃɔːkbɔːd] n (Am) pizarra f.

challenge [ˈtʃælɪndʒ] n desafío m ◆ vt (question) poner en tela de juicio; **to ~ sb (to sthg)** desafiar a alguien (a algo).

chamber [ˈtʃeɪmbər] n (room)

cámara f.

chambermaid ['tʃeɪmbəmeɪd] n camarera f.

champagne [ʃæm'peɪn] n champán m.

champion ['tʃæmpjən] n (of competition) campeón m (-ona f).

championship ['tʃæmpjənʃɪp] n campeonato m.

chance [tʃɑːns] n (luck) azar m; (possibility) posibilidad f; (opportunity) oportunidad f ◆ vt: to ~ it (inf) arriesgarse; **to take a** ~ correr un riesgo; **by** ~ por casualidad, on off the ~ por si acaso.

Chancellor of the Exchequer [,tʃɑːnsələrəvðəɪks'tʃekəʳ] n ministro de economía y hacienda en Gran Bretaña.

chandelier [,ʃændəˈlɪəʳ] n lámpara f de araña.

change [tʃeɪndʒ] n cambio m; (coins) suelto m ◆ vt cambiar; (on bus, train) hacer transbordo; (change clothes) cambiarse; a ~ **of clothes** una muda; **do you have** ~ **for a pound?** ¿tienes cambio de una libra?; **for a** ~ para variar; **to get** ~d cambiarse; **to** ~ **money** cambiar dinero; **to** ~ **a nappy** cambiar un pañal; **to** ~ **a wheel** cambiar una rueda; **to** ~ **trains/planes** cambiar de tren/avión; **all** ~! (on train) ¡cambio de tren!

changeable ['tʃeɪndʒəbl] adj (weather) variable.

change machine n máquina f de cambio.

changing room ['tʃeɪndʒɪŋ-] n (for sport) vestuario m; (in shop) probador m.

channel ['tʃænl] n canal m; **the (English) Channel** el Canal de la Mancha.

Channel Islands npl: **the** ~ las islas del Canal de la Mancha.

Channel Tunnel n: **the** ~ el túnel del Canal de la Mancha.

---

i	CHANNEL TUNNEL

La conexión férrea entre Cheriton (cerca de Folkestone) y Coquelles (cerca de Calais) a través del Eurotúnel se abrió en 1994. Un tren de carga, Le Shuttle, transporta los vehículos y frecuentes trenes para pasajeros conectan Londres con otras ciudades europeas.

---

chant [tʃɑːnt] vt (RELIG) cantar; (words, slogan) corear.

chaos ['keɪɒs] n caos m inv.

chaotic [keɪˈɒtɪk] adj caótico(-ca).

chap [tʃæp] n (Br: inf) chico m, tío m.

chapatti [tʃəˈpætɪ] n tipo de pan ázimo de origen indio.

chapel ['tʃæpl] n capilla f.

chapped [tʃæpt] adj agrietado(-da).

chapter ['tʃæptəʳ] n capítulo m.

character ['kærəktəʳ] n carácter m; (in film, book, play) personaje m; (inf: person, individual) tipo m.

characteristic [,kærəktəˈrɪstɪk] adj característico(-ca) ◆ n característica f.

charcoal ['tʃɑːkəʊl] n (for barbecue) carbón m (vegetal).

charge [tʃɑːdʒ] *n (price)* tarifa *f;* *(JUR)* cargo *m* ♦ *vt (money, customer)* cobrar; *(JUR)* acusar; *(battery)* cargar ♦ *vi (ask money)* cobrar; **she ~d** in entró en tromba; **to be in ~ (of)** ser el encargado (de); **to take ~ (of)** hacerse cargo (de); **extra ~** suplemento *m;* **free of ~** gratis; **there is no ~ for service** el servicio está incluido.

char-grilled [tʃɑːgrɪld] *adj* asado(-da) a la parrilla.

charity [tʃærətɪ] *n (organization)* entidad *f* benéfica; **to give to ~** hacer donaciones a entidades benéficas.

charity shop *n* tienda de objetos usados cuyas ventas se destinan a entidades benéficas.

charm [tʃɑːm] *n (attractiveness)* encanto *m* ♦ *vt* encantar, hechizar.

charming [tʃɑːmɪŋ] *adj* encantador(-ra).

chart [tʃɑːt] *n (diagram)* gráfico *m;* **the ~s** la lista de éxitos.

chartered accountant [ˌtʃɑːtəd-] *n* contable *m* colegiado (contable *f* colegiada).

charter flight [tʃɑːtə-] *n* vuelo *m* chárter.

chase [tʃeɪs] *n* persecución *f* ♦ *vt* perseguir.

chat [tʃæt] *n* charla *f* ♦ *vi* charlar; **to have a ~ (with)** charlar (con) ❑ **chat up** *vt sep (Br: inf)* ligarse.

chat show *n (Br)* programa *m* de entrevistas.

chatty [tʃætɪ] *adj (letter)* informal; *(person)* dicharrachero(-ra).

chauffeur [ʃəʊfəʳ] *n* chófer *mf.*

cheap [tʃiːp] *adj (inexpensive)* barato(-ta); *(pej: low-quality)* de

mala calidad.

cheap day return *n (Br)* billete de ida y vuelta más barato que se ha de utilizar en el mismo día y después de las 9.15.

cheaply [tʃiːplɪ] *adv* barato.

cheat [tʃiːt] *n* tramposo *m (-sa f)* ♦ *vi* hacer trampa ♦ *vt:* **to ~ sb (out of sthg)** estafar (algo) a alguien.

check [tʃek] *n (inspection)* inspección *f;* *(Am: bill)* cuenta *f;* *(Am: tick)* señal *f* de visto bueno; *(Am)* = **cheque** ♦ *vt (inspect)* revisar; *(verify)* comprobar ♦ *vi:* **to ~ for sthg** comprobar algo; **to ~ on sthg** comprobar algo; **to ~ with sb** consultar con alguien ❑ **check in** *vt sep (luggage)* facturar ♦ *vi (at hotel)* inscribirse; *(at airport)* facturar; **check off** *vt sep* ir comprobando (en una lista); **check out** *vi* dejar el hotel; **check up** *vi:* **to ~ up (on)** informarse (acerca de).

checked [tʃekt] *adj* a cuadros.

checkers [tʃekəz] *n (Am)* damas *fpl.*

check-in desk *n* mostrador *m* de facturación.

checkout [tʃekaʊt] *n* caja *f.*

checkpoint [tʃekpɔɪnt] *n* control *m.*

checkroom [tʃekrʊm] *n (Am)* consigna *f.*

checkup [tʃekʌp] *n* chequeo *m.*

cheddar (cheese) [tʃedəʳ-] *n* cheddar *m.*

cheek [tʃiːk] *n* mejilla *f;* **what a ~!** ¡qué cara!

cheeky [tʃiːkɪ] *adj* descarado(-da).

cheer [tʃɪəʳ] n aclamación f ◆ vi gritar con entusiasmo.

cheerful ['tʃɪəful] adj alegre.

cheerio [,tʃɪərɪ'əu] excl (Br: inf) ¡hasta luego!

cheers [tʃɪəz] excl (when drinking) ¡salud!; (Br: inf: thank you) ¡gracias!

cheese [tʃiːz] n queso m.

cheeseboard ['tʃiːzbɔːd] n (cheese and biscuits) tabla f de quesos.

cheeseburger ['tʃiːz,bɜːgəʳ] n hamburguesa f de queso.

cheesecake ['tʃiːzkeik] n tarta f de queso (fresco, sin hornear).

chef [ʃef] n jefe m de cocina.

chef's special n especialidad f de la casa.

chemical ['kemikl] adj químico(-ca) ◆ n sustancia f química.

chemist ['kemist] n (Br: pharmacist) farmacéutico m (-ca f); (scientist) químico m (-ca f); ~'s (Br: shop) farmacia f.

chemistry ['kemistri] n química f.

cheque [tʃek] n (Br) cheque m; **to pay by ~** pagar con cheque.

chequebook ['tʃekbuk] n talonario m de cheques.

cheque card n tarjeta f de identificación bancaria.

cherry ['tʃeri] n cereza f.

chess [tʃes] n ajedrez m.

chest [tʃest] n (of body) pecho m; (box) arca f.

chestnut ['tʃesnʌt] n castaña f ◆ adj (colour) castaño(-ña).

chest of drawers n cómoda f.

chew [tʃuː] vt masticar ◆ n (sweet)

gominola f.

chewing gum ['tʃuːɪn-] n chicle m.

chic [ʃiːk] adj elegante.

chicken ['tʃikɪn] n (bird) gallina f; (meat) pollo m.

chicken breast n pechuga f de pollo.

chicken Kiev [-'kiːev] n filete de pollo relleno con mantequilla, ajo y especias y rebozado con pan rallado.

chickenpox ['tʃikɪnpɒks] n varicela f.

chickpea ['tʃikpiː] n garbanzo m.

chicory ['tʃikəri] n achicoria f.

chief [tʃiːf] adj (highest-ranking) jefe(ta), (main) principal ◆ n jefe m (-fa f).

chiefly ['tʃiːfli] adv (mainly) principalmente; (especially) por encima de todo.

child [tʃaild] (pl children) n (young boy, girl) niño m (-ña f); (son, daughter) hijo m (-ja f).

child abuse n maltrato m de niños.

child benefit n subsidio pagado a todas las familias británicas por cada hijo.

childhood ['tʃaildhud] n infancia f.

childish ['tʃaildiʃ] adj (pej: immature) infantil.

childminder ['tʃaild,maindəʳ] n (Br) niñera f (durante el día).

children ['tʃildrən] pl → **child**.

childrenswear ['tʃildrənzweəʳ] n ropa f de niños.

child seat n asiento m de seguridad para niños.

Chile [ˈtʃɪlɪ] n Chile.

Chilean [ˈtʃɪlɪən] adj chileno(-na)
♦ n chileno m (-na f).

chill [tʃɪl] n (illness) resfriado m ♦
vt enfriar; **there's a ~ in the air**
hace un poco de fresco.

chilled [tʃɪld] adj frío(-a); "**serve
~**" "sírvase muy frío".

chilli [ˈtʃɪlɪ] (pl -ies) n (vegetable)
guindilla f; (dish) = **chilli con
carne**.

chilli con carne [-kɒnˈkɑːnɪ] n
picadillo de carne en una salsa picante
de guindilla con cebolla, tomate y
judías pintas.

chilly [ˈtʃɪlɪ] adj frío(-a).

chimney [ˈtʃɪmnɪ] n chimenea f.

chimneypot [ˈtʃɪmnɪpɒt] n
cañón m de chimenea.

chimpanzee [ˌtʃɪmpənˈziː] n
chimpancé mf.

chin [tʃɪn] n barbilla f.

china [ˈtʃaɪnə] n (material) porcelana f.

China [ˈtʃaɪnə] n la China.

Chinese [ˌtʃaɪˈniːz] adj chino(-na)
♦ n (language) chino m ♦ npl: **the ~**
los chinos; **a ~ restaurant** un restaurante chino.

chip [tʃɪp] n (small piece) pedacito
m; (mark) mella f; (counter) ficha f;
(COMPUT) chip m ♦ vt desportillar ❏
chips npl (Br: French fries) patatas
fpl fritas (de sartén) ; (Am: crisps)
patatas fpl fritas (de bolsa).

chiropodist [kɪˈrɒpədɪst] n
podólogo m (-ga f).

chisel [ˈtʃɪzl] n formón m.

chives [tʃaɪvz] npl cebollino m.

chlorine [ˈklɔːriːn] n cloro m.

choc-ice [ˈtʃɒkaɪs] n (Br) tipo de

bombón helado en forma de bloque y
sin palo.

chocolate [ˈtʃɒkələt] n (food,
drink) chocolate m; (sweet) bombón m ♦ adj de chocolate.

chocolate biscuit n galleta f
de chocolate.

choice [tʃɔɪs] n (option) elección f;
(person or thing chosen) opción f;
(variety) variedad f ♦ adj de primera calidad; "**pizzas with the topping of your ~**" "elija los ingredientes de su pizza".

choir [ˈkwaɪəʳ] n coro m.

choke [tʃəʊk] n (AUT) estárter m
♦ vt asfixiar ♦ vi (on fishbone etc)
atragantarse; (to death) asfixiarse.

cholera [ˈkɒlərə] n cólera m.

choose [tʃuːz] (pt chose, pp chosen) vt & vi elegir; **to ~ to do sthg**
decidir hacer algo.

chop [tʃɒp] n (of meat) chuleta f ♦
vt cortar ❏ **chop down** vt sep talar;
chop up vt sep picar.

chopper [ˈtʃɒpəʳ] n (inf: helicopter) helicóptero m.

chopping board [ˈtʃɒpɪŋ-] n
tabla f de cocina.

choppy [ˈtʃɒpɪ] adj picado(-da).

chopsticks [ˈtʃɒpstɪks] npl
palillos mpl (chinos).

chop suey [ˌtʃɒpˈsuːɪ] n plato
chino de brotes de soja, verdura, arroz
y carne de cerdo o pollo con salsa de
soja.

chord [kɔːd] n acorde m.

chore [tʃɔːʳ] n tarea f.

chorus [ˈkɔːrəs] n (part of song)
estribillo m; (group of singers, dancers)
coro m.

chose [tʃəʊz] pt → **choose**.

chosen ['tʃəʊzn] pp → choose.

choux pastry [ʃuː-] n pasta f brisa.

chowder ['tʃaʊdəʳ] n sopa espesa de pescado.

chow mein [,tʃaʊ'meɪn] n chow mein m.

Christ [kraɪst] n Cristo m.

christen ['krɪsn] vt (baby) bautizar.

Christian ['krɪstʃən] adj cristiano(-na) ♦ n cristiano m (-na f).

Christian name n nombre m de pila.

Christmas ['krɪsməs] n (day) Navidad f; (period) Navidades fpl; **Happy ~!** ¡Felices Navidades!

Christmas card n tarjeta f de Navidad.

Christmas carol [-'kærəl] n villancico m.

Christmas Day n día m de Navidad.

Christmas Eve n Nochebuena f.

Christmas pudding n pudín de frutas que se come caliente el día de Navidad.

Christmas tree n árbol m de Navidad.

chrome [krəʊm] n cromo m.

chuck [tʃʌk] vt (inf) (throw) tirar; (boyfriend, girlfriend) mandar a paseo, dejar ❑ **chuck away** vt sep tirar.

chunk [tʃʌŋk] n trozo m.

church [tʃɜːtʃ] n iglesia f; **to go to ~** ir a misa.

churchyard ['tʃɜːtʃjɑːd] n cementerio m.

chute [ʃuːt] n vertedor m.

chutney ['tʃʌtnɪ] n salsa agridulce y picante de fruta y semillas.

cider ['saɪdəʳ] n sidra f.

cigar [sɪ'gɑːʳ] n puro m.

cigarette [,sɪgə'ret] n cigarrillo m.

cigarette lighter n mechero m.

cinema ['sɪnəmə] n cine m.

cinnamon ['sɪnəmən] n canela f.

circle ['sɜːkl] n círculo m; (in theatre) anfiteatro m ♦ vt (draw circle around) rodear con un círculo; (move round) dar vueltas alrededor de ♦ vi dar vueltas.

circuit ['sɜːkɪt] n (track) circuito m; (lap) vuelta f.

circular ['sɜːkjʊləʳ] adj circular ♦ n circular f.

circulation [,sɜːkjʊ'leɪʃn] n (of blood) circulación f; (of newspaper, magazine) tirada f.

circumstances ['sɜːkəmstənsɪz] npl circunstancias fpl; **in** OR **under the ~** dadas las circunstancias.

circus ['sɜːkəs] n circo m.

cistern ['sɪstən] n (of toilet) cisterna f.

citizen ['sɪtɪzn] n (of country) ciudadano m (-na f); (of town) habitante mf.

city ['sɪtɪ] n ciudad f; **the City** la City.

city centre n centro m de la ciudad.

city hall n (Am) ayuntamiento m.

civilian [sɪ'vɪljən] n civil mf.

civilized ['sɪvɪlaɪzd] adj (society) civilizado(-da); (person, evening) agradable.

civil rights [ˌsɪvl-] *npl* derechos *mpl* civiles.

civil servant [ˌsɪvl-] *n* funcionario *m* (-ria *f*).

civil service [ˌsɪvl-] *n* administración *f* pública.

civil war [ˌsɪvl-] *n* guerra *f* civil.

cl *(abbr of centilitre)* cl.

claim [kleɪm] *n (assertion)* afirmación *f*, declaración *f*; *(demand)* demanda *f*, reivindicación *f*; *(for insurance)* reclamación *f* ♦ *vt (allege)* afirmar; *(demand)* reclamar; *(credit, responsibility)* reivindicar ♦ *vi (on insurance)* reclamar.

claimant [ˈkleɪmənt] *n (of benefit)* solicitante *mf*.

claim form *n* impreso *m* de solicitud.

clam [klæm] *n* almeja *f*.

clamp [klæmp] *n (for car)* cepo *m* ♦ *vt (car)* poner un cepo a.

clap [klæp] *vi* aplaudir.

claret [ˈklærət] *n* burdeos *m inv*.

clarinet [ˌklærəˈnet] *n* clarinete *m*.

clash [klæʃ] *n (noise)* estruendo *m*; *(confrontation)* enfrentamiento *m* ♦ *vi (colours)* desentonar; *(event, date)* coincidir.

clasp [klɑːsp] *n* cierre *m* ♦ *vt* agarrar.

class [klɑːs] *n* clase *f* ♦ *vt*: **to ~ sthg/sb (as)** clasificar algo/a alguien (de).

classic [ˈklæsɪk] *adj (typical)* clásico(-ca) ♦ *n* clásico *m*.

classical [ˈklæsɪkl] *adj* clásico(-ca).

classical music *n* música *f* clásica.

classification [ˌklæsɪfɪˈkeɪʃn] *n* clasificación *f*.

classified ads [ˌklæsɪfaɪd-] *npl* anuncios *mpl* por palabras.

classroom [ˈklɑːsrum] *n* aula *f*.

claustrophobic [ˌklɔːstrə-ˈfəʊbɪk] *adj* claustrofóbico(-ca).

claw [klɔː] *n (of bird, cat, dog)* garra *f*; *(of crab, lobster)* pinza *f*.

clay [kleɪ] *n* arcilla *f*.

clean [kliːn] *adj* limpio(-pia); *(page)* en blanco; *(driving licence)* sin sanciones ♦ *vt* limpiar; **to ~ one's teeth** lavarse los dientes.

cleaner [ˈkliːnəʳ] *n (person)* hombre *m* de la limpieza (mujer *f* de la limpieza); *(substance)* producto *m* de limpieza.

cleanse [klenz] *vt* limpiar.

cleanser [ˈklenzəʳ] *n* tónico *m*.

clear [klɪəʳ] *adj* claro(-ra); *(road, view, sky)* despejado(-da) ♦ *vt (remove obstructions from)* limpiar, despejar; *(jump over)* saltar; *(declare not guilty)* declarar inocente; *(authorize)* aprobar; *(cheque)* conformar ♦ *vi (weather, fog)* despejarse; **to be ~ (about sthg)** entender (algo); **to be ~ of sthg** *(not touching)* no estar en contacto con algo; **to ~ one's throat** carraspear; **to ~ the table** quitar la mesa ❑ **clear up** *vt sep (room, toys)* ordenar; *(problem, confusion)* aclarar ♦ *vi (weather)* despejarse; *(tidy up)* recoger.

clearance [ˈklɪərəns] *n (authorization)* permiso *m*; *(free distance)* distancia *f* de seguridad; *(for take-off)* autorización *f* (para despegar).

clearing [ˈklɪərɪŋ] *n* claro *m*.

clearly [ˈklɪəlɪ] *adv* claramente;

(obviously) obviamente.

clearway ['klɪəweɪ] *n* (Br) carretera donde no se puede parar.

clementine ['klemənti:n] *n* clementina *f*.

clerk [Br klɑːk, Am klɜːrk] *n* (in office) oficinista *mf*; (Am: in shop) dependiente *m* (-ta *f*).

clever ['klevə*r*] *adj* (person) listo(-ta); (idea, device) ingenioso(-sa).

click [klɪk] *n* chasquido *m* ◆ *vi* (make sound) hacer clic.

client ['klaɪənt] *n* cliente *m* (-ta *f*).

cliff [klɪf] *n* acantilado *m*.

climate ['klaɪmɪt] *n* clima *m*.

climax ['klaɪmæks] *n* clímax *m inv*.

climb [klaɪm] *vt* (tree) trepar a; (ladder) subir; (mountain) escalar ◆ *vi* (person) ascender; (plane) subir ❏ **climb down** *vt fus* (tree, mountain) descender de; (ladder) bajar ◆ *vi* bajar; **climb up** *vt fus* (tree) trepar a; (ladder) subir; (mountain) escalar.

climber ['klaɪmə*r*] *n* (person) escalador *m* (-ra *f*).

climbing ['klaɪmɪŋ] *n* montañismo *m*; **to go ~** ir de montañismo.

climbing frame *n* (Br) barras de metal para trepar los niños.

clingfilm ['klɪŋfɪlm] *n* (Br) film *m* de plástico adherente.

clinic ['klɪnɪk] *n* clínica *f*.

clip [klɪp] *n* (fastener) clip *m*; (of film, programme) fragmento *m* ◆ *vt* (fasten) sujetar; (cut) recortar; (ticket) picar.

cloak [kləʊk] *n* capa *f*.

cloakroom ['kləʊkrʊm] *n* (for coats) guardarropa *m*; (Br: toilet) servicios *mpl*.

clock [klɒk] *n* (for telling time) reloj *m*; (mileometer) cuentakilómetros *m inv*; **round the ~** día y noche.

clockwise ['klɒkwaɪz] *adv* en el sentido de las agujas del reloj.

clog [klɒg] *n* zueco *m* ◆ *vt* obstruir.

close¹ [kləʊs] *adj* (near) cercano(-na); (friend) íntimo(-ma); (relation, family) cercano(-na); (contact, cooperation, link) estrecho(-cha); (resemblance) grande; (examination) detallado(-da); (race, contest) reñido(-da) ◆ *adv* cerca; **~ by** cerca; **to (near) cerca de**; **~ to tears** a punto de llorar.

close² [kləʊz] *vt* cerrar ◆ *vi* (door, jar, eyes) cerrarse; (shop, office) cerrar; (deadline, offer, meeting) terminar ❏ **close down** *vt sep & vi* cerrar (definitivamente).

closed [kləʊzd] *adj* cerrado(-da).

closely ['kləʊslɪ] *adv* (related, involved) estrechamente; (follow, examine) atentamente.

closet ['klɒzɪt] *n* (Am: cupboard) armario *m*.

close-up ['kləʊs-] *n* primer plano *m*.

closing time ['kləʊzɪŋ-] *n* hora *f* de cierre.

clot [klɒt] *n* (of blood) coágulo *m*.

cloth [klɒθ] *n* (fabric) tela *f*; (piece of cloth) trapo *m*.

clothes [kləʊðz] *npl* ropa *f*.

clothesline ['kləʊðzlaɪn] *n* cuerda *f* para tender la ropa.

clothes peg *n* (Br) pinza *f* (para

la ropa).

clothespin [ˈkləʊðzpɪn] *(Am)* = clothes peg.

clothes shop *n* tienda *f* de ropa.

clothing [ˈkləʊðɪŋ] *n* ropa *f*.

clotted cream [ˈklɒtɪd-] *n* nata muy espesa típica de Cornualles.

cloud [klaʊd] *n* nube *f*.

cloudy [ˈklaʊdɪ] *adj (sky, day)* nublado(-da); *(liquid)* turbio(-bia).

clove [kləʊv] *n (of garlic)* diente *n* ▫ **cloves** *npl (spice)* clavos *mpl*.

clown [klaʊn] *n* payaso *m*.

club [klʌb] *n (organization)* club *m*; *(nightclub)* = sala *f* de fiestas *(abierta sólo por la noche)*; *(stick)* garrote *m* ▫ **clubs** *npl (in cards)* tréboles *mpl*.

clubbing [ˈklʌbɪŋ] *n:* **to go ~** *(inf)* ir de disco.

club class *n* clase *f* club.

club sandwich *n (Am)* sandwich *m* de tres pisos.

club soda *n (Am)* soda *f*.

clue [klu:] *n (information)* pista *f*; *(in crossword)* clave *f*; **I haven't got a ~** no tengo ni idea.

clumsy [ˈklʌmzɪ] *adj (person)* torpe.

clutch [klʌtʃ] *n (on car, motorbike)* embrague *m*; *(clutch pedal)* pedal *m* de embrague ◆ *vt* agarrar.

cm *(abbr of centimetre)* cm.

c/o *(abbr of care of)* c/d.

Co. *(abbr of company)* Cía.

coach [kəʊtʃ] *n (bus)* autocar *m*; *(of train)* vagón *m*; *(SPORT)* entrenador *m (tra f)*.

coach party *n (Br)* grupo de personas en un viaje organizado en autobús.

coach station *n* estación *f* de autocares.

coach trip *n (Br)* excursión *f* en autocar.

coal [kəʊl] *n* carbón *m*.

coal mine *n* mina *f* de carbón.

coarse [kɔ:s] *adj (rough)* áspero(-ra); *(vulgar)* ordinario(-ria).

coast [kəʊst] *n* costa *f*.

coaster [ˈkəʊstər] *n* posavasos *m inv*.

coastguard [ˈkəʊstgɑ:d] *n (person)* guardacostas *mf inv*; *(organization)* guardacostas *mpl*.

coastline [ˈkəʊstlaɪn] *n* litoral *m*.

coat [kəʊt] *n (garment)* abrigo *m*; *(of animal)* pelaje *m* ◆ *vt:* **to ~ sthg (with)** rebozar algo (en).

coat hanger *n* percha *f*.

coating [ˈkəʊtɪŋ] *n (of chocolate)* baño *m*; *(on surface)* capa *f*; **with a ~ of breadcrumbs** rebozado en pan rallado.

cobbled street [ˈkɒbld-] *n* calle *f* adoquinada.

cobbles [ˈkɒblz] *npl* adoquines *mpl*.

cobweb [ˈkɒbweb] *n* telaraña *f*.

Coca-Cola® [ˌkəʊkəˈkəʊlə] *n* Coca-Cola® *f*.

cocaine [kəʊˈkeɪn] *n* cocaína *f*.

cock [kɒk] *n (male chicken)* gallo *m*.

cock-a-leekie [ˌkɒkəˈliːkɪ] *n* sopa de pollo y puerros.

cockerel [ˈkɒkrəl] *n* gallo *m* joven.

cockles [ˈkɒklz] *npl* berberechos *mpl*.

cockpit [ˈkɒkpɪt] *n* cabina *f*.

cockroach [ˈkɒkrəʊtʃ] *n* cucaracha *f*.

cocktail [ˈkɒkteɪl] n cóctel m.

cocktail party n cóctel m.

cock-up n (Br: vulg): **to make a ~ of sthg** jorobar algo.

cocoa [ˈkəʊkəʊ] n (drink) chocolate m.

coconut [ˈkəʊkənʌt] n coco m.

cod [kɒd] (pl inv) n bacalao m.

code [kəʊd] n (system) código m; (dialling code) prefijo m.

cod-liver oil n aceite m de hígado de bacalao.

coeducational [ˌkəʊedjuːˈkeɪʃənl] adj mixto(-ta).

coffee [ˈkɒfɪ] n café m; **black/white ~** café solo/con leche; **ground/instant ~** café molido/instantáneo.

coffee bar n (Br) cafetería f (en aeropuerto, etc).

coffee break n descanso en el trabajo, por la mañana y por la tarde.

coffeepot [ˈkɒfɪpɒt] n cafetera f.

coffee shop n (cafe) cafetería f.

coffee table n mesita f baja.

coffin [ˈkɒfɪn] n ataúd m.

cog(wheel) [kɒg(wiːl)] n rueda f dentada.

coil [kɔɪl] n (of rope) rollo m; (Br: contraceptive) DIU m ◆ vt enrollar.

coin [kɔɪn] n moneda f.

coinbox [ˈkɔɪnbɒks] n (Br) teléfono m público.

coincide [ˌkəʊɪnˈsaɪd] vi: **to ~ (with)** coincidir (con)

coincidence [kəʊˈɪnsɪdəns] n coincidencia f.

Coke® [kəʊk] n Coca-Cola® f.

colander [ˈkʌləndəʳ] n colador m.

cold [kəʊld] adj frío(-a) ◆ n (illness) resfriado m; (low temperature) frío m; **I'm ~** tengo frío; **it's ~** hace frío; **to get ~** enfriarse; **to catch (a) ~** resfriarse.

cold cuts (Am) = **cold meats**.

cold meats npl fiambres mpl.

coleslaw [ˈkəʊlslɔː] n ensalada de col, zanahoria, cebolla y mayonesa.

colic [ˈkɒlɪk] n cólico m.

collaborate [kəˈlæbəreɪt] vi colaborar

collapse [kəˈlæps] vi (building, tent) desplomarse; (person) sufrir un colapso.

collar [ˈkɒləʳ] n (of shirt, coat) cuello m, (of dog, cat) collar m.

collarbone [ˈkɒləbəʊn] n clavícula f

colleague [ˈkɒliːg] n colega mf.

collect [kəˈlekt] vt (gather) reunir; (as a hobby) coleccionar; (go and get) recoger; (money) recaudar ◆ vi acumularse ◆ adv (Am): **to call (sb) ~** llamar (a alguien) a cobro revertido.

collection [kəˈlekʃn] n colección f; (of money) recaudación f; (of mail) recogida f.

collector [kəˈlektəʳ] n (as a hobby) coleccionista mf.

college [ˈkɒlɪdʒ] n (school) instituto m, escuela f; (Br: of university) colegio universitario que forma parte de ciertas universidades; (Am: university) universidad f.

collide [kəˈlaɪd] vi: **to ~ (with)** colisionar (con).

collision [kəˈlɪʒn] n colisión f.

cologne [kəˈləʊn] n colonia f.

Colombia [kə'lɒmbɪə] *n* Colombia.

Colombian [kə'lɒmbɪən] *adj* colombiano(-na) ♦ *n* colombiano *m* (-na *f*).

colon ['kəʊlən] *n* (GRAMM) dos puntos *mpl*.

colonel ['kɜːnl] *n* coronel *m*.

colony ['kɒlənɪ] *n* (country) colonia *f*.

color ['kʌlər] (Am) = **colour**.

colour ['kʌlər] *n* color *m* ♦ *adj* (photograph, film) en color ♦ *vt* (hair) teñir; (food) colorear ❏ **colour in** *vt sep* colorear.

colour-blind *adj* daltónico(-ca).

colourful ['kʌləful] *adj* (picture, garden, scenery) de vivos colores; (fig: person, place) pintoresco(-ca).

colouring ['kʌlərɪŋ] *n* (of food) colorante *m*; (complexion) tez *f*.

colouring book *n* libro *m* de colorear.

colour supplement *n* suplemento *m* en color.

colour television *n* televisión *f* en color.

column ['kɒləm] *n* columna *f*.

coma ['kəʊmə] *n* coma *m*.

comb [kəʊm] *n* peine *m* ♦ *vt*: **to ~ one's hair** peinarse (el pelo).

combination [ˌkɒmbɪ'neɪʃn] *n* combinación *f*.

combine [kəm'baɪn] *vt*: **to ~ sthg (with)** combinar algo (con).

combine harvester [ˌkɒmbaɪn'hɑːvɪstər] *n* cosechadora *f*.

come [kʌm] (*pt* **came**, *pp* **come**) *vi* 1. (move) venir; **we came by taxi** vinimos en taxi; **~ here!** ¡ven aquí!

2. (arrive) llegar; **they still haven't ~** todavía no han llegado; **"coming soon"** "próximamente".

3. (in order): **to ~ first/last** (in race) llegar el primero/el último; (in exam) quedar el primero/el último.

4. (reach): **the water ~s up to my ankles** el agua me llega hasta los tobillos.

5. (become): **to ~ loose** aflojarse; **to ~ undone** deshacerse.

6. (be sold) venir; **they ~ in packs of six** vienen en paquetes de seis.

❏ **come across** *vt fus* encontrarse con; **come along** *vi* (progress) ir; (arrive) venir; **~ along!** ¡venga!; **come apart** *vi* (book, clothes) deshacerse; **come back** *vi* (return) volver; **come down** *vi* (price) bajar; **come down with** *vt fus* (illness) coger, agarrar (Amér); **come from** *vt fus* (person) ser de; (noise, product) venir de; **come in** *vi* (enter) entrar; (arrive) llegar; (tide) crecer; **~ in!** ¡adelante!; **come off** *vi* (become detached) desprenderse; (succeed) salir bien; **come on** *vi* (progress) ir; (improve) mejorar; **~ on!** ¡venga!; **come out** *vi* salir; (film) estrenarse; (stain) quitarse; **come over** *vi* (visit) venir; **come round** *vi* (visit) venir; (regain consciousness) volver en sí; **come to** *vt fus* (subj: bill) ascender a; **come up** *vi* (go upstairs) subir; (be mentioned, arise) surgir; (sun, moon) salir; **come up with** *vt fus*: **she came up with a brilliant idea** se le ocurrió una idea estupenda.

comedian [kə'miːdɪən] *n* humorista *m*.

comedy ['kɒmədɪ] *n* (TV programme, film, play) comedia f; (humour) humor m.

comfort ['kʌmfət] n comodidad f; (consolation) consuelo m ♦ vt consolar.

comfortable ['kʌmftəbl] adj cómodo(-da); (after illness, operation) en estado satisfactorio; (financially) acomodado(-da).

comic ['kɒmɪk] adj cómico(-ca) ♦ n (person) humorista mf; (adult magazine) cómic m; (children's magazine) tebeo m.

comical ['kɒmɪkl] adj cómico(-ca).

comic strip n tira f cómica.

comma ['kɒmə] n coma f.

command [kə'mɑ:nd] n (order) orden f; (mastery) dominio m ♦ vt (order) ordenar; (be in charge of) estar al mando de.

commander [kə'mɑ:ndər] n comandante m.

commemorate [kə'meməreɪt] vt conmemorar.

commence [kə'mens] vi (fml) comenzar.

comment ['kɒment] n comentario m ♦ vi hacer comentarios.

commentary ['kɒməntrɪ] n (on TV, radio) comentario m.

commentator ['kɒmənteɪtər] n (on TV, radio) comentarista mf.

commerce ['kɒmɜ:s] n comercio m.

commercial [kə'mɜ:ʃl] adj comercial ♦ n anuncio m (televisivo o radiofónico).

commercial break n pausa f para la publicidad.

commission [kə'mɪʃn] n comi-

sión f.

commit [kə'mɪt] vt (crime, sin) cometer; to ~ o.s. (to sthg) comprometerse (a algo); to ~ suicide suicidarse.

committee [kə'mɪtɪ] n comité m.

commodity [kə'mɒdətɪ] n producto m.

common ['kɒmən] adj común; (pej: vulgar) ordinario(-ria) ♦ n (Br: land) zona de hierba abierta accesible a todo el mundo; in ~ en común.

commonly ['kɒmənlɪ] adv (generally) generalmente.

Common Market n Mercado m Común.

common room n sala f de estudiantes.

common sense n sentido m común.

Commonwealth ['kɒmənwelθ] n Commonwealth f.

communal ['kɒmjunl] adj comunal.

communicate [kə'mju:nɪkeɪt] vi: to ~ (with) comunicarse (con).

communication [kə,mju:nɪ'keɪʃn] n comunicación f.

communication cord n (Br) alarma f (de un tren o metro).

communist ['kɒmjunɪst] n comunista mf.

community [kə'mju:nətɪ] n comunidad f.

community centre n centro m social.

commute [kə'mju:t] vi viajar diariamente al lugar de trabajo, especialmente en tren.

commuter [kə'mju:tər] n perso-

na que viaja diariamente al lugar de trabajo, especialmente en tren.

compact [adj kəm'pækt, n 'kɒmpækt] *adj* compacto(-ta) ♦ *n (for make-up)* polvera *f*; *(Am: car)* utilitario *m*.

compact disc [,kɒmpækt-] *n* compact disc *m*.

compact disc player [,kɒmpækt-] *n* compact *m* (disc).

company ['kʌmpəni] *n* compañía *f*; **to keep sb ~** hacer compañía a alguien.

company car *n* coche *m* de la empresa.

comparatively [kəm'pærətɪvlɪ] *adv* relativamente.

compare [kəm'peəʳ] *vt*: **to ~ sthg (with)** comparar algo (con); **~d with** en comparación con.

comparison [kəm'pærɪsn] *n* comparación *f*; **in ~ with** en comparación con.

compartment [kəm'pɑːtmənt] *n* compartimento *m*.

compass ['kʌmpəs] *n* brújula *f*; **(a pair of) ~es** (un) compás.

compatible [kəm'pætəbl] *adj* compatible.

compensate ['kɒmpenseɪt] *vt* compensar ♦ *vi*: **to ~ for sthg** compensar algo; **to ~ sb for sthg** compensar a alguien por algo.

compensation [,kɒmpen'seɪʃn] *n (money)* indemnización *f*.

compete [kəm'piːt] *vi* competir; **to ~ with sb for sthg** competir con alguien por algo.

competent ['kɒmpɪtənt] *adj* competente.

competition [,kɒmpɪ'tɪʃn] *n*

(SPORT) competición *f*; *(of writing, music etc)* concurso *m*; *(rivalry)* competencia *f*; **the ~** la competencia.

competitive [kəm'petɪtɪv] *adj* competitivo(-va).

competitor [kəm'petɪtəʳ] *n (in race, contest)* participante *mf*; *(in game show)* concursante *mf*; *(COMM)* competidor *m* (-ra *f*).

complain [kəm'pleɪn] *vi*: **to ~ (about)** quejarse (de).

complaint [kəm'pleɪnt] *n (statement)* queja *f*; *(illness)* dolencia *f*.

complement ['kɒmplɪ,ment] *vt* complementar.

complete [kəm'pliːt] *adj (whole)* completo(-ta); *(finished)* terminado(-da); *(change, disaster)* total; *(idiot)* consumado(-da) ♦ *vt (finish)* terminar; *(a form)* rellenar; *(make whole)* completar; **~ with** con.

completely [kəm'pliːtlɪ] *adv* completamente.

complex ['kɒmpleks] *adj* complejo(-ja) ♦ *n* complejo *m*.

complexion [kəm'plekʃn] *n (of skin)* cutis *m inv*.

complicated ['kɒmplɪkeɪtɪd] *adj* complicado(-da).

compliment [*n* 'kɒmplɪmənt, *vb* 'kɒmplɪment] *n* cumplido *m* ♦ *vt* felicitar.

complimentary [,kɒmplɪ'mentərɪ] *adj (seat, ticket)* gratuito(-ta); *(words, person)* halagador(-ra).

compose [kəm'pəʊz] *vt* componer; **to be ~d of** estar compuesto de.

composed [kəm'pəʊzd] *adj* tranquilo(-la).

composer [kəm'pəʊzə*r*] *n* compositor *m* (-ra *f*).

composition [,kɒmpə'zɪʃn] *n* (essay) redacción *f*.

compound ['kɒmpaʊnd] *n* (substance) compuesto *m*; (word) palabra *f* compuesta.

comprehensive [,kɒmprɪ'hensɪv] *adj* amplio(-plia).

comprehensive (school) *n* (Br) instituto *de* enseñanza media no selectiva en Gran Bretaña.

compressed air [kəm'prest-] *n* aire *m* comprimido.

comprise [kəm'praɪz] *vt* comprender.

compromise ['kɒmprəmaɪz] *n* arreglo *m*, acuerdo *m*.

compulsory [kəm'pʌlsərɪ] *adj* obligatorio(-ria).

computer [kəm'pju:tə*r*] *n* ordenador *m*.

computer game *n* videojuego *m*.

computerized [kəm'pju:təraɪzd] *adj* informatizado(-da).

computer operator *n* operador *m* (-ra *f*) de ordenador.

computer programmer ['-prəʊgræmə*r*] *n* programador *m* (-ra *f*) (de ordenadores).

computing [kəm'pju:tɪŋ] *n* informática *f*.

con [kɒn] *n* (inf: trick) timo *m*, estafa *f*; **all mod ~s** con todas las comodidades.

conceal [kən'si:l] *vt* ocultar.

conceited [kən'si:tɪd] *adj* (pej) engreído(-da).

concentrate ['kɒnsəntreɪt] *vi* concentrarse ♦ *vt*: **to be ~d** (in one *place)* concentrarse; **to ~ on sthg** concentrarse en algo.

concentrated ['kɒnsəntreɪtɪd] *adj* concentrado(-da).

concentration [,kɒnsən'treɪʃn] *n* concentración *f*.

concern [kən'sɜ:n] *n* (worry) preocupación *f*; (matter of interest) asunto *m*; (COMM) empresa *f* ♦ *vt* (be about) tratar de; (worry) preocupar; (involve) concernir; **to be ~ed about** estar preocupado por; **to be ~ed with** tratar de; **to ~ o.s. with sthg** preocuparse por algo; **as far as I'm ~ed** por lo que a mí respecta.

concerned [kən'sɜ:nd] *adj* preocupado(-da).

concerning [kən'sɜ:nɪŋ] *prep* acerca de.

concert ['kɒnsət] *n* concierto *m*.

concession [kən'seʃn] *n* (reduced price) descuento *m*.

concise [kən'saɪs] *adj* conciso(-sa).

conclude [kən'klu:d] *vt* concluir ♦ *vi* (fml: end) concluir.

conclusion [kən'klu:ʒn] *n* (decision) conclusión *f*; (end) final *m*.

concrete ['kɒŋkri:t] *adj* (building, path) de hormigón; (idea, plan) concreto(-ta) ♦ *n* hormigón *m*.

concussion [kən'kʌʃn] *n* conmoción *f* cerebral.

condensation [,kɒndən'seɪʃn] *n* (on window) vaho *m*.

condensed milk [kən'denst-] *n* leche *f* condensada.

condition [kən'dɪʃn] *n* (state) estado *m*; (proviso) condición *f*; (illness) afección *f*; **to be out of ~** no estar en forma; **on ~ that** a condición de que ❑ **conditions** *npl (circumstances)* condiciones *fpl*.

conditioner [kən'dɪʃnəʳ] *n* suavizante *m*.

condo ['kɒndəʊ] *(Am: inf)* = **condominium**.

condom ['kɒndəm] *n* condón *m*.

condominium [,kɒndə'mɪnɪəm] *n (Am)* apartamento *m*.

conduct [*vb* kən'dʌkt, *n* 'kɒndʌkt] *vt (investigation, business)* llevar a cabo; *(MUS)* dirigir ◆ *n (fml)* conducta *f*; **to ~ o.s.** *(fml)* comportarse.

conductor [kən'dʌktəʳ] *n (MUS)* director *m* (-ra *f*); *(on bus)* cobrador *m* (-ra *f*); *(Am: on train)* revisor *m* (-ra *f*).

cone [kəʊn] *n (shape, on roads)* cono *m*; *(for ice cream)* cucurucho *m*.

confectioner's [kən'fekʃnəz] *n (shop)* confitería *f*.

confectionery [kən'fekʃnərɪ] *n* dulces *mpl*.

conference ['kɒnfərəns] *n* conferencia *f*, congreso *m*.

confess [kən'fes] *vi*: **to ~ (to sth)** confesar (algo).

confession [kən'feʃn] *n* confesión *f*.

confidence ['kɒnfɪdəns] *n (self-assurance)* seguridad *f* (en sí mismo); *(trust)* confianza *f*; **to have ~ in** tener confianza en.

confident ['kɒnfɪdənt] *adj (self-assured)* seguro de sí mismo (segura de sí misma); *(certain)* seguro(-ra).

confined [kən'faɪnd] *adj* limita-

do(-da).

confirm [kən'fɜːm] *vt* confirmar.

confirmation [,kɒnfə'meɪʃn] *n* confirmación *f*.

conflict [*n* 'kɒnflɪkt, *vb* kən'flɪkt] *n* conflicto *m* ◆ *vi*: **to ~ (with)** estar en desacuerdo (con).

conform [kən'fɔːm] *vi*: **to ~ (to)** ajustarse (a).

confuse [kən'fjuːz] *vt* confundir; **to ~ sthg with sthg** confundir algo con algo.

confused [kən'fjuːzd] *adj* confuso(-sa).

confusing [kən'fjuːzɪŋ] *adj* confuso(-sa).

confusion [kən'fjuːʒn] *n* confusión *f*.

congested [kən'dʒestɪd] *adj (street)* congestionado(-da).

congestion [kən'dʒestʃn] *n (traffic)* congestión *f*.

congratulate [kən'grætʃʊleɪt] *vt*: **to ~ sb (on sthg)** felicitar a alguien (por algo).

congratulations [kən,grætʃʊ-'leɪʃənz] *excl* ¡enhorabuena!

congregate ['kɒngrɪgeɪt] *vi* congregarse.

Congress ['kɒngres] *n (Am)* el Congreso.

conifer ['kɒnɪfəʳ] *n* conífera *f*.

conjunction [kən'dʒʌŋkʃn] *n (GRAMM)* conjunción *f*.

conjurer ['kʌndʒərəʳ] *n* prestidigitador *m* (-ra *f*).

connect [kə'nekt] *vt* conectar; *(caller on phone)* comunicar, poner ◆ *vi*: **to ~ with** *(train, plane)* enlazar con; **to ~ sthg with sthg** *(associate)* asociar algo con algo.

connecting flight [kə'nektɪŋ-] n vuelo m de enlace.

connection [kə'nekʃn] n (link) conexión f; (train, plane) enlace m; **a bad ~** (on phone) mala línea; **a loose ~** (in machine) un hilo suelto; **in ~ with** con relación a.

conquer ['kɒŋkəʳ] vt conquistar.

conscience ['kɒnʃəns] n conciencia f.

conscientious [,kɒnʃɪ'enʃəs] adj concienzudo(-da).

conscious ['kɒnʃəs] adj (awake) consciente; (deliberate) deliberado(-da); **to be ~ of** ser consciente de.

consent [kən'sent] n consentimiento m.

consequence ['kɒnsɪkwəns] n (result) consecuencia f.

consequently ['kɒnsɪkwəntlɪ] adv por consiguiente.

conservation [,kɒnsə'veɪʃn] n conservación f.

conservative [kən'sɜːvətɪv] adj conservador(-ra) □ **Conservative** adj conservador(-ra) ♦ n conservador m (-ra f).

conservatory [kən'sɜːvətrɪ] n pequeña habitación acristalada aneja a la casa.

consider [kən'sɪdəʳ] vt considerar; **to ~ doing sthg** pensarse si hacer algo.

considerable [kən'sɪdrəbl] adj considerable.

consideration [kən,sɪdə'reɪʃn] n consideración f; **to take sthg into ~** tener algo en cuenta.

considering [kən'sɪdərɪŋ] prep teniendo en cuenta.

consist [kən'sɪst]: **consist in** vt fus consistir en; **consist of** vt fus consistir en.

consistent [kən'sɪstənt] adj (coherent) coherente; (worker, performance) constante.

consolation [,kɒnsə'leɪʃn] n consuelo m.

console ['kɒnsəʊl] n consola f.

consonant ['kɒnsənənt] n consonante f.

conspicuous [kən'spɪkjʊəs] adj visible

constable ['kʌnstəbl] n (Br) policía mf.

constant ['kɒnstənt] adj constante.

constantly ['kɒnstəntlɪ] adv (all the time) constantemente.

constipated ['kɒnstɪpeɪtɪd] adj estreñido(-da).

constitution [,kɒnstɪ'tjuːʃn] n (health) constitución f.

construct [kən'strʌkt] vt construir.

construction [kən'strʌkʃn] n construcción f; **"under ~"** "en construcción".

consul ['kɒnsəl] n cónsul mf.

consulate ['kɒnsjʊlət] n consulado m.

consult [kən'sʌlt] vt consultar.

consultant [kən'sʌltənt] n (Br: doctor) especialista mf.

consume [kən'sjuːm] vt consumir.

consumer [kən'sjuːməʳ] n consumidor m (-ra f).

contact ['kɒntækt] n contacto m ♦ vt ponerse en contacto con; **in ~ with** en contacto con.

contact lens *n* lentilla *f*.

contagious [kən'teɪdʒəs] *adj* contagioso(-sa).

contain [kən'teɪn] *vt* contener.

container [kən'teɪnə^r] *n* (box etc) envase *m*.

contaminate [kən'tæmɪneɪt] *vt* contaminar.

contemporary [kən'tempərərɪ] *adj* contemporáneo(-a) ◆ *n* contemporáneo *m* (-a *f*).

contend [kən'tend]: **contend with** *vt fus* afrontar.

content [*adj* kən'tent, *n* 'kɒntent] *adj* contento(-ta) ◆ *n* (of vitamins, fibre etc) contenido *m* □ **contents** *npl* (things inside) contenido *m*; (at beginning of book) índice *m* (de materias).

contest [*n* 'kɒntest, *vb* kən'test] *n* (competition) competición *f*, concurso *m*; (struggle) contienda *f* ◆ *vt* (election, seat) presentarse como candidato a; (decision, will) impugnar.

context ['kɒntekst] *n* contexto *m*.

continent ['kɒntɪnənt] *n* continente *m*; **the Continent** (Br) la Europa continental.

continental [,kɒntɪ'nentl] *adj* (Br: European) de la Europa continental.

continental breakfast *n* desayuno *m* continental.

continental quilt *n* (Br) edredón *m*.

continual [kən'tɪnjʊəl] *adj* continuo(-nua).

continually [kən'tɪnjʊəlɪ] *adv* continuamente.

continue [kən'tɪnjuː] *vt & vi* continuar; **to ~ doing sthg** continuar haciendo algo; **to ~ with sthg** continuar con algo.

continuous [kən'tɪnjʊəs] *adj* continuo(-nua).

continuously [kən'tɪnjʊəslɪ] *adv* continuamente.

contraception [,kɒntrə'sepʃn] *n* anticoncepción *f*.

contraceptive [,kɒntrə'septɪv] *n* anticonceptivo *m*.

contract [*n* 'kɒntrækt, *vb* kən'trækt] *n* contrato *m* ◆ *vt* (fml: illness) contraer.

contradict [,kɒntrə'dɪkt] *vt* contradecir.

contraflow [*n* 'kɒntrəfləʊ] *n* (Br) estrechamiento en una autopista, a una vía de dos direcciones.

contrary ['kɒntrərɪ] *n*: **on the ~** al contrario.

contrast [*n* 'kɒntrɑːst, *vb* kən'trɑːst] *n* contraste *m* ◆ *vt* contrastar; **in ~ to** a diferencia de.

contribute [kən'trɪbjuːt] *vt* (help, money) contribuir ◆ *vi*: **to ~ to** contribuir a.

contribution [,kɒntrɪ'bjuːʃn] *n* contribución *f*.

control [kən'trəʊl] *n* control *m* ◆ *vt* controlar; (restrict) restringir; **to be in ~** estar al mando; **out of ~** fuera de control; **under ~** bajo control □ **controls** *npl* (for TV, video) botones *mpl* de mando; (of plane) mandos *mpl*.

control tower *n* torre *f* de control.

controversial [,kɒntrə'vɜːʃl] *adj* controvertido(-da).

convenience [kən'viːnjəns] *n (convenient nature)* conveniencia *f; (convenient thing)* comodidad *f;* **at your ~** cuando le venga bien.

convenient [kən'viːnjənt] *adj (suitable)* conveniente; *(well-situated)* bien situado(-da); **would tomorrow be ~?** ¿le viene bien mañana?

convent ['kɒnvənt] *n* convento *m.*

conventional [kən'venʃənl] *adj* convencional.

conversation [ˌkɒnvə'seɪʃn] *n* conversación *f.*

conversion [kən'vɜːʃn] *n (change)* conversión *f; (to building)* reforma *f.*

convert [kən'vɜːt] *vt* convertir; **to ~ sth into** convertir algo en.

converted [kən'vɜːtɪd] *adj (barn, loft)* acondicionado(-da).

convertible [kən'vɜːtəbl] *n* descapotable *m.*

convey [kən'veɪ] *vt (fml: transport)* transportar; *(idea, impression)* transmitir.

convict [*n* 'kɒnvɪkt, *vb* kən'vɪkt] *n* presidiario *m* (-ria *f*) ♦ *vt:* **to ~ sb (of)** declarar a alguien culpable (de).

convince [kən'vɪns] *vt:* **to ~ sb (of sth)** convencer a alguien (de algo); **to ~ sb to do sth** convencer a alguien para que haga algo.

convoy ['kɒnvɔɪ] *n* convoy *m.*

cook [kʊk] *n* cocinero *m* (-ra *f*) ♦ *vt (meal)* preparar; *(food)* guisar ♦ *vi (person)* guisar; *(food)* cocerse, hacerse.

cookbook ['kʊkbʊk] = **cookery book.**

cooker ['kʊkə^r] *n* cocina *f (aparato).*

cookery ['kʊkərɪ] *n* cocina *f (arte).*

cookery book *n* libro *m* de cocina.

cookie ['kʊkɪ] *n (Am)* galleta *f.*

cooking ['kʊkɪŋ] *n* cocina *f.*

cooking apple *n* manzana *f* para asar.

cooking oil *n* aceite *m* para cocinar.

cool [kuːl] *adj (temperature)* fresco(-ca); *(calm)* tranquilo(-la); *(unfriendly)* frío(-a); *(inf: great)* chachi ♦ *vt* refrescar ❑ **cool down** *vi (become colder)* enfriarse; *(become calmer)* calmarse.

cooperate [kəʊ'ɒpəreɪt] *vi* cooperar.

cooperation [kəʊˌɒpə'reɪʃn] *n* cooperación *f.*

cooperative [kəʊ'ɒpərətɪv] *adj* dispuesto(-ta) a cooperar.

coordinates [kəʊ'ɔːdɪnəts] *npl (clothes)* conjuntos *mpl.*

cope [kəʊp] *vi:* **to ~ with** *(problem, situation)* hacer frente a; *(work)* poder con.

copilot ['kəʊˌpaɪlət] *n* copiloto *mf.*

copper ['kɒpə^r] *n (metal)* cobre *m; (Br: inf: coin)* moneda de cobre de uno o dos peniques.

copy ['kɒpɪ] *n* copia *f; (of newspaper, book)* ejemplar *m* ♦ *vt (duplicate)* hacer una copia de; *(imitate)* copiar.

cord(uroy) ['kɔːd(ərɔɪ)] *n* pana *f.*

core [kɔː^r] *n (of fruit)* corazón *m.*

coriander [ˌkɒrɪˈændəʳ] n cilantro m.

cork [kɔːk] n (in bottle) corcho m.

corkscrew [ˈkɔːkskruː] n sacacorchos m inv.

corn [kɔːn] n (Br: crop) cereal m; (Am: maize) maíz m; (on foot) callo m.

corned beef [ˌkɔːnd-] n carne de vaca cocinada y enlatada.

corner [ˈkɔːnəʳ] n (outside angle, bend in road) esquina f; (inside angle) rincón m; (in football) córner m; **it's just around the ~** está a la vuelta de la esquina.

corner shop n (Br) pequeña tienda de ultramarinos de barrio.

cornet [ˈkɔːnɪt] n (Br: ice-cream cone) cucurucho m.

cornflakes [ˈkɔːnfleɪks] npl copos mpl de maíz.

corn-on-the-cob [-ˈkɒb] n mazorca f.

Cornwall [ˈkɔːnwɔːl] n Cornualles.

corporal [ˈkɔːpərəl] n cabo mf.

corpse [kɔːps] n cadáver m.

correct [kəˈrekt] adj correcto(-ta) ♦ vt corregir.

correction [kəˈrekʃn] n corrección f.

correspond [ˌkɒrɪˈspɒnd] vi: to ~ (to) (match) concordar (con); to ~ (with) (exchange letters) cartearse (con).

corresponding [ˌkɒrɪˈspɒndɪŋ] adj correspondiente.

corridor [ˈkɒrɪdɔːʳ] n pasillo m.

corrugated iron [ˈkɒrəgeɪtɪd-] n chapa f ondulada.

corrupt [kəˈrʌpt] adj corrup-to(-ta).

cosmetics [kɒzˈmetɪks] npl cosméticos mpl.

cost [kɒst] (pt & pp **cost**) n coste m ♦ vt costar; **how much does it ~?** ¿cuánto cuesta?

Costa Rica [ˌkɒstəˈriːkə] n Costa Rica.

Costa Rican [ˌkɒstəˈriːkən] adj costarricense ♦ n costarricense mf.

costly [ˈkɒstlɪ] adv (expensive) costoso(-a).

costume [ˈkɒstjuːm] n traje m.

cosy [ˈkəʊzɪ] adj (Br: room, house) acogedor(-ra).

cot [kɒt] n (Br: for baby) cuna f; (Am: camp bed) cama f plegable.

cottage [ˈkɒtɪdʒ] n casita f de campo.

cottage cheese n requesón m.

cottage pie n (Br) pastel de carne de vaca picada y cebollas con una capa de puré de patatas cocinado al horno.

cotton [ˈkɒtn] adj (dress, shirt) de algodón ♦ n (cloth) algodón m; (thread) hilo m (de algodón).

cotton candy n (Am) algodón m (de azúcar).

cotton wool n algodón m (hidrófilo).

couch [kaʊtʃ] n (sofa) sofá m; (at doctor's) camilla f.

couchette [kuːˈʃet] n (bed on train) litera f; (seat on ship) butaca f.

cough [kɒf] n tos f ♦ vi toser; **to have a ~** tener tos.

cough mixture n jarabe m para la tos.

could [kʊd] pt → **can**.

couldn't ['kʊdnt] = could not.

could've ['kʊdəv] = could have.

council ['kaʊnsl] n (Br: of town) ayuntamiento m; (of county) = diputación f; (organization) consejo m.

council house n (Br) = casa f de protección oficial.

councillor ['kaʊnsələr] n (Br) concejal mf.

council tax n (Br) = contribución f urbana.

count [kaʊnt] vt & vi contar ♦ n (nobleman) conde m □ **count on** vt fus contar con.

counter ['kaʊntər] n (in shop) mostrador m; (in bank) ventanilla f; (in board game) ficha f.

counterclockwise [,kaʊntə'klɒkwaɪz] adv (Am) en sentido opuesto a las agujas del reloj.

counterfoil ['kaʊntəfɔɪl] n matriz f.

countess ['kaʊntɪs] n condesa f.

country ['kʌntrɪ] n (state) país m; (countryside) campo m; (population) pueblo m ♦ adj campestre.

country and western n música f country.

country house n casa f de campo.

country road n camino m vecinal.

countryside ['kʌntrɪsaɪd] n campo m.

county ['kaʊntɪ] n (in Britain) condado m; (in US) división administrativa de un estado en EEUU.

couple ['kʌpl] n pareja f; **a ~ (of)** un par (de).

coupon ['kuːpɒn] n cupón m.

courage ['kʌrɪdʒ] n valor m.

courgette [kɔː'ʒet] n (Br) calabacín m.

courier ['kʊrɪər] n (for holidaymakers) guía mf; (for delivering letters) mensajero m (-ra f).

course [kɔːs] n curso m; (of meal) plato m; (of treatment, injections) tratamiento m; (for golf) campo m (de golf); **of ~** por supuesto, claro; **of ~ not** claro que no; **in the ~ of** en el curso de.

court [kɔːt] n (JUR: building, room) juzgado m; (SPORT) cancha f; (of king, queen) corte f.

courtesy coach ['kɜːtɪsɪ] n autocar gratuito fletado para llevar a invitados.

court shoes npl zapatos de señora de tacón alto y sin adornos.

courtyard ['kɔːtjɑːd] n patio m.

cousin ['kʌzn] n primo m (-ma f).

cover ['kʌvər] n (soft covering) funda f; (lid) tapa f; (of book, magazine) cubierta f; (blanket) manta f; (insurance) cobertura f ♦ vt cubrir; (travel) recorrer; (apply to) afectar; (discuss) abarcar; **to be ~ed in** estar cubierto de; **to ~ sthg with sthg** (food, tray, furniture etc) cubrir algo con algo; (hole, ears) tapar algo con algo; **to take ~** refugiarse □ **cover up** vt sep (put cover on) cubrir; (facts, truth) encubrir.

cover charge n precio m del cubierto.

cover note n (Br) póliza f provisional.

cow [kaʊ] n vaca f.

coward ['kaʊəd] n cobarde mf.

cowboy ['kaʊbɔɪ] n vaquero m.

crab [kræb] n cangrejo m.

crack [kræk] n (in cup, glass, wood) grieta f; (gap) rendija f ◆ vt (cup, glass, wood) agrietar, rajar; (nut, egg) cascar; (inf: joke) contar; (whip) chasquear ◆ vi agrietarse, rajarse.

cracker ['krækə^r] n (biscuit) galleta f salada; (for Christmas) tubo con sorpresa típico de Navidades que produce un pequeño restallido al ser abierto.

cradle ['kreɪdl] n cuna f.

craft [krɑːft] n (skill, trade) oficio m; (boat: pl inv) embarcación f.

craftsman ['krɑːftsmən] (pl -men [-mən]) n artesano m.

cram [kræm] vt: **to ~ sthg into** embutir algo en; **to be crammed with** estar atestado de.

cramp [kræmp] n calambres mpl; **stomach ~s** retortijones mpl.

cranberry ['krænbəri] n arándano m (agrio).

cranberry sauce n salsa de arándanos agrios que se suele comer con pavo.

crane [kreɪn] n (machine) grúa f.

crap [kræp] adj (vulg) de mierda ◆ n (vulg: excrement) mierda f.

crash [kræʃ] n (accident) colisión f; (noise) estruendo m ◆ vt (car) estrellar ◆ vi (two vehicles) chocar; (into wall, ground) estrellarse ❑ **crash into** vt fus estrellarse contra.

crash helmet n casco m protector.

crash landing n aterrizaje m forzoso.

crate [kreɪt] n caja f (para embalaje o transporte).

crawl [krɔːl] vi (baby) gatear; (person, insect) arrastrarse; (traffic) ir a paso de tortuga ◆ n (swimming stroke) crol m.

crawler lane ['krɔːlə-] n (Br) carril m de los lentos.

crayfish ['kreɪfɪʃ] (pl inv) n cangrejo m de río.

crayon ['kreɪɒn] n lápiz m de cera.

craze [kreɪz] n moda f.

crazy ['kreɪzɪ] adj loco(-ca); **to be ~ about** estar loco por.

crazy golf n minigolf m.

cream [kriːm] n (food) nata f; (for face, burns) crema f ◆ adj (in colour) crema inv.

cream cake n (Br) pastel m de nata.

cream cheese n queso m cremoso.

cream sherry n jerez m cream.

cream tea n (Br) merienda de té con bollos, nata cuajada y mermelada.

creamy ['kriːmɪ] adj cremoso(-sa).

crease [kriːs] n arruga f.

creased [kriːst] adj arrugado(-da).

create [kriː'eɪt] vt (make) crear; (impression, interest) producir.

creative [kriː'eɪtɪv] adj creativo(-va).

creature ['kriːtʃə^r] n criatura f.

crèche [kreʃ] n (Br) guardería f.

credit ['kredɪt] n (praise) mérito m; (money, for studies) crédito m; **to be in ~** estar con saldo acreedor ❑

credits npl (of film) rótulos mpl de

crédito.

credit card n tarjeta f de crédito; **to pay by ~** pagar con tarjeta de crédito; **"all major ~s accepted"** "se aceptan las principales tarjetas de crédito".

creek [kriːk] n (inlet) cala f; (Am: river) riachuelo m.

creep [kriːp] (pt & pp **crept**) vi arrastrarse ◆ n (inf: groveller) pelotillero m (-ra f).

cremate [krɪˈmeɪt] vt incinerar.

crematorium [ˌkremaˈtɔːrɪəm] n crematorio m.

crepe [kreɪp] n (thin pancake) crepe f.

crept [krept] pt & pp → **creep**

cress [kres] n berro m.

crest [krest] n (of hill) cima f; (of wave) cresta f; (emblem) blasón m.

crew [kruː] n (of ship, plane) tripulación f.

crew neck n cuello m redondo.

crib [krɪb] n (Am: cot) cuna f.

cricket [ˈkrɪkɪt] n (game) críquet m; (insect) grillo m

crime [kraɪm] n (serious offence) crimen m; (less serious offence) delito m; (illegal activity) delincuencia f.

criminal [ˈkrɪmɪnl] adj criminal ◆ n (serious) criminal mf; (less serious) delincuente mf; **~ offence** delito m.

cripple [ˈkrɪpl] n lisiado m (-da f) ◆ vt dejar inválido.

crisis [ˈkraɪsɪs] (pl **crises** [ˈkraɪsiːz]) n crisis f.

crisp [krɪsp] adj crujiente ❑ **crisps** npl (Br) patatas fpl fritas (de bolsa).

crispy [ˈkrɪspɪ] adj crujiente.

critic [ˈkrɪtɪk] n (reviewer) crítico m (-ca f).

critical [ˈkrɪtɪkl] adj crítico(-ca); (very serious, dangerous) grave.

criticize [ˈkrɪtɪsaɪz] vt criticar.

crockery [ˈkrɒkərɪ] n vajilla f.

crocodile [ˈkrɒkədaɪl] n cocodrilo m.

crocus [ˈkrəʊkəs] (pl **-es**) n azafrán m (flor).

crooked [ˈkrʊkɪd] adj torcido(-da).

crop [krɒp] n (kind of plant) cultivo m; (harvest) cosecha f ❑ **crop up** vi surgir.

cross [krɒs] adj enfadado(-da) ◆ n cruz f; (mixture) mezcla f ◆ vt cruzar ◆ vi cruzarse ❑ **cross out** vt sep tachar; **cross over** vt fus cruzar.

crossbar [ˈkrɒsbaː] n (of goal) larguero m; (of bicycle) barra f.

cross-Channel ferry n ferry que hace la travesía del Canal de la Mancha.

cross country (running) n cross m.

crossing [ˈkrɒsɪŋ] n (on road) cruce m; (sea journey) travesía f.

crossroads [ˈkrɒsrəʊdz] (pl inv) n cruce m.

crosswalk [ˈkrɒswɔːk] n (Am) paso m de peatones.

crossword (puzzle) [ˈkrɒswɜːd-] n crucigrama m.

crotch [krɒtʃ] n entrepierna f.

crouton [ˈkruːtɒn] n cuscurro m.

crow [krəʊ] n cuervo m.

crowbar [ˈkrəʊbaː] n palanca f.

crowd [kraʊd] n (large group of people) multitud f; (at match) público m.

crowded ['kraʊdɪd] adj atestado(-da).

crown [kraʊn] n corona f; (of head) coronilla f.

Crown Jewels npl joyas de la corona británica.

ⓘ CROWN JEWELS

Estas ricas joyas, que el monarca británico utiliza en ocasiones oficiales, se pueden admirar en la Torre de Londres, donde están expuestas en un edificio construido para tal fin. Las joyas de la antigua corona escocesa se pueden contemplar en el castillo de Edimburgo.

---

crucial ['kru:ʃl] adj crucial.

crude [kru:d] adj (rough) tosco(-ca); (rude) ordinario(-ria).

cruel [krʊəl] adj cruel.

cruelty ['krʊəltɪ] n crueldad f.

cruet (set) ['kru:ɪt-] n vinagreras fpl.

cruise [kru:z] n crucero m ♦ vi (car, plane, ship) ir a velocidad de crucero.

cruiser ['kru:zər] n crucero m.

crumb [krʌm] n miga f.

crumble ['krʌmbl] n compota de fruta cubierta con una masa de harina, azúcar y mantequilla que se sirve caliente ♦ vi (building, cliff) desmoronarse; (cheese) desmenuzarse.

crumpet ['krʌmpɪt] n bollo que se come tostado y con mantequilla.

crunchy ['krʌntʃɪ] adj crujiente.

crush [krʌʃ] n (drink) zumo con

agua añadida ♦ vt (flatten) aplastar; (garlic, ice) triturar.

crust [krʌst] n corteza f.

crusty ['krʌstɪ] adj crujiente.

crutch [krʌtʃ] n (stick) muleta f; (between legs) = **crotch**.

cry [kraɪ] n grito m ♦ vi (weep) llorar; (shout) gritar ❑ **cry out** vi gritar.

crystal ['krɪstl] n cristal m.

cub [kʌb] n (animal) cachorro m.

Cub [kʌb] n boy scout de entre 8 y 11 años.

Cuba ['kju:bə] n Cuba.

Cuban ['kju:bən] adj cubano(-na) ♦ n cubano m (-na f).

cube [kju:b] n (shape) cubo m; (of sugar) terrón m; (of ice) cubito m.

cubicle ['kju:bɪkl] n (at swimming pool) caseta f; (in shop) probador m.

Cub Scout = **Cub**.

cuckoo ['kʊku:] n cuclillo m.

cucumber ['kju:kʌmbər] n pepino m.

cuddle ['kʌdl] n abrazo m.

cuddly toy ['kʌdlɪ-] n muñeco m de peluche.

cue [kju:] n (in snooker, pool) taco m.

cuff [kʌf] n (of sleeve) puño m; (Am: of trousers) vuelta f.

cuff links npl gemelos mpl.

cuisine [kwɪ'zi:n] n cocina f.

cul-de-sac ['kʌldəsæk] n callejón m sin salida.

cult [kʌlt] n culto m ♦ adj de culto.

cultivate ['kʌltɪveɪt] vt cultivar.

cultivated ['kʌltɪveɪtɪd] adj (person) culto(-ta).

cultural [ˈkʌltʃərəl] *adj* cultural.

culture [ˈkʌltʃəʳ] *n* cultura *f*.

cumbersome [ˈkʌmbəsəm] *adj* aparatoso(-sa).

cumin [ˈkjuːmɪn] *n* comino *m*.

cunning [ˈkʌnɪŋ] *adj* astuto(-ta).

cup [kʌp] *n* (for drinking, cupful) taza *f*; (trophy, competition, of bra) copa *f*.

cupboard [ˈkʌbəd] *n* armario *m*.

curator [ˌkjʊəˈreɪtəʳ] *n* director *m* (-ra *f*) (de museo, biblioteca, etc).

curb [kɜːb] (*Am*) = **kerb**.

curd cheese [ˌkɜːd-] *n* requesón *m*.

cure [kjʊəʳ] *n* cura *f* ◆ *vt* curar.

curious [ˈkjʊərɪəs] *adj* curioso(-sa).

curl [kɜːl] *n* (of hair) rizo *m* ◆ *vt* (hair) rizar.

curler [ˈkɜːləʳ] *n* rulo *m*.

curly [ˈkɜːlɪ] *adj* rizado(-da).

currant [ˈkʌrənt] *n* pasa *f* de Corinto.

currency [ˈkʌrənsɪ] *n* (money) moneda *f*.

current [ˈkʌrənt] *adj* actual ◆ *n* corriente *f*.

current account *n* (*Br*) cuenta *f* corriente.

current affairs *npl* temas *mpl* de actualidad.

currently [ˈkʌrəntlɪ] *adv* actualmente.

curriculum [kəˈrɪkjələm] *n* temario *m*.

curriculum vitae [-ˈviːtaɪ] *n* (*Br*) currículum *m* (vitae).

curried [ˈkʌrɪd] *adj* al curry.

curry [ˈkʌrɪ] *n* curry *m*.

curse [kɜːs] *vi* maldecir.

cursor [ˈkɜːsəʳ] *n* cursor *m*.

curtain [ˈkɜːtn] *n* (in house) cortina *f*; (in theatre) telón *m*.

curve [kɜːv] *n* curva *f* ◆ *vi* torcer.

curved [kɜːvd] *adj* curvo(-va).

cushion [ˈkʊʃn] *n* cojín *m*.

custard [ˈkʌstəd] *n* natillas *fpl*.

custom [ˈkʌstəm] *n* (tradition) costumbre *f*; "**thank you for your ~**" "gracias por su visita".

customary [ˈkʌstəmərɪ] *adj* habitual.

customer [ˈkʌstəməʳ] *n* (of shop) cliente *m* (-ta *f*).

customer services *n* (department) servicio *m* de atención al cliente.

customs [ˈkʌstəmz] *n* aduana *f*; **to go through ~** pasar por la aduana.

customs duty *n* derechos *mpl* de aduana.

customs officer *n* empleado *m* (-da *f*) de aduana.

cut [kʌt] (*pt & pp* **cut**) *n* corte *m*; (reduction) reducción *f*, recorte *m* ◆ *vt* cortar; (reduce) reducir ◆ *vi* (knife, scissors) cortar; **to ~ a blowdry** corte y peinado; **to ~ one's finger** cortarse el dedo; **to ~ one's nails** cortarse las uñas; **to ~ o.s.** cortarse; **to have one's hair ~** cortarse el pelo; **to ~ the grass** cortar el césped; **to ~ sthg open** abrir algo (cortándolo) □ **cut back** *vi*: **to ~ back on sthg** reducir algo; **cut down** *vt sep* (tree) talar; **cut down on** *vt fus*: **to ~ down on sweets** comer menos golosinas; **cut off** *vt sep* (remove, disconnect) cortar; **I've been ~ off** (on phone) me han desconectado; **to be ~ off** *(isolated)* estar aislado; **cut out** *vt sep (newspaper article, photo)* recortar ♦ *vi (engine)* calarse; **to ~ out smoking** dejar de fumar; **~ it out!** *(inf)* ¡basta ya!; **cut up** *vt sep* desmenuzar.

cute [kju:t] *adj* mono(-na).

cut-glass *adj* de cristal labrado.

cutlery ['kʌtləri] *n* cubertería *f*.

cutlet ['kʌtlɪt] *n (of meat)* chuleta *f*; *(of nuts, vegetables)* ≃ croqueta *f*.

cut-price *adj* de oferta.

cutting ['kʌtɪŋ] *n (from newspaper)* recorte *m*.

CV *n (Br: abbr of curriculum vitae)* CV *m*.

cwt *abbr* = **hundredweight**.

cycle ['saɪkl] *n (bicycle)* bicicleta *f*; *(series)* ciclo *m* ♦ *vi* ir en bicicleta.

cycle hire *n* alquiler *m* de bicicletas.

cycle lane *n* carril-bici *m*.

cycle path *n* camino *m* para bicicletas.

cycling ['saɪklɪŋ] *n* ciclismo *m*; **to go ~** ir en bicicleta.

cycling shorts *npl* pantalones *mpl* de ciclista.

cyclist ['saɪklɪst] *n* ciclista *mf*.

cylinder ['sɪlɪndər] *n (container)* bombona *f*; *(in engine)* cilindro *m*.

cynical ['sɪnɪkl] *adj* cínico(-ca).

Czech [tʃek] *adj* checo(-ca) ♦ *n (person)* checo *m* (-ca *f*); *(language)* checo *m*.

Czechoslovakia [ˌtʃekəsləˈvækɪə] *n* Checoslovaquia.

Czech Republic *n*: **the ~** la República Checa.

dab [dæb] *vt (ointment, cream)* aplicar una pequeña cantidad de.

dad [dæd] *n (inf)* papá *m*.

daddy ['dædɪ] *n (inf)* papá *m*.

daddy longlegs [-ˈlɒŋlegz] *(pl inv)* *n* típula *f*.

daffodil ['dæfədɪl] *n* narciso *m*.

daft [dɑːft] *adj (Br: inf)* tonto (-ta).

daily ['deɪlɪ] *adj* diario(-ria) ♦ *adv* diariamente ♦ *n*: **a ~ (newspaper)** un diario.

dairy ['deərɪ] *n (on farm)* vaquería *f*; *(shop)* lechería *f*.

dairy product *n* producto *m* lácteo.

daisy ['deɪzɪ] *n* margarita *f*.

dam [dæm] *n* presa *f*.

damage ['dæmɪdʒ] *n (physical harm)* daño *m*; *(fig: to reputation, chances)* perjuicio *m* ♦ *vt (house, car)* dañar; *(back, leg)* hacerse daño en; *(fig: reputation, chances)* perjudicar.

damn [dæm] *excl (inf)* ¡maldita sea! ♦ *adj (inf)* maldito(-ta) ♦ *n*: **I don't give a ~** me importa un rábano.

damp [dæmp] *adj* húmedo(-da) ♦ *n* humedad *f*.

damson ['dæmzn] *n* ciruela *f* damascena.

dance [dɑːns] *n* baile *m* ♦ *vi* bailar; **to have a ~** bailar.

dance floor *n* pista *f* de baile.

dancer ['dɑ:nsəʳ] n bailarín m (-ina f).

dancing ['dɑ:nsɪŋ] n baile m; **to go ~** ir a bailar.

dandelion ['dændɪlaɪən] n diente m de león.

dandruff ['dændrʌf] n caspa f.

Dane [deɪn] n danés m (-esa f).

danger ['deɪndʒəʳ] n peligro m; **in ~** en peligro.

dangerous ['deɪndʒərəs] adj peligroso(-sa).

Danish ['deɪnɪʃ] adj danés(-esa) ♦ n (language) danés m.

Danish pastry n pasta de hojaldre con pasas, manzanas, etc.

dare [deəʳ] vt: **to ~ to do sthg** atreverse a hacer algo; **to ~ sb to do sthg** desafiar a alguien a hacer algo; **how ~ you!** ¡cómo te atreves?

daring ['deərɪŋ] adj atrevido(-da).

dark [dɑ:k] adj oscuro(-ra); (day, weather) sombrío(-a); (person, skin) moreno(-na) ♦ n: **after ~** después del anochecer; **the ~** la oscuridad.

dark chocolate n chocolate m amargo.

dark glasses npl gafas fpl oscuras.

darkness ['dɑ:knɪs] n oscuridad f.

darling ['dɑ:lɪŋ] n (term of affection) querido m (-da f).

dart [dɑ:t] n dardo m ❑ **darts** n (game) dardos mpl.

dartboard ['dɑ:tbɔ:d] n diana f.

dash [dæʃ] n (of liquid) gotas fpl; (in writing) guión m ♦ vi ir de prisa.

dashboard ['dæʃbɔ:d] n salpicadero m.

data ['deɪtə] n datos mpl.

database ['deɪtəbeɪs] n base f de datos.

date [deɪt] n (day) fecha f; (meeting) cita f; (Am: person) pareja f (con la que se sale); (fruit) dátil m ♦ vt (cheque, letter) fechar; (person) salir con ♦ vi (become unfashionable) pasar de moda; **what's the ~?** ¿qué fecha es?; **to have a ~ with sb** tener una cita con alguien.

date of birth n fecha f de nacimiento.

daughter ['dɔ:təʳ] n hija f.

daughter-in-law n nuera f.

dawn [dɔ:n] n amanecer m.

day [deɪ] n día m; **what ~ is it today?** ¿qué día es hoy?; **what a lovely ~!** ¡qué día más bonito!; **to have a ~ off** tomarse un día libre; **to have a ~ out** ir de excursión; **by ~** de día; **the ~ after tomorrow** pasado mañana; **the ~ before** el día anterior; **the ~ before yesterday** anteayer; **the following ~** el día siguiente; **have a nice ~!** ¡adiós y gracias!

daylight ['deɪlaɪt] n luz f del día.

day return n (Br) billete de ida y vuelta para un día.

dayshift ['deɪʃɪft] n turno m de día.

daytime ['deɪtaɪm] n día m.

day-to-day adj cotidiano(-na).

day trip n excursión f (de un día).

dazzle ['dæzl] vt deslumbrar.

DC (abbr of direct current) CC.

dead [ded] adj (not alive) muerto(-ta); (not lively) sin vida; (telephone, line) cortado(-da); (battery) descargado(-da) ♦ adv (precisely) justo; (inf: very) la mar de; **it's ~**

ahead está justo enfrente; "**~ slow**" "al paso".

dead end n *(street)* callejón m sin salida.

deadline ['dedlaɪn] n fecha f tope.

deaf [def] adj sordo(-da) ♦ npl: **the ~** los sordos.

deal [di:l] *(pt & pp dealt)* n *(agreement)* trato m ♦ vt *(cards)* repartir; **to be a good/bad ~** estar bien/mal de precio; **a great ~ of** mucho; **it's a ~!** ¡trato hecho! ◘ **deal in** vt fus comerciar en; **deal with** vt fus *(handle)* hacer frente a; *(be about)* tratar de.

dealer ['di:ləʳ] n *(COMM)* comerciante mf; *(in drugs)* traficante mf *(que vende)*.

dealt [delt] *pt & pp* → **deal**.

dear [dɪəʳ] adj *(loved)* querido(-da); *(expensive)* caro(-ra) ♦ n: **my ~** querido m (-da f); **Dear Sir** Muy señor mío; **Dear Madam** Estimada señora; **Dear John** Querido John; **oh ~!** ¡vaya por Dios!

death [deθ] n muerte f.

debate [dɪ'beɪt] n debate m ♦ vt *(wonder)* pensar, considerar.

debit ['debɪt] n debe m ♦ vt: **to ~ sb's account with an amount** deducir una cantidad de la cuenta de alguien.

debt [det] n deuda f; **to be in ~** tener deudas.

decaff ['di:kæf] n *(inf)* descafeinado m.

decaffeinated [di'kæfɪneɪtɪd] adj descafeinado(-da).

decanter [dɪ'kæntəʳ] n licorera f.

decay [dɪ'keɪ] n *(of building, wood)* deterioro m; *(of tooth)* caries f inv ♦ vi descomponerse.

deceive [dɪ'si:v] vt engañar.

decelerate [,di:'seləreɪt] vi desacelerar.

December [dɪ'sembəʳ] n diciembre m, → **September**.

decent ['di:snt] adj decente; *(kind)* amable.

decide [dɪ'saɪd] vt & vi decidir; **to ~ to do sthg** decidir hacer algo ◘ **decide on** vt fus decidirse por.

decimal ['desɪml] adj decimal.

decimal point n coma f decimal.

decision [dɪ'sɪʒn] n decisión f; **to make a ~** tomar una decisión.

decisive [dɪ'saɪsɪv] adj *(person)* decidido(-da); *(event, factor)* decisivo(-va).

deck [dek] n *(of ship)* cubierta f; *(of bus)* piso m; *(of cards)* baraja f.

deckchair ['dektʃeəʳ] n tumbona f.

declare [dɪ'kleəʳ] vt declarar; **to ~ that** declarar que; "**goods to ~**" cartel que indica la ruta para personas con objetos que declarar en la aduana; "**nothing to ~**" cartel que indica la ruta para personas sin objetos que declarar en la aduana.

decline [dɪ'klaɪn] n declive m ♦ vi *(get worse)* disminuir; *(refuse)* rehusar.

decorate ['dekəreɪt] vt *(with wallpaper)* empapelar; *(with paint)* pintar; *(make attractive)* decorar.

decoration [,dekə'reɪʃn] n *(wallpaper, paint, furniture)* decoración f; *(decorative object)* adorno m.

decorator ['dekəreɪtə^r] n *(painter)* pintor m (-ra f); *(paperhanger)* empapelador m (-ra f).

decrease [n 'di:kri:s, vb dɪ'kri:s] n disminución f ♦ vi disminuir.

dedicated ['dedɪkeɪtɪd] adj dedicado(-da).

deduce [dɪ'dju:s] vt deducir.

deduct [dɪ'dʌkt] vt deducir.

deduction [dɪ'dʌkʃn] n deducción f.

deep [di:p] adj profundo(-da); *(colour)* intenso(-sa); *(breath, sigh)* hondo(-da); *(voice)* grave ♦ adv hondo; **it's two metres ~** tiene dos metros de profundidad.

deep end n *(of swimming pool)* parte f honda.

deep freeze n congelador m.

deep-fried [-'fraɪd] adj frito(-ta) en aceite abundante.

deep-pan adj de masa doble.

deer [dɪə^r] *(pl inv)* n ciervo m.

defeat [dɪ'fi:t] n derrota f ♦ vt derrotar.

defect ['di:fekt] n defecto m.

defective [dɪ'fektɪv] adj defectuoso(-sa).

defence [dɪ'fens] n *(Br)* defensa f.

defend [dɪ'fend] vt defender.

defense [dɪ'fens] *(Am)* = **defence**.

deficiency [dɪ'fɪʃnsɪ] n *(lack)* deficiencia f.

deficit ['defɪsɪt] n déficit m inv.

define [dɪ'faɪn] vt definir.

definite ['defɪnɪt] adj *(answer, plans)* definitivo(-va); *(improvement)* claro(-ra); *(person)* concluyente; **it's not ~** no es seguro.

definite article n artículo m definido.

definitely ['defɪnɪtlɪ] adv *(certainly)* sin duda alguna.

definition [defɪ'nɪʃn] n *(of word)* definición f.

deflate [dɪ'fleɪt] vt *(tyre)* desinflar.

deflect [dɪ'flekt] vt desviar.

defogger [di:'fɒgə^r] n *(Am)* luneta f térmica.

deformed [dɪ'fɔ:md] adj deforme.

defrost [di:'frɒst] vt *(food, fridge)* descongelar; *(Am: demist)* desempañar.

degree [dɪ'gri:] n grado m; *(qualification)* = licenciatura f; **to have a ~ in sthg** tener una licenciatura en algo.

dehydrated [di:haɪ'dreɪtɪd] adj deshidratado(-da).

de-ice [di:'aɪs] vt descongelar.

de-icer [di:'aɪsə^r] n descongelante m.

dejected [dɪ'dʒektɪd] adj abatido(-da).

delay [dɪ'leɪ] n retraso m ♦ vt retrasar ♦ vi retrasarse; **without ~** sin demora.

delayed [dɪ'leɪd] adj: **to be ~** ir con retraso; **our train was ~ by two hours** nuestro tren llegó con dos horas de retraso.

delegate [n 'delɪgət, vb 'delɪgeɪt] n delegado m (-da f) ♦ vt *(person)* delegar.

delete [dɪ'li:t] vt borrar.

deli ['delɪ] n *(inf: abbr of delicatessen)* = charcutería f.

deliberate [dɪ'lɪbərət] adj *(inten-

tional) deliberado(-da).

deliberately [dɪ'lɪbərətlɪ] *adv (intentionally)* deliberadamente.

delicacy ['delɪkəsɪ] *n (food)* manjar *m.*

delicate ['delɪkət] *adj* delicado(-da); *(object, china)* frágil; *(taste, smell)* suave.

delicatessen [,delɪkə'tesn] *n* = charcutería *f.*

delicious [dɪ'lɪʃəs] *adj* delicioso(-sa).

delight [dɪ'laɪt] *n (feeling)* gozo *m* ♦ *vt* encantar; **to take (a) ~ in doing sthg** deleitarse haciendo algo.

delighted [dɪ'laɪtɪd] *adj* encantado(-da).

delightful [dɪ'laɪtfʊl] *adj* encantador(-ra).

deliver [dɪ'lɪvər] *vt (goods, letters, newspaper)* entregar; *(speech, lecture)* pronunciar; *(baby)* traer al mundo.

delivery [dɪ'lɪvərɪ] *n (of goods, letters)* entrega *f; (birth)* parto *m.*

delude [dɪ'lu:d] *vt* engañar.

de-luxe [də'lʌks] *adj* de lujo.

demand [dɪ'mɑːnd] *n* demanda *f; (requirement)* requisito *m* ♦ *vt (request forcefully)* exigir; *(require)* requerir; **to ~ to do sthg** exigir hacer algo; **in ~** solicitado.

demanding [dɪ'mɑːndɪŋ] *adj* absorbente.

demerara sugar [demə'reərə-] *n* azúcar *m* moreno.

demist [,di:'mɪst] *vt (Br)* desempañar.

demister [,di:'mɪstər] *n (Br)* luneta *f* térmica.

democracy [dɪ'mɒkrəsɪ] *n* democracia *f.*

Democrat ['deməkræt] *n (Am)* demócrata *mf.*

democratic [demə'krætɪk] *adj* democrático(-ca).

demolish [dɪ'mɒlɪʃ] *vt (building)* demoler.

demonstrate ['demənstreɪt] *vt (prove)* demostrar; *(machine, appliance)* hacer una demostración de ♦ *vi* manifestarse.

demonstration [demən'streɪʃn] *n (protest)* manifestación *f; (of machine, proof)* demostración *f.*

denial [dɪ'naɪəl] *n* negación *f.*

denim ['denɪm] *n* tela *f* vaquera ❑ **denims** *npl* vaqueros *mpl.*

denim jacket *n* cazadora *f* vaquera.

Denmark ['denmɑːk] *n* Dinamarca.

dense [dens] *adj (crowd, smoke, forest)* denso(-sa).

dent [dent] *n* abolladura *f.*

dental ['dentl] *adj* dental.

dental floss [-flɒs] *n* hilo *m* dental.

dental surgeon *n* odontólogo *m (-ga f).*

dental surgery *n (place)* clínica *f* dental.

dentist ['dentɪst] *n* dentista *mf;* **to go to the ~'s** ir al dentista.

dentures ['dentʃəz] *npl* dentadura *f* postiza.

deny [dɪ'naɪ] *vt (declare untrue)* negar; *(refuse)* denegar.

deodorant [di:'əʊdərənt] *n* desodorante *m.*

depart [dɪ'pɑːt] *vi* salir; **this train**

will ~ from platform 3 este tren efectuará su salida de la vía 3.

department [dɪˈpɑːtmənt] *n* departamento *m*; *(of government)* ministerio *m*.

department store *n* grandes almacenes *mpl*.

departure [dɪˈpɑːtʃəʳ] *n* salida *f*; **"~s"** "salidas".

departure lounge *n (at airport)* sala *f* de embarque; *(at coach station)* vestíbulo *m* de salidas.

depend [dɪˈpend] *vi:* **it ~s** depende □ **depend on** *vt fus (be decided by)* depender de; *(rely on)* confiar en; **~ing on** dependiendo de.

dependable [dɪˈpendəbl] *adj* fiable.

deplorable [dɪˈplɔːrəbl] *adj* deplorable.

deport [dɪˈpɔːt] *vt* deportar.

deposit [dɪˈpɒzɪt] *n (in bank)* ingreso *m*; *(part-payment)* entrada *f*; *(against damage)* depósito *m*; *(substance)* sedimento *m* ♦ *vt (put down)* depositar; *(money in bank)* ingresar.

deposit account *n (Br)* cuenta *f* de ahorro a plazo fijo.

depot [ˈdiːpəʊ] *n (Am: for buses, trains)* terminal *f*.

depressed [dɪˈprest] *adj* deprimido(-da).

depressing [dɪˈpresɪŋ] *adj* deprimente.

depression [dɪˈpreʃn] *n* depresión *f*.

deprive [dɪˈpraɪv] *vt:* **to ~ sb of sthg** privar a alguien de algo.

depth [depθ] *n* profundidad *f*; **I'm out of my ~** *(when swimming)* he perdido pie; *(fig: unable to cope)*

no puedo; **~ of field** profundidad de campo.

deputy [ˈdepjʊtɪ] *adj* suplente; **~ head** subdirector *m* (-ra *f*).

derailleur [dəˈreɪljəʳ] *n* cambio *m* de piñón.

derailment [dɪˈreɪlmənt] *n* descarrilamiento *m*.

derelict [ˈderəlɪkt] *adj* abandonado(-da).

derv [dɜːv] *n (Br)* gasóleo *m*.

descend [dɪˈsend] *vt* descender por ♦ *vi* descender.

descendant [dɪˈsendənt] *n* descendiente *mf*.

descent [dɪˈsent] *n (going down)* descenso *m*; *(downward slope)* pendiente *f*.

describe [dɪˈskraɪb] *vt* describir.

description [dɪˈskrɪpʃn] *n* descripción *f*.

desert [*n* ˈdezət, *vb* dɪˈzɜːt] *n* desierto *m* ♦ *vt* abandonar.

deserted [dɪˈzɜːtɪd] *adj* desierto(-ta).

deserve [dɪˈzɜːv] *vt* merecer.

design [dɪˈzaɪn] *n* diseño *m* ♦ *vt* diseñar; **to be ~ed for** estar diseñado para.

designer [dɪˈzaɪnəʳ] *n* diseñador *m* (-ra *f*) ♦ *adj (clothes, sunglasses)* de marca.

desirable [dɪˈzaɪərəbl] *adj* deseable.

desire [dɪˈzaɪəʳ] *n* deseo *m* ♦ *vt* desear; **it leaves a lot to be ~d** deja mucho que desear.

desk [desk] *n (in home, office)* escritorio *m*; *(in school)* pupitre *m*; *(at airport, station, hotel)* mostrador *m*.

desktop publishing ['desk-
,tɒp-] *n* autoedición *f* de textos.

despair [dɪ'speəʳ] *n* desesperación *f*.

despatch [dɪ'spætʃ] = dispatch.

desperate ['despərət] *adj* deses-
perado(-da); **to be ~ for** sthg necesitar algo desesperadamente.

despicable [dɪ'spɪkəbl] *adj* des-
preciable.

despise [dɪ'spaɪz] *vt* despreciar.

despite [dɪ'spaɪt] *prep* a pesar de.

dessert [dɪ'zɜːt] *n* postre *m*.

dessertspoon [dɪ'zɜːtspuːn] *n*
(spoon) cuchara *f* de postre; *(spoonful)* cucharada *f* (de postre).

destination [,destɪ'neɪʃn] *n* destino *m*.

destroy [dɪ'strɔɪ] *vt* destruir.

destruction [dɪ'strʌkʃn] *n* destrucción *f*.

detach [dɪ'tætʃ] *vt* separar.

detached house [dɪ'tætʃt-] *n*
casa *f* individual.

detail ['diːteɪl] *n* *(minor point)*
detalle *m*; *(facts, information)* deta-
lles *mpl*; **in ~** detalladamente ❑
details *npl* *(facts)* información *f*.

detailed ['diːteɪld] *adj* detalla-
do(-da).

detect [dɪ'tekt] *vt* detectar.

detective [dɪ'tektɪv] *n* detective
mf; **a ~ story** una novela policíaca.

detention [dɪ'tenʃn] *n* *(SCH)* castigo de permanecer en la escuela después de clase.

detergent [dɪ'tɜːdʒənt] *n* detergente *m*.

deteriorate [dɪ'tɪərɪəreɪt] *vi*
deteriorarse.

determination [dɪ,tɜːmɪ'neɪʃn]

n determinación *f*.

determine [dɪ'tɜːmɪn] *vt* determinar.

determined [dɪ'tɜːmɪnd] *adj*
decidido(-da); **to be ~ to do** sthg
estar decidido a hacer algo.

deterrent [dɪ'terənt] *n* fuerza *f*
disuasoria.

detest [dɪ'test] *vt* detestar.

detour ['diː,tuəʳ] *n* desvío *m*.

detrain [,diː'treɪn] *vi* *(fml)* apearse *(de un tren)*.

deuce [djuːs] *excl* *(in tennis)* cuarenta iguales.

devastate ['devəsteɪt] *vt* devas-
tar.

develop [dɪ'veləp] *vt* *(idea, company)* desarrollar; *(land)* urbanizar;
(film) revelar; *(machine, method)* elaborar; *(illness)* contraer; *(habit,
interest)* adquirir ◆ *vi* *(evolve)* desarrollarse.

developing country [dɪ-
'veləpɪŋ-] *n* país *m* en vías de desarrollo.

development [dɪ'veləpmənt] *n*
(growth) desarrollo *m*; *(new event)*
(nuevo) acontecimiento *m*; **a housing ~** una urbanización.

device [dɪ'vaɪs] *n* dispositivo *m*.

devil ['devl] *n* diablo *m*; **what the
~ ...?** *(inf)* ¿qué demonios ...?

devise [dɪ'vaɪz] *vt* diseñar.

devoted [dɪ'vəʊtɪd] *adj* dedica-
do(-da), leal.

dew [djuː] *n* rocío *m*.

diabetes [,daɪə'biːtiːz] *n* diabetes
f inv.

diabetic [,daɪə'betɪk] *adj* *(person)*
diabético(-ca); *(chocolate)* para dia-
béticos ◆ *n* diabético *m* (-ca *f*).

diagnosis [,daɪəg'nəʊsɪs] (*pl* **-oses** [-əʊsi:z]) *n* diagnóstico *m*.

diagonal [daɪ'ægənl] *adj* diagonal.

diagram ['daɪəgræm] *n* diagrama *m*.

dial ['daɪəl] *n* (*of telephone, radio*) dial *m*; (*of clock*) esfera *f* ♦ *vt* marcar.

dialling code ['daɪəlɪŋ-] *n* (*Br*) prefijo *m* (telefónico).

dialling tone ['daɪəlɪŋ-] *n* (*Br*) señal *f* de llamada.

dial tone (*Am*) = **dialling tone**.

diameter [daɪ'æmɪtəʳ] *n* diámetro *m*.

diamond ['daɪəmənd] *n* diamante *m* ❑ **diamonds** *npl* (*in cards*) diamantes *mpl*.

diaper ['daɪpəʳ] *n* (*Am*) pañal *m*.

diarrhoea [,daɪə'rɪə] *n* diarrea *f*.

diary ['daɪərɪ] *n* (*for appointments*) agenda *f*; (*journal*) diario *m*.

dice [daɪs] (*pl inv*) *n* dado *m*.

diced [daɪst] *adj* cortado(-da) en cuadraditos.

dictate [dɪk'teɪt] *vt* dictar.

dictation [dɪk'teɪʃn] *n* dictado *m*.

dictator [dɪk'teɪtəʳ] *n* dictador *m* (-ra *f*).

dictionary ['dɪkʃənrɪ] *n* diccionario *m*.

did [dɪd] *pt* → **do**.

die [daɪ] (*cont* **dying**) *vi* morir; **to be dying for sthg** (*inf*) morirse por algo; **to be dying to do sthg** (*inf*) morirse por hacer algo ❑ **die away** *vi* desvanecerse; **die out** *vi* extinguirse.

diesel ['di:zl] *n* (*fuel*) gasóleo *m*;

(*car*) vehículo *m* diesel.

diet ['daɪət] *n* (*for slimming, health*) dieta *f*, régimen *m*; (*food eaten*) dieta *f* ♦ *vi* estar a régimen ♦ *adj* bajo(-ja) en calorías.

diet Coke® *n* Coca-Cola® *f* light.

differ ['dɪfəʳ] *vi*: **to ~ (from)** (*be dissimilar*) ser distinto (de); (*disagree*) discrepar (de).

difference ['dɪfrəns] *n* diferencia *f*; **it makes no ~** da lo mismo; **a ~ of opinion** un desacuerdo

different ['dɪfrənt] *adj* distinto(-ta); **to be ~ (from)** ser distinto (de).

differently ['dɪfrəntlɪ] *adv* de otra forma.

difficult ['dɪfɪkəlt] *adj* difícil.

difficulty ['dɪfɪkəltɪ] *n* dificultad *f*.

dig [dɪg] (*pt & pp* **dug**) *vt* (*hole, tunnel*) excavar; (*garden, land*) cavar ♦ *vi* cavar ❑ **dig up** *vt sep* sacar; **dig up** *vt sep* desenterrar.

digest [dɪ'dʒest] *vt* digerir.

digestion [dɪ'dʒestʃn] *n* digestión *f*.

digestive (biscuit) [dɪ'dʒestɪv-] *n* (*Br*) galleta hecha con harina integral.

digit ['dɪdʒɪt] *n* (*figure*) dígito *m*; (*finger, toe*) dedo *m*.

digital ['dɪdʒɪtl] *adj* digital.

dill [dɪl] *n* eneldo *m*.

dilute [daɪ'lu:t] *vt* diluir.

dim [dɪm] *adj* (*light*) tenue; (*room*) sombrío(-a); (*inf: stupid*) torpe ♦ *vt* atenuar.

dime [daɪm] *n* (*Am*) moneda de diez

centavos.

dimensions [dɪˈmenʃnz] *npl (measurements)* dimensiones *fpl; (extent)* dimensión *f.*

din [dɪn] *n* estrépito *m.*

dine [daɪn] *vi* cenar ❑ **dine out** *vi* cenar fuera.

diner [ˈdaɪnər] *n (Am: restaurant)* restaurante *m* económico; *(person)* cliente *mf (en un restaurante).*

---

i DINER

Los "diners", pequeños restaurantes baratos donde se sirven comidas ligeras, suelen localizarse en las carreteras principales, aunque también se dan en ciudades. La mayoría de sus clientes son camioneros y gente de paso.

---

dinghy [ˈdɪŋgɪ] *n* bote *m.*

dingy [ˈdɪndʒɪ] *adj* lóbrego(-ga).

dining car [ˈdaɪnɪŋ-] *n* vagón *m* restaurante.

dining hall [ˈdaɪnɪŋ-] *n (SCH)* comedor *m.*

dining room [ˈdaɪnɪŋ-] *n* comedor *m.*

dinner [ˈdɪnər] *n (at lunchtime)* almuerzo *m; (in evening)* cena *f;* **to have ~** *(at lunchtime)* almorzar; *(in evening)* cenar.

dinner jacket *n* esmoquin *m.*

dinner party *n* cena *f (de amigos en casa).*

dinner set *n* vajilla *f.*

dinner suit *n* traje *m* de esmoquin.

dinnertime [ˈdɪnətaɪm] *n (at*

lunchtime) hora *f* del almuerzo; *(in evening)* hora *f* de la cena.

dinosaur [ˈdaɪnəsɔːr] *n* dinosaurio *m.*

dip [dɪp] *n (in road, land)* pendiente *f; (food)* salsa *f* ◆ *vt (into liquid)* mojar ◆ *vi* descender ligeramente; **to have a ~** darse un chapuzón; **to ~ one's headlights** *(Br)* poner las luces de cruce.

diploma [dɪˈpləʊmə] *n* diploma *m.*

dipstick [ˈdɪpstɪk] *n* varilla *f* (para medir el nivel) del aceite.

direct [dɪˈrekt] *adj* directo(-ta) ◆ *vt* dirigir; *(give directions to)* indicar el camino a ◆ *adv* directamente.

direct current *n* corriente *f* continua.

direction [dɪˈrekʃn] *n* dirección *f;* **to ask for ~s** pedir señas ❑ **directions** *npl (instructions)* instrucciones *fpl (de uso).*

directly [dɪˈrektlɪ] *adv (exactly)* directamente; *(soon)* pronto.

director [dɪˈrektər] *n* director *m* (-ra *f).*

directory [dɪˈrektərɪ] *n* guía *f* (telefónica).

directory enquiries *n (Br)* servicio *m* de información telefónica.

dirt [dɜːt] *n* suciedad *f; (earth)* tierra *f.*

dirty [ˈdɜːtɪ] *adj* sucio(-cia); *(joke)* verde.

disability [ˌdɪsəˈbɪlətɪ] *n* minusvalía *f.*

disabled [dɪsˈeɪbld] *adj* minusválido(-da) ◆ *npl:* **the ~** los minusválidos; **"~ toilet"** "aseo para minusválidos".

disadvantage [,dɪsəd'vɑːntɪdʒ] n desventaja f.

disagree [,dɪsə'griː] vi (people) discrepar; **to ~ with sb (about)** no estar de acuerdo con alguien (sobre); **those mussels ~d with me** los mejillones me sentaron mal.

disagreement [,dɪsə'griːmənt] n (argument) discusión f; (dissimilarity) discrepancia f.

disappear [,dɪsə'pɪə^r] vi desaparecer.

disappearance [,dɪsə'pɪərəns] n desaparición f.

disappoint [,dɪsə'pɔɪnt] vt decepcionar.

disappointed [,dɪsə'pɔɪntɪd] adj decepcionado(-da).

disappointing [,dɪsə'pɔɪntɪŋ] adj decepcionante.

disappointment [,dɪsə'pɔɪntmənt] n decepción f.

disapprove [,dɪsə'pruːv] vi: **to ~ of** censurar.

disarmament [dɪs'ɑːməmənt] n desarme m.

disaster [dɪ'zɑːstə^r] n desastre m.

disastrous [dɪ'zɑːstrəs] adj desastroso(-sa).

disc [dɪsk] n (Br)(circular object, record) disco m; (CD) disco compacto; **to slip a ~** sufrir una hernia discal.

discard [dɪ'skɑːd] vt desechar.

discharge [dɪs'tʃɑːdʒ] vt (prisoner) poner en libertad; (patient) dar de alta; (soldier) licenciar; (liquid, smoke, gas) emitir.

discipline ['dɪsɪplɪn] n disciplina f.

disc jockey n pinchadiscos mf inv.

disco ['dɪskəʊ] n (place) discoteca f; (event) baile m.

discoloured [dɪs'kʌləd] adj descolorido(-da).

discomfort [dɪs'kʌmfət] n (pain) malestar m.

disconnect [,dɪskə'nekt] vt (unplug) desenchufar; (telephone, gas supply, pipe) desconectar.

discontinued [,dɪskən'tɪnjuːd] adj (product) que ya no se fabrica.

discotheque ['dɪskətek] n (place) discoteca f; (event) baile m.

discount ['dɪskaʊnt] n descuento m.

discover [dɪ'skʌvə^r] vt descubrir.

discovery [dɪ'skʌvərɪ] n descubrimiento m.

discreet [dɪ'skriːt] adj discreto(-ta).

discrepancy [dɪ'skrepənsɪ] n discrepancia f.

discriminate [dɪ'skrɪmɪneɪt] vi: **to against sb** discriminar a alguien.

discrimination [dɪ,skrɪmɪ'neɪʃn] n discriminación f.

discuss [dɪ'skʌs] vt discutir.

discussion [dɪ'skʌʃn] n discusión f.

disease [dɪ'ziːz] n enfermedad f.

disembark [,dɪsɪm'bɑːk] vi desembarcar.

disgrace [dɪs'greɪs] n vergüenza f; **it's a ~!** ¡es una vergüenza!

disgraceful [dɪs'greɪsfʊl] adj vergonzoso(-sa).

disguise [dɪs'gaɪz] n disfraz m ♦ vt disfrazar; **in ~** disfrazado.

disgust

disgust [dɪsˈgʌst] n asco m ◆ vt asquear.

disgusting [dɪsˈgʌstɪŋ] adj asqueroso(-sa).

dish [dɪʃ] n (container) fuente f; (food) plato m; (Am: plate) plato; **to do the ~es** fregar los platos; **"~ of the day"** "plato del día" ❑ **dish up** vt sep servir.

dishcloth [ˈdɪʃklɒθ] n trapo m de fregar los platos.

disheveled [dɪˈʃevəld] (Am) = **dishevelled**.

dishevelled [dɪˈʃevəld] adj (Br: person) desaliñado(-da).

dishonest [dɪsˈɒnɪst] adj deshonesto(-ta).

dish towel n (Am) paño m de cocina.

dishwasher [ˈdɪʃˌwɒʃər] n (machine) lavavajillas m inv.

disinfectant [ˌdɪsɪnˈfektənt] n desinfectante m.

disintegrate [dɪsˈɪntɪgreɪt] vi desintegrarse.

disk [dɪsk] n (Am) = **disc**; (COM-PUT) disquete m.

disk drive n disquetera f.

dislike [dɪsˈlaɪk] n (poor opinion) aversión f ◆ vt tener aversión a; **to take a ~ to** cogerle manía a.

dislocate [ˈdɪsləkeɪt] vt dislocar.

dismal [ˈdɪzml] adj (weather, place) sombrío(-a); (terrible) lamentable.

dismantle [dɪsˈmæntl] vt desmontar.

dismay [dɪsˈmeɪ] n consternación f.

dismiss [dɪsˈmɪs] vt (not consider) desechar; (from job) despedir; (from classroom) echar.

disobedient [ˌdɪsəˈbiːdjənt] adj desobediente.

disobey [ˌdɪsəˈbeɪ] vt desobedecer.

disorder [dɪsˈɔːdər] n (confusion) desorden m; (violence) disturbios mpl; (illness) afección f.

disorganized [dɪsˈɔːgənaɪzd] adj desorganizado(-da).

dispatch [dɪˈspætʃ] vt enviar.

dispense [dɪˈspens]: **dispense with** vt fus prescindir de.

dispenser [dɪˈspensər] n máquina f expendedora.

dispensing chemist [dɪˈspensɪŋ-] n (Br) (person) farmacéutico m (-ca f); (shop) farmacia f.

disperse [dɪˈspɜːs] vt dispersar ◆ vi dispersarse.

display [dɪˈspleɪ] n (of goods in window) escaparate m; (public event) demostración f; (readout) pantalla f ◆ vt (goods, information) exponer; (feeling, quality) mostrar; **on ~** expuesto.

displeased [dɪsˈpliːzd] adj disgustado(-da).

disposable [dɪˈspəʊzəbl] adj desechable.

dispute [dɪˈspjuːt] n (argument) disputa f; (industrial) conflicto m ◆ vt cuestionar.

disqualify [ˌdɪsˈkwɒlɪfaɪ] vt descalificar; **he has been disqualified from driving** (Br) se le ha retirado el permiso de conducir.

disregard [ˌdɪsrɪˈgɑːd] vt hacer caso omiso de.

disrupt [dɪsˈrʌpt] vt trastornar.

disruption [dɪsˈrʌpʃn] n trastorno m.

dissatisfied [ˌdɪsˈsætɪsfaɪd] adj descontento(-ta).

dissolve [dɪˈzɒlv] vt disolver ♦ vi disolverse.

dissuade [dɪˈsweɪd] vt: **to ~ sb from doing sthg** disuadir a alguien de hacer algo.

distance [ˈdɪstəns] n distancia f; **from a ~** desde lejos; **in the ~** a lo lejos.

distant [ˈdɪstənt] adj lejano(-na); (reserved) distante.

distilled water [dɪˈstɪld-] n agua f destilada.

distillery [dɪˈstɪlərɪ] n destilería f.

distinct [dɪˈstɪŋkt] adj (separate) distinto(-ta); (noticeable) notable.

distinction [dɪˈstɪŋkʃn] n (difference) distinción f; (mark for work) sobresaliente m.

distinctive [dɪˈstɪŋktɪv] adj característico(-ca).

distinguish [dɪˈstɪŋgwɪʃ] vt distinguir; **to ~ sthg from sthg** distinguir algo de algo.

distorted [dɪˈstɔːtɪd] adj (figure, shape) deformado(-da); (sound) distorsionado(-da).

distract [dɪˈstrækt] vt distraer.

distraction [dɪˈstrækʃn] n distracción f.

distress [dɪˈstres] n (pain) dolor m; (anxiety) angustia f.

distressing [dɪˈstresɪŋ] adj angustioso(-sa).

distribute [dɪˈstrɪbjuːt] vt distribuir.

distributor [dɪˈstrɪbjʊtəʳ] n (COMM) distribuidor m (-ra f); (AUT)

delco m.

district [ˈdɪstrɪkt] n (region) región f; (of town) distrito m.

district attorney n (Am) fiscal mf (del distrito).

disturb [dɪˈstɜːb] vt (interrupt) molestar; (worry) inquietar; (move) mover; **"do not ~"** "no molestar".

disturbance [dɪˈstɜːbəns] n (riot) disturbio m; (small altercation) altercado m.

ditch [dɪtʃ] n zanja f.

ditto [ˈdɪtəʊ] adv ídem.

divan [dɪˈvæn] n diván m.

dive [daɪv] (pt Am -d OR dove, pt Br -d) n (of swimmer) zambullida f ♦ vi (from divingboard, rock) zambullirse; (under water) bucear; (bird, plane) bajar en picado; (rush) lanzarse.

diver [ˈdaɪvəʳ] n (from divingboard, rock) saltador m (-ra f); (under water) buceador m (-ra f).

diversion [daɪˈvɜːʃn] n (of traffic) desvío m; (amusement) diversión f.

divert [daɪˈvɜːt] vt (traffic, river) desviar; (attention) distraer.

divide [dɪˈvaɪd] vt dividir; (share out) repartir ❑ **divide up** vt sep (into two parts) dividir; (share out) repartir.

diving [ˈdaɪvɪŋ] n (from divingboard, rock) salto m; (under water) buceo m; **to go ~** bucear.

divingboard [ˈdaɪvɪŋbɔːd] n trampolín m.

division [dɪˈvɪʒn] n división f.

divorce [dɪˈvɔːs] n divorcio m ♦ vt divorciarse de.

divorced [dɪˈvɔːst] adj divorciado(-da).

DIY *n* (*abbr of* do-it-yourself) bricolaje *m*.

dizzy ['dɪzɪ] *adj* mareado(-da).

DJ *n* (*abbr of* disc jockey) pinchadiscos *mf inv*.

do [duː] (*pt* did, *pp* done, *pl* dos) *aux vb* 1. (*in negatives*): **don't ~ that!** ¡no hagas eso!; **she didn't listen** no hizo caso.

2. (*in questions*): **~ you like it?** ¿te gusta?; **how ~ you do it?** ¿cómo se hace?

3. (*referring to previous verb*): **I eat more than you** ~ yo como más que tú; **~ you smoke? - yes, I ~/no, I don't** ¿fumas? - sí/no; **so ~ I** yo también.

4. (*in question tags*): **so, you like Scotland, ~ you?** así que te gusta Escocia ¿no?

◆ *vt* 1. (*gen*) hacer; **to ~ one's homework** hacer los deberes; **what can I ~ for you?** ¿en qué puedo servirle?; **to ~ one's hair** peinarse; **to ~ one's teeth** lavarse los dientes; **to ~ damage** hacer daño; **to ~ sb good** sentarle bien a alguien.

2. (*have as job*): **what do you ~?** ¿a qué te dedicas?

3. (*provide, offer*) hacer; **we ~ pizzas for under £4** vendemos pizzas a menos de 4 libras.

4. (*study*) hacer.

5. (*subj: vehicle*) ir a.

6. (*inf: visit*) recorrer.

◆ *vi* 1. (*behave, act*) hacer; **~ as I say** haz lo que te digo.

2. (*progress, get on*) ir; **I did well/badly** me fue bien/mal.

3. (*be sufficient*) valer; **will £5 ~?** ¿llegará con cinco libras?

4. (*in phrases*): **how do you ~?** (*greeting*) ¿cómo está usted?;

(*answer*) mucho gusto; **what has that got to ~ with it?** ¿y eso qué tiene que ver?

◆ *n* (*party*) fiesta *f*; **~s and don'ts** normas *fpl* de conducta.

❑ **do out of** *vt sep* (*inf*) timar; **do up** *vt sep* (*shirt, buttons*) abrochar; (*shoes, laces*) atar; (*zip*) subir; (*decorate*) renovar; (*wrap up*) envolver; **do with** *vt fus*: **I could ~ with a drink** no me vendría mal una copa; **do without** *vt fus* pasar sin.

dock [dɒk] *n* (*for ships*) muelle *m*; (*JUR*) banquillo *m* (de los acusados) ◆ *vi* atracar.

doctor ['dɒktər] *n* (*of medicine*) médico *m* (-ca *f*); (*academic*) doctor *m* (-ra *f*); **to go to the ~'s** ir al médico.

document ['dɒkjʊmənt] *n* documento *m*.

documentary [,dɒkjʊ'mentərɪ] *n* documental *m*.

Dodgems® ['dɒdʒəmz] *npl* (*Br*) coches *mpl* de choque.

dodgy ['dɒdʒɪ] *adj* (*Br: inf: plan, car*) poco fiable; (*health*) delicado(-da).

does [weak form dəz, strong form dʌz] → **do**.

doesn't ['dʌznt] = does not.

dog [dɒg] *n* perro *m*.

dog food *n* comida *f* para perros.

doggy bag ['dɒgɪ] *n* bolsa que da el restaurante para llevarse las sobras.

do-it-yourself *n* bricolaje *m*.

dole [dəʊl] *n*: **to be on the ~** (*Br*) estar parado.

doll [dɒl] *n* muñeca *f*.

dollar ['dɒlər] *n* dólar *m*.

dolphin ['dɒlfɪn] n delfín m.

dome [dəʊm] n cúpula f.

domestic [də'mestɪk] adj (of house, family) doméstico(-ca); (of country) nacional.

domestic appliance n electrodoméstico m.

domestic flight n vuelo m nacional.

domestic science n hogar m (asignatura).

dominate ['dɒmɪneɪt] vt dominar.

dominoes ['dɒmɪnəʊz] n dominó m.

donate [də'neɪt] vt donar.

donation [də'neɪʃn] n donación f.

done [dʌn] pp → **do** ♦ adj (finished) listo(ta); (cooked) hecho (-cha).

donkey ['dɒŋkɪ] n burro m.

don't [dəʊnt] = **do not**.

door [dɔː] n puerta f.

doorbell ['dɔːbel] n timbre m.

doorknob ['dɔːnɒb] n pomo m.

doorman ['dɔːmən] (pl -men [-mən]) n portero m.

doormat ['dɔːmæt] n felpudo m.

doormen ['dɔːmən] pl → **door man**.

doorstep ['dɔːstep] n (in front of door) peldaño m de la puerta; (Br: piece of bread) rebanada de pan muy gruesa.

doorway ['dɔːweɪ] n portal m.

dope [dəʊp] n (inf) (any illegal drug) droga f; (marijuana) maría f.

dormitory ['dɔːmɪtrɪ] n dormitorio m.

Dormobile® ['dɔːmə,biːl] n autocaravana f.

dosage ['dəʊsɪdʒ] n dosis f inv.

dose [dəʊs] n (amount) dosis f inv; (of illness) ataque m.

dot [dɒt] n punto m; **on the ~** (fig) en punto.

dotted line ['dɒtɪd-] n línea f de puntos.

double ['dʌbl] adj doble ♦ n (twice the amount) el doble; (alcohol) doble m ♦ vt doblar ♦ vi doblarse ♦ adv: it's ~ the size es el doble de grande; **to bend sthg** ~ doblar algo; **a ~ whisky** un whisky doble; ~ **three, four, two** treinta y tres, cuarenta y dos; **it's spelt with a ~ "s"** se escribe con dos eses ❑ **doubles** n dobles mpl.

double bed n cama f de matrimonio.

double-breasted [-'brestɪd] adj cruzado(-da).

double cream n (Br) nata f enriquecida.

double-decker (bus) [-'dekə-] n autobús m de dos pisos.

double doors npl puerta f de dos hojas.

double-glazing [-'gleɪzɪŋ] n doble acristalamiento m.

double room n habitación f doble.

doubt [daʊt] n duda f ♦ vt (distrust) dudar de; **I** ~ **it** lo dudo; **I** ~ **she'll be there** dudo que esté ahí; **to be in** ~ (person) estar dudando; (matter, outcome) ser incierto; **no** ~ sin duda.

doubtful ['daʊtfʊl] adj (uncertain) dudoso(-sa); **it's** ~ **that ...** es improbable que ...

dough [dəʊ] n masa f.

doughnut ['dəʊnʌt] n (without hole) buñuelo m; (with hole) dónut® m.

dove¹ [dʌv] n (bird) paloma f.

dove² [dəʊv] pt (Am) → **dive**.

Dover sole ['dəʊvə-ˡ] n lenguado de gran calidad que proviene del Canal de la Mancha.

down [daʊn] adv 1. (towards the bottom) (hacia) abajo; ~ **here/there** aquí/allí abajo; **to fall** ~ caer. 2. (along) **I'm going** ~ **to the shops** voy a acercarme a las tiendas. 3. (downstairs) abajo; **I'll come** ~ **later** bajaré más tarde. 4. (southwards) hacia el sur; **we're going** ~ **to London** vamos a bajar a Londres. 5. (in writing): **to write sthg** ~ apuntar algo. 6. (in phrases): **to go** ~ **with** (illness) pillar.
♦ prep 1. (towards the bottom of) : **they ran** ~ **the hill** corrieron cuesta abajo. 2. (along) por; **I was walking** ~ **the street** iba andando por la calle.
♦ adj (inf: depressed) deprimido(-da).
♦ n (feathers) plumón m.
❑ **downs** npl (Br) montes m en el sur de Inglaterra.

downhill [ˌdaʊn'hɪl] adv cuesta abajo.

Downing Street ['daʊnɪŋ-] n Downing Street m.

---

i **DOWNING STREET**

E sta calle de Londres es famosa por ser la residencia del Primer Ministro británico (en el número 10) y del Ministro de Economía y Hacienda (en el número 11). El nombre "Downing Street" se utiliza también para referirse al Primer Ministro y sus asistentes.

---

downpour ['daʊnpɔːˡ] n chaparrón m.

downstairs [adj 'daʊnˌsteəz, adv ˌdaʊn'steəz] adj de abajo ♦ adv abajo; **to go** ~ bajar (la escalera).

downtown [adj 'daʊntaʊn, adv ˌdaʊn'taʊn] adj céntrico(-ca) ♦ adv (live) en el centro; (go) al centro; ~ **New York** el centro de Nueva York.

down under adv (Br: inf) en/a Australia.

downwards ['daʊnwədz] adv hacia abajo.

doz. abbr = **dozen**.

doze [dəʊz] vi dormitar.

dozen ['dʌzn] n docena f; **a** ~ **eggs** una docena de huevos.

Dr (abbr of Doctor) Dr.

drab [dræb] adj (clothes, wallpaper) deslustrado(-da).

draft [drɑːft] n (early version) borrador m; (money order) giro m; (Am) = **draught**.

drag [dræg] vt arrastrar ♦ vi (along ground) arrastrar; **what a** ~! ¡qué rollo! ❑ **drag on** vi ser interminable.

dragonfly ['drægnflaɪ] n libélula f.

drain [dreɪn] n (sewer) desagüe m; (grating in street) sumidero m ♦ vt (tank, radiator) vaciar ♦ vi (vegetables, washing-up) escurrirse.

draining board ['dreɪnɪŋ-] n

escurridero m.

drainpipe ['dreinpaip] n tubo m de desagüe.

drama ['dra:mə] n (play, excitement) drama m; (art) teatro m.

dramatic [drə'mætik] adj (impressive) dramático(-ca).

drank [dræŋk] pt → **drink**.

drapes [dreips] npl (Am) cortinas fpl.

drastic ['dræstik] adj (extreme) drástico(-ca); (change, improvement) radical.

drastically ['dræstikli] adv drásticamente.

draught [dra:ft] n (Br: of air) corriente f de aire.

draught beer n cerveza f de barril.

draughts [dra:fts] n (Br) damas fpl.

draughty ['dra:fti] adj: it's ~ hay corriente.

draw [dra:] (pt drew, pp drawn) vt (picture, map) dibujar; (line) trazar; (pull) tirar de; (attract) atraer; (comparison) señalar; (conclusion) llegar a ◆ vi (with pen, pencil) dibujar; (SPORT) empatar ◆ n (SPORT: result) empate m; (lottery) sorteo m; **to ~ the curtains** (open) descorrer las cortinas; (close) correr las cortinas ❏ **draw out** vt sep (money) sacar; **draw up** vt sep (list, plan) preparar ◆ vi (car, bus) pararse.

drawback ['drɔ:bæk] n desventaja f.

drawer [drɔ:r] n cajón m.

drawing ['drɔ:ɪŋ] n dibujo m.

drawing pin n (Br) chincheta f.

drawing room n cuarto m de estar.

drawn [drɔ:n] pp → **draw**.

dreadful ['dredful] adj terrible.

dream [dri:m] n sueño m ◆ vt (when asleep) soñar, (imagine) imaginar ◆ vi: **to ~ (of)** soñar (con); **a ~ house** una casa de ensueño.

dress [dres] n (for woman, girl) vestido m; (clothes) traje m ◆ vt (person, baby) vestir; (wound) vendar; (salad) aliñar ◆ vi (get dressed) vestirse; (in particular way) vestir; **to be ~ed in** ir vestido de, **to get ~ed** vestirse ❏ **dress up** vi (in costume) disfrazarse; (in best clothes) engalanarse.

dress circle n piso m principal.

dresser ['dresər] n (Br: for crockery) aparador m; (Am: chest of drawers) cómoda f.

dressing ['dresɪŋ] n (for salad) aliño m; (for wound) vendaje m.

dressing gown n bata f.

dressing room n vestuario m.

dressing table n tocador m.

dressmaker ['dres,meikər] n modisto m (-ta f).

dress rehearsal n ensayo m general.

drew [dru:] pt → **draw**.

dribble ['dribl] vi (liquid) gotear; (baby) babear.

drier ['draiər] = **dryer**.

drift [drift] n (of snow) ventisquero m ◆ vi (in wind) dejarse llevar por el viento; (in water) dejarse llevar por el agua.

drill [dril] n (tool) taladro m; (of dentist) fresa f ◆ vt (hole) taladrar.

drink [drɪŋk] (pt drank, pp drunk) n (of water, tea etc) bebida f;

drinkable 90

(alcoholic) copa f ♦ vt & vi beber; **to have a ~** (alcoholic) tomar una copa; **would you like a ~?** ¿quieres beber algo?

drinkable ['drɪŋkəbl] adj (safe to drink) potable; (wine) agradable.

drinking water ['drɪŋkɪŋ-] n agua f potable.

drip [drɪp] n (drop) gota f; (MED) gotero m ♦ vi gotear.

drip-dry adj de lava y pon.

dripping (wet) ['drɪpɪŋ-] adj empapado(-da).

drive [draɪv] (pt **drove**, pp **driven**) n (journey) viaje m (en coche); (in front of house) camino m (de entrada) ♦ vt (car, bus, train) conducir; (take in car) llevar (en coche); (operate, power) impulsar ♦ vi (drive car) conducir; (travel in car) ir en coche; **to ~ sb to do sthg** llevar a alguien a hacer algo; **to go for a ~** dar una vuelta en coche; **to ~ sb mad** volver loco a alguien.

drivel ['drɪvl] n tonterías fpl.

driven ['drɪvn] pp → **drive**.

driver ['draɪvəʳ] n (of car, bus) conductor m (-ra f); (of train) maquinista mf.

driver's license (Am) = **driving licence**.

driveshaft ['draɪvʃɑːft] n eje m de transmisión.

driveway ['draɪvweɪ] n camino m de entrada.

driving lesson ['draɪvɪŋ-] n clase f de conducir.

driving licence ['draɪvɪŋ-] n (Br) permiso m de conducir.

driving test ['draɪvɪŋ-] n examen m de conducir.

drizzle ['drɪzl] n llovizna f.

drop [drɒp] n (drip, small amount) gota f; (distance down) caída f; (decrease) descenso m; (in wages) disminución f ♦ vt (let fall) dejar caer; (reduce) reducir; (from vehicle) dejar; (omit) omitir ♦ vi (fall) caer; (decrease) disminuir; (price, temperature) bajar; **to ~ a hint** lanzar una indirecta; **to ~ sb a line** escribir unas líneas a alguien ❑ **drop in** vi (inf): **to ~ in on sb** pasarse por casa de alguien; **drop off** vt sep (from vehicle) dejar ♦ vi (fall asleep) quedarse dormido; (fall off) desprenderse; **drop out** vi (of college) abandonar los estudios; (of race) retirarse.

drought [draʊt] n sequía f.

drove [drəʊv] pt → **drive**.

drown [draʊn] vi ahogarse.

drug [drʌg] n (MED) medicamento m; (stimulant) droga f ♦ vt drogar.

drug addict n drogadicto m (-ta f).

druggist ['drʌgɪst] n (Am) farmacéutico m (-ca f).

drum [drʌm] n (MUS) tambor m; (container) bidón m; **~s** (in pop music) batería f.

drummer ['drʌməʳ] n (in pop music) batería mf.

drumstick ['drʌmstɪk] n (of chicken) muslo m.

drunk [drʌŋk] pp → **drink** ♦ adj borracho(-cha) ♦ n borracho m (-cha f); **to get ~** emborracharse.

dry [draɪ] adj seco(-ca); (day) sin lluvia ♦ vt secar ♦ vi secarse; **to ~ o.s.** secarse; **to ~ one's hair** secarse el pelo; **to ~ one's hands** secarse las manos ❑ **dry up** vi (become dry)

secarse; *(dry the dishes)* secar.
dry-clean *vt* limpiar en seco.
dry cleaner's *n* tintorería *f*.
dryer ['draɪə'] *n (for clothes)* secadora *f*; *(for hair)* secador *m*.
dry-roasted   peanuts
[-'rəustɪd-] *npl* cacahuetes *mpl* tostados y salados.
DSS *n (Br)* ministerio británico de la seguridad social.
DTP *n (abbr of desktop publishing)* autoed. *f*.
dual carriageway ['djuəl] *n (Br)* (tramo de) carretera con dos carriles en cada dirección.
dubbed [dʌbd] *adj (film)* doblado(-da).
dubious ['djuːbjəs] *adj (suspect)* sospechoso(-sa).
duchess ['dʌtʃɪs] *n* duquesa *f*
duck [dʌk] *n (bird)* pato *m* (-ta *f*); *(food)* pato *m* ◆ *vi* agacharse.
due [djuː] *adj (bill, rent)* pagadero(-ra); **when is the train ~?** ¿cuándo debería llegar el tren?; **the money ~ to me** el dinero que se me debe; **in ~ course** a su debido tiempo; **~ to** debido a.
duet [djuː'et] *n* dúo *m*.
duffel bag ['dʌfl-] *n* morral *m*.
duffel coat ['dʌfl-] *n* trenca *f*.
dug [dʌg] *pt & pp* → **dig.**
duke [djuːk] *n* duque *m*.
dull [dʌl] *adj (boring)* aburrido(-da); *(not bright)* torpe; *(weather)* gris; *(pain)* sordo(-da).
dumb [dʌm] *adj (inf: stupid)* estúpido(-da); *(unable to speak)* mudo (-da).
dummy ['dʌmɪ] *n (Br: for baby)* chupete *m*; *(for clothes)* maniquí *m*.

dump [dʌmp] *n (for rubbish)* vertedero *m*; *(inf: place)* tugurio *m* ◆ *vt (drop carelessly)* dejar; *(get rid of)* deshacerse de.
dumpling ['dʌmplɪŋ] *n* bola de masa que se guisa al vapor con carne y verduras.
dune [djuːn] *n* duna *f*.
dungarees [,dʌŋgə'riːz] *npl (Br: for work)* mono *m*; *(fashion item)* pantalones *mpl* de peto; *(Am: jeans)* vaqueros de tela gruesa utilizados para trabajar.
dungeon ['dʌndʒən] *n* mazmorra *f*.
duo ['djuːəu] *n*: **with a ~ of sauces** con dos salsas distintas.
duplicate ['djuːplɪkət] *n* copia *f*.
during ['djuərɪŋ] *prep* durante.
dusk [dʌsk] *n* crepúsculo *m*.
dust [dʌst] *n* polvo *m* ◆ *vt* quitar el polvo a.
dustbin ['dʌstbɪn] *n (Br)* cubo *m* de la basura.
dustcart ['dʌstkɑːt] *n (Br)* camión *m* de la basura.
duster ['dʌstə'] *n* trapo *m* (de quitar el polvo).
dustman ['dʌstmən] *(pl -men* [-mən]*) n (Br)* basurero *m*.
dustpan ['dʌstpæn] *n* recogedor *m*.
dusty ['dʌstɪ] *adj* lleno(-na) de polvo.
Dutch [dʌtʃ] *adj* holandés(-esa) ◆ *n (language)* holandés *m* ◆ *npl*: **the ~** los holandeses.
Dutchman ['dʌtʃmən] *(pl -men* [-mən]*) n* holandés *m*.
Dutchwoman ['dʌtʃ,wumən] *(pl -women* [-,wɪmɪn]*) n* holandesa *f*.

duty ['djuːtɪ] n (moral obligation) deber m; (tax) impuesto m; **to be on** ~ estar de servicio; **to be off** ~ no estar de servicio ❏ **duties** npl (job) tareas fpl.

duty chemist's n farmacia f de guardia.

duty-free adj libre de impuestos ♦ n (article) artículo m libre de impuestos.

duty-free shop n tienda f libre de impuestos.

duvet ['duːveɪ] n edredón m.

dwarf [dwɔːf] (pl **dwarves** [dwɔːvz]) n enano m (-na f).

dwelling ['dwelɪŋ] n (fml) morada f.

dye [daɪ] n tinte m ♦ vt teñir.

dying ['daɪɪŋ] cont → **die**.

dynamite ['daɪnəmaɪt] n dinamita f.

dynamo ['daɪnəməʊ] (pl **-s**) n dínamo f.

dyslexic [dɪs'leksɪk] adj disléxico(-ca).

E (abbr of east) E.

E111 n E111 m, impreso para obtener asistencia médica en otros países de la Unión Europea.

each [iːtʃ] adj cada ♦ pron cada uno m (cada una f); ~ **one** cada uno (cada una); ~ **of them** cada uno (cada una); ~ **other** el uno al otro; **they hate** ~ **other** se odian; **we know** ~ **other** nos conocemos; **one** ~ uno cada uno (una cada una); **one of** ~ uno de cada.

eager ['iːgəʳ] adj (pupil) entusiasta; (expression) de entusiasmo; **to be** ~ **to do sthg** estar deseoso(-sa) de hacer algo.

eagle ['iːgl] n águila f.

ear [ɪəʳ] n (of person, animal) oreja f; (of corn) espiga f.

earache ['ɪəreɪk] n: **to have** ~ tener dolor de oídos.

earl [ɜːl] n conde m.

early ['ɜːlɪ] adj temprano(-na) ♦ adv temprano; ~ **last year** a principios del año pasado; ~ **morning** la madrugada; **it arrived an hour** ~ llegó con una hora de adelanto; **at the earliest** como muy pronto; ~ **on** al principio; **to have an** ~ **night** irse a la cama temprano.

earn [ɜːn] vt (money) ganar; (praise, success) ganarse; **to** ~ **a living** ganarse la vida.

earnings ['ɜːnɪŋz] npl ingresos mpl.

earphones ['ɪəfəʊnz] npl auriculares mpl.

earplugs ['ɪəplʌgz] npl tapones mpl para los oídos.

earrings ['ɪərɪŋz] npl pendientes mpl.

earth [ɜːθ] n tierra f; (Br: electrical connection) toma f de tierra ♦ vt (Br) conectar a tierra; **how on** ~ ...? ¿cómo demonios ...?

earthenware ['ɜːθnweəʳ] adj de loza.

earthquake ['ɜːθkweɪk] n terremoto m.

ease [i:z] n facilidad f ◆ vt (pain) aliviar; (problem) atenuar; **at ~** cómodo; **with ~** con facilidad ❑ **ease off** vi (pain) calmarse; (rain) amainar.

easily ['i:zɪlɪ] adv (without difficulty) fácilmente; (by far) sin lugar a dudas

east [i:st] n este m ◆ adv hacia el este; **in the ~ of England** al este de Inglaterra; **the East** (Asia) el Oriente.

eastbound ['i:stbaund] adj con dirección este.

Easter ['i:stər] n (day) Domingo m de Resurrección; (period) Semana f Santa.

eastern ['i:stən] adj del este ❑ **Eastern** adj (Asian) oriental.

Eastern Europe n Europa del Este.

eastwards ['i:stwədz] adv hacia el este.

easy ['i:zɪ] adj (not difficult) fácil; (without problems) cómodo(-da); **to take it ~** (relax) relajarse.

easygoing ['i:zɪ'gəʊɪŋ] adj tranquilo(-la).

eat [i:t] (pt ate, pp eaten [i:tn]) vt & vi comer ❑ **eat out** vi comer fuera.

eating apple ['i:tɪŋ-] n manzana f (para comer).

ebony ['ebənɪ] n ébano m.

EC n (abbr of European Community) CE f.

eccentric [ɪk'sentrɪk] adj excéntrico(-ca).

echo ['ekəʊ] (pl -es) n eco m ◆ vi resonar.

ecology [ɪ'kɒlədʒɪ] n ecología f.

economic [,i:kə'nɒmɪk] adj (relating to the economy) económico(-ca); (profitable) rentable ❑ **economics** n economía f.

economical [,i:kə'nɒmɪkl] adj económico(-ca).

economize [ɪ'kɒnəmaɪz] vi economizar.

economy [ɪ'kɒnəmɪ] n economía f.

economy class n clase f turista.

economy size adj de tamaño económico.

ecstasy ['ekstəsɪ] n éxtasis m inv

ECU ['ekju:] n ECU m.

Ecuador ['ekwədɔ:r] n Ecuador m.

Ecuadoran [,ekwə'dɔ:rən] adj ecuatoriano(-na) ◆ n ecuatoriano m (-na f).

eczema ['eksɪmə] n eccema m.

edge [edʒ] n (border) borde m; (of table, coin, ruler) canto m; (of knife) filo m.

edible ['edɪbl] adj comestible.

Edinburgh ['edɪnbrə] n Edimburgo.

Edinburgh Festival n: the ~ el festival de Edimburgo.

ⓘ EDINBURGH FESTIVAL

El festival de Edimburgo es un festival internacional de música y teatro que tiene lugar cada año en la capital escocesa durante el mes de agosto. El festival oficial, con lo mejor en música, baile y teatro, se complementa con el "Fringe", que incluye cientos de producciones independientes representadas en pequeños locales por toda la ciudad.

---

edition [ɪˈdɪʃn] n edición f.

editor [ˈedɪtəʳ] n (of newspaper, magazine) director m (-ra f); (of book) autor m (-ra f) de la edición; (of film, TV programme) montador m (-ra f).

editorial [ˌedɪˈtɔːrɪəl] n editorial m.

educate [ˈedʒʊkeɪt] vt educar.

education [ˌedʒʊˈkeɪʃn] n (field) enseñanza f; (process or result of teaching) educación f.

EEC n CEE f.

eel [iːl] n anguila f.

effect [ɪˈfekt] n efecto m; **to put sthg into** ~ hacer entrar en vigor; **to take** ~ (medicine) hacer efecto; (law) entrar en vigor.

effective [ɪˈfektɪv] adj (successful) eficaz; (law, system) operativo(-va).

effectively [ɪˈfektɪvlɪ] adv (successfully) eficazmente; (in fact) de hecho.

efficient [ɪˈfɪʃənt] adj eficiente.

effort [ˈefət] n esfuerzo m; **to make an** ~ **to do sthg** hacer un esfuerzo por hacer algo; **it's not worth the** ~ no merece la pena.

e.g. adv p. ej.

egg [eg] n huevo m.

egg cup n huevera f.

egg mayonnaise n relleno de bocadillo consistente en huevo duro triturado con mayonesa.

eggplant [ˈeɡplɑːnt] n (Am) berenjena f.

egg white n clara f (de huevo).

egg yolk n yema f (de huevo).

Egypt [ˈiːdʒɪpt] n Egipto m.

eiderdown [ˈaɪdədaʊn] n edredón m.

eight [eɪt] num ocho, → **six**.

eighteen [ˌeɪˈtiːn] num dieciocho, → **six**.

eighteenth [ˌeɪˈtiːnθ] num decimoctavo(-va), → **sixth**.

eighth [eɪtθ] num octavo(-va), → **sixth**.

eightieth [ˈeɪtɪθ] num octogésimo(-ma), → **sixth**.

eighty [ˈeɪtɪ] num ochenta, → **six**.

Eire [ˈeərə] n Eire.

eisteddfod [aɪˈstedfɒd] n festival galés de cultura.

ℹ️ EISTEDDFOD

El "Eisteddfod" es un festival que tiene lugar cada agosto en Gales para celebrar el idioma y la cultura galeses, con competiciones de música, poesía, teatro y arte. Este festival se remonta al siglo XII.

---

either [ˈaɪðəʳ, ˈiːðəʳ] adj: ~ **book will do** cualquiera de los dos libros vale ◆ pron: **I'll take** ~ (of them) me llevaré cualquiera (de los dos); **I don't like** ~ (of them) no me gusta ninguno (de los dos). ◆ adv: **I can't** ~ yo tampoco (puedo); ~ **... or** o ... o; **I don't speak** ~ **French or Spanish** no hablo ni francés ni español; **on** ~ **side** a ambos lados.

eject [ɪˈdʒekt] vt (cassette) expulsar.

elaborate [ɪˈlæbrət] adj elaborado(-da).

elastic [ɪˈlæstɪk] n elástico m.

elastic band n (Br) goma f (elástica).

elbow ['elbəʊ] n codo m.

elder ['eldə'] adj mayor.

elderly ['eldəlɪ] adj anciano(-na)
♦ npl: **the ~ los** ancianos.

eldest ['eldɪst] adj mayor.

elect [ɪ'lekt] vt (by voting) elegir;
to ~ to do sthg (fml) optar por
hacer algo.

election [ɪ'lekʃn] n elección f.

electric [ɪ'lektrɪk] adj eléctri-
co(-ca).

electrical goods [ɪ'lektrɪkl-]
npl electrodomésticos mpl.

electric blanket n manta f
eléctrica.

electric drill n taladro m eléctrico.

electric fence n cercado m
electrificado.

electrician [ˌɪlek'trɪʃn] n electricista mf.

electricity [ˌɪlek'trɪsətɪ] n electricidad f.

electric shock n descarga f
eléctrica.

electrocute [ɪ'lektrəkjuːt] vt
electrocutar.

electronic [ˌɪlek'trɒnɪk] adj elec-
trónico(-ca).

elegant ['elɪgənt] adj elegante.

element ['elɪmənt] n (part, chemical) elemento m; (degree) toque m,
matiz m; (of fire, kettle) resistencia
f; **the ~s los** elementos.

elementary [ˌelɪ'mentərɪ] adj
elemental.

elephant ['elɪfənt] n elefante m.

elevator ['elɪveɪtə'] n (Am)
ascensor m.

eleven [ɪ'levn] num once, → **six**.

eleventh [ɪ'levnθ] num undéci-

mo(-ma), → **sixth**.

eligible ['elɪdʒəbl] adj elegible.

eliminate [ɪ'lɪmɪneɪt] vt eliminar.

Elizabethan [ɪˌlɪzə'biːθn] adj
isabelino(-na).

elm [elm] n olmo m.

El Salvador [ˌel'sælvədɔːʳ] n El
Salvador.

else [els] adv: **I don't want anything ~** no quiero nada más; **anything ~?** ¿algo más?; **everyone ~**
todos los demás (todas las
demás); **nobody ~** nadie más,
nothing ~ nada más; **somebody ~**
otra persona; **something ~** otra
cosa; **somewhere ~** a/en otra
parte; **what ~?** ¿qué más?; **who ~?**
¿quién más?; **or ~** si no.

elsewhere [els'weəʳ] adv a/en
otra parte.

embankment [ɪm'bæŋkmənt] n
(next to river) dique m; (next to road,
railway) terraplén m.

embark [ɪm'baːk] vi (board ship)
embarcar.

embarkation card [ˌembɑː-
'keɪʃn-] n tarjeta f de embarque.

embarrass [ɪm'bærəs] vt avergonzar.

embarrassed [ɪm'bærəst] adj: **I
was ~ me** daba vergüenza.

embarrassing [ɪm'bærəsɪŋ] adj
embarazoso(-sa).

embarrassment [ɪm'bærəs-
mənt] n vergüenza f.

embassy ['embəsɪ] n embajada f.

emblem ['embləm] n emblema
m.

embrace [ɪm'breɪs] vt abrazar.

embroidered [ɪm'brɔɪdəd] adj
bordado(-da).

embroidery [ɪmˈbrɔɪdərɪ] n bordado m.

emerald [ˈemərəld] n esmeralda f.

emerge [ɪˈmɜːdʒ] vi (from place) salir; (fact, truth) salir a la luz.

emergency [ɪˈmɜːdʒənsɪ] n emergencia f ◆ adj de emergencia; **in an ~** en caso de emergencia.

emergency exit n salida f de emergencia.

emergency landing n aterrizaje m forzoso.

emergency services npl servicios mpl de emergencia.

emigrate [ˈemɪɡreɪt] vi emigrar.

emit [ɪˈmɪt] vt emitir.

emotion [ɪˈməʊʃn] n emoción f.

emotional [ɪˈməʊʃənl] adj emotivo(-va).

emphasis [ˈemfəsɪs] (pl -ses [-siːz]) n énfasis m inv.

emphasize [ˈemfəsaɪz] vt enfatizar, subrayar.

empire [ˈempaɪəʳ] n imperio m.

employ [ɪmˈplɔɪ] vt emplear.

employed [ɪmˈplɔɪd] adj empleado(-da).

employee [ɪmˈplɔɪiː] n empleado m (-da f).

employer [ɪmˈplɔɪəʳ] n patrono m (-na f).

employment [ɪmˈplɔɪmənt] n empleo m.

employment agency n agencia f de trabajo.

empty [ˈemptɪ] adj vacío(-a); (threat, promise) vano(-na) ◆ vt vaciar.

EMU n UME f.

emulsion (paint) [ɪˈmʌlʃn-] n pintura f mate.

enable [ɪˈneɪbl] vt: **to ~ sb to do sthg** permitir a alguien hacer algo.

enamel [ɪˈnæml] n esmalte m.

enclose [ɪnˈkləʊz] vt (surround) rodear; (with letter) adjuntar.

enclosed [ɪnˈkləʊzd] adj (space) cerrado(-da).

encounter [ɪnˈkaʊntəʳ] vt encontrarse con.

encourage [ɪnˈkʌrɪdʒ] vt (person) animar; **to ~ sb to do sthg** animar a alguien a hacer algo.

encouragement [ɪnˈkʌrɪdʒmənt] n aliento m, ánimo m.

encyclopedia [ɪn,saɪkləˈpiːdjə] n enciclopedia f.

end [end] n fin m; (furthest point) extremo m; (of finger, toe) punta f ◆ vt terminar ◆ vi acabarse; **to come to an ~** acabarse; **to put an ~ to sthg** poner fin a algo; **for days on ~** día tras día; **in the ~** al final; **to make ~s meet** llegar al final de mes; **at the ~ of** (street, garden) al final de; **at the ~ of April** a finales de abril ❑ **end up** vi acabar, terminar; **to ~ up doing sthg** acabar por hacer algo.

endangered species [ɪnˈdeɪndʒəd-] n especie f en peligro.

ending [ˈendɪŋ] n (of story, film) final m; (GRAMM) terminación f.

endive [ˈendaɪv] n (curly) endibia f; (chicory) achicoria f.

endless [ˈendlɪs] adj interminable.

endorsement [ɪnˈdɔːsmənt] n (of driving licence) nota de sanción en el carné de conducir.

endurance [ɪnˈdjʊərəns] n resis-

tencia f.
endure [ɪnˈdjʊəʳ] vt soportar.
enemy [ˈenɪmɪ] n enemigo m (-ga f).
energy [ˈenədʒɪ] n energía f.
enforce [ɪnˈfɔːs] vt hacer cumplir.
engaged [ɪnˈɡeɪdʒd] adj (to be married) prometido(-da); (Br: phone) ocupado(-da), comunicando, (toilet) ocupado(-da), **to get ~** prometerse.
engaged tone n (Br) señal f de comunicando.
engagement [ɪnˈɡeɪdʒmənt] n (to marry) compromiso m; (appointment) cita f.
engagement ring n anillo m de compromiso.
engine [ˈendʒɪn] n (of vehicle) motor m; (of train) máquina f.
engineer [ˌendʒɪˈnɪəʳ] n ingeniero m (-ra f).
engineering [ˌendʒɪˈnɪərɪŋ] n ingeniería f.
engineering works npl (on railway line) trabajos mpl de mejora en la línea.
England [ˈɪŋɡlənd] n Inglaterra.
English [ˈɪŋɡlɪʃ] adj inglés(-esa) ♦ n (language) inglés m ♦ npl: **the ~** los ingleses.
English breakfast n desayuno m inglés.
English Channel n. the ~ el Canal de la Mancha.
Englishman [ˈɪŋɡlɪʃmən] (pl -men [-mən]) n inglés m.
Englishwoman [ˈɪŋɡlɪʃˌwʊmən] (pl -women [-ˌwɪmɪn]) n inglesa f.
engrave [ɪnˈɡreɪv] vt grabar.

engraving [ɪnˈɡreɪvɪŋ] n grabado m.
enjoy [ɪnˈdʒɔɪ] vt: **I ~ed the film** me gustó la película; **I ~ swimming** me gusta nadar; **to ~ o.s.** divertirse; **~ your meal!** ¡que aproveche!
enjoyable [ɪnˈdʒɔɪəbl] adj agradable.
enjoyment [ɪnˈdʒɔɪmənt] n placer m.
enlargement [ɪnˈlɑːdʒmənt] n (of photo) ampliación f.
enormous [ɪˈnɔːməs] adj enorme.
enough [ɪˈnʌf] adj, pron & adv bastante; **~ time** bastante tiempo; **is that ~?** ¿es bastante?; **it's not big ~** no es lo bastante grande, **to have had ~ (of)** estar harto (de).
enquire [ɪnˈkwaɪəʳ] vi informarse.
enquiry [ɪnˈkwaɪərɪ] n (question) pregunta f; (investigation) investigación f; "Enquiries" "Información".
enquiry desk n información f.
enrol [ɪnˈrəʊl] vi (Br) matricularse.
enroll [ɪnˈrəʊl] (Am) = **enrol**.
en suite bathroom [ɒnˈswiːt-] n baño m adjunto.
ensure [ɪnˈʃʊəʳ] vt asegurar.
entail [ɪnˈteɪl] vt conllevar.
enter [ˈentəʳ] vt (room, building) entrar en; (plane, bus) subir a; (college) matricularse a; (army) alistarse en; (competition) presentarse a; (on form) escribir ♦ vi (come in) entrar; (in competition) presentarse, participar.
enterprise [ˈentəpraɪz] n empresa f.

entertain [ˌentəˈteɪn] vt *(amuse)* entretener.

entertainer [ˌentəˈteɪnəʳ] n artista mf.

entertaining [ˌentəˈteɪnɪŋ] adj entretenido(-da).

entertainment [ˌentəˈteɪnmənt] n *(amusement)* diversión f; *(show)* espectáculo m.

enthusiasm [ɪnˈθjuːzɪæzm] n entusiasmo m.

enthusiast [ɪnˈθjuːzɪæst] n entusiasta mf.

enthusiastic [ɪnˌθjuːzɪˈæstɪk] adj entusiasta.

entire [ɪnˈtaɪəʳ] adj entero(-ra).

entirely [ɪnˈtaɪəlɪ] adv enteramente.

entitle [ɪnˈtaɪtl] vt: to ~ sb to sthg dar a alguien derecho a algo; to ~ sb to do sthg autorizar a alguien a hacer algo.

entrance [ˈentrəns] n entrada f.

entrance fee n precio m de entrada.

entry [ˈentrɪ] n entrada f; *(in competition)* respuesta f; **"no ~"** "prohibido el paso".

envelope [ˈenvələʊp] n sobre m.

envious [ˈenvɪəs] adj envidioso(-sa).

environment [ɪnˈvaɪərənmənt] n *(surroundings)* entorno m; **the ~** el medio ambiente.

environmental [ɪnˌvaɪərənˈmentl] adj medioambiental.

environmentally friendly [ɪnˌvaɪərənˈmentlɪ-] adj ecológico(-ca).

envy [ˈenvɪ] vt envidiar.

epic [ˈepɪk] n epopeya f.

epidemic [ˌepɪˈdemɪk] n epidemia f.

epileptic [ˌepɪˈleptɪk] adj epiléptico(-ca).

episode [ˈepɪsəʊd] n episodio m.

equal [ˈiːkwəl] adj igual ◆ vt *(number)* ser igual a; **to be ~ to** ser igual a.

equality [ɪˈkwɒlətɪ] n igualdad f.

equalize [ˈiːkwəlaɪz] vi marcar el empate.

equally [ˈiːkwəlɪ] adv igualmente; *(pay, treat)* equitativamente; *(share)* por igual.

equation [ɪˈkweɪʒn] n ecuación f.

equator [ɪˈkweɪtəʳ] n: **the ~** el ecuador.

equip [ɪˈkwɪp] vt: to ~ sb with proveer a alguien (de); to ~ sthg with equipar algo (con).

equipment [ɪˈkwɪpmənt] n equipo m.

equipped [ɪˈkwɪpt] adj: to be ~ with estar provisto(-ta) de.

equivalent [ɪˈkwɪvələnt] adj equivalente ◆ n equivalente m.

erase [ɪˈreɪz] vt borrar.

eraser [ɪˈreɪzəʳ] n goma f de borrar.

erect [ɪˈrekt] adj *(person, posture)* erguido(-da) ◆ vt *(tent)* montar; *(monument)* erigir.

ERM n mecanismo de tipos de cambio (del SME).

erotic [ɪˈrɒtɪk] adj erótico(-ca).

errand [ˈerənd] n recado m.

erratic [ɪˈrætɪk] adj irregular.

error [ˈerəʳ] n error m.

escalator [ˈeskəleɪtəʳ] n escalera f mecánica.

escalope ['eskǝlɒp] n escalope m.

escape [ɪ'skeɪp] n (flight) fuga f; (of gas, water) escape m ♦ vi: to ~ (from) (prison, danger) escaparse (de); (leak) fugarse (de).

escort [n 'eskɔːt, vb ɪ'skɔːt] n (guard) escolta f ♦ vt escoltar.

espadrilles ['espǝ,drɪlz] npl alpargatas fpl.

especially [ɪ'speʃǝlɪ] adv especialmente.

esplanade [,esplǝ'neɪd] n paseo m marítimo.

essay ['eseɪ] n (at school) redacción f; (at university) trabajo m.

essential [ɪ'senʃl] adj esencial □ **essentials** npl. **the (bare) ~s** lo (mínimo) indispensable.

essentially [ɪ'senʃǝlɪ] adv esencialmente.

establish [ɪ'stæblɪʃ] vt (set up, create) establecer; (fact, truth) verificar.

establishment [ɪ'stæblɪʃmǝnt] n (business) establecimiento m.

estate [ɪ'steɪt] n (land in country) finca f; (for housing) urbanización f; (Br: car) = estate car.

estate agent n (Br) agente m inmobiliario (agente f inmobiliaria).

estate car n (Br) coche m familiar, coche m ranchera.

estimate [n 'estɪmǝt, vb 'estɪmeɪt] n (guess) estimación f; (for job) presupuesto m ♦ vt calcular.

estuary ['estjʊǝrɪ] n estuario m.

ethnic minority ['eθnɪk-] n minoría f étnica.

EU n (abbr of European Union) UE f.

Eurocheque ['jʊǝrǝʊ,tʃek] n eurocheque m.

Europe ['jʊǝrǝp] n Europa.

European [,jʊǝrǝ'pɪǝn] adj europeo(-a) ♦ n europeo m (-a f).

European Community n Comunidad f Europea.

evacuate [ɪ'vækjʊeɪt] vt evacuar.

evade [ɪ'veɪd] vt eludir.

evaporated milk [ɪ'væpǝreɪtɪd-] n leche f evaporada.

eve [iːv] n: **on the ~ of** en la víspera de.

even [iːvn] adj (uniform) constante, uniforme; (level, flat) llano(-na), liso(-sa); (equal) igualado(-da), (number) par ♦ adv (emphasizing surprise) hasta; (in comparisons) aun; **to break ~** acabar sin ganar ni perder; **~ so** aun así; **~ though** aun que; **not ~** ni siquiera.

evening ['iːvnɪŋ] n (from 5 p.m. to 8 p.m.) tarde f; (from 9 p.m. onwards) noche f; (event) velada f; **good ~!** ¡buenas tardes!, ¡buenas noches!; **in the ~** por la tarde, por la noche.

evening classes npl clases fpl nocturnas.

evening dress n (formal clothes) traje m de etiqueta; (woman's garment) traje de noche.

evening meal n cena f.

event [ɪ'vent] n (occurrence) suceso m; (SPORT) prueba f; **in the ~ of** (fml) en caso de.

eventual [ɪ'ventʃʊǝl] adj final, definitivo(-va).

eventually [ɪ'ventʃʊǝlɪ] adv finalmente.

ever ['evǝr] adv (at any time) alguna vez; *(in negatives)* nunca; **I don't ~ do that** no hago eso nunca; **the best I've ~ seen** lo mejor que nunca he visto; **he was ~ so angry** estaba muy enfadado; **for ~** *(eternally)* para siempre; **we've been waiting for ~** hace siglos que esperamos; **hardly ~** casi nunca; **~ since** *adv* desde entonces ♦ *prep* desde ♦ *conj* desde que.

every ['evrɪ] *adj* cada; **~ day** cada día; **~ other day** un día sí y otro no; **one in ~ ten** uno de cada diez; **we make ~ effort ...** hacemos todo lo posible ...; **~ so often** de vez en cuando.

everybody ['evrɪˌbɒdɪ] = **everyone.**

everyday ['evrɪdeɪ] *adj* diario(-ria).

everyone ['evrɪwʌn] *pron* todo el mundo, todos *mpl* (-das *fpl*).

everyplace ['evrɪˌpleɪs] *(Am)* = **everywhere.**

everything ['evrɪθɪŋ] *pron* todo.

everywhere ['evrɪweəʳ] *adv (be, search)* por todas partes; *(with verbs of motion)* a todas partes; **~ you go** por todas partes.

evidence ['evɪdəns] *n (proof)* prueba *f*; *(JUR)* declaración *f*.

evident ['evɪdənt] *adj* evidente.

evidently ['evɪdəntlɪ] *adv (apparently)* aparentemente; *(obviously)* evidentemente.

evil ['iːvl] *adj* malvado(-da) ♦ *n* mal *m*.

ex [eks] *n (inf)* ex *mf*.

exact [ɪgˈzækt] *adj* exacto(-ta); **"~ fare ready please"** "tenga listo el precio exacto del billete".

exactly [ɪgˈzæktlɪ] *adv* exacta-

mente ♦ *excl* ¡exacto!

exaggerate [ɪgˈzædʒəreɪt] *vt & vi* exagerar.

exaggeration [ɪgˌzædʒəˈreɪʃn] *n* exageración *f*.

exam [ɪgˈzæm] *n* examen *m*; **to take an ~** examinarse, presentarse a un examen.

examination [ɪgˌzæmɪˈneɪʃn] *n (exam)* examen *m*; *(MED)* reconocimiento *m*.

examine [ɪgˈzæmɪn] *vt (inspect)* examinar; *(consider carefully)* considerar; *(MED)* reconocer.

example [ɪgˈzɑːmpl] *n* ejemplo *m*; **for ~** por ejemplo.

exceed [ɪkˈsiːd] *vt (be greater than)* exceder; *(go beyond)* rebasar.

excellent ['eksələnt] *adj* excelente.

except [ɪkˈsept] *prep & conj* salvo; **~ for** aparte de; **"~ for access"** cartel que indica que el tránsito no está permitido; **"~ for loading"** "salvo carga y descarga".

exception [ɪkˈsepʃn] *n* excepción *f*.

exceptional [ɪkˈsepʃnəl] *adj* excepcional.

excerpt ['eksɑːpt] *n* extracto *m*.

excess [ɪkˈses, *before noun* 'ekses] *adj* excedente ♦ *n* exceso *m*.

excess baggage *n* exceso *m* de equipaje.

excess fare *n (Br)* suplemento *m*.

excessive [ɪkˈsesɪv] *adj* excesivo(-va).

exchange [ɪksˈtʃeɪndʒ] *n (of telephones)* central *f* telefónica; *(of students)* intercambio *m* ♦ *vt* intercambiar; **to ~ sthg for sthg** cambiar algo por algo; **to be on an ~** estar de intercambio.

exchange rate n tipo m de cambio.

excited [ɪk'saɪtɪd] adj emocionado(-da).

excitement [ɪk'saɪtmənt] n emoción f; **~s** (exciting things) emociones fpl.

exciting [ɪk'saɪtɪŋ] adj emocionante.

exclamation mark [,eksklə'meɪʃn-] n (Br) signo m de admiración.

exclamation point [,eksklə'meɪʃn-] (Am) = **exclamation mark**.

exclude [ɪk'sklu:d] vt excluir.

excluding [ɪk'sklu:dɪŋ] prep excepto, con excepción de.

exclusive [ɪk'sklu:sɪv] adj (highclass) selecto(-ta); (sole) exclusivo(-va) ◆ n exclusiva f; **~ of** excluyendo.

excursion [ɪk'skɜ:ʃn] n excursión f.

excuse [n ɪk'skju:s, vb ɪk'skju:z] n excusa f ◆ vt (forgive) perdonar; (let off) dispensar; **~ me!** (attracting attention) ¡perdone!, (trying to get past) ¿me deja pasar, por favor?; (as apology) perdone.

ex-directory adj (Br) que no figura en la guía telefónica.

execute ['eksɪkju:t] vt ejecutar.

executive [ɪg'zekjʊtɪv] adj (desk, suite) para ejecutivos ◆ n (person) ejecutivo m (-va f).

exempt [ɪg'zempt] adj: **~ (from)** exento(-ta) (de).

exemption [ɪg'zempʃn] n exención f.

exercise ['eksəsaɪz] n ejercicio m ◆ vi hacer ejercicio; **to do ~s** hacer ejercicio.

exercise book n cuaderno m de ejercicios.

exert [ɪg'zɜ:t] vt ejercer.

exhaust [ɪg'zɔ:st] vt agotar ◆ n: **~ (pipe)** tubo m de escape.

exhausted [ɪg'zɔ:stɪd] adj agotado(-da).

exhibit [ɪg'zɪbɪt] n (in museum, gallery) objeto m expuesto ◆ vt (in exhibition) exponer.

exhibition [,eksɪ'bɪʃn] n (of art) exposición f.

exist [ɪg'zɪst] vi existir.

existence [ɪg'zɪstəns] n existencia f; **to be in ~** existir.

existing [ɪg'zɪstɪŋ] adj existente.

exit ['eksɪt] n salida f ◆ vi salir.

exotic [ɪg'zɒtɪk] adj exótico(-ca).

expand [ɪk'spænd] vi (in size) extenderse, expandirse; (in number) aumentarse, ampliarse.

expect [ɪk'spekt] vt esperar; **to ~ to do sthg** esperar hacer algo; **to ~ sb to do sthg** esperar que alguien haga algo; **to be ~ing** (be pregnant) estar embarazada.

expedition [,ekspɪ'dɪʃn] n (to explore etc) expedición f; (short outing) salida f

expel [ɪk'spel] vt (from school) expulsar.

expense [ɪk'spens] n gasto m; **at the ~ of** a costa de ❑ **expenses** npl (of business person) gastos mpl.

expensive [ɪk'spensɪv] adj caro(-ra).

experience [ɪkˈspɪərɪəns] n experiencia f ◆ vt experimentar.

experienced [ɪkˈspɪərɪənst] adj experimentado(-da).

experiment [ɪkˈsperɪmənt] n experimento m ◆ vi experimentar.

expert [ˈekspɜːt] adj experto(-ta) ◆ n experto m (-ta f).

expire [ɪkˈspaɪər] vi caducar.

expiry date [ɪkˈspaɪərɪ-] n fecha f de caducidad.

explain [ɪkˈspleɪn] vt explicar.

explanation [ˌekspləˈneɪʃn] n explicación f.

explode [ɪkˈspləʊd] vi estallar.

exploit [ɪkˈsplɔɪt] vt explotar.

explore [ɪkˈsplɔːr] vt explorar.

explosion [ɪkˈspləʊʒn] n explosión f.

explosive [ɪkˈspləʊsɪv] n explosivo m.

export [n ˈekspɔːt, vb ɪkˈspɔːt] n exportación f ◆ vt exportar.

exposed [ɪkˈspəʊzd] adj (place) al descubierto.

exposure [ɪkˈspəʊʒər] n exposición f; (MED) hipotermia f.

express [ɪkˈspres] adj (letter, delivery) urgente; (train) rápido(-da) ◆ n (train) expreso m ◆ vt expresar ◆ adv urgente.

expression [ɪkˈspreʃn] n expresión f.

expresso [ɪkˈspresəʊ] n café m exprés.

expressway [ɪkˈspresweɪ] n (Am) autopista f.

extend [ɪkˈstend] vt (visa, permit) prorrogar; (road, railway) prolongar; (hand) tender ◆ vi (stretch) extenderse.

extension [ɪkˈstenʃn] n (of building) ampliación f; (for phone, permit, essay) extensión f.

extension lead [-liːd] n alargador m.

extensive [ɪkˈstensɪv] adj (damage, area) extenso(-sa); (selection) amplio(-plia).

extent [ɪkˈstent] n (of damage, knowledge) extensión f; **to a certain ~** hasta cierto punto; **to what ~ ...?** ¿hasta qué punto ...?

exterior [ɪkˈstɪərɪər] adj exterior ◆ n (of car, building) exterior m.

external [ɪkˈstɜːnl] adj externo(-na).

extinct [ɪkˈstɪŋkt] adj extinto(-ta).

extinction [ɪkˈstɪŋkʃn] n extinción f.

extinguish [ɪkˈstɪŋgwɪʃ] vt (fire) extinguir; (cigarette) apagar.

extinguisher [ɪkˈstɪŋgwɪʃər] n extintor m.

extortionate [ɪkˈstɔːʃnət] adj exorbitante.

extra [ˈekstrə] adj (additional) extra inv; (spare) de más ◆ n (bonus) paga f extraordinaria; (optional thing) extra m ◆ adv (more) más; **an ~ special offer** una oferta muy especial; **be ~ careful** ten mucho cuidado; **I need some ~ help** necesito más ayuda; **~ charge** suplemento m; **~ large** extra-grande ❑ **extras** npl (in price) suplementos mpl.

extract [n ˈekstrækt, vb ɪkˈstrækt] n (of yeast, malt etc) extracto m; (from book, opera) fragmento m ◆ vt (tooth) extraer.

extractor fan [ɪkˈstræktər-] n

(Br) extractor *m* (de humos).

extraordinary [ɪkˈstrɔːdnrɪ] *adj* extraordinario(-ria).

extravagant [ɪkˈstrævəgənt] *adj (wasteful)* derrochador(-ra); *(expensive)* exorbitante.

extreme [ɪkˈstriːm] *adj* extremo(-ma) ◆ *n* extremo.

extremely [ɪkˈstriːmlɪ] *adv* extremadamente.

extrovert [ˈekstrəvɜːt] *n* extrovertido *m* (-da *f*).

eye [aɪ] *n* ojo *m* ◆ *vt* mirar detenidamente, **to keep an ~ on** vigilar.

eyebrow [ˈaɪbraʊ] *n* ceja *f*.

eye drops *npl* colirio *m*.

eyeglasses [ˈaɪglɑːsɪz] *npl (Am)* gafas *fpl*.

eyelash [ˈaɪlæʃ] *n* pestaña *f*.

eyelid [ˈaɪlɪd] *n* párpado *m*.

eyeliner [ˈaɪlaɪnəʳ] *n* lápiz *m* de ojos.

eye shadow *n* sombra *f* de ojos.

eyesight [ˈaɪsaɪt] *n* vista *f*.

eye test *n* prueba *f* de visión.

eyewitness [ˈaɪwɪtnɪs] *n* testigo *mf* presencial.

F *(abbr of Fahrenheit)* F.

fabric [ˈfæbrɪk] *n (cloth)* tejido *m*.

fabulous [ˈfæbjʊləs] *adj* fabuloso(-sa).

facade [fəˈsɑːd] *n* fachada *f*.

face [feɪs] *n* cara *f*; *(of clock, watch)* esfera *f* ◆ *vt (look towards)* mirar a; *(confront, accept)* hacer frente a; *(cope with)* soportar; **to be ~d with** enfrentarse con ❑ **face up to** *vt fus* hacer frente a.

facecloth [ˈfeɪsklɒθ] *n (Br)* toalla *f* de cara.

facial [ˈfeɪʃəl] *n* limpieza *f* de cutis.

facilitate [fəˈsɪlɪteɪt] *vt (fml)* facilitar.

facilities [fəˈsɪlɪtɪz] *npl* instalaciones *fpl*.

facsimile [fækˈsɪmɪlɪ] *n* facsímil *m*.

fact [fækt] *n (established truth)* hecho *m*; *(piece of information)* dato *m*; **in ~** *(in reality)* en realidad, *(moreover)* de hecho.

factor [ˈfæktəʳ] *n (condition)* factor *m*; *(of suntan lotion)* factor (de protección solar); **~ ten suntan lotion** bronceador *m* con factor de protección diez.

factory [ˈfæktərɪ] *n* fábrica *f*.

faculty [ˈfækltɪ] *n (at university)* facultad *f*.

FA Cup *n* copa de fútbol británica, ≈ Copa *f* del Rey

fade [feɪd] *vi (light, sound)* irse apagando; *(flower)* marchitarse, *(jeans, wallpaper)* descolorarse.

faded [ˈfeɪdɪd] *adj (jeans)* desteñido(-da).

fag [fæg] *n (Br: inf: cigarette)* pitillo *m*.

Fahrenheit [ˈfærənhaɪt] *adj* Fahrenheit *inv*.

fail [feɪl] *vt (exam)* suspender ◆ *vi*

(not succeed) fracasar; *(in exam)* suspender; *(engine)* fallar; **to ~ to do sthg** *(not do)* no hacer algo.

failing ['feɪlɪŋ] *n* defecto *m* ◆ *prep:* ~ **that** en su defecto.

failure ['feɪljə'] *n* fracaso *m*; *(unsuccessful person)* fracasado *m* (-da *f*); ~ **to comply with the regulations** el incumplimiento de las normas.

faint [feɪnt] *adj (sound, colour)* débil; *(outline)* impreciso(-sa); *(dizzy)* mareado(-da)* ◆ *vi* desmayarse; **I haven't the ~est idea** no tengo la más mínima idea.

fair [feə'] *adj (just)* justo(-ta); *(quite large)* considerable; *(quite good)* bastante bueno(-na); *(SCH)* satisfactorio(-ria); *(hair, person)* rubio(-bia); *(skin)* blanco(-ca); *(weather)* bueno(-na) ◆ *n* feria *f*; **~ enough!** ¡vale!

fairground ['feəgraund] *n* recinto *m* de la feria.

fair-haired [-'heəd] *adj* rubio (-bia).

fairly ['feəlɪ] *adv (quite)* bastante.

fairy ['feərɪ] *n* hada *f*.

fairy tale *n* cuento *m* de hadas.

faith [feɪθ] *n* fe *f*.

faithfully ['feɪθfʊlɪ] *adv:* **Yours ~** le saluda atentamente.

fake [feɪk] *n (false thing)* falsificación *f* ◆ *vt (signature, painting)* falsificar.

fall [fɔːl] *(pt* fell, *pp* fallen ['fɔːln]) *vi* caer; *(lose balance)* caerse; *(decrease)* bajar *n (accident)* caída *f; (decrease)* descenso *m; (of snow)* nevada *f; (Am: autumn)* otoño *m;* **to ~ asleep** dormirse; **to ~ ill** ponerse enfermo; **to ~ in love** enamorarse

❏ **falls** *npl (waterfall)* cataratas *fpl;* **fall behind** *vi (with work, rent)* retrasarse; **fall down** *vi (lose balance)* caerse; **fall off** *vi (person)* caerse; *(handle, branch)* desprenderse; **fall out** *vi (argue)* pelearse; **my tooth fell out** se me cayó un diente; **fall over** *vi* caerse; **fall through** *vi* fracasar.

false [fɔːls] *adj* falso(-sa); *(artificial)* postizo(-za).

false alarm *n* falsa alarma *f.*

false teeth *npl* dentadura *f* postiza.

fame [feɪm] *n* fama *f.*

familiar [fə'mɪljə'] *adj (known)* familiar; *(informal)* demasiado amistoso(-sa); **to be ~ with** *(know)* estar familiarizado(-da) con.

family ['fæmlɪ] *n* familia *f* ◆ *adj (large)* familiar; *(film, holiday)* para toda la familia.

family planning clinic [-'plænɪŋ-] *n* clínica *f* de planificación familiar.

family room *n (at hotel)* habitación *f* familiar; *(at pub, airport)* habitación para familias con niños pequeños.

famine ['fæmɪn] *n* hambruna *f.*

famished ['fæmɪʃt] *adj (inf)* muerto(-ta) de hambre.

famous ['feɪməs] *adj* famoso(-sa).

fan [fæn] *n (held in hand)* abanico *m; (electric)* ventilador *m; (enthusiast)* admirador *m* (-ra *f); (supporter)* aficionado *m* (-da *f*).

fan belt *n* correa *f* del ventilador.

fancy ['fænsɪ] *adj (elaborate)* recargado(-da); *(food)* elaborado(-da) ◆

vt (inf) : **I ~ an ice cream** me apetece tomar un helado; **he fancies Jane** él está por Jane; **~ (that)!** ¡fíjate!

fancy dress n disfraz m.

fan heater n convector m.

fanlight ['fænlaɪt] n (Br) montante m de abanico.

fantastic [fæn'tæstɪk] adj fantástico(-ca).

fantasy ['fæntəsɪ] n fantasía f.

far [fɑːʳ] (compar **farther** OR **farther**, superl **furthest** OR **farthest**) adv (in distance, time) lejos; (in degree) mucho ◆ adj (end) extremo(-ma); (side) opuesto(-ta); **have you come ~!** ¡vienes de lejos?; **how ~ is it?** ¿está lejos?; **how ~ is it to London?** ¿cuánto hay de aquí a Londres?; **as ~ as** (place) hasta; **as ~ as I'm concerned** por mí se refiere; **as ~ as I know** que yo sepa; **~ better** mucho mejor; **by ~** con mucho; **it's ~ too difficult** es demasiado difícil; **so ~** hasta ahora; **to go too ~** pasarse.

farce [fɑːs] n farsa f.

fare [feəʳ] n (on bus, train etc) precio m del billete; (fml: food) comida f ◆ vi: **she ~d well** le fue bien.

Far East n: **the ~** el Lejano Oriente.

fare stage n (Br) parada de autobús donde termina un tramo de línea con misma tarifa.

farm [fɑːm] n granja f.

farmer ['fɑːməʳ] n agricultor m (-ra f).

farmhouse ['fɑːmhaʊs, pl -haʊzɪz] n caserío m.

farming ['fɑːmɪŋ] n agricultura f.

farmland ['fɑːmlænd] n tierras fpl de labranza.

farmyard ['fɑːmjɑːd] n corral m.

farther ['fɑːðəʳ] compar → far.

farthest ['fɑːðəst] superl → far.

fascinating ['fæsɪneɪtɪŋ] adj fascinante.

fascination [,fæsɪ'neɪʃn] n fascinación f.

fashion ['fæʃn] n (trend, style) moda f; (manner) manera f; **to be in ~** estar de moda; **to be out of ~** estar pasado de moda.

fashionable ['fæʃnəbl] adj de moda.

fashion show n desfile m de moda.

fast [fɑːst] adj (quick) rápido(-da); (clock, watch) adelantado(-da) ◆ adv (quickly) rápidamente; (securely) firmemente; **~ asleep** profundamente dormido; **a ~ train** un tren rápido.

fasten ['fɑːsn] vt (belt, coat) abrochar; (two things) sujetar.

fastener ['fɑːsnəʳ] n (of window, box) cierre m; (of dress) corchete m.

fast food n comida f rápida.

fat [fæt] adj (person) gordo(-da); (meat) con mucha grasa ◆ n grasa f; (for cooking) manteca f.

fatal ['feɪtl] adj (accident, disease) mortal.

father ['fɑːðəʳ] n padre m.

Father Christmas n (Br) Papá m Noel.

father-in-law n suegro m.

fattening ['fætnɪŋ] adj que engorda.

fatty ['fætɪ] adj graso(-sa).

faucet ['fɔːsɪt] n (Am) grifo m.

fault [fɔːlt] n (responsibility) culpa f; (flaw) defecto m; (in machine) fallo m; **it's your ~** tú tienes la culpa.

faulty [ˈfɔːltɪ] adj defectuoso(-sa).

favor [ˈfeɪvər] (Am) = favour.

favour [ˈfeɪvər] n (Br: kind act) favor m ◆ vt (prefer) preferir; **to be in ~ of** estar a favor de; **to do sb a ~** hacerle un favor a alguien.

favourable [ˈfeɪvrəbl] adj favorable.

favourite [ˈfeɪvrɪt] adj favorito(-ta) ◆ n favorito m (-ta f).

fawn [fɔːn] adj beige inv.

fax [fæks] n fax m inv ◆ vt (document) enviar por fax; (person) enviar un fax a.

fear [fɪər] n (sensation) miedo m; (thing feared) temor m ◆ vt (be afraid of) temer; **for ~ of** por miedo a.

feast [fiːst] n banquete m.

feather [ˈfeðər] n pluma f.

feature [ˈfiːtʃər] n (characteristic) característica f; (of face) rasgo m; (in newspaper) artículo m de fondo; (on radio, TV) programa m especial ◆ vt (subj: film) estar protagonizado por.

feature film n largometraje m.

Feb [feb] (abbr of February) feb.

February [ˈfebruərɪ] n febrero m, → September.

fed [fed] pt & pp → feed.

fed up adj harto(-ta); **to be ~ with** estar harto de.

fee [fiː] n (for entry) precio m; (for service) tarifa f; (of doctor, lawyer) honorarios mpl.

feeble [ˈfiːbəl] adj (weak) débil.

feed [fiːd] (pt & pp fed) vt (person, animal) dar de comer a; (insert) introducir.

feel [fiːl] (pt & pp felt) vt (touch) tocar; (experience) sentir; (think) pensar que ◆ vi (tired, ill, better) encontrarse; (sad, angry, safe) sentirse ◆ n (of material) tacto m; **my nose ~s cold** tengo la nariz fría; **to ~ cold** tener frío; **to ~ hungry** tener hambre; **I ~ like a cup of tea** me apetece una taza de té; **to ~ up to doing sthg** sentirse con ánimos de hacer algo.

feeling [ˈfiːlɪŋ] n (emotion) sentimiento m; (sensation) sensación f; (belief) impresión f; **to hurt sb's ~s** herir los sentimientos de alguien.

feet [fiːt] pl → foot.

fell [fel] pt → fall ◆ vt talar.

fellow [ˈfeləʊ] n (man) tío m ◆ adj **my ~ students** mis compañeros de clase.

felt [felt] pt & pp → feel ◆ n fieltro m.

felt-tip pen n rotulador m.

female [ˈfiːmeɪl] adj (of animal) hembra; (person) femenino(-na) ◆ n hembra f.

feminine [ˈfemɪnɪn] adj femenino(-na).

feminist [ˈfemɪnɪst] n feminista mf.

fence [fens] n valla f.

fencing [ˈfensɪŋ] n (SPORT) esgrima f.

fend [fend] vi: **to ~ for o.s.** valerse por sí mismo(-ma).

fender [ˈfendər] n (for fireplace) guardafuego m; (Am: on car) guardabarros m inv.

fennel [ˈfenl] n hinojo m.

fern [fɜːn] n helecho m.

ferocious [fəˈrəʊʃəs] adj feroz.

ferry ['feri] n ferry m.

fertile ['fɜːtail] adj fértil.

fertilizer ['fɜːtɪlaɪzəʳ] n abono m.

festival ['festəvl] n (of music, arts etc) festival m; (holiday) día m festivo.

feta cheese ['fetə-] n queso blando de origen griego fabricado con leche de oveja.

fetch [fetʃ] vt (person) ir a buscar; (object) traer; (be sold for) alcanzar.

fete [feɪt] n fiesta al aire libre.

---

i **FETE**

Un n "fete" es una especie de fiesta al aire libre, generalmente en verano, que incluye concursos, espectáculos y venta de productos caseros. Se suele celebrar un "fete" para recolectar dinero destinado a fines benéficos o a proyectos locales.

---

fever ['fiːvəʳ] n fiebre f; **to have a ~** tener fiebre.

feverish ['fiːvərɪʃ] adj febril.

few [fjuː] adj pocos(-cas) ♦ pron pocos mpl (-cas fpl); **~ people** poca gente; **a ~** adj algunos(-nas) ♦ pron unos pocos mpl (unas pocas fpl); **quite a ~** bastantes.

fewer ['fjuːəʳ] adj & pron menos.

fiancé [fɪˈɒnseɪ] n prometido m.

fiancée [fɪˈɒnseɪ] n prometida f.

fib [fib] n (inf) bola f.

fiber ['faɪbəʳ] (Am) = **fibre**.

fibre ['faɪbəʳ] n (Br) fibra f.

fibreglass ['faɪbəglɑːs] n fibra f de vidrio.

fickle ['fikl] adj voluble.

fiction ['fikʃn] n ficción f.

fiddle ['fidl] n (violin) violín m ♦ vi: **to ~ with sthg** juguetear con algo.

fidget ['fidʒɪt] vi moverse inquietamente.

field [fiːld] n campo m.

field glasses npl prismáticos mpl.

fierce [fɪəs] adj (animal, person) feroz; (storm, heat) fuerte.

fifteen [fɪfˈtiːn] num quince, → **six**.

fifteenth [fɪfˈtiːnθ] num decimoquinto(-ta), → **sixth**.

fifth [fifθ] num quinto(-ta), → **sixth**.

fiftieth [ˈfiftiəθ] num quincuagésimo(-ma), → **sixth**.

fifty ['fiftɪ] num cincuenta, → **six**.

fig [fig] n higo m.

fight [faɪt] (pt & pp fought) n (physical clash, argument) pelea f; (struggle) lucha f ♦ vt (enemy, crime, illness) luchar contra; (in punch-up) pelearse con ♦ vi (in war, struggle) luchar; (quarrel) discutir; **to have a ~ with sb** pelearse con alguien ❑ **fight back** vi defenderse; **fight off** vt sep (attacker) rechazar; (illness) sanar de.

fighting ['faɪtɪŋ] n (at football match, in streets) violencia f; (in war) combate m.

figure [Br 'figəʳ, Am 'figjər] n (number, statistic) cifra f; (shape of body) tipo m; (outline of person) figura f; (diagram) gráfico m ❑ **figure out** vt sep (answer) figurar f; **I can't ~ out how to do it** no sé cómo hacerlo.

file [faɪl] n (document holder) carpeta f; (information on person) expediente m; (COMPUT) fichero m; (tool) lima f ◆ vt (complaint, petition) presentar; (nails) limar; **in single ~** in fila india.

filing cabinet ['faɪlɪŋ-] n archivador m.

fill [fɪl] vt (make full) llenar; (hole) rellenar; (role) desempeñar; (tooth) empastar ❑ **fill in** vt sep (form) rellenar; **fill out** vt sep = **fill in**; **fill up** vt sep llenar (hasta el tope); **~ her up!** (with petrol) ¡llénelo!

filled roll [,fɪld-] n bocadillo m (de bollo).

fillet ['fɪlɪt] n filete m.

fillet steak n filete m de carne de vaca.

filling ['fɪlɪŋ] n (of cake, sandwich) relleno m; (in tooth) empaste m ◆ adj que llena mucho.

filling station n estación f de servicio.

film [fɪlm] n película f ◆ vt rodar.

film star n estrella f de cine.

filter ['fɪltər] n filtro m.

filthy ['fɪlθɪ] adj (very dirty) sucísimo(-ma).

fin [fɪn] n (of fish) aleta f; (Am: of swimmer) aleta f.

final ['faɪnl] adj (last) último(-ma); (decision, offer) definitivo(-va) ◆ n final f.

finalist ['faɪnəlɪst] n finalista mf.

finally ['faɪnəlɪ] adv (at last) por fin; (lastly) finalmente.

finance [n 'faɪnæns, vb far'næns] n (money) fondos mpl; (management of money) finanzas fpl ◆ vt financiar ❑ **finances** npl finanzas fpl.

financial [fɪ'nænʃl] adj finan-

ciero(-ra).

find [faɪnd] (pt & pp found) vt encontrar; (find out) enterarse de ◆ n hallazgo m; **to ~ the time to do sthg** encontrar tiempo para hacer algo ❑ **find out** vt sep (fact, truth) averiguar ◆ vi: **to ~ out about sthg** averiguar algo.

fine [faɪn] adj (good) bueno(-na); (food, wine) excelente; (thin) fino (-na) ◆ adv (thinly) finamente; (well) bien ◆ n multa f ◆ vt multar ◆ excl vale; **I'm ~** estoy bien; **it's ~** está bien.

fine art n bellas artes fpl.

finger ['fɪŋgər] n dedo m.

fingernail ['fɪŋgəneɪl] n uña f de la mano.

fingertip ['fɪŋgətɪp] n yema f de la mano.

finish ['fɪnɪʃ] n (end) final m; (on furniture) acabado m ◆ vt & vi acabar; **to ~ doing sthg** terminar de hacer algo ❑ **finish off** vt sep (complete) acabar del todo; (eat or drink) acabar; **finish up** vi acabar; **to ~ up doing sthg** acabar haciendo algo.

Finland ['fɪnlənd] n Finlandia.

Finn [fɪn] n finlandés m (-esa f).

Finnan haddock ['fɪnən-] n tipo de eglefino ahumado escocés.

Finnish ['fɪnɪʃ] adj finlandés (-esa) ◆ n (language) finlandés m.

fir [fɜːr] n abeto m.

fire ['faɪər] n fuego m; (uncontrolled) incendio m; (device) estufa f ◆ vt (gun) disparar; (from job) despedir; **on ~** en llamas; **to catch ~** prender fuego; **to make a ~** encender un fuego.

fire alarm n alarma f antiincendios.

fire brigade n (Br) cuerpo m de bomberos.

fire department (Am) = **fire brigade**.

fire engine n coche m de bomberos.

fire escape n escalera f de incendios.

fire exit n salida f de incendios.

fire extinguisher n extintor m.

fire hazard n: it's a ~ podría causar un incendio.

fireman ['faɪəmən] (pl -men [-mən]) n bombero m.

fireplace ['faɪəpleɪs] n chimenea f.

fire regulations npl ordenanzas fpl en caso de incendio.

fire station n parque m de bomberos.

firewood ['faɪəwʊd] n leña f.

firework display ['faɪəwɜːk-] n espectáculo m de fuegos artificiales.

fireworks ['faɪəwɜːks] npl fuegos mpl artificiales.

firm [fɜːm] adj firme ◆ n firma f, empresa f.

first [fɜːst] adj primero(-ra) ◆ adv primero; (for the first time) por primera vez ◆ n (event) acontecimiento m sin precedentes ◆ pron: the ~ el primero (la primera); ~ (gear) primera f (marcha); ~ thing (in the morning) a primera hora (de la mañana); for the ~ time por primera vez; the ~ of January el uno de enero; at ~ al principio; ~ of all antes de nada.

first aid n primeros auxilios mpl.

first-aid kit n botiquín m (de primeros auxilios).

first class n (mail) correo que se distribuye al día siguiente; (on train, plane, ship) primera clase f.

first-class adj (stamp) para la UE o distribución al día siguiente; (ticket) de primera (clase); (very good) de primera.

first floor n (Br: floor above ground floor) primer piso m; (Am: ground floor) bajo m.

firstly ['fɜːstlɪ] adv en primer lugar.

First World War n: the ~ la Primera Guerra Mundial.

fish [fɪʃ] (pl inv) n (animal) pez m; (food) pescado m ◆ vi pescar.

fish and chips n filete de pescado blanco rebozado, con patatas fritas.

_i_ FISH AND CHIPS

La tradicional comida británica para llevar, "fish and chips", consiste en pescado rebozado y frito acompañado de patatas fritas, todo ello envuelto en papel de estraza y periódico. En las tiendas de "fish and chips", que son muy comunes en Gran Bretaña, se pueden encontrar otras frituras, tales como salchichas, pollo, morcilla y pasteles de carne. A menudo, "fish and chips" se come al aire libre directamente del envoltorio.

fishcake ['fɪʃkeɪk] n hamburguesa f de pescado.

fisherman ['fɪʃəmən] (*pl* **-men** [-mən]) *n* pescador *m*.

fish farm *n* piscifactoría *f*.

fish fingers *npl* (*Br*) palitos *mpl* de pescado.

fishing ['fɪʃɪŋ] *n* pesca *f*; **to go** ~ ir de pesca.

fishing boat *n* barco *m* de pesca.

fishing rod *n* caña *f* de pescar.

fishmonger's ['fɪʃ,mʌŋgəz] *n* (*shop*) pescadería *f*.

fish sticks (*Am*) = **fish fingers**.

fish supper *n* (*Scot*) filete de pescado blanco rebozado, con patatas fritas.

fist [fɪst] *n* puño *m*.

fit [fɪt] *adj* (*healthy*) en forma ◆ *vt* (*be right size for*) sentar bien a; (*a lock, kitchen, bath*) instalar; (*insert*) insertar ◆ *vi* (*clothes, shoes*) estar bien de talla; (*in space*) caber ◆ *n* ataque *m*; **to be ~ for sthg** ser apto(-ta) para algo; ~ **to eat** apto para el consumo; **it's a good ~** sienta bien; **it doesn't ~** no cabe; **to get ~** ponerse en forma; **to keep ~** mantenerse en forma ❑ **fit in** *vt sep* (*find time to do*) hacer un hueco a ◆ *vi* (*belong*) encajar.

fitness ['fɪtnɪs] *n* (*health*) estado *m* físico.

fitted carpet [,fɪtəd-] *n* moqueta *f*.

fitted sheet [,fɪtəd-] *n* sábana *f* ajustable.

fitting room ['fɪtɪŋ-] *n* probador *m*.

five [faɪv] *num* cinco, → **six**.

fiver ['faɪvə'] *n* (*Br*) (*inf*) (£5) cinco libras *fpl*; (£5 *note*) billete *m*

de cinco libras.

fix [fɪks] *vt* (*attach, decide on*) fijar; (*mend*) reparar; (*drink, food*) preparar; **have you ~ed anything for tonight?** ¿tienes planes para esta noche? ❑ **fix up** *vt sep*: **to ~ sb up with sthg** proveer a alguien de algo.

fixture ['fɪkstʃə'] *n* (*SPORT*) encuentro *m*; **~s and fittings** instalaciones *fpl* domésticas.

fizzy ['fɪzɪ] *adj* gaseoso(-sa).

flag [flæg] *n* bandera *f*.

flake [fleɪk] *n* (*of snow*) copo *m* ◆ *vi* descamarse.

flame [fleɪm] *n* llama *f*.

flammable ['flæməbl] *adj* inflamable.

flan [flæn] *n* tarta *f*.

flannel ['flænl] *n* (*material*) franela *f*; (*Br: for washing face*) toalla *f* de cara ❑ **flannels** *npl* pantalones *mpl* de franela.

flap [flæp] *n* (*of envelope, pocket*) solapa *f*; (*of tent*) puerta *f* ◆ *vt* (*wings*) batir.

flapjack ['flæpdʒæk] *n* (*Br*) torta *f* de avena.

flare [fleə'] *n* (*signal*) bengala *f*.

flared [fleəd] *adj* acampanado(-da).

flash [flæʃ] *n* (*of light*) destello *m*; (*for camera*) flash *m* ◆ *vi* (*light*) destellar; **a ~ of lightning** un relámpago; **to ~ one's headlights** dar las luces.

flashlight ['flæʃlaɪt] *n* linterna *f*.

flask [flɑːsk] *n* (*Thermos*) termo *m*; (*hip flask*) petaca *f*.

flat [flæt] *adj* (*level*) llano(na); (*battery*) descargado(-da); (*drink*) muerto(-ta); *(rate, fee)* único(-ca) ♦ *n (Br)* piso *m* ♦ *adv*: **to lie ~** estar extendido; **a ~ (tyre)** un pinchazo; **~ out** a toda velocidad.

flatter ['flætə'] *vt* adular.

flavor ['fleɪvər] *(Am)* = **flavour**.

flavour ['fleɪvə'] *n (Br)* sabor *m*.

flavoured ['fleɪvəd] *adj* de sabores.

flavouring ['fleɪvərɪŋ] *n* aroma *m*.

flaw [flɔ:] *n* fallo *m*.

flea [fli:] *n* pulga *f*.

flea market *n* mercado de objetos curiosos y de segunda mano, ≈ rastro *m*.

fleece [fli:s] *n (downy material)* vellón *m*

fleet [fli:t] *n* flota *f*.

Flemish ['flemɪʃ] *adj* flamenco(-ca) ♦ *n (language)* flamenco *m*.

flesh [fleʃ] *n (of person, animal)* carne *f*; *(of fruit, vegetable)* pulpa *f*

flew [flu:] *pt* → **fly**.

flex [fleks] *n* cable *m*.

flexible ['fleksəbl] *adj* flexible.

flick [flɪk] *n (of a switch)* apretar; *(with finger)* golpear rápidamente ♦ **flick through** *vt fus* hojear rápidamente.

flies [flaɪz] *npl* bragueta *f*.

flight [flaɪt] *n* vuelo *m*; **a ~ (of stairs)** un tramo de (escaleras).

flight attendant *n* auxiliar *mf* de vuelo.

flimsy ['flɪmzɪ] *adj (object)* frágil, poco sólido(da); *(clothes)* ligero(-ra).

fling [flɪŋ] *(pt & pp flung) vt* arrojar.

flint [flɪnt] *n (of lighter)* piedra *f*.

flip-flop ['flɪp-] *n (Br)* chancleta *f*.

flipper ['flɪpə'] *n (Br)* aleta *f*.

flirt [flɜ:t] *vi*: **to ~ (with sb)** coquetear (con alguien).

float [fləʊt] *n (for swimming)* flotador *m*; *(for fishing)* corcho *m*; *(in procession)* carroza *f*; *(drink)* bebida con una bola de helado flotando ♦ *vi* flotar.

flock [flɒk] *n (of birds)* bandada *f*; *(of sheep)* rebaño *m* ♦ *vi (people)* acudir en masa.

flood [flʌd] *n* inundación *f* ♦ *vt* inundar.

floodlight ['flʌdlaɪt] *n* foco *m*.

floor [flɔ:'] *n (of room)* suelo *m*; *(storey)* piso *m*; *(of nightclub)* pista *f* de baile.

floorboard ['flɔ:bɔ:d] *n* tabla *f* del suelo.

floor show *n* espectáculo *m* de cabaret.

flop [flɒp] *n (inf)* fracaso *m*.

floppy disk [,flɒpɪ-] *n* floppy disk *m*.

floral ['flɔ:rəl] *adj (pattern)* floreado(-da).

Florida Keys ['flɒrɪdə-] *npl*: **the ~** las Florida Keys.

FLORIDA KEYS

Un archipiélago de pequeñas islas que se extiende más de 100 millas frente a la costa sur de Florida, las Florida Keys incluyen lugares turísticos como las islas de Cayo Largo y Cayo Hueso. Un sistema de carreteras y puentes, la "Overseas Highway", comunica las distintas islas.

florist's ['flɒrɪsts] *n (shop)* floristería *f*.

flour ['flaʊə*r*] *n* harina *f*.

flow [fləʊ] *n* corriente *f* ♦ *vi* correr.

flower ['flaʊə*r*] *n* flor *f*.

flowerbed ['flaʊəbed] *n* arriate *m*.

flowerpot ['flaʊəppt] *n* tiesto *m*.

flown [fləʊn] *pp* → fly.

fl oz *abbr* = fluid ounce.

flu [flu:] *n* gripe *f*.

fluent ['flu:ənt] *adj:* to be ~ in/to speak ~ Spanish dominar el español.

fluff [flʌf] *n* pelusa *f*.

fluid ounce ['flu:ɪd-] *n = 0,03 litros*, onza *f* líquida.

flume [flu:m] *n* tobogán *m* acuático.

flung [flʌŋ] *pt & pp* → fling.

flunk [flʌŋk] *vt (Am: inf)* catear.

fluorescent [flʊə'resənt] *adj* fluorescente.

flush [flʌʃ] *vi (toilet)* funcionar ♦ *vt:* to ~ the toilet tirar de la cadena.

flute [flu:t] *n* flauta *f*.

fly [flaɪ] *(pt* flew, *pp* flown*) n (insect)* mosca *f; (of trousers)* bragueta *f* ♦ *vt (plane, helicopter)* pilotar; *(travel by)* viajar con; *(transport)* transportar en avión ♦ *vi* volar; *(pilot a plane)* pilotar; *(flag)* ondear.

fly-drive *n* paquete turístico que incluye vuelo *y* coche alquilado.

flying ['flaɪɪŋ] *n:* I like ~ me gusta volar.

flyover ['flaɪ,əʊvə*r*] *n (Br)* paso *m* elevado.

flypaper ['flaɪ,peɪpə*r*] *n* papel *m* insecticida.

flysheet ['flaɪʃi:t] *n* doble techo *m*.

FM *n* FM *f*.

foal [fəʊl] *n* potro *m*.

foam [fəʊm] *n (bubbles)* espuma *f; (foam rubber)* gomaespuma *f*.

focus ['fəʊkəs] *n (of camera)* foco *m* ♦ *vi (with camera, binoculars)* enfocar; **in ~** enfocado; **out of ~** desenfocado.

fog [fɒg] *n* niebla *f*.

fogbound ['fɒgbaʊnd] *adj (airport)* cerrado(-da) a causa de la niebla.

foggy ['fɒgi] *adj (weather)* brumoso(-sa).

fog lamp *n* faro *m* antiniebla.

foil [fɔɪl] *n* papel *m* de aluminio.

fold [fəʊld] *n* pliegue *m* ♦ *vt (paper, material)* doblar; *(wrap)* envolver; **to ~ one's arms** cruzarse de brazos ❑ **fold up** *vi* plegarse.

folder ['fəʊldə*r*] *n* carpeta *f*.

foliage ['fəʊlɪdʒ] *n* follaje *m*.

folk [fəʊk] *npl (people)* gente *f;* ~ **(music)** folk *m* ❑ **folks** *npl (inf: relatives)* familia *f*.

follow ['fɒləʊ] *vt* seguir; *(understand)* comprender ♦ *vi (go behind)* ir detrás; *(in time)* seguir; *(understand)* comprender; **~ed by** seguido de; **as ~s** como sigue ❑ **follow on** *vi* ir detrás.

following ['fɒləʊɪŋ] *adj* siguiente ♦ *prep* tras.

follow on call *n* nueva llamada con crédito restante, sin colgar.

fond [fɒnd] *adj:* to be ~ of *(person)* tener cariño a; *(thing)* ser aficionado(-da) a.

fondue ['fɒndu:] n fondue f.

food [fu:d] n (nourishment) comida f; (type of food) alimento m.

food poisoning [-,pɔɪznɪŋ] n intoxicación f alimenticia.

food processor [-,prəʊsesə^r] n robot m de cocina.

foodstuffs ['fu:dstʌfs] npl comestibles mpl.

fool [fu:l] n (idiot) tonto m (-ta f); (pudding) mousse de nata y fruta ◆ vt engañar.

foolish ['fu:lɪʃ] adj tonto(ta).

foot [fʊt] (pl **feet**) n pie m; (of animal, wardrobe, tripod) pata f; **by** ~ a pie; **on** ~ a pie.

football ['fʊtbɔ:l] n (Br: soccer) fútbol m; (Am: American football) fútbol americano; (Br: in soccer) balón m (de fútbol); (Am: in American football) balón (de fútbol americano).

footballer ['fʊtbɔ:lə^r] n (Br) futbolista mf.

football pitch n (Br) campo m de fútbol.

footbridge ['fʊtbrɪdʒ] n pasarela f.

footpath ['fʊtpɑ:θ, pl -pɑ:ðz] n sendero m.

footprint ['fʊtprɪnt] n huella f.

footstep ['fʊtstep] n paso m.

footwear ['fʊtweə^r] n calzado m.

for [fɔ:^r] prep 1. (expressing intention, purpose, destination) para; **this book is** ~ **you** este libro es para ti; **what did you do that** ~? ¿por qué hiciste eso?; **what's it** ~? ¿para qué es?; **to go** ~ **a walk** dar un paseo; **"~ sale"** "se vende"; **a ticket** ~

Edinburgh un billete para Edimburgo; **the train** ~ **London** el tren de Londres.

2. (expressing reason) por; **a town famous** ~ **its wine** una ciudad famosa por sus vinos; **the reason** ~ **it** el motivo de ello.

3. (during) durante; **I've lived here** ~ **ten years** llevo diez años viviendo aquí; **we've lived here** ~ **years** vivimos aquí desde hace años; **we talked** ~ **hours** estuvimos hablando durante horas y horas.

4. (by, before) para, para las ocho de la tarde.

5. (on the occasion of) por; **what's** ~ **dinner?** ¿qué hay de cena?; ~ **the first time** por primera vez.

6. (on behalf of) por; **to do sthg** ~ **sb** hacer algo por alguien; **to work** ~ **sb** trabajar para alguien.

7. (with time and space) para; **there's no room/time** ~ **it** no hay sitio/tiempo para eso.

8. (expressing distance): **road works** ~ **10 miles** obras por espacio de 20 millas; **we walked** ~ **miles** andamos millas y millas.

9. (expressing price) por; **I bought it** ~ **five pounds** lo compré por cinco libras; **they sell** ~ **a pound** se venden a una libra.

10. (expressing meaning): **what's the Spanish** ~ **"boy"?** ¿cómo se dice "boy" en español?

11. (with regard to) por; **it's cold** ~ **summer** hace frío para el verano; **I'm sorry** ~ **them** me dan pena.

12. (introducing more information) para; **it's too far** ~ **us to walk** nos queda demasiado lejos para ir andando; **it's time** ~ **dinner** es

hora de cenar.

forbid [fə'bɪd] (*pt* **-bade** [-'beɪd], *pp* **-bidden**) *vt* prohibir; **to ~ sb to do sthg** prohibir a alguien hacer algo.

forbidden [fə'bɪdn] *adj* prohibido(-da).

force [fɔ:s] *n* fuerza *f* ♦ *vt* forzar; **to ~ sb to do sthg** forzar a alguien a hacer algo; **to ~ one's way through** abrirse camino; **the ~s** las fuerzas armadas.

ford [fɔ:d] *n* vado *m*.

forecast ['fɔ:kɑ:st] *n* pronóstico *m*.

forecourt ['fɔ:kɔ:t] *n* patio *m*.

forefinger ['fɔ:ˌfɪŋgəʳ] *n* dedo *m* índice.

foreground ['fɔ:graʊnd] *n* primer plano *m*.

forehead ['fɔ:hed] *n* frente *f*.

foreign ['fɒrən] *adj* extranjero(-ra).

foreign currency *n* divisa *f*.

foreigner ['fɒrənəʳ] *n* extranjero *m* (-ra *f*).

foreign exchange *n* divisas *fpl*.

Foreign Secretary *n* (*Br*) ministro *m* (-tra *f*) de Asuntos Exteriores.

foreman ['fɔ:mən] (*pl* **-men** [-mən]) *n* capataz *m*.

forename ['fɔ:neɪm] *n* (*fml*) nombre *m* de pila.

foresee [fɔ:'si:] (*pt* **-saw** [-'sɔ:], *pp* **-seen** [-'si:n]) *vt* prever.

forest ['fɒrɪst] *n* bosque *m*.

forever [fə'revəʳ] *adv* (*eternally*) para siempre; (*continually*) siempre.

forgave [fə'geɪv] *pt* → **forgive**.

forge [fɔ:dʒ] *vt* falsificar.

forgery ['fɔ:dʒərɪ] *n* falsificación *f*.

forget [fə'get] (*pt* **-got**, *pp* **-gotten**) *vt* olvidar ♦ *vi* olvidarse; **to ~ about sthg** olvidarse de algo; **to ~ how to do sthg** olvidar cómo se hace algo; **to ~ to do sthg** olvidarse de hacer algo; **~ it!** ¡ni lo menciones!

forgetful [fə'getfʊl] *adj* olvidadizo(-za).

forgive [fə'gɪv] (*pt* **-gave**, *pp* **-given** [-'gɪvn]) *vt* perdonar.

forgot [fə'gɒt] *pt* → **forget**.

forgotten [fə'gɒtn] *pp* → **forget**.

fork [fɔ:k] *n* (*for eating with*) tenedor *m*; (*for gardening*) horca *f*; (*of road, path*) bifurcación *f* ❑ **forks** *npl* (*of bike, motorbike*) horquilla *f*.

form [fɔ:m] *n* (*type, shape*) forma *f*; (*piece of paper*) impreso *m*; (*SCH*) clase *f* ♦ *vt* formar ♦ *vi* formarse; **off ~** en baja forma; **on ~** en forma; **to ~ part of** formar parte de.

formal ['fɔ:ml] *adj* formal.

formality [fɔ:'mælətɪ] *n* formalidad *f*; **it's just a ~** es una pura formalidad.

format ['fɔ:mæt] *n* formato *m*.

former ['fɔ:məʳ] *adj* (*previous*) antiguo(-gua); (*first*) primero(-ra) ♦ *pron*: **the ~** el primero (la primera).

formerly ['fɔ:məlɪ] *adv* previamente, antiguamente.

formula ['fɔ:mjʊlə] (*pl* **-as** OR **-ae** [-i:]) *n* fórmula *f*.

fort [fɔ:t] *n* fortaleza *f*.

forthcoming [fɔːˈθkʌmɪŋ] adj (future) próximo(-ma).

fortieth [ˈfɔːtɪɪθ] num cuadragésimo(-ma), → sixth.

fortnight [ˈfɔːtnaɪt] n (Br) quincena f.

fortunate [ˈfɔːtʃnət] adj afortunado(-da).

fortunately [ˈfɔːtʃnətlɪ] adv afortunadamente.

fortune [ˈfɔːtʃuːn] n (money) fortuna f; (luck) suerte f; **it costs a ~** (inf) cuesta un riñón.

forty [ˈfɔːtɪ] num cuarenta, → six.

forward [ˈfɔːwəd] adv hacia adelante ♦ n delantero m (-ra f) ♦ vt reenviar; **to look ~ to** esperar (con ilusión).

forwarding address [ˈfɔːwədɪŋ-] n nueva dirección f para reenvío del correo.

fought [fɔːt] pt & pp → fight.

foul [faʊl] adj (unpleasant) asqueroso(-sa) ♦ n falta f.

found [faʊnd] pt & pp → find ♦ vt fundar.

foundation (cream) [faʊnˈdeɪʃn-] n base f (hidratante).

foundations [faʊnˈdeɪʃnz] npl cimientos mpl.

fountain [ˈfaʊntɪn] n fuente f.

fountain pen n pluma f.

four [fɔːʳ] num cuatro, → six.

four-star (petrol) n = súper f.

fourteen [ˌfɔːˈtiːn] num catorce, → six.

fourteenth [ˌfɔːˈtiːnθ] num decimocuarto(-ta), → sixth.

fourth [fɔːθ] num cuarto(-ta), → sixth.

four-wheel drive n coche m con tracción a las cuatro ruedas.

fowl [faʊl] (pl inv) n volatería f.

fox [fɒks] n zorro m.

foyer [ˈfɔɪeɪ] n vestíbulo m.

fraction [ˈfrækʃn] n fracción f.

fracture [ˈfræktʃəʳ] n fractura f ♦ vt fracturar, romper.

fragile [ˈfrædʒaɪl] adj frágil.

fragment [ˈfrægmənt] n fragmento m.

fragrance [ˈfreɪɡrəns] n fragancia f.

frail [freɪl] adj débil.

frame [freɪm] n (of window, photo, door) marco m; (of glasses) montura f; (of tent, bicycle, bed) armazón m ♦ vt (photo, picture) enmarcar.

France [frɑːns] n Francia.

frank [fræŋk] adj franco(-ca).

frankfurter [ˈfræŋkfɜːtəʳ] n salchicha f de Fráncfort.

frankly [ˈfræŋklɪ] adv francamente.

frantic [ˈfræntɪk] adj frenético(-ca).

fraud [frɔːd] n (crime) fraude m.

freak [friːk] adj estrafalario(-ria) ♦ n (inf: fanatic) fanático m (-ca f).

freckles [ˈfreklz] npl pecas fpl.

free [friː] adj libre; (costing nothing) gratis (inv) ♦ vt (prisoner) liberar ♦ adv (without paying) gratis; **for ~** gratis; **~ of charge** gratis; **to be ~ to do sthg** ser libre de hacer algo.

freedom [ˈfriːdəm] n libertad f.

freefone [ˈfriːfəʊn] n (Br) teléfono m gratuito.

free gift n obsequio m.

free house n (Br) "pub" no controlado por una compañía cervecera.

free kick n tiro m libre.

freelance [ˈfriːlɑːns] adj autónomo(-ma).

freely [ˈfriːlɪ] adv (available) fácilmente; (speak) francamente; (move) libremente.

free period n hora f libre.

freepost [ˈfriːpəʊst] n franqueo m pagado.

free-range adj de granja.

free time n tiempo m libre.

freeway [ˈfriːweɪ] n (Am) autopista f.

freeze [friːz] (pt froze, pp frozen) vt congelar ◆ vi helarse ◆ v impers helar.

freezer [ˈfriːzər] n (deep freeze) arcón m congelador; (part of fridge) congelador m.

freezing [ˈfriːzɪŋ] adj helado(-da); it's ~ hace un frío cortante.

freezing point n: below ~ bajo cero.

freight [freɪt] n (goods) mercancías fpl.

French [frentʃ] adj francés(-esa) ◆ n (language) francés m ◆ npl: the ~ los franceses.

French bean n judía f verde.

French bread n pan m de barra.

French dressing n (in UK) vinagreta f; (in US) salsa f rosa.

French fries npl patatas fpl fritas.

Frenchman [ˈfrentʃmən] (pl -men [-mən]) n francés m.

French toast n torrija f.

French windows npl puerta-ventanas fpl.

Frenchwoman [ˈfrentʃˌwʊmən] (pl -women [-ˌwɪmɪn]) n francesa f.

frequency [ˈfriːkwənsɪ] n frecuencia f.

frequent [ˈfriːkwənt] adj frecuente.

frequently [ˈfriːkwəntlɪ] adv frecuentemente.

fresh [freʃ] adj fresco(-ca); (bread) del día; (coffee) recién hecho; (refreshing) refrescante; (water) dulce; (developments, instructions, start) nuevo(-va); (news) reciente; to get some ~ air tomar el aire.

fresh cream n nata f (no artificial).

freshen [ˈfreʃn]: freshen up vi refrescarse.

freshly [ˈfreʃlɪ] adv recién.

fresh orange (juice) n zumo m de naranja.

Fri (abbr of Friday) v.

Friday [ˈfraɪdɪ] n viernes m inv, → Saturday.

fridge [frɪdʒ] n nevera f.

fried egg [fraɪd-] n huevo m frito.

fried rice [fraɪd-] n arroz frito, mezclado a veces con huevo, carne o verduras, servido como acompañamiento de platos chinos.

friend [frend] n amigo m (-ga f); to be ~s with sb ser amigo de alguien; to make ~s with sb hacerse amigo de alguien.

friendly [ˈfrendlɪ] adj (kind) amable; to be ~ with sb ser amigo(-ga) de alguien.

friendship [ˈfrendʃɪp] n amistad f.

fries [fraɪz] = French fries.

fright [fraɪt] *n* terror *m*; **to give sb a ~** darle un susto a alguien.

frighten ['fraɪtn] *vt* asustar.

frightened ['fraɪtnd] *adj* asustado(-da); **I'm ~ we won't finish it** temo que no vamos a acabar; **to be ~ of** tener miedo a.

frightening ['fraɪtnɪŋ] *adj* aterrador(-ra).

frightful ['fraɪtful] *adj* horrible.

frilly ['frɪlɪ] *adj* con volantes.

fringe [frɪndʒ] *n* (*Br: of hair*) flequillo *m*, (*of clothes, curtain etc*) fleco *m*.

frisk [frɪsk] *vt* cachear.

frittor ['frɪtəʳ] *n* buñuelo *m*.

fro [frəʊ] *adv* → **to**.

frog [frɒg] *n* rana *f*.

from [weak form frəm, strong form frɒm] *prep* 1. (*expressing origin, source*) de; **I'm ~ Spain** soy de España; **I bought it ~ a supermarket** lo compré en un supermercado; **the train ~ Manchester** el tren (procedente) de Manchester.
2. (*expressing removal, separation, deduction*) de; **away ~ home** fuera de casa; **to take sthg (away) ~ sb** quitarle algo a alguien; **10% will be deducted ~ the total** se descontará un 10% del total.
3. (*expressing distance*) de; **five miles ~ London** a cinco millas de Londres.
4. (*expressing position*) desde; **~ here you can see the valley** desde aquí se ve el valle.
5. (*expressing starting point*) desde; **~ now on** de ahora en adelante; **open ~ nine to five** abierto de nueve a cinco; **tickets are ~ £10** hay entradas desde 10 libras.
6. (*expressing change*) de; **the price has gone up ~ £1 to £2** el precio ha subido de 1 a 2 libras.
7. (*expressing range*): **it could take ~ two to six months** podría tardar entre dos y seis meses.
8. (*as a result of*) de; **I'm tired ~ walking** estoy cansado de haber andado tanto.
9. (*expressing protection*) de; **sheltered ~ the wind** resguardado del viento.
10. (*in comparisons*): **different ~** diferente a.

fromage frais [,frɒmɑːʒ'freɪ] *n* tipo de queso fresco.

front [frʌnt] *adj* delantero(-ra) ◆ *n* (*foremost part*) parte *f* delantera; (*of building*) fachada *f*; (*of weather*) frente *m*; (*by the sea*) paseo *m* marítimo; **in ~** delante; **to be in ~** ir ganando; **in ~ of** delante de.

front door *n* puerta *f* principal.

frontier [frʌn'tɪəʳ] *n* frontera *f*.

front page *n* portada *f*.

front seat *n* asiento *m* delantero.

frost [frɒst] *n* (*on ground*) escarcha *f*; (*cold weather*) helada *f*.

frosty ['frɒstɪ] *adj* (*morning, weather*) de helada.

froth [frɒθ] *n* espuma *f*.

frown [fraʊn] *n* ceño *m* ◆ *vi* fruncir el ceño.

froze [frəʊz] *pt* → **freeze**.

frozen [frəʊzn] *pp* → **freeze** ◆ *adj* helado(-da); (*food*) congelado(-da).

fruit [fruːt] *n* fruta *f*; **a piece of ~** una fruta; **~s of the forest** frutas del bosque.

fruit cake n pastel de pasas y frutas confitadas.

fruiterer ['fruːtərər] n (Br) frutero m (-ra f).

fruit juice n zumo m de fruta.

fruit machine n (Br) máquina f tragaperras.

fruit salad n macedonia f (de frutas).

frustrating [frʌ'streɪtɪŋ] adj frustrante.

frustration [frʌ'streɪʃn] n frustración f.

fry [fraɪ] vt freír.

frying pan ['fraɪɪŋ-] n sartén f.

ft abbr = **foot, feet.**

fudge [fʌdʒ] n caramelo fabricado con leche, azúcar y mantequilla.

fuel [fjʊəl] n combustible m.

fuel pump n surtidor m de gasolina.

fulfil [fʊl'fɪl] vt (Br) (promise, duty, conditions) cumplir; (need) satisfacer; (role) desempeñar.

fulfill [fʊl'fɪl] (Am) = **fulfil.**

full [fʊl] adj (filled) lleno(-na); (complete) completo(-ta); (maximum) máximo(-ma); (busy) atareado(-da); (flavour) rico(-ca) ◆ adv de lleno; **I'm ~ (up)** estoy lleno; **~ of** lleno de; **in ~** íntegramente.

full board n pensión f completa.

full-cream milk n leche f entera.

full-length adj (skirt, dress) largo(-ga) (hasta los pies).

full moon n luna f llena.

full stop n punto m.

full-time adj de jornada completa ◆ adv a tiempo completo.

fully ['fʊlɪ] adv (completely) completamente.

fully-licensed adj autorizado para vender bebidas alcohólicas durante el horario completo establecido legalmente.

fumble ['fʌmbl] vi: **to ~ for sthg** buscar algo a tientas.

fun [fʌn] n (amusement) diversión f; **it's good ~** es muy divertido; **for ~ de broma; to have ~** divertirse; **to make ~ of** burlarse de.

function ['fʌŋkʃn] n (role) función f; (formal event) acto m ◆ vi funcionar.

fund [fʌnd] n fondo m ◆ vt financiar ❑ **funds** npl fondos mpl.

fundamental [ˌfʌndə'mentl] adj fundamental.

funeral ['fjuːnərəl] n funeral m.

funfair ['fʌnfeər] n parque m de atracciones.

funky ['fʌŋkɪ] adj (inf: music) funky (inv).

funnel ['fʌnl] n (for pouring) embudo m; (on ship) chimenea f.

funny ['fʌnɪ] adj (person) gracioso(-sa); (thing) divertido(-da); (strange) raro(-ra); **to feel ~ (ill)** sentirse raro.

fur [fɜːr] n (on animal) pelaje m; (garment) piel f.

fur coat n abrigo m de piel.

furious ['fjʊərɪəs] adj furioso(-sa).

furnished ['fɜːnɪʃt] adj amueblado(-da).

furnishings ['fɜːnɪʃɪŋz] npl mobiliario m.

furniture ['fɜːnɪtʃər] n muebles mpl; **a piece of ~** un mueble.

furry ['fɜ:rɪ] adj peludo(-da).

further ['fɜ:ðəʳ] compar → **far** ◆ adv (in distance) más lejos; (more) más ◆ adj (additional) otro (otra); **until ~ notice** hasta nuevo aviso.

furthermore [,fɜ:ðə'mɔ:ʳ] adv además.

furthest ['fɜ:ðɪst] superl → **far** ◆ adj (most distant) más lejano(-na) ◆ adv (in distance) más lejos.

fuse [fju:z] n (of plug) fusible m; (on bomb) mecha f ◆ vi (plug) fundirse; (electrical device) estropearse

fuse box n caja f de fusibles

fuss [fʌs] n (agitation) jaleo m; (complaints) quejas fpl

fussy ['fʌsɪ] adj (person) quisquilloso(-sa)

future ['fju:tʃəʳ] n futuro m ◆ adj futuro(ra); **in ~** de ahora en adelante.

g (abbr of gram) g.

gable ['geɪbl] n aguilón m.

gadget ['gædʒɪt] n artilugio m.

Gaelic ['geɪlɪk] n gaélico m.

gag [gæg] n (inf: joke) chiste m.

gain [geɪn] vt (get more of) ganar; (achieve) conseguir; (subj: clock, watch) adelantarse ◆ vi (get benefit) beneficiarse ◆ n (improvement) mejora f; (profit) ganancia f.

gale [geɪl] n vendaval m.

gallery ['gælərɪ] n (for art etc) galería f; (at theatre) gallinero m.

gallon ['gælən] n (in UK) = 4,546 litros, galón m; (in US) = 3,785 litros, galón m.

gallop ['gæləp] vi galopar.

gamble ['gæmbl] n riesgo m ◆ vi (bet money) apostar.

gambling ['gæmblɪŋ] n juego m (de dinero).

game [geɪm] n juego m; (of football, tennis, cricket) partido m; (of chess, cards, snooker) partida f □ **games** n (SCH) deportes mpl ◆ npl (sporting event) juegos mpl.

gammon ['gæmən] n jamón m.

gang [gæŋ] n (of criminals) banda f; (of friends) pandilla f.

gangster ['gæŋstəʳ] n gángster m.

gangway ['gæŋweɪ] n (for ship) plancha f (de atraque); (Br: in bus, plane, theatre) pasillo m.

gaol [dʒeɪl] (Br) = **jail**.

gap [gæp] n (space) hueco m; (of time) intervalo m; (difference) discordancia f.

garage ['gærɑ:ʒ, 'gærɪdʒ] n (for keeping car) garaje m; (Br: for petrol) gasolinera f; (for repairs) taller m (de reparaciones); (Br: for selling cars) concesionario m (de automóviles).

garbage ['gɑ:bɪdʒ] n (Am: refuse) basura f.

garbage can n (Am) cubo m de la basura.

garbage truck n (Am) camión m de la basura.

garden ['gɑ:dn] n jardín m ◆ vi

trabajar en el jardín ❏ **gardens** npl (public park) jardines mpl.

garden centre n centro m de jardinería.

gardener ['gɑ:dnə^r] n jardinero m (-ra f).

gardening ['gɑ:dnɪŋ] n jardinería f.

garden peas npl guisantes mpl.

garlic ['gɑ:lɪk] n ajo m.

garlic bread n pan untado con mantequilla y ajo y cocido al horno.

garlic butter n mantequilla f con ajo.

garment ['gɑ:mənt] n prenda f (de vestir).

garnish ['gɑ:nɪʃ] n (herbs, vegetables) adorno m; (sauce) guarnición f ◆ vt adornar.

gas [gæs] n gas m; (Am: petrol) gasolina f.

gas cooker n (Br) cocina f de gas.

gas cylinder n bombona f de gas.

gas fire n (Br) estufa f de gas.

gasket ['gæskɪt] n junta f (de culata).

gas mask n máscara f antigás.

gasoline ['gæsəli:n] n (Am) gasolina f.

gasp [gɑ:sp] vi (in shock, surprise) ahogar un grito.

gas pedal n (Am) acelerador m.

gas station n (Am) gasolinera f.

gas stove (Br) = **gas cooker**.

gas tank n (Am) depósito m de gasolina.

gasworks ['gæswɜ:ks] (pl inv) n fábrica f de gas.

gate [geɪt] n (to garden, field) puer-

ta f; (at airport) puerta f de embarque.

gâteau ['gætəʊ] (pl **-x** [-z]) n (Br) tarta f (con nata).

gateway ['geɪtweɪ] n entrada f.

gather ['gæðə^r] vt (collect) recoger; (speed) ganar; (understand) deducir ◆ vi reunirse.

gaudy ['gɔ:dɪ] adj chillón(-ona).

gauge [geɪdʒ] n (for measuring) indicador m; (of railway track) ancho m de vía ◆ vt (calculate) calibrar.

gauze [gɔ:z] n gasa f.

gave [geɪv] pt → **give**.

gay [geɪ] adj (homosexual) homosexual.

gaze [geɪz] vi: **to ~ at** mirar fijamente.

GB (abbr of Great Britain) GB.

GCSE n examen final de enseñanza media en Gran Bretaña.

---

i **GCSE**

Los GCSE (General Certificate of Secondary Education) se introdujeron en Gran Bretaña en 1986 en lugar de los "O-levels". Se hacen a los 15 o 16 años y los estudiantes que deseen preparar "A-levels" han de aprobar al menos cinco asignaturas. A diferencia de los antiguos "O-levels", las notas se basan no sólo en el examen sino también en el trabajo a lo largo del curso.

---

gear [gɪə^r] n (wheel) engranaje m; (speed) marcha f; (equipment, clothes) equipo m; (belongings) cosas fpl; **in ~** con una marcha metida.

gearbox ['gɪəbɒks] n caja f de cambios.

gear lever n palanca f de cambios.

gear shift (Am) = gear lever.

gear stick (Br) = gear lever.

geese [gi:s] pl → goose.

gel [dʒel] n (for hair) gomina f; (for shower) gel m (de ducha).

gelatine ['dʒeləti:n] n gelatina f.

gem [dʒem] n piedra f preciosa.

Gemini ['dʒemɪnaɪ] n Géminis m inv.

gender ['dʒendər] n género m.

general ['dʒenərəl] adj general ◆ n general m; **in ~** (as a whole) en general; (usually) generalmente.

general anaesthetic n anestesia f general.

general election n elecciones fpl generales.

generally ['dʒenərəlɪ] adv en general.

general practitioner [-præk'tɪʃənər] n médico -a (m f) de cabecera.

general store n tienda f de ultramarinos.

generate ['dʒenəreɪt] vt generar.

generation [,dʒenə'reɪʃn] n generación f.

generator ['dʒenəreɪtər] n generador m.

generosity [,dʒenə'rɒsətɪ] n generosidad f.

generous ['dʒenərəs] adj generoso(-sa).

genitals ['dʒenɪtlz] npl genitales mpl.

genius ['dʒi:njəs] n genio m.

gentle ['dʒentl] adj (careful) cuidadoso(-sa); (kind) dulce, amable; (movement, breeze) suave.

gentleman ['dʒentlmən] (pl -men [-mən]) n (man) señor m; (well-behaved man) caballero m; **"gentlemen"** "caballeros".

gently ['dʒentlɪ] adv (carefully) con cuidado.

gents [dʒents] n (Br) caballeros mpl.

genuine ['dʒenjuɪn] adj (authentic) auténtico(-a); (sincere) sincero (-a).

geographical [dʒɪə'græfɪkl] adj geográfico(-a).

geography [dʒɪ'ɒgrəfɪ] n geografía f.

geology [dʒɪ'ɒlədʒɪ] n geología f.

geometry [dʒɪ'ɒmɪtrɪ] n geometría f.

Georgian ['dʒɔ:dʒən] adj georgiano(-na).

geranium [dʒɪ'reɪnjəm] n geranio m.

German ['dʒɜ:mən] adj alemán(-ana) ◆ n (person) alemán m (-ana f); (language) alemán m.

German measles n rubéola f.

Germany ['dʒɜ:mənɪ] n Alemania.

germs [dʒɜ:mz] npl microbios mpl.

gesture ['dʒestʃər] n (movement) gesto m.

get [get] (Br pt & pp got, Am pt got, pp gotten) vt 1. (obtain) conseguir; **I got some crisps from the shop** compré unas patatas fritas en la tienda; **she got a job** consiguió un trabajo; **I ~ a lot of enjoy-**

ment from it me gusta mucho (hacerlo).

2. *(receive)* recibir; **I got a book for Christmas** me regalaron un libro por Navidades.

3. *(means of transport)* coger, tomar *(Amér)*; **let's ~ a taxi** ¡vamos a coger un taxi!

4. *(fetch)* traer; **could you ~ me the boss?** *(in shop)* ¿puede ver al jefe?; *(on phone)* ¿puede ponerme con el jefe?; **~ me a drink** tráeme algo de beber.

5. *(illness)* coger, agarrar *(Amér)*; **I've got a cold** tengo un catarro.

6. *(cause to become, do)*: **to ~ sthg done** mandar hacer algo; **to ~ sb to do sthg** hacer que alguien haga algo; **can I ~ my car repaired here?** ¿pueden arreglarme el coche aquí?; **to ~ sthg ready** preparar algo.

7. *(move)*: **to ~ sthg out** sacar algo; **I can't ~ it through the door** no puedo meterlo por la puerta.

8. *(understand)* entender; **to ~ a joke** coger un chiste.

9. *(time, chance)* tener; **we didn't ~ the chance to see everything** no tuvimos la oportunidad de verlo todo.

10. *(phone)* contestar.

11. *(in phrases)*: **you ~ a lot of rain here in winter** aquí llueve mucho en invierno, → **have**.

◆ *vi* 1. *(become)* ponerse; **it's getting late** se está haciendo tarde; **to ~ dark** oscurecer; **to ~ lost** perderse; **to ~ ready** prepararse; **~ lost!** *(inf)* ¡vete a la porra!

2. *(into particular state, position)* meterse; **how do you ~ to Luton from here?** ¿cómo se puede ir a

Luton desde aquí?; **to ~ into the car** meterse en el coche.

3. *(arrive)* llegar; **when does the train ~ here?** ¿a qué hora llega el tren?

4. *(in phrases)*: **to ~ to do sthg** llegar a hacer algo.

◆ *aux vb*: **to ~ delayed** retrasarse; **to ~ killed** resultar muerto.

❑ **get back** *vi (return)* volver; **get in** *vi (arrive)* llegar; *(enter)* entrar; **get off** *vi (leave train, bus)* bajarse; *(depart)* salir; **get on** *vi (enter train, bus)* subirse; *(in relationship)* llevarse; **how are you getting on?** ¿cómo te va?; **get out** *vi (of car, bus, train)* bajarse; **get through** *vi (on phone)* conseguir comunicar; **get up** *vi* levantarse.

get-together *n (inf)* reunión *f*.

ghastly ['gɑːstlɪ] *adj (inf: very bad)* horrible.

gherkin ['gɜːkɪn] *n* pepinillo *m*.

ghetto blaster ['getəʊ,blɑːstə[r]] *n (inf)* radiocasete portátil de gran tamaño y potencia.

ghost [gəʊst] *n* fantasma *m*.

giant ['dʒaɪənt] *adj* gigantesco(-ca) ◆ *n (in stories)* gigante *m*.

giblets ['dʒɪblɪts] *npl* menudillos *mpl*.

giddy ['gɪdɪ] *adj (dizzy)* mareado(-da).

gift [gɪft] *n (present)* regalo *m*; *(talent)* don *m*.

gifted ['gɪftɪd] *adj (talented)* dotado(-da); *(very intelligent)* superdotado(-da).

gift shop *n* tienda *f* de souvenirs.

gift voucher *n (Br)* vale *m*

(para canjear por un regalo).

gig [gɪg] *n (inf)* concierto *m* (de música pop).

gigantic [dʒaɪˈgæntɪk] *adj* gigantesco(-ca).

giggle ['gɪgl] *vi* reírse a lo tonto.

gill [dʒɪl] *n (measurement)* – 0,142 litros.

gimmick ['gɪmɪk] *n* reclamo *m*.

gin [dʒɪn] *n* ginebra *f*; **~ and tonic** gin tonic *m*.

ginger ['dʒɪndʒəʳ] *n* jengibre *m* ◆ *adj (colour)* rojizo(-za).

ginger ale *n* ginger-ale *m*.

ginger beer *n* refresco de jengibre con bajo contenido en alcohol.

gingerbread ['dʒɪndʒəbred] *n* pan *m* de jengibre.

gipsy ['dʒɪpsɪ] *n* gitano *m* (-na *f*).

giraffe [dʒɪˈrɑːf] *n* jirafa *f*.

girdle ['gɜːdl] *n* faja *f*.

girl [gɜːl] *n (child, daughter)* niña *f*; *(young woman)* chica *f*.

girlfriend ['gɜːlfrend] *n (of boy, man)* novia *f*; *(of girl, woman)* amiga *f*.

Girl Guide *n (Br)* exploradora *f*.

Girl Scout *(Am)* = **Girl Guide**.

giro ['dʒaɪrəʊ] *(pl* **-s**) *n (system)* giro *m*.

give [gɪv] *(pt* **gave**, *pp* **given** ['gɪvn]) *vt* dar; *(a laugh, look)* echar; *(attention)* prestar; *(time)* dedicar; **to ~ sb sthg** *(hand over, convey)* dar algo a alguien; *(as present)* regalar algo a alguien; **to ~ sthg a push** empujar algo; **to ~ sb a kiss** besar a alguien; **~ or take** más o menos; **"~ way" "ceda el paso" ❏ give away** *vt sep (get rid of)* regalar; *(reveal)* revelar; **give back** *vt sep*

devolver; **give in** *vi* ceder; **give off** *vt fus* despedir; **give out** *vt sep (distribute)* repartir; **give up** *vt sep (seat)* ceder ◆ *vi (stop smoking)* dejar de fumar; *(admit defeat)* darse por vencido; **to ~ up cigarettes** OR **smoking** dejar de fumar.

glacier ['glæsjəʳ] *n* glaciar *m*.

glad [glæd] *adj* contento(-ta); **to be ~ to do sthg** tener mucho gusto en hacer algo.

gladly ['glædlɪ] *adv (willingly)* con mucho gusto.

glamorous ['glæmərəs] *adj* atractivo(-va).

glance [glɑːns] *n* vistazo *m* ◆ *vi:* **to ~ (at)** echar un vistazo (a).

gland [glænd] *n* glándula *f*.

glandular fever ['glændjʊlə-] *n* mononucleosis *f inv* infecciosa.

glare [gleəʳ] *vi (person)* lanzar una mirada asesina; *(sun, light)* brillar.

glass [glɑːs] *n (material)* cristal *m*; *(container, glassful)* vaso *m* ◆ *adj* de cristal ❏ **glasses** *npl* gafas *fpl*.

glassware ['glɑːsweəʳ] *n* cristalería *f*.

glen [glen] *n (Scot)* cañada *f*.

glider ['glaɪdəʳ] *n* planeador *m*.

glimpse [glɪmps] *vt* vislumbrar.

glitter ['glɪtəʳ] *vi* relucir.

global warming ['gləʊbl 'wɔːmɪŋ] *n* calentamiento *m* de la atmósfera.

globe [gləʊb] *n (with map)* globo *m (terráqueo)*; **the ~** *(Earth)* la Tierra.

gloomy ['gluːmɪ] *adj (room, day)* oscuro(-ra); *(person)* melancólico(-ca).

glorious ['glɔːrɪəs] *adj (weather,*

sight) espléndido(-da); (victory, history) glorioso(-sa).

glory ['glɔːrɪ] n gloria f.

gloss [glɒs] n (shine) brillo m; ~ (paint) pintura f de esmalte.

glossary ['glɒsərɪ] n glosario m.

glossy ['glɒsɪ] adj (magazine, photo) de papel satinado.

glove [glʌv] n guante m.

glove compartment n guantera f.

glow [gləʊ] n fulgor m ♦ vi brillar, lucir.

glucose ['gluːkəʊs] n glucosa f.

glue [gluː] n pegamento m ♦ vt pegar.

gnat [næt] n mosquito m.

gnaw [nɔː] vt roer.

go [gəʊ] (pt went, pp gone, pl goes) vi 1. (move, travel, attend) ir; to ~ home irse a casa; to ~ to Spain ir a España; to ~ by bus ir en autobús; to ~ to church/school ir a misa/la escuela; to ~ for a walk ir a dar una vuelta; to ~ and do sthg ir a hacer algo; to ~ shopping ir de compras; where does this path ~? ¿adónde lleva este camino?

2. (leave) irse; (bus) salir; it's time to ~ ya es hora de irse; ~ away! ¡largo de aquí!

3. (become) ponerse; she went pale se puso pálida; the milk has gone sour la leche se ha cortado.

4. (expressing intention, probability, certainty): to be going to do sthg ir a hacer algo.

5. (function) funcionar; the car won't ~ el coche no funciona.

6. (stop working) estropearse; the fuse has gone se ha fundido el plomo.

7. (pass) pasar.

8. (progress) ir; to ~ well ir bien; how's it going? ¿qué tal te va?

9. (bell, alarm) sonar.

10. (match, be appropriate): to ~ with ir bien con.

11. (be sold) venderse; "everything must ~" "liquidación total".

12. (fit) caber.

13. (belong) ir.

14. (in phrases): (do) ~ on! ¡venga!; to let ~ of sthg soltar algo; to ~ (Am: to take away) para llevar; there are three weeks to ~ quedan tres semanas.

♦ n 1. (turn) turno m; it's your ~ toca a ti.

2. (attempt) jugada f; to have a ~ at sthg probar algo; "50p a ~" "a 50 peniques la jugada".

❑ **go ahead** vi (take place) tener lugar; go ~! ¡adelante!; **go back** vi volver; **go down** vi (price, standard) bajar; (sun) ponerse; (tyre) deshincharse; **go down with** vt fus (inf) pillar; **go in** vi entrar; **go off** vi (alarm, bell) sonar; (food) estropearse; (milk) cortarse; (stop operating) apagarse; **go on** vi (happen) ocurrir, pasar; (start operating) encenderse; to ~ on doing sthg seguir haciendo algo; **go out** vi (leave house) salir; (light, fire, cigarette) apagarse; to ~ out with sb salir (con alguien); to ~ out for a meal cenar fuera; **go over** vt fus (check) repasar; **go round** vi (revolve) girar; there isn't enough to ~ round no hay bastante para todos; **go through** vt fus (experience) pasar (por); (spend) gastar; (search) registrar; **go up** vi (increase) subir; **go with** vt fus (be included with) venir con; **go without** vt fus pasar sin.

goal [gəʊl] n (posts) portería f; (point scored) gol m; (aim) objetivo m.

goalkeeper ['gəʊl,kiːpəʳ] n portero m (-ra f).

goalpost ['gəʊlpəʊst] n poste m (de la portería).

goat [gəʊt] n cabra f.

gob [gɒb] n (Br: inf: mouth) pico m.

god [gɒd] n dios m □ **God** n Dios m.

goddaughter ['gɒd,dɔːtəʳ] n ahijada f.

godfather ['gɒd,fɑːðəʳ] n padrino m.

godmother ['gɒd,mʌðəʳ] n madrina f.

gods [gɒdz] npl: **the** ~ (Br: inf: in theatre) el gallinero.

godson ['gɒdsʌn] n ahijado m.

goes [gəʊz] → go.

goggles ['gɒglz] npl (for swimming) gafas fpl submarinas; (for skiing) gafas de esquí.

going ['gəʊɪŋ] adj (available) disponible; **the** ~ **rate** el precio actual.

go-kart [-kɑːt] n kart m.

gold [gəʊld] n oro m ◆ adj de oro.

goldfish ['gəʊldfɪʃ] (pl inv) n pez m de colores.

gold-plated [-'pleɪtɪd] adj chapado(-da) en oro.

golf [gɒlf] n golf m.

golf ball n pelota f de golf.

golf club n (place) club m de golf; (piece of equipment) palo m de golf.

golf course n campo m de golf.

golfer ['gɒlfəʳ] n jugador m (-ra f)

de golf.

gone [gɒn] pp → go ◆ prep (Br): **it's** ~ **ten** ya pasa de las diez.

good [gʊd] (compar **better**, superl **best**) adj bueno(-na) ◆ n el bien; **that's very** ~ **of you** es muy amable por tu parte; **be** ~! ¡pórtate bien!; **to have a** ~ **time** pasarlo bien; **I'm** ~ **at maths** se me dan bien las matemáticas; **a** ~ **ten minutes** diez minutos por lo menos; **in** ~ **time** a tiempo de sobra; **to make** ~ **sthg** compensar algo; **for** ~ para siempre; **for the** ~ **of** en bien de; **to do sb** ~ sentarle bien a alguien; **it's no** ~ (there's no point) no vale la pena; ~ **afternoon!** ¡buenas tardes!; ~ **evening!** (in the evening) ¡buenas tardes!; (at night) ¡buenas noches!; ~ **morning!** ¡buenos días!; ~ **night!** ¡buenas noches! □ **goods** npl productos mpl.

goodbye [,gʊd'baɪ] excl ¡adiós!

Good Friday n Viernes m inv Santo.

good-looking ['lʊkɪŋ] adj guapo(-pa).

goods train [gʊdz-] n tren m de mercancías.

goose [guːs] (pl **geese**) n ganso m.

gooseberry ['gʊzbərɪ] n grosella f espinosa.

gorge [gɔːdʒ] n desfiladero m.

gorgeous ['gɔːdʒəs] adj (day, meal, countryside) magnífico(-ca); **to be** ~ (inf: good-looking) estar buení simo(-ma).

gorilla [gə'rɪlə] n gorila mf.

gossip ['gɒsɪp] n (talk) cotilleo m ◆ vi cotillear.

gossip column n ecos mpl de

sociedad.

got [gɒt] pt & pp → get.

gotten ['gɒtn] pp (Am) → get.

goujons ['gu:dʒɒnz] npl fritos mpl (rebozados).

goulash ['gu:læʃ] n gulasch m.

gourmet ['gʊəmeɪ] n gastrónomo m (-ma f) ♦ adj para gastrónomos.

govern ['gʌvən] vt gobernar.

government ['gʌvnmənt] n gobierno m.

gown [gaʊn] n (dress) vestido m (de noche).

GP n (abbr of general practitioner) médico de cabecera.

grab [græb] vt (grasp) agarrar; (snatch away) arrebatar.

graceful ['greɪsfʊl] adj elegante.

grade [greɪd] n (quality) clase f; (in exam) nota f; (Am: year at school) curso m.

gradient ['greɪdjənt] n pendiente f.

gradual ['grædʒʊəl] adj paulatino(-na).

gradually ['grædʒʊəlɪ] adv paulatinamente.

graduate [n 'grædʒʊət, vb 'grædʒʊeɪt] n (from university) licenciado m (-da f); (Am: from high school) = bachiller mf ♦ vi (from university) licenciarse; (Am: from high school) = obtener el título de bachiller.

graduation [ˌgrædʒʊ'eɪʃn] n (ceremony) graduación f.

graffiti [grə'fi:tɪ] n pintadas fpl.

grain [greɪn] n (seed, granule) grano m; (crop) cereales mpl.

gram [græm] n gramo m.

grammar ['græmər] n gramática f.

grammar school n (in UK) colegio de enseñanza secundaria tradicional para alumnos de 11 a 18 años, con examen de acceso.

gramme [græm] = gram.

gramophone ['græməfəʊn] n gramófono m.

gran [græn] n (Br: inf) abuelita f.

grand [grænd] adj (impressive) grandioso(-sa) ♦ n (inf) (£1,000) mil libras fpl; ($1,000) mil dólares mpl.

grandchild ['græntʃaɪld] (pl -children [-,tʃɪldrən]) n nieto m (-ta f).

granddad ['grændæd] n (inf) abuelito m.

granddaughter ['græn,dɔ:tər] n nieta f.

grandfather ['grænd,fɑ:ðər] n abuelo m.

grandma ['grænmɑ:] n (inf) abuelita f.

grandmother ['græn,mʌðər] n abuela f.

grandpa ['grænpɑ:] n (inf) abuelito m.

grandparents ['græn,peərənts] npl abuelos mpl.

grandson ['grænsʌn] n nieto m.

granite ['grænɪt] n granito m.

granny ['grænɪ] n (inf) abuelita f.

grant [grɑ:nt] n (for study) beca f; (POL) subvención f ♦ vt (fml: give) conceder; **to take sthg/sb for ~ed** no saber apreciar algo/a alguien por lo que vale.

grape [greɪp] n uva f.

grapefruit ['greɪpfru:t] n pomelo m.

grapefruit juice n zumo m de pomelo.

graph [grɑːf] n gráfico m.

graph paper n papel m cuadriculado.

grasp [grɑːsp] vt (grip) agarrar; (understand) entender.

grass [grɑːs] n (plant) hierba f; (lawn) césped m; **"keep off the ~"** "prohibido pisar el césped".

grasshopper ['grɑːsˌhɒpəʳ] n saltamontes m inv.

grate [greɪt] n parrilla f.

grated ['greɪtɪd] adj rallado(-da).

grateful ['greɪtful] adj agradecido(-da).

grater ['greɪtəʳ] n rallador m.

gratitude ['grætɪtjuːd] n agradecimiento m.

gratuity [grəˈtjuːɪtɪ] n (fml) propina f.

grave[1] [greɪv] adj (mistake, news, concern) grave ♦ n tumba f.

grave[2] [grɑːv] adj (accent) grave.

gravel ['grævl] n gravilla f.

graveyard ['greɪvjɑːd] n cementerio m.

gravity ['grævətɪ] n gravedad f.

gravy ['greɪvɪ] n salsa f de carne.

gray [greɪ] (Am) = grey.

graze [greɪz] vt (injure) rasguñar.

grease [griːs] n grasa f.

greaseproof paper ['griːsˌpruːf-] n (Br) papel m de cera.

greasy ['griːsɪ] adj (tools, clothes, food) grasiento(-ta); (skin, hair) graso(-sa).

great [greɪt] adj grande; (very good) estupendo(-da); **~ success**

gran éxito; **(that's) ~!** ¡genial!; **to have a ~ time** pasarlo genial.

Great Britain n Gran Bretaña.

GREAT BRITAIN

Gran Bretaña es la isla que comprende Inglaterra, Escocia y Gales. No debe confundirse con el Reino Unido, que incluye además Irlanda del Norte, ni tampoco con las islas Británicas, que incluyen además la República de Irlanda, la isla de Man, las Orcadas, las Shetland y las islas del Canal de la Mancha.

great-grandfather n bisabuelo m.

great-grandmother n bisabuela f.

greatly ['greɪtlɪ] adv enormemente.

Greece [griːs] n Grecia.

greed [griːd] n (for food) glotonería f; (for money) codicia f.

greedy ['griːdɪ] adj (for food) glotón(-ona); (for money) codicioso(-sa).

Greek [griːk] adj griego(-ga) ♦ n (person) griego m (-ga f); (language) griego m.

Greek salad n ensalada con lechuga, tomate, cebolla, pepino, aceitunas negras y queso de cabra.

green [griːn] adj verde; (inf: inexperienced) novato(-ta) ♦ n color verde m; (in village) pequeña zona de hierba accesible a todo el mundo; (on golf course) green m □ **greens** npl (vegetables) verduras fpl.

green beans npl judías fpl

verdes.

green card n (Br: for car) seguro de automóvil para viajar al extranjero; (Am: work permit) permiso m de trabajo (para EEUU).

green channel n pasillo en la aduana para la gente sin artículos que declarar.

greengage ['griːngeɪdʒ] n ciruela f claudia.

greengrocer's ['griːnɡrəʊsəz] n (shop) verdulería f.

greenhouse ['griːnhaʊs], pl -hauzɪz] n invernadero m.

greenhouse effect n efecto m invernadero.

green light n luz f verde.

green pepper n pimiento m verde.

Greens [griːnz] npl: **the ~** los Verdes.

green salad n ensalada f verde.

greet [griːt] vt (say hello to) saludar.

greeting ['griːtɪŋ] n saludo m.

grenade [ɡrəˈneɪd] n granada f.

grew [ɡruː] pt → **grow**.

grey [ɡreɪ] adj (in colour) gris; (weather) nublado(-da) ◆ n gris m; he's going ~ le están saliendo canas.

greyhound ['ɡreɪhaʊnd] n galgo m.

grid [ɡrɪd] n (grating) reja f; (on map etc) cuadrícula f.

grief [ɡriːf] n pena f, aflicción f; to come to ~ (plan) ir al traste.

grieve [ɡriːv] vi: to ~ for llorar por.

grill [ɡrɪl] n (on cooker) grill m; (for open fire, part of restaurant) parrilla f;

(beefburger) hamburguesa f ◆ vt asar a la parrilla.

grille [ɡrɪl] n (AUT) rejilla f.

grilled [ɡrɪld] adj asado(-da) a la parrilla.

grim [ɡrɪm] adj (expression) adusto(-ta); (news, reality) deprimente.

grimace ['ɡrɪməs] n mueca f.

grimy ['ɡraɪmɪ] adj mugriento(-ta).

grin [ɡrɪn] n sonrisa f (amplia) ◆ vi sonreír (ampliamente).

grind [ɡraɪnd] (pt & pp ground) vt (pepper, coffee) moler.

grip [ɡrɪp] n (hold) agarrar ◆ n (of tyres) adherencia f; (handle) asidero m; (bag) bolsa f de viaje; to have a ~ on sthg agarrar algo.

gristle ['ɡrɪsl] n cartílago m.

groan [ɡrəʊn] n gemido m ◆ vi (in pain) gemir; (complain) quejarse.

groceries ['ɡrəʊsərɪz] npl comestibles mpl.

grocer's ['ɡrəʊsəz] n (shop) tienda f de comestibles.

grocery ['ɡrəʊsərɪ] n (shop) tienda f de comestibles.

groin [ɡrɔɪn] n ingle f.

groove [ɡruːv] n ranura f.

grope [ɡrəʊp] vi: to ~ around for sthg buscar algo a tientas.

gross [ɡrəʊs] adj (weight, income) bruto(-ta).

grossly ['ɡrəʊslɪ] adv (extremely) enormemente.

grotty ['ɡrɒtɪ] adj (Br: inf) cochambroso(-sa).

ground [ɡraʊnd] pt & pp → **grind** ◆ n (surface of earth) suelo m; (soil) tierra f; (SPORT) campo m ◆ adj (coffee) molido(-da) ◆ vt: to be ~ed *(plane)* tener que permanecer en tierra; *(Am: electrical connection)* estar conectado a tierra; **below ~** bajo tierra ❏ **grounds** *npl (of building)* jardines *mpl; (of coffee)* poso *m; (reason)* razones *fpl.*

ground floor *n* planta *f* baja.

groundsheet ['graundʃiːt] *n* lona *f* impermeable *(para tienda de campaña).*

group [gruːp] *n* grupo *m.*

grouse [graus] *(pl inv)* *n* urogallo *m.*

grovel ['grɒvl] *vi (be humble)* humillarse.

grow [grəu] *(pt* grew, *pp* grown) *vi* crecer; *(become)* volverse ♦ *vt (plant, crop)* cultivar; *(beard)* dejarse crecer ❏ **grow up** *vi* hacerse mayor.

growl [graul] *vi (dog)* gruñir.

grown [grəun] *pp →* grow.

grown-up *adj* adulto(-ta) ♦ *n* persona *f* mayor.

growth [grəuθ] *n (increase)* aumento *m; (MED)* bulto *m.*

grub [grʌb] *n (inf: food)* papeo *m.*

grubby ['grʌbi] *adj* mugriento(-ta).

grudge [grʌdʒ] *n* rencor *m* ♦ *vt:* **to ~ sb sthg** dar algo a alguien de mala gana.

grueling ['gruəlɪŋ] *(Am)* = gruelling.

gruelling ['gruəlɪŋ] *adj (Br)* agotador(-ra).

gruesome ['gruːsəm] *adj* horripilante.

grumble ['grʌmbl] *vi* refunfuñar.

grumpy ['grʌmpi] *adj (inf)* cascarrabias *(inv).*

grunt [grʌnt] *vi* gruñir.

guarantee [,gærən'tiː] *n* garantía *f* ♦ *vt* garantizar.

guard [gɑːd] *n (of prisoner etc)* guardia *mf; (on train)* jefe *m* de tren; *(protective cover)* protector *m* ♦ *vt (watch over)* guardar; **to be on one's ~** estar en guardia.

Guatemala [,gwɑːtə'mɑːlə] *n* Guatemala.

Guatemalan [,gwɑːtə'mɑːlən] *adj* guatemalteco(-ca) ♦ *n* guatemalteco *m (-ca f).*

guess [ges] *n* suposición *f* ♦ *vt* adivinar ♦ *vi* suponer; **I ~ (so)** me imagino (que sí).

guest [gest] *n (in home)* invitado *m (-da f); (in hotel)* huésped *m f.*

guesthouse ['gesthaus] *pl* -hauziz] *n* casa *f* de huéspedes.

guestroom ['gestrum] *n* cuarto *m* de los huéspedes.

guidance ['gaɪdəns] *n* orientación *f.*

guide [gaɪd] *n (for tourists)* guía *mf; (guidebook)* guía *f* ♦ *vt* guiar ❏ **Guide** *n (Br)* exploradora *f.*

guidebook ['gaɪdbuk] *n* guía *f.*

guide dog *n* perro *m* lazarillo.

guided tour ['gaɪdɪd-] *n* visita *f* guiada.

guidelines ['gaɪdlaɪnz] *npl* directrices *fpl.*

guilt [gɪlt] *n (feeling)* culpa *f; (JUR)* culpabilidad *f.*

guilty ['gɪlti] *adj* culpable.

guinea pig ['gɪnɪ-] *n* conejillo *m* de Indias.

guitar [gɪ'tɑːr] *n* guitarra *f.*

guitarist [gɪ'tɑːrɪst] *n* guitarrista *mf.*

gulf [gʌlf] *n (of sea)* golfo *m*.

Gulf War *n*: **the ~** la Guerra del Golfo.

gull [gʌl] *n* gaviota *f*.

gullible ['gʌlɪbl] *adj* ingenuo (-nua).

gulp [gʌlp] *n* trago *m*.

gum [gʌm] *n (chewing gum, bubble gum)* chicle *m*; *(adhesive)* pegamento *m* ❑ **gums** *npl (in mouth)* encías *fpl*.

gun [gʌn] *n (pistol)* pistola *f*; *(rifle)* escopeta *f*; *(cannon)* cañón *m*.

gunfire ['gʌnfaɪəʳ] *n* disparos *mpl*.

gunshot ['gʌnʃɒt] *n* tiro *m*.

gust [gʌst] *n* ráfaga *f*.

gut [gʌt] *n (inf: stomach)* buche *m* ❑ **guts** *npl (inf) (intestines)* tripas *fpl*; *(courage)* agallas *fpl*.

gutter ['gʌtəʳ] *n (beside road)* cuneta *f*; *(of house)* canalón *m*.

guy [gaɪ] *n (inf: man)* tío *m* ❑ **guys** *npl (Am: inf: people)* tíos *mpl*.

Guy Fawkes Night [-'fɔːks-] *n (Br)* el 5 de noviembre.

En esta fiesta, que también se conoce como "Bonfire Night", se conmemora cada 5 de noviembre con hogueras y fuegos artificiales el descubrimiento del "Gunpowder Plot", una conjuración católica para volar el Parlamento y asesinar al rey Jaime I en 1605. Es tradicional que los niños hagan monigotes de uno de los conspiradores, Guy Fawkes, y

los lleven por las calles recolectando dinero. Estos monigotes se queman después en las hogueras del 5 de noviembre.

---

guy rope *n* cuerda *f (de tienda de campaña)*.

gym [dʒɪm] *n (place)* gimnasio *m*; *(school lesson)* gimnasia *f*.

gymnast ['dʒɪmnæst] *n* gimnasta *mf*.

gymnastics [dʒɪm'næstɪks] *n* gimnasia *f*.

gym shoes *npl* zapatillas *fpl* de gimnasia.

gynaecologist [,gaɪnə'kɒlədʒɪst] *n* ginecólogo *m* (-ga *f*).

gypsy ['dʒɪpsɪ] = **gipsy**.

H

H *(abbr of hot)* C *(en grifo)*; *(abbr of hospital)* H.

habit ['hæbɪt] *n* costumbre *f*.

hacksaw ['hæksɔː] *n* sierra *f* para metales.

had [hæd] *pt & pp* → **have**.

haddock ['hædək] *(pl inv) n* eglefino *m*.

hadn't ['hædnt] = **had not**.

haggis ['hægɪs] *n* plato típico escocés hecho con las asaduras del cordero, harina de avena y especias.

haggle ['hægl] *vi* regatear.

hall of residence

hail [heɪl] n granizo m ♦ v impers: it's ~ing está granizando.

hailstone ['heɪlstəʊn] n granizo m.

hair [heə^r] n pelo m; (on skin) vello m; **to have one's ~ cut** cortarse el pelo; **to wash one's ~** lavarse el pelo.

hairband ['heəbænd] n turbante m (banda elástica).

hairbrush ['heəbrʌʃ] n cepillo m (del pelo).

hairclip ['heəklɪp] n prendedor m (del pelo).

haircut ['heəkʌt] n (style) corte m (de pelo); **to have a ~** cortarse el pelo.

hairdo ['heəduː] (pl -s) n peinado m.

hairdresser ['heə,dresə^r] n peluquero m (-ra f); **~'s** (salon) peluquería f; **to go to the ~'s** ir a la peluquería.

hairdryer ['heə,draɪə^r] n secador m (del pelo).

hair gel n gomina f.

hairgrip ['heəgrɪp] n (Br) horquilla f.

hairnet ['heənet] n redecilla f (para el pelo).

hairpin bend ['heəpɪn-] n curva f muy cerrada.

hair remover [-rɪ,muːvə^r] n depilatorio m.

hair rollers [-'rəʊləz] npl tubos mpl (del pelo).

hair slide n prendedor m.

hairspray ['heəspreɪ] n laca f (para el pelo).

hairstyle ['heəstaɪl] n peinado m.

hairy ['heərɪ] adj peludo(-da).

half [Br hɑːf, Am hæf] (pl halves) n (50%) mitad f; (of match) tiempo m; (half pint) media pinta f; (child's ticket) billete m medio ♦ adj medio(-dia) ♦ adv: **~ cooked** a medio cocinar; **~ full** medio lleno; **I'm ~ Scottish** soy medio escocés; **four and a ~** cuatro y medio; **~ past seven** las siete y media; **~ as big as** la mitad de grande que; **an hour and a ~** una hora y media; **~ an hour** media hora; **~ a dozen** media docena; **~ price** a mitad de precio.

half board n media pensión f.

half-day n media jornada f.

half fare n medio billete m

half portion n media ración f.

half-price adj a mitad de precio.

half term n (Br) semana f de vacaciones escolares a mitad de cada trimestre.

half time n descanso m

halfway [hɑːf'weɪ] adv: **~ between** a mitad de camino entre; **~ through the film** a mitad de la película.

halibut ['hælɪbət] (pl inv) n halibut m.

hall [hɔːl] n (of house) vestíbulo m; (large room) sala f; (building) pabellón m; (country house) mansión f.

hallmark ['hɔːlmɑːk] n (on silver, gold) contraste m.

hallo [hə'ləʊ] = hello.

hall of residence n colegio m mayor.

Halloween [ˌhæləʊˈiːn] n el 31 de octubre.

---

i HALLOWEEN

E l 31 de octubre, también conocido como "All Hallows Eve" es tradicionalmente la noche en que los fantasmas y brujas se aparecen. Los niños se disfrazan y visitan a sus vecinos jugando a "trick or treat", un juego en que amenazan con gastar una broma si no se les da dinero o golosinas. En Gran Bretaña y Estados Unidos son tradicionales las linternas que consisten en una calabaza vaciada en cuyo interior se coloca una vela que ilumina a través de una cara tallada en la corteza.

halt [hɔːlt] vi detenerse ♦ n: to come to a ~ detenerse.

halve [Br hɑːv, Am hæv] vt (reduce by half) reducir a la mitad; (divide in two) partir por la mitad.

halves [Br hɑːvz, Am hævz] pl → **half**.

ham [hæm] n jamón m.

hamburger [ˈhæmbɜːgəʳ] n (beefburger) hamburguesa f; (Am: mince) carne f picada.

hamlet [ˈhæmlɪt] n aldea f.

hammer [ˈhæməʳ] n martillo m ♦ vt (nail) clavar.

hammock [ˈhæmək] n hamaca f.

hamper [ˈhæmpəʳ] n cesta f.

hamster [ˈhæmstəʳ] n hámster m.

hamstring [ˈhæmstrɪŋ] n tendón m de la corva.

hand [hænd] n mano f; (of clock, watch, dial) aguja f; **to give sb a ~** echar una mano a alguien; **to get out of ~** hacerse incontrolable; **by ~** a mano; **in ~** (time) de sobra; **on the one ~** por una parte; **on the other ~** por otra parte □ **hand in** vt sep entregar; **hand out** vt sep repartir; **hand over** vt sep (give) entregar.

handbag [ˈhændbæg] n bolso m.

handbasin [ˈhændbeɪsn] n lavabo m.

handbook [ˈhændbʊk] n manual m.

handbrake [ˈhændbreɪk] n freno m de mano.

hand cream n crema f de manos.

handcuffs [ˈhændkʌfs] npl esposas fpl.

handful [ˈhændfʊl] n (amount) puñado m.

handicap [ˈhændɪkæp] n (physical, mental) incapacidad f; (disadvantage) desventaja f.

handicapped [ˈhændɪkæpt] adj disminuido(-da) ♦ npl: **the ~** los minusválidos.

handkerchief [ˈhæŋkətʃɪf] (pl -chiefs OR -chieves [-tʃiːvz]) n pañuelo m.

handle [ˈhændl] n (round) pomo m; (long) manilla f; (of knife, pan) mango m; (of suitcase) asa f ♦ vt (touch) tocar; (deal with) encargarse de; "~ with care" "frágil".

handlebars [ˈhændlbɑːz] npl manillar m.

hand luggage n equipaje m de mano.

handmade [ˌhændˈmeɪd] adj hecho(-cha) a mano.

handout ['hændaʊt] n (leaflet) hoja f informativa.

handrail ['hændreɪl] n barandilla f.

handset ['hændset] n auricular m (de teléfono); **"please replace the ~"** mensaje que avisa que el teléfono está descolgado.

handshake ['hændʃeɪk] n apretón m de manos.

handsome ['hænsəm] adj (man) guapo.

handstand ['hændstænd] n pino m.

handwriting ['hænd,raɪtɪŋ] n letra f.

handy ['hændɪ] adj (useful) práctico(-ca); (good with one's hands) mañoso(-sa); (near) a mano; **to come in ~** (inf) venir de maravilla.

hang [hæŋ] (pt & pp hung) vt (on hook, wall etc) colgar; (execute: pt & pp hanged) ahorcar ◆ vi (be suspended) colgar ◆ n: **to get the ~ of sthg** coger el tranquillo a algo ⸺ **hang about** vi (Br: inf) pasar el rato; **hang around** (inf) = **hang about; hang down** vi caer, estar colgado; **hang on** vi (inf: wait) esperar; **hang out** vt sep tender ◆ vi (inf: spend time) pasar el rato; **hang up** vi (on phone) colgar.

hangar ['hæŋə^r] n hangar m.

hanger ['hæŋə^r] n percha f.

hang gliding [-'glaɪdɪŋ] n vuelo m con ala delta.

hangover ['hæŋ,əʊvə^r] n resaca f.

hankie ['hæŋkɪ] n (inf) pañuelo m.

happen ['hæpən] vi pasar; **I ~ed to be alone** dio la casualidad de que estaba solo.

happily ['hæpɪlɪ] adv (luckily) afortunadamente.

happiness ['hæpɪnɪs] n felicidad f.

happy ['hæpɪ] adj feliz; **to be ~ about sthg** (satisfied) estar contento(-ta) con algo; **to be ~ to do sthg** estar muy dispuesto(-ta) a hacer algo; **to be ~ with sthg** estar contento con algo; **Happy Birthday!** ¡Feliz Cumpleaños!, **Happy Christmas!** ¡Feliz Navidad!, **Happy New Year!** ¡Feliz Año Nuevo!

happy hour n (inf) tiempo en que las bebidas se venden a precio reducido en un bar.

harassment ['hærəsmənt] n acoso m.

harbor ['hɑːbər] (Am) = **harbour.**

harbour ['hɑːbə^r] n (Br) puerto m.

hard [hɑːd] adj duro(-ra); (difficult, strenuous) difícil; (blow, push, frost) fuerte ◆ adv (try, work, rain) mucho; (listen) atentamente; (hit) con fuerza.

hardback ['hɑːdbæk] n edición f en pasta dura.

hardboard ['hɑːdbɔːd] n aglomerado m.

hard-boiled egg [-bɔɪld] n huevo m duro.

hard disk n disco m duro.

hardly ['hɑːdlɪ] adv apenas; **~ ever** casi nunca.

hardship ['hɑːdʃɪp] n (difficult conditions) privaciones fpl; (difficult circumstance) dificultad f.

hard shoulder n (Br) arcén m.

hard up adj (inf) sin un duro.

hardware ['hɑ:dweəʳ] n (tools, equipment) artículos mpl de ferretería; (COMPUT) hardware m.

hardwearing [,hɑ:d'weərɪŋ] adj (Br) resistente.

hardworking [,hɑ:d'wɜ:kɪŋ] adj trabajador(-ra).

hare [heəʳ] n liebre f.

harm [hɑ:m] n daño m ♦ vt (person) hacer daño a; (object) dañar; (chances, reputation) perjudicar.

harmful ['hɑ:mful] adj perjudicial.

harmless ['hɑ:mlɪs] adj inofensivo(-va).

harmonica [hɑ:'mɒnɪkə] n armónica f.

harmony ['hɑ:mənɪ] n armonía f.

harness ['hɑ:nɪs] n (for horse) arreos mpl; (for child) andadores mpl.

harp [hɑ:p] n arpa f.

harsh [hɑ:ʃ] adj (conditions, winter) duro(-ra); (cruel) severo(-ra); (weather, climate) inclemente; (sound, voice) áspero(-ra).

harvest ['hɑ:vɪst] n cosecha f.

has [weak form həz, strong form hæz] → **have**.

hash browns [hæʃ-] npl (Am) patatas cortadas en trozos y fritas con cebolla en forma de bola.

hasn't ['hæznt] = **has not**.

hassle ['hæsl] n (inf: problems) jaleo m; (annoyance) fastidio m.

hastily ['heɪstɪlɪ] adv (rashly) a la ligera.

hasty ['heɪstɪ] adj (hurried) precipitado(-da); (rash) irreflexivo(-va).

hat [hæt] n sombrero m.

hatch [hætʃ] n (for serving food) ventanilla f ♦ vi (egg) romperse.

hatchback ['hætʃ,bæk] n coche m con puerta trasera.

hatchet ['hætʃɪt] n hacha f.

hate [heɪt] n odio m ♦ vt odiar; to ~ doing sthg odiar hacer algo.

hatred ['heɪtrɪd] n odio m.

haul [hɔ:l] vt arrastrar ♦ n: a long ~ un buen trecho.

haunted ['hɔ:ntɪd] adj (house) encantado(-da).

have [hæv] (pt & pp **had**) aux vb 1. (to form perfect tenses) haber; I ~ finished he terminado; ~ you been there? – No, I haven't ¿has estado allí? – No; we had already left ya nos habíamos ido.
2. (must): to ~ (got) to do sthg tener que hacer algo; do you ~ to pay? ¿hay que pagar?
♦ vt 1. (possess): to ~ (got) tener; do you ~ OR ~ you got a double room? ¿tiene una habitación doble?; she has (got) brown hair tiene el pelo castaño.
2. (experience) tener; to ~ a cold tener catarro; to ~ a good time pasarlo bien.
3. (replacing other verbs): to ~ breakfast desayunar; to ~ dinner cenar; to ~ lunch comer; to ~ a drink tomar algo; to ~ a shower ducharse; to ~ a swim ir a nadar; to ~ a walk dar un paseo.
4. (feel) tener; I ~ no doubt about it no tengo ninguna duda.
5. (invite): to ~ sb round for dinner invitar a alguien a cenar.
6. (cause to be): to ~ sthg done hacer que se haga algo; to ~ one's hair cut cortarse el pelo.

7. (be treated in a certain way): **I've had my wallet stolen** me han robado la cartera.

haversack ['hævəsæk] n mochila f.

havoc ['hævək] n estragos mpl.

hawk [hɔ:k] n halcón m.

hawker ['hɔ:kəʳ] n vendedor m (-ra f) ambulante.

hay [heɪ] n heno m.

hay fever n alergia f primaveral.

haystack ['heɪstæk] n almiar m.

hazard ['hæzəd] n riesgo m.

hazardous ['hæzədəs] adj arriesgado(-da).

hazard warning lights npl (Br) luces fpl de emergencia.

haze [heɪz] n neblina f.

hazel ['heɪzl] adj de color miel.

hazelnut ['heɪzl,nʌt] n avellana f.

hazy ['heɪzɪ] adj (misty) neblinoso(-sa).

he [hi:] pron él; **~'s tall** (él) es alto.

head [hed] n cabeza f; (of queue, page, letter, bed) principio m; (of table, bed) cabecera f; (of company, department, school) director m (-ra f); (of beer) espuma f ♦ vt estar a la cabeza de ♦ vi dirigirse hacia; **£10 a ~** diez libras por persona; **~s or tails?** ¿cara o cruz? □ **head for** vt fus (place) dirigirse a.

headache ['hedeɪk] n (pain) dolor m de cabeza; **I have a ~** me duele la cabeza.

heading ['hedɪŋ] n encabezamiento m.

headlamp ['hedlæmp] (Br) = **headlight**.

headlight ['hedlaɪt] n faro m.

headline ['hedlaɪn] n titular m.

headmaster [,hed'mɑ:stəʳ] n director m (de colegio).

headmistress [,hed'mɪstrɪs] n directora f (de colegio).

head of state n jefe m (-fa f) de estado.

headphones ['hedfəʊnz] npl auriculares mpl.

headquarters [,hed'kwɔ:təz] npl sede f central.

headrest ['hedrest] n apoyacabezas m inv.

headroom ['hedrʊm] n (under bridge) altura f libre.

headscarf ['hedskɑ:f] (pl -scarves [-skɑ:vz]) n pañoleta f.

head start n ventaja f (desde el comienzo).

head teacher n director m (-ra f) (de colegio).

head waiter n jefe m (de camareros).

heal [hi:l] vt curar ♦ vi cicatrizar.

health [helθ] n salud f; **to be in good ~** tener buena salud; **to be in poor ~** tener mala salud; **your (very) good ~!** ¡a tu salud!

health centre n centro m de salud.

health food n productos mpl de dietética.

health food shop n tienda f de dietética.

health insurance n seguro m médico.

healthy ['helθɪ] adj (person, skin) sano(-na); (good for one's health) saludable.

heap [hi:p] n montón m; **~s of**

(inf) montones de.

hear [hɪəʳ] *(pt & pp* **heard** [hɜːd]) *vt* oír; *(JUR)* ver ◆ *vi* oír; **to ~ about** sth enterarse de algo; **to ~ from** sb tener noticias de alguien; **to have heard of** haber oído hablar de.

hearing ['hɪərɪŋ] *n (sense)* oído *m; (at court)* vista *f;* **to be hard of ~** ser duro de oído.

hearing aid *n* audífono *m.*

heart [hɑːt] *n* corazón *m;* **to know sth (off) by ~** saberse algo de memoria; **to lose ~** desanimarse □ **hearts** *npl (in cards)* corazones *mpl.*

heart attack *n* infarto *m.*

heartbeat ['hɑːtbiːt] *n* latido *m.*

heartburn ['hɑːtbɜːn] *n* ardor *m* de estómago.

heart condition *n:* **to have a ~** padecer del corazón.

hearth [hɑːθ] *n* chimenea *f.*

hearty ['hɑːtɪ] *adj (meal)* abundante.

heat [hiːt] *n* calor *m; (specific temperature)* temperatura *f* □ **heat up** *vt sep* calentar.

heater ['hiːtəʳ] *n* calentador *m.*

heath [hiːθ] *n* brezal *m.*

heather ['heðəʳ] *n* brezo *m.*

heating ['hiːtɪŋ] *n* calefacción *f.*

heat wave *n* ola *f* de calor.

heave [hiːv] *vt (push)* empujar; *(pull)* tirar de.

Heaven ['hevn] *n* el cielo.

heavily ['hevɪlɪ] *adv* mucho.

heavy ['hevɪ] *adj (in weight)* pesado(-da); *(rain, fighting, traffic)* intenso(-sa); *(losses, defeat)* grave; *(food)* indigesto(-ta); **how ~ is it?** ¿cuánto

pesa?; **to be a ~ smoker** fumar mucho.

heavy cream *n (Am)* nata *f* para montar.

heavy goods vehicle *n (Br)* vehículo *m* pesado.

heavy industry *n* industria *f* pesada.

heavy metal *n* heavy metal *m.*

heckle ['hekl] *vt* reventar.

hectic ['hektɪk] *adj* ajetreado(-da).

hedge [hedʒ] *n* seto *m.*

hedgehog ['hedʒhɒg] *n* erizo *m.*

heel [hiːl] *n (of person)* talón *m; (of shoe)* tacón *m.*

hefty ['heftɪ] *adj (person)* fornido(-da); *(fine)* considerable.

height [haɪt] *n* altura *f; (of person)* estatura *f; (peak period)* punto *m* álgido; **what ~ is it?** ¿cuánto mide?

heir [eəʳ] *n* heredero *m.*

heiress ['eərɪs] *n* heredera *f.*

held [held] *pt & pp →* **hold.**

helicopter ['helɪkɒptəʳ] *n* helicóptero *m.*

Hell [hel] *n* el infierno.

he'll [hiːl] = **he will.**

hello [hə'ləʊ] *excl (as greeting)* ¡hola!; *(when answering phone)* ¡diga!, ¡bueno! *(Amér); (when phoning, to attract attention)* ¡oiga!

helmet ['helmɪt] *n* casco *m.*

help [help] *n* ayuda *f* ◆ *vt & vi* ayudar ◆ *excl* ¡socorro!; **I can't ~ it** no puedo evitarlo; **to ~ sb (to) do sth** ayudar a alguien a hacer algo; **to ~ o.s. (to sth)** servirse (algo); **can I ~ you?** *(in shop)* ¿en qué puedo servirle? □ **help out** *vi* echar una mano.

helper ['helpə^r] n (assistant) ayudante mf; (Am: cleaner) mujer f de la limpieza.

helpful ['helpful] adj (person) atento(-ta), servicial; (useful) útil.

helping ['helpɪŋ] n ración f.

helpless ['helplɪs] adj (person) indefenso(-sa).

hem [hem] n dobladillo m.

hemophiliac [,hi:məˈfɪlɪæk] n hemofílico m.

hemorrhage ['hemərɪdʒ] n hemorragia f.

hen [hen] n (chicken) gallina f.

hepatitis [,hepəˈtaɪtɪs] n hepatitis f inv.

her [hɜːr] adj su, sus (pl) ♦ pron: I know ~ la conozco; It's ~ es ella; send it to ~ envíaselo; tell ~ to come dile que venga; he's worse than ~ él es peor que ella.

herb [hɜːb] n hierba f.

herbal tea ['hɜːbl] n infusión f.

herd [hɜːd] n (of sheep) rebaño m; (of cattle) manada f

here [hɪə^r] adv aquí; ~'s your book aquí tienes tu libro; ~ you are aquí tienes.

heritage ['herɪtɪdʒ] n patrimonio m.

heritage centre n museo en un lugar de interés histórico.

hernia ['hɜːnjə] n hernia f.

hero ['hɪərəʊ] (pl -es) n héroe m.

heroin ['herəʊɪn] n heroína f.

heroine ['herəʊɪn] n heroína f.

heron ['herən] n garza f real.

herring ['herɪŋ] n arenque m.

hers [hɜːz] pron suyo m (-ya f), suyos mpl (-yas fpl); a friend of ~

un amigo suyo.

herself [hɜːˈself] pron (reflexive) se; (after prep) sí misma; she did it ~ lo hizo ella sola.

hesitant ['hezɪtənt] adj indeciso(-sa).

hesitate ['hezɪteɪt] vi vacilar.

hesitation [,hezɪˈteɪʃn] n vacilación f.

heterosexual [,hetərəʊˈsekʃʊəl] adj heterosexual ♦ n heterosexual mf.

hey [heɪ] excl (inf) ¡ch!, ¡oye!

HGV abbr = heavy goods vehicle.

hi [haɪ] excl (inf) ¡hola!

hiccup ['hɪkʌp] n: to have (the) ~s tener hipo.

hide [haɪd] (pt hid [hɪd], pp hidden ['hɪdn]) vt esconder, (truth, feelings) ocultar ♦ vi esconderse ♦ n (of animal) piel f.

hideous ['hɪdɪəs] adj horrible.

hi-fi ['haɪfaɪ] n equipo m de alta fidelidad.

high [haɪ] adj alto(-ta); (winds) fuerte; (good) bueno(-na); (position, rank) elevado(-da); (inf: from drugs) flipado(-da) ♦ n (weather front) zona f de altas presiones ♦ adv alto; how ~ is it? ¿cuánto mide?; it's 10 metres ~ mide 10 metros de alto.

high chair n silla f alta.

high-class adj de categoría.

Higher ['haɪə^r] n examen al final de la enseñanza secundaria en Escocia.

higher education n enseñanza f superior.

high heels npl tacones mpl

altos.
high jump n salto m de altura.
Highland Games [ˈhaɪlənd-]
npl festival típico de Escocia.

ℹ HIGHLAND GAMES

Estos festivales de música y deportes celebrados en Escocia eran originariamente reuniones de los clanes de las Highlands. Hoy en día, los juegos recogen eventos tales como carreras, salto de longitud y salto de altura así como competiciones de gaita y bailes tradicionales. Otro concurso es "tossing the caber", una prueba de fuerza en la que los participantes han de lanzar un pesado tronco de abeto.

Highlands [ˈhaɪləndz] npl: **the ~** las tierras altas del norte de Escocia.
highlight [ˈhaɪlaɪt] n (best part) mejor parte ♦ vt (emphasize) destacar ❏ **highlights** npl (of football match etc) momentos npl más interesantes; (in hair) mechas fpl, reflejos mpl.
highly [ˈhaɪlɪ] adv (extremely) enormemente; (very well) muy bien.
high-pitched [-ˈpɪtʃt] adj agudo (-da).
high-rise building n rascacielos m inv.
high school n = instituto m de bachillerato.
high season n temporada f alta.
high-speed train n tren m de alta velocidad.

high street n (Br) calle f mayor.
high tide n marea f alta.
highway [ˈhaɪweɪ] n (Am: between towns) autopista f; (Br: any main road) carretera f.
Highway Code n (Br) código m de la circulación.
hijack [ˈhaɪdʒæk] vt secuestrar.
hijacker [ˈhaɪdʒækəʳ] n secuestrador m (-ra f).
hike [haɪk] n caminata f ♦ vi ir de excursión.
hiking [ˈhaɪkɪŋ] n: **to go ~** ir de excursión.
hilarious [hɪˈleərɪəs] adj desternillante.
hill [hɪl] n colina f.
hillwalking [ˈhɪlwɔːkɪŋ] n senderismo m.
hilly [ˈhɪlɪ] adj montañoso(-sa).
him [hɪm] pron: **I know ~** le conozco, lo conozco; **it's ~** es él; **send it to ~** envíaselo; **tell ~ to come** dile que venga; **she's worse than ~** ella es peor que él.
himself [hɪmˈself] pron (reflexive) se; (after prep) sí mismo; **he did it ~** lo hizo él solo.
hinder [ˈhɪndəʳ] vt estorbar.
Hindu [ˈhɪnduː] (pl -s) adj hindú ♦ n (person) hindú mf.
hinge [hɪndʒ] n bisagra f.
hint [hɪnt] n (indirect suggestion) indirecta f; (piece of advice) consejo m; (slight amount) asomo m ♦ vi: **to ~ at sthg** insinuar algo.
hip [hɪp] n cadera f.
hippopotamus [ˌhɪpəˈpɒtəməs] n hipopótamo m.
hippy [ˈhɪpɪ] n hippy mf.

hollow

hire ['haɪəʳ] vt alquilar; **for ~** *(taxi)* libre; **"boats for ~"** "se alquilan barcos" ❏ **hire out** vt sep alquilar.

hire car n *(Br)* coche m de alquiler.

hire purchase n *(Br)* compra f a plazos.

his [hɪz] adj su, sus *(pl)* ♦ pron suyo m (-ya f), suyos mpl (-yas fpl); **a friend of ~** un amigo suyo.

historical [hɪ'stɒrɪkəl] adj histórico(-ca).

history ['hɪstərɪ] n historia f, *(record)* historial m.

hit [hɪt] *(pt & pp hit)* vt *(strike on purpose)* pegar; *(collide with)* chocar contra; *(bang)* golpearse; *(a target)* alcanzar ♦ n *(record, play, film)* éxito m.

hit-and-run adj *(accident)* en que el conductor se da a la fuga.

hitch [hɪtʃ] n obstáculo m ♦ vi hacer autoestop ♦ vt: **to ~ a lift** conseguir que le lleven a uno en coche.

hitchhike ['hɪtʃhaɪk] vi hacer autoestop.

hitchhiker ['hɪtʃhaɪkəʳ] n autoestopista mf.

hive [haɪv] n *(of bees)* colmena f.

HIV-positive adj seropositivo(-va).

hoarding ['hɔːdɪŋ] n *(Br: for adverts)* valla f publicitaria.

hoarse [hɔːs] adj ronco(-ca).

hoax [həʊks] n engaño m.

hob [hɒb] n encimera f.

hobby ['hɒbɪ] n hobby m.

hock [hɒk] n *(wine)* vino m blanco del Rin.

hockey ['hɒkɪ] n *(on grass)* hoc-

key m *(sobre hierba)*; *(Am: ice hockey)* hockey m sobre hielo.

hoe [həʊ] n azada f.

hold [həʊld] *(pt & pp held)* vt *(in hand, arms etc)* tener cogido; *(keep in position)* sujetar; *(organize)* celebrar; *(contain)* contener; *(number of people)* tener cabida para; *(possess)* poseer ♦ vi *(weather, luck)* mantenerse; *(offer)* seguir en pie; *(on telephone)* esperar ♦ n *(of ship, aircraft)* bodega f; **to have a ~ on sthg** agarrar algo; **to ~ sb prisoner** tener a alguien como prisionero; **~ the line, please** no cuelgue, por favor ❏ **hold back** vt sep *(restrain)* contener; *(keep secret)* ocultar; **hold on** vi *(wait)* esperar; *(on telephone)* no colgar; **to ~ on to sthg** *(grip)* agarrarse a algo; **hold out** vt sep *(extend)* extender; **hold up** vt sep *(delay)* retrasar.

holdall ['həʊldɔːl] n *(Br)* bolsa f de viaje.

holder ['həʊldəʳ] n *(of passport, licence)* titular mf; *(container)* soporte m.

holdup ['həʊldʌp] n *(delay)* retraso m.

hole [həʊl] n agujero m; *(in ground, in golf)* hoyo m.

holiday ['hɒlɪdeɪ] n *(Br: period of time)* vacaciones fpl; *(day off)* fiesta f, día m festivo ♦ vi *(Br)* veranear; **to be on ~** estar de vacaciones; **to go on ~** ir de vacaciones.

holidaymaker ['hɒlɪdɪˌmeɪkəʳ] n *(Br)* turista mf.

holiday pay n *(Br)* sueldo m de vacaciones.

Holland ['hɒlənd] n Holanda f.

hollow ['hɒləʊ] adj hueco(-ca).

holly ['hɒlɪ] *n* acebo *m*.
Hollywood ['hɒlɪwʊd] *n* Hollywood *m*.

---

i **HOLLYWOOD**

Hollywood es un barrio de Los Ángeles que a partir de 1911 se convirtió en el centro de la industria cinematográfica estadounidense. Alcanzó su punto máximo en los años cuarenta y cincuenta, cuando los grandes estudios como 20th Century Fox, Paramount y Warner Brothers producían cientos de películas por año. Hoy en día, Hollywood es una de las principales atracciones turísticas de Estados Unidos.

---

holy ['həʊlɪ] *adj (sacred)* sagrado(-da), santo(-ta).
home [həʊm] *n (house)* casa *f; (own country)* tierra *f; (one's family)* hogar *m; (for old people)* residencia *f* de ancianos ◆ *adv (to one's house)* a casa; *(in one's house)* en casa ◆ *adj (not foreign)* nacional; *(cooking)* casero(-ra); **at ~** en casa; **make yourself at ~** estás como en casa; **to go ~** ir a casa; **~ address** domicilio *m* particular; **~ number** número *m* particular.
home economics *n* economía *f* doméstica.
home help *n (Br)* asistente que ayuda en las tareas domésticas a enfermos y ancianos.
homeless ['həʊmlɪs] *npl:* **the ~** los sin hogar.
homemade [,həʊm'meɪd] *adj* casero(-ra).

homeopathic [,həʊmɪəʊ'pæθɪk] *adj* homeopático(-ca).
Home Secretary *n (Br)* Ministro *m* del Interior.
homesick ['həʊmsɪk] *adj:* **to be ~** tener morriña.
homework ['həʊmwɜːk] *n* deberes *mpl*.
homosexual [,həʊmə'sekʃʊəl] *adj* homosexual ◆ *n* homosexual *mf*.
Honduran [hɒn'djʊərən] *adj* hondureño(-ña) ◆ *n* hondureño *m* (-ña *f*).
Honduras [hɒn'djʊərəs] *n* Honduras.
honest ['ɒnɪst] *adj (trustworthy)* honrado(-da); *(frank)* sincero(-ra).
honestly ['ɒnɪstlɪ] *adv (truthfully)* honradamente; *(frankly)* sinceramente.
honey ['hʌnɪ] *n* miel *f*.
honeymoon ['hʌnɪmuːn] *n* luna *f* de miel.
honor ['ɒnər] *(Am)* = **honour**.
honour ['ɒnər] *n (Br)* honor *m*.
honourable ['ɒnrəbl] *adj* honorable.
hood [hʊd] *n (of jacket, coat)* capucha *f; (on convertible car)* capota *f; (Am: car bonnet)* capó *m*.
hoof [huːf] *n (of horse)* casco *m; (of cow, goat)* pezuña *f*.
hook [hʊk] *n (for picture, coat)* gancho *m; (for fishing)* anzuelo *m*; **off the ~** *(telephone)* descolgado.
hooligan ['huːlɪgən] *n* gamberro *m* (-rra *f*).
hoop [huːp] *n* aro *m*.
hoot [huːt] *vi (driver)* sonar.
Hoover® ['huːvər] *n (Br)* aspiradora *f*.

hop [hɒp] vi saltar a la pata coja.

hope [həʊp] n esperanza f ◆ vt esperar que; **to ~ for** sthg esperar algo; **to ~ to do** sthg esperar hacer algo; **I ~ so** espero que sí.

hopeful ['həʊpfʊl] adj (optimistic) optimista.

hopefully ['həʊpfəlɪ] adv (with luck) con suerte.

hopeless ['həʊplɪs] adj (inf: useless) inútil, (without any hope) desesperado(-da).

hops [hɒps] npl lúpulo m.

horizon [hə'raɪzn] n horizonte m.

horizontal [ˌhɒrɪ'zɒntl] adj horizontal.

horn [hɔːn] n (of car) claxon m; (on animal) cuerno m.

horoscope ['hɒrəskəʊp] n horóscopo m.

horrible ['hɒrəbl] adj horrible.

horrid ['hɒrɪd] adj (person) antipático(-ca); (place) horroroso(-sa).

horrific [hɒ'rɪfɪk] adj horrendo(-da).

hors d'oeuvres [ɔː'dɜːvr] npl entremeses mpl.

horse [hɔːs] n caballo m.

horseback ['hɔːsbæk] n: **on ~** a caballo.

horse chestnut n castaña f de Indias.

horse-drawn carriage n calesa f.

horsepower ['hɔːsˌpaʊər] n caballos mpl de vapor.

horse racing n carreras fpl de caballos.

horseradish (sauce) ['hɔːsˌrædɪʃ-] n salsa picante de rábano silvestre, que se suele servir con rosbif.

horse riding n equitación f.

horseshoe ['hɔːsʃuː] n herradura f.

hose [həʊz] n manguera f.

hosepipe ['həʊzpaɪp] n manguera f.

hosiery ['həʊzɪərɪ] n medias fpl y calcetines.

hospitable [hɒ'spɪtəbl] adj hospitalario(-ria).

hospital ['hɒspɪtl] n hospital m; **in ~** en el hospital.

hospitality [ˌhɒsprɪ'tælɪu] n hospitalidad f.

host [həʊst] n (of party, event) anfitrión m (-ona f); (of show, TV programme) presentador m (-ra f).

hostage ['hɒstɪdʒ] n rehén m.

hostel ['hɒstl] n (youth hostel) albergue m.

hostess ['həʊstes] n (on plane) azafata f; (of party, event) anfitriona f.

hostile [Br 'hɒstaɪl, Am 'hɒstl] adj hostil.

hostility [hɒ'stɪlɪtɪ] n hostilidad f.

hot [hɒt] adj caliente; (spicy) picante; **to be ~** (person) tener calor; **it's ~** (weather) hace calor.

hot chocolate n chocolate m (bebida).

hot-cross bun n bollo con pasas y dibujo en forma de cruz que se come en Semana Santa.

hot dog n perrito m caliente.

hotel [həʊ'tel] n hotel m.

hot line n teléfono m rojo.

hotplate ['hɒtpleɪt] n calentador m.

hotpot ['hɒtpɒt] n estofado de cabrito cubierto con patatas en rodajas y cocido al horno.

hot-water bottle n bolsa f de agua caliente.

hour ['auə^r] n hora f; **I've been waiting for ~s** llevo horas esperando.

hourly ['auəlɪ] adj por hora ◆ adv (pay, charge) por hora; (depart) cada hora.

house [n haus, pl 'hauzız, vb hauz] n casa f; (SCH) división de los alumnos de una escuela para actividades extraacadémicas ◆ vt (person) alojar.

household ['haushəuld] n hogar m.

housekeeping ['haus,ki:pɪŋ] n quehaceres mpl domésticos.

House of Commons n Cámara f de los Comunes.

House of Lords n Cámara f de los Lores.

Houses of Parliament npl (Br) Parlamento m británico.

---

i HOUSES OF PARLIAMENT

El Parlamento británico se halla en Londres a orillas del Támesis. Conocido también como el Palacio de Westminster, el Parlamento consta de dos cámaras: la de los Comunes y la de los Lores. Los edificios donde hoy se alojan fueron construidos a mediados del siglo XIX para reemplazar el antiguo Palacio, destruido por un incendio en 1834.

---

housewife ['hauswaif] (pl -wives [ˌwaivz]) n ama f de casa.

house wine n vino m de la casa.

housework ['hauswɜ:k] n quehaceres mpl domésticos.

housing ['hauzɪŋ] n (houses) vivienda f.

housing estate n (Br) urbanización de viviendas de protección oficial.

housing project (Am) = housing estate.

hovercraft ['hɒvəkrɑ:ft] n aerodeslizador m.

hoverport ['hɒvəpɔ:t] n terminal f de aerodeslizador.

how [hau] adv 1. (asking about way or manner) cómo; ~ **does it work?** ¿cómo funciona?; **tell me ~ to do it** dime cómo se hace.
2. (asking about health, quality, event) cómo; ~ **are you?** ¿cómo estás?; ~ **are you doing?** ¿qué tal estás?; ~ **are things?** ¿cómo van las cosas?; ~ **do you do?** (greeting) ¿cómo está usted?; (answer) mucho gusto; ~ **is your room?** ¿qué tal es tu habitación?
3. (asking about degree, amount): ~ **far?** ¿a qué distancia?; ~ **long?** ¿cuánto tiempo?; ~ **many?** ¿cuántos?; ~ **much?** ¿cuánto?; ~ **much is it?** ¿cuánto es?
4. (in phrases): ~ **about a drink?** ¿qué tal si tomamos algo?; ~ **lovely!** ¡qué precioso!

however [hau'evə^r] adv (nevertheless) sin embargo; ~ **hard I try** por mucho que lo intente; ~ **easy it may be** por muy fácil que sea.

howl [haul] vi (dog) aullar; (person) gritar; (wind) bramar.

HP abbr (Br) = hire purchase.

HQ *abbr* = **headquarters**.

hub airport [hʌb-] *n* aeropuerto *m* principal.

hubcap ['hʌbkæp] *n* tapacubos *m inv*.

hug [hʌg] *vt* abrazar ◆ *n*: **to give sb a ~** abrazar a alguien.

huge [hju:dʒ] *adj* enorme.

hull [hʌl] *n* casco *m*.

hum [hʌm] *vi* (*bee, machine*) zumbar; (*person*) canturrear.

human ['hju:mən] *adj* humano(-na) ◆ *n*: **~ (being)** ser *m* humano.

humanities [hju:'mænətɪz] *npl* humanidades *fpl*.

human rights *npl* derechos *mpl* humanos.

humble ['hʌmbl] *adj* humilde.

humid ['hju:mɪd] *adj* húmedo(-da).

humidity [hju:'mɪdətɪ] *n* humedad *f*.

humiliating [hju:'mɪlɪeɪtɪŋ] *adj* humillante.

humiliation [hju:,mɪlɪ'eɪʃn] *n* humillación *f*.

hummus ['huməs] *n* puré de garbanzos, ajo y pasta de sésamo.

humor ['hju:mər] (*Am*) = **humour**.

humorous ['hju:mərəs] *adj* humorístico(-ca).

humour ['hju:mər] *n* humor *m*; **a sense of ~** un sentido del humor.

hump [hʌmp] *n* (*bump*) montículo *m*; (*of camel*) joroba *f*.

humpbacked bridge ['hʌmpbækt-] *n* puente *m* peraltado.

hunch [hʌntʃ] *n* presentimiento *m*.

hundred ['hʌndrəd] *num* cien; **a ~ cien**; **a ~ and ten** ciento diez, → **six**.

hundredth ['hʌndrətθ] *num* centésimo(-ma), → **sixth**.

hundredweight ['hʌndrədweɪt] *n* (*in UK*) = 50,8 kg; (*in US*) = 45,3 kg.

hung [hʌŋ] *pt & pp* → **hang**.

Hungarian [hʌŋ'geərɪən] *adj* húngaro(-ra) ◆ *n* (*person*) húngaro *m* (-ra *f*); (*language*) húngaro *m*.

Hungary ['hʌŋgərɪ] *n* Hungría.

hunger ['hʌŋgər] *n* hambre *f*.

hungry ['hʌŋgrɪ] *adj* hambriento(-ta); **to be ~** tener hambre.

hunt [hʌnt] *n* (*Br: for foxes*) caza *f* (del zorro) ◆ *vt* (*animals*) cazar ◆ *vi* (*for animals*) cazar; **to ~ (for sthg)** (*search*) buscar (algo).

hunting ['hʌntɪŋ] *n* (*for animals*) caza *f*; (*Br: for foxes*) caza del zorno.

hurdle ['hɜ:dl] *n* (*SPORT*) valla *f*.

hurl [hɜ:l] *vt* arrojar.

hurricane ['hʌrɪkən] *n* huracán *m*.

hurry ['hʌrɪ] *vt* (*person*) meter prisa a ◆ *vi* apresurarse ◆ *n*: **to be in a ~** tener prisa; **to do sthg in a ~** hacer algo de prisa ❏ **hurry up** *vi* darse prisa.

hurt [hɜ:t] (*pt & pp* **hurt**) *vt* hacerse daño en; (*emotionally*) herir ◆ *vi* doler; **my arm ~s** me duele el brazo; **to ~ o.s.** hacerse daño.

husband ['hʌzbənd] *n* marido *m*.

hustle ['hʌsl] *n*: **~ and bustle** bullicio *m*.

hut [hʌt] *n* cabaña *f*.

hyacinth ['haɪəsɪnθ] *n* jacinto *m*.

hydrofoil ['haɪdrəfɔɪl] *n* hidrofoil *m*.

hygiene ['haɪdʒiːn] *n* higiene *f*.

hygienic [haɪ'dʒiːnɪk] *adj* higiénico(-ca).

hymn [hɪm] *n* himno *m*.

hypermarket ['haɪpə,mɑːkɪt] *n* hipermercado *m*.

hyphen ['haɪfn] *n* guión *m*.

hypocrite ['hɪpəkrɪt] *n* hipócrita *mf*.

hypodermic needle [,haɪpə'dɜːmɪk-] *n* aguja *f* hipodérmica.

hysterical [hɪs'terɪkl] *adj* histérico(-ca); *(inf: very funny)* tronchante.

I [aɪ] *pron* yo; **I'm a doctor** soy médico.

ice [aɪs] *n* hielo *m*; *(ice cream)* helado *m*.

iceberg ['aɪsbɜːg] *n* iceberg *m*.

iceberg lettuce *n* lechuga *f* iceberg.

icebox ['aɪsbɒks] *n* (*Am*) refrigerador *m*.

ice-cold *adj* helado(-da).

ice cream *n* helado *m*.

ice cube *n* cubito *m* de hielo.

ice hockey *n* hockey *m* sobre hielo.

Iceland ['aɪslənd] *n* Islandia.

ice lolly *n* (*Br*) polo *m*.

ice rink *n* pista *f* de hielo.

ice skates *npl* patines *mpl* de

cuchilla.

ice-skating *n* patinaje *m* sobre hielo; **to go ~** ir a patinar.

icicle ['aɪsɪkl] *n* carámbano *m*.

icing ['aɪsɪŋ] *n* glaseado *m*.

icing sugar *n* azúcar *m* glas.

icy ['aɪsɪ] *adj* helado(-da).

I'd [aɪd] = **I would, I had**.

ID *n (abbr of identification)* documentos *mpl* de identificación.

ID card *n* carné *m* de identidad.

IDD code *n* prefijo *m* internacional automático.

idea [aɪ'dɪə] *n* idea *f*; **I've no ~** no tengo ni idea.

ideal [aɪ'dɪəl] *adj* ideal ◆ *n* ideal *m*.

ideally [aɪ'dɪəlɪ] *adv* idealmente; *(suited)* perfectamente.

identical [aɪ'dentɪkl] *adj* idéntico(-ca).

identification [aɪ,dentɪfɪ'keɪʃn] *n* identificación *f*.

identify [aɪ'dentɪfaɪ] *vt* identificar.

identity [aɪ'dentətɪ] *n* identidad *f*.

idiom ['ɪdɪəm] *n (phrase)* locución *f*.

idiot ['ɪdɪət] *n* idiota *mf*.

idle ['aɪdl] *adj (lazy)* perezoso(-sa); *(not working)* parado(-da) ◆ *vi (engine)* estar en punto muerto.

idol ['aɪdl] *n (person)* ídolo *m*.

idyllic [ɪ'dɪlɪk] *adj* idílico(-ca).

i.e. *(abbr of id est)* i.e.

if [ɪf] *conj* si; **~ I were you** yo que tú; **~ not** *(otherwise)* si no.

ignition [ɪg'nɪʃn] *n (AUT)* ignición *f*.

ignorant ['ɪɡnərənt] *adj (pej)* ignorante; **to be ~ of** desconocer.

ignore [ɪg'nɔ:ʳ] *vt* ignorar.

ill [ɪl] *adj* enfermo(-ma); *(bad)* malo(-la).

I'll [aɪl] = I will, I shall.

illegal [ɪ'li:gl] *adj* ilegal.

illegible [ɪ'ledʒəbl] *adj* ilegible.

illegitimate [ɪlɪ'dʒɪtɪmət] *adj* ilegítimo(-ma).

illiterate [ɪ'lɪtərət] *adj* analfabeto(-ta).

illness ['ɪlnɪs] *n* enfermedad *f*.

illuminate [ɪ'lu:mɪneɪt] *vt* iluminar.

illusion [ɪ'lu:ʒn] *n (false idea)* ilusión *f*; *(visual)* ilusión óptica.

illustration [ɪlə'streɪʃn] *n* ilustración *f*.

I'm [aɪm] = I am.

image ['ɪmɪdʒ] *n* imagen *f*.

imaginary [ɪ'mædʒɪnrɪ] *adj* imaginario(-ria).

imagination [ɪmædʒɪ'neɪʃn] *n* imaginación *f*.

imagine [ɪ'mædʒɪn] *vt* imaginar; *(suppose)* imaginarse que.

imitate ['ɪmɪteɪt] *vt* imitar.

imitation [ɪmɪ'teɪʃn] *n* imitación *f* ♦ *adj* de imitación.

immaculate [ɪ'mækjʊlət] *adj (very clean)* inmaculado(-da); *(perfect)* impecable.

immature [ɪmə'tjʊəʳ] *adj* inmaduro(-ra).

immediate [ɪ'mi:djət] *adj (without delay)* inmediato(-ta).

immediately [ɪ'mi:djətlɪ] *adv (at once)* inmediatamente ♦ *conj (Br)* en cuanto.

immense [ɪ'mens] *adj* inmenso(-sa).

immersion heater [ɪ'mɜ:ʃn] *n* calentador *m* de inmersión.

immigrant ['ɪmɪɡrənt] *n* inmigrante *mf*.

immigration [ɪmɪ'ɡreɪʃn] *n* inmigración *f*.

imminent ['ɪmɪnənt] *adj* inminente.

immune [ɪ'mju:n] *adj*: **to be ~ to** *(MED)* ser inmune a.

immunity [ɪ'mju:nɪtɪ] *n (MED)* inmunidad *f*.

immunize ['ɪmjʊnaɪz] *vt* inmunizar.

impact ['ɪmpækt] *n* impacto *m*.

impair [ɪm'peəʳ] *vt (sight)* dañar; *(ability)* mermar; *(movement)* entorpecer.

impatient [ɪm'peɪʃnt] *adj* impaciente; **to be ~ to do sthg** estar impaciente por hacer algo.

imperative [ɪm'perətɪv] *n* imperativo *m*.

imperfect [ɪm'pɜ:fɪkt] *n* imperfecto *m*.

impersonate [ɪm'pɜ:səneɪt] *vt (for amusement)* imitar.

impertinent [ɪm'pɜ:tɪnənt] *adj* impertinente.

implement [*n* 'ɪmplɪmənt, *vb* 'ɪmplɪment] *n* herramienta *f* ♦ *vt* llevar a cabo.

implication [ɪmplɪ'keɪʃn] *n (consequence)* consecuencia *f*.

imply [ɪm'plaɪ] *vt (suggest)* insinuar.

impolite [ɪmpə'laɪt] *adj* maleducado(-da).

import [*n* 'ɪmpɔ:t, *vb* ɪm'pɔ:t] *n*

importance

146

importación f ◆ vt importar.

importance [ɪm'pɔːtns] n importancia f.

important [ɪm'pɔːtnt] adj importante.

impose [ɪm'pəʊz] vt imponer ◆ vi abusar; **to ~ sthg on** imponer algo a.

impossible [ɪm'pɒsəbl] adj imposible; (person, behaviour) inaguantable.

impractical [ɪm'præktɪkl] adj poco práctico(-ca).

impress [ɪm'pres] vt impresionar.

impression [ɪm'preʃn] n impresión f.

impressive [ɪm'presɪv] adj impresionante.

improbable [ɪm'prɒbəbl] adj improbable.

improper [ɪm'prɒpəʳ] adj (incorrect, illegal) indebido(-da); (rude) indecoroso(-sa).

improve [ɪm'pruːv] vt & vi mejorar ❑ **improve on** vt fus mejorar.

improvement [ɪm'pruːvmənt] n mejora f; (to home) reforma f.

improvise ['ɪmprəvaɪz] vi improvisar.

impulse ['ɪmpʌls] n impulso m; **on ~** sin pensárselo dos veces.

impulsive [ɪm'pʌlsɪv] adj impulsivo(-va).

in [ɪn] prep 1. (expressing location, position) en; **it comes ~ a box** viene en una caja; **~ the bedroom** en la habitación; **~ Scotland** en Escocia; **~ the sun** al sol; **~ here** aquí/allí dentro; **~ the middle** en el medio; **I'm not ~ the photo** no

estoy en la foto.
2. (participating in) en; **who's ~ the play?** ¿quién actúa?
3. (expressing arrangement): **~ a row** en fila; **they come ~ packs of three** vienen en paquetes de tres.
4. (with time) en; **~ April** en abril; **~ the afternoon** por la tarde; **~ the morning** por la mañana; **at ten o'clock ~ the morning** a las diez de la mañana; **~ 1994** en 1994; **it'll be ready ~ an hour** estará listo en una hora; **they're arriving ~ two weeks** llegarán dentro de dos semanas.
5. (expressing means) en; **~ writing** por escrito; **they were talking ~ English** estaban hablando en inglés; **write ~ ink** escribe a bolígrafo.
6. (wearing) de; **the man ~ the suit** el hombre del traje.
7. (expressing condition) en; **~ good health** bien de salud; **to be ~ pain** tener dolor; **~ ruins** en ruinas; **a rise ~ prices** una subida de precios; **to be 50 metres ~ length** medir 50 metros de largo; **she's ~ her twenties** tiene unos veintitantos años.
8. (with numbers): **one ~ ten** uno de cada diez.
9. (with colours): **it comes ~ green or blue** viene en verde o en azul.
10. (with superlatives): **the best ~ the world** el mejor del mundo.
◆ adv 1. (inside) dentro; **you can go ~ now** puedes entrar ahora.
2. (at home, work): **she's not ~** no está; **to stay ~** quedarse en casa.
3. (train, bus, plane): **the train's not ~ yet** el tren todavía no ha llegado.
4. (tide): **the tide is ~** la marea es-

tá alta.

◆ adj (inf: fashionable) de moda.

inability [,ɪnə'bɪlətɪ] n: ~ **(to do sthg)** incapacidad f (de hacer algo).

inaccessible [,ɪnək'sesəbl] adj inaccesible.

inaccurate [ɪn'ækjʊrət] adj incorrecto(-ta).

inadequate [ɪn'ædɪkwət] adj (insufficient) insuficiente.

inappropriate [,ɪnə'prəʊprɪət] adj impropio(-pia).

inauguration [ɪ,nɔ:gjʊ'reɪʃn] n (of leader) investidura f; (of building) inauguración f.

incapable [ɪn'keɪpəbl] adj: **to be ~ of doing sthg** ser incapaz de hacer algo.

incense ['ɪnsens] n incienso m.

incentive [ɪn'sentɪv] n incentivo m.

inch [ɪntʃ] n = 2,5 cm, pulgada f.

incident ['ɪnsɪdənt] n incidente m.

incidentally [,ɪnsɪ'dentəlɪ] adv por cierto.

incline ['ɪnklaɪn] n pendiente f.

inclined [ɪn'klaɪnd] adj (sloping) inclinado(-da); **to be ~ to do sthg** tener tendencia a hacer algo.

include [ɪn'klu:d] vt incluir.

included [ɪn'klu:dɪd] adj incluido(-da); **to be ~ in sthg** estar incluido en algo.

including [ɪn'klu:dɪŋ] prep inclusive.

inclusive [ɪn'klu:sɪv] adj: **from the 8th to the 16th ~** del ocho al dieciseis inclusive; **~ of VAT** incluido IVA.

income ['ɪŋkʌm] n ingresos mpl.

income support n (Br) subsidio para personas con muy bajos ingresos o desempleados sin derecho a subsidio de paro.

income tax n impuesto m sobre la renta.

incoming ['ɪn,kʌmɪŋ] adj (train, plane) que efectúa su llegada; "~ **calls only**" cartel que indica que sólo se pueden recibir llamadas en un teléfono.

incompetent [ɪn'kɒmpɪtənt] adj incompetente.

incomplete [,ɪnkəm'pli:t] adj incompleto(-ta).

inconsiderate [,ɪnkən'sɪdərət] adj desconsiderado(-da).

inconsistent [,ɪnkən'sɪstənt] adj inconsecuente.

incontinent [ɪn'kɒntɪnənt] adj incontinente.

inconvenient [,ɪnkən'vi:njənt] adj (time) inoportuno(-na); (place) mal situado(-da); **tomorrow's ~** mañana no me viene bien.

incorporate [ɪn'kɔ:pəreɪt] vt incorporar.

incorrect [,ɪnkə'rekt] adj incorrecto(-ta)

increase [n 'ɪnkri:s, vb ɪn'kri:s] n aumento m ◆ vt & vi aumentar; **an ~ in sthg** un aumento en algo.

increasingly [ɪn'kri:sɪŋlɪ] adv cada vez más.

incredible [ɪn'kredəbl] adj increíble.

incredibly [ɪn'kredəblɪ] adv increíblemente.

incur [ɪn'kɜ:r] vt incurrir en.

indecisive [,ɪndɪ'saɪsɪv] adj indeciso(-sa).

indeed [ɪn'diːd] *adv (for emphasis)* verdaderamente; *(certainly)* ciertamente.

indefinite [ɪn'defɪnɪt] *adj (time, number)* indefinido(-da); *(answer, opinion)* impreciso(-sa).

indefinitely [ɪn'defɪnətlɪ] *adv (closed, delayed)* indefinidamente.

independence [,ɪndɪ'pendəns] *n* independencia *f*.

independent [,ɪndɪ'pendənt] *adj* independiente.

independently [,ɪndɪ'pendəntlɪ] *adv* independientemente.

independent school *n (Br)* colegio *m* privado.

index ['ɪndeks] *n (of book)* índice *m*; *(in library)* catálogo *m*.

index finger *n* dedo *m* índice.

India ['ɪndjə] *n* India.

Indian ['ɪndjən] *adj* indio(-dia) *(de India)* ♦ *n* indio *m* (-dia *f*) *(de India)*; ~ **restaurant** restaurante indio.

Indian Ocean *n* océano *m* Índico.

indicate ['ɪndɪkeɪt] *vt & vi* indicar.

indicator ['ɪndɪkeɪtər] *n (AUT)* intermitente *m*.

indifferent [ɪn'dɪfrənt] *adj* indiferente.

indigestion [,ɪndɪ'dʒestʃn] *n* indigestión *f*.

indigo ['ɪndɪgəʊ] *adj* añil.

indirect [,ɪndɪ'rekt] *adj* indirecto(-ta).

individual [,ɪndɪ'vɪdʒʊəl] *adj (tuition, case)* particular; *(portion)* individual ♦ *n* individuo *m*.

individually [,ɪndɪ'vɪdʒʊəlɪ] *adv* individualmente.

Indonesia [,ɪndə'niːzjə] *n* Indonesia.

indoor ['ɪndɔːʳ] *adj (swimming pool)* cubierto(-ta); *(sports)* en pista cubierta.

indoors [ɪn'dɔːz] *adv* dentro.

indulge [ɪn'dʌldʒ] *vi*: **to ~ in sthg** permitirse algo.

industrial [ɪn'dʌstrɪəl] *adj* industrial.

industrial estate *n (Br)* polígono *m* industrial.

industry ['ɪndəstrɪ] *n* industria *f*.

inedible [ɪn'edɪbl] *adj* no comestible.

inefficient [,ɪnɪ'fɪʃnt] *adj* ineficaz.

inequality [,ɪnɪ'kwɒlətɪ] *n* desigualdad *f*.

inevitable [ɪn'evɪtəbl] *adj* inevitable.

inevitably [ɪn'evɪtəblɪ] *adv* inevitablemente.

inexpensive [,ɪnɪk'spensɪv] *adj* barato(-ta).

infamous ['ɪnfəməs] *adj* infame.

infant ['ɪnfənt] *n (baby)* bebé *m*; *(young child)* niño *m* pequeño (niña *f* pequeña).

infant school *n (Br)* colegio *m* preescolar.

infatuated [ɪn'fætjʊeɪtɪd] *adj*: **to be ~ with** estar encaprichado(-da) con.

infected [ɪn'fektɪd] *adj* infectado(-da).

infectious [ɪn'fekʃəs] *adj* contagioso(-sa).

inferior [ɪn'fɪərɪəʳ] *adj* inferior.

infinite [ˈɪnfɪnət] *adj* infinito(-ta).

infinitely [ˈɪnfɪnətlɪ] *adv* infinitamente.

infinitive [ɪnˈfɪnɪtɪv] *n* infinitivo *m*.

infinity [ɪnˈfɪnətɪ] *n* infinito *m*.

infirmary [ɪnˈfɜːmərɪ] *n* hospital *m*.

inflamed [ɪnˈfleɪmd] *adj* inflamado(-da).

inflammation [ˌɪnfləˈmeɪʃn] *n* inflamación *f*.

inflatable [ɪnˈfleɪtəbl] *adj* hinchable.

inflate [ɪnˈfleɪt] *vt* inflar.

inflation [ɪnˈfleɪʃn] *n* inflación *f*.

inflict [ɪnˈflɪkt] *vt* infligir.

in-flight *adj* proporcionado (-da) durante el vuelo.

influence [ˈɪnfluəns] *vt* influenciar ♦ *n*: ~ **(on)** influencia *f* (en).

inform [ɪnˈfɔːm] *vt* informar.

informal [ɪnˈfɔːml] *adj* (occasion, dress) informal.

information [ˌɪnfəˈmeɪʃn] *n* información *f*; **a piece of** ~ un dato.

information desk *n* información *f*.

information office *n* oficina *f* de información.

informative [ɪnˈfɔːmətɪv] *adj* informativo(-va).

infuriating [ɪnˈfjʊərɪeɪtɪŋ] *adj* exasperante.

ingenious [ɪnˈdʒiːnjəs] *adj* ingenioso(-sa).

ingredient [ɪnˈgriːdjənt] *n* ingrediente *m*.

inhabit [ɪnˈhæbɪt] *vt* habitar.

inhabitant [ɪnˈhæbɪtənt] *n* habitante *mf*.

inhale [ɪnˈheɪl] *vi* respirar.

inhaler [ɪnˈheɪləʳ] *n* inhalador *m*.

inherit [ɪnˈherɪt] *vt* heredar.

inhibition [ˌɪnhɪˈbɪʃn] *n* inhibición *f*.

initial [ɪˈnɪʃl] *adj* inicial ♦ *vt* poner las iniciales a □ **initials** *npl* iniciales *fpl*.

initially [ɪˈnɪʃəlɪ] *adv* inicialmente.

initiative [ɪˈnɪʃətɪv] *n* iniciativa *f*.

injection [ɪnˈdʒekʃn] *n* inyección *f*.

injure [ˈɪndʒəʳ] *vt* herir; (leg, arm) lesionarse; **to** ~ **o.s.** hacerse daño.

injured [ˈɪndʒəd] *adj* herido(-da).

injury [ˈɪndʒərɪ] *n* lesión *f*.

ink [ɪŋk] *n* tinta *f*.

inland [adj ˈɪnlənd, adv ɪnˈlænd] *adj* interior ♦ *adv* hacia el interior.

Inland Revenue *n* (Br) = Hacienda *f*.

inn [ɪn] *n* pub decorado a la vieja usanza.

inner [ˈɪnəʳ] *adj* (on inside) interior.

inner city *n* núcleo *m* urbano.

inner tube *n* cámara *f* (de aire).

innocence [ˈɪnəsəns] *n* inocencia *f*.

innocent [ˈɪnəsənt] *adj* inocente.

inoculate [ɪˈnɒkjʊleɪt] *vt*: **to** ~ **sb (against sthg)** inocular a alguien (contra algo).

inoculation [ɪˌnɒkjʊˈleɪʃn] *n* inoculación *f*.

input [ˈɪnpʊt] (pt & pp **input** OR

-ted] vt *(COMPUT)* entrar.
inquire [ɪnˈkwaɪəʳ] = enquire.
inquiry [ɪnˈkwaɪərɪ] = enquiry.
insane [ɪnˈseɪn] *adj* demente.
insect [ˈɪnsekt] *n* insecto *m*.
insect repellent [-rəˈpelənt] *n* loción *f* antiinsectos.
insensitive [ɪnˈsensətɪv] *adj* insensible.
insert [ɪnˈsɜːt] *vt* introducir.
inside [ɪnˈsaɪd] *prep* dentro de ♦ *adv (be, remain)* dentro; *(go, run)* adentro ♦ *adj* interior ♦ *n*: **the ~** *(interior)* el interior; *(AUT: in UK)* el carril de la izquierda; *(AUT: in Europe, US)* el carril de la derecha; **~ out** *(clothes)* al revés.
inside lane *n (AUT: in UK)* carril *m* de la izquierda; *(in Europe, US)* carril de la derecha.
inside leg *n* medida *f* de la pernera.
insight [ˈɪnsaɪt] *n (glimpse)* idea *f*.
insignificant [ˌɪnsɪgˈnɪfɪkənt] *adj* insignificante.
insinuate [ɪnˈsɪnjʊeɪt] *vt* insinuar.
insist [ɪnˈsɪst] *vi* insistir; **to ~ on doing sthg** insistir en hacer algo.
insole [ˈɪnsəʊl] *n* plantilla *f*.
insolent [ˈɪnsələnt] *adj* insolente.
insomnia [ɪnˈsɒmnɪə] *n* insomnio *m*.
inspect [ɪnˈspekt] *vt* examinar.
inspection [ɪnˈspekʃn] *n* examen *m*.
inspector [ɪnˈspektəʳ] *n (on bus, train)* revisor *m* (-ra *f*); *(in police force)* inspector *m* (-ra *f*).
inspiration [ˌɪnspəˈreɪʃn] *n (quality)* inspiración *f*; *(source of*

inspiration) fuente *f* de inspiración.
instal [ɪnˈstɔːl] *(Am)* = **install**.
install [ɪnˈstɔːl] *vt (Br: equipment)* instalar.
installment [ɪnˈstɔːlmənt] *(Am)* = **instalment**.
instalment [ɪnˈstɔːlmənt] *n (payment)* plazo *m*; *(episode)* episodio *m*.
instamatic (camera) [ˌɪnstəˈmætɪk-] *n* Polaroid® *f*.
instance [ˈɪnstəns] *n* ejemplo *m*; **for ~** por ejemplo.
instant [ˈɪnstənt] *adj* instantáneo(-nea) ♦ *n* instante *m*.
instant coffee *n* café *m* instantáneo.
instead [ɪnˈsted] *adv* en cambio; **~ of** en vez de.
instep [ˈɪnstep] *n* empeine *m*.
instinct [ˈɪnstɪŋkt] *n* instinto *m*.
institute [ˈɪnstɪtjuːt] *n* instituto *m*.
institution [ˌɪnstɪˈtjuːʃn] *n (organization)* institución *f*.
instructions [ɪnˈstrʌkʃnz] *npl (for use)* instrucciones *fpl*.
instructor [ɪnˈstrʌktəʳ] *n* monitor *m* (-ra *f*).
instrument [ˈɪnstrʊmənt] *n* instrumento *m*.
insufficient [ˌɪnsəˈfɪʃnt] *adj* insuficiente.
insulating tape [ˈɪnsjʊˌleɪtɪŋ-] *n* cinta *f* aislante.
insulation [ˌɪnsjʊˈleɪʃn] *n* aislamiento *m*.
insulin [ˈɪnsjʊlɪn] *n* insulina *f*.
insult [*n* ˈɪnsʌlt, *vb* ɪnˈsʌlt] *n* insulto *m* ♦ *vt* insultar.
insurance [ɪnˈʃʊərəns] *n* seguro *m*.

insurance certificate n certificado m de seguro.

insurance company n compañía f de seguros.

insurance policy n póliza f de seguros.

insure [ɪnˈʃʊəʳ] vt asegurar.

insured [ɪnˈʃʊəd] adj: **to be ~** estar asegurado(-da).

intact [ɪnˈtækt] adj intacto(-ta).

intellectual [ɪntəˈlektjʊəl] adj intelectual ♦ n intelectual mf.

intelligence [ɪnˈtelɪdʒəns] n (cleverness) inteligencia f.

intelligent [ɪnˈtelɪdʒənt] adj inteligente.

intend [ɪnˈtend] vt: **it's ~ed as a** handbook esta pensado como un manual; **to ~ to do sthg** tener la intención de hacer algo.

intense [ɪnˈtens] adj intenso(-sa).

intensity [ɪnˈtensətɪ] n intensidad f.

intensive [ɪnˈtensɪv] adj intensivo(-va).

intensive care n cuidados mpl intensivos.

intent [ɪnˈtent] adj: **to be ~ on** doing sthg estar empeñado(-da) en hacer algo.

intention [ɪnˈtenʃn] n intención f.

intentional [ɪnˈtenʃənl] adj deliberado(-da).

intentionally [ɪnˈtenʃənlɪ] adv deliberadamente.

interchange [ˈɪntətʃeɪndʒ] n (on motorway) cruce m.

Intercity® [ɪntəˈsɪtɪ] n (Br) tren rápido de largo recorrido en Gran Bretaña.

intercom [ˈɪntəkɒm] n portero m automático.

interest [ˈɪntrəst] n interés m ♦ vt interesar; **to take an ~ in sthg** interesarse en algo.

interested [ˈɪntrəstɪd] adj interesado(-da); **to be ~ in sthg** estar interesado en algo.

interesting [ˈɪntrəstɪŋ] adj interesante.

interest rate n tipo m de interés.

interfere [ɪntəˈfɪəʳ] vi (meddle) entrometerse; **to ~ with sthg** (damage) interferir en algo.

interference [ɪntəˈfɪərəns] n (on TV, radio) interferencia f.

interior [ɪnˈtɪərɪəʳ] adj interior ♦ n interior m.

intermediate [ɪntəˈmiːdjət] adj intermedio(-dia).

intermission [ɪntəˈmɪʃn] n descanso m.

internal [ɪnˈtɜːnl] adj (not foreign) nacional; (on the inside) interno(-na).

internal flight n vuelo m nacional.

international [ɪntəˈnæʃənl] adj internacional.

international flight n vuelo m internacional.

interpret [ɪnˈtɜːprɪt] vi hacer de intérprete.

interpreter [ɪnˈtɜːprɪtəʳ] n intérprete mf.

interrogate [ɪnˈterəgeɪt] vt interrogar.

interrupt [ɪntəˈrʌpt] vt interrumpir.

intersection [ɪntəˈsekʃn] n

intersección f.

interval ['ɪntəvl] n intervalo m; *(Br: at cinema, theatre)* intermedio m.

intervene [ˌɪntə'viːn] vi *(person)* intervenir; *(event)* interponerse.

interview ['ɪntəvjuː] n entrevista f ◆ vt entrevistar.

interviewer ['ɪntəvjuːə'] n entrevistador m (-ra f).

intestine [ɪn'testɪn] n intestino m.

intimate ['ɪntɪmət] adj íntimo(-ma).

intimidate [ɪn'tɪmɪdeɪt] vt intimidar.

into ['ɪntʊ] prep *(inside)* en; *(against)* con; *(concerning)* en relación con; **4 ~ 20 goes 5 (times)** veinte entre cuatro a cinco; **to translate ~ Spanish** traducir al español; **to change ~ sthg** transformarse en algo; **I'm ~ music** *(inf)* lo mío es la música.

intolerable [ɪn'tɒlrəbl] adj intolerable.

intransitive [ɪn'trænzətɪv] adj intransitivo(-va).

intricate ['ɪntrɪkət] adj intrincado(-da).

intriguing [ɪn'triːgɪn] adj intrigante.

introduce [ˌɪntrə'djuːs] vt presentar; **I'd like to ~ you to Fred** me gustaría presentarle a Fred.

introduction [ˌɪntrə'dʌkʃn] n *(to book, programme)* introducción f; *(to person)* presentación f.

introverted ['ɪntrə,vɜːtɪd] adj introvertido(-da).

intruder [ɪn'truːdə'] n intruso

m (-sa f).

intuition [ˌɪntjuː'ɪʃn] n intuición f.

invade [ɪn'veɪd] vt invadir.

invalid *[adj* ɪn'vælɪd, *n* 'ɪnvəlɪd] adj nulo(-la) ◆ n inválido m (-da f).

invaluable [ɪn'væljuəbl] adj inestimable.

invariably [ɪn'veərɪəblɪ] adv siempre.

invasion [ɪn'veɪʒn] n invasión f.

invent [ɪn'vent] vt inventar.

invention [ɪn'venʃn] n invención f.

inventory ['ɪnvəntrɪ] n *(list)* inventario m; *(Am: stock)* existencias fpl.

inverted commas [ɪn'vɜːtɪd-] npl comillas fpl.

invest [ɪn'vest] vt invertir ◆ vi: **to ~ in sthg** invertir en algo.

investigate [ɪn'vestɪgeɪt] vt investigar.

investigation [ɪn,vestɪ'geɪʃn] n investigación f.

investment [ɪn'vestmənt] n inversión f.

invisible [ɪn'vɪzɪbl] adj invisible.

invitation [ˌɪnvɪ'teɪʃn] n invitación f.

invite [ɪn'vaɪt] vt invitar; **to ~ sb to do sthg** invitar a alguien a hacer algo; **to ~ sb round** invitar a alguien.

invoice ['ɪnvɔɪs] n factura f.

involve [ɪn'vɒlv] vt *(entail)* conllevar; **what does it ~?** ¿qué implica?; **to be ~d in sthg** *(scheme, activity)* estar metido en algo; *(accident)* verse envuelto en algo.

involved [ɪn'vɒlvd] adj: **what is**

~? ¿qué supone?

inwards ['ɪnwədz] *adv* hacia dentro.

IOU *n* pagaré *m*.

IQ *n* C.I. *m*.

Iran [ɪ'rɑːn] *n* Irán.

Iraq [ɪ'rɑːk] *n* Irak.

Ireland ['aɪələnd] *n* Irlanda.

iris ['aɪrɪs] *(pl* **-es**) *n (flower)* lirio *m*.

Irish ['aɪrɪʃ] *adj* irlandés(-esa) ♦ *n (language)* irlandés *m* ♦ *npl* **the ~** los irlandeses.

Irish coffee *n* café *m* irlandés.

Irishman ['aɪrɪʃmən] *(pl* **-men** [-mən]) *n* irlandés *m*.

Irish stew *n* estofado de carne de cordero, patatas y cebolla.

Irishwoman ['aɪrɪʃ,wʊmən] *(pl* **-women** [-,wɪmɪn]) *n* irlandesa *f*.

iron ['aɪən] *n (metal, golf club)* hierro *m*; *(for clothes)* plancha *f* ♦ *vt* planchar.

ironic [aɪ'rɒnɪk] *adj* irónico(-ca).

ironing board ['aɪənɪŋ-] *n* tabla *f* de planchar.

ironmonger's ['aɪən,mʌŋgəz] *n (Br)* ferretería *f*.

irrelevant [ɪ'reləvənt] *adj* irrelevante.

irresistible [,ɪrɪ'zɪstəbl] *adj* irresistible.

irrespective [,ɪrɪ'spektɪv]: **irrespective of** *prep* con independencia de.

irresponsible [,ɪrɪ'spɒnsəbl] *adj* irresponsable.

irrigation [,ɪrɪ'geɪʃn] *n* riego *m*.

irritable ['ɪrɪtəbl] *adj* irritable.

irritate ['ɪrɪteɪt] *vt* irritar.

irritating ['ɪrɪteɪtɪŋ] *adj* irritante.

IRS *n (Am)* = Hacienda *f*.

is [ɪz] → **be**.

Islam ['ɪzlɑːm] *n* islam *m*.

island ['aɪlənd] *n (in water)* isla *f*; *(in road)* isleta *f*.

isle [aɪl] *n* isla *f*.

isolated ['aɪsəleɪtɪd] *adj* aislado(-da).

Israel ['ɪzreɪəl] *n* Israel.

issue ['ɪʃuː] *n (problem, subject)* cuestión *f*; *(of newspaper, magazine)* edición *f* ♦ *vt (statement)* hacer público; *(passport, document)* expedir; *(stamps, bank notes)* emitir.

it [ɪt] *pron* **1.** *(referring to specific thing: subj)* él *m* (ella *f*); *(direct object)* lo *m* (la *f*); *(indirect object)* le *m*f; **~'s big** es grande; **she hit ~** lo golpeó; **give ~ to me** dámelo.
2. *(nonspecific)* ello; **~'s nice here** se está bien aquí; **I can't remember ~** no me acuerdo (de ello); **tell me about ~** cuéntamelo; **~'s me** soy yo; **who is ~?** ¿quién es?
3. *(used impersonally)* **~'s hot** hace calor; **~'s six o'clock** son las seis; **~'s Sunday** es domingo.

Italian [ɪ'tæljən] *adj* italiano(-na) ♦ *n (person)* italiano *m* (-na *f*); *(language)* italiano *m*; **~ restaurant** restaurante italiano.

Italy ['ɪtəlɪ] *n* Italia.

itch [ɪtʃ] *vi*: **my arm is ~ing** me pica el brazo.

item ['aɪtəm] *n* artículo *m*; *(on agenda)* asunto *m*; **a news ~** una noticia.

itemized bill ['aɪtəmaɪzd-] *n* factura *f* detallada.

its [ɪts] *adj* su, sus *(pl)*.

it's [ɪts] = **it is, it has**.

itself [ɪt'self] *pron (reflexive)* se; *(after prep)* sí mismo(-ma); **the house ~ is fine** la casa en sí está bien.

I've [aɪv] = **I have**.

ivory ['aɪvərɪ] *n* marfil *m*.

ivy ['aɪvɪ] *n* hiedra *f*.

J

jab [dʒæb] *n (Br: inf: injection)* pinchazo *m*.

jack [dʒæk] *n (for car)* gato *m*; *(playing card)* = sota *f*.

jacket ['dʒækɪt] *n (garment)* chaqueta *f*; *(of book)* sobrecubierta *f*; *(Am: of record)* cubierta *f*; *(of potato)* piel *f*.

jacket potato *n* patata *f* asada con piel.

jack-knife *vi* derrapar la parte delantera.

Jacuzzi® [dʒə'ku:zɪ] *n* jacuzzi® *m*.

jade [dʒeɪd] *n* jade *m*.

jail [dʒeɪl] *n* cárcel *f*.

jam [dʒæm] *n (food)* mermelada *f*; *(of traffic)* atasco *m*; *(inf: difficult situation)* apuro *m* ♦ *vt (pack tightly)* apiñar ♦ *vi* atascarse; **the roads are jammed** las carreteras están atascadas.

jam-packed [-'pækt] *adj (inf)*

a tope.

Jan. [dʒæn] *(abbr of January)* ene.

janitor ['dʒænɪtər] *n (Am & Scot)* conserje *m*.

January ['dʒænjʊərɪ] *n* enero *m*, → **September**.

Japan [dʒə'pæn] *n* Japón *m*.

Japanese [,dʒæpə'ni:z] *adj* japonés(-esa) ♦ *n (language)* japonés *m* ♦ *npl*: **the ~** los japoneses.

jar [dʒɑ:ʳ] *n* tarro *m*.

javelin ['dʒævlɪn] *n* jabalina *f*.

jaw [dʒɔ:] *n (of person)* mandíbula *f*.

jazz [dʒæz] *n* jazz *m*.

jealous ['dʒeləs] *adj* celoso(-sa).

jeans [dʒi:nz] *npl* vaqueros *mpl*.

Jeep® [dʒi:p] *n* jeep *m*.

Jello® ['dʒeləʊ] *n (Am)* gelatina *f*.

jelly ['dʒelɪ] *n (dessert)* gelatina *f*; *(Am: jam)* mermelada *f*.

jellyfish ['dʒelɪfɪʃ] *(pl inv)* *n* medusa *f*.

jeopardize ['dʒepədaɪz] *vt* poner en peligro.

jerk [dʒɜ:k] *n (movement)* movimiento *m* brusco; *(inf: idiot)* idiota *mf*.

jersey ['dʒɜ:zɪ] *(pl -s)* *n (garment)* jersey *m*.

jet [dʒet] *n (aircraft)* reactor *m*; *(of liquid, gas)* chorro *m*; *(outlet)* boquilla *f*.

jetfoil ['dʒetfɔɪl] *n* hidroplano *m*.

jet lag *n* jet lag *m*.

jet-ski *n* moto *f* acuática.

jetty ['dʒetɪ] *n* embarcadero *m*.

Jew [dʒu:] *n* judío *m* (-a *f*).

jewel ['dʒu:əl] *n* piedra *f* preciosa

❏ **jewels** *npl (jewellery)* joyas *fpl.*

jeweler's ['dʒuːələz] *(Am)* = **jeweller's**.

jeweller's ['dʒuːələz] *n (Br: shop)* joyería *f.*

jewellery ['dʒuːəlrɪ] *n (Br)* joyas *fpl.*

jewelry ['dʒuːəlrɪ] *(Am)* = **jewellery**.

Jewish ['dʒuːɪʃ] *adj* judío(-a).

jigsaw (puzzle) ['dʒɪgsɔː-] *n* puzzle *m,*

jingle ['dʒɪŋgl] *n (of advert)* sintonía *f (de anuncio).*

job [dʒɒb] *n* trabajo *m; (function)* cometido *m;* **to lose one's ~** perder el trabajo.

job centre *n (Br)* oficina *f* de empleo.

jockey ['dʒɒkɪ] *(pl -s) n* jockey *mf.*

jog [dʒɒg] *vt (bump)* golpear ligeramente ◆ *vi* hacer footing ◆ *n:* **to go for a ~** hacer footing.

jogging ['dʒɒgɪŋ] *n* footing *m;* **to go ~** hacer footing.

join [dʒɔɪn] *vt (club, organization)* hacerse socio de; *(fasten together)* unir, juntar; *(come together with, participate in)* unirse a; *(connect)* conectar ❏ **join in** *vt fus* participar en ◆ *vi* participar.

joint [dʒɔɪnt] *adj (responsibility, effort)* compartido(-a); *(bank account, ownership)* conjunto(-ta) ◆ *n (of body)* articulación *f; (Br: of meat)* corte *m; (in structure)* juntura *f.*

joke [dʒəʊk] *n* chiste *m* ◆ *vi* bromear.

joker ['dʒəʊkər] *n (playing card)* comodín *m.*

jolly ['dʒɒlɪ] *adj (cheerful)* alegre ◆ *adv (Br: inf)* muy.

jolt [dʒəʊlt] *n* sacudida *f.*

jot [dʒɒt]: **jot down** *vt sep* apuntar.

journal ['dʒɜːnl] *n (magazine)* revista *f; (diary)* diario *m.*

journalist ['dʒɜːnəlɪst] *n* periodista *mf.*

journey ['dʒɜːnɪ] *(pl -s) n* viaje *m.*

joy [dʒɔɪ] *n (happiness)* alegría *f.*

joypad ['dʒɔɪpæd] *n (of video game)* mando *m.*

joyrider ['dʒɔɪraɪdər] *n persona que se pasea en un coche robado y luego lo abandona.*

joystick ['dʒɔɪstɪk] *n (of video game)* joystick *m.*

judge [dʒʌdʒ] *n* juez *mf* ◆ *vt (competition)* juzgar; *(evaluate)* calcular.

judg(e)ment ['dʒʌdʒmənt] *n* juicio *m; (JUR)* fallo *m.*

judo ['dʒuːdəʊ] *n* judo *m.*

jug [dʒʌg] *n* jarra *f.*

juggernaut ['dʒʌgənɔːt] *n (Br)* camión *m* grande.

juggle ['dʒʌgl] *vi* hacer malabarismo.

juice [dʒuːs] *n* zumo *m; (from meat)* jugo *m.*

juicy ['dʒuːsɪ] *adj (food)* jugoso(-a).

jukebox ['dʒuːkbɒks] *n* máquina *f* de discos.

Jul. *(abbr of July)* jul.

July [dʒuːˈlaɪ] *n* julio *m,* → **September**.

jumble sale ['dʒʌmbl-] n (Br) rastrillo m benéfico.

---

i JUMBLE SALE

Las "jumble sales" son mercadillos muy baratos de ropa, libros y objetos domésticos de segunda mano. Normalmente se celebran en locales pertenecientes a iglesias o en centros sociales, para recaudar dinero con fines benéficos.

---

jumbo ['dʒʌmbəʊ] adj (inf) (pack) familiar; (sausage, sandwich) gigante.

jumbo jet n jumbo m.

jump [dʒʌmp] n salto m ◆ vi (through air) saltar; (with fright) sobresaltarse; (increase) aumentar de golpe ◆ vt (Am: train, bus) montarse sin pagar en; **to ~ the queue** (Br) colarse.

jumper ['dʒʌmpə'] n (Br: pullover) jersey m; (Am: dress) pichi m.

jump leads npl cables mpl de empalme.

junction ['dʒʌŋkʃn] n (of roads) cruce m; (of railway lines) empalme m.

June [dʒuːn] n junio m, → September.

jungle ['dʒʌŋgl] n selva f.

junior ['dʒuːnjə'] adj (of lower rank) de rango inferior; (Am: after name) júnior (inv) ◆ n: **she's my ~** es más joven que yo.

junior school n (Br) escuela f primaria.

junk [dʒʌŋk] n (inf: unwanted things) trastos mpl.

junk food n (inf) comida preparada poco nutritiva o saludable.

junkie ['dʒʌŋkɪ] n (inf) yonqui mf.

junk shop n tienda f de objetos de segunda mano.

jury ['dʒʊərɪ] n jurado m.

just [dʒʌst] adj justo(-ta) ◆ adv (exactly) justamente; (only) sólo; **I'm ~ coming** ahora voy; **we were ~ leaving** justo íbamos a salir; **a bit more** un poquito más; **~ as good** igual de bueno; **~ over an hour** poco más de una hora; **passengers ~ arriving** los pasajeros que acaban de llegar; **to be ~ about to do sthg** estar a punto de hacer algo; **to have ~ done sthg** acabar de hacer algo; **~ about** casi; **(only) ~** (almost not) por los pelos; **~ a minute!** ¡un minuto!

justice ['dʒʌstɪs] n justicia f.

justify ['dʒʌstɪfaɪ] vt justificar.

jut [dʒʌt]: **jut out** vi sobresalir.

juvenile ['dʒuːvənaɪl] adj (young) juvenil; (childish) infantil.

K

kangaroo [ˌkæŋgəˈruː] (pl -s) n canguro m.

karaoke [ˌkærˈəʊkɪ] n karaoke m.

karate [kəˈrɑːtɪ] n kárate m.

kebab [kɪˈbæb] n (shish kebab) pincho m moruno; (doner kebab) pan árabe relleno de ensalada y carne de cordero, con salsa.

keel [ki:l] n quilla f.

keen [ki:n] adj (enthusiastic) entusiasta; (eyesight, hearing) agudo (-da); **to be ~ on** ser aficionado(-da) a; **to be ~ to do sthg** tener ganas de hacer algo.

keep [ki:p] (pt & pp **kept**) vt (change, book, object loaned) quedarse con; (job, old clothes) conservar; (store, not tell) guardar; (cause to remain) mantener; (promise) cumplir; (appointment) acudir a; (delay) retener; (record, diary) llevar ◆ vi (food) conservarse; (remain) mantenerse; **to ~ (on) doing sthg** (do continuously) seguir haciendo algo, (do repeatedly) no dejar de hacer algo; **to ~ sb from doing sthg** impedir a alguien hacer algo; **~ back!** ¡atrás!; **"~ in lane!"** señal que advierte a los conductores que se mantengan en el carril; **"~ left"** "circula por la izquierda!"; **"~ off the grass!"** "no pisar la hierba"; **"~ out!"** "prohibida la entrada"; **"~ your distance!"** señal que incita a mantener la distancia de prudencia (de coches) ❑ **keep up** vt sep mantener ◆ vi (maintain pace, level etc) mantener el ritmo.

keep-fit n (Br) ejercicios mpl de mantenimiento.

kennel ['kenl] n caseta f del perro.

kept [kept] pt & pp → **keep**.

kerb [kɜ:b] n (Br) bordillo m.

kerosene ['kerəsi:n] n (Am) queroseno m.

ketchup ['ketʃəp] n catsup m.

kettle ['ketl] n tetera f para hervir; **to put the ~ on** poner a hervir la tetera.

key [ki:] n (for lock) llave f; (of piano, typewriter) tecla f; (of map) clave f ◆ adj clave (inv).

keyboard ['ki:bɔ:d] n teclado m.

keyhole ['ki:həʊl] n ojo m de la cerradura.

keypad ['ki:pæd] n teclado m.

key ring n llavero m.

kg (abbr of kilogram) kg.

kick [kɪk] n (of foot) patada f ◆ vt (with foot) dar una patada.

kickoff ['kɪkɒf] n saque m inicial.

kid [kɪd] n (inf) (child) crío m (-a f); (young person) chico m (-ca f) ◆ vi bromear.

kidnap ['kɪdnæp] vt secuestrar.

kidnaper ['kɪdnæpər] (Am) = **kidnapper**.

kidnapper ['kɪdnæpər] n (Br) secuestrador m (-ra f).

kidney ['kɪdnɪ] (pl -s) n riñón m.

kidney bean n judía f pinta.

kill [kɪl] vt matar; **my feet are ~ing me!** ¡los pies me están matando!

killer ['kɪlər] n asesino m (-na f).

kilo ['ki:ləʊ] (pl -s) n kilo m.

kilogram ['kɪləgræm] n kilogramo m.

kilometre ['kɪləmi:tər] n kilómetro m.

kilt [kɪlt] n falda f escocesa.

kind [kaɪnd] adj amable ◆ n tipo m; **~ of** (Am: inf) un poco, algo.

kindergarten ['kɪndəgɑ:tn] n jardín m de infancia.

kindly ['kaɪndlɪ] adv: **would you ~ ...?** ¿sería tan amable de ...?

kindness ['kaındnıs] n amabilidad f.

king [kıŋ] n rey m.

kingfisher ['kıŋ,fıʃə'] n martín m pescador.

king prawn n langostino m.

king-size bed n cama f gigante.

kiosk ['ki:ɒsk] n (for newspapers etc) quiosco m; (Br: phone box) cabina f.

kipper ['kıpə'] n arenque m ahumado.

kiss [kıs] n beso m ◆ vt besar.

kiss of life n boca a boca m inv.

kit [kıt] n (set, clothes) equipo m; (for assembly) modelo m para armar.

kitchen ['kıtʃın] n cocina f.

kitchen unit n módulo m de cocina.

kite [kaıt] n (toy) cometa f.

kitten ['kıtn] n gatito m.

kitty ['kıtı] n (for regular expenses) fondo m común.

kiwi fruit ['ki:wi:-] n kiwi m.

Kleenex® ['kli:neks] n kleenex® m inv.

km (abbr of kilometre) km.

km/h (abbr of kilometres per hour) km/h.

knack [næk] n: **I've got the ~ (of it)** he cogido el tranquillo.

knackered ['nækəd] adj (Br: inf) hecho(-cha) polvo.

knapsack ['næpsæk] n mochila f.

knee [ni:] n rodilla f.

kneecap ['ni:kæp] n rótula f.

kneel [ni:l] (Br pt & pp knelt [nelt], Am pt & pp knelt OR -ed) vi (be on one's knees) estar de rodillas; (go down on one's knees) arrodillarse.

knew [nju:] pt → know.

knickers ['nıkəz] npl (Br: underwear) bragas fpl.

knife [naıf] (pl knives) n cuchillo m.

knight [naıt] n (in history) caballero m; (in chess) caballo m.

knit [nıt] vt tejer.

knitted ['nıtıd] adj de punto.

knitting ['nıtıŋ] n (thing being knitted) punto m; (activity) labor f de punto.

knitting needle n aguja f de hacer punto.

knitwear ['nıtweə'] n género m de punto.

knives [naıvz] pl → knife.

knob [nɒb] n (on door etc) pomo m; (on machine) botón m.

knock [nɒk] n (at door) golpe m ◆ vt (hit) golpear; (one's head, leg) golpearse ◆ vi (at door etc) llamar □ **knock down** vt sep (pedestrian) atropellar; (building) derribar; (price) bajar; **knock out** vt sep (make unconscious) dejar sin conocimiento; (of competition) eliminar; **knock over** vt sep (glass, vase) volcar; (pedestrian) atropellar.

knocker ['nɒkə'] n (on door) aldaba f.

knot [nɒt] n nudo m.

know [nəʊ] (pt knew, pp known) vt (have knowledge of) saber; (language) saber hablar; (person, place) conocer; **to get to ~ sb** llegar a conocer a alguien; **to ~ about sthg**

(understand) saber de algo; *(have heard)* saber algo; **to ~ how to do sthg** saber hacer algo; **to ~ of** conocer; **to be ~n as** ser conocido como; **to let sb ~ sthg** avisar a alguien de algo; **you ~** *(for emphasis)* ¿sabes?

knowledge ['nɒlɪdʒ] *n* conocimiento *m*; **to my ~** que yo sepa.

known [nəʊn] *pp* ▸ **know**.

knuckle ['nʌkl] *n (of hand)* nudillo *m*; *(of pork)* jarrete *m*.

Koran [kɒ'rɑːn] *n*: **the ~** el Corán.

l *(abbr of litre)* l.

L *(abbr of learner)* L.

lab [læb] *n (inf)* laboratorio *m*.

label ['leɪbl] *n* etiqueta *f*.

labor ['leɪbər] *(Am)* = **labour**.

laboratory [*Br* lə'bɒrətrɪ, *Am* 'læbrə,tɔːrɪ] *n* laboratorio *m*.

labour ['leɪbər] *n (Br) (work)* trabajo *m*; **in ~** *(MED)* de parto.

labourer ['leɪbərər] *n* obrero *m* (-ra *f*).

Labour Party *n (Br)* partido *m* Laborista.

labour-saving *adj* que ahorra trabajo.

lace [leɪs] *n (material)* encaje *m*; *(for shoe)* cordón *m*.

lace-ups *npl* zapatos *mpl* con cordones.

lack [læk] *n* falta *f* ◆ *vt* carecer de ◆ *vi*: **to be ~ing** faltar.

lacquer ['lækər] *n* laca *f*.

lad [læd] *n (inf)* chaval *m*.

ladder ['lædər] *n (for climbing)* escalera *f* (de mano); *(Br: in tights)* carrera *f*.

ladies ['leɪdɪz] *n (Br)* lavabo *m* de señoras.

ladies' room *(Am)* = **ladies**.

ladieswear ['leɪdɪz,weər] *n* ropa *f* de señoras.

ladle ['leɪdl] *n* cucharón *m*.

lady ['leɪdɪ] *n (woman)* señora *f*; *(woman of high status)* dama *f*.

ladybird ['leɪdɪbɜːd] *n* mariquita *f*.

lag [læg] *vi* retrasarse; **to ~ behind** *(move more slowly)* rezagarse.

lager ['lɑːgər] *n* cerveza *f* rubia.

lagoon [lə'guːn] *n* laguna *f*.

laid [leɪd] *pt & pp* → **lay**.

lain [leɪn] *pp* → **lie**.

lake [leɪk] *n* lago *m*.

Lake District *n*: **the ~** el Distrito de los Lagos al noroeste de Inglaterra.

lamb [læm] *n* cordero *m*.

lamb chop *n* chuleta *f* de cordero.

lame [leɪm] *adj* cojo(-ja).

lamp [læmp] *n (light)* lámpara *f*; *(in street)* farola *f*.

lamppost ['læmppəʊst] *n* farol *m*.

lampshade ['læmpʃeɪd] *n* pantalla *f*.

land [lænd] *n* tierra *f*; *(property)* tierras *fpl* ◆ *vi (plane)* aterrizar;

(passengers) desembarcar; *(fall)* caer.

landing ['lændɪŋ] n *(of plane)* aterrizaje m; *(on stairs)* rellano m.

landlady ['lænd,leɪdɪ] n *(of house)* casera f; *(of pub)* dueña f.

landlord ['lændlɔːd] n *(of house)* casero m; *(of pub)* dueño m.

landmark ['lændmɑːk] n punto m de referencia.

landscape ['lændskeɪp] n paisaje m.

landslide ['lændslaɪd] n *(of earth, rocks)* desprendimiento m de tierras.

lane [leɪn] n *(in town)* calleja f; *(in country, on road)* camino m; **"get in ~"** señal que advierte a los conductores que tomen el carril adecuado.

language ['læŋgwɪdʒ] n *(of a people, country)* idioma m; *(system of communication, words)* lenguaje m.

Lanzarote [,lænzə'rɒtɪ] n Lanzarote.

lap [læp] n *(of person)* regazo m; *(of race)* vuelta f.

lapel [lə'pel] n solapa f.

lapse [læps] vi *(passport, membership)* caducar.

lard [lɑːd] n manteca f de cerdo.

larder ['lɑːdə'] n despensa f.

large [lɑːdʒ] adj grande.

largely ['lɑːdʒlɪ] adv en gran parte.

large-scale adj de gran escala.

lark [lɑːk] n alondra f.

laryngitis [,lærɪn'dʒaɪtɪs] n laringitis f inv.

lasagne [lə'zænjə] n lasaña f.

laser ['leɪzə'] n láser m.

lass [læs] n *(inf)* chavala f.

last [lɑːst] adj último(-ma) ◆ adv *(most recently)* por última vez; *(at the end)* en último lugar ◆ pron: the **~ to come** el último en venir; the **~ but one** el penúltimo (la penúltima); **the time before ~** la penúltima vez; **~ year** el año pasado; **the ~ year** el año pasado; **at ~** por fin.

lastly ['lɑːstlɪ] adv por último.

last-minute adj de última hora.

latch [lætʃ] n pestillo m; **to be on the ~** tener el pestillo echado.

late [leɪt] adj *(not on time)* con retraso; *(after usual time)* tardío(-a); *(dead)* difunto(-ta) ◆ adv *(not on time)* con retraso; *(after usual time)* tarde; **in ~ June** a finales de junio; **in the ~ afternoon** al final de la tarde; **~ in June** a finales de junio; **to be (running) ~** ir con retraso.

lately ['leɪtlɪ] adv últimamente.

late-night adj de última hora, de noche.

later ['leɪtə'] adj posterior ◆ adv: **~ (on)** más tarde; **at a ~ date** en una fecha posterior.

latest ['leɪtɪst] adj: **the ~ fashion** la última moda; **the ~** lo último; **at the ~** como muy tarde.

lather ['lɑːðə'] n espuma f.

Latin ['lætɪn] n latín m.

Latin America n América Latina.

Latin American adj latinoamericano(-na) ◆ n latinoamericano m *(-na f)*.

latitude ['lætɪtjuːd] n latitud f.

latter ['lætə'] n: **the ~** éste m *(-ta f)*.

laugh [lɑːf] n risa f ◆ vi reírse; **to have a ~** (Br: inf) pasarlo bomba ❑ **laugh at** vt fus reírse de.

laughter ['lɑːftər] n risa f.

launch [lɔːntʃ] vt (boat) botar; (new product) lanzar.

laund(e)rette [lɔːn'dret] n lavandería f.

laundry ['lɔːndrɪ] n (washing) ropa f sucia; (place) lavandería f.

lavatory ['lævətrɪ] n servicio m.

lavender ['lævəndər] n lavanda f.

lavish ['lævɪʃ] adj (meal, decoration) espléndido(-da).

law [lɔː] n ley f; (study) derecho m; **the ~** (JUR: set of rules) la ley, **to be against the ~** estar en contra de la ley.

lawn [lɔːn] n césped m.

lawnmower ['lɔːnmaʊər] n cortacésped m.

lawyer ['lɔːjər] n abogado m (-da f).

laxative ['læksətɪv] n laxante m.

lay [leɪ] (pt & pp laid) vt → **lie** ◆ vt (place) colocar; (egg) poner; **to ~ the table** poner la mesa ❑ **lay off** vt sep (worker) despedir; **lay on** vt sep proveer; **lay out** vt sep (display) disponer.

lay-by (pl lay-bys) n área f de descanso.

layer ['leɪər] n capa f.

layman ['leɪmən] (pl -men [-mən]) n lego m (-ga f).

layout ['leɪaʊt] n (of building, streets) trazado m.

lazy ['leɪzɪ] adj perezoso(-sa).

lb (abbr of pound) lb.

lead¹ [liːd] (pt & pp led) vt (take) llevar; (be in charge of) estar al frente de; (be in front of) encabezar ◆ vi (be winning) ir en cabeza ◆ n (for dog) correa f; (cable) cable m; **to ~ sb to do sthg** llevar a alguien a hacer algo; **to ~ to** (go to) conducir a; (result in) llevar a; **to ~ the way** guiar; **to be in the ~** llevar la delantera.

lead² [led] n (metal) plomo m; (for pencil) mina f ◆ adj de plomo.

leaded petrol ['ledɪd-] n gasolina f con plomo.

leader ['liːdər] n líder mf.

leadership ['liːdəʃɪp] n (position of leader) liderazgo m.

lead-free [led-] adj sin plomo.

leading ['liːdɪŋ] adj (most important) destacado(-da).

lead singer [liːd-] n cantante mf (de un grupo).

leaf [liːf] (pl leaves) n (of tree) hoja f.

leaflet ['liːflɪt] n folleto m.

league [liːg] n liga f.

leak [liːk] n (hole) agujero m; (of gas, water) escape m ◆ vi (roof, tank) tener goteras.

lean [liːn] (pt & pp leant [lent] OR -ed) adj (meat) magro(-gra); (person, animal) delgado y musculoso (delgada y musculosa) ◆ vi (bend) inclinarse ◆ vt: **to ~ sthg against sthg** apoyar algo contra algo, **to ~ on** apoyarse en; **to ~ forward** inclinarse hacia delante; **to ~ over** inclinarse.

leap [liːp] (pt & pp leapt [lept] OR -ed) vi saltar.

leap year n año m bisiesto.

learn [lɜːn] (pt & pp learnt OR -ed) vt aprender; **to ~ (how) to do**

sthg aprender a hacer algo; **to ~ about sthg** *(hear about)* enterarse de algo; *(study)* aprender algo.
learner (driver) ['lɜːnəʳ-] *n* conductor *m* principiante.
learnt [lɜːnt] *pt & pp →* **learn**.
lease [liːs] *n* arriendo *m* ◆ *vt* arrendar; **to ~ sthg from sb** arrendar algo de alguien; **to ~ sthg to sb** arrendar algo a alguien.
leash [liːʃ] *n* correa *f*.
least [liːst] *adj & adv* menos ◆ *pron:* **(the) ~** menos; **I have ~ food** soy la que menos comida tiene; **I like him ~** él es el que menos me gusta; **he paid (the) ~** es el que menos pagó; **it's the ~ you could do** es lo menos que puedes hacer; **at ~** *(with quantities, numbers)* por lo menos; *(to indicate an advantage)* al menos.
leather ['leðəʳ] *n* piel *f* ❑
leathers *npl* cazadora y pantalón de cuero utilizados por motociclistas.
leave [liːv] *(pt & pp* **left**) *vt* dejar; *(go away from)* salir de; *(not take away)* dejarse ◆ *vi (person)* marcharse; *(train, bus etc)* salir ◆ *vt (time off work)* permiso *m*; **to ~ a message** dejar un mensaje, ► **left** *vt* **leave behind** *vt sep (not take away)* dejar; **leave out** *vt sep* omitir.
leaves [liːvz] *pl →* **leaf**.
Lebanon ['lebənən] *n* Líbano.
lecture ['lektʃəʳ] *n (at university)* clase *f*; *(at conference)* conferencia *f*.
lecturer ['lektʃərəʳ] *n* profesor *m* (-ra *f*) (de universidad).
lecture theatre *n* aula *f*.
led [led] *pt & pp →* **lead¹**.
ledge [ledʒ] *n (of window)* alféizar *m*.

leek [liːk] *n* puerro *m*.
left [left] *pt & pp →* **leave** ◆ *adj (not right)* izquierdo(-da) ◆ *adv* a la izquierda ◆ *n* izquierda *f*; **on the ~** a la izquierda; **there are none ~** no queda ninguno (más).
left-hand *adj* izquierdo(-da).
left-hand drive *n* vehículo *m* con el volante a la izquierda.
left-handed [-'hændɪd] *adj (person)* zurdo(-da); *(implement)* para zurdos.
left-luggage locker *n (Br)* consigna *f* automática.
left-luggage office *n (Br)* consigna *f*.
left-wing *adj* de izquierdas.
leg [leg] *n (of person)* pierna *f*; *(of animal, table, chair)* pata *f*; *(of trousers)* pernera *f*; **~ of lamb** pierna de cordero.
legal ['liːgl] *adj* legal.
legal aid *n* ayuda financiera para personas que no poseen posibilidades económicas para pagar a un abogado.
legalize ['liːgəlaɪz] *vt* legalizar.
legal system *n* sistema *m* jurídico.
legend ['ledʒənd] *n* leyenda *f*.
leggings ['legɪŋz] *npl* mallas *fpl*.
legible ['ledʒɪbl] *adj* legible.
legislation [ledʒɪs'leɪʃn] *n* legislación *f*.
legitimate [lɪ'dʒɪtɪmət] *adj* legítimo(-ma).
leisure [*Br* 'leʒəʳ, *Am* 'liːʒəʳ] *n* ocio *m*.
leisure centre *n* centro *m* deportivo y cultural.
leisure pool *n* piscina *f* (recreativa).

lemon ['leman] n limón m.

lemonade [,lema'neɪd] n gaseosa f.

lemon curd [-kɜːd] n (Br) dulce para untar hecho con limón, huevos, mantequilla y azúcar.

lemon juice n zumo m de limón.

lemon meringue pie n tarta de masa quebrada con crema de limón y una capa de merengue.

lemon sole n platija f.

lemon tea n té m con limón.

lend [lend] (pt & pp lent) vt prestar; **to ~ sb sthg** prestarle algo a alguien.

length [leŋθ] n (in distance) longitud f, (in time) duración f; (of swimming pool) largo m.

lengthen ['leŋθən] vt alargar.

lens [lenz] n (of camera) objetivo m; (of glasses) lente f; (contact lens) lentilla f.

lent [lent] pt & pp → **lend**.

Lent [lent] n Cuaresma f.

lentils ['lentlz] npl lentejas fpl.

leopard ['lepəd] n leopardo m.

leopard-skin adj estampado(-da) en piel de leopardo.

leotard ['liːətɑːd] n body m.

leper ['lepəʳ] n leproso m (-sa f).

lesbian ['lezbɪən] adj lesbiano(-na) ◆ n lesbiana f.

less [les] adj, adv, & pron menos; **~ than 20** menos de 20; **I eat ~ than her** yo como menos que ella.

lesson ['lesn] n (class) clase f.

let [let] (pt & pp **let**) vt (allow) dejar; (rent out) alquilar; **to ~ sb do sthg** dejar hacer algo a alguien; **to ~ go of sthg** soltar algo; **to ~ sb**

have sthg prestar algo a alguien; **to ~ sb know sthg** avisar a alguien de algo; **~'s go!** ¡vamos!; **"to ~"** "se alquila" □ **let in** vt sep dejar entrar; **let off** vt sep (not punish) perdonar; **she ~ me off doing it** me dejó no hacerlo; **can you ~ me off at the station?** ¿puede dejarme en la estación?; **let out** vt sep (allow to go out) dejar salir.

letdown ['letdaʊn] n (inf) desilusión f.

lethargic [lə'θɑːdʒɪk] adj aletargado(-da).

letter ['letəʳ] n (written message) carta f; (of alphabet) letra f.

letterbox ['letəbɒks] n (Br) buzón m.

lettuce ['letɪs] n lechuga f.

leuk(a)emia [luː'kiːmɪə] n leucemia f.

level ['levl] adj (horizontal) plano(-na) ◆ n nivel m; (storey) planta f; **to be ~ with** (in height) estar a nivel de; (in standard) estar al mismo nivel que.

level crossing n (Br) paso m a nivel.

lever [Br 'liːvəʳ, Am 'levəʳ] n palanca f.

liability [,laɪə'bɪlətɪ] n (responsibility) responsabilidad f.

liable ['laɪəbl] adj: **to be ~ to do sthg** tener tendencia a hacer algo; **to be ~ for sthg** ser responsable de algo.

liaise [lɪ'eɪz] vi: **to ~ with** mantener contacto con.

liar ['laɪəʳ] n mentiroso m (-sa f).

liberal ['lɪbərəl] adj (tolerant) liberal; (generous) generoso(-sa).

Liberal Democrat Party *n* partido *m* demócrata liberal.

liberate ['lɪbəreɪt] *vt* liberar.

liberty ['lɪbətɪ] *n* libertad *f*.

librarian [laɪ'breərɪən] *n* bibliotecario *m* (-ria *f*).

library ['laɪbrərɪ] *n* biblioteca *f*.

Libya ['lɪbɪə] *n* Libia.

lice [laɪs] *npl* piojos *mpl*.

licence ['laɪsəns] *n* (*Br*) permiso *m* ♦ *vt* (*Am*) = **license**.

license ['laɪsəns] *vt* (*Br*) autorizar ♦ *n* (*Am*) = **licence**.

licensed ['laɪsənst] *adj* (*restaurant, bar*) autorizado(-da) para vender bebidas alcohólicas.

licensing hours ['laɪsənsɪŋ-] *npl* (*Br*) horario en que se autoriza la venta de bebidas alcohólicas al público en un "*pub*".

lick [lɪk] *vt* lamer.

lid [lɪd] *n* (*cover*) tapa *f*.

lie [laɪ] (*pt* **lay**, *pp* **lain**, *cont* **lying**) *n* mentira *f* ♦ *vi* (*tell lie: pt & pp* **lied**) mentir; (*be horizontal*) estar echado; (*lie down*) echarse; (*be situated*) encontrarse; **to tell ~s** contar mentiras; **to ~ about sthg** mentir respecto a algo ❑ **lie down** *vi* acostarse.

lieutenant [*Br* lef'tenənt, *Am* luː'tenənt] *n* teniente *m*.

life [laɪf] (*pl* **lives**) *n* vida *f*.

life assurance *n* seguro *m* de vida.

life belt *n* salvavidas *m inv*.

lifeboat ['laɪfbəʊt] *n* (*launched from shore*) bote *m* salvavidas; (*launched from ship*) lancha *f* de salvamento.

lifeguard ['laɪfɡɑːd] *n* soco-

rrista *mf*.

life jacket *n* chaleco *m* salvavidas.

lifelike ['laɪflaɪk] *adj* realista.

life preserver [-prɪ'zɜːvər] *n* (*Am*) (*life belt*) salvavidas *m inv*; (*life jacket*) chaleco *m* salvavidas.

life-size *adj* de tamaño natural.

lifespan ['laɪfspæn] *n* vida *f*.

lifestyle ['laɪfstaɪl] *n* estilo *m* de vida.

lift [lɪft] *n* (*Br: elevator*) ascensor *m* ♦ *vt* (*raise*) levantar ♦ *vi* (*in colour*) claro(-ra); (*rain*) fino(-na) ♦ *n* luz *f*; (*for cigarette*) fuego *m* ♦ *vt* (*fire, cigarette*) encender; (*room, stage*) iluminar; **have you got a ~?** ¿tienes fuego?; **to set ~ to sthg** prender fuego a algo ❑ **lights** (*traffic lights*) semáforo *m*;

light up *vt sep* (*house, road*) iluminar ♦ *vi* (*inf: light a cigarette*) encender un cigarrillo.

light bulb *n* bombilla *f*.

lighter ['laɪtər] *n* mechero *m*.

light-hearted [-'hɑːtɪd] *adj* alegre.

lighthouse ['laɪthaʊs, *pl* -haʊzɪz] *n* faro *m*.

lighting ['laɪtɪŋ] *n* iluminación *f*.

light meter *n* contador *m* de la luz.

lightning ['laɪtnɪŋ] *n* relámpagos *mpl*.

lightweight ['laɪtweɪt] *adj* (*clothes, object*) ligero(-ra).

like [laɪk] *prep* como; (*typical of*)

típico de ◆ *vt (want)* querer; **I ~ beer** me gusta la cerveza; **I ~ them** me gustan; **I ~ doing it** me gusta hacerlo; **what's it ~?** ¿cómo es?; **~ that** así; **~ this** así; **to look ~ sb/sthg** parecerse a algo/a algo; **I'd ~ to come** me gustaría venir; **I'd ~ to sit down** quisiera sentarme; **I'd ~ a drink** me apetece tomar algo.

likelihood ['laɪklɪhʊd] *n* probabilidad *f.*

likely ['laɪklɪ] *adj* probable.

likeness ['laɪknɪs] *n (similarity)* parecido *m.*

likewise ['laɪkwaɪz] *adv* del mismo modo.

lilac ['laɪlək] *adj* lila *(inv).*

Lilo® ['laɪləʊ] *(pl* **-s)** *n (Br)* colchoneta *f.*

lily ['lɪlɪ] *n* azucena *f.*

lily of the valley *n* lirio *m* de los valles.

limb [lɪm] *n* miembro *m.*

lime [laɪm] *n (fruit)* lima *f,* **(juice)** refresco *m* de lima.

limestone ['laɪmstəʊn] *n* piedra *f* caliza.

limit ['lɪmɪt] *n* límite *m* ◆ *vt* limitar; **the city ~s** los límites de la ciudad.

limited ['lɪmɪtɪd] *adj* limitado(-da).

limp [lɪmp] *adj* flojo(-ja) ◆ *vi* cojear.

line [laɪn] *n* línea *f*; *(row)* fila *f*; *(Am: queue)* cola *f*; *(of words on page)* renglón *m*; *(of poem, song)* verso *m*; *(for fishing)* sedal *m*; *(for washing, rope)* cuerda *f*; *(railway track)* vía *f*; *(of business, work)* especialidad *f*;

(type of food) surtido *m* ◆ *vt (coat, drawers)* forrar; **in ~** *(aligned)* alineado(-da); **it's a bad ~** hay interferencias; **the ~ is engaged** está comunicando; **to drop sb a ~** *(inf)* escribir unas letras a alguien; **to stand in ~** *(Am)* hacer cola ❑ **line up** *vt sep (arrange)* programar ◆ *vi* alinearse.

lined [laɪnd] *adj (paper)* de rayas.

linen ['lɪnɪn] *n (cloth)* lino *m*; *(tablecloths, sheets)* ropa *f* blanca.

liner ['laɪnər] *n (ship)* transatlántico *m.*

linesman ['laɪnzmən] *(pl* **-men** [-mən]) *n* juez *mf* de línea.

linger ['lɪŋgər] *vi (in place)* rezagarse.

lingerie ['lænʒərɪ] *n* lencería *f.*

lining ['laɪnɪŋ] *n* forro *m.*

link [lɪŋk] *n (connection)* conexión *f*; *(between countries, companies)* vínculo *m* ◆ *vt (connect)* conectar; **rail ~** enlace *m* ferroviario; **road ~** conexión de carreteras.

lino ['laɪnəʊ] *n (Br)* linóleo *m.*

lion ['laɪən] *n* león *m.*

lioness ['laɪənes] *n* leona *f.*

lip [lɪp] *n* labio *m.*

lip salve [-sælv] *n* protector *m* labial.

lipstick ['lɪpstɪk] *n* barra *f* de labios.

liqueur [lɪˈkjʊər] *n* licor *m.*

liquid ['lɪkwɪd] *n* líquido *m.*

liquor ['lɪkər] *n (Am)* bebida *f* alcohólica.

liquorice ['lɪkərɪs] *n* regaliz *m.*

lisp [lɪsp] *n* ceceo *m.*

list [lɪst] *n* lista *f* ◆ *vt* hacer una lista de.

listen ['lɪsn] *vi*: **to ~ (to)** *(to person, sound, radio)* escuchar; *(to advice)* hacer caso (de).

listener ['lɪsnəʳ] *n (to radio)* oyente *mf*.

lit [lɪt] *pt & pp* → **light**.

liter ['liːtəʳ] *(Am)* = **litre**.

literally ['lɪtərəlɪ] *adv* literalmente.

literary ['lɪtərərɪ] *adj* literario(-ria).

literature ['lɪtrətʃəʳ] *n* literatura *f*; *(printed information)* folletos *mpl* informativos.

litre ['liːtəʳ] *n (Br)* litro *m*.

litter ['lɪtəʳ] *n* basura *f*.

litterbin ['lɪtəbɪn] *n (Br)* papelera *f (en la calle)*.

little ['lɪtl] *adj* pequeño(-ña); *(distance, time)* corto(-ta); *(not much)* poco(-ca) ◆ *adv* poco ◆ *pron*: **I have very ~** tengo muy poco; **as ~ as possible** lo menos posible; **~ by ~** poco a poco; **a ~** *pron & adv* un poco; **a ~ sugar** un poco de azúcar; **a ~ while** un rato.

little finger *n* meñique *m*.

live[1] [lɪv] *vi* vivir; **to ~ with sb** vivir con alguien ❏ **live together** *vi* vivir juntos.

live[2] [laɪv] *adj (alive)* vivo(-va); *(programme, performance)* en directo; *(wire)* cargado(-da) ◆ *adv* en directo.

lively ['laɪvlɪ] *adj (person)* vivaz; *(place, atmosphere)* animado(-da).

liver ['lɪvəʳ] *n* hígado *m*.

lives [laɪvz] *pl* → **life**.

living ['lɪvɪŋ] *adj (alive)* vivo(-va) ◆ *n*: **to earn a ~** ganarse la vida; **what do you do for a ~?** ¿en qué

trabajas?

living room *n* sala *f* de estar.

lizard ['lɪzəd] *n* lagartija *f*.

load [ləʊd] *n (thing carried)* carga *f* ◆ *vt* cargar; **~s of** *(inf)* un montón de.

loaf [ləʊf] *(pl* **loaves)** *n*: **~ (of bread)** barra *f* de pan.

loan [ləʊn] *n* préstamo *m* ◆ *vt* prestar.

loathe [ləʊð] *vt* detestar.

loaves [ləʊvz] *pl* → **loaf**.

lobby ['lɒbɪ] *n (hall)* vestíbulo *m*.

lobster ['lɒbstəʳ] *n* langosta *f*.

local ['ləʊkl] *adj* local ◆ *n (inf) (local person)* vecino *m* (del lugar); *(Br: pub)* = bar *m* del barrio; *(Am: bus)* autobús *m* urbano; *(Am: train)* tren *m* de cercanías.

local anaesthetic *n* anestesia *f* local.

local call *n* llamada *f* urbana.

local government *n* administración *f* local.

locate [*Br* ləʊˈkeɪt, *Am* ˈləʊkeɪt] *vt (find)* localizar; **to be ~d** estar situado.

location [ləʊˈkeɪʃn] *n (place)* situación *f*.

loch [lɒk] *n (Scot)* lago *m*.

lock [lɒk] *n (on door, drawer)* cerradura *f*; *(for bike)* candado *m*; *(on canal)* esclusa *f* ◆ *vt (fasten with key)* cerrar con llave; *(keep safely)* poner bajo llave ◆ *vi (become stuck)* bloquearse ❏ **lock in** *vt sep (accidentally)* dejar encerrado; **lock out** *vt sep (accidentally)* dejar fuera accidentalmente; **lock up** *vt sep (imprison)* encarcelar ◆ *vi* cerrar con llave.

locker [ˈlɒkəʳ] n taquilla f.

locker room n (Am) vestuario m (con taquillas).

locket [ˈlɒkɪt] n guardapelo m.

locomotive [ˌləʊkəˈməʊtɪv] n locomotora f.

locum [ˈləʊkəm] n interino m (-na f).

locust [ˈləʊkəst] n langosta f (insecto).

lodge [lɒdʒ] n (for hunters, skiers) refugio m ♦ vi alojarse.

lodger [ˈlɒdʒəʳ] n huésped mf.

lodgings [ˈlɒdʒɪnz] npl habitación f alquilada.

loft [lɒft] n desván m.

log [lɒg] n tronco m.

logic [ˈlɒdʒɪk] n lógica f.

logical [ˈlɒdʒɪkl] adj lógico(-ca).

logo [ˈləʊgəʊ] (pl -s) n logotipo m.

loin [lɔɪn] n lomo m.

loiter [ˈlɔɪtəʳ] vi merodear.

lollipop [ˈlɒlɪpɒp] n chupachús m inv.

lolly [ˈlɒlɪ] n (inf) (lollipop) chupachús m inv; (Br: ice lolly) polo m.

London [ˈlʌndən] n Londres.

Londoner [ˈlʌndənəʳ] n londinense mf.

lonely [ˈləʊnlɪ] adj (person) solo(-la), (place) solitario(-ria).

long [lɒŋ] adj largo(-ga) ♦ adv mucho (tiempo); it's 2 metres ~ mide 2 metros de largo; it's two hours ~ dura dos horas; how ~ is it? (in distance) ¿cuánto mide (de largo)?; (in time) ¿cuánto tiempo dura?; a ~ time mucho tiempo; all day ~ todo el día; as ~ as mientras (que); for ~ mucho tiempo; I'm no ~er interested ya no me interesa;

so ~! (inf) ¡hasta luego! ❑ **long for** vt fus desear vivamente.

long-distance call n conferencia f (telefónica).

long drink n combinado de alcohol y refresco.

long-haul adj de larga distancia.

longitude [ˈlɒndʒɪtjuːd] n longitud f.

long jump n salto m de longitud.

long-life adj de larga duración.

longsighted [ˌlɒŋˈsaɪtɪd] adj présbita.

long-term adj a largo plazo.

long wave n onda f larga.

longwearing [ˌlɒŋˈweərɪŋ] adj (Am) duradero(-ra).

loo [luː] (pl -s) n (Br: inf) wáter m.

look [lʊk] n (act of looking) mirada f; (appearance) aspecto m ♦ vi (with eyes, search) mirar; (seem) parecer; you mustn't ~ well no tienes muy buen aspecto; to ~ onto dar a; to have a ~ (see) echar un vistazo; (search) buscar; (good) ~s atractivo m (físico); I'm just ~ing (in shop) solamente estoy mirando; ~ out! ¡cuidado! ❑ **look after** vt fus (person) cuidar; (matter, arrangements) encargarse de; **look at** vt fus (observe) mirar; (examine) examinar; **look for** vt fus buscar; **look forward to** vt fus esperar (con ilusión); **look out for** vt fus estar atento a; **look round** vt fus (city, museum) visitar; (shop) mirar ♦ vi volver la cabeza; **look up** vt sep (in dictionary, phone book) buscar.

loony [ˈluːnɪ] n (inf) chiflado m (-da f).

loop [lu:p] n lazo m.

loose [lu:s] adj (not fixed firmly) flojo(-ja); (sweets, sheets of paper) suelto(-ta); (clothes) ancho(-cha); **to let sthg/sb ~** soltar algo/a alguien.

loosen ['lu:sn] vt aflojar.

lop-sided [-'saɪdɪd] adj ladeado(-da).

lord [lɔ:d] n (member of nobility) lord m, título de nobleza británica.

lorry ['lɒrɪ] n (Br) camión m.

lorry driver n (Br) camionero m (-ra f).

lose [lu:z] (pt & pp lost) vt perder; (subj: watch, clock) atrasarse ◆ vi perder; **to ~ weight** adelgazar.

loser ['lu:zə'] n (in contest) perdedor m (-ra f).

loss [lɒs] n pérdida f.

lost [lɒst] pt & pp → **lose** ◆ adj perdido(-da); **to get ~** (lose way) perderse.

lost-and-found office n (Am) oficina f de objetos perdidos.

lost property office n (Br) oficina f de objetos perdidos.

lot [lɒt] n (group of things) grupo m; (at auction) lote m; (Am: car-park) aparcamiento m; **a ~** (large amount) mucho(-cha), muchos(-chas) (pl); (to a great extent, often) mucho; **a ~ of time** mucho tiempo; **a ~ of problems** muchos problemas; **~s (of)** mucho(-cha), muchos(-chas) (pl); **the ~** (everything) todo.

lotion ['ləʊʃn] n loción f.

lottery ['lɒtərɪ] n lotería f.

loud [laʊd] adj (voice, music, noise) alto(-ta); (colour, clothes) chillón(-ona).

loudspeaker [ˌlaʊd'spi:kə'] n altavoz m.

lounge [laʊndʒ] n (in house) salón m; (at airport) sala f de espera.

lounge bar n (Br) salón-bar m.

lousy ['laʊzɪ] adj (inf: poor-quality) cochambroso(-sa).

lout [laʊt] n gamberro m (-rra f).

love [lʌv] n amor m; (strong liking) pasión f; (in tennis) cero m ◆ vt querer; **I ~ music** me encanta la música; **I'd ~ a coffee** un café me vendría estupendamente; **I ~ playing tennis** me encanta jugar al tenis; **to be in ~ (with)** estar enamorado (de); **(with) ~ from** (in letter) un abrazo (de).

love affair n aventura f amorosa.

lovely ['lʌvlɪ] adj (very beautiful) guapísimo(-ma); (very nice) precioso(-sa).

lover ['lʌvə'] n amante mf.

loving ['lʌvɪŋ] adj cariñoso(-sa).

low [ləʊ] adj bajo(-ja); (quality, opinion) malo(-la); (sound, note) grave; (supply) escaso(-sa); (depressed) deprimido(-da) ◆ n (area of low pressure) zona f de baja presión (atmosférica); **we're ~ on petrol** se está terminando la gasolina.

low-alcohol adj bajo(-ja) en alcohol.

low-calorie adj bajo(-ja) en calorías.

low-cut adj escotado(-da).

lower ['ləʊə'] adj inferior ◆ vt (move downwards) bajar; (reduce) reducir.

lower sixth n (Br) primer curso de enseñanza secundaria pre-

universitaria para alumnos de 17 años
que preparan sus "A-levels".

low-fat *adj* de bajo contenido graso.

low tide *n* marea *f* baja.

loyal ['lɔɪəl] *adj* leal.

loyalty ['lɔɪəltɪ] *n* lealtad *f*.

lozenge ['lɒzɪndʒ] *n (sweet)* caramelo *m* para la tos.

LP *n* LP *m*.

L-plate ['el-] *n (Br)* placa *f* de la L *(de prácticas)*.

Ltd *(abbr of limited)* S L.

lubricate ['lu:brɪkeɪt] *vt* lubricar.

luck [lʌk] *n* suerte *f*; **bad ~** mala suerte; **good ~!** ¡buena suerte!; **with ~** con un poco de suerte.

luckily ['lʌkɪlɪ] *adv* afortunadamente.

lucky ['lʌkɪ] *adj (person, escape)* afortunado(-da); *(event, situation)* oportuno(-na); *(number, colour)* de la suerte; **to be ~** tener suerte.

ludicrous ['lu:dɪkrəs] *adj* ridículo(-la).

lug [lʌg] *vt (inf)* arrastrar.

luggage ['lʌgɪdʒ] *n* equipaje *m*.

luggage compartment *n* maletero *m (en tren)*.

luggage locker *n* consigna *f* automática.

luggage rack *n (on train)* redecilla *f (para equipaje)*.

lukewarm ['lu:kwɔ:m] *adj* tibio(-bia).

lull [lʌl] *n* intervalo *m*.

lullaby ['lʌləbaɪ] *n* nana *f*.

lumbago [lʌm'beɪgəʊ] *n* lumbago *m*.

lumber ['lʌmbər] *n (Am: timber)*

maderos *mpl*.

luminous ['lu:mɪnəs] *adj* luminoso(-sa).

lump [lʌmp] *n (of coal, mud, butter)* trozo *m*; *(of sugar)* terrón *m*; *(on body)* bulto *m*.

lump sum *n* suma *f* global.

lumpy ['lʌmpɪ] *adj (sauce)* grumoso(-sa); *(mattress)* lleno(-na) de bultos.

lunatic ['lu:nətɪk] *n (pej)* loco *m* (-ca *f*).

lunch [lʌntʃ] *n* comida *f*, almuerzo *m*; **to have ~** comer, almorzar.

luncheon ['lʌntʃən] *n (fml)* almuerzo *m*.

luncheon meat *n* conserva *f* de carne de cerdo y cereales.

lunch hour *n* hora *f* del almuerzo.

lunchtime ['lʌntʃtaɪm] *n* hora *f* del almuerzo.

lung [lʌŋ] *n* pulmón *m*.

lunge [lʌndʒ] *vi*: **to ~ at** arremeter contra.

lurch [lɜ:tʃ] *vi* tambalearse.

lure [ljʊər] *vt* atraer con engaños.

lurk [lɜ:k] *vi (person)* estar al acecho.

lush [lʌʃ] *adj* exuberante.

lust [lʌst] *n (sexual desire)* lujuria *f*.

Luxembourg ['lʌksəmbɜ:g] *n* Luxemburgo.

luxurious [lʌg'zʊərɪəs] *adj* lujoso(-sa).

luxury ['lʌkʃərɪ] *adj* de lujo ◆ *n* lujo *m*.

lying ['laɪɪŋ] *cont* → **lie**.

lyrics ['lɪrɪks] *npl* letra *f*.

m 170

m (abbr of metre) m ◆ abbr = **mile**.

M (Br: abbr of motorway) A; (abbr of medium) M.

MA n (abbr of Master of Arts) máster en letras.

mac [mæk] n (Br: inf) gabardina f.

macaroni [,mækə'rəʊnɪ] n macarrones mpl.

macaroni cheese n macarrones mpl con queso.

machine [mə'ʃi:n] n máquina f.

machinegun [mə'ʃi:ngʌn] n ametralladora f.

machinery [mə'ʃi:nərɪ] n maquinaria f.

machine-washable adj lavable a máquina.

mackerel ['mækrəl] (pl inv) n caballa f.

mackintosh ['mækɪntɒʃ] n (Br) gabardina f.

mad [mæd] adj loco(-ca); (angry) furioso(-sa); (uncontrolled) desenfrenado(-da); **to be ~ about** (inf: like a lot) estar loco por; **like ~** (run) como un loco.

Madam ['mædəm] n señora f.

made [meɪd] pt & pp → **make**.

madeira [mə'dɪərə] n madeira m.

made-to-measure adj hecho(-cha) a medida.

madness ['mædnɪs] n locura f.

magazine [,mægə'zi:n] n revista f.

maggot ['mægət] n gusano m (larva).

magic ['mædʒɪk] n magia f.

magician [mə'dʒɪʃn] n (conjurer) prestidigitador m (-ra f).

magistrate ['mædʒɪstreɪt] n magistrado m (-da f).

magnet ['mægnɪt] n imán m.

magnetic [mæg'netɪk] adj magnético(-ca).

magnificent [mæg'nɪfɪsənt] adj magnífico(-ca).

magnifying glass ['mægnɪfaɪɪŋ-] n lupa f.

mahogany [mə'hɒgənɪ] n caoba f.

maid [meɪd] n (servant) criada f.

maiden name ['meɪdn-] n nombre m de soltera.

mail [meɪl] n (letters) correspondencia f; (system) correo m ◆ vt (Am) enviar por correo.

mailbox ['meɪlbɒks] n (Am) buzón m.

mailman ['meɪlmən] (pl -men [-mən]) n (Am) cartero m.

mail order n pedido m por correo.

main [meɪn] adj principal.

main course n plato m principal.

main deck n cubierta f principal.

mainland ['meɪnlənd] n: **the ~** el continente.

main line n línea f férrea principal.

mainly ['meɪnlɪ] adv principalmente.

main road n carretera f principal.

mains [meɪnz] npl: **the ~** (for electricity) la red eléctrica; (for gas, water) la tubería principal.

main street n (Am) calle f principal.

maintain [meɪn'teɪn] vt mantener.

maintenance ['meɪntənəns] n (of car, machine) mantenimiento m; (money) pensión f de manutención.

maisonctte [ˌmeɪzə'net] n (Br) piso m dúplex.

maize [meɪz] n maíz m.

major ['meɪdʒəʳ] adj (important) importante, (most important) principal ◆ n (MIL) comandante m ◆ vi (Am): **to ~ in** especializarse en.

Majorca [mə'jɔːkə, mə'dʒɔːkə] n Mallorca f.

majority [mə'dʒɒrɪtɪ] n mayoría f.

major road n carretera f principal.

make [meɪk] (pt & pp made) vt 1. (produce, construct) hacer; **to be made of** estar hecho de; **to ~ lunch/supper** hacer la comida/cena; **made in Japan** fabricado en Japón.
2. (perform, do) hacer; **to ~ a mistake** cometer un error; **to ~ a phone call** hacer una llamada.
3. (cause to be, do) hacer; **to ~ sb sad** poner triste a alguien; **to ~ sb happy** hacer feliz a alguien; **the ice made her slip** el hielo le hizo res-

balar; **to ~ sb do sthg** (force) obligar a alguien a hacer algo.
4. (amount to, total) hacer; **that ~s £5** eso hace 5 libras.
5. (calculate) calcular; **I ~ it seven o'clock** calculo que serán las siete.
6. (money) ganar; (profit) obtener; (loss) sufrir.
7. (inf: arrive in time for): **I don't think we'll ~ the 10 o'clock train** no creo que lleguemos para el tren de las diez.
8. (friend, enemy) hacer.
9. (have qualities for) ser, **this would ~ a lovely bedroom** esta habitación sería preciosa como dormitorio.
10. (bed) hacer.
11. (in phrases): **to ~ do** arreglárselas; **to ~ good** (compensate for) indemnizar; **to ~ it** (arrive in time) llegar a tiempo; (be able to go) poder ir.
◆ n (of product) marca f.
❑ **make out** vt sep (form) rellenar; (cheque, receipt) extender; (see) divisar; (hear) entender; **make up** vt sep (invent) inventar; (comprise) formar; (difference) cubrir; **make up for** vt fus compensar.

makeshift ['meɪkʃɪft] adj improvisado(-da).

make-up n maquillaje m.

malaria [mə'leərɪə] n malaria f.

Malaysia [mə'leɪzɪə] n Malasia f.

male [meɪl] adj (person) masculino(-na); (animal) macho ◆ n (animal) macho m.

malfunction [mæl'fʌŋkʃn] vi (fml) funcionar mal.

malignant [mə'lɪgnənt] adj (disease, tumour) maligno(-na).

mall 172

mall [mɔːl] n zona f comercial peatonal.

i MALL

Una gran zona ajardinada en el centro de Washington DC, "the Mall" se extiende desde el Capitolio al Monumento a Lincoln. A lo largo de ello se encuentran los distintos museos del Smithsonian Institute, varios museos de arte, la Casa Blanca y los monumentos a Washington y a Jefferson. En el extremo oeste se halla "the Wall", donde se han inscrito los nombres de los soldados muertos en la guerra de Vietnam.
En el Reino Unido, "the Mall" es el nombre de la larga avenida londinense que va desde el Palacio de Buckingham hasta Trafalgar Square.

mallet ['mælɪt] n mazo m.
malt [mɔːlt] n malta f.
maltreat [,mæl'triːt] vt maltratar.
malt whisky n whisky m de malta.
mammal ['mæml] n mamífero m.
man [mæn] (pl **men**) n hombre m; (mankind) el hombre ♦ vt: **the lines are manned 24 hours a day** las líneas están abiertas las 24 horas.
manage ['mænɪdʒ] vt (company, business) dirigir; (suitcase, job, food) poder con ♦ vi (cope) arreglárselas; **can you ~ Friday?** ¿te viene bien el viernes?; **to ~ to do sthg** conseguir hacer algo.
management ['mænɪdʒmənt] n

(people in charge) dirección f; (control, running) gestión f.
manager ['mænɪdʒər] n (of business, bank) director m (-ra f); (of shop) jefe m (-fa f); (of sports team) = entrenador m (-ra f).
manageress [,mænɪdʒə'res] n (of business, bank) directora f; (of shop) jefa f.
managing director ['mænɪdʒɪŋ-] n director m (-ra f) general.
mandarin ['mændərɪn] n (fruit) mandarina f.
mane [meɪn] n crin f.
maneuver [mə'nuːvər] (Am) = manoeuvre.
mangetout [,mɒnʒ'tuː] n vaina de guisante tierna que se come entera.
mangle ['mæŋgl] vt aplastar.
mango ['mæŋgəʊ] (pl **-es** OR **-s**) n mango m.
Manhattan [,mæn'hætn] n Manhattan m.

i MANHATTAN

Manhattan es el distrito central de Nueva York y se divide en los tres barrios llamados "Downtown", "Midtown" y "Upper". Allí se encuentran rascacielos tan famosos como el Empire State Building y el Chrysler Building y lugares tan conocidos como Central Park, la Quinta Avenida, Broadway, la Estatua de la Libertad y Greenwich Village.

manhole ['mænhəʊl] n registro m (de alcantarillado).
maniac ['meɪnɪæk] n (inf: wild per-

son) maníaco *m* (-ca *f*).

manicure ['mænɪkjʊəʳ] *n* manicura *f*.

manifold ['mænɪfəʊld] *n* colector *m*.

manipulate [məˈnɪpjʊleɪt] *vt (person)* manipular; *(machine, controls)* manejar.

mankind [ˌmænˈkaɪnd] *n* la humanidad.

manly ['mænlɪ] *adj* varonil.

man-made *adj* artificial.

manner ['mænəʳ] *n (way)* manera *f* □ **manners** *npl* modales *mpl*.

manoeuvre [məˈnuːvəʳ] *n (Br)* maniobra *f* ♦ *vt (Br)* maniobrar.

manor ['mænəʳ] *n* casa *f* solariega.

mansion ['mænʃn] *n* casa *f* solariega.

manslaughter ['mænˌslɔːtəʳ] *n* homicidio *m* no premeditado.

mantelpiece ['mæntlpiːs] *n* repisa *f* de la chimenea.

manual ['mænjʊəl] *adj* manual ♦ *n* manual *m*.

manufacture [ˌmænjʊˈfæktʃəʳ] *n* fabricación *f* ♦ *vt* fabricar.

manufacturer [ˌmænjʊˈfæktʃərəʳ] *n* fabricante *mf*.

manure [məˈnjʊəʳ] *n* estiércol *m*.

many ['menɪ] *(compar* **more**, *superl* **most**) *adj* muchos(-chas) ♦ *pron* muchos *mpl* (-chas *fpl*); **as** ... tantos(-tas) como ... ; **twice as ~ as** el doble que; **how ~?** ¿cuántos(-tas)?; **so ~** tantos; **too ~** demasiados(-das).

map [mæp] *n (of town)* plano *m*; *(of country)* mapa *m*.

maple syrup ['meɪpl-] *n* jarabe

de arce que se come con crepes, etc.

Mar. *(abbr of* March) mar.

marathon ['mærəθən] *n* maratón *m*.

marble ['mɑːbl] *n (stone)* mármol *m*; *(glass ball)* canica *f*.

march [mɑːtʃ] *n (demonstration)* manifestación *f* ♦ *vi (walk quickly)* dirigirse resueltamente.

March [mɑːtʃ] *n* marzo *m*, → **September**.

mare [meəʳ] *n* yegua *f*.

margarine [ˌmɑːdʒəˈriːn] *n* margarina *f*.

margin ['mɑːdʒɪn] *n* margen *m*.

marina [məˈriːnə] *n* puerto *m* deportivo.

marinated ['mærɪneɪtɪd] *adj* marinado(-da).

marital status ['mærɪtl-] *n* estado *m* civil.

mark [mɑːk] *n* marca *f*; *(SCH)* nota *f* ♦ *vt (blemish)* manchar; *(put symbol on)* marcar; *(correct)* corregir; *(show position of)* señalar; **(gas) ~ five** número cinco (del horno).

marker pen ['mɑːkə-] *n* rotulador *m*.

market ['mɑːkɪt] *n* mercado *m*.

marketing ['mɑːkɪtɪŋ] *n* marketing *m*.

marketplace ['mɑːkɪtpleɪs] *n* mercado *m*.

markings ['mɑːkɪŋz] *npl (on animal, plant)* manchas *fpl*; *(on road)* marcas *fpl* viales.

marmalade ['mɑːməleɪd] *n* mermelada *f (de frutos cítricos)*.

marquee [mɑːˈkiː] *n* carpa *f*.

marriage ['mærɪdʒ] *n (event)* boda *f*; *(time married)* matrimonio *m*.

married ['mærɪd] *adj* casado(-da); **to get ~** casarse.

marrow ['mærəʊ] *n* (*vegetable*) calabacín *m* grande.

marry ['mærɪ] *vt* casarse con ◆ *vi* casarse.

marsh [mɑːʃ] *n* (*area*) zona *f* pantanosa.

martial arts [ˌmɑːʃl-] *npl* artes *fpl* marciales.

marvellous ['mɑːvələs] *adj* (*Br*) maravilloso(-sa).

marvelous ['mɑːvələs] (*Am*) = **marvellous**.

marzipan ['mɑːzɪpæn] *n* mazapán *m*.

mascara [mæs'kɑːrə] *n* rímel *m*.

masculine ['mæskjʊlɪn] *adj* masculino(-na); (*woman*) hombruno(-na).

mashed potatoes ['mæʃt-] *npl* puré *m* de patatas.

mask [mɑːsk] *n* máscara *f*.

masonry ['meɪsnrɪ] *n*: **falling ~** materiales que se desprenden de un edificio.

mass [mæs] *n* (*large amount*) montón *m*; (*RELIG*) misa *f*; **~es (of)** (*inf*) montones (de).

massacre ['mæsəkər] *n* masacre *f*.

massage [*Br* 'mæsɑːʒ, *Am* mə'sɑːʒ] *n* masaje *m* ◆ *vt* dar masajes a.

masseur [mæ'sɜːr] *n* masajista *m*.

masseuse [mæ'sɜːz] *n* masajista *f*.

massive ['mæsɪv] *adj* enorme.

mast [mɑːst] *n* (*on boat*) mástil *m*.

master ['mɑːstər] *n* (*at primary*

school) maestro *m*; (*at secondary school*) profesor *m*; (*of servant, dog*) amo *m* ◆ *vt* (*skill, language*) dominar.

masterpiece ['mɑːstəpiːs] *n* obra *f* maestra.

mat [mæt] *n* (*small rug*) esterilla *f*; (*for plate*) salvamanteles *m inv*; (*for glass*) posavasos *m inv*.

match [mætʃ] *n* (*for lighting*) cerilla *f*; (*game*) partido *m* ◆ *vt* (*in colour, design*) hacer juego con; (*be the same as*) coincidir con; (*be as good as*) competir con ◆ *vi* (*in colour, design*) hacer juego.

matchbox ['mætʃbɒks] *n* caja *f* de cerillas.

matching ['mætʃɪŋ] *adj* a juego.

mate [meɪt] *n* (*inf*) colega *mf* ◆ *vi* aparearse.

material [mə'tɪərɪəl] *n* (*substance*) material *m*; (*cloth*) tela *f*; (*information*) información *f* ❏ **materials** *npl*: **writing ~s** objetos *mpl* de escritorio.

maternity leave [mə'tɜːnətɪ-] *n* baja *f* por maternidad.

maternity ward [mə'tɜːnətɪ-] *n* sala *f* de maternidad.

math [mæθ] (*Am*) = **maths**.

mathematics [ˌmæθə'mætɪks] *n* matemáticas *fpl*.

maths [mæθs] *n* (*Br*) mates *fpl*.

matinée ['mætɪneɪ] *n* (*at cinema*) primera sesión *f*; (*at theatre*) función *f* de tarde.

matt [mæt] *adj* mate.

matter ['mætər] *n* (*issue, situation*) asunto *m*; (*physical material*) materia *f* ◆ *vi*: **winning is all that ~s** lo único que importa es ganar;

it doesn't ~ no importa; **no ~ what happens** pase lo que pase; **there's something the ~ with my car** algo le pasa a mi coche; **what's the ~?** ¿qué pasa?; **as a ~ of course** rutinariamente; **as a ~ of fact** en realidad.

mattress ['mætrɪs] n colchón m.

mature [mə'tjʊəʳ] adj (person, behaviour) maduro(-ra); (cheese) curado(-da); (wine) añejo(-ja).

mauve [məʊv] adj malva (inv).

max. [mæks] (abbr of maximum) máx.

maximum ['mæksɪməm] adj máximo(-ma) ◆ n máximo m.

may [meɪ] aux vb 1. (expressing possibility): **with the ~ it** rain puede que llueva; **they ~ have** lost puede que se hayan perdido.
2. (expressing permission): **~ I smoke?** ¿puedo fumar?; **you ~ sit, if you wish** puede sentarse si lo desea.
3. (when conceding a point): **it ~ be a long walk, but it's worth it** puede que sea una caminata, pero merece la pena.

May [meɪ] n mayo m, → September.

maybe ['meɪbi:] adv quizás.

mayonnaise [,meɪə'neɪz] n mayonesa f.

mayor [meəʳ] n alcalde m.

mayoress ['meəris] n esposa f del alcalde.

maze [meɪz] n laberinto m.

me [mi:] pron me; **she knows ~** me conoce; **it's ~** soy yo; **send it to ~** envíamelo; **tell ~** dime; **he's worse than ~** él aún es peor que yo; **with ~** conmigo; **without ~** sin mí.

meadow ['medəʊ] n prado m.

meal [mi:l] n comida f.

mealtime ['mi:ltaɪm] n hora f de comer.

mean [mi:n] (pt & pp meant) adj (miserly) tacaño(-ña); (unkind) mezquino(-na) ◆ vt (signify, matter) significar; (intend) querer decir; (be a sign of) indicar; **I ~ it** hablo en serio; **to ~ to do sthg** pensar hacer algo; **I didn't ~ to hurt you** no quería hacerte daño; **to be meant to do sthg** deber hacer algo; **it's meant to be good** dicen que es bueno.

meaning ['mi:nɪŋ] n (of word, phrase) significado m, (intention) sentido m.

meaningless ['mi:nɪŋlɪs] adj (irrelevant) sin importancia.

means [mi:nz] (pl inv) n (method) medio m ◆ npl (money) medios mpl; **by all ~!** ¡por supuesto!; **by ~ of** por medio de.

meant [ment] pt & pp → mean.

meantime ['mi:ntaɪm]: **in the meantime** adv mientras tanto.

meanwhile ['mi:nwaɪl] adv mientras tanto.

measles ['mi:zlz] n sarampión m.

measure ['meʒəʳ] vt medir ◆ n medida f; **the room ~s 10 m²** la habitación mide 10 m².

measurement ['meʒəmənt] n medida f □ **measurements** npl (of person) medidas fpl.

meat [mi:t] n carne f; **red ~** carnes rojas; **white ~** carnes blancas.

meatball ['mi:tbɔ:l] n albóndiga f.

mechanic [mɪ'kænɪk] n mecánico *m* (-ca *f*).

mechanical [mɪˈkænɪkl] *adj* (*device*) mecánico(-ca).

mechanism [ˈmekənɪzm] *n* mecanismo *m*.

medal [medl] *n* medalla *f*.

media [ˈmiːdjə] *n or npl*: **the ~** los medios de comunicación.

medical [ˈmedɪkl] *adj* médico(-ca) ◆ *n* chequeo *m* (médico).

medication [ˌmedrˈkeɪʃn] *n* medicación *f*.

medicine [ˈmedsɪn] *n* (*substance*) medicamento *m*; (*science*) medicina *f*.

medicine cabinet *n* botiquín *m*.

medieval [ˌmedrˈiːvl] *adj* medieval.

mediocre [ˌmiːdrˈəʊkəʳ] *adj* mediocre.

Mediterranean [ˌmedɪtəˈreɪnjən] *n*: **the ~** (*region*) el Mediterráneo; **the ~ (Sea)** el (Mar) Mediterráneo.

medium [ˈmiːdjəm] *adj* (*middle-sized*) mediano(-na); (*wine*) suave, semi; (*sherry*) medium.

medium-dry *adj* semiseco (-ca).

medium-sized [-saɪzd] *adj* de tamaño mediano.

medley [ˈmedlɪ] *n* (CULIN) selección *f*.

meet [miːt] (*pt & pp* met) *vt* (*by arrangement*) reunirse con; (*by chance*) encontrarse con; (*get to know*) conocer; (*go to collect*) ir a buscar; (*need, requirement*) satisfacer; (*cost, expenses*) cubrir ◆ *vi* (*by arrangement*) reunirse; (*by chance*)

encontrarse; (*get to know each other*) conocerse; (*intersect*) unirse; **~ me at the bar** espérame en el bar ❑ **meet up** *vi* reunirse; **meet with** *vt fus* (*problems, resistance*) encontrarse con; (*Am: by arrangement*) reunirse con.

meeting [ˈmiːtɪŋ] *n* (*for business*) reunión *f*.

meeting point *n* punto *m* de encuentro.

melody [ˈmelədɪ] *n* melodía *f*.

melon [ˈmelən] *n* melón *m*.

melt [melt] *vi* derretirse.

member [ˈmembəʳ] *n* (*of group, party, organization*) miembro *mf*; (*of club*) socio *m* (-cia *f*).

Member of Congress *n* miembro *mf* del Congreso (*de EEUU*).

Member of Parliament *n* diputado *m* (-da *f*) (*del parlamento británico*).

membership [ˈmembəʃɪp] *n* (*state of being a member*) afiliación *f*; (*members*) miembros *mpl*; (*of club*) socios *mpl*.

memorial [mɪˈmɔːrɪəl] *n* monumento *m* conmemorativo.

memorize [ˈmeməraɪz] *vt* memorizar.

memory [ˈmemərɪ] *n* (*ability to remember, of computer*) memoria *f*; (*thing remembered*) recuerdo *m*.

men [men] *pl* → **man**.

menacing [ˈmenəsɪn] *adj* amenazador(-ra).

mend [mend] *vt* arreglar.

menopause [ˈmenəpɔːz] *n* menopausia *f*.

men's room *n* (*Am*) servicio *m*

de caballeros.

menstruate ['menstruert] *vi* tener la menstruación.

menswear ['menzweə^r] *n* confección *f* de caballeros.

mental ['mentl] *adj* mental.

mental hospital *n* hospital *m* psiquiátrico.

mentally handicapped ['mentlɪ-] *adj* disminuido *m* psíquico (disminuida *f* psíquica) ◆ *npl*: **the ~** los disminuidos psíquicos.

mentally ill ['mentlɪ-] *adj*: to be **~** ser un enfermo mental (ser una enferma mental).

mention ['menʃn] *vt* mencionar; **don't ~ it!** ¡no hay de que!

menu ['menju:] *n* menú *m*; **children's ~** menú infantil.

merchandise ['mɜːtʃəndaɪz] *n* géneros *mpl*.

merchant marine [,mɜːtʃənt-mə'ri:n] *(Am)* = merchant navy.

merchant navy [,mɜːtʃənt-] *n (Br)* marina *f* mercante.

mercury ['mɜːkjʊrɪ] *n* mercurio *m*.

mercy ['mɜːsɪ] *n* compasión *f*.

mere [mɪə^r] *adj* simple; **a ~ two pounds** tan sólo dos libras.

merely ['mɪəlɪ] *adv* solamente.

merge [mɜːdʒ] *vi (combine)* mezclarse; **"merge"** *(Am)* cartel que indica que los coches que acceden a una autopista deben entrar en el carril de la derecha.

merger ['mɜːdʒə^r] *n* fusión *f*.

meringue [mə'ræŋ] *n* merengue *m*.

merit ['merɪt] *n* mérito *m*; *(in exam)* = notable *m*.

merry ['merɪ] *adj (cheerful)* alborozado(-da); *(inf: tipsy)* achispado(-da); **Merry Christmas!** ¡Feliz Navidad!

merry-go-round *n* tiovivo *m*.

mess [mes] *n (untidiness)* desorden *m*; *(difficult situation)* lío *m*; **in a ~** *(untidy)* desordenado ❑ **mess about** *vi (inf) (have fun)* divertirse; *(behave foolishly)* hacer el tonto; **to ~ about with sthg** *(interfere)* manosear algo; **mess up** *vt sep (inf: ruin, spoil)* estropear.

message ['mesɪdʒ] *n* mensaje *m*.

messenger ['mesɪndʒə^r] *n* mensajero *m* (-ra *f*).

messy ['mesɪ] *adj* desordenado(-da).

met [met] *pt & pp* → **meet**.

metal ['metl] *adj* metálico(-ca) ◆ *n* metal *m*.

metalwork ['metəlwɜːk] *n (craft)* metalistería *f*.

meter ['mi:tə^r] *n (device)* contador *m*; *(Am)* = metre.

method ['meθəd] *n* método *m*.

methodical [mɪ'θɒdɪkl] *adj* metódico(-ca).

meticulous [mɪ'tɪkjʊləs] *adj* meticuloso(-sa).

metre ['mi:tə^r] *n (Br)* metro *m*.

metric ['metrɪk] *adj* métrico(-ca).

mews [mju:z] *(pl inv)* *n (Br)* calle o patio de casas de lujo reconvertidas a partir de antiguas caballerizas.

Mexican ['meksɪkn] *adj* mejicano(-na) ◆ *n* mejicano *m* (-na *f*).

Mexico ['meksɪkəʊ] *n* Méjico *m*.

mg *(abbr of milligram)* mg.

miaow [mi:'aʊ] *vi (Br)* maullar.

mice [maɪs] pl → **mouse.**

microchip ['maɪkrəʊtʃɪp] n microchip m.

microphone ['maɪkrəfəʊn] n micrófono m.

microscope ['maɪkrəskəʊp] n microscopio m.

microwave (oven) ['maɪkrə-weɪv-] n microondas m inv.

midday [ˌmɪd'deɪ] n mediodía m.

middle ['mɪdl] n (in space) centro m; (in time) medio m ♦ adj del medio; **in the ~ of the road** en (el) medio de la carretera; **in the ~ of April** a mediados de abril; **to be in the ~ of doing sthg** estar haciendo algo.

middle-aged adj de mediana edad.

middle-class adj de clase media.

Middle East n: **the ~** el Oriente Medio.

middle name n segundo nombre m (de pila) (en un nombre compuesto).

middle school n etapa de la enseñanza secundaria británica para niños de 14 y 15 años.

midge [mɪdʒ] n mosquito m.

midget ['mɪdʒɪt] n enano m (-na f).

Midlands ['mɪdləndz] npl: **the ~** la región del centro de Inglaterra.

midnight ['mɪdnaɪt] n medianoche f.

midsummer [ˌmɪd'sʌmər] n pleno verano m.

midway [ˌmɪd'weɪ] adv (in space) a medio camino; (in time) a la mitad.

midweek [adj 'mɪdwiːk, adv mɪd'wiːk] adj de entre semana ♦ adv entre semana.

midwife ['mɪdwaɪf] (pl -wives) n comadrona f.

midwinter [ˌmɪd'wɪntər] n pleno invierno m.

midwives ['mɪdwaɪvz] pl → **midwife.**

might [maɪt] aux vb 1. (expressing possibility): poder; **I suppose they ~ still come** supongo que aún podrían venir.
2. (fml: expressing permission): **~ I have a few words?** ¿podría hablarle un momento?
3. (when conceding a point): **it ~ be expensive, but it's good quality** puede que sea caro, pero es de buena calidad.
4. (would): **I'd hoped you ~ come too** esperaba que tú vinieras también.
♦ n fuerzas fpl.

migraine ['miːgreɪn, 'maɪgreɪn] n jaqueca f.

mild [maɪld] adj (taste, weather, detergent) suave; (illness, discomfort) leve; (slight) ligero(-ra); (person, nature) apacible ♦ n (Br) cerveza de sabor suave.

mile [maɪl] n milla f; **it's ~s away** está muy lejos.

mileage ['maɪlɪdʒ] n distancia f en millas, ≈ kilometraje m.

mileometer [maɪ'lɒmɪtər] n cuentamillas m inv, ≈ cuentakilómetros m inv.

military ['mɪlɪtrɪ] adj militar.

milk [mɪlk] n leche f ♦ vt (cow) ordeñar.

milk chocolate n chocolate m

con leche.

milkman ['mɪlkmən] (*pl* -men [-mən]) *n* lechero *m*.

milk shake *n* batido *m*.

milky ['mɪlkɪ] *adj* (*drink*) con mucha leche.

mill [mɪl] *n* (*flour-mill*) molino *m*; (*for grinding*) molinillo *m*; (*factory*) fábrica *f*.

milligram ['mɪlɪɡræm] *n* miligramo *m*.

millilitre ['mɪlɪ,liːtəʳ] *n* mililitro *m*.

millimetre ['mɪlɪ,miːtəʳ] *n* milímetro *m*.

million ['mɪljən] *n* millón *m*; **~s of** (*fig*) millones de

millionaire [,mɪljə'neəʳ] *n* millonario *m* (-ria *f*).

mime [maɪm] *vi* hacer mímica.

min. [mɪn] (*abbr of minute*) min.; (*abbr of minimum*) mín.

mince [mɪns] *n* (*Br*) carne *f* picada.

mincemeat ['mɪnsmiːt] *n* (*sweet filling*) dulce de fruta confitada con especias; (*Am: mince*) carne *f* picada.

mince pie *n* pastelillo navideño de pasta quebrada, rellena de fruta confitada y especias.

mind [maɪnd] *n* mente *f*; (*memory*) memoria *f* ◆ *vt* (*look after*) cuidar de ◆ *vi*: **do you ~ if ...?** ¿le importa si ...?; **I don't ~** (*it won't disturb me*) no me molesta; (*I'm indifferent*) me da igual; **it slipped my ~** se me olvidó; **state of ~** estado *m* de ánimo; **to my ~** en mi opinión; **to bear sthg in ~** tener algo en cuenta; **to change one's ~** cambiar de opinión; **to have sthg in ~** tener

algo en mente; **to have sthg on one's ~** estar preocupado por algo; **do you ~ the noise?** ¿te molesta el ruido?; **to make one's ~ up** decidirse; **I wouldn't ~ a drink** no me importaría tomar algo; **"~ the gap!"** advertencia a los pasajeros de tener cuidado con el hueco entre el andén y el metro; **"~ the step"** "cuidado con el peldaño"; **never ~!** (*don't worry*) ¡no importa!

mine[1] [maɪn] *pron* mío *m* (-a *f*); **a friend of ~** un amigo mío.

mine[2] *n* mina *f*.

miner ['maɪnəʳ] *n* minero *m* (-ra *f*).

mineral ['mɪnərəl] *n* mineral *m*.

mineral water *n* agua *f* mineral.

minestrone [,mɪnɪ'strəʊnɪ] *n* minestrone *f*.

mingle ['mɪŋɡl] *vi* (*combine*) mezclarse; (*with other people*) alternar.

miniature ['mɪnətʃəʳ] *adj* en miniatura ◆ *n* (*bottle of alcohol*) botellín *m* (*de bebida alcohólica*).

minibar ['mɪnɪbɑːʳ] *n* minibar *m*.

minibus ['mɪnɪbʌs] (*pl* -es) *n* microbús *m*.

minicab ['mɪnɪkæb] *n* (*Br*) radiotaxi *m*.

minimal ['mɪnɪml] *adj* mínimo(-ma).

minimum ['mɪnɪməm] *adj* mínimo(-ma) ◆ *n* mínimo *m*.

miniskirt ['mɪnɪskɜːt] *n* minifalda *f*.

minister ['mɪnɪstəʳ] *n* (*in government*) ministro *m* (-tra *f*); (*in Church*) pastor *m*.

ministry ['mɪnɪstrɪ] *n* (*of govern-*

minor

180

ment) ministerio *m*.

minor ['maɪnəʳ] *adj* menor ◆ *n (fml)* menor *mf* de edad.

Minorca [mɪˈnɔːkə] *n* Menorca.

minority [maɪˈnɒrɪtɪ] *n* minoría *f*.

minor road *n* carretera *f* secundaria.

mint [mɪnt] *n (sweet)* caramelo *m* de menta; *(plant)* menta *f*.

minus ['maɪnəs] *prep (in subtraction)* menos; **it's ~ 10°C** estamos a 10°C bajo cero.

minuscule ['mɪnəskjuːl] *adj* minúsculo(-la).

minute[1] ['mɪnɪt] *n* minuto *m*; **any ~** en cualquier momento; **just a ~!** ¡espera un momento!

minute[2] [maɪˈnjuːt] *adj* diminuto(-ta).

minute steak ['mɪnɪt-] *n* filete muy fino que se hace rápido al cocinarlo.

miracle ['mɪrəkl] *n* milagro *m*.

miraculous [mɪˈrækjʊləs] *adj* milagroso(-sa).

mirror ['mɪrəʳ] *n (on wall, handheld)* espejo *m*; *(on car)* retrovisor *m*.

misbehave [ˌmɪsbɪˈheɪv] *vi* portarse mal.

miscarriage [ˌmɪsˈkærɪdʒ] *n* aborto *m* (natural).

miscellaneous [ˌmɪsəˈleɪnjəs] *adj* diverso(-sa).

mischievous ['mɪstʃɪvəs] *adj* travieso(-sa).

misconduct [ˌmɪsˈkɒndʌkt] *n* mala conducta *f*.

miser ['maɪzəʳ] *n* avaro *m* (-ra *f*).

miserable ['mɪzrəbl] *adj (un-*

happy) infeliz; *(depressing, small)* miserable; *(weather)* horrible.

misery ['mɪzərɪ] *n (unhappiness)* desdicha *f*; *(poor conditions)* miseria *f*.

misfire [ˌmɪsˈfaɪəʳ] *vi (car)* no arrancar.

misfortune [mɪsˈfɔːtʃuːn] *n (bad luck)* mala suerte *f*.

mishap ['mɪshæp] *n* contratiempo *m*.

misjudge [ˌmɪsˈdʒʌdʒ] *vt (distance, amount)* calcular mal; *(person, character)* juzgar mal.

mislay [ˌmɪsˈleɪ] *(pt & pp* -laid [-leɪd]) *vt* extraviar.

mislead [ˌmɪsˈliːd] *(pt & pp* -led [-led]) *vt* engañar.

miss [mɪs] *vt* perder; *(not notice)* no ver; *(regret absence of)* echar de menos; *(appointment)* faltar a; *(programme)* perderse ◆ *vi* fallar; **you can't ~ it** no tiene pérdida ❑ **miss out** *vt sep* pasar por alto ❑ *vi*: **to ~ out on sthg** perderse algo.

Miss [mɪs] *n* señorita *f*.

missile [*Br* 'mɪsaɪl, *Am* 'mɪsl] *n (weapon)* misil *m*; *(thing thrown)* proyectil *m*.

missing ['mɪsɪŋ] *adj (lost)* perdido(-da); **to be ~** *(not there)* faltar.

missing person *n* desaparecido *m* (-da *f*).

mission ['mɪʃn] *n* misión *f*.

missionary ['mɪʃənrɪ] *n* misionario *m* (-ria *f*).

mist [mɪst] *n* neblina *f*.

mistake [mɪˈsteɪk] *(pt* -took, *pp* -taken [-ˈteɪkn]) *n* error *m* ◆ *vt (misunderstand)* malentender; **by ~** por error; **to make a ~** equivocarse; **to ~ sthg/sb for** confundir algo/a alguien con.

Mister ['mɪstə'] n señor m.

mistook [mɪ'stuk] pp → **mistake**.

mistress ['mɪstrɪs] n (lover) amante f; (Br: primary teacher) maestra f; (Br: secondary teacher) profesora f.

mistrust [,mɪs'trʌst] vt desconfiar de.

misty ['mɪstɪ] adj neblinoso(-sa).

misunderstanding [,mɪsʌndə-'stændɪŋ] n malentendido m.

misuse [,mɪs'juːs] n uso m indebido

mitten ['mɪtn] n manopla f.

mix [mɪks] vt mezclar ◆ vi (socially) alternar ◆ n (for cake, sauce) mezcla f; **to ~ sthg with sthg** mezclar algo con algo ❏ **mix up** vt sep (confuse) confundir; (put into disorder) mezclar.

mixed [mɪkst] adj (school) mixto(-ta).

mixed grill n parrillada mixta de carne, champiñones y tomate.

mixed salad n ensalada f mixta.

mixed vegetables npl selección f de verduras.

mixer ['mɪksə'] n (for food) batidora f; (drink) bebida no alcohólica que se mezcla con las bebidas alcohólicas.

mixture ['mɪkstʃə'] n mezcla f.

mix-up n (inf) confusión f.

ml (abbr of millilitre) ml.

mm (abbr of millimetre) mm.

moan [məʊn] vi (in pain, grief) gemir; (inf: complain) quejarse.

moat [məʊt] n foso m.

mobile ['məʊbaɪl] adj móvil.

mobile phone n teléfono m portátil.

mock [mɒk] adj fingido(-da) ◆ vt burlarse de ◆ n (Br: exam) simulacro m de examen.

mode [məʊd] n modo m.

model ['mɒdl] n modelo m; (small copy) maqueta f; (fashion model) modelo mf.

moderate ['mɒdərət] adj moderado(-da).

modern ['mɒdən] adj moderno(-na).

modernized ['mɒdənaɪzd] adj modernizado(-da).

modern languages npl lenguas fpl modernas.

modest ['mɒdɪst] adj modesto(-ta); (price) módico(-ca); (increase, improvement) ligero(-ra).

modify ['mɒdɪfaɪ] vt modificar.

mohair ['məʊheə'] n mohair m.

moist [mɔɪst] adj húmedo(-da).

moisture ['mɔɪstʃə'] n humedad f.

moisturizer ['mɔɪstʃəraɪzə'] n crema f hidratante.

molar ['məʊlə'] n muela f.

mold [məʊld] (Am) = **mould**.

mole [məʊl] n (animal) topo m; (spot) lunar m.

molest [mə'lest] vt (child) abusar sexualmente; (woman) acosar.

mom [mɒm] n (Am: inf) mamá f.

moment ['məʊmənt] n momento m; **at the ~** en este momento; **for the ~** de momento.

Mon. (abbr of Monday) lun.

monarchy ['mɒnəkɪ] n: **the ~** la familia real.

monastery ['mɒnəstrɪ] n monasterio m.

Monday ['mʌndɪ] n lunes m inv, → **Saturday**.

money ['mʌnɪ] n dinero m.

money belt n riñonera f.

money order n giro m postal.

mongrel ['mʌŋgrəl] n perro m cruzado.

monitor ['mɒnɪtər] n (computer screen) monitor m ◆ vt (check, observe) controlar.

monk [mʌŋk] n monje m.

monkey ['mʌŋkɪ] n (pl monkeys) mono m.

monkfish ['mʌŋkfɪʃ] n rape m.

monopoly [mə'nɒpəlɪ] n monopolio m.

monorail ['mɒnəʊreɪl] n monorraíl m.

monotonous [mə'nɒtənəs] adj monótono(-na).

monsoon [mɒn'su:n] n monzón m.

monster ['mɒnstər] n monstruo m.

month [mʌnθ] n mes m; **every ~** cada mes; **in a ~'s time** en un mes.

monthly ['mʌnθlɪ] adj mensual ◆ adv mensualmente.

monument ['mɒnjʊmənt] n monumento m.

mood [mu:d] n humor m; **to be in a (bad) ~** estar de mal humor; **to be in a good ~** estar de buen humor.

moody ['mu:dɪ] adj (bad-tempered) malhumorado(-da); (changeable) de humor variable.

moon [mu:n] n luna f.

moonlight ['mu:nlaɪt] n luz f de luna.

moor [mɔ:r] n páramo m ◆ vt amarrar.

moose [mu:s] n (pl inv) n alce m.

mop [mɒp] n (for floor) fregona f ◆ vt (floor) pasar la fregona por □ **mop up** vt sep (clean up) limpiar.

moped ['məʊped] n ciclomotor m.

moral ['mɒrəl] adj moral ◆ n (lesson) moraleja f.

morality [mə'rælɪtɪ] n moralidad f.

more [mɔ:r] adj 1. (a larger amount of) más; **there are ~ tourists than usual** hay más turistas que de costumbre.

2. (additional) más; **are there any ~ cakes?** ¿hay más pasteles?; **there's no ~ wine** no hay más vino; **have some ~ rice** come un poco más de arroz.

3. (in phrases): **~ and more** cada vez más.

◆ adv 1. (in comparatives) más; **it's ~ difficult than before** es más difícil que antes; **speak ~ clearly** habla con más claridad.

2. (to a greater degree) más; **we ought to go to the cinema ~** deberíamos ir más al cine.

3. (longer) más; **I don't go there any ~** ya no voy más allí.

4. (again): **once ~** una vez más.

5. (in phrases): **~ or less** más o menos; **we'd be ~ than happy to help** estaríamos encantados de ayudarle.

◆ pron 1. (a larger amount) más; **I've got ~ than you** tengo más que tú;

motorcar

~ **than 20 types of pizza** más de 20 clases de pizzas.

2. *(an additional amount)* más; **is there any ~?** ¿hay más?

moreover [mɔː'rəʊvəʳ] *adv* (fml) además.

morning ['mɔːnɪŋ] *n* mañana *f*; **two o'clock in the ~** las dos de la mañana; **good ~!** ¡buenos días!; **in the ~** *(early in the day)* por la mañana; *(tomorrow morning)* mañana por la mañana.

morning-after pill *n* píldora *f* del día siguiente.

morning sickness *n* náuseas *fpl* de por la mañana.

Morocco [mə'rɒkəʊ] *n* Marruecos.

moron ['mɔːrɒn] *n* (inf) imbécil *mf*.

Morse (code) [mɔːs-] *n* Morse *m*.

mortgage ['mɔːgɪdʒ] *n* hipoteca *f*.

mosaic [mə'zeɪɪk] *n* mosaico *m*.

Moslem ['mɒzləm] = **Muslim**.

mosque [mɒsk] *n* mezquita *f*.

mosquito [mə'skiːtəʊ] *(pl* -es*)* *n* mosquito *m*.

mosquito net *n* mosquitero *m*.

moss [mɒs] *n* musgo *m*.

most [məʊst] *adj* **1.** *(the majority of)* la mayoría de; ~ **people** la mayoría de la gente.

2. *(the largest amount of)* más; **I drank (the) ~ beer** yo fui el que bebió más cerveza.

♦ *adv* **1.** *(in superlatives)* más; **the ~ expensive hotel** el hotel más caro.

2. *(to the greatest degree)* más; **I like**

this one ~ éste es el que más me gusta.

3. *(fml: very)* muy; **we would be ~ grateful** les agradeceríamos mucho.

♦ *pron* **1.** *(the majority)* la mayoría; ~ **of the villages** la mayoría de los pueblos; ~ **of the time** la mayor parte del tiempo.

2. *(the largest amount)*: **she earns (the) ~** es la que más gana.

3. *(in phrases)*: **at ~** como máximo; **to make the ~ of sthg** aprovechar algo al máximo.

mostly ['məʊstlɪ] *adv* principalmente.

MOT *n* (Br: test) revisión anual obligatoria para todos los coches de más de tres años, = ITV *f*.

motel [məʊ'tel] *n* motel *m*.

moth [mɒθ] *n* polilla *f*.

mother ['mʌðəʳ] *n* madre *f*.

mother-in-law *n* suegra *f*.

mother-of-pearl *n* nácar *m*.

motif [məʊ'tiːf] *n* motivo *m*.

motion ['məʊʃn] *n* (movement) movimiento *m* ♦ *vi*: **to ~ to sb** hacer una señal a alguien.

motionless ['məʊʃənlɪs] *adj* inmóvil.

motivate ['məʊtɪveɪt] *vt* motivar.

motive ['məʊtɪv] *n* motivo *m*.

motor ['məʊtəʳ] *n* motor *m*.

Motorail® ['məʊtəreɪl] *n* motorraíl *m*.

motorbike ['məʊtəbaɪk] *n* moto *f*.

motorboat ['məʊtəbəʊt] *n* lancha *f* motora.

motorcar ['məʊtəkɑːʳ] *n* automóvil *m*.

motorcycle [ˈməʊtəˌsaɪkl] *n*
motocicleta *f*.

motorcyclist [ˈməʊtəˌsaɪklɪst] *n*
motociclista *mf*.

motorist [ˈməʊtərɪst] *n* automovilista *mf*.

motor racing *n* automovilismo *m* (deporte).

motorway [ˈməʊtəweɪ] *n* (Br)
autopista *f*.

motto [ˈmɒtəʊ] (pl **-s**) *n* lema *m*.

mould [məʊld] *n* (Br) (shape)
molde *m*; (substance) moho *m* ◆ *vt*
(Br) moldear.

mouldy [ˈməʊldɪ] *adj* (Br) mohoso(-sa).

mound [maʊnd] *n* (hill) montículo *m*; (pile) montón *m*.

mount [maʊnt] *n* (for photo)
marco *m*; (mountain) monte *m* ◆ *vt*
(horse) montar en; (photo) enmarcar ◆ *vi* (increase) aumentar.

mountain [ˈmaʊntɪn] *n* montaña *f*.

mountain bike *n* bicicleta *f*
de montaña.

mountaineer [ˌmaʊntɪˈnɪəʳ] *n*
montañero *m* (-ra *f*).

mountaineering [ˌmaʊntɪˈnɪərɪŋ] *n*: **to go ~** hacer montañismo.

mountainous [ˈmaʊntɪnəs] *adj*
montañoso(-sa).

Mount Rushmore [-ˈrʌʃmɔːʳ]
n el monte Rushmore.

MOUNT RUSHMORE

Este gigantesco relieve de los bustos de los presidentes Washington, Jefferson, Lincoln y
Theodore Roosevelt, excavado en un lado del Monte Rushmore (Dakota del Sur), es un monumento nacional y una popular atracción turística.

---

mourning [ˈmɔːnɪŋ] *n*: **to be in
~** estar de luto.

mouse [maʊs] (pl **mice**) *n* ratón *m*.

moussaka [muːˈsɑːkə] *n* plato
griego de berenjenas, tomate, salsa de
queso y carne picada.

mousse [muːs] *n* (food) mousse
m; (for hair) espuma *f*.

moustache [məˈstɑːʃ] *n* (Br)
bigote *m*.

mouth [maʊθ] *n* boca *f*; (of river)
desembocadura *f*.

mouthful [ˈmaʊθfʊl] *n* (of food)
bocado *m*; (of drink) trago *m*.

mouthorgan [ˈmaʊθˌɔːgən] *n*
armónica *f*.

mouthpiece [ˈmaʊθpiːs] *n* (of
telephone) micrófono *m*; (of musical
instrument) boquilla *f*.

mouthwash [ˈmaʊθwɒʃ] *n* elixir *m* bucal.

move [muːv] *n* (change of house)
mudanza *f*; (movement) movimiento *m*; (in games) jugada *f*; (turn to
play) turno *m*; (course of action)
medida *f* ◆ *vt* (shift) mover; (emotionally) conmover ◆ *vi* (shift)
moverse; **to ~ (house)** mudarse; **to
make a ~** (leave) irse ❑ **move
along** *vi* hacerse a un lado; **move
in** *vi* (to house) instalarse; **move off**
vi (train, car) ponerse en marcha;
move on *vi* (after stopping) reanudar la marcha; **move out** *vi* (from
house) mudarse; **move over**

hacer sitio; **move up** vi hacer sitio.

movement ['mu:vmənt] n movimiento m.

movie ['mu:vɪ] n película f.

movie theater n (Am) cine m.

moving ['mu:vɪŋ] adj (emotionally) conmovedor(-ra).

mow [məʊ] vt: **to ~ the lawn** cortar el césped.

mozzarella [ˌmɒtsə'relə] n mozzarella f.

MP abbr = **Member of Parliament**.

mph (abbr of miles per hour) mph.

Mr ['mɪstə'] abbr Sr.

Mrs ['mɪsɪz] abbr Sra.

Ms [mɪz] abbr abreviatura que se utiliza delante del apellido cuando no se quiere decir el estado civil de la mujer.

MSc n (abbr of Master of Science) título postuniversitario de dos años en ciencias.

much [mʌtʃ] (compar **more**, superl **most**) adj mucho(-cha); **I haven't got ~ money** no tengo mucho dinero; **as ~ food as you can eat** tanta comida como puedas comer; **how ~ time is left?** ¿cuánto tiempo queda?; **they have so ~ money** tienen tanto dinero; **we have too ~ food** tenemos demasiada comida.

♦ adv mucho; **it's ~ better** es mucho mejor; **he's ~ too good** es demasiado bueno; **I like it very ~** me gusta muchísimo; **it's not ~ good** no vale mucho; **thank you very ~** muchas gracias; **we don't go there ~** no vamos mucho allí.

♦ pron mucho; **I haven't got ~** no tengo mucho; **as ~ as you like** tanto como quieras; **how ~ is it?** ¿cuánto es?; **you've got so ~** tienes tanto; **you've got too ~** tienes demasiado.

muck [mʌk] n mugre f ❑ **muck about** vi (Br: inf) hacer el indio; **muck up** vt sep (Br: inf) fastidiar.

mud [mʌd] n barro m.

muddle ['mʌdl] n: **to be in a ~** estar hecho un lío.

muddy ['mʌdɪ] adj lleno(-na) de barro.

mudguard ['mʌdgɑːd] n guardabarros m inv.

muesli ['mju:zlɪ] n muesli m.

muffin ['mʌfɪn] n (roll) panecillo m; (cake) especie de bollo que se come caliente.

muffler ['mʌflə'] n (Am: silencer) silenciador m.

mug [mʌg] n (cup) tanque m, taza f grande (cilíndrica) ♦ vt asaltar.

mugging ['mʌgɪŋ] n atraco m.

muggy ['mʌgɪ] adj bochornoso(-sa).

mule [mju:l] n mula f.

multicoloured ['mʌltɪˌkʌləd] adj multicolor.

multiple ['mʌltɪpl] adj múltiple.

multiplex cinema [ˌmʌltɪpleks-] n multicine m.

multiplication [ˌmʌltɪplɪ'keɪʃn] n multiplicación f.

multiply ['mʌltɪplaɪ] vt multiplicar ♦ vi multiplicarse.

multistorey (car park) [ˌmʌltɪ'stɔːrɪ-] n aparcamiento m de muchas plantas.

mum [mʌm] n (Br: inf) mamá f.

mummy ['mʌmɪ] *n (Br: inf: mother)* mamá *f*.

mumps [mʌmps] *n* paperas *fpl*.

munch [mʌntʃ] *vt* masticar.

municipal [mju:'nɪsɪpl] *adj* municipal.

mural ['mjʊərəl] *n* mural *m*.

murder ['mɜ:dər] *n* asesinato *m* ♦ *vt* asesinar.

murderer ['mɜ:dərər] *n* asesino *m* (-na *f*).

muscle ['mʌsl] *n* músculo *m*.

museum [mju:'zi:əm] *n* museo *m*.

mushroom ['mʌʃrʊm] *n (small and white)* champiñón *m; (darker and flatter)* seta *f*.

music ['mju:zɪk] *n* música *f*.

musical ['mju:zɪkl] *adj (connected with music)* musical; *(person)* con talento para la música ♦ *n* musical *m*.

musical instrument *n* instrumento *m* musical.

musician [mju:'zɪʃn] *n* músico *m* (-ca *f*).

Muslim ['mʊzlɪm] *adj* musulmán(-ana) ♦ *n* musulmán *m* (-ana *f*).

mussels ['mʌslz] *npl* mejillones *mpl*.

must [mʌst] *aux vb* deber, tener que ♦ *n (inf)*: **it's a ~** no te lo puedes perder; **I ~ go** debo irme; **the room ~ be vacated by ten** la habitación debe dejarse libre para las diez; **you ~ have seen it** tienes que haberlo visto; **you ~ see that film** no te puedes perder esa película; **you ~ be joking!** estás de broma ¿no?

mustache ['mʌstæʃ] *(Am)* = **moustache**.

mustard ['mʌstəd] *n* mostaza *f*.

mustn't ['mʌsənt] = **must not**.

mutter ['mʌtər] *vt* musitar.

mutton ['mʌtn] *n* oveja *f*.

mutual ['mju:tʃʊəl] *adj (feeling)* mutuo(-tua); *(friend, interest)* común.

muzzle ['mʌzl] *n (for dog)* bozal *m*.

my [maɪ] *adj* mi, mis *(pl)*.

myself [maɪ'self] *pron (reflexive)* me; *(after prep)* mi mismo(-ma); **I did it ~** lo hice yo solo.

mysterious [mɪ'stɪərɪəs] *adj* misterioso(-sa).

mystery ['mɪstərɪ] *n* misterio *m*.

myth [mɪθ] *n* mito *m*.

N *(abbr of north)* N.

nag [næg] *vt* regañar.

nail [neɪl] *n (of finger, toe)* uña *f; (metal)* clavo *m* ♦ *vt (fasten)* clavar.

nailbrush ['neɪlbrʌʃ] *n* cepillo *m* de uñas.

nail file *n* lima *f* de uñas.

nail scissors *npl* tijeras *fpl* para las uñas.

nail varnish *n* esmalte *m* de uñas.

nail varnish remover [-rɪ'mu:vər] *n* quitaesmaltes *m inv*.

naive [naɪ'i:v] *adj* ingenuo(-nua).

naked ['neɪkɪd] *adj (person)* desnudo(-da).

name [neɪm] *n* nombre *m*; *(surname)* apellido *m*; *(reputation)* reputación *f* ♦ *vt (date, price)* fijar; **they ~d him John** le pusieron John de nombre; **first ~** nombre *m*; **last ~** apellido; **what's your ~?** ¿cómo te llamas?; **my ~ is ...** me llamo ...

namely ['neɪmlɪ] *adv* a saber.

nan bread ['næn-] *n* tipo de pan indio en forma de torta, condimentado normalmente con especias.

nanny ['nænɪ] *n (childminder)* niñera *f*; *(inf: grandmother)* abuelita *f*.

nap [næp] *n*: **to have a ~** echar una siesta.

napkin ['næpkɪn] *n* servilleta *f*.

nappy ['næpɪ] *n* pañal *m*.

nappy liner *n* parte desechable de un pañal de gasa.

narcotic [nɑː'kɒtɪk] *n* narcótico *m*.

narrow ['nærəʊ] *adj (road, gap)* estrecho(-cha) ♦ *vi (road, gap)* estrecharse.

narrow-minded [-'maɪndɪd] *adj* estrecho(-cha) de miras.

nasty ['nɑːstɪ] *adj (spiteful)* malintencionado(-da); *(accident, fall)* grave, *(unpleasant)* desagradable.

nation ['neɪʃn] *n* nación *f*.

national ['næʃənl] *adj* nacional ♦ *n* súbdito *m* (-ta *f*).

national anthem *n* himno *m* nacional.

National Health Service *n* organismo gestor de la salud pública en Gran Bretaña.

National Insurance *n (Br: contributions)* = Seguridad *f* Social.

nationality [,næʃə'nælətɪ] *n* nacionalidad *f*.

national park *n* parque *m* nacional.

---

i | **NATIONAL PARK**

L os parques nacionales en Gran Bretaña y Estados Unidos son grandes extensiones naturales abiertas al público que están protegidas para conservar su interés paisajístico. Snowdonia, el Lake District y el Peak District son conocidos parques nacionales británicos; los más conocidos de Estados Unidos son Yellowstone y Yosemite. En todos ellos hay lugares donde se puede hacer camping.

---

nationwide ['neɪʃənwaɪd] *adj* a escala nacional.

native ['neɪtɪv] *adj (country)* natal; *(customs, originario (ria), (population)* indígeno(-na) ♦ *n* natural *mf*; **a ~ speaker of English** un hablante nativo de inglés.

NATO ['neɪtəʊ] *n* OTAN *f*.

natural ['nætʃrəl] *adj (ability, charm)* natural; *(swimmer, actor)* nato(-ta).

natural gas *n* gas *m* natural.

naturally ['nætʃrəlɪ] *adv (of course)* naturalmente.

natural yoghurt *n* yogur *m* natural.

nature ['neɪtʃər] *n* naturaleza *f*.

nature reserve *n* reserva *f* natural.

naughty ['nɔːtɪ] *adj (child)* travieso(-sa).

nausea ['nɔːzɪə] *n* náusea *f*.

navigate ['nævɪɡeɪt] *vi (in boat, plane)* dirigir; *(in car)* guiar.

navy ['neɪvɪ] *n (ships)* armada *f* ♦ *adj*: ~ (blue) azul marino.

NB *(abbr of nota bene)* N.B.

near [nɪəʳ] *adj (place, object)* cerca; *(relation)* cercano(-na) ♦ *prep*: ~ (to) cerca de, cerca de; **in the ~ future** en el futuro próximo.

nearby [nɪə'baɪ] *adv* cerca ♦ *adj* cercano(-na).

nearly ['nɪəlɪ] *adv* casi.

neat [niːt] *adj (writing, work)* bien hecho(-cha); *(room)* ordenado(-da); *(whisky, vodka etc)* solo(-la).

neatly ['niːtlɪ] *adv (placed, arranged)* con pulcritud; *(written)* con buena letra.

necessarily [ˌnesə'serɪlɪ, *Br* 'nesəsrəlɪ] *adv*: **not** ~ no necesariamente.

necessary ['nesəsrɪ] *adj* necesario(-ria); **it is** ~ **to do it** es necesario hacerlo.

necessity [nɪ'sesətɪ] *n* necesidad *f* ❑ **necessities** *npl* artículos *mpl* de primera necesidad.

neck [nek] *n (of person, jumper, shirt)* cuello *m*; *(of animal)* pescuezo *m*.

necklace ['neklɪs] *n (long)* collar *m*; *(short)* gargantilla *f*.

nectarine ['nektərɪn] *n* nectarina *f*.

need [niːd] *n* necesidad *f* ♦ *vt* necesitar; **to ~ to do sthg** *(require)* necesitar hacer algo; *(be obliged)* tener que hacer algo.

needle ['niːdl] *n* aguja *f*.

needlework ['niːdlwɜːk] *n (SCH)* costura *f*.

needn't ['niːdənt] = need not.

needy ['niːdɪ] *adj* necesitado (-da).

negative ['negətɪv] *adj* negativo(-va) ♦ *n (in photography)* negativo *m*; *(GRAMM)* negación *f*.

neglect [nɪ'glekt] *vt (child, garden, work)* descuidar.

negligence ['neglɪdʒəns] *n* negligencia *f*.

negotiations [nɪˌgəʊʃɪ'eɪʃnz] *npl* negociaciones *fpl*.

negro ['niːgrəʊ] *(pl* -es) *n* negro *m* (-gra *f*).

neighbor ['neɪbər] *(Am)* = neighbour.

neighbour ['neɪbəʳ] *n* vecino *m* (-na *f*).

neighbourhood ['neɪbəhʊd] *n* barrio *m*.

neighbouring ['neɪbərɪŋ] *adj* vecino(-na).

neither ['naɪðəʳ, 'niːðəʳ] *adj*: ~ **bag is big enough** ninguna de las dos bolsas es bastante grande. ♦ *pron*: ~ **of us** ninguno *m* de nosotros (ninguna *f* de nosotras). ♦ *conj*: ~ **do I** yo tampoco; ~ ... **nor** ... ni ... ni ...

neon light ['niːɒn-] *n* luz *f* de neón.

nephew ['nefjuː] *n* sobrino *m*.

nerve [nɜːv] *n (in body)* nervio *m*; *(courage)* coraje *m*; **what a ~!** ¡qué caradura!

nervous ['nɜːvəs] *adj (tense by nature)* nervioso(-sa); *(apprehensive)* aprensivo(-va); *(uneasy)* preocupa-

nervous breakdown n crisis f inv nerviosa.

nest [nest] n nido m.

net [net] n red f ♦ adj neto(-ta).

netball ['netbɔːl] n deporte parecido al baloncesto femenino.

Netherlands ['neðələndz] npl: the ~ los Países Bajos.

nettle ['netl] n ortiga f.

network ['netwɜːk] n (of streets, trains) red f; (RADIO & TV) cadena f.

neurotic [ˌnjʊəˈrɒtɪk] adj neurótico(-ca).

neutral ['njuːtrəl] adj (country, person) neutral; (in colour) incoloro(-ra) ♦ n (AUT): **in** ~ en punto muerto.

never ['nevər] adv nunca; **I've been to Berlin** no he estado nunca en Berlín; **she's** ~ **late** (ella) nunca llega tarde; ~ **mind!** ¡no importa!

nevertheless [ˌnevəðəˈles] adv sin embargo.

new [njuː] adj nuevo(-va).

newly ['njuːlɪ] adv recién.

new potatoes npl patatas fpl nuevas.

news [njuːz] n noticias fpl; **a piece of** ~ una noticia.

newsagent ['njuːzeɪdʒənt] n (shop) = quiosco m de periódicos.

newspaper ['njuːzˌpeɪpər] n periódico m.

New Year n Año m Nuevo.

NEW YEAR

En Nochevieja en Gran Bretaña se celebran fiestas públicas y la gente se reúne en la calle. Tradicionalmente, se canta "Auld Lang Syne" mientras el reloj da las doce. En Escocia, donde se conoce como "Hogmanay", es particularmente importante. El día siguiente, Año Nuevo, es fiesta en toda Gran Bretaña.

New Year's Day n día m de Año Nuevo.

New Year's Eve n Nochevieja f.

New Zealand [-ˈziːlənd] n Nueva Zelanda.

next [nekst] adj (in the future, following) próximo(-ma); (room, house) de al lado ♦ adv (afterwards) después; (on next occasion) la próxima vez; **when does the** ~ **bus leave?** ¿a qué hora sale el próximo autobús?; ~ **year/Monday** el año/el lunes que viene; ~ **to** (by the side of) junto a; **the week after** ~ la semana que viene, la otra.

next door adv en la casa de al lado.

next of kin [-kɪn] n pariente m más próximo (pariente f más próxima).

NHS abbr = **National Health Service.**

nib [nɪb] n plumilla f.

nibble ['nɪbl] vt mordisquear.

Nicaragua [ˌnɪkəˈræɡjʊə] n Nicaragua.

Nicaraguan [ˌnɪkəˈræɡjʊən] adj nicaragüense ♦ n nicaragüense mf.

nice [naɪs] adj (pleasant) agradable; (pretty) bonito(-ta); (kind) amable; **to have a** ~ **time** pasarlo bien; ~ **to see you!** ¡encantado(-da) de verle!

nickel ['nɪkl] n (metal) níquel m; (Am: coin) moneda f de cinco centavos.

nickname ['nɪkneɪm] n apodo m.

niece [niːs] n sobrina f.

night [naɪt] n (time when asleep) noche f; (evening) tarde f; **at ~** de noche; **by ~** por la noche; **last ~** anoche.

nightclub ['naɪtklʌb] n = sala f de fiestas (abierta sólo por las noches).

nightdress ['naɪtdres] n camisón m.

nightie ['naɪtɪ] n (inf) camisón m.

nightlife ['naɪtlaɪf] n vida f nocturna.

nightly ['naɪtlɪ] adv cada noche.

nightmare ['naɪtmeər] n pesadilla f.

night safe n caja f nocturna (en un banco).

night school n escuela f nocturna.

nightshift ['naɪtʃɪft] n turno m de noche.

nil [nɪl] n (SPORT) cero m.

Nile [naɪl] n: **the ~** el Nilo.

nine [naɪn] num nueve, → **six**.

nineteen [,naɪn'tiːn] num diecinueve, → **six**; **~ ninety-five** mil novecientos noventa y cinco.

nineteenth [,naɪn'tiːnθ] num decimonoveno(-na), → **sixth**.

ninetieth ['naɪntɪəθ] num nonagésimo(-ma), → **sixth**.

ninety ['naɪntɪ] num noventa, → **six**.

ninth [naɪnθ] num noveno(-na), → **sixth**.

nip [nɪp] vt (pinch) pellizcar.

nipple ['nɪpl] n (of breast) pezón m; (of bottle) tetilla f.

nitrogen ['naɪtrədʒən] n nitrógeno m.

no [nəʊ] adv no ◆ adj ninguno(-na) ◆ n no m; **I've got ~ time** no tengo tiempo; **I've got ~ money left** no me queda (ningún) dinero.

noble ['nəʊbl] adj noble.

nobody ['nəʊbədɪ] pron nadie.

nod [nɒd] vi (in agreement) asentir con la cabeza.

noise [nɔɪz] n ruido m.

noisy ['nɔɪzɪ] adj ruidoso(-sa).

nominate ['nɒmɪneɪt] vt proponer.

nonalcoholic [,nɒnælkə'hɒlɪk] adj sin alcohol.

none [nʌn] pron ninguno m (-na f); **there's ~ left** no queda nada.

nonetheless [,nʌnðə'les] adv no obstante.

nonfiction [,nɒn'fɪkʃn] n no ficción f.

non-iron adj que no necesita plancha.

nonsense ['nɒnsəns] n tonterías fpl.

nonsmoker [,nɒn'sməʊkər] n no fumador m (-ra f).

nonstick [,nɒn'stɪk] adj antiadherente.

nonstop [,nɒn'stɒp] adj (talking, arguing) continuo(-nua); (flight) sin escalas ◆ adv (run, rain) sin parar; (fly, travel) directamente.

noodles ['nuːdlz] npl fideos mpl.

noon [nuːn] n mediodía m.

no one = **nobody**.

nor [nɔːr] conj tampoco; **~ do I** yo

tampoco, → **neither**.

normal ['nɔ:ml] *adj* normal.

normally ['nɔ:məlɪ] *adv* normalmente.

north [nɔ:θ] *n* norte *m* ♦ *adv* (fly, walk) hacia el norte; (be situated) al norte; **in the ~ of England** en el norte de Inglaterra.

North America *n* Norteamérica.

northbound ['nɔ:θbaʊnd] *adj* con dirección norte.

northeast [,nɔ:θ'i:st] *n* nordeste *m*.

northern ['nɔ:ðən] *adj* del norte.

Northern Ireland *n* Irlanda del Norte.

North Pole *n* Polo *m* Norte.

North Sea *n* Mar *m* del Norte.

northwards ['nɔ:θwədz] *adv* hacia el norte.

northwest [,nɔ:θ'west] *n* noroeste *m*.

Norway ['nɔ:weɪ] *n* Noruega.

Norwegian [nɔ:'wi:dʒən] *adj* noruego(-ga) ♦ *n* (person) noruego *m* (-ga *f*); (language) noruego *m*.

nose [nəʊz] *n* (of person) nariz *f*; (of animal) hocico *m*; (of plane, rocket) morro *m*.

nosebleed ['nəʊzbli:d] *n*: **he had a ~** le sangraba la nariz.

nostril ['nɒstrəl] *n* (of person) ventana *f* de la nariz; (of animal) orificio *m* nasal.

nosy ['nəʊzɪ] *adj* fisgón(-ona).

not [nɒt] *adv* no; **she's ~ there** no está allí; **I hope ~** espero que no; **~ yet** todavía no; **~ at all** (pleased, interested) en absoluto; (in reply to

thanks) no hay de qué.

notably ['nəʊtəblɪ] *adv* especialmente.

note [nəʊt] *n* nota *f*; (bank note) billete *m* ♦ *vt* (notice) notar; (write down) anotar; **to take ~s** tomar apuntes.

notebook ['nəʊtbʊk] *n* libreta *f*.

noted ['nəʊtɪd] *adj* célebre.

notepaper ['nəʊtpeɪpə[r]] *n* papel *m* de escribir (para cartas).

nothing ['nʌθɪŋ] *pron* nada; **he did ~ no hizo nada**; **~ new/interesting** nada nuevo/interesante; **for ~** (for free) gratis; (in vain) para nada.

notice ['nəʊtɪs] *vt* notar ♦ *n* (written announcement) anuncio *m*; (warning) aviso *m*; **to take ~ of** hacer caso de; **to hand in one's ~** presentar la dimisión.

noticeable ['nəʊtɪsəbl] *adj* perceptible.

notice board *n* tablón *m* de anuncios

notion ['nəʊʃn] *n* noción *f*.

notorious [nəʊ'tɔ:rɪəs] *adj* de mala reputación.

nougat ['nu:gɑ:] *n* turrón de frutos secos y frutas confitadas.

nought [nɔ:t] *n* cero *m*.

noun [naʊn] *n* nombre *m*, sustantivo *m*.

nourishment ['nʌrɪʃmənt] *n* alimento *m*.

novel ['nɒvl] *n* novela *f* ♦ *adj* original.

novelist ['nɒvəlɪst] *n* novelista *mf*.

November [nə'vembə[r]] *n* noviembre *m*, → **September**.

now [nau] adv ahora ♦ conj: ~ (that) ahora que; just ~ ahora mismo; right ~ (at the moment) en este momento; (immediately) ahora mismo; by ~ ya; from ~ on de ahora en adelante.

nowadays ['nauədeɪz] adv hoy en día.

nowhere ['nəuwɛəʳ] adv en ninguna parte.

nozzle ['nɒzl] n boquilla f.

nuclear ['njuːklɪəʳ] adj nuclear.

nude [njuːd] adj desnudo(-da).

nudge [nʌdʒ] vt dar un codazo a.

nuisance ['njuːsns] n: it's a real ~! ¡es una lata!; he's such a ~! ¡es tan pelma!

numb [nʌm] adj (person) entumecido(-da); (leg, arm) dormido(-da).

number ['nʌmbəʳ] n número ♦ vt (give number to) numerar.

numberplate ['nʌmbəpleɪt] n matrícula f.

numeral ['njuːmərəl] n número m.

numerous ['njuːmərəs] adj numeroso(-sa).

nun [nʌn] n monja f.

nurse [nɜːs] n enfermera f ♦ vt (look after) cuidar de; male ~ enfermero m.

nursery ['nɜːsərɪ] n (in house) cuarto m de los niños; (for plants) vivero m.

nursery (school) n escuela f de párvulos.

nursery slope n pista f para principiantes.

nursing ['nɜːsɪŋ] n (profession) enfermería f.

nut [nʌt] n (to eat) nuez f (frutos secos en general); (of metal) tuerca f.

nutcrackers ['nʌt,krækəz] npl cascanueces m inv.

nutmeg ['nʌtmeg] n nuez f moscada.

nylon ['naɪlɒn] n nylon m ♦ adj de nylon.

o' [ə] abbr = of.

O [əu] n (zero) cero m.

oak [əuk] n roble m ♦ adj de roble.

OAP abbr = old age pensioner.

oar [ɔːʳ] n remo m.

oatcake ['əutkeɪk] n galleta f de avena.

oath [əuθ] n (promise) juramento m.

oatmeal ['əutmiːl] n harina f de avena.

oats [əuts] npl avena f.

obedient [ə'biːdjənt] adj obediente.

obey [ə'beɪ] vt obedecer.

object [n 'ɒbdʒɪkt, vb əb'dʒekt] n objeto m; (GRAMM) objeto m, complemento m ♦ vi: to ~ (to) oponerse (a).

objection [əb'dʒekʃn] n objeción f.

objective [əb'dʒektɪv] n objetivo m.

obligation [,ɒblɪ'geɪʃn] n obligación f.

obligatory [ə'blɪgətrɪ] *adj* obligatorio(-ria).

oblige [ə'blaɪdʒ] *vt*: **to ~ sb to do sthg** obligar a alguien a hacer algo.

oblique [ə'bliːk] *adj* oblicuo (-cua).

oblong ['ɒblɒŋ] *adj* rectangular ◆ *n* rectángulo *m*.

obnoxious [əb'nɒkʃəs] *adj* detestable.

oboe ['əʊbəʊ] *n* oboe *m*.

obscene [əb'siːn] *adj* obsceno(-na).

obscure [əb'skjʊə^r] *adj* (*difficult to understand*) oscuro(-ra); (*not well-known*) desconocido(-da).

observant [əb'zɜːvnt] *adj* observador(-ra).

observation [ˌɒbzə'veɪʃn] *n* observación *f*.

observatory [əb'zɜːvətrɪ] *n* observatorio *m*.

observe [əb'zɜːv] *vt* observar.

obsessed [əb'sest] *adj* obsesionado(-da).

obsession [əb'seʃn] *n* obsesión *f*.

obsolete ['ɒbsəliːt] *adj* obsoleto(-ta).

obstacle ['ɒbstəkl] *n* obstáculo *m*.

obstinate ['ɒbstənət] *adj* obstinado(-da).

obstruct [əb'strʌkt] *vt* (*road, path*) obstruir.

obstruction [əb'strʌkʃn] *n* (*in road, path*) obstáculo *m*.

obtain [əb'teɪn] *vt* obtener.

obtainable [əb'teɪnəbl] *adj* asequible.

obvious ['ɒbvɪəs] *adj* obvio(-via).

obviously ['ɒbvɪəslɪ] *adv* (*of course*) evidentemente; (*clearly*) claramente.

occasion [ə'keɪʒn] *n* (*instance*) vez *f*; (*important event*) acontecimiento *m*; (*opportunity*) ocasión *f*.

occasional [ə'keɪʒənl] *adj* esporádico(-ca).

occasionally [ə'keɪʒnəlɪ] *adv* de vez en cuando.

occupant ['ɒkjʊpənt] *n* (*of house*) inquilino *m* (-na *f*); (*of car, plane*) ocupante *mf*.

occupation [ˌɒkjʊ'peɪʃn] *n* (*job*) empleo *m*; (*pastime*) pasatiempo *m*.

occupied ['ɒkjʊpaɪd] *adj* (*toilet*) ocupado(-da).

occupy ['ɒkjʊpaɪ] *vt* ocupar; (*building*) habitar.

occur [ə'kɜː^r] *vi* (*happen*) ocurrir; (*exist*) encontrarse.

occurrence [ə'kʌrəns] *n* acontecimiento *m*.

ocean ['əʊʃn] *n* océano *m*; **the ~** (*Am: sea*) el mar.

o'clock [ə'klɒk] *adv*: **it's one ~** es la una; **it's two ~** son las dos; **at one/two ~** a la una/las dos.

Oct. (*abbr of October*) oct.

October [ɒk'təʊbə^r] *n* octubre *m*, → **September**.

octopus ['ɒktəpəs] *n* pulpo *m*.

odd [ɒd] *adj* (*strange*) raro(-ra), (*number*) impar; (*not matching*) sin pareja; (*occasional*) ocasional; **sixty ~ miles** sesenta y pico millas; **some ~ bits of paper** algunos que otros cachos de papel; **~ jobs** chapuzas *fpl*.

odds [ɒdz] *npl* (*in betting*) apuestas *fpl; (chances)* probabilidades *fpl;* ~ **and ends** chismes *mpl.*

odor ['əʊdər] *(Am)* = **odour.**

odour ['əʊdər] *n (Br)* olor *m.*

of [ɒv] *prep* 1. *(gen)* de; **the handle** ~ **the door** el pomo de la puerta; **fear** ~ **spiders** miedo a las arañas; **he died** ~ **cancer** murió de cáncer; **the city** ~ **Glasgow** la ciudad de Glasgow; **that was very kind** ~ **you** fue muy amable por tu parte.

2. *(describing amounts, contents)* de; **a piece** ~ **cake** un trozo de pastel; **a glass** ~ **beer** un vaso de cerveza; **a fall** ~ **20%** un descenso del 20%.

3. *(made from)* de; **it's made** ~ **wood** es de madera.

4. *(referring to time)* de; **the summer** ~ **1969** el verano de 1969; **the 26th** ~ **August** el 26 de agosto.

5. *(Am: in telling the time)*: **it's ten** ~ **four** son las cuatro menos diez.

off [ɒf] *adv* 1. *(away)*: **to drive/walk** ~ alejarse; **to get** ~ *(bus, train etc)* bajarse; **we're** ~ **to Austria next week** nos vamos a Austria la semana que viene.

2. *(expressing removal)*: **to take sthg** ~ *(clothes, shoes)* quitarse algo; *(lid, wrapper)* quitar algo; *(money)* descontar algo.

3. *(so as to stop working)*: **to turn sthg** ~ *(TV, radio, engine)* apagar; *(tap)* cerrar.

4. *(expressing distance or time away)*: **it's a long way** ~ *(in distance)* está muy lejos; **Christmas is a long way** ~ queda mucho para las Navidades.

5. *(not at work)* libre; **I'm taking a week** ~ voy a tomar una semana libre; **she's** ~ **ill** está de baja por enfermedad.

6. *(expressing completion)*: **to finish sthg** ~ terminar algo.

◆ *prep* 1. *(away from)*: **to get** ~ **sthg** bajarse de algo; **she fell** ~ **the chair** se cayó de la silla.

2. *(indicating removal)*: **take the lid** ~ **the jar** quita la tapa del tarro; **we'll take £20** ~ **the price** le descontaremos 20 libras del precio.

3. *(adjoining)*: **it's just** ~ **the main road** está al lado de la carretera principal.

4. *(absent from)*: **to be** ~ **work** no estar en el trabajo.

5. *(inf: from)*: **I bought it** ~ **her** se lo compré (a ella).

6. *(inf: no longer liking)*: **I'm** ~ **my food** no me apetece comer estos días.

◆ *adj* 1. *(meat, cheese)* pasado(-da); *(milk)* cortado(-da); *(beer)* agrio (-gria).

2. *(not working)* apagado(-da); *(tap)* cerrado(-da).

3. *(cancelled)* suspendido(-da).

4. *(not available)*: **the soup's** ~ no hay sopa.

offence [ə'fens] *n (Br) (crime)* delito *m; (upset)* ofensa *f.*

offend [ə'fend] *vt* ofender.

offender [ə'fendər] *n* delincuente *mf.*

offense [ə'fens] *(Am)* = **offence.**

offensive [ə'fensɪv] *adj (insulting)* ofensivo(-va).

offer ['ɒfər] *n* oferta *f* ◆ *vt* ofrecer; **on** ~ *(available)* disponible; *(reduced)* en oferta; **to** ~ **to do sthg** ofrecerse a hacer algo; **to** ~ **sb sthg** ofrecer algo a alguien.

office ['ɒfɪs] *n* oficina *f.*

office block *n* bloque *m* de oficinas.

officer [ˈɒfɪsəʳ] *n* (MIL) oficial *mf*; (policeman) agente *mf* de policía.

official [əˈfɪʃl] *adj* oficial ♦ *n* (of government) funcionario *m* (-ria *f*).

officially [əˈfɪʃəlɪ] *adv* oficialmente.

off-licence *n* (Br) tienda de bebidas alcohólicas para llevar.

off-peak *adj* de tarifa reducida.

off sales *npl* (Br) venta de bebidas alcohólicas para llevar en un pub.

off-season *n* temporada *f* baja.

offshore [ˈɒfʃɔːʳ] *adj* (breeze) costero(-ra).

off side *n* (for right hand drive) lado *m* izquierdo, (for left hand drive) lado derecho.

off-the-peg *adj* confeccionado(-da).

often [ˈɒfn, ˈɒftn] *adv* a menudo, con frecuencia; **how ~ do the buses run?** ¿cada cuánto tiempo pasan los autobuses?; **every so ~** cada cierto tiempo.

oh [əʊ] *excl* ¡ah!, ¡oh!

oil [ɔɪl] *n* aceite *m*; (fuel) petróleo *m*.

oilcan [ˈɔɪlkæn] *n* aceitera *f*.

oil filter *n* filtro *m* del aceite.

oil rig *n* plataforma *f* petrolífera.

oily [ˈɔɪlɪ] *adj* (cloth, hands) grasiento(-ta); (food) aceitoso(-sa).

ointment [ˈɔɪntmənt] *n* pomada *f*.

OK [ˌəʊˈkeɪ] (inf) *adv* (expressing agreement) vale; (satisfactorily, well) bien ♦ *adj*: **is that ~ with you?** ¿te parece bien?; **everyone's ~** todos están bien; **the film was ~** la película estuvo bien.

okay [ˌəʊˈkeɪ] = **OK.**

old [əʊld] *adj* viejo(-ja); (former) antiguo(-gua); **how ~ are you?** ¿cuántos años tienes?; **I'm 36 years ~** tengo 36 años; **to get ~** hacerse viejo.

old age *n* vejez *f*.

old age pensioner *n* pensionista *mf*.

O-level *n* antiguo examen estatal en una materia que se solía hacer a los 16 años en Inglaterra y Gales.

olive [ˈɒlɪv] *n* aceituna *f*.

olive oil *n* aceite *m* de oliva.

Olympic Games [əˈlɪmpɪk] *npl* Juegos *mpl* Olímpicos.

omelette [ˈɒmlɪt] *n* tortilla *f*; **mushroom ~** tortilla de champiñones.

ominous [ˈɒmɪnəs] *adj* siniestro(-tra).

omit [əˈmɪt] *vt* omitir.

on [ɒn] *prep* 1. (indicating position) en, sobre; **it's ~ the table** está en OR sobre la mesa; **~ the floor** está en el suelo; **a picture ~ the wall** un cuadro en la pared; **the exhaust ~ the car** el tubo de escape del coche; **~ the left/right** a la izquierda/derecha; **we stayed ~ a farm** estuvimos en una granja; **~ the banks of the river** a orillas del río; **the instructions ~ the packet** las instrucciones en el paquete.
2. (with forms of transport): **~ the train/plane** en el tren/avión; **to get ~ a bus** subirse a un autobús.
3. (expressing means, method) en; **~ foot** a pie; **to lean ~ one's elbows** apoyarse en los codos; **~ the radio** en la radio; **~ TV** en la televisión;

it runs ~ unleaded petrol funciona con gasolina sin plomo.
4. *(about)* sobre, acerca de; **a book ~ Germany** un libro sobre Alemania.
5. *(expressing time)*: **~ arrival** al llegar; **~ Tuesday** el martes; **~ Tuesdays** los martes; **~ 25th August** el 25 de agosto.
6. *(with regard to)* en, sobre; **a tax ~ imports** un impuesto sobre las importaciones; **the effect ~ Britain** el impacto en Gran Bretaña.
7. *(describing activity, state)*: **~ holiday** de vacaciones; **~ offer** *(reduced)* en oferta; **~ sale** en venta.
8. *(in phrases)*: **do you have any money ~ you?** *(inf)* ¿llevas dinero?; **the drinks are ~ me** (a las copas) invito yo.
◆ *adv* 1. *(in place, covering)*: **put the lid ~** pon la tapa; **to put one's clothes ~** vestirse.
2. *(film, play, programme)*: **the news is ~** están dando las noticias; **what's ~ at the cinema?** ¿qué ponen en el cine?
3. *(with transport)*: **to get ~** subirse.
4. *(functioning)*: **to turn sthg ~** *(TV, radio, engine)* encender algo; *(tap)* abrir algo.
5. *(taking place)*: **the match is already ~** ya ha empezado el partido.
6. *(indicating continuing action)*: **to keep ~ doing sthg** seguir haciendo algo; **to drive ~** seguir (conduciendo).
7. *(in phrases)*: **have you anything ~ tonight?** ¿haces algo esta noche?
◆ *adj* *(TV, radio, light, engine)* encendido(-da); *(tap)* abierto(-ta); **is the game ~?** ¿se va a celebrar el partido?

once [wʌns] *adv* *(one time)* una vez; *(in the past)* en otro tiempo ◆ *conj* una vez que; **at ~** *(immediately)* inmediatamente; *(at the same time)* a la vez; **for ~** por una vez; **~ a month** una vez al mes; **~ more** *(one more time)* una vez más; *(again)* otra vez.

oncoming [ˈɒnˌkʌmɪŋ] *adj* *(traffic)* que viene en dirección contraria.

one [wʌn] *num* uno (una) ◆ *adj* *(only)* único(-ca) ◆ *pron* *(fml: you)* uno (una *f*); **the green ~** el verde (la verde); **I want a blue ~** quiero uno azul; **thirty-~** treinta y uno; **a hundred and ~** ciento uno; **~ fifth** un quinto; **that ~** ése *m* (ésa *f*); **this ~** éste *m* (ésta *f*); **which ~?** ¿cuál?; **the ~ I told you about** aquél que te conté; **~ of my friends** uno de mis amigos; **~ day** *(in past)* un día; *(in future)* algún día.

one-piece (swimsuit) *n* traje *m* de baño de una pieza.

oneself [wʌnˈself] *pron* *(reflexive)* se; *(after prep)* uno mismo *m* (una misma *f*); **to wash ~** lavarse.

one-way *adj* *(street)* de dirección única; *(ticket)* de ida.

onion [ˈʌnjən] *n* cebolla *f*.

onion bhaji [-ˈbɑːdʒɪ] *n* buñuelo de cebolla picada, rebozada y muy frita preparado al estilo indio.

onion rings *npl* anillos *mpl* de cebolla rebozados.

only [ˈəʊnlɪ] *adj* único(-ca) ◆ *adv* sólo; **an ~ child** hijo único; **I ~ want one** sólo quiero uno; **we've ~ just arrived** acabamos de llegar; **there's ~ just enough** apenas hay lo justo; **"members ~"** "miembros sólo"; **not ~** no sólo.

onto ['ɒntuː] *prep (with verbs of movement)* encima de, sobre; **to get ~ sb** *(telephone)* ponerse en contacto con alguien.

onward ['ɒnwəd] *adv* = **onwards** ♦ *adj*: **your ~ journey** el resto de su viaje.

onwards ['ɒnwədz] *adv (forwards)* adelante; **from now ~** de ahora en adelante; **from October ~** de octubre en adelante.

opal ['əupl] *n* ópalo *m*.

opaque [əu'peɪk] *adj* opaco(-ca).

open ['əupn] *adj* abierto(-ta), *(honest)* sincero(-ca) ♦ *vt* abrir; *(start)* dar comienzo a ♦ *vi (door, window, lock)* abrirse; *(shop, office, bank)* abrir; *(start)* dar comienzo; **are you ~ at the weekend?** ¿abres el fin de semana?; **wide ~** abierto de par en par; **in the ~ (air)** al aire libre ❏ **open onto** *vi fus* dar a; **open up** *vi* abrir.

open-air *adj* al aire libre.

opening ['əupnɪŋ] *n (gap)* abertura *f*; *(beginning)* comienzo *m*; *(opportunity)* oportunidad *f*.

opening hours *npl* horario *m* de apertura.

open-minded [-'maɪndɪd] *adj* sin prejuicios.

open-plan *adj* de plano abierto.

open sandwich *n* rebanada de pan cubierta con relleno habitual de bocadillos.

opera ['ɒprə] *n* ópera *f*.

opera house *n* teatro *m* de la ópera.

operate ['ɒpəreɪt] *vt (machine)* hacer funcionar ♦ *vi (work)* funcionar; **to ~ on sb** operar a alguien.

operating room ['ɒpəreɪtɪŋ-] *n (Am)* = **operating theatre**.

operating theatre ['ɒpəreɪtɪŋ-] *n (Br)* quirófano *m*.

operation [ˌɒpə'reɪʃn] *n* operación *f*; **to be in ~** *(law, system)* estar en vigor; **to have an ~** operarse.

operator ['ɒpəreɪtə'] *n (on phone)* operador *m* (-ra *f*).

opinion [ə'pɪnjən] *n* opinión *f*; **in my ~** en mi opinión.

opponent [ə'pəunənt] *n (SPORT)* contrincante *mf*; *(of idea, policy, party)* adversario *m* (-ria *f*).

opportunity [ˌɒpə'tjuːnəti] *n* oportunidad *f*.

oppose [ə'pəuz] *vt* oponerse a.

opposed [ə'pəuzd] *adj*: **to be ~ to** oponerse a.

opposite ['ɒpəzɪt] *adj (facing)* de enfrente; *(totally different)* opuesto(-ta) ♦ *prep* enfrente de ♦ *n*: **the ~ (of)** lo contrario (de).

opposition [ˌɒpə'zɪʃn] *n (objections)* oposición *f*; *(SPORT)* oponentes *mfpl*; **the Opposition** la oposición.

opt [ɒpt] *vt*: **to ~ to do sthg** optar por hacer algo.

optician's [ɒp'tɪʃnz] *n (shop)* óptica *f*.

optimist ['ɒptɪmɪst] *n* optimista *mf*.

optimistic [ˌɒptɪ'mɪstɪk] *adj* optimista.

option ['ɒpʃn] *n* opción *f*.

optional ['ɒpʃənl] *adj* opcional.

or [ɔː'] *conj* o, u *(before "o" or "ho")*;

(after negative) ni; **I can't read ~ write** no sé (ni) leer ni escribir.

oral ['ɔːrəl] *adj (spoken)* oral; *(of the mouth)* bucal ◆ *n* examen *m* oral.

orange ['ɒrɪndʒ] *adj* naranja *(inv)* ◆ *n* naranja *f.*

orange juice *n* zumo *m* de naranja.

orange squash *n (Br)* naranjada *f.*

orbit ['ɔːbɪt] *n* órbita *f.*

orbital (motorway) ['ɔːbɪtl-] *n (Br)* ronda *f* de circunvalación.

orchard ['ɔːtʃəd] *n* huerto *m.*

orchestra ['ɔːkɪstrə] *n* orquesta *f.*

ordeal [ɔːˈdiːl] *n* calvario *m.*

order ['ɔːdəʳ] *n (sequence, neatness, discipline)* orden *m; (command, in restaurant)* orden *f; (COMM)* pedido *m* ◆ *vt (command)* ordenar; *(food, drink, taxi)* pedir; *(COMM)* encargar ◆ *vi (in restaurant)* pedir; **in ~ to** para; **out of ~** *(not working)* estropeado; **in working ~** en funcionamiento; **to ~ sb to do sthg** ordenar a alguien que haga algo.

order form *n* hoja *f* de pedido.

ordinary ['ɔːdənrɪ] *adj* corriente.

ore [ɔːʳ] *n* mineral *m.*

oregano [ˌɒrɪˈgɑːnəʊ] *n* orégano *m.*

organ ['ɔːgən] *n* órgano *m.*

organic [ɔːˈgænɪk] *adj* orgánico(-ca).

organization [ˌɔːgənaɪˈzeɪʃn] *n* organización *f.*

organize ['ɔːgənaɪz] *vt* organizar.

organizer ['ɔːgənaɪzəʳ] *n (person)* organizador *m* (-ra *f); (diary)*

agenda *f.*

oriental [ˌɔːrɪˈentl] *adj* oriental.

orientate ['ɔːrɪenteɪt] *vt:* **to ~ o.s.** orientarse.

origin ['ɒrɪdʒɪn] *n* origen *m.*

original [əˈrɪdʒənl] *adj (first)* originario(-ria); *(novel)* original.

originally [əˈrɪdʒənəlɪ] *adv* originalmente.

originate [əˈrɪdʒəneɪt] *vi:* **to ~ (from)** nacer (de).

ornament ['ɔːnəmənt] *n* adorno *m.*

ornamental [ˌɔːnəˈmentl] *adj* ornamental.

ornate [ɔːˈneɪt] *adj* recargado(-da).

orphan ['ɔːfn] *n* huérfano *m* (-na *f*).

orthodox ['ɔːθədɒks] *adj* ortodoxo(-xa).

ostentatious [ˌɒsten'teɪʃəs] *adj* ostentoso(-sa).

ostrich ['ɒstrɪtʃ] *n* avestruz *m.*

other ['ʌðəʳ] *adj* otro (otra) ◆ *adv:* **~ than** excepto; **the ~ (one)** el otro (la otra); **the ~ day** el otro día; **one after the ~** uno después del otro ❑ **others** *pron (additional ones)* otros *mpl* (otras *fpl*); **the ~s** *(remaining ones)* los demás (las demás), los otros (las otras).

otherwise ['ʌðəwaɪz] *adv (or else)* sino; *(apart from that)* por lo demás; *(differently)* de otra manera.

otter ['ɒtəʳ] *n* nutria *f.*

ought [ɔːt] *aux vb* deber; **it ~ to be ready** debería de estar listo; **you ~ to do it** deberías hacerlo.

ounce [aʊns] *n = 28,35g,* onza *f.*

our ['aʊəʳ] *adj* nuestro(-tra).

ours ['aʊəz] *pron* nuestro *m* (-tra *f*); **a friend of ~** un amigo nuestro.

ourselves [aʊə'selvz] *pron* (*reflexive*) nos; (*after prep*) nosotros *mpl* mismos (nosotras *fpl* mismas); **we did it ~** lo hicimos nosotros mismos

out [aʊt] *adj* (*light, cigarette*) apagado(-da).
♦ *adv* 1. (*outside*) fuera; **to get ~ (of)** (*car*) bajar (de); **to go ~ (of)** salir (de); **it's cold ~ today** hace frío hoy.
2. (*not at home, work*) fuera; **to go ~** salir; **she's ~** está fuera.
3. (*extinguished*): **put your cigarette ~** apaga tu cigarrillo
4. (*expressing removal*): **to take sthg ~ (of)** sacar algo (de); **to pour sthg ~** (*liquid*) echar algo.
5. (*outwards*) hacia fuera; **to stick ~** sobresalir.
6. (*expressing exclusion*) fuera; **"keep ~"** "prohibido el paso"
7 (*wrong*): **the bill's £10 ~** hay un error de 10 libras en la cuenta
8. (*in phrases*): **stay ~ of the sun** no te expongas al sol; **made ~ of wood** (hecho) de madera; **five ~ of ten women** cinco de cada diez mujeres; **I'm ~ of cigarettes** no tengo (más) cigarrillos.

outback ['aʊtbæk] *n*: **the ~** los llanos del interior australiano.

outboard (motor) ['aʊtbɔːd-] *n* fueraborda *m*.

outbreak ['aʊtbreɪk] *n* (*of war*) comienzo *m*; (*of illness*) epidemia f.

outburst ['aʊtbɜːst] *n* explosión f.

outcome ['aʊtkʌm] *n* resultado *m*.

outcrop ['aʊtkrɒp] *n* afloramiento *m*.

outdated [,aʊt'deɪtɪd] *adj* anticuado(-da).

outdo [,aʊt'duː] *vt* aventajar.

outdoor ['aʊtdɔːr] *adj* (*swimming pool, activities*) al aire libre.

outdoors [,aʊt'dɔːz] *adv* al aire libre.

outer ['aʊtər] *adj* exterior.

outer space *n* el espacio exterior.

outfit ['aʊtfɪt] *n* (*clothes*) traje *m*.

outing ['aʊtɪŋ] *n* excursión f.

outlet ['aʊtlet] *n* (*pipe*) desagüe *m*; **"no ~"** (*Am*) señal que indica que una carretera no tiene salida.

outline ['aʊtlaɪn] *n* (*shape*) contorno *m*; (*description*) esbozo *m*.

outlook ['aʊtlʊk] *n* (*for future*) perspectivas *fpl*; (*of weather*) pronóstico *m*; (*attitude*) enfoque *m*.

out-of-date *adj* (*old-fashioned*) anticuado(-da); (*passport, licence*) caducado(-da).

outpatients' (department) ['aʊt,peɪʃnts-] *n* departamento *m* de pacientes externos.

output ['aʊtpʊt] *n* (*of factory*) producción f; (*COMPUT: printout*) impresión f.

outrage ['aʊtreɪdʒ] *n* (*cruel act*) atrocidad f.

outrageous [aʊt'reɪdʒəs] *adj* (*shocking*) indignante.

outright [,aʊt'raɪt] *adv* (*tell, deny*) categóricamente; (*own*) totalmente.

outside [*adv* ,aʊt'saɪd, *adj, prep &* *n* 'aʊtsaɪd] *adv* fuera ♦ *prep* fuera de ♦ *adj* (*exterior*) exterior; (*help, ad-*

vice) independiente ◆ *n*: the ~ *(of building, car, container)* el exterior; *(AUT: in UK)* carril *m* de adelantamiento; *(AUT: in Europe, US)* carril lento; **an ~ line** una línea exterior; **~ of** *(Am) (on the outside of)* fuera de; *(apart from)* aparte de.

outside lane *n (in UK)* carril *m* de adelantamiento; *(in Europe, US)* carril lento.

outsize ['autsaiz] *adj (clothes)* de talla grande.

outskirts ['autskɜːts] *npl* afueras *fpl*.

outstanding [,aut'stændɪŋ] *adj (remarkable)* destacado(-da); *(problem, debt)* pendiente.

outward ['autwəd] *adj (journey)* de ida; *(external)* visible.

outwards ['autwədz] *adv* hacia afuera.

oval ['əuvl] *adj* oval.

ovation [əu'veɪʃn] *n* ovación *f*.

oven ['ʌvn] *n* horno *m*.

oven glove *n* guante *m* de horno.

ovenproof ['ʌvnpruːf] *adj* refractario(-ria).

oven-ready *adj* listo(-ta) para hornear.

over ['əuvə^r] *prep* **1.** *(above)* encima de; **a lamp ~ the table** una lámpara encima de la mesa.
2. *(across)* por encima de; **to walk/drive ~ sthg** cruzar algo; **it's just ~ the road** está enfrente.
3. *(covering)* sobre; **to smear the cream ~ the wound** untar la herida con la crema.
4. *(more than)* más de; **it cost ~ £1,000** costó más de mil libras.
5. *(during)* durante; **~ the past two**

years en los dos últimos años.
6. *(with regard to)* sobre; **an argument ~ the price** una discusión sobre el precio.
◆ *adv* **1.** *(downwards)*: **to fall ~** caerse; **to push sthg ~** empujar algo.
2. *(referring to position, movement)*: **to drive/walk ~** cruzar; **~ here** aquí; **~ there** allí.
3. *(round to other side)*: **to turn sthg ~** dar la vuelta a algo.
4. *(more)*: **children aged 12 and ~** niños de 12 años en adelante.
5. *(remaining)*: **to be (left) ~** quedar.
6. *(to one's house)*: **to invite sb ~ for dinner** invitar a alguien a cenar.
7. *(in phrases)*: **all ~** *adj (finished)* terminado(-da) ◆ *prep (throughout)* por todo.
◆ *adj (finished)*: **to be ~** haber terminado.

overall [*adv* ,əuvə'rɔːl, *n* 'əuvərɔːl] *adv* en conjunto ◆ *n (Br: coat)* guardapolvo *m*; *(Am: boiler suit)* mono *m*; **how much does it cost ~?** ¿cuánto cuesta en total? ❑ **overalls** *npl (Br: boiler suit)* mono *m*; *(Am: dungarees)* pantalones *mpl* de peto.

overboard ['əuvəbɔːd] *adv (from ship)* por la borda.

overbooked [,əuvə'bukt] *adj*: **to be ~** tener overbooking.

overcame [,əuvə'keɪm] *pt* → **overcome**.

overcast [,əuvə'kɑːst] *adj* cubierto(-ta).

overcharge [,əuvə'tʃɑːdʒ] *vt* cobrar en exceso.

overcoat ['əuvəkəut] *n* abrigo *m*.

overcome [,əuvə'kʌm] *(pt* **-came**,

pp **-come**) *vt (defeat)* vencer.

overcooked [,əʊvə'kʊkt] *adj* demasiado hecho(-cha).

overcrowded [,əʊvə'kraʊdɪd] *adj* atestado(-da).

overdo [,əʊvə'duː] *(pt* **-did** [-'dɪd], *pp* **-done**) *vt (exaggerate)* exagerar; **to ~ it** exagerar.

overdone [,əʊvə'dʌn] *pp* → **overdo** ◆ *adj (food)* demasiado hecho(-cha).

overdose ['əʊvədəʊs] *n* sobredosis *f inv*.

overdraft ['əʊvədrɑːft] *n (money owed)* saldo *m* deudor; *(credit limit)* descubierto *m*.

overdue [,əʊvə'djuː] *adj (bus, flight)* retrasado(-da); *(rent, payment)* vencido(-da).

over easy *adj (Am:* egg) frito(-ta) por ambos lados.

overexposed [,əʊvərɪk'spəʊzd] *adj* sobreexpuesto(-ta).

overflow [*vb* ,əʊvə'fləʊ, *n* 'əʊvəfləʊ] *vi* desbordarse ◆ *n (pipe)* cañería *f* de desagüe.

overgrown [,əʊvə'grəʊn] *adj* cubierto(-ta) de matojos.

overhaul [,əʊvə'hɔːl] *n (of machine, car)* revisión *f*.

overhead [*adj* 'əʊvəhed, *adv* ,əʊvə'hed] *adj* aéreo(-a) ◆ *adv* por lo alto.

overhead locker *n* maletero *m* superior.

overhear [,əʊvə'hɪə*r*] *(pt & pp* **-heard** [-'hɜːd]) *vt* oír por casualidad.

overheat [,əʊvə'hiːt] *vi* recalentarse.

overland ['əʊvəlænd] *adv* por vía

terrestre.

overlap [,əʊvə'læp] *vi* superponerse.

overleaf [,əʊvə'liːf] *adv* al dorso.

overload [,əʊvə'ləʊd] *vt* sobrecargar.

overlook [*vb* ,əʊvə'lʊk, *n* 'əʊvəlʊk] *vt (subj: building, room)* dar a; *(miss)* pasar por alto ◆ *n: (scenic)* ~ *(Am)* mirador *m*.

overnight [*adv* ,əʊvə'naɪt, *adj* 'əʊvənaɪt] *adv (during the night)* durante la noche, *(until next day)* toda la noche ◆ *adj (train, journey)* de noche.

overnight bag *n* bolso *m* de mano.

overpass ['əʊvəpɑːs] *n* paso *m* elevado.

overpowering [,əʊvə'paʊərɪŋ] *adj* arrollador(-ra).

oversaw [,əʊvə'sɔː] *pt* → **oversee**.

overseas [*adv* ,əʊvə'siːz, *adj* 'əʊvəsiːz] *adv (go)* al extranjero; *(live)* en el extranjero ◆ *adj (holiday, branch)* en el extranjero; *(student)* extranjero(-ra).

oversee [,əʊvə'siː] *(pt* **-saw**, *pp* **-seen** [-'siːn]) *vt* supervisar.

overshoot [,əʊvə'ʃuːt] *(pt & pp* **-shot** [-'ʃɒt]) *vt* pasarse.

oversight ['əʊvəsaɪt] *n* descuido *m*.

oversleep [,əʊvə'sliːp] *(pt & pp* **-slept** [-'slept]) *vi* dormirse, no despertarse a tiempo.

overtake [,əʊvə'teɪk] *(pt* **-took**, *pp* **-taken** [-'teɪkən]) *vt & vi* adelantar; **"no overtaking"** "prohibido adelantar".

overtime 202

overtime ['əʊvətaɪm] *n* horas *fpl* extra.

overtook [,əʊvə'tʊk] *pt* → **overtake**.

overture ['əʊvə,tjʊəʳ] *n* (MUS) obertura *f*.

overturn [,əʊvə'tɜːn] *vi* volcar.

overweight [,əʊvə'weɪt] *adj* gordo(-da).

overwhelm [,əʊvə'welm] *vt* abrumar.

owe [əʊ] *vt* deber; **to ~ sb sthg** deber algo a alguien; **owing to** debido a.

owl [aʊl] *n* búho *m*.

own [əʊn] *adj* propio(-pia) ◆ *vt* poseer ◆ *pron*: **my ~** el mío (la mía); **her ~** la suya; **his ~** el suyo; **on my ~** solo(-la); **to get one's ~ back** tomarse la revancha ❑ **own up** *vi*: **to ~ up (to sthg)** confesar (algo).

owner ['əʊnəʳ] *n* propietario *m* (-ria *f*).

ownership ['əʊnəʃɪp] *n* propiedad *f*.

ox [ɒks] (*pl* **oxen** ['ɒksən]) *n* buey *m*.

oxtail soup ['ɒksteɪl-] *n* sopa *f* de rabo de buey.

oxygen ['ɒksɪdʒən] *n* oxígeno *m*.

oyster ['ɔɪstəʳ] *n* ostra *f*.

oz *abbr* = **ounce**.

ozone-friendly ['əʊzəʊn-] *adj* que no daña la capa de ozono.

p *abbr* = **penny**, **pence**; (*abbr of page*) pág.

pace [peɪs] *n* paso *m*.

pacemaker ['peɪs,meɪkəʳ] *n* (for heart) marcapasos *m inv*.

Pacific [pə'sɪfɪk] *n*: **the ~ (Ocean)** el (océano) Pacífico *m*.

pacifier ['pæsɪfaɪəʳ] *n* (Am: for baby) chupete *m*.

pacifist ['pæsɪfɪst] *n* pacifista *mf*.

pack [pæk] *n* (packet) paquete *m*; (of crisps) bolsa *f*; (Br: of cards) baraja *f*; (rucksack) mochila *f* ◆ *vt* (suitcase, bag) hacer; (clothes, camera etc) meter en la maleta; (to package) empaquetar ◆ *vi* hacer la maleta; **a ~ of lies** una sarta de mentiras; **to ~ sthg into sthg** meter algo en algo; **to ~ one's bags** hacerse las maletas ❑ **pack up** *vi* (pack case) hacer las maletas; (tidy up) recoger; (Br: inf: machine, car) fastidiarse.

package ['pækɪdʒ] *n* paquete *m* ◆ *vt* envasar.

package holiday *n* vacaciones *fpl* con todo incluido.

package tour *n* tour *m* con todo incluido.

packaging ['pækɪdʒɪŋ] *n* embalaje *m*.

packed [pækt] *adj* (crowded) repleto(-ta).

packed lunch *n* almuerzo preparado que se lleva al colegio, trabajo, etc.

packet ['pækɪt] n paquete m; **it cost a ~** (Br: inf) costó un dineral.

packing ['pækɪŋ] n (material) embalaje m; **to do one's ~** hacer el equipaje.

pad [pæd] n (of paper) bloc m; (of cloth, cotton wool) almohadilla f; **shoulder ~s** hombreras fpl.

padded ['pædɪd] adj acolchado(-a).

padded envelope n sobre m acolchado.

paddle ['pædl] (pole) pala f ◆ vi (wade) pasear por la orilla; (in canoe) remar.

paddling pool ['pædlɪŋ] n (in park) estanque m para chapotear.

paddock ['pædək] n (at racecourse) paddock m.

padlock ['pædlɒk] n candado m.

page [peɪdʒ] n página f ◆ vt llamar por megafonía; **"paging Mr Hill"** "llamando a Mr Hill".

paid [peɪd] pt & pp → **pay** ◆ adj pagado(-a).

pain [peɪn] n (physical) dolor m; (emotional) pena f; **to be in ~** sufrir dolor; **he's such a ~!** (inf) ¡es un plasta! □ **pains** npl (trouble) esfuerzos mpl.

painful ['peɪnful] adj doloroso(-a); **my leg is ~** me duele la pierna.

painkiller ['peɪn,kɪlər] n calmante m.

paint [peɪnt] n pintura f ◆ vt & vi pintar; **to ~ one's nails** pintarse las uñas □ **paints** npl (tubes, pots etc) pinturas fpl.

paintbrush ['peɪntbrʌʃ] n (of decorator) brocha f; (of artist) pincel m.

painter ['peɪntər] n pintor m (-ra f).

painting ['peɪntɪŋ] n (picture) cuadro m; (artistic activity, trade) pintura f.

pair [peər] n (of two things) par m; **in ~s** pose pares; **a ~ of pliers** unos alicates; **a ~ of scissors** unas tijeras; **a ~ of shorts** unos pantalones cortos; **a ~ of tights** un par de medias; **a ~ of trousers** unos pantalones.

pajamas [pə'dʒɑːməz] (Am) = **pyjamas**

Pakistan [Br ,pɑːkɪ'stɑːn, Am ,pækɪ'stæn] n Paquistán.

Pakistani [Br ,pɑːkɪ'stɑːnɪ, Am ,pækɪ'stænɪ] adj paquistaní ◆ n paquistaní mf.

pakora [pə'kɔːrə] npl verduras rebozadas muy fritas y picantes, al estilo indio.

pal [pæl] n (inf) colega mf.

palace ['pælɪs] n palacio m

palatable ['pælətəbl] adj sabroso(-a).

palate ['pælət] n paladar m.

pale [peɪl] adj (not bright) claro (-ra); (skin) pálido(-da).

pale ale n tipo de cerveza rubia.

palm [pɑːm] n (of hand) palma f; **~ (tree)** palmera f.

palpitations [,pælpɪ'teɪʃnz] npl palpitaciones fpl.

pamphlet ['pæmflɪt] n folleto m.

pan [pæn] n cazuela f.

Panama [,pænə'mɑː] n Panamá.

Panamanian [,pænə'meɪnjən] adj panameño(-ña) ◆ n panameño m (-ña f).

pancake ['pæŋkeɪk] n crepe f.

pancake roll n rollito m de primavera.

panda ['pændə] n panda m.

panda car n (Br) coche m patrulla.

pane [peɪn] n cristal m.

panel ['pænl] n (of wood, on TV, radio) panel m; (group of experts) equipo m.

paneling ['pænəlɪŋ] (Am) = panelling.

panelling ['pænəlɪŋ] n (Br) paneles mpl.

panic ['pænɪk] (pt & pp **-ked**, cont **-king**) n pánico m ◆ vi aterrarse.

panniers ['pænɪəz] npl (for bicycle) bolsas fpl para equipaje.

panoramic [,pænə'ræmɪk] adj panorámico(-ca).

pant [pænt] vi jadear.

panties ['pæntɪz] npl (inf) bragas fpl.

pantomime ['pæntəmaɪm] n (Br) musical humorístico infantil de Navidades.

---

i PANTOMIME

Inspiradas normalmente en cuentos de hadas tradicionales, las "pantomimes" son musicales cómicos para niños que se representan durante las Navidades. Es costumbre que una actriz joven haga el papel del héroe y un actor cómico el de anciana.

---

pantry ['pæntrɪ] n despensa f.

pants [pænts] npl (Br: underwear) calzoncillos mpl; (Am: trousers) pantalones mpl.

panty hose ['pæntɪ-] npl (Am) medias fpl.

paper ['peɪpər] n (material) papel m; (newspaper) periódico m; (exam) examen m ◆ adj de papel ◆ vt empapelar; **a piece of ~** (sheet) un papel; (scrap) un trozo de papel ◻ **papers** npl (documents) documentación f.

paperback ['peɪpəbæk] n libro m en rústica.

paper bag n bolsa f de papel.

paperboy ['peɪpəbɔɪ] n repartidor m de periódicos.

paper clip n clip m.

papergirl ['peɪpəgɜ:l] n repartidora f de periódicos.

paper handkerchief n pañuelo m de papel.

paper shop n = quiosco m de periódicos.

paperweight ['peɪpəweɪt] n pisapapeles m inv.

paprika ['pæprɪkə] n pimentón m.

par [pɑ:r] n (in golf) par m.

paracetamol [,pærə'si:təmɒl] n paracetamol m.

parachute ['pærəʃu:t] n paracaídas m inv.

parade [pə'reɪd] n (procession) desfile m; (of shops) hilera f.

paradise ['pærədaɪs] n paraíso m.

paraffin ['pærəfɪn] n parafina f.

paragraph ['pærəgrɑ:f] n párrafo m.

Paraguay ['pærəgwaɪ] n (el) Paraguay.

Paraguayan [,pærə'gwaɪən] adj

paraguayo(-ya) ◆ *n* paraguayo *m* (-ya *f*).

parallel ['pærəlel] *adj*: ~ **(to)** paralelo(-la) (a).

paralysed ['pærəlaızd] *adj* (*Br*) paralizado(-da).

paralyzed ['pærəlaızd] (*Am*) = **paralysed**.

paramedic [,pærə'medık] *n* auxiliar *m* sanitario (auxiliar *f* sanitaria).

paranoid ['pærənɔɪd] *adj* paranoico(-ca).

parasite ['pærəsaɪt] *n* (*animal*) parásito *m*; (*pej: person*) parásito *m* (-ta *f*).

parasol ['pærəsɒl] *n* sombrilla *f*.

parcel ['pɑːsl] *n* paquete *m*

parcel post *n* servicio *m* de paquete postal.

pardon ['pɑːdn] *excl*: ~? ¿perdón?; ~ **(me)!** ¡perdone!; **I beg your** ~! (*apologizing*) ¡le ruego me perdone!; **I beg your** ~? (*asking for repetition*) ¿cómo dice?

parents ['peərənts] *npl* padres *mpl*.

parish ['pærɪʃ] *n* (*of church*) parroquia *f*; (*village area*) municipio *m*.

park [pɑːk] *n* parque *m* ◆ *vt & vi* aparcar.

park and ride *n* aparcamiento *m* en las afueras de la ciudad en donde hay autobuses al centro.

parking ['pɑːkɪŋ] *n* aparcamiento *m*.

parking brake *n* (*Am*) freno *m* de mano.

parking lot *n* (*Am*) aparcamiento *m* (al aire libre).

parking meter *n* parquí-

metro *m*.

parking space *n* sitio *m* (para aparcar).

parking ticket *n* multa *f* por aparcamiento indebido.

parkway ['pɑːkweɪ] *n* (*Am*) avenida *f* (con zona ajardinada en el medio).

parliament ['pɑːləmənt] *n* parlamento *m*.

Parmesan (cheese) [,pɑːmɪ'zæn-] *n* parmesano *m*.

parrot ['pærət] *n* loro *m*.

parsley ['pɑːslɪ] *n* perejil *m*.

parsnip ['pɑːsnɪp] *n* chirivía *f*.

parson ['pɑːsn] *n* párroco *m*.

part [pɑːt] *n* parte *f*; (*of machine, car*) pieza *f*; (*in play, film*) papel *m*; (*Am: in hair*) raya *f* ◆ *adv* en parte ◆ *vi* (*couple*) separarse; **in this** ~ **of France** en esta parte de Francia; **to form** ~ **of** formar parte de; **to play a** ~ **in** desempeñar un papel en; **to take** ~ **in** tomar parte en; **for my** ~ por mi parte; **for the most** ~ en su mayoría; **in these** ~**s** por aquí.

partial ['pɑːʃl] *adj* (*not whole*) parcial; **to be** ~ **to sthg** ser aficionado(-da) a algo.

participant [pɑː'tɪsɪpənt] *n* participante *mf*.

participate [pɑː'tɪsɪpeɪt] *vi*: **to** ~ **(in)** participar (en).

particular [pə'tɪkjʊləʳ] *adj* (specific, fussy) particular; (special) especial; **in** ~ en particular; **nothing in** ~ nada en particular ❑ **particulars** *npl* (details) datos *mpl* personales.

particularly [pə'tɪkjʊləlɪ] *adv* especialmente.

parting ['pɑːtɪŋ] n (Br: in hair) raya f.

partition [pɑːˈtɪʃn] n (wall) tabique m.

partly ['pɑːtlɪ] adv en parte.

partner ['pɑːtnəʳ] n pareja f; (COMM) socio m (-cia f).

partnership ['pɑːtnəʃɪp] n asociación f.

partridge ['pɑːtrɪdʒ] n perdiz f.

part-time ['pɑːt] adj & adv a tiempo parcial.

party ['pɑːtɪ] n (for fun) fiesta f; (POL) partido m; (group of people) grupo m; **to have a ~** hacer una fiesta.

pass [pɑːs] vt pasar; (house, entrance etc) pasar por delante de; (person in street) cruzarse con; (test, exam) aprobar; (overtake) adelantar; (law) aprobar ◆ vi pasar; (overtake) adelantar; (in test, exam) aprobar ◆ n (document, SPORT) pase m; (in mountain) desfiladero m; (in exam) aprobado m; **to ~ sb sthg** pasarle algo a alguien ❑ **pass by** vt fus (building, window etc) pasar por ◆ vi pasar cerca; **pass on** vt sep transmitir; **pass out** vi (faint) desmayarse; **pass up** vt sep (opportunity) dejar pasar.

passable ['pɑːsəbl] adj (road) transitable; (satisfactory) pasable.

passage ['pæsɪdʒ] n (corridor) pasadizo m; (in book) pasaje m; (sea journey) travesía f.

passageway ['pæsɪdʒweɪ] n pasadizo m.

passenger ['pæsɪndʒəʳ] n pasajero m (-ra f).

passerby [ˌpɑːsəˈbaɪ] n transeúnte mf.

passing place ['pɑːsɪŋ-] n (for cars) apartadero m.

passion ['pæʃn] n pasión f.

passionate ['pæʃənət] adj apasionado(-da).

passive ['pæsɪv] n pasiva f.

passport ['pɑːspɔːt] n pasaporte m.

passport control n control m de pasaportes.

passport photo n foto f de pasaporte.

password ['pɑːswɜːd] n contraseña f.

past [pɑːst] adj (at earlier time) anterior; (finished) terminado(-da); (last) último(-ma); (former) antiguo(-gua) ◆ prep (further than) más allá de; (in front of) por delante de ◆ n pasado m ◆ adv: **to run ~** pasar corriendo; **~ (tense)** pasado; **the ~ month** el mes pasado; **twenty ~ four** las cuatro y veinte; **in the ~** en el pasado.

pasta ['pæstə] n pasta f.

paste [peɪst] n (spread) paté m; (glue) engrudo m.

pastel ['pæstl] n pastel m.

pasteurized ['pæstʃəraɪzd] adj pasteurizado(-da).

pastille ['pæstɪl] n pastilla f.

pastime ['pɑːstaɪm] n pasatiempo m.

pastry ['peɪstrɪ] n (for pie) pasta f; (cake) pastel m.

pasture ['pɑːstʃəʳ] n pasto m.

pasty ['pæstɪ] n (Br) empanada f.

pat [pæt] vt golpear ligeramente.

patch [pætʃ] n (for clothes) remiendo m; (of colour, damp, for eye) parche m; (for skin) esparadrapo m; **a bad ~** (fig) un mal momento.

pâté ['pæteɪ] n paté m.

patent [Br 'peɪtənt, Am 'pætənt] n patente f.

path [pɑːθ, pl pɑːðz] n (in garden, park, country) camino m.

pathetic [pə'θetɪk] adj (pej: useless) inútil.

patience ['peɪʃns] n (quality) paciencia f; (Br: card game) solitario m.

patient ['peɪʃnt] adj paciente ◆ n paciente mf.

patio ['pætɪəʊ] n patio m.

patriotic [Br ˌpætrɪ'ɒtɪk, Am ˌpeɪtrɪ'ɒk] adj patriótico(-ca).

patrol [pə'trəʊl] vt patrullar ◆ n patrulla f.

patrol car n coche m patrulla.

patron ['peɪtrən] n (fml: customer) cliente mf; "~s only" "sólo para clientes".

patronizing ['pætrənaɪzɪŋ] adj paternalista.

pattern ['pætn] n (of shapes, colours) diseño m; (for sewing) patrón m.

patterned ['pætənd] adj estampado(-da).

pause [pɔːz] n pausa f ◆ vi (when speaking) hacer una pausa; (in activity) detenerse.

pavement ['peɪvmənt] n (Br: beside road) acera f; (Am: roadway) calzada f.

pavilion [pə'vɪljən] n pabellón m.

paving stone ['peɪvɪŋ-] n losa f.

pavlova [pæv'ləʊvə] n postre de merengue relleno de fruta y nata montada.

paw [pɔː] n pata f.

pawn [pɔːn] vt empeñar ◆ n (in chess) peón m.

pay [peɪ] (pt & pp **paid**) vt pagar ◆ vi (give money) pagar; (be profitable) ser rentable ◆ n paga f; **to ~ sb for sthg** pagar a alguien por algo; **to ~ money into an account** ingresar dinero en una cuenta; **to ~ attention (to)** prestar atención (a); **to ~ sb a visit** hacer una visita a alguien; **to ~ by credit card** pagar con tarjeta de crédito ❑ **pay back** vt sep (money) devolver, (person) devolver el dinero a; **pay for** vt fus pagar; **pay in** vt sep ingresar; **pay out** vt sep (money) pagar; **pay up** vi pagar.

payable ['peɪəbl] adj (bill) pagadero(-ra); **~ to** (cheque) a favor de.

payment ['peɪmənt] n pago m

payphone ['peɪfəʊn] n teléfono m público.

PC n (abbr of personal computer) ordenador personal, PC m; (Br: abbr of police constable) policía mf.

PE abbr = **physical education**.

pea [piː] n guisante m.

peace [piːs] n paz f; **to leave sb in ~** dejar a alguien en paz; **~ and quiet** tranquilidad f.

peaceful ['piːsfʊl] adj (place, day, feeling) tranquilo(-la); (demonstration) pacífico(-ca)

peach [piːtʃ] n melocotón m.

peach melba [-'melbə] n postre de melocotones en almíbar con helado y jarabe de frambuesa.

peacock ['piːkɒk] n pavo m real.

peak [piːk] n (of mountain) pico m; (of hat) visera f; (fig: highest point) apogeo m.

peak hours *npl* horas *fpl* punta.

peak rate *n* (on telephone) tarifa *f* de hora punta.

peanut ['pi:nʌt] *n* cacahuete *m*.

peanut butter *n* manteca *f* de cacahuete.

pear [peəʳ] *n* pera *f*.

pearl [pɜ:l] *n* perla *f*.

peasant ['peznt] *n* campesino *m* (-na *f*).

pebble ['pebl] *n* guijarro *m*.

pecan pie [pɪ'kæn-] *n* tartaleta *f* de pacanas.

peck [pek] *vi* picotear.

peculiar [pɪ'kju:ljəʳ] *adj* (strange) peculiar; **to be ~ to** ser propio(-pia) de.

peculiarity [pɪ,kju:lɪ'ærətɪ] *n* (special feature) peculiaridad *f*.

pedal ['pedl] *n* pedal *m* ◆ *vi* pedalear.

pedal bin *n* cubo *m* de basura con tapadera de pedal.

pedalo ['pedələʊ] (*pl* -**S**) *n* patín *m* (de agua).

pedestrian [pɪ'destrɪən] *n* peatón *m*.

pedestrian crossing *n* paso *m* de peatones.

pedestrianized [pɪ'destrɪənaɪzd] *adj* peatonal.

pedestrian precinct *n* (Br) zona *f* peatonal.

pedestrian zone (Am) = **pedestrian precinct**.

pee [pi:] *vi* (inf) mear ◆ *n*: **to have a ~** (inf) echar una meada.

peel [pi:l] *n* piel *f* ◆ *vt* pelar ◆ *vi* (paint) descascarillarse; (skin) pelarse.

peep [pi:p] *n*: **to have a ~** echar una ojeada.

peer [pɪəʳ] *vi* mirar con atención.

peg [peg] *n* (for tent) estaca *f*; (hook) gancho *m*; (for washing) pinza *f*.

pelican crossing ['pelɪkən-] *n* (Br) paso de peatones con semáforo que el usuario puede accionar apretando un botón.

pelvis ['pelvɪs] *n* pelvis *f*.

pen [pen] *n* (ballpoint pen) bolígrafo *m*; (fountain pen) pluma *f* (estilográfica); (for animals) corral *m*.

penalty ['penltɪ] *n* (fine) multa *f*; (in football) penalty *m*.

pence [pens] *npl* (Br) peniques *mpl*.

pencil ['pensl] *n* lápiz *m*.

pencil case *n* estuche *m*.

pencil sharpener [-'ʃɑ:pnəʳ] *n* sacapuntas *m inv*.

pendant ['pendənt] *n* colgante *m*.

pending ['pendɪŋ] *prep* (fml) a la espera de.

penetrate ['penɪtreɪt] *vt* (pierce) penetrar en.

penfriend ['penfrend] *n* amigo *m* (-ga *f*) por correspondencia.

penguin ['peŋgwɪn] *n* pingüino *m*.

penicillin [,penɪ'sɪlɪn] *n* penicilina *f*.

peninsula [pə'nɪnsjʊlə] *n* península *f*.

penis ['pi:nɪs] *n* pene *m*.

penknife ['pennaɪf] (*pl* -**knives** [-naɪvz]) *n* navaja *f*.

penny ['penɪ] (*pl* **pennies**) *n* (in UK) penique *m*; (in US) centavo *m*.

pension ['penʃn] n pensión f.

pensioner ['penʃənər] n pensionista mf.

penthouse ['penthaus, pl -hauziz] n ático m.

penultimate [pe'nʌltɪmət] adj penúltimo(-ma).

people ['pi:pl] npl (persons) personas fpl; (in general) gente f ◆ n (nation) pueblo m; **the ~** (citizens) el pueblo.

pepper ['pepər] n (spice) pimienta f; (vegetable) pimiento m.

peppercorn ['pepəkɔ:n] n grano m de pimienta.

peppermint ['pepəmɪnt] adj de menta ◆ n (sweet) caramelo m de menta.

pepper pot n pimentero m.

pepper steak n bistec m a la pimienta.

Pepsi® ['pepsi] n Pepsi-Cola f.

per [pɜ:r] prep por; **~ person** por persona; **~ week** por semana; **£20 ~ night** 20 libras por noche.

perceive [pə'si:v] vt percibir.

per cent adv por ciento.

percentage [pə'sentɪdʒ] n porcentaje m.

perch [pɜ:tʃ] n (for bird) percha f.

percolator ['pɜ:kəleɪtər] n percolador m.

perfect [adj & n 'pɜ:fɪkt, vb pə'fekt] adj perfecto(-ta) ◆ vt perfeccionar ◆ n: **the ~** (tense) el perfecto.

perfection [pə'fekʃn] n: **to do sthg to ~** hacer algo a la perfección.

perfectly ['pɜ:fɪktlɪ] adv (very well) perfectamente.

perform [pə'fɔ:m] vt (task, operation) realizar; (play) representar; (concert) interpretar ◆ vi (actor, singer) actuar.

performance [pə'fɔ:məns] n (of play, concert, film) función f; (by actor, musician) actuación f; (of car) rendimiento m.

performer [pə'fɔ:mər] n intérprete mf.

perfume ['pɜ:fju:m] n perfume m.

perhaps [pə'hæps] adv quizás.

perimeter [pə'rɪmɪtər] n perímetro m.

period ['pɪərɪəd] n periodo m; (SCH) hora f; (Am: full stop) punto m ◆ adj de época; **sunny ~s** intervalos mpl de sol.

periodic [,pɪərɪ'ɒdɪk] adj periódico(-ca).

period pains npl dolores mpl menstruales.

periphery [pə'rɪfərɪ] n periferia f.

perishable ['perɪʃəbl] adj perecedero(-ra).

perk [pɜ:k] n beneficio m adicional.

perm [pɜ:m] n permanente f ◆ vt: **to have one's hair ~ed** hacerse una permanente.

permanent ['pɜ:mənənt] adj permanente.

permanent address n domicilio m fijo.

permanently ['pɜ:mənəntlɪ] adv permanentemente.

permissible [pə'mɪsəbl] adj (fml) lícito(-ta).

permission [pə'mɪʃn] n permiso *m*.

permit [*vb* pə'mɪt, *n* 'pɜ:mɪt] *vt* permitir ♦ *n* permiso *m*; **to ~ sb to do sthg** permitir a alguien hacer algo; **"~ holders only"** "aparcamiento prohibido a personas no autorizadas".

perpendicular [,pɜ:pən'dɪkjʊləʳ] *adj* perpendicular.

persevere [,pɜ:sɪ'vɪəʳ] *vi* perseverar.

persist [pə'sɪst] *vi* persistir; **to ~ in doing sthg** empeñarse en hacer algo.

persistent [pə'sɪstənt] *adj* persistente; *(person)* tenaz.

person ['pɜ:sn] (*pl* **people**) *n* persona *f*; **in ~** en persona.

personal ['pɜ:sənl] *adj* personal; *(life, letter)* privado(-da); *(rude)* ofensivo(-va); **a ~ friend** un amigo íntimo.

personal assistant *n* asistente *m* (-ta *f*) personal.

personal belongings *npl* efectos *mpl* personales.

personal computer *n* ordenador *m* personal.

personality [,pɜ:sə'næləti] *n* personalidad *f*.

personally ['pɜ:snəlɪ] *adv* personalmente.

personal property *n* bienes *mpl* muebles.

personal stereo *n* walkman® *m*.

personnel [,pɜ:sə'nel] *npl* personal *m*.

perspective [pə'spektɪv] *n* perspectiva *f*.

Perspex® ['pɜ:speks] *n* (*Br*) ≃

plexiglás® *m inv*.

perspiration [,pɜ:spə'reɪʃn] *n* transpiración *f*.

persuade [pə'sweɪd] *vt*: **to ~ sb (to do sthg)** persuadir a alguien (para que haga algo); **to ~ sb that** ... persuadir a alguien de que ...

persuasive [pə'sweɪsɪv] *adj* persuasivo(-va).

Peru [pə'ru:] *n* Perú.

Peruvian [pə'ru:vjən] *adj* peruano(-na) ♦ *n* peruano *m* (-na *f*).

pervert ['pɜ:vɜ:t] *n* pervertido *m* (-da *f*).

pessimist ['pesɪmɪst] *n* pesimista *mf*.

pessimistic [,pesɪ'mɪstɪk] *adj* pesimista.

pest [pest] *n* *(insect)* insecto *m* nocivo; *(animal)* animal *m* nocivo; *(inf: person)* pelma *mf*.

pester ['pestəʳ] *vt* incordiar.

pesticide ['pestɪsaɪd] *n* pesticida *m*.

pet [pet] *n* animal *m* de compañía; **the teacher's ~** el favorito (la favorita) del maestro.

petal ['petl] *n* pétalo *m*.

pet food *n* alimentos *mpl* para animales de compañía.

petition [pɪ'tɪʃn] *n* petición *f*.

petits pois [,pətɪ'pwa] *npl* guisantes *mpl* pequeños.

petrified ['petrɪfaɪd] *adj* *(frightened)* aterrado(-da).

petrol ['petrəl] *n* (*Br*) gasolina *f*.

petrol can *n* (*Br*) lata *f* de gasolina.

petrol cap *n* (*Br*) tapón *m* del depósito.

petrol gauge *n* (*Br*) indicador

physics

m del nivel de carburante.

petrol pump *n (Br)* surtidor *m* de gasolina.

petrol station *n (Br)* gasolinera *f*.

petrol tank *n (Br)* depósito *m* de gasolina.

pet shop *n* tienda *f* de animales de compañía.

petticoat ['petɪkəʊt] *n* combinación *f*.

petty ['petɪ] *adj (pej: person, rule)* mezquino(-na).

petty cash *n* dinero *m* para pequeños gastos.

pew [pju:] *n* banco *m (de iglesia)*.

pewter ['pju:tə'] *n* peltre *m*.

PG *(abbr of parental guidance)* con algunas escenas no aptas para menores de 15 años.

pharmacist ['fɑ:məsɪst] *n* farmacéutico *m* (-ca *f*).

pharmacy ['fɑ:məsɪ] *n (shop)* farmacia *f*.

phase [feɪz] *n* fase *f*.

PhD *n (degree)* doctorado *m*.

pheasant ['feznt] *n* faisán *m*.

phenomena [fɪ'nɒmɪnə] *pl →* phenomenon.

phenomenal [fɪ'nɒmɪnl] *adj* fenomenal.

phenomenon [fɪ'nɒmɪnən] *(pl* -mena*)* *n* fenómeno *m*.

Philippines ['fɪlɪpi:nz] *npl:* the ~ (las) Filipinas.

philosophy [fɪ'lɒsəfɪ] *n* filosofía *f*.

phlegm [flem] *n (in throat)* flema *f*.

phone [fəʊn] *n* teléfono *m* ♦ *vt & vi (Br)* telefonear; **on the ~** *(talking)*

al teléfono; **to be on the ~** *(connected)* tener teléfono ❑ **phone up** *vt sep & vi* llamar (por teléfono).

phone book *n* guía *f* telefónica.

phone booth *n* teléfono *m* público.

phone box *n (Br)* cabina *f* de teléfono.

phone call *n* llamada *f* telefónica.

phonecard ['fəʊnkɑ:d] *n* tarjeta *f* telefónica.

phone number *n* número *m* de teléfono.

photo ['fəʊtəʊ] *n* foto *f*; **to take a ~ of** *(person)* sacar una foto a; *(thing)* sacar una foto de.

photo album *n* álbum *m* de fotos.

photocopier [ˌfəʊtəʊ'kɒpɪə'] *n* fotocopiadora *f*.

photocopy ['fəʊtəʊˌkɒpɪ] *n* fotocopia *f* ♦ *vt* fotocopiar.

photograph ['fəʊtəgrɑ:f] *n* fotografía *f* ♦ *vt* fotografiar.

photographer [fə'tɒgrəfə'] *n* fotógrafo *m* (-fa *f*).

photography [fə'tɒgrəfɪ] *n* fotografía *f*.

phrase [freɪz] *n* frase *f*.

phrasebook ['freɪzbʊk] *n* libro *m* de frases.

physical ['fɪzɪkl] *adj* físico(-ca) ♦ *n* reconocimiento *m* médico.

physical education *n* educación *f* física.

physically handicapped ['fɪzɪklɪ-] *adj* disminuido físico (disminuida física).

physics ['fɪzɪks] *n* física *f*.

physiotherapy [ˌfɪzɪəʊˈθerəpɪ] *n* fisioterapia *f*.

pianist [ˈpɪənɪst] *n* pianista *mf*.

piano [pɪˈænəʊ] (*pl* -s) *n* piano *m*.

pick [pɪk] *vt (select)* escoger; *(fruit, flowers)* coger ◆ *n (pickaxe)* piqueta *f*; **to ~ a fight** buscar camorra; **to ~ one's nose** hurgarse la nariz; **to take one's ~** escoger lo que uno quiera ❑ **pick on** *vt fus* meterse con; **pick out** *vt sep (select)* escoger; *(see)* distinguir; **pick up** *vt sep* recoger; *(lift up)* recoger (del suelo); *(bargain, habit)* adquirir; *(language, hints)* aprender; *(inf: woman, man)* ligar con ◆ *vi (improve)* mejorar.

pickaxe [ˈpɪkæks] *n* piqueta *f*.

pickle [ˈpɪkl] *n (Br: food)* condimento hecho con trozos de frutas y verduras maceradas hasta formar una salsa agridulce; *(Am: pickled cucumber)* pepinillo *m* encurtido.

pickled onion [ˌpɪkld-] *n* cebolleta *f* en vinagre.

pickpocket [ˈpɪkˌpɒkɪt] *n* carterista *mf*.

pick-up (truck) *n* camioneta *f*.

picnic [ˈpɪknɪk] *n* comida *f* campestre.

picnic area *n* = área *f* de descanso.

picture [ˈpɪktʃəʳ] *n (painting)* cuadro *m*; *(drawing)* dibujo *m*; *(photograph)* foto *f*; *(on TV)* imagen *f*; *(film)* película *f* ❑ **pictures** *npl*: **the ~s** *(Br)* el cine.

picture frame *n* marco *m* (para fotos).

picturesque [ˌpɪktʃəˈresk] *adj* pintoresco(-ca).

pie [paɪ] *n (savoury)* empanada *f*; *(sweet)* tarta *f (cubierta de hojaldre).*

piece [piːs] *n (part, bit)* trozo *m*; *(component, in chess, of music)* pieza *f*; **a 20p ~** una moneda de 20 peniques; **a ~ of advice** un consejo; **a ~ of clothing** una prenda de vestir; **a ~ of furniture** un mueble; **a ~ of paper** una hoja de papel; **to fall to ~s** deshacerse; **in one ~** *(intact)* intacto; *(unharmed)* sano y salvo.

pier [pɪəʳ] *n* paseo *m* marítimo *(sobre malecón).*

pierce [pɪəs] *vt* perforar; **to have one's ears ~d** hacerse agujeros en las orejas.

pig [pɪg] *n (animal)* cerdo *m*; *(inf: greedy person)* tragón *m* (-ona *f*).

pigeon [ˈpɪdʒɪn] *n* paloma *f*.

pigeonhole [ˈpɪdʒɪnhəʊl] *n* casilla *f*.

pigskin [ˈpɪgskɪn] *adj* de piel de cerdo.

pigtail [ˈpɪgteɪl] *n* trenza *f*.

pike [paɪk] *n (fish)* lucio *m*.

pilau rice [pɪˈlaʊ-] *n* arroz de distintos colores, condimentado con especias orientales.

pilchard [ˈpɪltʃəd] *n* sardina *f*.

pile [paɪl] *n (heap)* montón *m*; *(neat stack)* pila *f* ◆ *vt* amontonar; **~s of** *(inf: a lot)* un montón de ❑ **pile up** *vt sep* amontonar ◆ *vi (accumulate)* acumularse.

piles [paɪlz] *npl (MED)* almorranas *fpl*.

pileup [ˈpaɪlʌp] *n* colisión *f* en cadena.

pill [pɪl] *n* pastilla *f*; **the ~** la píldora.

pillar [ˈpɪləʳ] *n* pilar *m*.

pillar box n (Br) buzón m.

pillion ['pɪljən] n: **to ride ~** ir sentado atrás (en moto).

pillow ['pɪləʊ] n (for bed) almohada f; (Am: on chair, sofa) cojín m.

pillowcase ['pɪləʊkeɪs] n funda f de la almohada.

pilot ['paɪlət] n piloto mf.

pilot light n piloto m.

pimple ['pɪmpl] n grano m.

pin [pɪn] n (for sewing) alfiler m; (drawing pin) chincheta f; (safety pin) imperdible m; (Am: brooch) broche m; (Am: badge) chapa f, pin m ♦ vt (fasten) prender; **a two-~ plug** un enchufe de dos clavijas; **~s and needles** hormigueo m.

pinafore ['pɪnəfɔːʳ] n (apron) delantal m; (Br: dress) pichi m.

pinball ['pɪnbɔːl] n flipper m.

pincers ['pɪnsəz] npl (tool) tenazas fpl.

pinch [pɪntʃ] vt (squeeze) pellizcar; (Br: inf: steal) mangar ♦ n (of salt) pizca f.

pine [paɪn] n pino m ♦ adj de pino.

pineapple ['paɪnæpl] n piña f.

pink [pɪŋk] adj rosa inv ♦ n (colour) rosa m.

pinkie ['pɪŋkɪ] n (Am) dedo m meñique.

PIN number ['pɪn-] n número m personal.

pint [paɪnt] n (in UK) = 0,568 litros, pinta f; (in US) = 0,473 litros, pinta; **a ~ (of beer)** (Br) una jarra de cerveza.

pip [pɪp] n (of fruit) pepita f.

pipe [paɪp] n (for smoking) pipa f; (for gas, water) tubería f.

pipe cleaner n limpiapipas m inv.

pipeline ['paɪplaɪn] n (for oil) oleoducto m.

pipe tobacco n tabaco m de pipa.

pirate ['paɪrət] n pirata m.

Pisces ['paɪsiːz] n Piscis m inv.

piss [pɪs] vi (vulg) mear ♦ n: **to have a ~** (vulg) echar una meada; **it's ~ing down** (vulg) está lloviendo que te cagas.

pissed [pɪst] adj (Br: vulg: drunk) mamado(-da); (Am: vulg: angry) cabreado(-da).

pissed off adj (vulg) cabreado(-da).

pistachio [pɪ'stɑːʃɪəʊ] n pistacho m ♦ adj de pistacho.

pistol ['pɪstl] n pistola f.

piston ['pɪstən] n pistón m.

pit [pɪt] n (hole) hoyo m; (coalmine) mina f; (for orchestra) foso m de la orquesta; (Am: in fruit) hueso m.

pitch [pɪtʃ] n (Br: SPORT) campo m ♦ vt (throw) lanzar; **to ~ a tent** montar una tienda de campaña.

pitcher ['pɪtʃəʳ] n (large jug) cántaro m; (Am: small jug) jarra f.

pitfall ['pɪtfɔːl] n escollo m.

pith [pɪθ] n (of orange) parte blanca de la corteza.

pitta (bread) ['pɪtə-] n fina torta de pan ácimo.

pitted ['pɪtɪd] adj (olives) deshuesado(-da).

pity ['pɪtɪ] n (compassion) lástima f; **to have ~ on sb** compadecerse de alguien; **it's a ~ (that) ...** es una pena que ...; **what a ~!** ¡qué pena!

pivot ['pɪvət] n eje m.

pizza ['piːtsə] n pizza f.

pizzeria [ˌpiːtsə'rɪə] n pizzería f.

Pl. (abbr of Place) nombre de ciertas calles en Gran Bretaña.

placard ['plækɑːd] n pancarta f.

place [pleɪs] n (location) sitio m, lugar m; (house, flat) casa f; (seat) asiento m; (proper position) sitio m; (in race, list) lugar m; (at table) cubierto m ◆ vt (put) colocar; (an order, bet) hacer; **in the first ~** ... en primer lugar ...; **to take** ~ tener lugar; **to take sb's** ~ sustituir a alguien; **all over the** ~ por todas partes; **in** ~ **of** en lugar de.

place mat n mantel m individual.

placement ['pleɪsmənt] n colocación f temporal.

place of birth n lugar m de nacimiento.

plague [pleɪg] n peste f.

plaice [pleɪs] n platija f.

plain [pleɪn] adj (not decorated) liso(-sa); (simple) sencillo(-lla); (clear) claro(-ra); (paper) sin rayas; (pej: not attractive) sin ningún atractivo ◆ n llanura f.

plain chocolate n chocolate m amargo.

plainly ['pleɪnlɪ] adv (obviously) evidentemente; (distinctly) claramente.

plait [plæt] n trenza f ◆ vt trenzar.

plan [plæn] n (scheme, project) plan m; (drawing) plano m ◆ vt (organize) planear; **have you any plans for tonight?** ¿tienes algún plan para esta noche?; **according to** ~ según

lo previsto; **to** ~ **to do sthg, to** ~ **on doing sthg** pensar hacer algo.

plane [pleɪn] n (aeroplane) avión m; (tool) cepillo m.

planet ['plænɪt] n planeta m.

plank [plæŋk] n tablón m.

plant [plɑːnt] n planta f ◆ vt (seeds, tree) plantar; (land) sembrar; **"heavy ~ crossing"** cartel que indica peligro por salida de vehículos pesados.

plantation [plæn'teɪʃn] n plantación f.

plaque [plɑːk] n placa f.

plaster ['plɑːstər] n (Br: for cut) tirita® f; (for walls) escayola f; **in** ~ escayolado.

plaster cast n (for broken bones) escayola f.

plastic ['plæstɪk] n plástico m ◆ adj de plástico.

plastic bag n bolsa f de plástico.

Plasticine® ['plæstɪsiːn] n (Br) plastilina® f.

plate [pleɪt] n (for food) plato m; (of metal) placa f.

plateau ['plætəʊ] n meseta f.

plate-glass adj de vidrio cilindrado.

platform ['plætfɔːm] n (at railway station) andén m; (raised structure) plataforma f; ~ **12** la vía 12.

platinum ['plætɪnəm] n platino m.

platter ['plætər] n (CULIN) combinado, especialmente de mariscos, servido en una fuente alargada.

play [pleɪ] vt (sport, game) jugar a; (music, instrument) tocar; (opponent) jugar contra; (CD, tape, record) poner; *(role, character)* representar ♦ *vi (child, in sport, game)* jugar; *(musician)* tocar ♦ *n (in theatre, on TV)* obra *f* (de teatro); *(button on CD, tape recorder)* botón *m* del "play" ❏ **play back** *vt sep* volver a poner; **play up** *vi* dar guerra.

player ['pleɪə'] *n (of sport, game)* jugador *m* (-ra *f*); *(of musical instrument)* intérprete *mf*.

playful ['pleɪfʊl] *adj* juguetón (-ona).

playground ['pleɪgraʊnd] *n (in school)* patio *m* de recreo; *(in park etc)* zona *f* recreativa.

playgroup ['pleɪgruːp] *n* guardería *f*.

playing card ['pleɪɪŋ-] *n* carta *f*.

playing field ['pleɪɪŋ-] *n* campo *m* de deportes.

playroom ['pleɪrʊm] *n* cuarto *m* de los juguetes.

playschool ['pleɪskuːl] = **playgroup**.

playtime ['pleɪtaɪm] *n* recreo *m*.

playwright ['pleɪraɪt] *n* dramaturgo *m* (-ga *f*).

plc *(abbr of public limited company)* = S.A.

pleasant ['plezənt] *adj* agradable.

please [pliːz] *adv* por favor ♦ *vt* complacer; **yes ~!** ¡sí, gracias!; **whatever you ~** lo que desee.

pleased [pliːzd] *adj* contento(-ta); **to be ~ with** estar contento con; **~ to meet you!** ¡encantado(-da) de conocerle!

pleasure ['pleʒə'] *n* placer *m*; **with ~** con mucho gusto; **it's a ~!** ¡es un placer!

pleat [pliːt] *n* pliegue *m*.

pleated ['pliːtɪd] *adj* plisado (-da).

plentiful ['plentɪfʊl] *adj* abundante.

plenty ['plentɪ] *pron* de sobra; **~ of money** dinero de sobra; **~ of chairs** sillas de sobra.

pliers ['plaɪəz] *npl* alicates *mpl*.

plimsoll ['plɪmsəl] *n (Br)* playera *f*.

plonk [plɒŋk] *n (Br: inf: wine)* vino *m* peleón.

plot [plɒt] *n (scheme)* complot *m*; *(of story, film, play)* trama *f*; *(of land)* parcela *f*.

plough [plaʊ] *n (Br)* arado *m* ♦ *vt (Br)* arar.

ploughman's (lunch) ['plaʊmənz-] *n (Br)* tabla de queso servida con pan, cebolla, ensalada y salsa agridulce.

plow [plaʊ] *(Am)* = **plough**.

ploy [plɔɪ] *n* estratagema *f*.

pluck [plʌk] *vt (eyebrows)* depilar *(con pinzas)*, *(chicken)* desplumar.

plug [plʌg] *n (ELEC)* enchufe *m*, *(for bath, sink)* tapón *m* ❏ **plug in** *vt sep* enchufar.

plughole ['plʌghəʊl] *n* agujero *m* del desagüe.

plum [plʌm] *n* ciruela *f*.

plumber ['plʌmə'] *n* fontanero *m*.

plumbing ['plʌmɪŋ] *n (pipes)* tuberías *fpl*.

plump [plʌmp] *adj* regordete.

plunge [plʌndʒ] *vi (fall, dive)* zambullirse; *(decrease)* caer vertiginosamente.

plunge pool *n* piscina *f* (muy pequeña).

plunger ['plʌndʒəʳ] n (for unblocking pipe) desatascador m.

pluperfect (tense) [,plu:-'pɜ:fɪkt-] n: **the ~** el pluscuamperfecto.

plural ['pluərəl] n plural m; **in the ~** en plural.

plus [plʌs] prep más ♦ adj: **30 ~** treinta o más.

plush [plʌʃ] adj lujoso(-sa).

Pluto ['plu:təu] n Plutón m.

plywood ['plaɪwud] n contrachapado m.

p.m. (abbr of post meridiem): **at 4 ~** a las cuatro de la tarde; **at 10 ~** a las diez de la noche.

PMT n (abbr of premenstrual tension) SPM m.

pneumatic drill [nju:'mætɪk-] n taladradora f neumática.

pneumonia [nju:'məunjə] n pulmonía f.

poached egg [pəutʃt-] n huevo m escalfado.

poached salmon [pəutʃt-] n salmón m hervido.

poacher ['pəutʃəʳ] n (hunting) cazador m furtivo; (fishing) pescador m furtivo.

PO Box n (abbr of Post Office Box) apdo. m.

pocket ['pokɪt] n bolsillo m; (in car door) bolsa f ♦ adj de bolsillo.

pocketbook ['pokɪtbuk] n (notebook) libreta f; (Am: handbag) bolso m.

pocket money n (Br) propina f semanal.

podiatrist [pə'daɪətrɪst] n (Am) podólogo m (-ga f).

poem ['pəuɪm] n poema m.

poet ['pəuɪt] n poeta m (-tisa f).

poetry ['pəuɪtrɪ] n poesía f.

point [pɔɪnt] n punto m; (tip) punta f; (most important thing) razón f; (Br: electric socket) enchufe m ♦ vi: **to ~ to** señalar; **five ~ seven** cinco coma siete; **what's the ~?** ¿para qué?; **there's no ~** no vale la pena; **to be on the ~ of doing sthg** estar a punto de hacer algo; **to come to the ~** ir al grano ❑ **points** npl (Br: on railway) agujas fpl; **point out** vt sep (object, person) señalar; (fact, mistake) hacer notar.

pointed ['pɔɪntɪd] adj (in shape) puntiagudo(-da).

pointless ['pɔɪntlɪs] adj sin sentido.

point of view n punto m de vista.

poison ['pɔɪzn] n veneno m ♦ vt (intentionally) envenenar; (unintentionally) intoxicar.

poisoning ['pɔɪzn̩ɪŋ] n (intentional) envenenamiento m; (unintentional) intoxicación f.

poisonous ['pɔɪznəs] adj (food, gas, substance) tóxico(-ca); (snake, spider) venenoso(-sa).

poke [pəuk] vt (with finger, stick) dar; (with elbow) dar un codazo.

poker ['pəukəʳ] n (card game) póker m.

Poland ['pəulənd] n Polonia f.

polar bear ['pəulə-] n oso m polar.

Polaroid® ['pəulərɔɪd] n (photograph) fotografía f polaroid; (camera) cámara f polaroid.

pole [pəul] n (of wood) palo m.

Pole [pəul] n (person) polaco m

(-ca f).

police [pə'liːs] npl: **the ~** la policía.

police car n coche m patrulla.

police force n cuerpo m de policía.

policeman [pə'liːsmən] (pl -men [-mən]) n policía m.

police officer n agente mf de policía.

police station n comisaría f de policía.

policewoman [pə'liːswʊmən] (pl -women [-wɪmɪn]) n mujer f policía.

policy ['pɒləsɪ] n (approach, attitude) política f; (for insurance) póliza f.

policy-holder n asegurado m (-da f).

polio ['pəʊlɪəʊ] n polio f.

polish ['pɒlɪʃ] n (for cleaning) abrillantador m ◆ vt sacar brillo a.

Polish ['pəʊlɪʃ] adj polaco(-ca) ◆ n (language) polaco m ◆ npl: **the ~** los polacos.

polite [pə'laɪt] adj educado(-da).

political [pə'lɪtɪkl] adj político(-ca).

politician [ˌpɒlɪ'tɪʃn] n político m (-ca f).

politics ['pɒlətɪks] n política f.

poll [pəʊl] n (survey) encuesta f; **the ~s** (election) los comicios.

pollen ['pɒlən] n polen m.

Poll Tax n (Br: formerly) = contribución f urbana.

pollute [pə'luːt] vt contaminar.

pollution [pə'luːʃn] n (of sea, air) contaminación f; (substances) agentes mpl contaminantes.

polo neck ['pəʊləʊ-] n (Br: jumper) jersey m de cuello de cisne.

polyester [ˌpɒlɪ'estəʳ] n poliéster m.

polystyrene [ˌpɒlɪ'staɪriːn] n poliestireno m.

polytechnic [ˌpɒlɪ'teknɪk] n centro de enseñanza superior especialmente de materias técnicas que concede diplomas universitarios; casi todos los "polytechnics" se han convertido en universidades.

polythene ['pɒlɪθiːn] n polietileno m.

pomegranate ['pɒmɪˌgrænɪt] n granada f.

pompous ['pɒmpəs] adj (person) engreído(-da).

pond [pɒnd] n estanque m.

pontoon [pɒn'tuːn] n (Br: card game) veintiuna f.

pony ['pəʊnɪ] n poni m.

ponytail ['pəʊnɪteɪl] n cola f de caballo (peinado).

pony-trekking [ˌ-trekɪŋ] n (Br) excursión f en poni.

poodle ['puːdl] n caniche m.

pool [puːl] n (for swimming) piscina f; (of water, blood, milk) charco m; (small pond) estanque m; (game) billar m americano ❑ **pools** npl (Br): **the ~s** las quinielas.

poor [pɔːʳ] adj pobre; (bad) malo(-la) ◆ npl: **the ~** los pobres.

poorly ['pɔːlɪ] adj (Br) pachucho(-cha) ◆ adv mal.

pop [pɒp] n (music) música f pop ◆ vt (inf: put) meter ◆ vi (balloon) reventar; **my ears popped** me estallaron los oídos ❑ **pop in** vi (Br)

entrar un momento.
popcorn ['pɒpkɔːn] n palomitas fpl (de maíz).
Pope [pəʊp] n: the ~ el Papa.
pop group n grupo m de música pop.
poplar (tree) ['pɒplər-] n álamo m.
pop music n música f pop.
poppadom ['pɒpədəm] n torta fina de pan indio, frito y crujiente.
popper ['pɒpər] n (Br) corchete m.
poppy ['pɒpɪ] n amapola f.
Popsicle® ['pɒpsɪkl] n (Am) polo m.
pop socks npl calcetines cortos de cristal.
pop star n estrella f del pop.
popular ['pɒpjʊlər] adj (person, activity) popular; (opinion, ideas) generalizado(-da).
popularity [,pɒpjʊ'lærɪtɪ] n popularidad f.
populated ['pɒpjʊleɪtɪd] adj poblado(-da).
population [,pɒpjʊ'leɪʃn] n población f.
porcelain ['pɔːsəlɪn] n porcelana f.
porch [pɔːtʃ] n porche m.
pork [pɔːk] n carne f de cerdo.
pork chop n chuleta f de cerdo.
pork pie n empanada redonda de carne de cerdo.
pornographic [,pɔːnə'græfɪk] adj pornográfico(-ca).
porridge ['pɒrɪdʒ] n papilla f de avena.
port [pɔːt] n (town, harbour) puer-

to m; (drink) oporto m.
portable ['pɔːtəbl] adj portátil.
porter ['pɔːtər] n (at hotel, museum) conserje mf; (at station, airport) mozo m.
porthole ['pɔːthəʊl] n ojo m de buey.
portion ['pɔːʃn] n (part) porción f; (of food) ración f.
portrait ['pɔːtreɪt] n retrato m.
Portugal ['pɔːtʃʊgl] n Portugal.
Portuguese [,pɔːtʃʊ'giːz] adj portugués(-esa) ♦ n (language) portugués m ♦ npl: the ~ los portugueses.
pose [pəʊz] vt (problem) plantear; (threat) suponer ♦ vi (for photo) posar.
posh [pɒʃ] adj (inf) (person, accent) de clase alta; (hotel, restaurant) de lujo.
position [pə'zɪʃn] n posición f; (situation) situación f; (rank, importance) rango m; (fml: job) puesto m; "~ closed" "cerrado".
positive ['pɒzətɪv] adj positivo(-va); (certain, sure) seguro(-ra); (optimistic) optimista.
possess [pə'zes] vt poseer.
possession [pə'zeʃn] n posesión f.
possessive [pə'zesɪv] adj posesivo(-va).
possibility [,pɒsə'bɪlətɪ] n posibilidad f.
possible ['pɒsəbl] adj posible; it's ~ that we may be late puede (ser) que lleguemos tarde; would it be ~ for me to use the phone? ¿podría usar el teléfono?; as much as ~ tanto como sea posible; if ~

si es posible.

possibly ['pɒsəblɪ] *adv (perhaps)* posiblemente.

post [pəʊst] *n (system, letters etc)* correo *m; (delivery)* reparto *m; (pole)* poste *m; (fml: job)* puesto *m* ◆ *vt (letter, parcel)* echar al correo; **by ~** por correo.

postage ['pəʊstɪdʒ] *n* franqueo *m;* **~ and packing** gastos *mpl* de envío; **~ paid** franqueo pagado.

postage stamp *n (fml)* sello *m.*

postal order ['pəʊstl-] *n* giro *m* postal.

postbox ['pəʊstbɒks] *n (Br)* buzón *m.*

postcard ['pəʊstkɑːd] *n* postal *f.*

postcode ['pəʊstkəʊd] *n (Br)* código *m* postal.

poster ['pəʊstə'] *n* póster *m.*

poste restante [,pəʊst-'restɑːnt] *n (Br)* lista *f* de correos.

post-free *adv* con porte pagado.

postgraduate [,pəʊst-'grædʒʊət] *n* posgraduado *m* (-da *f*).

postman ['pəʊstmən] (*pl* -men [-mən]) *n* cartero *m.*

postmark ['pəʊstmɑːk] *n* matasellos *m inv.*

post office *n (building)* oficina *f* de correos; **the Post Office** ≃ Correos *m inv.*

postpone [,pəʊst'pəʊn] *vt* aplazar.

posture ['pɒstʃə'] *n* postura *f.*

postwoman ['pəʊst,wʊmən] (*pl* -women [-,wɪmɪn]) *n* cartera *f.*

pot [pɒt] *n (for cooking)* olla *f; (for*

jam) tarro *m; (for paint)* bote *m; (for tea)* tetera *f; (for coffee)* cafetera *f; (inf: cannabis)* maría *f;* **a ~ of tea** una tetera.

potato [pə'teɪtəʊ] (*pl* -es) *n* patata *f.*

potato salad *n* ensalada *f* de patatas.

potential [pə'tenʃl] *adj* potencial ◆ *n* potencial *m.*

pothole ['pɒthəʊl] *n (in road)* bache *m.*

pot plant *n* planta *f* de interior.

pot scrubber [-'skrʌbə'] *n* estropajo *m.*

potted ['pɒtɪd] *adj (meat, fish)* en conserva; *(plant)* en maceta.

pottery ['pɒtərɪ] *n* cerámica *f.*

potty ['pɒtɪ] *adj* chalado(-da).

pouch [paʊtʃ] *n (for money)* monedero *m* de atar; *(for tobacco)* petaca *f.*

poultry ['pəʊltrɪ] *n (meat)* carne *f* de pollería ◆ *npl (animals)* aves *fpl* de corral.

pound [paʊnd] *n (unit of money)* libra *f; (unit of weight)* = 453,6 g, libra ◆ *vi (heart, head)* palpitar.

pour [pɔː'] *vt (liquid etc)* verter; *(drink)* servir ◆ *vi (flow)* manar; **it's ~ing (with rain)** está lloviendo a cántaros ❑ **pour out** *vt sep (drink)* servir.

poverty ['pɒvətɪ] *n* pobreza *f.*

powder ['paʊdə'] *n* polvo *m.*

power ['paʊə'] *n (control, authority)* poder *m; (ability)* capacidad *f; (strength, force)* fuerza *f; (energy)* energía *f; (electricity)* corriente *f* ◆ *vt* impulsar; **to be in ~** estar en el poder.

power cut n apagón m.

power failure n corte m de corriente.

powerful ['pauəful] adj (having control) poderoso(-sa); (physically strong, forceful) fuerte; (machine, drug, voice) potente; (smell) intenso(-sa).

power point n (Br) toma f de corriente.

power station n central f eléctrica.

power steering n dirección f asistida.

practical ['præktɪkl] adj práctico(-ca).

practically ['præktɪklɪ] adv (almost) prácticamente.

practice ['præktɪs] n (training, training session) práctica f; (SPORT) entrenamiento m; (of doctor) consulta f; (of lawyer) bufete m; (regular activity, custom) costumbre f ◆ vt (Am) = **practise**; **to be out of ~** tener falta de práctica.

practise ['præktɪs] vt (sport, music, technique) practicar ◆ vi (train) practicar; (doctor, lawyer) ejercer ◆ n (Am) = **practice**.

praise [preɪz] n elogio m ◆ vt elogiar.

pram [præm] n (Br) cochecito m de niño.

prank [præŋk] n travesura f.

prawn [prɔːn] n gamba f.

prawn cocktail n cóctel m de gambas.

prawn cracker n pan m de gambas.

pray [preɪ] vi rezar; **to ~ for sthg** (fig) rogar por algo.

prayer [preəʳ] n (to God) oración f.

precarious [prɪ'keərɪəs] adj precario(-ria).

precaution [prɪ'kɔːʃn] n precaución f.

precede [prɪ'siːd] vt (fml) preceder.

preceding [prɪ'siːdɪŋ] adj precedente.

precinct ['priːsɪŋkt] n (Br: for shopping) zona f comercial peatonal; (Am: area of town) distrito m.

precious ['preʃəs] adj precioso(-sa); (memories) entrañable; (possession) de gran valor sentimental.

precious stone n piedra f preciosa.

precipice ['presɪpɪs] n precipicio m.

precise [prɪ'saɪs] adj preciso(-sa), exacto(-ta).

precisely [prɪ'saɪslɪ] adv (accurately) con precisión; (exactly) exactamente.

predecessor ['priːdɪsesəʳ] n predecesor m (-ra f).

predicament [prɪ'dɪkəmənt] n apuro m.

predict [prɪ'dɪkt] vt predecir.

predictable [prɪ'dɪktəbl] adj (foreseeable) previsible; (pej: unoriginal) poco original.

prediction [prɪ'dɪkʃn] n predicción f.

preface ['prefɪs] n prólogo m.

prefect ['priːfekt] n (Br: at school) alumno de un curso superior elegido por los profesores para mantener el orden fuera de clase.

prefer [prɪˈfɜːʳ] vt: **to ~ sthg (to)** preferir algo (a); **to ~ to do sthg** preferir hacer algo.

preferable [ˈprefrəbl] adj preferible.

preferably [ˈprefrəblɪ] adv preferiblemente.

preference [ˈprefərəns] n preferencia f.

prefix [ˈpriːfɪks] n prefijo m.

pregnancy [ˈpregnənsɪ] n embarazo m.

pregnant [ˈpregnənt] adj embarazada.

prejudice [ˈpredʒʊdɪs] n prejuicio m.

prejudiced [ˈpredʒʊdɪst] adj parcial.

preliminary [prɪˈlɪmɪnərɪ] adj preliminar.

premature [ˈpremətjʊəʳ] adj prematuro(-ra); (arrival) anticipado(-da).

premier [ˈpremjəʳ] adj primero(-ra) ◆ n primer ministro m (primera ministra f).

premiere [ˈpremɪeəʳ] n estreno m.

premises [ˈpremɪsɪz] npl local m.

premium [ˈpriːmjəm] n (for insurance) prima f.

premium-quality adj (meat) de calidad superior.

preoccupied [priːˈɒkjʊpaɪd] adj preocupado(-da).

prepacked [priːˈpækt] adj preempaquetado(-da).

prepaid [ˈpriːpeɪd] adj (envelope) con porte pagado.

preparation [ˌprepəˈreɪʃn] n (preparing) preparación f ❑ **preparations** npl (arrangements) preparativos mpl.

preparatory school [prɪˈpærətrɪ-] n (in UK) colegio privado que prepara a alumnos de 7 a 12 años para la enseñanza secundaria; (in US) colegio privado de enseñanza media que prepara a sus alumnos para estudios superiores.

prepare [prɪˈpeəʳ] vt preparar ◆ vi prepararse.

prepared [prɪˈpeəd] adj (ready) preparado(-da); **to be ~ to do sthg** estar dispuesto(-ta) a hacer algo.

preposition [ˌprepəˈzɪʃn] n preposición f.

prep school [ˈprep-] = **preparatory school**.

prescribe [prɪˈskraɪb] vt prescribir.

prescription [prɪˈskrɪpʃn] n receta f.

presence [ˈprezns] n presencia f; **in sb's ~** en presencia de alguien.

present [adj & n ˈpreznt, vb prɪˈzent] adj (in attendance) presente; (current) actual ◆ n (gift) regalo m ◆ vt (give as present) obsequiar; (problem, challenge, play) representar; (portray, on radio or TV) presentar; **the ~ (tense)** el presente m; **at ~** actualmente; **the ~** el presente; **to ~ sb to sb** presentar a alguien a alguien.

presentable [prɪˈzentəbl] adj presentable.

presentation [ˌpreznˈteɪʃn] n (way of presenting) presentación f; (ceremony) ceremonia f de entrega.

presenter [prɪˈzentəʳ] n (of TV, radio programme) presentador m (-ra f).

presently ['prezntlɪ] adv (soon) dentro de poco; (now) actualmente.

preservation [,prezə'veɪʃn] n conservación f.

preservative [prɪ'zɜːvətɪv] n conservante m.

preserve [prɪ'zɜːv] n (jam) confitura f ♦ vt conservar.

president ['prezɪdənt] n presidente m (-ta f).

press [pres] vt (push) apretar; (iron) planchar ♦ n: the ~ la prensa; to ~ sb to do sthg presionar a alguien para que haga algo.

press conference n rueda f de prensa.

press-stud n automático m.

press-up n flexión f.

pressure ['preʃə'] n presión f.

pressure cooker n olla f exprés.

prestigious [pre'stɪdʒəs] adj prestigioso(-sa).

presumably [prɪ'zjuːməblɪ] adv probablemente.

presume [prɪ'zjuːm] vt suponer.

pretend [prɪ'tend] vt: to ~ to do sthg fingir hacer algo.

pretentious [prɪ'tenʃəs] adj pretencioso(-sa).

pretty ['prɪtɪ] adj (person) guapo(-pa); (thing) bonito(-ta) ♦ adv (inf) (quite) bastante; (very) muy.

prevent [prɪ'vent] vt prevenir; to ~ sb/sthg from doing sthg impedir que alguien/algo haga algo.

prevention [prɪ'venʃn] n prevención f.

preview ['priːvjuː] n (of film) preestreno m; (short description) repor-

taje m (sobre un acontecimiento futuro).

previous ['priːvjəs] adj (earlier) previo(-via); (preceding) anterior.

previously ['priːvjəslɪ] adv anteriormente.

price [praɪs] n precio m ♦ vt: **attractively ~d** con un precio atractivo.

priceless ['praɪslɪs] adj (expensive) de un valor incalculable; (valuable) valiosísimo(-ma).

price list n lista f de precios.

pricey ['praɪsɪ] adj (inf) caro(-ra).

prick [prɪk] vt (skin, finger) pinchar; (sting) picar.

prickly ['prɪklɪ] adj (plant, bush) espinoso(-sa).

prickly heat n sarpullido causado por el calor.

pride [praɪd] n orgullo m ♦ vt: to ~ o.s. on sthg estar orgulloso de algo.

priest [priːst] n sacerdote m.

primarily ['praɪmərɪlɪ] adv primordialmente.

primary school ['praɪmərɪ-] n escuela f primaria.

prime [praɪm] adj (chief) primero(-ra); (quality, beef, cut) de calidad superior.

prime minister n primer ministro m (primera ministra f).

primitive ['prɪmɪtɪv] adj (simple) rudimentario(-ria).

primrose ['prɪmrəʊz] n primavera f.

prince [prɪns] n príncipe m.

Prince of Wales n Príncipe m de Gales.

princess [prɪn'ses] n princesa f.

principal ['prɪnsəpl] *adj* principal ◆ *n* (of school, university) director *m* (-ra *f*).

principle ['prɪnsəpl] *n* principio *m*; **in ~** en principio.

print [prɪnt] *n* (words) letras *fpl* (de imprenta); (photo) foto *f*; (of painting) reproducción *f*; (mark) huella *f* ◆ *vt* (book, newspaper, photo) imprimir; (publish) publicar; (write) escribir en letra de imprenta; **out of ~** agotado ❑ **print out** *vt sep* imprimir.

printed matter [ˌprɪntɪd-] *n* impresos *mpl*.

printer ['prɪntəᵣ] *n* (machine) impresora *f*; (person) impresor *m* (-ra *f*).

printout ['prɪntaʊt] *n* copia *f* de impresora.

prior ['praɪəᵣ] *adj* (previous) anterior; **~ to** (fml) con anterioridad a.

priority [praɪ'ɒrətɪ] *n* prioridad *f*; **to have ~ over** tener prioridad sobre.

prison ['prɪzn] *n* cárcel *f*.

prisoner ['prɪznəᵣ] *n* preso *m* (-sa *f*).

prisoner of war *n* prisionero *m* (-ra *f*) de guerra.

prison officer *n* funcionario *m* (-ria *f*) de prisiones.

privacy [*Br* 'prɪvəsɪ, *Am* 'praɪvəsɪ] *n* intimidad *f*.

private ['praɪvɪt] *adj* privado(-da); (class, lesson) particular; (matter, belongings) personal; (quiet) retirado(-da) ◆ *n* (MIL) soldado *m* raso; **in ~** en privado.

private health care *n* asistencia *f* sanitaria privada.

private property *n* propiedad *f* privada.

private school *n* colegio *m* privado.

privilege ['prɪvɪlɪdʒ] *n* privilegio *m*; **it's a ~!** ¡es un honor!

prize [praɪz] *n* premio *m*.

prize-giving [-ˌgɪvɪŋ] *n* entrega *f* de premios.

pro [prəʊ] (*pl* **-s**) *n* (inf: professional) profesional *mf* ❑ **pros** *npl*: **the ~s and cons** los pros y los contras.

probability [ˌprɒbə'bɪlətɪ] *n* probabilidad *f*.

probable ['prɒbəbl] *adj* probable.

probably ['prɒbəblɪ] *adv* probablemente.

probation officer [prə'beɪʃn-] *n* oficial encargado de la vigilancia de presos en libertad condicional.

problem ['prɒbləm] *n* problema *m*; **no ~!** (inf) ¡no hay problema!

procedure [prə'siːdʒəᵣ] *n* procedimiento *m*.

proceed [prə'siːd] *vi* (fml) (continue) proseguir; (act) proceder; (advance) avanzar; **"~ with caution"** "conduzca con precaución".

proceeds ['prəʊsiːdz] *npl* recaudación *f*.

process ['prəʊses] *n* proceso *m*; **to be in the ~ of doing sthg** estar haciendo algo.

processed cheese ['prəʊsest-] *n* queso *m* para sandwiches.

procession [prə'seʃn] *n* desfile *m*.

prod [prɒd] *vt* empujar repetidamente.

produce [vb prə'dju:s, n 'prɒdju:s] vt producir; (show) mostrar; (play) poner en escena ♦ n productos mpl agrícolas.

producer [prə'dju:sə[r]] n (manufacturer) fabricante mf; (of film) productor m (-ra f); (of play) director m (-ra f) de escena.

product ['prɒdʌkt] n producto m.

production [prə'dʌkʃn] n (manufacture) producción f; (of film, play) realización f; (play) representación f.

productivity [,prɒdʌk'tɪvətɪ] n productividad f.

profession [prə'feʃn] n profesión f.

professional [prə'feʃənl] adj profesional ♦ n profesional mf.

professor [prə'fesə[r]] n (in UK) catedrático m (-ca f); (in US) profesor m (-ra f) de universidad.

profile ['prəʊfaɪl] n (silhouette, outline) perfil m; (description) corta biografía f.

profit ['prɒfɪt] n (financial) beneficio m ♦ vi: to ~ (from) sacar provecho (de).

profitable ['prɒfɪtəbl] adj rentable.

profiteroles [prə'fɪtə,rəʊlz] npl profiteroles mpl.

profound [prə'faʊnd] adj profundo(-da).

program ['prəʊgræm] n (COMPUT) programa m; (Am) = programme ♦ vt (COMPUT) programar.

programme ['prəʊgræm] n programa m.

progress [n 'prəʊgres, vb prə'gres] n (improvement) progreso m; (forward movement) avance m ♦ vi (work, talks, student) progresar; (day, meeting) avanzar; to make ~ (improve) progresar; (in journey) avanzar; in ~ en curso.

progressive [prə'gresɪv] adj (forward-looking) progresista.

prohibit [prə'hɪbɪt] vt prohibir; "smoking strictly ~ed" "está terminantemente prohibido fumar".

project ['prɒdʒekt] n (plan) proyecto m; (at school) trabajo m.

projector [prə'dʒektə[r]] n proyector m.

prolong [prə'lɒŋ] vt prolongar.

prom [prɒm] n (Am: dance) baile m de gala (en colegios).

promenade [,prɒmə'nɑːd] n (Br: by the sea) paseo m marítimo.

prominent ['prɒmɪnənt] adj (person) eminente; (noticeable) prominente.

promise ['prɒmɪs] n promesa f ♦ vt prometer ♦ vi: I ~ te lo prometo; to show ~ ser prometedor; I ~ (that) I'll come te prometo que vendré; to ~ sb sthg prometer algo a alguien; to ~ to do sthg prometer hacer algo.

promising ['prɒmɪsɪŋ] adj prometedor(-ra).

promote [prə'məʊt] vt (in job) ascender.

promotion [prə'məʊʃn] n (in job) ascenso m; (of product) promoción f.

prompt [prɒmpt] adj inmediato(-ta) ♦ adv: at six o'clock ~ a las seis en punto.

prone [prəʊn] adj: to be ~ to sthg ser propenso(-sa) a algo; to

225

be ~ to do sthg tender a hacer algo.

prong [prɒŋ] *n* diente *m*.

pronoun ['prəʊnaʊn] *n* pronombre *m*.

pronounce [prə'naʊns] *vt* (word) pronunciar.

pronunciation [prə,nʌnsɪ'eɪʃn] *n* pronunciación *f*.

proof [pruːf] *n* (evidence) prueba *f*; **it's 12% ~** tiene 12 grados.

prop [prɒp]: **prop up** *vt sep* (support) apuntalar.

propeller [prə'pelər] *n* hélice *f*.

proper ['prɒpər] *adj* (suitable) adecuado(-da); (correct, socially acceptable) correcto(-ta).

properly ['prɒpəlɪ] *adv* (suitably) bien; (correctly) correctamente.

property ['prɒpətɪ] *n* propiedad *f*; (land) finca *f*; (fml: building) inmueble *m*.

proportion [prə'pɔːʃn] *n* proporción *f*.

proposal [prə'pəʊzl] *n* (suggestion) propuesta *f*.

propose [prə'pəʊz] *vt* (suggest) proponer ◆ *vi*: **to ~ to sb** pedir la mano a alguien.

proposition [,prɒpə'zɪʃn] *n* (offer) propuesta *f*.

proprietor [prə'praɪətər] *n* (fml) propietario *m* (-ria *f*).

prose [prəʊz] *n* (not poetry) prosa *f*; (SCH) traducción *f* inversa.

prosecution [,prɒsɪ'kjuːʃn] *n* (JUR: charge) procesamiento *m*.

prospect ['prɒspekt] *n* (possibility) posibilidad *f*; **I don't relish the ~** no me apasiona la perspectiva ❑

prospects *npl* (for the future) perspectivas *fpl*.

prospectus [prə'spektəs] *n* folleto *m* informativo.

prosperous ['prɒspərəs] *adj* próspero(-ra).

prostitute ['prɒstɪtjuːt] *n* prostituta *f*.

protect [prə'tekt] *vt* proteger; **~ sthg/sb against** proteger algo/a alguien contra; **~ sthg/sb from** proteger algo/a alguien de.

protection [prə'tekʃn] *n* protección *f*.

protection factor *n* factor *m* de protección solar.

protective [prə'tektɪv] *adj* protector(-ra).

protein ['prəʊtiːn] *n* proteína *f*.

protest [*n* 'prəʊtest, *vb* prə'test] *n* (complaint) protesta *f*; (demonstration) manifestación *f* ◆ *vt* (Am: protest against) protestar contra ◆ *vi*: **to ~ (against)** protestar (contra).

Protestant ['prɒtɪstənt] *n* protestante *mf*.

protester [prə'testər] *n* manifestante *mf*.

protractor [prə'træktər] *n* transportador *m*.

protrude [prə'truːd] *vi* sobresalir.

proud [praʊd] *adj* (pleased) orgulloso(-sa); (pej: arrogant) soberbio(-bia); **to be ~ of** estar orgulloso de.

prove [pruːv] (*pp* -d OR **proven** [pruːvn]) *vt* (show to be true) probar; (turn out to be) resultar.

proverb ['prɒvɜːb] *n* proverbio *m*.

provide [prə'vaɪd] *vt* proporcio-

~ sb with sthg proporcio-
~go a alguien ❑ **provide for**
~ (person) mantener.

provided (that) [prə'vaɪdɪd-]
onj con tal de que.
providing (that) [prə'vaɪdɪŋ-]
= **provided (that)**.
province ['prɒvɪns] *n* provincia
f.
provisional [prə'vɪʒənl] *adj* provisional.
provisions [prə'vɪʒnz] *npl* provisiones *fpl*.
provocative [prə'vɒkətɪv] *adj*
provocador(-ra).
provoke [prə'vəʊk] *vt* provocar.
prowl [praʊl] *vi* merodear.
prune [pru:n] *n* ciruela *f* pasa ♦
vt podar.
PS (*abbr of* postscript) P.D.
psychiatrist [saɪ'kaɪətrɪst] *n* psiquiatra *mf*.
psychic ['saɪkɪk] *adj* clarividente.
psychological [ˌsaɪkə'lɒdʒɪkl]
adj psicológico(-ca).
psychologist [saɪ'kɒlədʒɪst] *n*
psicólogo *m* (-ga *f*).
psychology [saɪ'kɒlədʒɪ] *n* psicología *f*.
psychotherapist [ˌsaɪkəʊ-
'θerəpɪst] *n* psicoterapeuta *mf*.
pt *abbr* = pint.
PTO (*abbr of* please turn over)
sigue.
pub [pʌb] *n* = bar *m*.

ⓘ PUB

El "pub" es una institución muy
importante en la vida social británica, y es el principal lugar de
encuentro en las comunidades rura-
les. El acceso para menores es restringido, aunque las condiciones
varían de un "pub" a otro. Hasta
recientemente, su horario de apertura estaba estrictamente regulado,
pero hoy día la mayoría de los
"pubs" abre de las once de la mañana a las once de la noche. Además
de bebidas, los "pubs" suelen ofrecer
comidas ligeras.

puberty ['pju:bətɪ] *n* pubertad *f*.
public ['pʌblɪk] *adj* público(-ca)
♦ *n*: the ~ el público; in ~ en
público.
publican ['pʌblɪkən] *n* (Br) patrón
de un "pub".
publication [ˌpʌblɪ'keɪʃn] *n* publicación *f*.
public bar *n* (Br) bar cuya decoración es más sencilla y cuyos precios
son más bajos.
public convenience *n* (Br)
aseos *mpl* públicos.
public footpath *n* (Br) camino *m* público.
public holiday *n* fiesta *f*
nacional.
public house *n* (Br: fml) = bar
m.
publicity [pʌb'lɪsɪtɪ] *n* publicidad *f*.
public school *n* (in UK) colegio *m* privado; (in US) escuela *f*
pública.
public telephone *n* teléfono
m público.
public transport *n* transporte *m* público.
publish ['pʌblɪʃ] *vt* publicar.

publisher ['pʌblɪʃər] n (person) editor m (-ra f); (company) editorial f.

publishing ['pʌblɪʃɪŋ] n (industry) industria f editorial.

pub lunch n almuerzo generalmente sencillo en un "pub".

pudding ['pʊdɪŋ] n (sweet dish) pudín m; (Br: course) postre m.

puddle ['pʌdl] n charco m.

puff [pʌf] vi (breathe heavily) resollar ♦ n (of air) soplo m; (of smoke) bocanada f; to ~ at dar caladas a.

puff pastry n hojaldre m.

pull [pʊl] vt tirar de; (tow) arrastrar; (trigger) apretar ♦ vi tirar ♦ n: to give sthg a ~ dar algo un tirón; to ~ a face hacer muecas, to ~ a muscle dar un tirón en un músculo; "pull" (on door) "tirar" ❑ **pull apart** vt sep (machine) desmontar; **pull down** vt sep (lower) bajar; (demolish) derribar; **pull in** vi pararse; **pull out** vt sep sacar ♦ vi (train, car) salir; (withdraw) retirarse; **pull over** vi (car) hacerse a un lado; **pull up** vt sep (socks, trousers, sleeve) subirse ♦ vi parar.

pulley ['pʊlɪ] (pl **pulleys**) n polea f.

pull-out n (Am) área f de descanso.

pullover ['pʊl,əʊvər] n jersey m.

pulpit ['pʊlpɪt] n púlpito m.

pulse [pʌls] n (MED) pulso m.

pump [pʌmp] n (device, bicycle pump) bomba f; (for petrol) surtidor m ❑ **pumps** npl (sports shoes) zapatillas fpl de tenis; **pump up** vt sep inflar.

pumpkin ['pʌmpkɪn] n calabaza f.

pun [pʌn] n juego m de palabras.

punch [pʌntʃ] n (blow) puñetazo m; (drink) ponche m ♦ vt (hit) dar un puñetazo; (ticket) picar.

Punch and Judy show [-'dʒuːdɪ] n teatro de guiñol para niños que se representa en la playa.

punctual ['pʌŋktʃʊəl] adj puntual.

punctuation [,pʌŋktʃʊ'eɪʃn] n puntuación f.

puncture ['pʌŋktʃər] n pinchazo m ♦ vt pinchar.

punish ['pʌnɪʃ] vt: to ~ sb (for sthg) castigar a alguien (por algo).

punishment ['pʌnɪʃmənt] n castigo m.

punk [pʌŋk] n (person) punki mf; (music) punk m.

punnet ['pʌnɪt] n (Br) canasta f pequeña.

pupil ['pjuːpl] n (student) alumno m (-na f); (of eye) pupila f.

puppet ['pʌpɪt] n títere m.

puppy ['pʌpɪ] n cachorro m.

purchase ['pɜːtʃəs] vt (fml) comprar ♦ n (fml) compra f.

pure [pjʊər] adj puro(-ra).

puree ['pjʊəreɪ] n puré m.

purely ['pjʊəlɪ] adv puramente.

purity ['pjʊərətɪ] n pureza f.

purple ['pɜːpl] adj morado(-da).

purpose ['pɜːpəs] n propósito m; on ~ a propósito.

purr [pɜːr] vi (cat) ronronear.

purse [pɜːs] n (Br: for money) monedero m; (Am: handbag) bolso m.

pursue [pə'sjuː] vt (follow) perseguir; (study, inquiry, matter) continuar con.

pus [pʌs] n pus m.

push [pʊʃ] vt *(shove)* empujar; *(press)* apretar; *(product)* promocionar ◆ vi *(shove)* empujar ◆ n: to give sb/sthg a ~ dar un empujón a alguien/algo; to ~ sb into doing sthg obligar a alguien a hacer algo; "push" *(on door)* "empujar" □ **push in** vi *(in queue)* colarse; **push off** vi *(inf: go away)* largarse.

push-button telephone n teléfono m de botones.

pushchair ['pʊʃtʃeəʳ] n *(Br)* silla f (de paseo).

pushed [pʊʃt] adj *(inf)*: to be ~ **(for time)** andar corto(-ta) de tiempo.

push-ups npl flexiones fpl.

put [pʊt] *(pt & pp* put*)* vt poner; *(pressure)* ejercer; *(blame)* echar; *(express)* expresar; *(a question)* hacer; to ~ sthg at *(estimate)* estimarse algo en; to ~ a child to bed acostar a un niño; to ~ money into sthg invertir dinero en algo □ **put aside** vt sep *(money)* apartar; **put away** vt sep *(tidy up)* poner en su sitio; **put back** vt sep *(replace)* volver a poner en su sitio; *(postpone)* aplazar; *(clock, watch)* atrasar; **put down** vt sep *(on floor, table, from vehicle)* dejar; *(Br: animal)* matar; *(deposit)* pagar como depósito; **put forward** vt sep *(clock, watch)* adelantar; *(suggest)* proponer; **put in** vt sep *(insert)* meter; *(install)* instalar; **put off** vt sep *(postpone)* posponer; *(distract)* distraer; *(repel)* repeler; *(passenger)* dejar; **put on** vt sep *(clothes, glasses, make-up)* ponerse; *(weight)* ganar; *(television, light, radio)* encender; *(CD, tape, record)* poner; *(play, show)* representar; to ~ the kettle on poner la tetera a

hervir; **put out** vt sep *(cigarette, fire, light)* apagar; *(publish)* hacer público; *(hand, arm, leg)* extender; *(inconvenience)* causar molestias a; to ~ one's back out fastidiarse la espalda; **put together** vt sep *(assemble)* montar; *(combine)* juntar; **put up** vt sep *(tent, statue, building)* construir; *(umbrella)* abrir; *(a notice, sign)* pegar; *(price, rate)* subir; *(provide with accommodation)* alojar ◆ vi *(Br: in hotel)* alojarse; **put up with** vt fus aguantar.

putter ['pʌtəʳ] n *(club)* putt m.

putting green ['pʌtɪŋ-] n minigolf m *(con césped y sin obstáculos)*.

putty ['pʌtɪ] n masilla f.

puzzle ['pʌzl] n *(game)* rompecabezas m inv; *(jigsaw)* puzzle m; *(mystery)* misterio m ◆ vt desconcertar.

puzzling ['pʌzlɪŋ] adj desconcertante.

pyjamas [pə'dʒɑːməz] npl *(Br)* pijama m.

pylon ['paɪlən] n torre f de alta tensión.

pyramid ['pɪrəmɪd] n pirámide f.

Pyrenees [,pɪrə'niːz] npl: the ~ los Pirineos.

Pyrex® ['paɪreks] n pírex® m.

quail [kweɪl] *n* codorniz *f*.

quail's eggs *npl* huevos *mpl* de codorniz.

quaint [kweɪnt] *adj* pintoresco(-ca).

qualification [ˌkwɒlɪfɪ'keɪʃn] *n* (diploma) título *m*; (ability) aptitud *f*.

qualified ['kwɒlɪfaɪd] *adj* (having qualifications) cualificado(-da).

qualify ['kwɒlɪfaɪ] *vi* (for competition) clasificarse; (pass exam) sacar el título.

quality ['kwɒlɪtɪ] *n* (standard, high standard) calidad *f*; (feature) cualidad *f* ◆ *adj* de calidad.

quarantine ['kwɒrəntiːn] *n* cuarentena *f*.

quarrel ['kwɒrəl] *n* riña *f* ◆ *vi* reñir.

quarry ['kwɒrɪ] *n* (for stone, sand) cantera *f*.

quart [kwɔːt] *n* cuarto *m* de galón.

quarter ['kwɔːtə'] *n* (fraction) cuarto *m*; (Am: coin) cuarto de dólar; (4 ounces) cuatro onzas *fpl*; (three months) trimestre *m*; (part of town) barrio *m*; **(a) ~ to five** (Br) las cinco menos cuarto; **(a) ~ of five** (Am) las cinco menos cuarto; **(a) ~ past five** (Br) las cinco y cuarto; **(a) ~ after five** (Am) las cinco y cuarto; **(a) ~ of an hour** un cuarto de hora.

quarterpounder [ˌkwɔːtə-'paʊndə'] *n* hamburguesa *f* de un cuarto de libra.

quartet [kwɔː'tet] *n* cuarteto *m*.

quartz [kwɔːts] *adj* de cuarzo.

quay [kiː] *n* muelle *m*.

queasy ['kwiːzɪ] *adj* (inf) mareado(-da).

queen [kwiːn] *n* reina *f*; (in cards) dama *f*.

queer [kwɪə'] *adj* (strange) raro(-ra); (inf: ill) pachucho(-cha) ◆ *n* (inf) marica *m*.

quench [kwentʃ] *vt*: **to ~ one's thirst** apagar la sed.

query ['kwɪərɪ] *n* pregunta *f*.

question ['kwestʃn] *n* (query, in exam, on questionnaire) pregunta *f*; (issue) cuestión *f* ◆ *vt* (person) interrogar; **it's out of the ~** es imposible.

question mark *n* signo *m* de interrogación.

questionnaire [ˌkwestʃə'neə'] *n* cuestionario *m*.

queue [kjuː] *n* (Br) cola *f* ◆ *vi* (Br) hacer cola ❑ **queue up** *vi* (Br) hacer cola.

quiche [kiːʃ] *n* quiche *f*.

quick [kwɪk] *adj* rápido(-da) ◆ *adv* rápidamente.

quickly ['kwɪklɪ] *adv* de prisa.

quid [kwɪd] (*pl inv*) *n* (Br: inf) libra *f*.

quiet ['kwaɪət] *adj* (silent, not noisy) silencioso(-sa); (calm, peaceful) tranquilo(-la); (voice) bajo(-ja) ◆ *n* tranquilidad *f*; **keep ~!** ¡silencio!; **to keep ~** quedarse callado(-da); **to keep ~ about sthg** callarse algo.

quieten ['kwaɪətn]: **quieten**

down *vi* tranquilizarse.

quietly ['kwaɪətlɪ] *adv* (*silently*) silenciosamente; (*not noisily*) sin hacer ruido; (*calmly*) tranquilamente.

quilt [kwɪlt] *n* (*duvet*) edredón *m*; (*eiderdown*) colcha *f*.

quince [kwɪns] *n* membrillo *m*.

quirk [kwɜːk] *n* manía *f*, rareza *f*.

quit [kwɪt] (*pt & pp* **quit**) *vi* (*resign*) dimitir; (*give up*) rendirse ◆ *vt* (*Am: school, job*) abandonar; **to ~ doing sthg** dejar de hacer algo.

quite [kwaɪt] *adv* (*fairly*) bastante; (*completely*) totalmente; **there's not ~ enough** no alcanza por poco; **~ a lot (of children)** bastantes (niños); **~ a lot of money** bastante dinero.

quiz [kwɪz] (*pl* **-zes**) *n* concurso *m*.

quota ['kwəʊtə] *n* cuota *f*.

quotation [kwəʊ'teɪʃn] *n* (*phrase*) cita *f*; (*estimate*) presupuesto *m*.

quotation marks *npl* comillas *fpl*.

quote [kwəʊt] *vt* (*phrase, writer*) citar; (*price*) dar ◆ *n* (*phrase*) cita *f*; (*estimate*) presupuesto *m*.

R

rabbit ['ræbɪt] *n* conejo *m*.
rabies ['reɪbiːz] *n* rabia *f*.
RAC *n* asociación británica del auto-

móvil, = RACE *m*.

race [reɪs] *n* (*competition*) carrera *f*; (*ethnic group*) raza *f* ◆ *vi* (*compete*) competir; (*go fast*) ir corriendo; (*engine*) acelerarse ◆ *vt* (*compete against*) competir con.

racecourse ['reɪskɔːs] *n* hipódromo *m*.

racehorse ['reɪshɔːs] *n* caballo *m* de carreras.

racetrack ['reɪstræk] *n* (*for horses*) hipódromo *m*.

racial ['reɪʃl] *adj* racial.

racing ['reɪsɪŋ] *n*: (*horse*) **~** carreras *fpl* de caballos.

racing car *n* coche *m* de carreras.

racism ['reɪsɪzm] *n* racismo *m*.

racist ['reɪsɪst] *n* racista *mf*.

rack [ræk] *n* (*for coats*) percha *f*; (*for plates*) escurreplatos *m inv*; (*for bottles*) botellero *m*; (*luggage*) **~** portaequipajes *m inv*; **~ of lamb** costillar *m* de cordero.

racket ['rækɪt] *n* (*SPORT*) raqueta *f*; (*noise*) jaleo *m*.

racquet ['rækɪt] *n* raqueta *f*.

radar ['reɪdɑːʳ] *n* radar *m*.

radiation [ˌreɪdɪ'eɪʃn] *n* radiación *f*.

radiator ['reɪdɪeɪtəʳ] *n* radiador *m*.

radical ['rædɪkl] *adj* radical.

radii ['reɪdɪaɪ] *pl* → **radius**.

radio ['reɪdɪəʊ] (*pl* **-s**) *n* radio *f* ◆ *vt* radiar; **on the ~** (*hear, be broadcast*) por la radio.

radioactive [ˌreɪdɪəʊ'æktɪv] *adj* radiactivo(-va).

radio alarm *n* radiodespertador *m*.

radish [ˈrædɪʃ] n rábano m.

radius [ˈreɪdɪəs] (pl **radii**) n radio m.

raffle [ˈræfl] n rifa f.

raft [rɑːft] n (of wood) balsa f; (inflatable) bote m.

rafter [ˈrɑːftəʳ] n par m.

rag [ræg] n (old cloth) trapo m.

rage [reɪdʒ] n rabia f.

raid [reɪd] n (attack) incursión f; (by police) redada f; (robbery) asalto m ◆ vt (subj: police) hacer una redada en; (subj: thieves) asaltar.

rail [reɪl] n (bar) barra f; (for curtain, train) carril m; (on stairs) barandilla f ◆ adj ferroviario(-ria); **by ~** por ferrocarril.

railcard [ˈreɪlkɑːd] n (Br) tarjeta que da derecho a un descuento al viajar en tren.

railings [ˈreɪlɪŋz] npl reja f.

railroad [ˈreɪlrəʊd] (Am) = **railway**.

railway [ˈreɪlweɪ] n (system) ferrocarril m; (track) vía f (férrea).

railway line n (route) línea f de ferrocarril; (track) vía f (férrea).

railway station n estación f de ferrocarril.

rain [reɪn] n lluvia f ◆ v impers llover; **it's ~ing** está lloviendo.

rainbow [ˈreɪnbəʊ] n arco m iris.

raincoat [ˈreɪnkəʊt] n impermeable m.

raindrop [ˈreɪndrɒp] n gota f de lluvia.

rainfall [ˈreɪnfɔːl] n pluviosidad f.

rainy [ˈreɪnɪ] adj lluvioso(-sa).

raise [reɪz] vt (lift) levantar; (increase) aumentar; (money) recaudar; (child, animals) criar; (question,

subject) plantear ◆ n (Am: pay increase) aumento m.

raisin [ˈreɪzn] n pasa f.

rake [reɪk] n (tool) rastrillo m.

rally [ˈrælɪ] n (public meeting) mitin m; (motor race) rally m; (in tennis, badminton, squash) peloteo m.

ram [ræm] n carnero m ◆ vt (bang into) chocar con.

Ramadan [ˌræməˈdæn] n Ramadán m.

ramble [ˈræmbl] n paseo m por el campo.

ramp [ræmp] n (slope) rampa f; (Br: in roadworks) rompecoches m inv; (Am: to freeway) acceso m; "**ramp**" (Br) "rampa".

ramparts [ˈræmpɑːts] npl murallas fpl.

ran [ræn] pt → **run**.

ranch [rɑːntʃ] n rancho m.

ranch dressing n (Am) aliño cremoso y algo picante.

rancid [ˈrænsɪd] adj rancio(-cia).

random [ˈrændəm] adj fortuito(-ta); **at ~** al azar.

rang [ræŋ] pt → **ring**.

range [reɪndʒ] n (of radio, telescope) alcance m; (of aircraft) autonomía f; (of prices, temperatures, ages) escala f; (of goods, services) variedad f, (of hills, mountains) sierra f; (for shooting) campo m de tiro; (cooker) fogón m ◆ vi (vary) oscilar.

ranger [ˈreɪndʒəʳ] n guardabosques m inv.

rank [ræŋk] n (in armed forces, police) grado m ◆ adj (smell, taste) pestilente.

ransom [ˈrænsəm] n rescate m.

rap [ræp] n (music) rap m.

rape [reɪp] n (crime) violación f ◆ vt violar.

rapid ['ræpɪd] adj rápido(-da) □ **rapids** npl rápidos mpl.

rapidly ['ræpɪdlɪ] adv rápidamente.

rapist ['reɪpɪst] n violador m.

rare [reər] adj (not common) raro(-ra); (meat) poco hecho(-cha).

rarely ['reəlɪ] adv raras veces.

rash [ræʃ] n (on skin) sarpullido m ◆ adj precipitado(-da).

rasher ['ræʃər] n loncha f.

raspberry ['rɑːzbərɪ] n frambuesa f.

rat [ræt] n rata f.

ratatouille [,rætə'twiː] n guiso de tomate, cebolla, pimiento, calabacín, berenjenas, etc.

rate [reɪt] n (level) índice m; (of interest) tipo m; (charge) precio m; (speed) velocidad f ◆ vt (consider) considerar; (deserve) merecer; ~ of exchange tipo de cambio; **at any** ~ de todos modos; **at this** ~ a este paso.

rather ['rɑːðər] adv (quite) bastante; **I'd ~ have a beer** prefiero tomar una cerveza; **I'd ~ not** mejor que no; **would you ~ ...?** ¿preferirías ...?; ~ **a lot** bastante; ~ **than** antes que.

ratio ['reɪʃɪəʊ] (pl -s) n proporción f.

ration ['ræʃn] n ración f □ **rations** npl (food) víveres mpl.

rational ['ræʃnl] adj racional.

rattle ['rætl] n (of baby) sonajero m ◆ vi golpetear.

rave [reɪv] n (party) fiesta multitudinaria en locales muy amplios con música bakalao y, generalmente, drogas.

raven ['reɪvn] n cuervo m.

ravioli [,rævɪ'əʊlɪ] n raviolis mpl.

raw [rɔː] adj (uncooked) crudo (-da); (sugar) sin refinar.

raw material n materia f prima.

ray [reɪ] n rayo m.

razor ['reɪzər] n (with blade) navaja f; (electric) maquinilla f de afeitar.

razor blade n hoja f de afeitar.

Rd abbr = Road.

re [riː] prep con referencia a.

RE n (abbr of religious education) religión f (materia).

reach [riːtʃ] vt llegar a; (manage to touch) alcanzar; (contact) contactar con ◆ n: **out of** ~ fuera de alcance; **within** ~ **of the beach** a poca distancia de la playa □ **reach out** vi: **to** ~ **out** (for) alargar la mano (para).

react [rɪ'ækt] vi reaccionar.

reaction [rɪ'ækʃn] n reacción f.

read [riːd] (pt & pp **read** [red]) vt leer; (subj: sign, note) decir; (subj: meter, gauge) marcar ◆ vi leer; **I read about it in the paper** lo leí en el periódico □ **read out** vt sep leer en voz alta.

reader ['riːdər] n (of newspaper, book) lector m (-ra f).

readily ['redɪlɪ] adv (willingly) de buena gana; (easily) fácilmente.

reading ['riːdɪŋ] n lectura f.

reading matter n lectura f.

ready ['redɪ] adj (prepared) listo (-ta); **to be ~ for sthg** (prepared) estar listo para algo; **to be ~ to do sthg** (willing) estar dispuesto(-ta) a hacer algo; *(likely)* estar a punto de hacer algo; **to get ~** prepararse; **to get sthg ~** preparar algo.

ready cash *n* dinero *m* contante.

ready-cooked [-kʊkt] *adj* precocinado(-da).

ready-to-wear *adj* confeccionado(-da).

real ['rɪəl] *adj (existing)* real; *(genuine)* auténtico(-ca), *(for emphasis)* verdadero(-ra) ◆ *adv (Am)* muy.

real ale *n (Br)* cerveza criada en toneles, a la manera tradicional.

real estate *n* propiedad *f* inmobiliaria.

realistic [rɪəˈlɪstɪk] *adj* realista.

reality [rɪˈælətɪ] *n* realidad *f*; **in ~** en realidad.

realize ['rɪəlaɪz] *vt (become aware of, know)* darse cuenta de; *(ambition, goal)* realizar.

really ['rɪəlɪ] *adv* realmente, not **~** en realidad no; **~?** *(expressing surprise)* ¿de verdad?

realtor ['rɪəltɔː] *n (Am)* agente *m* inmobiliario (agente *f* inmobiliaria).

rear [rɪə'] *adj* trasero(-ra) ◆ *n (back)* parte *f* de atrás.

rearrange [ˌriːəˈreɪndʒ] *vt (room, furniture)* colocar de otro modo; *(meeting)* volver a concertar.

rearview mirror ['rɪəvjuː-] *n* espejo *m* retrovisor.

rear-wheel drive *n* coche *m* con tracción trasera.

reason ['riːzn] *n (motive, cause)* razón *f*; *(justification)* razones *fpl*; **for some ~** por alguna razón.

reasonable ['riːznəbl] *adj* razo-

nable.

reasonably ['riːznəblɪ] *adv (quite)* razonablemente.

reasoning ['riːznɪŋ] *n* razonamiento *m*.

reassure [ˌriːəˈʃɔː'] *vt* tranquilizar.

reassuring [ˌriːəˈʃɔːrɪŋ] *adj* tranquilizador(-ra).

rebate ['riːbeɪt] *n* devolución *f*.

rebel [*n* 'rebl, *vb* rɪ'bel] *n* rebelde *mf* ◆ *vi* rebelarse.

rebound [rɪ'baʊnd] *vi* rebotar.

rebuild [ˌriː'bɪld] *(pt & pp* rebuilt [ˌriː'bɪlt]) *vt* reconstruir.

rebuke [rɪ'bjuːk] *vt* reprender.

recall [rɪ'kɔːl] *vt (remember)* recordar.

receipt [rɪ'siːt] *n (for goods, money)* recibo *m*; **on ~ of** al recibo de.

receive [rɪ'siːv] *vt* recibir.

receiver [rɪ'siːvə'] *n (of phone)* auricular *m*.

recent ['riːsnt] *adj* reciente.

recently ['riːsntlɪ] *adv* recientemente.

receptacle [rɪ'septəkl] *n (fml)* receptáculo *m*.

reception [rɪ'sepʃn] *n* recepción *f*.

reception desk *n* recepción *f*.

receptionist [rɪ'sepʃənɪst] *n* recepcionista *mf*.

recess ['riːses] *n (in wall)* hueco *m*; *(Am: SCH)* recreo *m*.

recession [rɪ'seʃn] *n* recesión *f*.

recipe ['resɪpɪ] *n* receta *f*.

recite [rɪ'saɪt] *vt (poem)* recitar; *(list)* enumerar.

reckless ['reklɪs] *adj* imprudente.

reckon ['rekn] *vt (inf: think)* pensar ❏ **reckon on** *vt fus* contar con; **reckon with** *vt fus (expect)* contar con.

reclaim [rɪ'kleɪm] *vt (baggage)* reclamar.

reclining seat [rɪ'klaɪnɪŋ-] *n* asiento *m* reclinable.

recognition [,rekəg'nɪʃn] *n* reconocimiento *m*.

recognize ['rekəgnaɪz] *vt* reconocer.

recollect [,rekə'lekt] *vt* recordar.

recommend [,rekə'mend] *vt* recomendar; **to ~ sb to do sthg** recomendar a alguien hacer algo.

recommendation [,rekəmen-'deɪʃn] *n* recomendación *f*.

reconsider [,riːkən'sɪdər] *vt* reconsiderar.

reconstruct [,riːkən'strʌkt] *vt* reconstruir.

record [*n* 'rekɔːd, *vb* rɪ'kɔːd] *n (MUS)* disco *m; (best performance, highest level)* récord *m; (account)* anotación *f* ◆ *vt (keep account of)* anotar; *(on tape)* grabar.

recorded delivery [rɪ'kɔːdɪd-] *n (Br)* = correo *m* certificado.

recorder [rɪ'kɔːdər] *n (tape recorder)* magnetófono *m; (instrument)* flauta *f*.

recording [rɪ'kɔːdɪŋ] *n* grabación *f*.

record player *n* tocadiscos *m inv*.

record shop *n* tienda *f* de música.

recover [rɪ'kʌvər] *vt (stolen goods,* lost property) recuperar ◆ *vi* recobrarse.

recovery [rɪ'kʌvərɪ] *n* recuperación *f*.

recovery vehicle *n (Br)* grúa *f* remolcadora.

recreation [,rekrɪ'eɪʃn] *n* recreo *m*.

recreation ground *n* campo *m* de deportes.

recruit [rɪ'kruːt] *n (to army)* recluta *mf* ◆ *vt (staff)* contratar.

rectangle ['rek,tæŋgl] *n* rectángulo *m*.

rectangular [rek'tæŋgjʊlər] *adj* rectangular.

recycle [,riː'saɪkl] *vt* reciclar.

red [red] *adj* rojo(-ja) ◆ *n (colour)* rojo *m*; **she has ~ hair** es pelirroja; **in the ~** en números rojos.

red cabbage *n* lombarda *f*.

Red Cross *n* Cruz *f* Roja.

redcurrant ['redkʌrənt] *n* grosella *f*.

redecorate [,riː'dekəreɪt] *vt* cambiar la decoración de.

redhead ['redhed] *n* pelirrojo *m* (-ja *f*).

red-hot *adj* al rojo vivo.

redial [,riː'daɪəl] *vi* volver a marcar.

redirect [,riːdɪ'rekt] *vt (letter)* reexpedir; *(traffic, plane)* redirigir.

red pepper *n* pimiento *m* rojo.

reduce [rɪ'djuːs] *vt (make smaller)* reducir; *(make cheaper)* rebajar ◆ *vi (Am: slim)* adelgazar.

reduced price [rɪ'djuːst-] *n* precio *m* rebajado.

reduction [rɪ'dʌkʃn] *n (in size)* reducción *f; (in price)* descuento *m*.

redundancy [rɪ'dʌndənsɪ] n (Br: job loss) despido m.

redundant [rɪ'dʌndənt] adj (Br): to be made ~ perder el empleo.

red wine n vino m tinto.

reed [riːd] n carrizo m.

reef [riːf] n arrecife m.

reek [riːk] vi apestar.

reel [riːl] n carrete m.

refectory [rɪ'fektərɪ] n refectorio m.

refer [rɪ'fɜːʳ]: **refer to** vt fus (speak about, relate to) referirse a; (consult) consultar.

referee [,refə'riː] n (SPORT) árbitro m.

reference ['refrəns] n (mention) referencia f; (letter for job) referencias fpl ♦ adj (book, library) de consulta; **with ~** con referencia a.

referendum [,refə'rendəm] n referéndum m.

refill [n 'riːfɪl, vb ,riː'fɪl] n (for pen) cartucho m de recambio; **would you like a ~!** (inf) ¿quieres tomar otra copa de lo mismo?

refinery [rɪ'faɪnərɪ] n refinería f.

reflect [rɪ'flekt] vt reflejar ♦ vi (think) reflexionar.

reflection [rɪ'flekʃn] n (image) reflejo m.

reflector [rɪ'flektəʳ] n reflector m.

reflex ['riːfleks] n reflejo m.

reflexive [rɪ'fleksɪv] adj reflexivo(-va).

reform [rɪ'fɔːm] n reforma f ♦ vt reformar.

refresh [rɪ'freʃ] vt refrescar.

refreshing [rɪ'freʃɪŋ] adj refres-

cante.

refreshments [rɪ'freʃmənts] npl refrigerios mpl.

refrigerator [rɪ'frɪdʒəreɪtəʳ] n refrigerador m.

refugee [,refjʊ'dʒiː] n refugiado m (-da f).

refund [n 'riːfʌnd, vb rɪ'fʌnd] n reembolso m ♦ vt reembolsar.

refundable [rɪ'fʌndəbl] adj reembolsable.

refusal [rɪ'fjuːzl] n negativa f.

refuse[1] [rɪ'fjuːz] vt (not accept) rechazar; (not allow) denegar ♦ vi negarse; **to ~ to do sthg** negarse a hacer algo.

refuse[2] ['refjuːs] n (fml) basura f.

refuse collection ['refjuːs-] n (fml) recogida f de basuras.

regard [rɪ'gɑːd] vt (consider) considerar ♦ n: **with ~ to** respecto a; **as ~s** por lo que se refiere a ☐ **regards** npl (in greetings) recuerdos mpl; **give them my ~s** saludales de mi parte.

regarding [rɪ'gɑːdɪŋ] prep respecto a.

regardless [rɪ'gɑːdlɪs] adv a pesar de todo; **~ of** sin tener en cuenta.

reggae ['regeɪ] n reggae m.

regiment ['redʒɪmənt] n regimiento m.

region ['riːdʒən] n región f; **in the ~ of** alrededor de.

regional ['riːdʒənl] adj regional.

register ['redʒɪstəʳ] n (official list) registro m ♦ vt registrar ♦ vi (be officially recorded) inscribirse; (at hotel) registrarse.

registered ['redʒɪstəd] adj (letter,

parcel) certificado(-da).

registration [ˌredʒɪ'streɪʃn] *n (for course)* inscripción *f; (at conference)* entrega *f* de documentación.

registration (number) *(of car)* número *m* de matrícula.

registry office ['redʒɪstrɪ-] *n* registro *m* civil.

regret [rɪ'gret] *n* pesar *m* ♦ *vt* lamentar; **to ~ doing sth** lamentar haber hecho algo; **we ~ any inconvenience caused** lamentamos las molestias ocasionadas.

regrettable [rɪ'gretəbl] *adj* lamentable.

regular ['regjʊləʳ] *adj* regular; *(frequent)* habitual; *(normal, of normal size)* normal ♦ *n* cliente *mf* habitual.

regularly ['regjʊləlɪ] *adv* con regularidad.

regulate ['regjʊleɪt] *vt* regular.

regulation [ˌregjʊ'leɪʃn] *n (rule)* regla *f*.

rehearsal [rɪ'hɜːsl] *n* ensayo *m*.

rehearse [rɪ'hɜːs] *vt* ensayar.

reign [reɪn] *n* reinado *m* ♦ *vi* reinar.

reimburse [ˌriːɪm'bɜːs] *vt (fml)* reembolsar.

reindeer ['reɪndɪəʳ] *(pl inv)* reno *m*.

reinforce [ˌriːɪn'fɔːs] *vt* reforzar.

reinforcements [ˌriːɪn'fɔːsmənts] *npl* refuerzos *mpl*.

reins [reɪnz] *npl (for horse)* riendas *fpl; (for child)* andadores *mpl*.

reject [rɪ'dʒekt] *vt* rechazar.

rejection [rɪ'dʒekʃn] *n* rechazo *m*.

rejoin [ˌriː'dʒɔɪn] *vt (motorway)* reincorporarse a.

relapse [rɪ'læps] *n* recaída *f*.

relate [rɪ'leɪt] *vt (connect)* relacionar ♦ *vi*: **to ~ to** *(be connected with)* estar relacionado con; *(concern)* referirse a.

related [rɪ'leɪtɪd] *adj (of same family)* emparentado(-da); *(connected)* relacionado(-da).

relation [rɪ'leɪʃn] *n (member of family)* pariente *mf; (connection)* relación *f*; **in ~ to** en relación con ❏ **relations** *npl (international etc)* relaciones *fpl*.

relationship [rɪ'leɪʃnʃɪp] *n* relación *f*.

relative ['relətɪv] *adj* relativo (-va) ♦ *n* pariente *mf*.

relatively ['relətɪvlɪ] *adv* relativamente.

relax [rɪ'læks] *vi* relajarse.

relaxation [ˌriːlæk'seɪʃn] *n* relajación *f*.

relaxed [rɪ'lækst] *adj (person)* tranquilo(-la); *(atmosphere)* desenfadado(-da).

relaxing [rɪ'læksɪŋ] *adj* relajante.

relay ['riːleɪ] *n (race)* carrera *f* de relevos.

release [rɪ'liːs] *vt (set free)* liberar; *(hand, brake, catch)* soltar; *(film)* estrenar; *(record)* sacar ♦ *n (film)* estreno *m; (record)* lanzamiento *m*.

relegate ['relɪgeɪt] *vt*: **to be ~d** *(SPORT)* descender.

relevant ['reləvənt] *adj (connected, appropriate)* pertinente; *(important)* importante.

reliable [rɪ'laɪəbl] *adj (person, machine)* fiable.

relic ['relɪk] *n (vestige)* reliquia *f*.

relief [rɪ'liːf] n (gladness) alivio m; (aid) ayuda f.

relief road n carretera f auxiliar de descongestión.

relieve [rɪ'liːv] vt (pain, headache) aliviar.

relieved [rɪ'liːvd] adj aliviado(-da).

religion [rɪ'lɪdʒn] n religión f.

religious [rɪ'lɪdʒəs] adj religioso(-sa).

relish ['relɪʃ] n (sauce) salsa f picante.

reluctant [rɪ'lʌktənt] adj reacio(-cia).

rely [rɪ'laɪ]: **rely on** vt fus (trust) contar con; (depend on) depender de.

remain [rɪ'meɪn] vi (stay) permanecer; (continue to exist) quedar □ **remains** npl restos mpl.

remainder [rɪ'meɪndər] n resto m.

remaining [rɪ'meɪnɪŋ] adj restante.

remark [rɪ'mɑːk] n comentario m ◆ vt comentar.

remarkable [rɪ'mɑːkəbl] adj excepcional.

remedy ['remədɪ] n remedio m.

remember [rɪ'membər] vt recordar ◆ vi acordarse; **to ~ doing sthg** acordarse de haber hecho algo; **to ~ to do sthg** acordarse de hacer algo.

remind [rɪ'maɪnd] vt: **to ~ sb of** sb recordarle a alguien a alguien; **to ~ sb to do sthg** recordar a alguien hacer algo.

reminder [rɪ'maɪndər] n (for bill, library book) notificación f.

remittance [rɪ'mɪtns] n giro m.

remnant ['remnənt] n resto m.

remote [rɪ'məʊt] adj remoto(-ta).

remote control n (device) mando m (de control remoto).

removal [rɪ'muːvl] n (taking away) extracción f.

removal van n camión m de mudanzas.

remove [rɪ'muːv] vt quitar.

renew [rɪ'njuː] vt renovar.

renovate ['renəveɪt] vt reformar.

renowned [rɪ'naʊnd] adj renombrado(-da).

rent [rent] n alquiler m ◆ vt alquilar.

rental ['rentl] n alquiler m.

repaid [riː'peɪd] pt & pp → repay.

repair [rɪ'peər] vt reparar ◆ n: in good ~ en buen estado □ **repairs** npl reparaciones fpl.

repair kit n caja f de herramientas.

repay [riː'peɪ] (pt & pp repaid) vt (money, favour) devolver.

repayment [riː'peɪmənt] n devolución f.

repeat [rɪ'piːt] vt repetir ◆ n (on TV, radio) reposición f.

repetition [ˌrepɪ'tɪʃn] n repetición f.

repetitive [rɪ'petɪtɪv] adj repetitivo(-va).

replace [rɪ'pleɪs] vt (substitute) sustituir; (faulty goods) reemplazar; (put back) poner en su sitio.

replacement [rɪ'pleɪsmənt] n (substitute) sustituto m (-ta f).

replay ['riːpleɪ] n (rematch) partido *m* de desempate; *(on TV)* repetición *f*.

reply [rɪ'plaɪ] *n* respuesta *f* ◆ *vt & vi* responder.

report [rɪ'pɔ:t] *n (account)* informe *m*; *(in newspaper, on TV, radio)* reportaje *m*; *(Br: SCH)* boletín de evaluación ◆ *vt (announce)* informar; *(theft, disappearance, person)* denunciar ◆ *vi* informar; **to ~ to sb** *(go to)* presentarse a alguien.

report card *n* boletín *m* de evaluación.

reporter [rɪ'pɔ:tər] *n* reportero *m* (-ra *f*).

represent [,reprɪ'zent] *vt* representar.

representative [,reprɪ'zentətɪv] *n* representante *mf*.

repress [rɪ'pres] *vt* reprimir.

reprieve [rɪ'pri:v] *n (delay)* tregua *f*.

reprimand ['reprɪmɑ:nd] *vt* reprender.

reproach [rɪ'prəʊtʃ] *vt* reprochar.

reproduction [,ri:prə'dʌkʃn] *n* reproducción *f*.

reptile ['reptaɪl] *n* reptil *m*.

republic [rɪ'pʌblɪk] *n* república *f*.

Republican [rɪ'pʌblɪkən] *n (in US)* republicano *m* (-na *f*) ◆ *adj (in US)* republicano(-na).

repulsive [rɪ'pʌlsɪv] *adj* repulsivo(-va).

reputable ['repjʊtəbl] *adj* de buena reputación.

reputation [,repjʊ'teɪʃn] *n* reputación *f*.

reputedly [rɪ'pju:tɪdlɪ] *adv* según se dice.

request [rɪ'kwest] *n* petición *f* ◆ *vt* solicitar; **to ~ sb to do sthg** rogar a alguien que haga algo; **available on ~** disponible a petición del interesado.

request stop *n (Br)* parada *f* discrecional.

require [rɪ'kwaɪər] *vt (need)* necesitar; **passengers are ~d to show their tickets** los pasajeros han de mostrar los billetes.

requirement [rɪ'kwaɪəmənt] *n* requisito *m*.

resat [,ri:'sæt] *pt & pp* → **resit**.

rescue ['reskju:] *vt* rescatar.

research [,rɪ'sɜ:tʃ] *n* investigación *f*.

resemblance [rɪ'zembləns] *n* parecido *m*.

resemble [rɪ'zembl] *vt* parecerse a.

resent [rɪ'zent] *vt* tomarse a mal.

reservation [,rezə'veɪʃn] *n (booking)* reserva *f*; *(doubt)* duda *f*; **to make a ~** hacer una reserva.

reserve [rɪ'zɜ:v] *n (SPORT)* suplente *mf*; *(for wildlife)* reserva *f* ◆ *vt* reservar.

reserved [rɪ'zɜ:vd] *adj* reservado(-da).

reservoir ['rezəvwɑ:r] *n* pantano *m*.

reset [,ri:'set] *(pt & pp* **reset)** *vt (watch, meter, device)* reajustar.

reside [rɪ'zaɪd] *vi (fml)* residir.

residence ['rezɪdəns] *n (fml)* residencia *f*; **place of ~** *(fml)* domicilio *m*.

residence permit *n* permiso *m* de residencia.

resident ['rezɪdənt] *n (of country)*

residente *mf*; *(of hotel)* huésped *mf*; *(of area, house)* vecino *m* (-na *f*); "~s only" *(for parking)* "sólo para residentes".

residential [ˌrezɪ'denʃl] *adj (area)* residencial.

residue ['rezɪdjuː] *n* residuo *m*.

resign [rɪ'zaɪn] *vi* dimitir ◆ *vt*: to ~ o.s. to sthg resignarse a algo.

resignation [ˌrezɪg'neɪʃn] *n (from job)* dimisión *f*.

resilient [rɪ'zɪlɪənt] *adj* resistente.

resist [rɪ'zɪst] *vt (fight against)* resistir a; *(temptation)* resistir; I can't ~ cream cakes me encantan los pasteles de nata; to ~ doing sthg resistirse a hacer algo.

resistance [rɪ'zɪstəns] *n* resistencia *f*.

resit [ˌriː'sɪt] *(pt & pp* resat*)* *vt* volver a presentarse a.

resolution [ˌrezə'luːʃn] *n (promise)* propósito *m*.

resolve [rɪ'zɒlv] *vt (solve)* resolver.

resort [rɪ'zɔːt] *n (for holidays)* lugar *m* de vacaciones; as a last ~ como último recurso ❑ resort to *vt fus* recurrir a; to ~ to doing sthg recurrir a hacer algo.

resource [rɪ'sɔːs] *n* recurso *m*.

resourceful [rɪ'sɔːsful] *adj* habilidoso(-sa).

respect [rɪ'spekt] *n* respeto *m*; *(aspect)* aspecto *m* ◆ *vt* respetar; in some ~s en algunos aspectos; with ~ to con respecto a.

respectable [rɪ'spektəbl] *adj* respetable.

respective [rɪ'spektɪv] *adj* respectivo(-va).

respond [rɪ'spɒnd] *vi* responder.

response [rɪ'spɒns] *n* respuesta *f*.

responsibility [rɪˌspɒnsə'bɪlətɪ] *n* responsabilidad *f*.

responsible [rɪ'spɒnsəbl] *adj* responsable; to be ~ (for) *(accountable)* ser responsable (de).

rest [rest] *n (relaxation, for foot)* descanso *m*; *(for head)* respaldo *m* ◆ *vi (relax)* descansar; the ~ el resto; to have a ~ descansar; to ~ against apoyarse contra.

restaurant ['restərɒnt] *n* restaurante *m*.

restaurant car *n (Br)* vagón *m* restaurante.

restful ['restful] *adj* tranquilo(-la).

restless ['restlɪs] *adj (bored, impatient)* impaciente; *(fidgety)* inquieto(-ta).

restore [rɪ'stɔː] *vt (reintroduce)* restablecer; *(renovate)* restaurar.

restrain [rɪ'streɪn] *vt* controlar.

restrict [rɪ'strɪkt] *vt* restringir.

restricted [rɪ'strɪktɪd] *adj* limitado(-da).

restriction [rɪ'strɪkʃn] *n (rule)* restricción *f*; *(limitation)* limitación *f*.

rest room *n (Am)* aseos *mpl*.

result [rɪ'zʌlt] *n* resultado *m* ◆ *vi*: to ~ in resultar en, as a ~ of como resultado de ❑ results *npl (of test, exam)* resultados *mpl*.

resume [rɪ'zjuːm] *vi* volver a empezar.

résumé ['rezjuːmeɪ] *n (summary)* resumen *m*; *(Am: curriculum vitae)* currículum m.

retail ['ri:teil] n venta f al por menor ♦ vt vender (al por menor) ♦ vi: **to ~ at** venderse a.

retailer ['ri:teilə'] n minorista mf.

retail price n precio m de venta al público.

retain [rɪ'teɪn] vt (fml) retener.

retaliate [rɪ'tælieɪt] vi desquitarse.

retire [rɪ'taɪə'] vi (stop working) jubilarse.

retired [rɪ'taɪəd] adj jubilado(-da).

retirement [rɪ'taɪəmənt] n (leaving job) jubilación f; (period after retiring) retiro m.

retreat [rɪ'triːt] vi retirarse ♦ n (place) refugio m.

retrieve [rɪ'triːv] vt recobrar.

return [rɪ'tɜːn] n (arrival back) vuelta f; (Br: ticket) billete m de ida y vuelta ♦ vt (put back) volver a poner; (ball, serve) restar; (give back) devolver ♦ vi (go back, come back) volver; (happen again) reaparecer ♦ adj (journey) de vuelta; **to ~ sthg (to sb)** devolver algo (a alguien); **by ~ of post** (Br) a vuelta de correo; **many happy ~s!** ¡que cumplas muchos más!; **in ~ (for)** en recompensa (por).

return flight n vuelo m de regreso.

return ticket n (Br) billete m de ida y vuelta.

reunite [,riːjuː'naɪt] vt reunir.

reveal [rɪ'viːl] vt revelar.

revelation [,revə'leɪʃn] n revelación f.

revenge [rɪ'vendʒ] n venganza f.

reverse [rɪ'vɜːs] adj inverso(-sa) ♦ n (AUT) marcha f atrás; (of coin) reverso m; (of document) dorso m ♦ vt (car) dar marcha atrás a; (decision) revocar ♦ vi dar marcha atrás; **the ~** (opposite) lo contrario; **in ~ order** al revés; **to ~ the charges** (Br) llamar a cobro revertido.

reverse-charge call n (Br) llamada f a cobro revertido.

review [rɪ'vjuː] n (of book, record, film) reseña f; (examination) repaso m ♦ vt (Am: for exam) repasar.

revise [rɪ'vaɪz] vt revisar ♦ vi (Br) repasar.

revision [rɪ'vɪʒn] n (Br) repaso m.

revive [rɪ'vaɪv] vt (person) reanimar; (economy, custom) resucitar.

revolt [rɪ'vəʊlt] n rebelión f.

revolting [rɪ'vəʊltɪŋ] adj asqueroso(-sa).

revolution [,revə'luːʃn] n revolución f.

revolutionary [,revə'luːʃnərɪ] adj revolucionario(-ria).

revolver [rɪ'vɒlvə'] n revólver m.

revolving door [rɪ'vɒlvɪŋ-] n puerta f giratoria.

revue [rɪ'vjuː] n revista f teatral.

reward [rɪ'wɔːd] n recompensa f ♦ vt recompensar.

rewind [,riː'waɪnd] (pt & pp **rewound** [,riː'waʊnd]) vt rebobinar.

rheumatism ['ruːmətɪzm] n reumatismo m.

rhinoceros [raɪ'nɒsərəs] (pl inv OR **-es**) n rinoceronte m.

rhubarb ['ruːbɑːb] n ruibarbo m.

rhyme [raɪm] n (poem) rima f ♦ vi rimar.

rhythm ['rɪðm] n ritmo m.

rib [rɪb] n costilla f.

ribbon ['rɪbən] n cinta f.

rice [raɪs] n arroz m.

rice pudding n arroz m con leche.

rich [rɪtʃ] adj rico(-ca) ♦ npl: **the ~** los ricos; **to be ~ in sthg** abundar en algo.

ricotta cheese [rɪ'kɒtə] n queso m de ricotta.

rid [rɪd] vt: **to get ~ of** deshacerse de.

ridden ['rɪdn] pp → ride.

riddle ['rɪdl] n (puzzle) acertijo m; (mystery) enigma m.

ride [raɪd] (pt rode, pp ridden) n (on horse, bike) paseo m; (in vehicle) vuelta f ♦ vt (horse) montar a; (bike) montar en ♦ vi (on horse) montar a caballo; (bike) ir en bici; (in car) ir en coche; **to go for a ~** (in car) darse una vuelta en coche.

rider ['raɪdər] n (on horse) jinete m (amazona f); (on bike) ciclista mf.

ridge [rɪdʒ] n (of mountain) cresta f; (raised surface) rugosidad f.

ridiculous [rɪ'dɪkjʊləs] adj ridículo(-la).

riding ['raɪdɪŋ] n equitación f.

riding school n escuela f de equitación.

rifle ['raɪfl] n fusil m.

rig [rɪg] n torre f de perforación ♦ vt amañar.

right [raɪt] adj 1. (correct) correcto(-ta); **to be ~** tener razón; **have you got the ~ time?** ¿tienes buena hora?; **to be ~ to do sthg** hacer bien en hacer algo.

2. (most suitable) adecuado(-da); **is this the ~ way?** ¿así está bien?

3. (fair) justo(-ta); **that's not ~!** ¡eso no es justo!

4. (on the right) derecho(-cha); **the ~ side of the road** la derecha de la carretera.

♦ n 1. (side): **the ~** la derecha.

2. (entitlement) derecho m; **to have the ~ to do sthg** tener el derecho a hacer algo.

♦ adv 1. (towards the right) a la derecha; **turn ~** tuerza a la derecha.

2. (correctly) bien; **am I pronouncing it ~?** ¿lo pronuncio bien?

3. (for emphasis) justo; **~ here** aquí mismo; **~ the way down the road** por toda la calle abajo.

4. (immediately): **I'll be ~ back** vuelvo enseguida; **~ after** justo después; **~ away** enseguida.

right angle n ángulo m recto.

right-hand adj derecho(-cha).

right-hand drive n vehículo m con el volante a la derecha.

right-handed ['-hændɪd] adj (person) diestro(-tra); (implement) para personas diestras.

rightly ['raɪtlɪ] adv (correctly) correctamente; (justly) debidamente.

right of way n (AUT) prioridad f; (path) camino m público.

right-wing adj derechista.

rigid ['rɪdʒɪd] adj rígido(-da).

rim [rɪm] n borde m.

rind [raɪnd] n corteza f.

ring [rɪŋ] (pt rang, pp rung) n (for finger) anillo m, (circle) círculo m; (sound) timbrazo m; (on cooker) quemador m; (for boxing) cuadrilátero m; (in circus) pista f ♦ vt (Br: on phone) llamar (por teléfono); (bell) tocar ♦ vi (bell, telephone) sonar; (Br: make *phone call)* llamar (por teléfono); **to give sb a ~** llamar a alguien (por teléfono); **to ~ the bell** tocar el timbre ❑ **ring back** *vt sep & vi (Br)* volver a llamar; **ring off** *vi (Br)* colgar; **ring up** *vt sep & vi (Br)* llamar (por teléfono).

ringing tone ['rɪŋɪŋ-] *n* tono *m* de llamada.

ring road *n* carretera *f* de circunvalación.

rink [rɪŋk] *n* pista *f*.

rinse [rɪns] *vt* aclarar ❑ **rinse out** *vt sep* enjuagar.

riot ['raɪət] *n* disturbio *m*.

rip [rɪp] *n* rasgón *m* ◆ *vt* rasgar ◆ *vi* rasgarse ❑ **rip up** *vt sep* desgarrar.

ripe [raɪp] *adj* maduro(-ra).

ripen ['raɪpn] *vi* madurar.

rip-off *n (inf)* estafa *f*.

rise [raɪz] *(pt* rose, *pp* risen ['rɪzn]) *vi (move upwards)* elevarse; *(sun, moon)* salir; *(increase)* aumentar; *(stand up)* levantarse ◆ *n (increase)* ascenso *m; (Br: pay increase)* aumento *m; (slope)* subida *f*.

risk [rɪsk] *n (danger)* peligro *m; (in insurance)* riesgo *m* ◆ *vt* arriesgar; **to take a ~** arriesgarse; **at your own ~** bajo su cuenta y riesgo; **to ~ doing sthg** exponerse a hacer algo; **to ~ it** arriesgarse.

risky ['rɪskɪ] *adj* peligroso(-sa).

risotto [rɪ'zɒtəʊ] *(pl* -s) *n* arroz con carne, marisco o verduras.

ritual ['rɪtʃʊəl] *n* ritual *m*.

rival ['raɪvl] *adj* rival ◆ *n* rival *mf*.

river ['rɪvəʳ] *n* río *m*.

river bank *n* orilla *f* del río.

riverside ['rɪvəsaɪd] *n* ribera *f* del río.

Riviera [ˌrɪvɪ'eərə] *n:* **the (French) ~** la Riviera (francesa).

roach [rəʊtʃ] *n (Am)* cucaracha *f*.

road [rəʊd] *n (major, roadway)* carretera *f; (minor) camino m; (street)* calle *f;* **by ~** por carretera.

road book *n* libro *m* de carreteras.

road map *n* mapa *m* de carreteras.

road safety *n* seguridad *f* en carretera.

roadside ['rəʊdsaɪd] *n:* **the ~** el borde de la carretera.

road sign *n* señal *f* de tráfico.

road tax *n* impuesto *m* de circulación.

roadway ['rəʊdweɪ] *n* calzada *f*.

road works *npl* obras *fpl* (en la carretera).

roam [rəʊm] *vi* vagar.

roar [rɔːʳ] *n (of crowd, aeroplane)* estruendo *m* ◆ *vi* rugir.

roast [rəʊst] *n* asado *m* ◆ *vt* asar ◆ *adj* asado(-da); **~ beef** rosbif *m;* **~ chicken** pollo *m* asado; **~ lamb** cordero *m* asado; **~ pork** cerdo *m* asado; **~ potatoes** patatas *fpl* asadas.

rob [rɒb] *vt* robar; **to ~ sb of sthg** robar a alguien algo.

robber ['rɒbəʳ] *n* ladrón *m* (-ona *f*).

robbery ['rɒbərɪ] *n* robo *m*.

robe [rəʊb] *n (Am: bathrobe)* bata *f*.

robin ['rɒbɪn] *n* petirrojo *m*.

robot ['rəʊbɒt] *n* robot *m*.

rock [rɒk] *n (boulder)* peñasco *m; (Am: stone)* guijarro *m; (substance)* roca *f; (music)* rock *m; (Br: sweet)* palo *m* de caramelo ◆ *vt (baby, boat)* mecer; **on the ~s** *(drink)* con hielo.

rock climbing *n* escalada *f* (de rocas); **to go ~** ir de escalada.

rocket ['rɒkɪt] *n* cohete *m*.

rocking chair ['rɒkɪŋ-] *n* mecedora *f*.

rock 'n' roll [,rɒkən'rəʊl] *n* rock and roll *m*.

rocky ['rɒkɪ] *adj* rocoso(-sa).

rod [rɒd] *n* (wooden) vara *f*, (metal) barra *f*; *(for fishing)* caña *f*.

rode [rəʊd] *pt* → **ride**.

roe [rəʊ] *n* hueva *f*.

role [rəʊl] *n* papel *m*.

roll [rəʊl] *n* (of bread) bollo *m*, panecillo *m*; (of film, paper) rollo *m* ♦ *vi* (ball, rock) rodar; (vehicle) avanzar; (ship) balancearse ♦ *vt* (ball, rock) hacer rodar; (cigarette) liar; (dice) rodar ❑ **roll over** *vi* (person, animal) darse la vuelta; (car) volcar; **roll up** *vt sep* (map, carpet) enrollar; (sleeves, trousers) remangarse.

roller coaster ['rəʊlə,kəʊstə] *n* montaña *f* rusa.

roller skate ['rəʊlə-] *n* patín *m* (de ruedas).

roller-skating ['rəʊlə-] *n* patinaje *m* sobre ruedas.

rolling pin ['rəʊlɪŋ-] *n* rodillo *m*.

Roman ['rəʊmən] *adj* romano(-na) ♦ *n* romano *m* (-na *f*).

Roman Catholic *n* católico *m* romano (católica *f* romana).

romance [rəʊ'mæns] *n* (love) lo romántico, (love affair) amorío *m*, (novel) novela *f* romántica.

Romania [ru:'meɪnjə] *n* Rumanía *f*.

romantic [rəʊ'mæntɪk] *adj* romántico(-ca).

romper suit ['rɒmpə-] *n* pe-

lele *m*.

roof [ru:f] *n* (of building, cave) tejado *m*; (of car, caravan, tent) techo *m*.

roof rack *n* baca *f*.

room [ru:m, rʊm] *n* habitación *f*; (larger) sala *f*; (space) sitio *m*.

room number *n* número *m* de habitación.

room service *n* servicio *m* de habitación.

room temperature *n* temperatura *f* ambiente.

roomy ['ru:mɪ] *adj* espacioso(-sa).

root [ru:t] *n* raíz *f*.

rope [rəʊp] *n* cuerda *f* ♦ *vt* atar con cuerda.

rose [rəʊz] *pt* → **rise** ♦ *n* rosa *f*.

rosé ['rəʊzeɪ] *n* rosado *m*.

rosemary ['rəʊzmərɪ] *n* romero *m*.

rot [rɒt] *vi* pudrirse.

rota ['rəʊtə] *n* lista *f* (de turnos).

rotate [rəʊ'teɪt] *vi* girar.

rotten ['rɒtn] *adj* (food, wood) podrido(-da); *(inf: not good)* malísimo(-ma); **I feel ~** (ill) me siento fatal.

rouge [ru:ʒ] *n* colorete *m*.

rough [rʌf] *adj* (surface, skin, wine) áspero(ra); (sea, crossing) agitado(-da); (person) bruto(-ta); (approximate) aproximado(-da); (conditions) básico(-ca); (area, town) peligroso(-a) ♦ *n* (in golf) rough *m*; **to have a ~ time** pasar por un momento difícil.

roughly ['rʌflɪ] *adv* (approximately) aproximadamente; (push, handle) brutalmente.

roulade [ru:'lɑ:d] *n* rollo *m*.

roulette [ru:'let] *n* ruleta *f*.

round [raʊnd] adj redondo(-da).

♦ n 1. (of drinks) ronda f; **it's my ~** es mi ronda.

2. (of sandwiches) sándwich cortado en cuartos.

3. (of toast) tostada f.

4. (of competition) vuelta f.

5. (in golf) partido m.

6. (in boxing) asalto m.

7. (of policeman, milkman) recorrido m.

♦ adv 1. (in a circle) en redondo; **to spin ~** girar.

2. (surrounding) alrededor; **it had a wall all (the way) ~** estaba todo rodeado por un muro; **all ~** por todos lados.

3. (near): **~ about** alrededor.

4. (to one's house): **to ask some friends ~** invitar a unos amigos a casa.

5. (continuously): **all year ~** durante todo el año.

♦ prep 1. (surrounding) alrededor de; **they stood ~ the car** estaban alrededor del coche.

2. (circling) alrededor de; **to go ~ the corner** doblar la esquina; **we walked ~ the lake** fuimos andando alrededor del lago.

3. (visiting): **to go ~ a town** recorrer una ciudad.

4. (approximately) sobre; **~ (about) 100** unos 100; **~ ten o'clock** a eso de las diez.

5. (near): **~ here** por aquí.

6. (in phrases): **it's just ~ the corner** (nearby) está a la vuelta de la esquina; **~ the clock** las 24 horas.

❏ **round off** vt sep (meal, day, visit) terminar.

roundabout ['raʊndəbaʊt] n (Br) (in road) raqueta f (de tráfico); (in playground) plataforma giratoria donde juegan los niños; (at fairground) tiovivo m.

rounders ['raʊndəz] n (Br) juego parecido al béisbol.

round trip n viaje m de ida y vuelta.

route [ru:t] n ruta f ♦ vt dirigir.

routine [ru:'ti:n] n rutina f ♦ adj rutinario(-ria).

row[1] [rəʊ] n fila f ♦ vt (boat) remar ♦ vi remar; **four in a ~** cuatro seguidos.

row[2] [raʊ] n (argument) pelea f; (inf: noise) estruendo m; **to have a ~** tener una pelea.

rowboat ['rəʊbəʊt] (Am) = **rowing boat**.

rowdy ['raʊdɪ] adj ruidoso(-sa).

rowing ['rəʊɪŋ] n remo m.

rowing boat n (Br) bote m de remos.

royal ['rɔɪəl] adj real.

royal family n familia f real.

Este es el nombre que reciben el monarca británico y su familia; la actual cabeza de la Familia Real es la reina Isabel. Otros miembros importantes son su esposo el príncipe Felipe (duque de Edimburgo), sus hijos los príncipes Carlos (Príncipe de Gales), Andrés y Eduardo, la princesa Ana y la reina madre. El himno nacional británico se toca cuando alguno de sus miembros acude a un acontecimiento oficial y la bandera británica se despliega en sus palacios cuando se encuentran ahí.

royalty [ˈrɔɪəltɪ] n realeza f.

RRP (abbr of recommended retail price) P.V.P.

rub [rʌb] vt (back, eyes) frotar; (polish) sacar brillo a ◆ vi (with hand, cloth) frotar; (shoes) rozar □ **rub in** vt sep (lotion, oil) frotar; **rub out** vt sep borrar.

rubber [ˈrʌbə] adj de goma ◆ n (material) goma f; (Br: eraser) goma f de borrar; (Am: inf: condom) goma f.

rubber band n goma f elástica.

rubber gloves npl guantes mpl de goma.

rubber ring n flotador m.

rubbish [ˈrʌbɪʃ] n (refuse) basura f; (inf: worthless thing) porquería f; (inf: nonsense) tonterías fpl.

rubbish bin n (Br) cubo m de la basura.

rubbish dump n (Br) vertedero m de basura.

rubble [ˈrʌbl] n escombros mpl.

ruby [ˈruːbɪ] n rubí m.

rucksack [ˈrʌksæk] n mochila f.

rudder [ˈrʌdə] n timón m.

rude [ruːd] adj (person) maleducado(-da); (behaviour, joke, picture) grosero(-ra).

rug [rʌɡ] n (for floor) alfombra f; (Br: blanket) manta f de viaje.

rugby [ˈrʌɡbɪ] n rugby m.

ruin [ˈruːɪn] vt estropear □ **ruins** npl ruinas fpl.

ruined [ˈruːɪnd] adj (building) en ruinas; (clothes, meal, holiday) estropeado(-da).

rule [ruːl] n regla f ◆ vt gobernar; **to be the ~** ser la norma; **against the ~s** contra las normas; **as a ~** por regla general □ **rule out** vt sep descartar.

ruler [ˈruːlə] n (of country) gobernante mf; (for measuring) regla f.

rum [rʌm] n ron m.

rumor [ˈruːmər] (Am) = rumour.

rumour [ˈruːmə] n (Br) rumor m.

rump steak [ˌrʌmp-] n filete m (grueso) de lomo.

run [rʌn] (pt ran, pp run) vi 1. (on foot) correr.
2. (train, bus) circular; **the bus ~s every hour** hay un autobús cada hora; **the train is running an hour late** el tren va con una hora de retraso.
3. (operate) funcionar; **to ~ on sthg** funcionar con algo; **leave the engine running** deja el motor en marcha.
4. (tears, liquid) correr.
5. (road, river, track) pasar; **the path ~s along the coast** el camino sigue la costa.
6. (play) estar en cartelera; (event) durar; **"now running at the Palladium"** "en cartelera en el Palladium".
7. (tap): **to leave the tap running** dejar el grifo abierto.
8. (nose) moquear; (eyes) llorar.
9. (colour, dye, clothes) desteñir.
10. (remain valid) ser válido.
◆ vt 1. (on foot) correr; **to ~ a race** participar en una carrera.
2. (manage, organize) llevar.
3. (car) mantener; **it's cheap to ~ es** económico.
4. (bus, train): **we're running a special bus to the airport** hemos puesto un autobús especial al aeropuerto.
5. (take in car) llevar en coche.
6. (bath): **to ~ a bath** llenar la bañera.

~ n 1. *(on foot)* carrera f; **to go for a ~** ir a correr.

2. *(in car)* paseo m en coche; **to go for a ~** dar un paseo en coche.

3. *(of play, show)*: **it had a two-year ~** estuvo dos años en cartelera.

4. *(for skiing)* pista f.

5. *(of success)* racha f.

6. *(Am: in tights)* carrera f.

7. *(in phrases)*: **in the long ~** a largo plazo.

❑ **run away** vi huir; **run down** vt sep *(run over)* atropellar; *(criticize)* hablar mal de ◆ vi *(clock)* pararse; *(battery)* acabarse; **run into** vt fus *(meet)* tropezarse con; *(hit)* chocar con; *(problem, difficulty)* encontrarse con; **run out** vi *(be used up)* acabarse; **run out of** vt fus quedarse sin; **run over** vt sep atropellar.

runaway ['rʌnəweɪ] n fugitivo m (-va f).

rung [rʌŋ] pp → **ring** ◆ n escalón m.

runner ['rʌnə'] n *(person)* corredor m (-ra f); *(for door, drawer)* corredera f; *(of sledge)* patín m.

runner bean n judía f escarlata.

runner-up *(pl* **runners-up)** n subcampeón m (-ona f).

running ['rʌnɪŋ] n *(SPORT)* carreras fpl; *(management)* dirección f ◆ adj: **three days ~** durante tres días seguidos; **to go ~** hacer footing.

running water n agua f corriente.

runny ['rʌnɪ] adj *(egg, omelette)* poco hecho(-cha); *(sauce)* líquido(-da); *(nose)* que moquea; *(eye)* lloroso(-sa).

runway ['rʌnweɪ] n pista f.

rural ['rʊərəl] adj rural.

rush [rʌʃ] n *(hurry)* prisa f; *(of crowd)* tropel m de gente ◆ vi *(move quickly)* ir de prisa; *(hurry)* apresurarse ◆ vt *(work)* hacer de prisa; *(meal)* comer de prisa; *(transport quickly)* llevar urgentemente; **to be in a ~** tener prisa; **there's no ~!** ¡no corre prisa!; **don't ~ me!** ¡no me metas prisa!

rush hour n hora f punta.

Russia ['rʌʃə] n Rusia.

Russian ['rʌʃn] adj ruso(-sa) ◆ n *(person)* ruso m (-sa f); *(language)* ruso m.

rust [rʌst] n óxido m ◆ vi oxidarse.

rustic ['rʌstɪk] adj rústico(-ca).

rustle ['rʌsl] vi susurrar.

rustproof ['rʌstpruːf] adj inoxidable.

rusty ['rʌstɪ] adj oxidado(-da).

RV n *(Am: abbr of recreational vehicle)* casa remolque.

rye [raɪ] n centeno m.

rye bread n pan m de centeno.

S

S *(abbr of south)* S.; *(abbr of small)* P.

saccharin ['sækərɪn] n sacarina f.

sachet ['sæʃeɪ] n bolsita f.

sack [sæk] n saco m ◆ vt despedir; **to get the ~** ser despedido.

sacrifice ['sækrɪfaɪs] n *(fig)* sacrificio m.

sad [sæd] adj triste; *(unfortunate)*

lamentable.

saddle ['sædl] n (on horse) silla f de montar; (on bicycle, motorbike) sillín m.

saddlebag ['sædlbæg] n (on bicycle, motorbike) cartera f; (on horse) alforja f.

sadly ['sædlı] adv (unfortunately) desgraciadamente; (unhappily) tristemente.

sadness ['sædnıs] n tristeza f.

s.a.e. n (Br: abbr of stamped addressed envelope) sobre con señas y franqueo.

safari park [sə'fɑːrı-] n safari m (reserva).

safe [seıf] adj (not dangerous, risky) seguro(-ra); (out of harm) a salvo ◆ n caja f de caudales; **a ~ place** un lugar seguro; **(have a) ~ journey!** ¡feliz viaje!; **~ and sound** sano y salvo.

safe-deposit box n caja f de seguridad.

safely ['seıflı] adv (not dangerously) sin peligro; (arrive) a salvo; (out of harm) seguramente.

safety ['seıftı] n seguridad f.

safety belt n cinturón m de seguridad.

safety pin n imperdible m.

sag [sæg] vi combarse.

sage [seıdʒ] n (herb) salvia f.

Sagittarius [,sædʒɪ'teərıəs] n Sagitario m.

said [sed] pt & pp → say.

sail [seıl] n vela f ◆ vi (boat, ship) navegar; (person) ir en barco; (depart) zarpar ◆ vt: **to ~ a boat** gobernar un barco; **to set ~** zarpar.

sailboat ['seılbəut] (Am) = sailing boat.

sailing ['seılıŋ] n (activity) vela f; (departure) salida f; **to go ~** ir a practicar la vela.

sailing boat n barco m de vela.

sailor ['seılər] n marinero m (-ra f).

saint [seınt] n santo m (-ta f).

sake [seık] n: **for my/their ~** por mí/ellos; **for God's ~!** ¡por el amor de Dios!

salad ['sæləd] n ensalada f.

salad bar n (Br: area in restaurant) bufé m de ensaladas; (restaurant) restaurante que sirve platos de ensaladas variadas.

salad bowl n ensaladera f.

salad cream n (Br) salsa parecida a la mayonesa, aunque de sabor más dulce, utilizada para aderezar ensaladas.

salad dressing n aliño m.

salami [sə'lɑːmı] n salami m.

salary ['sælərı] n sueldo m.

sale [seıl] n (selling) venta f; (at reduced prices) liquidación f; **"for ~"** "se vende"; **on ~** en venta ◘ **sales** npl (COMM) ventas fpl; **the ~s** las rebajas.

sales assistant ['seılz-] n dependiente m (-ta f).

salesclerk ['seılzklɑːrk] (Am) = sales assistant.

salesman ['seılzmən] (pl -men [-mən]) n (in shop) dependiente m; (rep) representante m de ventas.

sales rep(resentative) n representante mf de ventas.

saleswoman ['seılz,wumən] (pl -women [-,wımın]) n dependienta f.

saliva [sə'laıvə] n saliva f.

salmon ['sæmən] (pl inv) n salmón *m*.

salon ['sælɒn] *n* salón *m*.

saloon [sə'lu:n] *n* (*Br: car*) turismo *m*; (*Am: bar*) bar *m*; ~ (**bar**) (*Br*) bar de un hotel o "pub", decorado lujosamente, que sirve bebidas a precios más altos que en el "public bar".

salopettes [,sælə'pets] *npl* pantalones *mpl* de peto para esquiar.

salt [sɔ:lt, sɒlt] *n* sal *f*.

saltcellar ['sɔ:lt,selə'] *n* (*Br*) salero *m*.

salted peanuts ['sɔ:ltɪd-] *npl* cacahuetes *mpl* salados.

salt shaker [-,ʃeɪkə'] (*Am*) = saltcellar.

salty ['sɔ:ltɪ] *adj* salado(-da).

salute [sə'lu:t] *n* saludo *m* ◆ *vi* hacer un saludo.

Salvadorean [,sælvə'dɔ:rɪən] *adj* salvadoreño(-ña) ◆ *n* salvadoreño *m* (-ña *f*).

same [seɪm] *adj* mismo(-ma) ◆ *pron*: **the** ~ (*unchanged*) el mismo (la misma); (*in comparisons*) lo mismo; **they look the** ~ parecen iguales; **I'll have the** ~ **as her** yo voy a tomar lo mismo que ella; **you've got the** ~ **book as me** tienes el mismo libro que yo; **it's all the** ~ **to me** me da igual.

samosa [sə'məʊsə] *n* empanadilla india picante en forma triangular, rellena de carne picada y verduras.

sample ['sɑ:mpl] *n* muestra *f* ◆ *vt* probar.

sanctions ['sæŋkʃnz] *npl* sanciones *fpl*.

sanctuary ['sæŋktʃʊərɪ] *n* (*for birds, animals*) reserva *f*.

sand [sænd] *n* arena *f* ◆ *vt* lijar ❑

sands *npl* playa *f*.

sandal ['sændl] *n* sandalia *f*.

sandcastle ['sænd,kɑ:sl] *n* castillo *m* de arena.

sandpaper ['sænd,peɪpə'] *n* papel *m* de lija.

sandwich ['sænwɪdʒ] *n* (*made with roll*) bocadillo *m*; (*made with freshly sliced bread*) sándwich *m* frío.

sandwich bar *n* tienda donde se venden bocadillos y refrescos.

sandy ['sændɪ] *adj* (*beach*) arenoso(-sa); (*hair*) de color rubio rojizo.

sang [sæŋ] *pt* → **sing**.

sanitary ['sænɪtrɪ] *adj* (*conditions, measures*) sanitario(-ria); (*hygienic*) higiénico(-ca).

sanitary napkin (*Am*) = sanitary towel.

sanitary towel *n* (*Br*) compresa *f*.

sank [sæŋk] *pt* → **sink**.

sapphire ['sæfaɪə'] *n* zafiro *m*.

sarcastic [sɑ:'kæstɪk] *adj* sarcástico(-ca).

sardine [sɑ:'di:n] *n* sardina *f*.

SASE *n* (*Am: abbr of self-addressed stamped envelope*) sobre con señas y franqueo.

sat [sæt] *pt & pp* → **sit**.

Sat. (*abbr of Saturday*) sáb.

satchel ['sætʃəl] *n* cartera *f* (*para escolares*).

satellite ['sætəlaɪt] *n* (*in space*) satélite *m*; (*at airport*) sala *f* de embarque auxiliar.

satellite dish *n* antena *f* parabólica.

satellite TV *n* televisión *f* por vía satélite.

satin ['sætɪn] *n* raso *m*.

satisfaction [ˌsætɪsˈfækʃn] n satisfacción f.

satisfactory [ˌsætɪsˈfæktərɪ] adj satisfactorio(-ria).

satisfied [ˈsætɪsfaɪd] adj satisfecho(-cha).

satisfy [ˈsætɪsfaɪ] vt satisfacer.

satsuma [ˌsætˈsuːmə] n (Br) satsuma f.

saturate [ˈsætʃəreɪt] vt (with liquid) empapar.

Saturday [ˈsætədɪ] n sábado m; it's ~ es sábado; ~ morning el sábado por la mañana; **on** ~ el sábado; **on** ~s los sábados; **last** ~ el sábado pasado; **this** ~ este sábado; **next** ~ el sábado de la semana que viene; ~ **week, a week on** ~ del sábado en ocho días.

sauce [sɔːs] n salsa f.

saucepan [ˈsɔːspən] n (with one long handle) cazo m; (with two handles) cacerola f.

saucer [ˈsɔːsər] n platillo m.

Saudi Arabia [ˌsaʊdɪˈreɪbjə] n Arabia Saudí.

sauna [ˈsɔːnə] n sauna f.

sausage [ˈsɒsɪdʒ] n salchicha f.

sausage roll n salchicha pequeña envuelta en hojaldre y cocida al horno.

sauté [Br ˈsauteɪ, Am sauˈteɪ] adj salteado(-da).

savage [ˈsævɪdʒ] adj salvaje.

save [seɪv] vt (rescue) salvar; (money) ahorrar; (time, space) ganar; (reserve) reservar; (SPORT) parar; (COMPUT) guardar ◆ n parada f □ **save up** vi ahorrar; **to** ~ **up (for sthg)** ahorrar (para comprarse algo).

saver [ˈseɪvər] n (Br: ticket) billete m

económico.

savings [ˈseɪvɪŋz] npl ahorros mpl.

savings and loan association n (Am) = caja f de ahorros.

savings bank n = caja f de ahorros.

savory [ˈseɪvərɪ] (Am) = **savoury**.

savoury [ˈseɪvərɪ] adj (Br) salado(-da).

saw [sɔː] (Br pt -ed, pp sawn, Am pt & pp -ed) pt → **see** ◆ n sierra f ◆ vt serrar.

sawdust [ˈsɔːdʌst] n serrín m.

sawn [sɔːn] pp → **saw**.

saxophone [ˈsæksəfəʊn] n saxofón m.

say [seɪ] (pt & pp said) vt decir; (subj: clock, meter) marcar ◆ n: **to have a** ~ **in sthg** tener voz y voto en algo; **could you** ~ **that again?** ¿puede repetir?; ~ **we met at nine?** ¿ponemos que nos vemos a las nueve?; **to** ~ **yes** decir que sí; **what did you** ~? ¿qué has dicho?

saying [ˈseɪɪŋ] n dicho m.

scab [skæb] n postilla f.

scaffolding [ˈskæfəldɪŋ] n andamios mpl.

scald [skɔːld] vt escaldar.

scale [skeɪl] n escala f; (extent) extensión f; (of fish, snake) escama f; (in kettle) costra f caliza ❑ **scales** npl (for weighing person) báscula f; (for weighing food) balanza f.

scallion [ˈskæljən] n (Am) cebolleta f.

scallop [ˈskɒləp] n vieira f.

scalp [skælp] n cuero m cabelludo.

scampi [ˈskæmpɪ] n: (breaded) ~ gambas fpl rebozadas.

scan [skæn] vt (consult quickly)

scandal 250

echar un vistazo a ◆ n (MED) escáner m.

scandal ['skændl] n (disgrace) escándalo m; (gossip) habladurías fpl.

Scandinavia [,skændɪ'neɪvjə] n Escandinavia f.

scar [skɑːʳ] n cicatriz f.

scarce [skeəs] adj escaso(-sa).

scarcely ['skeəslɪ] adv apenas.

scare [skeəʳ] vt asustar.

scarecrow ['skeəkrəʊ] n espantapájaros m inv.

scared [skeəd] adj asustado(-da).

scarf [skɑːf] (pl **scarves**) n (woollen) bufanda f; (for women) pañoleta f.

scarlet ['skɑːlət] adj escarlata.

scarves [skɑːvz] pl → scarf.

scary ['skeərɪ] adj (inf) espeluznante.

scatter ['skætəʳ] vt (seeds, papers) esparcir; (birds) dispersar ◆ vi dispersarse.

scene [siːn] n (in play, film, book) escena f; (of crime, accident) lugar m; (view) panorama m; **the music ~** el mundo de la música; **to make a ~** armar un escándalo.

scenery ['siːnərɪ] n (countryside) paisaje m; (in theatre) decorado m.

scenic ['siːnɪk] adj pintoresco(-ca).

scent [sent] n (smell) fragancia f; (of animal) rastro m; (perfume) perfume m.

sceptical ['skeptɪkl] adj (Br) escéptico(-ca).

schedule [Br 'ʃedjuːl, Am 'skedʒʊl] n (of work, things to do) plan m; (timetable) horario m; (list) lista f ◆ vt programar; **according to ~** según lo previsto; **behind ~** con retraso; **on**

~ a la hora prevista.

scheduled flight [Br 'ʃedjuːld-, Am 'skedʒʊld-] n vuelo m regular.

scheme [skiːm] n (plan) proyecto m; (pej: dishonest plan) estratagema f.

scholarship ['skɒləʃɪp] n (award) beca f.

school [skuːl] n escuela f (institute) academia f; (university department) facultad f; (Am: university) universidad f ◆ adj escolar; **at ~** en la escuela.

schoolbag ['skuːlbæg] n cartera f.

schoolbook ['skuːlbʊk] n libro m de texto.

schoolboy ['skuːlbɔɪ] n alumno m.

school bus n autobús m escolar.

schoolchild ['skuːltʃaɪld] (pl -children [-tʃɪldrən]) n alumno m (-na f).

schoolgirl ['skuːlgɜːl] n alumna f.

schoolmaster ['skuːlmɑːstəʳ] n (Br) (primary) maestro m; (secondary) profesor m.

schoolmistress ['skuːlmɪstrɪs] n (Br) (primary) maestra f; (secondary) profesora f.

schoolteacher ['skuːltiːtʃəʳ] n (primary) maestro m (-tra f); (secondary) profesor m (-ra f).

school uniform n uniforme m escolar.

science ['saɪəns] n ciencia f; (SCH) ciencias fpl.

science fiction n ciencia f ficción.

scientific [,saɪən'tɪfɪk] adj científico(-ca).

scientist ['saɪəntɪst] n científico m (-ca f).

scissors ['sɪzəz] npl: **(a pair of) ~** unas tijeras.

scold [skəʊld] vt regañar.

scone [skɒn] n pastelillo redondo hecho con harina, manteca y a veces pasas, que suele tomarse a la hora del té.

scoop [sku:p] n (for ice cream) pinzas fpl de helado; (for flour) paleta f; (of ice cream) bola f; (in media) exclusiva f.

scooter ['sku:tər] n (motor vehicle) Vespa® f.

scope [skəʊp] n (possibility) posibilidades fpl; (range) alcance m.

scorch [skɔ:tʃ] vt chamuscar.

score [skɔ:r] n (final result) resultado m; (points total) puntuación f; (in exam) calificación f ◆ vt (SPORT) marcar; (in test) obtener una puntuación de ◆ vi (SPORT) marcar; **what's the ~?** ¿cómo van?

scorn [skɔ:n] n desprecio m.

Scorpio ['skɔ:pɪəʊ] n Escorpión m.

scorpion ['skɔ:pjən] n escorpión m.

Scot [skɒt] n escocés m (-esa f).

scotch [skɒtʃ] n whisky m escocés.

Scotch broth n sopa espesa con caldo de carne, verduras y cebada.

Scotch tape® n (Am) celo® m.

Scotland ['skɒtlənd] n Escocia f.

Scotsman ['skɒtsmən] (pl -men [-mən]) n escocés m.

Scotswoman ['skɒtswʊmən] (pl -women [-wɪmɪn]) n escocesa f.

Scottish ['skɒtɪʃ] adj escocés (-esa).

scout [skaʊt] n (boy scout) explorador m.

Los "scouts" son miembros de la "Scouting Association", fundada en Gran Bretaña en 1908 por Lord Baden-Powell para promover el sentido de la responsabilidad y de la aventura entre la juventud. Pequeños grupos de niños de 11 a 16 años se organizan bajo el mando de un adulto. Sus miembros adquieren conocimientos de primeros auxilios y técnicas de supervivencia al aire libre. Los niños de menos de 11 años pueden hacerse miembros de los "Cub Scouts", y también existen organizaciones paralelas para niñas, llamadas "Girl Guides" y "Brownies".

scowl [skaʊl] vi fruncir el ceño.

scrambled eggs [,skræmbld-] npl huevos mpl revueltos.

scrap [skræp] n (of paper, cloth) trozo m; (old metal) chatarra f.

scrapbook ['skræpbʊk] n álbum m de recortes.

scrape [skreɪp] vt (rub) raspar; (scratch) rasguñar.

scrap paper n (Br) papel m usado.

scratch [skrætʃ] n (cut) arañazo m; (mark) rayazo m ◆ vt (cut) arañar; (mark) rayar; (rub) rascar; **to be up to ~** tener un nivel aceptable; **to start from ~** empezar desde el principio.

scratch paper (Am) = scrap paper.

scream [skri:m] n grito m ◆ vi gritar.

screen [skri:n] n (of TV, computer,

for film) pantalla f; *(hall in cinema)* sala f (de proyecciones); *(panel)* biombo m ♦ vt *(film)* proyectar; *(programme)* emitir.

screening ['skri:nɪŋ] n *(of film)* proyección f.

screen wash n líquido m limpiaparabrisas.

screw [skru:] n tornillo m ♦ vt *(fasten)* atornillar; *(twist)* enroscar.

screwdriver ['skru:ˌdraɪvəʳ] n destornillador m.

scribble ['skrɪbl] vi garabatear.

script [skrɪpt] n *(of play, film)* guión m.

scrub [skrʌb] vt restregar.

scruffy ['skrʌfɪ] adj andrajoso(-sa).

scrumpy ['skrʌmpɪ] n sidra de alta graduación procedente del suroeste de Inglaterra.

scuba diving ['sku:bə-] n buceo m (con botellas de oxígeno).

sculptor ['skʌlptəʳ] n escultor m (-ra f).

sculpture ['skʌlptʃəʳ] n *(statue)* escultura f.

sea [si:] n mar m o f; **by ~** en barco; **by the ~** a orillas del mar.

seafood ['si:fu:d] n mariscos mpl.

seafront ['si:frʌnt] n paseo m marítimo.

seagull ['si:gʌl] n gaviota f.

seal [si:l] n *(animal)* foca f; *(on bottle, container)* precinto m; *(official mark)* sello m ♦ vt *(envelope, container)* cerrar.

seam [si:m] n *(in clothes)* costura f.

search [sɜ:tʃ] n búsqueda f ♦ vt *(place)* registrar; *(person)* cachear ♦ vi: **to ~ for** buscar.

seashell ['si:ʃel] n concha f (marina).

seashore ['si:ʃɔ:ʳ] n orilla f del mar.

seasick ['si:sɪk] adj mareado(-da) *(en barco)*.

seaside ['si:saɪd] n: **the ~** la playa.

seaside resort n lugar m de veraneo *(junto al mar)*.

season ['si:zn] n *(division of year)* estación f; *(period)* temporada f ♦ vt sazonar; **in ~** *(holiday)* en temporada alta; **strawberries are in ~** ahora es la época de las fresas; **out of ~** *(fruit, vegetables)* fuera de temporada; *(holiday)* en temporada baja.

seasoning ['si:znɪŋ] n condimento m.

season ticket n abono m.

seat [si:t] n *(place, chair)* asiento m; *(for show)* entrada f; *(in parliament)* escaño m ♦ vt *(subj: building, vehicle)* tener cabida para; **"please wait to be ~ed"** cartel que ruega a los clientes que esperen hasta que les sea asignada una mesa.

seat belt n cinturón m de seguridad.

seaweed ['si:wi:d] n alga f marina.

secluded [sɪ'klu:dɪd] adj aislado(-da).

second ['sekənd] n segundo m ♦ num segundo(-da), → **sixth**; **~ gear** segunda marcha f ☐ **seconds** npl *(goods)* artículos mpl defectuosos; **who wants ~s?** *(inf: food)* ¿quién quiere repetir?

secondary school ['sekəndrɪ-] n instituto m de enseñanza media.

second-class adj *(ticket)* de segunda clase; *(stamp)* para el correo *nacional ordinario; (inferior) de segunda categoría.*

second-hand *adj* de segunda mano.

Second World War *n*: the ~ la segunda Guerra Mundial.

secret ['si:krɪt] *adj* secreto(-ta) ♦ *n* secreto *m*.

secretary [Br 'sekrətrɪ, Am 'sekrə,teri] *n* secretario *m* (-ria *f*).

Secretary of State *n* (Am: foreign minister) ministro *m* (-tra *f*) de Asuntos Exteriores; (Br: government minister) ministro *m* (-tra *f*).

section ['sekʃn] *n* sección *f*.

sector ['sektə'] *n* sector *m*.

secure [sɪ'kjʊə'] *adj* seguro(-ra) ♦ *vt* (fix) fijar, (fml: obtain) conseguir.

security [sɪ'kjʊərətɪ] *n* seguridad *f*.

security guard *n* guardia *mf* jurado.

sedative ['sedətɪv] *n* sedante *m*.

seduce [sɪ'dju:s] *vt* seducir.

see [si:] (*pt* saw, *pp* seen) *vt* ver; (friends) visitar; (understand) entender; (accompany) acompañar; (find out) ir a ver; (undergo) experimentar ♦ *vi* ver; **I ~** ya veo; **to ~ if one can do sthg** ver si uno puede hacer algo; **to ~ to sthg** (deal with) encargarse de algo; (repair) arreglar algo; **~ you!** ¡hasta la vista!; **~ you later!** ¡hasta luego!, ~ **you soon!** ¡hasta pronto!; **~ p 14** véase p. 14 ❑ **see off** *vt sep* (say goodbye to) despedir.

seed [si:d] *n* semilla *f*.

seedy ['si:dɪ] *adj* sórdido(-da).

seeing (as) ['si:ɪŋ-] *conj* en vista de que.

seek [si:k] (*pt & pp* sought) *vt* (fml)

(look for) buscar; (request) solicitar.

seem [si:m] *vi* parecer ♦ *v impers*: **it ~s (that) ...** parece que ...; **to ~ like** parecer.

seen [si:n] *pp* → see.

seesaw ['si:sɔ:] *n* balancín *m*.

segment ['segmənt] *n* (of fruit) gajo *m*.

seize [si:z] *vt* (grab) agarrar; (drugs, arms) incautarse de ❑ **seize up** *vi* agarrotarse.

seldom ['seldəm] *adv* rara vez.

select [sɪ'lekt] *vt* seleccionar ♦ *adj* selecto(-ta).

selection [sɪ'lekʃn] *n* (selecting) selección *f*; (range) surtido *m*.

self-assured [,selfə'ʃʊəd] *adj* seguro de sí mismo (segura de sí misma).

self-catering [,self'keɪtərɪŋ] *adj* con alojamiento sólo.

self-confident [,self-] *adj* seguro de sí mismo (segura de sí misma).

self-conscious [,self-] *adj* cohibido(-da).

self-contained [,selfkən'teɪnd] *adj* (flat) autosuficiente.

self-defence [,self-] *n* defensa *f* personal.

self-employed [,self-] *adj* autónomo(-ma).

selfish ['selfɪʃ] *adj* egoísta.

self-raising flour [,self'reɪzɪŋ-] *n* (Br) harina *f* con levadura.

self-rising flour [,self'raɪzɪŋ-] (Am) = **self-raising flour**.

self-service [,self-] *adj* de autoservicio.

sell [sel] (*pt & pp* sold) *vt & vi* vender; **to ~ for** venderse a; **to ~ sb**

sth vender algo a alguien.

sell-by date n fecha f de caducidad.

seller ['selə'] n vendedor m (-ra f).

Sellotape® ['seləteɪp] n (Br) ≈ celo® m.

semester [sɪ'mestə'] n semestre m.

semicircle ['semɪˌsɜːkl] n semicírculo m.

semicolon [ˌsemɪ'kəʊlən] n punto m y coma.

semidetached [ˌsemɪdɪ'tætʃt] adj adosado(-da).

semifinal [ˌsemɪ'faɪnl] n semifinal f.

seminar [ˈsemɪnɑː'] n seminario m.

semolina [ˌseməˈliːnə] n sémola f.

send [send] (pt & pp sent) vt mandar; (TV or radio signal) transmitir; **to ~ sthg to sb** mandar algo a alguien ❑ **send back** vt sep devolver; **send off** vt sep (letter, parcel) mandar (por correo); (SPORT) expulsar ❋ vi: **to ~ off (for sthg)** solicitar (algo) por escrito.

sender ['sendə'] n remitente mf.

senile ['siːnaɪl] adj senil.

senior ['siːnjə'] adj superior ❋ n (SCH) senior mf.

senior citizen n persona f de la tercera edad.

sensation [sen'seɪʃn] n sensación f.

sensational [sen'seɪʃənl] adj sensacional.

sense [sens] n sentido m ❋ vt sentir; **to make ~** tener sentido; **~ of direction** sentido de la orientación; **~ of humour** sentido del humor.

sensible ['sensəbl] adj (person) sensato(-ta); (clothes, shoes) práctico(-ca).

sensitive ['sensɪtɪv] adj (skin, eyes, device) sensible; (easily offended) susceptible; (emotionally) comprensivo(-va); (subject, issue) delicado(-da).

sent [sent] pt & pp → send.

sentence ['sentəns] n (GRAMM) oración f; (for crime) sentencia f ❋ vt condenar.

sentimental [ˌsentɪ'mentl] adj (pej) sentimental.

Sep. (abbr of September) sep.

separate [adj 'seprət, vb 'sepəreɪt] adj (different, individual) distinto(-ta); (not together) separado(-da) ❋ vt (divide) dividir; (detach) separar ❋ vi separarse ❑ **separates** npl (Br) prendas de vestir femeninas combinables.

separately ['seprətlɪ] adv (individually) independientemente; (alone) por separado.

separation [ˌsepə'reɪʃn] n separación f.

September [sep'tembə'] n septiembre m; **at the beginning of ~** a principios de septiembre; **at the end of ~** a finales de septiembre; **during ~** en septiembre; **every ~** todos los años en septiembre; **in ~** en septiembre; **last ~** en septiembre del año pasado; **next ~** en septiembre del próximo año; **this ~** en septiembre de este año; **2 ~ 1994** (in letters etc) 2 de septiembre de 1994.

septic ['septɪk] adj séptico(-ca).

septic tank n fosa f séptica.

sequel ['siːkwəl] n continuación f.

sequence ['siːkwəns] n (series)

sucesión f; *(order)* orden m.

sequin ['si:kwɪn] n lentejuela f.

sergeant ['sɑ:dʒənt] n *(in police force)* = subinspector m (-ra f) de policía; *(in army)* sargento mf.

serial ['sɪərɪəl] n serial m.

series ['sɪəri:z] *(pl inv)* n serie f.

serious ['sɪərɪəs] adj serio(-ria); *(very bad)* grave; **I'm ~** hablo en serio.

seriously ['sɪərɪəslɪ] adv *(really)* en serio; *(badly)* gravemente.

sermon ['sɜ:mən] n sermón m.

servant ['sɜ:vənt] n sirviente m (-ta f).

serve [sɜ:v] vt servir ♦ vi *(SPORT)* sacar; *(work)* servir ♦ n saque m; **to ~ as** *(be used for)* servir de; **the town is ~d by two airports** la ciudad está provista de dos aeropuertos; **"~s two"** "para dos personas"; **it ~s you right** te está bien empleado.

service ['sɜ:vɪs] n servicio m; *(at church)* oficio m; *(of car)* revisión f ♦ vt *(car)* revisar; **"out of ~"** "no funciona"; **"~ included"** "servicio incluido"; **"~ not included"** "servicio no incluido"; **to be of ~ to sb** *(fml)* ayudar a alguien □ **services** npl *(on motorway)* área f de servicios; *(of person)* servicios mpl.

service area n área f de servicios.

service charge n servicio m.

service department n departamento m de servicio al cliente.

service station n estación f de servicio.

serviette [,sɜ:vɪ'et] n servilleta f.

serving ['sɜ:vɪŋ] n ración f.

serving spoon n cucharón m.

sesame seeds ['sesəmɪ-] npl sésamo m.

session ['seʃn] n sesión f.

set [set] *(pt & pp set)* adj 1. *(fixed)* fijo(-ja); **a ~ lunch** el menú del día. 2. *(text, book)* obligatorio(-ria). 3. *(situated)* situado(-da).
♦ n 1. *(collection)* juego m; *(of stamps, stickers)* colección f.
2. *(TV)* aparato m; **a TV ~** un televisor.
3. *(in tennis)* set m.
4. *(of play)* decorado m.
5. *(at hairdresser's)*: **a shampoo and ~** lavado m y marcado.
♦ vt 1. *(put)* colocar, poner.
2. *(cause to be)*: **to ~ a machine going** poner una máquina en marcha; **to ~ fire to** prender fuego a.
3. *(clock, alarm, controls)* poner; **~ the alarm for 7 a.m.** pon el despertador para las 7 de la mañana.
4. *(fix)* fijar.
5. *(essay, homework, the table)* poner.
6. *(a record)* marcar.
7. *(broken bone)* componer.
8. *(play, film, story)*: **to be ~ in** desarrollarse en.
♦ vi 1. *(sun)* ponerse.
2. *(glue)* secarse; *(jelly)* cuajar.
□ **set down** vt sep *(Br passengers)* dejar; **set off** vt sep *(alarm)* hacer saltar ♦ vi ponerse en camino; **set out** vt sep *(arrange)* disponer ♦ vi ponerse en camino; **set up** vt sep *(barrier, cordon)* levantar; *(equipment)* preparar; *(meeting, interview)* organizar; *(committee)* crear.

set meal n menú m *(plato)*.

set menu n menú m del día.

settee [se'ti:] n sofá m.

setting ['setɪŋ] n (on machine) posición f; (surroundings) escenario m.

settle ['setl] vt (argument) resolver; (bill) saldar; (stomach) asentar; (nerves) calmar; (arrange, decide on) acordar ♦ vi (start to live) establecerse; (come to rest) posarse; (sediment, dust) depositarse ❑ **settle down** vi (calm down) calmarse; (sit comfortably) acomodarse; **settle up** vi saldar las cuentas.

settlement ['setlmənt] n (agreement) acuerdo m; (place) asentamiento m.

seven ['sevn] num siete, → **six**.

seventeen [,sevn'tiːn] num diecisiete, → **six**.

seventeenth [,sevn'tiːnθ] num decimoséptimo(-ma), → **sixth**.

seventh ['sevnθ] num séptimo(-ma), → **sixth**.

seventieth ['sevntɪəθ] num septuagésimo(-ma), → **sixth**.

seventy ['sevntɪ] num setenta, → **six**.

several ['sevrəl] adj varios(-rias) ♦ pron varios mpl (-rias fpl).

severe [sɪ'vɪər] adj severo(-ra); (illness) grave; (pain) fuerte.

Seville [sə'vɪl] n Sevilla.

sew [səʊ] (pp sewn) vt & vi coser.

sewage ['suːɪdʒ] n aguas fpl residuales.

sewing ['səʊɪŋ] n costura f.

sewing machine n máquina f de coser.

sewn [səʊn] pp → **sew**.

sex [seks] n sexo m; **to have ~ (with)** tener relaciones sexuales (con).

sexist ['seksɪst] n sexista mf.

sexual ['sekʃʊəl] adj sexual.

sexy ['seksɪ] adj sexi inv.

shabby ['ʃæbɪ] adj (clothes, room) desastrado(-da); (person) desharrapado(-da).

shade [ʃeɪd] n (shadow) sombra f; (lampshade) pantalla f; (of colour) tonalidad f ♦ vt (protect) proteger ❑ **shades** npl (inf: sunglasses) gafas fpl de sol.

shadow ['ʃædəʊ] n (dark shape) sombra f; (darkness) oscuridad f.

shady ['ʃeɪdɪ] adj (place) sombreado(-da); (inf: person) sospechoso(-sa); (inf: deal) turbio(-bia).

shaft [ʃɑːft] n (of machine) eje m; (of lift) pozo m.

shake [ʃeɪk] (pt shook, pp shaken ['ʃeɪkn]) vt (tree, rug, packet, etc) sacudir; (bottle) agitar; (person) zarandear; (dice) mover; (shock) conmocionar ♦ vi temblar; **to ~ hands with sb** estrechar la mano a alguien; **to ~ one's head** (saying no) negar con la cabeza.

shall [weak form ʃəl, strong form ʃæl] aux vb 1. (expressing future): **I ~ be ready soon** estaré listo enseguida.
2. (in questions): **~ I buy some wine?** ¿compro vino?; **where ~ we go?** ¿adónde vamos?
3. (fml: expressing order): **payment ~ be made within a week** debe efectuarse el pago dentro de una semana.

shallot [ʃə'lɒt] n chalote m.

shallow ['ʃæləʊ] adj poco profundo(-da).

shallow end n (of swimming pool) parte f poco profunda.

shambles ['ʃæmblz] n desbarajuste m.

shame [ʃeɪm] n (remorse) vergüenza f; (disgrace) deshonra f; **it's a ~** es una lástima; **what a ~!** ¡qué lástima!

shampoo [ʃæm'pu:] n (liquid) champú m; (wash) lavado m.

shandy ['ʃændɪ] n cerveza f con gaseosa.

shape [ʃeɪp] n (form) forma f; (object, person, outline) figura f; **to be in good/bad ~** estar en (buena) forma/baja forma.

share [ʃeəʳ] n (part) parte f; (in company) acción f ◆ vt (room, work, cost) compartir; (divide) repartir □ **share out** vt sep repartir.

shark [ʃɑːk] n tiburón m.

sharp [ʃɑːp] adj (knife, razor, teeth) afilado(-da); (pin, needle) puntiagudo(-da); (clear) nítido(-da); (quick, intelligent) inteligente; (rise, bend) marcado(-da); (change) brusco(-ca); (painful) agudo(-da); (food, taste) ácido(-da) ◆ adv (exactly) en punto.

sharpen ['ʃɑːpn] vt (knife) afilar; (pencil) sacar punta a.

shatter ['ʃætəʳ] vt (break) hacer añicos ◆ vi hacerse añicos.

shattered ['ʃætəd] adj (Br: inf: tired) hecho(-cha) polvo.

shave [ʃeɪv] vt afeitar ◆ vi afeitarse ◆ n: **to have a ~** afeitarse.

shaver ['ʃeɪvəʳ] n maquinilla f de afeitar.

shaver point n enchufe m para maquinilla de afeitar.

shaving brush ['ʃeɪvɪŋ-] n brocha f de afeitar.

shaving cream ['ʃeɪvɪŋ-] n crema f de afeitar.

shaving foam ['ʃeɪvɪŋ-] n espuma f de afeitar.

shawl [ʃɔːl] n chal m.

she [ʃiː] pron ella f; **~'s tall** (ella) es alta.

sheaf [ʃiːf] (pl sheaves) n (of paper, notes) fajo m.

shears [ʃɪəz] npl (for gardening) tijeras fpl de podar.

sheaves [ʃiːvz] pl → **sheaf**.

shed [ʃed] (pt & pp shed) n cobertizo m ◆ vt (tears, blood) derramar.

she'd [weak form ʃɪd, strong form ʃiːd] = **she had, she would**.

sheep [ʃiːp] (pl inv) n oveja f.

sheepdog ['ʃiːpdɒg] n perro m pastor.

sheepskin ['ʃiːpskɪn] adj piel f de carnero; **~ jacket** zamarra f.

sheer [ʃɪəʳ] adj (pure, utter) puro(-ra); (cliff) escarpado(-da); (stockings) fino(-na).

sheet [ʃiːt] n (for bed) sábana f; (of paper) hoja f; (of glass, metal, wood) lámina f.

shelf [ʃelf] (pl shelves) n estante m.

shell [ʃel] n (of egg, nut) cáscara f; (on beach) concha f; (of animal) caparazón m; (bomb) proyectil m.

she'll [ʃiːl] = **she will, she shall**.

shellfish ['ʃelfɪʃ] n (food) mariscos mpl.

shell suit n (Br) chándal m de Táctel®.

shelter ['ʃeltəʳ] n refugio m ◆ vt (protect) proteger ◆ vi resguardarse; **to take ~** cobijarse.

sheltered ['ʃeltəd] adj protegido(-da).

shelves [ʃelvz] pl → shelf.

shepherd ['ʃepəd] n pastor m.

shepherd's pie ['ʃepədz-] n plato consistente en carne picada de vaca, cebolla y especias cubierta con una capa de puré de patata dorada al grill.

sheriff ['ʃerɪf] n sheriff m.

sherry ['ʃerɪ] n jerez m.

she's [ʃiːz] = she is, she has.

shield [ʃiːld] n escudo m ◆ vt proteger.

shift [ʃɪft] n (change) cambio m; (period of work) turno m ◆ vt mover ◆ vi (move) moverse; (change) cambiar.

shin [ʃɪn] n espinilla f.

shine [ʃaɪn] (pt & pp shone) vi brillar ◆ vt (shoes) sacar brillo a; (torch) enfocar.

shiny ['ʃaɪnɪ] adj brillante.

ship [ʃɪp] n barco m; **by ~** en barco.

shipwreck ['ʃɪprek] n (accident) naufragio m; (wrecked ship) barco m náufrago.

shirt [ʃɜːt] n camisa f.

shit [ʃɪt] n (vulg) mierda f ◆ excl (vulg) ¡mierda!

shiver ['ʃɪvəʳ] vi temblar.

shock [ʃɒk] n (surprise) susto m; (force) sacudida f ◆ vt (surprise) conmocionar; (horrify) escandalizar; **to be in ~** (MED) estar en estado de shock.

shock absorber [-əb,zɔːbəʳ] n amortiguador m.

shocking ['ʃɒkɪŋ] adj (very bad) horroroso(-sa).

shoe [ʃuː] n zapato m.

shoelace ['ʃuːleɪs] n cordón m (de zapato).

shoe polish n betún m.

shoe repairer's [-rɪ,peərəz] n zapatero m (remendón).

shoe shop n zapatería f.

shone [ʃɒn] pt & pp → shine.

shook [ʃʊk] pt → shake.

shoot [ʃuːt] (pt & pp shot) vt (kill) matar a tiros; (injure) herir (con arma de fuego); (gun, arrow) disparar; (film) rodar ◆ vi (with gun) disparar; (move quickly) pasar disparado; (SPORT) chutar ◆ n (of plant) brote m.

shop [ʃɒp] n tienda f ◆ vi hacer compras.

shop assistant n (Br) dependiente m (-ta f).

shop floor n (place) taller m.

shopkeeper ['ʃɒp,kiːpəʳ] n tendero m (-ra f).

shoplifter ['ʃɒp,lɪftəʳ] n ratero m (-ra f) de tiendas.

shopper ['ʃɒpəʳ] n comprador m (-ra f).

shopping ['ʃɒpɪŋ] n compras fpl; **I hate ~** odio hacer las compras; **to do the ~** hacer las compras; **to go ~** ir de compras.

shopping bag n bolsa f de la compra.

shopping basket n cesta f de la compra.

shopping centre n centro m comercial.

shopping list n lista f de la compra.

shopping mall n centro m comercial.

shop steward n enlace m sindical.

shop window n escaparate m.

shore [ʃɔːr] n orilla f; **on ~** en tierra.

short [ʃɔːt] adj (not tall) bajo(-ja); (in length, time) corto(-a) ◆ adv (cut hair) corto ◆ n (Br: drink) licor m; (film) cortometraje m; **to be ~ of sthg** andar escaso de algo; **to be ~ for sthg** (be abbreviation of) ser el diminutivo de algo; **I'm ~ of breath** me falta el aliento; **in ~** en resumen ❑ **shorts** npl (short trousers) pantalones mpl cortos; (Am: underpants) calzoncillos mpl.

shortage [ˈʃɔːtɪdʒ] n escasez f.

shortbread [ˈʃɔːtbred] n especie de torta dulce y quebradiza hecha con harina, azúcar y mantequilla.

short-circuit vi tener un cortocircuito.

shortcrust pastry [ˈʃɔːtkrʌst-] n pasta f quebrada.

short cut n atajo m.

shorten [ˈʃɔːtn] vt acortar.

shorthand [ˈʃɔːthænd] n taquigrafía f.

shortly [ˈʃɔːtlɪ] adv (soon) dentro de poco; **~ before** poco antes de.

shortsighted [ˌʃɔːtˈsaɪtɪd] adj miope.

short-sleeved [-ˌsliːvd] adj de manga corta.

short-stay car park n aparcamiento m para estancias cortas.

short story n cuento m.

short wave n onda f corta.

shot [ʃɒt] pt & pp → **shoot** ◆ n (of gun, in football) tiro m; (in tennis, golf) golpe m; (photo) foto f; (in film)

plano m; (inf: attempt) intento m; (drink) trago m.

shotgun [ˈʃɒtgʌn] n escopeta f.

should [ʃʊd] aux vb 1. (expressing desirability) deber; **we ~ leave now** deberíamos irnos ahora. 2. (asking for advice): **~ I go too?** ¿yo también voy? 3. (expressing probability) deber de; **she ~ arrive soon** debe de estar a punto de llegar. 4. (ought to have) deber; **they ~ have won the match** deberían haber ganado el partido. 5. (in clauses with "that"): **we decided that you ~ do it** decidimos que lo hicieras tú. 6. (fml: in conditionals): **~ you need anything, call reception** si necesita alguna cosa, llame a recepción. 7. (fml: expressing wish): **I ~ like to come with you** me gustaría ir contigo.

shoulder [ˈʃəʊldər] n (of person) hombro m; (of meat) espaldilla f; (Am: of road) arcén m.

shoulder pad n hombrera f.

shouldn't [ˈʃʊdnt] = **should not.**

should've [ˈʃʊdəv] = **should have.**

shout [ʃaʊt] n grito m ◆ vt & vi gritar ❑ **shout out** vt sep gritar.

shove [ʃʌv] vt (push) empujar; (put carelessly) poner de cualquier manera.

shovel [ˈʃʌvl] n pala f.

show [ʃəʊ] (pp **-ed** OR **shown**) n (at theatre) función f; (on TV, radio) programa m; (exhibition) exhibición f ◆ vt mostrar; (undergo) registrar; (represent, depict) representar; (ac-

company) acompañar; *(film)* proyectar; *(TV programme)* emitir ◆ *vi (be visible)* verse; *(film)* proyectarse; **to ~ sthg to sb** enseñar algo a alguien; **to ~ sb how to do sthg** enseñar a alguien cómo se hace algo ❏ **show off** *vi* presumir; **show up** *vi (come along)* aparecer; *(be visible)* resaltar.

shower ['ʃaʊəʳ] *n (for washing)* ducha *f*; *(of rain)* chubasco *m* ◆ *vi* ducharse; **to have a ~** darse una ducha.

shower gel *n* gel *m* de baño.

shower unit *n* ducha *f (cubículo)*.

showing ['ʃəʊɪŋ] *n (of film)* proyección *f*.

shown [ʃəʊn] *pp* → show.

showroom ['ʃəʊrʊm] *n* sala *f* de exposición.

shrank [ʃræŋk] *pt* → shrink.

shrimp [ʃrɪmp] *n* camarón *m*.

shrine [ʃraɪn] *n* santuario *m*.

shrink [ʃrɪŋk] *(pt* shrank, *pp* shrunk) *n (inf)* loquero *m* (-ra *f*) ◆ *vi (become smaller)* encoger; *(diminish)* reducirse.

shrub [ʃrʌb] *n* arbusto *m*.

shrug [ʃrʌg] *vi* encogerse de hombros ◆ *n*: **she gave a ~** se encogió de hombros.

shrunk [ʃrʌŋk] *pp* → shrink.

shuffle ['ʃʌfl] *vt (cards)* barajar ◆ *vi* andar arrastrando los pies.

shut [ʃʌt] *(pt & pp* shut) *adj* cerrado(-da) ◆ *vt* cerrar ◆ *vi (door, mouth, eyes)* cerrarse; *(shop, restaurant)* cerrar ❏ **shut down** *vt sep* cerrar; **shut up** *vi (inf)* callarse la boca.

shutter ['ʃʌtəʳ] *n (on window)*

contraventana *f*; *(on camera)* obturador *m*.

shuttle ['ʃʌtl] *n (plane)* avión *m* de puente aéreo; *(bus)* autobús *m* de servicio regular.

shuttlecock ['ʃʌtlkɒk] *n* volante *m*.

shy [ʃaɪ] *adj* tímido(-da).

sick [sɪk] *adj (ill)* enfermo(-ma); *(nauseous)* mareado(-da); **to be ~** *(vomit)* devolver; **to feel ~** estar mareado; **to be ~ of** estar harto (-ta) de.

sick bag *n* bolsa *f* para el mareo.

sickness ['sɪknɪs] *n* enfermedad *f*.

sick pay *n* = subsidio *m* de enfermedad.

side [saɪd] *n* lado *m*; *(of hill, valley)* ladera *f*; *(of river)* orilla *f*; *(of paper, coin, tape, record)* cara *f*; *(team)* equipo *m*; *(Br: TV channel)* canal *m*; *(page of writing)* página *f* ◆ *adj* lateral; **at the ~ of** al lado de; **on the other ~** al otro lado; **on this ~** en este lado; **~ by ~** juntos.

sideboard ['saɪdbɔːd] *n* aparador *m*.

sidecar ['saɪdkɑːʳ] *n* sidecar *m*.

side dish *n* plato *m* de acompañamiento.

side effect *n* efecto *m* secundario.

sidelight ['saɪdlaɪt] *n (Br)* luz *f* lateral.

side order *n* guarnición *f (no incluida en el plato)*.

side salad *n* ensalada *f* de acompañamiento.

side street *n* travesía *f*.

sidewalk ['saɪdwɔːk] *n (Am)* acera *f*.

sideways ['saɪdweɪz] *adv (move)* de lado; *(look)* de reojo.

sieve [sɪv] *n* tamiz *m*.

sigh [saɪ] *n* suspiro *m* ♦ *vi* suspirar.

sight [saɪt] *n (eyesight)* vista *f*; *(thing seen)* imagen *f*; at first ~ a primera vista; to catch ~ of divisar; in ~ a la vista; to lose ~ of perder de vista; out of ~ fuera de vista □ sights *npl (of city, country)* lugares *mpl* de interés turístico.

sightseeing ['saɪt,siːɪŋ] *n*: to go ~ ir a visitar los lugares de interés turístico.

sign [saɪn] *n* señal *f*; *(on shop)* letrero *m*; *(symbol)* signo *m* ♦ *vt & vi* firmar; there's no ~ of her no hay señales de ella □ sign in *vi* firmar en el registro de entrada.

signal ['sɪgnl] *n* señal *f*; *(Am: traffic lights)* semáforo *m* ♦ *vi* señalizar.

signature ['sɪgnətʃə'] *n* firma *f*.

significant [sɪg'nɪfɪkənt] *adj* significativo(-va).

signpost ['saɪnpəʊst] *n* letrero *m* indicador.

Sikh [siːk] *n* sij *mf*.

silence ['saɪləns] *n* silencio *m*.

silencer ['saɪlənsə'] *n (Br)* silenciador *m*.

silent ['saɪlənt] *adj* silencioso(-sa).

silk [sɪlk] *n* seda *f*.

sill [sɪl] *n* alféizar *m*.

silly ['sɪlɪ] *adj* tonto(-ta).

silver ['sɪlvə'] *n (substance)* plata *f*; *(coins)* monedas *fpl* plateadas ♦ *adj* de plata.

silver foil *n* papel *m* de aluminio.

silver-plated [-'pleɪtɪd] *adj* chapado(-da) en plata.

similar ['sɪmɪlə'] *adj* similar; to be ~ to ser parecido(-da) a.

similarity [,sɪmɪ'lærətɪ] *n (resemblance)* parecido *m*; *(similar point)* similitud *f*.

simmer ['sɪmə'] *vi* hervir a fuego lento.

simple ['sɪmpl] *adj* sencillo(-lla).

simplify ['sɪmplɪfaɪ] *vt* simplificar.

simply ['sɪmplɪ] *adv (just)* simplemente; *(easily, not elaborately)* sencillamente.

simulate ['sɪmjʊleɪt] *vt* simular.

simultaneous [Br ,sɪml'teɪnjəs, Am ,saɪml'teɪnjəs] *adj* simultáneo (-a).

simultaneously [Br ,sɪml'teɪnjəslɪ, Am ,saɪml'teɪnjəslɪ] *adv* simultáneamente.

sin [sɪn] *n* pecado *m* ♦ *vi* pecar.

since [sɪns] *adv* desde entonces ♦ *prep* desde ♦ *conj (in time)* desde que; *(as)* ya que; ever ~ *prep* desde ♦ *conj* desde que.

sincere [sɪn'sɪə'] *adj* sincero(-ra).

sincerely [sɪn'sɪəlɪ] *adv* sinceramente; Yours ~ (le saluda) atentamente.

sing [sɪŋ] *(pt sang, pp sung) vt & vi* cantar.

singer ['sɪŋə'] *n* cantante *mf*.

single ['sɪŋgl] *adj (just one)* solo (la); *(not married)* soltero(-ra) ♦ *n (Br: ticket)* billete *m* de ida; *(record)* disco *m* sencillo; every ~ cada uno (una) de □ singles *n* modalidad *f* individual ♦ *adj (bar, club)* para solteros.

single bed *n* cama *f* individual.

single cream *n (Br)* nata *f* líquida.

single parent n padre m soltero (madre f soltera).

single room n habitación f individual.

single track road n carretera f de una sola vía.

singular ['sɪŋgjʊləʳ] n singular m; **in the ~** en singular.

sinister ['sɪnɪstəʳ] adj siniestro(-tra).

sink [sɪŋk] (pt sank, pp sunk) n (in kitchen) fregadero m; (washbasin) lavabo m ◆ vi (in water, mud) hundirse; (decrease) descender.

sink unit n fregadero m (con mueble debajo).

sinuses ['saɪnəsɪz] npl senos mpl frontales.

sip [sɪp] n sorbo m ◆ vt beber a sorbos.

siphon ['saɪfn] n sifón m ◆ vt sacar con sifón.

sir [sɜːʳ] n señor m; **Dear Sir** Muy Señor mío; **Sir Richard Blair** Sir Richard Blair.

siren ['saɪərən] n sirena f.

sirloin steak [sɜːlɔɪn-] n solomillo m.

sister ['sɪstəʳ] n hermana f; (Br: nurse) enfermera f jefe.

sister-in-law n cuñada f.

sit [sɪt] (pt & pp sat) vi sentarse; (be situated) estar situado ◆ vt (place) poner; (Br: exam) presentarse a; **to be sitting** estar sentado ❑ **sit down** vi sentarse; **to be sitting down** estar sentado; **sit up** vi (after lying down) incorporarse; (stay up late) quedarse levantado.

site [saɪt] n (place) sitio m; (building site) obra f de construcción.

sitting room ['sɪtɪŋ-] n sala f de estar.

situated ['sɪtjʊeɪtɪd] adj: **to be ~** estar situado(-da).

situation [ˌsɪtjʊ'eɪʃn] n situación f; **"~s vacant"** "ofertas de empleo".

six [sɪks] num adj seis inv ◆ num n seis m inv; **to be ~ (years old)** tener seis años (de edad); **it's ~ (o'clock)** son las seis; **a hundred and ~** ciento seis; **~ Hill St** Hill St, número seis; **it's minus ~ (degrees)** hay seis grados bajo cero; **~ out of ten** seis sobre diez.

sixteen [sɪks'tiːn] num dieciséis, → **six**.

sixteenth [sɪks'tiːnθ] num decimosexto(-ta), → **sixth**.

sixth [sɪksθ] num adj sexto(-ta) ◆ pron sexto m (-ta f) ◆ num n (fraction) sexto m ◆ num adv sexto; **a ~ (of)** la sexta parte (de); **the ~ (of September)** el seis (de septiembre).

sixth form n (Br) curso de enseñanza media que prepara a alumnos de 16 a 18 años para los "A-levels".

sixth-form college n (Br) centro de enseñanza que prepara a alumnos de 16 a 18 años para los "A-levels" o exámenes de formación profesional.

sixtieth ['sɪkstɪəθ] num sexagésimo(-ma), → **sixth**.

sixty ['sɪkstɪ] num sesenta, → **six**.

size [saɪz] n tamaño m; (of clothes, hats) talla f; (of shoes) número m; **what ~ do you take?** ¿qué talla/número usas?; **what ~ is this?** ¿de qué talla es esto?

sizeable ['saɪzəbl] adj considerable.

skate [skeɪt] n (ice skate, roller skate) patín m; (fish) raya f ◆ vi patinar.

skateboard ['skeɪtbɔːd] n monopatín m.

skater ['skeɪtə'] n (ice-skater) patinador m (-ra f).

skating ['skeɪtɪŋ] n: **to go ~** ir a patinar.

skeleton ['skelɪtn] n esqueleto m.

skeptical ['skeptɪkl] (Am) = sceptical.

sketch [sketʃ] n (drawing) bosquejo m; (humorous) sketch m ◆ vt hacer un bosquejo de.

skewer ['skjuə'] n brocheta f.

ski [skiː] (pt & pp **skied**, cont **skiing**) n esquí m ◆ vi esquiar.

ski boots npl botas fpl de esquí.

skid [skɪd] n derrape m ◆ vi derrapar.

skier ['skiːə'] n esquiador m (-ra f).

skiing ['skiːɪŋ] n esquí m; **to go ~** ir a esquiar; **a ~ holiday** unas vacaciones de esquí.

skilful ['skɪlful] adj (Br) experto(-ta).

ski lift n telesilla m.

skill [skɪl] n (ability) habilidad f, (technique) técnica f.

skilled [skɪld] adj (worker, job) especializado(-da); (driver, chef) cualificado(-da).

skillful ['skɪlful] (Am) = skilful.

skimmed milk [ˌskɪmd-] n leche f desnatada.

skin [skɪn] n piel f; (on milk) nata f.

skin freshener [-ˌfreʃnə'] n tónico m.

skinny ['skɪnɪ] adj flaco(-ca).

skip [skɪp] vi (with rope) saltar a la comba, (jump) ir dando brincos ◆ vt saltarse ◆ n (container) contenedor m

ski pants npl pantalones mpl de esquí.

ski pass n forfait m.

ski pole n bastón m para esquiar.

skipping rope ['skɪpɪŋ-] n cuerda f de saltar.

skirt [skɜːt] n falda f.

ski slope n pista f de esquí.

ski tow n remonte m.

skittles ['skɪtlz] n bolos mpl.

skull [skʌl] n (of living person) cráneo m; (of skeleton) calavera f.

sky [skaɪ] n cielo m.

skylight ['skaɪlaɪt] n tragaluz m.

skyscraper ['skaɪˌskreɪpə'] n rascacielos m inv.

slab [slæb] n (of stone, concrete) losa f.

slack [slæk] adj (rope) flojo(-ja); (careless) descuidado(-da); (not busy) inactivo(-va).

slacks [slæks] npl pantalones mpl (holgados).

slam [slæm] vt cerrar de golpe ◆ vi cerrarse de golpe.

slander ['slɑːndə'] n calumnia f.

slang [slæŋ] n argot m.

slant [slɑːnt] n (slope) inclinación f ◆ vi inclinarse.

slap [slæp] n bofetada f ◆ vt abofetear.

slash [slæʃ] vt (cut) cortar; (fig:

prices) recortar drásticamente ◆ n (*written symbol*) barra f (oblicua).

slate [sleɪt] n pizarra f.

slaughter ['slɔːtəʳ] vt (*kill*) matar; (*fig: defeat*) dar una paliza.

slave [sleɪv] n esclavo m (-va f).

sled [sled] = **sledge**.

sledge [sledʒ] n trineo m.

sleep [sliːp] (*pt & pp* **slept**) n (*rest*) descanso m; (*nap*) siesta f ◆ vi dormir ◆ vt: **the house ~s six** la casa tiene seis plazas; **did you ~ well?** ¿dormiste bien?; **I couldn't get to ~** no pude conciliar el sueño; **to go to ~** dormirse; **to ~ with sb** acostarse con alguien.

sleeper ['sliːpəʳ] n (*train*) tren m nocturno (con literas); (*sleeping car*) coche-cama m; (*Br: on railway track*) traviesa f; (*Br: earring*) aro m.

sleeping bag ['sliːpɪŋ-] n saco m de dormir.

sleeping car ['sliːpɪŋ-] n coche-cama m.

sleeping pill ['sliːpɪŋ-] n pastilla f para dormir.

sleeping policeman ['sliːpɪŋ-] n (*Br*) rompecoches m inv.

sleepy ['sliːpɪ] adj soñoliento(-ta).

sleet [sliːt] n aguanieve f ◆ vi impers: **it's ~ing** cae aguanieve.

sleeve [sliːv] n (*of garment*) manga f; (*of record*) cubierta f.

sleeveless ['sliːvlɪs] adj sin mangas.

slept [slept] pt & pp → **sleep**.

slice [slaɪs] n (*of bread*) rebanada f; (*of meat*) tajada f; (*of cake, pizza*) trozo m; (*of lemon, sausage, cucumber*) rodaja f; (*of cheese, ham*) loncha f ◆ vt cortar.

sliced bread [,slaɪst-] n pan m en rebanadas.

slide [slaɪd] (*pt & pp* **slid** [slɪd]) n (*in playground*) tobogán m; (*of photograph*) diapositiva f; (*Br: hair slide*) prendedor m ◆ vi (*slip*) resbalar.

sliding door [,slaɪdɪŋ-] n puerta f corredera.

slight [slaɪt] adj (*minor*) leve; **the ~est** el menor (la menor); **not in the ~est** en absoluto.

slightly ['slaɪtlɪ] adv ligeramente.

slim [slɪm] adj delgado(-da) ◆ vi adelgazar.

slimming ['slɪmɪŋ] n adelgazamiento m.

sling [slɪŋ] (*pt & pp* **slung**) n (*for arm*) cabestrillo m ◆ vt (*inf*) tirar.

slip [slɪp] vi resbalar ◆ n (*mistake*) descuido m; (*of paper*) papelito m; (*petticoat*) enaguas fpl ❑ **slip up** vi (*make a mistake*) cometer un error.

slipper ['slɪpəʳ] n zapatilla f.

slippery ['slɪpərɪ] adj resbaladizo(-za).

slip road n (*Br*) (*for joining motorway*) acceso m; (*for leaving motorway*) salida f.

slit [slɪt] n ranura f.

slob [slɒb] n (*inf*) guarro m (-rra f).

slogan ['sləʊgən] n eslogan m.

slope [sləʊp] n (*incline*) inclinación f; (*hill*) cuesta f; (*for skiing*) pista f ◆ vi inclinarse.

sloping ['sləʊpɪŋ] adj inclinado(-da).

slot [slɒt] n (*for coin*) ranura f; (*groove*) muesca f.

slot machine n (*vending machine*) máquina f automática; (*for*

gambling) máquina *f* tragaperras.
Slovakia [sləˈvækɪə] *n* Eslovaquia.
slow [sləʊ] *adj (not fast)* lento(-ta); *(clock, watch)* atrasado(-da); *(business)* flojo(-ja); *(in understanding)* corto(-ta) ♦ *adv* despacio; **"slow"** cartel que aconseja a los automovilistas ir despacio; **a ~ train** = un tren tranvía ❑ **slow down** *vt sep* reducir la velocidad de ♦ *vi (vehicle)* reducir la velocidad; *(person)* reducir el paso.
slowly [ˈsləʊlɪ] *adv (not fast)* despacio; *(gradually)* poco a poco.
slug [slʌɡ] *n* babosa *f*.
slum [slʌm] *n (building)* cuchitril *m* ❑ **slums** *npl (district)* barrios *mpl* bajos.
slung [slʌŋ] *pt & pp* → **sling**.
slush [slʌʃ] *n* nieve *f* medio derretida.
sly [slaɪ] *adj (cunning)* astuto(-ta); *(deceitful)* furtivo(-va).
smack [smæk] *n (slap)* cachete *m* ♦ *vt* dar un cachete.
small [smɔːl] *adj* pequeño(-ña).
small change *n* cambio *m*.
smallpox [ˈsmɔːlpɒks] *n* viruela *f*.
smart [smɑːt] *adj (elegant, posh)* elegante; *(clever)* inteligente.
smart card *n* tarjeta *f* con banda magnética.
smash [smæʃ] *n (SPORT)* mate *m*; *(inf: car crash)* choque *m* ♦ *vt (plate, window)* romper ♦ *vi (plate, vase etc)* romperse.
smashing [ˈsmæʃɪŋ] *adj (Br: inf)* fenomenal.
smear test [ˈsmɪə-] *n* citología *f*.
smell [smel] *(pt & pp* **-ed** OR

smelt) *n* olor *m* ♦ *vt & vi* oler; **to ~ of sthg** oler a algo.
smelly [ˈsmelɪ] *adj* maloliente.
smelt [smelt] *pt & pp* → **smell**.
smile [smaɪl] *n* sonrisa *f* ♦ *vi* sonreír.
smoke [sməʊk] *n* humo *m* ♦ *vt & vi* fumar; **to have a ~** echarse un cigarro.
smoked [sməʊkt] *adj* ahumado(-da).
smoked salmon *n* salmón *m* ahumado.
smoker [ˈsməʊkər] *n* fumador *m* (-ra *f*).
smoking [ˈsməʊkɪŋ] *n* el fumar; **"no -"** "prohibido fumar".
smoking area *n* área *f* de fumadores.
smoking compartment *n* compartimento *m* de fumadores.
smoky [ˈsməʊkɪ] *adj (room)* lleno (-na) de humo.
smooth [smuːð] *adj (surface, road)* liso(-sa); *(skin)* terso(-sa); *(flight, journey)* tranquilo(-la); *(mixture, liquid)* sin grumos; *(wine, beer)* suave; *(pej: suave)* meloso(-sa) ❑ **smooth down** *vt sep* alisar.
smother [ˈsmʌðər] *vt (cover)* cubrir.
smudge [smʌdʒ] *n* mancha *f*.
smuggle [ˈsmʌɡl] *vt* pasar de contrabando.
snack [snæk] *n* piscolabis *m inv*.
snack bar *n* cafetería *f*.
snail [sneɪl] *n* caracol *m*.
snake [sneɪk] *n (smaller)* culebra *f*; *(larger)* serpiente *f*.
snap [snæp] *vt (break)* partir (en dos) ♦ *vi (break)* partirse (en dos) ♦

n (inf: photo) foto *f*; *(Br: card game)* guerrilla *f*.

snare [sneə^r] *n* trampa *f*.

snatch [snætʃ] *vt (grab)* arrebatar; *(steal)* dar el tirón.

sneakers ['sni:kəz] *npl (Am)* zapatos *mpl* de lona.

sneeze [sni:z] *n* estornudo *m* ◆ *vi* estornudar.

sniff [snɪf] *vi (from cold, crying)* sorber ◆ *vt* oler.

snip [snɪp] *vt* cortar con tijeras.

snob [snɒb] *n* esnob *mf*.

snooker ['snu:kə^r] *n* snooker *m*, juego parecido al billar.

snooze [snu:z] *n* cabezada *f*.

snore [snɔ:^r] *vi* roncar.

snorkel ['snɔ:kl] *n* tubo *m* respiratorio.

snout [snaʊt] *n* hocico *m*.

snow [snəʊ] *n* nieve *f* ◆ *v impers:* it's ~ing está nevando.

snowball ['snəʊbɔ:l] *n* bola *f* de nieve.

snowdrift ['snəʊdrɪft] *n* montón *m* de nieve.

snowflake ['snəʊfleɪk] *n* copo *m* de nieve.

snowman ['snəʊmæn] *(pl* **-men** [-men]*)* *n* muñeco *m* de nieve.

snowplough ['snəʊplaʊ] *n* quitanieves *m inv*.

snowstorm ['snəʊstɔ:m] *n* tormenta *f* de nieve.

snug [snʌg] *adj (person)* cómodo y calentito (cómoda y calentita); *(place)* acogedor(-ra).

so [səʊ] *adv* **1.** *(emphasizing degree)* tan; **it's ~ difficult (that ...)** es tan difícil (que ...); **~ many** tantos; **~**

much tanto.

2. *(referring back):* **~ you knew already** así que ya lo sabías; **I don't think ~** no creo; **I'm afraid ~** me temo que sí; **if ~** en ese caso.

3. *(also)* también: **~ do I** yo también.

4. *(in this way)* así.

5. *(expressing agreement):* **~ I see** ya lo veo.

6. *(in phrases):* **or ~** más o menos; **~ as to do sthg** para hacer algo; **come here ~ that I can see you** ven acá para que te vea.

◆ *conj* **1.** *(therefore)* así que.

2. *(summarizing)* entonces; **~ what have you been up to?** entonces ¿qué has estado haciendo?

3. *(in phrases):* **~ what?** *(inf)* ¿y qué?; **~ there!** *(inf)* ¡y si no te gusta te aguantas!

soak [səʊk] *vt (leave in water)* poner en remojo; *(make very wet)* empapar ◆ *vi:* **to ~ through sthg** calar algo ❏ **soak up** *vt sep* absorber.

soaked [səʊkt] *adj* empapado (-da).

soaking ['səʊkɪŋ] *adj* empapado(-da).

soap [səʊp] *n* jabón *m*.

soap opera *n* culebrón *m*.

soap powder *n* detergente *m* en polvo.

sob [sɒb] *n* sollozo *m* ◆ *vi* sollozar.

sober ['səʊbə^r] *adj (not drunk)* sobrio(-bria).

soccer ['sɒkə^r] *n* fútbol *m*.

sociable ['səʊʃəbl] *adj* sociable.

social ['səʊʃl] *adj* social.

social club *n* club *m* social.

socialist ['səʊʃəlɪst] *adj* socialista *m* ◆ *n* socialista *mf*.

social life *n* vida *f* social.

social security n seguridad f social.

social worker n asistente m (-ta f) social.

society [sə'saɪətɪ] n sociedad f.

sociology [,səʊsɪ'ɒlədʒɪ] n sociología f.

sock [sɒk] n calcetín m.

socket ['sɒkɪt] n (for plug, light bulb) enchufe m.

sod [sɒd] n (Br: vulg) cabrón m (-ona f).

soda ['səʊdə] n (soda water) soda f; (Am: fizzy drink) gaseosa f.

soda water n soda f.

sofa ['səʊfə] n sofá m.

sofa bed n sofá-cama m

soft [sɒft] adj (not firm, stiff) blando(-da); (not rough, loud) suave; (not forceful) ligero(ra).

soft cheese n queso m blando.

soft drink n refresco m.

software ['sɒftweə] n software m.

soil [sɔɪl] n tierra f.

solarium [sə'leərɪəm] n solario m.

solar panel ['səʊlə-] n panel m solar.

sold [səʊld] pt & pp → sell.

soldier ['səʊldʒə] n soldado m.

sold out adj agotado(-da)

sole [səʊl] adj (only) único(-ca); (exclusive) exclusivo(-va) ♦ n (of shoe) suela f; (of foot) planta f; (fish: pl inv) lenguado m.

solemn ['sɒləm] adj solemne.

solicitor [sə'lɪsɪtə] n (Br) abogado que actúa en los tribunales de primera instancia y prepara casos para los tribunales superiores.

solid ['sɒlɪd] adj sólido(-da); (table,

gold, oak) macizo(-za).

solo ['səʊləʊ] (pl -s) n solo m; "~ m/cs" (traffic sign) "sólo motocicletas".

soluble ['sɒljʊbl] adj soluble.

solution [sə'luːʃn] n solución f.

solve [sɒlv] vt resolver.

some [sʌm] adj 1. (certain amount of): would you like ~ coffee? ¿quieres café?; can I have ~ cheese? ¿me dejas un poco de queso?; ~ money algo de dinero.
2. (certain number of) unos (unas); ~ sweets unos caramelos; have ~ grapes coge uvas; ~ people alguna gente.
3. (large amount of) bastante; I had ~ difficulty getting here me resultó bastante difícil llegar aquí.
4. (large number of) bastante; I've known him for ~ years hace bastantes años que lo conozco.
5. (not all) algunos(-nas); ~ jobs are better paid than others algunos trabajos están mejor pagados que otros.
6. (in imprecise statements) un (una); ~ man phoned llamó un hombre.
♦ pron 1. (certain amount) un poco; can I have ~? ¿puedo coger un poco?
2. (certain number) algunos mpl (-nas fpl); can I have ~? ¿puedo coger algunos?; ~ (of them) left early algunos (de ellos) se fueron pronto.
♦ adv aproximadamente; there were ~ 7,000 people there había unas 7.000 personas allí.

somebody ['sʌmbədɪ] = someone.

somehow ['sʌmhaʊ] adv (some way or other) de alguna manera; (for some reason) por alguna razón.

someone [ˈsʌmwʌn] *pron* alguien.

someplace [ˈsʌmpleɪs] *(Am)* = **somewhere**.

somersault [ˈsʌməsɔːlt] *n* salto *m* mortal.

something [ˈsʌmθɪŋ] *pron* algo; **it's really ~** es algo impresionante; **or ~** *(inf)* o algo así; **~ like** algo así como.

sometime [ˈsʌmtaɪm] *adv* en algún momento.

sometimes [ˈsʌmtaɪmz] *adv* a veces.

somewhere [ˈsʌmweə] *adv* (in or to unspecified place) en/a alguna parte; (approximately) aproximadamente.

son [sʌn] *n* hijo *m*.

song [sɒŋ] *n* canción *f*.

son-in-law *n* yerno *m*.

soon [suːn] *adv* pronto; **how ~ can you do it?** ¿para cuándo estará listo?; **as ~ as** tan pronto como; **as ~ as possible** cuanto antes; **~ after** poco después; **~er or later** tarde o temprano.

soot [sʊt] *n* hollín *m*.

soothe [suːð] *vt* (pain, sunburn) aliviar; (person, anger, nerves) calmar.

sophisticated [səˈfɪstɪkeɪtɪd] *adj* sofisticado(-da).

sorbet [ˈsɔːbeɪ] *n* sorbete *m*.

sore [sɔː] *adj* (painful) dolorido (-da); (Am: inf: angry) enfadado (-da) ◆ *n* úlcera *f*; **to have a ~ throat** tener dolor de garganta.

sorry [ˈsɔːrɪ] *adj*: **I'm ~!** ¡lo siento!; **I'm ~ I'm late** siento llegar tarde; **I'm ~ you failed** lamento que hayas suspendido; **~?** (pardon?) ¿perdón?; **to feel ~ for sb** sentir lástima por alguien; **to be ~ about sthg** sentir algo.

sort [sɔːt] *n* tipo *m*, clase *f* ◆ *vt* clasificar; **~ of** más o menos; **it's ~ of difficult** es algo difícil □ **sort out** *vt sep* (classify) clasificar; (resolve) resolver.

so-so *adj & adv* (inf) así así.

soufflé [ˈsuːfleɪ] *n* suflé *m*.

sought [sɔːt] *pt & pp* → **seek**.

soul [səʊl] *n* (spirit) alma *f*; (soul music) música *f* soul.

sound [saʊnd] *n* sonido *m*; (individual noise) ruido *m* ◆ *vt* (horn, bell) hacer sonar ◆ *vi* (make a noise) sonar; (seem to be) parecer ◆ *adj* (health, person) bueno(-na); (heart) sano(-na); (building, structure) sólido(-da); **to ~ like** (make a noise like) sonar como; (seem to be) sonar.

soundproof [ˈsaʊndpruːf] *adj* insonorizado(-da).

soup [suːp] *n* sopa *f*.

soup spoon *n* cuchara *f* sopera.

sour [ˈsaʊə] *adj* (taste) ácido(-da); (milk) agrio(agria); **to go ~** agriarse.

source [sɔːs] *n* (supply, origin) fuente *f*; (cause) origen *m*; (of river) nacimiento *m*.

sour cream *n* nata *f* amarga.

south [saʊθ] *n* sur *m* ◆ *adv* al sur; **in the ~ of England** en el sur de Inglaterra.

South Africa *n* Sudáfrica.

South America *n* Sudamérica.

southbound [ˈsaʊθbaʊnd] *adj* con rumbo al sur.

southeast [ˌsaʊθˈiːst] *n* sudeste *m*.

southern ['sʌðən] *adj* del sur.
South Pole *n* Polo *m* Sur.
southwards ['saʊθwədz] *adv*
hacia el sur.
southwest [,saʊθ'west] *n* suroeste *m*.
souvenir [,suːvə'nɪəʳ] *n* recuerdo
m.
Soviet Union [,səʊvɪət-] *n*: the
~ la Unión Soviética.
sow[1] [səʊ] (*pp* **sown** [səʊn]) *vt*
sembrar.
sow[2] [aʊ] *n* (*pig*) cerda *f*.
soya ['sɔɪə] *n* soja *f*.
soya bean *n* semilla *f* de soja.
soy sauce [,sɔɪ-] *n* salsa *f* de soja.
spa [spaː] *n* balneario *m*.
space [speɪs] *n* espacio *m* ♦ *vt*
espaciar.
spaceship ['speɪsʃɪp] *n* nave *f*
espacial.
space shuttle *n* transbordador *m* espacial.
spacious ['speɪʃəs] *adj* espacio-
so(-sa)
spade [speɪd] *n* (*tool*) pala *f* □
spades *npl* (*in cards*) picas *fpl*.
spaghetti [spə'geti] *n* espaguetis
mpl.
Spain [speɪn] *n* España *f*.
span [spæn] *pt* → **spin** ♦ *n* (*length*)
duración *f*; (*of time*) período *m*.
Spaniard ['spænjəd] *n* español *m*
(-la *f*).
spaniel ['spænjəl] *n* perro *m* de
aguas.
Spanish ['spænɪʃ] *adj* espa-
ñol(-la) ♦ *n* (*language*) español *m*.
spank [spæŋk] *vt* zurrar.
spanner ['spænəʳ] *n* llave *f* (de

tuercas).
spare [speəʳ] *adj* (*kept in reserve*)
de sobra; (*not in use*) libre ♦ *n* (*spare
part*) recambio *m*; (*spare wheel*)
rueda *f* de recambio ♦ *vt*: **I can't ~
the time** no tengo tiempo; **with
ten minutes to ~** con diez minutos
de sobra.
spare part *n* pieza *f* de recambio.
spare ribs *npl* costillas *fpl*
(sueltas).
spare room *n* habitación *f* de
invitados.
spare time *n* tiempo *m* libre.
spare wheel *n* rueda *f* de
repuesto.
spark [spaːk] *n* chispa *f*.
sparkling ['spaːklɪŋ] *adj* (*drink*)
con gas.
sparkling wine *n* vino *m*
espumoso.
spark plug *n* bujía *f*.
sparrow ['spærəʊ] *n* gorrión *m*.
spat [spæt] *pt & pp* (*Br*) → **spit**.
speak [spiːk] (*pt* **spoke**, *pp* **spoken**) *vt* (*language*) hablar; (*say*)
decir ♦ *vi* hablar; **who's ~ing?** (*on
phone*) ¿quién es?; **can I ~ to Sarah?
- ~ing!** ¿puedo hablar con Sara? -
¡soy yo!; **to ~ to sb about sthg**
hablar con alguien sobre algo □
speak up *vi* (*more loudly*) hablar
más alto.
speaker ['spiːkəʳ] *n* (*at conference*)
conferenciante *mf*; (*loudspeaker, of
stereo*) altavoz *m*; **a Spanish ~** un
hispanohablante.
spear [spɪəʳ] *n* lanza *f*.
special ['speʃl] *adj* (*not ordinary*)
especial; (*particular*) particular ♦ *n*

(dish) plato *m* del día; **"today's ~"** "plato del día".

special delivery *n (Br)* = correo *m* urgente.

special effects *npl* efectos *mpl* especiales.

specialist ['speʃəlɪst] *n (doctor)* especialista *mf*.

speciality [ˌspeʃɪ'ælətɪ] *n* especialidad *f*.

specialize ['speʃəlaɪz] *vi*: **to ~ (in)** especializarse (en).

specially ['speʃəlɪ] *adv* especialmente; *(particularly)* particularmente.

special offer *n* oferta *f* especial.

special school *n (Br)* escuela *f* especial.

specialty ['speʃltɪ] *(Am)* = **speciality**.

species ['spiːʃiːz] *(pl inv)* *n* especie *f*.

specific [spə'sɪfɪk] *adj* específico(-a).

specifications [ˌspesɪfɪ'keɪʃnz] *npl (of machine, building etc)* datos *mpl* técnicos.

specimen ['spesɪmən] *n (MED)* espécimen *m*; *(example)* muestra *f*.

specs [speks] *npl (inf)* gafas *fpl*.

spectacle ['spektəkl] *n* espectáculo *m*.

spectacles ['spektəklz] *npl* gafas *fpl*.

spectacular [spek'tækjulər] *adj* espectacular.

spectator [spek'teɪtər] *n* espectador *m* (-ra *f*).

sped [sped] *pt & pp* → **speed**.

speech [spiːtʃ] *n (ability to speak)* habla *f*; *(manner of speaking)* manera *f* de hablar; *(talk)* discurso *m*.

speech impediment [-ɪmˌpedɪmənt] *n* impedimento *m* al hablar.

speed [spiːd] *(pt & pp* **-ed** OR **sped)** *n* velocidad *f* ♦ *vi (move quickly)* moverse de prisa; *(drive too fast)* conducir con exceso de velocidad; **"reduce ~ now"** "reduzca su velocidad" ❑ **speed up** *vi* acelerarse.

speedboat ['spiːdbəʊt] *n* lancha *f* motora.

speeding ['spiːdɪŋ] *n* exceso *m* de velocidad.

speed limit *n* límite *m* de velocidad.

speedometer [spɪ'dɒmɪtər] *n* velocímetro *m*.

spell [spel] *(Br pt & pp* **-ed** OR **spelt,** *Am pt & pp* **-ed)** *vt (word, name)* deletrear; *(subj: letters)* significar ♦ *n (time spent)* temporada *f*; *(of weather)* racha *f*; *(magic)* hechizo *m*.

spelling ['spelɪŋ] *n* ortografía *f*.

spelt [spelt] *pt & pp (Br)* → **spell**.

spend [spend] *(pt & pp* **spent** [spent]) *vt (money)* gastar; *(time)* pasar.

sphere [sfɪər] *n* esfera *f*.

spice [spaɪs] *n* especia *f* ♦ *vt* condimentar.

spicy ['spaɪsɪ] *adj* picante.

spider ['spaɪdər] *n* araña *f*.

spider's web *n* telaraña *f*.

spike [spaɪk] *n (metal)* clavo *m*.

spill [spɪl] *(Br pt & pp* **-ed** OR **spilt** [spɪlt], *Am pt & pp* **-ed)** *vt* derramar ♦ *vi* derramarse.

spin [spɪn] (pt **span** OR **spun**, pp **spun**) vt (wheel, coin, chair) hacer girar; (washing) centrifugar ◆ n (on ball) efecto m; **to go for a ~** (inf) ir a dar una vuelta.

spinach ['spɪnɪdʒ] n espinacas fpl.

spine [spaɪn] n (of back) espina f dorsal; (of book) lomo m.

spinster ['spɪnstəʳ] n soltera f.

spiral ['spaɪərəl] n espiral f.

spiral staircase n escalera f de caracol.

spire ['spaɪəʳ] n aguja f.

spirit ['spɪrɪt] n (soul) espíritu m; (energy) vigor m; (courage) valor m; (mood) humor m ❑ **spirits** npl (Br) (alcohol) licores mpl.

spit [spɪt] (Br pt & pp **spat**, Am pt & pp **spit**) vi ocupar ◆ n (saliva) saliva f; (for cooking) asador m ◆ v impers: **it's spitting** está chispeando.

spite [spaɪt] n: **in spite of** prep a pesar de.

spiteful ['spaɪtful] adj rencoroso(-sa).

splash [splæʃ] n (sound) chapoteo m ◆ vt salpicar.

splendid ['splendɪd] adj (beautiful) magnífico(-ca); (very good) espléndido(-da).

splint [splɪnt] n tablilla f.

splinter ['splɪntəʳ] n astilla f.

split [splɪt] (pt & pp **split**) n (tear) rasgón m; (crack) grieta f; (in skirt) abertura f ◆ vt (wood, stone) agrietar; (tear) rasgar; (bill, profits, work) dividir ◆ vi (wood, stone) agrietarse; (tear) rasgarse ❑ **split up** vi (group, couple) separarse.

spoil [spɔɪl] (pt & pp **-ed** OR **spoilt** [spɔɪlt]) vt (ruin) estropear; (child) mimar.

spoke [spəʊk] pt → **speak** ◆ n radio m.

spoken ['spəʊkn] pp → **speak**.

spokesman ['spəʊksmən] (pl **-men** [-mən]) n portavoz m.

spokeswoman ['spəʊks-ˌwʊmən] (pl **-women** [-ˌwɪmɪn]) n portavoz f.

sponge [spʌndʒ] n (for cleaning, washing) esponja f.

sponge bag n (Br) neceser m.

sponge cake n bizcocho m.

sponsor ['spɒnsəʳ] n (of event, TV programme) patrocinador m (-ra f).

sponsored walk [spɒnsəd-] n marcha f benéfica.

spontaneous [spɒn'teɪnjəs] adj espontáneo(-nea).

spoon [spuːn] n cuchara f.

spoonful ['spuːnful] n cucharada f.

sport [spɔːt] n deporte m.

sports car [spɔːts-] n coche m deportivo.

sports centre [spɔːts-] n centro m deportivo.

sports jacket [spɔːts-] n chaqueta f de sport.

sportsman ['spɔːtsmən] (pl **-men** [-mən]) n deportista m.

sports shop [spɔːts-] n tienda f de deporte.

sportswoman ['spɔːtsˌwʊmən] (pl **-women** [-ˌwɪmɪn]) n deportista f.

spot [spɒt] n (of paint, rain) gota f; (on clothes) lunar m; (on skin) grano m; (place) lugar m ◆ vt notar; **on the**

~ *(at once)* en el acto; *(at the scene)* en el lugar.

spotless ['spɒtlɪs] *adj* inmaculado(-da).

spotlight ['spɒtlaɪt] *n* foco *m*.

spotty ['spɒtɪ] *adj (skin, person, face)* lleno(-na) de granos.

spouse [spaʊs] *n (fml)* esposo *m* (-sa *f*).

spout [spaʊt] *n* pitorro *m*.

sprain [spreɪn] *vt* torcerse.

sprang [spræŋ] *pt* → **spring**.

spray [spreɪ] *n (of aerosol, perfume)* espray *m; (droplets)* rociada *f; (of sea)* espuma *f* ◆ *vt* rociar.

spread [spred] *(pt & pp* **spread**) *vt (butter, jam, glue)* untar; *(map, tablecloth, blanket)* extender; *(legs, fingers, arms)* estirar; *(disease)* propagar; *(news, rumour)* difundir ◆ *vi (disease, fire, stain)* propagarse; *(news, rumour)* difundirse ◆ *n (food)* pasta *f* para untar ❑ **spread out** *vi (disperse)* dispersarse.

spring [sprɪŋ] *(pt* **sprang**, *pp* **sprung**) *n (season)* primavera *f; (coil)* muelle *m; (of water)* manantial *m* ◆ *vi (leap)* saltar; **in (the)** ~ en (la) primavera.

springboard ['sprɪŋbɔ:d] *n* trampolín *m*.

spring-cleaning [-'kli:nɪŋ] *n* limpieza *f* general.

spring onion *n* cebolleta *f*.

spring roll *n* rollito *m* de primavera.

sprinkle ['sprɪŋkl] *vt* rociar.

sprinkler ['sprɪŋklər] *n* aspersor *m*.

sprint [sprɪnt] *n (race)* esprint *m* ◆ *vi (run fast)* correr a toda velocidad.

Sprinter® ['sprɪntər] *n (Br: train)* tren *m* de corto recorrido.

sprout [spraʊt] *n (vegetable)* col *f* de Bruselas.

spruce [spru:s] *n* picea *f*.

sprung [sprʌŋ] *pp* → **spring** ◆ *adj (mattress)* de muelles.

spud [spʌd] *n (inf)* patata *f*.

spun [spʌn] *pt & pp* → **spin**.

spur [spɜ:r] *n (for horse rider)* espuela *f*; **on the** ~ **of the moment** sin pensarlo dos veces.

spurt [spɜ:t] *vi* salir a chorros.

spy [spaɪ] *n* espía *mf*.

squall [skwɔ:l] *n* turbión *m*.

squalor ['skwɒlər] *n* miseria *f*.

square [skweər] *adj (in shape)* cuadrado(-da) ◆ *n (shape)* cuadrado *m; (in town)* plaza *f; (of chocolate)* onza *f; (on chessboard)* casilla *f*; **2** ~ **metres** 2 metros cuadrados; **it's 2 metres** ~ tiene 2 metros cuadrados; **we're (all)** ~ **now** quedamos en paz.

squash [skwɒʃ] *n (game)* squash *m; (Br: drink)* refresco *m; (Am: vegetable)* calabaza *f* ◆ *vt* aplastar.

squat [skwɒt] *adj* achaparrado(-da) ◆ *vi (crouch)* agacharse.

squeak [skwi:k] *vi* chirriar.

squeeze [skwi:z] *vt (orange)* exprimir; *(hand)* apretar; *(tube)* estrujar ❑ **squeeze in** *vi* meterse.

squid [skwɪd] *n (food)* calamares *mpl*.

squint [skwɪnt] *n* estrabismo *m* ◆ *vi* bizquear.

squirrel [*Br* 'skwɪrəl, *Am* 'skwɜ:rəl] *n* ardilla *f*.

squirt [skwɜ:t] *vi* salir a chorro.

St (abbr of Street) c; (abbr of Saint) Sto., Sta.

stab [stæb] vt (with knife) apuñalar.

stable ['steɪbl] adj (unchanging) estable; (firmly fixed) fijo(-ja) ◆ n cuadra f.

stack [stæk] n (pile) pila f; ~s of (inf: lots) montones de.

stadium ['steɪdjəm] n estadio m.

staff [stɑːf] n (workers) empleados mpl.

stage [steɪdʒ] n (phase) etapa f; (in theatre) escenario m.

stagger ['stægəʳ] vt (arrange in stages) escalonar ◆ vi tambalearse.

stagnant ['stægnənt] adj estancado(-da).

stain [steɪn] n mancha f ◆ vt manchar.

stained glass window [.steɪnd] n vidriera f.

stainless steel ['steɪnlɪs] n acero m inoxidable.

staircase ['steəkeɪs] n escalera f.

stairs [steəz] npl escaleras fpl.

stairwell ['steəwel] n hueco m de la escalera.

stake [steɪk] n (share) participación f; (in gambling) apuesta f; (post) estaca f; **at** ~ en juego.

stale [steɪl] adj (food) pasado(-da); (bread) duro(-ra).

stalk [stɔːk] n (of flower, plant) tallo m; (of fruit, leaf) pecíolo m.

stall [stɔːl] n (in market, at exhibition) puesto m ◆ vi (car, plane, engine) calarse ❑ **stalls** npl (Br: in theatre) platea f.

stamina ['stæmɪnə] n resistencia f.

stammer ['stæməʳ] vi tartamudear.

stamp [stæmp] n sello m ◆ vt (passport, document) sellar ◆ vi: **to** ~ **on sthg** pisar algo; **to** ~ **one's foot** patear.

stamp-collecting [-kə,lektɪŋ] n filatelia f.

stamp machine n máquina f expendedora de sellos.

stand [stænd] (pt & pp stood) vi (be on feet) estar de pie; (be situated) estar (situado); (get to one's feet) ponerse de pie ◆ vt (place) colocar; (bear, withstand) soportar ◆ n (stall) puesto m; (for coats) perchero m; (for umbrellas) paragüero m; (for bike, motorbike) patín m de apoyo; (at sports stadium) tribuna f; **to be** ~**ing** estar de pie; **to** ~ **sb a drink** invitar a alguien a beber algo; "no ~ing" (Am: AUT) "prohibido aparcar" ❑ **stand back** vi echarse para atrás; **stand for** vt fus (mean) significar; (tolerate) tolerar; **stand in** vi: **to** ~ **in for sb** sustituir a alguien; **stand out** vi (be conspicuous) destacar; (be superior) sobresalir; **stand up** vi (be on feet) levantarse ◆ vt sep (inf: boyfriend, girlfriend etc) dejar plantado; **stand up for** vt fus salir en defensa de.

standard ['stændəd] adj (normal) normal ◆ n (level) nivel m; (point of comparison) criterio m; **up to** ~ al nivel requerido ❑ **standards** npl (principles) valores mpl morales.

standard-class adj (Br) de segunda clase.

standby ['stændbaɪ] adj sin

reserva.

stank [stæŋk] pt → stink.

staple ['steɪpl] n (for paper) grapa f.

stapler ['steɪpləʳ] n grapadora f.

star [stɑːʳ] n estrella f ♦ vt (subj: film, play etc) estar protagonizado por ❏ **stars** npl (horoscope) horóscopo m.

starboard ['stɑːbəd] adj de estribor.

starch [stɑːtʃ] n (for clothes) almidón m; (in food) fécula f.

stare [steəʳ] vi mirar fijamente; **to ~ at** mirar fijamente.

starfish ['stɑːfɪʃ] (pl inv) n estrella f de mar.

starling ['stɑːlɪŋ] n estornino m.

Stars and Stripes n: the ~ la bandera de las barras y estrellas.

---

i STARS AND STRIPES

Esto es uno de los muchos nombres que recibe la bandera estadounidense, junto con "Old Glory", "Star-Spangled Banner" y "Stars and Bars". Las 50 estrellas representan los 50 estados de hoy día y las 13 barras rojas y blancas los 13 estados fundadores de la Unión. Los estadounidenses están muy orgullosos de su bandera y muchos particulares la hacen ondear frente a su casa.

---

start [stɑːt] n (beginning) principio m; (starting place) salida f ♦ vt (begin) empezar; (car, engine) arrancar; (business, club) montar ♦ vi (begin) empezar; (car, engine) arrancar; (begin journey) salir; **at the ~ of**

the year a principios del año; **prices ~ at** OR **from £5** precios desde cinco libras; **to ~ doing sthg** OR **to do sthg** empezar a hacer algo; **to ~ with** (in the first place) para empezar; (when ordering meal) de primero ❏ **start out** vi (on journey) salir; (be originally) empezar; **start up** vt sep (car, engine) arrancar; (business, shop) montar.

starter ['stɑːtəʳ] n (Br: of meal) primer plato m; (of car) motor m de arranque; **for ~s** (in meal) de primero.

starter motor n motor m de arranque.

starting point ['stɑːtɪŋ-] n punto m de partida.

startle ['stɑːtl] vt asustar.

starvation [stɑːˈveɪʃn] n hambre f.

starve [stɑːv] vi (have no food) pasar hambre; **I'm starving!** ¡me muero de hambre!

state [steɪt] n estado m ♦ vt (declare) declarar; (specify) indicar; **the State** el Estado; **the States** los Estados Unidos.

statement ['steɪtmənt] n (declaration) declaración f; (from bank) extracto m.

state school n = instituto m.

statesman ['steɪtsmən] (pl -men [-mən]) n estadista m.

static ['stætɪk] n interferencias fpl.

station ['steɪʃn] n estación f; (on radio) emisora f.

stationary ['steɪʃnərɪ] adj inmóvil.

stationer's ['steɪʃnəz] n (shop) papelería f.

stationery ['steɪʃnərɪ] n objetos mpl de escritorio.

station wagon n (Am) furgoneta f familiar.

statistics [stəˈtɪstɪks] npl datos mpl.

statue ['stætʃuː] n estatua f.

Statue of Liberty n: the ~ la Estatua de la Libertad.

ⓘ STATUE OF LIBERTY

Esta gigantesca estatua de una mujer con una antorcha en la mano se alza sobre una pequeña isla situada a la entrada del puerto de Nueva York y puede ser visitada por el público. La estatua es un obsequio que Francia hizo a Estados Unidos en 1884.

---

status ['steɪtəs] n (legal position) estado m; (social position) condición f; (prestige) prestigio m.

stay [steɪ] n estancia f ◆ vi (remain) quedarse; (as guest) alojarse; (Scot: reside) vivir; **to ~ the night** pasar la noche ❑ **stay away** vi (not attend) no asistir; (not go near) no acercarse; **stay in** vi quedarse en casa; **stay out** vi (from home) quedarse fuera; **stay up** vi quedarse levantado.

STD code n (abbr of subscriber trunk dialling) prefijo para llamadas interurbanas.

steady ['stedɪ] adj (not shaking, firm) firme; (gradual) gradual; (stable) constante; (job) estable ◆ vt (stop from shaking) mantener firme.

steak [steɪk] n (type of meat) bis-

tec m; (piece of meat, fish) filete m.

steak and kidney pie n empanada de bistec y riñones.

steakhouse ['steɪkhaʊs, pl -haʊzɪz] n parrilla f (restaurante).

steal [stiːl] (pt stole, pp stolen) vt robar; **to ~ sthg from sb** robar algo a alguien.

steam [stiːm] n vapor m ◆ vt (food) cocer al vapor.

steamboat ['stiːmbəʊt] n buque m de vapor.

steam engine n máquina f de vapor.

steam iron n plancha f de vapor.

steel [stiːl] n acero m ◆ adj de acero.

steep [stiːp] adj (hill, path) empinado(-da); (increase, drop) considerable.

steeple ['stiːpl] n torre f coronada con una aguja.

steer [stɪəʳ] vt (car, boat, plane) conducir, dirigir.

steering ['stɪərɪŋ] n dirección f.

steering wheel n volante m.

stem [stem] n (of plant) tallo m; (of glass) pie m.

step [step] n paso m; (stair, rung) peldaño m; (measure) medida f ◆ vi: **to ~ on sthg** pisar algo; **"mind the ~"** "cuidado con el escalón" ❑ **steps** npl (stairs) escaleras fpl; **step aside** vi (move aside) apartarse; **step back** vi (move back) echarse atrás.

step aerobics n step m.

stepbrother ['step,brʌðəʳ] n hermanastro m.

stepdaughter ['step,dɔːtəʳ] n

hijastra f.

stepfather ['step,fɑːðəʳ] n padrastro m.

stepladder ['step,lædəʳ] n escalera f de tijera.

stepmother ['step,mʌðəʳ] n madrastra f.

stepsister ['step,sɪstəʳ] n hermanastra f.

stepson ['stepsʌn] n hijastro m.

stereo ['steriəʊ] (pl -s) adj estéreo inv ◆ n (hi-fi) equipo m estereofónico; (stereo sound) estéreo m.

sterile ['sterail] adj (germ-free) esterilizado(-da).

sterilize ['sterilaiz] vt esterilizar.

sterling ['stɜːlɪŋ] adj (pound) esterlina ◆ n la libra esterlina.

sterling silver n plata f de ley.

stern [stɜːn] adj severo(-ra) ◆ n popa f.

stew [stjuː] n estofado m.

steward ['stjʊəd] n (on plane) auxiliar m de vuelo; (on ship) camarero m; (at public event) ayudante mf de organización.

stewardess ['stjʊədis] n auxiliar f de vuelo.

stewed [stjuːd] adj (fruit) en compota.

stick [stɪk] (pt & pp stuck) n (of wood, for sport) palo m; (thin piece) barra f; (walking stick) bastón m ◆ vt (glue) pegar; (push, insert) meter; (inf: put) poner ◆ vi (become attached) pegarse; (jam) atrancarse ☐ **stick out** vi sobresalir; **stick to** vt fus (decision) atenerse a; (principles) ser fiel a; (promise) cumplir con; **stick up** vt sep (poster, notice) pegar ◆ vi salir; **stick up for** vt fus defender.

sticker ['stɪkəʳ] n pegatina f.

sticking plaster ['stɪkɪŋ-] n esparadrapo m.

stick shift n (Am: car) coche m con palanca de cambios.

sticky ['stɪki] adj (substance, hands, sweets) pegajoso(-sa); (label, tape) adhesivo(-va); (weather) húmedo(-da).

stiff [stɪf] adj (firm) rígido(-da); (back, neck) agarrotado(-da); (door, latch, mechanism) atascado(-da) ◆ adv: **to be bored ~** (inf) estar muerto de aburrimiento; **to feel ~** tener agujetas.

stile [stail] n escalones mpl para pasar una valla.

stiletto heels [sti'letəʊ-] npl (shoes) tacones mpl de aguja.

still [stil] adv todavía; (despite that) sin embargo; (even) aún ◆ adj (motionless) inmóvil; (quiet, calm) tranquilo(-la); (not fizzy) sin gas; **we've ~ got ten minutes** aún nos quedan diez minutos; **~ more** aún más; **to stand ~** estarse quieto.

Stilton ['stiltn] n queso inglés de sabor fuerte y amargo.

stimulate ['stimjʊleit] vt (encourage) estimular; (make enthusiastic) excitar.

sting [stiŋ] (pt & pp stung) vt picar ◆ vi: **my eyes are ~ing** me pican los ojos.

stingy ['stindʒi] adj (inf) roñoso(-sa).

stink [stiŋk] (pt stank OR stunk, pp stunk) vi (smell bad) apestar.

stipulate ['stipjʊleit] vt estipular.

stir [stɜːʳ] *vt (move around, mix)* remover.

stir-fry *n* plato que se fríe en aceite muy caliente y removiendo constantemente.

stirrup ['stɪrəp] *n* estribo *m*.

stitch [stɪtʃ] *n (in sewing, knitting)* punto *m*; **to have a ~** sentir pinchazos ❏ **stitches** *npl (for wound)* puntos *mpl*.

stock [stɒk] *n (of shop, business)* existencias *fpl*; *(supply)* reserva *f*; *(FIN)* capital *m*; *(in cooking)* caldo *m* ◆ *vt (have in stock)* tener, vender; **in ~** en existencia; **out of ~** agotado.

stock cube *n* pastilla *f* de caldo.

stock exchange *n* bolsa *f*.

stocking ['stɒkɪŋ] *n* media *f*.

stock market *n* mercado *m* de valores.

stodgy ['stɒdʒɪ] *adj (food)* indigesto(-ta).

stole [stəʊl] *pt* → **steal**.

stolen ['stəʊln] *pp* → **steal**.

stomach ['stʌmək] *n (organ)* estómago *m*; *(belly)* vientre *m*.

stomachache ['stʌməkeɪk] *n* dolor *m* de estómago.

stomach upset [-'ʌpset] *n* trastorno *m* gástrico.

stone [stəʊn] *n (substance, pebble)* piedra *f*; *(in fruit)* hueso *m*; *(measurement)* = 6,35 kilos; *(gem)* piedra *f* preciosa ◆ *adj* de piedra.

stonewashed ['stəʊnwɒʃt] *adj* lavado(-da) a la piedra.

stood [stʊd] *pt & pp* → **stand**.

stool [stuːl] *n* taburete *m*.

stop [stɒp] *n* parada *f* ◆ *vt* parar; *(prevent)* impedir ◆ *vi* pararse;

(cease) parar; *(stay)* quedarse; **to ~ sb/sthg from doing sthg** impedir que alguien/algo haga algo; **to ~ doing sthg** dejar de hacer algo; **to put a ~ to sthg** poner fin a algo; **"stop"** *(road sign)* "stop"; **"stopping at ..."** *(train, bus)* "con paradas en ..." ❏ **stop off** *vi* hacer una parada.

stopover ['stɒpˌəʊvəʳ] *n* parada *f*.

stopper ['stɒpəʳ] *n* tapón *m*.

stopwatch ['stɒpwɒtʃ] *n* cronómetro *m*.

storage ['stɔːrɪdʒ] *n* almacenamiento *m*.

store [stɔːʳ] *n (shop)* tienda *f*; *(supply)* provisión *f* ◆ *vt* almacenar.

storehouse ['stɔːhaʊs] *pl* -houses] *n* almacén *m*.

storeroom ['stɔːrʊm] *n* almacén *m*.

storey ['stɔːrɪ] *(pl* -s) *n (Br)* planta *f*.

stork [stɔːk] *n* cigüeña *f*.

storm [stɔːm] *n* tormenta *f*.

stormy ['stɔːmɪ] *adj (weather)* tormentoso(-sa).

story ['stɔːrɪ] *n (account, tale)* cuento *m*; *(news item)* artículo *m*; *(Am)* = **storey**.

stout [staʊt] *adj (fat)* corpulento(-ta) ◆ *n (drink)* cerveza *f* negra.

stove [stəʊv] *n (for cooking)* cocina *f*; *(for heating)* estufa *f*.

straight [streɪt] *adj (not curved)* recto(-ta); *(upright, level)* derecho(-cha); *(hair)* liso(-sa); *(consecutive)* consecutivo(-va); *(drink)* solo(-la) ◆ *adv (in a straight line)* en línea recta; *(upright)* derecho;

(directly) directamente; *(without delay)* inmediatamente; **~ ahead** todo derecho; **~ away** enseguida.

straightforward [ˌstreɪt-ˈfɔːwəd] *adj (easy)* sencillo(-lla).

strain [streɪn] *n (force)* presión *f*; *(nervous stress)* tensión *f* nerviosa; *(tension)* tensión; *(injury)* torcedura *f* ◆ *vt (muscle)* torcerse; *(eyes)* cansar; *(food, tea)* colar.

strainer [ˈstreɪnəʳ] *n* colador *m*.

strait [streɪt] *n* estrecho *m*.

strange [streɪndʒ] *adj (unusual)* raro(-ra); *(unfamiliar)* extraño(-ña).

stranger [ˈstreɪndʒəʳ] *n (unfamiliar person)* extraño *m* (-ña *f*); *(person from different place)* forastero *m* (-ra *f*).

strangle [ˈstræŋgl] *vt* estrangular.

strap [stræp] *n (of bag, camera, watch)* correa *f*; *(of dress, bra)* tirante *m*.

strapless [ˈstræplɪs] *adj* sin tirantes.

strategy [ˈstrætɪdʒɪ] *n* estrategia *f*.

Stratford-upon-Avon [ˌstrætfədəpɒnˈeɪvn] *n* Stratford-upon-Avon.

STRATFORD-UPON-AVON

Esta localidad en Warwickshire es famosa por ser el lugar de origen del dramaturgo y poeta William Shakespeare (1564-1616). Hoy, la Royal Shakespeare Company tiene allí su sede y sus representaciones de obras de Shakespeare y otros auto-

res hacen del lugar un centro del teatro británico.

straw [strɔː] *n* paja *f*.

strawberry [ˈstrɔːbərɪ] *n* fresa *f*.

stray [streɪ] *adj (ownerless)* callejero(-ra) ◆ *vi* vagar.

streak [striːk] *n (stripe, mark)* raya *f*; *(period)* racha *f*.

stream [striːm] *n (river)* riachuelo *m*; *(of traffic, people, blood)* torrente *m*.

street [striːt] *n* calle *f*.

streetcar [ˈstriːtkɑːʳ] *n (Am)* tranvía *m*.

street light *n* farola *f*.

street plan *n* callejero *m (mapa)*.

strength [streŋθ] *n (of person, food, drink)* fuerza *f*; *(of structure)* solidez *f*; *(influence)* poder *m*; *(strong point)* punto *m* fuerte; *(of feeling, wind, smell)* intensidad *f*; *(of drug)* potencia *f*.

strengthen [ˈstreŋθn] *vt* reforzar.

stress [stres] *n (tension)* estrés *m inv*; *(on word, syllable)* acento *m* ◆ *vt (emphasize)* recalcar; *(word, syllable)* acentuar.

stretch [stretʃ] *n (of land, water)* extensión *f*; *(of road)* tramo *m*; *(of time)* periodo *m* ◆ *vt (rope, material, body)* estirar; *(elastic, clothes)* estirar *(demasiado)* ◆ *vi (land, sea)* extenderse; *(person, animal)* estirarse; **to ~ one's legs** *(fig)* dar un paseo ◆ *vi (lie down)* tumbarse.

stretch out *vt sep (hand)* alargar ◆ *vi (lie down)* tumbarse.

stretcher [ˈstretʃəʳ] *n* camilla *f*.

strict [strɪkt] *adj* estricto(-ta).

(exact) exacto(-ta).

strictly ['strɪktlɪ] *adv (absolutely)* terminantemente; *(exclusively)* exclusivamente; **~ speaking** realmente.

stride [straɪd] *n* zancada *f*.

strike [straɪk] *(pt & pp* struck*) n (of employees)* huelga *f* ♦ *vt (fml: hit)* pegar; *(fml: collide with)* chocar contra; *(a match)* encender ♦ *vi (refuse to work)* estar en huelga; *(happen suddenly)* sobrevenir; **the clock struck eight** el reloj dio las ocho.

striking ['straɪkɪŋ] *adj (noticeable)* chocante; *(attractive)* atractivo(-va).

string [strɪŋ] *n* cuerda *f*; *(of pearls, beads)* sarta *f*; *(series)* serie *f*; **a piece of ~** una cuerda.

strip [strɪp] *n (of paper, cloth etc)* tira *f*; *(of land, water)* franja *f* ♦ *vt (paint, wallpaper)* quitar ♦ *vi (undress)* desnudarse.

stripe [straɪp] *n (of colour)* raya *f*.

striped [straɪpt] *adj* a rayas.

strip-search *vt* registrar exhaustivamente, haciendo que se quite la ropa.

strip show *n* espectáculo *m* de striptease.

stroke [strəʊk] *n (MED)* derrame *m* cerebral; *(in tennis, golf)* golpe *m*; *(swimming style)* estilo *m* ♦ *vt* acariciar, **a ~ of luck** un golpe de suerte.

stroll [strəʊl] *n* paseo *m*.

stroller ['strəʊlər] *n (Am: pushchair)* sillita *f* de niño).

strong [strɒŋ] *adj* fuerte; *(structure, bridge, chair)* resistente; *(influential)* poderoso(-sa); *(possibility)* serio(-ria); *(drug)* potente;

(accent) marcado(-da); *(point, subject)* mejor.

struck [strʌk] *pt & pp* → **strike**.

structure ['strʌktʃər] *n (arrangement, organization)* estructura *f*; *(building)* construcción *f*.

struggle ['strʌgl] *n (great effort)* lucha *f* ♦ *vi (fight)* luchar; *(in order to get free)* forcejear; **to ~ to do sthg** esforzarse en hacer algo.

stub [stʌb] *n (of cigarette)* colilla *f*; *(of cheque)* matriz *f*; *(of ticket)* resguardo *m*.

stubble ['stʌbl] *n (on face)* barba *f* de tres días.

stubborn ['stʌbən] *adj* terco (-ca).

stuck [stʌk] *pt & pp* → **stick** ♦ *adj (jammed, unable to continue)* atascado(-da); *(stranded)* colgado(-da).

stud [stʌd] *n (on boots)* taco *m*; *(fastener)* automático *m*; *(earring)* pendiente *m* (pequeño).

student ['stjuːdnt] *n* estudiante *mf*.

student card *n* carné *m* de estudiante.

students' union [,stjuːdnts-] *n (place)* club *m* de alumnos.

studio ['stjuːdɪəʊ] *(pl* -s*) n* estudio *m*.

studio apartment *(Am)* = **studio flat**.

studio flat *n (Br)* estudio *m*.

study ['stʌdɪ] *n* estudio *m* ♦ *vt (learn about)* estudiar; *(examine)* examinar ♦ *vi* estudiar.

stuff [stʌf] *n (inf) (substance)* cosa *f*, sustancia *f*; *(things, possessions)* cosas *fpl* ♦ *vt (put roughly)* meter; *(fill)* rellenar.

stuffed [stʌft] adj (food) relleno(-na); (inf: full up) lleno(-na); (dead animal) disecado(-da).

stuffing ['stʌfɪŋ] n relleno m.

stuffy ['stʌfɪ] adj (room, atmosphere) cargado(-da).

stumble ['stʌmbl] vi (when walking) tropezar.

stump [stʌmp] n (of tree) tocón m.

stun [stʌn] vt aturdir.

stung [stʌŋ] pt & pp → **sting**.

stunk [stʌŋk] pt & pp → **stink**.

stunning ['stʌnɪŋ] adj (very beautiful) imponente; (very surprising) pasmoso(-sa).

stupid ['stju:pɪd] adj (foolish) estúpido(-da); (inf: annoying) puñetero(-ra).

sturdy ['stɜ:dɪ] adj robusto(-ta).

stutter ['stʌtəʳ] vi tartamudear.

sty [staɪ] n pocilga f.

style [staɪl] n (manner) estilo m; (elegance) clase f; (design) modelo m ♦ vt (hair) peinar.

stylish ['staɪlɪʃ] adj elegante.

stylist ['staɪlɪst] n (hairdresser) peluquero m (-ra f).

sub [sʌb] n (inf) (substitute) reserva mf; (Br: subscription) suscripción f.

subdued [səb'dju:d] adj (person, colour) apagado(-da); (lighting) tenue.

subject [n 'sʌbdʒekt, vb səb'dʒekt] n (topic) tema m; (at school, university) asignatura f; (GRAMM) sujeto m; (fml: of country) ciudadano m (-na f) ♦ vt: **to ~ sb to sthg** someter a alguien a algo; **~ to availability** hasta fin de existencias;

they are ~ **to an additional charge** están sujetos a un suplemento.

subjunctive [səb'dʒʌŋktɪv] n subjuntivo m.

submarine [,sʌbmə'ri:n] n submarino m.

submit [səb'mɪt] vt presentar ♦ vi rendirse.

subordinate [sə'bɔ:dɪnət] adj (GRAMM) subordinado(-da).

subscribe [səb'skraɪb] vi (to magazine, newspaper) suscribirse.

subscription [səb'skrɪpʃn] n suscripción f.

subsequent ['sʌbsɪkwənt] adj subsiguiente.

subside [səb'saɪd] vi (ground) hundirse; (noise, feeling) apagarse.

substance ['sʌbstəns] n sustancia f.

substantial [səb'stænʃl] adj (large) sustancial.

substitute ['sʌbstɪtju:t] n (replacement) sustituto m (-ta f); (SPORT) suplente mf.

subtitles ['sʌb,taɪtlz] npl subtítulos mpl.

subtle ['sʌtl] adj (difference, change) sutil; (person, plan) ingenioso(-sa).

subtract [səb'trækt] vt restar.

subtraction [səb'trækʃn] n resta f.

suburb ['sʌbɜ:b] n barrio m residencial; **the ~s** las afueras.

subway ['sʌbweɪ] n (Br: for pedestrians) paso m subterráneo; (Am: underground railway) metro m.

succeed [sək'si:d] vi (be successful) tener éxito ♦ vt (fml) suceder a; **to ~ in doing sthg** conseguir hacer algo.

success [sək'ses] *n* éxito *m*.

successful [sək'sesful] *adj (plan, attempt)* afortunado(-da); *(film, book, person)* de éxito; *(politician, actor)* popular.

succulent ['sʌkjulənt] *adj* suculento(-ta).

such [sʌtʃ] *adj (of stated kind)* tal, semejante; *(so great)* tal ♦ *adv*: ~ **a lot** tanto; ~ **a lot of books** tantos libros; **it's ~ a lovely day** hace un día tan bonito; ~ **a thing should never have happened** tal cosa nunca debería de haber pasado; ~ **as** tales como.

suck [sʌk] *vt* chupar.

sudden ['sʌdn] *adj* repentino(-na); **all of a ~** de repente.

suddenly ['sʌdnlɪ] *adv* de repente.

sue [su:] *vt* demandar.

suede [sweɪd] *n* ante *m*.

suffer ['sʌfə*r*] *vt* sufrir ♦ *vi* sufrir; *(experience bad effects)* salir perjudicado; **to ~ from** *(illness)* padecer.

suffering ['sʌfrɪŋ] *n (mental)* sufrimiento *m*; *(physical)* dolor *m*.

sufficient [sə'fɪʃnt] *adj (fml)* suficiente.

sufficiently [sə'fɪʃntlɪ] *adv (fml)* suficientemente.

suffix ['sʌfɪks] *n* sufijo *m*.

suffocate ['sʌfəkeɪt] *vi* asfixiarse.

sugar ['ʃugə*r*] *n* azúcar *m*.

suggest [sə'dʒest] *vt (propose)* sugerir; **to ~ doing sthg** sugerir hacer algo.

suggestion [sə'dʒestʃn] *n (proposal)* sugerencia *f*; *(hint)* asomo *m*.

suicide ['suɪsaɪd] *n* suicidio *m*; **to commit ~** suicidarse.

suit [su:t] *n (man's clothes)* traje *m*; *(woman's clothes)* traje de chaqueta; *(in cards)* palo *m*; *(JUR)* pleito *m* ♦ *vt (subj: clothes, colour, shoes)* favorecer; *(be convenient for)* convenir; *(be appropriate for)* ser adecuado para; **to be ~ed to** ser apropiado para.

suitable ['su:təbl] *adj* adecuado(-da); **to be ~ for** ser adecuado para.

suitcase ['su:tkeɪs] *n* maleta *f*.

suite [swi:t] *n (set of rooms)* suite *f*; *(furniture)* juego *m*.

sulk [sʌlk] *vi* estar de mal humor.

sultana [səl'tɑ:nə] *n (Br: raisin)* pasa *f* de Esmirna.

sultry ['sʌltrɪ] *adj (weather, climate)* bochornoso(-sa).

sum [sʌm] *n* suma *f* ❑ **sum up** *vt sep (summarize)* resumir.

summarize ['sʌmaraɪz] *vt* resumir.

summary ['sʌmərɪ] *n* resumen *m*.

summer ['sʌmə*r*] *n* verano *m*; **in (the) ~** en verano; ~ **holidays** *fpl* vacaciones *fpl* de verano.

summertime ['sʌmətaɪm] *n* verano *m*.

summit ['sʌmɪt] *n (of mountain)* cima *f*; *(meeting)* cumbre *f*.

summon ['sʌmən] *vt (send for)* llamar; *(JUR)* citar.

sumptuous ['sʌmptʃʊəs] *adj* suntuoso(-sa).

sun [sʌn] *n* sol *m* ♦ *vt*: **to ~ o.s.** tomar el sol; **to catch the ~** coger color; **in the ~** al sol; **out of the ~** en la sombra.

Sun. *(abbr of Sunday)* dom.

sunbathe ['sʌnbeɪð] *vi* tomar el sol.

sunbed ['sʌnbed] *n* camilla *f* de rayos ultravioletas.

sun block *n* pantalla *f* solar.

sunburn ['sʌnbɜːn] *n* quemadura *f* de sol.

sunburnt ['sʌnbɜːnt] *adj* quemado(-da) (por el sol).

sundae ['sʌndeɪ] *n* helado con salsa, nata montada y nueces.

Sunday ['sʌndɪ] *n* domingo *m*, → Saturday.

Sunday school *n* catequesis *f* inv.

sundress ['sʌndres] *n* vestido *m* de playa.

sundries ['sʌndrɪz] *npl* artículos *mpl* diversos.

sunflower ['sʌnˌflaʊəʳ] *n* girasol *m*.

sunflower oil *n* aceite *m* de girasol.

sung [sʌŋ] *pt* → sing.

sunglasses ['sʌnˌglɑːsɪz] *npl* gafas *fpl* de sol.

sunhat ['sʌnhæt] *n* pamela *f*.

sunk [sʌŋk] *pp* → sink.

sunlight ['sʌnlaɪt] *n* luz *f* del sol.

sun lounger [-ˌlaʊndʒəʳ] *n* tumbona *f*.

sunny ['sʌnɪ] *adj* soleado(-da); it's ~ hace sol.

sunrise ['sʌnraɪz] *n* amanecer *m*.

sunroof ['sʌnruːf] *n* (on car) techo *m* corredizo.

sunset ['sʌnset] *n* anochecer *m*.

sunshine ['sʌnʃaɪn] *n* luz *f* del sol; in the ~ al sol.

sunstroke ['sʌnstrəʊk] *n* insolación *f*.

suntan ['sʌntæn] *n* bronceado *m*.

suntan cream *n* crema *f* bronceadora.

suntan lotion *n* loción *f* bronceadora.

super ['suːpəʳ] *adj* fenomenal ♦ *n* (petrol) gasolina *f* súper.

superb [suː'pɜːb] *adj* excelente.

superficial [ˌsuːpə'fɪʃl] *adj* superficial.

superfluous [suː'pɜːfluəs] *adj* superfluo(-flua).

Superglue® ['suːpəgluː] *n* pegamento *m* rápido.

superior [suː'pɪərɪəʳ] *adj* superior ♦ *n* superior *mf*.

supermarket ['suːpəˌmɑːkɪt] *n* supermercado *m*.

supernatural [ˌsuːpə'nætʃrəl] *adj* sobrenatural.

Super Saver® *n* (Br) billete de tren de precio muy reducido.

superstitious [ˌsuːpə'stɪʃəs] *adj* supersticioso(-sa).

superstore ['suːpəstɔːʳ] *n* hipermercado *m*.

supervise ['suːpəvaɪz] *vt* supervisar.

supervisor ['suːpəvaɪzəʳ] *n* supervisor *m* (-ra *f*).

supper ['sʌpəʳ] *n* cena *f*.

supple ['sʌpl] *adj* flexible.

supplement [*n* 'sʌplɪmənt, *vb* 'sʌplɪment] *n* suplemento *m*; (of diet) complemento *m* ♦ *vt* complementar.

supplementary [ˌsʌplɪ'mentərɪ] *adj* suplementario(-ria).

supply [sə'plaɪ] *n* suministro *m* ♦

283

vt suministrar; **to ~ sb with sthg** proveer a alguien de algo ❑ **supplies** *npl* provisiones *fpl*.

support [sə'pɔ:t] *n (backing, encouragement)* apoyo *m; (supporting object)* soporte *m* ◆ *vt (cause, campaign, person)* apoyar; *(SPORT)* seguir; *(hold up)* soportar; *(financially)* financiar.

supporter [sə'pɔ:tə^r] *n (SPORT)* hincha *mf; (of cause, political party)* partidario *m* (-ria *f*).

suppose [sə'pəʊz] *vt* suponer ◆ *conj* = **supposing; I ~ so** supongo que sí; **it's ~d to be good** se dice que es bueno; **it was ~d to arrive yesterday** debería haber llegado ayer.

supposing [sə'pəʊzɪŋ] *conj* si, suponiendo que.

supreme [sʊ'pri:m] *adj* supremo(-ma).

surcharge ['sɜ:tʃɑ:dʒ] *n* recargo *m*.

sure [ʃʊə^r] *adj* seguro(-ra) ◆ *adv (inf)* por supuesto; **to be ~ of o.s.** estar seguro de sí mismo; **to make ~ (that)** asegurarse de que; **for ~** a ciencia cierta.

surely ['ʃʊəlɪ] *adv* sin duda.

surf [sɜ:f] *n* espuma *f* ◆ *vi* hacer surf.

surface ['sɜ:fɪs] *n* superficie *f*.

surface area *n* área *f* de la superficie.

surface mail *n* correo *m* por vía terrestre y marítima.

surfboard ['sɜ:fbɔ:d] *n* tabla *f* de surf.

surfing ['sɜ:fɪŋ] *n* surf *m*; **to go ~** hacer surf.

surgeon ['sɜ:dʒən] *n* cirujano *m* (-na *f*).

surgery ['sɜ:dʒərɪ] *n (treatment)* cirugía *f; (Br: building)* consultorio *m; (Br: period)* consulta *f*.

surname ['sɜ:neɪm] *n* apellido *m*.

surplus ['sɜ:pləs] *n* excedente *m*.

surprise [sə'praɪz] *n* sorpresa *f* ◆ *vt (astonish)* sorprender.

surprised [sə'praɪzd] *adj* asombrado(-da).

surprising [sə'praɪzɪŋ] *adj* sorprendente.

surrender [sə'rendə^r] *vi* rendirse ◆ *vt (fml: hand over)* entregar.

surround [sə'raʊnd] *vt* rodear.

surrounding [sə'raʊndɪŋ] *adj* circundante ❑ **surroundings** *npl* alrededores *mpl*.

survey ['sɜ:veɪ] *(pl -s) n (investigation)* investigación *f; (poll)* encuesta *f; (of land)* medición *f; (Br: of house)* inspección *f*.

surveyor [sə'veɪə^r] *n (Br: of houses)* perito *m* tasador de la propiedad; *(of land)* agrimensor *m* (-ra *f*).

survival [sə'vaɪvl] *n* supervivencia *f*.

survive [sə'vaɪv] *vi* sobrevivir ◆ *vt* sobrevivir a.

survivor [sə'vaɪvə^r] *n* superviviente *mf*.

suspect [*vb* sə'spekt, *n & adj* 'sʌspekt] *vt (believe)* imaginar, *(mistrust)* sospechar ◆ *n* sospechoso *m* (-sa *f*) ◆ *adj* sospechoso(-sa); **to ~ sb of sthg** considerar a alguien sospechoso de algo.

suspend [sə'spend] *vt* suspender; *(from team, school, work)* expulsar temporalmente.

suspender belt [sə'spendə-] n liguero m.

suspenders [sə'spendəz] npl (Br: for stockings) ligas fpl; (Am: for trousers) tirantes mpl.

suspense [sə'spens] n suspense m.

suspension [sə'spenʃn] n (of vehicle) suspensión f; (from team, school, work) expulsión f temporal.

suspicion [sə'spiʃn] n (mistrust) recelo m; (idea) sospecha f; (trace) pizca f.

suspicious [sə'spiʃəs] adj (behaviour, situation) sospechoso(-sa); to be ~ (of) ser receloso(-sa) (de).

swallow ['swɒləʊ] n (bird) golondrina f ◆ vt & vi tragar.

swam [swæm] pt → swim.

swamp [swɒmp] n pantano m.

swan [swɒn] n cisne m.

swap [swɒp] vt (possessions, places) cambiar; (ideas, stories) intercambiar; to ~ sthg for sthg cambiar algo por algo.

swarm [swɔːm] n (of bees) enjambre m.

swear [sweəʳ] (pt swore, pp sworn) vi jurar ◆ vt: to ~ to do sthg jurar hacer algo.

swearword ['sweəwɜːd] n palabrota f.

sweat [swet] n sudor m ◆ vi sudar.

sweater ['swetəʳ] n suéter m.

sweatshirt ['swetʃɜːt] n sudadera f.

swede [swiːd] n (Br) nabo m sueco.

Swede [swiːd] n sueco m (-ca f).

Sweden ['swiːdn] n Suecia.

Swedish ['swiːdiʃ] adj sueco(-ca) ◆ n (language) sueco m ◆ npl: the ~ los suecos.

sweep [swiːp] (pt & pp swept) vt (with brush, broom) barrer.

sweet [swiːt] adj (food, drink) dulce; (smell) fragante; (person, nature) amable ◆ n (Br) (candy) caramelo m; (dessert) postre m.

sweet-and-sour adj agridulce.

sweet corn n maíz m.

sweetener ['swiːtnəʳ] n (for drink) edulcorante m.

sweet potato n batata f.

sweet shop n (Br) confitería f.

swell [swel] (pt -ed, pp swollen OR -ed) vi (ankle, arm etc) hincharse.

swelling ['swelɪŋ] n hinchazón f.

swept [swept] pt & pp → sweep.

swerve [swɜːv] vi virar bruscamente.

swig [swɪg] n (inf) trago m.

swim [swɪm] (pt swam, pp swum) n baño m ◆ vi nadar; to go for a ~ ir a nadar.

swimmer ['swɪməʳ] n nadador m (-ra f).

swimming ['swɪmɪŋ] n natación f; to go ~ ir a nadar.

swimming baths npl (Br) piscina f municipal.

swimming cap n gorro m de baño.

swimming costume n (Br) traje m de baño.

swimming pool n piscina f.

swimming trunks npl bañador m.

swimsuit ['swɪmsuːt] n traje m

de baño.

swindle ['swɪndl] n estafa f.

swing [swɪŋ] (pt & pp swung) n (for children) columpio m ◆ vt (move from side to side) balancear ◆ vi (move from side to side) balancearse.

swipe [swaɪp] vt (credit card etc) pasar por el datáfono.

Swiss [swɪs] adj suizo(-za) ◆ n (person) suizo m (-za f) ◆ npl: **the ~** los suizos.

Swiss cheese n queso m suizo.

swiss roll n brazo m de gitano.

switch [swɪtʃ] n (for light, power, television) interruptor m ◆ vt (change) cambiar de; (exchange) intercambiar ◆ vi cambiar □ **switch off** vt sep apagar, **switch on** vi sep encender.

switchboard ['swɪtʃbɔːd] n centralita f.

Switzerland ['swɪtsələnd] n Suiza.

swivel ['swɪvl] vi girar.

swollen ['swəʊln] pp → swell ◆ adj hinchado(-da).

swop [swɒp] = swap.

sword [sɔːd] n espada f.

swordfish ['sɔːdfɪʃ] (pl inv) n pez m espada.

swore [swɔːr] pt → swear.

sworn [swɔːn] pp → swear.

swum [swʌm] pp → swim.

swung [swʌŋ] pt & pp → swing.

syllabi ['sɪləbaɪ] pl → syllabus.

syllable ['sɪləbl] n sílaba f.

syllabus ['sɪləbəs] (pl -buses OR -bi) n programa m (de estudios).

symbol ['sɪmbl] n símbolo m.

sympathetic [,sɪmpə'θetɪk] adj (understanding) comprensivo(-va).

sympathize ['sɪmpəθaɪz] vi: **to ~ (with)** (feel sorry) compadecerse (de); (understand) comprender.

sympathy ['sɪmpəθɪ] n (understanding) comprensión f; (compassion) compasión f.

symphony ['sɪmfənɪ] n sinfonía f.

symptom ['sɪmptəm] n síntoma m.

synagogue ['sɪnəgɒg] n sinagoga f.

synthesizer ['sɪnθəsaɪzər] n sintetizador m.

synthetic [sɪn'θetɪk] adj sintético(-ca).

syringe [sɪ'rɪndʒ] n jeringa f.

syrup ['sɪrəp] n (for fruit etc) almíbar m.

system ['sɪstəm] n sistema m; (for gas, heating etc) instalación f.

ta [taː] excl (Br: inf) ¡gracias!

tab [tæb] n (of cloth, paper etc) lengüeta f; (bill) cuenta f; **put it on my ~** póngalo en mi cuenta.

table ['teɪbl] n (piece of furniture) mesa f; (of figures etc) tabla f.

tablecloth ['teɪblklɒθ] n mantel m.

tablemat ['teɪblmæt] n salvamanteles m inv.

tablespoon ['teɪblspuːn] n

tablet

(spoon) cuchara *f* grande (para servir); *(amount)* cucharada *f* grande.

tablet ['tæblɪt] *n* pastilla *f*.

table tennis *n* tenis *m* de mesa.

table wine *n* vino *m* de mesa.

tabloid ['tæblɔɪd] *n* periódico *m* sensacionalista.

tack [tæk] *n (nail)* tachuela *f*.

tackle ['tækl] *n (SPORT)* entrada *f*; *(for fishing)* aparejos *mpl* ◆ *vt (SPORT)* entrar; *(deal with)* abordar.

tacky ['tækɪ] *adj (inf: jewellery, design etc)* cutre.

taco ['tækəʊ] *(pl* -s*) n* taco *m*.

tact [tækt] *n* tacto *m*.

tactful ['tæktful] *adj* discreto(-ta).

tactics ['tæktɪks] *npl* táctica *f*.

tag [tæg] *n (label)* etiqueta *f*.

tagliatelle [ˌtæɡljə'telɪ] *n* tallarines *mpl*.

tail [teɪl] *n* cola *f* (□ **tails** *n (of coin)* cruz *f* ◆ *npl (formal dress)* frac *m*.

tailgate ['teɪlɡeɪt] *n* portón *m*.

tailor ['teɪlə'] *n* sastre *m*.

Taiwan [ˌtaɪ'wɑːn] *n* Taiwán.

take [teɪk] *(pt* took*, pp* taken*) vt*
1. *(gen)* tomar.
2. *(carry, drive)* llevar.
3. *(hold, grasp)* coger, agarrar *(Amér)*.
4. *(do, make):* **to ~ a bath** bañarse; **to ~ an exam** hacer un examen; **to ~ a photo** sacar una foto.
5. *(require)* requerir; **how long will it ~?** ¿cuánto tiempo tardará?
6. *(steal)* quitar.
7. *(size in clothes, shoes)* usar; **what size do you ~?** ¿qué talla/número usas?

8. *(subtract)* restar.
9. *(accept)* aceptar; **do you ~ traveller's cheques?** ¿acepta cheques de viaje?; **to ~ sb's advice** seguir los consejos de alguien.
10. *(contain)* tener cabida para.
11. *(react to)* tomarse.
12. *(tolerate)* soportar.
13. *(assume):* **I ~ it that ...** supongo que ...
14. *(rent)* alquilar.
□ **take apart** *vt sep (remove)* desmontar.
take away *vt sep (remove)* quitar; *(subtract)* restar; **take back** *vt sep (return)* devolver; *(accept)* aceptar la devolución de; *(statement)* retirar.
take down *vt sep (picture, curtains)* descolgar; **take in** *vt sep (include)* abarcar; *(understand)* entender; *(deceive)* engañar; **~ this dress in** mete un poco en este vestido; **take off** *vt sep (remove)* quitar; *(clothes)* quitarse; *(as holiday)* tomarse libre ◆ *vi (plane)* despegar; **take out** *vt sep (from container, pocket, library)* sacar; *(insurance policy)* hacerse; *(loan)* conseguir; **to ~ sb out to dinner** invitar a alguien a cenar; **take over** *vi* tomar el relevo; **take up** *vt sep (begin)* dedicarse a; *(use up)* ocupar; *(trousers, skirt, dress)* acortar.

takeaway ['teɪkəˌweɪ] *n (Br) (shop)* tienda *f* de comida para llevar; *(food)* comida *f* para llevar.

taken ['teɪkn] *pp* → **take**.

takeoff ['teɪkɒf] *n (of plane)* despegue *m*.

takeout ['teɪkaʊt] *(Am)* = **takeaway**.

takings ['teɪkɪŋz] *npl* recaudación *f*.

talcum powder ['tælkəm-] *n*

taxi rank

talco m.

tale [teɪl] n (story) cuento m; (account) anécdota f.

talent ['tælənt] n talento m.

talk [tɔːk] n (conversation) conversación f; (speech) charla ♦ vi hablar; **to ~ to sb** (about sth) hablar con alguien (sobre algo); **to ~ with sb** hablar con alguien ❑ **talks** npl conversaciones fpl.

talkative ['tɔːkətɪv] adj hablador(-ra).

tall [tɔːl] adj alto(-ta); **how ~ are you?** ¿cuánto mides?; **I'm 2 metres ~** mido dos metros.

tame [teɪm] adj (animal) doméstico(-ca).

tampon ['tæmpɒn] n tampón m.

tan [tæn] n (suntan) bronceado m ♦ vi broncearse ♦ adj (colour) de color marrón claro.

tangerine [ˌtændʒəˈriːn] n mandarina f.

tank [tæŋk] n (container) depósito m; (vehicle) tanque m.

tanker ['tæŋkəʳ] n (truck) camión m cisterna.

tanned [tænd] adj (suntanned) bronceado(-da).

tap [tæp] n (for water) grifo m ♦ vt (hit) golpear ligeramente.

tape [teɪp] n cinta f; (adhesive material) cinta adhesiva ♦ vt (record) grabar; (stick) pegar.

tape measure n cinta f métrica.

tape recorder n magnetófono m.

tapestry ['tæpɪstrɪ] n tapiz m.

tap water n agua f del grifo.

tar [tɑːʳ] n alquitrán m.

target ['tɑːgɪt] n (in archery, shooting) blanco m; (MIL) objetivo m.

tariff ['tærɪf] n (price list) tarifa f, lista f de precios; (Br: menu) menú m; (at customs) arancel m.

tarmac ['tɑːmæk] n (at airport) pista f ❑ **Tarmac®** n (on road) alquitrán m.

tarpaulin [tɑːˈpɔːlɪn] n lona f alquitranada.

tart [tɑːt] n (sweet) tarta f.

tartan ['tɑːtn] n tartán m.

tartare sauce [ˌtɑːtə-] n salsa f tártara.

task [tɑːsk] n tarea f.

taste [teɪst] n (flavour) sabor m; (discernment, sense) gusto m ♦ vt (sample) probar; (detect) notar un sabor a ♦ vi: **to ~ of sth** saber a algo; **it ~s bad** sabe mal; **it ~s good** sabe bien; **to have a ~ of sth** probar algo; **bad ~** mal gusto; **good ~** buen gusto.

tasteful ['teɪstfʊl] adj de buen gusto.

tasteless ['teɪstlɪs] adj (food) soso(-sa); (comment, decoration) de mal gusto.

tasty ['teɪstɪ] adj sabroso(-sa).

tattoo [tæˈtuː] n (pl -s) n (on skin) tatuaje m; (military display) desfile m militar.

taught [tɔːt] pt & pp → **teach**.

Taurus ['tɔːrəs] n Tauro m.

taut [tɔːt] adj tenso(-sa).

tax [tæks] n impuesto m ♦ vt (goods, person) gravar.

tax disc n (Br) pegatina del impuesto de circulación.

tax-free adj libre de impuestos.

taxi ['tæksɪ] n taxi m ♦ vi (plane) rodar por la pista.

taxi driver n taxista mf.

taxi rank n (Br) parada f de taxis.

taxi stand *(Am)* = taxi rank.

T-bone steak ['ti:-] *n* chuleta de carne de vaca con un hueso en forma de T.

tea [ti:] *n* té *m*; *(herbal)* infusión *f*; *(afternoon meal)* = merienda *f*; *(evening meal)* = merienda cena.

tea bag *n* bolsita *f* de té.

teacake ['ti:keɪk] *n* bollo *m* con pasas.

teach [ti:tʃ] *(pt & pp* **taught)** *vt* enseñar ◆ *vi* ser profesor; **to ~ sb sthg, to ~ sthg to sb** enseñar algo a alguien; **to ~ sb (how) to do sthg** enseñar a alguien a hacer algo.

teacher ['ti:tʃər] *n (in secondary school)* profesor *m* (-ra *f*); *(in primary school)* maestro *m* (-ra *f*).

teaching ['ti:tʃɪŋ] *n* enseñanza *f*.

tea cloth = tea towel.

teacup ['ti:kʌp] *n* taza *f* de té.

team [ti:m] *n* equipo *m*.

teapot ['ti:pɒt] *n* tetera *f*.

tear[1] [teər] *(pt* **tore,** *pp* **torn)** *vt (rip)* rasgar ◆ *vi (rip)* romperse; *(move quickly)* ir a toda pastilla ◆ *n (rip)* rasgón *m* ❏ **tear up** *vt sep* hacer pedazos.

tear[2] [tɪər] *n* lágrima *f*.

tearoom ['tɪrum] *n* salón *m* de té.

tease [ti:z] *vt* tomar el pelo.

tea set *n* juego *m* de té.

teaspoon ['ti:spu:n] *n (utensil)* cucharilla *f*; *(amount)* = teaspoonful.

teaspoonful ['ti:spu:n,fʊl] *n* cucharadita *f*.

teat [ti:t] *n (of animal)* teta *f*; *(Br: of bottle)* tetina *f*.

teatime ['ti:taɪm] *n* hora *f* de la merienda cena.

tea towel *n* paño *m* de cocina.

technical ['teknɪkl] *adj* técnico(-ca).

technical drawing *n* dibujo *m* técnico.

technicality [,teknɪ'kælətɪ] *n (detail)* detalle *m* técnico.

technician [tek'nɪʃn] *n* técnico *m* (-ca *f*).

technique [tek'ni:k] *n* técnica *f*.

technological [,teknə'lɒdʒɪkl] *adj* tecnológico(-ca).

technology [tek'nɒlədʒɪ] *n* tecnología *f*.

teddy (bear) ['tedɪ-] *n* oso *m* de peluche.

tedious ['ti:djəs] *adj* tedioso(-sa).

tee [ti:] *n* tee *m*.

teenager ['ti:n,eɪdʒər] *n* adolescente *mf*.

teeth [ti:θ] *pl* → tooth.

teethe [ti:ð] *vi*: **to be teething** estar echando los dientes.

teetotal [ti:'təʊtl] *adj* abstemio(-mia).

telegram ['telɪgræm] *n* telegrama *m*.

telegraph ['telɪgrɑ:f] *n* telégrafo *m* ◆ *vt* telegrafiar.

telegraph pole *n* poste *m* de telégrafos.

telephone ['telɪfəʊn] *n* teléfono *m* ◆ *vt & vi* telefonear; **to be on the ~** *(talking)* estar al teléfono; *(connected)* tener teléfono.

telephone booth *n* teléfono *m* público.

telephone box *n* cabina *f* telefónica.

telephone call *n* llamada *f* telefónica.

telephone directory *n* guía *f* telefónica.

telephone number *n* número m de teléfono.

telephonist [tɪˈlefənɪst] n (Br)
telefonista mf.

telephoto lens [ˌtelɪˈfəʊtəʊ-] n
teleobjetivo m.

telescope [ˈtelɪskəʊp] n telescopio m.

television [ˈtelɪˌvɪʒn] n televisión f; **on (the) ~** en la televisión.

telex [ˈteleks] n télex m inv.

tell [tel] (pt & pp **told**) vt decir;
(story, joke) contar ◆ vi: **I can't ~** no
lo sé; **can you ~ me the time?** ¿me
puedes decir la hora?; **to ~ sb sthg**
decir algo a alguien; **to ~ sb about**
sthg contar a alguien acerca de
algo; **to ~ sb how to do sthg** decir
a alguien cómo hacer algo; **to ~ sb**
to do sthg decir a alguien que
haga algo; **to be able to ~ sthg**
saber algo ❑ **tell off** vt sep reñir.

teller [ˈtelər] n (in bank) cajero m
(-ra f)

telly [ˈtelɪ] n (Br: inf) tele f.

temp [temp] n secretario m eventual (secretaria f eventual) ◆ vi trabajar de eventual.

temper [ˈtempər] n (character)
temperamento m; **to be in a ~**
estar de mal humor; **to lose one's**
~ perder la paciencia.

temperature [ˈtemprətʃər] n
(heat, cold) temperatura f; (MED) fiebre f; **to have a ~** tener fiebre.

temple [ˈtempl] n (building) templo m; (of forehead) sien f.

temporary [ˈtempərərɪ] adj
temporal.

tempt [tempt] vt tentar; **to be**
~ed to do sthg sentirse tentado de
hacer algo.

temptation [tempˈteɪʃn] n tentación f.

tempting [ˈtemptɪŋ] adj tenta-
dor(-ra).

ten [ten] num diez, → **six**.

tenant [ˈtenənt] n inquilino m
(-na f).

tend [tend] vi: **to ~ to do sthg**
soler hacer algo.

tendency [ˈtendənsɪ] n (trend)
tendencia f; (inclination) inclinación f.

tender [ˈtendər] adj tierno(-na);
(sore) dolorido(-da) ◆ vt (fml: pay)
pagar.

tendon [ˈtendən] n tendón m.

tenement [ˈtenəmənt] n bloque
de viviendas modestas.

Tenerife [ˌtenəˈriːf] n Tenerife.

tennis [ˈtenɪs] n tenis m.

tennis ball n pelota f de tenis.

tennis court n pista f de tenis.

tennis racket n raqueta f de
tenis.

tenpin bowling [ˈtenpɪn-] n
(Br) bolos mpl.

tenpins [ˈtenpɪnz] (Am) = **tenpin**
bowling.

tense [tens] adj tenso(-sa) ◆ n
tiempo m.

tension [ˈtenʃn] n tensión f.

tent [tent] n tienda f de campaña.

tenth [tenθ] num décimo(-ma),
→ **sixth**.

tent peg n estaca f.

tepid [ˈtepɪd] adj tibio(-bia).

tequila [tɪˈkiːlə] n tequila m.

term [tɜːm] n (word, expression)
término m; (at school, university) trimestre m; **in the long ~** a largo
plazo; **in the short ~** a corto
plazo; **in ~s of** por lo que se refiere a; **in business ~s** en términos de
negocios ❑ **terms** npl (of contract)

condiciones *fpl*; *(price)* precio *m*.

terminal ['tɜːmɪnl] *adj* terminal ♦ *n (for buses, at airport)* terminal *f*; *(COMPUT)* terminal *m*.

terminate ['tɜːmɪneɪt] *vi (train, bus)* finalizar el trayecto.

terminus ['tɜːmɪnəs] *(pl* **-ni** [-naɪ] OR **-nuses)** *n* terminal *f*.

terrace ['terəs] *n (patio)* terraza *f*; **the ~s** *(at football ground)* las gradas.

terraced house ['terəst-] *n (Br)* casa *f* adosada.

terrible ['terəbl] *adj (very bad, very ill)* fatal; *(very great)* terrible.

terribly ['terəblɪ] *adv (extremely)* terriblemente; *(very badly)* fatalmente.

terrier ['terɪəʳ] *n* terrier *m*.

terrific [təˈrɪfɪk] *adj (inf) (very good)* estupendo(-da); *(very great)* enorme.

terrified ['terɪfaɪd] *adj* aterrorizado(-da).

territory ['terɪtrɪ] *n (political area)* territorio *m*; *(terrain)* terreno *m*.

terror ['terəʳ] *n (fear)* terror *m*.

terrorism ['terərɪzm] *n* terrorismo *m*.

terrorist ['terərɪst] *n* terrorista *mf*.

terrorize ['terəraɪz] *vt* aterrorizar.

test [test] *n (exam)* examen *m*; *(check)* prueba *f*; *(of blood)* análisis *m inv*; *(of eyes)* revisión *f* ♦ *vt (check, try out)* probar; *(give exam to)* examinar.

testicles ['testɪklz] *npl* testículos *mpl*.

tetanus ['tetənəs] *n* tétanos *m inv*.

text [tekst] *n (written material)* texto *m*; *(textbook)* libro *m* de texto.

textbook ['tekstbʊk] *n* libro *m* de texto.

textile ['tekstaɪl] *n* textil *m*.

texture ['tekstʃəʳ] *n* textura *f*.

Thai [taɪ] *adj* tailandés(-esa).

Thailand ['taɪlænd] *n* Tailandia.

Thames [temz] *n*: **the ~** el Támesis.

than [weak form ðən, strong form ðæn] *prep, conj* que; **you're better** ~ **me** eres mejor que yo; **I'd rather stay in** ~ **go out** prefiero quedarme antes que salir; **more** ~ **ten** más de diez.

thank [θæŋk] *vt*: **to** ~ **sb (for sthg)** agradecer a alguien (algo) □ **thanks** *npl* agradecimiento *m* ♦ *excl* ¡gracias!; ~**s to** gracias a; **many** ~**s** muchas gracias.

Thanksgiving ['θæŋks,gɪvɪŋ] *n* Día *m* de Acción de Gracias.

ⓘ THANKSGIVING

El cuarto jueves de cada noviembre se celebra en EEUU la fiesta nacional del Día de Acción de Gracias como signo de gratitud de la cosecha y otros beneficios recibidos a lo largo del año. Sus orígenes se remontan al año 1621 cuando los "Pilgrims" (colonizadores británicos) recogieron su primera cosecha. El menú tradicional de Acción de Gracias consiste en pavo asado y pastel de calabaza.

---

thank you *excl* ¡gracias!; ~ **very much** muchísimas gracias; **no** ~ no gracias.

that [ðæt, *weak form of pron sense* 3 & *conj* ðət] *adj* (*pl* **those**) *adj* (*referring to thing, person mentioned*) ese (esa), esos (esas) (*pl*); (*referring to thing, person further away*) aquel (aquella), aquellos (aquellas) (*pl*); **I prefer ~ book** prefiero ese libro; **~ book at the back** aquel libro del fondo; **~ one** ése (ésa)/aquél (aquélla).

♦ *pron* **1.** (*referring to thing, person mentioned*) ése *m* (ésa *f*), ésos *mpl* (ésas *fpl*); (*indefinite*) eso; **who's ~?** ¿quién es?; **is ~ Lucy?** (*on the phone*) ¿eres Lucy?; **what's ~?** ¿qué es eso?; **~'s interesting** qué interesante.
2. (*referring to thing, person further away*) aquél *m* (aquélla *f*), aquéllos *mpl* (aquéllas *fpl*); (*indefinite*) aquello; **I want those at the back** quiero aquéllos del fondo.
3. (*introducing relative clause*) que; **a shop ~ sells antiques** una tienda que vende antigüedades; **the film ~ I saw** la película que vi; **the room ~ I sleep in** el cuarto en (el) que duermo.

♦ *adv* tan; **it wasn't ~ bad/good** no estuvo tan mal/bien; **it doesn't cost ~ much** no cuesta tanto.

♦ *conj* que; **tell him ~ I'm going to be late** dile que voy a llegar tarde.

thatched [θætʃt] *adj* (*building*) con techo de paja.

that's [ðæts] = **that is**.

thaw [θɔː] *vi* (snow, ice) derretir ♦ *vt* (*frozen food*) descongelar.

the [*weak form* ðə, *before vowel* ðɪ, *strong form* ðiː] *definite article* **1.** (*gen*) el (la), los (las) (*pl*); **~ book** el libro; **~ woman** la mujer; **~ girls** las chicas; **~ Wilsons** los Wilson; **to play ~ piano** tocar el piano; **give it to ~**

man dáselo al hombre; **the cover of ~ book** la tapa del libro.
2. (*with an adjective to form a noun*) el (la); **~ British** los británicos; **~ impossible** lo imposible.
3. (*in dates*): **~ twelfth of May** el doce de mayo; **~ forties** los cuarenta
4. (*in titles*): **Elizabeth ~ Second** Isabel segunda.

theater [θiːətəʳ] *n* (*Am*) (for plays, drama) = **theatre**; (for films) cine *m*.

theatre [θiːətəʳ] *n* (*Br*) teatro *m*.

theft [θeft] *n* robo *m*.

their [ðeəʳ] *adj* su, sus (*pl*).

theirs [ðeəz] *pron* suyo *m* (-ya *f*), suyos *mpl* (-yas *fpl*); **a friend of ~** un amigo suyo.

them [*weak form* ðəm, *strong form* ðem] *pron*: **I know ~** los conozco; **it's ~** son ellos; **send it to ~** envíaselo; **tell ~ to come** diles que vengan; **he's worse than ~** él es peor que ellos.

theme [θiːm] *n* (*topic*) tema *m*; (*tune*) sintonía *f*.

theme park *n* parque de atracciones basado en un tema específico.

themselves [ðəmˈselvz] *pron* (*reflexive*) se; (*after prep*) sí; **they did it ~** lo hicieron ellos mismos.

then [ðen] *adv* entonces; (*next, afterwards*) luego; **from ~ on** desde entonces; **until ~** hasta entonces.

theory [θɪərɪ] *n* teoría *f*; **in ~** en teoría.

therapist [θerəpɪst] *n* terapeuta *mf*.

therapy [θerəpɪ] *n* terapia *f*.

there [ðeəʳ] *adv* ahí; (*further away*) allí ♦ *pron*: **~ is** hay; **~ are**

hay; **is Bob ~, please?** (on phone)
¿está Bob?; **over ~** por allí; **~ you
are** (when giving) aquí lo tienes.

thereabouts [ˌðeərə'baʊts] adv:
or ~ o por ahí.

therefore [ˈðeəfɔːʳ] adv por lo
tanto.

there's [ðeəz] = there is.

thermal   underwear
[ˌθɜːml-] n ropa f interior térmica.

thermometer [θəˈmɒmɪtəʳ] n
termómetro m.

Thermos (flask)® [ˈθɜːməs-] n
termo m.

thermostat [ˈθɜːməstæt] n termostato m.

these [ðiːz] pl → this.

they [ðeɪ] pron ellos mpl (ellas
fpl); **~'re good** son buenos.

thick [θɪk] adj (in size) grue-
so(-sa); (dense) espeso(-sa); (inf:
stupid) necio(-cia); **it's 3 metres ~**
tiene 3 metros de grosor.

thicken [ˈθɪkn] vt espesar ◆ vi
espesarse.

thickness [ˈθɪknɪs] n espesor m.

thief [θiːf] (pl **thieves** [θiːvz]) n
ladrón m (-ona f).

thigh [θaɪ] n muslo m.

thimble [ˈθɪmbl] n dedal m.

thin [θɪn] adj (in size) fino(-na);
(not fat) delgado(-da); (soup, sauce)
claro(-ra).

thing [θɪŋ] n cosa f; **the ~ is** el
caso es que ❑ **things** npl (clothes,
possessions) cosas fpl; **how are ~s?**
(inf) ¿qué tal van las cosas?

thingummyjig [ˈθɪŋəmɪdʒɪg] n
(inf) chisme m.

think [θɪŋk] (pt & pp **thought**) vt
(believe) creer, pensar; (have in

mind, expect) pensar ◆ vi pensar; **to
~ that** creer que; **to ~ about** (have
in mind) pensar en; (consider) pensar; **to ~ of** (have in mind, consider)
pensar en; (invent) pensar; (remember) acordarse de; **to ~ of doing
sthg** pensar en hacer algo; **I ~ so**
creo que sí; **I don't ~ so** creo que
no; **do you ~ you could ...?** ¿crees
que podría ...?; **to ~ highly of sb**
apreciar mucho a alguien ❑ **think
over** vt sep pensarse; **think up** vt
sep idear.

third [θɜːd] num (after noun, as
pronoun) tercero(-ra); (before noun)
tercer(-ra), → sixth.

third party insurance n
seguro m a terceros.

Third World n: **the ~** el Tercer
Mundo.

thirst [θɜːst] n sed f.

thirsty [ˈθɜːstɪ] adj: **to be ~** tener
sed.

thirteen [ˌθɜːˈtiːn] num trece, →
six.

thirteenth [ˌθɜːˈtiːnθ] num deci-
motercero(-ra), → sixth.

thirtieth [ˈθɜːtɪəθ] num trigési-
mo(-ma), → sixth.

thirty [ˈθɜːtɪ] num treinta, → six.

this [ðɪs] (pl **these**) adj 1. (referring
to thing, person) este (esta), estos
(estas) (pl); **I prefer ~ book** prefiero este libro; **these chocolates are
delicious** estos bombones son
riquísimos; **~ morning/week** esta
mañana/semana; **~ one** éste
(ésta).
2. (inf: when telling a story): **~ big
dog appeared** apareció un perro
grande.

◆ pron éste m (ésta f), éstos mpl

(éstas *fpl*); (indefinite) esto; ~ **is for you** esto es para ti; **what are these?** ¿qué son estas cosas?; ~ **is David Gregory** (introducing someone) te presento a David Gregory; (on telephone) soy David Gregory.
◆ *adv*: **it was** ~ **big** era así de grande; **I need** ~ **much** necesito un tanto así; **I don't remember it being** ~ **hard** no recordaba que fuera tan difícil.

thistle [ˈθɪsl] *n* cardo *m*.

thorn [θɔ:n] *n* espina *f*.

thorough [ˈθʌrə] *adj* (check, search) exhaustivo(-va); (person) minucioso(-sa).

thoroughly [ˈθʌrəlɪ] *adv* (completely) completamente.

those [ðəuz] *pl* → **that**.

though [ðəu] *conj* aunque ◆ *adv* sin embargo; **even** ~ aunque.

thought [θɔ:t] *pt & pp* → **think**
◆ *n* (idea) idea *f*; **I'll give it some** ~ lo pensaré □ **thoughts** *npl* (opinion) opiniones *fpl*

thoughtful [ˈθɔ:tful] *adj* (quiet and serious) pensativo(-va); (considerate) considerado(-da).

thoughtless [ˈθɔ:tlɪs] *adj* desconsiderado(-da).

thousand [ˈθauznd] *num* mil; **a** OR **one** ~ mil; **two** ~ dos mil; ~**s of** miles de, → **six**.

thrash [θræʃ] *vt* (inf: defeat heavily) dar una paliza a.

thread [θred] *n* (of cotton etc) hilo *m* ◆ *vt* (needle) enhebrar.

threadbare [ˈθredbeəʳ] *adj* raído(-da).

threat [θret] *n* amenaza *f*.

threaten [ˈθretn] *vt* amenazar;

to ~ **to do sthg** amenazar con hacer algo.

threatening [ˈθretnɪŋ] *adj* amenazador(-ra).

three [θri:] *num* tres, → **six**.

three-D [-ˈdi:] *adj* en tres dimensiones.

three-piece suite *n* tresillo *m*.

three-quarters [-ˈkwɔ:təz] *n* tres cuartos *mpl*; ~ **of an hour** tres cuartos de hora.

threshold [ˈθreʃhəuld] *n* (fml: of door) umbral *m*.

threw [θru:] *pt* → **throw**.

thrifty [ˈθrɪftɪ] *adj* (person) ahorrativo(-va).

thrilled [θrɪld] *adj* encantado(-da).

thriller [ˈθrɪləʳ] *n* (film) película *f* de suspense.

thrive [θraɪv] *vi* (plant, animal) crecer mucho; (person, business, place) prosperar.

throat [θrəut] *n* garganta *f*.

throb [θrɒb] *vi* (head, pain) palpitar; (noise, engine) vibrar.

throne [θrəun] *n* trono *m*.

throttle [ˈθrɒtl] *n* (of motorbike) válvula *f* reguladora.

through [θru:] *prep* (to other side of, by means of) a través de; (because of) a causa de, (from beginning to end of) durante; (across all of) por todo ◆ *adv* (from beginning to end) hasta el final ◆ *adj*: **to be** ~ (with sthg) (finished) haber terminado (algo); **you're** ~ (on phone) ya puedes hablar; **Monday** ~ **Thursday** (Am) de lunes a jueves; **to let sb** ~ dejar pasar a alguien; **to go** ~

(sthg) pasar (por algo); **to soak ~** penetrar; **~ traffic** tráfico m de tránsito; **a ~ train** tren directo; **"no ~ road"** (Br) "carretera cortada".

throughout [θruːˈaut] prep (day, morning, year) a lo largo de; (place, country, building) por todo ♦ adv (all the time) todo el tiempo; (everywhere) por todas partes.

throw [θrəu] (pt threw, pp thrown [θrəun]) vt tirar; (ball, javelin, person) lanzar; (a switch) apretar; **to ~ sthg in the bin** tirar algo a la basura ❏ **throw away** vt sep (get rid of) tirar □ **throw out** vt sep (get rid of) tirar; (person) echar; **throw up** vi (inf: vomit) echar la pastilla.

thru [θruː] (Am) = through.

thrush [θrʌʃ] n tordo m.

thud [θʌd] n golpe m seco.

thug [θʌg] n matón m.

thumb [θʌm] n pulgar m ♦ vt: **to ~ a lift** hacer dedo.

thumbtack [ˈθʌmtæk] n (Am) chincheta f.

thump [θʌmp] n (punch) puñetazo m; (sound) golpe m seco ♦ vt dar un puñetazo a.

thunder [ˈθʌndər] n truenos mpl.

thunderstorm [ˈθʌndəstɔːm] n tormenta f.

Thurs. (abbr of Thursday) jue.

Thursday [ˈθɜːzdɪ] n jueves m inv, → Saturday.

thyme [taɪm] n tomillo m.

tick [tɪk] n (written mark) marca f de visto bueno; (insect) garrapata f ♦ vt marcar (con una señal de visto bueno) ♦ vi hacer tictac ❏

tick off vt sep (mark off) marcar (con una señal de visto bueno).

ticket [ˈtɪkɪt] n (for travel) billete m; (for cinema, theatre, match) entrada f; (label) etiqueta f; (speeding ticket, parking ticket) multa f.

ticket collector n revisor m (-ra f).

ticket inspector n revisor m (-ra f).

ticket machine n máquina f automática de venta de billetes.

ticket office n taquilla f, boletería f (Amér).

tickle [ˈtɪkl] vt (touch) hacer cosquillas a ♦ vi hacer cosquillas.

ticklish [ˈtɪklɪʃ] adj (person) cosquilloso(-sa).

tick-tack-toe n (Am) tres fpl en raya.

tide [taɪd] n (of sea) marea f.

tidy [ˈtaɪdɪ] adj (room, desk, person) ordenado(-da); (hair, clothes) arreglado(-da) ❏ **tidy up** vt sep ordenar.

tie [taɪ] (pt & pp tied, cont tying) n (around neck) corbata f; (draw) empate m; (Am: on railway track) traviesa f ♦ vt (knot) hacer ♦ vi (draw) empatar ❏ **tie up** vt sep atar; (delay) retrasar.

tiepin [ˈtaɪpɪn] n alfiler m de corbata.

tier [tɪər] n (of seats) hilera f.

tiger [ˈtaɪgər] n tigre m.

tight [taɪt] adj (difficult to move) apretado(-da); (clothes, shoes) estrecho(-cha); (rope, material) tirante; (bend, turn) cerrado(-da); (schedule) ajustado(-da); (inf: drunk) cocido(-da) ♦ adv (hold) con fuerza; **my**

chest feels ~ tengo el pecho cogido.

tighten ['taɪtn] vt apretar.

tightrope ['taɪtrəʊp] n cuerda f floja.

tights [taɪts] npl medias fpl; **a pair of ~** unas medias.

tile [taɪl] n (for roof) teja f; (for floor) baldosa f; (for wall) azulejo m.

till [tɪl] n caja f registradora ◆ prep hasta ◆ conj hasta que.

tiller ['tɪləʳ] n caña f del timón.

tilt [tɪlt] vt inclinar ◆ vi inclinarse.

timber ['tɪmbəʳ] n (wood) madera f (para construir); (of roof) viga f.

time [taɪm] n tiempo m; (measured by clock) hora f; (moment) momento m; (occasion) vez f; (in history) época f ◆ vt (measure) cronometrar; (arrange) programar; **I haven't got (the) ~** no tengo tiempo; **it's ~ to go** es hora de irse; **what's the ~?** ¿qué hora es?; **do you have the ~?** ¿tiene hora?; **two ~s** two dos por dos; **five ~s as much** cinco veces más; **in a month's ~** dentro de un mes; **to have a good ~** pasárselo bien; **all the ~** todo el tiempo; **every ~** cada vez; **from ~ to ~** de vez en cuando; **for the being** de momento; **in ~ (arrive)** a tiempo; **in good ~** con tiempo de sobra; **last ~** la última vez; **most of the ~** la mayor parte del tiempo; **on ~** puntualmente; **some of the ~** parte del tiempo; **this ~** esta vez; **two at a ~** de dos en dos.

time difference n diferencia f horaria.

time limit n plazo m.

timer ['taɪməʳ] n temporizador m.

time share n copropiedad f.

timetable ['taɪm,teɪbl] n horario m; (of events) programa m.

time zone n huso m horario.

timid ['tɪmɪd] adj tímido(-da).

tin [tɪn] n (metal) estaño m; (container) lata f ◆ adj de hojalata.

tinfoil ['tɪnfɔɪl] n papel m de aluminio.

tinned food [tɪnd-] n (Br) conservas fpl.

tin opener [-ˌəʊpnəʳ] n (Br) abrelatas m inv.

tinsel ['tɪnsl] n oropel m.

tint [tɪnt] n tinte m.

tinted glass [ˌtɪntɪd-] n cristal m ahumado.

tiny ['taɪnɪ] adj diminuto(-ta).

tip [tɪp] n (point, end) punta f; (to waiter, taxi driver etc) propina f; (piece of advice) consejo m; (rubbish dump) vertedero m ◆ vt (waiter, taxi driver etc) dar una propina; (tilt) inclinar; (pour) vaciar ❑ **tip over** vt sep volcar ◆ vi volcarse.

tire ['taɪəʳ] vi cansarse ◆ n (Am) = tyre.

tired ['taɪəd] adj (sleepy) cansado(-da); **to be ~ of** estar cansado de.

tired out adj agotado(-da).

tiring ['taɪərɪŋ] adj cansado(-da).

tissue ['tɪʃuː] n (handkerchief) pañuelo m de papel.

tissue paper n papel m de seda.

tit [tɪt] n (vulg: breast) teta f.

title ['taɪtl] n título m; (Dr, Mr, Lord etc) tratamiento m.

T-junction ['tiː-] n cruce m (en

forma de T).

to [unstressed before consonant tə, unstressed before vowel tʊ, stressed tuː] *prep* **1.** (indicating direction, position) a; **to go ~ France** ir a Francia; **to go ~ school** ir a la escuela; **the road ~ Leeds** la carretera de Leeds; **~ the left/right** a la izquierda/derecha.

2. (expressing indirect object) a; **to give sthg ~ sb** dar algo a alguien; **give it ~ me** dámelo; **to listen ~ the radio** escuchar la radio.

3. (indicating reaction, effect): **~ my surprise** para sorpresa mía; **it's ~ your advantage** va en beneficio tuyo.

4. (until) hasta; **to count ~ ten** contar hasta diez; **we work from 9 ~ 5** trabajamos de 9 a 5.

5. (in stating opinion): **~ me, he's lying** para mí que miente.

6. (indicating change of state): **it could lead ~ trouble** puede ocasionar problemas.

7. (Br: in expressions of time) menos; **it's ten ~ three** son las tres menos diez.

8. (in ratios, rates) por; **40 miles ~ the gallon** un galón por cada 40 millas.

9. (of, for): **the key ~ the car** la llave del coche; **a letter ~ my daughter** una carta a mi hija.

10. (indicating attitude) con; **to be rude ~ sb** tratar a alguien con grosería.

♦ with infinitive **1.** (forming simple infinitive): **~ walk** andar.

2. (following another verb): **to begin ~ do sthg** empezar a hacer algo; **to try ~ do sthg** intentar hacer algo.

3. (following an adjective) de; **difficult ~ do** difícil de hacer; **ready ~ go** listo para marchar.

4. (indicating purpose) para; **we came here ~ look at the castle** vinimos a ver el castillo; **I'm phoning ~ ask you something** te llamo para preguntarte algo.

toad [təʊd] *n* sapo *m*.

toadstool [ˈtəʊdstuːl] *n* seta *f* venenosa.

toast [təʊst] *n* (bread) pan *m* tostado; (when drinking) brindis *m inv* ♦ *vt* (bread) tostar; **a piece** OR **slice of ~** una tostada.

toasted sandwich [ˌtəʊstɪd-] *n* sandwich *m* (a la plancha).

toaster [ˈtəʊstər] *n* tostador *m*.

toastie [ˈtəʊstɪ] (inf) = **toasted sandwich**.

tobacco [təˈbækəʊ] *n* tabaco *m*.

tobacconist's [təˈbækənɪsts] *n* (shop) estanco *m*.

toboggan [təˈbɒgən] *n* tobogán *m* (de deporte).

today [təˈdeɪ] *n* hoy *m* ♦ *adv* hoy.

toddler [ˈtɒdlər] *n* niño *m* pequeño (niña *f* pequeña).

toe [təʊ] *n* (of person) dedo *m* del pie.

toe clip *n* calzapiés *m inv*.

toenail [ˈtəʊneɪl] *n* uña *f* del dedo del pie.

toffee [ˈtɒfɪ] *n* tofe *m*.

together [təˈgeðər] *adv* juntos(-tas); **~ with** junto con.

toilet [ˈtɔɪlɪt] *n* (in public place) servicios *mpl*; (at home) wáter *m*; (bowl) retrete *m*; **to go to the ~** ir al wáter; **where's the ~?** ¿dónde está el servicio?

toilet bag *n* neceser *m*.

toilet paper n papel m higiénico.

toiletries ['tɔɪlɪtrɪz] npl artículos mpl de tocador.

toilet roll n (paper) papel m higiénico.

toilet water n agua f de colonia.

token ['təʊkn] n (metal disc) ficha f.

told [təʊld] pt & pp → **tell**.

tolerable ['tɒlərəbl] adj tolerable.

tolerant ['tɒlərənt] adj tolerante.

tolerate ['tɒləreɪt] vt tolerar.

toll [təʊl] n (for road, bridge) peaje m.

tollbooth ['təʊlbu:θ] n cabina f de peaje.

toll-free adj (Am) gratuito(-ta).

tomato [Br tə'mɑ:təʊ, Am tə'meɪtəʊ] (pl -es) n tomate m.

tomato juice n zumo m de tomate.

tomato ketchup n ketchup m.

tomato puree n puré m de tomate concentrado.

tomato sauce n ketchup m.

tomb [tu:m] n tumba f.

tomorrow [tə'mɒrəʊ] n mañana f ♦ adv mañana; **the day after ~** pasado mañana; **~ afternoon** mañana por la tarde; **~ morning** mañana por la mañana; **~ night** mañana por la noche.

ton [tʌn] n (in Britain) = 1016 kilos; (in U.S.) = 907 kilos; (metric tonne) tonelada f; **~s of** (inf) un montón de.

tone [təʊn] n tono m; (on phone) señal f.

tongs [tɒŋz] npl (for hair) tenazas fpl; (for sugar) pinzas fpl.

tongue [tʌŋ] n lengua f.

tonic ['tɒnɪk] n (tonic water) tónica f; (medicine) tónico m.

tonic water n agua f tónica.

tonight [tə'naɪt] n esta noche f ♦ adv esta noche.

tonne [tʌn] n tonelada f (métrica).

tonsillitis [ˌtɒnsɪ'laɪtɪs] n amigdalitis f inv.

too [tu:] adv (excessively) demasiado; (also) también; **it's not ~ good** no está muy bien; **it's ~ late to go out** es demasiado tarde para salir; **~ many** demasiados(-das); **~ much** demasiado(-da).

took [tʊk] pt → **take**.

tool [tu:l] n herramienta f.

tool kit n juego m de herramientas.

tooth [tu:θ] (pl **teeth**) n diente m.

toothache ['tu:θeɪk] n dolor m de muelas.

toothbrush ['tu:θbrʌʃ] n cepillo m de dientes.

toothpaste ['tu:θpeɪst] n pasta f de dientes.

toothpick ['tu:θpɪk] n palillo m.

top [tɒp] adj (highest) de arriba; (best, most important) mejor ♦ n (highest part) parte f superior; (best point) cabeza f; (of box, jar) tapa f; (of bottle, tube) tapón m; (of pen) capuchón m; (garment) camiseta f; (of street, road) final m; **at the ~ (of)** (stairway, pile) en lo más alto (de);

(list, page) al principio (de); **on ~ of** *(on highest part of)* encima de; *(of hill, mountain)* en lo alto de; *(in addition to)* además de; **at ~ speed** a toda velocidad; **~ gear** directa f ❑ **top up** vt sep *(glass, drink)* volver a llenar ◆ vi *(with petrol)* repostar.

top floor *n* último piso *m*.

topic ['tɒpɪk] *n* tema *m*.

topical ['tɒpɪkl] *adj* actual.

topless ['tɒplɪs] *adj* topless *(inv)*.

topped [tɒpt] *adj*: **~ with** cubierto(-ta) con.

topping ['tɒpɪŋ] *n*: **with a ~ of** cubierto con; **the ~ of your choice** los ingredientes que Vd. elija.

torch [tɔːtʃ] *n* *(Br: electric light)* linterna f.

tore [tɔːʳ] *pt* → **tear.**

torment [tɔː'ment] *vt* *(annoy)* fastidiar.

torn [tɔːn] *pp* → **tear** ◆ *adj* *(ripped)* desgarrado(-da).

tornado [tɔː'neɪdəʊ] *(pl* -es OR -s) *n* tornado *m*.

torrential rain [tə,renʃl-] *n* lluvia f torrencial.

tortoise ['tɔːtəs] *n* tortuga f *(de tierra)*.

tortoiseshell ['tɔːtəʃel] *n* carey *m*.

torture ['tɔːtʃəʳ] *n* tortura f ◆ *vt* torturar.

Tory ['tɔːrɪ] *n* conservador *m* (-ra f).

toss [tɒs] *vt* *(throw)* tirar; *(salad)* mezclar; **to ~ a coin** echar a cara o cruz; **~ed in butter** con mantequilla.

total ['təʊtl] *adj* total ◆ *n* total *m*; **in ~** en total.

touch [tʌtʃ] *n* *(sense)* tacto *m*; *(small amount)* pizca f; *(detail)* toque *m* ◆ *vt* tocar; *(move emotionally)* conmover ◆ *vi* tocarse; **to get in ~ (with sb)** ponerse en contacto (con alguien); **to keep in ~ (with sb)** mantenerse en contacto (con alguien) ❑ **touch down** vi aterrizar.

touching ['tʌtʃɪŋ] *adj* *(moving)* conmovedor(-ra).

tough [tʌf] *adj* *(resilient)* fuerte; *(hard, strong)* resistente; *(meat, regulations, policies)* duro(-ra); *(difficult)* difícil.

tour [tʊəʳ] *n* *(journey)* viaje *m*; *(of city, castle etc)* recorrido *m*; *(of pop group, theatre company)* gira f ◆ *vt* recorrer; **on ~** en gira.

tourism ['tʊərɪzm] *n* turismo *m*.

tourist ['tʊərɪst] *n* turista *mf*.

tourist class *n* clase f turista.

tourist information office *n* oficina f de turismo.

tournament ['tɔːnəmənt] *n* torneo *m*.

tour operator *n* touroperador *m* (-ra f).

tout [taʊt] *n* revendedor *m* (-ra f).

tow [təʊ] *vt* remolcar.

toward [tə'wɔːd] *(Am)* = **towards.**

towards [tə'wɔːdz] *prep* *(Br)* hacia; *(to help pay for)* para.

towaway zone ['təʊəweɪ-] *n* *(Am)* zona en la que está prohibido estacionarse y los vehículos son retirados por la grúa.

towel ['taʊəl] *n* toalla f.

toweling ['taʊəlɪŋ] *(Am)* = **tow-**

elling.

towelling ['taʊəlɪŋ] n (Br) toalla f (tejido).

towel rail n toallero m.

tower ['taʊəʳ] n torre f.

tower block n (Br) bloque m alto de pisos.

Tower Bridge n puente londinense.

---

i TOWER BRIDGE

Construido en el siglo XIX, este puente neogótico extiende sobre el Támesis sus características ramas gemelas que se izan para permitir el paso de los barcos de mayor altura.

Tower of London n: the ~ la Torre de Londres.

---

i TOWER OF LONDON

Situada al norte del Támesis, la Torre de Londres es una fortaleza construida en el siglo XI que fue utilizada como residencia real hasta el siglo XVII. Hoy en día, la Torre y el museo que alberga son una popular atracción turística.

---

town [taʊn] n (smaller) pueblo m; (larger) ciudad f; (town centre) centro m.

town centre n centro m.

town hall n ayuntamiento m.

towpath ['taʊpɑːθ, pl -pɑːðz] n camino m de sirga.

towrope ['taʊrəʊp] n cuerda f de

remolque.

tow truck n (Am) grúa f.

toxic ['tɒksɪk] adj tóxico(-ca).

toy [tɔɪ] n juguete m.

toy shop n juguetería f.

trace [treɪs] n (sign) rastro m; (small amount) pizca f ♦ vt (find) localizar.

tracing paper ['treɪsɪŋ] n papel m de calco.

track [træk] n (path) sendero m; (of railway) vía f; (SPORT) pista f; (song) canción f ❑ **track down** vt sep localizar.

tracksuit ['træksuːt] n chándal m.

tractor ['træktəʳ] n tractor m.

trade [treɪd] n (COMM) comercio m; (job) oficio m ♦ vt cambiar ♦ vi comerciar.

trade-in n artículo viejo que se da como entrada al comprar uno nuevo.

trademark ['treɪdmɑːk] n marca f (comercial).

trader ['treɪdəʳ] n comerciante mf.

tradesman ['treɪdzmən] (pl -men [-mən]) n (deliveryman) repartidor m; (shopkeeper) tendero m.

trade union n sindicato m.

tradition [trəˈdɪʃn] n tradición f.

traditional [trəˈdɪʃənl] adj tradicional.

traffic ['træfɪk] (pt & pp -ked) n tráfico m ♦ vi: to ~ in traficar con.

traffic circle n (Am) raqueta f.

traffic island n isla f de peatones.

traffic jam n atasco m.

traffic lights npl semáforos mpl.

traffic warden *n* (Br) = guardia *mf* de tráfico.

tragedy ['trædʒədɪ] *n* tragedia *f*.

tragic ['trædʒɪk] *adj* trágico(-ca).

trail [treɪl] *n* (path) sendero *m*; (marks) rastro *m* ♦ *vi* (be losing) ir perdiendo.

trailer ['treɪləʳ] *n* (for boat, luggage) remolque *m*; (Am: caravan) caravana *f*; (for film, programme) trailer *m*.

train [treɪn] *n* tren *m* ♦ *vt* (teach) enseñar ♦ *vi* (SPORT) entrenar; **by ~** en tren.

train driver *n* maquinista *mf* (de tren).

trainee [treɪ'ni:] *n* aprendiz *m* (-za *f*).

trainer ['treɪnəʳ] *n* (of athlete etc) entrenador *m* (-ra *f*) ❑ **trainers** *npl* (Br) zapatillas *fpl* de deporte.

training ['treɪnɪŋ] *n* (instruction) formación *f*; (exercises) entrenamiento *m*.

training shoes *npl* (Br) zapatillas *fpl* de deporte.

tram [træm] *n* (Br) tranvía *m*.

tramp [træmp] *n* vagabundo *m* (-da *f*).

trampoline ['træmpəliːn] *n* cama *f* elástica.

trance [trɑːns] *n* trance *m*.

tranquilizer ['træŋkwɪlaɪzəʳ] (Am) = **tranquillizer**.

tranquillizer ['træŋkwɪlaɪzəʳ] *n* (Br) tranquilizante *m*.

transaction [træn'zækʃn] *n* transacción *f*.

transatlantic [ˌtrænzət'læntɪk] *adj* transatlántico(-ca).

transfer [*n* 'trænsfɜːʳ, *vb* træns-

'fɜːʳ] *n* (of money, power) transferencia *f*; (of sportsman) traspaso *m*; (picture) calcomanía *f*; (Am: ticket) clase de billete que permite hacer transbordos durante un viaje ♦ *vt* transferir ♦ *vi* (change bus, plane etc) hacer transbordo; **"~s"** (in airport) "transbordos".

transfer desk *n* mostrador *m* de tránsito.

transform [træns'fɔːm] *vt* transformar.

transfusion [træns'fjuːʒn] *n* transfusión *f*.

transistor radio [træn'zɪstəʳ-] *n* transistor *m*.

transit ['trænzɪt]: **in transit** *adv* de tránsito.

transitive ['trænzɪtɪv] *adj* transitivo(-va).

transit lounge *n* sala *f* de tránsito.

translate [træns'leɪt] *vt* traducir.

translation [træns'leɪʃn] *n* traducción *f*.

translator [træns'leɪtəʳ] *n* traductor *m* (-ra *f*).

transmission [trænz'mɪʃn] *n* transmisión *f*.

transmit [trænz'mɪt] *vt* transmitir.

transparent [træns'pærənt] *adj* transparente.

transplant [træns'plɑːnt] *n* trasplante *m*.

transport [*n* 'trænspɔːt, *vb* træn-'spɔːt] *n* transporte *m* ♦ *vt* transportar.

transportation [ˌtrænspɔː-'teɪʃn] *n* (Am) transporte *m*.

trap [træp] *n* trampa *f* ♦ *vt*: **to be**

trapped estar atrapado.

trapdoor ['træp,dɔːⁱ] n trampilla f.

trash [træʃ] n (Am) basura f.

trashcan ['træʃkæn] n (Am) cubo m de la basura.

trauma ['trɔːma] n trauma m.

traumatic [trɔː'mætɪk] adj traumático(-ca).

travel ['trævl] n viajes mpl ♦ vt (distance) recorrer ♦ vi viajar.

travel agency n agencia f de viajes.

travel agent n empleado m (-da f) m de una agencia de viajes; **~'s (shop)** agencia f de viajes.

Travelcard ['trævlkɑːd] n billete, normalmente de un día, para el metro, tren y autobús de Londres.

travel centre n oficina f de información al viajero.

traveler ['trævlⁱ] (Am) = **traveller**.

travel insurance n seguro m de viaje.

traveller ['trævlⁱ] n (Br) viajero m (-ra f).

traveller's cheque ['trævləz-] n cheque m de viaje.

travelsick ['trævlsɪk] adj mareado(-da) por el viaje.

trawler ['trɔːlⁱ] n trainera f.

tray [treɪ] n bandeja f.

treacherous ['tretʃərəs] adj (person) traidor(-ra); (roads, conditions) peligroso(-sa).

treacle ['triːkl] n (Br) melaza f.

tread [tred] (pt trod, pp trodden) n (of tyre) banda f ♦ vi: to ~ on sthg pisar algo.

treasure ['treʒⁱ] n tesoro m.

treat [triːt] vt tratar ♦ n: he bought me a meal para a ~ me invitó a cenar; **to ~ sb to sthg** invitar a alguien a algo.

treatment ['triːtmənt] n (MED) tratamiento m; (of person, subject) trato m.

treble ['trebl] adj triple.

tree [triː] n árbol m.

trek [trek] n viaje m largo y difícil.

tremble ['trembl] vi temblar.

tremendous [trɪ'mendəs] adj (very large) enorme; (inf: very good) estupendo(-da).

trench [trentʃ] n zanja f.

trend [trend] n (tendency) tendencia f; (fashion) moda f.

trendy ['trendɪ] adj (inf) (person) moderno(-na); (clothes, bar) de moda.

trespasser ['trespəsⁱ] n intruso m (-sa f); **"~s will be prosecuted"** "los intrusos serán sancionados por la ley".

trial ['traɪəl] n (JUR) juicio m; (test) prueba f; **a ~ period** un periodo de prueba.

triangle ['traɪæŋgl] n triángulo m.

triangular [traɪ'æŋgjulⁱ] adj triangular.

tribe [traɪb] n tribu f.

tributary ['trɪbjutrɪ] n afluente m.

trick [trɪk] n (deception) truco m; (in magic) juego m (de manos) ♦ vt engañar; **to play a ~ on sb** gastarle una broma a alguien.

trickle ['trɪkl] vi resbalar (formando un hilo).

tricky ['trɪkɪ] *adj* difícil.

tricycle ['traɪsɪkl] *n* triciclo *m*.

trifle ['traɪfl] *n* (*dessert*) postre de bizcocho con frutas, nata, natillas y gelatina.

trigger ['trɪgəʳ] *n* gatillo *m*.

trim [trɪm] *n* (*haircut*) recorte *m* ◆ *vt* recortar.

trinket ['trɪŋkɪt] *n* baratija *f*.

trio ['triːəʊ] (*pl* -s) *n* trío *m*.

trip [trɪp] *n* viaje *m* ◆ *vi* tropezar ❑ **trip up** *vi* tropezar.

triple ['trɪpl] *adj* triple.

tripod ['traɪpɒd] *n* trípode *m*.

triumph ['traɪəmf] *n* triunfo *m*.

trivial ['trɪvɪəl] *adj* (*pej*) trivial.

trod [trɒd] *pt* → **tread**.

trodden ['trɒdn] *pp* → **tread**.

trolley ['trɒlɪ] (*pl* -s) *n* (*Br*: in supermarket, at airport, for food etc) carrito *m*; (*Am*: tram) tranvía *m*.

trombone [trɒm'bəʊn] *n* trombón *m*.

troops [truːps] *npl* tropas *fpl*.

trophy ['trəʊfɪ] *n* trofeo *m*.

tropical ['trɒpɪkl] *adj* tropical.

trot [trɒt] *vi* trotar ◆ *n*: **three on the ~** (*inf*) tres seguidos.

trouble ['trʌbl] *n* (*difficulty, problems, malfunction*) problemas *mpl*; (*pain*) dolor *m*; (*illness*) enfermedad *f* ◆ *vt* (*worry*) preocupar; (*bother*) molestar; **to be in ~** tener problemas; **to get into ~** meterse en líos; **to take the ~ to do sthg** tomarse la molestia de hacer algo; **it's no ~** no es molestia.

trough [trɒf] *n* (*for drinking*) abrevadero *m*.

trouser press ['traʊzəʳ-] *n* prensa *f* para pantalones.

trousers ['traʊzəz] *npl* pantalones *mpl*; **a pair of ~** un pantalón.

trout [traʊt] (*pl inv*) *n* trucha *f*.

trowel ['traʊəl] *n* (*for gardening*) desplantador *m*.

truant ['truːənt] *n*: **to play ~** hacer novillos.

truce [truːs] *n* tregua *f*.

truck [trʌk] *n* camión *m*.

true [truː] *adj* verdadero(-ra); (*genuine, sincere*) auténtico(-ca); **it's ~** es verdad.

truly ['truːlɪ] *adv*: **yours ~** le saluda atentamente.

trumpet ['trʌmpɪt] *n* trompeta *f*.

trumps [trʌmps] *npl* triunfo *m*.

truncheon ['trʌntʃən] *n* porra *f*.

trunk [trʌŋk] *n* (*of tree*) tronco *m*; (*Am: of car*) maletero *m*; (*case, box*) baúl *m*; (*of elephant*) trompa *f*.

trunk call *n* (*Br*) llamada *f* interurbana.

trunk road *n* (*Br*) = carretera *f* nacional.

trunks [trʌŋks] *npl* bañador *m* (*de hombre*).

trust [trʌst] *n* (*confidence*) confianza *f* ◆ *vt* (*believe, have confidence in*) confiar en; (*fml: hope*) confiar.

trustworthy ['trʌst,wɜːðɪ] *adj* digno(-na) de confianza.

truth [truːθ] *n* (*true facts*) verdad *f*; (*quality of being true*) veracidad *f*.

truthful ['truːθfʊl] *adj* (*statement, account*) verídico(-ca); (*person*) sincero(-ra).

try [traɪ] *n* (*attempt*) intento *m* ◆ *vt* (*attempt*) intentar; (*experiment with, test*) probar; (*seek help from*) acudir a; (*JUR*) procesar ◆ *vi* intentar; **to do sthg** intentar hacer algo ❑

303 **turn**

try on vt sep probarse; **try out** vt sep poner a prueba.

T-shirt ['tiː-] n camiseta f.

tub [tʌb] n (of margarine etc) tarrina f; (inf: bath) bañera f.

tube [tjuːb] n tubo m; (Br: inf: underground) metro m; **by ~** en metro.

tube station n (Br: inf) estación f de metro.

tuck [tʌk]: **tuck in** vt sep (shirt) meterse; (child, person) arropar ◆ vi (inf) comer con apetito.

tuck shop n (Br) confitería f (en un colegio).

Tudor ['tjuːdəʳ] adj (architecture) Tudor.

Tues. (abbr of Tuesday) mar.

Tuesday ['tjuːzdɪ] n martes m inv, → **Saturday**.

tuft [tʌft] n (of grass) matojo m; (of hair) mechón m.

tug [tʌg] vt tirar de.

tuition [tjuːˈɪʃn] n clases fpl.

tulip ['tjuːlɪp] n tulipán m.

tumble-dryer ['tʌmbldraɪəʳ] n secadora f.

tumbler ['tʌmbləʳ] n (glass) vaso m.

tummy ['tʌmɪ] n (inf) barriga f.

tummy upset n (inf) dolor m de barriga.

tumor ['tuːmər] (Am) = **tumour**.

tumour ['tjuːməʳ] n (Br) tumor m.

tuna (fish) [Br 'tjuːnə, Am 'tuːnə] n atún m.

tuna melt n (Am) tostada con atún y queso suizo fundido.

tune [tjuːn] n melodía f ◆ vt (radio, TV) sintonizar; (engine) poner a punto; (instrument) afinar;

in ~ afinado; out of ~ desafinado.

tunic ['tjuːnɪk] n túnica f.

Tunisia [tjuːˈnɪzɪə] n Túnez m.

tunnel ['tʌnl] n túnel m.

turban ['tɜːbən] n turbante m.

turbo ['tɜːbəʊ] (pl -s) n (car) turbo m.

turbulence ['tɜːbjʊləns] n turbulencia f.

turf [tɜːf] n (grass) césped m.

Turk [tɜːk] n turco m (-ca f).

turkey ['tɜːkɪ] (pl -s) n pavo m.

Turkey ['tɜːkɪ] n Turquía.

Turkish ['tɜːkɪʃ] adj turco(-ca) ◆ n (language) turco m ◆ npl: **the ~** los turcos.

Turkish delight n rahat lokum m, dulce gelatinoso cubierto de azúcar glas.

turn [tɜːn] n (in road) curva f; (of knob, key, switch) vuelta f; (go, chance) turno m ◆ vt (car, page, omelette) dar la vuelta a; (head) volver; (knob, key, switch) girar; (corner, bend) doblar; (become) volverse; (cause to become) poner ◆ vi girar; (milk) cortarse; **to ~ into sthg** convertirse en algo; **to ~ sthg into sthg** transformar algo en algo; **to ~ left/right** torcer a la derecha/izquierda; **it's your ~** te toca (a ti); **at the ~ of the century** a finales de siglo; **to take it in ~s** to do sthg hacer algo por turnos, **to ~ sthg inside out** darle la vuelta a algo (de dentro para afuera) ❑ **turn back** vt sep volver ◆ vi volver; **turn down** vt sep (radio, volume, heating) bajar; (offer, request) rechazar; **turn off** vt sep (light, TV) apagar; (water, gas, tap) cerrar; (engine) parar ◆ vi (leave road) salir;

turn on vt sep (light, TV, engine) encender; (water, gas, tap) abrir; **turn out** vt fus (be in the end) resultar ◆ vt sep (light, fire) apagar ◆ vi (come, attend) venir; **to ~ out to be sthg** resultar ser algo; **turn over** vi (in bed) darse la vuelta; (Br: change channels) cambiar ◆ vt sep (page, card, omelette) dar la vuelta a; **turn round** vt sep dar la vuelta a ◆ vi (person) darse la vuelta; **turn up** vt sep (radio, volume, heating) subir ◆ vi aparecer.

turning ['tɜːnɪŋ] n bocacalle f.

turnip ['tɜːnɪp] n nabo m.

turn-up n (Br: on trousers) vuelta f.

turps [tɜːps] n (Br: inf) trementina f.

turquoise ['tɜːkwɔɪz] adj turquesa (inv).

turtle ['tɜːtl] n tortuga f (marina).

turtleneck ['tɜːtlnek] n jersey m de cuello de cisne.

tutor ['tjuːtəʳ] n (private teacher) tutor m (-ra f).

tuxedo [tʌkˈsiːdəʊ] (pl -s) n (Am) esmoquin m.

TV n televisión f; **on ~** en la televisión.

tweed [twiːd] n tweed m.

tweezers ['twiːzəz] npl pinzas fpl.

twelfth [twelfθ] num duodécimo(-ma), → sixth.

twelve [twelv] num doce, → six.

twentieth ['twentɪəθ] num vigésimo(-ma); **the ~ century** el siglo XX, → sixth.

twenty ['twentɪ] num veinte, → six.

twice [twaɪs] adj & adv dos veces; **it's ~ as good** es el doble de bueno; **~ as much** el doble.

twig [twɪɡ] n ramita f.

twilight ['twaɪlaɪt] n crepúsculo m.

twin [twɪn] n gemelo m (-la f).

twin beds npl dos camas fpl.

twine [twaɪn] n bramante m.

twin room n habitación f con dos camas.

twist [twɪst] vt (wire) torcer; (thread, rope) retorcer; (hair) enroscar; (bottle top, lid, knob) girar; **to ~ one's ankle** torcerse el tobillo.

twisting ['twɪstɪŋ] adj con muchos recodos.

two [tuː] num dos, → six.

two-piece adj de dos piezas.

tying ['taɪɪŋ] cont → tie.

type [taɪp] n (kind) tipo m ◆ vt teclear ◆ vi escribir a máquina.

typewriter ['taɪpˌraɪtəʳ] n máquina f de escribir.

typhoid ['taɪfɔɪd] n fiebre f tifoidea.

typical ['tɪpɪkl] adj típico(-ca).

typist ['taɪpɪst] n mecanógrafo m (-fa f).

tyre ['taɪəʳ] n (Br) neumático m.

U [juː] adj (Br: film) para todos los públicos.

UFO n (abbr of unidentified flying

object) OVNI m.

ugly [ˈʌglɪ] adj feo(-a).

UHT adj (abbr of ultra heat treated) uperizado(-da).

UK n: the ~ el Reino Unido.

ulcer [ˈʌlsəʳ] n úlcera f.

ultimate [ˈʌltɪmət] adj (final) final; (best, greatest) máximo (-ma).

ultraviolet [ˌʌltrəˈvaɪələt] adj ultravioleta.

umbrella [ʌmˈbrelə] n paraguas m inv.

umpire [ˈʌmpaɪəʳ] n árbitro m.

UN n (abbr of United Nations): the ~ la ONU.

unable [ʌnˈeɪbl] adj: to be ~ to do sthg ser incapaz de hacer algo.

unacceptable [ˌʌnəkˈseptəbl] adj inaceptable.

unaccustomed [ˌʌnəˈkʌstəmd] adj: to be ~ to sthg no estar acostumbrado(-da) a algo.

unanimous [juːˈnænɪməs] adj unánime.

unattended [ˌʌnəˈtendɪd] adj desatendido(-da).

unattractive [ˌʌnəˈtræktɪv] adj poco atractivo(-va).

unauthorized [ˌʌnˈɔːθəraɪzd] adj no autorizado(-da).

unavailable [ˌʌnəˈveɪləbl] adj no disponible.

unavoidable [ˌʌnəˈvɔɪdəbl] adj inevitable.

unaware [ˌʌnəˈweəʳ] adj inconsciente; to be ~ of sthg no ser consciente de algo.

unbearable [ʌnˈbeərəbl] adj insoportable.

unbelievable [ˌʌnbɪˈliːvəbl] adj increíble.

unbutton [ˌʌnˈbʌtn] vt desabrocharse.

uncertain [ʌnˈsɜːtn] adj (not definite) incierto(-ta); (not sure) indeciso(-sa).

uncertainty [ʌnˈsɜːtntɪ] n incertidumbre f.

uncle [ˈʌŋkl] n tío m.

unclean [ˌʌnˈkliːn] adj sucio (-cia).

unclear [ˌʌnˈklɪəʳ] adj poco claro (-ra); (not sure) poco seguro(-ra).

uncomfortable [ˌʌnˈkʌmftəbl] adj incómodo(-da).

uncommon [ʌnˈkɒmən] adj poco común.

unconscious [ʌnˈkɒnʃəs] adj: to be ~ (after accident) estar inconsciente; (unaware) ser inconsciente.

unconvincing [ˌʌnkənˈvɪnsɪŋ] adj poco convincente.

uncooperative [ˌʌnkəʊˈɒpərətɪv] adj que no quiere cooperar.

uncork [ˌʌnˈkɔːk] vt descorchar.

uncouth [ʌnˈkuːθ] adj grosero(-ra).

uncover [ʌnˈkʌvəʳ] vt (discover) descubrir; (swimming pool) dejar al descubierto; (car) descapotar.

under [ˈʌndəʳ] prep (beneath) debajo de; (less than) menos de; (according to) según; (in classification) en; ~ the water bajo el agua; children ~ ten niños menores de diez años; ~ the circumstances dadas las circunstancias; to be ~ pressure (from a person) estar presionado; (stressed) estar en tensión.

underage [ʌndər'eɪdʒ] *adj* menor de edad.

undercarriage ['ʌndəˌkærɪdʒ] *n* tren *m* de aterrizaje.

underdone [ʌndə'dʌn] *adj* poco hecho(-cha).

underestimate [ʌndər'estɪmeɪt] *vt* subestimar.

underexposed [ʌndərɪk'spəʊzd] *adj (photograph)* subexpuesto(-ta).

undergo [ʌndə'gəʊ] (*pt* -went, *pp* -gone [-'gɒn]) *vt (change, difficulties)* sufrir; *(operation)* someterse a.

undergraduate [ʌndə'grædjʊət] *n* estudiante *m* universitario (no licenciado) (estudiante *f* universitaria (no licenciada)).

underground ['ʌndəgraʊnd] *adj (below earth's surface)* subterráneo(-a); *(secret)* clandestino(-na) ◆ *n (Br: railway)* metro *m*.

undergrowth ['ʌndəgrəʊθ] *n* maleza *f*.

underline [ʌndə'laɪn] *vt* subrayar.

underneath [ʌndə'ni:θ] *prep* debajo de ◆ *adv* debajo ◆ *n* superficie *f* inferior.

underpants ['ʌndəpænts] *npl* calzoncillos *mpl*.

underpass ['ʌndəpɑ:s] *n* paso *m* subterráneo.

undershirt ['ʌndəʃɜ:t] *n (Am)* camiseta *f*.

underskirt ['ʌndəskɜ:t] *n* enaguas *fpl*.

understand [ʌndə'stænd] (*pt & pp* -stood) *vt* entender; *(believe)* tener entendido ◆ *vi* entender; **I don't ~** no entiendo; **to**

make o.s. understood hacerse entender.

understanding [ʌndə'stændɪŋ] *adj* comprensivo(-va) ◆ *n (agreement)* acuerdo *m*; *(knowledge)* entendimiento *m*; *(interpretation)* impresión *f*; *(sympathy)* comprensión *f* mutua.

understatement [ʌndə'steɪtmənt] *n*: **that's an ~** eso es quedarse corto.

understood [ʌndə'stʊd] *pt & pp* → **understand**.

undertake [ʌndə'teɪk] (*pt* -took, *pp* -taken [-'teɪkn]) *vt* emprender; **to ~ to do sthg** comprometerse a hacer algo.

undertaker ['ʌndəˌteɪkər] *n* director *m* (-ra *f*) de funeraria.

undertaking [ʌndə'teɪkɪŋ] *n (promise)* promesa *f*; *(task)* empresa *f*.

undertook [ʌndə'tʊk] *pt* → **undertake**.

underwater [ʌndə'wɔ:tər] *adj* submarino(-na) ◆ *adv* bajo el agua.

underwear ['ʌndəweər] *n* ropa *f* interior.

underwent [ʌndə'went] *pt* → **undergo**.

undesirable [ʌndɪ'zaɪərəbl] *adj* indeseable.

undo [ʌn'du:] (*pt* -did [-'dɪd], *pp* -done) *vt (coat, shirt)* desabrocharse; *(tie, shoelaces)* desatarse; *(parcel)* abrir.

undone [ʌn'dʌn] *adj (coat, shirt)* desabrochado(-da); *(tie, shoelaces)* desatado(-da).

undress [ʌn'dres] *vi* desnudarse ◆ *vt* desnudar.

undressed [ʌn'drest] *adj* desnudo(-da); **to get ~** desnudarse.

uneasy [ʌn'iːzɪ] *adj* intranquilo(-la).

uneducated [ʌn'edjʊkeɪtɪd] *adj* inculto(-ta).

unemployed [ʌnɪm'plɔɪd] *adj* desempleado(-da) ◆ *npl*: **the ~** los parados.

unemployment [ʌnɪm'plɔɪmənt] *n* paro *m*.

unemployment benefit *n* subsidio *m* de desempleo.

unequal [ʌn'iːkwəl] *adj* desigual.

uneven [ʌn'iːvn] *adj* desigual; *(road)* lleno(-na) de baches.

uneventful [ʌnɪ'ventfʊl] *adj* sin incidentes destacables.

unexpected [ʌnɪk'spektɪd] *adj* inesperado(-da).

unexpectedly [ʌnɪk'spektɪdlɪ] *adv* inesperadamente.

unfair [ʌn'feəʳ] *adj* injusto(-ta).

unfairly [ʌn'feəlɪ] *adv* injustamente.

unfaithful [ʌn'feɪθfʊl] *adj* infiel.

unfamiliar [ʌnfə'mɪljəʳ] *adj* desconocido(-da); **to be ~ with** no estar familiarizado(-da) con.

unfashionable [ʌn'fæʃnəbl] *adj* pasado(-da) de moda.

unfasten [ʌn'fɑːsn] *vt (button, belt)* desabrochar; *(tie, knot)* desatarse.

unfavourable [ʌn'feɪvrəbl] *adj* desfavorable.

unfinished [ʌn'fɪnɪʃt] *adj* incompleto(-ta).

unfit [ʌn'fɪt] *adj*: **to be ~** *(not healthy)* no estar en forma; **to be ~**

for sthg no ser apto(-ta) para algo.

unfold [ʌn'fəʊld] *vt* desdoblar.

unforgettable [ʌnfə'getəbl] *adj* inolvidable.

unforgivable [ʌnfə'gɪvəbl] *adj* imperdonable.

unfortunate [ʌn'fɔːtʃnət] *adj (unlucky)* desgraciado(-da); *(regrettable)* lamentable.

unfortunately [ʌn'fɔːtʃnətlɪ] *adv* desgraciadamente.

unfriendly [ʌn'frendlɪ] *adj* huraño(-ña).

unfurnished [ʌn'fɜːnɪʃt] *adj* sin amueblar.

ungrateful [ʌn'greɪtfʊl] *adj* desagradecido(-da).

unhappy [ʌn'hæpɪ] *adj (sad)* triste; *(wretched)* desgraciado(-da); *(not pleased)* descontento(-ta); **I'm ~ about that idea** no me gusta esa idea.

unharmed [ʌn'hɑːmd] *adj* ileso(-sa).

unhealthy [ʌn'helθɪ] *adj (person)* enfermizo(-za); *(food, smoking)* perjudicial para la salud; *(place)* insalubre.

unhelpful [ʌn'helpfʊl] *adj (person)* poco servicial; *(advice)* inútil.

unhurt [ʌn'hɜːt] *adj* ileso(-sa).

unhygienic [ʌnhaɪ'dʒiːnɪk] *adj* antihigiénico(-ca).

unification [juːnɪfɪ'keɪʃn] *n* unificación *f*.

uniform ['juːnɪfɔːm] *n* uniforme *m*.

unimportant [ʌnɪm'pɔːtənt] *adj* sin importancia.

unintelligent [ʌnɪn'telɪdʒənt] *adj* poco inteligente.

unintentional [ˌʌnɪnˈtenʃənl] *adj* no intencionado(-da).

uninterested [ʌnˈɪntrəstɪd] *adj* indiferente.

uninteresting [ʌnˈɪntrəstɪŋ] *adj* poco interesante.

union [ˈjuːnjən] *n (of workers)* sindicato *m*.

Union Jack *n:* the ~ la bandera del Reino Unido.

unique [juːˈniːk] *adj* único(-ca); to be ~ to ser peculiar de.

unisex [ˈjuːnɪseks] *adj* unisex *(inv)*.

unit [ˈjuːnɪt] *n* unidad *f; (department, building)* sección *f; (piece of furniture)* módulo *m; (group)* equipo *m*.

unite [juːˈnaɪt] *vt (people)* unir; *(country, party)* unificar ◆ *vi* unirse.

United Kingdom [juːˈnaɪtɪd-] *n:* the ~ el Reino Unido.

United Nations [juːˈnaɪtɪd-] *npl:* the ~ las Naciones Unidas.

United States (of America) [juːˈnaɪtɪd-] *npl:* the ~ los Estados Unidos (de América).

unity [ˈjuːnətɪ] *n* unidad *f*.

universal [ˌjuːnɪˈvɜːsl] *adj* universal.

universe [ˈjuːnɪvɜːs] *n* universo *m*.

university [ˌjuːnɪˈvɜːsətɪ] *n* universidad *f*.

unjust [ˌʌnˈdʒʌst] *adj* injusto(-ta).

unkind [ʌnˈkaɪnd] *adj* desagradable.

unknown [ʌnˈnəʊn] *adj* desconocido(-da).

unleaded (petrol) [ʌnˈledɪd-] *n* gasolina *f* sin plomo.

unless [ənˈles] *conj* a menos que.

unlike [ʌnˈlaɪk] *prep (different to)* diferente a; *(in contrast to)* a diferencia de; *(not typical of)* poco característico de.

unlikely [ʌnˈlaɪklɪ] *adj (not probable)* poco probable; she's ~ to do it es poco probable que lo haga.

unlimited [ʌnˈlɪmɪtɪd] *adj* ilimitado(-da); ~ mileage sin límite de recorrido.

unlisted [ʌnˈlɪstɪd] *adj (Am: phone number)* que no figura en la guía telefónica.

unload [ʌnˈləʊd] *vt* descargar.

unlock [ʌnˈlɒk] *vt* abrir (con llave).

unlucky [ʌnˈlʌkɪ] *adj (unfortunate)* desgraciado(-da); *(bringing bad luck)* de la mala suerte.

unmarried [ʌnˈmærɪd] *adj* no casado(-da).

unnatural [ʌnˈnætʃrəl] *adj (unusual)* poco normal; *(behaviour, person)* afectado(-da).

unnecessary [ʌnˈnesəsərɪ] *adj* innecesario(-ria).

unobtainable [ˌʌnəbˈteɪnəbl] *adj* inasequible.

unoccupied [ʌnˈɒkjʊpaɪd] *adj (place, seat)* libre.

unofficial [ˌʌnəˈfɪʃl] *adj* extraoficial.

unpack [ʌnˈpæk] *vt* deshacer ◆ *vi* deshacer el equipaje.

unpleasant [ʌnˈpleznt] *adj (smell, weather, surprise etc)* desagradable; *(person)* antipático(-ca).

unplug [ʌnˈplʌg] *vt* desenchufar.

unpopular [ʌnˈpɒpjʊləʳ] *adj* impopular.

unpredictable [ˌʌnprɪ'dɪktəbl] *adj* imprevisible.

unprepared [ˌʌnprɪ'peəd] *adj*: to be ~ no estar preparado(-da).

unprotected [ˌʌnprə'tektɪd] *adj* desprotegido(-da).

unqualified [ˌʌn'kwɒlɪfaɪd] *adj* (person) no cualificado(-da).

unreal [ˌʌn'rɪəl] *adj* irreal.

unreasonable [ˌʌn'riːznəbl] *adj* (unfair) poco razonable; (excessive) excesivo(-va).

unrecognizable [ˌʌnrekəg-'naɪzəbl] *adj* irreconocible.

unreliable [ˌʌnrɪ'laɪəbl] *adj* poco fiable.

unrest [ˌʌn'rest] *n* malestar *m*.

unroll [ˌʌn'rəʊl] *vt* desenrollar.

unsafe [ˌʌn'seɪf] *adj* (dangerous) peligroso(-sa); (in danger) inseguro(-ra).

unsatisfactory [ˌʌnsætɪs-'fæktərɪ] *adj* insatisfactorio(-ria).

unscrew [ˌʌn'skruː] *vt* (lid, top) desenroscar.

unsightly [ˌʌn'saɪtlɪ] *adj* feo(-a).

unskilled [ˌʌn'skɪld] *adj* (worker) no cualificado(-da).

unsociable [ˌʌn'səʊʃəbl] *adj* insociable.

unsound [ˌʌn'saʊnd] *adj* (building, structure) inseguro(-ra); (argument, method) erróneo(-a).

unspoiled [ˌʌn'spɔɪlt] *adj* no erosionado(-da) (por el hombre).

unsteady [ˌʌn'stedɪ] *adj* inestable; (hand) tembloroso(-sa).

unstuck [ˌʌn'stʌk] *adj*: to come ~ despegarse.

unsuccessful [ˌʌnsək'sesfʊl] *adj* fracasado(-da).

unsuitable [ˌʌn'suːtəbl] *adj* inadecuado(-da).

unsure [ˌʌn'ʃɔːʳ] *adj*: to be ~ (about) no estar muy seguro(-ra) (de).

unsweetened [ˌʌn'swiːtnd] *adj* no edulcorado(-da).

untidy [ˌʌn'taɪdɪ] *adj* (person) desaliñado(-da); (room, desk) desordenado(-da).

untie [ˌʌn'taɪ] (cont untying) *vt* desatar.

until [ən'tɪl] *prep* hasta ♦ *conj* hasta que; don't start ~ I tell you no empieces hasta que no te lo diga.

untrue [ˌʌn'truː] *adj* falso(-sa).

untrustworthy [ˌʌn'trʌst-wɜːðɪ] *adj* poco fiable.

untying [ˌʌn'taɪɪŋ] *cont* → untie.

unusual [ˌʌn'juːʒl] *adj* (not common) poco común; (distinctive) peculiar.

unusually [ˌʌn'juːʒəlɪ] *adv* (more than usual) extraordinariamente.

unwell [ˌʌn'wel] *adj* indispuesto(-ta); to feel ~ sentirse mal.

unwilling [ˌʌn'wɪlɪŋ] *adj*: to be ~ to do sthg no estar dispuesto(-ta) a hacer algo.

unwind [ˌʌn'waɪnd] (pt & pp **unwound** [ˌʌn'waʊnd]) *vt* desenrollar ♦ *vi* (relax) relajarse.

unwrap [ˌʌn'ræp] *vt* desenvolver.

unzip [ˌʌn'zɪp] *vt* abrir la cremallera de.

up [ʌp] *adv* 1. (towards higher position, level) hacia arriba; we walked ~ to the top fuimos andando hasta arriba del todo; to pick sthg ~ coger algo; prices are going ~ los

precios están subiendo.
2. *(in higher position)* arriba; she's ~ **in her bedroom** está arriba, en su cuarto; ~ **there** allí arriba.
3. *(into upright position)*: **to sit** ~ sentarse derecho; **to stand** ~ ponerse de pie.
4. *(northwards)*: **we're going** ~ **to Dewsbury** vamos a subir a Dewsbury.
5. *(in phrases)*: **to walk** ~ **and down** andar de un lado para otro; **to jump** ~ **and down** dar brincos; ~ **to six weeks/ten people** hasta seis semanas/diez personas; **are you** ~ **to travelling?** ¿estás en condiciones de viajar?; **what are you** ~ **to?** ¿qué andas tramando?; **it's** ~ **to you** depende de ti; ~ **until ten o'clock** hasta las diez.
◆ *prep* 1. *(towards higher position)*: **to walk** ~ **a hill** subir por una colina; **I went** ~ **the stairs** subí las escaleras.
2. *(in higher position)* en lo alto de; ~ **a hill** en lo alto de una colina.
3. *(at end of)*: **they live** ~ **the road from us** viven al final de nuestra calle.
◆ *adj* 1. *(out of bed)* levantado(-da); **I was** ~ **at six today** hoy, me levanté a las seis.
2. *(at an end)* terminado(-da); **time's** ~ se acabó el tiempo.
3. *(rising)*: **the** ~ **escalator** el ascensor que sube.
◆ *n*: ~**s and downs** altibajos *mpl*.

update [ʌp'deɪt] *vt* actualizar.

uphill [ʌp'hɪl] *adv* cuesta arriba.

upholstery [ʌp'həʊlstərɪ] *n* tapicería *f*.

upkeep [ʌpkiːp] *n* mantenimiento *m*.

up-market *adj* de mucha categoría.

upon [ə'pɒn] *prep (fml: on)* en, sobre; ~ **hearing the news** ... al oír la noticia ...

upper [ʌpə^r] *adj* superior ◆ *n (of shoe)* pala *f*.

upper class *n* clase *f* alta.

uppermost [ʌpəməʊst] *adj (highest)* más alto(-ta).

upper sixth *n (Br: SCH)* segundo año del curso optativo de dos que prepara a los alumnos de 18 años para los "A-levels".

upright [ʌpraɪt] *adj (person)* erguido(-da); *(object)* vertical ◆ *adj* derecho.

upset [ʌp'set] *(pt & pp upset) adj* disgustado(-da) ◆ *vt (distress)* disgustar; *(cause to go wrong)* estropear; *(knock over)* volcar; **to have an** ~ **stomach** tener el estómago revuelto.

upside down [ʌpsaɪd-] *adj & adv* al revés.

upstairs [ʌp'steəz] *adj* arriba ◆ *adv* arriba; **to go** ~ ir arriba.

up-to-date *adj (modern)* moderno(-na); *(well-informed)* al día.

upwards [ʌpwədz] *adv* hacia arriba; ~ **of 100 people** más de 100 personas.

urban [ˈɜːbən] *adj* urbano(-na).

urban clearway *n (Br)* carretera donde no está permitido parar ni estacionar.

Urdu [ˈʊədu:] *n* urdu *m*.

urge [ɜːdʒ] *vt*: **to** ~ **sb to do sthg** incitar a alguien a hacer algo.

urgent [ˈɜːdʒənt] *adj* urgente.

urgently [ˈɜːdʒəntlɪ] *adv (im-*

mediately) urgentemente.

urinal [juəˈraɪnl] n (*apparatus*) orinal m; (*fml: place*) urinario m.

urinate [ˈjuərɪneɪt] vi (*fml*) orinar.

urine [ˈjuərɪn] n orina f.

Uruguay [ˈjuərəgwaɪ] n Uruguay.

Uruguayan [ˌjuərəˈgwaɪən] adj uruguayo(-ya) ♦ n uruguayo m (-ya f).

us [ʌs] pron nos; **they know ~** nos conocen; **it's ~** somos nosotros; **send it to ~** envíanoslo; **tell ~** dinos; **they're worse than ~** son peores que nosotros.

US n (abbr of United States): **the ~** los EEUU.

USA n (abbr of United States of America): **the ~** los EEUU.

usable [ˈjuːzəbl] adj utilizable.

use [n juːs, vb juːz] n uso m ♦ vt usar; (*exploit*) utilizar; **to be of ~** ser útil; **to have the ~ of sthg** poder hacer uso de algo; **to make ~ of sthg** aprovechar algo; **"out of ~"** "no funciona"; **to be in ~** usarse; **it's no ~** es inútil; **what's the ~?** ¿de qué vale?; **to ~ sthg as sthg** usar algo como algo; **"~ before ..."** "consumir preferentemente antes de ..." ❑ **use up** vt sep agotar.

used [adj juːzd, aux vb juːst] adj usado(-da) ♦ aux vb: **to ~ to live near here** antes vivía cerca de aquí; **I ~ to go there every day** solía ir allí todos los días; **to be ~ to sthg** estar acostumbrado(-da) a algo; **to get ~ to sthg** acostumbrarse a algo.

useful [ˈjuːsfʊl] adj útil.

useless [ˈjuːslɪs] adj inútil; (*inf: very bad*) pésimo(-ma).

user [ˈjuːzər] n usuario m (-ria f).

usher [ˈʌʃər] n (at cinema, theatre) acomodador m.

usherette [ˌʌʃəˈret] n acomodadora f.

USSR n: **the (former) ~** la (antigua) URSS.

usual [ˈjuːʒəl] adj habitual; **as ~** (in the normal way) como de costumbre; (as often happens) como siempre.

usually [ˈjuːʒəlɪ] adv normalmente.

utensil [juːˈtensl] n utensilio m.

utilize [ˈjuːtəlaɪz] vt (fml) utilizar.

utmost [ˈʌtməʊst] adj mayor ♦ n: **to do one's ~** hacer todo cuanto sea posible.

utter [ˈʌtər] adj completo(-ta) ♦ vt (word) pronunciar; (sound) emitir.

utterly [ˈʌtəlɪ] adv completamente.

U-turn n giro m de 180°.

vacancy [ˈveɪkənsɪ] n (job) vacante f; **"vacancies"** "hay camas"; **"no vacancies"** "completo".

vacant [ˈveɪkənt] adj libre; **"vacant"** "libre".

vacate [vəˈkeɪt] vt (fml: room, house) desocupar.

vacation [vəˈkeɪʃn] n (Am) vacaciones *fpl* ♦ *vi* (Am) estar de vacaciones; **to go on** ~ ir de vacaciones.

vacationer [vəˈkeɪʃənər] *n* (Am) (throughout the year) persona *f* de vacaciones; (in summer) veraneante *mf*.

vaccination [ˌvæksɪˈneɪʃn] *n* vacunación *f*.

vaccine [Br ˈvæksiːn, Am vækˈsiːn] *n* vacuna *f*.

vacuum [ˈvækjʊəm] *vt* pasar la aspiradora por.

vacuum cleaner *n* aspiradora *f*.

vague [veɪg] *adj* (plan, letter, idea) vago(-ga); (memory, outline) borroso(-sa); (person) impreciso(-sa).

vain [veɪn] *adj* (pej: conceited) engreído(-da); **in** ~ en vano.

Valentine card [ˈvæləntaɪn-] *n* tarjeta *f* del día de San Valentín.

Valentine's Day [ˈvæləntaɪnz-] *n* día *m* de San Valentín.

valet [ˈvæleɪ, ˈvælɪt] *n* ayuda *m* de cámara.

valet service *n* (in hotel) servicio *m* de ayuda de cámara; (for car) servicio *m* de limpieza de automóviles.

valid [ˈvælɪd] *adj* (ticket, passport) valedero(-ra).

validate [ˈvælɪdeɪt] *vt* validar.

Valium® [ˈvælɪəm] *n* Valium® *m*.

valley [ˈvælɪ] (*pl* -s) valle *m*.

valuable [ˈvæljʊəbl] *adj* valioso(-sa) □ **valuables** *npl* objetos *mpl* de valor.

value [ˈvæljuː] *n* (financial) valor *m*; (usefulness) sentido *m*; **a** ~ **pack** un paquete económico; **to be**

good ~ **(for money)** estar muy bien de precio □ **values** *npl* valores *mpl* morales.

valve [vælv] *n* válvula *f*.

van [væn] *n* furgoneta *f*.

vandal [ˈvændl] *n* vándalo *m* (-la *f*).

vandalize [ˈvændəlaɪz] *vt* destrozar.

vanilla [vəˈnɪlə] *n* vainilla *f*.

vanish [ˈvænɪʃ] *vi* desaparecer.

vapor [ˈveɪpər] (Am) = **vapour**.

vapour [ˈveɪpər] *n* vapor *m*.

variable [ˈveərɪəbl] *adj* variable.

varicose veins [ˈværɪkəʊs-] *npl* varices *fpl*.

varied [ˈveərɪd] *adj* variado(-da).

variety [vəˈraɪətɪ] *n* variedad *f*.

various [ˈveərɪəs] *adj* varios (-rias).

varnish [ˈvɑːnɪʃ] *n* (for wood) barniz *m* ♦ *vt* (wood) barnizar.

vary [ˈveərɪ] *vt & vi* variar; **to** ~ **from sthg to sthg** variar entre algo y algo; **"prices** ~**"** "los precios varían".

vase [Br vɑːz, Am veɪz] *n* florero *m*.

Vaseline® [ˈvæsəliːn] *n* vaselina® *f*.

vast [vɑːst] *adj* inmenso(-sa).

vat [væt] *n* cuba *f*.

VAT [væt, viːeɪˈtiː] *n* (abbr of value added tax) IVA *m*.

vault [vɔːlt] *n* (in bank) cámara *f* acorazada; (in church) cripta *f*; (roof) bóveda *f*.

VCR *n* (abbr of video cassette recorder) vídeo *m*.

VDU *n* (abbr of visual display unit) monitor *m*.

veal [viːl] n ternera f.

veg [vedʒ] n (abbr of vegetable) verdura f.

vegan ['viːgən] adj de tipo vegetariano puro ◆ n persona vegetariana que no consume ningún producto de procedencia animal, como leche, huevos, etc.

vegetable ['vedʒtəbl] n vegetal m; ~s verduras fpl.

vegetable oil n aceite m vegetal.

vegetarian [,vedʒɪ'teərɪən] adj vegetariano(-na) ◆ n vegetariano m (-na f).

vegetation [,vedʒɪ'teɪʃn] n vegetación f.

vehicle ['viːəkl] n vehículo m.

veil [veɪl] n velo m.

vein [veɪn] n vena f.

Velcro® ['velkrəʊ] n velcro® m.

velvet ['velvɪt] n terciopelo m.

vending machine ['vendɪŋ-] n máquina f de venta automática.

venetian blind [vɪ,niːʃn-] n persiana f veneciana.

Venezuela [,venɪz'weɪlə] n Venezuela.

Venezuelan [,venɪz'weɪlən] adj venezolano(-na) ◆ n venezolano m (-na f).

venison ['venɪzn] n carne f de venado.

vent [vent] n (for air, smoke etc) rejilla f de ventilación.

ventilation [,ventɪ'leɪʃn] n ventilación f.

ventilator ['ventɪleɪtə'] n ventilador m.

venture ['ventʃə'] n empresa f ◆ vi (go) aventurarse a ir.

venue ['venjuː] n lugar m (de un acontecimiento).

veranda [və'rændə] n porche m.

verb [vɜːb] n verbo m.

verdict ['vɜːdɪkt] n (JUR) veredicto m; (opinion) juicio m.

verge [vɜːdʒ] n (of road, lawn, path) borde m; "soft ~s" señal que avisa del peligro de estancarse en los bordes de la carretera.

verify ['verɪfaɪ] vt verificar.

vermin ['vɜːmɪn] n bichos mpl.

vermouth ['vɜːməθ] n vermut m.

versa → vice versa.

versatile ['vɜːsətaɪl] adj (person) polifacético(-ca); (machine, food) que tiene muchos usos.

verse [vɜːs] n (of song, poem) estrofa f; (poetry) versos mpl.

version [vɜːʃn] n versión f.

versus ['vɜːsəs] prep contra.

vertical ['vɜːtɪkl] adj vertical.

vertigo ['vɜːtɪgəʊ] n vértigo m.

very ['verɪ] adv muy ◆ adj mismísimo(-ma); ~ much mucho; not ~ big no muy grande; my ~ own room mi propia habitación; the ~ best el mejor de todos; the ~ person justo la persona.

vessel ['vesl] n (fml: ship) nave f.

vest [vest] n (Br: underwear) camiseta f; (Am: waistcoat) chaleco m.

vet [vet] n (Br) veterinario m (-ria f).

veteran ['vetrən] n veterano m (-na f).

veterinarian [,vetrɪ'neərɪən] (Am) = **vet**.

veterinary surgeon ['vetərɪnrɪ-] (Br: fml) = **vet**.

F n (abbr of very high frequency) vHF m.

VHS n (abbr of video home system) VHS m.

via ['vaɪə] prep (place) pasando por; (by means of) por medio de.

viaduct ['vaɪədʌkt] n viaducto m.

vibrate [vaɪ'breɪt] vi vibrar.

vibration [vaɪ'breɪʃn] n vibración f.

vicar ['vɪkəʳ] n párroco m (-ca f).

vicarage ['vɪkərɪdʒ] n casa f parroquial.

vice [vaɪs] n vicio m; (Br: tool) torno m de banco.

vice-president n vicepresidente m (-ta f).

vice versa [,vaɪs'vɜ:sə] adv viceversa.

vicinity [vɪ'sɪnətɪ] n: in the ~ en las proximidades.

vicious ['vɪʃəs] adj (attack) brutal; (animal) sañoso(-sa); (comment) hiriente.

victim ['vɪktɪm] n víctima f.

Victorian [vɪk'tɔ:rɪən] adj victoriano(-na).

victory ['vɪktərɪ] n victoria f.

video ['vɪdɪəʊ] (pl -s) n vídeo m ◆ vt (using video recorder) grabar en vídeo; (using camera) hacer un vídeo de; on ~ en vídeo.

video camera n videocámara f.

video game n videojuego m.

video recorder n vídeo m.

video shop n tienda f de vídeos.

videotape ['vɪdɪəʊteɪp] n cinta f de vídeo.

Vietnam [Br ,vjet'næm, Am ,vjet'nɑ:m] n Vietnam.

view [vju:] n (scene, line of sight) vista f; (opinion) opinión f; (attitude) visión f ◆ vt (look at) observar; in my ~ desde mi punto de vista; in ~ of (considering) en vista de; to come into ~ aparecer; you're blocking my ~ no me dejas ver nada.

viewer ['vju:əʳ] n (of TV) telespectador m (-ra f).

viewfinder ['vju:,faɪndəʳ] n visor m.

viewpoint ['vju:pɔɪnt] n (opinion) punto m de vista; (place) mirador m.

vigilant ['vɪdʒɪlənt] adj (fml) alerta.

villa ['vɪlə] n (in countryside, by sea) casa f de campo; (Br: in town) chalé m.

village ['vɪlɪdʒ] n (larger) pueblo m; (smaller) aldea f.

villager ['vɪlɪdʒəʳ] n aldeano m (-na f).

villain ['vɪlən] n (of book, film) malo m (-la f); (criminal) criminal mf.

vinaigrette [,vɪnɪ'gret] n vinagreta f.

vine [vaɪn] n (grapevine) vid f; (climbing plant) parra f.

vinegar ['vɪnɪgəʳ] n vinagre m.

vineyard ['vɪnjəd] n viña f.

vintage ['vɪntɪdʒ] adj (wine) añejo(-ja) ◆ n (year) cosecha f (de vino).

vinyl ['vaɪnɪl] n vinilo m.

viola [vɪ'əʊlə] n viola f.

violence ['vaɪələns] n violencia f.

violent ['vaɪələnt] adj violento(-ta); *(storm)* fuerte.

violet ['vaɪələt] *adj* violeta *(inv)* ◆ *n (flower)* violeta *f*.

violin [,vaɪə'lɪn] *n* violín *m*.

VIP *n (abbr of very important person)* gran personalidad *f*.

virgin ['vɜːdʒɪn] *n* virgen *mf*.

Virgo ['vɜːgəʊ] *(pl -s)* *n* Virgo *m*.

virtually ['vɜːtʃʊəlɪ] *adv* prácticamente.

virtual reality [,vɜːtʃʊəl-] *n* realidad *f* virtual.

virus ['vaɪrəs] *n* virus *m inv*

visa ['viːzə] *n* visado *m*.

viscose ['vɪskəʊs] *n* viscosa *f*.

visibility [,vɪzɪ'bɪlətɪ] *n* visibilidad *f*.

visible ['vɪzəbl] *adj* visible.

visit ['vɪzɪt] *vt* visitar ◆ *n* visita *f*.

visiting hours ['vɪzɪtɪŋ-] *npl* horas *fpl* de visita.

visitor ['vɪzɪtər] *n (to person)* visita *f*; *(to place)* visitante *mf*.

visitor centre *n* establecimiento en un lugar de interés turístico donde suele haber una exhibición, cafetería, tienda, etc.

visitors' book ['vɪzɪtəz-] *n* libro *m* de visitas.

visitor's passport ['vɪzɪtəz-] *n (Br)* pasaporte *m* provisional.

visor ['vaɪzər] *n* visera *f*.

vital ['vaɪtl] *adj* esencial.

vitamin [*Br* 'vɪtəmɪn, *Am* 'vaɪtəmɪn] *n* vitamina *f*.

vivid ['vɪvɪd] *adj* vivo(-va).

V-neck ['viː-] *n (design)* cuello *m* de pico.

vocabulary [və'kæbjʊlərɪ] *n* vocabulario *m*.

vodka ['vɒdkə] *n* vodka *m*.

voice [vɔɪs] *n* voz *f*.

volcano [vɒl'keɪnəʊ] *(pl -es* OR *-s) n* volcán *m*.

volleyball ['vɒlɪbɔːl] *n* voleibol *m*.

volt [vəʊlt] *n* voltio *m*.

voltage ['vəʊltɪdʒ] *n* voltaje *m*.

volume ['vɒljuːm] *n* volumen *m*.

voluntary ['vɒləntrɪ] *adj* voluntario(-ria).

volunteer [,vɒlən'tɪər] *n* voluntario *m* (ria *f*) ◆ *vt*: **to ~ to do sthg** ofrecerse voluntariamente a hacer algo.

vomit ['vɒmɪt] *n* vómito *m* ◆ *vi* vomitar.

vote [vəʊt] *n (choice)* voto *m*; *(process)* votación *f*; *(number of votes)* votos *mpl* ◆ *vi*: **to ~ (for)** votar (a).

voter ['vəʊtər] *n* votante *mf*.

voucher ['vaʊtʃər] *n* bono *m*.

vowel ['vaʊəl] *n* vocal *f*.

voyage ['vɔɪɪdʒ] *n* viaje *m*.

vulgar ['vʌlgər] *adj (rude)* grosero(-ra); *(in bad taste)* chabacano(-na).

vulture ['vʌltʃər] *n* buitre *m*.

W *(abbr of west)* O.

wad [wɒd] *n (of paper)* taco *m*; *(of banknotes)* fajo *m*; *(of cotton)* bola *f*.

waddle ['wɒdl] *vi* anadear.

wade [weɪd] *vi* caminar dentro del agua.

wading pool [weɪdɪŋ-] *n* (*Am*) piscina *f* infantil.

wafer [weɪfə'] *n* barquillo *m*.

waffle [wɒfl] *n* (*pancake*) gofre *m* ♦ *vi* (*inf*) enrollarse.

wag [wæg] *vt* menear.

wage [weɪdʒ] *n* (*weekly*) salario *m* ❑ **wages** *npl* (*weekly*) salario *m*.

wagon [wægən] *n* (*vehicle*) carro *m*; (*Br: of train*) vagón *m*.

waist [weɪst] *n* cintura *f*.

waistcoat [weɪskəʊt] *n* chaleco *m*.

wait [weɪt] *n* espera *f* ♦ *vi* esperar; **to ~ for sb to do sthg** esperar a que alguien haga algo; **I can't ~!** ¡me muero de impaciencia! ❑ **wait for** *vt fus* esperar.

waiter [weɪtə'] *n* camarero *m*.

waiting room [weɪtɪŋ-] *n* sala *f* de espera.

waitress [weɪtrɪs] *n* camarera *f*.

wake [weɪk] (*pt* woke, *pp* woken) *vt* despertar ♦ *vi* despertarse ❑ **wake up** *vt sep* despertar ♦ *vi* despertarse.

Waldorf salad [wɔːldɔːf-] *n* ensalada de manzana, nueces y apio con mayonesa.

Wales [weɪlz] *n* (el país de) Gales.

walk [wɔːk] *n* (*journey on foot*) paseo *m*; (*path*) ruta *f* paisajística (a pie) ♦ *vi* andar; (*as hobby*) caminar ♦ *vt* (*distance*) andar; (*dog*) pasear; **to go for a ~** ir a dar un paseo; **it's a short ~** está a poca distancia a pie; **to take the dog for a ~** pasear el perro; **"walk"** (*Am*) señal que autoriza a los peatones a cruzar;

"don't ~" (*Am*) señal que prohíbe cruzar a los peatones ❑ **walk away** *vi* marcharse; **walk in** *vi* entrar; **walk out** *vi* (*leave angrily*) marcharse enfurecido.

walker [wɔːkə'] *n* caminante *mf*.

walking boots [wɔːkɪŋ-] *n* botas *fpl* de montaña.

walking stick [wɔːkɪŋ-] *n* bastón *m*.

Walkman® [wɔːkmən] *n* walkman® *m*.

wall [wɔːl] *n* (*of building, room*) pared *f*; (*in garden, countryside, street*) muro *m*.

wallet [wɒlɪt] *n* billetero *m*.

wallpaper [wɔːl,peɪpə'] *n* papel de pared.

wally [wɒlɪ] *n* (*Br: inf*) imbécil *mf*.

walnut [wɔːlnʌt] *n* (*nut*) nuez *f* (de nogal).

waltz [wɔːls] *n* vals *m*.

wander [wɒndə'] *vi* vagar.

want [wɒnt] *vt* (*desire*) querer; (*need*) necesitar; **to ~ to do sthg** querer hacer algo; **to ~ sb to do sthg** querer que alguien haga algo.

war [wɔː'] *n* guerra *f*.

ward [wɔːd] *n* (*in hospital*) sala *f*.

warden [wɔːdn] *n* (*of park*) guarda *mf*; (*of youth hostel*) encargado *m* (-da *f*).

wardrobe [wɔːdrəʊb] *n* armario *m*, guardarropa *m*.

warehouse [weəhaʊs, *pl* -haʊzɪz] *n* almacén *m*.

warm [wɔːm] *adj* (*pleasantly hot*) caliente; (*lukewarm*) templado (-da); (*day, weather, welcome*) caluroso(-sa); (*clothes, blankets*) que abriga; *(person, smile)* afectuoso(-sa) ◆ *vt* calentar; **I'm ~** tengo calor; **it's ~** hace calor; **are you ~ enough?** no tendrás frío ¿verdad? □ **warm up** *vt sep* calentar ◆ *vi (get warmer)* entrar en calor; *(do exercises)* hacer ejercicios de calentamiento; *(machine, engine)* calentarse.

war memorial *n* monumento *m* a los caídos de una guerra.

warmth [wɔːmθ] *n* calor *m*.

warn [wɔːn] *vt* advertir; **to ~ sb about sthg** prevenir a alguien sobre algo; **to ~ sb not to do sthg** advertir a alguien que no haga algo.

warning [wɔːnɪŋ] *n* aviso *m*.

warranty [wɒrəntɪ] *n (fml)* garantía *f*.

warship [wɔːʃɪp] *n* buque *m* de guerra.

wart [wɔːt] *n* verruga *f*.

was [wɒz] *pt →* **be**.

wash [wɒʃ] *vt* lavar ◆ *vi* lavarse ◆ *n*: **to give sthg a ~** lavar algo; **to have a ~** lavarse; **to ~ one's hands/face** lavarse las manos/la cara □ **wash up** *vi (Br: do washing-up)* fregar los platos; *(Am: clean o.s.)* lavarse.

washable [wɒʃəbl] *adj* lavable.

washbasin [wɒʃ,beɪsn] *n* lavabo *m*.

washbowl [wɒʃbəʊl] *n (Am)* lavabo *m*.

washer [wɒʃər] *n (ring)* arandela *f*.

washing [wɒʃɪŋ] *n (activity, clean clothes)* colada *f*; *(dirty clothes)* ropa *f* sucia.

washing line *n* tendedero *m*.

washing machine *n* lavadora *f*.

washing powder *n* detergente *m* (en polvo).

washing-up *n (Br)*: **to do the ~** fregar los platos.

washing-up bowl *n (Br)* barreño *m*.

washing-up liquid *n (Br)* lavavajillas *m inv*.

washroom [wɒʃrum] *n (Am)* aseos *mpl*.

wasn't [wɒznt] = **was not**.

wasp [wɒsp] *n* avispa *f*.

waste [weɪst] *n (rubbish)* desperdicios *mpl*; *(toxic, nuclear)* residuos *mpl* ◆ *vt (energy, opportunity)* desperdiciar; *(money)* malgastar; *(time)* perder; **a ~ of money** un derroche de dinero; **a ~ of time** una pérdida de tiempo.

wastebin [weɪstbɪn] *n* cubo *m* de la basura.

waste ground *n* descampado *m*.

wastepaper basket [weɪst-ˈpeɪpə-] *n* papelera *f*.

watch [wɒtʃ] *n (wristwatch)* reloj *m* (de pulsera) ◆ *vt (observe)* ver; *(spy on)* vigilar; *(be careful with)* tener cuidado con □ **watch out** *vi (be careful)* tener cuidado; **~ out for a big hotel** estate al tanto de un hotel grande.

watchstrap [wɒtʃstræp] *n* correa *f* de reloj.

water [wɔːtər] *n* agua *f* ◆ *vt* regar ◆ *vi*: **my eyes are ~ing** me lloran los ojos; **my mouth is ~ing** se me está haciendo la boca agua.

water bottle n cantimplora f.

watercolour ['wɔːtəˌkʌlər] n acuarela f.

watercress ['wɔːtəkres] n berro m.

waterfall ['wɔːtəfɔːl] n (small) cascada f; (large) catarata f.

watering can ['wɔːtərɪŋ-] n regadera f.

watermelon ['wɔːtəˌmelən] n sandía f.

waterproof ['wɔːtəpruːf] adj impermeable.

water purification tablets [-pjʊərɪfɪˈkeɪʃn-] npl pastillas fpl para depurar el agua.

water skiing n esquí m acuático.

watersports ['wɔːtəspɔːts] npl deportes mpl acuáticos.

water tank n depósito m del agua.

watertight ['wɔːtətaɪt] adj hermético(-ca).

watt [wɒt] n vatio m; **a 60-~ bulb** una bombilla de 60 vatios.

wave [weɪv] n (in sea, of crime) ola f; (in hair, of light, sound) onda f ◆ vt (hand) saludar con; (flag) agitar ◆ vi (when greeting) saludar con la mano; (when saying goodbye) decir adiós con la mano.

wavelength ['weɪvleŋθ] n longitud f de onda.

wavy ['weɪvɪ] adj ondulado(-da).

wax [wæks] n cera f.

way [weɪ] n (manner, means) modo m, manera f; (route, distance travelled) camino m; (direction) dirección f; **it's the wrong ~ round** es al revés; **which ~ is the station?** ¿por

dónde se va a la estación?; **the town is out of our ~** la ciudad no nos queda de camino; **to be in the ~** estar en medio; **to be on the ~** (coming) estar de camino; **to get out of the ~** quitarse de en medio; **to get under ~** dar comienzo; **there's a long ~ to go** nos queda mucho camino; **a long ~ away** muy lejos; **to lose one's ~** perderse; **on the ~ back** a la vuelta; **on the ~ there** a la ida; **that ~** (like that) así; (in that direction) por allí; **this ~** (like this) así; (in this direction) por aquí; **"give ~"** "ceda el paso"; **"~ in"** "entrada"; **"~ out"** "salida"; **no ~!** (inf) ¡ni hablar!

WC n (abbr of water closet) aseos mpl.

we [wiː] pron nosotros mpl (-tras fpl); **we're young** (nosotros) somos jóvenes.

weak [wiːk] adj débil; (not solid) frágil; (drink) poco cargado(-a); (soup) líquido(-da); (poor, not good) mediocre.

weaken ['wiːkn] vt debilitar.

weakness ['wiːknɪs] n (weak point) defecto m; (fondness) debilidad f.

wealth [welθ] n riqueza f.

wealthy ['welθɪ] adj rico(-ca).

weapon ['wepən] n arma f.

wear [weər] (pt **wore**, pp **worn**) vt llevar ◆ n (clothes) ropa f; **wear and tear** desgaste m ☐ **wear off** vi desaparecer; **wear out** vi gastarse.

weary ['wɪərɪ] adj fatigado(-da).

weasel ['wiːzl] n comadreja f.

weather ['weðər] n tiempo m; **what's the ~ like?** ¿qué tiempo hace?; **to be under the ~** *(inf)* no encontrarse muy bien.

weather forecast *n* pronóstico *m* del tiempo.

weather forecaster [-fɔː-kɑːstəʳ] *n* hombre *m* del tiempo (mujer *f* del tiempo).

weather report *n* parte *m* meteorológico.

weather vane [-veɪn] *n* veleta *f.*

weave [wi:v] *(pt* **wove,** *pp* **woven)** *vt* tejer.

web [web] *n* telaraña *f.*

Wed. *(abbr of Wednesday)* miér.

wedding [wedɪŋ] *n* boda *f.*

wedding anniversary *n* aniversario *m* de boda.

wedding dress *n* vestido *m* de novia.

wedding ring *n* anillo *m* de boda.

wedge [wedʒ] *n (of cake)* trozo *m; (of wood etc)* cuña *f.*

Wednesday [wenzdɪ] *n* miércoles *m inv,* → **Saturday.**

wee [wi:] *adj (Scot)* pequeño(-ña) ♦ *n (inf)* pipí *m.*

weed [wi:d] *n* mala hierba *f.*

week [wi:k] *n* semana *f; (weekdays)* días *mpl* laborables; **a ~ today** de hoy en ocho días; **in a ~'s time** dentro de una semana

weekday [wi:kdeɪ] *n* día *m* laborable.

weekend [ˌwi:kˈend] *n* fin *m* de semana.

weekly [wi:klɪ] *adj* semanal ♦ *adv* cada semana ♦ *n* semanario *m.*

weep [wi:p] *(pt & pp* **wept)** *vi* llorar.

weigh [weɪ] *vt* pesar; **how much does it ~?** ¿cuánto pesa?

weight [weɪt] *n* peso *m;* **to lose ~** adelgazar; **to put on ~** engordar ❏ **weights** *npl (for weight training)* pesas *fpl.*

weightlifting [weɪtˌlɪftɪŋ] *n* halterofilia *f.*

weight training *n* ejercicios *mpl* de pesas.

weir [wɪəʳ] *n* presa *f.*

weird [wɪəd] *adj* raro(-ra).

welcome [welkəm] *adj (guest)* bienvenido(-da); *(freely allowed)* muy libre; *(appreciated)* grato(-ta) ♦ *n* bienvenida *f* ♦ *vt (greet)* dar la bienvenida a; *(be grateful for)* agradecer ♦ *excl* ¡bienvenido!; **to make sb feel ~** recibir bien a alguien; **you're ~!** de nada.

weld [weld] *vt* soldar.

welfare [welfeəʳ] *n (happiness, comfort)* bienestar *m; (Am: money)* subsidio *m* de la Seguridad Social.

well [wel] *(compar* **better,** *superl* **best)** *adj & adv* bien ♦ *n* pozo *m;* **to get ~** reponerse, **to go ~** ir bien; **~ before** the start mucho antes del comienzo; **~ done!** ¡muy bien!; **it may ~ happen** es muy probable que ocurra; **it's ~ worth it** sí que merece la pena; **as ~** también; **as ~ as** además de.

we'll [wi:l] = **we shall, we will.**

well-behaved [-brˈheɪvd] *adj* bien educado(-da).

well-built *adj* fornido(-da).

well-done *adj* muy hecho (-cha).

well-dressed [-ˈdrest] *adj* bien vestido(-da).

wellington (boot) [ˈwelɪŋtən-] n bota f de agua.

well-known adj conocido (-da).

well-off adj (rich) adinerado(-da).

well-paid adj bien remunerado(-da).

welly [ˈwelɪ] n (Br: inf) bota f de agua.

Welsh [welʃ] adj galés(-esa) ◆ n (language) galés m ◆ npl: the ~ los galeses.

Welshman [ˈwelʃmən] (pl -men [-mən]) n galés m.

Welsh rarebit [-ˈreəbɪt] n tostada con queso gratinado.

Welshwoman [ˈwelʃˌwʊmən] (pl -women [-ˌwɪmɪn]) n galesa f.

went [went] pt → go.

wept [wept] pt & pp → weep.

were [wɜːr] pt → be.

we're [wɪər] = we are.

weren't [wɜːnt] = were not.

west [west] n oeste m ◆ adv (fly, walk) hacia el oeste; (be situated) al oeste; in the ~ of England en el oeste de Inglaterra.

westbound [ˈwestbaʊnd] adj con dirección oeste.

West Country n: the ~ el sudoeste de Inglaterra, especialmente los condados de Somerset, Devon y Cornualles.

West End n: the ~ (of London) zona occidental del centro de Londres, muy conocida por sus tiendas, cines y teatros.

western [ˈwestən] adj occidental ◆ n película f del oeste.

West Indies [-ˈɪndiːz] npl: the ~ las Antillas.

Westminster [ˈwestmɪnstər] n Westminster.

i **WESTMINSTER**

En esta zona de Londres cercana al río Támesis se hallan el Parlamento y la abadía de Westminster. La palabra "Westminster" también se usa para referirse al propio parlamento británico.

Westminster Abbey n la abadía de Westminster.

i **WESTMINSTER ABBEY**

La abadía de Westminster es una iglesia londinense donde se corona al monarca británico. Varios personajes ilustres están ahí enterrados, y hay una zona especial conocida como "Poets' Corner" que alberga los sepulcros de escritores como Chaucer, Dickens y Hardy.

westwards [ˈwestwədz] adv hacia el oeste.

wet [wet] (pt & pp wet OR -ted) adj (soaked) mojado(-da); (damp) húmedo(-da); (rainy) lluvioso(-sa) ◆ vt (soak) mojar; (dampen) humedecer; to get ~ mojarse; "~ paint" "recién pintado".

wet suit n traje m de submarinista.

we've [wiːv] = we have.

whale [weɪl] n ballena f.

wharf [wɔːf] (pl -s OR wharves

[wɔːvz]) *n* muelle *m*.

what [wɒt] *adj* 1. *(in questions)* qué; ~ **colour is it?** ¿de qué color es?; ~ **shape is it?** ¿qué forma tiene?; **he asked me** ~ **colour it was** me preguntó de qué color era. 2. *(in exclamations)* qué; ~ **a surprise!** ¡qué sorpresa!; ~ **a beautiful day!** ¡qué día más bonito!

♦ *pron* 1. *(in questions)* qué; ~ **is going on?** ¿qué pasa?; ~ **are they doing?** ¿qué hacen?; ~ **is it called?** ¿cómo se llama?; ~ **are they talking about?** ¿de qué están hablando?; **she asked me** ~ **happened** me preguntó qué había pasado. 2. *(introducing relative clause)* lo que; **I didn't see** ~ **happened** no vi lo que pasó; **take** ~ **you want** coge lo que quieras. 3. *(in phrases)*: ~ **for?** ¿para qué?; ~ **about going out for a meal?** ¿qué tal si salimos a cenar?

♦ *excl* ¡qué!

whatever [wɒt'evəʳ] *pron*: **take** ~ **you want** coge lo que quieras; ~ **I do, I'll lose** haga lo que haga, saldré perdiendo; ~ **that may be** sea lo que sea eso.

wheat [wiːt] *n* trigo *m*.

wheel [wiːl] *n* rueda *f*, *(steering wheel)* volante *m*.

wheelbarrow [ˈwiːlˌbærəʊ] *n* carretilla *f*.

wheelchair [ˈwiːltʃeəʳ] *n* silla *f* de ruedas.

wheelclamp [ˌwiːlˈklæmp] *n* cepo *m*.

wheezy [ˈwiːzɪ] *adj*: **to be** ~ resollar.

when [wen] *adv* cuándo ♦ *conj* cuando.

whenever [wen'evəʳ] *conj* siempre que; ~ **you like** cuando quieras.

where [weəʳ] *adv* dónde ♦ *conj* donde.

whereabouts [ˈweərəbaʊts] *adv* (por) dónde ♦ *npl* paradero *m*.

whereas [weərˈæz] *conj* mientras que.

wherever [weərˈevəʳ] *conj* dondequiera que; ~ **that may be** dondequiera que esté eso; ~ **you like** donde quieras.

whether [ˈweðəʳ] *conj* si; ~ **you like it or not** tanto si te gusta como si no.

which [wɪtʃ] *adj* qué; ~ **room do you want?** ¿qué habitación quieres?; **she asked me** ~ **room I wanted** me preguntó qué habitación quería o ~ **one?** ¿cuál?

♦ *pron* 1. *(in questions)* cuál; ~ **is the cheapest?** ¿cuál es el más barato?; **he asked me** ~ **was the best** me preguntó cuál era el mejor. 2. *(introducing relative clause)* que; **the house** ~ **is on the corner** la casa que está en la esquina; **the television** ~ **I bought** la televisión que compré; **the settee on** ~ **I'm sitting** el sofá en el que estoy sentado. 3. *(referring back)* lo cual; **she denied it,** ~ **surprised me** lo negó, lo cual me sorprendió.

whichever [wɪtʃ'evəʳ] *pron* el que *m* (la que *f*) ♦ *adj*: **take** ~ **chocolate you like best** coge el bombón que prefieras; ~ **way you do it** lo hagas como lo hagas.

while [waɪl] *conj (during the time that)* mientras; *(although)* aunque; *(whereas)* mientras que ♦ *n*: **a** ~ un rato; **a ~ ago** hace tiempo; **for a ~** un rato; **in a ~** dentro de un rato.

whim [wɪm] n capricho m.

whine [waɪn] vi (make noise) gimotear; (complain) quejarse.

whip [wɪp] n látigo m ♦ vt azotar.

whipped cream [wɪpt-] n nata f montada.

whirlpool [ˈwɜːlpuːl] n (Jacuzzi) jacuzzi® m.

whisk [wɪsk] n batidor m (de varillas) ♦ vt (eggs, cream) batir.

whiskers [ˈwɪskəz] npl (of person) patillas fpl; (of animal) bigotes mpl.

whiskey [ˈwɪskɪ] (pl -s) n whisky m (de Irlanda o EEUU).

whisky [ˈwɪskɪ] n whisky m (de Escocia).

ℹ️ **WHISKY**

El whisky, considerado la bebida nacional escocesa, es un fuerte licor elaborado con cebada y malta. El whisky siempre madura en barriles de madera y presenta distintas características dependiendo de los métodos de producción y tipos de agua utilizados. El whisky de malta conocido como "single malt", que en muchos casos se elabora en pequeñas destilerías regionales, se considera superior a otros tipos normalmente más baratos, llamados "blended".

---

whisper [ˈwɪspər] vt susurrar ♦ vi cuchichear.

whistle [ˈwɪsl] n (instrument) silbato m; (sound) silbido m ♦ vi silbar.

white [waɪt] adj blanco(-ca); (coffee, tea) con leche ♦ n (colour) blanco m; (of egg) clara f; (person) blanco m (-ca f).

white bread n pan m blanco.

White House n: **the ~** la Casa Blanca.

white sauce n salsa f bechamel.

white spirit n especie de aguarrás.

whitewash [ˈwaɪtwɒʃ] vt blanquear.

white wine n vino m blanco.

whiting [ˈwaɪtɪŋ] (pl inv) n pescadilla f.

Whitsun [ˈwɪtsn] n Pentecostés m.

who [huː] pron (in questions) quién, quiénes (pl); (in relative clauses) que.

whoever [huːˈevər] pron quienquiera que; **~ it is** quienquiera que sea; **~ you like** quien quieras.

whole [həʊl] adj entero(-ra) ♦ n: **the ~ of the journey** todo el viaje; **on the ~** en general.

wholefoods [ˈhəʊlfuːdz] npl alimentos mpl integrales.

wholemeal bread [ˈhəʊlmiːl-] n (Br) pan m integral.

wholesale [ˈhəʊlseɪl] adv al por mayor.

wholewheat bread [ˈhəʊl-ˌwiːt-] (Am) = **wholemeal bread**.

whom [huːm] pron (fml: in questions) quién, quiénes (pl); (in relative clauses) que.

whooping cough [ˈhuːpɪŋ-] n tos f ferina.

whose [huːz] adj (in questions) de

quién; *(in relative clauses)* cuyo(-ya)
♦ *pron* de quién; ~ **book is this?** ¿de quién es este libro?

why [waɪ] *adv & conj* por qué; **this is ~ we can't do it** esta es la razón por la que no podemos hacerlo; **explain the reason ~** explícame por qué; **~ not?** *(in suggestions)* ¿por qué no?; *(all right)* por supuesto (que sí).

wick [wɪk] *n* mecha *f*.

wicked ['wɪkɪd] *adj (evil)* perverso(-sa); *(mischievous)* travieso(-sa).

wicker ['wɪkə^r] *adj* de mimbre.

wide [waɪd] *adj (make distance)* ancho(-cha); *(range, variety)* amplio (-plia); *(difference, gap)* grande ♦ *adv:* **to open sth** ~ abrir bien algo; **how ~ is the road?** ¿cómo es de ancha la carretera?; **it's 12 metres** ~ tiene 12 metros de ancho; ~ **open** *(door, window)* abierto de par en par.

widely ['waɪdlɪ] *adv (known, found)* generalmente; *(travel)* extensamente.

widen ['waɪdn] *vt (make broader)* ensanchar ♦ *vi (gap, difference)* aumentar.

widespread ['waɪdspred] *adj* general.

widow ['wɪdəʊ] *n* viuda *f*.

widower ['wɪdəʊə^r] *n* viudo *m*.

width [wɪdθ] *n* anchura *f*; *(of swimming pool)* ancho *m*.

wife [waɪf] *(pl* **wives)** *n* mujer *f*.

wig [wɪg] *n* peluca *f*.

wild [waɪld] *adj (plant)* silvestre; *(animal)* salvaje; *(land, area)* agreste; *(uncontrolled)* frenético(-ca); *(crazy)* alocado(-da); **to be ~ about** *(inf)* estar loco(-ca) por.

wild flower *n* flor *f* silvestre.

wildlife ['waɪldlaɪf] *n* fauna *f*.

will¹ [wɪl] *aux vb* **1.** *(expressing future tense):* **I ~ see you next week** te veré la semana que viene; ~ **you be here next Friday?** ¿vas a venir el próximo viernes?; **yes I ~** sí; **no I won't** no.

2. *(expressing willingness):* **I won't do it** no lo haré; **no one ~ do it** nadie quiere hacerlo.

3. *(expressing polite question):* ~ **you have some more tea?** ¿le apetece más té?

4. *(in commands, requests):* ~ **you please be quiet!** ¿queréis hacer el favor de callaros?; **close the window, ~ you?** cierra la ventana, por favor.

will² [wɪl] *n (document)* testamento *m*; **against one's** ~ contra la voluntad de uno.

willing ['wɪlɪŋ] *adj:* **to be ~ (to do sth)** estar dispuesto(-ta) (a hacer algo).

willingly ['wɪlɪŋlɪ] *adv* de buena gana.

willow ['wɪləʊ] *n* sauce *m*.

win [wɪn] *(pt & pp* **won)** *n* victoria *f* ♦ *vt & vi* ganar.

wind¹ [wɪnd] *n* viento *m*; *(in stomach)* gases *mpl*.

wind² [waɪnd] *(pt & pp* **wound)** *vi* serpentear ♦ *vt:* **to ~ sth round sth** enrollar algo alrededor de algo ❑ **wind up** *vt sep (Br: inf: annoy)* vacilar; *(car window)* subir; *(clock, watch)* dar cuerda a.

windbreak ['wɪndbreɪk] *n* lona *f* de protección contra el viento.

windmill ['wɪndmɪl] *n* molino *m* de viento.

...ndow ['wɪndəʊ] *n* ventana *f*; *(of car, plane)* ventanilla *f*; *(of shop)* escaparate *m*.

window box *n* jardinera *f* (de ventana).

window cleaner *n* limpiacristales *mf inv*.

windowpane ['wɪndəʊpeɪn] *n* cristal *m*.

window seat *n* asiento *m* junto a la ventanilla.

window-shopping *n*: to go ~ mirar los escaparates.

windowsill ['wɪndəʊsɪl] *n* alféizar *m*.

windscreen ['wɪndskri:n] *n* (Br) parabrisas *m inv*.

windscreen wipers *npl* (Br) limpiaparabrisas *m inv*.

windshield ['wɪndʃi:ld] *n* (Am) parabrisas *m inv*.

Windsor Castle ['wɪnzə^r-] *n* el castillo de Windsor.

ⓘ WINDSOR CASTLE

Los orígenes del castillo de Windsor, en Berkshire, se remontan al siglo XI cuando Guillermo el Conquistador inició su construcción. Hoy, es una de las residencias oficiales del monarca británico, y una parte está abierta al público.

---

windsurfing ['wɪnd,sɜ:fɪŋ] *n* windsurf *m*; to go ~ ir a hacer windsurf.

windy ['wɪndɪ] *adj (day, weather)* de mucho viento; it's ~ hace viento.

wine [waɪn] *n* vino *m*.

wine bar *n* (Br) bar de cierta distinción, especializado en la venta de vinos y que suele servir comidas.

wineglass ['waɪnglɑ:s] *n* copa *f* (de vino).

wine list *n* lista *f* de vinos.

wine tasting [-'teɪstɪŋ] *n* cata *f* de vinos.

wine waiter *n* sommelier *m*.

wing [wɪŋ] *n* ala *f*; (Br: of car) guardabarros *m inv* ❑ **wings** *npl*: the ~s los bastidores.

wink [wɪŋk] *vi* guiñar el ojo.

winner ['wɪnə^r] *n* ganador *m* (-ra *f*).

winning ['wɪnɪŋ] *adj (person, team)* vencedor(-ra); (ticket, number) premiado(-da).

winter ['wɪntə^r] *n* invierno *m*; in (the) ~ en invierno.

wintertime ['wɪntətaɪm] *n* invierno *m*.

wipe [waɪp] *vt* limpiar; to ~ one's feet limpiarse los zapatos (en el felpudo); to ~ one's hands limpiarse las manos ❑ **wipe up** *vt sep (liquid)* secar; (dirt) limpiar ◆ *vi (dry the dishes)* secar (los platos).

wiper ['waɪpə^r] *n (windscreen wiper)* limpiaparabrisas *m inv*.

wire [waɪə^r] *n* alambre *m*; (electrical wire) cable *m* ◆ *vt (plug)* conectar el cable a.

wireless ['waɪəlɪs] *n* radio *f*.

wiring ['waɪərɪŋ] *n* instalación *f* eléctrica.

wisdom tooth ['wɪzdəm-] *n* muela *f* del juicio.

wise [waɪz] *adj (person)* sabio(-bia); *(decision, idea)* sensato(-ta).

wish [wɪʃ] *n* deseo *m* ♦ *vt* desear; **I ~ I was younger** ¡ojalá fuese más joven!; **best ~es** un saludo; **to ~ for sthg** pedir algo (como deseo); **to ~ to do sthg** *(fml)* desear hacer algo; **to ~ sb luck/happy birthday** desear a alguien buena suerte/feliz cumpleaños; **if you ~** *(fml)* si usted lo desea.

witch [wɪtʃ] *n* bruja *f*.

with [wɪð] *prep* 1. *(in company of)* con; **I play tennis ~ her** juego al tenis con ella; **~ me** conmigo; **~ you** contigo; **~ himself/herself** consigo; **we stayed ~ friends** estuvimos en casa de unos amigos.
2. *(in descriptions)* con; **the man ~ the beard** el hombre de la barba; **a room ~ a bathroom** una habitación con baño.
3. *(indicating means, manner)* con; **I washed it ~ detergent** lo lavé con detergente; **they won ~ ease** ganaron con facilidad; **topped ~ cream** cubierto de nata; **to tremble ~ fear** temblar de miedo.
4. *(regarding)* con; **be careful ~ that!** ¡ten cuidado con eso!
5. *(indicating opposition)* contra; **to argue ~ sb** discutir con alguien.

withdraw [wɪð'drɔː] *(pt* -drew, *pp* -drawn) *vt (take out)* retirar; *(money)* sacar ♦ *vi* retirarse.

withdrawal [wɪð'drɔːəl] *n (from bank account)* reintegro *m*.

withdrawn [wɪð'drɔːn] *pp* → withdraw.

withdrew [wɪð'druː] *pt* → withdraw.

wither [wɪðə^r] *vi* marchitarse.

within [wɪ'ðɪn] *prep (inside)* dentro de; *(certain distance)* a menos de; *(certain time)* en menos de ♦ *adv* dentro; **it's ~ ten miles of ...** está a menos de diez millas de ...; **it's ~ walking distance** se puede ir andando; **it arrived ~ a week** llegó en menos de una semana; **~ the next week** durante la próxima semana.

without [wɪð'aʊt] *prep* sin; **~ me knowing** sin que lo supiera.

withstand [wɪð'stænd] *(pt & pp* -stood [-'stʊd]) *vt* resistir.

witness [wɪtnɪs] *n* testigo *mf* ♦ *vt (see)* presenciar.

witty [wɪtɪ] *adj* ocurrente.

wives [waɪvz] *pl* → wife.

wobbly [wɒblɪ] *adj (table, chair)* cojo(-ja).

wok [wɒk] *n* sartén china profunda de base redondeada para cocinar con fuego intenso.

woke [wəʊk] *pt* → wake.

woken [wəʊkn] *pp* → wake.

wolf [wʊlf] *(pl* wolves [wʊlvz]) *n* lobo *m*.

woman [wʊmən] *(pl* women) *n* mujer *f*.

womb [wuːm] *n* matriz *f*.

women [wɪmɪn] *pl* → woman.

won [wʌn] *pt & pp* → win.

wonder [wʌndə^r] *vi (ask o.s.)* preguntarse ♦ *n (amazement)* asombro *m*; **to ~ if** preguntarse si; **I ~ if I could ask you a favour?** ¿le importaría hacerme un favor?

wonderful [wʌndəful] *adj* maravilloso(-sa).

won't [wəʊnt] = will not.

wood [wʊd] *n (substance)* madera

f; (small forest) bosque m; (golf club) palo m de madera.

wooden ['wʊdn] adj de madera.

woodland ['wʊdlənd] n bosque m.

woodpecker ['wʊd,pekər] n pájaro m carpintero.

woodwork ['wʊdwɜːk] n carpintería f.

wool [wʊl] n lana f.

woolen ['wʊlən] (Am) = **woollen**.

woollen ['wʊlən] adj (Br) de lana.

woolly ['wʊlɪ] adj de lana.

wooly ['wʊlɪ] (Am) = **woolly**.

Worcester sauce ['wʊstər-] n salsa f Perrins®.

word [wɜːd] n palabra f; **in other ~s** es decir; **to have a ~ with sb** hablar con alguien.

wording ['wɜːdɪŋ] n formulación f.

word processing [-'prəʊsesɪŋ] n procesamiento m de textos.

word processor [-'prəʊsesər] n procesador m de textos.

wore [wɔːr] pt → **wear**.

work [wɜːk] n trabajo m; (painting, novel etc) obra f ◆ vi trabajar; (operate, have desired effect) funcionar; (take effect) hacer efecto ◆ vt (machine, controls) hacer funcionar; **out of ~** desempleado; **to be at ~** (at workplace) estar en el trabajo; (working) estar trabajando; **to be off ~** estar ausente del trabajo; **the ~s** (inf: everything) todo; **how does it ~?** ¿cómo funciona?; **it's not ~ing** no funciona; **to ~ as** trabajar ▸ **work out** vt sep (price, total) cular; (solution, reason) deducir; thod, plan) dar con; (understand)

entender ◆ vi (result, turn out) salir; (be successful) funcionar; (do exercise) hacer ejercicio; **it ~s out at £20 each** sale a 20 libras cada uno.

worker ['wɜːkər] n trabajador m (-ra f).

working class ['wɜːkɪŋ-] n: **the ~** la clase obrera.

working hours ['wɜːkɪŋ-] npl horario m de trabajo.

workman ['wɜːkmən] (pl -men [-mən]) n obrero m.

work of art n obra f de arte.

workout ['wɜːkaʊt] n sesión f de ejercicios.

work permit n permiso m de trabajo.

workplace ['wɜːkpleɪs] n lugar m de trabajo.

workshop ['wɜːkʃɒp] n taller m.

work surface n encimera f.

world [wɜːld] n mundo m ◆ adj mundial; **the best in the ~** el mejor del mundo.

worldwide [,wɜːld'waɪd] adv a escala mundial.

worm [wɜːm] n gusano m.

worn [wɔːn] pp → **wear** ◆ adj gastado(-da).

worn-out adj (tired) agotado(-da); **to be ~** (clothes, shoes etc) ya estar para tirar.

worried ['wʌrɪd] adj preocupado(-da).

worry ['wʌrɪ] n preocupación f ◆ vt preocupar ◆ vi: **to ~ (about)** preocuparse (por).

worrying ['wʌrɪɪŋ] adj preocupante.

worse [wɜːs] adj & adv peor; **to get ~** empeorar; **~ off** (in worse *position)* en peor situación; *(poorer)* peor de dinero.

worsen [ˈwɜːsn] *vi* empeorar.

worship [ˈwɜːʃɪp] *n (church service)* oficio *m* ◆ *vt* adorar.

worst [wɜːst] *adj & adv* peor ◆ *n:* the ~ *(person)* el peor (la peor); *(thing)* lo peor.

worth [wɜːθ] *prep:* how much is it ~? ¿cuánto vale?; it's ~ £50 vale 50 libras; it's ~ seeing merece la pena verlo; it's not ~ it no vale la pena; £50 ~ of traveller's cheques cheques de viaje por valor de 50 libras.

worthless [ˈwɜːθlɪs] *adj* sin valor.

worthwhile [ˌwɜːθˈwaɪl] *adj* que vale la pena.

worthy [ˈwɜːðɪ] *adj* digno(-na); to be ~ of sthg merecer algo.

would [wʊd] *aux vb* **1.** *(in reported speech):* she said she ~ come dijo que vendría.

2. *(indicating condition):* what ~ you do? ¿qué harías?; what ~ you have done? ¿qué habrías hecho?; I ~ be most grateful le estaría muy agradecido.

3. *(indicating willingness):* she ~n't go no quería irse; he ~ do anything for her haría cualquier cosa por ella.

4. *(in polite questions):* ~ you like a drink? ¿quieres tomar algo?; ~ you mind closing the window? ¿le importaría cerrar la ventana?

5. *(indicating inevitability):* he ~ say that y él ¿qué va a decir?

6. *(giving advice):* I ~ report it if I were you yo en tu lugar lo denunciaría.

7. *(expressing opinions):* I ~ prefer yo preferiría; I ~ have thought (that) ... hubiera pensado que ...

wound[1] [wuːnd] *n* herida *f* ◆ *vt* herir.

wound[2] [waʊnd] *pt & pp* → **wind**[2].

wove [wəʊv] *pt* → **weave**.

woven [ˈwəʊvn] *pp* → **weave**.

wrap [ræp] *vt (package)* envolver; to ~ sthg round sthg liar algo alrededor de algo ❑ **wrap up** *vt sep (package)* envolver ◆ *vi* abrigarse.

wrapper [ˈræpər] *n* envoltorio *m*.

wrapping [ˈræpɪŋ] *n* envoltorio *m*.

wrapping paper *n* papel *m* de envolver.

wreath [riːθ] *n* corona *f* (de flores).

wreck [rek] *n (of plane, car)* restos *mpl* del siniestro; *(of ship)* restos *mpl* del naufragio ◆ *vt (destroy)* destrozar; *(spoil)* echar por tierra; to be ~ed *(ship)* naufragar.

wreckage [ˈrekɪdʒ] *n (of plane, car)* restos *mpl*; *(of building)* escombros *mpl*.

wrench [rentʃ] *n (Br: monkey wrench)* llave *f* inglesa; *(Am: spanner)* llave *f* de tuercas.

wrestler [ˈreslər] *n* luchador *m* (-ra *f*).

wrestling [ˈreslɪŋ] *n* lucha *f* libre.

wretched [ˈretʃɪd] *adj (miserable)* desgraciado(-da); *(very bad)* pésimo(-ma).

wring [rɪŋ] *(pt & pp* **wrung**) *vt* retorcer.

wrinkle 328

wrinkle ['rɪŋkl] *n* arruga *f*.

wrist [rɪst] *n* muñeca *f*.

wristwatch ['rɪstwɒtʃ] *n* reloj *m* de pulsera.

write [raɪt] (*pt* **wrote**, *pp* **written**) *vt* escribir; (*cheque*) extender; (*prescription*) hacer; (*Am: send letter to*) escribir a ♦ *vi* escribir; **to ~ (to sb)** (*Br*) escribir (a alguien) ❑ **write back** *vi* contestar; **write down** *vt sep* apuntar; **write off** *vt sep* (*Br: inf: car*) cargarse ♦ *vi*: **to ~ off for sthg** hacer un pedido de algo (por escrito); **write out** *vt sep* (*list, essay*) escribir; (*cheque, receipt*) extender.

write-off *n*: **the car was a ~** el coche quedó hecho un estropicio.

writer ['raɪtər] *n* (*author*) escritor *m* (-ra *f*).

writing ['raɪtɪŋ] *n* (*handwriting*) letra *f*; (*written words*) escrito *m*; (*activity*) escritura *f*.

writing desk *n* escritorio *m*.

writing pad *n* bloc *m*.

writing paper *n* papel *m* de escribir.

written ['rɪtn] *pp* → **write** ♦ *adj* (*exam*) escrito(-ta); (*notice, confirmation*) por escrito.

wrong [rɒŋ] *adj* (*incorrect*) equivocado(-da); (*unsatisfactory*) malo (-la); (*moment*) inoportuno(-na); (*person*) inapropiado(-da) ♦ *adv* mal; **to be ~** (*person*) estar equivocado; (*immoral*) estar mal; **what's ~?** ¿qué pasa?; **something's ~ with the car** el coche no marcha bien; **to be in the ~** haber hecho mal; **to ~ sthg** ~ confundirse con algo; **to ~ (machine)** estropearse; **"~** señal que indica a los conducto-

res que existe el peligro de ir en la dirección contraria.

wrongly ['rɒŋlɪ] *adv* equivocadamente.

wrong number *n*: **sorry, I've got the ~** perdone, me he equivocado de número.

wrote [rəʊt] *pt* → **write**.

wrought iron [rɔːt-] *n* hierro *m* forjado.

wrung [rʌŋ] *pt & pp* → **wring**.

xing (*Am: abbr of crossing*): **"ped ~"** señal que indica un paso de peatones.

XL (*abbr of extra-large*) XL.

Xmas ['eksməs] *n* (*inf*) Navidad *f*.

X-ray ['eks-] *n* (*picture*) radiografía *f* ♦ *vt* hacer una radiografía a; **to have an ~** hacerse una radiografía.

yacht [jɒt] *n* (*for pleasure*) yate *m*; (*for racing*) balandro *m*.

yard [jɑːd] *n* (*unit of measurement*)

= *91,44 cm,* yarda *f; (enclosed area)*
patio *m; (Am: behind house)* jardín
m.

yard sale *n (Am)* venta de objetos
de segunda mano organizada por una
sola persona frente a su casa.

yarn [jɑːn] *n* hilo *m.*

yawn [jɔːn] *vi* bostezar.

yd *abbr* = **yard**.

yeah [jɛə] *adv (inf)* sí.

year [jɪəʳ] *n* año *m; (at school)*
curso *m;* **next** ~ el año que viene;
this ~ este año; **I'm 15** ~**s old**
tengo 15 años; **I haven't seen her
for** ~**s** *(inf)* hace siglos que no la
veo.

yearly [ˈjɪəlɪ] *adj* anual.

yeast [jiːst] *n* levadura *f.*

yell [jel] *vi* chillar.

yellow [ˈjeləʊ] *adj* amarillo(-lla)
♦ *n* amarillo *m.*

yellow lines *npl* líneas *fpl* amarillas (de tráfico).

yes [jes] *adv* sí; **to say** ~ decir que
sí.

yesterday [ˈjestədɪ] *n* ayer *m* ♦
adv ayer; **the day before** ~ anteayer; ~ **afternoon** ayer por la
tarde; ~ **evening** anoche; ~ **morning** ayer por la mañana.

yet [jet] *adv* aún, todavía ♦ *conj*
sin embargo; **have they arrived** ~?
¿ya han llegado?; **the best one** ~ el
mejor hasta ahora; **not** ~ todavía
no; **I've** ~ **to do it** aún no lo he
hecho; ~ **again** otra vez más; ~
another delay otro retraso más.

yew [juː] *n* tejo *m.*

yield [jiːld] *vt (profit, interest)* producir ♦ *vi (break, give way)* ceder;
"yield" *(Am. AUT)* "ceda el paso".

YMCA *n* asociación internacional
de jóvenes cristianos.

yob [jɒb] *n (Br: inf)* gamberro *m*
(-rra *f*).

yoga [ˈjəʊgə] *n* yoga *m.*

yoghurt [ˈjɒgət] *n* yogur *m.*

yoik [jɔʊk] *n* yema *f.*

York Minster [ˌjɔːkˈmɪnstəʳ] *n* la
catedral de York.

ⓘ YELLOW LINES

En Gran Bretaña, líneas amarillas
dobles o individuales pintadas a
lo largo del borde de una carretera
indican una zona de aparcamiento
restringido. Una única línea prohíbe
aparcar entre las 8 de la mañana y
las 6.30 de la tarde en días laborables, y una línea amarilla doble prohíbe aparcar en todo momento. Se
puede aparcar sobre una línea amarilla después de las 6.30 de la tarde o
en domingo.

Yellow Pages® *n:* **the** ~ las
Páginas Amarillas®.

ⓘ YORK MINSTER

Esta catedral, famosa por sus
paredes de piedra clara y su
rosetón, está situada en la amuralla-
da ciudad de York, en el norte de
Inglaterra. Fue construida en el siglo
XII, y ha sido recientemente restaura-
da tras unos daños producidos en
1984 por un rayo.

Yorkshire pudding [ˈjɔːkʃə-]
n masa de harina, huevos y leche, coci-

da al horno hasta formar un pastel ligero y esponjoso, que se sirve tradicionalmente con el rosbif.

you [ju:] *pron* **1.** *(subject: singular)* tú, vos *(Amér)*; *(subject: plural)* vosotros *mpl* (-tras *fpl*), ustedes *mfpl (Amér)*; *(subject: polite form)* usted, ustedes *(pl)*; ~ **French** vosotros sois franceses.
2. *(direct object: singular)* te; *(direct object: plural)* os, les *(Amér)*; *(direct object: polite form)* lo *m* (la *f)*; **I hate ~!** te odio.
3. *(indirect object: singular)* te; *(indirect object: plural)* os, les *(Amér)*; *(indirect object: polite form)* le, les *(pl)*; **I told ~** te lo dije.
4. *(after prep: singular)* ti; *(after prep: plural)* vosotros *mpl* (-tras *fpl*), ustedes *mfpl (Amér)*; *(after prep: polite form)* usted, ustedes *(pl)*; **we'll go without ~** iremos sin ti.
5. *(indefinite use)* uno *m* (una *f)*; ~ **never know** nunca se sabe.

young [jʌŋ] *adj* joven ◆ *npl*: **the ~** los jóvenes.

younger [ˈjʌŋgəʳ] *adj (brother, sister)* menor.

youngest [ˈjʌŋgəst] *adj (brother, sister)* menor.

youngster [ˈjʌŋstəʳ] *n* joven *mf*.

your [jɔːʳ] *adj* **1.** *(singular subject)* tu; *(plural subject)* vuestro(-tra); *(polite form)* su; ~ **dog** tu perro; ~ **children** tus hijos.
2. *(indefinite subject)*: **it's good for ~ teeth** es bueno para los dientes.

yours [jɔːz] *pron (singular subject)* tuyo *m* (-ya *f)*; *(plural subject)* vuestro *m* (-tra *f)*; *(polite form)* suyo *m* (...); **a friend of ~** un amigo

yourself [jɔːˈself] *(pl* **-selves** [-ˈselvz]) *pron* **1.** *(reflexive: singular)* te; *(reflexive: plural)* os; *(reflexive: polite form)* se.
2. *(after prep: singular)* ti mismo (-ma); *(after prep: plural)* vosotros mismos (vosotras mismas); *(after prep: polite form)* usted mismo (-ma), ustedes mismos (-mas) *(pl)*; **did you do it ~?** *(singular)* ¿lo hiciste tú mismo?; *(polite form)* ¿lo hizo usted mismo?; **did you do it yourselves?** ¿lo hicisteis vosotros/ustedes mismos?

youth [ju:θ] *n* juventud *f*; *(young man)* joven *m*.

youth club *n* club *m* juvenil.

youth hostel *n* albergue *m* juvenil.

Yugoslavia [ˌjuːgəˈslɑːvɪə] *n* Yugoslavia.

yuppie [ˈjʌpɪ] *n* yuppy *mf*.

YWCA *n* asociación internacional de jóvenes cristianas.

zebra [Br ˈzebrə, Am ˈziːbrə] *n* cebra *f*.

zebra crossing *n (Br)* paso *m* de cebra.

zero [ˈzɪərəʊ] *(pl* **-es)** *n* cero *m*; **five degrees below ~** cinco grados bajo cero.

zest [zest] *n (of lemon, orange)* ralladura *f*.

zigzag [ˈzɪgzæg] *vi* zigzag *m*.

zinc [zɪŋk] n zinc m.

zip [zɪp] n (Br) cremallera f ♦ vt cerrar la cremallera de ❑ **zip up** vt sep subir la cremallera de.

zip code n (Am) código m postal.

zipper ['zɪpə'] n (Am) cremallera f.

zit [zɪt] n (inf) grano m.

zodiac ['zəʊdɪæk] n zodiaco m.

zone [zəʊn] n zona f.

zoo [zu:] (pl -s) n zoo m.

zoom (lens) [zu:m-] n zoom m.

zucchini [zu:'ki:nɪ] (pl inv) n (Am) calabacín m.